FOURTH EDITION *

# A History of MUSIC in Western Culture

## Mark Evan Bonds

Department of Music
University of North Carolina at Chapel Hill

**PEARSON**

Boston   Columbus   Indianapolis   New York   San Francisco   Upper Saddle River
Amsterdam   Cape Town   Dubai London   Madrid   Milan   Munich   Paris   Montreal   Toronto
Delhi   Mexico City   Sao Paulo   Sydney   Hong Kong   Seoul   Singapore   Taipei   Tokyo

# To Dorothea, Peter, Andrew

President: *Yolanda de Rooy*
Editorial Director: *Craig Campanella*
Editor-in-Chief: *Sarah Touborg*
Senior Publisher: *Roth Wilkofsky*
Editorial Project Manager: *Nesin Osman*
Editorial Assistant: *Christopher Fegan*
Director of Marketing: *Brandy Dawson*
Executive Marketing Manager: *Kate Mitchell*
Marketing Assistant: *Paige Patunas*
Managing Editor: *Melissa Feimer*
Production Liaison: *Joe Scordato*
Full-Service Management: *GEX Publishing Services*
Production Editor: *GEX Publishing Services*

Photo Research and Permissions: *Ben Ferrini*
Senior Operations Specialist: *Diane Peirano*
Creative Director: *Pat Smythe*
Interior Design: *Delgado and Company*
Cover Design: *Delgado and Company*
Cover Image: *Thomas Rowlandson, "John Bull at the Italian Opera". © Newberry Library/SuperStock*
Senior Digital Media Editor: *David Alick*
Digital Media Project Manager: *Rich Barnes*
Composition: *GEX Publishing Services*
Printer/Binder: *R. R. Donnelley & Sons*
Cover Printer: *Lehigh-Phoenix Color Corp.*

Credits and acknowledgments borrowed from other sources and reproduced, with permission, in this textbook appear on the appropriate page within text.

**Library of Congress Cataloging-in-Publication Data**

Bonds, Mark Evan.
  A history of music in Western culture / Mark Evan Bonds. — 4th ed.
    p. cm.
  Includes bibliographical references and index.
  ISBN-13: 978-0-205-86722-6
  ISBN-10: 0-205-86722-7
  I. Title.
ML160.B75 2012
780.9—dc23

2012039346

Student Edition
ISBN 10: 0-205-86722-7
ISBN 13: 978-0-205-86722-6

Instructor's Resource Copy
ISBN 10: 0-205-93233-9
ISBN-13: 978-0-205-93233-7

10 9 8 7 6 5 4 3 2 1

# Contents

# Preface

Undergraduates studying music history may or may not be passionate about history, but they are always passionate about music. For this reason, I have structured *A History of Music in Western Culture* around a carefully selected repertory of music that reflects the development of the art from antiquity to the present. My goal has been to help students gain a broad understanding of the nature of music, its role in society, and the ways in which these have changed over time. Students who become familiar with the repertory of works in the accompanying *Anthology of Scores* and the corresponding set of recordings will be well equipped to understand this history: the requisite names, dates, and terms will be far more memorable when associated with specific works of music. Perhaps even more importantly, students will have a sound basis from which to explore musical works and repertories beyond those covered in the present book, including the musics of other cultures.

*A History of Music in Western Culture* seeks to challenge students to think critically about the nature of music and its past. Music history is too often presented (and learned) as one long series of indisputable facts. I have tried to integrate into this text enough primary source documents—excerpts from composers' letters, contemporary reviews, theoretical treatises, and the like—to demonstrate the ways in which the raw materials of history can be open to conflicting interpretations. Indeed, the most interesting historical issues tend to be precisely those about which experts disagree.

## FEATURES OF THE TEXT

*A History of Music in Western Culture* builds its narrative around the two-volume *Anthology of Scores* and a set of accompanying sound recordings, which are available both as compact discs and as streaming audio available through the *MySearchLab*, an online learning environment designed specifically for this text. Every work in the *Anthology* gets a discussion in the text, called out with an icon in the margin cross-referenced to both the scores and recordings.

Following a prologue on the music of antiquity, the text is divided into six parts, each corresponding to a major era in music history: Medieval, Renaissance, Baroque, Classical, 19th century, and 20th century. The text concludes with a brief epilogue on music today. Each part begins with a **prelude**—with one or more **maps**—that summarizes the historical and social background of each era, and the first chapter in each part provides an overview of the major stylistic characteristics and theoretical concerns of the music of the era.

The text also offers a variety of features and pedagogical tools:

- An **outline** at the beginning of each chapter gives students an overview of the content of the chapter.

- The opening pages of each prelude include a **comparative timeline** that lists major musical events side-by-side with other significant historical events.

- A graphic **summary of style differences** in each part highlights the principal differences in musical style between each era and the one immediately preceding (Renaissance versus Medieval, Baroque versus Renaissance, etc.).

- **Key terms** are highlighted in each chapter and defined in a **glossary** at the end of the book.

- Significant composers are featured in extended **Composer Profiles** that include key biographical information and a survey of principal works.

- **Primary Evidence** boxes contain excerpts from relevant contemporary documents, exposing students to some of the raw materials of music history. A brief introduction places each selection in its context and challenges students to think about the interpretation of historical evidence.

- **Focus** boxes highlight important information that expands on aspects of the core narrative.

- **Performance Practice** boxes examine in detail an alternative performance of the same work.

Students will thereby have the opportunity to compare and discuss strikingly different ways of bringing to life the same notes on a page. In the Baroque era, for example, students can hear excerpts from Bach's "Goldberg" Variations as performed by Trevor Pinnock, playing on a harpsichord such as the composer would have played, and as performed by Glenn Gould, playing on his 20th-century concert grand piano.

- Numerous **examples, tables,** and **diagrams** help students grasp key points and visualize musical structures.

- The last chapter in each part concludes with a set of **discussion questions** designed to stimulate reflection on broad issues in music history.

# NEW FEATURES OF THE FOURTH EDITION

This text has been expanded, corrected, and updated, particularly in the sections on Medieval and Renaissance music. New repertory has been introduced throughout the text in response to feedback from instructors on what works elicit the best responses from students in the classroom. Improved graphics make the material more readily comprehensible. Other key changes include the following:

- The all new *MySearchLab* online learning environment provides a variety of tools to help instructors access lecture materials, and help students understand the material found in the book, including
  - An **interactive eText**, fully page compatible with the printed version, that allows students to highlight passages and make notes, as well as access other *MySearchLab* features.
  - **Scrolling Translations** online that allow students to follow original texts and English translations simultaneously. No more flipping back and forth to the end of a score to follow a translation of the text in the score!
  - **Streaming audio** so that students and instructors can access music easily anywhere with an internet connection.
  - **Quizzes** that offer students the opportunity to test their understanding of each chapter's materials.

- A variety of other learning materials, including Term Flashcards, Inside the Orchestra videos, documentaries, and more.

# FEATURES OF THE SCORE ANTHOLOGY

The works in the *Anthology of Scores to A History of Music in Western Culture* have been carefully selected to represent the developments in music history discussed in the text. Every selection in the *Anthology of Scores* is discussed in the text. Volume I covers antiquity through the Baroque era; Volume II covers music of the Classical era to the present.

Key features of the Score Anthology include

- **Integrated commentary.** Excerpts from the text are integrated into the score anthology at the end of each selection, providing students with basic information and a brief discussion of every work.

- **Cross-referencing to text and recordings.** Each selection in the anthology opens with a clear cross-reference to the recorded version of the work (disc and track number) and to the discussion of the work within the text (page number). In addition, the score and recordings in the anthology correspond exactly within their chronological span (Volume One of each through the Baroque era; Volume Two of each since the Classical era).

## New to the Score Anthology

- **New works and improved editions.** New and authoritative editions of 12th-century organum, 15th-century chanson, 19th-century ballet, band music, and three new compositions written since 2000.

- All new **Scrolling Translations** on *MySearchLab*, which provide both students and instructors with easy access to real-time English translations of foreign-language vocal works in the Anthology.

# FEATURES OF THE RECORDED ANTHOLOGY

Fifteen compact discs complement the text and *Anthology of Scores*. These recordings draw on the resources of many different recording labels and feature some of the most distinguished artists and ensembles of our time, such as Sequentia, Anonymous 4, Hilliard Ensemble, Orlando Consort, Les Arts Florissants, Huelgas Ensemble, Gothic Voices, La Chapelle Royale, Consort of Musicke, Tashi, La Petite Band, Tallis Scholars, Concentus Musicus Wien, Theatre of Voices, English Baroque Soloists, Orchestre Révolutionnaire et Romantique, and Concerto Köln. Representative soloists include Paul O'Dette, Emma Kirkby, Davitt Moroney, Thomas Quasthoff, Trevor Pinnock, Malcolm Bilson, Ruggiero Raimondi, Kiri Te Kanawa, Roberto Alagna, and Jessye Norman.

The discs are arranged chronologically and mirror the content and structure of the *Anthology of Scores*:

- Volume I: Antiquity through the Baroque Era (6 discs).
- Volume II: The Classical Era to the Present (9 discs).

# AN EXPANDED LIBRARY OF RESOURCES FOR STUDENTS AND INSTRUCTORS

*A History of Music in Western Culture* comes with a variety of supplementary print and multimedia materials for both instructors and students.

## Instructor's Manual

*The Instructor's Resource Manual with Tests* provides the following:

- Sample syllabi, including suggestions for how best to incorporate *MySearchLab* materials into your course.
- Chapter outlines and summaries to help you organize and structure your lectures.
- Key terms found throughout the book.
- Discussion Questions, Essay Questions, and Class Projects, each designed to both spur in-class conversations on important topics and provide the opportunity for outside assignments for your students.
- A list of online resources and publications that can be used for research.
- Other media sources that can be helpful such as movies and DVDs of live concerts/performances.

## Test Item File and Pearson *MyTest*

The all-new Test Item File is filled with dozens of multiple choice and essay questions per chapter, allowing instructors to create their own custom exams. The Test Item File is available in a variety of formats, including BlackBoard and WebCT, as well as in Pearson's own *MyTest* format, which allows instructors to build and randomize tests, save multiple versions across semesters, and print their exams and answer keys from any computer.

## PowerPoint Lecture Slides

Mirroring the organization and content of the text, a set of PowerPoint slides provides a useful tool for lectures and classroom presentations. The value of the slides is further enhanced by the inclusion of some of the book's photos, maps, tables and charts, as well as links to all of the *MySearchLab* assets so that instructors can seamlessly access streaming audio and videos during their lectures.

## Acknowledgments

I am grateful to the many scholars who reviewed the manuscript for this book and its revisions at various points in its development. Their thoughtful and often detailed comments were invaluable at every stage in the process:

Roberto Catalano, San Bernardino Valley College; Alice Clark, Loyola University New Orleans; Vincent Corrigan, Bowling Green State University; Jim Davis, SUNY Fredonia; Alicia Doyle, California State University, Long Beach; Rachel Golden, University of Tennessee; Margaret Hasselman, Virginia Polytechnic Institute and State University; Karl Hinterbichler, University of New Mexico; Michael Long, University at Buffalo; Alyson McLamore, California Polytechnic State University, San Luis Obispo; Kevin N. Moll, East Carolina University; James Randall, The University of Montana; Christina Reitz, Western Carolina University; Matthew Steel, Western Michigan University; Sarah Waltz, University of the Pacific; Eric Wood, University of the Pacific. For the fourth edition in particular, I am especially indebted to Sean Gallagher (Boston University) for his thorough review and thoughtful suggestions for strengthening the Medieval and Renaissance portions of the text and anthology. Rob Deemer (SUNY-Fredonia) was a great help in selecting three representative works of music written since 2000. Thanks, Rob.

I am also grateful to many colleagues and students at the University of North Carolina at Chapel Hill for their help at many points along the way. Fellow faculty members Tim Carter, John Covach, Annegret Fauser, Jon Finson, Anne MacNeil, Jocelyn Neal, Severine Neff, and Tom Warburton all offered helpful advice (and an ear) at various stages of the project. I was also fortunate to be able to draw on the able help of several students in preparing the manuscript: Christina Tuskey, Jennifer Germann, Michelle Oswell, Seth Coluzzi, Ethan Lechner, Joseph Singleton, Douglas Shadle, and above all Peter Lamothe. Samuel Brannon prepared new musical examples and anthology scores for the fourth edition with great efficiency. The staff of the Music Library—particularly Dan Zager, Phil Vandermeer, Diane Steinhaus, Eva Boyce, Carrie Monette, and Bradshaw Lentz—were unfailingly helpful and efficient.

Thanks, too, to Ruell Tyson and his staff at the Humanities Institute at the University of North Carolina at Chapel Hill. My fellowship there in the spring of 1999 provided the time and mental space needed to launch this project, and my weekly conversations with the other fellows that semester helped me think through some of the more basic issues associated with writing a textbook of this kind.

I am grateful as well to Massimo Ossi (Indiana University) for his comments on an early version of the Baroque section of the text; to Suzanne Cusick (New York University) for her help in matters pertaining to Francesca Caccini; and to Diane Parr Walker and Jane Edmister Penner (University of Virginia) for their help in securing a reproduction of Thomas Jefferson's request for music by Carlo Antonio Campioni. J. Samuel Hammond (Duke University Libraries) and Jeremy Yudkin (Boston University) also provided help and advice at many points along the way. Margaret Murata (UC-Irvine) and Barbara Haggh-Huglo (University of Maryland) were very generous in suggesting improvements for earlier editions.

My editors at Pearson have been a delight to work with from the very beginning. I first discussed the project with Bud Therien. Bud's successor as music editor, Chris Johnson, was the prime mover in this enterprise, as was Richard Carlin for the third edition. The current team at Pearson Education—Music Editor, Roth Wilkofsky; Editorial Assistant, Chris Fegan; and Production Manager, Joe Scordato—has been indispensable in making the fourth edition that much better. Teresa Nemeth provided many useful ideas for improving early drafts of the manuscript. Elsa Peterson helped with the development of the 20th-century chapters and coordinated the compilation of the anthology manuscript. Francelle Carapetyan and Diana Gongora were unflagging in their effort to track down the needed illustrations. Tom Laskey (Sony BMG Music Entertainment) expertly coordinated the revised package of recordings.

Finally, my deepest thanks go to my family. My parents were not directly involved in producing this book, but they made it possible in ways that go well beyond the obvious. My brother Bob gave invaluable advice at an early stage of the process. And it is to Dorothea, Peter, and Andrew that I dedicate this book, with love.

# About the Author

✴———✴

Mark Evan Bonds is the Cory C. Boshamer Distinguished Professor of Music at the University of North Carolina at Chapel Hill, where he has taught since 1992. He holds degrees from Duke University (BA), Christian-Albrechts-Universität Kiel (MA), and Harvard University (PhD). His publications include *Wordless Rhetoric: Musical Form and the Metaphor of the Oration* (1991), *After Beethoven: Imperatives of Symphonic Originality* (1996), and *Music as Thought: Listening to the Symphony in the Age of Beethoven* (2006). He has also published essays on the music of Haydn and Mozart and has served as editor-in-chief of *Beethoven Forum*.

# Why Study Music History?

**W**hy study music history? This is a fair question, one you have likely asked yourself, particularly if you happen to be using this book as part of a required course. Here are a few reasons:

- **A greater understanding of music's emotional power and its role in society.** Music is one of the most powerful yet least understood of all the arts. It has played a significant role in every known culture in human history. In the Western world, people have used it in widely varying contexts. It has provided entertainment, played a central role in many forms of religious worship, and has long been considered important to a well-rounded education. It has been admired since ancient times for its therapeutic benefits and it is used in shopping malls today for its ability to put people in the mood to buy. Political candidates identify themselves with theme songs, and patriotic music helps promote feelings of national unity. Music has even been used for torture. Entire generations have defined themselves according to the music they have enjoyed. And today, music drives a multibillion-dollar industry.

- **A richer understanding of music's basic elements.** Composers and musicians have combined a few basic elements—rhythm, melody, harmony, texture, timbre, and form—in a remarkable variety of ways since ancient times. The polyphony of the 13th century sounds quite different from early-20th-century ragtime, but both are composed from the same building blocks. Studying music history helps us understand how these elements have been manipulated over time to create such a diversity of effects. And in the process, it can make us better listeners.

- **A sense of changing musical styles across time.** Why, within the space of less than a hundred years, did Bach write in one style, Mozart in another, and Chopin in yet another? Why is so much of the music written after 1900 difficult to grasp on first listening? Why do musical styles change at all? Although we do not have to be able to answer these kinds of questions to enjoy the music of any composer or period, our attempts to do so can increase our understanding of it and deepen the pleasure it brings us.

- **A basis for exploring new works and repertories.** Familiarity with a wide range of representative works from different historical periods enhances our ability to learn and understand new works and repertories of different kinds, including those of non-Western cultures. All of us are looking to expand our playlists in one way or another.

- **A greater ability to talk and write about music.** Music, the most abstract of all the arts, is notoriously difficult to describe in words. If we could identify exactly what a work of music is "about" or translate its meaning into words, why would we bother with the music at all? Still, the fact that we can never capture in prose the essence of music does not mean that we should remain silent on the subject. The very process of trying to write about music can help us appreciate what distinguishes it from fiction, poetry, drama, painting, dance, architecture, or any other form of human expression.

# Prologue

# Antiquity

J.D. Dallet/age fotostock/SuperStock

Every known civilization has had music of some kind. The human voice is as old as the species itself, and a recorder-like object crafted from the thigh bones of a bear may have been made as long as 50,000 years ago by Neanderthals living in what is now Slovenia, in eastern Europe. The earliest indisputable musical instrument—a kind of flute made from the wing bone of a vulture—dates from about 34,000 B.C.E. and was found in what is now southwestern France. The ancient civilizations of Egypt and Sumeria, which emerged between 4000 and 3000 B.C.E., left behind many images of people singing and playing instruments, particularly in connection with religious rituals.

## MUSIC IN THE BIBLICAL WORLD

The Old Testament makes repeated references to music. Immediately after crossing the Red Sea in the exodus from Egypt, Miriam the prophetess, the sister of Moses and Aaron, used her tambourine to lead the Israelite women in song and dance to praise God for delivering her people (Exodus 15:20–21). The young David cured Saul's melancholy by playing the harp (1 Samuel 16:14–23), one of the earliest recorded instances of music therapy. David went on to write many of the Psalms, and as king of Israel (about 1055–1015 B.C.E.), he played a key role in establishing the order of worship, including the singing of psalms and hymns. The temple he envisioned in Jerusalem—completed by his son Solomon but destroyed by the Babylonians in 586 B.C.E.—is reported to have been attended by 4,000 instrumentalists (1 Chronicles 23:5) and a cadre of 288 singers (1 Chronicles 25:7). A passage that reveals the importance of music in worship describes how, at the moment when the Ark of the Covenant was brought into the temple, the singers

arrayed in fine linen, with cymbals, harps, and lyres, stood east of the altar with a hundred and twenty priests who were trumpeters; and it was the duty of the trumpeters and singers to make themselves heard in unison in praise and thanksgiving to the Lord, and when the song was raised, with trumpets and cymbals and other musical instruments, in praise to the Lord. "For he is good, for his

◀ Orpheus was the paradigmatic musician of ancient times. In this late-Roman mosaic from the 3rd century C.E., Orpheus charms wild beasts through his music. In other legends, he used music—and not words—to move rivers, stones, and even the hearts of the gods of the underworld, who had heard (and ignored) the verbal pleas of mortals countless times. All of these stories reflect the ancient belief in the transcendental power of music and its ability to overcome the limitations and realities of ordinary life and death.

## Chapter Outline

Music in the Biblical World

Ancient Greece
Music in Ancient Greek Society
Greek Musical Theory

Music in the Roman Empire

The Musical Legacies of Antiquity
Music and the Cosmos
Music and the Soul
Music and the State
Vocal versus Instrumental Music
Theory versus Practice

steadfast love endures for ever," the house, the house of the Lord, was filled with a cloud, so that the priests could not stand to minister because of the cloud; for the glory of the Lord filled the house of God. (2 Chronicles 5:12–14)

The precise nature of the music described in the Old Testament remains largely a matter of speculation, for none of it has survived in notated form. From written accounts, we know that psalms and hymns were sung in unison, either antiphonally (two choirs alternating) or responsorially (soloist alternating with one choir). The words were chanted primarily to simple melodic formulas in a way that helped project the text across large spaces. Traditions of Jewish psalmody and hymnody played a vital role in the emergence of plainchant in the Christian church (see Chapter 1). More important still is the enduring association they created between music and feelings of intense spirituality.

# ANCIENT GREECE

Many of the concepts that form the roots of the Western musical tradition derive from the works of the ancient Greeks. Some time around the 8th century B.C.E., the people of ancient Greece began to develop patterns of thought and social organization that differed in fundamental ways from those of other civilizations. Mythic explanations of the cosmos gave way to rational, more scientific modes of thought. Philosophy emerged as a means of reconciling abstract reason with empirical reality. Personal self-knowledge became the central goal in the life of the individual, a goal reflected in the famous dictum of the 5th-century B.C.E. philosopher Socrates: "The unexamined life is not worth living."

The characteristic social and political unit of the ancient Greeks, the city-state, or *polis*, was a forge for many fundamental concepts about civic duty, social justice, and

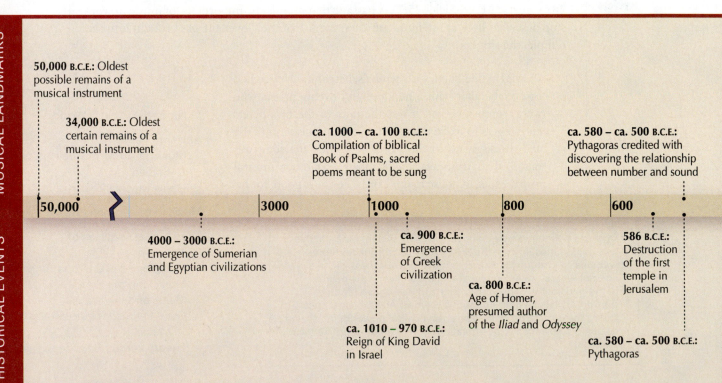

**PROLOGUE TIMELINE**

**MUSICAL LANDMARKS**

**50,000 B.C.E.:** Oldest possible remains of a musical instrument

**34,000 B.C.E.:** Oldest certain remains of a musical instrument

**ca. 1000 – ca. 100 B.C.E.:** Compilation of biblical Book of Psalms, sacred poems meant to be sung

**ca. 580 – ca. 500 B.C.E.:** Pythagoras credited with discovering the relationship between number and sound

50,000    3000    1000    800    600

**HISTORICAL EVENTS**

**4000 – 3000 B.C.E.:** Emergence of Sumerian and Egyptian civilizations

**ca. 900 B.C.E.:** Emergence of Greek civilization

**ca. 800 B.C.E.:** Age of Homer, presumed author of the *Iliad* and *Odyssey*

**586 B.C.E.:** Destruction of the first temple in Jerusalem

**ca. 1010 – 970 B.C.E.:** Reign of King David in Israel

**ca. 580 – ca. 500 B.C.E.:** Pythagoras

individual liberty that have had an enduring legacy in Western society. The democracy that emerged in ancient Athens, however limited, was an approach to government no society had yet attempted.

Athens attained its political, commercial, and cultural height—its Golden Age—under the leadership of the statesman Pericles in the 5th century B.C.E. This was an era whose accomplishments included the construction of the Parthenon, the plays of Sophocles, Euripides, Aeschylus, and Aristophanes, and the philosophy of Socrates as transmitted by his student Plato. Toward the end of the 4th century B.C.E., the Greek city-states, weakened by incessant warfare, succumbed to the armies of Philip of Macedon and his son Alexander (whose tutor was the philosopher Aristotle). Alexander went on to conquer vast territories from the eastern Mediterranean to the Ganges in present-day India. This empire did not survive Alexander's death intact. Its successor states, however, spread Greek, or Hellenistic, culture widely in the eastern Mediterranean and in western Asia.

## Music in Ancient Greek Society

Relatively little notated music has survived from ancient Greece, and most of the surviving 45 pieces are fragments. The musical culture of this era relied heavily on memory and improvisation. Yet we know from written accounts, archaeological evidence, and the surviving notated fragments that music played a central role in Greek culture.

The most important public venue for music in ancient Greece was the theater. Greek drama accorded a significant role to the chorus, which provided a running commentary and response to the actions unfolding on the stage, and we know from written accounts and internal evidence within the plays themselves that these choruses were sung. Ensembles could consist of men or women, or occasionally both. Choruses gave voice to the feelings of the community through a combination of word, music, and dance—all of which were considered inseparable in the ancient Greek view of music.

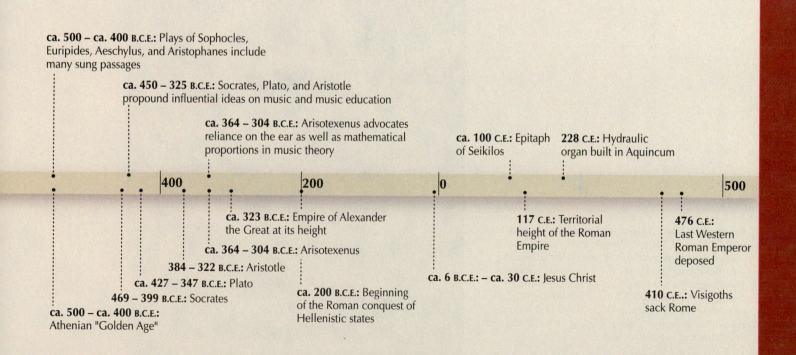

ca. 500 – ca. 400 B.C.E.: Plays of Sophocles, Euripides, Aeschylus, and Aristophanes include many sung passages

ca. 450 – 325 B.C.E.: Socrates, Plato, and Aristotle propound influential ideas on music and music education

ca. 364 – 304 B.C.E.: Arisotexenus advocates reliance on the ear as well as mathematical proportions in music theory

ca. 100 C.E.: Epitaph of Seikilos

228 C.E.: Hydraulic organ built in Aquincum

400 | 200 | 0 | 500

ca. 323 B.C.E.: Empire of Alexander the Great at its height

117 C.E.: Territorial height of the Roman Empire

476 C.E.: Last Western Roman Emperor deposed

ca. 364 – 304 B.C.E.: Arisotexenus

384 – 322 B.C.E.: Aristotle

ca. 427 – 347 B.C.E.: Plato

469 – 399 B.C.E.: Socrates

ca. 200 B.C.E.: Beginning of the Roman conquest of Hellenistic states

ca. 6 B.C.E.: – ca. 30 C.E.: Jesus Christ

410 C.E.: Visigoths sack Rome

ca. 500 – ca. 400 B.C.E.: Athenian "Golden Age"

Music also played a central role in religious and civic rituals. Homer's *Iliad* describes how the Greeks propitiated the god Apollo by singing a "splendid hymn" in his honor for an entire day. The *Iliad* and *Odyssey* themselves are believed to have been sung to formulaic melodies. And the odes written by the 5th-century B.C.E. poet Pindar to commemorate the victors in the Olympic games were clearly intended to be sung; "ode" and "song" were virtually synonymous in the Greek world. Singing was itself one of the competitive events in the Pythian games, held every four years at Delphi in honor of Apollo, a god closely associated with music.

The ancient Greeks also developed repertories of songs and instrumental music for specific social functions: weddings, banquets, funerals, working, and marching, for example. Writers of the time repeatedly warned against mixing genres of song and had a strong sense of which pieces were appropriate in certain settings and which were not.

Greek music, as best we can tell, was largely **monophonic**—consisting of a single melodic line—with the possibility of an accompanimental line that either doubled or modestly embellished the principal voice. The Greeks apparently did not cultivate **polyphony** of any kind, at least not in the conventional sense of the term—the simultaneous sounding of independent parts of equal importance. Their vocal music emphasized instead the fusion of word, rhythm, and melody, which is precisely how Plato defined song (*melos*).

## Greek Musical Theory

The musical system used in ancient Greece was based on a series of interlocking **tetrachords**, descending successions of four notes spanning the interval of a fourth. The inner notes within a tetrachord could be distributed according to one of three

**An ancient bard.** This small bronze statue was crafted around 700 B.C.E. and is thus roughly contemporary with the poet Homer, to whom the epic poems of the *Iliad* and *Odyssey* are ascribed. These verses are believed to have been sung to the accompaniment of a lyre or other harp-like instrument, very much in the manner of the figure shown here, who is clearly singing as he plucks the strings of his instrument.

**Source:** Erich Lessing/Archaeological Museum, Heraklion, Crete, Greece/Art Resource, NY

**Community theater in ancient Greece.** The dramas of Aeschylus, Euripides, Aristophanes, and other Greek playwrights were sung either in whole or in part in settings like the one shown here, the Theater of Dionysus, built in Athens between 342 and 326 B.C.E. The semicircular construction around the large stage area brings the audience close to the theater. The drama's chorus, in turn, gave voice to the community as a whole, at least symbolically.

**Source:** akg-images/Newscom

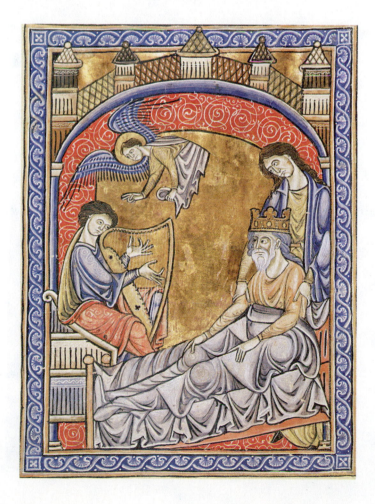

**Music therapy in the ancient world.** This illustration from an English psalter prepared around 1225 shows David playing the harp to cure Saul of his melancholy. According to the biblical text 1 Samuel 16:14–23, "Now the Spirit of the Lord departed from Saul, and an evil spirit from the Lord tormented him. And Saul's servants said to him, 'Let our lord now command your servants . . . to seek out a man who is skilful in playing the lyre; and when the evil spirit from God is upon you, he will play it, and you will be well.' So Saul said to his servants, 'Provide for me a man who can play well, and bring him to me.' . . . And whenever the evil spirit from God was upon Saul, David took the lyre and played it with his hand; so Saul was refreshed, and was well, and the evil spirit departed from him."

**Source:** The Pierpont Morgan Library/Art Resource, NY

*genera* (the plural of *genus*, a class or category): diatonic, chromatic, or enharmonic. Only the outer pitches of each tetrachord were fixed; the exact pitches of the inner notes were variable and depended on the *genus*. In modern-day terms, a diatonic tetrachord (Example A–1a) consisted of two whole-tone intervals followed by a halftone. A chromatic tetrachord began with a minor third and continued with two halftones (Example A–1b). And an enharmonic tetrachord moved downward by a major third, then by two microtones, intervals smaller than a half step (Example A–1c).

A series of four interlocking tetrachords plus one additional note combined to create the Greater Perfect System, a span of two octaves that encompassed the notes used in actual music. Melodies were organized according to the characteristics of one of several *tonoi* (singular *tonos*). Writers of the time disagreed on the precise nature and number of *tonoi*, but their names refer to Greek ethnic groups and regions, indicating that at some distant time they were associated with the musical practices of those groups and regions: the Dorian *tonos* with southern Greece, the Ionian with southwestern Greece, the Phrygian and Lydian with Asia Minor, and the Aeolian with the Greek islands. (The names used to classify modes much later, in the late Middle Ages, were taken from these names, but the pitches and structures of the medieval modes were altogether different from those of the original Greek *tonoi*. See Chapter 1.)

**EXAMPLE A–1** The Greek *genera:* diatonic (a), chromatic (b), and enharmonic (c).

**Greek musical notation.** The inscription on this 1st-century C.E. gravestone includes a song that was apparently an epitaph for the deceased. It begins with the words "I am a tombstone, an image. Seikilos placed me here as an everlasting sign of deathless remembrance." The song begins in the sixth line of text. The signs between the lines indicate rhythm—notated with an unusual degree of clarity—and pitch.

**Source:** National Museum of Denmark, Copenhagen - Dept. of Classical and Near Eastern Antiquities/inv. no. 14987

## Focus    INSTRUMENTS OF ANCIENT GREECE

From written accounts and from the archaeological record—especially illustrations on pottery—scholars have been able to identify a wide range of musical instruments cultivated in ancient Greece.

The most important stringed instruments were the many types of lyres, each with its own characteristic sound and symbolic significance. A lyre consisted of a sound box from which curved arms extended, joined by a crossbar. Strings, attached between the crossbar and the sound box, were often played with a plectrum (a "pick"). Lyres were used either as solo instruments or to accompany voices.

The most prominent wind instrument was the aulos, a pair of pipes, one held in each hand, with a single or double reed. Like the instruments of the lyre family, the aulos could be used either as a solo instrument or to accompany a singer. Other wind instruments include the syrinx, a single reed pipe or panpipe, and various kinds of horns, made either from animal horns or from metal.

Percussion instruments included drums of many kinds, as well as the krotala (hollowed-out blocks of wood played in the manner of castanets) and kumbala (finger cymbals).

**Music education in ancient Greece.** These images, from an Athenian vase made about 480 B.C.E., depict a variety of ancient Greek instruments and reflect the important place of music in the education of Athenian youth. In the top panel, the larger, older figures teach youths how to read and play the lyre. The bottom panel shows a figure playing an aulos (on the left) and another writing on a tablet (center). Plato, who recognized music's power but was deeply suspicious of its hold on the mind and spirit, recommended that youths learn just enough music to use it in society and to appreciate it as an art, but not to cultivate it as a profession. Although young women received education in music as well, schooling of all kinds separated the sexes entirely.

**Source:** Johannes Laurentius/bpk, Berlin/Art Resource, NY

One of the works to have survived in ancient Greek notation is the *Epitaph of Seikilos*, so called because it appears on a tombstone inscription. This brief piece, dating from the 1st century C.E., is in the Ionian *tonos*, occupying an octave on E that includes C♯ and F♯, with special prominence given to the pitch A. This last pitch, the middle note of the octave on E, constitutes the *mese* ("mean") of the range. "In all good music," comments the author of the *Problems* (possibly Aristotle), "*mese* occurs frequently, and all good composers have frequent recourse to *mese*, and, if they leave it, they soon return to it, as they do to no other note."[1] Songs like this are known to have been accompanied on the lyre or some similar instrument, but the accompaniment itself was never notated and remains a matter of considerable speculation.

((•● **Listen**

**CD1    Track 1**
**mysearchlab** (with scrolling translation)
EPITAPH OF SEIKILOS
Score Anthology I/1

# MUSIC IN THE ROMAN EMPIRE

Between the 2nd century B.C.E. and the early 1st century C.E., the Greek homeland and the Hellenistic kingdoms of the eastern Mediterranean succumbed to the armies of Rome. By 117 C.E., when it reached its greatest extent, the Roman Empire controlled

## Focus INSTRUMENTS OF ANCIENT ROME

The Romans made significant advances over the Greeks in instrument building. Brass instruments like the tuba and cornu (horn) featured detachable mouthpieces and figured prominently in military life, providing signals to troops in battle. Roman society valued the hydraulic organ in particular. Powered by water pressure created with a bellows, this instrument was used in civic ceremonies and even gladiatorial fights. The statesman and poet Cicero (106–43 B.C.E.) compared the sound of the organ to fine food and associated it with the most sensual feelings.

In 1931, archaeologists working in Budapest, Hungary, discovered substantial portions of a hydraulic organ built in 228 C.E. that had been presented to a company of fire-fighters in the Roman colony of Aquincum. Careful study of the remains of this instrument have shown it to reflect a level of technological sophistication that would not be equaled again until the late Middle Ages. For a modern reconstruction of another hydraulis, discovered recently in Dion, Greece, see http://www.archaeologychannel.org/hydraulisint.html.

**Source:** Strolling masked musicians, scene from a comedy play by Dioskourides of Samos (2nd century BC), found in Villa of Cicero Pompeii (mosaic)/Museo Archeologico Nazionale, Naples, Italy/The Bridgeman Art Library

the entire Mediterranean world and western Europe into Britain. For some 200 years, beginning with the reign of Augustus (27 B.C.E.–14 C.E.), Roman dominion brought stability and prosperity to this region.

Even before they conquered Greece, the Romans had absorbed many aspects of Greek culture, including its music. No Roman music has survived in notated form, yet we know from written accounts that music played an important role in many aspects of Roman life, including the theater and civic ritual. Every religious cult had its own particular repertory of music and instruments. The poet Lucretius (99–55 B.C.E.) described a procession in honor of the goddess Cybele as accompanied by the sound of "tightly stretched drums" that "thunder out as they are struck by the hands of her attendants. Curved cymbals clash, and horns threaten with their harsh wailing. And the hollow flute stirs the heart with Phrygian Tune." Apuleius,

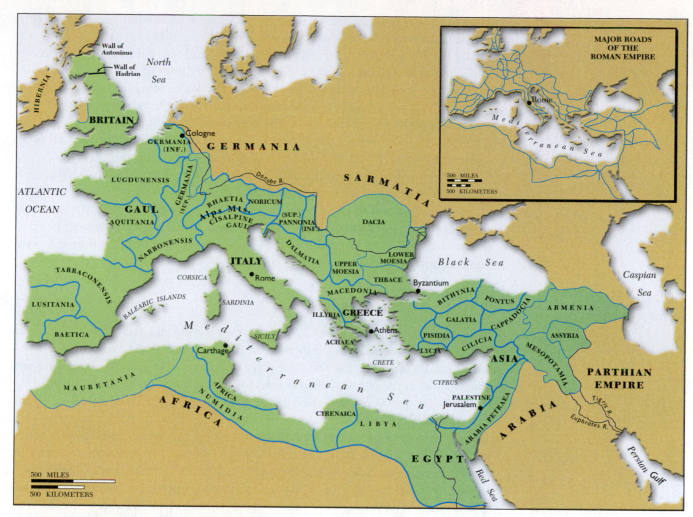

**The Roman Empire at its greatest extent, 117 C.E.**

writing in the 2nd century C.E., left this account of an initiation ritual for the cult of Isis:

> Flutes and pipes and piccolos sounded a very soothing harmony. An attractive choir of carefully chosen boys, radiant in their white vestments, followed, singing a hymn which had been composed by a skillful poet, inspired by the Muses, and which explained the processional rites of this important ceremony. Then came the pipe players dedicated to the cult of mighty Serapis [the Greek equivalent of the Egyptian god Osiris]. Holding their pipes out to the side, toward their right ears, they played a tune usually heard in a temple, by the god.[2]

# THE MUSICAL LEGACIES OF ANTIQUITY

Beginning in the late 3rd century C.E., the Roman Empire entered a long period of decline. Pressured by Germanic invaders on its borders and stagnating economically, it fragmented into two major regions, eastern and western. During this time, Christianity rose to dominance within the empire, ultimately displacing the Greek and Roman pantheon to become the state religion. In 410, the Visigoths sacked Rome, and in 476, with the overthrow of its last emperor, the Western Roman Empire all but vanished.

The Greek-speaking Eastern, or Byzantine, Empire would endure until the fall of its capital, Constantinople (modern Istanbul), to the Turks in 1453.

By the 5th century C.E., the music of antiquity and the oral tradition that accompanied it had also all but vanished. The theoretical writings of antiquity about music, however, continued to be transmitted through the works of such writers as Ptolemy (2nd century C.E.), Aristides Quintilianus (3rd century C.E.), and Alypius (4th century C.E.). These authors were known to such later figures as Boethius (ca. 480–524 C.E.; see Chapter 1) and Cassiodorus (ca. 490–ca. 583 C.E.), who transmitted the basic elements and terminology of Greek and Roman music theory to the medieval era.

Thus, although the music of antiquity was essentially lost to the medieval era, the attitudes of the ancient Greeks and Romans toward music have exerted an unbroken influence on Western thinking about the art down to the present day. Many of these attitudes and beliefs found their expression in myth. Other aspects of ancient perspectives toward music can be gleaned from philosophy, drama, poetry, and through writings concerned directly with music itself.

## Music and the Cosmos

Pythagoras (6th century B.C.E.) is credited with having discovered the relationship between musical sound and number. According to legend, Pythagoras was passing by a blacksmith's forge one day and noticed that hammers of different weights were creating sounds in the intervals of an octave, a fifth, and a fourth. When he weighed the hammers, he discovered that their weight fell into the ratio 2:1 (octave), 3:2 (fifth), and 4:3 (fourth). Because of their mathematical simplicity, these intervals were considered "perfect" consonances. Pythagoras considered the mathematical basis of sound a fundamental law governing the relationship of all physical bodies in the universe. Music, according to this view, is what prevents planets and stars from colliding with one another. The followers of Pythagoras ascribed to him the assertion that "there is a geometry in the humming of the strings; there is music in the spacings of the spheres." There is, in other words, a "harmony of the spheres" based on the mathematical ratios of movement and distance among the heavenly bodies that creates a music of its own—inaudible on earth, unfortunately, but no less real. This belief in the music of the spheres would permeate Western thought for more than 2,000 years. In the late 16th century, for example, William Shakespeare could count on his audiences to understand it in a passage like the following, from *The Merchant of Venice* (Act V, Scene i):

> There's not the smallest orb which thou behold'st
> But in his motion like an angel sings,
> Still quiring to the young ey'd cherubins;
> Such harmony is in immortal souls;
> But, whilst this muddy vesture of decay
> Doth grossly close it in, we cannot hear it.

## Music and the Soul

The same forces perceived to govern the cosmos, including music, were also understood by the ancients to govern the human soul. Music thus had the power to alter behavior in the most fundamental way, creating either harmony or discord within the spirit of the individual.

The myth of Orpheus and Euridice gives powerful expression to this belief. Orpheus was a celebrated musician capable of calming wild beasts with his playing.

When his wife, Euridice, died on their wedding day, he attempted to retrieve her from the underworld, Hades. To do so, he had to persuade the guardians of Hades to allow him—a mortal—to cross into the realm of the dead and then return to life. Charon, the boatman who ferries dead souls across the River Styx, refused this absurd request, but Orpheus's skill on the lyre was so powerful that Charon was overwhelmed and fell into a deep sleep. Orpheus similarly used music to persuade Pluto, god of the underworld, to release Euridice. The story thus suggests that through music, humans can bridge the otherwise unbridgeable divide between life and death.

Like the god Pluto, even the most powerful mortals are helpless to resist the spell of music. Not even the great Odysseus could resist the sirens, whose seductive song lured sailors to dash their boats to pieces on their rock. The goddess Circe warned Odysseus that he could safely pass the sirens only by plugging the ears of his crew with thick wax. Odysseus permitted himself to hear the sirens' song after commanding his men to bind him to the mast of his ship. And according to legend, Alexander the Great, after defeating the Persians, was himself conquered by the power of music. At the banquet celebrating Alexander's victory, the musician Timotheus sang a series of contrasting songs that took the great warrior through a succession of widely different emotional states, from erotic passion to sorrow to fury to joy. The English poet John Dryden captured this story in verse in his ode *Alexander's Feast*, written in 1697, which George Frideric Handel set to music in 1736.

The belief that music has the power to elevate or debase the soul, to enlighten or degrade the mind, was widespread in antiquity and is still current today. The **doctrine of ethos** held that music was capable of arousing listeners to certain kinds of emotions and behaviors. Plato, in the late 4th century B.C.E., recommended that youths learn to make music in the Dorian and Phrygian modes: the former because it imparted courage, the latter because it imparted thoughtfulness. The important point here is not so much exactly what Plato meant by "Dorian" or "Phrygian" as his firm belief that each embodied its own ethical powers that could directly affect human behavior. Plato was by no means alone in this view. Aristotle observed that some modes "make men noticeably mournful and restrained in mood, like the so-called Mixolydian," whereas other modes "soften the temper of the active intelligence. . . . It is the same with rhythms:

**Odysseus and the sirens.** Book 12 of Homer's *Odyssey* emphasizes the overwhelming power of music, both for good and for ill. The sirens—part woman, part bird—sing so beautifully that seafarers forget all worldly concerns and die when their ships strike the nearby rocks. To succumb to the beauty of music means to turn one's back on life. "But if you wish to listen," Circe tells Odysseus, "let the men tie you . . . hand and foot, back to the mast, lashed to the mast, so you may hear those harpies' thrilling voices; shout as you will, begging to be untied, your crew must only twist more line around you and keep their stroke up, till the singers fade." As his crew members continue to row with beeswax in their ears, Odysseus gains wisdom by hearing the sirens' song, all the while straining against and begging to be freed from the ropes.

**Source:** Erich Lessing/British Museum, London, Great Britain/ Art Resource, NY

some have a remarkably stable ethos, others an ethos which stirs the emotions; and of this latter class some are notably vulgar in their emotional effects while others better suit freeborn persons."[3]

## Music and the State

The same powers that affect the individual also affect the state—which is, after all, a collection of individuals. Music education was thus an element of good citizenship in ancient Greece, for youth of both sexes. "Music has the power of producing a certain effect on the moral character of the soul," Aristotle declared, "and if it has the power to do this, it is clear that the young must be directed to music and must be educated in it." His teacher Plato had taken a far more restrictive approach to music education, even while acknowledging its importance:

> The overseers of our state must . . . be watchful against innovations in music and gymnastics counter to the established order, and to the best of their power guard against them. . . . For a change to a new type of music is something to beware of as a hazard of all our fortunes. For the modes of music are never disturbed without unsettling of the most fundamental political and social conventions.[4]

This fear of the subversive power of unfamiliar music (or any music) has cropped up countless times over the centuries. In the 20th century alone, older generations have condemned ragtime (in the 1910s), jazz (1920s), rock and roll (1950s and 1960s), heavy metal (1980s), and rap (1990s) as threats to the morals of American youth. The danger was seen to reside not only in the lyrics but also in the music itself, either because of its rhythm (ragtime, jazz, rock and roll) or volume and timbre (heavy metal). In one way or another, all of these repertories created anxiety about the disruption of the established order.

## Theory versus Practice

One of the most enduring legacies of classical antiquity was its division of music into two distinct categories: theory and practice. This dichotomy still pervades Western attitudes toward music.

Pythagoras and his followers represent the earliest, most extreme, and most influential form of an essentially theoretical approach to the discipline. They were concerned not with the creation or performance of music, but with the discovery of music's essence, its mathematical basis in sound. This conception of music as a means of understanding the cosmos is evident in the ancient world's classification of the discipline within the seven liberal arts.

The liberal arts were those disciplines practiced by individuals who were free— *liber* is the root of our word "liberty"—as opposed to those who were limited by the demands of a particular profession, such as carpentry or blacksmithing. (In later times, it was believed these disciplines could actually make individuals free by liberating them from base instincts and fostering critical thought.) Music in this sense was not the profession of making music, but rather of contemplating it, above all its mathematical proportions. The liberal arts themselves were divided into two categories: the language arts of the *trivium* (grammar, rhetoric, and dialectic) and the mathematical *quadrivium* (arithmetic, geometry, astronomy, and music). The *trivium* comprised the arts of expression and persuasion, but as part of the *quadrivium*, music was considered an art of measurement.

Not all ancient philosophers were as convinced as Pythagoras and his followers that music should be conceived only as a sounding manifestation of abstract number. Aristoxenus (ca. 364 B.C.E.–304 B.C.E.) preferred to base his theories on a mixture of abstract reason and empirical perception. Aristoxenus, a pupil of Aristotle, judged the size of musical intervals by relying to a large extent on his ears, rejecting the exclusively abstract calculations of the Pythagoreans. But Aristoxenus was in the decided minority in his time, and the Pythagorean approach to theory would dominate for many centuries.

## Vocal versus Instrumental Music

In Greek, the word *mousike* was understood to encompass not only elements of melody and rhythm, but also the words being sung and even the dance that might accompany them. Poetry and song, in Greek culture, were virtually indistinguishable. Instrumental music was thus seen as an inherently lesser art than vocal music. It was welcomed in its place but held in lower esteem. Aristotle, for example, argued that vocal music was superior to instrumental music because voices, whether human or animal, are found only in creatures that have a soul.

At the same time, instrumental music was regarded with a certain mixture of awe and suspicion, precisely because it was able to move listeners without recourse to words. Its power, in other words, was inexplicable and in this sense irrational. When Orpheus persuaded the gods of the underworld to breach the boundary between death and life, he did so through the power of melody and rhythm, not through the words of his song. And when this same Orpheus charmed the savage beasts, it was again without recourse to words. A parallel episode can be found in the biblical story of David, who cures Saul of melancholy not with song, but with the music of the harp alone.

Practicing musicians, although widely admired for their performances, were not considered among the intellectual elite: they could entertain, but they could not edify their audiences. Demodocus, who entertained at one of the banquets in the *Odyssey*, held a place of special honor at the Phaeacian court, but he was not among its rulers or leading statesmen.

Instrumental music is so elemental that it works at a level not fully susceptible to rational explanation. This helps explain the uneasy mix of attitudes toward instrumental music—condescension mixed with an acute awareness of its powers—that would characterize Western attitudes for the next 2,000 years.

## SUMMARY

Although the musical repertories of classical antiquity were largely lost to subsequent eras, Greek attitudes toward music established basic patterns of thought that still hold. The Greeks perceived music as both an art and a science, a means of providing pleasure as well as insight into the nature of the universe. They recognized music's ethical and spiritual power and its ability to transcend reason, yet they also recognized its scientific basis in the principles of mathematical proportions. The legacy of classical antiquity would provide a strong foundation for the development of musical thought and practice in the medieval era.

 Study and Review on mysearchlab.com

# Part One
# The Medieval Era

W hat we now call the medieval era spans almost an entire millennium, from the fall of the Western Roman Empire in 476 C.E. until the beginnings of the Renaissance in the early 15th century. *Medieval* means literally "between the ages," and the term was coined by later historians who looked back on these "middle ages" as an era of darkness between two periods of light, classical antiquity and the Renaissance. Those who lived in the medieval era did not see themselves as living "between" anything, of course, and this period was scarcely one of unbroken darkness. To the contrary: the legacies of the Roman Empire were far too deep and widespread to have disappeared entirely, and the architects, painters, poets, and musicians of the medieval era created some of the most breathtaking achievements in human history.

Still, the concept of a medieval era has persisted and it continues to provide a useful shorthand designation for an era that in many ways was undeniably different from what had come before. The five centuries after the fall of Rome were particularly difficult: western Europe experienced a marked decline in political stability, populations declined, infrastructure decayed, and learning of all kinds was lost. Basic engineering skills known in antiquity would not be recovered for almost 1,000 years. Entire libraries disappeared through fire or pillage. The collection of the great library at Alexandria, Egypt, with perhaps as many as 400,000 manuscripts during its glory years, would not be rivaled again for almost 2,000 years. For most of the medieval era, almost no one in western Europe could read ancient Greek; as a result, even those manuscripts by such philosophers as Plato and Aristotle that survived in the West could not be deciphered and were for all practical purposes lost until the later centuries of the era, when Latin translations began to appear. Although scholars in the Greek-speaking Byzantine Empire and in the Islamic world continued to cultivate Greek, contact between Eastern and Western scholars was extremely limited until the late medieval era.

The medieval world was also a dangerous place. Infant mortality was high, and most of those who survived childhood died before age 30. Diseases like dysentery, typhus, and smallpox posed a constant threat, and plagues were a recurring feature

◄ **The three varieties of music.** This frontispiece to one of the most important sources of early polyphony, the Florence manuscript of the 13th-century *Magnus liber organi*, illustrates what medieval thinkers believed to be the three varieties of music. The figure on the left in each of the three panels is Musica. In the top panel, she points with her fully extended wand to an illustration of the four elements—earth, water, air, and fire (the stars)—representing music in its highest form: *musica mundana*, the "harmony of the spheres," created by the mathematical ratios of movement and distance among the heavenly bodies. The belief in this kind of music, inaudible to the human ear, dates back to the ancient Greeks. In the middle panel, Musica points with her partially extended wand to four figures with their hands intertwined. These represent *musica humana* ("human music"), a harmonizing force that unites reason with the body, spirit with matter. *Musica humana* is also inaudible to human ears. In the bottom panel, Musica, with her wand retracted, gestures admonishingly to a man surrounded by musical instruments and playing a vielle. This image represents *musica instrumentalis* ("sounding music"), music in its lowest form, but also the only one of the three that can be heard by mortals.

**Source:** Firenze, Biblioteca Medicea Laurenziana/Ministry for Cultural Affairs/Med. Palat. 87, c. 121v.

of life. Travelers moved in large groups whenever they could to protect themselves against vagabonds and brigands. The rule of law was little more than an abstract idea in many corners of the continent.

Many men and women withdrew from the secular world altogether and devoted themselves to the church. Self-sufficient monastic communities dotted the European countryside. In England alone there were some 500 monasteries by the beginning of the 14th century. The Benedictines, Carmelites, Dominicans, Franciscans, and other orders varied in their forms of worship and routines, but all were devoted to the principle of monasticism, a way of life based on a vow of poverty, chastity, and obedience. Monastic communities served as the primary repositories of learning in the medieval world. Devoting themselves to lives of prayer and labor, monks and nuns prepared, collected, and preserved manuscripts of all kinds, including treatises on philosophy, medicine, law, astronomy, and mathematics—topics having little or nothing to do with religion or theology.

New political entities arose to fill the vacuum left by the collapse of Rome. The most powerful of these was that of Charlemagne, the ruler of the Franks. His realm extended across what is now France, western and central Germany, Austria, Switzerland, and northern Italy. Charlemagne consolidated his powers through a strategic alliance with the papacy and, on Christmas Day in 800, he was crowned in Rome by Pope Leo III as "Sovereign of the Roman Empire." He ruled from Aix-la-Chapelle (now Aachen, in western Germany), where he sought to follow the Roman model and reimpose strong centralized authority with a single set of laws within his dominions. As part of this effort, he sought to standardize the forms of Christian worship, and in the process exerted a profound effect on the development of sacred music (see Chapter 1).

But Charlemagne's empire did not survive him. By the end of the 9th century his domain had been divided in three, with the Kingdom of France to the west, the Kingdom of Italy to the south, and the East Frankish Kingdom to the east. The last of

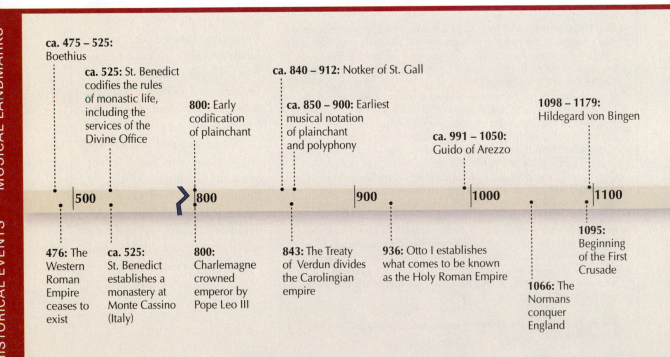

**MEDIEVAL TIMELINE**

**MUSICAL LANDMARKS**

ca. 475 – 525: Boethius

ca. 525: St. Benedict codifies the rules of monastic life, including the services of the Divine Office

800: Early codification of plainchant

ca. 840 – 912: Notker of St. Gall

ca. 850 – 900: Earliest musical notation of plainchant and polyphony

ca. 991 – 1050: Guido of Arezzo

1098 – 1179: Hildegard von Bingen

500 | 800 | 900 | 1000 | 1100

**HISTORICAL EVENTS**

476: The Western Roman Empire ceases to exist

ca. 525: St. Benedict establishes a monastery at Monte Cassino (Italy)

800: Charlemagne crowned emperor by Pope Leo III

843: The Treaty of Verdun divides the Carolingian empire

936: Otto I establishes what comes to be known as the Holy Roman Empire

1066: The Normans conquer England

1095: Beginning of the First Crusade

these emerged as the center of the Holy Roman Empire, a loose confederation of states that, as the 18th-century French philosopher Voltaire famously quipped, was "neither holy, nor Roman, nor an Empire." It was an essentially German entity that extended into what is now northern Italy. Weakened by a conflict with the papacy over the control of the territory around Rome and over the power to designate high-ranking church officials, the empire soon lost its cohesion. The emperor himself exercised only nominal authority and was elected by a small group of princes. The empire had no fixed capital but was ruled instead from whatever happened to be the home of the monarch at the time. Charles IV, for example, ruled from Prague in the years 1355 to 1378, and various emperors were crowned in such diverse places as Aix-la-Chapelle, Rome, and Mainz.

The looseness of this confederation was a political liability, but it proved an enormous boon to the arts, including music. Every one of the hundreds of duchies, principalities, and kingdoms across central and southern Europe employed its share of painters, poets, and musicians. By the end of the medieval era, the courts rivaled and in some respects even surpassed the church in the composition and consumption of new music.

While Germany fragmented, France and England began to emerge as centralized nation-states under the leadership of increasingly powerful monarchies. Here too, the arts flourished under the courts of kings and powerful nobles. The Duchy of Burgundy in eastern France was particularly hospitable to painting, poetry, and music in the 14th and 15th centuries before being absorbed into the Kingdom of France in 1477.

Medieval society was shaped by the system of feudalism, whose economic foundation was the self-sufficient estate, or manor. The peasants who worked the lands of the manor swore allegiance and service to the lord of the manor, who might in turn be the vassal of a more powerful noble. The peasants kept a portion of the harvest and submitted the remainder to the lord. In this highly decentralized system, economic and legal authority resided in a nearby castle rather than at some distant court. The steady growth of population and prosperity in the centuries after 1000 would ultimately spell

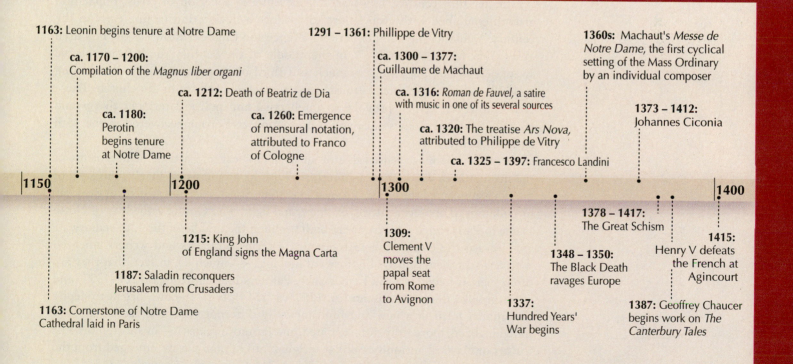

**1163:** Leonin begins tenure at Notre Dame

**ca. 1170 – 1200:** Compilation of the *Magnus liber organi*

**ca. 1180:** Perotin begins tenure at Notre Dame

**ca. 1212:** Death of Beatriz de Dia

**ca. 1260:** Emergence of mensural notation, attributed to Franco of Cologne

**1291 – 1361:** Phillippe de Vitry

**ca. 1300 – 1377:** Guillaume de Machaut

**ca. 1316:** *Roman de Fauvel*, a satire with music in one of its several sources

**ca. 1320:** The treatise *Ars Nova*, attributed to Philippe de Vitry

**ca. 1325 – 1397:** Francesco Landini

**1360s:** Machaut's *Messe de Notre Dame*, the first cyclical setting of the Mass Ordinary by an individual composer

**1373 – 1412:** Johannes Ciconia

1150      1200      1300      1400

**1215:** King John of England signs the Magna Carta

**1187:** Saladin reconquers Jerusalem from Crusaders

**1163:** Cornerstone of Notre Dame Cathedral laid in Paris

**1309:** Clement V moves the papal seat from Rome to Avignon

**1337:** Hundred Years' War begins

**1348 – 1350:** The Black Death ravages Europe

**1378 – 1417:** The Great Schism

**1387:** Geoffrey Chaucer begins work on *The Canterbury Tales*

**1415:** Henry V defeats the French at Agincourt

the demise of the feudal system. As agricultural productivity increased and trade began to expand, towns and cities replaced the castle as the central marketplace for goods and services.

Courtly life revolved around a highly stylized code of conduct. In public, love could be expressed passionately but only from a distance: the ideal knight paid homage to a lady of noble birth by dedicating himself to her service and offering lavish poetry and song in her praise—but never directly. The idea of courtly love in its purest form always involved self-contained torment. The object of desire was either a maiden or a married woman, but in either case unattainable by the strictures of social convention. In this context, love took on a kind of abstract, almost religious quality. Indeed, many poems and songs in praise of "my lady" can be understood as being directed toward either the Virgin Mary or an earthly noblewoman.

The year 1000 proved to be a milestone in history. Many feared the millennium would bring the end of the world. Instead, it marked the beginning of a wave of energy and optimism. The later centuries of the medieval era witnessed notable advancements in technology, architecture, education, and the arts. The horizontal loom, operated by foot treadles and vastly more efficient than its predecessors, came into widespread use in the 11th century; magnetic compasses and windmills first appeared in the 12th century; and paper, already common in Arabic lands for several centuries, was being produced in quantity in Europe by the 13th century.

Increasing prosperity and confidence combined with an upsurge in religious zeal in the late 11th century inspired a series of military ventures to reclaim the Holy Land from Muslim rule. The First Crusade, launched by Pope Urban II in 1095, succeeded in capturing Jerusalem, if only for a short time. Over the next 300 years various Christian rulers would try repeatedly to duplicate this feat, but without success. Although a failure from a military point of view, the Crusades had the unintended benefit of bringing the West into closer contact with Islamic culture, which for centuries had been cultivating such disciplines as philosophy, astronomy, mathematics (particularly algebra), and medicine.

In the 14th century, however, Europe entered a period of crisis. Population growth combined with crop failure to produce a devastating famine early in the century. A debilitating conflict between France and England known as the Hundred Years' War broke out in 1337. In the middle of the century the bubonic plague swept across Europe, killing as much as a third of its population. And beginning in 1378, conflicting claimants to the papacy created a schism in the church. These crises, however, helped provoke an intellectual and political ferment that would contribute to the Renaissance and Reformation as Europe recovered in the 15th and 16th centuries.

Perhaps the most remarkable of all technological and artistic achievements of the medieval era was Gothic architecture. With its emphasis on height, this style of building supplanted the earlier Romanesque style. Squat, compact structures gave way to buildings of unprecedented size, grace, and light. The Gothic cathedrals of Notre Dame in Paris and in Chartres were both begun in the middle of the 12th century.

Toward the end of the 13th century, a series of artists and writers emerged whose works seem remarkably forward looking—so much so, in fact, that they are often seen as heralds of the Renaissance. Painters like Giotto (ca. 1267–1337) and sculptors like Giovanni Pisano (ca. 1250–ca. 1314), both Italians, began to depict the human form in a new and fundamentally different way. The faces are more individualized, more fully differentiated, and far more realistic—in short, more like the art of classical antiquity. Similar insights into human nature emerged from the work of poets like Dante Alighieri (1265–1321), Giovanni Boccaccio (1313–1375),

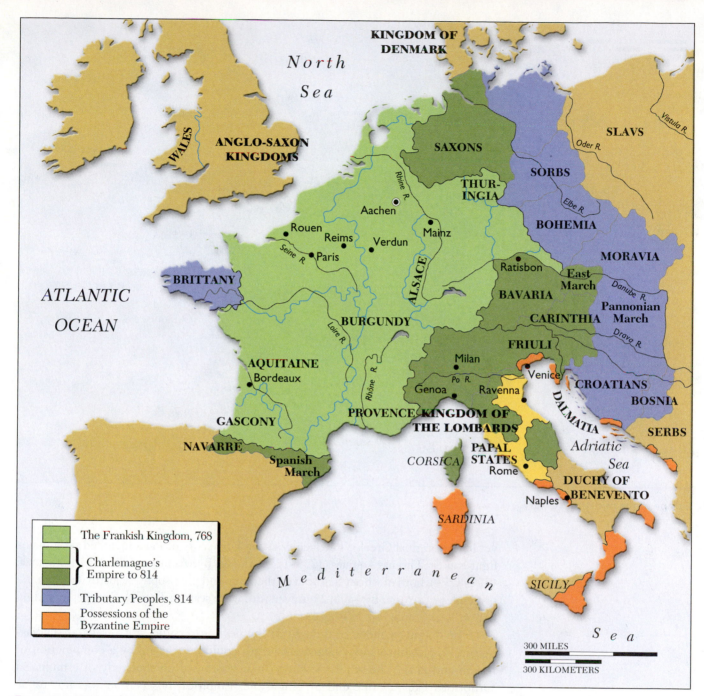

**Europe, ca. 768–814.**

and Geoffrey Chaucer (1342–1400), who produced works of striking originality not in the international language of Latin, but in the vernacular languages of Italian and English.

The pace of learning as a whole gradually accelerated from the 12th century onward. The chief centers of scholarship began to shift from the church to newly emerging universities, many of which grew out of cathedral schools. The earliest universities—most notably in Bologna and Paris, both founded around the middle of the 12th century—focused chiefly on the study of theology, law, and medicine, but students in different fields often read the same authors. The most important of these was Aristotle, whose works were becoming more widely known at this time (although not

**Europe in the mid-14th century.**

yet in the original Greek). The faculty at the University of Paris included such major figures as St. Thomas Aquinas (1225–1274) and St. Bonaventure (Giovanni di Fidanza, 1221–1274), both of whom synthesized theology and philosophy to justify faith on the principles of reason. By 1300, 23 universities were scattered across Europe, including Oxford and Cambridge in England.

The dominant mode of thought in the new universities was known as scholasticism. Its proponents maintained that truth could be reached by a combination of reason and faith. The scholastic curriculum was based on the study of established authorities like Aristotle and St. Augustine. Empirical observation was not to be trusted, for the medieval mind was deeply suspicious of worldly appearances. Life on earth, after all, was considered transitory and decidedly inferior to the higher truths of divine eternity. Music was an important object of study in the new universities, but not musical performance. In the tradition of Pythagoras and the quadrivium, music was understood as a mathematical discipline—related more to geometry and astronomy than poetry or drama—that provided a source of insight into the relationship between numbers and the cosmos.

This preoccupation with theory at the expense of performance undermined the unwritten traditions of performance that might otherwise have survived between the musical practices of ancient and medieval worlds. The phenomenon of the sung drama was gone by the 5th century, as was the ability to read ancient musical notation. A new system of notation would not begin to emerge until the 9th century, and

**The two sides of music.** This miniature from an early-12th-century manuscript shows two contrasting approaches to the art of music. King David (top) represents musicians who understand their art. The figure at the top left plays chime bells of varying sizes, suggesting Pythagorean proportions; with his right hand he plucks a monochord, a device with a single string used to measure the ratios of sound according to the mathematical divisions of the string. Below him, two men provide the wind for a medieval organ by alternating pressure on the paired bellows; the organ itself is played on a set of levers, a precursor to the keyboard. The singers to the right read from notated music. In the image at bottom, a beast makes music, beating on a simple drum. No written music is in sight, and the acrobats in the lower left do somersaults. The two scenes reflect the medieval belief in the superiority of theory over practice. They conjure up Guido of Arezzo's derisive distinction between a *musicus* and a *cantor*: "There is a great distance between a musician and singer/The latter says, the former understands what constitutes music./ For whoever does things without understanding them, is by definition a beast."

**Source:** Reprinted by permission of the Master and Fellows of St. John's College, Cambridge University Library

although elements of ancient musical theory endured through the writings of a few authors, their works were known to only a few and understood by fewer. The writings of the single most important theorist of the early medieval period, Manlius Severinus Boethius (480–524), for example, remained in obscurity until the 9th century.

The musical practices of the medieval era are thus difficult to reconstruct. Not until the late 9th century do we have notated sources of any kind, and even these are rare. Few manuscripts have survived the ravages of time. One very important early source of liturgical music, a manuscript known as Chartres 47, was destroyed by fire as recently as World War II. Fortunately, its contents had already been photographed. Yet we know any number of medieval works by the thread of a single source, and we can imagine all too easily the quantity of music that has been lost. And much of medieval music was never written down at all. From all that we know about the music of the minstrels, it seems clear that most of this repertory was improvised, produced on the spot for the lords and ladies of a particular court as the occasion demanded.

The medieval era covers almost 1,000 years. Not surprisingly, the music of this period is extremely diverse, ranging from monophonic plainchant, first consolidated sometime around the 6th or 7th century, to the intricate polyphony of the 13th and early 14th centuries. And the range of music that has survived is amply sufficient to reveal a richly varied musical culture that established basic concepts and techniques we take for granted today: notation, polyphony, and an elaborate theory by which to rationalize both the art and science of music.

## *Primary Evidence*　THREE CATEGORIES OF MUSICIANS

*In his* De institutione musica *("Fundamentals of Music"), written in the early 6th century and widely read from the 9th century onward, Boethius answers the question "What is a musician?" by dividing those who deal with music into three classes. His distinction between theory and practice is a legacy of antiquity that would continue to influence the subsequent history of music.*

■ ■ ■

Thus, there are three classes of those who are engaged in the musical art. The first class consists of those who perform on instruments, the second of those who compose songs, and the third of those who judge instrumental performance and song.

But those of the class which is dependent upon instruments and who spend their entire effort there—such as kitharists and those who prove their skill on the organ and other musical instruments—are excluded from comprehension of musical knowledge, since, as was said, they act as slaves. None of them makes use of reason; rather, they are totally lacking in thought.

The second class of those practicing music is that of the poets, a class led to song not so much by thought and reason as by a certain natural instinct. For this reason this class, too, is separated from music.

The third class is that which acquires an ability for judging, so that it can carefully weigh rhythms and melodies and the composition as whole. This class, since it is totally grounded in reason and thought, will rightly be esteemed as musical. That person is a musician who exhibits the faculty of forming judgments according to speculation or reason relative and appropriate to music concerning modes and rhythms, the genera of songs, consonances, and all the things which are to be explained subsequently, as well as concerning the songs of the poets.

**Source:** Ancius Manlius Severinus Boethius, *Fundamentals of Music,* trans. Calvin M. Bower, ed. Claude V. Palisca (New Haven: Yale University Press, 1989), p. 51.

# Plainchant and Secular Monophony

The earliest notated repertories of medieval music are monophonic. The oldest sources of **plainchant**—the monophonic sacred music of the Christian church—date from the last quarter of the 9th century; the first notated secular monophonic songs are found in manuscripts written about a century later. Both repertories flourished long before the emergence of notation, however, which makes it difficult to reconstruct their early history.

## THE EMERGENCE OF PLAINCHANT

Although it is often called **Gregorian chant,** after its supposed creator, Pope Gregory I, plainchant existed well before his reign (590–604), and its development continued long afterward.

The origins and evolution of plainchant are inextricably linked to the development of the Christian liturgy—that is, the body of texts and actions prescribed for Christian worship services. Christianity originated as a sect of Judaism, and the earliest Christians preserved many of the traditions and practices of Jewish worship: the offering of prayers, the singing of hymns, and the systematic recitation or singing of psalms and other passages from Holy Scripture. The Eucharistic **Mass**, or celebration of Holy Communion, although a distinctively Christian practice, also has Jewish roots. It is a ritual-istic reenactment of the Last Supper, Christ's celebration of the Jewish feast of Passover with his disciples the day before his crucifixion.

The singing of psalms was particularly important in the early church. Indeed the Old Testament Book of Psalms itself demands this practice, as a few examples make clear:

> O come, let us sing unto the Lord; let us make a joyful noise to the rock of our salvation. Let us come before his presence with thanksgiv-ing, and make a joyful noise unto him with psalms. (Psalm 95)

> O sing unto the Lord a new song. . . . Sing unto the Lord with the harp; with the harp and the voice of a psalm. (Psalm 98)

> O give thanks unto the Lord. . . . Sing unto him, sing psalms unto him. (Psalm 105)

The New Testament reinforced this tradition. Saint Paul admonishes the faith-ful to "Let the word of Christ dwell in you richly in all wisdom; teaching and admonishing one another in psalms and hymns and spiritual songs, singing with grace in your hearts to the Lord" (Colossians 3:16).

The patriarchs of the early church recognized the power of music to project the words of psalms and hymns with heightened intensity. "To chant well is to pray twice," observed Saint Augustine (354–430), the bishop of the North African city of Hippo and a major figure in the early church.

At the same time, church leaders had qualms about mixing words and music in worship. The music, they worried, could distract listeners from the message of the text. Such ambivalence toward music in the liturgy would emerge repeatedly throughout the history of Christianity. Saint Basil (ca. 330–379), addressing this concern, rationalized the singing of psalms in this manner:

> What did the Holy Spirit do when he saw that the human race was not led easily to virtue, and that due to our penchant for pleasure we gave little heed to an upright life? He mixed sweetness of melody with doctrine so that inadvertently we would absorb the benefit of the words through gentleness and ease of hearing, just as clever physicians frequently smear the cup with honey when giving the fastidious some rather bitter medicine to drink. Thus he contrived for us these harmonious psalm tunes, so that those who are children in actual age as well as those who are young in behavior, while appearing only to sing would in reality be training their souls. For not one of these many indifferent people ever leaves church easily retaining in memory some maxim of either the Apostles or the Prophets, but they do sing the texts of the Psalms at home and circulate them in the marketplace.[1]

"Even a forceful lesson does not always endure," Saint Basil concluded, "but what enters the mind with joy and pleasure somehow becomes more firmly impressed upon it." Saint Augustine was not quite so optimistic. Music could indeed uplift the spirit, he argued, but it could also seduce listeners with its easy pleasure (see Primary Evidence: The Seductive Power of Music).

In spite of such misgivings, most leaders of the early church acknowledged the power of rhythm and melody to reinforce the word and cultivated liturgical song. But none of this earliest chant was notated, and we have only tantalizing references to it. We know much more about the texts that were set to music than we do about the music itself, which was passed on from one generation to the next in a process of oral transmission. As Isidore of Seville (ca. 560–636) observed, "Because sound is a sense impression, it vanishes as time passes and is imprinted upon the memory. . . . If a man does not remember sounds they perish, for they cannot be written down."[2]

Surviving accounts document a wide diversity of liturgical and musical practices during Christianity's first 600 years. The church lacked a strong central authority, and liturgical and musical practices varied considerably from place to place. By the 7th century, several distinct rites had established themselves in the West. The most important of these were the Roman, the Ambrosian (used in northern Italy and named after Saint Ambrose, who died in 397), the Gallican (in Frankish lands of what is now France and western Germany), and the Mozarabic or Visigothic (on the Iberian Peninsula). Each of these rites maintained its own liturgy and repertory of chants.

How, then, did a comprehensive and unified repertory of plainchant come into existence? The answer is inextricably linked to the establishment of the Roman rite as the primary liturgy of the church. From the early 7th century onward, successive popes—the bishops of Rome—asserted their primacy within the Western church,

## Primary Evidence    THE SEDUCTIVE POWER OF MUSIC

*Saint Augustine (354–430) was the bishop of the North African city of Hippo from 391 until his death. A prolific writer and influential thinker, he is considered a founder of Christian theology. In this passage from his autobiographical Confessions, he struggles with the role of music in worship, remaining ambivalent about it. To the extent that it opens the mind of the worshipper to the meaning of the text it conveys—"the words which give it life"—it is, he admits, good. But to the extent that it enthralls the worshipper with its own seductive sensuousness, he condemns it as an invitation to sin.*

■ ■ ■

I used to be much more fascinated by the pleasures of sound than the pleasures of smell. I was enthralled by them, but you [God] broke my bonds and set me free. I admit that I still find some enjoyment in the music of hymns, which are alive with your praises, when I hear them sung by well trained, melodious voices. But I do not enjoy it so much that I cannot tear myself away. I can leave it when I wish. But if I am not to turn a deaf ear to music, which is the setting for the words which give it life, I must allow it a position of some honor in my heart, and I find it difficult to assign it to its proper place. For sometimes I feel that I treat it with more honor than it deserves. I realize that when they are sung these sacred words stir my mind to greater religious fervor and kindle in me a more ardent flame of piety than they would if they were not sung; and I also know that there are particular modes in song and in the voice, corresponding to my various emotions and able to stimulate them because of some mysterious relationship between the two. But I ought not to allow my mind to be paralyzed by the gratification of my senses, which often leads it astray. For the senses are not content to take second place. Simply because I allow them their due, as adjuncts to reason, they attempt to take precedence and forge ahead of it, with the result that I sometimes sin in this way but am not aware of it until later.

Sometimes, too, from over-anxiety to avoid this particular trap I make the mistake of being too strict. When this happens, I have no wish but to exclude from my ears, and from the ears of the Church as well, all the melody of those lovely chants to which the Psalms of David are habitually sung; and it seems safer to me to follow the precepts which I remember often having heard ascribed to Athanasius, bishop of Alexandria, who used to oblige the lectors to recite the psalms with such slight modulation of the voice that they seemed to be speaking rather than chanting. But when I remember the tears that I shed on hearing the songs of the Church in the early days, soon after I had recovered my faith, and when I realized that nowadays it is not the singing that moves me but the meaning of the words when they are sung in a clear voice to the most appropriate tune, I again acknowledge the great value of this practice. So I waver between the danger that lies in gratifying the senses and the benefits which, as I know from experience, can accrue from singing. Without committing myself to an irrevocable opinion, I am inclined to approve of the custom of singing in church, in order that by indulging the ears weaker spirits may be inspired with feelings of devotion. Yet when I find the singing itself more moving than the truth which it conveys, I confess that this is a grievous sin, and at those times I would prefer not to hear the singer.

**Source:** Saint Augustine, *Confessions*, Book X, 33, trans. and ed. R. S. Pine-Coffin (London: Penguin Books, 1961), pp. 238–9.

and in so doing vigorously promoted the export of the Roman liturgy and with it a standardized body of chant. In the absence of musical notation, the popes relied on specially trained singer-clerics to carry this repertory of chant to distant realms. By the late 9th century, the legend had emerged that Pope Gregory I (Saint Gregory the Great), who reigned from 590 to 604, had been responsible not only for promoting the diffusion of the Roman liturgy, but for composing the chants himself, inspired by the Holy Spirit. Like all myths, this one had a basis in reality, for unquestionably an earlier pope had brought a substantial degree of order to what must have been a widely diverse body of melodies and texts. Possibly it was Gregory I, who had indeed been instrumental in establishing papal authority and who had sponsored a mission to distant England. Or it may have been another Gregory, Pope Gregory II, also a

**Pope Gregory and the Holy Spirit.** Pope Gregory I, according to legend, received the corpus of plainchant through the agency of the Holy Spirit, who visited him in the form of a dove and whispered the chant melodies into his ear. To the medieval mind, the legend was a reality and a cornerstone of the belief that the repertory of plainchant was a sacred gift. The image here is anachronistic insofar as no system of musical notation existed during the time of Pope Gregory I's reign (590–604). The earliest surviving notated sources date from about 300 years later. The curtain represents the distance between the simple scribe and the pope who would later become a saint. According to the legend, the scribe, puzzled by the pope's long intervals of silence while dictating the chant, peeked behind the screen and saw Gregory receiving the chant from the Holy Spirit.

**Source:** Universitätsbibliothek/akg-images

strong promoter of Roman primacy, who reigned from 715 to 731. Without notated sources, and in the absence of further documentation, we will probably never know with certainty exactly who played what role in the early dissemination of a unified plainchant repertory.

We do know, however, that this early consolidation of the chant was not universally accepted, at least not immediately. The Gallican, Ambrosian, and Mozarabic rites and their associated plainchant repertories continued to flourish alongside the Roman liturgy and its chants. It was ultimately not a pope, but a secular ruler, Charlemagne, who realized the papal goal of a primarily Roman liturgy in the West.

Charlemagne's coronation as emperor by Pope Leo III in Rome in 800 consummated an alliance between the papacy and the most powerful secular kingdom in the West. The church, in effect, validated Charlemagne's power, and Charlemagne, in turn, supported the authority of the church. The emperor devoted considerable energy to the administration of his far-flung territories. He recognized that a unified liturgy—along with a unified body of music—would go a long way toward solidifying both the idea and practice of central authority. With the aid of the papacy, Charlemagne eventually succeeded in imposing a single, more or less standard liturgy—the Roman liturgy—throughout his empire. The Mozarabic and Ambrosian liturgies never disappeared entirely, but their use declined significantly.

Although the evidence is sketchy, most scholars now believe that Charlemagne instigated an even more comprehensive codification of the core repertory of plainchant than that accomplished under earlier popes. One prominent scholar has recently argued that a notated form of these chants must have been prepared by the end of Charlemagne's life, but that it and the subsequent sources from the next century or more have since been lost. This hypothesis has merit. Certainly a great many manuscripts have been lost, and these could have included ones with notated chant. Yet it seems equally plausible that the chant repertory continued to be transmitted entirely by word of mouth for well over a century.

In either case, the absence of written plainchant melodies from Charlemagne's time prevents us from understanding the early history of plainchant with much precision. The liturgical books, decrees, and accounts that have survived suggest the repertory Charlemagne had distributed throughout his empire was not the original Roman chant but rather a Frankish reworking of it. In promulgating the Roman liturgy, in other words, Charlemagne's administrators substantially modified the music of that liturgy. We also know that Charlemagne established several singing schools to teach the chant to choirmasters, who in turn took these melodies (either memorized or notated) back to their home churches. The most important of these singing schools were in Metz (in what is now eastern France) and St. Gall (in what is now eastern Switzerland). Charlemagne further ordered that "in every bishop's see instruction shall be given in the psalms, musical notation, chant, the computation of the years and seasons, and grammar."[3]

To judge from the earliest preserved notated chant sources, which date from the beginning of the 10th century, Charlemagne largely succeeded in his attempt to unify the corpus of liturgical music used throughout his realm. Notation emerged gradually in different forms in different places—an Aquitanian manuscript from southern France, for example, uses a set of note shapes unlike those found in Beneventan manuscripts of southern Italy—yet the repertory transcribed by these apparently independent sources is remarkably consistent from place to place. In the oldest known layer of plainchant melodies, disagreements among sources tend to be insignificant. One source might fill in an interval of a third that others leave open, but this hardly constitutes a substantial change to the nature of the melody.

If these chants were indeed disseminated by word of mouth, as most scholars believe, their preservation represents a remarkable feat of collective memory. It may seem unlikely that thousands of chants could be learned and transmitted orally for two centuries or more without any significant deterioration of their integrity. Memory, however, was a skill cultivated far more intensively in medieval times than in our own. The monks and clerics who transmitted these chants sang them on a regular basis week after week, month after month, year after year. They viewed them not merely as a repertory of songs to be learned but as objects of intense devotion—sacred relics—passed down from none other than Saint Gregory himself. A single chant melody, moreover, might serve more than 50 different liturgical texts, reducing the total number of melodies to be memorized. Finally, many chants rest on melodic fragments that are formulaic in one way or another—that is, they are made up of subunits whose shape follows an established pattern.

The ability of singers to learn and memorize the chant repertory without musical notation helps explain why notation itself was so slow to develop. In this sense, the real puzzle is why notation ever emerged at all. Perhaps it resulted from the desire to set down in writing an object—the chant—considered to be divinely inspired. It seems not to have been connected with the rise of polyphony, whose earliest forms were apparently also performed without the aid of notation. Whatever the reason, the emergence of notation changed the way in which music was both created and transmitted.

Early chant notation was based on signs known as **neumes** that indicate the pitches or groups of pitches in a chant melody. The word derives from the Greek *neuma* meaning "gesture," and most of the signs do in fact point, or gesture, in the direction of the pitches they represent, either singly or in groups of two, three, or four. Various forms of neumes used throughout Europe resembled one another fairly closely. The following diagram gives the Latin names of seven neume forms and compares the way they appear in manuscripts from two different early sources: the monastery of St. Gall in Switzerland and the Aquitaine region of France. The fourth column shows how the same neumes appear in modern plainchant notation as presented in the 19th century by the monks of Solesmes, France, and sanctioned by the Vatican. The last column shows the pitch contours transcribed in conventional modern notation.

In the earliest notated chant manuscripts, like the 10th-century example from St. Gall shown here, the neumes indicate only relative movement—three notes up, a skip downward, an ascent of four notes—not specific pitches. They are thus at best memory aids for singers already familiar with the melodies they record. These manuscripts almost certainly were not used in performance because they show none of the telltale wear that would have resulted from such use, such as finger smudges or candle wax.

During the 11th century, some scribes began to align neumes according to their pitch above and below an imaginary line. At about this same time, still other scribes began to add a single line or a pair of lines to indicate a fixed pitch or pitches. In a Gradual copied in the 11th or 12th century, for example, we find a much more careful placement of neumes around two lines, the upper one labeled as C (middle C), the lower one labeled as F (below middle C). These early **diastematic**, or **heightened neumes**, provide a far better sense of pitches, although even this kind of notation is still not entirely unambiguous. Only much later, in the 13th and 14th centuries, do we begin to see sources with pitches clearly notated on a full set of staff lines. These later diastematic sources nevertheless confirm the remarkable consistency of the plainchant repertory throughout medieval Europe.

### Selected neumes found in chant manuscripts

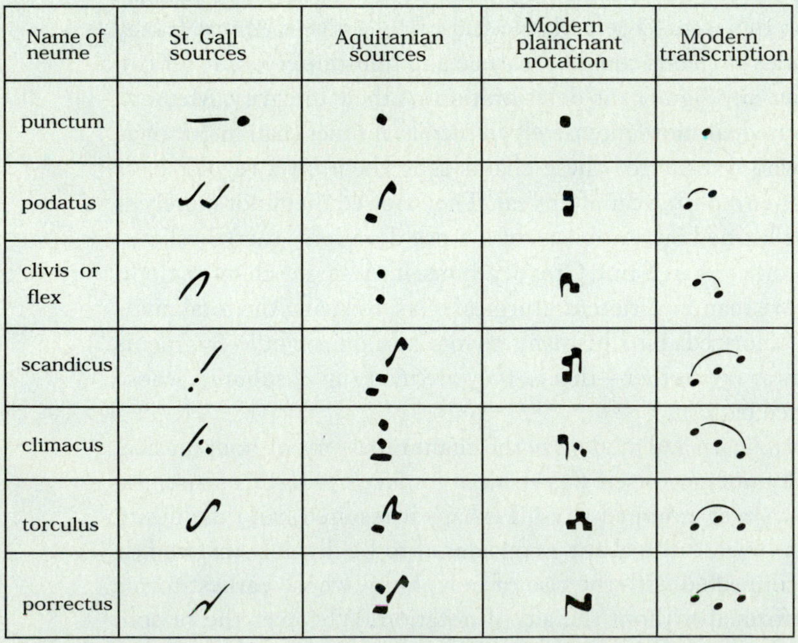

| Name of neume | St. Gall sources | Aquitanian sources | Modern plainchant notation | Modern transcription |
|---|---|---|---|---|
| punctum | | | | |
| podatus | | | | |
| clivis or flex | | | | |
| scandicus | | | | |
| climacus | | | | |
| torculus | | | | |
| porrectus | | | | |

*Focus* continued

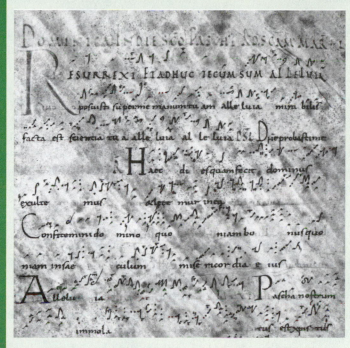

**Non-diastematic chant notation.** The neumes of the earliest notated sources, originally from the Benedictine abbey of St. Gall (now Switzerland), indicate the general contours but not the actual pitches of the chants. Shown here is the Introit, Gradual, and Alleluia for the Mass for Easter Sunday from one of the earliest notated chant manuscripts that has survived in its entirety—Laon 239—believed to have been copied in eastern France some time around 930.

**Source:** Bibliotheque Municipale de Laon, France/Ms 239, folio 52

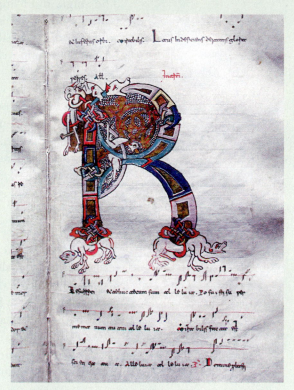

**Partially diastematic chant notation.** The opening of the Easter Sunday Introit *Resurrexi* in this chant manuscript copied in southern Italy in the 11th or 12th century illustrates the emerging technique of diastematic chant notation. The scribe has used a straight line labeled with an F-clef to indicate a fixed pitch and has meticulously arranged the Beneventan neumes to reflect their relative position in relation to this pitch. The spectacularly elaborate initial "R" (for "Resurrexi") reflects the special importance of the feast day of Easter.

**Source:** Biblioteca Capitolare, Benevento, Italy, Codex VI-34, fol. 123 recto/photo © 2002 Antonio Citrigno

# THE ELEMENTS OF PLAINCHANT

Plainchant is pure melody, with no harmony, accompaniment, or added voices. Analyzing it requires a different set of criteria than that used for most other kinds of music. Five elements in particular are key to understanding plainchant:

- Liturgical function
- The relationship of words and music
- Mode
- Melodic structure
- Rhythm

Let us consider each of these elements in detail.

## Liturgical Function

The single most important factor defining the nature of any given chant melody is its function within the liturgy. A basic understanding of the Christian liturgy is therefore essential to understanding the musical styles of chant. The two main forms of worship were the Divine Office, a series of services held at specified times throughout the day, and the Mass, a ritual reenactment of Christ's Last Supper with his disciples.

In its broadest outlines, the liturgy of Western Christianity remained essentially consistent throughout western Europe from the time of Charlemagne's imposition of the Roman liturgy early in the 9th century until the Reformation in the 16th century. Variations in local custom notwithstanding, a Mass celebrated in Paris followed basically the same format as one celebrated in London or Rome. A Vespers service sung in Antwerp was essentially the same as one sung in Madrid. Even the language—Latin—was universal.

**The Divine Office.** The **Divine Office** (also known as simply the **Office;** the term derives from the Latin *officium*, meaning "duty") owes much to the traditions of Jewish worship, which featured a fixed daily schedule of prayer and the singing of psalms. The Rule of Saint Benedict—the regulations governing monastic life promulgated by Saint Benedict (ca. 480–ca. 547)—codified the basic structure and content of the eight services that comprise the Office. The Office was observed primarily by cloistered monks and nuns rather than the laity. Local practices varied considerably and changed over time, but here is the general outline:

| | |
|---|---|
| Matins: during the night (2 or 3 A.M.) | Sext: at noon |
| Lauds: at dawn | None: at 3 P.M. |
| Prime: at 6 A.M. | Vespers: at sunset |
| Terce: at 9 A.M. | Compline: before bedtime |

These services varied considerably in length, from as little as 20 minutes (Prime, Terce, Sext, None) to as much as 2 or 3 hours (Matins); Lauds, Vespers, and Compline generally ran from a half hour to an hour. Regardless of length, every service centered on the recitation of psalms and included the singing of at least one **strophic** hymn (a hymn with each stanza set to the same melody) as well as readings from the scripture, which in turn were followed by a sung response. Some Offices included canticles, biblical passages not from the Psalms but recited or sung as such. Under the Rule of Saint Benedict, the entire Book of Psalms—all 150 of them—was recited once each week over the course of the Divine Office.

**The Mass.** Mass was celebrated in monasteries and convents every day between Prime and Terce and in all churches every day in the early morning. It was open to any baptized member of the community in good standing with the church. The Mass consisted of a mixture of spoken, recited, and sung elements, some of which took place in every celebration of Mass (the Ordinary), some of which were specific to particular Sundays or feast days (the Propers). An easy way to remember the difference between the Ordinary and the Proper is that the Ordinary was sung at every Mass, hence its content was unchanging or "ordinary"; the Proper consisted of those items suitable or "proper" only to particular days.

The full text of the Mass Ordinary is given in Appendix 5. The table here outlines the structure of the service as a whole.

## THE STRUCTURE OF THE MASS

| SUNG | | RECITED OR SPOKEN | |
|---|---|---|---|
| Ordinary | Proper | Ordinary | Proper |
| | 1. Introit | | |
| 2. Kyrie | | | |
| 3. Gloria | | | |
| | | | 4. Collect |
| | | | 5. Epistle |
| | 6. Gradual | | |
| | 7. Alleluia (or Tract) | | |
| | (7a. Sequence) | | |
| | | | 8. Gospel |
| 9. Credo | | | |
| | 10. Offertory | | |
| | | 11. Offertory Prayers | |
| | | | 12. Secret |
| | | | 13. Preface |
| 14. Sanctus | | | |
| | | 15. Canon | |
| | | 16. Lord's Prayer | |
| 17. Agnus Dei | | | |
| | 18. Communion | | |
| | | | 19. Post-Communion |
| 20. Ite missa est | | | |

**The liturgical year.**    The church year revolves around two major feasts: Christmas, which celebrates Christ's birth, and Easter, which celebrates Christ's resurrection. Each of these feasts is preceded by a season of penitence—Advent before Christmas and Lent before Easter—and each is followed by a season of variable length—Epiphany after Christmas, Pentecost after Easter. The church year begins with Advent, and the cycle as a whole, in somewhat simplified form, follows this order:

- **Advent**—From the fourth Sunday before Christmas until Christmas Day.

- **Christmas**—December 25 and the 12 days following.

- **Epiphany**—January 6 (the visit of the Magi) until the beginning of Lent.

- **Lent**—From Ash Wednesday (40 days—not counting Sundays—before Easter) to Maundy Thursday (the Thursday before Easter). The 40 days commemorate Christ's period of time in the wilderness. Maundy Thursday, which commemorates the Last Supper, is followed by Good Friday, which marks the day of Christ's crucifixion, and Holy Saturday, the Easter Vigil.

## Focus  A GUIDE TO THE LITURGICAL BOOKS CONTAINING PLAINCHANT

The Vatican has always played an active role in editing and publishing the official chant books used in the Office and Mass. During the 19th century, however, the Benedictine monks of the Abbey of Solesmes, in northern France, began to take an active role in recovering the earliest forms of the chant by carefully comparing the notation preserved in early medieval manuscripts. The resulting "Solesmes editions" of chant—published by the firm of Desclee in Tournai, working in conjunction with the monks of Solesmes—were soon recognized by the Vatican as the official chant books of the Roman Catholic Church. After the wide-scale reform of the liturgy during the Second Vatican Council from 1962 to 1965, however, these books fell out of widespread active use and were for many years out of print. Scholars who specialize in the study of chant generally work from the original notation on medieval manuscripts (see Focus: Early Chant Notation, p. 30).

The most important chant books are as follows:

- The **Gradual** (*Graduale*), which contains the complete chants for the Mass, both Ordinary and Propers

- The **Antiphoner** (*Antiphonale*), which contains chants for the Office, except Matins

- The **Liber usualis,** a useful 20th-century anthology of many different kinds of chants from both the Mass and the Office.

- **Easter**—The first Sunday after the first full moon on or after March 21 (the beginning of spring). Eastertide continues for 40 days, concluding with the Feast of the Ascension, marking Christ's entry into heaven.

- **Pentecost**—From 50 days after Easter until Advent. The Feast of Pentecost commemorates the descent of the Holy Spirit on Christ's disciples. Lasting from 5 to 6 months, the season after Pentecost is the longest in the church year.

## Relationship of Words and Music

Plainchant is a wonderfully effective way of projecting a text. From a purely practical point of view, the sung chant resonates longer, carries much farther, and is more readily audible in a large space like a church than a text that is merely read. Syllabic recitations of chant, with one note per syllable on a single pitch, are especially effective in this regard. Yet the urge to embellish such recitations musically—to deviate from the standard formulas of recitation on a fixed pitch—ultimately led to the creation of new chants that went well beyond merely practical needs. Simple and elaborate chants thus exist side by side in the liturgy, depending on the nature and function of the texts to be sung. From a musical perspective, chants fall into three broad stylistic categories: syllabic, neumatic, and melismatic (Example 1–1). In **syllabic** passages, each syllable of text has its own note. In the more embellished **neumatic** passages, each syllable is sung to between two and six notes. And in the most florid **melismatic** passages, a single syllable is sung to many notes.

**Syllabic chant in the Mass.**   Certain elements of the Mass, such as the Epistle or the Gospel, must convey relatively long texts, and for this reason they do not afford time for embellishment. The Epistle and Gospel for Christmas Day, for example, both follow prescribed formulas and feature little melodic motion. The priest intoning these texts need only adjust the number of notes on a basic **recitation tone** to the number of syllables, deviating in a formulaic way from this central pitch at points corresponding to the grammatical middle and end of each sentence. These slight deviations allow

**EXAMPLE 1–1** Syllabic, neumatic, and melismatic chant.

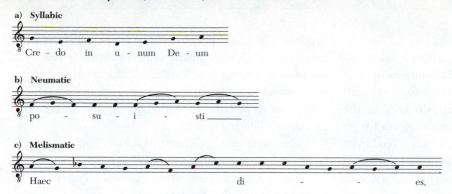

a) **Syllabic**

Cre - do    in    u - num De - um

b) **Neumatic**

po -    su - i -    sti _____

c) **Melismatic**

Haec                di -    -    es,

the listener to hear the text as a series of distinct syntactic units. Closure at the end of the text is indicated by a distinctive drop in pitch, a **cadence** (a term derived from the Latin word *cadere*, meaning "to fall"). Similar patterns of recitation are evident in the Collect (a prayer; the word is pronounced with the accent on the first syllable), the Preface (so called because it leads into the Sanctus), and the Post-Communion (a prayer of thanks). The Secret is a prayer said silently by the priest at the high altar with a concluding Amen sung aloud to a reciting tone.

Other chants with relatively long texts are syllabic without centering on a recitation tone. These include the various forms of the Gloria and Credo, as well as the Lord's Prayer (*Pater noster*) and the Sequence, a kind of hymn that appears after the Alleluia on special feast days.

### Neumatic Chant in the Mass.

Whereas syllabic chants tend to be functional but not of great interest from a musical point of view, other portions of the liturgy—those that do not incorporate so much text—receive more elaborate music. The Introit, Offertory, and Communion are sometimes called action chants because they accompany actions of the priest and his attendants who are celebrating Mass. The Introit is sung during the procession into the church, the Offertory during the presentation of the bread and wine, and the Communion during the distribution of the bread and wine.

These chants are typically built around a psalm verse. *Puer natus est notbis*, the Introit for the Mass on Christmas Day, for example, incorporates a psalm verse (*Cantate Domino canticum novum . . .* from Psalm 98) that is essentially recitational. But the introduction to the psalm verse (from *Puer natus* through *magni consilii*) is freely composed in terms of both its text and its music. The setting is neumatic, with melismas of three, four, or five notes distributed liberally throughout. The Offertory and Communion for Christmas Day are even more elaborate. The remaining items of the Ordinary—the Kyrie, Sanctus, Agnus Dei, and Ite missa est, all of which feature relatively brief texts—are also predominantly neumatic with a mixture of syllabic and mildly melismatic passages.

### Melismatic Chant in the Mass.

The most elaborate chants in the Mass are the Gradual and Alleluia, along with the Tract, which replaces the Alleluia during the penitential seasons of Advent and Lent. These chants feature relatively brief texts, and to recite such a short text in the same manner as the Epistle or Gospel would create an exceptionally brief unit of music. This kind of text thus not only allows but virtually demands a more musically elaborate presentation, and the Alleluia repertory in particular

((•─**Listen**

CD1    Track 2

**mysearchlab** (with scrolling translation)
INTROIT *PUER NATUS EST NOBIS* FROM THE MASS FOR CHRISTMAS DAY
Score Anthology I/2a

((•─**Listen**

CD1    Tracks 5/6

**mysearchlab** (with scrolling translation)
OFFERTORY AND COMMUNION FROM THE MASS FOR CHRISTMAS DAY
Score Anthology I/2g & 2j

((•─**Listen**

CD1    Track 3

**mysearchlab** (with scrolling translation)
GRADUAL *VIDERUNT OMNES* FROM THE MASS FOR CHRISTMAS DAY
Score Anthology I/2d

((•─**Listen**

CD1    Track 4

**mysearchlab** (with scrolling translation)
ALLELUIA *DIES SANCTIFICATUS* FROM THE MASS FOR CHRISTMAS DAY
Score Anthology I/2e

## Focus  MODERN CHANT NOTATION

The modern editions of plainchant produced by the monks of Solesmes retain certain elements of the medieval neumes but can nevertheless be read quite easily with the knowledge of a few simple rules. Each four-line staff is marked with a clef indicating either middle C or the F below middle C. The individual neumes are read from left to right, except for the podatus (♪), which is read from bottom to top. Groupings of notes are sometimes indicated by ligatures (such as ♣ or ♫). What looks like half a neume at the end of each staff line is in fact an indication of the first pitch of the next line. This *custos* ("guardian") makes it easier for the eye to move from one staff to the next.

The rhythmic interpretation of chant has long been a controversial issue. Even the monks of Solesmes did not agree among themselves about whether the chant was rhythmically fixed (proportionally long and short durations) or "free," with all the notes of more or less equal duration but shaded in length according to the length of the syllable being sung. Most performances nowadays tend toward the latter approach, giving the music a supple, almost floating quality.

The Solesmes editions of chant include several additional markings to distinguish among the individual sections of a given chant. In the Gradual *Viderunt omnes* from the Mass for Christmas Day, for example, vertical lines of varying length in the middle of the staff indicate major divisions within the text (and thus also the music) of the chant. The dot at the end of the last note of each such unit reinforces the demarcation of that portion of the text; the dot itself has no rhythmic significance.

Graudal *Viderunt omnes*, from the Liber usualis (Paris: Deslée, 1964), p. 409.

**Source:** Gradual *Viderunt omnes* From The Liber usualis. Ed. by the Benedictines of Solesmes. Tournai (Belgium): Desclee, 1959. Page 409.

is known for its florid, exuberant melodies, especially on the final syllable of the word *alleluia*, a passage known as the **jubilus** (derived from the same root as "jubilation").

The Gradual, Alleluia, and Tract are called **responsorial chants** because the chorus alternates with ("responds to") the soloist. In the Gradual for Christmas Day, *Viderunt omnes*, the soloist intones the opening two words (up to the asterisk marked in the score), at which point the chorus enters (*fines terrae* . . .). This entire unit is known as the **respond.** The subsequent psalm verse, also taken from Psalm 98 (*Notum fecit Dominus* . . .), is then sung by the soloist. In earlier times, the chorus's part of the respond would be repeated, but this practice had disappeared by the 13th century.

**Nuns chanting.** Plainchant was sung with equal fervor in convents as well as monasteries. This scene is from a miniature in an early-15th-century English manuscript.

**Source:** Master of St. Jerome: Nuns in choir, Cotton Domitian A XVII, f.177v, 7/10340, © The British Library Board. All Rights Reserved

Alleluias are performed in a slightly different manner. The soloist intones the opening word (up to the asterisk in the score); then the chorus repeats this same passage exactly. The chorus proceeds to sing the *jubilus*, an elaborate melisma, and the soloist then sings the verse (*Dies sanctificatus . . .*), with the chorus joining in on the final phrase (here, *super terram*). Finally, the soloist sings the opening "alleluia" and the chorus enters directly with the *jubilus*.

**Word and Music in the Chants of the Divine Office.** The chants for the Divine Office reflect the nature of their texts in a similar fashion. Psalms, with their lengthy texts, are recited syllabically to one of the eight melodic formulas known as **psalm tones**. Each psalm tone corresponds to one of the eight musical modes (discussed in the next section). The eighth psalm tone (Example 1–2) is typical of the various formulas used to recite these texts: it begins with a very brief gesture that brings the singer to the recitation tone, which serves to project any number of syllables. Psalm verses typically divide into two units, and a cadential formula provides a mediant cadence; the second half of the psalm verse is recited to the same recitation tone, and a final cadence marks the end of the verse. This pattern is repeated for as many verses as are to be sung. The two halves of the psalm tone were often sung antiphonally, between a soloist and the chorus, or between two halves of the chorus. The psalm tone is repeated until all the appointed verses of the psalm have been sung. The ninth psalm tone, the *Tonus peregrinus* ("wandering tone"), has two different recitation tones but is limited largely to the singing of a single text, Psalm 113.

**EXAMPLE 1–2** The eighth psalm tone.

Psalm and psalm-related recitations in the Divine Office were preceded and followed by a more musically varied **antiphon**. Antiphons tend to be relatively brief; although syllabic, they are more melodically varied than the psalm recitations they frame. On Whit Tuesday (two days after Pentecost Sunday) at Vespers, for example, the antiphon *Pacem relinquo vobis* (Peace I leave with you; John 14:27) is followed by Psalm 116 (Vulgate), *Laudate Dominum omnes gentes* (O praise the Lord, all ye nations), a short text to which is added the Gloria Patri (the Lesser Doxology). Then the antiphon is repeated in its entirety. In performance the antiphon creates what might be thought of as a set of bookends for the psalm. Originally, the antiphon was repeated after each verse of the psalm; in modern practice, the initial antiphon is followed by only one verse of the psalm and the Doxology (*Gloria Patri*), with the antiphon repeated a second time at the very end.

Most of the thousands of antiphons are performed in conjunction with the psalms, but a few dozen are used in processions on certain important feast days. A group of four antiphons in honor of the Blessed Virgin Mary—*Alma Redemptoris Mater*, *Ave Regina caelorum*, *Regina caeli laetare*, and *Salve Regina*—also function as independent chants and are sung at the end of Compline, one for each season of the liturgical year.

**Hymns**—whose texts are not scriptural—tend to be syllabic in style. They typically feature multiple strophes, as in the hymn for the Feast of Corpus Christi, *Pange lingua gloriosi corporis mysterium*.

## Mode

**Modes** are scale types characterized by a specific pattern of whole steps and half steps. Melodies in any of the eight medieval modes end on a characteristic pitch (the **finalis** or final) and move up and down within a particular range (**ambitus**). Thus a melody in the first mode will typically end on the finalis D and be built from the pattern of pitches D-E-F-G-A-B-C-D, or to put it in terms of intervals (W = whole step, H = half step): W-H-W-W-W-H-W. A melody in the second mode will be built on the same pitches but range a fifth above to a fourth below the finalis, D. These intervallic relationships are in fact the basis of how medieval musicians would have thought of the modes, for there was no way at the time to ascertain the frequency of any one fixed pitch. Thus an A in one monastery might sound like a G in another 50 miles down the road. Intervals, however—half-steps, whole-steps, and even microtones—could be measured quite precisely on a monochord, a single-stringed instrument used to measure the ratios of sound according to the mathematical divisions of the string (see illustration on p. 23).

The eight modes used in the classification of plainchant (Example 1–3) are based on the pitches D, E, F, and G, with each pitch supporting two modes, one called **authentic** (with an ambitus running an octave above the finalis), the other **plagal** (with an ambitus running a fifth above and a fourth below the finalis). In practice, the question of ambitus was fairly flexible. An authentic-mode chant, for example, might easily dip down a note or two below its finalis. Each of the modes featured its own particular recitation tone (also called a *repercussio*) used to recite long passages of text on a single note. Recitation tones play a particularly important role in the psalm tone associated with each of the eight modes.

**EXAMPLE 1–3** The medieval plainchant modes.

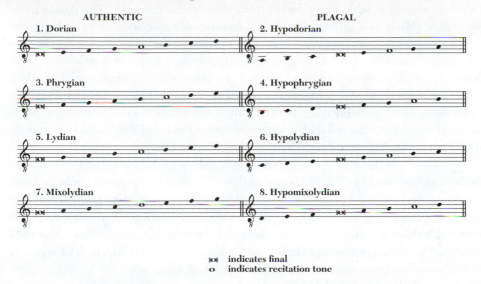

AUTHENTIC                  PLAGAL

1. Dorian        2. Hypodorian

3. Phrygian        4. Hypophrygian

5. Lydian        6. Hypolydian

7. Mixolydian        8. Hypomixolydian

|◖◗|    indicates final
o    indicates recitation tone

The names that came to be connected with these modes much later—Dorian, Phrygian, Lydian, Mixolydian—derive from Greek place names thought to be associated with each of the modes, rather in the same manner as the Greek *tonoi*. The Greek prefix *hypo* means "under" (as in "hypotenuse") and was applied to those modes with an ambitus that ranged under (and over) the finalis. But these designations are more appropriately reserved for discussions of 16th- and 17th-century polyphony. When speaking of medieval plainchant, it is preferable to apply the simple numerical designations (Mode 1, Mode 2, etc.) actually used in the original sources of this music.

Although early chant manuscripts give evidence of at least some organization of their contents by mode, it was not until the 11th century that we find a systematic and consistent application of the eight-mode system, thanks in large part to the work of the Italian monk Guido of Arezzo (991–after 1033) and the German monk Hermannus Contractus (1013–1054). Most later chant manuscripts—from about the middle of the 11th century onward—assign every chant to a particular mode.

## Melodic Structure

Plainchant melodies generally follow a limited number of intervallic patterns. In keeping with the function of projecting the text at hand, most chants feature a high percentage of stepwise intervals, punctuated by thirds and an occasional fourth or fifth (the fifths almost always ascending, not descending). Intervals greater than a fifth are quite rare, especially in the oldest layers of the chant repertory. Octave leaps might occasionally occur between two separate phrases of a chant but almost never within a musical or linguistic phrase.

The melody of the Introit for the Mass on Christmas Day, *Puer natus est nobis*, is fairly typical. The intervals are mostly conjunct with an occasional leap of a fifth or third. The range is limited largely to a sixth (G below middle C to E above), with an occasional extension to the F above the E. This is a standard range for a melody in Mode 7. The middle section (the psalm verse, beginning with *Cantate Domino*) explores a slightly higher range and centers on the Mode 7 recitation tone, D.

The Gradual *Viderunt omnes* (Mode 5) ranges somewhat farther afield, as might be expected of the more musically elaborate genre of the Gradual. Like most chant melodies, it features a series of distinctive contours. The opening section moves through a succession of gently rising and falling arches. The verse (*Notum fecit Dominus . . .*) covers an unusually wide range before returning to the finalis, F. The Alleluia *Dies sanctificatus* (Mode 2) is equally elaborate in its series of rising and falling melodic arcs.

In theoretical terms, the pitches used in plainchant melodies do not derive from a system of successive diatonic octaves, but rather from a series of interlocking hexachords. In medieval theory, a **hexachord** is a group of six notes, all separated by whole steps except the third and fourth notes, which are separated by a half step. The individual notes of the hexachord are known by their **solmization syllables**—*ut, re, mi, fa, sol, la*—derived from the syllables and corresponding notes of the first six lines in the plainchant hymn *Ut queant laxis* (Example 1–4).

We must not think of these solmization syllables as the equivalent of our fixed pitches (such as "middle C" or "G below middle C"). Instead, the system of hexachords provided singers with a framework of pitch relationships: from *mi* to *fa* is always a half step, and it can always be found between the third and fourth pitches above *ut*, which itself was a movable pitch. Only much later did the solmization syllables come to be associated with fixed pitches in certain languages such as French, in which *ut, re, mi, fa, sol, la* are used today to indicate the pitches C, D, E, F, G, and A.

The entire range of available pitches—the **gamut**—was conceived of as a series of seven interlocking hexachords beginning on C, F, or G (Example 1–5).

Hexachords were considered "hard" if they included a B♮, "soft" if they included a B♭, and "natural" if they included no B at all (that is, running from C to A). Individual notes within the hexachord system were identified unambiguously by combining the names of all the various solmization syllables each could sustain. Thus the lowest note in the system, the *gamma*, could only be an *ut* and was thus known as *gamma ut* (which in turn gave the name to the gamut). The F a seventh higher, in turn, could function

**EXAMPLE 1–4** The opening of the hymn *Ut queant laxis:* the source of the solmization syllables.

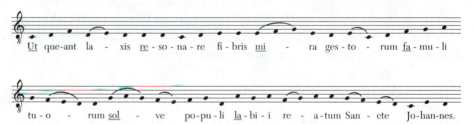

That your servants may sing with deeper notes of your wondrous deeds, St. John, cleanse the guilt of unclean lips.

**EXAMPLE 1–5** The gamut.

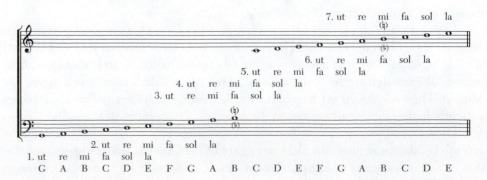

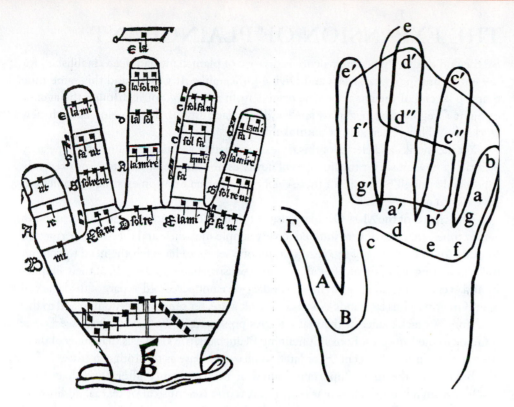

either as a *fa* in the second hexachord or as an *ut* in the third; it was thus identified as *F fa ut*. To help students remember this system, medieval theorists developed a mnemonic device known as the **Guidonian hand** (see the illustration), so called because it was believed to have been developed by Guido of Arezzo, although it in fact appears in none of his surviving writings. For a chant like *Ut queant laxis* (Example 1–4), solmization was simple, because it stays within a single hexachord. For more elaborate chants, singers were required to apply a technique known as **mutation**, whereby a particular note within the course of a chant would function as a pivot to a new syllable in a different hexachord. With years of training and experience, such changes became second nature to the singers, most if not all of whom presumably knew an enormous repertory of melodies and their words by heart. Indeed, words and music reinforced one another and made both more readily memorable.

## Rhythm

Rhythm is the most controversial issue in reconstructing medieval performance practices of plainchant. The official Vatican editions prepared by the monks of Solesmes advocate (and transmit) a style of chant in which all notes are of essentially equal value, with only slight degrees of variation—longer notes at the end of phrases, for example. But strong evidence in at least some of the earliest manuscripts and in the theoretical writings of the medieval era suggests that not all notes were performed evenly. Some scholars interpret certain markings, such as a short horizontal line over a note, to indicate a doubling of the note value. The precise meaning of such indications, however, is unknown, so the "equalist" approach has predominated in modern plainchant performances and recordings. Singers seek to project the rhythms of the words of the chants, but flexibly rather than in any systematic way.

**A medieval monastery at high tide.** The Benedictine Abbey of Mont St. Michel, built on the coast of Normandy in northern France, reflects both the harshness and beauty of medieval monastic life. Protected from the outside world by rock, sand, and tides, it grew by accretion over many centuries. Founded in 708, the monastery's oldest surviving buildings date from around 1000; further construction continued off and on for another 500 years. The abbey at the very top represents the physical and spiritual center of the monastery, the place where plainchant was recited in the eight daily services of the Divine Office and the daily celebration of the Mass until the French Revolution.

**Source:** Cotton Coulson/National Geographic Stock

# THE EXPANSION OF PLAINCHANT

By the end of the 9th century, a core repertory of plainchant had been established for the entire liturgical year, Mass and Divine Office alike. It was around this same time that the legend of the chant's divine origins from the Holy Spirit through the agency of Saint Gregory first began to appear. To replace any of these melodies with new works would have been almost unthinkable.

Yet the monks and clerics of this time continued to add to the plainchant repertory by writing new music for the liturgies of newly established feast days to honor recently canonized saints. The music for these celebrations often drew on existing melodies but gave rise to new ones as well.

The chants of the Mass Ordinary also continued to expand after the 9th century. In earlier times, these texts were intoned to very simple melodies, and they were performed so often (once every day of the year) that no one seems to have felt the need to commit them to writing: parchment, after all, was an expensive material. Because of their simplicity and everyday use, moreover, these melodies were not perceived as part of the legacy of Saint Gregory. Thus later monks and clerics felt a greater sense of freedom to add to this repertory. A quick glance at the many Kyries preserved in the *Liber usualis* (see Focus: A Guide to the Liturgical Books Containing Plainchant, p. 34) reveals that many of them were written in the 10th century or later, some even as late as the 16th century.

But by far the most important source of new repertory after the 9th century resulted from a process known as **troping**. A **trope** is a musical or textual addition to an existing chant. The term comes from the Latin *tropus*, meaning "a turn of phrase," and is used here in the sense of embellishing or elaborating an otherwise plain statement. Tropes could be added to the beginning or end of a chant, or they could be interpolated into the chant itself. The original chant, in any event, remained intact, even if it was now framed or interrupted by new material.

One category of tropes added words to an existing melisma. These interpolated texts, known as *prosulae* (singular, *prosula*, from the same root as the English word "prose"), also served as a kind of commentary on the original text. Textual troping was especially prevalent in the extended melismas of the Gradual, the Alleluia, and the Offertory, as well as those sections of the Mass Ordinary with brief texts, such as the Kyrie. The Sequence, authorized for special feast days, began life as a texted trope on the jubilus, the extended melisma at the end of the Alleluia. It eventually became a separate element of the liturgy in its own right and was cultivated with special intensity in the 10th century.

## Primary Evidence · SPARE THE ROD, SPOIL THE CHANT

*Singing chant was a serious business. Regulations in place during the 11th century at the Cathedral of St. Benigne in Dijon (France) prescribed a variety of techniques for dealing with choirboys—students at the cathedral school—whose demeanor or performance fell short of established standards.*

■ ■ ■

At Nocturns, and indeed at all the Hours [of the Divine Office], if the boys commit any fault in the psalmody or other singing, either by sleeping or such like transgression, let there be no sort of delay, but let them be stripped forthwith of frock and cowl, and beaten in their shirt only . . . with pliant and smooth osier rods provided for that special purpose. If any of them, weighed down with sleep, sing ill at Nocturns, then the master giveth into his hand a reasonably great book, to hold until he be well awake. At Matins the principal master standeth before them with a rod until all are in their seats and their faces well covered. At their uprising likewise, if they rise too slowly, the rod is straightway over them.

**Source:** *The Oxford History of Music,* introductory volume (Oxford: Oxford University Press, 1901), pp. 190–1.

The Kyrie *Cunctipotens Genitor Deus* (Example 1–6) is a later (post-9th-century) chant that, during the 12th century, was troped with a new text. Between the two original words—the simple plea for mercy, *Kyrie eleison*—are interpolated the words *Cunctipotens Genitor Deus omni creator* ("All-powerful Father, God, creator of all things"). The troping process (with added words indicated in italics) thus leads to this:

Kyrie *Cunctipotens Genitor Deus omni creator* eleison

Lord, *All-powerful Father, God, creator of all things*, have mercy

Aside from the textual trope, the melody itself exhibits several characteristic features of late chant. The earliest melodies tend to float without a strong sense of

**EXAMPLE 1–6** Kyrie *Cunctipotens Genitor Deus*: (a) untexted trope; (b) texted trope.

## Primary Evidence — WORDS, MUSIC, AND MEMORY: THE *PROSULA*

*Long before the advent of musical notation, the monks who sang plainchant on a daily basis had begun to embellish at least some melodies both musically and textually. Melismatic chants—the various intonations of the Kyrie and the jubilus of the Alleluia in particular—proved especially inviting for the addition of interpolated texts. In one of the earliest accounts of such a trope, Notker of St. Gall (ca. 840–912, also known as Notker Balbulus, "The Stammerer") explains that the practice arose from a need to make the chants easier to memorize. Notker was a monk who worked at the Benedictine abbey of St. Gall in what is now eastern Switzerland. He eventually collected the prosulae he had written in a* Liber hymnorum *(Book of Hymns), which he organized according to the cycle of the liturgical year.*

■ ■ ■

When I was still young, and very long melodies—repeatedly entrusted to memory—escaped from my poor little head, I began to reason with myself how I could bind them fast.

In the meantime it happened that a certain priest from Jumièges (recently laid waste by the Normans) came to us, bringing with him his antiphonary, in which some verses had been set to sequences; but they were in a very corrupt state. Upon closer inspection I was as bitterly disappointed in them as I had been delighted at first glance.

Nevertheless, in imitation of them I began to write *Laudes Deo concinat orbis universus, qui gratis est redemptus*, and further on *Coluber adae deceptor*. When I took these lines to my teacher Iso, he, commending my industry while taking pity on my lack of experience, praised what was pleasing, and what was not he set about to improve, saying, "The individual motions of the melody should receive separate syllables." Hearing that, I immediately corrected those which fell under *ia*; those under *le* or *lu*, however, I left as too difficult; but later, with practice, I managed it easily—for example in "Dominus in Sina" and "Mater." Instructed in this manner, I soon composed my second piece, *Psallat ecclesia mater illibata*.

When I showed these little verses to my teacher Marcellus, he, filled with joy, had them copied as a group on a roll; and he gave out different pieces to different boys to be sung. And when he told me that I should collect them in a book and offer them as a gift to some eminent person, I shrank back in shame, thinking I would never be able to do that.

**Source:** Notker Balbulus, Preface to *Liber hymnorum* (Book of Hymns), trans. in Richard Crocker, *The Early Medieval Sequence* (Berkeley and Los Angeles: University of California Press, 1977), p. 1.

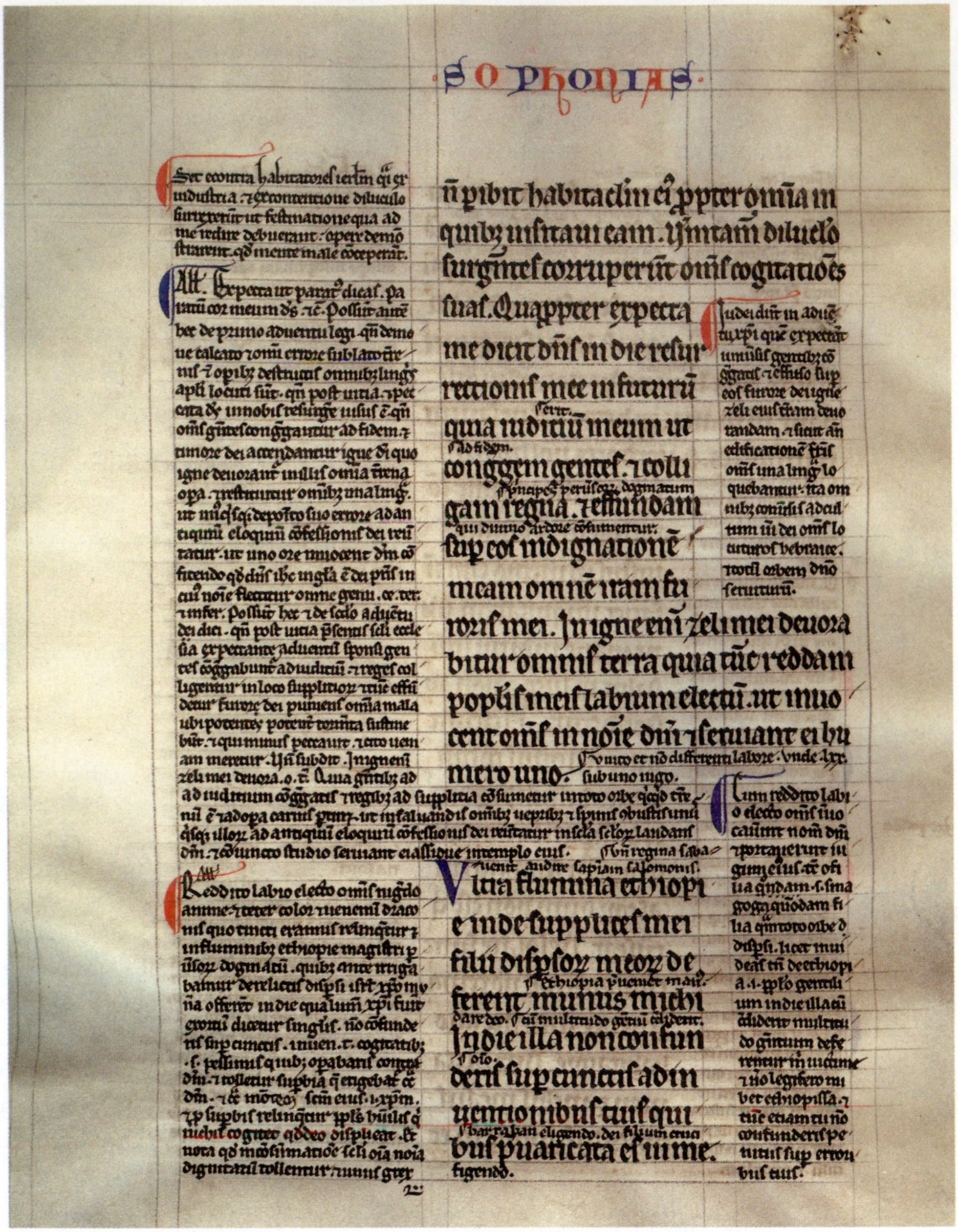

**The art of glossing.** In the medieval era, anything worth reading was worth glossing. The original text shown here—a 13th-century manuscript copy of the Old Testament's Book of Zephaniah, in Latin—was prepared from the very start with a gloss of its own in both the right and left margins. Still further commentary was inserted between some of the lines in the main text: these additions interpret specific words or phrases. The practice of adding successive layers of commentary to an original source lies behind the medieval impetus to create textual and musical tropes for existing chants, and eventually to add new voices to an established plainchant melody.

**Source:** Bridwell Library Special Collections. Perkins School of Theology. Southern Methodist University.

contour or direction, whereas later ones often have a much stronger sense of movement toward the cadences at the end of each grammatical unit and especially toward the finalis. The prominence of the interval of the fifth, particularly the rising fifth, is also typical of later chant. A relatively higher degree of melodic repetition within a chant also characterizes the later repertory, although even the earliest Kyrie settings tend to feature musical repetitions that mirror the repetitive nature of the text.

Another kind of trope adds both words and new music to an existing chant. In one manuscript from the late 10th or 11th century (Example 1–7), the Introit for the Mass on Easter Sunday, *Resurrexi*, is preceded by an extended trope consisting of both words and music, with a series of similar tropes interpolated into the course of the Introit itself. The troped text (indicated in italics here) comments on the words of the original Introit. The introductory trope sets the mood ("Rejoice and be glad . . ."), and subsequent interpolations comment on the original Introit text (in roman type),

**EXAMPLE 1–7** Beginning of the troped Introit *Resurrexi*: original antiphon (b, d) alternating with trope (a, c, e).

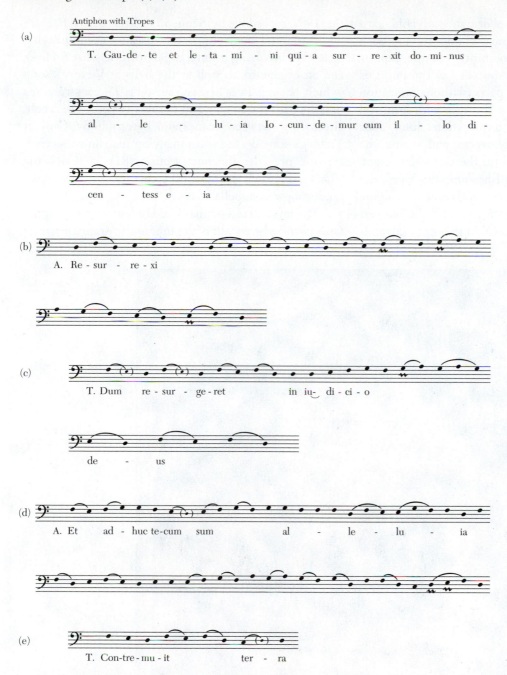

Christ's pronouncement to the visitors to his tomb on the morning of Easter Sunday ("I have risen . . .").

| | |
|---|---|
| *Gaudete et letamini quia surrexit dominus alleluia* | *Rejoice and be glad, for the Lord has risen, alleluia.* |
| *Iocundemur cum illo dicentes eia* | *Let us delight in that, saying "Eia."* |
| Resurrexi | I have risen |
| *Dum resurgeret in iudicio deus* | *Until in judgment God would rise* |
| Et adhuc tecum sum alleluia. | And I am still with you, alleluia. |
| *Contremuit terra xpisto surgente Christ a mortuis . . .* | *The earth trembled when rose from the dead . . .* |

## Focus   BEYOND NOTATION

Any ensemble that plans a performance of Hildegard von Bingen's *Ordo virtutum* must choose an approach both compatible with and committed to the expression of the notated score. The sources that transmit this work provide only the voice parts, without indication of rhythmic values (much as is the case with liturgical chant manuscripts). Some interpretations limit their scope accordingly, using only voices and basing the rhythms on the accents built into the melodic line and text meaning. The version by Ensemble für Musik des Mittelalters, led by Stefan Morent, adds only the ringing of bells at the climactic song of Victory ("the old serpent has been bound," section 80). At the other extreme, the 1982 recording by Sequentia, directed by Barbara Thornton and Benjamin Bagby, uses an accompanying ensemble involving a flute, a pair of fidels (or fiddles), and an organetto, as well as the bells at Victory's song (which is sung in a higher register). The instruments breathe with the singers and follow the vocal line freely, alternating between drones and heterophony. Only at Victory's song do the accompanying instruments cease; a pause precedes the next section (81), in which the Virtues sing their praises in the customary lower register, but now a cappella.

Medieval sacred dramas like Hildegard von Bingen's *Ordo virtutum* grew out of the inherently dramatic nature

Erich Lessing / Museo di S. Marco, Florence, Italy/Art Resource, NY

of the Mass itself, and in particular such dramatic tropes as *Quem quaeritis in sepolcro*. The scene between the women and the angel at the tomb of Jesus Christ is depicted in this Fra Angelico fresco, "Holy Women at the Sepulchre."

Is it legitimate to take such liberties with the notated score? From the evidence available to us through contemporary accounts and depictions of music-making, we know that notated sources do not always reflect the full range of resources used in performance. Yet how far is too far? The historical record for a work like Hildegard's *Ordo virtutum* is too thin to say with any degree of certainty that it was always performed in a certain way

and by certain forces but not by others. Some will find the present performance excessive in its interpolations; others will maintain that it creates a greater degree of sonic variety that makes *Ordo virtutum* more appealing to modern-day audiences. Still others will hold that attempts to achieve historically "authentic" performances impinge excessively on the demands of musicianship, and that the very concept of authenticity itself is anachronistic: it is entirely possible that Hildegard herself may well not have thought in terms of any one correct manner of performance. (Sequentia, when it issued a second recording of *Ordo virtutum* in 1998, took a very different approach from its first one.) The debate continues.

**Manuscript of the "Quem quaeritis" trope.** This Easter trope, first found in 10th-century manuscripts in St. Martial, Limoges, France, evolved at a time when church officials were encouraging dramatizations of liturgical events to make them more tangible for congregants. The "Quem quaeritis" trope was successful enough to be part of the Sarum (English) liturgy by the end of the century. From there, the English developed the nonliturgical mystery play, collected in regional cycles that have remained a part of the British theatrical repertory. This version comes from a *processionale*, a collection of chants and prayers for processionals, from 14th-century Dublin.

**Source:** Bodleian Library, Oxford University

## Composer Profile

# Hildegard von Bingen (1098–1179)

We can securely attribute more compositions to Hildegard von Bingen than to any other musician, male or female, who worked before the early 14th century. In spite of her impressive output, Hildegard did not consider herself a professional composer or musician. Born into a noble family in what is now western Germany, she entered a Benedictine convent at the age of 7 and took vows when she was 16. In her early 30s she began to experience visions and revelations, which she recorded in a series of books. Hildegard was the first woman to receive explicit permission from a pope to write on theology. She also wrote on such diverse subjects as medicine, plants, and lives of the saints, all while directing the life of a thriving convent as its abbess.

Hildegard's devotion to music is clearly evident in a letter of protest she wrote toward the end of her life. The laws of the church dictate that individuals who have been excommunicated—barred from receiving communion because of a grave offense against the church—cannot be buried on consecrated ground. Hildegard was accused of having permitted just such a person to be buried on the hallowed ground of her convent's cemetery, and as punishment the prelates of Mainz forbade the nuns there from celebrating the Divine Office with music, permitted only to speak the liturgy. In a letter to those prelates, Hildegard eloquently defends the practice of music as something that goes beyond aesthetics and penetrates the most basic issues of faith.

In obedience to you we have until now given up the singing of the Divine Office, celebrating it only by quiet reading—and I heard a voice coming from the living light, telling of those various kinds of praise concerning which David speaks in the Psalms: "Praise him with the sound of the trumpet, praise him with the psaltery and the cithara, praise him with the tympanum and the chorus, praise him with strings and the organ, praise him with the well-sounding cymbals, praise him with the cymbals of jubilation. Let every spirit praise the Lord" [Psalm 150: 3–6]. In these words we are taught about inward concerns by external objects, how according to the makeup of material things (the properties of musical instruments)

we ought best to convert and to refashion the workings of our interior man to the praise of the Creator. . . .

Thus it is just that God be praised in everything. And since man sighs and moans with considerable frequency upon hearing some song, as he recalls in his soul the quality of celestial harmony, the prophet David, considering with understanding the nature of what is spiritual (because the soul is harmonious), exhorts us in the psalm, "Let us confess the Lord on the cithara, let us play to him on the psaltery of ten strings" [Psalm 32:1], intending that the cithara, which sounds from below, pertains to the discipline of the body; that the psaltery, which sounds from above, pertains to the striving of the spirit; and that the ten strings refer to the contemplation of the Law. Thus they who without the weight of sure reason impose silence upon a church in the matter of songs in praise of God, and thereby unjustly deprive God of the honor of his praise on earth, will be deprived themselves of the participation in the angelic praises heard in Heaven, unless they make amends by true regret and humble penitence.

Church officials eventually relented.

| KEY DATES IN THE LIFE OF HILDEGARD VON BINGEN | |
| --- | --- |
| 1098 | Born in Bermersheim near Worms (now western Germany). |
| 1106 | Enters a Benedictine convent. |
| 1136 | Becomes prioress of the abbey of St. Disibod in Diessenberg. |
| 1147 | Establishes a new convent on the Rupertsberg, within the bishopric of Mainz. |
| 1152 | Finishes her decade-long work on *Scivias* ("Know the Ways"), a manuscript that records and interprets her visions. |
| 1179 | Dies on 17 September at her convent in Rupertsberg near Bingen (western Germany). |

# PRINCIPAL WORKS

Hildegard herself organized her compositions into two large collections: the *Symphonia armonie celestium revelationum* ("Symphony of the Harmony of Celestial Revelations") and the *Ordo virtutum* ("Play of the Virtues"). The *Symphonia armonie* is a cycle of liturgical works partly for the Mass (an Alleluia, a Kyrie, and seven Sequences) but mostly for the Office (43 antiphons, 18 responsory chants, 3 hymns, and 4 devotional songs). The *Ordo virtutum* is a morality play consisting of 82 monophonic songs that depict a struggle between the devil and the 16 Virtues (Charity, Obedience, Humility, Chastity, and so on). The settings of the poetry are predominantly syllabic; the cycle may have been performed in connection with the services of the Office or in celebration of a newly opened church.

**Hildegard von Bingen.** This image comes from a 12th-century manuscript copy of Hildegard's works. Looking toward heaven, Hildegard receives divine inspiration and writes on a tablet. The similarity to images of Saint Gregory receiving the plainchant from the Holy Spirit is striking (see p. 28).

**Source:** Biblioteca Governativa Statale/LUCCA/akg-images

This kind of troping reflects a much broader medieval phenomenon that permeated virtually every field, from theology to philosophy to astronomy to law: the desire to comment, to embellish, to gloss. Providing new commentary on an existing text was considered one of the most basic ways to advance knowledge. If enough viewpoints and arguments were taken into account, medieval thinkers reasoned, the truth of any given matter would surely come out in the end. Thus we have countless medieval manuscripts in which an original text is glossed and in which the glosses themselves become an object of still further commentary.

Certain passages in the liturgy became special favorites for troping because of their inherently dramatic nature. In its original state, the Introit *Resurrexi* begins with Christ's first words to Mary and those who seek his body in the tomb: "I have risen. . . ." The trope known as *Quem quaeritis in sepulcro* recreates the drama leading up to this moment. It begins with the angel asking Mary and her companions, *Quem quaeritis in sepulcro, o Cristicole?* ("Whom do you seek in the sepulchre, O followers of Christ?"). The dialogue continues:

**Trope** [MARY]:  The crucified Nazarene, Jesus, O heavenly one.

[ANGEL]:  He is not here; he has risen as he foretold. Go and announce that he is risen.

[MARY AND HER COMPANIONS]:  Alleluia, the angel at the tomb announces that Christ has risen.

And behold, that which had been foretold by the prophet is fulfilled. To the father in this manner he says:

**Introit** I have risen and am still with you, alleluia . . . [etc.]

This scene and others like it were occasionally staged as **liturgical dramas**—dramas because the parts were represented by individuals, liturgical because the presentation was part of the service of worship. One medieval account describes the staging of the *Quem quaeritis in sepolcro* scene in some detail. A monk representing the angel at the tomb of Christ assumes his position "quietly, with a palm-branch in his hand" while a group of three others, representing "the women coming with spices to anoint the body of Jesus," move through the church "slowly, in the manner of seeking something. When therefore that one seated shall see the three, as if straying about and seeking something . . . let him begin in a dulcet voice of medium pitch to sing: 'Whom do you seek in the sepulchre, O followers of Christ?'" The dialogue continues from there.

Dramatized performances of such dialogues varied widely by time and location, as well as by their place in the liturgy. They were sometimes presented as tropes of the Introit at Mass, sometimes as additions to Matins. Hildegard von Bingen's *Ordo virtutum* is an example of a freely composed drama not connected with any existing chant or ritual but rather composed to texts and melodies entirely of Hildegard's own creation. The plot of this morality play—a dramatized allegory of good versus evil—centers on a series of disputes between the devil and 16 Virtues, each of which is represented by a different singer. Significantly, the devil has no music: he shouts all his lines. It would seem that hell, for Hildegard, was a world without music (see Composer Profile: Hildegard von Bingen).

New saints and new feast days also created a demand for new texts and new music. During the late medieval era and well into the Renaissance, more than a thousand rhymed offices—so called because their music and poetic text followed a strict metrical and rhyming pattern—were established for use in services in honor of particular saints or feasts. Hymns offered yet another outlet for the creative impulses of composers

((•─**Listen**

**CD1    Track 9**
**mysearchlab** (with scrolling translation)
HILDEGARD VON BINGEN
*Ordo virtutum*
Score Anthology I/5

working within the medieval church, who produced more than a thousand melodies to these freely composed strophic texts. The melody of *Pange lingua gloriosi corporis mysterium*, to a text written by St. Thomas Aquinas in the 13th century for the Feast of Corpus Christi, exemplifies this repertory. It bears the melodic hallmarks of a later chant style, with a strong sense of melodic symmetry and direction.

Composers continued to write chants well into the Renaissance. No less a figure than Guillaume Du Fay (see Chapter 4) composed a plainchant office in honor of the Virgin Mary as late as the 1450s. Other, less prominent composers were still writing chants in the 16th century. By this point, however, many of these later accretions to the repertory of liturgical plainchant—troped portions of the Ordinary, Introits, Offertories, and the like—had come to be viewed as unauthorized and corrupt. The reform-minded Council of Trent (1545–1563), reacting to the challenge of the Protestant Reformation, eliminated all troped texts and all but four Sequences from the liturgy (*Victimae paschali laudes* was one of the few to survive). For this reason, these textual tropes and most Sequences are not included in modern editions of the church's liturgical books. At least some of the melodies associated with these tropes have remained, however, like the Kyrie *Cunctipotens Genitor Deus*, whose music (without the troped words) can still be found in the *Liber usualis*.

Chant nevertheless continued to be performed in services regularly for more than 1,000 years, often in heavily modified form, including harmonized versions in the 18th and 19th centuries. Only with the Second Vatican Council of 1963–1965 did the tradition of plainchant as a vital element of the Roman Catholic liturgy come to an end.

# SECULAR MONOPHONY

Plainchant had secular parallels in every European culture of the medieval era. As with plainchant, word and music were considered inseparable. Poet, composer, and singer were often one in the same person, and most of this repertory was transmitted orally long before any of it was ever committed to writing. Although the surviving sources preserve only a single line of music for any given work, images and written accounts suggest that these songs could also be accompanied by one or more instruments. The exact nature of such performances remains a matter of speculation, although it seems clear that the essence of this repertory rests in its melody rather than in any polyphonic elaboration that may or may not have been added to it in performance.

## Songs in Latin

Songs in Latin passed easily across linguistic boundaries. The most famous collection of this kind is the *Carmina Burana*—"Songs of Benediktbeuern"—a name given in the 19th century in honor of the Benedictine monastery in Bavaria where the manuscript containing these songs was housed for many years. (Carl Orff's 1937 oratorio *Carmina Burana* is a more recent setting of 25 of the more than 200 texts in the collection.) The original manuscript, compiled in the late 13th century, is notorious for its songs about gambling, drinking, and erotic love. It also includes songs that satirize the moral teachings of the church and point out the shortcomings of priests and monks, as in the following:

> I am the abbot of Cockaigne
> and my assembly is one of drinkers,
> and I wish to be in the Order of Decius,
> and whoever searches me out at the tavern in the morning,
> after Vespers he will leave naked,

and thus stripped of his clothes he will call out:
Woe! Woe!
what have you done, vilest Fate?
the joys of my life
you have taken all away!

Such texts would have had great appeal to the wandering minstrels who went from town to town and court to court providing entertainment to any and all who would pay for it. One such group called itself the Order of the Goliards, after a nonexistent patron Golias (Goliath). They owed their allegiance to no particular court, but earned their living by performing on the road. Other minstrels did more than sing: they juggled, danced, and performed acrobatic feats and magic tricks.

## France

The *troubadours* (in southern France) and *trouvères* (in northern France) derive their names from the same root as the modern French *trouver* ("to find"). These poet-composers "found"—or as we would say today, created—new texts and melodies alike. The trouvères wrote their songs in medieval French, the troubadours in Occitan (also known as Provençal), a language related to both French and Spanish. A substantial repertory of some 2,100 trouvère songs—both texts and music—has been preserved. Music to lyrics by the troubadours, in contrast, is available for only about a tenth of the more than 2,500 known poems.

The troubadours and trouvères were at their most active in the 12th and 13th centuries. Their repertories included love songs, laments, pastorals, and dialogues. The relationship between noblemen and noblewomen in the texts of these songs is consistently governed by the elaborate etiquette of courtly love, which called for the woman to be idolized and praised from afar. Most of these works, regardless of subject matter, are strophic, both musically and textually. The longest form is the *chanson de geste* (literally, a "song of deed"), an epic account of chivalrous accomplishments. The popular *Chanson de Roland*, from the second half of the 11th century, for example, recounts the heroic adventures of one of Charlemagne's knights. This lengthy poem of more than 4,000 lines could be recited by a singer according to a formulaic pattern not unlike that of the psalm tones. The performers of this repertory—usually minstrels and *jongleurs*, members of a lower social order—were expected to embellish and improvise on this basic pattern; as a result, individual songs transmitted in more than one source often show significant variants. Unlike plainchant, secular songs were not considered gifts of the Holy Spirit and were not regarded as objects of veneration. Stylistically, though, this repertory is not unlike plainchant in its melodic structure: text settings are primarily syllabic and only occasionally melismatic. The rhythmic interpretation of the notated songs remains a particular matter of debate among modern-day scholars. As in the case of chant, most performers today prefer a flexible approach that allows the words to be declaimed in a fluid, natural manner.

Although some troubadours and trouvères were of noble birth, most were not, and these tended to be an itinerant lot. One of the most famous and prolific of all troubadours, Bernart de Ventadorn (ca. 1140–ca. 1190), was banished from two different courts for becoming too emotionally attached to the ladies of those courts; he spent the last years of his life in a monastery.

Forbidden love also seems to have shaped the life (or at least the writings) of the Countess (Beatriz) de Dia (d. ca. 1212), a **trobairitz** (female troubadour) whose *A chantar m'es al cor* (I must sing from the heart), in Occitan, may well be autobiographical.

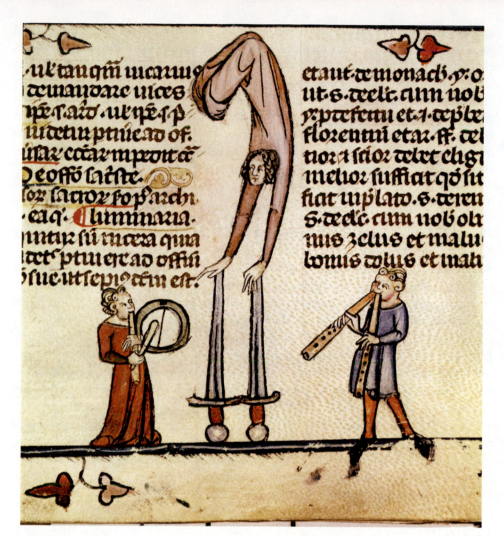

**Music and social status.** For many centuries, wind and percussion instruments were more closely associated with outdoor activities and the lower classes than were stringed instruments. The musicians shown here belong to the social class of acrobats, actors, and *jongleurs* whose skills were widely enjoyed in the medieval era but whose personal status in society was quite low. The double flute on the right is an indirect descendant of the ancient Greek aulos; the pipe and tabor were typically played by a single instrumentalist who fingered the pipe with one hand and beat the drum with the other.

**Source:** Royal 10 E. IV ©The British Library Board. All Rights Reserved

It is a moving lament written from a woman's perspective, and the only poem of the Countess to have survived in manuscript with music. The music of *A chantar* moves within a relatively narrow ambitus, but its steady rise and fall, culminating in a climb to the melody's highest pitch in the penultimate line, imparts a sense of intense emotion to the words. According to an account (*vida*) written about a century after the Countess's death, she was married to Guillaume, Count of Poitiers, but fell in love with a certain Raimbaut d'Orange (Raimbaut d'Aurenga, d. 1173), also a troubadour, and "made about him many good and beautiful songs"; but chronology and lack of positive evidence make it unlikely that Guillaume or Raimbaut was involved with the Countess.

Regarded highly by his contemporaries and successors, Peire Vidal (fl. ca. 1175–ca. 1215), the son of a furrier from Toulouse in what is now southern France, is credited with around 50 surviving texts; 12 of these have melodies. Many courts sought his talents: he served at the courts of Toulouse, Marseilles, Aragon, Castile, and Montferrat, and he may have accompanied his patron Richard I (Richard the Lion-Hearted) on the Third Crusade (1193–1194). His tempestuous character was far different from that of the Countess, indeed from most troubadours. *Baros, de mon dan covit* ("My lord, he who wishes [my downfall]") begins with typically prodigious praise of a lady, but over the course of the poem Peire compares his behavior at court favorably with others, boasts of his skills in seduction and fighting (which he loves more than monks love peace), and touches on the gossip that surrounds lovers and the imperative

((•┤**Listen**

**CD1     Track 10**
**mysearchlab** (with scrolling translation)
BEATRIZ DE DIA
*A chantar*
Score Anthology I/6

((•┤**Listen**

**CD1     Track 11**
**mysearchlab** (with scrolling translation)
PEIRE VIDAL
*Baros, de mon dan covet*
Score Anthology I/7

to wander. *Baros, de mon dan covit*, like *A chantar*, follows the AAB structure referred to as "bar form" in German medieval secular monophony (discussed earlier in this chapter). Its conjunct melody stays within a fourth for its opening four lines, but then leaps upward dramatically for the fifth and sixth lines ("I love her completely, without falsehood/And am entirely hers, if she will be mine") before returning to the lowest part of the song's ambitus for the final three lines. *A chantar* has seven lines in each stanza and has a tighter melodic structure (a b a b c d b) than *Baros, de mon dan covit*, which after its initial four lines (a a1 a a1) is relatively varied. (See Performance Perspective: Interpreting the Troubadour and Trobairitz Repertory.)

## The Iberian Peninsula

((•-Listen

**CD1    Track 12**
**mysearchlab** (with scrolling translation)
ALFONSO EL SABIO (?)
*Cantigas de Santa Maria*, no. 140
Score Anthology I/8

The preserved repertory of *cantigas* ("songs") from the Iberian peninsula—present-day Spain and Portugal—is quite small. Only two sources transmit the poetry with melodies. One is a set of six songs by Martin Codax, an otherwise obscure composer working around 1230 in what is now northwestern Spain. The other source is a large and sumptuously illustrated manuscript containing more than 400 *Cantigas de Santa Maria*, songs in honor of the Virgin Mary, prepared for (and possibly composed in part by) Alfonso el Sabio ("The Wise"), king of Castille and Leon from 1252 until 1284. Although sacred in subject matter, these songs were not liturgical. Their poetic and musical style, moreover, is consistent with what we know of the secular songs that were written in this place and time. The texts of the *cantigas* are written in Gallo-Portuguese, and most are set syllabically in strophic form with a refrain.

Scholars have debated the extent of Arabic influence on the music of this repertory. Large portions of the Iberian peninsula had been under Muslim rule since the 8th century, and the impact of this culture on Spain and Portugal extended to virtually every aspect of life. Exactly how much musical influence is to be found in the *Cantigas de Santa Maria* remains unclear, however.

## Germany

In German-speaking lands, the **Minnesinger** (literally, singers of *Minne*, or courtly love) developed their own repertory of songs. The most famous of these poet-composer-performers were Tannhäuser (ca. 1230–1280), the central character in Wagner's 19th-century opera of the same name; Walther von der Vogelweide (ca. 1170–1230);

**Knight music.** A combatant prepares for a jousting tournament to the accompaniment of a lute (played with a plectrum) and a vielle in this image from a 14th-century French manuscript.

**Source:** Bibliothèque nationale de France

## Performance Perspective

# Interpreting the Troubadour and Trobairitz Repertory

Our knowledge of the troubadour and trobairitz repertory is sketchy at best. What few written sources survive convey only words and pitches, but no rhythms. Iconographic evidence and verbal accounts suggest that these songs were performed with instrumental accompaniment, but we have no idea of what form that accompaniment might have taken. In short, we have very little evidence of how these works were actually performed. This leaves contemporary performers with considerable latitude in interpreting these works. The performances of the two *cansos* in the Anthology represent just a sampling of possibilities. Both use instrumental accompaniments that are wholly speculative, and both reflect the influence of Arabic music on European secular musicians of the medieval era, the result not only of the various Christian crusades to Islamic Palestine but also the occupation of the Iberian peninsula by the Moors from the 8th century on. Libby Crabtree, the soprano of the Martin Best Consort, sings *A chantar m'es al cor* with a relatively pure sound to the accompaniment of an ensemble of instruments: a fiddle, which provides sustained drones in a manner that recalls the practice of organum (to be discussed in Chapter 2); an *oud*, the Middle Eastern forerunner to the lute; and a psaltery, a plucked string instrument resembling a small zither. The group brings a strong sense of organization to the piece, although pulse is never allowed to dominate the flow.

The Clemencic Consort, by contrast, uses only a psaltery accompaniment, and the tenor, Frederick Urrey, employs a more declamatory and slightly nasal style of singing reminiscent of traditional Middle Eastern performance practice even today: he "slides" into and out of notes, and the intonation is intentionally flexible. The group adds a brief improvised segment on the recorder between verses. Among the most recorded of Vidal's songs, *Baros* (or *Baron* or *Barons* as it has been transmitted in some sources) has been performed in a variety of singing styles and with a wide range of accompanying instruments, including flute and hand drum as well as the instruments mentioned previously. There is even one recording of *Baros* for solo *vielle* (fiddle), without a singer. As with performances of Hildegard's *Ordo virtutum*, these ensembles and others have only their imaginations to limit their aesthetic choices.

**Countess (Beatriz) de Dia.** Her precise identity remains uncertain, but this trobairitz probably penned many more songs than *A chantar*, the only one securely ascribed to her.

**Source:** Bibliothèque nationale de France

**Peire Vidal.** One contemporary described this celebrated troubadour as "the best singer in the world and a good finder [creator]; but he was the most foolish man in the world, because he thought everything tiresome except verse."

**Source:** Bibliothèque nationale de France

**The Cantigas de Santa Maria.**
Although ascribed to Alfonso el Sabio
("Alfonso the Wise"), who ruled
the Kingdom of Castile and León I,
scholars now believe that if Alfonso
wrote any of the words or music at
all, he probably wrote a relatively
small number of them. In this image,
from one of the several 13th-century
manuscripts that preserve the
*Cantigas de Santa Maria*, Alfonso
(center right) listens to musicians
performing a song in praise of the
Virgin Mary (right). The instruments
include three psalteries of varying
shapes, a recorder, and a *vielle*
(fiddle). Dancers perform in the
background.

**Source:** Album/Oronoz/Newscom

**((•• Listen**
**CD1   Track 13**
**mysearchlab** (with scrolling translation)
WALTHER VON DER VOGELWEIDE
*Palästinalied*
Score Anthology I/9

**✓•─ Study** and **Review**
on **mysearchlab.com**

and Wolfram von Eschenbach (1170–1220), author of the epic *Parzifal*. Chivalry, the praise of God, and the praise of noblewomen are recurrent themes in their songs. Many *Minnelieder* (*Lieder* means "songs") are written in **bar Δ17form**, consisting of two musically identical statements (called *Stollen*) and a final closing statement (the *Abgesang*), creating the pattern of AAB.

Walther von der Vogelweide's *Palästinalied* provides a good example of this repertory. In bar form and largely syllabic, it tells of a crusader knight's thrill at standing on the same ground as Christ had during his lifetime. (The First Crusade had captured Jerusalem, permitting Christians to make pilgrimages to the holy city.) Like the songs of the troubadours and trouvères, the Minnelieder were almost certainly performed to the accompaniment of instruments, but no notated source of this accompaniment has been preserved.

## SUMMARY

By the time the repertories of secular monophony reached their peak in the 11th and 12th century, polyphony had already established itself in the realms of both the sacred and secular. The repertory of liturgical plainchant would continue as an integral element of the Christian liturgy for many centuries, supplemented by newer works for multiple voices. Secular monophony, however, would gradually be supplanted by polyphonic genres by the end of the 14th century.

# Polyphony to 1300

The emergence of polyphony sometime around the 8th or 9th century is one of the most important stylistic developments in the history of music. The simultaneous juxtaposition of contrasting voices opened entirely new dimensions for composers, allowing them to move beyond the single line of plainchant to explore sonorities of two or more voices. Counterpoint, harmony, and texture became standard elements of Western music.

No one knows exactly when polyphony first began to be cultivated. The earliest notated sources date from the latter part of the 9th century, although it seems almost certain that this kind of texture was already in use in at least some areas before this time. As in the case of plainchant, practice preceded notation. But clearly the same drives that led to the monophonic troping of plainchants helped foster polyphony as well.

## ORGANUM

The earliest known polyphonic compositions were based on existing plainchants and thus we can think of them, in effect, as vertical tropes. The original "text"—the combined words and melody of the chant—remained intact but was now elaborated and amplified through the addition of a new voice or voices layered on top of the chant.

The first preserved reference to polyphony in medieval times appears in a manuscript treatise known as the *Musica enchiriadis* ("Musical Handbook"), written during the middle or second half of the 9th century by an unknown author or authors, possibly in what is now eastern France. This instructional manual includes examples of what we now call **organum** (plural, **organa**), a polyphonic work consisting of an original plainchant melody in one voice along with at least one additional voice above or below. (The exact origin of the term *organum* is unclear: the word means "instrument" in Latin and could be applied to any instrument, although it later came to be associated specifically with the organ.) The *Musica enchiriadis* offers several examples of **parallel organum**, in which an additional voice runs parallel to an established plainchant melody at a constant interval. The plainchant melody is called the *vox principalis* (principal voice); the additional voice is called the *vox organalis* (the organal, or added, voice). In the simplest parallel organum, a single organal voice runs a fourth or fifth below the principal voice (Example 2–1). Other examples include four voices, with the principal voice doubled an octave down and the organal voice doubled an octave up (Example 2–2).

**EXAMPLE 2–1**  Parallel organum.
The solid notes indicate the principal voice; the hollow notes indicate the organal voice.

Tu  Pa - tris  sem - pi - ter - nus  es  fi - li - us.

You are the eternal son of the Father.

**Source:** *Te Deum,* phrase in parallel fifths, from *Musica Enchiriadis.* Text edition by Hans Schmid, *Musica et Scolica Enchiriadis,* Veröffentlichungen der musikhistorischen Kommission, vol. 3 (Munich: Bayerische Akademie der Wissenschaften, 1981). Used by permission of the publisher.

**EXAMPLE 2–2**  Four-part parallel organum.
The solid notes indicate the principal voice; the hollow notes indicate the organal voice.

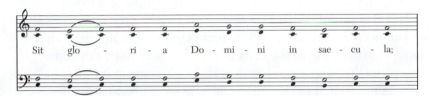

Sit  glo - ri - a  Do - mi - ni  in  sae - cu - la;

lae - ta - bi - tur  Do - mi - nus  in  o - pe - ri - bus  su - is.

May the glory of the Lord last forever;
the Lord will rejoice in his works.

**Source:** Four-part parallel polyphony from *Musica Enchiriadis.* Text edition by Hans Schmid, *Musica et Scolica Enchiriadis,* Veröffentlichungen der musikhistorischen Kommission, vol. 3 (Munich: Bayerische Akademie der Wissenschaften, 1981). Used by permission of the publisher.

Not all organa in the *Musica enchiriadis* are so mechanical. In some cases (Example 2–3), the *vox organalis* begins on the same pitch as the *vox principalis* but remains fixed until the plainchant melody has climbed to the interval of a fourth above, returning to a unison at the ends of phrases. The second phrase of Example 2–3 is particularly interesting because it has more intervallic variety than the first, with two thirds and one fifth alongside the fourths.

## Innovations in Organum

In later sources, more elaborate organum like that in the second phrase of Example 2–3 becomes increasingly common, a trend that coincides with the growing prominence of organum within the liturgy for certain feast days in some regions. This more intricate style characterizes many Alleluias, Sequences, Tracts, and responsary chants from the Divine Office in the Winchester Troper, compiled at Winchester Cathedral, England, sometime around 1000.

**EXAMPLE 2–3** Two-part organum.
The solid notes indicate the principal voice; the hollow notes indicate the organal voice.

Rex    cae - li,    Do - mi - ne,    ma - ris    un - di - so - ni,
Ti - ta - nis    ni - ti - di    squa - li - di - que    so - li.

> O Lord, King of Heaven, and of the sounding sea,
> Of the shining sun and the dark earth.

Te   hu - mi - les   fa - mu - li,   mo - du - lis   ve - ne - ran - do   pi - is,
Su   iu - be - as   fla - gi - tant   va - ri - is   li - be - ra - re   ma - lis.

> Your humble servants worship you in sacred songs,
> And urge you to agree to free them from all their evils.

**Source:** *Rex Caeli,* two-part polyphony, from *Musica Enchiriadis.* Text edition by Hans Schmid, *Musica et Scolica Enchiriadis,* Veröffentlichungen der musikhistorischen Kommission, vol. 3 (Munich: Bayerische Akademie der Wissenschaften, 1981). Used by permission of the publisher.

Another important stylistic innovation in organum appears in *Ad organum faciendum* ("On the Making of Organum"), a treatise written around 1100. Here, the *vox organalis* is placed above the *vox principalis.* This relationship—plainchant below, added voice above—would soon become standard. Around this same time, contrary motion between voices begins to be preferred over parallel motion. One 12th-century writer (formerly known as John Cotton, now simply as John) recommended that "whenever there is an ascent in the original melody"—that is, in the chant—there should be "at that point a descent in the organal part and vice versa."[1] He illustrates this principle with the brief but striking passage shown in Example 2–4.

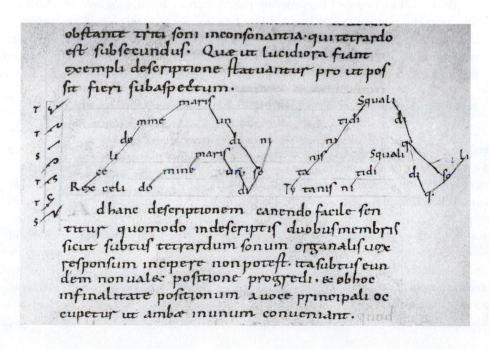

**Early organum.** It is no coincidence that one of the earliest sources of polyphony, the treatise entitled *Musica enchiriadis,* should also be one of the first to indicate fixed, unambiguously identifiable pitches. At this early stage of notation, the scribe of the *Musica enchiriadis* has not attempted to give any rhythmic signs beyond the words of the chant being sung, but the pitches are indicated quite precisely through the daseian signs in the margin at the left. Adapted from grammatical accent marks in ancient Greek, each of these corresponds to a specific pitch; the passage shown here is transcribed in Example 2–3.

**Source:** Staatsbibliothek Bamberg/Msc. Var 1. fol. 57r

**EXAMPLE 2–4** Organum in contrary motion.

Praise God in Heaven.

**Source:** *HUCBALD, GUIDO, AND JOHN ON MUSIC: THREE MEDIEVAL TREATISES,* translated by Warren Babb and edited by Claude Palisca. Copyright ©1978 Yale University Press. Reprinted by permission.

This innovation transformed the organal voice from a derivative of the original—running parallel to it at the interval of a fourth, a fifth, or an octave—into a distinctive and independent line of its own. Organum thus includes the earliest known instances of *counterpoint*, the simultaneous combination of independent musical lines. Contrapuntal texture allowed for the vertical expansion of sound through multiple voices of essentially equal weight. It also prompted medieval theorists to reevaluate what intervals might or might not be considered consonant. Octaves, fifths, and fourths had long been considered "perfect" intervals within the Pythagorean system because they could be expressed as mathematically simple ratios: octave = 2:1; fifth = 3:2; fourth = 4:3. Thirds and sixths were deemed "imperfect consonances," although some writers were reluctant to accept various forms of these intervals, particularly the major and minor sixth. Important cadences always resolved to fifths, octaves, or unisons.

Yet another step in the development of organum was the introduction of multiple notes in the *vox organalis* over a single note in the chant. The resulting **melismatic organum** allowed for a much wider use of dissonance between the organal voice and the chant. This type of organum is particularly prevalent in manuscripts from northern Spain and from southwestern France, particularly the abbey of St. Martial (see Focus: St. Martial). The two-part organum on the plainchant Kyrie *Cunctipotens genitor deus* illustrates this new style of melismatic organum (for the original plainchant version, see the Anthology). This particular organum comes from the Codex Calixtinus, a text written around 1120 to 1130 as a guide and songbook for pilgrims on their way to Santiago de Compostela in northwestern Spain, the site of the shrine of Saint James the Apostle.

((•• **Listen**

**CD1    Track 14**

**mysearchlab** (with scrolling translation)

KYRIE *CUNCTIPOTENS GENITOR DEUS*

Score Anthology I/10

## *Focus*  ST. MARTIAL

One of the most important centers for the production and collection of medieval chant and early polyphony was the Abbey of St. Martial de Limoges, in the region in south-central France known as Aquitaine. Like every abbey of any size, it had its own *scriptorium*, a scribal workshop in which monks with special calligraphic skills would copy old manuscripts and prepare new ones. The repertory of chant manuscripts using Aquitanian neumes is considerable. The librarians of St. Martial, moreover, seem to have gone out of their way to acquire manuscripts from smaller institutions, amassing one of the most impressive libraries of chant manuscripts in late medieval Europe. St. Martial was for the most part spared the ravages of war that damaged or destroyed so many of the monasteries in northern France. But like many French monasteries, it was closed in the wake of the French Revolution and demolished shortly afterward, in 1792. Fortunately, its manuscripts had been sold to the French royal library in 1730, and scholars today can consult this remarkable collection in the National Library of France, in Paris.

An important effect of melismatic organum was to force performers to slow the pace of the chant melody in the lower voice to allow time for those singing the orgainal line to get in all their notes. As a result, the lower voice came to be designated the **tenor**, from the Latin *tenere*, meaning "to hold." For several more centuries at least, the term *tenor* would refer to the voice of a polyphonic work that "held" the chant; until the middle of the 15th century, this was usually the lowest voice. Only later did it become associated with a particular range. The added second voice in organum and later forms of polyphony came to be known as the **duplum**.

## Notre Dame Organum

The most elaborate forms of organa appeared from a circle of largely anonymous composers working in and around the Cathedral of Notre Dame in Paris in the 12th century. Although a church had existed on this site for some time before, builders laid the cornerstone of the magnificent structure we now know as Notre Dame in 1163, and it was at just about this same time that a composer identified only as Léonin (or Leoninus, in the Latinized form) began to write large quantities of organa for the chants of the liturgical year. Although other contemporary composers were undoubtedly involved in this process, we may take Léonin as the prototypical composer of what is now called Notre Dame organum.

Léonin and his colleagues turned their attention primarily to the responsorial chants—that is, those plainchants performed in part by a soloist (or small group of soloists singing in unison), to which a chorus responds. Léonin left unchanged the choral portions of these chants, which continued to be performed monophonically by the chorus, but he wrote lengthy two-voice organa for those portions of the chants performed by the soloists. His organum setting of the Christmas plainchant Gradual *Viderunt omnes* (Anthology) may be diagrammed as follows:

| RESPOND | | VERSE | |
|---|---|---|---|
| **Soloists** | **Chorus** | **Soloists** | **Chorus** |
| Two-part organum | Plainchant | Two-part organum | Plainchant |
| *Viderunt omnes* | fines terrae... | *Notum fecit...* | iustitiam. |

Léonin's organal sections are either in melismatic organum (also known as **free organum** or **unmeasured organum**) or in **measured organum** (also known as **discant organum**). In free organum, the duplum voice moves rapidly against the slower moving notes of the original chant. It was used in passages that in the original chant are neumatic, as on the opening word *Viderunt*. In measured organum, the two voices move at about the same speed in what is essentially a note-against-note style. This type of organum was used in passages that are melismatic in the original chant, such as on the word *omnes* (in *Viderunt omnes*) and, in the verse, on the word *Dominus*.

Any given piece of organum in the style of Léonin thus consists of up to three different kinds of texture, determined by the nature of the original plainchant:

- Unison plainchant, unchanged from the original, in those sections of a responsorial chant sung by the chorus.

((•• **Listen**

CD1    Track 15
**mysearchlab** (with scrolling translation)
LÉONIN (?)
Two-voice Organum on *Viderunt omnes*
Score Anthology I/11

**The Cathedral of Notre Dame, Paris.**
For more than 600 years—from the completion of its towers in the first half of the 13th century until 1889, when the Eiffel Tower was built—the Cathedral of Notre Dame was the tallest building in Paris. It dominated the city in more than just size, however. Occupying a prominent space on the Ile de la Cité on the River Seine, Notre Dame stands at the very center of the French capital.

**Source:** Andy Marshal/Alamy

(((•►[Listen

**CD1    Track 16**
**mysearchlab** (with scrolling translation)
PÉROTIN
*Four-voice Organum on* Viderunt omnes
Score Anthology I/12

- Free organum in those sections sung by the soloists that are predominantly neumatic in the original chant.

- Measured organum in those sections sung by the soloists that are predominantly melismatic in the original chant.

Measured organum required a new kind of notation, one that could show the temporal relationship of the various voices. This new system of **rhythmic modes** allowed composers to distinguish between long and short notes in various combinations (see Focus: The Rhythmic Modes). Any given voice tended to stay within a single rhythmic mode for a fairly long period of time; composers rarely switched from one rhythmic mode to another in quick succession. It was standard practice, however, to set different voices in contrasting rhythmic modes at the same time. Tenors, for example, frequently adhere to the fifth rhythmic mode under an upper voice or voices moving in the first, second, or third modes.

Once these basic principles of composition and notation had been established, composers were able to add still further layers of musical commentary to their original glosses on a given chant. The composer known only as Pérotin (Perotinus), a younger contemporary of Léonin, is credited with having added a third voice (**triplum**) and on rare occasions even a fourth voice (**quadruplum**) to organa for feasts of special significance. These are works of astonishing length. Even in a fairly lively performance, Pérotin's four-voice organum for the Gradual *Viderunt omnes* (Anthology) runs more than 11 minutes.

The scale of time here expands enormously. In the recording used in the Anthology, the ensemble dwells on the first word of the text—*Viderunt*—for more than two full minutes. The original melody of the plainchant, in the tenor voice, is sung to extremely long notes that serve as a foundation to the superstructure of the three upper voices, which intertwine in a higher and relatively narrow range and at a far more rapid pace. Each syllable of the first word brings out a new vowel sound—*Vi* ("ee")-*de* ("eh")-*runt* (short "u")—which in turn changes the sonority of the whole. The tenor voice also shifts pitch with each new syllable, furthering a sense of forward motion. In this way, a single word of three syllables intoned over a span of more than two minutes conveys a sense of enormous variety and momentum.

The return to plainchant at the words *finis terr[a]e* corresponds to the point of the original plainchant Gradual at which the chorus begins its response to the opening words of the soloist (*Viderunt omnes*). The organal portions of Pérotin's setting were probably sung by soloists or a small ensemble of singers with only a few voices to each part: this is rhythmically intricate music that demands a higher level of musical skill than that possessed by the average monk. Polyphony returns with the verse *Notum fecit. . . .* At the word *Dominus*, the tenor voice assumes a strict rhythmic pattern for this first time; this corresponds to the similar change from free to strict rhythm at the same point in the earlier two-voice organum. This change, too, helps propel the music forward and give it a sense of ever-building energy, even as it seems to otherwise operate somehow outside the parameters of time. If we can imagine ourselves back in the 12th century, hearing polyphony for the first time, and in a setting as grand and vast as the Cathedral of Notre Dame in Paris, we can begin to appreciate the power of this music to enhance the spiritual qualities of the liturgy. And we can understand why such extraordinary works like Pérotin's four-voice organum on *Viderunt omnes* were reserved for special feasts of the liturgical year, such as Christmas Day.

Within only a few decades during the second half of the 12th century, the composers working in and around the Cathedral of Notre Dame in Paris had assembled a sizable collection of polyphony for use throughout the liturgical year. They committed these new works to writing in a compendium that came to be known as the *Magnus liber organi* ("The Great Book of Organum"). Although the earliest version (or perhaps versions) of this compilation have been lost, large portions of it were distributed widely throughout Europe, and those that have survived transmit a sizable repertory of two-, three-, and four-part organa and clausula (see Focus: The *Magnus liber organi*).

## Clausula

The drive to gloss did not end with the composition of organa, not even for three and four voices. Composers like Pérotin also composed many **clausulae**—brief polyphonic sections of discant organum—that could be substituted at will into the appropriate section of a larger existing work of organum. The **clausula** (to use its singular form) is thus not an independent composition that can be performed on its own. The tenor voice of a typical clausula in fact often consists of only a single word or even just a syllable or two of a longer word.

A single source typically provides clausulae for several different passages within the same organum and sometimes even multiple clausulae for the same passage. The Florence manuscript of the *Magnus liber organi*, for example, contains no fewer than nine different two-voice clausulae for the passage on the words *Dominus* within the Gradual *Viderunt omnes*. Clausulae could be longer, shorter, or about the same length as the passage they were written to replace. Stylistically, however, clausulae are always in the same style of organum as the passage into which they could be inserted. In the complete two-voice organum of the Gradual *Viderunt omnes*, for example, the word *Dominus* is set in measured organum, and the many clausulae that might be substituted for this passage are also in measured organum.

In performing organum, singers were free to substitute whichever clausula or clausulae they desired in any combination. Alternatively, they could use no clausulae at all and sing the organum in its original form. What is important here from a liturgical point of view is that regardless of the clausulae chosen (or not chosen), all the notes and words of the original chant would be present in one form or another. The impetus for clausulae, as for organa, it would seem, lay in the desire to write new music that would gloss the original plainchant by providing different layers of musical "commentary" above the plainchant.

((•●[ **Listen**

**CD1    Track 17**
**mysearchlab**
CLAUSULA ON *DOMINUS*
Score Anthology I/13

## Focus THE RHYTHMIC MODES

When faced with the challenge of notating rhythm precisely for passages of measured organum, 12th-century composers built on concepts and terms already in place for analyzing the rhythmic structure of poetry. Each of the six medieval rhythmic modes corresponds to a poetic meter, a specific pattern of long and short syllables, as in the first of the following tables.

To notate these modes, composers used a system of ligatures adopted from traditional chant notation. Ligatures are neumes or notes combined in groupings of two, three,

or four; no more than one syllable may be set to an individual ligature. But what had formerly been used merely to indicate pitch now took on rhythmic significance as well. In modal notation, specific combinations of ligatures and simple notes were used to indicate the prevailing rhythmic mode. A group of three (a ternary) followed by groups of two (binaries), for example, signaled the first mode. A passage beginning with a binary, followed by binaries, and closing with a ternary signaled the second mode. All six patterns are shown in the second of the following tables.

### THE RHYTHMIC MODES

| Mode | Medieval Notation | Poetic Meter Equivalent | Rhythm | Modern Notation |
|---|---|---|---|---|
| 1 | | Trochaic | Long-Short | |
| 2 | | Iambic | S-L | |
| 3 | | Dactylic | L-S-S | |
| 4 | | Anapestic | S-S-L | |
| 5 | | Spondaic | L-L | |
| 6 | | Tribrachic | S-S-S | |

### LIGATURES

| Mode | Ligature Sequence | Medieval Notation | Modern Notation |
|---|---|---|---|
| 1 | Ternary, binary, binary . . . | | |
| 2 | Binary, binary . . . ternary | | |
| 3 | simple, ternary, ternary . . . | | |
| 4 | Ternary, ternary . . . simple | | |
| 5 | Ternary, ternary, ternary . . . | | |
| 6 | Quaternary, ternary, ternary . . . | | |

## Focus THE *MAGNUS LIBER ORGANI*

The "Great Book of Organum" was a 13th-century repository of notated polyphonic works or portions of works that could be interpolated into existing chants of the liturgy throughout the church year. Portions of this repertory were copied and distributed in various manuscripts. The most important of those to have survived are known to scholars by the briefest of abbreviations: F, W1, W2, and Ma. These names are based on the first letter of the cities in which the manuscripts now reside.

**F** is located in the Biblioteca Mediceo-Laurenziana in Florence, Italy. The largest and oldest source, it consists of 441 leaves. Probably copied in Paris around 1245 to 1255, it contains more than 1,000 pieces of music and includes an elaborate illustration on its opening page (see page 16) that depicts the three varieties of music.

**W1** and **W2** are both located in the Herzog-August-Bibliothek in Wolfenbüttel, Germany. W1 is a relatively modest copy (197 leaves) that was prepared in Scotland in the mid-13th century for the Augustinian priory at St. Andrews. W2 (225 leaves)

was copied in France—but not at Notre Dame—in the middle of the 13th century.

**Ma** is located in the Biblioteca Nacional in Madrid, Spain. This manuscript contains 142 leaves. It was copied in Spain during the mid- to late 13th century.

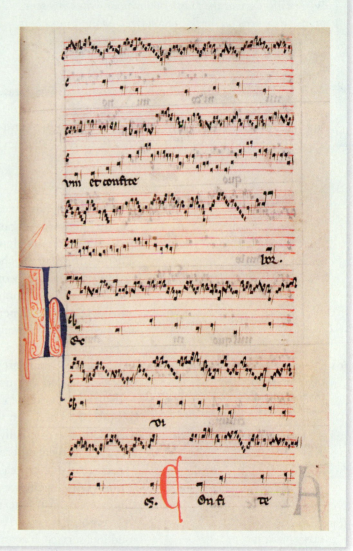

The *Magnus liber organi*. This page, from W1, contains the beginning of the Easter Sunday Gradual *Haec dies*. The alignment of the two voices is only approximate, leaving room for legitimate disagreement about the precise placement of notes at times. Only the polyphonic portion of the organum, which was to be performed by a small group of soloists, appears here, not the plainchant portion, which was to be performed monophonically by the chorus. This is, after all, the "Great Book of Polyphony," not of chant. The polyphony resumes with the beginning of the verse on the last system (with *Confitemini*); this, too, was music for the soloists. The faint notes visible on this page are from the ink that has bled through from the reverse side of the parchment.

Source: Herzog August Bibliothek

## Motet

Although clausulae may have been fragmentary from a liturgical point of view, consisting of only a few syllables or words, the longer ones constituted a musical whole that began and ended in the same mode; the very word clausula itself comes from a Latin root meaning "to cadence" or "conclude." The only thing many clausulae lacked to be performed separately was a text.

## Primary Evidence — LÉONIN AND PÉROTIN

*The identification of Léonin and Pérotin as the chief composers of the Magnus liber organi hangs by the thread of a single document, an account—excerpted here—written in the late 13th century by an English student at the University of Paris. Ironically, we do not know the identity of the student, who since the 19th century has been known as "Anonymous IV" because he was the fourth anonymous writer in a series of medieval texts on music anthologized by the 19th-century French scholar Charles-Henri-Edmond de Coussemaker.*

■ ■ ■

And note that Master Léonin, according to what was said, was the best composer of organa, who made the great book of organum from the gradual and antiphonary to elaborate the divine service. And it was in use up to the time of Pérotin the Great, who edited it and made very many better *clausulae* or *puncta*, since he was the best composer of discant, and better than Léonin. But this is not to be said about the subtlety of the organum, etc.

But Master Pérotin himself made excellent *quadrupla*, like "Viderunt" and "Sederunt," with an abundance of colors of the harmonic art; and also several very noble *tripla* like "Alleluia Posui Adiutorium," "Nativitas," etc.

**Source:** *THE MUSIC TREATISE OF ANONYMOUS IV: A NEW TRANSLATION* by Jeremy Yudkin. Copyright © 1985 Jeremy Yudkin. Reprinted by permission.

**((•— Listen**
**CD1    Track 18**
**mysearchlab** (with scrolling translation)
MOTET *FACTUM EST SALUTARE / DOMINUS*
Score Anthology I/14

**((•— Listen**
**CD1    Track 19**
**mysearchlab** (with scrolling translation)
MOTET *SUPER TE / SED FULSIT / PRIMUS TENOR / DOMINUS*
Score Anthology I/15

In the venerable medieval tradition of troping, some unknown individual or group of individuals working in the late 12th or early 13th century had the idea of underlaying a new text to the duplum of an existing clausula and performing the new work outside the liturgy of the church. Thus was born the genre of the **motet** (from the French word *mot*, meaning "word"). The term was fitting because the text for the duplum in many of the earliest motets was in the vernacular, not Latin. It is the presence of a contrasting text in the upper voice or voices that distinguishes the motet from its immediate ancestor, the clausula. The texted duplum was known as the **motetus** because it had words.

Musically, there are only minor differences between the aforementioned clausula on *Dominus* and the motet *Factum est salutare/Dominus*. (By convention, the titles of 13th-century motets consist of the first word or words of each voice in order from top to bottom.) The Latin text for the motetus is a trope on the longer text in which the word *Dominus* originally appeared, the plainchant Gradual for the Mass on Christmas Day. The musical differences between the original clausula and the motet are so minor, in fact, that one can easily follow a performance of the latter using the score of the former. Once again, we see the urge of medieval minds to gloss an existing text (or in this case, an existing text and melody) by adding new layers.

A motet, however, is not a prescribed element of a sacred liturgy: while it might be used in a service, it is not obligatory in the way that a Gradual or Alleluia is. Separated from its liturgical context, then, the tenor of a motet was no longer a sacred object—a portion of a larger plainchant—and composers were quick to take advantage of this fact. They began to manipulate the musical content of the tenor in various ways. The movement in this direction is evident in the four-part motet *Super te / Sed fulsit / Primus tenor / Dominus* (Anthology): its lowest voice is based on the familiar *Dominus* tenor but with the rhythms and even some of the pitches treated rather freely at points. Someone—an anonymous composer, possibly working in England around 1270—also added a second, untexted tenor to create a four-voice texture. The upper two voices (in Latin) sing two different texts, each of which is a gloss on the Christmas story, with emphasis on the miracle of the virgin birth of Christ. The end result is a self-contained

## *Focus*  SOURCES OF 13TH-CENTURY MOTETS

Most of the surviving 13th-century motets are preserved in three important manuscripts of the time: the Montpellier Codex, the Bamberg Codex, and the Las Huelgas Codex.

**The Montpellier Codex,** at the Bibliothèque Inter-Universitaire in Montpellier, France, is by far the largest extant collection of medieval polyphony. The codex consists of 397 leaves and contains 336 works of music, mostly motets. Its various fascicles (gatherings of parchment leaves) were not all copied at the same time: the oldest layer of the manuscript dates from the 1270s, with additions dating from as late as the early 14th century.

**The Bamberg Codex,** although now housed at the Staatliche Bibliothek in Bamberg, Germany, was, like the Montpellier Codex, prepared in Paris, probably during the last quarter of the 13th century. It contains 100 double motets, of which 44 are in Latin, 47 are in French, and 9 are polylingual.

**The Las Huelgas Codex,** at the Monasterio de Las Huelgas in Burgos, was copied at the Cistercian monastery of Las Huelgas in north-central Spain around 1300. This manuscript contains 186 pieces, including organa and sequences, as well as motets.

***Huic main/Haec dies* from the Montpellier Codex.** The upper of the two voices begins on the second line, with the elaborate initial H. The tenor, untexted in this source, begins about a third of the way into the next-to-last system. *Mulierum* at the bottom marks the beginning of a different motet that continues on the next leaf of the manuscript.

**Source:** IAM/akg-images

whole, a set of multiple glosses on a single theme, both from the literary and musical point of view. This **polytextual motet** is typical of the genre in the second half of the 13th century: different voices sing different texts simultaneously.

Other 13th-century motets bear no relationship at all to any preexistent work. The anonymous *A Paris/On parole/Frese nouvele* is based on an apparently newly composed tenor with its own self-contained (if very brief) text in French. The tenor states its eight-measure unit of text and music a total of four times. At least one of the two upper voices, in turn, overlaps the cadential points of the tenor, thus creating a sense of forward momentum even while articulating points of rest within the three-voice texture. The text of the tenor—*Frese nouvele, muere france* ("Fresh strawberries! Nice blackberries!")—simulates (or may actually quote) a street vendor's call, the 13th-century equivalent of a peanut vendor's cry in a baseball stadium. As such, it justifies both the

((•• Listen
**CD1  Track 20**
**mysearchlab** (with scrolling translation)
MOTET *A PARIS/ON PAROLE/FRESE NOUVELE*
Score Anthology I/16

musical and textual repetition it receives here. The multiple repetition of rhythmic and melodic ideas would in fact become a central feature of *isorhythm*, a structural device found in many motets in the 14th century (see Chapter 3).

The motetus and triplum of this motet present two texts different from each other and different yet again from that presented in the tenor. The three texts of *A Paris/ On parole/Frese nouvele* are all related in content. Above the street vendor's cry in the tenor, the triplum and duplum extol the virtues of Paris: good bread, good wine, good friends, even good prices to "to suit a poor man's purse." The texts of many other 13th-century polytextual motets are more diverse; some are even polylingual, with a motetus in Latin and a triplum in French, or vice versa. Subject matter is often equally unrelated. It is not unusual, for example, to find a sacred Latin motetus juxtaposed with a French triplum whose text is a love poem. The distinction between sacred and secular was not nearly so sharp in the medieval era as it would be in later centuries. Still, we sense in at least some of these compositions a real delight in the contrasting images they evoke. It is also likely they contain references that would have been familiar in the 13th century but are no longer readily grasped today.

By about 1230, motets had become so popular that no one seems to have been particularly interested in writing clausulae anymore. We are not altogether sure just who performed motets and under what circumstances. Given the nature of the sources and their notational sophistication, it seems most likely that they were sung by the same clerics who cultivated plainchant and organum. Johannes de Grocheo, a theorist writing around 1300, observed that a motet "ought not to be performed in the presence of common people, for they would not perceive its subtlety, nor take pleasure in its sound." Instead, motets should be performed only "in the presence of learned persons and those who seek after subtleties in art."

We also lack firm evidence on how these works were performed. The absence of any substantial quantity of text in most of the tenors has led some scholars to speculate that the tenor line may have been performed on instruments. But it seems equally plausible that this part could have been **vocalized**—that is, sung to a vowel sound, without a text. Another possibility of performance would have been to have instruments double the tenor line.

## Conductus

The **conductus** (plural, **conductus** or **conducti**) offered yet another outlet for composers wishing to write either monophonic or polyphonic music in the late 12th and early 13th centuries. These works, for one, two, three, or occasionally four voices, are not based on borrowed material of any kind. The texts consist of freely composed poems written in metered verse that lend themselves to syllabic and strongly metrical musical settings. In the polyphonic conductus, all voices move in roughly the same rhythm. The note-against-note part writing in this genre is so distinctive in fact that this manner of composition in medieval music has since come to be called "conductus style."

Rhythmically, the notation of these pieces is ambiguous. They do not follow the system of modal rhythm evident in the measured sections of organum, clausula, and motet, but they probably adhere to the modal rhythm of the texts themselves. Most sources align the voices with some care, using vertical lines to clarify the relationship of the different parts. The long melisma at the end of the last strophe of *Flos ut rosa floruit* is a characteristic feature of the genre known as a *cauda*, a term derived from the Latin word for "tail," the same root word from which *coda* would eventually evolve.

**Gothic heights.** The interior of the Cathedral at Amiens, in northern France, is three times as high (43 meters, or about 142 feet) as it is wide. Begun in 1220, this masterpiece of Gothic architecture reflects certain parallels to the rhythmic strata of motets in this era: a wide base (comparable to a slow-moving tenor), with a smaller series of arches in the middle (the faster-moving duplum) and a series of still smaller arches at the top, just below the vaulted ceiling (the triplum). Although such parallels are in one sense superficial, they correspond in a deeper way to the medieval penchant for variety and contrast within layered structures.

**Source:** Anthony Scibilia/Art Resource, NY

Conducti (or conductus; either plural is correct) derive their name from the Latin word *conducere*, meaning "to escort," and these pieces were probably first used as processionals—that is, as music to be performed while a priest and his attendants entered and left the church. The conductus repertory is sizable: about 200 polyphonic works of this kind are found side by side with the organa and clausulae in the various manuscripts associated with the *Magnus liber organi*. Another, separate repertory of conducti survives in manuscripts from southwestern France and the Iberian peninsula. The writing of conductus continued in Germany and England into the second half of the 13th century but had largely ceased by the beginning of the 14th.

# MENSURAL NOTATION

By the middle of the 13th century, the notational system using ligature groupings to indicate rhythmic modes (see Focus: The Rhythmic Modes) could no longer accommodate the increasing rhythmic variety of the latest motets. In response, a new, more precise system emerged. The writer most widely credited with setting down the principles of this system—known as **mensural notation** (from the Latin *mensurata*, meaning "measured," in the sense of a division into units)—was Franco of Cologne. In his *Ars cantus mensurabilis* ("The Art of Measurable Song"), written sometime between 1260 and 1280, Franco codified a system that retained the note shapes and many of the conventions of the rhythmic modes but that introduced one important modification in particular: Franco's system assigned specific rhythmic meanings to each of the various note shapes. The significance of this innovation can scarcely be underestimated, for it provided composers with a system capable of vastly greater flexibility, one that is essentially still in place today in spite of many subsequent modifications.

## Franconian Notation

In the earliest variety of mensural notation, now known as **Franconian notation**, the main note values were the **long**, the **breve**, and the **semibreve** (Example 2–5). The breve took its name from the Latin word for "brief," for this described its relationship to the long. In modern editions, the long is usually transcribed as a dotted half note or half note, depending on the context, and the breve as a quarter note, but these values are less important than the temporal relationships.

Each of these notes could be divided into smaller units of two or three. Triple divisions, which Franco associated with the perfection of the Holy Trinity (God the Father, God the Son, God the Holy Spirit), were considered perfect. Duple divisions, in turn, were considered imperfect. The basic unit of measurement was the *tempus* ("time"; plural, *tempora*) and was associated with the duration of the breve. Perfect division of the long resulted in three breves of equal duration—three tempora, that is—but imperfect division resulted in two notes of unequal value, the first of which was known as an "altered" breve and consisted of a duration of two tempora. The breve, in turn, could be divided into three equal semibreves (perfect) or two unequal breves (imperfect), transcribed in modern notation as a half note followed by a quarter note.

Franconian notation indicated perfection or imperfection by the patterned grouping of ligatures (for example, a three-note ligature followed by a series of two-note ligatures) in much the same way that the rhythmic modes had been indicated. Under Franco's system, the final note in any succession of ligatures must be perfect. (For those first learning this system of notation, it is therefore sometimes easier to work from right to left in interpreting these units; musicians of the time were of course adept at discerning such patterns at sight.) A notated long, in other words, could be understood as a dotted half note or as a half note (followed by a quarter-note breve) depending on its context. Example 2–6 (a, b, c, and d) indicates how this system worked. The final long in (a) and (b) is understood to be perfect—that is, the equivalent of three breves. But in (b), the initial long must be imperfected to accommodate the breve in the middle. In (c), in which three breves separate two longs, the opening long is read as

**EXAMPLE 2–5** Franconian notation: the long, the breve, and the semibreve.

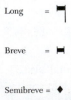

Long =

Breve =

Semibreve = ◆

**EXAMPLE 2–6** Interpreting Franconian notation.

a)

b)

c)

d)

perfect because the last long must also be perfect. In (d), however, in which four breves separate two longs, the opening long must be imperfected to mesh with the remaining breves and the concluding perfect long.

Seemingly complicated, the system was in fact perfectly suited to the music it represents, for it provided a smooth and supple sense of rhythm and syncopation that avoids the accented downbeat implicit in the concept of the bar line.

## Petronian Notation

Franco's system did not gain immediate acceptance, but by the end of the 13th century his principles were in widespread use. Around 1280, Petrus de Cruce (Pierre de la Croix), a French composer and theorist, refined the Franconian system to allow for greater subdivision of the breve. **Petronian notation** allowed for as many as nine semibreves within the duration of a single breve, accommodating the increasingly rapid movement of motet tripla. (Motets notated in this new fashion, which typically feature a very rapidly moving triplum, are sometimes called Petronian motets.) The basic pulse of the music, in turn, shifted from the breve to the shorter semibreve. Petrus also introduced the **minim** and **semiminim**, so named because of their very short—minimal—duration (Example 2–7). A minim could be either a third or half the duration of a semibreve, but a semiminim was always equal to half a minim, never a third.

Another Petronian innovation was the *punctus divisionis*, a small "dot of division" used in perfect mensurations to separate groups of notes, making it easier for performers to determine exactly which notes should be altered in their rhythmic value. In Example 2–8 (a), the dot after the first long indicates it is separate—and thus perfect—thereby making it clear that the two following notes (a breve and a long) must together

**EXAMPLE 2–7** Petronian notation: the minim and semiminim.

Minim =

Semiminim =

**EXAMPLE 2–8** Interpreting the *punctus divisionis.*

a)

b)

constitute a perfection of three tempora. In Example 2–8 (b), the *punctus divisionis* indicates that the initial long and breve together comprise one perfection, necessitating the alteration of the long to the value of a half note in transcription.

## SUMMARY

By the end of the 13th century, polyphony and a comprehensive system of notation were well established. A considerable repertory of organa (with substitute clausulae), motets, and conductus enjoyed wide distribution throughout Europe. Within a few decades, however, this music would soon be regarded as an *ars antiqua*—an "old" art—that would give way to the *ars nova*—the "new art" of the 14th century.

✓●—**Study** and **Review**
on **mysearchlab.com**

# Music in the 14th Century

Until the middle or end of the 13th century, the prevailing musical style of western Europe was essentially international. No distinctively regional styles of composition existed. Indeed, the organa, motets, and conductus emanating from Paris, as we have seen, were copied and distributed throughout the continent and even across the English Channel.

In the 14th century, by contrast, important regional differences began to emerge. Vernacular poetry—that is, poetry written in the native language of the poet, be it English, French, Spanish, or Italian—replaced Latin poetry in importance, and composers responded to this development by setting to music an increasing number of texts written in their own tongue. Composers themselves became more prominent and less anonymous, actively connecting their names with their works with far greater frequency than in previous centuries (see Focus: The Rise of the Composer).

## FRANCE: THE *ARS NOVA*

In France, there was a growing sense that music had entered a new era in the early decades of the 14th century. Composers self-consciously called what they were doing the ***ars nova***, or "new art." This term, which has become a label for much of 14th-century French music in general, is the title of a treatise written around 1320 and attributed to the theorist-composer Philippe de Vitry (1291–1361). At about the same time, Johannes de Muris (ca. 1300–1350) wrote his *Ars novae musicae* ("The New Art of Music"). In 1324–1325, Pope John XXII acknowledged the influence of the *ars nova* and condemned it as decadent and dangerous in a papal bull (see Primary Evidence: The Pope Condemns the *Ars nova*). The theorist Jacques de Liège (ca. 1260–after 1330), in his *Speculum musicae* ("The Mirror of Music," 1330), also criticized the new practices.

What was this new art? Its chief characteristic was enhanced rhythmic flexibility. Much of Philippe de Vitry's treatise *Ars nova* is in fact devoted to issues of rhythmic notation, including the following:

- The increased use of the minim and semiminim.

- The legitimization of duple meter as fully equal to triple. Prior to the 13th century, duple meter was used to a far more limited extent.

- Imperfection by notes of more remote values instead of by notes of the next shorter value.

- The use of red ink ("coloration") to make otherwise perfect rhythmic values imperfect. A breve written in red ink, for example, was understood as having two-thirds the duration of a breve in the same context written in black ink.

## Focus    THE RISE OF THE COMPOSER

Medieval art in all its forms—painting, sculpture, architecture, music—has for the most part been transmitted anonymously. Medieval artists, as a rule, sublimated their own fame to what they often referred to as "the greater glory of God."

Toward the end of the medieval era, attitudes began gradually to change. We can connect the names of Léonin and Pérotin with the *Magnus liber organi* of the 13th century through only a single surviving account. But beginning in the 13th century, the master builders responsible for the great Gothic cathedrals began to be buried in the structures, their names inscribed on the floor. By the early 14th century, more and more artists were associating their names with their creations. Painters—at least some of them—began to sign their works, and composers followed suit. Although plenty of

musical works continued to be transmitted anonymously for many subsequent centuries, the surviving sources from the 14th century onward preserve a far greater number of composers' names than ever before. Some composers even went out of their way to assemble collections of their work. The French poet and composer Guillaume de Machaut (ca. 1300–1377) compiled what amounts to a complete edition of his poetry and music. The Squarcialupi Codex, a sumptuous musical manuscript copied in Italy during the first half of the 15th century, provides not only the names but even portraits of several of the 14th-century composers whose works it includes. (One of them is Francesco Landini, ca. 1325–1397, whose portrait appears on page 86.) Composers were beginning to be acknowledged as artists rather than as artisans, as creators rather than craftsmen.

Vitry also played an important role in codifying the use of **mensuration signs**. These signs indicated whether the subdivision of breves and semibreves should be understood as perfect or imperfect. Two temporal relationships are relevant here: the *tempus* and the *prolatio*.

- The *tempus* is the relationship of the breve to the semibreve. When perfect, there are three semibreves to each breve; when imperfect there are two.

- The *prolatio* is the relationship of the semibreve to the minim. When perfect ("major"), there are three minims to each semibreve; when imperfect ("minor") there are two.

There are thus four possible combinations of perfect and imperfect *tempus* and *prolatio*. Each of the four basic mensuration signs indicates one of these four combinations, as Example 3–1 summarizes.

The system codified by Philippe de Vitry increased the clarity and flexibility of mensural notation. With only minor modifications, this system would stay in effect throughout the Renaissance and gradually develop into the modern system of notation in the 17th century. The modern-day time signature known as *alla breve*—a semicircle often corrupted into a stylized "C" with a line down the middle—is a vestige of early-14th-century mensural notation; even though we no longer use breves, we understand the sign to mean a beat of two half notes in each measure, the half note being the descendant of the medieval breve.

### The *Roman de Fauvel*

The *ars nova* style is amply evident in a number of works composed in or around 1316 for the satirical allegory *Le Roman de Fauvel* ("The Story of Fauvel"). The author of this allegory, Gervais de Bus, was a clerk who worked at the French court from 1313

## Primary Evidence — THE POPE CONDEMNS THE *ARS NOVA*

*The rhythmic flexibility of the* Ars nova, *according to Pope John XXII, promoted wantonness at the expense of devotion. The "notes of . . . small values," he declared in the papal bull* Docta sanctorum patrum *of 1324–1325, were "disturbing" the Divine Office. The document gives eloquent witness to the church's ongoing ambivalence about the role of music in worship. The pope acknowledges the need for polyphony, "particularly on feast days," but argues that the original melodies of the plainchant are to be left intact and recognizable as such. The hockets to which the pope further objects—rapid-fire passages in which a melodic line bounces back and forth between different voices—had actually been in use long before the* ars nova.

■ ■ ■

Certain disciples of the new school, much occupying themselves with the measured dividing of the *tempora*, display their prolation in notes that are new to us, preferring to devise new methods of their own rather than to continue singing in the old way. Therefore the music of the Divine Office is disturbed with notes of these small values. Moreover, they hinder the melody with hockets, they deprave them with descants, and sometimes they pad them out with upper parts made out of secular songs. The result is that they often seem to be losing sight of the fundamental sources of our melodies in the Antiphoner and Gradual, and forget what it is that they are burying under their superstructures. They may become entirely ignorant of the ecclesiastical modes, which they have already ceased to distinguish and the limits of which they abuse in the prolixity of their notes. The modest rise and temperate descents of plainsong, by which the modes themselves are recognized, are entirely obscured. The voices move incessantly to and fro, intoxicating rather than soothing the ear, while the singers themselves try to convey the emotion of the music by their gestures. The consequence of all this is that devotion, the true aim of all worship, is neglected, and wantonness, which ought to be eschewed, increases.

This state of things, which has become the common one, we and our brethren have come to regard as needing correction. Therefore we hasten to forbid these methods, or rather to drive them more effectively out of the house of God than has been done in the past. For this reason, having taken counsel with our brethren, we strictly command that no one shall henceforth consider himself at liberty to use these methods, or methods like them, in the singing of the canonical Office or in solemn celebrations of the Mass. . . .

Nevertheless, it is not our wish to forbid the occasional use—especially on feast days or in solemn celebration of the Mass and the Divine Office—of some consonances, for example, the octave, the fifth, and the fourth, which heighten the beauty of the melody. Such intervals, therefore, may be sung above the ecclesiastical chant, but in such a way that the integrity of the chant remains intact and that nothing in the prescribed music be changed. Used thus, the consonances would, more than any other music is able to do, both soothe the hearer and inspire his devotion without destroying religious feeling in the minds of the singers.

**Source:** Henry Raynor, *A Social History of Music from the Middle Ages to Beethoven* (London: Barrie & Jenkins, 1972), pp. 36–37.

**EXAMPLE 3–1** Mensuration signs.

until 1338. A commentary on the dangers of corrupt and incompetent government ministers, it tells the story of a donkey named Fauvel who, through the intercession of the goddess Fortuna, ascends to the throne of France. He marries Vainglory, and together they produce new Fauvels, bringing ruin to France and the world. The name *Fauvel* derives from the first letter of the following vices:

| | |
|---|---|
| **Flaterie** | Flattery |
| **Avarice** | Avarice, greed |
| **Uialanie** | Villainy ("U" and "V" were interchangeable at the time) |
| **Variété** | Inconstancy, fickleness |
| **Envie** | Envy |
| **Lacheté** | Cowardice |

*Fauve*, moreover, was the name of a color—a dark yellow—that was widely associated with evil, deceit, and vanity.

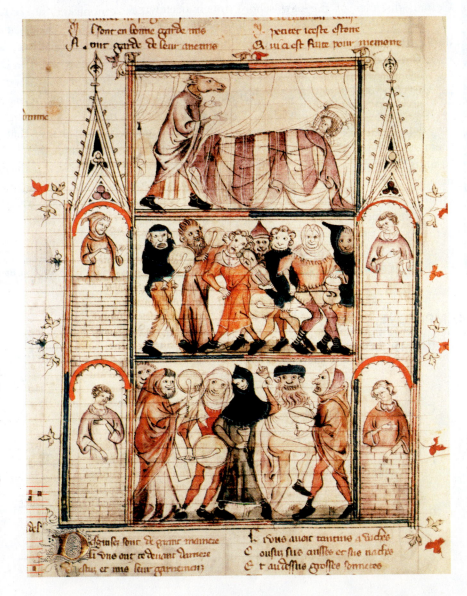

**The *Roman de Fauvel*.** In the 14th-century *Roman de Fauvel*, the donkey Fauvel (top) marries Vainglory, and on their wedding night they are visited by noisy (and masked) music makers, as part of the tradition of charivari, in which revelers strive to disrupt the newlyweds. The instruments (see Focus: Instruments of the Medieval Era) are mostly "high" (loud) ones: bells, cymbals, and many varieties of drums, along with a lone vielle.

**Source:** Ms Fr 146 f.34 'Le Charivari', discordant musicians from the Story of Fauvel written by Gervais du Bois (vellum), French School, (14th century)/Bibliotheque Nationale, Paris, France/Flammarion/The Bridgeman Art Library

One of the 12 surviving manuscripts of *Le Roman de Fauvel* includes a number of interpolated musical compositions, ranging from short monophonic pieces to large-scale polyphonic motets. The motet *Garrit gallus/In nova fert/Neuma* may be by Philippe de Vitry himself, who refers to it in his treatise *Ars nova* to illustrate certain features of the new art.

The untexted tenor of *Garrit gallus/In nova fert/Neuma* is freely composed and bears the simple indication *Neuma*, a kind of generic designation for a melisma. The tenor is structured according to the principle of **isorhythm**, a term coined in the 20th century to describe a technique common to many motets and Mass movements written between roughly 1300 and 1450. An isorhythmic tenor is one based on a fixed rhythmic and melodic pattern that is repeated at least once (and usually more often) over the course of an entire work. Although the tenors of many clausulae of the 12th and 13th century featured repeating rhythmic patterns, the isorhythmic units of the 14th century are far longer and not so closely tied to the basic units of the rhythmic modes. Isorhythm became the preferred structure of the motet in the 14th century: most of the 34 motets in the *Roman de Fauvel* are isorhythmic, as are most of Guillaume de Machaut's 23 motets.

The rhythmic pattern of an isorhythmic tenor is called its **talea** (meaning "cutting" or "segment"); the melodic pattern is called its **color** (a term borrowed from rhetoric and used to describe certain techniques of repetition). Although *talea* and *color* are sometimes of the same length within a given tenor, more often they are not. The *talea* of the tenor of *Garrit gallus/In nova fert/Neuma* (Example 3–2) is stated six times in succession, beginning at measures 1, 26, 51, 76, 101, and 126. The *color*, in contrast, is three times as long and stated in its entirety only twice, beginning at measures 1 and 76.

The tenor of this motet also illustrates the legitimization of duple meter in the *ars nova*. The *talea* is rhythmically symmetrical, and its central notes (marked in Example 3–2 in small brackets) are written in red in the original manuscript, signifying they are to be imperfected, that is, lose one-third of their normal value. The resulting alternation between triple and duple meters is one of the rhythmic novelties that so agitated Pope John XXII, who condemned the mixture of perfect and imperfect mensurations (see Primary Evidence: The Pope Condemns the *Ars nova*).

## Polyphonic Settings of the Mass Ordinary

Composers of the 14th century devoted relatively little energy to polyphonic settings of the complete Mass Ordinary, limiting themselves largely to individual movements or pairs of movements (the Gloria and Credo, for example, or the Sanctus and Agnus Dei). The idea of composing a polyphonic setting of the entire Mass Ordinary would become important in the 15th century but remained largely unexplored in the 14th. Three polyphonic cycles that have survived from the 14th century—known by the location of their various sources as the Mass of Tournai and the Mass of Barcelona—are almost certainly miscellanies gathered after the fact. These are not, in other words, musically integrated cycles of the Ordinary as a whole.

(••─Listen
CD1    Track 22
**mysearchlab** (with scrolling translation)
PHILIPPE DE VITRY (?)
*Garrit Gallus/In nova fert/Neuma*
Score Anthology I/18

**EXAMPLE 3–2**  The *talea* of the tenor in *Garrit gallus/In nova fert/Neuma*.

## Composer Profile

# Philippe de Vitry (1291–1361)

Philippe de Vitry was a man of many talents: composer, music theorist, poet, counselor at the French court, and bishop. He was a friend of the great Italian poet Francesco Petrarca (Petrarch), who called him "the only true poet among the French."

Unlike Guillaume de Machaut, who carefully guarded and organized his musical works, Philippe de Vitry rarely associated his name with his music. The motet *Garrit gallus/In nova fert/Neuma*, for example (Anthology I/16), is attributed to him because an example of it appears in another work attributed to him, the treatise *Ars nova*. Yet the evidence that he wrote the *Ars nova* (and, by extension, the motet) is quite thin, and some scholars have argued that neither is his. Philippe de Vitry nevertheless enjoyed great renown during his lifetime as both a composer and music theorist. Which compositions and treatises were in fact his is a question that scholars will continue to wrestle with for some time, seeking out further references to him from other 14th-century documents and perhaps even new sources of 14th-century music not yet known.

# PRINCIPAL WORKS

Philippe de Vitry's works are plagued by questions of authorship and attribution; he appears to have devoted himself primarily to the genre of the motet, of which he composed perhaps as many as two dozen.

| KEY DATES IN THE LIFE OF PHILIPPE DE VITRY | |
|---|---|
| 1291 | Born October 31 in Vitry (eastern France). |
| ca. 1320 | Begins 20 years of service to Louis de Bourbon, who later becomes the Duke of Bourbon. |
| 1327 | Serves as Louis's representative to the papal court in Avignon. |
| 1340 | Holds a series of positions at the French royal court. |
| 1351 | Appointed Bishop of Meaux, in northern France. |

((•⊷[ **Listen**

**CD1    Track 23**
**mysearchlab**
GUILLAUME DE MACHAUT
*Messe de Nostre Dame*
Score Anthology I/19

One possible exception to this pattern is Guillaume de Machaut's *Messe de Nostre Dame* ("Mass of Our Lady"). Composed sometime during the early 1360s, the work is the only 14th-century polyphonic setting of the complete Mass Ordinary known to have been written by a specific composer. Yet even here, the musical connections among the various movements are subtle and do not revolve around shared musical material or a particular technique. The Gloria and Credo are clearly linked through extended passages that are closely similar, as are the Sanctus and Agnus Dei, but the brief melodic gestures that have been interpreted by some critics as a kind of thread running through the entire cycle seem fairly inconsequential by comparison.

This lack of thematic unity, however, in no way detracts from the remarkable force of the music. Machaut differentiates between movements with large quantities of text and those with relatively little text. The former are set in a predominantly syllabic, conductus-like fashion (note against note), whereas the latter are set in the style of an isorhythmic motet.

Whatever their differences in style, all the movements are based on a plainchant version of the appropriate element of the Ordinary. Thus the tenor of the Kyrie derives from the plainchant Kyrie *Cunctipotens Genitor Deus* (see Example 1–6). The *talea* of the tenor in the first Kyrie is extremely brief (only four measures in modern transcription), and the only rest comes at the very end, which helps articulate each successive return of the *talea*. The *color*, adhering to the pitches of the chant exactly, is stated only once. In a practice that became common around the middle of the 14th century, Machaut includes a voice known as the **contratenor** (meaning "against the tenor") that occupies the same range as the tenor. The contratenor, like the tenor, is isorhythmic, but its *talea* in the first Kyrie is longer. It is fully stated twice—in measures 1–12 and 13–25—then

## Composer Profile

# Guillaume de Machaut (ca. 1300–1377)

In the tradition of the 12th-century trouvères, Guillaume de Machaut was a poet as well as a musician. His texts abound with puns, extended imagery, and possibly encryptions. The formal structures can be complex at times, using rhyme and meter in ways that are far from ordinary. His *Livre du voir dit* ("Book of the True Poem") is a sprawling, quasi-autobiographical collection of letters, lyrics, and song settings written in praise of a young woman, Péronne d'Armentières, with whom Machaut was deeply infatuated late in his life.

Machaut's accomplishments in the realm of music are even more significant. He elevated the *formes fixes* of virelai, rondeau, and ballade to new heights and inspired subsequent generations of poets and composers to cultivate these genres. He also wrote what is apparently the first polyphonic setting of the Mass Ordinary as a coherent cycle.

Machaut always moved in elite circles, working at the courts of the Duke of Berry, the king of Navarre, and the king of Cyprus, as well as the French royal court. He kept tight control over the copying and distribution of his music: only 22 of his 143 musical works are preserved in sources known to have originated outside his immediate circle. The 6 "Machaut Manuscripts," consisting of some 2,100 leaves, were prepared under his supervision and transmit almost all his music in multiple copies, each with the inevitable variant versions associated with the process of copying by hand. The differences in the readings are sometimes slight, sometimes not.

**Guillaume de Machaut.** Love introduces his three children, *Doux Penser* (Sweet Thoughts), *Plaisance* (Pleasure), and *Espérance* (Hope) to the elderly composer at work in his study. This image is from one of the six "Machaut Manuscripts" containing the composer's musical and poetic works and prepared directly under his supervision.

**Source:** Bibliotheque Nationale de France

## PRINCIPAL WORKS

The large majority of Machaut's works are secular. He cultivated all the *formes fixes* of his day, and his output includes some 42 ballades, 22 rondeaux, and 33 virelais. He also wrote 19 *lais*, lengthy monophonic works of 12 strophes but through-composed rather than strophic, reflecting the variety of different poetic forms from strophe to strophe. Almost all of Machaut's 24 motets are isorhythmic; 19 of them are for 3 voices, the remainder for 4.

| KEY DATES IN THE LIFE OF GUILLAUME DE MACHAUT | |
|---|---|
| ca. 1300 | Born in northern France, possibly in Rheims. |
| ca. 1323 | Becomes royal secretary to King John of Luxembourg, king of Bohemia; travels with him as far east as Russia before the king's death in 1346. |
| 1335 | Appointed a canon of the cathedral at Rheims but travels widely over the next 40 years, serving a variety of rulers. |
| 1377 | Dies at Rheims. |

restated partially in the last two measures. By virtue of its length and internal rests, it keeps the motion of the lower voices moving forward. The *color* of the contratenor, unrelated to any preexisting melody, is stated only once. The motetus (duplum) and triplum move freely in more rapid rhythms. In the Christe and the final Kyrie, the *talea* of the tenor and of the contratenor voices coincide.

The addition of the contratenor provided composers with a greatly expanded range of options for **voice leading**—that is, the manner in which two or more voices move in relationship to one another. By the middle of the 14th century, only the third, fifth, sixth, and octave were considered acceptable intervals above the lowest sounding note. Given these restrictions, a fourth voice moving in the same range as the tenor—at times above it, at times below it—greatly increases the number of possible simultaneously sounding pitch combinations. Consider the opening of the Kyrie of Machaut's Mass, for example. Without a contratenor, the A of the tenor could be harmonized in only one of the three basic ways shown in Example 3–3. Adding a contratenor a fifth or a major third below the tenor's A, however, creates the four additional possibilities shown in Example 3–4, more than doubling the number of potential sonorities from three to seven.

The melodic character of Machaut's Kyrie is typical of mid-14th-century polyphony: somewhat angular, with large leaps (an upward seventh in the contratenor of Kyrie I in measure 17, an upward major sixth in measures 21–22), **hockets** (from the Latin word for "hiccough") in measures 10 and 22, and a good deal of syncopation throughout.

The principal cadences follow the standard formulas of the day, with the two structural voices—the highest sounding voice and the tenor, which together provide the basic harmonic intervals—moving from a sixth to an octave (Example 3–5a) or from a third to a fifth (Example 3–5b). Such cadences are found in Machaut's Kyrie at measure 80 (sixth to an octave in the tenor and the triplum, the highest sounding voice at this point) and at measure 27 (third to fifth in the tenor and triplum).

Under certain circumstances, performers were expected to sharpen leading tones that were not notated as such (for a fuller discussion of this convention, part of what is known as *musica ficta*, see Focus: Musica Ficta in Chapter 5). In the cadence at measure 27 of the Kyrie (and in Example 3–6), we can be certain that performers would have sharpened the G in the triplum that precedes the closing A. Otherwise they would be singing a tritone—a forbidden interval—against the C♯ that Machaut explicitly specified in the duplum. The combination of G♯ and C♯ here is part of a **double leading-tone cadence**, a favorite device of 14th-century composers in which a sharped seventh leads to the octave and a sharped fourth leads to the fifth. (In modern transcriptions of music of this period, accidentals the performer would have applied are marked above the notes; accidentals indicated in the original source are notated beside the notes.)

**EXAMPLE 3–3** Possible sonorities with three voices.

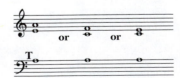

**EXAMPLE 3–4** Additional sonorities possible with four voices.

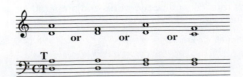

**EXAMPLE 3–5** Cadential patterns in the Kyrie of Machaut's *Messe de Nostre Dame.*

**EXAMPLE 3–6** Double leading-tone cadence at the end of Kyrie I in Machaut's *Messe de Nostre Dame.*

Double leading-tone cadences are also found at the end of the Kyrie II and III. All of these cadences include parallel octaves and fifths. The theorist Johannes de Garlandia had recommended against the use of such parallel movement as early as 1300, but it would continue to be used well into the 15th century, especially at cadences.

## Secular Song

By the middle of the 14th century, three *formes fixes*—literally "fixed forms," or structural patterns—had established themselves as the most important varieties of secular song in France: the ballade, virelai, and rondeau. These were at once both poetic and musical forms, each with its own characteristic pattern of rhyme and musical repetition, with at least one line of refrain—that is, the same words sung to the same music in every strophe (or verse). Musically, each of these forms consists of two parts, conventionally labeled A and B. The first ending of a repeated part (A, B, or both) is known as its *ouvert* ("open"), and the second ending as its *clos* ("close").

The text of the **ballade** usually consists of three strophes of seven or eight lines, the last of which is a refrain. The rhyme pattern varies. That of Machaut's *Je puis trop bien ma dame comparer* ("I May Well Compare My Lady") is ababccdD. (Lowercase letters indicate lines of text that are different in each strophe; uppercase letters indicate the refrain, which is identical throughout, both textually and musically.) Other typical rhyme patterns for the ballade include ababbcbC, ababcdE, and ababcdeF.

Musically, the ballade falls into two distinct sections, the first of which is always repeated and the second of which is sometimes repeated. The music thus unfolds in the pattern AAB (like Machaut's *Je puis trop bien ma dame comparer*; see the following table) or AABB.

Ballades tend to be the most melismatic of all the *formes fixes* used in 14th-century France, with a rhythmically active uppermost voice. Machaut's *Je puis trop* is highly florid, yet the cadences are carefully aligned to the structure of the poetry. As in Machaut's four-part setting of the Mass, the tenor and contratenor lines weave in and out of one another.

The **virelai** follows the pattern AbbaA. The refrain, in other words, is sung at the beginning and end of each strophe. Virelais are typically set in a syllabic fashion, as in Machaut's *Douce dame jolie* ("Sweet Pretty Lady"; see the following table). About three-fourths of Machaut's 33 virelais have come down to us as monophonic works, although this does not preclude the possibility that other voices were added, either as accompaniment or in the form of improvised counterpoint. Virelais, like all songs of this period, could also be performed instrumentally, without any text at all.

((•• Listen
CD1   Track 24
**mysearchlab** (with scrolling translation)
GUILLAUME DE MACHAUT
*Je puis trop bien ma dame comparer*
Score Anthology I/20

((•• Listen
CD1   Track 25
**mysearchlab** (with scrolling translation)
GUILLAUME DE MACHAUT
*Douce dame jolie*
Score Anthology I/21

The **rondeau** (plural, **rondeaux**) consists of eight lines of text set to music following the scheme ABaAabAB. Machaut's rondeau *Ma fin est mon commencement* ("My End Is My Beginning") is a particularly ingenious application of the form. The cantus (the highest voice) and the tenor—in a direct musical representation of the text—are exact retrogrades of each other. In other words, the cantus line, sung backward from end to beginning, is exactly the same as what the tenor sings forward from beginning to end. The contratenor line, in turn, reverses itself at midpoint: it moves forward from measure 1 to the cadence at measure 20, then retraces its steps backward from measure 21 to the end. The idea that beginnings and endings are one and the same is deeply rooted in Christian theology, which connects death to physical and spiritual rebirth.

## The *Ars subtilior* at the End of the 14th Century

The kind of ingenuity evident in Machaut's *Ma fin est mon commencement* was part of a broader fascination with musical puzzles that occupied many composers in the last quarter of the 14th century, particularly in France. Much of this repertory has been called mannered or mannerist because it is self-conscious, complex, and sometimes

### GUILLAUME DE MACHAUT'S BALLADE *JE PUIS TROP BIEN MA DAME COMPARER*: THE RELATION OF TEXT AND MUSICAL STRUCTURE

| Strophe 1 | Rhyme Scheme | Musical Structure |
|---|---|---|
| *Je puis trop bien ma dame comparer* | a | A, first ending (*ouvert*) |
| *A l'ymage que fist Pymalion.* | b | |
| *D'yvoire fu, tant belle et si sans per* | a | A, second ending (*clos*) |
| *Que plus l'ama que Medea Jazon.* | b | |
| *Li folz toudis la prioit,* | c | |
| *Mais l'ymage riens nelie respondoit.* | c | B |
| *Einsi me fait celle qui mon cuer font.* | d | |
| *Qu'ades la pri et riens ne me respont.* | D (refrain) | |

### GUILLAUME DE MACHAUT'S VIRELAI *DOUCE DAME JOLIE*: THE RELATION OF TEXT AND MUSICAL STRUCTURE

| Rhyme Scheme | Musical Structure |
|---|---|
| A (refrain) | A |
| b | B, first ending (*ouvert*) |
| b | B, second ending (*clos*) |
| a | A |
| A (refrain) | A |

downright obscure. But the term *mannered* has negative connotations that are unfair to this fascinating repertory, and most scholars working in this field today prefer the newly coined designation of *ars subtilior* (Latin for "the more subtle art") to acknowledge the central roles that subtlety, understatement, and misdirection play in this music. Composers writing in this style viewed music not only as an art of sound but also as an object of contemplation that could engage and challenge the intellect as well as the soul.

The notational conventions that composers used to record this music present some formidable challenges. Among them are these:

- Special note shapes that sometimes occur in only a single source, such as semibreves with added swirls on their flags or semiminims with flags going both up and down from the same note head.

- Special kinds of coloration used to indicate unusual varieties of syncopation, such as half-colored notes (half red, half black) or hollow red notes, which indicate yet another kind of rhythmic change.

- Obscure verbal canons—rules—given as clues to guide the realization of a puzzling passage, although the rules themselves turn out to be part of the puzzle.

- Notational inconsistencies, with the meaning of certain note values, for example, changing within the course of a single work.

Deciphering these works is an often delightful intellectual challenge, rather like doing an extremely difficult crossword puzzle. The manuscript originals can also be quite visually arresting. Jacob de Senleches's virelai *La harpe de mélodie* ("The Harp of Melody") is notated on staff lines embedded in the frame of a harp; Baude Cordier's *Belle, bonne, sage* ("Beautiful, Good, Wise"), a love song, is notated in the shape of a stylized heart. In this same tradition, Cordier's rondeau *Tout par compas* ("In a Circle I Am Composed") is notated in a circle (see illustration). The two upper voices constitute a **canon**, in which one voice follows the other in strict imitation. The notational difficulties of these works, however, should not obscure their emotional intensity.

Cordier, like many composers of the *ars subtilior*, worked for a time at the papal court in Avignon, in southern France, at the time of the Great Schism. This was the period from 1378 to 1417 when rival popes claimed power over the church, one in Rome, the other in Avignon. (There was even a third pope for a brief time in Pisa.) As if to legitimize itself and increase its prestige, the court at Avignon spared no expense to attract the best available talent in many fields. The Italian poet Petrarch worked there for a time, as did a number of gifted (if now slightly obscure) composers such as Cordier, Jacob de Senleches, Anthonello de Caserta, a certain Grimace, and one Trebor ("Robert" spelled backward?).

The composer known only as Solage appears to have been one of these figures in and around Avignon. His polyphonic virelai *Joieux de cuer* ("Heart's Joy") exemplifies the sophisticated part-writing found in the *ars subtilior* chanson repertory of the late 14th century. In the work's sole source, the Chantilly Codex, only the cantus voice is texted. It is certainly the most melodic of the four parts and the one with the widest range, spanning the interval of an eleventh at one point in a relatively short time (m. 5–10), but the other voices weave themselves around it and around each other in an astonishingly intricate manner so that in the end each voice seems to carry equal weight, even as each goes its own way with its own distinctive melodic ideas.

((•• **Listen**

**CD2 Track 1**

**mysearchlab** (with scrolling translation)
SOLAGE
*Joieux de cuer*
Score Anthology I/23

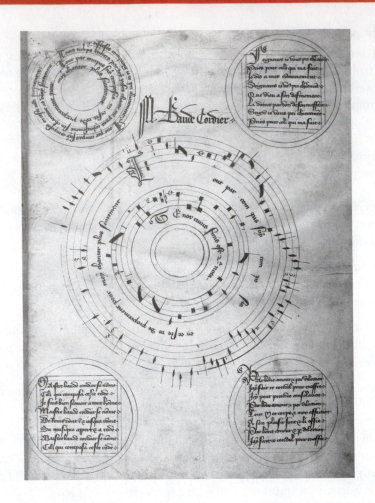

**Baude Cordier, *Tout par compas*.** In the Chantilly Codex, Baude Cordier's rondeau *Tout par compas* assumes the visual form of its text ("In a Circle I Am Composed"). The visual pun goes even further: *compas* also means the drafting instrument of the compass, which is clearly the tool used to prepare the staves of this manuscript. The single line that generates the two canonic upper voices is notated in the outer circle; the tenor part is notated on the inner circle. The texts of the additional strophes are written in the circles at the four corners.

**Source:** Ms 564/1047 fol.12, 'Tout par compas suy composés', illuminated composition by Baude Cordier, from a collection of Medieval ballads, motets, and songs (ink on vellum), French School, (15th century)/Musée Condé, Chantilly, France/Giraudon/The Bridgeman Art Library

The early 15th century in France witnessed a turn away from the rhythmic complexities of the *ars subtilior* and toward a more straightforward style. This shift is generally associated with the beginning of the Renaissance era in music.

# ITALY: THE TRECENTO

Many of the developments in French music during the 14th century have their counterparts in Italian music—so many, in fact, that some scholars speak of an Italian *ars nova*. The more common designation for Italian music of this period, however, is **trecento**. (The term means, literally, the 1300s, or the 14th century. **Quattrocento** is similarly used to designate Italian music of the 15th century.)

The principal secular vocal genres of the trecento are the ballata, the caccia, and the madrigal. As with the *formes fixes* in France, each of these had its own particular textual and musical characteristics.

The **ballata** (plural, **ballate**) is formally similar to the French virelai of the same period (not, as we might expect, to the ballade). The poetic form of the ballata is AbbaA, with a refrain framing the internal lines of each strophe. Most ballate have three strophes, but some have only one; most are polyphonic (usually for two or three voices), but a few monophonic ones exist as well.

Francesco Landini's *Ecco la primavera* ("Behold, Spring"), for two voices, exemplifies the ballata genre. It features smooth melodic lines that project the text syllabically. Not all ballate are quite this syllabic, however. The openings of the first and second section of the music are said to "rhyme," in that they share certain features of rhythm

((•⊸Listen

**CD2    Track 2**
**mysearchlab** (with scrolling translation)
LANDINI
*Ecco la primavera*
Score Anthology I/24

and melody, as do the corresponding cadential measures of the two sections. This kind of musical rhyme can be found in many ballate.

The 14th-century Italian **madrigal** began as a literary form that by the 1340s had crystallized into a series of two or three strophes, each consisting of three lines, with a two-line **ritornello** at the very end. Musical settings of this poetry clearly reflect its textual structure. The ritornello is almost invariably set in a contrasting meter, as in Jacopo da Bologna's *Non al suo amante* ("Never to Her Lover"). Composers of madrigals often set the end (and sometimes the beginning) of individual lines to elaborate melismas. Almost all the trecento madrigal repertory is for two voices, with the upper voice the more florid of the two. Although the tenor is often texted, it lends itself equally well to instrumental performance.

By the end of the 14th century, the madrigal was in decline. The new vocal genre of the same name that arose in the 1520s (see Chapter 6) had no direct connection to it.

The **caccia** (plural, **cacce**) takes its name from the same root word as the English word "chase." Caccia texts often deal, aptly, with hunting, although they can also depict such lively scenes as fires, street vendors' cries, and the bustle of the marketplace. The music, usually for three voices, features two canonic upper parts and an independent tenor. Many (but not all) cacce conclude with a ritornello that can be monophonic, polyphonic, or canonic. Although written monophonically, the ritornello in Lorenzo da Firenze's *A poste messe* ("In Their Positions") can also be realized canonically.

Johannes Ciconia (ca. 1370–1412) is the leading composer of early-15th-century Italy. His *Doctorum principem/Melodia suavissima/Vir mitis* is an example of a new kind of work, the civic motet, written in praise of a particular person or place—in this case Francesco Zabarella, an important authority on canon law from Padua in northern Italy and Ciconia's protector and patron. The *color* of the isorhythmic tenor is stated three times, each time in a different mensuration; thus, although the pitches of the tenor line repeat, the rhythmic pattern changes with each statement. The optional contratenor is constructed in the same way. The voice leading—with many hockets, a relatively free treatment of dissonance (especially in the contratenor), and cadential parallel fifths—is typical of the late 14th and early 15th centuries.

((•• Listen

CD2    Track 3
**mysearchlab** (with scrolling translation)
JACOPO DA BOLOGNA
*Non al suo amante*
Score Anthology I/25

((•• Listen

CD2    Track 4
**mysearchlab** (with scrolling translation)
LORENZO DA FIRENZE
*A poste messe*
Score Anthology I/26

((•• Listen

CD2    Track 5
**mysearchlab** (with scrolling translation)
CICONIA
*Doctorum principem/Melodia suavissima/Vir mitis*
Score Anthology I/27

## *Focus*  COMPOSERS OF THE TRECENTO

**FRANCESCO LANDINI** (ca. 1325–1397), blinded by smallpox as a child, served as organist at various churches in his native Florence. His works feature prominently in the Squarcialupi Codex, where he is portrayed with a portative organ on his knee. The bulk of his surviving music consists of 140 ballate, of which about two-thirds are for 2 voices, the remainder for 3. He also wrote 9 madrigals, 1 caccia, and 1 virelai.

**JACOPO DA BOLOGNA** (flourished 1340–1360) wrote mostly madrigals, 25 of them for 2 voices, 7 for 3 voices. He was active at the courts of Milan and Verona and wrote a treatise on mensuration, but little else is known about him.

**LORENZO DA FIRENZE** (d. 1372 or 1373) was active at the church of San Lorenzo in Florence, where he may have studied with Landini. His surviving works include 7 monophonic ballate, 10 madrigals, a 3-voice caccia (Anthology), and 2 Mass movements.

**JOHANNES CICONIA** (ca. 1370–1412) was born in Liège (now in Belgium) but spent most of his career in Italy, first in Rome, then at the Visconti court in Milan and Pavia, and finally in the northern city of Padua. We possess more (and more varied) music by him than by any other composer active around 1400. These include motets, Mass movements, and songs with both French (virelais) and Italian texts (ballate and madrigals).

# A CLOSER LOOK

✳ Explore on **mysearchlab**

**THE SQUARCIALUPI CODEX**, assembled in Florence ca. 1410–1415, is the single most important surviving source of trecento music. The manuscript takes its name from a later owner, Antonio Squarcialupi (1416–1480), who was an organist and composer in Florence. This enormous collection comprises more than 350 works, including ballate, cacce, and madrigals by Landini, Jacopo da Bologna, and others.

**Composers' works** are grouped together in the Squarcialupi Codex: all of Landini's 146 compositions appear together in a continuous sequence, as do the 28 by Jacopo da Bologna, and so on. Each composer's portion of the manuscript, moreover, includes a portrait and his name: visible here is the beginning of Landini's name, which continues on the next page of the manuscript. The care with which the compiler of the manuscript has identified the authorship of each work reflects the growing awareness of the role of the composer as an individual.

**Francesco Landini** is shown here playing a portative organ. His right hand is on the keyboard, while his left hand operates the bellows behind the instrument that force air through the pipes.

Images of **instruments**, overlaid with gold leaf—actual gold beaten extremely thin—adorn the manuscript. The instruments shown on this page include a lute, a vielle (fiddle), a psaltery, recorders, shawms, and at bottom center, yet another portative organ.

The **parchment** leaves are far more durable than paper, but also far more expensive to produce. A piece of parchment is made from the prepared skin of a sheep or goat; it is cleaned, dried, and stretched thin to form a smooth surface for writing.

The **six-line staff** is typical of trecento sources; the **black notation** of the Medieval era would eventually give way around the middle of the 15th century to white notation.

**Source:** Topham/The Image Works.

# ENGLAND

A small but impressive repertory of English song survives from the 13th and 14th centuries. These works are roughly contemporary with the great English poet Geoffrey Chaucer (1342–1400), whose *Canterbury Tales* are full of musical imagery and references to music making.

Stylistically, English composers and theorists were more inclined to use the interval of a third in practice than composers on the continent. As the early-14th-century commentator Walter Odington noted, although thirds could not be considered consonant "in number"—that is, on the basis of their numerical ratios—"the voices of men" with their "subtlety" could use thirds to create a "smooth mixture and full consonance." The oldest known canon in Western music, a setting of the poem *Sumer is icumen in* ("Summer has Come In"), testifies to this English predilection for thirds. Believed to have been written around 1250, it consists of a *rota*—or round for two notated voices—that unfolds over a two-part **rondellus**, in which the two voices exchange phrases (A and B) continuously, following this scheme:

A   B   A   B

B   A   B   A

The work is preserved in a manuscript that includes both Latin and English texts; which is the older version of the text is debatable, but they seem in any event to be separate—this is not, in other words, a polylingual motet. The original manuscript's instructions for performing the work direct that it be "sung by four companions, but it should not be sung by fewer than three, or two at the least, in addition to those who sing the *pes* [that is, the rondellus in the two lower voices]."

The anonymous song *Edi be thu, heven-queene* ("Blessed Be Thou, Heaven-Queen") also makes liberal use of thirds and sixths as consonant intervals. The rhythmic interpretation of this and similar songs of the 14th century is open to debate. Although the original source for this song carefully aligns the two parts, it leaves ambiguous the duration of the notes. The version in the anthology follows the regular meters of the text, although this is only one of several possibilities. Either or both parts could be performed vocally or instrumentally.

((•• Listen

CD2   Track 6

**mysearchlab** (with scrolling translation)
ANONYMOUS
*Sumer is icumen in*
Score Anthology I/28

((•• Listen

CD2   Track 7

**mysearchlab** (with scrolling translation)
ANONYMOUS
*Edi be thu, heven-queene*
Score Anthology I/29

# INSTRUMENTAL MUSIC

From written accounts and visual images—paintings and statues—we know that instruments played an important role in medieval music. They were routinely used to accompany or double vocal lines, and they were often used on their own, independently of voices. Purely instrumental music entertained guests at banquets, accompanied dancers, and signaled troops in battle. Instruments also found a place in religious music. The Book of Psalms provided ample justification for their use within the liturgy, particularly this often-quoted passage from Psalm 150:

Praise him with the sound of the trumpet: praise him with the psaltery and harp. Praise him with the timbrel and dance: praise him with stringed instruments and organs. Praise him upon the loud cymbals: praise him upon the high sounding cymbals.

At least some church patriarchs were nevertheless uneasy about purely instrumental music. They considered music without a text to be transient and empty. A passage long attributed to Saint Basil (ca. 330–379), but probably written by a different author, reflects a dismissive attitude toward purely instrumental music that would prevail for many centuries:

> Now among the arts which are necessary to life, the goal of which is plain to see, there is carpentry and the chair, architecture and the house, shipbuilding and the ship, weaving and the cloak, forging and the blade; among the useless arts are cithara playing, dancing, aulos playing and all others whose product disappears when the activity ceases.[1]

Visual evidence nevertheless confirms that instruments—either alone or as accompaniment to singing—played an important role in medieval worship. Many medieval churches are adorned with carved images of musicians playing such diverse instruments as the vielle and rebec (bowed stringed instruments), lute, bells, trumpet, and organistrum (hurdy-gurdy). And at least some medieval manuscripts include illustrations that show singers and instrumentalists performing together.

Unfortunately, very little medieval instrumental music was ever written down. It operated instead within an unwritten tradition, one that relied on memory and improvisation. Composers rarely wrote music to be performed on specific instruments or by specific combinations of voices and instruments. Indeed, it would be difficult (and pointless) to draw a sharp distinction between vocal and instrumental music in medieval times. With the exception of plainchant and liturgical polyphony—elements of a sacred ritual whose words were of central importance—vocal and instrumental lines were essentially interchangeable. Instruments could double voice lines or substitute for them altogether, as could voices for instruments. Musicians made ready use of whatever instruments happened to be available at any given moment. In this sense it is impossible to reconstruct a single "correct" performance force for any given piece of medieval music. Issues of medieval performance practice are better approached by taking into account the extraordinarily wide range of options open to musicians of this time—to ask, in effect, whether or not a particular realization of a work is one that *might* have taken place in this era.

Among the earliest works that may have been conceived specifically for instruments are a series of untexted hockets that appear at the end of a 13th-century manuscript known as the Bamberg Codex. Scholars believe these works may have been written with an eye toward instrumental performance because they lack a text in the upper voices. Several of these hockets are based on a tenor line derived from the same *In saeculum* passage of the Easter Gradual *Haec dies* used in a number of early clausulae.

The oldest surviving source of notated keyboard music—intended for the organ—dates from the early 14th century. The Robertsbridge Codex, a few sheets tucked into a larger manuscript, appears to have been copied in France sometime around 1320 and consists of several dances, along with ornamented intabulations of some motets from *Le Roman de Fauvel*. An **intabulation** is an arrangement for keyboard or plucked string instrument (such as the lute) of a work originally written for voices. The Faenza Codex is a considerably more substantial collection of 96 folios copied in the early 15th century. It includes dances and intabulations of Mass movements, chansons, and Italian madrigals. The highly embellished arrangement of Jacopo da Bologna's *Non al suo amante* (Example 3–7) gives some idea of the elaborate figuration to be found in this source.

**EXAMPLE 3–7** Early notated keyboard music from the Faenza Codex.

Jacopo da Bologna

**Source:** Opening of keyboard arrangement of Jacopo da Bologna's *Non al suo amante.* Dragan Plamenac, ed., *Keyboard Music of the Late Middle Ages in the Codex Faenza 117* (American Institute of Musicology, 1972), p. 94. Copyright American Musicological Society, 1972.

The notated dance music of the medieval era is characterized by short repeated sections called *puncta* ("points"). These modular units could be repeated, varied, and embellished at will according to the needs of the dance. The *Quinte estampie real* ("Fifth Royal *Estampie*"), preserved in a French manuscript copied in the second half of the 13th century, illustrates the structural principles of medieval dance music in general. Each *punctum* ("point") is repeated immediately, with a first and then a second ending comparable to the *ouvert* and *clos* of contemporary vocal forms. Here, the same pair of endings serves for all four *puncta*. Dances of this era were highly stylized, with elaborate steps executed at times by individual couples, at times by large groups dancing as a unit. The round dance is an example of the latter category: it called for a group of dancers to hold hands and move in a circle with lively stepping. Dancing was a social activity practiced at all levels of society, from the nobles of the royal courts to the lowliest peasants.

By all accounts, the medieval ear relished contrasting timbres. This penchant for a mixture of sound colors matches well the layered counterpoint of 12th- and 13th-century vocal polyphony, with its clear delineation between a slow-moving tenor in the lowest register and faster-moving voices in the higher ranges. This tendency toward differentiation continued in the polyphony of the 14th century. Not until the second half of the 15th century did a shift toward timbral homogeneity begin to emerge.

((•• **Listen**

**CD2  Track 8**
**mysearchlab**
ANONYMOUS
*La quinte estampie real*
Score Anthology I/30

## Focus  INSTRUMENTS OF THE MEDIEVAL ERA

The basic instrument families that had been established in antiquity—strings, winds, percussion, and keyboard—continued to evolve in the medieval era. Returning crusaders introduced many instruments from the Islamic world to the West, including the lute, guitar, rebec, and shawm.

**STRINGS.** The two most common bowed string instruments of the medieval era were the vielle and the rebec. The vielle was a distant forerunner of the violin but with a longer body and a fifth string that provided a drone. The rebec was a small pear-shaped instrument with three to five strings, sometimes with frets; it produced a rather thin, nasal sound. Plucked string instruments included many varieties of harps, the lute, and the psaltery, a box zither of Arabic origin whose bronze strings could be plucked with the fingers or with quills.

**WINDS.** Medieval wind instruments, like those of the ancient world, were made from animal horns, wood, or metal. The shawm, a double-reed instrument, played a prominent role in processions and dances. Recorders and flutes took a variety of forms, including panpipes, whistles, and double pipes. The medieval trumpet was a straight piece of tubing without slides, valves, or finger holes. With a relatively restricted range, it was probably used mostly for fanfares. The slide trumpet, which appeared in the late medieval era, allowed the player to alter the length of the tubing by sliding the instrument back and forth against the stationary mouthpiece. This instrument, along with the shawm, is often seen in contemporary illustrations of medieval dancing.

**PERCUSSION.** Medieval musicians used a variety of percussion instruments, including individual bells and sets of bells hung from a wooden frame and struck by hammers. Cymbals, timbrels, and other jingling instruments were also quite popular. With a membrane stretched across its frame, the timbrel became a tambourine. Musicians also used drums of many shapes and sizes, from nakers (bowl-shaped drums rather like small kettledrums) to long drums (taller than they were wide) and side drums (wider than they were tall). The tabor was a small drum often played in conjunction with a pipe (whistle) by a single musician.

**KEYBOARD.** The earliest known notated organ music, found in the Robertsbridge Codex of 1325, requires a full chromatic octave—that is, an octave divided into 12 half-steps. But the medieval organ had no **stops**—levers that could control the passage of air through different combinations of pipes—and thus could not project the kind of timbral variety associated with later organs. The

portative organ, which could be transported easily, was the most common form of the instrument. The organistrum (also known as the *symphonia*, or, more commonly, hurdy-gurdy), a stringed keyboard instrument, was smaller and less complicated than the organ, and for that reason more widely used. Its strings were activated by a rotating cylinder of wood turned by a handle at one end; the length of the strings (and thus their pitch) was controlled by a simple keyboard mechanism at the other end. Larger versions of the instrument required two players, one to turn the handle, the other to manipulate the keys. The organistrum was capable of playing both a drone bass and a melody at the same time.

**HIGH AND LOW INSTRUMENTS.** From the 14th century onward, writers often distinguished between two main categories of instruments, "high" (*alta*) and "low" (*bas*), referring not to their register but to their dynamic level. High instruments included trumpets and horns, shawms, bagpipes, and drums. Low instruments included stringed instruments like the lute, vielle, and rebec, of which only the former would survive into the Renaissance.

**King David and his musicians.** In this image from an early-12th-century psalter, King David, inspired by the Holy Spirit in the form of a dove, plays the harp while the musicians surrounding him play the vielle (a bowed string instrument) and various wind instruments.

**Source:** British Library/akg-images

# SUMMARY

The music of the 14th century varied widely from place to place: France, Italy, and England all developed and cultivated their own distinctive idioms and genres. No single historical or musical event marks the end of the medieval era. But the second quarter of the 15th century witnessed a growing tendency toward simplified and homogeneous textures and a more carefully controlled use of dissonance. Isorhythm, although still cultivated, declined in importance as a structural device, and polytextual motets gradually became the exception rather than the norm. All these stylistic developments would eventually come to be associated with the era of music history we now think of as the Renaissance.

✓●—[ **Study** and **Review**
on **mysearchlab.com**

# Part Two
# The Renaissance

The Renaissance was both a cultural movement and a historical period. Its chronological range and defining characteristics are matters of ongoing debate, but in music the term is conventionally applied to the period from about 1420 to 1600.

The term *Renaissance*—"rebirth" in French—was coined by later historians to designate what they saw as an era marked by the revival, or rebirth, of attitudes and ideals rooted in classical antiquity. Many of the philosophical, technological, and artistic innovations of the Renaissance were inspired by the recovery of ancient works, particularly from Greece, that had for all practical purposes been lost to western Europe for almost a thousand years. Medieval scholars were familiar with only scattered works of Plato and other Greek writers, and even then only in Latin translations; Aristotle's works were better known but not in their original Greek. But Greek versions of the writings of these and many other ancient authors had been preserved to the east, in Islamic and Byzantine libraries, especially in and around the Byzantine capital Constantinople (modern-day Istanbul, in Turkey).

By the late 14th century, Western scholars were beginning to find and bring home many of these sources. When Constantinople fell to the Turks in 1453, a new wave of manuscripts arrived in the luggage of scholars seeking refuge in the West. This influx of ancient works—and the ideas they contained—coincided with significant transformations in European society and its economy. By the early 15th century, the population was rising again after the devastations of the Black Death. Increased trade and prosperity challenged feudal structures and promoted the growth of cities and city-states, regions ruled from a single urban center. Banks and insurance companies, which had first appeared toward the end of the medieval era, became increasingly common over the course of the 15th century.

The Italian peninsula proved particularly hospitable to the growth of cities and city-states based on industry, commerce, and banking. This environment nurtured a new type of leader, as exemplified by Cosimo de' Medici (1389–1464) of the city-state of Florence. Born into a family of bankers, Cosimo parlayed his wealth into political power. He never held office himself but used his influence to shape the growth of Florence, enhancing its economic and political power and promoting its reputation as a vital cultural center. He assembled what is believed to have been the largest library in all of Europe, including many

◄ **Performance practice.** A four-voice chanson being performed by three musicians reminds us that musicians of earlier times did not think in terms of "right" and "wrong" ways of performing a given repertory, but instead made creative use of whatever musical resources they had at their disposal. The anonymous artist of this painting from the second quarter of the 16th century took great pains to depict the actual music being played here: the notation of Claudin de Sermisy's chanson *Joyssance vous donneray* is so precise it can be easily read against modern editions of the work. The flute player is reading from the superius part book while the singer is performing the tenor part from what appears to be a separate sheet. The lutenist is probably filling in the other two voices.

**Source:** Master of Female Half Lengths (ca. 1490–ca. 1540) "The Concert"/ Private Collection/The Bridgeman Art Library

newly recovered manuscripts in Greek. Cosimo also founded the Platonic Academy, modeled after Plato's school in ancient Athens, and he was patron to many of the leading artists of his day. His grandson, Lorenzo de' Medici (1449–1492; known as Lorenzo the Magnificent), continued to promote Florentine political and economic power and to increase the city's reputation as a center for poetry, painting, architecture, and music. Lorenzo was himself a poet and scholar as well as a statesman, the archetypal "Renaissance man" whose abilities ranged from politics to the arts.

North of the Alps, cities of the region known as the Low Countries—roughly equivalent to modern-day Belgium and the Netherlands—also emerged as powerful centers of trade, finance, and culture in the 15th century. As in Italy, growing affluence in such cities as Antwerp, Ghent, Bruges, and Liège provided a source of patronage for the production of great masterpieces of painting, architecture, and music. In France, the Hundred Years' War between England and France finally came to an end in 1453 with the expulsion of the English from all but a small corner of what is now northern France. Joan of Arc, burned at the stake in 1431, had rallied the French army and populace and in so doing helped create a sense of French nationality. In England, the War of the Roses (a decades-long struggle for the throne between the houses of York and Lancaster) was finally decided at the Battle of Bosworth Field in 1485, in which Henry Tudor (later Henry VII) defeated Richard III. The Tudors would rule England until the death of Elizabeth I in 1603.

The Holy Roman Empire—a loose confederation of principalities, duchies, and kingdoms across north-central Europe in the area of what is now Germany, Austria, and portions of northern Italy—expanded greatly in the late 15th and 16th centuries under the rule of the Habsburg dynasty. In 1477, Emperor Maximilian I married Mary of Burgundy, the daughter of Charles the Bold, thereby adding the Burgundian lands to the empire's already considerable holdings. Thanks to a series of strategic

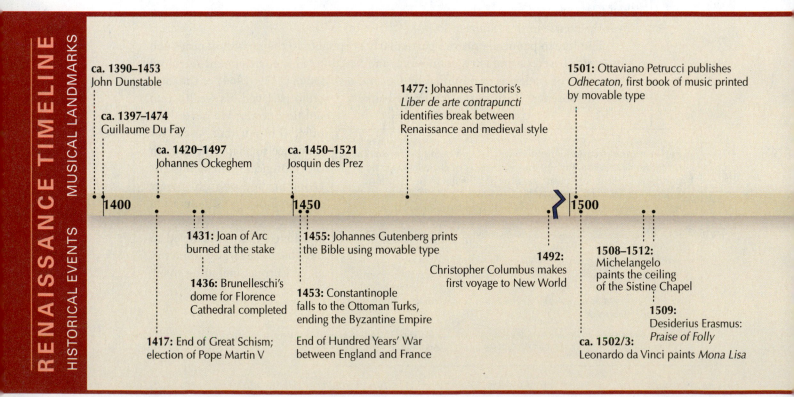

RENAISSANCE TIMELINE

MUSICAL LANDMARKS

**ca. 1390–1453**
John Dunstable

**ca. 1397–1474**
Guillaume Du Fay

**ca. 1420–1497**
Johannes Ockeghem

**ca. 1450–1521**
Josquin des Prez

**1477:** Johannes Tinctoris's *Liber de arte contrapuncti* identifies break between Renaissance and medieval style

**1501:** Ottaviano Petrucci publishes *Odhecaton*, first book of music printed by movable type

1400          1450          1500

HISTORICAL EVENTS

**1431:** Joan of Arc burned at the stake

**1436:** Brunelleschi's dome for Florence Cathedral completed

**1417:** End of Great Schism; election of Pope Martin V

**1455:** Johannes Gutenberg prints the Bible using movable type

**1453:** Constantinople falls to the Ottoman Turks, ending the Byzantine Empire

End of Hundred Years' War between England and France

**1492:** Christopher Columbus makes first voyage to New World

**1508–1512:** Michelangelo paints the ceiling of the Sistine Chapel

**1509:** Desiderius Erasmus: *Praise of Folly*

**ca. 1502/3:** Leonardo da Vinci paints *Mona Lisa*

marriages, the family's influence grew still further over the next century. The realm of Maximilian's grandson and successor, Charles V (reigned 1519–1556), extended to Spain, Portugal, and the Low Countries.

Spain itself was united in the late 15th century following the marriage of the rulers of its two most powerful kingdoms, Ferdinand of Aragon and Isabella of Castille. In 1492, they conquered Granada, the last center of Muslim rule in Spain. That same year, under the influence of the notorious Spanish Inquisition, Spain expelled all Jews who refused to convert to Christianity, and, after 1502, required Muslims to convert.

Also in 1492, the Spanish royal couple funded the first of several voyages of discovery led by the mariner Christopher Columbus, a Genoan by birth. Throughout the 15th century, Portuguese navigators had extended the reach of European shipping eastward, around the southern tip of Africa, but Columbus argued that Asia could be reached more readily by sailing west. In the process, he stumbled across the Americas. In 1519, the Portuguese explorer Ferdinand Magellan, under Spanish patronage, began the first circumnavigation of the globe, which took three years to complete and cost Magellan his life.

Through subsequent voyages of discovery and conquest, Spain acquired an immense empire that extended from what is now the southern and southwestern United States to Tierra del Fuego in South America. Flush with gold and silver from these lands, Spain enjoyed unprecedented wealth and power in the 16th century. Philip II (son of the Holy Roman Emperor Charles V), who ruled Spain from 1556 to 1598, presided over a court of remarkable accomplishments in literature, architecture, painting, and music.

Other countries were quick to follow Spain's lead in colonizing the Americas and exploiting its rich natural resources. Portugal established extensive settlements in what is now Brazil; the English set up their first (unsuccessful) colony in North Carolina in 1587, and their first permanent colony in Jamestown, Virginia, in 1607. The Pilgrims, seeking relief from religious persecution, settled farther to the north in Massachusetts in 1620.

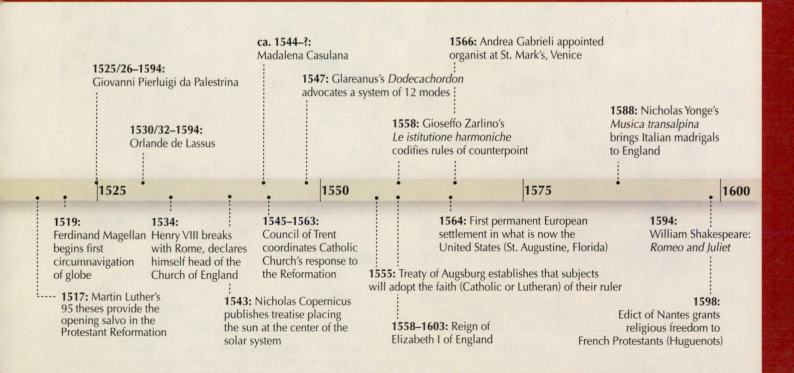

**1525/26–1594:**
Giovanni Pierluigi da Palestrina

**1530/32–1594:**
Orlande de Lassus

**ca. 1544–?:**
Madalena Casulana

**1547:** Glareanus's *Dodecachordon* advocates a system of 12 modes

**1566:** Andrea Gabrieli appointed organist at St. Mark's, Venice

**1558:** Gioseffo Zarlino's *Le istitutione harmoniche* codifies rules of counterpoint

**1588:** Nicholas Yonge's *Musica transalpina* brings Italian madrigals to England

1525     1550     1575     1600

**1519:** Ferdinand Magellan begins first circumnavigation of globe

**1517:** Martin Luther's 95 theses provide the opening salvo in the Protestant Reformation

**1534:** Henry VIII breaks with Rome, declares himself head of the Church of England

**1545–1563:** Council of Trent coordinates Catholic Church's response to the Reformation

**1543:** Nicholas Copernicus publishes treatise placing the sun at the center of the solar system

**1564:** First permanent European settlement in what is now the United States (St. Augustine, Florida)

**1555:** Treaty of Augsburg establishes that subjects will adopt the faith (Catholic or Lutheran) of their ruler

**1558–1603:** Reign of Elizabeth I of England

**1594:** William Shakespeare: *Romeo and Juliet*

**1598:** Edict of Nantes grants religious freedom to French Protestants (Huguenots)

# RENAISSANCE HUMANISM

The discovery of what was for Europeans a New World in 1492 opened up not only new territories but also new ways of thinking about the universe, prompting fundamental changes in the very perception of humanity's place in the world. The discovery of previously unknown but advanced civilizations like those of the Aztecs and Incas would help inspire emerging scientific theories that the earth was not the center of the universe.

The sudden abundance of pre-Christian sources from classical antiquity introduced Western minds to yet another new—or rather, very old—way of looking at the world. The ancient Greeks had measured the universe in terms of human values and reason, and many scholars of the early 15th century, adopting this "new" outlook for themselves, created a philosophical movement known as **humanism**. Renaissance humanists were committed to independent reasoning, careful study of the ancient classics in their original languages (particularly Greek), and a reliance on original sources rather than secondhand commentary about those sources. They also believed in the basic dignity of humankind. Humanists did not reject religion—indeed, many of them were among the most eloquent advocates of the church—but they sought understanding through a process guided as much by reason as faith.

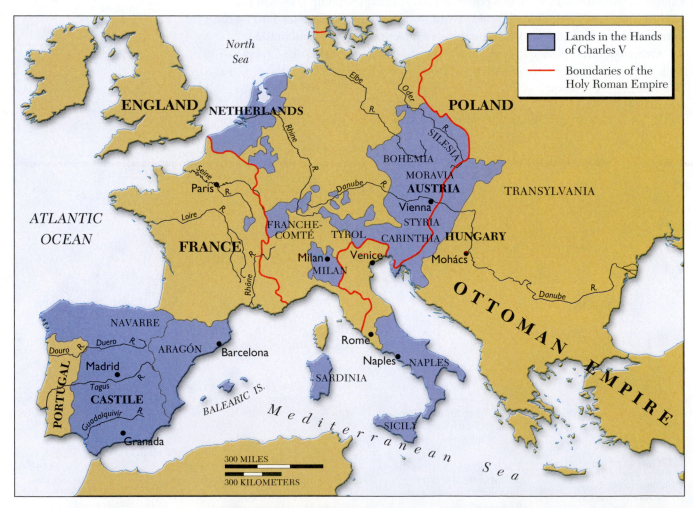

**The Holy Roman Empire and the Domains of Charles V.** Crowned in 1519, Charles V ruled over the Holy Roman Empire until his death in 1556. Through a series of strategic alliances and marriage, he also gained control of additional lands outside the Empire.

Humanism was a sharp departure from the scholasticism that had dominated late medieval intellectual life. Scholasticism relied almost entirely on abstract thought and the accumulation of wisdom through disputation. Commentaries—and commentaries on commentaries—were an important venue of scholastic thought, provided they came from the pens of acknowledged authorities. Scholasticism harbored deep suspicions about the reliability of the human senses and therefore had little place for empirical evidence or observation. Humanism, in contrast, combined reason with empirical evidence with results that often challenged the received wisdom of even the greatest authorities.

The Italian scholar Lorenzo Valla (ca. 1407–1457) is in many respects the prototypical Renaissance humanist. A poet and scholar who produced important Latin translations of the Greek historians Thucydides and Herodotus, he also wrote several treatises on philosophy that responded to the rediscovery of certain Aristotelian sources. But Valla is best known for *De falso credita et ementita Constantini donatione* (1440), which exposed as a forgery the Donation of Constantine. This document, purportedly a grant of lands and authority to the pope by the Roman emperor Constantine (d. 337), had buttressed the claims of the papacy to supremacy over secular rulers as well as the church. By examining the language of the document carefully, Valla demonstrated conclusively that it could not possibly have been written during the reign of Constantine; subsequent research has shown that the document was in fact written between 750 and 800. Valla's revelation disturbed church authorities, who summoned him before a court of inquisition (he was later released). The importance of *De falso credita*, however, went beyond its immediate impact. Valla's

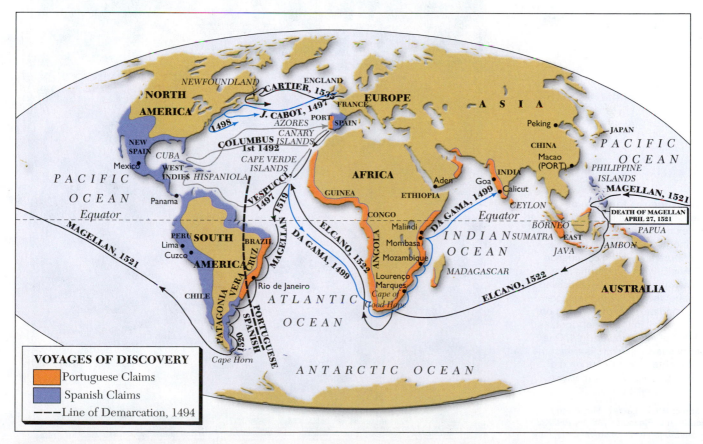

**Voyages of discovery and Spanish and Portuguese colonial claims in the 15th and 16th centuries.**

willingness to question the most basic premises of institutional power and his methods of discovering and applying rational evidence embodied Renaissance humanism. His work was an example for countless others who followed him in the new conviction that tradition was not in itself a source of truth.

One of Valla's staunchest supporters was the Dutch scholar Desiderius Erasmus (1466–1536), perhaps the single most influential humanist of his time. An ordained priest, Erasmus was devoutly religious and never openly questioned the authority of the church. He nevertheless defended Valla's efforts to arrive at the truth by means of evidence and reason. When Erasmus made a pilgrimage to the shrine of the martyred St. Thomas Becket (ca. 1118–1170) in Canterbury in the early 16th century, he was repelled by the veneration of saintly relics like St. Thomas's shoe, the arm of St. George, and a rag said to have been dipped in St. Thomas's blood. Only a little more than a hundred years before, Geoffrey Chaucer had written in *The Canterbury Tales* of pilgrims

**Music and the fountain of pleasure.** From a lavishly illustrated codex on astronomy produced in northern Italy around 1470, this miniature shows the confluence of music, wine, and erotic love. Three different types of musician are shown: singers in the upper left, wind players (performing on the shawm) in the upper right, and a lutenist in the lower right. One of the shawm players is overcome by laughter, a comment on the ludicrousness of this otherwise terribly earnest scene.

**Source:** "De Sphaera" (Music and the Fountain of Pleasure), MS. lat 209, X.2.14. Scala/Biblioteca Estense, Modena, Italy/ Art Resource, NY

# A CLOSER LOOK

✳ Explore on mysearchlab

**BEFORE THE INVENTION** of the printing press, in the mid-fifteenth century, the only way to reproduce a text was to copy it by hand. The end result of this laborious process was a single copy. The printing press made it possible to create hundreds and even thousands of copies of a text in a single process. By 1500, printing had become a major enterprise, countless presses, big and small, were springing up across Europe.

The **manuscript** of the text to be set is clipped to the wall.

Two **typesetters** set the type, pulling individual metal-cast letters one by one out of cases before them. Each case is divided into an upper half and a lower half: the one above stores the capital letters, hence the term "upper case" for capital letters, even today.

This worker is one of two carrying out the process of **proofreading**. His colleague, standing to his side, reads aloud from a sheet of type that just came off the printing press, while the seated worker corrects any errors by rearranging the type. The corrected type for that sheet will then go back to the press to be run off in multiple copies.

A delivery man brings fresh paper to the shop. **Paper mills** made large sheets of paper by straining fibers, usually derived from old rags. This process was much cheaper than working with animal skin to make parchment.

A workman applies **ink** to the set type, using two sponge-like applicators ("ink balls"). He will then lay a sheet of clean paper over the inked type and slide both into the wooden press.

The **pressman** pulls the press: the screw mechanism (adopted from wine-making technology) exerts the enormous pressure needed to affix the ink to the paper. Printed sheets are then hung up to dry on a line nearby.

A young boy (known as the "**printer's devil**") assists with miscellaneous tasks. If he proves himself trustworthy, he will eventually be given one of the more responsible jobs in the printshop.

The **owner** of the printshop supervises the operation. He pays the workers, negotiates contracts with authors, and invests the capital needed to run his small business.

✳ Explore on **mysearchlab**

to Canterbury who accepted the genuineness of such relics without a second thought. The contrast between these two outlooks—the ready credulity of the characters in *The Canterbury Tales* and the skepticism of Erasmus—neatly captures an essential difference between medieval and Renaissance mentalities.

The impact of humanism extended well beyond the fields of philosophy, theology, and science. Renaissance writers as a whole were deeply influenced by humanism and its efforts to explore the human mind. Following the lead of such late medieval figures as Dante Alighieri (1265–1321), Giovanni Boccaccio (1313–1375), and Geoffrey Chaucer (1342–1400), more and more writers began to produce works in the vernacular—Italian, French, English, Spanish—which in turn contributed to an ever-growing sense of national identity in the various regions of Europe.

The speed with which ideas could be disseminated in Renaissance Europe accelerated exponentially with the invention of movable type and the printing press in the mid-15th century. The significance of this new technology can scarcely be overstated. Before printing, the written word was scarce and remote. Even Bibles were a rarity. Manuscripts were expensive to produce and inconsistent in their texts; because they were produced by hand, no two manuscripts were identical, no matter how careful the scribes who copied them. But after Johannes Gutenberg produced the first printed Bible in Mainz (Germany) around 1455, it became possible to generate multiple and essentially identical copies of the same work in a relatively short period of time at only a fraction of the cost of a comparable number of manuscripts.

Printing spread swiftly across Europe. By 1500, the city of Venice was home to no fewer than 150 presses, including that of Aldus Manutius (1449–1515), who made a handsome profit producing elegant yet relatively inexpensive editions of Plato, Aristotle, and other ancient authors in the original Greek. It has been estimated that between the invention of the printing press in the mid-1450s and the end of the 15th century, some 25,000 different books were printed in Germany alone; with an average press run of 250 copies, this would mean a total of about 6 million printed books. The first music printed with movable type appeared in Venice in 1501.

# THE PROTESTANT REFORMATION

Humanism and printing combined to ignite the Protestant Reformation in the early 16th century. When a German monk named Martin Luther (1483–1546) nailed a list of grievances to the door of the castle church in Wittenberg in 1517, he was only the latest in a long line of individuals to voice objections to various church practices. The immediate object of Luther's protest was the sale of indulgences—certificates from the pope or a bishop promising forgiveness in the next life for sins committed in this one. But if Luther was not the first to protest what he saw as church corruption, he was among the first with access to the power of the printing press to promulgate his views. Between 1517 and 1520, Luther's books sold an estimated 300,000 copies in some 370 different editions in both Latin and German.

The Protestant Reformation, as its name implies, arose as an expression of protest against corrupt church practices and a desire to reform them. Luther and his followers emphasized the individual's personal relationship to God and preached a doctrine of salvation based on faith rather than on works. Protestants also encouraged worship in the vernacular, although Luther himself upheld the importance of Latin both in the liturgy and in the education of youth.

Such views did not sit well with the established church. Luther was declared a heretic, and his published writings against church doctrine were used as evidence against him when he was excommunicated in 1521. Later that year, at the Diet of Worms (*Diet* is an archaic word for an assembly; Worms, a city on the Rhine in western Germany), he refused to recant his position before the assembled leaders of the Holy Roman Empire. The political ramifications of Luther's stand were far reaching. The German people eventually split along Protestant and Catholic lines according to the professed faith of their local ruler.

Luther himself was challenged on matters of doctrine by other Protestants as early as 1521, and a host of Protestant sects emerged over the ensuing decades. Ulrich Zwingli (1484–1531) and Jean Calvin (1509–1564) were among the first to break with Luther over various theological issues and establish their own denominations. Henry VIII, chafing at the authority of the pope in Rome, declared himself head of the Church of England. Over the course of the next century, Anabaptists, Mennonites, Puritans, Methodists, Baptists, and Presbyterians all rejected the authority of Rome, each group establishing its own course on matters of doctrine, liturgy, and music.

The Roman Catholic Church, as it gradually came to be known—prior to the Reformation, there had been only one church in the West—did not sit idly by in the face of this religious revolution. It responded first by subjecting suspected heretics to trial, excommunication, and sometimes imprisonment or even death. The Counter-Reformation of the mid-16th century was a more systematic and positive attempt to retain or win back believers to the Roman Catholic Church, in part through a modification of doctrine and practices, in part through music.

**MAJOR ARTISTS OF THE RENAISSANCE ERA**

- Donatello
- Jan van Eyck
- Leonardo da Vinci
- Albrecht Dürer
- Michelangelo Buonarotti
- Raphael

✴ Explore on **mysearchlab**

# RENAISSANCE PAINTING AND SCULPTURE

The contrast between medieval and Renaissance perceptions of the world are particularly evident in the realm of painting and sculpture. Renaissance painters differed from their earlier counterparts in a number of important ways. One of the most striking of these was the use of linear perspective, a method for creating the illusion of three-dimensional depth on a two-dimensional surface. The technique had been familiar in an intuitive way to the ancient Greeks but was almost entirely lost over subsequent centuries. The Florentine artist Filippo Brunelleschi (1377–1446) was one of the first to reestablish the importance of linear perspective and articulate its geometric basis.

Another characteristic of Renaissance art was a renewed interest in the human body. Medieval artists had, for the most part, used nudity for depicting lasciviousness on earth or the torments of the damned in hell. In contrast, Renaissance artists, like the artists of antiquity, became interested in the human body as an object of admiration. They also display an unprecedented interest in the scientific details of human anatomy.

This interest in human anatomy accompanied one of the most distinctive characteristics of Renaissance art, a desire to capture individual character in portraiture. The seven figures in the 12th-century depiction of King David and his musicians in the St. Alban's Psalter (p. 90) all have essentially the same visage. Except for his size and ornate robes, David looks no different from the others. In contrast, each of the seven choir boys in Luca della Robbia's 1431 sculpture for the choir gallery of the Florence Cathedral (p. 103) has a distinctive appearance and personality.

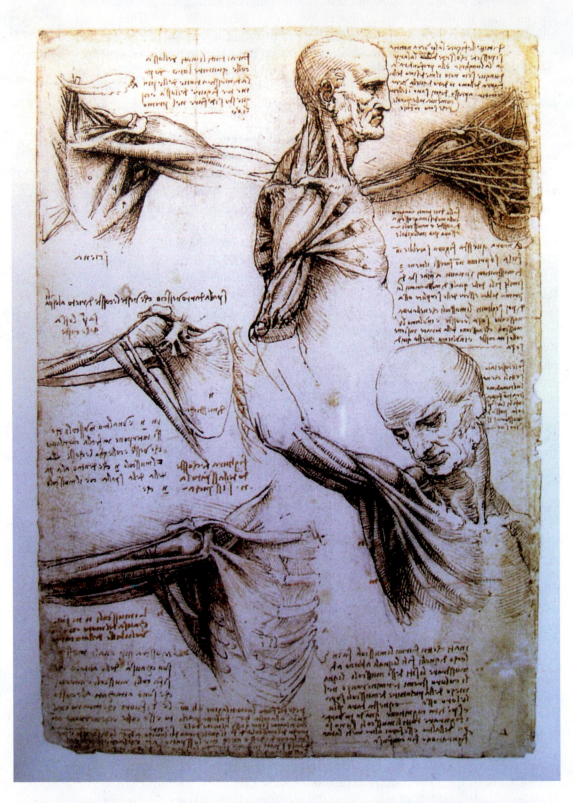

**Arts and sciences.** Leonardo da Vinci's anatomical sketches could not possibly have been made during the medieval era. They attend too closely to anatomical accuracy and detail and betray a connection between draftsmanship and science—in terms of both anatomy and the geometry of perspective—that had been unknown since the time of the ancient Greeks.

**Source:** Bildagentur-online/Alamy

**Humanist sculpture.** Humanism manifests itself in the arts in many ways. The seven marble figures here are all engaged in singing, yet each projects a sense of individuality. This sculpture is a part of a larger set that Luca della Robbia was commissioned to carve in the organ loft (the *Cantoria*) of the Florence Cathedral between 1431 and 1438. They are thus almost exactly contemporaneous with Du Fay's *Nuper rosarum flores,* also commissioned for the consecration of the Florence Cathedral in 1436 (see Chapter 4).

**Source:** Ted Spiegel/Corbis

# MUSIC IN THE RENAISSANCE

Composers and musicians of the Renaissance, unlike the philosophers, poets, and painters of their time, did not strive to emulate the ideals of their art in antiquity. No one at the time really knew very much about the music of ancient Greece, and it was not until the last quarter of the 16th century that anyone made a serious attempt to recreate it. By convention, however, music historians have called the period between roughly 1420 and 1600 the Renaissance on the grounds that the music of this time, like all the other arts of the period, shows decided stylistic changes over and against what we now think of as the medieval era.

These new stylistic developments are examined in Chapter 4. For the moment, it is important to remember that many older practices, including the basics of notation and many genres, continued without interruptions. We must also keep in mind that new developments took hold at different times and in different places. Many of the most important musical innovations of the 15th century began north of the Alps, particularly in the region that is now the Netherlands, Belgium, and northern France. Many of the greatest composers of the era, including Guillaume Du Fay, Josquin des Prez, Jacob Obrecht, Adrian Willaert, Cipriano de Rore, and Orlande de Lassus, to name only a few, were born in this part of Europe and eventually made their way to different musical centers across the continent.

The importance and value of music at secular courts grew steadily throughout the Renaissance. More and more rulers began to measure their greatness not just by their territory, treasury, and military might, but also by what might be called their cultural capital. The arts as a whole benefited enormously from this newfound concern for cultural prestige. The Medici in Florence, the Este dynasty in Ferrara, the Sforza dynasty in Milan, the collective leadership of the Republic of Venice, the Vatican in Rome, the royal court of Naples—all these and other principalities, duchies, and kingdoms throughout Italy, and eventually throughout Europe, placed great value on having talented poets, painters, sculptors, architects, and musicians active at their courts. Any court with pretensions to cultural importance maintained its own roster of musicians to perform during services in the court chapel as well as for banquets, dances, and other festivities of a more secular nature. The size and quality of these musical organizations varied greatly; a well-funded *cappella*, as such an ensemble was called, typically consisted of between 12 and 20 musicians but could be larger or smaller according to the resources of the court treasury at any given time. Affluent courts actively recruited the best musical talent they could afford. Composers and musicians were considerably more mobile in the Renaissance than before.

The church remained an important source of patronage as well. The surviving repertory indicates that the demand for new polyphonic liturgical music—from settings of the Mass Ordinary to hymns to motets—was enormous. Many affluent churches maintained resident composers, providing them with housing and a fixed income in exchange for music on demand.

The invention of the printing press provided yet another source of income for composers of all varieties of music, from secular songs to settings of the Mass Ordinary. Music that had once circulated in relatively scarce manuscripts could now be sold in quantity to a much wider audience.

As during the medieval era, only a fraction of the music of the Renaissance was the work of professional composers and musicians. Most music was performed in the context of an unwritten tradition that operated outside any system of notation. For those who pretended to gentility, however, the ability to read music, sing, and play at least one if not more instruments was considered an essential grace (see Primary Evidence: Music and Manners). Royals themselves set the standard. The English king Henry VIII took great pride in his abilities both as a composer and singer. His daughter, Elizabeth I, was renowned as a lutenist and keyboard player (see p. 164).

## Primary Evidence  MUSIC AND MANNERS

*Baldassare Castiglione's Il cortegiano ("The Courtier"), a guide to the proper behavior of a gentleman at court, was written between 1508 and 1516 and first published in 1528; it appeared in many translations and editions during the 16th century. According to Castiglione, the ideal courtier was expected to be conversant with the use of arms in battle as well as with the arts, including music. In the passage here, a fictionalized version of the author's friend Count Ludovico da Canossa (1476–1532), Castiglione's ideal gentleman, extols the virtues of music.*

■ ■ ■

Here everyone laughed, and the Count began again, "Gentlemen, you must know that I am not satisfied with our Courtier unless he be also a musician, and unless, besides understanding and being able to read music, he can play various instruments. For, if we rightly consider, no rest from toil and no medicine for ailing spirits can be found more decorous or praiseworthy in time of leisure than this; and especially in courts where, besides the release from vexations which music gives to all, many things are done to please the ladies, whose tender and delicate spirits are readily penetrated with harmony and filled with sweetness. Hence, it is no wonder that in both ancient and modern times they have always been particularly fond of musicians, finding music a most welcome food for the spirit."

Then signor Gasparo [Pallavicino (1486–1511), another Castiglione friend] said: "I think that music, along with many other vanities, is indeed well suited to women, and perhaps also to others who have the appearance of men, but not to real men; for the latter ought not to render their minds effeminate and afraid of death."

"Say not so," replied the Count, "or I shall launch upon a great sea of praise for music, reminding you how greatly music was always celebrated by the ancients and held to be a sacred thing; and how it was the opinion of very wise philosophers that the world is made up of music, that the heavens in their motion make harmony, and that even the human soul was formed on the same principle, and is therefore awakened and has its virtues brought to life, as it were, through music. Wherefore it is recorded that Alexander was sometimes so passionately excited by music that, almost in spite of himself, he was obliged to quit the banquet table and rush off to arms; whereupon the musician would change the kind of music, and he would then grow calm and return from arms to the banquet. And, I tell you, grave Socrates learned to play the cithara when he was very old. I remember also having heard once that both Plato and Aristotle wish a man who is well constituted to be a musician; and with innumerable reasons they show that music's power over us is very great; and (for many reasons which would be too long to tell now) that music must of necessity be learned from childhood, not so much for the sake of that outward melody which is heard, but because of the power it has to induce a good new habit of mind and an inclination to virtue, rendering the soul more capable of happiness, just as corporal exercise makes the body more robust; and that not only is music not harmful to the pursuits of peace and of war, but greatly to their advantage."

# Chapter

# 4

# The Emergence of Renaissance Style

## Chapter Outline

In their quest to revive ancient practices, most Renaissance scholars and artists had actual models to study and imitate. Ancient buildings and sculpture were close at hand in Italy for painters, sculptors, and architects. Writers had a growing body of ancient texts to emulate. But the sounds of ancient music had not been preserved, so for musicians, the imitation of models from classical antiquity was effectively impossible.

Not until the closing decades of the 16th century did scholars and musicians attempt to recreate the musical practices of ancient Greece. Most Renaissance musicians were nevertheless firmly convinced that the music of their own time was inferior to that of the distant past. They reached this conclusion from the many references in ancient literature to music's miraculous power. In the words of the Spanish composer and theorist Bartolomé Ramos de Pareja (ca. 1440–ca. 1491),

> Without a doubt, music has immense effect upon and mighty power over the human soul, whether to calm or to rouse it. If in our time music does not work so many miracles, it is to be attributed not to the art, whose perfection exceeds that of nature, but to those who use the art badly. If those excellent [Greek] musicians . . . were called back to life they would deny that our music was invented by them—so inept, unharmonious, and dissipated has it been rendered through the corruption of certain singers.[1]

## CONSONANCE AND DISSONANCE: TRUSTING THE EAR

Although they may have felt inferior to their ancient counterparts, Renaissance musicians felt confidently superior to their immediate predecessors. Commentators of the 15th century, influenced by humanism, by new ways of thinking about the arts in general, and by the still broader sense that they were part of a cultural rebirth, drew a clear distinction between what we now think of as medieval music and the music of their own time. Johannes Tinctoris (1435–1511), a renowned composer and the most prominent theorist of his generation, expressed this view bluntly. "[A]lthough it seems beyond belief," he declared in 1477, "there does not exist a single piece of music, not composed within the last forty years, that is regarded by the learned as worth hearing" (see Primary Evidence: A New Way of Hearing New Music).

Significantly, Tinctoris based his historical evaluation on actual composers and on works he knew. He did not rely on or even refer to the commentaries

## Primary Evidence    A NEW WAY OF HEARING NEW MUSIC

*This brief passage, from Johannes Tinctoris's Liber de arte contrapuncti ("Book on the Art of Counterpoint," 1477) is remarkable in two respects: first, because Tinctoris identifies a break in musical tradition that had occurred about 40 years before—that is, at what we now think of as the beginning of the Renaissance era in music—and second, because he bases his judgment not on the testimony of past authorities, in the manner of the medieval scholastics, but, following the humanist preference for direct evidence from original sources over received wisdom, on the study of actual works of music. Both the manner and nature of his observations signal the emergence of the Renaissance era in music.*

■ ■ ■

Concords of sounds and melodies, from whose sweetness . . . the pleasure of the ear is derived, are produced, then, not by heavenly bodies, but by earthly instruments with the cooperation of nature. To these concords the ancient musicians—Plato, Pythagoras, Nicomachus, Aristoxenus, Philolaus, Archytas, Ptolemy, and many others, including even Boethius—most assiduously applied themselves, yet how they were accustomed to arrange and to form them is almost unknown to our generation. And if I may refer to my own experience, I have had in my hands certain old songs . . . of unknown origin [that were] so ineptly, so stupidly composed that they rather offended than pleased the ear.

Further, although it seems beyond belief, there does not exist a single piece of music, not composed within the last forty years, that is regarded by the learned as worth hearing. Yet at this present time, not to mention innumerable singers of the most beautiful diction, there flourish, whether by the effect of some celestial influence or by the force of assiduous practice, countless composers, among them Jean Ockeghem, Jean Regis, Antoine Busnoys, Firmin Caron, and Guillaume Faugues, who glory in having studied this divine art under John Dunstable, Gilles Binchois, and Guillaume Du Fay, recently deceased. Nearly all the works of these men exhale such sweetness that in my opinion they are to be considered most suitable, not only for men and heroes, but even for the immortal gods. Indeed, I never hear them, I never examine them, without coming away happier and more enlightened. As Virgil took Homer for his model in that divine work the *Aeneid*, so I, by Hercules, have used these composers as models for my modest works, and especially in the arrangement of the concords I have plainly imitated their admirable style of composing.

**Source:** "Johannes Tinctoris's Liber de arte contrapunct" from *SOURCE READINGS IN MUSIC HISTORY*, edited by Oliver Struck. Copyright © 1950 by W.W. Norton & Company, Inc. Copyright renewed 1978 by Oliver Strunck. Reprinted by permission of the publisher.

of past authorities. In short, he trusted "the judgment of my ears" over tradition. This may not seem particularly striking now, but in Tinctoris's time, the practice of deferring to the judgment of established authority was still deeply ingrained.

A case in point involves an issue central to the difference between medieval and Renaissance music: the question of consonance and dissonance. Medieval theorists, drawing on the authority of Boethius and through him Pythagoras, gave priority to number and reason over sound in defining a consonant interval. They thus considered as consonant only those intervals that could be expressed as mathematically simple ratios: the octave (2:1), the fifth (3:2), and the fourth (4:3). Although the 4th-century B.C.E. Greek philosopher Aristoxenus had maintained, against Pythagoras, that thirds should be considered consonant because they *sound* consonant, Boethius had dismissed this appeal to the evidence of the senses. Aristoxenus, he complained, "left all judgment up to the ear," whereas Pythagoras, "having left behind the judgment of the ear, having proceeded to the underlying causes, mistrusting any human ear . . . and setting no store by instruments . . . inquired how one could explore the true cause of consonance through reason in a solid and reliable fashion."[2]

Tinctoris and other Renaissance theorists rejected this anti-empirical tradition. Tinctoris speaks of the "sweetness" of the third, praising it in what he describes as "Aristoxenian fashion," that is, "by the judgment of the ear."[3] Bartolomé Ramos de

Pareja similarly marshaled empirical evidence in favor of the third. According to traditional Pythagorean theory, the mathematical ratios for the thirds—81:64 for the major and 32:27 for the minor—were distinctly inelegant, justifying the classification of these intervals as dissonant. Ramos de Pareja maintained, however, that the ear could not in fact distinguish between the intervals of 81:64 and 80:64 (reducible to 5:4). He therefore argued that the major third of 5:4 should be considered consonant, along with the interval of the minor third as 30:25 (6:5).

This empirical and practical challenge to traditional music theory manifested itself in other ways as well. The 11th-century theorist Guido of Arezzo, following Boethius, had drawn a sharp distinction between a *musicus*—one who understands the essential, mathematical nature of music—and a *cantor* ("singer")—a mere performer, little better than a beast, "for whoever does things without understanding them, is by definition a beast"[4] (see illustration "The two sides of music," p. 23). Tinctoris endorsed the distinction, but with a practical twist. In his *Dictionary of Music* (published in 1473, the first such work of its kind), he defines a *musicus* as someone who "after careful rational investigation" of music "through benefit of thought, assumes the office of singer."[5] Ramos de Pareja, in a treatise pointedly entitled *Musica practica* ("Practical Music"), dismissed the authority of Guido altogether on the grounds that he was "perhaps a better monk than a musician."[6] This dig at Guido roused the clergy, who denounced Ramos de Pareja as a virtual heretic. One writer attacked him as a "Spanish prevaricator of the truth" and asked him publicly,

> If [Pope] Gregory [the Great, believed at the time to be the composer of all liturgical chant] wished to use only these seven Latin letters [A, B, C, etc.] and repeat them as often as needed, and if [Saint] Ambrose and [Saint] Augustine preferred to follow in his footsteps rather than in foreign ones, why don't you blush to pervert this order and deprave it with your arrogant censorship? Are you perhaps more saintly than these pillars of the church or more cultivated or more experienced? . . . The doctrine of that pious monk [Guido of Arezzo], spread throughout the world, will last forever, notwithstanding your malice.[7]

As this response suggests, more was at stake here than a difference of opinion about consonance and dissonance. Indeed, the Renaissance challenge to medieval scholasticism—in all areas of study, not just music—frightened many as a threat to the authority of the church and its teachings. The struggle between the acceptance of tradition and the new methods of critical thought would play itself out on many fronts over the course of succeeding centuries in the realms of astronomy, geography, theology, as well as music. The new attitude, exemplified by the willingness to question or even dismiss a large body of music and musical thought of the past, marks a significant shift in outlook and one that more than any single stylistic element characterizes the musical Renaissance.[8]

# SONORITY: THE *CONTENANCE ANGLOISE*

According to Tinctoris, the "fountain and origin" of what he and his contemporaries perceived to be a distinctly new musical style "lies with the English, whose leading master was [John] Dunstable." From Dunstable (ca. 1390–1453), he traces it to the French composers Gilles Binchois (1400–1460) and Guillaume Du Fay (ca. 1397–1474), and from them to the leading composers of his own day, most notably Johannes Ockeghem (ca. 1420–1497), Johannes Regis (1425–1496), and Antoine Busnoys (ca. 1430–1492). Little is known about Dunstable's life, but it is likely he spent time in France in the service of the Duke of Bedford, who was fighting the French in the Hundred Years' War. If so, he would have been well situated to influence French composers. And, indeed, almost all of his music is preserved in continental rather than English manuscripts.

Tinctoris was not the first to perceive something new in the music of Dunstable, Binchois, and Du Fay. As early as 1442, the French poet Martin le Franc had singled out these composers as exemplars of what he called the **contenance angloise**, the "English guise," which he characterized as a "new way of composing with lively consonances." Although le Franc does not describe this style in any detail, he seems to have been responding to a new kind of sonority, in which the music is dominated by thirds, fifths, and sixths. The English predilection for thirds had already been evident in music of the late medieval era (see Chapter 3). Dunstable and his followers used these intervals in a manner that has since been described as one of **panconsonance**, a harmonic idiom that makes ample use of **triads** (vertical alignments of three notes whose basic pitches are separated by major or minor thirds in close position) and limits the use of dissonance considerably.

Dunstable's *Quam pulchra es* ("How Fair You Are"), a motet written sometime before 1430 on a text from the Song of Solomon, illustrates these characteristics. Its three voices are of more or less equal weight; none of them derives from preexistent material. They all have the same rhythmic profile, and they combine repeatedly to form triads that move in blocks, almost like a chorale or hymn. The intervals resulting from the interrelationship of the three voices are overwhelmingly consonant: dissonances, such as the "E" in the uppermost voice in measure 2, are few in number and rhythmically brief. The texture here is similar to that of the polyphonic conductus (see Chapter 2), yet the rhythms and vertical alignment of sonorities clearly distinguish Dunstable's motet from that earlier form. The influence of the *contenance angloise* on Du Fay is apparent in that vertical intervals are strongly oriented toward thirds and triads, with an increasing number of triadic cadences; the fifth nevertheless retains its traditional pride of place as the final cadential interval, as in Dunstable's *Quam pulchra es*.

## Fauxbourdon and Faburden

Du Fay was an important figure in the development of **fauxbourdon**, another compositional technique that favored triadic sonorities and that emerged around 1430. A fauxbourdon is an unnotated line that runs parallel to the uppermost of two notated lines, usually at the interval of a fourth below, creating a harmonic texture rich in thirds and sixths. The Advent hymn *Conditor alme siderum* ("Bountiful Creator of the Stars") alternates between plainchant (in the odd-numbered strophes) and three-voiced polyphony. In the polyphonic sections, the two higher voices sing an embellished version of the original plainchant. Interestingly, the earliest preserved version of this work transmits the plainchant melody in mensural notation, bringing it into alignment with the rhythm of the alternating polyphony. This source also transcribes only one of the two upper voices in the polyphonic sections. The third voice is indicated simply by the word *fauxbourdon* written in the margin.

In the related contemporary English technique of **faburden**, musicians would interpolate lines both above and below a preexisting melody. The upper line would parallel the notated melody a fourth above, and the lower line would vary between thirds and fifths below it. This resulted in what we might today think of as sixth chords (that is, first-inversion chords, with the sixth scale degree in the root), although theorists of the time would not have perceived them as such. The net effect, however, as with fauxbourdon, was to reinforce the idea of thirds and sixths as consonant intervals.

**Listen**
CD2   Track 9
**mysearchlab** (with scrolling translation)
DUNSTABLE
*Quam pulchra es*
Score Anthology I/31

**Listen**
CD2   Track 10
**mysearchlab** (with scrolling translation)
DU FAY
*Conditor alme siderum*
Score Anthology I/32

## Focus SOURCES OF EARLY RENAISSANCE POLYPHONY

We know of many 15th-century works today only from a single surviving source, and we can only speculate about how many sources have been lost. Scholars have inventoried most sources, but work continues on almost all of them to determine when, where, and under what circumstances they were produced, what music they contain, and who composed them. The answers to many such questions often depend on small but crucial pieces of evidence. The type of paper used, the binding, the hand of a particular scribe, payment records in court archives—any and all of these can help unravel the mysteries of these fascinating documents.

Listed here are the most important collections of 15th-century polyphony that include a mixture of sacred and secular works. For a listing of 15th-century sources consisting primarily or exclusively of chansons, see Focus: Chanson Manuscripts of the 15th Century, in Chapter 5.

The **Old Hall Manuscript**, now in the British Library, London, but named after the library in St. Edmund's College in which it was originally housed, was prepared in England during the early decades of the 15th century. A sizable manuscript, it preserves a repertory that dates from ca. 1350 to ca. 1420. It contains about 150 Mass movements and motets by Leonel Power and other (mostly English) composers of the late 14th and early 15th centuries written in isorhythm, in English descant style (note against note), or in the style of contemporary chansons. The later works in this source display the panconsonance of the *contenance angloise*, with its plentiful use of thirds and sixths.

**Canonici Misc. 213**, now in the Bodleian Library, Oxford, was copied in northern Italy ca. 1420 to 1440. A large manuscript of 146 leaves, it contains some 325 compositions by Italian and Netherlandish composers, including Du Fay and Binchois. The repertory is both sacred (Mass movements, motets) and secular (chansons, ballate).

The massive collection of seven volumes known as the **Trent Codices** ("codices" is the plural of "codex") is housed in Trent, Italy, six volumes in the Museo Provinciale d'Arte and one in the Museo Diocesano. Compiled in the region of what is now southern Germany, Austria, and northern Italy between roughly 1430 and 1480, they contain more than 1,500 compositions, both sacred and secular, by composers from England, the Low Countries, Germany, France, and Italy, including Dunstable, Du Fay, and Binchois.

## New Sonority, Old Structure: Du Fay's *Nuper rosarum flores*

The new sonority characteristic of Renaissance style was not at first accompanied by new approaches to musical structure. Indeed, some of Du Fay's most significant early works are organized according to the medieval technique of isorhythm even as they explore new sonorities. The motet *Nuper rosarum flores* ("The Rose Blossoms"), written for the consecration of the newly completed dome of the cathedral in Florence on March 25, 1436, provides a revealing example of this mixing of old and new.

The dome—designed by Filippo Brunelleschi (1377–1446), who also oversaw its construction—is a triumph of Renaissance engineering. Brunelleschi's contemporaries marveled at it. "Who could ever be so cold or envious," asked Leon Battista Alberti, the author of an important treatise on perspective, "as to fail to recognize the genius of an architect capable of creating such an enormous structure, rising in the sky, big enough to cover all the people of Tuscany in its shadow—and all done without the aid of centering or even much scaffolding?"[9]

The consecration of the dome, then, was an event in honor of an architectural masterpiece, so it is no coincidence that the structure of the cathedral is reflected in Du Fay's motet. The **cantus firmus**—the term composers of the time were now using for the "fixed melody" that served as the basis of a composition—derives from

**EXAMPLE 4–1** Opening of the Introit *Terribilis est locus iste.*

A - ve Ma - ri - a, gra - ti - a ple - na Do - mi - nus te - cum, vir - go se - re - na.

the opening of the Introit *Terribilis est locus iste* ("Awesome Is This Place"), a chant employed (appropriately enough) in ceremonies for the dedication of a new church (see Example 4–1). Du Fay applies the cantus firmus in an unusual way here, stating it canonically in two voices (m. 29ff.). The melody in the Tenor II line is stated a fifth above the melody in the Tenor, and each voice is based on a different isorhythm, so the two voices move at different speeds.

It has been suggested that this two-voiced canonic cantus firmus structure may relate to the novel structure of Brunelleschi's dome, which consists of an inner frame supporting a separate outer skin. This technical innovation made the construction of such a large dome possible, and it may be that the double cantus firmus is Du Fay's musical counterpart to Brunelleschi's dome.

Less speculative is the relationship of the work's general proportions to Solomon's Temple in Jerusalem, which theologians had long viewed as the prototypical church. As described in I Kings, the Temple was laid out in the proportions 6:4:2:3, with 6 the total length of the building, 4 the length of the nave, 2 the width of the building and the length of the sanctuary, and 3 the height of the building. The Cathedral of Florence followed these same proportions, and Du Fay mirrors them precisely in the temporal presentation of the cantus firmus, which is stated four times in the proportions of 6:4:2:3. We can readily see these relationships by comparing the duration of the first note of the tenor line—a breve in the original notation—within each statement of the cantus firmus. Using a modern-day quarter note as the basic unit of measurement, the successive statements rest on an underlying value of 6 units per breve (measures 29–56, beginning with a dotted whole note in transcription), then 4 units (measures 85–112, beginning with a whole note), 2 units (measures 127–140, beginning with a half note), and finally 3 units (measures 155–168, beginning with a dotted half note). The motet concludes with a two-measure "Amen" that stands outside this scheme.

The number symbolism in Du Fay's motet goes further still. The numbers 4 and 7 dominate throughout. The text consists of four strophes of seven lines, and the music is divided into four sections, one for each strophe, corresponding to the changes in the rhythm of the cantus firmus just outlined. Finally, each of these sections has a duration of 28 breves; the length of each section varies according to the mensuration sign used for each section. The number 28, the product of 4 × 7, is also a perfect number, that is, a number that is the sum of all its factors, excluding itself (1 + 2 + 4 + 7 + 14 = 28).

In spite of its archaic isometric structure, the sonorities of *Nuper rosarum flores* are decidedly progressive. The music is full of what would now be called **root position triads**. The lowest line of Du Fay's motet is not always the basis—or root—of the harmony, but the lowest sounding voice usually is, whether it occurs in the Tenor, Tenor II, or motetus part. Thus the lowest sounding voice consistently provides the root of the triad sounding above it.

Even the sections for only two voices exhibit a sonority quite different from that of earlier music. In the two-voiced Italian caccia of the 14th century, for example (see Chapter 3), parallel seconds, fourths, fifths, sevenths, and octaves predominate. The most common intervals in the duo sections in Du Fay's work, in comparison, are thirds, sixths, and tenths, and each voice maintains its own distinct melodic profile.

**EXAMPLE 4–2** The isomelic structure of the upper voices in analogous passages from Du Fay's *Nuper rosarum flores.*

**Source:** From Howard Mayer Brown, *Music in the Renaissance,* 2nd ed. (Prentice-Hall, 1976, 1999), pp. 41–42. © 1999. Reprinted by permission of Pearson Education, Inc., Upper Saddle River, NJ.

112

The sections featuring four voices—that is, those sections containing the double cantus firmus in the Tenor and Tenor II lines—follow the outline of a consistent harmonic progression, moving from the principal tonal center (on G) to a fifth higher (on D) and then to a minor third above the tonal center (on B♭) before concluding on G. Although it would be anachronistic to speak in terms of a harmonic progression here—like their medieval counterparts, Renaissance composers thought of harmony as a by-product of polyphonic voice leading—this kind of patterned sonority would certainly have struck contemporary listeners as quite different from the motets of the previous generation.

The melodic materials in these four- and five-voice sections also follow a basic pattern. Each section is an embellished version of the one before—a series of variations, in effect (see Example 4–2). The variations are at times so elaborate that only the basic contour and cadential points remain, but these connections contribute to the overall structure of the work. Later commentators have called this kind of structural device **isomelic** (*melos* is Greek for "melody"), a melodic counterpart to the metrical patterns of isorhythm.

# JOSQUIN'S *AVE MARIA . . . VIRGO SERENA* AND THE STYLE OF THE RENAISSANCE

Judging from the many printed and manuscript sources in which it circulated, Josquin des Prez's *Ave Maria . . . virgo serena* was among the best-known and most widely admired musical works of its time. This motet was probably written during the 1470s or early 1480s. When the Venetian music printer Ottaviano Petrucci published his first collection of motets in 1502, he gave this work pride of place at the head of the volume. Indeed, it has been reproduced and discussed so often that it has been referred to (not altogether kindly) as the "Mona Lisa of Renaissance music." But even the Mona Lisa has something to reveal to those who stop to contemplate it in its original context. And like the Mona Lisa for Renaissance painting, Josquin's motet can serve as an exemplar for many of the characteristic features of Renaissance musical style.

((•●[Listen

CD2     Track 12
**mysearchlab** (with scrolling translation)
JOSQUIN DES PREZ
*Ave Maria . . . virgo serena*
Score Anthology I/34

---

## Primary Evidence | MUSIC AT THE CONSECRATION OF THE DOME OF THE FLORENCE CATHEDRAL

*Giovanni Manetti, an eyewitness to the consecration of the Florence Cathedral's dome in 1436, described the music in almost mystical terms. We do not know if Du Fay's* Nuper rosarum flores *was the work played at the elevation, but Manetti's account is certainly consistent with the nature of the music.*

■ ■ ■

[A]t the elevation of the Most Sacred Host, the whole space of the temple was filled with such choruses of harmony and such a concert of diverse instruments that it seemed (not without reason) as though the symphonies and songs of the angels and of divine paradise had been set forth from Heaven to whisper in our ears an unbelievable celestial sweetness. Therefore, in that moment, I was so possessed by ecstasy that I seemed to enjoy the life of the blessed here on earth; whether it happened so to others present I know not, but concerning myself I can bear witness.

**Source:** Guillaume Du Fay, *Opera omnia*, ed. G. De Van, Corpus mensurabilis musicae 1 (Rome, 1947–1949), II, p. xxvii.

## Composer Profile

# Guillaume Du Fay (1397–1474)

Guillaume Du Fay (or Dufay) was widely acknowledged during his lifetime as the leading composer of his day. Admired for both the quantity and quality of his compositions, he traveled widely throughout Europe. His musical output embodies the transition from medieval to Renaissance style. He was also among the first of the so-called northern composers to spend a good portion of his career in Italy. At his death the noted composer Loyset Compère called Du Fay "the moon of all music, and the light of all singers."

# PRINCIPAL WORKS

## Masses and Mass Movements

Most of Du Fay's half-dozen complete settings of the Ordinary are based on a single cantus firmus. Du Fay also wrote more than two dozen settings of individual Mass movements, pairs of movements (such as Gloria and Credo), or groups of three movements (Kyrie, Gloria, Credo). Most of these derive at least some portion of their melodic material from plainchant.

## Motets

Du Fay wrote a wide range of polyphonic vocal music that falls under the designation of motet, including isorhythmic motets, cantilena motets, and simple fauxbourdon antiphons. He also wrote four different settings of the Magnificat.

## Plainchant

Du Fay was the last prominent composer to contribute to the plainchant repertory. He was commissioned in 1457 to write the music for both the Mass and Office for an entire feast day dedicated to the Virgin Mary. The monophonic music for this service, lost for centuries, came to light only in 1988 when a scholar working in a Belgian archive discovered it.

## Chansons

Other than a handful of Italian-language songs, all of Du Fay's secular music is in French. It includes 8 ballades, more than 60 rondeaux (not all of which have survived in their entirety), and 4 virelais.

### KEY DATES IN THE LIFE OF DU FAY

| | |
|---|---|
| 1397 | Born at Hainault (now in Belgium). |
| 1419–1424 | In Rimini and Pesaro (Italy); returns north to Cambrai (northern France). |
| 1426–1428 | In Bologna (Italy). |
| 1428 | Joins the Papal Chapel in Rome as a singer. |
| 1434–1435 | Maestro di cappella (music director) at the court of Savoy (northwestern Italy). |
| 1435–1437 | Serves in Papal Chapel again, this time in Florence and Bologna. |
| 1439 | Returns to Cambrai as canon of the cathedral; travels widely in subsequent decades. |
| 1474 | Dies in Cambrai on November 27. |

**Guillaume Du Fay and Gilles Binchois.** This double portrait, from a manuscript version of Martin le Franc's *Le champion des dames* ("The Champion of Women," 1440–1442), is directly connected to the text beneath it, which praises the two composers for having developed "a new way of composing with lively consonances," presumably a reference to their frequent use of thirds and sixths. The dieresis over Du Fay's name suggests it is correctly pronounced as three syllables (Du Fa-ee). In other sources, the composer's name is given in three parts, with a "fa" in musical notation between the syllables "Du" and "y."

**Source:** Bibliotheque Nationale, Paris, France/Bridgeman-Giraudon/Art Resource, NY

## Treatment of Text

By the middle of the 15th century, composers had generally abandoned polyglot texts in favor of a single text and an increasingly direct connection between words and music. The text of Josquin's motet extols the Virgin Mary. Although its five internal strophes allude to five major feasts in honor of Mary (see table "Liturgical Allusions in the Text of Josquin's *Ave Maria . . . virgo serena*"), the text itself is not liturgical.

Josquin organizes *Ave Maria . . . virgo serena* around the structure of this text. Each strophe has its own thematic material, and each varies from the others in terms of texture, cadences, and the number of voices. The opening and closing sections feature a symmetrical use of all four voices. The five interior strophes move fluidly between imitative counterpoint and a more chordal texture (see next section). The texts of the first and second strophes are closely linked—both begin with the same two words (*Ave cuius . . .*)—and Josquin gives them appropriately similar settings. In the original notation, both are exactly 23½ breves long, and both move from duet to four-voiced texture.

## Texture

By the 1470s, many composers were making greater and greater use of a technique known as **pervading imitation**, in which a series of musical ideas are stated imitatively in all voices throughout an entire work or section of a work. By its very nature, pervading imitation requires all voices to sing essentially the same musical ideas, making all voices more or less equal in their melodic and rhythmic profiles. The resulting homogeneity of texture is a characteristic feature of much Renaissance music written from the late 15th century onward.

The motet *Ave Maria . . . virgo serena* by Josquin des Prez illustrates this new approach. The work opens with a series of imitative entries that move systematically from the highest to the lowest voice. A new theme (m. 8) enters before the Bassus has finished its statement of the first idea. This new theme, in turn, is taken up by each of the other voices in succession. Yet another theme enters in the Superius (m. 16), overlapping once again with the Bassus. The process repeats yet again beginning in m. 23,

| JOSQUIN'S *AVE MARIA . . . VIRGO SERENA*: LITURGICAL ALLUSIONS IN THE TEXT | | | |
|---|---|---|---|
| **Section** | **Measure Number** | **Feast** | **Liturgical Significance** |
| Salutation *Ave Maria, gratia plena* | 1–30 | | |
| Strophe 1 *Ave cuius conceptio* | 31–54 | Conception | Celebrates the Immaculate Conception of the Virgin Mary (December 8) |
| Strophe 2 *Ave cuius nativitas* | 54–77 | Nativity | Celebrates the birth of Christ to Mary (December 25) |
| Strophe 3 *Ave pia humilitas* | 78–93 | Annunciation | Celebrates the archangel Gabriel's announcement to Mary that she will give birth to Christ (March 25) |
| Strophe 4 *Ave vera virginitas* | 94–110 | Purification | Celebrates the presentation of the infant Jesus in the Temple of Jerusalem 40 days after his birth (February 2) |
| Strophe 5 *Ave praeclara omnibus* | 111–42 | Assumption | Celebrates the ascension of Mary into heaven (August 15) |
| Petition *O Mater Dei* | 143–55 | | |

| JOSQUIN'S *AVE MARIA . . . VIRGO SERENA*: TEXTURAL STRUCTURE | | |
|---|---|---|
| **Text Section** | **Measure Number** | **Texture** |
| Salutation | 1 | Pervading imitation; four voices together only at the very end |
| Strophe 1 | 31 | High vs. low, followed by full chordal texture |
| Strophe 2 | 54 | High vs. low, followed by full imitative texture |
| Strophe 3 | 78 | High vs. low, nonimitative |
| Strophe 4 | 94 | Fully voiced, note-against-note counterpoint |
| Strophe 5 | 111 | Four voices, pervading imitation |
| Petition | 143 | Four voices, note against note, long rhythmic values |

this time beginning in the Altus and overlapping with both Tenor and Bassus. Each of these distinctive thematic units is known as a **point of imitation**. Successive points of imitation and cadences of varying weight help articulate the individual sections even while moving the whole work forward.

Yet the work does not consist entirely of points of imitation using all four voices. Like most Renaissance composers, Josquin is careful to provide textural variety. He differentiates each unit of the text—an opening salutation to the Virgin, five strophes in praise of the Virgin, and a closing petition, a brief prayer invoking the protection of the Virgin—through a series of contrasting textures that are sometimes imitative and sometimes not. He also uses only two voices at certain junctures, at times playing off high against low registers (see table "Textural Structure of Josquin's *Ave Maria . . . virgo serena*").

## Cadential Structure

As in a great many musical works of the Renaissance, cadences play an important role in articulating the form of this motet. Each of its sections is more or less self-contained, depending on the strength of its closing cadence. Josquin calibrated the sequence of cadences with great care (see table "Cadential Structure of Josquin's *Ave Maria . . . virgo serena*"), moving from the weakest at the very beginning (two voices on the interval of a third, with rhythmic overlap into the next section) to the strongest at the end (four voices on the interval of a fifth, sustained for a duration of four full breves).

| JOSQUIN'S *AVE MARIA . . . VIRGO SERENA*: CADENTIAL STRUCTURE | | | | |
|---|---|---|---|---|
| **Section** | **Measure Number** | **Number of Voices** | **Intervals in Cadence** | **Rhythmic Features** |
| Salutation | 30–31 | 4 → 2 | Third → Octave | Overlaps into strophe 1 |
| Strophe 1 | 53–54 | 4 → 3 | Third | Overlaps into strophe 2 |
| Strophe 2 | 77 | 3 | Unison | No overlap |
| Strophe 3 | 93 | 2 | Unison | No overlap |
| Strophe 4 | 110 | 3 | Unison | No overlap |
| Strophe 5 | 141 | 3 | Fifth | Followed by one breve rest |
| Petition | 154–55 | 4 | Fifth | Sustained over four breves |

This kind of structure, based on discrete units that are more or less independent from one another, is known as **paratactic form**. Musically, no unifying themes or rhythmic patterns run throughout the work as a whole; instead, the structure consists of a succession of essentially closed, unconnected, and unrelated units (A, B, C, D, E, etc.). Paratactic form is characteristic of a great deal of Renaissance music, vocal as well as instrumental.

## Mode

Like other composers of the Renaissance, Josquin worked within the framework of the eight-mode system that had been in use since medieval times (see Chapter 1). Individual voices would generally move within the confines of a particular mode. Identifying the mode of a work consisting of many voices was sometimes a challenge. Most theorists agreed, however, that the mode of any given polyphonic composition could be determined primarily by the range and final of the tenor voice. According to this system, *Ave Maria . . . virgo serena* is written in transposed hypolydian (on C). Some theorists in the generations after Josquin recognized additional modes based on A and C. Thus the 16th-century theorist Heinrich Glarean cited this motet as an example of the hypoionian mode, which, according to his 12-mode system, is based on C with an ambitus from the G below to the G above.

## Melody

Melody in Renaissance music is generally characterized by **conjunct motion**—that is, stepwise progressions, with only occasional leaps of more than a fifth, and even then rarely anything other than a sixth or an octave. As in plainchant, large leaps are generally followed by a move in the opposite direction, further contributing to the broader sense of balance between upward and downward movement. The opening motive of *Ave Maria . . . virgo serena* in fact derives from the plainchant melody associated with the Sequence *Ave Maria* used in the Feast of the Annunciation. The Sequence varies from source to source—this was a late addition to the chant repertory—but in one German manuscript of Josquin's time it reads as in Example 4–3. Beginning with the nonliturgical portion of the text, however (*Ave cuius conceptio. . .*), Josquin abandons the Sequence as a source of melodic material and moves ahead with freely composed ideas. The musical style of these lines nevertheless preserves the same basic melodic character found in the opening motive.

**EXAMPLE 4–3** Sequence *Ave Maria.*

A - ve Ma - ri - a, gra - ti - a ple - na Do - mi - nus te - cum, vir - go se - re - na.

## Rhythm

Most Renaissance music lacks a sense of stressed downbeats and is organized rhythmically around a steady pulse called the *tactus* (Latin for "touch"). One theorist of the late 15th century claimed that the rate of the *tactus* was equivalent to the heartbeat of an

## Composer Profile

# Josquin des Prez (ca. 1450–1521)

Josquin, hailed by his contemporaries as one of the greatest composers of his time, was also one of the first composers whose reputation endured well past his death. "Josquin," wrote Martin Luther, "is master of the notes, which must express what he desires."[10] Thirty years after his death, theorists and pedagogues were still recommending his works as models for aspiring young composers. So great was Josquin's reputation, in fact, that some publishers sought to profit from it fraudulently. Several dozen works attributed to him in 16th-century prints are now known to have been written by others.

Indeed, it seems the more we learn about Josquin's life, the less we know with certainty. Only within the past ten years have scholars discovered his true family name was Lebloitte and that "des Prez" was a nickname of sorts. Archival research has further revealed that two "Josquins" were working at the cathedral of Milan in the 1470s: the composer we know as Josquin des Prez, and another Josquin who served in the ducal chapel for some 40 years and was also a singer and composer.

We nevertheless have enough to know that Josquin was a highly self-confident individual, well aware of his talents. In 1502, a member of the court of Duke Ercole d'Este of Ferrara wrote to his master about two potential employees, Josquin and Henricus Isaac:

I must notify Your Lordship that Isaac the singer has been in Ferrara and has written a motet on a fantasy entitled "La mi la so la so la mi" which is very good, and he wrote it in two days. From this one can only judge that he is very rapid in the art of composition; besides, he is good-natured and easy to get along with, and it seems to me that he is the right man for Your Lordship. Signor Don Alfonso bade me ask him if he would like to join Your Lordship's service, and he replied that he would rather be in your service than in that of any other lord whom he knows, and that he does not reject the proposal; and he has taken the period of one month to reply as to whether he will serve or not. We have accepted that term for taking him into service (only in order to advise you about it) and we have promised him 10 ducats a month, provided that you approve, and we ask you if you will deign to let us know if you approve of this or not. To me he seems well suited to serve Your Lordship, more so than Josquin, because he is of a better disposition among his companions, and he will compose new works more often. It is true that Josquin composes better, but he composes when he wants to, and not when one wants him to, and he is asking 200 ducats in salary while Isaac will come for 120— but Your Lordship will decide.[11]

His Lordship eventually decided in favor of the more difficult—and expensive—Josquin.

adult man breathing at a normal speed—that is, roughly 60 to 70 beats per minute. Dance music, of necessity, was organized around a fixed and regular meter with a relatively strong downbeat. But composers of vocal music for the most part avoided strong rhythmic accents within any given line, creating a kind of fluidity that allows each individual voice to "float." Syncopation emerges largely from the interplay of the various lines within a polyphonic texture. *Ave Maria . . . virgo serena* is thus typical of its time, for it avoids any strong sense of meter or consistently patterned rhythm. Each section of the work establishes its own characteristic rhythmic profile. Also typical of Renaissance music is the manner in which each section becomes somewhat more animated as it progresses, then slows down again toward its close. This same rhythmic pattern holds for the composition as a whole, with the final strophe the rhythmically fastest of all, and the petition at the very end the slowest, emphasizing its function of closure.

# PRINCIPAL WORKS

Josquin wrote in virtually every vocal genre of his time. He composed some 18 Masses and 6 individual Mass movements, almost 100 motets, and about 70 chansons, most of which are in French, some in Italian, and others with no text at all. These numbers are approximate because of the uncertain status of some of the works attributed to him.

IOSQVINVS PRATENSIS.

**Josquin des Prez**. Although first published in 1611, some 90 years after the composer's death, this woodcut was based on an earlier portrait destroyed by fire in the 16th century. No other even remotely authentic image of the composer has survived.

**Source:** akg-images

| KEY DATES IN THE LIFE OF JOSQUIN DES PREZ | |
|---|---|
| ca. 1450 | Born in what is now northern France or Belgium, possibly in Saint-Quentin. |
| 1475–ca. 1480 | Member of the chapel of King René of Anjou in Aix-en-Provence (southern France). |
| 1484–1485 | In the service of Cardinal Ascanio Sforza in Milan and Rome. |
| 1489–ca. 1495 | Serves in the Papal Chapel in Rome. |
| 1503–1504 | Serves in the chapel of Ercole d'Este in Ferrara. |
| 1504–1521 | Provost of the collegiate church of Notre-Dame in Condé-sur-Escaut, in what is now northern France. |
| 1521 | Dies in Condé-sur-Escaut. |

## *Focus* TINCTORIS'S EIGHT RULES FOR GOOD COUNTERPOINT

Tinctoris concludes his *Liber de arte contrapuncti* ("Treatise on the Art of Counterpoint," 1477) with "Eight Rules to Be Observed in All Counterpoint." These can be summarized as follows:

1. All counterpoint ought to begin and end with a perfect consonance (i.e., a fifth or octave).

2. Avoid parallel fifths and octaves.

3. Successive consonances of the same kind are permitted if the tenor remains on the same note.

4. Individual lines must be as conjunct as possible, with leaps used in moderation.

5. Cadences should never fall outside of the mode of the work at hand.

6. Individual lines should not repeat the same notes over and over unless for special effect, as in imitating the sound of bells or trumpets.

7. Avoid successive cadences on the same pitches.

8. Variety must be sought in all counterpoint.

## Primary Evidence  SUCCESSIVE VERSUS SIMULTANEOUS COMPOSITION

*Conceptions of the compositional process changed fundamentally over the course of the Renaissance. In the medieval era, composers were often able to layer voices one on top of the other, as in organa, clausulae, and isorhythmic motets. Cantus firmus compositions continued this tradition of successive composition to some extent. But the more homogeneous texture evident in a work like Josquin's* Ave Maria . . . virgo serena *suggests a different approach to writing. This kind of texture, based on interlocking points of imitation, required composers to work out the implications of any given idea for all the voices more or less at once. Here, the theorist Pietro Aron (1489–1545) describes this process of simultaneous conception in an account first published in 1529.*

■ ■ ■

Many composers were of the opinion that the soprano should be composed first, then the tenor, and after the tenor the bass. This happened because they lacked the order and understanding of what was necessary to compose the alto. Thus they had many awkward places in their compositions because they had to insert unisons, pauses, and ascending and descending leaps that were difficult for the singer or performer, so that those works had little sweetness and harmony. For in composing the soprano first and then the tenor, once the tenor was made there was sometimes no room for the bass, and once the bass was made, there was no place for many notes in the alto. Therefore, in considering only part by part, that is when the tenor is being composed, if you pay attention only to harmonizing this tenor [with the soprano], and the same with the bass, it is inevitable that each part will suffer where they come together. Therefore the modern composers had a better idea, which is apparent from their compositions in four, five, six, and more voices, in which each part has a comfortable, easy and agreeable place, because they take all the parts into consideration at once and not as described above. And if you prefer to compose the soprano, tenor, or bass first, you are free to follow that method and rule, as some at present do, who often begin with the bass, sometimes with the tenor, and sometimes with the alto. But because this will be awkward and uncomfortable for you at first, you will begin part by part; nevertheless, once you have gained some experience, you will follow the order and method described before.

**Source:** "On Compositional Process in the Fifteenth Century" by Bonnie J. Blackburn, from *JOURNAL OF THE AMERICAN MUSICOLOGICAL SOCIETY,* Summer 1987, Volume 40 (2). Copyright © 1987 by the American Musicological Society. Reprinted by permission of the University of California Press.

## Harmony

Although the works of Du Fay and his contemporaries resorted increasingly to triadic sonorities and carefully controlled dissonance, harmony in the Renaissance continued to be perceived as a by-product of voice leading, not as an end in its own right. It is therefore anachronistic to speak of Renaissance compositions in terms of later concepts of tonal harmony—to analyze them, say, in terms of the effects of a progression from a V chord to an I chord, as in the closing measures of Josquin's *Ave Maria . . . virgo serena*. Yet composers and listeners of the time were certainly aware of the effects of successive vertical sonorities. As early as 1477, Johannes Tinctoris could delineate "rules for good counterpoint" that would apply to all music to the end of the Renaissance (see Focus: Tinctoris's Eight Rules for Good Counterpoint). Consonance tables began to appear regularly in compositional treatises during the 1490s, an important indication that composers were thinking about their art—and teaching it—more and more in terms of what we today call harmony. In a treatise published in 1516, Pietro Aaron explicitly discussed the means of moving from one chord to another.[12] Privately, the theorist Giovanni Spataro complained as early as 1529 that "even without studying the precepts of counterpoint everyone is a master of composing harmony."[13]

## SUMMARY OF STYLE DIFFERENCES BETWEEN MEDIEVAL AND RENAISSANCE MUSIC

| TEXTURE | MEDIEVAL | RENAISSANCE |
|---|---|---|
| | Layered, with voices moving at different speeds in most genres. | More homogeneous textures, with all voices of essentially equal importance; pervading imitation dominates from the latter decades of the 15th century onward. |
| Rhythm | Sharp differentiation among various voices in certain genres (motet, chanson). Dominance of the rhythmic modes. | Generally balanced and evenly flowing. A steady pulse (the *tactus*) governs performance, and although this may change within the course of a work, it remains steady for long stretches at a time. |
| Melody | Often angular, without a strong sense of a larger-scale shape. | Generally lyrical ("vocal"). Relatively less use of melodic material from preexistent sources. |
| Harmony | Octaves, fifths, and fourths are consonant; thirds begin to emerge only gradually as consonant. | Thirds and sixths now considered consonant, fourths less so, particularly in practice. Relatively limited and carefully controlled use of dissonance. |
| Form | Cantus firmus structures, isorhythm, *formes fixes* predominate. | Cantus firmus, isorhythm, *formes fixes* all continue until ca. 1490; afterward, chansons and motets are more likely to be paratactic (A, B, C, D, etc.), with individual subunits of a work more or less sharply demarcated from one another. |
| Instrumentation | Extremely limited repertory for instruments alone; great flexibility in doubling or re- placing voices in vocal music. | Vocal works adhere to the a cappella (voice only) ideal, with the option of instruments doubling voices. Vocal and instrumental idioms are essentially interchangeable, with only a limited number of works written specifically and exclusively for instruments. |

## White Notation

Though not audible, the notation of Josquin's motet in the manuscripts of its time reflect the new practice of what we now call "white notation," a development that had begun to take hold around the middle of the 15th century. In white notation, standard longs and breves—instead of being filled in, or black—are left unfilled, or "white." The impetus for this change was largely practical: it eliminated the time required to fill in the note heads and it caused less wear and tear on paper, which was rapidly replacing parch- ment as the standard medium for books and manuscripts. (A well-developed paper industry had established itself in France, southern Germany, and Switzerland by the end of the 14th century.) The essential elements of mensural notation remained otherwise unchanged (see Chapters 2 and 3).

## SUMMARY

The characteristic style of Renaissance music emerged gradually over the course of the 15th century and continued to evolve throughout the 16th. None of its features appeared overnight: each asserted itself only incrementally, often against resistance. As is so often the case in the history of any art, these stylistic transformations were often generational. At any given time, older musicians might be maintaining tradi- tional practices while their younger colleagues were embracing new attitudes and new approaches.

✓•⎯ **Study** and **Review**
on **mysearchlab.com**

# The Genres of Renaissance Music, 1420–1520

The development of musical style during the first one hundred years of the Renaissance—from roughly 1420 to 1520—can best be traced by considering exemplary works from those genres of central importance to composers of this period. In the realm of sacred vocal music, these genres were the Mass and motet; in secular vocal music, the chanson and frottola. Instrumental music, although committed to writing only infrequently, preserves the keyboard and dance repertories of the time.

## SACRED VOCAL MUSIC

The principal genres of sacred music in the Renaissance were the Mass and the motet. Composers of the 15th and early 16th centuries cultivated both these genres with unprecedented intensity. From a stylistic perspective, both the Mass and the motet reflect all of the most important developments that occurred over the course of roughly three generations, from Dunstable (in the early 15th century) through Du Fay and Ockeghem (in the middle of the 15th century) to Josquin des Prez and his contemporaries (in the late 15th and early 16th centuries). Within the span of a generation—roughly the middle decades of the 15th century—cantus firmus technique supplanted isorhythm as the chief structural device in the composition of large-scale vocal works, including both Mass and motet. Although isorhythmic technique persisted for some time into the second half of the 15th century, it had largely disappeared by 1500. Pervading imitation, in turn, had become an important structural device by the beginning of the 16th century.

### The Mass: Du Fay and Ockeghem

Composers of the late medieval era were not particularly interested in polyphonic settings of the complete Mass Ordinary. Guillaume de Machaut's *Messe de Nostre Dame* (Anthology; see Chapter 3), written in the late 1360s, remained the only work of its kind for almost a century. The cycle as a whole, moreover, lacked any distinctive unifying musical element. Not until the early decades of the 15th century do we begin to find pairs of movements (Gloria and Credo, or Sanctus and Agnus Dei) linked by a single cantus firmus or shared thematic ideas. Sometime around the 1440s, the English composers Leonel Power (d. 1445) and John Dunstable began to write entire cycles of the Mass Ordinary based on a single cantus firmus. All the movements of Power's *Missa Alma redemptoris mater*, for example, are based on the same cantus firmus, which is stated once in its entirety in the same rhythm in the tenor (the lowest voice) of every movement.

The emergence of the **cyclic Mass**—a cycle of all movements of the Mass Ordinary integrated by a common cantus firmus or other musical device—signals an important shift in musical aesthetics. Composers now began to place issues of musical coherence above questions of liturgical propriety or the projection of the text. Machaut had based each movement of his Mass—Kyrie, Gloria, and so forth—on a different but liturgically appropriate plainchant. The result, in true medieval fashion, subordinated the polyphony to the chant. Renaissance composers were far more inclined to create Mass cycles connected by a common musical thread that may or may not have been liturgically appropriate.

Guillaume Du Fay is credited with six complete settings of the Mass. What is believed to be the first of these, the *Missa Se la face ay pale*, was written around 1450. The Mass takes its name from the ballade *Se la face ay pale* ("If My Face Is Pale"), which Du Fay himself had composed sometime during the 1430s. Two features of this Mass are significant: it is the first by any composer based on a cantus firmus from a secular source, and it is one of the first in which the tenor—the line carrying the cantus firmus—is no longer the lowest voice. This second feature is of particular importance, for with the lowest voice no longer bound to the cantus firmus, composers were free to exercise a wider range of vertical sonorities—what we now think of as harmony.

The cantus firmus, derived from the tenor of Du Fay's ballade (Example 5–1), appears repeatedly throughout the Mass. It is absent only in internal sections in some movements, such as the Christe section within the Kyrie, for example, and the section beginning *Pleni sunt caeli* in the Sanctus.

The composer wrote a verbal canon (meaning "rule" or "law") at the beginning of each movement of the Mass to indicate the rhythmic value of the cantus firmus in that movement. At the opening of the Kyrie, for example, we find the notation *Canon: Tenor crescit in duplo*, which means the rhythmic value of the notes of the tenor as set down in

((•– **Listen**
CD2    Track 13
**mysearchlab** (with scrolling translation)
DU FAY
*Se la face ay pale*
Score Anthology I/35

((•– **Listen**
CD2    Track 14
**mysearchlab** (with scrolling translation)
DU FAY
*Missa Se la face ay pale*
Score Anthology I/36

**EXAMPLE 5–1** The structure of the cantus firmus for Du Fay's *Missa Se la face ay pale*.

**Source:** Dufay, *Se la face ay pale*: structure of cantus firmus, from Howard Mayer Brown *Music in the Renaissance* 2/e (Prentice-Hall, 1976, 1999), p. 45. © 1999. Reprinted by permission of Pearson Education, Inc., Upper Saddle River, NJ

## DU FAY'S *MISSA SE LA FACE AY PALE*: FORMAL LAYOUT

| | SECTION OF CANTUS FIRMUS USED | RELATIVE SPEED OF CANTUS FIRMUS |
|---|---|---|
| **Kyrie** | | |
| Kyrie I | AB | 2 × original value |
| Christe | Cantus firmus omitted | |
| Kyrie II | C | 2 × original value |
| **Gloria** | | |
| Et in terra pax | Complete | 3 × original value |
| Qui tollis | Complete | 2 × original value |
| Cum sancto spiritu | Complete | Original value |
| **Credo** | | |
| Patrem omnipotentem | Complete | 3 × original value |
| Et iterum venturus est | Complete | 2 × original value |
| Confiteor | Complete | Original value |
| **Sanctus** | | |
| Sanctus | A | 2 × original value |
| Pleni sunt caeli | Cantus firmus omitted | |
| Osanna | B | 2 × original value |
| Benedictus | Cantus firmus omitted | |
| Osanna | C | 2 × original value |
| **Agnus Dei** | | |
| Agnus Dei I | AB | 2 × original value |
| Agnus Dei II | Cantus firmus omitted | |
| Agnus Dei III | C | 2 × original value |

**Source:** H. M. Brown, *Music in the Renaissance* 2/e (Prentice-Hall, 1976, 1999), p. 46. Reprinted by permission of Pearson Education, Inc., Upper Saddle River, NJ

the original notation of the chanson are to be doubled. Other canons are not quite so straightforward. At the head of both the Gloria and Credo we read (in translation from the original Latin), "The tenor is stated three times. The first time it grows by three, the second by two, the third as set down." In other words, the tenor is sung three times in succession, the first time at three times the value of the notated original, the second at twice the value, the third at the original of the notated value. The preceding table shows how Du Fay structured the Mass around the cantus firmus.

Although the cantus firmus is the most obvious and important of the devices unifying the various movements of this Mass, other elements also contribute to a sense of musical coherence. The thematic idea found in the opening measures of the top line in the Kyrie, for example, reappears at many points in subsequent movements, such as the beginning of the Christe and the beginning of the Gloria. Every movement except the opening Kyrie begins with a duet essentially identical to that found in the opening four measures of the Gloria. This **head motif**—a thematic idea in multiple voices placed prominently at the beginning of a movement or section of a movement—provides yet another element of coherence to the work as a whole.

Du Fay's Masses appear to have inspired an entire generation of composers to construct artful ways of unifying the movements of a Mass cycle. Many pursued the idea of manipulating a cantus firmus; others focused on the device of the unifying head motif. Still others used the musical canon as a unifying device. Easily the most remarkable of all works in this last category is Johannes Ockeghem's *Missa prolationum* ("Mass of the Prolations"), preserved in the sumptuous Chigi Codex. In this, the oldest surviving source of the work, only two of the four voices are actually notated: the other two can be derived from them, for every movement is a double canon in which each pair of voices presents the same material moving in different prolations, which are transcribed in modern editions as different meters (see Example 3–1 and the accompanying discussion of mensuration signs in Chapter 3). In almost every movement, each voice has its own unique mensuration. When all four voices are present, so too are all four of the basic mensurations ("prolations")—hence the name of the Mass. Throughout, the upper voices are in imperfect prolation, the lower voices in perfect prolation. The two upper voices in the opening of the Kyrie, for example, share exactly the same sequence of pitches, but one is in duple meter (2/4), the other in triple (3/4). The two lower voices, which share a different melodic line, move in the equivalent of modern-day compound duple and compound triple meter (6/8 and 9/8, respectively).

As if all this were not complex enough, Ockeghem varies the intervallic as well as the rhythmic relationship of the canonic lines across the Mass as a whole, creating an elaborate series of canons at successively higher intervals:

(((•–Listen

CD2   Track 15

mysearchlab (with scrolling translation)
OCKEGHEM
*Missa prolationum*
Score Anthology I/37

**Kyrie**

| | |
|---|---|
| Kyrie I | Canon at the unison |
| Christe | Canon at second above (not a true canon) |
| Kyrie II | Canon at the unison |

| | |
|---|---|
| **Gloria** | Canon at fourth below |
| **Credo** | Canon at fifth below |

**Sanctus**

| | |
|---|---|
| Sanctus | Canon at sixth above |
| Pleni | Canon for upper two voices only at seventh below |
| Osanna | Canon at octave |
| Benedictus | Canon at fourth below (not a true canon) |

**Agnus Dei**

| | |
|---|---|
| Agnus Dei I | Canon at fourth below |
| Agnus Dei II | Canon for upper two voices only at fifth below |
| Agnus Dei III | Canon at fifth above |

Ockeghem's fascination with canon and other elaborate structural devices is typical of the Franco-Flemish composers who flourished in the late 15th and early 16th centuries. In his *Missa Ecce ancilla Domini-Ne timeas Maria*, Johannes Regis (1425–1496) combines two cantus firmi simultaneously in the lower voices at the beginning of each movement and uses no fewer than seven cantus firmi throughout, all drawn from Marian antiphons, giving the work a total of seven cantus firmi. Although no more than two cantus firmi sound simultaneously at any given time, the combinatorial

**Ockeghem's *Missa prolationum*.** The Chigi Codex is remarkable not only for its opulence, its illuminations, and its often bizarre marginal illustrations, but also for preserving so many works by a single composer, Johannes Ockeghem. Scholars have recently suggested that it may have been compiled as a memorial volume shortly after the composer's death in 1497. The manuscript is known by the name of one of its early owners, Favio Chigi, who later became Pope Alexander VII. These pages, from the Kyrie of Ockeghem's *Missa prolationum* (discussed in this chapter), show music for only two voices, but each voice generates the other, creating a double mensuration canon for four voices. At the beginning of the superius on the left-hand side are two different signs of mensuration: the circle (perfect *tempus,* imperfect *prolatio*) and a half circle (imperfect *tempus,* imperfect *prolatio*). This is the only indication to singers that each of the two voices is to sing the same notes in a different mensuration. The same holds true for the two voices on the right-hand side of the opening: the dot in the middle of the full circle indicates perfect *tempus* and perfect *prolatio*; while the dot in the middle of the half circle indicates imperfect *tempus* and perfect *prolatio*. The blackened notes on the page show that the notes lose one-third of their normal value; thus, a blackened breve is the equivalent of two-thirds of a standard breve. Blackened notes are always imperfect.

**Source:** Biblioteca Apostolica Vaticana, Vatican City, Ms. Chigi Cod. c. VIII.234, 105v-106r

feat remains impressive. Ockeghem's *Missa cuiusvis toni* ("Mass in Any Mode") does not rely on any cantus firmus at all but is constructed to be performable in any of four different modes—Dorian, Phrygian, Lydian, or Mixolydian—by changing the clef signs in various combinations. Yet it is unlikely that Ockeghem, Regis, or any of their contemporaries expected listeners to be aware of the artifice of their works in performance. Even with a score, it is difficult to hear something as temporally complex as the double mensuration canons in Ockeghem's *Missa prolationum*. And no one would have ever heard the modal flexibility of the *Missa cuiusvis toni* in performance, for within the liturgy, each movement would be sung only once, in a single mode. Such artifices are nevertheless present in the music for those who take the trouble to study and unlock the intricacies of this repertory.

## Focus MASS SETTINGS ON THE "L'HOMME ARMÉ" MELODY: MYSTERIES AND MIRACLES

The melody known as "L'homme armé" ("The Armed Man") provided more than a dozen major composers of the 15th and 16th centuries with material for their own polyphonic settings of the Mass Ordinary. The melody figures in various settings by Du Fay, Busnoys, Caron, Ockeghem, Obrecht, Tinctoris, and Josquin. In more recent times, scholars have proposed a variety of theories to explain the symbolic significance of the melody and the unusually close relationship among many of the various compositions that draw on it in one way or another.

Recent scholarship has shown that one of the earliest settings to use the tune, the *Missa L'homme armé/Dum sacrum mysterium* (1462) by Johannes Regis, was written for the Feast of Saint Michael, suggesting a strong connection of the "armed man" to that dragon-slaying saint, who was often depicted in armor. Other scholars have identified the "armed man" as Charles the Bold of Burgundy, with the Christian armed with virtue, and with even Christ himself. Still other theories associate the early history of the "L'homme armé" Masses with the Order of the Golden Fleece, a fraternity of knights who were planning a crusade against the Turks shortly after the fall of Constantinople in 1453.

Whatever the identity—or identities—of the "armed man," many of the most significant composers working between roughly 1460 and 1520 took up the challenge of using the melody in ingenious ways and even seem to have been in competition to outdo one another. Du Fay, for example, set it in retrograde at one point, while Johannes Regis used it canonically at many points in his setting. Busnoys, in turn, manipulated the melody's various subsections according to what appears to be an elaborate set of Pythagorean durational proportions. Josquin wrote not one but two complete Masses on the tune: the *Missa L'homme armé super voces musicales* transposes the melody systematically over the course of all five movements, with a three-voice mensuration canon in the Agnus Dei; the *Missa L'homme armé sexti toni* incorporates canon, retrograde, and transposition, among other devices. The Agnus Dei of the latter setting is particularly elaborate, expanding from four to six voices, with the upper four presenting two different canons at the distance of minim, while two lower voices sing the "B" and "A" sections of the melody with the additional twist that one sings it from beginning to end, while the other sings the same music in retrograde. That Josquin succeeds in combining this canon with the two others going on simultaneously above—and with everything sounding effortless all the while—is one of those minor miracles of the 15th century.

**EXAMPLE 5–2** The *L'homme armé* melody.

L'Hom - me, l'hom - me, l'homme ar - mé, l'homme ar - mé, L'homme ar - mé doibt

on doub - ter, doibt on doub - ter. On a fait par - tout cri - er

*da capo al* 𝄐

Que chas - cun se viegne ar - mer D'un hau - bre - gon de fer.

## Primary Evidence  SIX RULES FOR SINGING IN ENSEMBLE (1473)

*In his* De modo bene cantandi *("On the Manner of Singing Well"), first published in 1473 and reissued in 1509, the German theorist Conrad von Zabern (d. ca. 1480) identifies the requirements for good singing in ensemble.*

■ ■ ■

Six requirements for good singing:

*Concorditer* (to sing with one spirit and accord)

*Mensuraliter* (to sing in proper measure)

*Mediocriter* (to sing in middle range)

*Differentialiter* (to sing with discrimination)

*Devotionaliter* (to sing with devotion)

*Satis urbaniter* (to sing with beauty and refinement)

1. To sing with one accord: each singer must put forth his voice at the same moment and in the same degree, without anyone anticipating or holding back. As examples, the angels sang together the night of Christ's birth; also, the three children in the fiery furnace who with their three voices praised God as with one. To acquire this habit, the singers should observe one another carefully, especially when the choir is large and the place of performance spacious.

2. To sing in proper tempo it is necessary that one give each note its value and not hold one longer than another. This is often wrong because the singers often hold the higher tones excessively long.

3. To choose a medium range for each song is reasonable, because in a large choir it usually happens that it is difficult for all to sing the very high or very low notes, and therefore one must do without some of the voices. It is therefore important that the leader should give the starting note in the proper range, so that a melody may lie in a range about eight or nine steps above or below it.

4. To sing with discrimination means to observe fittingly the necessary requirements for the church services and the church year . . .

5. To sing with devotion it is necessary . . . for each singer to maintain the notes firmly, as they are written and handed down from the blessed Father. Also, one should not divide single notes into several parts, nor leap to the upper fifth or lower fourth

or some other consonance, nor deviate from the written notes in a kind of discant. All such digressions destroy the devotion of the hearer and easily cause confusion in the choir. . .

6. The beautiful and well-bred manner of singing has the title of *urbanus* (urbane) and *urbanitas* in contrast to *rusticus* (rustic) and *rusticitas*, because city people ordinarily have more delicate manners than do country people.

**Source:** Conrad von Zabern, *De modo bene cantandi* (Mainz, ca. 1473), trans. Carol MacClintock in *Readings in the History of Music in Performance* (Bloomington: Indiana University Press, 1979), pp. 12–13, 13–14.

**Johannes Ockeghem.** Johannes Ockeghem (ca. 1420–1497), wearing eyeglasses (not new but still fairly rare at the time), leads his choristers in singing from a large choir book. The practice of singing from a single source reflects the expense of preparing manuscripts by hand.

**Source:** Ms Fr 1537 f.58v Illustration from 'Chants Royaux sur la Conception Couronnee du Puy de Rouan', depicting the choir singing the Gloria, conducted by Jean Ockeghem (1410–97), 1519–26 (vellum), French School, 16th century) / Bibliothèque Nationale, Paris, France / The Bridgeman Art Library

Composers clearly enjoyed demonstrating the variety of ways in which they could treat a single cantus firmus. Between the middle of the 15th century and the 17th century, more than two dozen composers based works on a tune known as *L'homme armé* ("The Armed Man"). Part of the melody's appeal lay in its clear three-part structure, upward trajectory, straightforward rhythm, and strong sense of a tonal center. But there was something more at work here. It was not just the melody alone that offered possibilities, but also the opportunity for composers to show what they could do with this melody that was new, different, and often quite ingenious (see Focus Box: "Mass Settings on the "L'homme armé" Melody: Mysteries and Miracles").

## The Mass: Josquin des Prez and His Contemporaries

Written over a span of some five decades, from the 1470s through the 1510s, the Masses of Josquin des Prez provide a compendium of the structural options available to composers in this genre in the late 15th and early 16th centuries. Josquin's Masses fall into one of four categories defined by the structural techniques that characterize them:

1. Cantus firmus

2. Canon

3. Imitation (or parody)

4. Paraphrase

The cantus firmus masses derive their structuring melodies from a variety of sources and apply them in many different ways. Josquin's cantus firmus sources include the following:

- Plainchant, either a single chant in all movements, as in the *Missa Gaudeamus* (from an Introit melody), or from the plainchant Ordinary cycle, as in the *Missa De beata vergine*, each of whose movements is based on a different cantus firmus derived from appropriate chants of the Ordinary (Kyrie, Gloria, etc.).

- Secular song, as in the two Masses on the *L'homme armé* or the Credo movement on Hayne van Ghizeghem's chanson *De tous biens pleine*.

- The more or less arbitrary arrangement of solmization syllables, as in the *Missa La sol fa re mi*, which is based on a cantus firmus consisting of the notes A-G-F-D-E.

- *Soggetto cavato*, in which the cantus firmus "subject" (*soggetto*) is "carved" (*cavato*) out of a given word or name. The *Missa Hercules Dux Ferrariae*, for example, derives its cantus firmus from the solmization syllables corresponding to the Duke of Ferrara's name (Example 5–3):

| Her- | cu- | les | Dux | Fer- | ra- | ri- | ae |
|------|-----|-----|-----|------|-----|-----|-----|
| Re | ut | re | ut | re | la | mi | Re |
| D | C | D | C | D | F | E | D |

The techniques by which Josquin applies a cantus firmus include strict, ostinato, and free:

- In strict technique, the cantus firmus remains consistently in the tenor, in keeping with earlier practice, although it may sometimes appear in additional voices as well. Examples of this technique include *Missa L'homme armé super voces musicales*, *Missa L'ami Baudichon*, and *Missa Hercules Dux Ferrariae*.

- In **ostinato** technique, the cantus firmus is repeated so consistently that it always appears in at least one voice at all times. An ostinato is a thematic idea repeated without interruption many times within the course of a section or entire work. Examples of an ostinato cantus firmus in Josquin's Masses may be found in the *Missa La sol fa re mi* and in the opening Kyrie of the *Missa Hercules Dux Ferrariae* (see Example 5–3).

- In free technique the cantus firmus migrates from voice to voice or may drop out altogether from time to time, as in the *Missa Faisant regretz*.

Canonic Masses are structured according to the principle of strict canon, in which at least one of the notated voices generates a second. In Josquin's *Missa ad fugam*, for example, the superius and tenor voices are canonic throughout the entire Mass, and the other two voices are freely composed. The *Missa sine nomine* ("The Nameless Mass," so called because it bears no relationship to any earlier musical source) is Josquin's other canonic Mass.

Imitation Masses (also known as parody Masses) incorporate all the voices of an existing work—not just a single voice—into the fabric of the new work, or at the very least into the opening sections of key movements. Examples by Josquin include the *Missa Fortuna desperata* and the *Missa Malheur me bat*, both of which are based on popular chansons. The opening of the *Missa Fortuna desperata*, for example, is derived from all three voices of a chanson attributed to Antoine Busnoys but more likely the work of one Ser Felice, a Florentine composer of the late 15th century. The opening measures of the superius and bassus parts of the Kyrie of Josquin's Mass are little more than lightly embellished versions of the original chanson. Yet Josquin also makes important modifications to the existing work. He shifts the music from duple to triple meter and reworks the rhythm of the tenor voice to make it move at a slower speed— that is, to function more like a strict cantus firmus. The added fourth voice in Josquin's work—the altus—also takes the tenor of the original as its point of departure.

Josquin carries the idea of reworking multiple voices a step further in subsequent movements of the *Missa Fortuna desperata*. In the Agnus Dei I, for example, he shifts the **inversion** (melodic mirror image) of the superius of the chanson to the bass line and **augments** it (increases the length of the note values) fourfold. This bizarre twist is a musical commentary on the fickleness of the goddess Fortuna, who is forever turning her wheel, bringing down the mighty and raising the lowly in a never-ending cycle. In keeping with this symbolism, the tenor melody, having been turned upside down, returns in its original form in the bass line of the final Agnus Dei.

By the middle of the 16th century, imitation—also known as *parody*, but without any suggestion of the comedy we now associate with the term—would become the predominant structural principle for Mass settings. Giovanni Pierluigi da Palestrina (1525 or 1526–1594) would use this device in about half of his 104 Masses, and Orlande de Lassus (1532–1594) would use it in more than two-thirds of his 74 Mass settings (see Chapter 6). Sacred motets and secular songs both provided musical material for such works. Cantus firmus settings, in turn, would become increasingly rare over the course of the 16th century.

((•—Listen

**CD2    Track 16**
**mysearchlab** (with scrolling translation)
SER FELICE (?) / BUSNOYS (?)
*Fortuna desperata*
Score Anthology I/38

((•—Listen

**CD1    Tracks 17–18**
**mysearchlab** (with scrolling translation)
JOSQUIN
*Missa Fortuna desperata*
Score Anthology I/39

**EXAMPLE 5–3** Josquin, *Missa Hercules Dux Ferrariae*, Kyrie (opening).

**Source:** Josquin, *Missa Hercules Dux Ferrariae,* Kyrie (mm. 1–17). From Josquin, *Werke,* ed. A. Smijers (Leipzig: C.F.W. Siegel, 1935), p. 19. Used by permission of KVNM [Koninklijke Vereniging voor Nederlandse Muziekgeschiedenis], Utrecht.

**Paraphrase,** in contrast to imitation, involves borrowing an existing melodic idea from a different work but elaborating it freely in all voices of a new work. In the *Missa Pange lingua,* Josquin's last Mass, written sometime after 1513, all four voices use melodic material derived from the plainchant hymn of the same name (Anthology I/40) but often in highly embellished form, with substantial interpolations between pitches. In the opening Kyrie, the composer distributes the six phrases of

((•─ **Listen**

**CD2    Track 19**
**mysearchlab**
JOSQUIN
*Missa Pange lingua*
Score Anthology I/40

**The original wheel of fortune.** In this image from Giovanni Boccaccio's *De Casibus Virorum Illustrium* (Paris, 1467), the author points toward the goddess Fortune (center), who seems to be rotating a wheel upon which her victims rise and fall. Traditionally depicted as a woman, Fortune personifies the medieval belief that personal misfortune was less the result of individual action than a reflection of the inevitable turning of her wheel. The *De Casibus Virorum Illustrium* ("On the Fates of Famous Men," 1355–1374) is one of several medieval writings modeled on Ovid's *Metamorphoses*. This manuscript is a copy of the 1409 French translation by Laurent de Premierfait, secretary to Jean, Duc de Berry. The image is roughly contemporary with the chanson *Fortuna desperata* and Josquin's Mass setting based on this chanson.

**Source:** Ms Hunter 371 f.1r Dame Fortune and victims falling from her wheel, from Boccaccio's 'The Fall of Princes', 1467 (vellum), French School, (15th century) / © Glasgow University Library, Scotland /The Bridgeman Art Library

the plainchant hymn across a series of corresponding points of imitation (see table on page 133). The texture is almost entirely homogeneous: no one voice stands out rhythmically or motivically. Later movements of the Mass do not adhere so closely to the structure of the hymn; at times, in fact, the plainchant is abandoned, but it returns in its entirety in the final Agnus Dei.

Josquin's Masses and other works were printed and distributed widely during his lifetime. The Venetian publisher Ottaviano Petrucci (1466–1539) published three books devoted exclusively to his Masses, in 1502, 1505, and 1514. The only known Mass missing from these collections is the last, *Missa Pange lingua* (first published in 1539), which either did not exist or had been only recently composed when the third volume was printed. (Two other masses published with the *Missa Pange lingua* are either misattributed or doubtful.) Indeed, thanks both to the nature of his music and the new technology of music printing, Josquin was one of the first composers of polyphonic music whose works continued to be widely performed long after his death.

Josquin's contemporaries were no less ingenious in their settings of the Mass Ordinary. A few examples will serve to convey some sense of the variety of solutions they devised to the challenge of setting the same text to music over and over again.

In his *Missa Sub tuum praesidium*, Jacob Obrecht (ca. 1457/8–1505) uses the same cantus firmus throughout but adds a new voice in each successive movement, starting with a Kyrie for three voices and then moving to a Gloria for four voices, a Credo for five, a Sanctus for six, and concluding with a seven-voice Agnus Dei. An increasing number of chants, all of them associated with the Virgin Mary, are also worked into each successive movement. And in his *Missa carminum* ("Mass of Songs"), Henricus Isaac (ca. 1450–1517) incorporated a whole series of German popular songs.

**Josquin's *Missa Pange lingua*.** This lavish manuscript was produced in the Low Countries by the workshop of Petrus Alamire during the early 1520s for the Fuggers, a wealthy family of merchants and bankers in Augsburg (in present-day Germany), and recalls the beautiful music manuscripts of previous centuries. It is a far cry from the contemporary books published by Petrucci and others of this repertoire (see Focus: "The Rise of Music Printing"). The illuminated "K" (the first letter of the text "Kyrie") is so elaborate as to be barely recognizable. It shows an altar with candles and a monstrance, the vessel that holds the consecrated communion wafer. The wafer, in turn, symbolizes the body of Christ and is thus of special importance for the feast of Corpus Christi, at which the plainchant hymn *Pange lingua* was always sung. This sacred image, carefully connected to Josquin's *Missa Pange lingua,* is framed by two bizarre visages, one of which seems to be emerging from the middle of a tree.

**Source:** Josquin Desprez/Bildarchiv der Osterreichische Nationalbibliothek/E23.999-C

| JOSQUIN'S *MISSA PANGE LINGUA*: DISTRIBUTION OF PHRASES FROM THE PLAINCHANT HYMN *PANGE LINGUA* IN THE KYRIE | |
| --- | --- |
| **PHRASE OF PLAINCHANT** | **MEASURE OF KYRIE** |
| 1 Pange lingua . . . | 1 |
| 2 Corporis mysterium . . . | 9 |
| 3 Sanguinisque . . . | 17 (transposed); 25 (original pitch) |
| 4 Quem in mundi . . . | 35 |
| 5 Fructus ventris . . . | 53 |
| 6 Rex effudit . . . | 61 |

## The Motet

For all their work in the realm of the Mass, composers of Josquin's generation devoted even more of their energies toward the genre of the motet, a prayer text set to music. These works were written to fulfill one of three principal functions:

- *Liturgical.* Motets continued to function within the liturgy of the Mass Proper but were limited largely to Offertory texts. Motets were rarely connected with the Office, which typically used less elaborate music, either plainchant or simple hymns.

- *Devotional.* Religious gatherings outside the liturgy became increasingly common during the 15th and 16th centuries. Groups called confraternities met on a regular basis for devotional (that is, nonliturgical) services to pray, sing hymns, and engage in contemplation. Some of these confraternities are known to have commissioned polyphonic settings of such texts as the sequence *Salve Regina*. Josquin's *Ave Maria . . . virgo serena*, based largely on nonliturgical poetry, is another example of this kind of motet (see Chapter 4). Memorial services for the deceased were another important venue for the motet during the Renaissance.

- *Occasional*. Motets were often commissioned for specific occasions, such as Du Fay's *Nuper rosarum flores*, written for the dedication of the Cathedral of Florence (see Chapter 4). Other texts seem to have been written in response to specific events in the lives of monarchs, such as *Absalon, fili mi* (discussed later, possibly by Josquin, possibly by Pierre de la Rue), apparently written as a consolation to a monarch on the death of his son.

As in the case of the Mass, Josquin's motets demonstrate virtually the entire range of options open to motet composers of the late 15th and early 16th centuries. He always used a plainchant in some way—either as a cantus firmus or as the basis of a melodic paraphrase—whenever he set a text associated with a chant. In his *Ave Maria . . . virgo serena*, as we have seen, he used the opening section of the corresponding plainchant

---

## Primary Evidence — JOSQUIN THE EXEMPLARY

*In his massive* Dodecachordon *of 1547, Henricus Glareanus refers repeatedly to Josquin as the composer most worthy of emulation by younger artists. Here, he summarizes the reasons for his admiration.*

■ ■ ■

No one has more effectively expressed the passions of the soul in music than this symphonist, no one has more felicitously begun, no one has been able to compete in grace and facility on an equal footing with him, just as there is no Latin poet superior in the epic to Maro [i.e., the Roman poet Virgil, author of the *Aeneid*]. For just as Maro, with his natural facility, was accustomed to adapt his poem to his subject so as to set weighty matters before the eyes of his readers with close-packed spondees, fleeting ones with unmixed dactyls, to use words suited to his every subject, in short, to undertake nothing inappropriately . . . so our Josquin, where his matter requires it, now advances with impetuous and precipitate notes, now intones his subject in long-drawn tones, and, to sum up, has brought forth nothing that was not delightful to the ear and approved as ingenious by the learned, nothing, in short, that was not acceptable and pleasing, even when it seemed less erudite, to those who listened to it with judgment. In most of his works he is the magnificent virtuoso, as in the *Missa [L'homme armé] super voces musicales* and the *Missa ad fugam*; in some he is the mocker, as in the *Missa La sol fa re mi*; in some he extends himself in rivalry, as in the *Missa de Beata Virgine* [written on the same cantus firmus as Antoine Brumel's Mass of the same name]; although others have also frequently attempted all these things, they have not with the same felicity met with a corresponding success in their undertakings.

This was for us the reason why in this, the consummation of our work, we have by preference cited examples by this man. And although his talent is beyond description, more easily admired than properly explained, he still seems preferable to others, not only for his talent, but also for his diligence in emending his works. For those who have known him say that he brought his things forth with much hesitation and with corrections of all sorts, and that he gave no composition to the public unless he had kept it by him for several years, the opposite of what we said Jacob Obrecht is reported to have done.

Sequence. In both of his two settings of the antiphon *Salve Regina* (one for four voices, the other for five), he used the distinctive opening motive of the chant.

Josquin's motets abound in complex devices; even the texts are cunningly crafted at times. The first letter of the first word of the first seven lines of text in *Illibata Dei virgo nutrix* ("Incomparable Virgin, Nurse of God") together spell out "IOSQVIN"; the eighth line begins with the word "Des"; and the final four lines begin with the letters "PREZ." The composer thus embeds his name into the text of one of his Marian motets as an acrostic.

*Ut phoebi radiis* ("As Through the Rays [of the moon, sister of] Phoebus") is even more extraordinary. Its anonymous Latin text combines images from pagan sources as well as Christian poetry in praise of the Virgin Mary. Each line of text adds one more solmization syllable to its opening. Thus the first line begins with the word "Ut" ("As"), the second with "Ut re," the third with "Ut remi," and so on, through a complete hexachord ("Ut remi fas sola Petri currere prora"). Remarkably, the poetry makes sense, even if the syntax and imagery are a bit forced at times. The last line of the text's first part translates roughly: "As it is the destiny of the oar of Peter to navigate by means of one ship," referring to the disciple Peter, who was also a fisherman. The second half of the poem reverses the entire process, working backward from "La" to "La sol fa me re ut"—again, with each line of the text making linguistic sense. Josquin responds to these musical cues with melodic material corresponding to each line's implied musical pitches.

The motet *Absalon, fili mi* ("Absalom, My Son"), ascribed to Josquin but possibly by Pierre de la Rue (ca. 1452–1518), illustrates the expressive power of the motet and at the same time reminds us of just how many questions remain to be answered about much of Renaissance music. The text is pieced together from three separate biblical passages, each of which deals with a father's lament on the death of his son: 2 Samuel 18:33, in which King David mourns the death of Absalom; Job 7:16, in which Job mourns the death of his son; and Genesis 37:35, in which Jacob mourns the death of Joseph.

The motivation behind this patchwork text is uncertain. Some scholars believe it was written in response to the murder of Juan Borja, Duke of Gandía and eldest son of Pope Alexander VI, in June 1497. Other scholars have pointed to the death of Emperor Maximilian I's son Philip the Fair in 1506. Still other candidates include the English princes Arthur (son of Henry VII) and Henry (son of Henry VIII), both of whom died in infancy in the early years of the 16th century.

The distribution of the voices and their notation, at least in the earliest surviving source of this work, are striking: the upper two voices carry a sign of two flats, the tenor three, and the bass four. All four voices, moreover, occupy an extremely low range, in keeping with the textual theme of lamentation. The bass, which in vocal literature rarely descends below the F that lies an octave and a half below middle C, hits the E♭ below it many times and eventually descends to D♭ and even the B♭ below that, a full fifth below what is normally the lowest note of the range. Scholars have debated this notation for many years without reaching a consensus about what it means or how the music should be performed. It may be that the work was sung in transposition at a higher pitch. One later version of *Absalon* (from the mid-16th century) transposes the work upward by a ninth (which makes the uppermost voice difficult to sing). But if the work was meant to be transposed, why was it notated in such a low range in the first place? Surely this had something to do with the text's theme of loss and mourning. The bass hits its lowest note at the very end of the piece, on the word *plorans* ("weeping"), concluding a line set to the words *non vivam*

((•• Listen

CD2   Track 20
**mysearchlab** (with scrolling translation)
JOSQUIN (?) / DE LA RUE (?)
*Absalon, fili mi*
Score Anthology I/41

## Focus  MUSICA FICTA

Unquestionably the most controversial issue in Renaissance notation is **musica ficta**, a term applied to the practice of sharpening or flattening certain notes even though they are not notated as such. *Ficta* ("imagined") comes from the same root word as our "fictive" or "fiction" and refers to the "feigned" notes that lie outside the Guidonian hand, or gamut (see Chapter 1). Rules for the application of musica ficta can be divided into two categories: melodic and harmonic.

- Melodic rules were intended to avoid certain linear tritones. A singsong rhyme ("Una nota sopra *la* semper est canendum *fa*") helped students of the time remember that "the note above *la*"—that is, the sixth scale degree in the hexachord being used at any given moment—"is always to be sung as *fa*." In other words, an excursion of one note above the top note of the hexachord, the *la*, should always be a half step. In a hexachord on C, for example (C-D-E-F-G-A), the notated B above A (*la*) would be sung as if it were a *fa*, that is, as a half step above *la*—in short, as a B♭. In a hexachord on F (F-G-A-B-C-D), a notated E would be sung as an E♭.

- Harmonic rules were intended to avoid vertical tritones, semitones, and cross-relations. To make the required adjustments, singers had to listen carefully to the lines of others, a practice that was a basic part of musical training in the Renaissance. The student's rhyme here was "Mi contra fa est diabolus in musica"—that is, the interval of a half step ("*mi* against *fa*") sounding simultaneously was considered "the devil in music."

According to Renaissance theorists, the conventions of musica ficta were driven in some cases by necessity (*causa necessitatis*), and in some cases by beauty (*causa pulchritudinis*). Necessity required the avoidance of tritones and cross-relations. Beauty required that certain cadences be approached by half steps. Thus performers approaching a perfect consonance (an octave or fifth) by means of an imperfect consonance (a third or a sixth) were expected to use musica ficta to create a half step—what we today would call a leading tone. A notated minor sixth moving to an octave, for example, would be performed as in Example 5–4a, and a notated minor third moving to a fifth would be performed as in Example 5–4b.

In modern editions, an accidental above the note indicates that it has been placed there by the editor; an accidental in its normal place, on the staff, indicates that it was notated as such in the original source.

Although writers of the time agreed on these core conventions, it is not always clear how musicians actually applied them. Making a change in one voice could sometimes set in motion a cascading series of subsequent changes in the same and other voices. Flattening a note, for example, might help avoid one linear or vertical tritone but create the danger of another soon afterward. It is also unclear just how much dissonance the Renaissance ear could tolerate. Cross-relations may well have been acceptable at times. And strong evidence suggests an occasional tritone was not only tolerated but welcomed. Thus editors and performers who apply the rules of musica ficta mechanically run the risk of interpretations that are blander than Renaissance composers or performers would have expected.

Renaissance musicians certainly did not always agree about the practice of musica ficta. Pietro Aaron noted in 1523 that "there are, among students of music, many arguments as to flats and sharps,"[1] that is, over whether composers should mark such accidentals. The noted theorist and composer Gioseffo Zarlino (1517–1590), writing a generation later, observed, "There are some who in singing sharpen or flatten a melody in a manner the composer never intended."[2] Others, in turn, took a more relaxed attitude toward the whole matter. "Because I thought it better flat than sharpe," Thomas Morley declared in his *Plaine and Easie Introduction to Practicall Musicke* (London, 1597), "I have set it flat, but if anie man like the other way better, let him use his discretion."[3]

Given so many disagreements and ambiguities, why did the practice of musica ficta persist as long as it did? The system may strike us today as cumbersome and ambiguous, but the need to introduce certain unnotated accidentals was apparently so self-evident to Renaissance musicians that they would have felt insulted had composers notated them. Tinctoris, writing in the late 15th century, contemptuously called a notated flat to avoid a linear tritone in the Lydian mode an "ass's mark." Only unusually chromatic passages were marked as such. Eventually, however, with the gradual decline of the hexachordal system and the growing dissemination of printed music, composers and publishers became increasingly specific about their instructions to performers in all aspects of music, from text underlay to tempo to the addition and cancellation of accidentals, no matter how conventional. As a result, by 1600 musica ficta had largely disappeared.

**EXAMPLE 5–4** Musica ficta for leading tones to octaves and fifths.

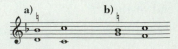

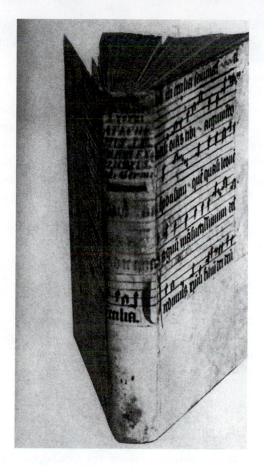

**Recycling music manuscripts.** Until well into the 19th century, manuscripts that were no longer useful were often recycled. Parchments, which were made from animal skins and thus both expensive and durable, were sometimes scraped down—their surfaces erased, in effect—to make way for a new layer of writing. The parchment shown here was in fact so sturdy that it could be reworked to provide a cover to an entirely different book. The original owner of this German-Latin edition of Martin Luther's *Catechism*, published in 1610, used a 16th-century chant manuscript to bind his or her new purchase.

**Source:** Mark Evan Bonds, UNC Libraries Photographic Services

*ultra, sed descendam in infernum plorans* ("Let me live no longer but descend into hell, weeping"). In an early instance of **word painting**—the use of musical elements to imitate the meaning of a specific passage of a text—the pain and depths of hell are represented by an unusual and unusually low pitch. Still other commentators have pointed out that the concept of fixed pitch did not exist in Josquin's time—a low "F" in Milan was not necessarily the same as a low "F" in Rome—and they have suggested the notation is effectively an instruction to the performers to sing the music as low as they possibly can.

The notation of *Absalon, fili mi* also raises the vexing issue of *musica ficta* (see Focus: "Musica ficta"). As a look at specific passages reveals, it is one thing to learn the conventions of *ficta*, quite another to apply them to a network of polyphonic voices in which changes in one melodic line frequently affect other lines as well. Consider, for example, the explicitly notated D♭ in the tenor in measure 58. This requires a flattened A in the superius to avoid an augmented fifth, which in turn demands another flattened A in the altus later in the same measure to avoid a **cross-relation** (the simultaneous or nearly simultaneous sounding of two pitches a half step apart) between the A♭ in the superius and the notated A♭ in the altus. The A in the altus should remain unflattened, however, at the end of measure 59 to provide a half-step resolution to the cadential B♭ that follows. Matters get even more convoluted as the work progresses, as for example with the cascading consequences of the notated G♭ in measure 66 and in measure 83.

Finally, a very basic question: who wrote *Absalon, fili mi*? The earliest extant source, a manuscript copied some time between 1509 and 1523, cites no composer at all—not an unusual phenomenon for the time, to be sure. The first attribution to Josquin appears in a German collection printed in 1540—well after the composer's death and far from where he lived and worked. Raising additional red flags, this same source also attributes other works of questionable authorship to Josquin. The attribution to Pierre de la Rue, however, rests entirely on circumstantial evidence. No print or manuscript of the motet from the period identifies him as the composer, but the earliest known source comes from the workshop of Petrus Alamire (ca. 1470–after 1534), a scribe closely associated with la Rue. The low range of voices, combined with signatures of more than one flat in all the voices, moreover, is a stylistic trait found in other works by la Rue but not in any other composition by Josquin. On the whole, the attribution to la Rue seems more plausible than the attribution to Josquin, but lacking more reliable evidence, it is impossible to be entirely certain who wrote this remarkable work.

# SECULAR VOCAL MUSIC

A good deal of the secular vocal music of the 15th century was never committed to writing. Many of the songs current during this period were performed through a combination of memory, embellishment, and improvisation. The surviving sources nevertheless document the approximately parallel stylistic developments in the sacred and secular repertories of this time.

## Chanson

Stylistic developments in the chanson during the period ca. 1420 to 1520 parallel those in the Mass and motet. These include the move from a layered to a more homogeneous texture, the rhythmic equalization of parts, and the increasing use of pervading imitation as the principal structural device. Of the *formes fixes* so prevalent in the 14th and early 15th centuries (see Chapter 3), only the rondeau survived through the end of the 15th. More than survive, however, it flourished, accounting for about three-fourths of the chanson repertory from the period 1450 to 1500.

To trace the evolution of the chanson in the 15th century, we will look at three representative works, each written by a different composer at a different time within the century: Du Fay's *Adieu ces bons vins de Lannoys* (1426), Busnoys' *Je ne puis vivre ainsy* (ca. 1470), and Henricus Isaac's *Innsbruck, ich muss dich lassen* (ca. 1490).

Du Fay's rondeau *Adieu ces bons vins de Lannoys* ("Farewell These Good Wines of Lannoys") illustrates the composer's early style and is typical of many chansons written between around 1425 and 1450. It opens and closes with brief untexted passages that may have been performed instrumentally. Only the uppermost line, the superius, is texted in the sources, and the tenor and contratenor were probably performed on instruments. Indeed, many Renaissance sources transmit chansons with no text at all, suggesting this repertory might well have been performed at times entirely on instruments, with no singing at all. The three voices in this particular chanson move in more or less the same rhythms throughout, with little syncopation. The tenor and the superius are the structural voices, providing all necessary consonances at openings and cadences. The contratenor is a filler voice: it cannot substitute for either the superius or the tenor to provide needed points of consonance. And in contrast to the other two voices, characterized by conjunct motion, the contratenor features several octave leaps.

((•► **Listen**

**CD2    Track 21**
**mysearchlab** (with scrolling translation)
DU FAY
*Adieu ces bons vins de Lannoys*
Score Anthology I/42

Antoine Busnoys' *Je ne puis vivre ainsy*, composed ca. 1470, is a lover's lament ("I cannot live like this forever/Unless I have in my distress/Some comfort,/Just an hour, or less—or more. . . ."). The text forms an acrostic: the first letter of each line of the text spells out the name of the woman who has caused such anguish: Jaqueline d'Aquevile. We do not know the biographical details of who she was or on whom she inflicted such torment, but the nature of the pain is clear enough.

Busnoys' setting of this French text gives equal importance to all three voices, with a good deal of imitative counterpoint. This is typical of the chanson repertory in the later decades of the 15th century. The music follows the pattern of a virelai (ABBAA), with the text of the opening and closing "A" section—the refrain—identical both textually and musically. (A virelai consisting of a single stanza was also known in

((•—)) **Listen**

**CD3**　　**Track 1**
**mysearchlab** (with scrolling translation)
BUSNOYS
*Je ne puis vivre ainsy*
Score Anthology I/43

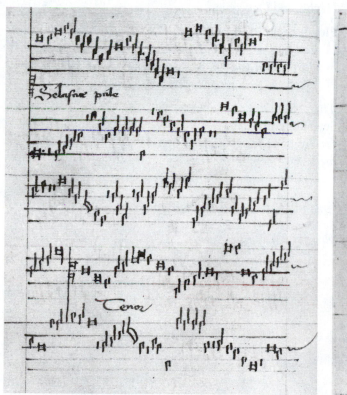 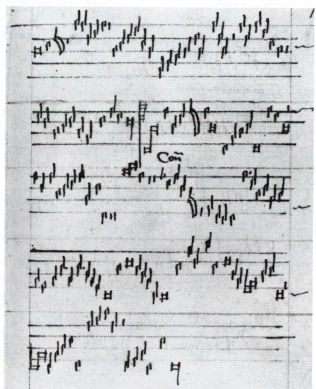

**A chansonnier for personal use.** In contrast to lavish chansonniers like Cordiforme (see page 140), Hartmann Schedel's songbook was compiled strictly for his own private use. The repertory is a mixture of German Lieder, French chansons, a *basse danse,* and a few sacred pieces—in short, a typical miscellaneous collection for a 15th-century medical student. Schedel gathered much of his music in his native Nuremberg but probably also collected a number of the chansons while studying in Italy in the early 1460s.

We can only speculate as to how many personal chansonniers of this kind existed during the 15th century. Schedel's has been preserved by virtue of the fact that he later gained fame as the author of the *Nuremberg Chronicles,* a massive history of the world and one of the most ambitious book-publishing projects undertaken before 1500. Schedel's enormous personal library, including his modest songbook, was purchased by the Bavarian Royal Library, which in turn formed the nucleus of today's Bavarian State Library in Munich. But many other songbooks compiled by less famous individuals must certainly have perished over time.

The opening here shows Guillaume Du Fay's *Se la face ay pale,* one of the most widely transmitted chansons of the 15th century. Typically for chansonniers of this era, there is no text, nor is the composer named. The notes are distributed in such a way as to maximize the use of paper, an expensive commodity at the time. The superius begins in the upper left, the tenor voice in the middle of the next-to-last system on the left-hand page, and the contratenor ("Con") in the middle of the second system on the right-hand page.

**Source:** Bayerische Staatsbibliothek Munich, fol. 69v–70

## Focus  CHANSON MANUSCRIPTS OF THE 15TH CENTURY

The repertory of 15th-century chansons is preserved in a surprisingly small number of manuscripts known as *chansonniers*, regardless of whether they come from France, Italy, or Germany. Only about two dozen or so have survived from the period between 1440 and 1500. Some of these, like the Chansonnier Cordiforme and the Mellon Chansonnier, were clearly meant as presentation copies: they are works of art in their own right, with richly illuminated initial letters and elaborate figures in the margins. Others, like the Schedel Liederbuch, were compiled for personal use and are quite modest in appearance.

The **Chansonnier Cordiforme,** now in Paris in the Bibliothèque nationale, is a lavishly illustrated manuscript in the shape of a heart (see the accompanying illustration). Compiled in Savoy (now northwestern Italy and southeastern France) between 1470 and 1477, it contains works by Busnoys, Du Fay, Hayne, and Ockeghem.

The **Dijon Chansonnier,** in the Bibliothèque municipale, in Dijon, France, was compiled in central France in the 1470s. It contains works by Binchois, Busnoys, Compère, Du Fay, Hayne, and Ockeghem.

The **Mellon Chansonnier,** named after the American industrialist Andrew Mellon, who purchased it in the early 20th century, is housed today in Yale University's Beinecke Library in New Haven, Connecticut. Produced in Naples in the 1470s, possibly under the supervision of Johannes Tinctoris, it includes works by Binchois, Busnoys, Du Fay, Hayne, and Ockeghem.

The **Laborde Chansonnier** is in the collection of the Library of Congress in Washington, D.C. The bulk of this manuscript was compiled in central France in the 1470s, with additional material added around 1490. It contains works by Binchois, Busnoys, Compère, Du Fay, Hayne, and Ockeghem.

**Florence 229,** in the Biblioteca nazionale centrale in Florence, is a large manuscript of 325 leaves prepared in Florence in the 1490s. It contains works by Du Fay, Hayne, Isaac, Josquin, Martini, Obrecht, and others.

The **Schedel Liederbuch,** in the Bayerische Staatsbibliothek, in Munich, Germany, is a small book prepared in the 1460s for personal use by a young German medical student. It includes a mixture of German, French, and Italian works, as well as a few sacred pieces.

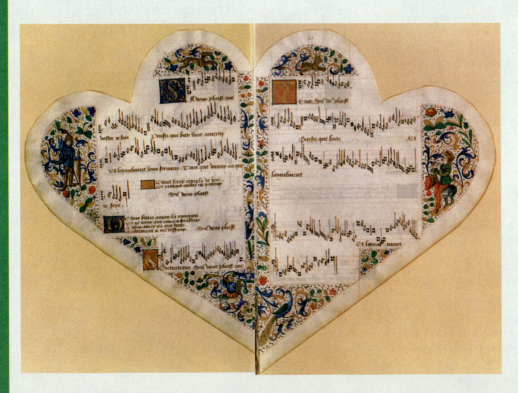

**The Chansonnier Cordiforme.** The most famous of all 15th-century chansonniers, this manuscript consists entirely of love songs. It is shaped like a heart when closed, a double heart when opened. None of the works is attributed to a composer in the manuscript, but we know from other sources that it includes music by Du Fay, Binchois, Busnoys, and Ockeghem. The work shown here is *S'il vous plaist,* a three-voice rondeau by the composer Johannes Regis.

**Source:** Bibliothèque nationale de France

the 15th century as a *bergerette*.) The mensuration changes from triple in the A section to double in the B section, and the inflections on E♭ and B♭ in the second half of the B section are particularly effective in creating contrast with the opening A section.

Henricus Isaac was an internationally known musician who served the Habsburgs in Austria, the Medici in Florence, Emperor Maximilian, and the elector of Saxony and traveled freely in Germany and Italy. He brought the Franco-Flemish style to the imperial court chapel, and his influence on German composers was considerable. He was deemed worthy of comparison to Josquin, as the correspondence concerning the hiring of a composer by the Estes in Ferrara shows (see the Composer Profile for Josquin de Prez in Chapter 4). Most of Isaac's surviving music was written for liturgical use; besides more than 35 masses there are the nearly completed cycles of Proper settings for the Habsburgs and the Konstanz Cathedral (the *Choralis Constantinus*) as well as other Propers and motets.

But like his contemporary Josquin, Isaac wrote or arranged numerous examples of the French chanson, the Italian frottola (discussed later in this chapter), and the German Tenorlied (see Chapter 6). His best-known work may be the Lied *Innsbruck, ich muss dich lassen* ("Innsbruck, I must leave you"; originally "Insprugk" or "Isbruck"); its melody may or may not have been composed by Isaac. He set it twice, once with the tune in the tenor (typical of a Tenorlied) in canon with the altus, the other with the tune in the soprano, in a more Italian manner (termed a *Diskantlied*). Even then, Isaac was not finished with *Innsbruck*; it is one of several cantus firmi in the Kyrie of his *Missa carminum*. Furthermore, besides arrangements by other composers, the tune was set to the Lutheran chorale *O Welt, ich muss dich lassen* in 1642, and as such appears in Bach's Cantata BWV 97, *In allen meinen Taten*, and the *St. Matthew Passion*; Telemann, Liszt, Brahms, and Hugo Distler also borrowed it.

((•• **Listen**

CD3    Track 2
**mysearchlab** (with scrolling translation)
ISAAC
*Innsbruck, ich muss dich lassen*
Score Anthology I/44

## Frottola

For most of the 15th century, the song repertory in Italy was dominated by the French chanson. Only in the 1480s did native composers begin setting texts in their own language once again, in a genre broadly known as the **frottola** (plural **frottole**). The texts for these songs include freely structured poems as well as poems in a variety of established Italian literary forms. In contrast to the preoccupation with courtly love that predominates in chanson texts, frottola poetry tends to be lighthearted and often sarcastic or ironic. Musically, frottole tend to avoid imitation and contrapuntal artifice, again in contrast to contemporary chansons. Frottole are characterized instead by chordal textures and lively, dancelike rhythms with frequent use of syncopation and **hemiola** (a brief passage of duple-meter rhythms within an otherwise triple-meter context). Many frottole use formulaic rhythmic units like the one in Example 5–5.

Harmonic progressions in the frottola are often simple. In modern terminology, the genre makes frequent use of patterns like I-IV-V-I. The music could be performed entirely vocally, entirely by instruments, or by any of various combinations of voices and instruments. Many frottole were arranged for solo voice and lute, or for keyboard alone, for frottole were in high demand. The Venetian publisher Petrucci (see Focus: The Rise of Music Printing) produced no fewer than 11 books of them between 1504 and 1514—a rate of roughly 1 a year.

**EXAMPLE 5–5** A typical frottola rhythmic pattern.

## Focus  THE RISE OF MUSIC PRINTING

Printing in various forms—most notably by woodblock—had existed long before Johannes Gutenberg printed his first book in the mid-1450s. Carving a block of wood, however, was time consuming, the blocks did not stand up well to repeated pressure, and they could not be reused for anything other than the particular pages for which they had been created. By using many separate pieces of small metal type, each consisting of a single letter or mark of punctuation, Gutenberg created a far more efficient process. A page of movable type could be assembled in fairly short order; the metal could withstand the intense pressure needed to create a clean image on many copies; and the pieces of type could be disassembled and reused to print another, entirely different page. Suddenly, the distribution of written knowledge was no longer limited to what could be produced by scribes, one handwritten copy at a time. Now thousands of essentially identical copies of a book could be produced cheaply and economically.

Printing music, however, presented a technical challenge not faced in the printing of text. It required the alignment of two elements occupying the same space: staff lines and notes. The earliest printed books containing music used woodblocks or other comparable methods, but these were mostly plainchant graduals and missals with only single lines of music. A few theoretical treatises contained brief musical examples.

The printing of polyphonic mensural music did not begin until the early 16th century. Ottaviano Petrucci of Venice (1466–1539) printed his music in three steps: first the staves, then the underlaid text, and finally the notes. His first publication, a collection of mostly three- and four-voice chansons and a few motets, was issued in 1501 under the title *Harmonice musices odhecaton A*. This "Hundred Songs of Polyphonic Music" actually contains only 96 pieces. The "A" points to a series of subsequent volumes that appeared under the simpler titles of *Canti B* ("Songs B," 1502) and *Canti C* ("Songs C," 1504).

Petrucci was equally important in establishing the business of music publishing. He recognized the market for collections of both sacred and secular music and fulfilled an ongoing demand for chansons, frottole, motets, and Masses. Petrucci himself, or more likely his editor—a Dominican friar who was also a singer and later maestro di cappella at a church in Venice—collected and prepared for publication the works of outstanding contemporary composers, most notably Josquin, Obrecht, and Ockeghem. Publication made this music suddenly accessible to a vastly wider audience than before. And to judge by the number of editions Petrucci produced, this music, particularly Josquin's, sold well.

Scribes nevertheless continued to play an important role in the copying of music throughout the 16th century. Indeed, for certain kinds of music, hand-copying remained more economical than printing well into the 18th century.

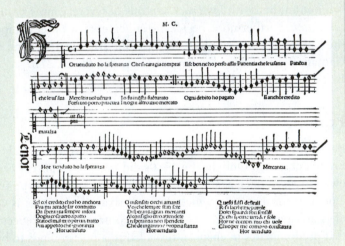

**Petrucci's printed music.** A portion of Marchetto Cara's frottola *Hor venduto ho la speranza* in its original four-voice version, as it appeared in Petrucci's *Frottole*, Book 1 (1504). Only two of the four voices are shown here, the cantus and the tenor. Petrucci's editions are beautifully printed. The music rarely seems cramped on the page, and the type is consistently crisp and elegant. Although this print is in choir book form, publishers often issued separate part books for each voice.

**Source:** Bayerische Staatsbibliothek Munich, Musikabteilung, Rar. 878-1

((•─ **Listen**

**CD3  Track 3**
**mysearchlab** (with scrolling translation)
CARA
*Hor venduto ho la speranza*
Score Anthology I/45

The frottola was cultivated with greatest intensity by Italian-born composers, most notably Bartolomeo Tromboncino (ca. 1470–ca. 1535) and Marchetto Cara (ca. 1470–1525). Both were active in the northern Italian city of Mantua. Cara's *Hor venduto ho la speranza* appeared in the first book of frottole published by Petrucci in

1504 in a four-voice version and then later in a version for solo voice and lute in 1509, also published by Petrucci. The lute part of this later version, which is the one that appears in the Anthology, is essentially polyphonic, in two voices.

**The instrument as a voice.** Silvestro Ganassi's *Fontegara* (Venice, 1535) is an important Renaissance manual on playing the recorder. The illustration on the title page shows two singers and three recorder players reading from part books. This kind of ensemble was typical in its day: instruments routinely substituted for voices or doubled them. The singer at the right, in fact, holds a sopranino recorder in his left hand, ready to move back to his instrument at any moment. Ganassi himself maintained that the voice was the ideal instrument and that the recorder (and for that matter all wind instruments) should strive to imitate the voice. He proudly proclaimed that his advice on ornamentation, articulation, and improvisation was applicable to all "wind and string players, as well as those who take delight in singing."

**Source:** Lebrecht Music & Arts/The Image Works

**The frottola.** Lorenzo Costa (1459–1535) was at one time the chief painter at the court of Mantua, which, along with Ferrara, was one of the main centers of frottola composition. This particular painting, dating from ca. 1485–1495, captures the spirit of this popular genre. The two singers on the outside seem to be beating time with their hands or perhaps even adding a percussive element to the music. The lutenist, who is also singing, keeps his eye on the open music book before him. The pocket fiddle and recorder stand at the ready, perhaps to be played in place of the voices at various points in the performance to provide variety.

**Source:** A Concert (oil on panel), Costa, Lorenzo (1459/60–1535) / National Gallery, London, UK / The Bridgeman Art Library

## Performance Perspective

### From Part Song to Solo Song

◀•▶ Listen on mysearchlab     CD3   Track 3

Although typically notated for multiple voices, Renaissance songs were also routinely performed either on a single instrument, such as the lute or harpsichord, or as a solo song with instrumental accompaniment. This rendition of *El grillo* represents a typical Renaissance performance scenario, with the lutenist herself singing as she plays. All the voices of the original four-part version are present—one in the voice, three in the lute—and the texture thus remains polyphonic. But the clear prominence of the voice against the lute gives the strong impression of a solo song with subsidiary accompaniment. True homophonic texture, notated as such, would not emerge until the very end of the sixteenth century. But the sound of a solo voice partnered with an instrument was already familiar to audiences well before this time.

Even when performed by a solo voice with lute accompaniment, the four parts of *El grillo* combine to create a polyphonic texture.

◀•▶ Listen
CD3   Tracks 4/5
mysearchlab (with scrolling translation)
JOSQUIN (?)
*El grillo*
Score Anthology I/46

Italians may have been the principal composers of frottola, but others also contributed to the genre, including, possibly, Josquin. The very title of *El grillo* ("The Cricket"), attributed to Josquin, tells us we are far from the realm of courtly love in which the poetry of the chanson usually dwells. The musical style of this brief piece also contrasts sharply with that of contemporary chansons. *El grillo* is predominantly chordal in texture, occasionally **antiphonal** (in the back-and-forth between high and low voices in m. 11–14), and not at all imitative. Its authorship, however, is unclear. In the only contemporary source in which it appears—Petrucci's third book of frottole, published in Venice in 1505—it is ascribed to "Josquin d'Ascanio." This may or may not be Josquin des Prez; recent research suggests it may have been the "other" Josquin in the service of Cardinal Ascanio Sforza of Milan from 1459 to 1498. Whoever wrote the piece had a wonderful knack for translating animal sounds into music, however.

## INSTRUMENTAL MUSIC

We know from paintings and written accounts that instrumental music in the Renaissance, as in the medieval era, was cultivated far more than notated sources would indicate. Performers routinely played from memory and often improvised. Notated vocal works, in turn, lent themselves to easy adaptation on any of a variety of instruments, and ample evidence suggests that chansons were routinely performed either in whole or in part on instruments.

Still, it is fair to say that composers of the 15th century rarely wrote music intended to be performed exclusively on instruments. The process of transforming vocal models into instrumental arrangements was left to performing musicians. A distinctly instrumental idiom would not begin to emerge until well into the 16th century.

## ENGLAND

The tombstone of **JOHN DUNSTABLE** (ca. 1390–1453) describes him as a mathematician, astronomer, and musician. He traveled for many years in the service of the Duke of Bedford throughout northern France in the 1420s and 1430s and may well have met Du Fay, Binchois, and other French composers. His output consists largely of motets and Mass movements, along with a few songs.

Less is known about **LEONEL (LIONEL) POWER**, who died in 1445 and seems to have been slightly older than Dunstable. He served in the Household Chapel of Thomas, Duke of Clarence, who was the brother of Henry V. In the last decade of his life, Power was master of the Lady Chapel Choir in Canterbury. Many of his works are included in the Old Hall Manuscript, and his settings of the Mass are among the earliest to use a single cantus firmus in all movements.

## FRANCE AND THE LOW COUNTRIES

**GILLES BINCHOIS** (ca. 1400–1460) was a contemporary of **GUILLAUME DU FAY** (ca. 1400–1474; see Composer Profile: Guillaume Du Fay in Chapter 4); the two composers cultivated many of the same genres. Binchois worked mostly in southern Belgium and northern France and did not travel nearly so widely as Du Fay. **ANTOINE BUSNOYS** (ca. 1430–1492) composed Masses, motets, and chansons, and like Binchois spent most of his career in Burgundian lands.

**JOHANNES OCKEGHEM** (ca. 1420–1497) was the eldest of a remarkable series of composers to come from an area known as the Low Countries, now consisting of the Netherlands, Belgium, and the northernmost part of France. (These composers as a group are sometimes referred to as "Franco-Flemish" or "Franco-Netherlandish.") Ockeghem is remembered today in large part for his remarkably complex polyphony, and contemporaries praised his music for its subtlety. The composer and theorist **JOHANNES TINCTORIS** (ca. 1435–?1511) dedicated his treatise on modes to Ockeghem and Busnoys; his *Terminorum musicae diffinitorium* ("Dictionary of Musical Terms," Naples, 1473) was the first separately published book of its kind. He served for many years at the court of the king of Naples.

**JOSQUIN DES PREZ** (ca. 1450–1521; see Composer Profile: "Josquin des Prez," in Chapter 4) was the most illustrious member of the next generation from this region. **JACOB OBRECHT** (ca. 1457/8–1505) and **HENRICUS ISAAC** (ca. 1450–1517) also spent considerable portions of their careers in Italy. Obrecht was music director at the Cathedral of Antwerp for a time but also worked at the court of Ferrara, where he died of the plague. He was a prolific composer of Masses and motets, many of extraordinary complexity and artifice. Isaac served as organist and maestro di cappella at the court of Lorenzo de Medici in Florence, then later at the court of Emperor Maximilian I in Vienna. He wrote some 36 Masses as well as 15 individual Mass movements and more than 40 motets. His *Choralis Constantinus*, written for the cathedral of Konstanz in southern Germany, contains polyphonic settings for all the Mass Propers of the entire church year. A truly international composer, Isaac also wrote French chansons, German Lieder, and Italian frottole.

## Renaissance Instruments

The Renaissance inherited and expanded on the rich variety of instruments used during the medieval era. Indeed, it is fair to say that a greater variety of sound was probably available to musicians in the Renaissance than at any other time in the history of music before the 20th century. Many instruments have disappeared since then, such as the *lira da braccio* (a large viol-like instrument held on the shoulder), the crumhorn (literally, a "bent horn," a kind of J-shaped double-reed instrument), the bladder pipe (a type of bagpipe), and the racket (see illustration "Renaissance forerunners of the bassoon" on page 149), affectionately known in colloquial German of the time as

**Sight and sound.** The lira da braccio (*lira* = lyre; *braccio* = arm) is one of many Renaissance instruments that have been revived only recently with the renewed interest in historically informed performance practice. Roughly the size of a very large viola and played with a bow, the lira da braccio features an additional set of drone strings to the left of the fingerboard; these resonate while the fingered strings are played and create an aura of sound around the melodic line. This particular instrument, made by Giovanni d'Andrea of Venice in 1511, exemplifies the drive to combine the pleasures of sight and sound. Harpsichord lids were often embellished even more elaborately.

**Source:** Erich Lessing / Kunsthistorisches Museum, Vienna, Austria/Art Resource, NY

the *Wurstfagott*—"sausage bassoon." Although these and other instruments of the time may seem exotic to us today, they were integral in creating a rich fabric of sound in a culture that reveled in timbral variety and contrast.

**Keyboard.**   The organ expanded steadily in size, range of pitches, number of pipes, and variety of timbres over the course of the Renaissance. By the early 16th century, most church organs of any size had multiple registers (sets of pipes). In addition to the main register (*Hauptwerk*, to use the German term by which it is often known), the most common additional register was the *Rückpositiv*, or Chair, a separate set of pipes situated behind or underneath the player.

Stops—manually operated knobs—allowed players to control the mixture of air flowing to an instrument's various registers and gave performers the ability to create a far greater variety of sound than had been possible in previous times. A reed stop, for example, could create a relatively raspy sound; others could create timbres approximating the sound of a flute. Another important development during the 15th and 16th centuries was the introduction of multiple keyboards connected to separate registers. The number of pedal notes available to the performer also increased steadily over time.

The smaller portative (portable) organ was popular for use in the home. The smallest of these, which had a range of only about two octaves and required the performer to pump the bellows with one hand while playing with the other, were strictly for melodies. Larger instruments, known as positive organs, rested on the floor or on a table. A second person worked the bellows on these instruments, leaving the performer free to play with both hands.

The clavichord evolved out of the monochord in the early 15th century, although the earliest surviving examples date from almost 150 years later. It was an ideal domestic instrument: portable, quiet, and capable of being played by a single individual, without the aid of a bellows operator. The clavichord also offered the

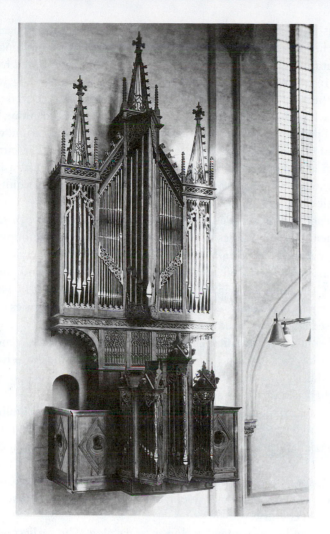

**The Renaissance organ.** Like almost all surviving Renaissance organs, this instrument is the product of many additions and alterations over an extended period of time. The original instrument, by Peter Gerritz, was built in 1479–1480 for the Nicolaïkerk in Utrecht (now in the Netherlands). The back positive, which obscures the bench where the player sits, was added in 1590, the pedals around 1600. The entire organ was later moved to the Koorkerk in Middelburg (also in the present-day Netherlands).

**Source:** Zeeuws Archief [Middelburgse Kerken] HTAM-B-1631 III

advantage of allowing the player to control the struck note from beginning to end, because the metal tangent hitting the string was directly connected to the key pressed down by the player.

The harpsichord also emerged in the late 14th century, although again, the earliest surviving instruments date from a good bit later, in the late 15th century. Early accounts refer to the instrument as a *clavicymbalum*, a key psaltery, with a mechanism that plucks the string rather than striking it. The typical Renaissance harpsichord is a single-manual (single-keyboard) instrument of four octaves with double stringing. The lower end of the keyboard often featured a "short octave" in which the last three or four keys do not actually correspond to the standard pitches with which they are associated in a higher range. Thus what on the keyboard looks like a low "E" might actually sound as "C," and the nearby keys that would normally produce F♯ and G♯ would actually sound as D and E, respectively, while the key used for F would sound its true pitch. Accidentals in this low range were seldom needed, and the short octave helped save space and cost.

Smaller varieties of the harpsichord emerged during the 15th century. The strings of the virginal run at right angles to the keys; the strings of the spinet run at an oblique angle. These smaller instruments were generally limited to a single set of strings and jacks and a single keyboard.

**Stringed Instruments.** The lute, with its pear-shaped body and backward-angled peg box, was the most common plucked stringed instrument in the Renaissance. Most early lutes featured four or five courses (single strings, or pairs tuned in octaves), but by the early 16th century, six courses had become standard. Tuning was usually by fourths, with the interval of a third between the middle courses. Related instruments—without the backward-sloping peg box—included the vihuela and guitar, both of which originated in Spain, and the cittern, bandore (pandora), and orpharion, which differed in the shape of the body and the material used for the courses. The cittern, bandore, and orpharion all used wire strings; the cittern and orpharion had a flat back. The mandora and mandolin (similar to today's instrument) were also quite popular for domestic music making.

The publisher Ottaviano Petrucci, sensing a ready market for printed music for these instruments, issued a series of publications for the lute beginning in 1507 with Francesco Spinacino's *Intabolatura de lauto, Libro primo*. The collection opens with a series of vocal works arranged for lute—including chansons and motets by such composers as Ockeghem, Josquin, and Isaac and a Mass movement by Isaac—together with an anonymous basse danse (see p. 152). It concludes with a series of 15 ricercars, freely composed works unrelated to any vocal model.

The viol and violin families emerged at roughly the same time, in the late 15th century. Viols came in many shapes and sizes. Any viol meant to be played while being held in the arm was called a *viola da braccio* ("viol of the arm"); one held upright on the lap or between the legs was called a *viola da gamba* ("viol of the leg"). Whatever their size or manner of performance, viols are distinguishable from violins by virtue of their sloped shoulders, flat backs, fretted fingerboards, and six strings tuned in fourths, except for a major third between the two middle strings. The viol emerged in Spain during the late 15th century, and the first treatises on playing it also came from Spain: Silvestro Ganassi's *Regola rubertina* (1542) and Diego Ortiz's *Trattado de glosas* (1553). The instrument enjoyed particular popularity in Elizabethan England and in France well into the 18th century.

The violin family was somewhat slower to develop. The earliest account of four matched instruments with the same tuning dates from the middle of the 16th century. By 1564, Andrea Amati had opened his workshop in Cremona and within less than one hundred years the violin family had become the standard bowed stringed instrument across the continent.

The difference in sound between viols and violins resulted from differences in their construction and the way each was played. In general, viols were softer, because they had no sound bar or sound post and were bowed underhand, reducing the overall force of the bow on the string and the difference in force between up- and down-bowing. The violin, viola, and cello, in contrast, were bowed overhand, and the structure of the instruments was such that the strings exerted greater pressure on the bridge. As a result, the violin could produce a sound of greater volume with a more penetrating attack.

**Winds and Percussion.** The earliest known recorder dates from the late 14th century. By the end of the 15th century, this family of instruments had developed into four standard varieties, each corresponding to a human voice range: soprano, alto, tenor, and bass. The sopranino recorder, pitched an octave higher than the soprano, was also available. Recorders evolved from earlier pipe instruments with the addition of a thumbhole on the upper back part of the instrument. Renaissance recorders were made in a single piece, which created problems of tuning and pitch control.

The shawm and crumhorn remained the principal double-reed instruments throughout the Renaissance. These, too, developed in a variety of ranges from high to low. Shawms, often played in groups of three, were popular for dances and processions.

Another double-reed instrument was the curtal, which in spite of its various shapes and sizes always corresponded to the range of the tenor or bass voice (see illustration "Renaissance forerunners of the bassoon"). The racket, a related instrument with a deep, reedy sound, achieved its effect through a system of tightly wound cylindrical tubing that bent back on itself up to 9 times in a space of only 11 inches or so.

Most Renaissance brass instruments, like those of the medieval era, were limited to the natural harmonics of a single note, determined by the shape of the player's lips (embouchure). The first instrument intended to negotiate notes outside the overtone series was the slide trumpet. The mouthpiece of this instrument was attached to a piece of movable tubing; the player held the mouthpiece firmly in one hand while pushing and pulling the rest of the instrument according to the desired pitch. The principle of sliding was applied with greater success on the trombone, also known as the sackbut, in which only a portion of the instrument, the slide, moved in and out.

It was during the Renaissance that the straight trumpet—a single long instrument—began to be doubled back on itself, making it less awkward to hold. Although straight trumpets continued to be used for heraldic functions, the folded form of the instrument had become fairly common by the end of the 15th century.

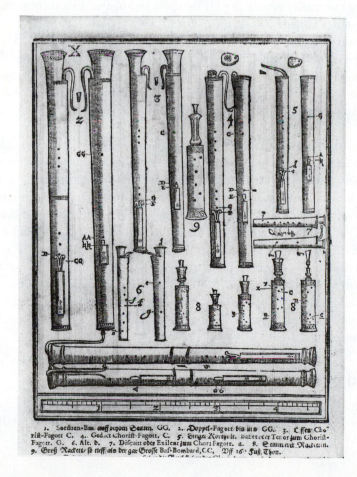

**Renaissance forerunners of the bassoon.** Our knowledge of late-16th-century instruments depends heavily on a treatise by the German composer Michael Praetorius (1571–1621). The second volume of his *Syntagma musicum* (1614) is devoted entirely to instruments and contains detailed illustrations and measurements. The image shown here includes examples of the sordun (lengthwise across the bottom), various varieties of the curtal (numbered 2–7), and rackets of different shapes and sizes (8–9). The only remaining modern descendants of these various instruments are the bassoon and double bassoon. Praetorius's treatise and others like it remind us of the remarkable variety of instruments from which Renaissance musicians could choose.

**Source:** Bodleian Library, University of Oxford/Plate 10 "musical instruments" from volume 2 of Syntagma Musicum by Michael Praetorius, 1614/Douce P 710 Plate 10

Psal. 150. Laudate Dominum in tympano & choro: laudate eum in chordis & organo.

**Dinner Music.** The ensemble here, consisting of organ, singers, trumpet, sackbut, flute, and curtal, provides music for the diners in the background to the right. This image is from Elias Nikolaus Ammerbach's *Orgel oder Instrument Tabulatur* ("Intabulations for Organ or Instruments"), published in Leipzig in 1571. The wind for the portative organ (on the right) is supplied by the young man in the center who operates the bellows by hand. A conductor (left center), holding a long stick, appears to be leading the musicians. The inscription at the top is from Psalm 150, 4: "Praise the Lord with timbrel and choir; praise him with strings and organs."

**Source:** Elias Nikolaus Ammerbach, Orgel oder Instrument Tabulatur (Leipzig, 1571)

Crooks were eventually added as well to allow the instrument to negotiate at least some of the notes outside its overtone series.

Percussion instruments of the Renaissance included a wide range of drums, cymbals of many shapes and sizes, tambourines, triangles, and even wooden xylophones. Judging from paintings and accounts of this period, these were used far more frequently than the surviving musical notation would suggest. The psaltery (hammered dulcimer) was also a favorite domestic instrument.

**Instrumental Ensembles.** The orchestra as we know it today did not exist during the Renaissance, and what little music seems to have been written specifically for ensembles rarely suggests specific combinations of instruments. A great deal of instrumental music was originally written for voices, and performers typically distributed instrumentation on the basis of range. Writers of the time distinguished between "high" (loud) and "low" (soft) instruments, but even these could be mixed as the occasion demanded (see illustration "'High' versus 'low' instruments").

Small ensembles of matched instruments, such as a set of four recorders, crumhorns, or viols, were often used in the Renaissance. With ranges corresponding to soprano, alto, tenor, and bass, these **consorts** of instruments could readily emulate the sounds of a four- or five-part vocal group, making them suited to perform vocal music instrumentally.

## Keyboard Music

Only a few manuscripts of any size containing music intended specifically for keyboard performance have come down to us from the 15th century. The most notable of these are three German sources.

- The *Ileborgh Tablature* (1448), now housed at the Curtis Institute of Music in Philadelphia, contains five preambles and three arrangements of a German song, *Frowe al my hoffen an dyr lyed* ("Lady, All My Hope Rests on Thee"), in different mensurations, suggesting it was intended as a vehicle for musical instruction. The manuscript takes its name from the organist who compiled it, Adam Ileborgh.

- *Fundamentum organisandi* (1452, "The Fundamentals of Composition") by Conrad Paumann is a pedagogical collection that has been transmitted in several different versions but consists primarily of cantus firmi embellished by passagework in a higher or lower voice. Vocal models predominate in this collection. Paumann (ca. 1410/15–1473) was a blind organist who held positions in his native Nuremberg and then later at the Bavarian court in Munich. He also traveled to Mantua and Ferrara in the 1470s.

- The *Buxheim Organ Book* (1460s), probably compiled in Munich by one of Paumann's students, is a massive collection of some 256 works, including 40 liturgical pieces, 16 preludes, basse danses (see "Dance Music," below), and keyboard arrangements of chansons by such composers as Dunstable, Du Fay, and Binchois, and arrangements of German songs.

## Dance Music

Dance music, by its very nature, was rarely committed to writing in the early Renaissance. Performers instead typically worked from memory, embellishing new lines above standard bass patterns in much the same way as jazz ensembles do today. Notated manuscripts with the melodies for one type of dance—the **basse danse**—have come down to us, but these convey little more than an outline of the improvised polyphony they supported, rather like a cheat book or fake book in modern-day popular music and jazz. The basse danse of the 15th century was a slow, stately couples' dance in compound triple meter, executed with smooth, gliding steps. Melodies were typically notated in even-note values (usually breves), with letters underneath that identify the sequence of associated dance steps. Example 5–6, a modern transcription of the 15th-century manuscript of the *Basse danse du roy d'Espaigne* ("Basse Danse of the King of Spain") illustrated here, gives some idea how these dances worked. The letters underneath each breve indicate the appropriate dance step:

r = *desmarche* (one step backward)
b = *branle* (a two-step motion, beginning with the left foot and ending with the right)
s = *pas simple* (advance the left foot; if followed by another, advance on the right foot)
d = *pas double* (three steps forward)

Each note of the basse danse melody corresponds to one complete unit of the dance step. If, as dance historians maintain, each unit of the dance took three or four seconds to perform, then the corresponding notes of the melody would have been held for a very long time indeed, making it all the easier for other instruments to perform in counterpoint against them.

**EXAMPLE 5–6** The *Basse danse du roy d'Espaigne*.

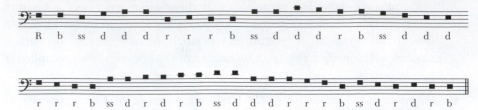

Source: *Basse danse du roy d'Espaigne* from Frederick Crane, *Materials for the Study of the Fifteenth Century Basse Danse* (Institute of Medieval Music [Dr. Luther A. Dittmer, Henryville, PA], 1968), p. 49.

**A basse danse manuscript (1471).**
This page comes from one of the most unusual musical manuscripts of the Renaissance. It was written on black paper with white ink. There are two dances on this page. The one on the bottom is entitled *La basse danse du roy d'Espaigne* ("The Basse Danse of the King of Spain"), transcribed in Example 5–6.

Source: Ms. 9.085 drom a facsimilie edition, Le manuscript dit les Basses danses de la Bibliothèque de Bourgogne, ed. Ernest Closson (Brussels: Societe des Bibliophiles at Iconophiles de Belgique, 1912; reprint edition: Geneva, Minkoff, 1976); reproduced with permission of the Royal Library of Belgium

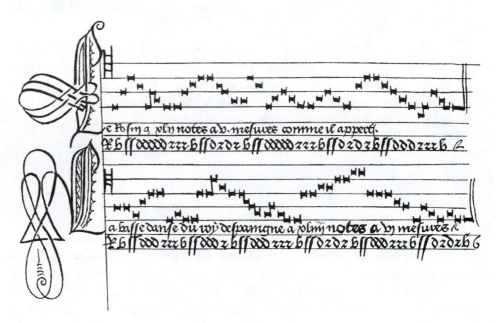

# SUMMARY

The first hundred years of the Renaissance witnessed important changes in musical style. The standard sonority moved from a layered to a homogeneous texture. Cantus firmus technique replaced isorhythm as the predominant structural principle in large-scale works in the second half of the 15th century; by the beginning of the 16th century, pervading imitation had become a standard feature in almost all genres of music.

The rise of music printing in the early 16th century, in turn, fundamentally altered the way in which music could be distributed and consumed. Compositions that once circulated either through oral transmission or through a mere handful of manuscripts (or even just a single source) could now be reproduced and distributed by the hundreds. By 1520, the music printing industry was poised to play a central role in both sacred and secular music. The rapid rise of new genres of secular song in the 1530s—the Parisian chanson in France and the madrigal in Italy—owes much to the ready availability of this repertory through print. In the realm of sacred music, printing played an equally significant role in both the Reformation and Counter-Reformation of the 16th century.

# Music in the 16th Century

The years between 1520 and 1600 witnessed remarkable changes in Europe's musical landscape. Distinct secular repertories flourished in France, Italy, Spain, Germany, and England. Sacred music became an important weapon in the ongoing struggle between Protestants and Catholics. Composers began writing specifically for instruments for the first time. And in the closing decades of the century, an artistic phenomenon known as mannerism began to make itself felt in music, leading composers to explore new extremes in the setting of texts.

Rapid advances in music printing in the early decades of the 16th century played a key role in these changes, helping expand the range of consumers for music beyond the court and those few who had the resources to copy out large quantities of music. Less rhythmically intricate genres like the frottola (Chapter 5) and Parisian chanson supplanted the more complex chanson of the late 15th century. Arrangements of vocal music for lute and keyboard began to appear in large numbers. A growing movement to write poetry in the vernacular, especially in Italy, led to the emergence of a new genre, the madrigal. The Reformation and Counter-Reformation, in turn, inspired Protestants and Roman Catholics alike to rethink the relationship between words and music within their respective liturgies.

## SECULAR VOCAL MUSIC

By the early 16th century, the rondeau, the last of the surviving *formes fixes* from the medieval era, had largely disappeared, replaced by more freely structured chansons based on the principle of pervading imitation. What emerged during the 1520s and 1530s were new approaches to setting vernacular texts: the Parisian chanson in France and the madrigal in Italy.

### The Parisian Chanson

During the 1520s, a new genre of song now known as the **Parisian chanson** emerged in the French capital. Among its most notable composers were Claudin de Sermisy (ca. 1490–1562) and Clément Janequin (ca. 1485–ca. 1560), whose works were widely disseminated by the Parisian music publisher Pierre Attaingnant. Reflecting the influence of the Italian frottola, the Parisian chanson is lighter and more chordally oriented than earlier chansons. Like the frottola, it is generally homorhythmic and dominated by vertical sonorities that we would now think of as tonic, subdominant, and dominant chords. Although the works are notated polyphonically, their melodies, in the manner of songs for solo voice with lute accompaniment, are generally confined to the upper-most line.

((•─ Listen

CD3   Track 6
mysearchlab (with scrolling translation)
SERMISY
*Tant que vivray*
Score Anthology I/47

Sermisy's *Tant que vivray* ("As Long As I Live") is a typical Parisian chanson. First published in 1528, it provided fodder for dozens of subsequent arrangements and reworkings (some with new texts) and was still being printed in anthologies more than one hundred years later. *Tant que vivray* is modest in dimension, with a lyrical melody that lies squarely in the uppermost voice. The text is conventional and unpretentious, a love song in praise first of love itself and then of the beloved. The rhythms and cadences of the music largely mirror those of the text, with one syllable per note except for a few discreet melismas toward the very ends of phrases, as in measure 10. Except for a hint of imitation on the words *Son coeur est mien. Le mien est sien* ("Her heart is mine, mine is hers") in m. 14–16, the text is declaimed in a predominantly chordal fashion.

Not all Parisian chansons were as simple as *Tant que vivray*. Janequin's *La guerre* ("The War") is a much longer work with greater independence among the voices and an extraordinary amount of onomatopoeia, in which the singers are asked to mimic the sounds of war: the sound of cannon, the clash of swords. *La guerre* is only one of several onomatopoeic songs by Janequin. The others are *Le chant des oiseaux* ("The Song of the Birds"), *La chasse* ("The Hunt"), *Les cris de Paris* ("The Cries of Paris"), and *Le caquet des femmes* ("The Women's Gossip").

## The Italian Madrigal

By the 1530s, a new genre of vocal music was emerging in Italy with the **madrigal**, a vocal composition for three or more voices, setting mostly secular texts. The 16th-century madrigal has no direct musical connection to the 14th-century genre also known as the madrigal (see Chapter 3). The term was revived in the 1530s for a new type of polyphonic song, similar in some respects to the frottola but more ambitious in tone, both textually and musically. Early madrigals (from the 1530s and 1540s) often share with the frottola a characteristically chordal texture, but with time, true contrapuntal writing became increasingly prevalent in the genre. And whereas the frottola is almost invariably strophic, with different words sung to the same music, the madrigal is **through-composed**, setting each line of text to essentially new music. This approach allowed for the kind of explicit word painting that became increasingly popular in the 16th century.

The impetus for the rise of the 16th-century madrigal was a revival of interest in the 14th-century poetry of Francesco Petrarca (Petrarch, 1304–1374). Pietro Bembo (1470–1547), a poet in his own right, championed Petrarch's work and urged his contemporaries to emulate Petrarch's combination of *piacevolezza* ("pleasingness") and *gravità* ("seriousness" or "weight") along with his attention to the rhymes, rhythms, and sonorities of the Italian language. Among the most notable to respond to Bembo's call—and to provide, together with Petrarch himself, a rich source of texts for madrigal composers—were Jacopo Sannazaro, Ludovico Ariosto, Torquato Tasso, and Giovanni Battista Guarini (see Focus: Poets of the Italian Madrigal). Madrigal texts of the 16th century follow no fixed form, but they tend to consist of a single stanza, with a free rhyme scheme. One of the more widespread poetic forms of the madrigal consists of lines that alternate between 7 and 11 syllables. Many madrigals incorporate some kind of conceit—a striking image—that reveals itself only at the very end of the poem.

Madrigals were performed in many settings, from banquets to private homes. For most of the 16th century, the style of the music is relatively undemanding, accessible to the well-trained amateur. And judging by the number of published madrigal collections that have survived, the appeal of this music was enormous.

Some 2,000 collections—most consisting of at least a dozen madrigals—were published between 1530 and 1600. This works out to about 30 publications a year, or roughly 1 every 12 days. A single composer, Philippe de Monte (1521–1603), published 34 books of madrigals between 1554 and 1603, yet in spite of their consistently high quality these works are scarcely known today. The same is true for the madrigals of other outstanding composers of the Renaissance, such as Adrian Willaert (ca. 1490–1562), Cipriano de Rore (1516–1565), Orlande de Lassus (1532–1594), and Andrea Gabrieli (1532 or 1533–1585).

With its clear declamation, modest dimensions, limited use of word painting, and predominantly chordal texture, Jacob Arcadelt's *Il bianco e dolce cigno* ("The White and Gentle Swan," first published in 1539) exemplifies the early madrigal. The text plays on two poetic conceits. One is the legend that swans, otherwise mute, sing just before they die. The other is a pun on the word *death*, used in one sense literally and in another as a euphemism (popular among Renaissance poets) for sexual climax. The poem's narrator contrasts the literal death of the swan, which sings yet is disconsolate, with his own desire for a euphemistic death "a thousand times a day." "Death," he explains, "fills me wholly with joy and desire."

Arcadelt's setting of this poem is at once tasteful and graphic. His music is more rhythmically supple than that of the typical frottola and he attends to the projection of individual words—the unexpected inflection on *piagendo* ("weeping") in m. 6–7, for example—without diverting the flow of the music as a whole. Toward the very end, however, on the words *di mille mort' il dì* ("a thousand deaths a day"), he introduces a suggestively rapid-fire imitative counterpoint that resolves chordally on the words *sarei contento* ("would make me happy").

Cipriano de Rore's *Da le belle contrade d'oriente* ("From the Fair Regions of the East"), first published in 1566, exemplifies the stylistic changes that distinguish the midcentury madrigal from earlier manifestations of the genre. The part writing is more imitative and less chordal, and with five voices, the texture is fuller. By the 1560s, five voices had become the norm for madrigals, although works for four and even three voices continued to appear through the end of the century.

((•• [Listen
**CD3 Track 7**
**mysearchlab** (with scrolling translation)
ARCADELT
*Il bianco e dolce cigno*
Score Anthology I/48

((•• [Listen
**CD3 Track 8**
**mysearchlab** (with scrolling translation)
RORE
*Da le belle contrade d'oriente*
Score Anthology I/49

---

## *Focus*    POETS OF THE ITALIAN MADRIGAL

Poet, scholar, statesman, and later cardinal, the nobleman **PIETRO BEMBO** (1470–1547) played a key role in reviving interest in the poetry of **FRANCESCO PETRARCA** (1304–1374). Many 16th-century composers in fact drew directly from Petrarch himself, setting to music words that had been written almost two hundred years before.

**JACOPO SANNAZARO** (1457–1530) was the author of *L'Arcadia* (1504), which helped establish the modern genre of the pastoral romance. Works in this genre are populated by shepherds and shepherdesses who display a simple nobility despite their rustic lives.

**LUDOVICO ARIOSTO'S** *Orlando furioso* (1516; final version 1532), an epic poem about the adventures of the crusaders, was a favorite source of texts for madrigal composers. Ariosto (1474–1533) served for many years at the Este court in Ferrara.

**TORQUATO TASSO** (1544–1595), who served for many years at the Este court in Ferrara, also wrote an epic poem about the crusades, *Gerusalemme liberata* ("Jerusalem Liberated," 1581), that would provide material for many madrigal composers and, after them, a long line of opera composers, including Lully, Handel, Gluck, Haydn, and Rossini.

**GIOVANNI BATTISTA GUARINI** (1538–1612), active at the Mantuan court, is best known as author of *Il pastor fido* ("The Faithful Shepherd"), a pastoral drama published in 1590 that combines tragic and romantic elements.

The text of Rore's madrigal, by an unknown poet, draws on the age-old image of two lovers parting at dawn. The young man describes himself as musing contentedly in the arms of his beloved when she cries out in anguish over his impending departure. She then embraces him even more tightly, so they become entwined like ivy and acanthus vines. Rore creates a distinctive musical profile for each line or pair of lines of this text, using melodic material with more internal contrasts than did Arcadelt. Rore also devotes more attention to individual words and phrases. He articulates the anxiety in the beloved's words *sola me lasci* ("you are leaving me alone")—and mimics their meaning—by setting them in a passage that the cantus (superius) voice sings entirely alone for a full measure (33). He conveys the meaning of the phrase *iterando gl'amplessi* ("repeating her embraces") with many repetitions (measure 62 onward). And he captures the image of acanthus entwining itself around ivy by setting the word *edra* ("ivy") to relatively slow notes and *acanto* ("acanthus") to a sinuously rapid melisma (m. 72–81).

It is easy to see why almost 40 years later Claudio Monteverdi (see Chapter 8) would point specifically to this composition (among others) in defending an aesthetic in which the "harmony obeys [the] words exactly." Monteverdi considered Rore one of the true founders of what he called "modern music" precisely because of the way he had shaped his compositions around the text at hand.

Still, it would be a mistake to conclude that earlier madrigalists—or, for that matter, chanson composers of the 15th century—were unconcerned with issues of text setting. Any composer of vocal music has to grapple with the relationship between words and music. The difference between Rore's *Da le belle contrade d'oriente* and Arcadelt's *Il bianco e dolce cigno* is one of degree. Both composers were moved to animate their respective texts through music, although in different ways.

Maddalena Casulana's *Morir non può il mio cuore* ("My Heart Cannot Die"), first published in 1566, is another representative mid-century madrigal that also happens to be among the earliest printed vocal works by a professional woman composer (see Composer Profile: Maddalena Casulana). The poetic text plays on the idea of a lover "owning" the heart of his or her beloved. But the relationship here has obviously gone sour, and the imagery is quite violent. The narrator would like to drive a stake through his (or her) own heart, because it causes so much pain, "but it cannot be dragged out from your breast where it has lain for so long." The narrator also recognizes that to commit suicide would also kill the beloved. Whether this is a good thing or not remains wonderfully ambiguous.

Casulana's music projects the despairing tone of this poem in measured but effective terms. The music is sometimes contrapuntal (as in measures 1–3), sometimes chordal (as in measures 4–5). The rising chromatic progression at the end of the text on the line *so che morreste voi* ("I know that you would die"), beginning at measure 15 and repeated at measure 21, is particularly effective. The major third of the final cadence conveys the idea of death as a means of achieving peace.

In the later decades of the 16th century, madrigal composers took word painting to still greater extremes than before. Luca Marenzio's *Solo e pensoso* ("Alone and Pensive"), published in 1599 to a text by none other than Petrarch himself, illustrates the lengths to which composers were willing to go to capture the meaning and emotion of a text. The opening measure is harmonically extraordinary, moving from the outline of a G major triad to one on E major, with a spectacularly exposed octave leap in the alto that reverses the motion of the previously steady downward skips. The piece proceeds to unfold in an even more bizarre fashion. The whole notes in the uppermost line that progress from G to G♯ in measure 1 turn out to be the beginning of a long chromatic ascent that will span a ninth (to A in measure 15) and then descend chromatically back down a fifth by measure 22.

(a)

**The cut-throat business of music publishing.**
Music publishing was a highly competitive business in the 16th century.

(a) In 1538, Antonio Gardano opened in Venice what would eventually become one of the leading music publishing houses in all of Europe. Gardano's first anthology of motets was issued under the title *Mottetti del frutto*. The title page, appropriately enough, depicts a still life of fruit.

**Source:** Dover Publications, Inc.

(b)

(b) Shortly afterward, the rival publishing firm of Buglhat, Campis, and Hucher of Ferrara issued a set of motets entitled *Moteti de la Simia* ("Motets of the Monkey"). The fruit-eating monkey on the title page of the cantus part symbolically refers to Gardano, whose shop in Venice was located in the Calle de la scimia ("Monkey Alley").

**Source:** Bayerische Staatsbibliothek Munich, Musikabtteilung, 4 Mus. pr. 194/8

(c)

(c) Another installment in Gardano's *Mottetti del frutto* series, published in 1539, features on its title page a lion and a bear (the two chief elements of what we would now call Gardano's logo) who are in the process of eating a monkey, who is himself surrounded by half-eaten pieces of fruit. It seems that Buglhat, Campis, and Hucher had preempted Gardano in the publication of some motets that it had been Gardano's intention to publish first.

**Source:** Dover Publications, Inc.

## Primary Evidence    OBLIGATIONS OF THE SINGER

*In his* Le istitutioni harmoniche *("The Foundations of Music," 1558), Gioseffo Zarlino reminds singers of their duties in performance.*

■ ■ ■

Matters for the singer to observe are these: First of all he must aim diligently to perform what the composer has written. He must not be like those who, wishing to be thought worthier and wiser than their colleagues, indulge in certain divisions (*diminutio*) that are so savage and so inappropriate that they not only annoy the hearer but are ridden with thousands of errors, such as many dissonances, consecutive unisons, octaves, fifths, and other similar progressions absolutely intolerable in composition. Then there are singers who substitute higher or lower tones for those intended by the composer, singing for instance a whole tone instead of a semitone, or vice versa, leading to countless errors as well as offense to the ear. Singers should aim to render faithfully what is written to express the composer's intent, intoning the correct steps in the right places. They should seek to adjust to the consonances and to sing in accord with the nature of the words of the composition; happy words will be sung happily and at a lively pace whereas sad texts call for the opposite. Above all, in order that the words may be understood, they should take care not to fall into the common error of changing the vowel sounds, singing *a* in place of *e*, *i* in place of *o*, or *u* in place of one of these; they should form each vowel in accord with its true pronunciation. It is truly reprehensible and shameful for certain oafs in choirs and public chapels as well as in private chambers to corrupt the words when they should be rendering them clearly, easily, and accurately. For example, if we hear singers shrieking certain songs—I cannot call it singing—with such crude tones and grotesque gestures that they appear to be apes, pronouncing the words *Aspro core, e selvaggio, e cruda voglia* ["Harsh heart and savage, and a cruel will"] so that we hear *Aspra cara, e salvaggia e croda vaglia*, ["Harsh beloved, savage and cruel Vaglia"—a town near Florence] are we not compelled to laugh? Or more truthfully who would not become enraged upon hearing such horrible, ugly counterfeits?

A singer should also not force the voice into a raucous, bestial tone. He should strive to moderate his tone and blend it with the other singers' so that no voice is heard above the others. Such pushed singing produces more noise than harmony. For harmony results only when many things are tempered so that no one exceeds the other. The singer should know too that in church and in public chapels he should sing with full voice, moderated of course as I have just said, while in private chambers he should use a subdued and sweet voice and avoid clamor. Singers in such places should use good taste, so as not to leave themselves open to rightful censure. Further, they should refrain from bodily movements and gestures that will incite the audience to laughter as some do who move—and this is also true of certain instrumentalists—as if they were dancing.

**Source:** *The Art of Counterpoint* by Gioseffo Zarlino. Copyright © 1968 Yale University Press. Reprinted by permission.

Paratactic in form like almost every other madrigal of its time, Marenzio's *Solo e pensoso* uses musical means to emphasize key points in each line of the text. The following table spells out how this works for the first part of the madrigal. The second part of the madrigal—by this time it was common for madrigals to have multiple parts—continues in this same vein.

*T'amo mia vita* ("I Love You, My Life"), by Luzzasco Luzzaschi (ca. 1545–1607), illustrates another growing trend in the madrigal toward the end of the 16th century: the increasing importance of virtuosity. The florid embellishments in each of the three voices seem for the most part unconnected to the text at hand. They cannot be considered word painting, for a similar figure serves for a wide variety of individual words. The same cadential gesture, for example, appears on *parola* ("word"), *amore* ("love"), *mia* ("mine"), *core* ("heart"), and *signore* ("lady").

((•—[Listen

**CD3    Track 11**
**mysearchlab** (with scrolling translation)
LUZZASCHI
*T'amo mia vita*
Score Anthology I/52

## Composer Profile

# Maddalena Casulana (ca. 1544–?)

Maddalena Casulana was the first professional woman composer to see her vocal music in print. Four of her madrigals (including *Morir non può il mio cuore*) appeared in an anthology of 1566 entitled *Il Desiderio* ("The Desire"), published by Girolamo Scotto of Venice. Two years later Casulana published these four madrigals and a fifth new one in her own *First Book of Madrigals for Four Voices*. The collection was successful enough to warrant a second edition in 1583, by which time she had issued two more books of madrigals, one for four voices, the other for five. Orlande de Lassus performed one of her pieces at the festivities for the marriage of Archduke Wilhelm of Bavaria in Munich in 1568. And in 1582, the music publisher Antonio Gardano dedicated to her Philippe de Monte's first book of madrigals for three voices—Gardano was trying to revive this earlier medium—and hailed Casulana as "the Muse and Siren of our age."

In an age when women had little if any access to professional training in the art of composition, Casulana's achievements are all the more remarkable. She was well aware of her pioneering role, and it is no coincidence that she dedicated her first book of madrigals to Isabella de' Medici Orsina, a patron of music who may also have been a composer in her own right. The self-deprecatory tone with which Casulana begins her letter of dedication is typical for this form—artists did not want to appear immodest when seeking the attention of potential patrons. But her subsequent outburst is anything but conventional, and it testifies to the frustration she surely felt in a profession overwhelmingly dominated by men:

I know truly, Most Illustrious and Excellent Signora, that these my first fruits, because of their weakness, cannot produce the effect that I would like, which would be not only to give you some testimony of my devotion but also to show the world (to the extent of my knowledge in the art of music) the vain error of men, who so much believe themselves to be the masters of the highest gifts of the intellect, that they think those gifts cannot be shared equally by women.[1]

The documentary evidence on Casulana's life is lamentably scant. She was composing, singing, and teaching both music and composition in Venice in the late 1560s, but we know little of her whereabouts in the 1570s or 1580s, and it is not known exactly when or where she died. She is believed to have married sometime after 1570 and moved away from Venice.

No evidence suggests Casulana ever held an official position at any church, court, or other institution. Still, her example paved the way for subsequent madrigal publications by other women, including Paola Massarenghi of Parma (1585), Vittoria Aleotti of Ferrara (1591 and 1593), and Cesarina Ricci di Tingoli (1597). By the 17th century, as the careers of Francesca Caccini, Barbara Strozzi, Isabella Leonarda, and Elisabeth Jacquet de la Guerre attest (see Chapters 8 and 10), the publication of music by women would no longer be quite so unusual.

# PRINCIPAL WORKS

Casulana's known works consist exclusively of madrigals—67 altogether—all but 1 of which were issued in her 3 published books of madrigals (1566, 1568, 1583).

| KEY DATES IN THE LIFE OF MADDALENA CASULANA | |
|---|---|
| ca. 1544 | Born in northern Italy, possibly near Siena. |
| 1560s | Sings, composes, and teaches composition in Venice. |
| 1566 | Publishes her first madrigals in an anthology of works by several composers. |
| 1568 | Publishes her first book of madrigals for four voices, followed by a second book two years later. |
| 1583 | Publishes her first book of madrigals for five voices. |
| After 1583 | Date and place of death unknown. |

Although not published until 1601, the work almost certainly dates from the 1590s if not earlier. It is part of a larger collection of "Madrigals for One, Two, or Three Sopranos" written expressly for the celebrated "Three Ladies of Ferrara," a group of extraordinarily talented singers whose performances were something of a legend throughout musical Europe (see Primary Evidence: The Three Ladies of Ferrara). Luzzaschi's published score includes a fully written-out harpsichord accompaniment that doubles the structural pitches of the vocal parts but also adds independent pitches of its own. By the end of the Renaissance, composers were exploring the possibilities of integrating voices and instruments to an unprecedented degree.

The Italian madrigal had its lighter side as well. Alongside the serious texts, polyphonic textures, and through-composed settings, composers also cultivated a number of subgenres that were decidedly less literary and less musically elaborate. These works often feature bawdy texts full of suggestive imagery and double entendres. They were frequently written in a local dialect (such as Neapolitan or Venetian) rather than Tuscan, the form of the language we now associate with Italian. The *napolitane*, for example, was written in Neapolitan dialect, the *giustiniana* in Venetian, the *gregescha* in a mixture of Venetian and Greek. Several subgenres emphasized chordal textures with little or no imitation. The works, often for only three voices, are strophic and mostly syllabic in their declamation. One common term for these subgenres as a whole was **villanella**, which originally meant a "country girl" but ultimately derives from the same root word as our "vile," suggesting something commonplace or vulgar. Other terms are *villanesca*, *villotta*, *canzonetta*, and *balletto*. Some of the most prominent madrigal composers of the 16th century, including Willaert, Lassus, and Marenzio, wrote works in these lighter subgenres. And the leading music publishers of the day were not shy about printing them, for they sold well.

## MARENZIO'S *SOLO E PENSOSO*, PART I: WORD PAINTING

| Italian Text | English Translation | Starting Measure | Textual Emphasis and Musical Effect |
|---|---|---|---|
| *Solo e pensoso i più deserti campi* | Alone and pensive through the most deserted fields | 1 | Solitude and pain, conveyed by the isolation and extraordinary chromaticism of the uppermost voice |
| *vo misurando a passi tardi e lenti,* | I go with measured steps, dragging and slow | 9 | Slow steps, conveyed by long note values |
| *e gl'occhi porto per fuggir intenti* | And my eyes intently watch in order to flee | 25 | Running, conveyed by points of temporally close imitation |
| *dove vestiggio human l'arenastampi.* | From any spot where the trace of a man the sand imprints. | 33 | A fixed spot, conveyed by relatively static melody and rhythm |
| *Altro schermo non trovo che mescampi* | No other defense do I find to escape | 44 | Escape, conveyed by the rapid imitative figure on *scampi* ("escape") |
| *dal manifesto accorger de le genti,* | From the plain knowledge of people, | 56 | Commonplace people and knowledge, conveyed by a relatively indistinctive passage, stated only once |
| *perché ne gl'atti d'allegrezza spenti* | Because in my actions, of joy devoid | 63 | The absence of joy, conveyed by a thinner texture of mostly three voices |
| *di fuor si legge com'iodentr'avampi.* | From without one may read how I blaze within. | 66 | The contrast between external calm and inward agitation, conveyed by the juxtaposition of slow and rapid rhythms |

Lassus's *Matona mia cara* ("My Dear Lady"), published in 1581, offers a witty example of this repertory. It is a *todesca*, a German soldier's song that like others of its kind pokes fun at the heavy accent of a German mercenary, who in this particular instance is serenading a young woman in broken Italian. The text is difficult to translate into English because it derives much of its humor from the way the German accent mangles the Italian, such as the tendency to pronounce a "v" at the beginning of a word as if it were an "f." The text also lampoons the more universal tendency of all speakers struggling with a foreign language to limit themselves to the infinitive form of verbs, no matter what the context. Thus the opening line, translated into a correspondingly corrupted English, might read something like "My tear leddy, I vant make song under vindow . . ." And like many songs of this lighter variety, *Matona mia cara* is full of nonsense syllables that can be heard as either meaningless or suggestive, depending on the listener's perspective ("Lancer makes good companion. Don, don, don, diri diri don. . . ."). When Lassus's lancer pleads toward the end that he "knows no Petrarch," we recognize we are dealing here with what might be called an anti-madrigal, one that intentionally adopts a lowbrow approach to its poetry. The music, too, is less intricate than what we find in the madrigals that Lassus otherwise wrote by the dozens. Yet *Matona mia cara*, and the hundreds of other works like it, are nonetheless marvelously compelling.

((•─ **Listen**

**CD3    Track 12**
**mysearchlab** (with scrolling translation)
LASSUS
*Matona mia cara*
Score Anthology I/53

## Secular Song in Germany, Spain, and England

Germany, Spain, and England all developed their own repertories of secular song over the course of the 16th century.

---

### *Primary Evidence*    THE THREE LADIES OF FERRARA

*Luzzaschi's T'amo mia vita is one of many works written by various composers for the resident* Concerto delle donne *("Ensemble of the Ladies") at the court of Ferrara, in northern Italy. The ensemble's most famous members were Laura Peverara (d. 1601), Livia d'Arco (d. 1611), and Anna Guarini (d. 1598). This group and others like it, especially in Mantua, attracted considerable attention and comment from visiting dignitaries. The account here, by the nobleman Vincenzo Giustiniani, was written sometime around 1628 and thus describes events that had occurred about 30 years before.*

■ ■ ■

The ladies of Mantua and Ferrara were highly competent, and vied with each other not only in regard to the timbre and training of their voices but also, in the design of exquisite passages delivered at opportune points, but not in excess. . . . Furthermore, they moderated or increased their voices, loud or soft, heavy or light, according to the demands of the piece they were singing; now slow, breaking off with sometimes a gentle sigh, now singing long passages legato or detached, now groups, now leaps, now with long trills, now with short, and again with sweet running passages sung softly, to which sometimes one heard an echo answer unexpectedly. They accompanied the music and the sentiment with appropriate facial expressions, glances and gestures, with no awkward movements of the mouth or hands or body which might not express the feeling of the song. They made the words clear in such a way that one could hear even the last syllable of every word, which was never interrupted or suppressed by passages and other embellishments. They used many other particular devices which will be known to persons more experienced than I. And under these favorable circumstances the above-mentioned musicians made every effort to win fame and the favor of the Princes their patrons, who were their principal support.

**Source:** *Readings in the History of Music in Performance,* trans. by Carol MacClintock (Bloomington: Indiana University Press, 1979). Reprinted by permission of Indiana Press.

**Listen**

CD3    Track 13

**mysearchlab** (with scrolling translation)
SENFL
*Zwischen Berg und tiefem Tal*
Score Anthology I/54

**Germany.** The most prominent varieties of song in 16th-century Germany were the **Lied** ("Song") and **Tenorlied** ("Tenor Song"). The Tenorlied was so called because it typically incorporated a well-known tune in the tenor or other voice, making it, in effect, a secular cantus firmus genre. Henricus Isaac put the melody for his *Innsbruck, ich muss dich lassen* ("Innsbruck, I Must Leave You") in the uppermost voice, whereas Ludwig Senfl put it in the slower moving tenor in his *Zwischen Berg und tiefem Tal* ("Between the Mountain and the Deep Valley").

Another type of German song was cultivated by members of what were called *Meistersinger* ("Master Singer") guilds. These were not professional musicians but rather tradesmen and craftsmen who formed societies and schools throughout Germany to foster the cultivation of music, poetry, and singing. (The 19th-century composer Richard Wagner made the most famous of all meistersingers, the cobbler Hans Sachs [1494–1576], the central figure in his 1868 opera *Die Meistersinger von Nürnberg*.) The guilds were governed by an elaborate system of rules and ranks and held regular competitions. Judges kept constant vigil against the violation of established norms. The songs were often written in bar form (AAB) in emulation of the medieval *Minnelieder* (see Chapter 1) and were performed by voice alone, with no accompaniment. Despite the old-fashioned nature of the genre and the rigid rules that governed the composing of the melodies, many found in this repertory are memorable. One, Sachs's *Silberweise* ("Silver Melody"), has been thought by some scholars to have provided the model for the roughly contemporary melody of Martin Luther's most famous chorale, *Ein feste Burg ist unser Gott*. More likely, however, the two works emerged from a common fund of German popular song.

**Spain.** The principal genre of Spanish song in the Renaissance was the **villancico**. The term was first used in the late 15th century to identify a poetic form equivalent to the French virelai (AbbaA). The Spanish composer Luis Milán (ca. 1500–after 1561) published 12 villancicos in his *El Maestro* (Valencia, 1536), a large collection of works for solo vihuela—a guitarlike instrument with 5 to 7 courses of gut strings tuned in the same manner as a lute—and for voice and vihuela.

**Listen**

CD3    Track 14

**mysearchlab** (with scrolling translation)
MILÁN
*Al amor quiero vencer*
Score Anthology I/55

Milán presents two different versions of *Al amor quiero vencer* ("I Want to Conquer Love"). In the first of these, notated in simple note-against-note fashion, Milán asks the singer to embellish his or her part. In the second, the vihuela line is written out in a more elaborate form, and here the composer asks the instrumentalist *not* to embellish. In either fashion, the texture of this and other villancicos in Milán's collection is similar to that of the frottola: the uppermost voice dominates while the lower voices fill out the polyphonic framework.

*El Maestro* is important not only as the first collection of printed music for the vihuela, but also as the first publication of any kind to indicate performance tempos. Milán uses markings in Italian that range from molto lento to molto allegro.

**England.** The Italian madrigal was transplanted to England first through manuscripts in the 1560s and then in a series of publications. The first of these, *Musica Transalpina* ("Music from Across the Alps"), published in 1588, was an anthology of 57 late-16th-century Italian madrigals with texts translated into English. The most notable among the composers represented were Marenzio, Palestrina, de Monte, and Alfonso Ferrabosco the elder (1543–1588), who served in Queen Elizabeth's court during the 1560s and 1570s. The English, at the time, were in the midst of an infatuation with things Italian. Shakespeare, for example, wrote a number of plays in the 1590s that are set in Italy, including *The Taming of the Shrew*, *The Two Gentlemen of Verona*, *Romeo and Juliet*, and *The Merchant of Venice*.

## Focus ITALIAN MADRIGALISTS IN THE 16TH CENTURY

Composers of Italian madrigals in the 16th century span roughly four generations. The early and middle decades of the century were dominated by northerners, mostly from the Low Countries, such as Arcadelt, Willaert, Rore, and Lassus. By the end of the century, however, an impressive group of native-born Italians—the Gabrielis, Luzzaschi, Marenzio, Monteverdi—had established leadership in the genre.

## 1520s–1530s

**JACOB ARCADELT** (ca. 1505–1568) and **PHILIPPE VERDELOT** (?–ca. 1552), both from the Low Countries, were among the earliest composers to cultivate the Italian madrigal. Arcadelt spent most of his career in Rome and in France; Verdelot worked primarily in Venice and Florence. **COSTANZO FESTA** (ca. 1480–1545), the most important native Italian of the first generation of madrigalists, was a member of the Papal Chapel in Rome.

## 1540s–1550s

**ADRIAN WILLAERT** (ca. 1490–1562), born in what is now Belgium, studied with Jean Mouton in Paris and then moved to Ferrara, where he served at the court of the Este dynasty. He was appointed maestro di cappella at San Marco in Venice in 1527, and he held this prestigious post for the rest of his career. His pupils include Gioseffo Zarlino, Cipriano de Rore, and Andrea Gabrieli. **CIPRIANO DE RORE** (1516–1565), also born in the region of present-day Belgium, succeeded Willaert at San Marco in Venice in 1562. He published eight books of madrigals in his lifetime.

## 1560s–1570s

**PHILIPPE DE MONTE** (1521–1603), born in the Low Countries, was the most prolific of all madrigalists, issuing some 34 books of madrigals during his career. He traveled widely early in life, holding positions in Naples, Antwerp, and London. In 1567, he was appointed maestro di cappella to Emperor Maximilian II in Vienna.

**GIOVANNI PIERLUIGI DA PALESTRINA** (1525 or 1526–1594; see the Composer Profile on page 171), although best known for his sacred music, composed more than 140 madrigals, many of which are based on spiritual texts. Two of his secular madrigals, *Io son ferito* and *Vestiva i colli*, however, were among the most popular works of their kind. **ORLANDE DE LASSUS** wrote a Mass based on the former, Palestrina himself one on the latter. Lassus (1532–1594; see the Composer Profile on page 175) published his first book of madrigals (for 5 voices) in 1555, his last in 1587. Altogether he wrote some 300 Italian madrigals, about 150 French chansons, and 150 German Lieder.

**ANDREA GABRIELI** (1532 or 1533–1585), a native of Venice, studied with Willaert at San Marco. After an extended period in Germany, he returned to Venice in 1566 and eventually became first organist at San Marco. Gabrieli published madrigals for five voices (three books), six voices (two books), three voices (one book), as well as many other madrigals in various anthologies. His nephew and pupil **GIOVANNI GABRIELI** (ca. 1553/56–1612) composed madrigals as well. **GIACHES DE WERT** (1535–1596), also from the Flemish-speaking region of what is now Belgium, was a student of Cipriano de Rore in Ferrara but spent most of his career in Mantua, where he served as maestro di cappella. He was a prolific composer, publishing 13 books of madrigals, 11 of them for 5 voices.

## 1580s–1590s

**LUZZASCO LUZZASCHI** (ca. 1545–1607), a native of Ferrara, studied with Cipriano de Rore and was himself a teacher of Girolamo Frescobaldi (see Chapter 10). Renowned as both an organist and composer, Luzzaschi published seven books of madrigals for five voices, along with many individual pieces that appeared in anthologies. **LUCA MARENZIO** (1553 or 1554–1599) worked at various times in both Rome and Ferrara. He published books of madrigals for three to six voices, including nine books of madrigals for five voices and six books for six voices. He also published five books of villanelle. **CLAUDIO MONTEVERDI** (1567–1643), although associated primarily with the music of the Baroque era (see Chapter 8), published one book of canzonette for three voices and four books of madrigals prior to 1605 that stand squarely in the Renaissance tradition.

In 1597, the English composer Thomas Morley (1557–1602) complained that the Italian fad was preventing his compatriots from appreciating the work of English composers. He expressed disgust with "the new-fangled opinions of our countrymen who will highly esteem whatsoever cometh from beyond the seas (and specially from Italy) be it never so simple, condemning that which is done at home though it be never so excellent."[2]

Morley, though, had an axe to grind—or more precisely, music to sell. He had already established himself as a composer of English madrigals and was eager to see the public taste move away from Italian music. He conveniently failed to mention that he had based a number of his own madrigals on Italian models. What's more, he adopted Anglicized versions of Italian terminology for his own lighter, dance-inspired madrigals. His early publications include *Canzonets, or Little Short Songs to Three Voyces* (1593) and a *First Book of Balletts to Five Voyces* (1595). The "ballett" *Now Is the Month of Maying* from the 1595 collection is almost entirely chordal in texture, very much in the style of Lassus's *Matona mia cara*. And perhaps a bit bawdy: the "barley break" in the last line refers to an old English game of mixed-sex tag in which the "losing" couple often wound up kissing.

Other English composers delighted in the word painting that Italian madrigalists such as Rore, Marenzio, and (later) Gesualdo made a stylistic signpost of the genre. John Farmer (ca. 1570–ca. 1605) worked as a cathedral organist in Dublin before coming to London, where he published a book of four-part madrigals in 1599. This volume

((•– **Listen**

**CD3    Track 15**
**mysearchlab**
MORLEY
*Now Is the Month of Maying*
Score Anthology I/56

**The unwritten tradition.** Certain instruments, such as the bagpipe and hurdy-gurdy, were invariably associated with the lower classes and the tradition of unwritten music, in contrast to the composed and notated music of the elite. The blind peasant accompanying himself on the hurdy-gurdy is portrayed here with powerful dignity, enhanced by the carefully lit setting and the strategic placement of his hat; one senses respect for the emotional power of this music. The scene would probably have reminded many viewers of the blind poet Homer who, according to legend, related the *Iliad* and *Odyssey* in the form of sung verse long before the words were ever written down.

**Source:** The Hurdy Gurdy Player, 1620s (oil on canvas), Tour, Georges de la (1593–1652) / Musee des Beaux-Arts, Nantes, France / Giraudon / The Bridgeman Art Libary

includes *Fair Phyllis I saw sitting all alone*, whose pastoral protagonists, the shepherdess Phyllis and her lover Amyntas, can be traced back to Virgil's *Eclogues* and who reappear in the Latin epics *Amintee Gaudia* and *Amyntas* (1585) of Thomas Watson. Farmer takes up the numerical ("sitting all alone"), geographical ("up and down"), and active ("fell a-kissing") in a playful and pithy manner that makes explicit what Morley only suggests.

Not all English madrigals are of this light, "fa la la" variety, however. Like the Italian madrigal, the English manifestation of the genre featured both a lighter and more serious side. Morley's own output includes works of a serious mood, some of which incorporate a chromaticism worthy of Lassus or Marenzio.

Another English song type, closely related to the madrigal, is the **lute song**, whose chief proponent was the composer John Dowland (1563–1626). Lute songs are strophic songs notated for lute and any combination of one or more voices. In practice, the uppermost voice is consistently the most melodic, although this should not exclude other arrangements that distribute voices and instruments among any of various combinations of parts. Dowland's setting of *Come, Heavy Sleep* plays on the perennial image of sleep as "the image of true death" both in its poetry and music. The long, languid arch of the cantus line conveys an almost palpable sense of fatigue in its measured rhythms and repeated downward progressions. It can be performed with voices on all parts or on only one part. When performed with a solo voice, the lute part picks up at least two of the three voices above it, preserving the essentially polyphonic texture of the whole.

((•• Listen

CD3    Track 16
**mysearchlab**
FARMER
*Fair Phyllis*
Score Anthology I/57

((•• Listen

CD3    Tracks 17–18
**mysearchlab**
DOWLAND
*Come, Heavy Sleep*
Score Anthology I/58

**Elizabeth I, lutenist.** England's Queen Elizabeth I put great store on her abilities as a lutenist and keyboard player but chose not to play in public, or at least before men. "The same day after dinner," recalled the diplomat Sir James Melville (1535–1617) of a day at court, "my Lord of Hunsdean drew me up to a quiet gallery . . . where I might hear the Queen play upon the virginals. After I had hearkened a while, I took by the tapestry that hung before the door of the chamber, and seeing her back was toward the door, I entered within the chamber, and stood a pretty space hearing her play excellently well. But she left off immediately, so soon as she turned her about and saw me. She appeared to be surprised to see me, and came forward, seeming to strike me with her hand; alleging she used not to play before men, but when she was solitary, to shun melancholy. She asked how I came there. I answered, 'As I was walking with my Lord of Hunsdean, as we passed by the chamber-door, I heard such melody as ravished me, whereby I was drawn in ere I knew how; excusing my fault of homeliness, as being brought up in the Court of France, where such freedom was allowed.' . . . She enquired whether my Queen or she played best. In that I found myself obliged to give her the praise."

**Source:** Queen Elizabeth I playing the lute (w/ c on paper) (see also 3912), Hilliard, Nicholas (1547–1619) / Berkeley Castle, Gloucestershire, UK /The Bridgeman Art Library

# SACRED VOCAL MUSIC

Until the early 16th century, western Europe had only one church, one central liturgy, and one liturgical language. No matter how great the local variations in practice, all parishes ultimately bowed to the authority of Rome and followed its Latin liturgy. The Reformation brought an abrupt end to this unity and created demands for a new kind of music. The Counter-Reformation, in turn, produced its own musical responses to the Protestant revolution.

## Music of the Reformation

In an age before newspapers and readily available printed books, it was not uncommon for individuals to post their ideas in a public place for all to see. When Martin Luther, following this practice, nailed his long list of complaints about objectionable church practices to the door of the castle church in Wittenberg, Germany, in 1517, he set in motion a religious revolution that would soon sweep across all of northern Europe.

From the very beginning, Luther recognized the power of music to spread the Protestant faith. He was himself a skilled lutenist, flutist, singer, and composer, and he deeply admired the works of Josquin des Prez. Luther never objected to polyphonic music or even works with Latin texts. Indeed, the new Protestant liturgy, although it increasingly emphasized worship in the vernacular, was closely patterned after the traditional Roman liturgy. Protestant composers still had cause to write motets that could serve as Introits, Graduals, and the like, and they could still set the Ordinary of the Mass, although no longer exclusively in Latin. Luther placed special emphasis on communal participation in worship and to that end encouraged the congregational singing of hymns—known in the German repertory as **chorales**—which in turn spawned a vast new repertory of melodies and texts.

*Focus* ENGLISH MADRIGALISTS

The English madrigal enjoyed a brief but intense flowering during the last decade of the 16th century and the first decade of the 17th—roughly the same period in which Shakespeare was writing many of his greatest works. The genre's popularity was due in part to the advocacy of English song by Queen Elizabeth I, who was herself an accomplished musician.

**THOMAS MORLEY** (1557–1602) was organist at Saint Paul's Cathedral and later a Gentleman of the Chapel Royal. He was one of the first native-born English composers to adopt the style of the Italian madrigal and author of an important treatise, *A Plaine and Easie Introduction to Practicall Musicke* (1597). He was also responsible for commissioning and publishing *The Triumphs of Oriana* (1601), an anthology of madrigals honoring Elizabeth I (identified metaphorically with the mythological shepherd queen Oriana).

**THOMAS WEELKES** (ca. 1574–1623) was organist at Chichester Cathedral. His madrigal *As Vesta Was from Latmos Hill Descending* (published in Morley's *The Triumphs of Oriana*) is an exemplar of word painting. But Weelkes stopped composing madrigals and devoted himself to sacred music at some point around 1600.

**JOHN WILBYE** (1574–1638) served as a musician to Sir Thomas Kytson most of his life. He issued two books of madrigals, each for three to six voices, one in 1598 and the other in 1609.

**JOHN DOWLAND** (1563–1626) was a self-described melancholic whose motto was *Semper Dowland, semper dolens* ("Always Dowland, always doleful")—he even pronounced the "o" in his last name in the same way as the "o" in "doleful." Many of his songs explore the theme of melancholy, and he based a set of consort variations on the melody of his *Lachrimae* ("Tears").

**EXAMPLE 6–1** (a) The Latin hymn *Veni Redemptor gentium* and (b) Luther's chorale *Nun komm, der Heiden Heiland.*

Come, redeemer of the peoples, show through the birth by the Virgin
Let every age marvel that such a birth is worthy of God.

Now come, ye savior of the heathen, child born of a virgin,
that all the world might marvel, that God should give him such a birth.

Many of the earliest chorales were derived from existing melodies, both liturgical and secular. Luther's *Nun komm, der Heiden Heiland* ("Now Come, Savior of the Heathen"), for example, adapts both the text and music of the plainchant Advent hymn *Veni, Redemptor gentium* ("Come, Savior of the People") (Example 6–1a and b). In the late 16th century, the melody of Isaac's Tenorlied, *Innsbruck, ich muss dich lassen* ("Innsbruck, I Must Leave You"), became the basis for the chorale *O Welt, Ich muss dich lassen* ("O World, I Must Leave You"). Johann Sebastian Bach would later use the same melody twice (for different texts) in his *St. Matthew Passion* of 1728. Still other chorales were newly composed to new texts, including the chorale that became the unofficial anthem of the Reformation, *Ein feste Burg ist unser Gott* ("A Mighty Fortress Is Our God"). Luther himself wrote the melody and adapted the text from Psalm 46 ("God is our refuge and our strength . . .").

Originally intended to be sung in unison by a congregation, chorale melodies soon began to be harmonized in increasingly sophisticated polyphonic settings. Johann Walter's setting of *Ein feste Burg ist unser Gott*, published in 1551, looks very much like a contemporary Tenorlied, with the principal melody in the tenor, surrounded by three other voices that move at a somewhat faster speed. The setting is well within reach of a moderately proficient choir. Walter (1496–1570) was the most prominent of the first generation of composers who wrote specifically for the Protestant liturgy.

Luther embraced this polyphonic elaboration of chorale melodies. "We marvel when we hear music in which one voice sings a simple melody, while three, four, or five other voices play and trip heartily around it and adorn the tune wonderfully with artistic musical effect, thus reminding us of a heavenly dance where all meet in a spirit of friendliness, caress, and embrace."[3] Other Protestant leaders were not so receptive to polyphony. The Calvinists, under Jean Calvin, banned instrumental music of any kind from church and limited sacred music to the unaccompanied unison singing of the

Psalms. Ulrich Zwingli (1484–1531) limited the use of music in the liturgy still further and even went so far as to order the organ of the main church in Zürich to be dismantled. Luther deplored such extremes. "I am not satisfied with him who despises music, as all fanatics do," Luther declared. "Music is . . . a gift of God, not a gift of men."[4]

In England, the Reformation was driven by the monarchy. Henry VIII (1491–1547; reigned 1509–1547) wanted to have his marriage to Catherine of Aragon annulled because she had produced no male heir, but the pope refused to accommodate him. In response, Henry declared the Church of England, with himself at its head, to be independent of Rome. Liturgical reforms were slow to follow this rupture of 1527. With the publication of the first *Book of Common Prayer* in 1549, English began to replace Latin as the language of the liturgy, but the Communion Service continued to follow the basic outline of the Mass. This permitted musicians to maintain their existing repertory by converting the texts of existing Mass settings and motets into English.

Not surprisingly, composers soon took up the challenge and opportunity to write motets in the English language. These works, which eventually came to be known as **anthems**, took two forms: full and verse. The full anthem is for chorus throughout. The verse anthem alternates choral passages with passages for solo voice and instrumental accompaniment.

The most outstanding composers of anthems during the 16th century were Christopher Tye (1500–1573), Thomas Tallis (ca. 1505–1585), and William Byrd (1542–1623). Tallis's *Verily, Verily I Say Unto You* exemplifies the earliest full anthems. The declamation is almost entirely chordal except for a few cadences (m. 11, 17–18) and a bit of word painting on the rising figure that sets the phrase "and I will raise him up" (m. 19–20). The style recalls that of the four-part settings of the Calvinist Genevan Psalter by composers such as Loys Bourgeois (ca. 1510–ca. 1559).

As the 16th century progressed, anthems became more elaborate. The composer William Byrd was a devout Catholic and as such had to be careful in his dealings with royal patrons. He wrote several settings of the Latin Mass as well as many widely admired settings of English texts that were used in Anglican services—that is, services of the Church of England. His full anthem *Sing Joyfully Unto God* features the six-voice texture so characteristic of choral music in the late 16th century. In many respects, the work resembles a sacred madrigal for chorus. It is paratactic in form and through-composed with discreet but unmistakable instances of word painting. Note the rising figure on "Sing joyfully" in measure 1, for example, the long note values and upward leaps on "Sing loud" at measure 10, and the triadic, fanfare-like figure to the words "Blow the trumpet" at measure 30.

## Music of the Counter-Reformation

After excommunicating Luther for heresy in 1521, the Roman Catholic Church began to reassess its stance toward the Protestant Reformation. The pope could not afford to alienate all of his German allies, and as a result Rome grew cautious and ambivalent in its response to changes north of the Alps in the 1520s and 1530s. By the 1540s, when it had become clear that Protestantism was firmly entrenched, Pope Paul III convened a special council to formulate a coordinated counteroffensive to the challenges of the Reformation.

The Council of Trent met in three sessions (1545–1547, 1551–1552, 1562–1563) in Trento (Trent), Italy, to formulate doctrines of faith, revise the liturgy, and generally purge the Roman Catholic Church of various practices that had accrued over many centuries—including the sale of indulgences. In the realm of music, the council eliminated a number of plainchants that had been added to the liturgy since medieval times

((•• Listen

CD3    Track 19
mysearchlab
TALLIS
*Verily, Verily I Say Unto You*
Score Anthology I/59

((•• Listen

CD3    Track 20
mysearchlab
BYRD
*Sing Joyfully Unto God*
Score Anthology I/60

## Primary Evidence    LUTHER ON MUSIC

*Like the church fathers of the 4th and 5th centuries, Luther felt compelled to justify the use of music in worship, for there were those who maintained the art was too frivolous for such a serious matter. The passage here is from Luther's preface to Georg Rhau's* Symphoniae iucundae *("Delightful Symphonies," 1538), a collection of 52 motets, one for each Sunday of the liturgical year.*

■ ■ ■

Here it must suffice to discuss the benefit of this great art [i.e., music]. But even that transcends the greatest eloquence of the most eloquent, because of the infinite variety of its forms and benefits. We can mention only one point (which experience confirms), namely, that next to the Word of God, music deserves the highest praise. She is a mistress and governess of those human emotions—to pass over the animals—which as masters govern men or more often overwhelm them. No greater commendation than this can be found—at least not by us. For whether you wish to comfort the sad, to terrify the happy, to encourage the despairing, to humble the proud, to calm the passionate, or to appease those full of hate—and who could number all these masters of the human heart, namely, the emotions, inclinations, and affections that impel men to evil or good?—what more effective means than music could you find? The Holy Ghost himself honors her as an instrument for his proper work when in his Holy Scriptures he asserts that through her his gifts were instilled in the prophets, namely, the inclination to all virtues, as can be seen in Elisha [II Kings 3:15]. On the other hand, she serves to cast out Satan, the instigator of all sins, as is shown in Saul, the king of Israel [I Samuel 16:23].

Thus it was not without reason that the fathers and prophets wanted nothing else to be associated as closely with the Word of God as music. Therefore, we have so many hymns and Psalms where message and music join to move the listener's soul, while in other living beings and [sounding] bodies music remains a language without words. After all, the gift of language combined with the gift of song was only given to man to let him know that he should praise God with both word and music, namely, by proclaiming [the Word of God] through music and by providing sweet melodies with words. For even a comparison between different men will show how rich and manifold our glorious Creator proves himself in distributing the gifts of music, how much men differ from each other in voice and manner of speaking so that one amazingly excels the other. No two men can be found with exactly the same voice and manner of speaking, although they often seem to imitate each other, the one as it were being the ape of the other.

But when [musical] learning is added to all this and artistic music which corrects, develops, and refines the natural music, then at last it is possible to taste with wonder (yet not to comprehend) God's absolute and perfect wisdom in his wondrous work of music. Here it is most remarkable that one single voice continues to sing the tenor, while at the same time many other voices play around it, exulting and adorning it in exuberant strains and, as it were, leading it forth in a divine roundelay, so that those who are the least bit moved know nothing more amazing in this world. But any who remain unaffected are unmusical indeed and deserve to hear a certain filth poet [*merdipoeta*] or the music of the pigs.

**Source:** Martin Luther, *Liturgy and Hymns*, ed. Ulrich S. Leupold (*Luther's Works*, vol. 53) (Philadelphia: Fortress Press, 1965), pp. 323–4.

(such as the Sequence on which Josquin had based the opening of his *Ave Maria . . . virgo serena*; see Chapter 4). The council further declared that the function of sacred music was to serve the text and the text should be clear and intelligible to listeners. "The whole plan of singing," according to a report issued by the council in 1562,

> should be constituted not to give empty pleasure to the ear, but in such a way that the words be clearly understood by all, and thus the hearts of the listeners be drawn to the desire of heavenly harmonies, in the contemplation of the joys of the blessed. . . . They shall also banish from church all music that contains, whether in the singing or in the organ playing, things that are lascivious or impure.[5]

## Primary Evidence PALESTRINA ON TEXT SETTING

*In 1570, the Duke of Mantua, Guglielmo Gonzaga, asked Palestrina to evaluate a motet and a madrigal that he had written. Palestrina's answer is tactful yet revealing: besides putting the motet into score (as would be the norm today), he places great weight on the intelligibility of text and gently criticizes the density of the Duke's part writing, advocating in its place a more transparent texture so the words of the text might emerge more clearly.*

■ ■ ■

Most Excellent and Esteemed Lord and Master:
After your Excellency's virtuoso had done me the courtesy of letting me hear the motet and madrigal, he ordered me on your behalf to give my opinion freely. So I say that just as your Excellency surpasses nature in each of your endeavors, so in music you surpass those who worthily serve it as a profession. In order to study it more satisfactorily I have set the motet into score, and have observed its beautiful workmanship, far removed from the common run, and the vital impulse given to its words, according to their meaning. I have indicated certain passages in which it seems to me that if one can do with less, the harmony will sound better—such as the sixth and unison, when both parts are moving with sixth and fifth ascending and at the same time certain unisons are descending; since the imitations cause the parts to move in this way, it seems to me that because of the dense interweaving of the imitations, the words are somewhat obscured to the listeners, who do not enjoy them as in ordinary music. Needless to say, your Excellency will understand these details much better than I, but I have said this in order to obey you, and thus I will always obey you when you do me the favor to give me orders, as your affectionate and most faithful servant. And as I pray our Lord to keep your Excellency, so I humbly kiss your hand.

Rome, March 3, 1570
From your Excellency's humble and devoted servant,
Giovanni Petraloysio [Pierluigi]

**Source:** "Letter of March 3, 1570," translated by Lewis Lockwood, from *Pope Marcellus Mass: Norton Critical Score* by Giovanni Pierluigi da Palestrina, edited by Lewis Lockwood. Copyright © 1975 by W. W. Norton & Company, Inc. Used by permission of W.W. Norton & Company, Inc.

The council's stance in this regard was scarcely revolutionary: composers of secular and sacred music alike had been wrestling with the challenge of textual intelligibility for centuries. Still, sacred sources from the first half of the 16th century tend on the whole to be little concerned with issues of text underlay—the exact placement of words under the notes—in part because professional singers were expected to be able to place a text to any given line of music at sight in much the same way that they were expected to apply the principles of musica ficta, and in part because audiences were already familiar with many if not most of the liturgical texts being sung. The opening phrase of *Gloria in excelsis Deo*, for example, conjured up the entire text in virtually every listener's mind. The ideal of textual intelligibility nonetheless exercised a powerful hold on the imaginations of those dealing with musical issues at the Council of Trent, and in pursuit of this ideal, some council members advocated a return to exclusively monophonic music—plainchant—in place of polyphony.

The council rejected this radical move, and legend has it that it did so because of a work by the composer Giovanni Pierluigi da Palestrina—his *Missa Papae Marcelli* ("Mass for Pope Marcellus," published in 1567). Although appealing, this story is not true. However, participants at the Council might very well have pointed to the straightforward and nonvirtuosic text setting in at least some of Palestrina's Masses in their defense of polyphony. The Credo of the *Missa Papae Marcelli*, for example, presents large amounts of text in a relatively short time in a way that allows the words to stand out clearly, particularly at the beginnings of phrases. Palestrina introduces musical variety and relieves the mostly chordal declamation of the text with discreet melismas from time to time.

**Composer Profile**

# Giovanni Pierluigi da Palestrina (1525 or 1526–1594)

From his time to ours, Palestrina's music—with its equal voices, seamless rhythmic flow, carefully controlled use of dissonance, and flawless part writing—has been hailed as quintessentially representative of Renaissance polyphonic style. This well-earned reputation was enhanced still further by the legend, not true but believed by music lovers for centuries, that his *Missa Papae Marcelli* convinced the Council of Trent not to ban polyphonic music from the Roman Catholic liturgy. Not surprisingly, given his renown, Palestrina was the first 16th-century composer to have his complete works published; the release of this collection began in 1862.

The reputation of Palestrina's music as an ideal pedagogical model was first established by Johann Joseph Fux in his *Gradus ad Parnassum* (1725; see Chapter 9) and reinforced by generations of later theorists, historians, and even composers: in 1917, the German composer Hans Pfitzner wrote an entire opera (*Palestrina*) based on the Council of Trent legend. But this image of Palestrina as conservative is one-dimensional and obscures a more complex individual whose music continues to repay careful study.

# PRINCIPAL WORKS

Palestrina wrote 104 settings of the Mass Ordinary (for from 4 to 8 voices), about 375 motets, 35 Magnificats, 68 offertories, 11 litanies, about 80 hymns, 49 sacred madrigals (for 5 voices), and more than 90 secular madrigals (for 3 to 6 voices).

**Giovanni Pierluigi da Palestrina.** The title page of Palestrina's *Missarum liber primus* ("First Book of Masses") published in Rome in 1554 shows the composer presenting his music to Pope Julius III. Palestrina's publication was the first of its kind by an Italian composer and as such marks the beginning of a gradual shift away from the predominance of northern composers and toward native-born artists in Italy in the second half of the 16th century.

**Source:** Bettmann/Corbis

| KEY DATES IN THE LIFE OF PIERLUIGI DA PALESTRINA | |
|---|---|
| ca. 1525 | Born in Palestrina, near Rome. |
| 1537 | Serves as choirboy at Santa Maria Maggiore, Rome. |
| 1544 | Becomes organist at San Agapito, in Palestrina. |
| 1551 | Appointed maestro di cappella of the Cappella Giulia in Rome. |
| 1555–1566 | Serves as maestro di cappella first at St. John Lateran, then at Santa Maria Maggiore. |
| 1571 | Returns to the Cappella Giulia as maestro di cappella. |
| 1594 | Dies in Rome on February 2. |

Palestrina's *Missa Papae Marcelli* also reflects the routine acceptance of thirds and sixths as fully consonant intervals in practice by the middle of the 16th century. Although the Spanish theorist Bartolomé Ramos de Pareja had argued in the 1480s that these intervals should be considered consonant (see Chapter 4), it was not until the second half of the 16th century that this view became widely accepted.

((•• **Listen**

**CD3 Track 21**
**mysearchlab**
PALESTRINA
*Missa Papae Marcelli*
Score Anthology I/61

Although it did not condemn polyphony, the Council of Trent discouraged using secular music as a model for sacred compositions. In so doing, it drew a distinction between sacred and secular musical sources that had not been apparent before. Du Fay and Josquin had routinely used secular music as a basis for at least some of their Masses, and even Palestrina in his earlier years composed half a dozen imitation Masses on secular madrigals or chansons. By the middle of the 16th century, however, attitudes toward this practice had begun to change. As one writer of the day put it, whenever Masses based on secular songs or even on battle pieces were performed in church, "they impel everyone to laughter, so that it appears almost as if the temple of God had become a place for the recitation of lascivious and ridiculous things."[6]

The motet assumed many of the characteristics of the madrigal in the 16th century, often interpreting and projecting its texts with great ingenuity. Lassus's six-voice motet *Cum essem parvulus* ("When I Was a Child"), published in 1579, sets Saint Paul's famous declaration from I Corinthians 13:11:

When I was a child, I spoke as a child,

I understood as a child, I thought as a child.

But when I became a man I put away childish things.

Now we see through a mirror, in riddles;

But then we shall see face to face.

## Primary Evidence THE SINGER AS ORATOR

*Renaissance writers, in imitation of classical antiquity, liked to compare musicians to orators, implicitly giving primacy to the text being sung. Here, Nicola Vicentino advocates performing from memory and with a certain flexibility in rhythm and tempo, techniques commonly recommended to orators as well.*

■ ■ ■

The tempo [*moto della misura*] should move according to the words; slower and faster, and one will consider that in the middle and end of compositions the measure may be changed by the proportion of equality, even though it may be that some have the opinion that when beating the measure *alla breve* one would not change the tempo; yet in singing, it *is* changed. And this is not a great error, for just as when the proportion of equality ceases one returns to another tempo, so for the manner just described changes of tempo are not inconvenient in any composition. The practice of the orator teaches this, for one sees how he proceeds in an oration—now he speaks loudly, now softly, and slower and faster; and this way of changing the tempo has an effect on the mind. So one sings music *alla mente* [literally "from the mind," that is, as if improvised] to imitate the accents and effects of the parts of the oration—for what effect would the orator make if he recited a fine speech without arranging his accents and pronunciation, with fast and slow movements, and speaking softly and loudly? That would not move his hearers. The same should occur in music; for if the orator moves his auditors with the aforesaid manners, how much more would music, recited in the same manner, accompanied by harmony and well united, make a greater effect.

And music sung *alla mente* will be more welcome than that sung *sopra le carte* ["from the page"]. Let them take the example of the preachers and the orators. If they recited a sermon or oration from the written page it would not have any grace, nor be well received by the audience, for the [expressive] glances together with the embellishments greatly move an audience when they are used together; and beautiful and learned compositions move even more those who are expert in the profession than those who are not practicing musicians and only natural, and deprived of artistic judgment, which can be gained only with effort. And let the bass singer take care to accord well with the octave of all the parts so the concentus of all will be perfect, for in this is contained perfect harmony.

**Source:** Nicola Vicentino, *L'antica musica* (Rome, 1555), Book 4, Chapter 42; trans Carol MacClintock, *Readings in the History of Music in Performance* (Bloomington: Indiana University Press, 1979), pp. 76–7, 78–9.

Lassus sets the opening words *Cum essem parvulus* ("When I was a child") in descending figures in the two uppermost voices, thereby reinforcing the meaning of the words through their sonority. In the late 16th century these parts would almost invariably have been sung by boys. These lines are answered by *loquebar*—"I spoke"—intoned by the four lower voices; the narrator is now a man, "speaking" in a lower voice. The last phrase of the opening statement—*ut parvulus* ("as a child")—returns to the boys' voices, a touching bit of superrealism; this pattern repeats in the next line. In line 3, the turning point comes after *Quando autem factus sum vir* ("But when I became a man"), intoned by the men alone: on *factus sum vir* ("became a man") all the voices enter for the first time; personal and musical goals have been achieved. The boys' voices with the descending figures at the reference to putting away "childish things." At the end of the *Prima pars,* when we are presented with the promise of seeing God face to face (*facie ad faciem*), the music moves from fragmented counterpoint (on *aenigmate*— "in riddles") to simple note-against-note counterpoint. The secunda pars begins with more word painting on abstract thereafter, and the music settles into a full six-voice imitative texture. One can well understand the reaction of one of the composer's contemporaries, who lauded Lassus' ability to "express the force of the affections" and to "place the object before the eyes, as if it were alive."[7]

At least some of Lassus' works make their objects come alive to such a degree that they have been described by later scholars as "mannerist." **Mannerism** is a term from art history that designates a style of painting and sculpture characterized by the use of distortion, exaggeration, and unsettling juxtaposition for dramatic effect. Mannerist

((•—**Listen**

**CD3    Track 22**
**mysearchlab** (with scrolling translation)
LASSUS
*Cum essem parvulus*
Score Anthology I/62

**Visual mannerism.** *The Virgin of the Long Neck,* by the Italian painter Parmigianino (Francesco Mazzola, 1503–1540), illustrates many elements of mannerism. The basic proportions of the central figures are wildly distorted: the Madonna's neck, hands, and fingers are all extraordinarily elongated, as is the Christ child. To confuse matters even further, the angels to the left seem perfectly proportioned while the figure of Saint Jerome in the background seems almost comically tiny in relation to his positioning. The columns supporting nothing at all add to the enigmatic quality of this curious—mannerist—image.

**Source:** Madonna with the Long Neck, 1534–40 (oil on canvas), Parmigianino (Francesco Mazzola) (1503–40)/Galleria degli Uffizi, Florence, Italy/Alinari/The Bridgeman Art Library

painters include Parmigianino (1503–1540; see illustration), Tintoretto (1518–1594), and El Greco (1541–1614). In music it applies to a small but important repertory of works (both sacred and secular) written in the second half of the 16th century and characterized by a comparable process of distortion, including extreme dissonance, unusual harmonic progressions, and exaggerated word painting.

The Prologue to Lassus's *Prophetiae sibyllarum*, composed ca. 1550–1552, is a good example of musical mannerism. The Sibylline Prophecies of the title are the work of 2nd-century authors apocryphally attributed to the legendary Sibyls, ancient Greek prophetesses. The texts, which purport to foretell the birth of Christ, were accepted as genuine by Saint Augustine and other early Christian thinkers, giving the Sibyls a status equal to that of Old Testament prophets. Michelangelo painted five of the Sibyls onto the ceiling of the Sistine Chapel in the Vatican in 1508–1512. The Prologue, whose text may have been written by Lassus himself, reads (in translation): "Polyphonic songs which you hear with a chromatic tenor/these are they, in which our twice-six sibyls once sang with fearless mouth the secrets of salvation."[8]

Lassus first focuses on the "chromatic" idea, introducing a series of jarring progressions. Within the opening 9 measures, he uses all 12 chromatic pitches and builds triads on 9 different roots. The piece is ostensibly in Mixolydian mode on G; in modern terminology, the work begins with a plagal (IV-I) cadence, C major to G major; proceeds through harmonies as remote as B major (V/vi), C♯ minor (♯iv, and E major (VI); returns to C major (IV); and travels through a circle of fifths to B♭ major (♭III) before finally cadencing on G major (I) at measure 9.

By straining against the boundaries of modality, the Prologue to *Prophetiae sibyllarum* not only renders 16th-century theory essentially inapplicable, but obscures any attempt by later tonal theorists to "make sense" of the voice leading. Even in the concluding eight measures, the music wavers between E and E♭ before finally cadencing on G.

Lassus presented the *Prophetiae sibyllarum* to his patron in a carefully prepared manuscript but never published it. These works are demanding for performers and listeners alike and were in all likelihood never intended for wide distribution. They belong to a category of music known at the time as ***musica reservata***—that is, music "reserved" for a select audience of noble-born or aristocratic listeners. These members of the cultural elite often gathered to debate the pressing philosophical, scientific, and artistic questions of their time, and in the closing decades of the sixteenth century, at least some of these groups turned their attention to the music of ancient Greece in an attempt to create music that could create the same miraculous effects (see Chapter 7).

## INSTRUMENTAL MUSIC

The tradition of performing vocal music on instruments continued unabated throughout the 16th century, but for the first time in the history of music, composers also began to write substantial quantities of specifically instrumental music. The genres of 16th-century instrumental music fall into four broad categories:

- Intabulations
- Variations
- Abstract works, freely composed and adhering to no established scheme or vocal model
- Dance music

((•– Listen

CD3    Track 23
mysearchlab (with scrolling translation)
LASSUS
*Prophetiae sibyllarum*
Score Anthology I/63

## Composer Profile

# Orlande de Lassus (1530 or 1532–1594)

One of the most cosmopolitan composers who ever lived, Lassus—also known by the Italianized form of his name, Orlando di Lasso—moved easily between north and south, holding important positions in both Italy and Bavaria. His letters are sometimes written in a mixture of different languages—Italian, French, German, and Latin—and at times full of puns and wordplay. His music ranges from the deeply serious and even mystic (the *Prophetiae sibyllarum*, for example) to the ribald (*Matona mia cara*). The kinds of honors he received in the 1570s—he was ennobled by the Holy Roman Emperor and made a Knight of the Golden Spur by the pope—were rarely conferred on musicians.

## PRINCIPAL WORKS

Lassus was one of the most prolific composers in the history of music, writing more than 2,000 works in virtually every genre of his era, both sacred and secular. Most of his approximately 70 Masses are "imitation" Masses based on polyphonic models. He also composed more than 500 motets for 2 to 12 voices, about 100 settings of the Magnificat for 4 to 10 voices, and various psalms and hymns for the church. He wrote songs in 3 languages: about 200 Italian madrigals and *villanelle*, some 150 French chansons, and about 90 German Lieder.

**Orlande de Lassus.** This copperplate engraving, made in 1593, shows the composer toward the end of his career as music director to the Duke of Bavaria in Munich. The chain around his neck holds the medallion of the Knight of the Golden Spur, an honor conferred on him by Pope Gregory XIII in 1574.

**Source:** Sadeler, Jean or Johann (1550–1600)/The Art Gallery Collection/Alamy

| KEY DATES IN THE LIFE OF ORLANDE DE LASSUS | |
|---|---|
| 1530 or 1532 | Born in Mons (now Belgium). |
| ca. 1544 | Enters the service of the Gonzagas in Mantua; holds various positions throughout Italy over the subsequent decade. |
| 1553 | Appointed maestro di cappella of St. John Lateran, Rome. |
| 1556 | Joins the court chapel of Duke Albrecht V of Bavaria in Munich. |
| 1563 | Becomes Kapellmeister to Duke Albrecht V of Bavaria and serves in this position for the remainder of his life while traveling frequently all the while. |
| 1570 | Receives a patent of nobility from Emperor Maximilian II. |
| 1574 | Made Knight of the Golden Spur by Pope Gregory XIII. |
| 1594 | Dies in Munich on June 14. |

**The Capirola Lute Book.** Many Italian nobleman of the Renaissance learned to play the lute, but Vincenzo Capirola (1474–after 1548) cultivated the instrument to an unusual degree. Sometime around 1515–1520, one of his pupils in Venice compiled a collection of his compositions that is today housed in the Newberry Library, Chicago, and known as the "Capirola Lute Book." The notation, in lute tabulature, indicates finger placements through numbers superimposed on the individual courses (strings) of the instrument; rhythms are indicated through the flagged stems above. The manuscript is full of fanciful marginal illustrations.

**Source:** Newberry Library / SuperStock

## Intabulations

Vocal and instrumental genres were in many respects interchangeable. As in the 15th century, chansons were often performed either wholly by instruments or by a combination of voices and instruments. Almost half of all the pieces published during this time for plucked stringed instruments—lute, guitar, vihuela, cittern, pandora—are **intabulations**, a term used to cover any arrangement of an existing vocal work for a plucked string instrument or keyboard. The first publication ever devoted entirely to keyboard music—*Frottole intabulate da sonare organi*, published in Rome by Andrea Antico in 1517—consists entirely of intabulations of frottole. This was a repertory that sold well. The pieces themselves were already known to a wide public, and solo arrangements reduced the forces needed to perform them to a single musician.

## Variations

Orators of the Renaissance, following the ancient models of Cicero and Quintilian, placed great value on the ability of public speakers to embellish the expression of an idea in different guises, varied in such a way as to both please and move an audience. Composers went about their task with much the same goal, shaping each restatement of a given theme in such a way as to delight and move listeners.

Antonio de Cabezón's *Diferencias sobre el canto de la Dama le demanda* ("Variations on the Song 'The Lady Demands It'") takes as its theme the popular melody known in France as *Belle, qui tient ma vie* ("Beautiful One, Who Holds My Life"). Cabezón (ca. 1510–1566) first presents the melody in the uppermost voice and then takes it through a series of five variations. Typically for keyboard music of the mid-16th century, the register remains fairly narrow throughout, the melody is never far from the surface, and the technical demands on the player are relatively modest.

## Freely Composed Works

Freely composed instrumental works adhere to no established scheme or vocal model. The most important genres of the 16th century include the ricercar, fantasia, toccata, canzona, and prelude.

In Italian, *ricercare* means "to research, to seek out," and the **ricercar** of the early 16th century is a freely composed work that "seeks out" a particular mode or thematic idea. The typical ricercar of this era is full of runs and passagework. Vincenzo Capirola's *Recercar quinto* ("Fifth Ricercar"), composed probably around 1515–1520, has all the hallmarks of improvisation: a dramatic pause after the opening strokes, the gradual accumulation of speed, and the eventual transformation of passagework into more tangible thematic ideas. The end result is a sense of generative energy, with a trajectory that moves from obscurity to focus, from generalities to specifics. The rhythms and metrical patterns are typically fluid and shift repeatedly from duple to triple; indeed, the necessity of so many meter changes in the modern transcription (including several passages in 5/4) underscores just how anachronistic our current-day conceptions of meter can be for music like this.

At least some ricercars of this era, including perhaps Capirola's *Recercar quinto*, appear introductory in function, serving to establish the mode of a subsequent work. Each of the ricercars in Marc' Antonio Cavazzoni's keyboard collection of 1523, *Recerchari motetti canzoni* ("Ricercars, Motets, Canzonas"), for example, is followed by an intabulation of a preexistent motet in the same mode.

A generation later, however, the essence of the ricercar had changed fundamentally. By the middle of the 16th century, the genre had become primarily imitative; the sense of "seeking out" was now being applied to the exploration of the contrapuntal possibilities inherent in a theme or series of themes. The ricercars in the *Intavolatura*

((•— **Listen**

**CD3    Track 25**

**mysearchlab**

CAPIROLA
*Recercar quinto*
Score Anthology I/65

**Interior of the Basilica of San Marco, Venice.** From about the 1520s onward, the directorship of music at San Marco was one of the most prestigious positions in all of Italy if not all of Europe. The position was held at various times by such prominent composers as Adrian Willaert, Cipriano de Rore, Gioseffo Zarlino, and, in the 17th century, Claudio Monteverdi, Francesco Cavalli, and Giovanni Legrenzi. Venice had strong commercial and cultural ties to the east, and the architecture of San Marco reflects the influence of the Byzantine style. Many of the composers associated with San Marco, particularly Andrea Gabrieli (1532/33–1585) and his nephew Giovanni Gabrieli (ca. 1553/56–1612), cultivated a style of performances involving antiphonal choirs (*cori spezzati*). These groups—choral, instrumental, or a mixture of the two—were in all likelihood not placed at opposite ends of the basilica's transept, as is often thought, but closer together at ground level.

**Source:** Michelle Grant/Rough Guides/DK Images

## Primary Evidence  KEYS TO LOVE

*Shakespeare's Sonnet 128 is one of many Renaissance poems that uses images of music and musical instruments to convey the idea of erotic love. Here, the references to "wood" and "jacks that leap" identify the instrument in question as a harpsichord or clavichord. The persona of the poem envies the keys for being "tickled" by the fingers of the desired.*

■ ■ ■

How oft when thou, my music, music play'st
Upon that blessed wood whose motion sounds
With thy sweet fingers when thou gently sway'st
The wiry concord that mine ear confounds,

Do I envy those jacks that nimble leap
To kiss the tender inward of thy hand,
Whilst my poor lips, which should that
   harvest reap,
At the wood's boldness by thee blushing stand.
To be so tickled they would change their state
And situation with those dancing chips,
O'er whom thy fingers walk with gentle gait,
Making dead wood more blest than living lips:
   Since saucy jacks so happy are in this,
   Give them thy fingers, me thy lips to kiss.

(•●) Listen

**CD3    Track 26**
**mysearchlab**
GABRIELI
*Ricercar del duodecimo tuono*
Score Anthology I/66

*cioè Ricercari, Canzoni, Hinni, Magnificati* (Venice, 1542) by Girolamo Cavazzoni (ca. 1525–after 1577), Marc'Antonio's son, are structurally identical to the motets of their day and are based on the principle of pervading imitation.

The *Ricercar del duodecimo tuono* by Andrea Gabrieli (1532/33–1585), published in 1589, stands squarely in the tradition of the polyphonic ricercar. The "duodecimo tuono" ("twelfth tone") of the title corresponds to the Ionian mode on C, which happens to be the equivalent of the modern-day major scale. The work can be performed by any combination of appropriate instruments with the needed ranges—strings, winds, brass. The writing here is not idiomatic to any particular instrument or for that matter to instruments at all; with an appropriately underlaid text, the parts could just as easily be sung. The practice of writing in a manner unique to a specific instrument is something that would not emerge until the 17th century, and even then only gradually.

Like the early ricercar, the **toccata** (from the Italian *toccare*, "to touch") is a sectional, freely constructed work unrelated to any preexistent material. The toccatas of Claudio Merulo (1533–1604) are typical of the genre in the second half of the 16th century. They abound in rapid passages that "touch" lightly on the keys and move freely between nonimitative and imitative sections. The **fantasia** of this era is structured according to the same principles. As its name implies, it allows for free flights of the composer's imaginative fantasy—what the English called "fancy." Thomas Morley, writing in 1597, characterized the genre in these terms:

> The most principal and chiefest kind of music which is made without a ditty [i.e., without words to be sung] is the Fantasy, that is when a musician taketh a point [i.e., theme] at his pleasure and wresteth and turneth it as he list, making either much or little of it according as shall seem best in his own conceit. In this may more art be shown than in any other music because the composer is tied to nothing, but that he may add, diminish, and alter at his pleasure. And this kind will bear any allowances whatsoever tolerable in other music except changing the air [i.e., the mode] and leaving the key, which in Fantasie may never be suffered. Other things you may use at your pleasure, bindings with discords, quick motions, slow motions, Proportions, and what you list. Likewise this kind of music is, with them who practise instruments of parts [i.e., play in an ensemble], in greatest use, but for voices it is but seldom used.[9]

## Focus  RENAISSANCE TUNING SYSTEMS

The Pythagorean system of tuning, developed in ancient Greece and based on mathematically pure fifths (3:2), served Western music well for more than one thousand years—at least in theory. In practice the system was problematic, in that a series of only four perfect fifths would produce a major third one fifth of a semitone too large. In other words, although fifths were consistently perfect, thirds were not. Moreover, the cycle of fifths did not create a closed system. Starting with a low note—say, the C two octaves below middle C—and moving up by fifths should eventually lead us, at the twelfth fifth, to the C five octaves above middle C. But this very high note sounds about a quarter of a semitone too sharp. This discrepancy is known as the "Pythagorean comma." The discrepancy was small enough to be worked around, because in practice, the predominance of the voice allowed performers to "bend" intervals enough to make them sonically satisfying as well.

With the growing importance of keyboard instruments in the Renaissance, however—particularly the organ—the problem of tuning became increasingly acute. Keyboard instruments, after all, have fixed pitches, and their tones cannot be manipulated in the same way as notes that are sung. From about 1300 onward, a number of systems were developed to moderate the discrepancies of Pythagorean tuning. The most widely used system, **mean-tone tuning**, shaved away slightly at perfect fifths in order to create thirds that were more pleasing to the ear. Mean-tone tuning was not without its own problems, however, and by the middle of the 18th century, yet another compromise—**equal temperament**—would gradually begin to supplant various compromise configurations of mean-tone tuning. (For more on tuning systems of the Renaissance and Baroque eras, see Focus: Systems of Temperament in Chapter 10.)

Morley's definition captures an important technical element that characterizes many (but by no means all) instrumental compositions of the 16th century: the technique of intense thematic manipulation, what Morley calls the "wresting" and "turning" of the musical idea.

## Dance Music

The quantity of sources that preserve dance music increased dramatically in the 16th century. The skeletal, single-line notation of the 15th-century basse danse (see Chapter 5) gave way to a notation that fills in other voices as well. Published intabulations of dance music for lute and keyboard in the early 16th century help give us a much better picture of the kinds of dance music in the later part of the Renaissance.

Tielman Susato's *Het derde musyck boexken* (1551, "The Third Little Book of Music") and Michael Praetorius's *Terpsichore* (published 1612, named after the ancient Greek muse of dancing) contain many kinds of dances popular during the second half of the 16th century and the early decades of the 17th century. Each of these dances has its own distinctive steps, meter, tempo, and musical character. These are the most common dance types:

- **pavane:** slow, courtly dance in duple meter
- **passamezzo:** similar to the pavane, but with a lighter step
- **bourrée:** lively dance in duple meter with a prominent upbeat at the beginning of each section
- **saltarello:** lively dance that often follows a slower one
- **galliarde:** like a saltarello but even more vigorous, with larger leaps by the dancers

((•• Listen
CD3    Track 27
BYRD
*Pavana, the Earle of Salisbury*
Score Anthology I/67

((•• Listen
CD4    Tracks 1–2
**mysearchlab**
PRAETORIUS
*Dances from Terpsichore*
Score Anthology I/68

- **volta:** vigorous "turning" dance (*voltare* means "to turn" in Italian), often in compound duple meter

- **branle:** "line dance," sometimes in duple meter (*branle simple*), sometimes triple (*branle gay*)

- **moresca:** "Moorish" dance, supposedly influenced by the Arabic cultures of northern Africa and Spain

- **rondo:** "round dance" performed by a large group moving in a circle at a lively tempo

Whatever their differences, all of these dances are built on the principle of **periodic phrase structure**—that is, they consist of many modular units of equal length. This structure derives from the basic function of social dance, which by its very nature consists of a prescribed pattern of steps that are repeated over and over again. The pavane, the waltz, the cha cha, the tango, the fox-trot, square dancing,

## *Primary Evidence*    MEN, WOMEN, AND DANCING

*From the Renaissance onward, dancing was an essential social skill in polite European society. Books on dance method were popular, and the dancing master was as much (or more) sought after for instruction as the music master. One of the most comprehensive and popular dance manuals of the Renaissance was Thoinot Arbeau's* Orchésographie *of 1589. In this dialogue from* Orchésographie, *Arbeau explains the social necessity of dance to his student Capriol.*

■ ■ ■

**CAPRIOL:** I much enjoyed fencing and tennis, and this placed me upon friendly terms with young men. But, without knowledge of dancing, I could not please the damsels, upon whom, it seems to me, the entire reputation of an eligible young man depends.

**ARBEAU:** You are quite right, as naturally the male and female seek one another, and nothing does more to stimulate a man to acts of courtesy, honor, and generosity than love. And if you desire to marry you must realize that a mistress is won by the good temper and grace displayed while dancing, because ladies do not like to be present at fencing or tennis, lest a splintered sword or a blow from a tennis ball cause them injury. . . . And there is more to it than this, for dancing is practiced to reveal whether lovers are in good health and sound of limb, after which they are permitted to kiss their mistresses in order that they may touch and savor one another thus to ascertain if they are shapely or emit an unpleasant odor as of bad meat. Therefore, from this

standpoint, quite apart from the many other advantages to be derived from dancing, it becomes an essential to a well-ordered society.

**Source:** *Orchesography* by Thoinot Arbeau translated by Mary Stewart Evans. Copyright © 1967 Dover Publications. Reprinted by permission.

Ru de vache droict.    Ru de vache gaulche.

Quand les deux pieds font gettez & posez à terre, l'vn deũat & l'aultre derrier, fupportans tous deux enfemblément le corps

**The Cow-Step, 1589.** Dancing was an essential social skill for any Renaissance gentleman or gentlewoman. In polite society, the dancing master was sought out for instruction even more often than the music master. The steps shown here—literally, the "Cow Step Right" and "Cow Step Left"—come from one of the most comprehensive and popular dance manuals of the 16th century, Thoinot Arbeau's *Orchésographie* of 1589. In this particular dance, Arbeau (ca. 1519–ca. 1595) urges the dancers to bring the rear foot down to the ground a moment before the one in front. "For when they both come down together," he observes, "it looks as if a sack of grain had been dumped on the ground."

**Source:** The New York Public Library Photographic Services/Art Resource, NY

**MARC'ANTONIO CAVAZZONI** (ca. 1490–ca. 1570) was active in both Venice and Rome. His *Recerchari, motetti, canzoni, Libro I* (Venice, 1523) is the first set of independently composed keyboard music ever published. His son **GIROLAMO CAVAZZONI** (ca. 1525–after 1577) wrote the first polyphonic ricercars in a collection published in Venice in 1542.

**ANTONIO DE CABEZÓN** (ca. 1510–1566) was organist at the court of the Spanish king and Holy Roman Emperor Charles V and later in the service of Prince Philip (who became Philip II of Spain). He traveled widely throughout Europe but returned to Spain for the final ten years of his life. His works were published posthumously under the editorship of his son Hernando (1541–1602), who succeeded his father as organist to Philip II. Antonio de Cabezón's organ music includes *tientos* (predominantly contrapuntal works), arrangements of motets by other composers, and variation sets.

**CLAUDIO MERULO** (1533–1604) served as organist at San Marco in Venice and then moved to Mantua and later to Parma, where he became court organist. Most of his music circulated in manuscript during his lifetime and was published only after his death. He is particularly renowned for his toccatas and ricercars.

**JAN PIETERSZOON SWEELINCK** (1562–1621) was born in Amsterdam and remained there as organist of the Oude Kerk (the "Old Church") for most of his life. He nevertheless exerted a tremendous influence throughout Europe both as a composer and teacher. Sweelinck greatly expanded the use of the pedal as an independent part and was one of the first to write extended fugues on a single subject.

**WILLIAM BYRD** (1543–1623), arguably the greatest of the many keyboard composers active in England in the late 16th and early 17th centuries, was organist at Lincoln Cathedral, then later at the Chapel Royal in London. He won fame for his choral music as well as his keyboard works, which are preserved in two major manuscripts, *My Ladye Nevells Booke* and the *Fitzwilliam Virginal Book*. His music also appears in the *Parthenia* of 1613 (see illustration), the source for his *Pavana, The Earle of Salisbury*.

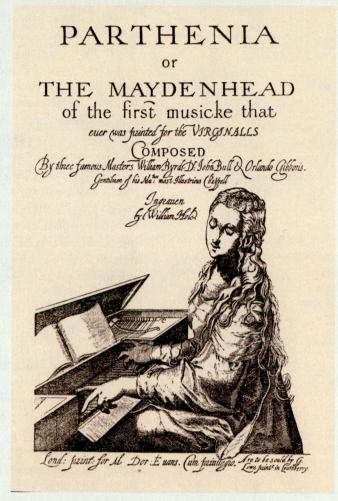

**Music for the virginal.** As its title page proudly proclaims, *Parthenia* (London, 1613) was the first keyboard music to be printed—at least in England. It contains music by three of the greatest English composers of its time: William Byrd (1543–1623), John Bull (ca. 1562–1628), and Orlando Gibbons (1583–1625). Like the contemporaneous plays of William Shakespeare (1564–1616), the title page is full of puns. "Parthenia" are the dances of Greek maidens from classical antiquity, and the demure young woman shown here exudes the modesty that befits a maiden or virgin. She is playing a virginal, a small harpsichord with a single keyboard and a single set of strings running at right angles to the keys. And the subtitle—"The Maydenhead of the First Musicke"—refers to the novelty of this publication in England. The collection was presented to Princess Elizabeth and Prince Frederick on the occasion of their marriage in 1613.

**Source:** Lebrecht Music and Arts Photo Library/Alamy

line dancing: no matter what the era or repertory, all of these dances require participants to execute a basic step—a modular unit—and repeat it many times. It is only natural that the music for this kind of dancing should rest on a correspondingly modular musical construction, with small units of equal size combining to make a larger whole.

In Byrd's minor-key *Pavana, The Earle of Salisbury*, for example, the phrasing falls very clearly into a 4 + 4 pattern that corresponds harmonically to what we would today think of as tonic moving to dominant (m. 1–4), followed by four measures that begin in the relative major before cadencing in the tonic. These smaller units of periodic phrase structure are based on a combination of melodic, harmonic, and rhythmic elements. Phrases that move from tonic to dominant (I–V) are called **antecedent** phrases (antecedent meaning "to come before"); phrases that move from the dominant back to the tonic (V–I) are called **consequent** phrases (consequent meaning "to follow as a result of something that has come before"). (In Byrd's *Pavana*, the mediant on C substitutes for the dominant on E.) In the simplest kind of periodic phrase structure, a four-measure antecedent phrase is followed by a four-measure consequent phrase; this larger eight-measure unit, in turn, can be juxtaposed with another unit of eight measures (4 + 4), as in Byrd's *Pavana*. Some pieces utilize more complex juxtapositions, as in the first Bouree of Praetorius's *Terpsichore* (2 + 4 repeated, 6 + 6 repeated).

Dance music abounds in repetition, and in performance, the individual **reprises**—the larger sections to be repeated—can be played as often as desired. Two reprises together constitute a **binary form**. Binary form represents one of the earliest instances of **syntactic form**, in which a central idea is presented and varied over the course of an entire movement, in contrast to paratactic form, in which each new section presents an essentially new idea. Binary form takes its name from the fact that it always consists of two reprises, that is, sections to be repeated ("reprised"). Binary form provides the basis for a great many dance types and would eventually be incorporated into instrumental music not written expressly for dancing. During the course of the 18th century, in fact, binary form would provide the structural basis for sonata form (see Chapter 11).

Susato promised his audiences that these dances "could be played quite delightfully and easily on all musical instruments," and his claim goes beyond mere salesmanship.

**Lassus's *Prophetiae Sibyllarum*.** The elaborate initial at the beginning (the *C* in the first word of the text, "Carmina") is typical of Renaissance manuscripts. This source, copied around 1558, illustrates the use of accidentals in music of this time. For such a chromatic work, Lassus and other composers could not—and for the most part did not—rely on performers to supply the necessary musica ficta but instead notated the accidentals explicitly. By the middle of the 16th century, the round note heads shown here were beginning to replace the old-fashioned lozenge-shaped note heads that had been standard in earlier notation, both in manuscripts and in printed scores.

**Source:** Bildarchiv der Österreichische Nationalbibliothek

The lines are so straightforward that they could in fact just as easily be sung. As with Andrea Gabrieli's ricercar, no idiom specific to a particular instrument is evident here, or even some 60 years later in the instrumental dances of Michael Praetorius.

## SUMMARY

Composers and musicians of the 16th century cultivated a rich variety of genres in both secular and sacred vocal music, most notably the chanson and madrigal (secular) and the Mass and motet (sacred). Expanding textures, increasingly intricate voicings, and an ever-growing attention to word painting characterize the music of this time. The mannerist tendencies of certain composers toward the end of the century were driven by a desire to enrich the poetic content of any given text through any musical means available, no matter how unusual or radical. As such, mannerism embodies many of the ideals that would find an ever-growing acceptance in the music of the Baroque. Instrumental music also became increasingly idiomatic over the course of the 16th century.

✓● Study and Review
on mysearchlab.com

# Part Three
# The Baroque Era

# Prelude

The Baroque era in music—the period between roughly 1600 and 1750—coincides with what is often called the Age of Absolutism, during which many of Europe's monarchs consolidated or laid claim to complete and sole authority over their dominions. Louis XIV, king of France from 1643 until his death in 1715, set the standard. He vigorously advocated the divine right of kings—the doctrine that rulers derive their authority not only through their ancestors but ultimately from God—and quashed the claims of the aristocracy to a share of power. "I am the state," he once famously declared. Along with military force, the French king used outward displays of material and cultural wealth to reinforce his hold on power. He built a magnificent new palace on the site of a royal hunting lodge in Versailles, west of Paris, and made it the site of lavish entertainments, including fireworks, tournaments, dramas, ballets, and operas.

Whatever its consequences as a political system, absolutism proved a boon to the arts. The French king patronized the greatest French composer of the 17th century, Jean-Baptiste Lully (1632–1687; see Chapter 9), as well as the equally celebrated playwrights Molière (1622–1673) and Jean Racine (1639–1699). Dozens of smaller palaces modeled after Versailles sprang up across Europe as other rulers—even those of the most modest duchies and principalities—vied with one another to follow the lead of France and cultivate a comparably brilliant cultural life at their own courts. As far away as Russia, Peter I (1672–1725; known as "The Great") transformed his nation into a European power, partly through military conquest and partly through cultural means. He established his capital in St. Petersburg in 1703 and built another palace nearby, the Peterhof, which soon became known as the "Russian Versailles." Poets, playwrights, composers, musicians, and dancers soon followed.

◀ **A view of the musical cosmos, 1650.** The frontispiece to Athanasius Kircher's *Musurgia universalis* (Rome, 1650) represents the many ways in which music was seen to manifest itself throughout the cosmos, from the heavens on high to the earth below. At the very top is the Holy Trinity, symbolized by a triangle surrounding the all-seeing eye. Angels sing a canon on the word "Sanctus" ("Holy") for 36 voices divided among 9 choruses of 4 voices each. In the center, Apollo, the Greek god of music and poetry, straddles the globe, which is ringed by the symbols of the zodiac. To the right, the winged horse Pegasus stands atop the steps leading to Mount Parnassus, home of the muses and the oracle of Delphi, sacred to Apollo. In the left foreground, Pythagoras, leaning against an engraving of his geometric theorem, points to blacksmiths pounding away at anvils. According to legend, it was by observing such activity that Pythagoras conceived the fundamental relationship between music and mathematics: the hammers created pitches whose intervals were proportional to their weight (2:1 for an octave, 3:2 for a perfect fifth, and so on). These same ratios were widely thought to govern not only the harmony of music but the harmony of the cosmos as well. In the right foreground, an allegorical figure of music, with a nightingale perched on top of her head, sits at the foot of Parnassus surrounded by several 17th-century musical instruments.

**Source:** George Olms Verlag AG

# WAR, REVOLUTION, AND COLONIAL EXPANSION

Against this backdrop of splendor, Europe was engulfed in religious strife and a series of seemingly endless wars. The last, longest, and bloodiest of these, the Thirty Years' War (1618–1648), was fought largely on German territory but involved at different times France, Spain, Sweden, Denmark, and Holland, as well as the various central European entities that together constituted the Holy Roman Empire. What began as a conflict between Catholic and Protestant realms eventually became indistinguishable from a struggle for territory among competing nation-states. The results of this war were disastrous for German-speaking lands and ushered in a long period of economic depression and political disarray. France, which emerged from the Thirty Years' War in a relatively strong position, undermined its own cause with the revocation of the Edict of Nantes in 1685. This edict, issued in 1598, had brought peace between French Catholics and Protestants after an earlier religious war. By revoking it, Louis XIV prompted some 500,000 Protestants to emigrate to Holland, Prussia, and North America, depriving France of a badly needed source of skilled labor.

England, which remained on the sidelines throughout the Thirty Years' War, was undergoing its own political and religious turmoil all the while. Absolutism never took hold to the same degree in the British Isles as it did on the Continent. As far back as the Magna Carta of 1215, the English king had been forced to share power with other members of the nobility. England's Parliament, in which the House of Lords represented the nobility and the House of Commons represented the wealthy landed gentry, had long been a counterweight to the monarchy. In the early 17th century, Parliament and crown found themselves increasingly at odds. This struggle came to a head in the English Civil War (1642–1649), which ended in the death of King Charles I (reigned 1625–1649). From 1649 to 1660, England, nominally a republic, was in effect

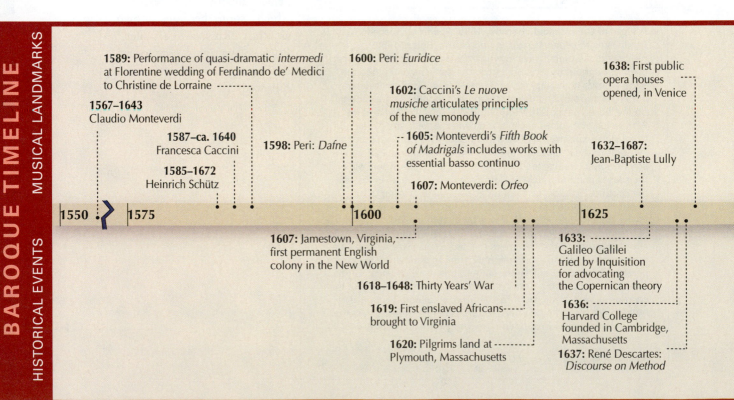

**BAROQUE TIMELINE**

**MUSICAL LANDMARKS**

**1589:** Performance of quasi-dramatic *intermedi* at Florentine wedding of Ferdinando de' Medici to Christine de Lorraine

**1600:** Peri: *Euridice*

**1638:** First public opera houses opened, in Venice

**1567–1643** Claudio Monteverdi

**1602:** Caccini's *Le nuove musiche* articulates principles of the new monody

**1587–ca. 1640** Francesca Caccini

**1598:** Peri: *Dafne*

**1605:** Monteverdi's *Fifth Book of Madrigals* includes works with essential basso continuo

**1632–1687:** Jean-Baptiste Lully

**1585–1672** Heinrich Schütz

**1607:** Monteverdi: *Orfeo*

1550 · 1575 · 1600 · 1625

**HISTORICAL EVENTS**

**1607:** Jamestown, Virginia, first permanent English colony in the New World

**1633:** Galileo Galilei tried by Inquisition for advocating the Copernican theory

**1618–1648:** Thirty Years' War

**1619:** First enslaved Africans brought to Virginia

**1636:** Harvard College founded in Cambridge, Massachusetts

**1620:** Pilgrims land at Plymouth, Massachusetts

**1637:** René Descartes: *Discourse on Method*

a military dictatorship dominated by Oliver Cromwell (1599–1658), the Lord Protector. In 1660, the monarchy was restored with the coronation of Charles II (reigned 1660–1685). The country's political stability was further enhanced with the bloodless "Glorious Revolution" of 1688–1689, which saw the ouster of the absolutist-inclined and pro-Catholic James II (reigned 1685–1688) and the enthronement of his daughter Mary and her husband William of Orange (for whom the second-oldest college in the United States, William and Mary, is named). Their reign (1689–1702) marked the formal establishment of England as a constitutional monarchy in which the power of the throne depended on the consent of Parliament.

The puritanical Cromwell had been no friend to the arts, but with the restoration of the monarchy, they began to thrive again. Under the constitutional monarchy of the 18th century, the arts developed in significantly different ways than under the absolutist regimes that dominated much of the rest of Europe. Public support emerged as an important alternative to the patronage of church and court. Theaters and opera houses flourished in London to an extent rivaled only in Hamburg and Venice, both of which, significantly, were governed by essentially republican governments. All three cities were also centers of trade and commerce with a spirit of enterprise that extended to the arts as well. The result was the emergence of forms of entertainment calculated to appeal to a paying public as opposed to a private ruler.

In their ongoing quest for wealth and territory, many European powers colonized new domains abroad. In the Western Hemisphere, England and France focused largely on North America; Spain and Portugal turned their attentions to Central and South America. All four nations, along with the newly independent (1648) and increasingly powerful Holland, made significant inroads in Africa, the Middle East, southern Asia, and the Pacific as well. Raw materials from throughout the world—gold and silver from South America, furs from French Canada, tobacco from English North America, sugar and cocoa from the Caribbean—provided new capital for what was slowly becoming a

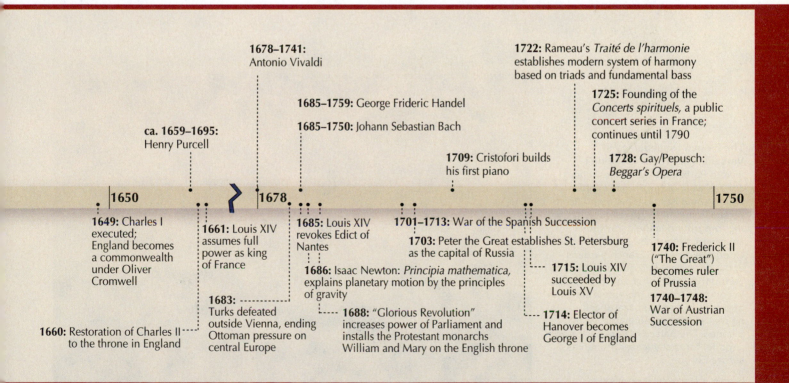

**1678–1741:** Antonio Vivaldi

**1722:** Rameau's *Traité de l'harmonie* establishes modern system of harmony based on triads and fundamental bass

**1685–1759:** George Frideric Handel

**1685–1750:** Johann Sebastian Bach

**1725:** Founding of the *Concerts spirituels,* a public concert series in France; continues until 1790

**ca. 1659–1695:** Henry Purcell

**1709:** Cristofori builds his first piano

**1728:** Gay/Pepusch: *Beggar's Opera*

| 1650 | 1678 | | 1750 |

**1649:** Charles I executed; England becomes a commonwealth under Oliver Cromwell

**1661:** Louis XIV assumes full power as king of France

**1685:** Louis XIV revokes Edict of Nantes

**1701–1713:** War of the Spanish Succession

**1703:** Peter the Great establishes St. Petersburg as the capital of Russia

**1740:** Frederick II ("The Great") becomes ruler of Prussia

**1686:** Isaac Newton: *Principia mathematica,* explains planetary motion by the principles of gravity

**1715:** Louis XIV succeeded by Louis XV

**1683:** Turks defeated outside Vienna, ending Ottoman pressure on central Europe

**1688:** "Glorious Revolution" increases power of Parliament and installs the Protestant monarchs William and Mary on the English throne

**1714:** Elector of Hanover becomes George I of England

**1740–1748:** War of Austrian Succession

**1660:** Restoration of Charles II to the throne in England

global economy. But the wealth that flowed to Europe as a consequence of this expansion came at an enormous cost. The native peoples of the Americas, displaced from their lands and exploited in gold and silver mines, declined precipitously in population. And European planters, desperate for laborers to work their plantations, began a brutal trade in human beings, enslaving millions of Africans over the course of several centuries.

# THE SCIENTIFIC REVOLUTION

The expansion of commerce during the 17th and early 18th centuries was aided by the remarkable scientific advances of the age, particularly in the realms of astronomy and navigation. The careful observations of the Danish astronomer Tycho Brahe (1546–1601) led to a far more accurate mapping of the skies than ever before. In 1609, Johannes Kepler (1571–1630), working with Brahe's data, determined that planetary orbits are elliptical rather than circular. Also in 1609, Galileo Galilei (1564–1642) turned the recently invented telescope on the heavens to make astonishing new discoveries, including the existence of mountains on the moon, the moons of Jupiter, and sunspots. These findings challenged fundamental beliefs, enshrined in religious doctrine, about the relationships among the heavenly bodies. Nicolaus Copernicus had already proposed, in 1543, that all planets orbit the sun and that the earth is not the center of the universe. It was not until the 17th century, however, that astronomers like Kepler and Galileo began to explore the wider implications of this theory. Galileo was eventually condemned by the Inquisition for advocating the Copernican view, which the church had censured in 1616.

Galileo's astronomical arguments combine empirical observation with a view that nature is subject to mathematical regularity. This combination of empiricism and mathematical analysis is characteristic of the scientific approach to knowledge and the natural world that rose to dominance in the 17th century. The English statesman, philosopher, and scientist Francis Bacon (1561–1626), for example, pointed to the induction of general principles from empirical evidence as a surer path to knowledge than

**The French royal palace at Versailles.** All roads that didn't lead to Paris led to Versailles, about 6 miles west of the French capital, where Louis XIV built his magnificent palace in the mid-17th century. In the foreground is the enormous courtyard; behind the palace are the extensive gardens. French gardens at the time were laid out in a strict geometrical fashion; English gardens, in contrast, tried to recreate a sense of wildness and haphazardness, no matter how carefully they were planned. The palace of Versailles was a model for many lesser monarchs across Europe.

**Source:** Topham/The Image Works

**Louis XIV as the Sun King**. Louis XIV styled himself *le roi soleil* ("The Sun King"), and here, dressed in gold from head to toe, he plays the part of the center of the solar system, the monarch around whom all subjects revolved. Louis XIV was an accomplished dancer in his own right, and the costume he wears here is from the intermezzo *Ballet de la Nuit* ("Ballet of the Night"), with vocal music by Jean de Cambefort (ca. 1605–1661), first performed in 1653. Louis XIV was passionate about the arts, particularly music and dance, and he commanded the financial resources to mount lavish productions of ballet and opera. Like many monarchs, he saw music and theater as a means of projecting his nation's cultural power.

**Source:** Lebrecht Music & Arts Photo Library

the reliance on received knowledge that had been characteristic of medieval philosophy. The French philosopher and mathematician René Descartes (1590–1650) advocated the rational investigation of the natural world and developed several powerful mathematical tools for doing so. Gottfried Wilhelm Leibniz (1646–1716) and Isaac Newton (1642–1727) further expanded the possibilities of mathematical analysis with their independent discovery of calculus. Leibniz also laid the foundations of symbolic logic, probability theory, and combinatorial analysis. Newton's laws of motion and his law of gravity laid the foundation of modern physics. He also made important contributions in optics and developed the first reflecting telescope.

The nation-states of 17th- and 18th-century Europe followed these advances in science with great interest and eventually began to sponsor their own national academies of science. In England, the Royal Society of London for the Improving of Natural Knowledge received its first royal charter in 1662; its *Philosophical Transactions*, which began publication in 1665, was the first scientific journal to appear on a regular basis. Louis XIV transformed the private Academy of Sciences into the Royal Academy of Sciences in 1699. In Prussia, a society founded by Leibniz in 1700 became the Royal Academy of Sciences in 1744.

## THE MUSICAL BAROQUE

The term *Baroque* derives from the Portuguese *barroco*, originally used to describe a misshapen pearl. The adjective *baroque* was at first almost always used in a negative sense to convey the idea of the distorted or grotesque. For example, the philosopher and part-time composer Jean-Jacques Rousseau, in his *Dictionary of Music* published in Paris in 1768, declared: "A baroque music is that in which the harmony is confused, charged

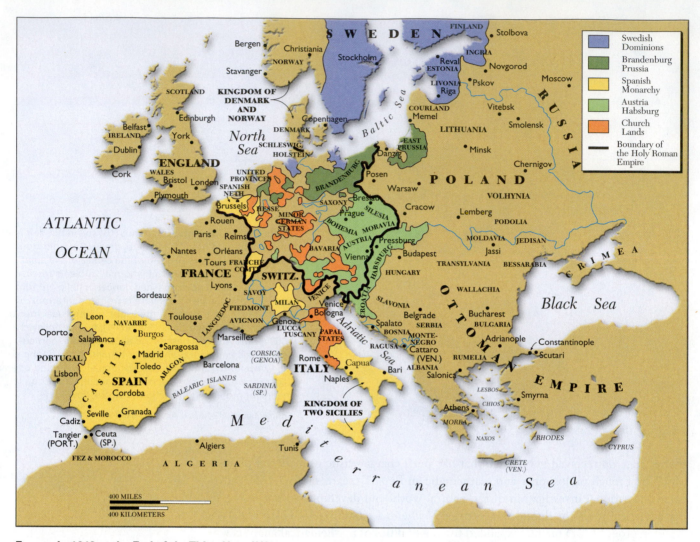

**Europe in 1648 at the End of the Thirty Years' War**

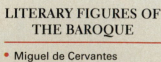

| LITERARY FIGURES OF THE BAROQUE |
| :--- |
| • Miguel de Cervantes |
| • John Donne |
| • Ben Jonson |
| • John Milton |
| • John Dryden |
| • Jonathan Swift |
| • Alexander Pope |
| • Peirre Corneille |
| • Moliere |
| • Jean Racine |

✳ Explore on **mysearchlab**

with modulations and dissonances, the melody is harsh and little natural, the intonation difficult, and the movement constrained." But Rousseau was writing in an age when "naturalness" had become the new aesthetic ideal (see Chapter 11). He was, moreover, using the term to characterize specific pieces of music rather than an entire period.

The application of the term *Baroque* to the era encompassing the 17th and early 18th centuries dates to the 19th century, when art historians used it to identify what they considered an age of decadence between the Renaissance and the Classical era. By the early 20th century, when music historians adopted it to designate the same era, the term had shed its negative connotations.

Stylistically, the music of the early Baroque era owes much to the late-Renaissance phenomenon of mannerism, in which composers set individual words of a text with exuberant and at times extreme gestures (see Chapter 6). As we will see, however, it is difficult to distill the essence of Baroque style into a single set of characteristics. The music of the era encompasses a wide range of harmonic practices and textures, as individual composers often wrote in both old and new styles according to the circumstances at hand. Still, one common trait comes through: the premise that every work or movement of music can and should convey a single predominant emotion, known at the time as its **affect** (with the accent on the first syllable). Baroque musicians and performers were committed to representing the passions through music. These passions are not to be understood as personal self-expression, but rather as a means for creating in the mind and spirit of listeners a corresponding emotional state. Like good actors, Baroque musicians tried to move their audience by the artful representation of emotion.

From a social perspective, the music of the Baroque era is as diverse as the society that nurtured it. Opera, which began and flourished under political absolutism, reinvented itself as a genre in the more public theaters that opened in Venice, Hamburg, and London over the course of the 17th century. What had originally been used to impress a small audience of elite listeners was recalibrated to appeal to a broad public. Novelty was a key element of this appeal. To be financially successful, opera houses had to present new works every season. Catholic and Protestant churches, in turn, vied to outdo one another in the opulence of their music, constantly demanding new works for their services.

This demand for the new was characteristic of the era as a whole and would persist well after 1750. Performers rarely played music by composers of a previous generation. As a result, composers who lived to a ripe age had the questionable privilege of seeing their own earlier works go out of fashion. By the time Monteverdi died in 1643, his opera *Orfeo* of 1607 was all but forgotten; by 1650, even his later operas like *Poppea* (1642) had dropped out of the repertory. Johann Sebastian Bach (1685–1750) seems not to have known a single note of music by Heinrich Schütz (1585–1672), the greatest German composer of sacred vocal music in the 17th century, even though Schütz had spent the majority of his career in the same general region of Germany in which Bach lived and worked. Most of Bach's own music, particularly his vocal music, would become scarce within 50 years of his death and would not be widely rediscovered until the 19th century.

The church and the court remained the primary musical institutions of the Baroque era. These were, after all, the institutions with the financial resources to hire the best talent of the day. And there was significant competition between church and court: when Monteverdi was lured away from his job at the court of Mantua to assume the directorship of music at the Basilica of San Marco in Venice, he received a substantial increase in salary, not to mention far better working conditions (see Composer Profile: Claudio Monteverdi, in Chapter 8).

Europe's expanding economy contributed to the increasing demand for new music. Publishers recognized a lucrative market for printed music aimed at amateurs. London, Paris, and Amsterdam emerged as the three most important centers for the music-publishing industry. In London, John Walsh established an important firm that would remain in his family from 1695 until 1766 and would publish works by Arcangelo Corelli (1653–1713), Henry Purcell (ca. 1659–1695), and above all George Frideric Handel (1685–1759). In Amsterdam, Estienne Roger was publishing Italian instrumental music of the day, including works by Giuseppe Torelli (1658–1709) and Corelli. The chief Parisian music publisher was the Ballard family firm, which held a royal monopoly until the French Revolution in 1789.

Developments in metallurgy made possible a new and more efficient music printing technology—engraving—that replaced music typesetting by the early 18th century. Unlike typeset forms, engraved plates could be stored for long periods, and publishers could pull them out of storage to run off new copies as demand warranted. Engraved music, without the broken lines characteristic of the earlier technology, was almost always superior to typeset music in quality.

Still, most music-making in the Baroque era, as in previous eras, took place within an unwritten tradition in streets and fields, coffeehouses and taverns, private homes and barracks rather than in church, court, or opera house. This repertory—songs, dance tunes, variations, and simple melodies—is difficult to reconstruct, for musicians performed it from memory or improvised it on the spot (see "The Hurdy Gurdy Player," page 164). We have no payment records for these kinds of musicians, for if they were

---

**MAJOR ARTISTS OF THE BAROQUE**

- Peter Paul Rubens
- Frans Hals
- Rembrandt
- Jan Vermeer
- Gianlorenzo Bernini
- Artemisia Gentileschi
- Diego Valasquez

✳ Explore on **mysearchlab**

paid at all, it was unlikely to be with money. As in the case of previous eras, however, we can glean some idea of this repertory through written descriptions of this music and through artists' renditions of street scenes (see A Closer Look: William Hogarth's "The Enraged Musician"). Most people learned music simply by ear, in the same way we learn a song like "The Star-Spangled Banner" or "Happy Birthday to You"—not from printed notes, but from repeated performances in which we ourselves have participated. The number of tunes transmitted in this fashion in the era before recordings was legion. Many of them were preserved in writing only when they caught the ear of a composer who incorporated them into a notated work (variations on a folk tune, for example). This repertory was, in effect, the popular music of its day.

**Popular versus elite music: Hogarth's "The Enraged Musician."** In this engraving of 1741, the English satirist William Hogarth (1697–1764) pits the written repertory against the unwritten one and raises the question of where music stops and noise begins. The angry violinist, indoors and above street level, dressed in a wig and fancy clothes, represents the written tradition of the upper classes. Note the printed music on his stand. On the wall to the far left is a poster for a revival of *The Beggar's Opera* (see Chapter 9), a work that notoriously lambastes the upper classes. The lower-class crowd below the window generates a welter of sounds that the spiked iron fence cannot keep at bay: the baby cries, the boy urinates, the astonished girl holds a rattle. The itinerant oboist (playing without notes) seems to be angling for a donation from the violinist. The woman holding the baby on the far left is singing and selling a ballad entitled "The Ladies' Fall," a commentary on her own state; anyone buying her wares will soon be adding his or her own voice to the fray. The knife sharpener, traveling up and down the street with his equipment, makes a living (and a sound) scraping, just like the violinist. The post horn, the merchants with bells, the street sweeper, the drummer boy: music (or is it noise?) is everywhere, and the professional musician cannot eliminate it.

**Source:** V&A Images/London/Art Resource, NY

# The New Practice

Many of the innovations we associate with Baroque music were driven by the continuing desire, evident already in the Renaissance, to recover the music of classical antiquity. The ancient Greeks had written repeatedly of music's miraculous powers. Their legendary hero Orpheus so charmed the gods of the underworld with song and lyre that he won the release of his beloved Euridice from death. How could it be that the effect of modern music seemed so tame in comparison?

## SEARCHING FOR THE SECRETS OF ANCIENT GREEK MUSIC

Beginning around the middle of the 16th century, composers and theorists began to seek in earnest for an answer to this question. Recovering the music of classical antiquity was no easy task, however. The few sources of ancient Greek musical notation known at the time were poorly understood and left commentators ample room for speculation.

And speculate they did. They debated endlessly about the music of the ancient Greeks: their scales, their instruments, their manner of singing, and above all their manner of combining poetry and music in drama. On this last issue, most commentators concurred that the dramas of Euripides, Aristophanes, and others had been sung, either in whole or in part, and that the words had taken priority over melody. Plato himself, after all, had described music as a form of heightened speech in which rhythm and pitch embellish a text.

Following this line of thought, a number of influential 16th-century writers and musicians began to reassess the balance between words and music. Composers increasingly embraced the ideas that (1) music should be driven by the word and (2) the **affect** of a text—its predominant emotion—should be heightened by expressive musical devices. As early as 1555, the composer and theorist Nicola Vicentino declared in his treatise *Ancient Music Adapted to Modern Practice* that "the composer's sole obligation is to animate the words, and, with harmony, to represent their passions—now harsh, now sweet, now cheerful, now sad—in accordance with their subject matter." To this end, Vicentino advocated any musical means that might help produce the desired effect. "This is why every bad leap and every poor consonance, depending on their effects, may be used to set the words. As a consequence, on such words you may write any sort of step or harmony, abandon the mode, and govern yourself by the subject matter of the . . . words."[1]

As we saw in Chapter 6, many late-16th-century composers did indeed exploit unusual effects—including "bad leaps" and "poor consonances"—to animate the texts they set. Look again, for example, at the extreme word-painting in Luca Marenzio's *Solo e pensoso* (Anthology). Yet for all the musical expressivity of this work, its polyphonic texture obscures the comprehensibility of its text as projected in performance. When multiple voices of more or less equal importance sing the same words at different times, or different words at the same time, listeners may not readily grasp the sense of the text as a whole.

To address this problem, some of the leading composers and theorists of the late 16th century advocated a transparent polyphonic style that would allow for clear projection of the text. In his highly esteemed *Le istitutioni harmoniche* ("The Foundations of Music," 1558), Gioseffo Zarlino acknowledged that contrapuntal intricacies often made the words of vocal music hard to understand. And the composer Giovanni Pierluigi da Palestrina, as we have seen, was particularly concerned not to obscure sacred texts in his motets and settings of the Mass. Yet Zarlino, Palestrina, and most of their contemporaries stopped short of advocating anything less than a fully polyphonic texture (see Primary Evidence: "Text versus Polyphony").

## *Primary Evidence*   TEXT VERSUS POLYPHONY

*Musicians and writers of all kinds have long speculated about the nature of music in classical antiquity, particularly the kinds of music used in ancient Greek drama. Even Gioseffo Zarlino, author of* Le istitutioni harmoniche *("The Foundations of Music"), the most important treatise on counterpoint in the 16th century, recognized that ancient Greek audiences had been moved by a combination of music and intelligible words—that is, words declaimed not by a multitude of voices in a polyphonic style, but rather by some method more nearly approaching solo song. Still, Zarlino remained ambivalent. In this passage from* Le istitutioni harmoniche, *he praises artistic simplicity yet continues to favor polyphony, provided the words being sung are presented intelligibly.*

■ ■ ■

Even in our times we see that music induces in us various passions in the way that it did in antiquity. For occasionally, it is observed, when some beautiful, learned, and elegant poem is recited by someone to the sound of some instrument, the listeners are greatly stirred and moved to do different things, such as to laugh [or] weep, or to similar actions. This has been experienced through the beautiful, learned, and graceful compositions of [the poet] Ariosto: when among other passages, the sad death of Zerbino and the tearful lament of his Isabella are recited, the listeners, moved with compassion, cried no less than did Ulysses hearing the excellent musician and poet Demodocus sing. Thus, if we do not hear that the music of today works on diverse subjects the effects that it did on Alexander, this may be because the causes are different, and not alike, as some assume. For, if such effects were wrought by music in

antiquity, it was recited as described above and not in the way that is used at present, with a multitude of parts and so many singers and instruments that at times nothing is heard but a jumbled din of voices and diverse instrumental sounds, singing without taste or discretion, and an unseemly pronunciation of words, so that we hear only a tumult and uproar. Music practiced in this way cannot have any effect on us worth remembering. But when music is recited with taste, staying close to the usage of the ancients, that is, to a simple style, singing to the sound of the lyre, lute, or other similar instruments texts of comic or tragic nature, or similar subjects, where there are long narrations, then the effects are observed. Those songs in which brief matters are related in a few words, as is customary today in certain canzonets called madrigals, truly are able to move the soul but little. Although these delight us greatly, they do not have the force alluded to above. That it is true that music universally pleases more when it is simple than when fashioned with much artifice and sung by many parts may be understood from this: that we listen to a solo singer accompanied by the sound of an organ, lyre, lute, or similar instrument with greater pleasure than to many. Although many singing together stir the soul, there is no doubt that songs in which the singers pronounce the words together are generally heard with greater pleasure than the learned compositions in which the words are interrupted by many voices.

**Source**: *Humanism in Italian Renaissance Musical Thought* by Claude Palisca. Copyright © 1986 Yale University Press. Reprinted by permission.

A few musicians took a more radical view, however, and maintained that polyphony itself was responsible for the failure of contemporary music to match the power of the music of the ancients. The composer and lutenist Vincenzo Galilei (ca. 1520–1591), father of the celebrated astronomer Galileo Galilei, acknowledged in his *Dialogue on Ancient and Modern Music* of 1581 that Zarlino's rules of counterpoint were "excellent and necessary for the simple delight of hearing harmonies in all their variety; but for the expression of ideas they are pestilent."[2] The problem, according to Galilei, was that the elaborate nature of polyphonic music obscured the intelligibility (and thus the force) of the words. Galilei maintained that words sung by four or five voices could not equal the power of ancient practice—a single voice supported by a lyre. He advocated a turn away from counterpoint and a move toward greater simplicity.

Like many radicals, Galilei was better at criticizing existing practices than suggesting a workable alternative. The "primitive simplicity" he called for did not include true monophony—a single line with no accompaniment—for this kind of texture was considered barbaric, at least for the chamber or the stage. (Plainchant by this time seems to have been treated as an isolated phenomenon, appropriate for liturgical use but not for "modern" music.) Equal-voiced polyphony was so deeply ingrained in 16th-century musical practice that musicians and listeners would have regarded any other texture as strange and foreign. Galilei's own surviving works consist mostly of lute intabulations of polyphonic songs.

# THE FLORENTINE CAMERATA

The real question, then, was how to allow a single voice to predominate in a texture that was not essentially polyphonic. Between roughly 1573 and 1587, a group of poets, musicians, and noblemen gathered informally at the house of Count Giovanni de' Bardi (1534–1612) in Florence to discuss this and other issues relating to the arts. This group, which later came to be known as the **Florentine Camerata** (*camerata* means "club" or "society"), debated ways to recreate the style of singing used by the ancient Greeks in their dramas. In addition to Bardi and Vincenzo Galilei, the group included the composer Giulio Caccini (1545–1618) and the poet Ottavio Rinuccini (1562–1621).

Although the members of the Camerata did not keep a record of their proceedings, we can glean some idea of the conclusions they reached from the musical and theatrical entertainments Bardi was asked to organize for the 1589 Florentine wedding of Ferdinando de' Medici, grand duke of Tuscany, to Christine de Lorraine, princess of France. The centerpiece of these entertainments was a spoken comedy entitled *La Pellegrina* ("The Pilgrim Woman"). Between the acts of this play the audience was treated to a series of six **intermedi** (what we today might call "entr'actes" or "intermezzos"), each centered on classical myths illustrating the miraculous powers of music:

- In Intermedio I, "The Harmony of the Spheres," Harmony, accompanied by Sirens, Fates, and the Planets, descends to join the mortals in their celebration of the wedding.

- In Intermedio II, "The Contest between the Muses and the Pierians," the daughters of King Pierus of Macedonia challenge the Muses to a singing contest and lose.

- In Intermedio III, "The Combat of Apollo and Python," the god Apollo slays the storied monster. The scene ends with a dance of victory.

- In Intermedio IV, "The Realm of the Demons," the spirits of the underworld lament that in the future they will have no souls to torment, for the marriage of Ferdinando and Christine portends an era of pure joy.

- In Intermedio V, "The Song of Arion," the poet Arion, about to be thrown into the sea by pirates, sings a lament so moving that Apollo summons a dolphin to rescue him and carry him to shore.

- In Intermedio VI, "The Descent of Apollo and Bacchus with Rhythm and Harmony," the gods join in a grand finale to sing the praises of the bride and groom.

((•●—Listen

**CD4    Track 3**
**mysearchlab** (with scrolling translation)
PERI
*Dunque fra torbide onde*
Score Anthology I/69

Each of the intermedi consists of four or five movements (at least one of them instrumental) and features a mixture of traditional polyphony and newer styles of composition. The poetry was by Ottavio Rinuccini, Giovambattisto Strozzi, and Bardi himself, the music by Emilio de' Cavalieri, Giacopo Peri, Giulio Caccini, and Luca Marenzio. The lavish production spared no expense on stage design, machinery, and costumes.

In the fifth intermedio, *Il Canto d'Arione* ("The Song of Arion"), the composer Jacopo Peri sang the title role himself. His aria "Dunque fra torbide onde ("Thus over Troubled Waters") recreates Arion's farewell to the world before being thrown overboard by pirates. (Attracted by his song, dolphins will carry him safely to shore.) The work is scored for four stringed instruments and three solo voice parts. Arion's line is labeled *parte principale* because it is clearly more important than the other two voices, which echo in response ("riposta") to Arion's melody and words. Except for some brief moments of overlap, however, the echoing voices do not sing simultaneously with Arion or even with each other. All three voices stand out from the instrumental accompaniment by virtue of their rhythmic freedom and melodic virtuosity. In this respect,

**Giacopo Peri as Arion.** Giacopo Peri sings the title role of his *Il Canto d'Arione* ("The Song of Arion"), the fifth intermedio of *La pellegrina,* presented at the wedding festivities of the Medici court in Florence in 1589. Peri's work includes an extended aria ("Dunque fra torbide onde") for solo baritone, two echoing voices, and accompanying strings. The singer's posture here is significant: he is shown in a relaxed, almost informal stance, emphasizing the quality of naturalness that was so dear to the proponents of the *seconda prattica*.

**Source:** Foto Marburg/Biblioteca, Nazionale, Florence, Italy/Art Resource, NY

we can see Peri moving toward a texture that is **homophonic**—consisting, that is, of a principal melodic line with subordinate accompanying voices. Homophony is particularly well suited to the clear projection of a text in the principal melodic voice. Yet the instrumental accompaniment here consists of four-part counterpoint and, on closer inspection, it turns out that the tenor, the principal singing voice, adheres in its outline to the tenor voice of the instrumental ensemble. Thus, even though the tenor's line is elaborately embellished, it functions structurally within the framework of traditional four-part polyphony.

# THE *SECONDA PRATTICA*

Peri and others continued to search for a means of more nearly matching the ancient Greek ideal of music as "naught but speech, with rhythm and tone coming after; not vice versa," to use the formulation of Giulio Caccini. The rhythms of music, according to this approach, should be modeled on the rhythms of speech—at times flowing, at times halting, full of various points of punctuation articulated through cadences of varying degrees of strength. This emphasis on the projection of the text lies at the heart of a new musical style that its advocates later called the *seconda prattica* (the "second," or later practice), to distinguish it from the *prima prattica* ("first," or earlier practice), the traditional style of Renaissance polyphony.

The *seconda prattica* emerged gradually over the course of the 1580s and 1590s as Peri, Caccini, and Cavalieri began to write works that placed a solo vocal line above an instrumental line that was conceived less as a polyphonic equal to the solo line than as a subordinate accompaniment to it. This supporting instrumental line was known as the **basso continuo**, a "continuous bass" that provided the harmonic framework for the solo voice above it. In notation, the basso continuo consists of a single bass line; in practice, the performer or performers playing it add upper voices as needed to fill out the harmonies implied by the bass. Through a series of numbers ("figures"), composers could indicate deviations from root-position harmonies—hence the term **figured bass**, often used synonymously with basso continuo.

The instrumentation of the basso continuo was flexible and rarely specified by composers: performers were expected to use whatever instruments happened to be available and suitable to the size and character of the performance venue. At a minimum, the basso continuo could consist of a single instrument capable of playing chords, such as a harpsichord, organ, or lute. Ideally it would combine a sustaining bass instrument, such as a viol or bassoon, with one or more chordal instruments, thereby providing both contrapuntal (horizontal) and chordal (vertical) support to the solo voice. The basso continuo created, in effect, a polarized texture between a melodic upper voice and a harmony-driven bass line, with the inner lines substantially reduced in prominence and volume. Performers often doubled the bass line with multiple instruments but left the inner voices to the improvisatory skills of only one member of the ensemble, such as the lutenist or keyboard player. This doubling of the bass line enhanced the sense of polarity between the lowermost and uppermost voices.

The range of stylistic possibilities opened up by the use of basso continuo was enormous. Functionally, the device provided a harmonic framework for a solo voice above it, thereby freeing composers from the obligation of writing in a consistently polyphonic manner. More important still, it allowed composers to project a sung text through a single voice, thereby bringing the music closer to what was perceived to be the ancient Greek manner of using melody and rhythm to project the words being sung and to enhance their meaning. Solo singing, in turn, allowed for the emergence

PRIMO INTERMEDIO DELLA VEGLIA DELLA LIBERATIONE DI TIRRENO FATTA NELLA SALA DELLE COM
DIE DEL SER.ᵐᵒ GRAN DVCA DI TOSCANA IL CARNOVALE DEL 1616. DOVE SI RAP.ᵗᵃ IL MONTE D'ISCHIA CON IL GIGANTE
TIFEO SOTTO.

**Dancing with the gods.** Presented between the acts of a play, intermedi often brought spectators and actors together in performance. At the end of the intermedi in Florence in 1589, audience members could dance with the gods, who descended from the stage to mingle with the mortals. The scene shown here is from the Florentine intermedi of 1617 as performed in the Uffizi theater, but the principle of actors and audience mingling remains the same. Note the stairs descending from either side of the stage into the audience.

**Source:** Scala/Gabinetto dei Disegni e delle Stampe, Uffizi, Florence, Italy/Art Resources, NY

of the new genre of **opera**—sung drama—in which individual singers could assume the role of individual characters. Opera, too, was believed to be a part of the long-sought realization of ancient Greek musical practices.

In the preface to his opera *Euridice* (1600), Peri provided a remarkable account of how he had arrived at this new manner of projecting a text:

> I judged that the ancient Greeks and Romans (who, according to the opinion of many, sang their tragedies throughout on the stage) used a harmony which, going beyond that of ordinary speech, fell so short of the melody of song that it assumed an intermediate form. I realized, similarly, that in our speech some words are intoned in such a manner that harmony can be founded upon them, and that while speaking one passes through many others which are not intoned, until one returns to another capable of movement through a new consonance. And taking note of these manners and those accents that serve us in grief, joy, and in similar states, I made the bass move in time to these, now faster, now slower, according to the emotions, and I held it firm through the dissonances and consonances until the voice of the speaker, passing through various notes, arrived at that which, being intoned in ordinary speech, opens the way to a new harmony. And I did this not only so that the flow of the speech would not offend the ear (as if stumbling in encountering the repeated notes because of the more frequent consonances) or that it might not seem in a way to dance to the movement of the bass, and chiefly in sad or serious subjects, since happier subjects require by their nature more frequent

movements, but also because the use of dissonances would either diminish or mask that advantage thereby gained because of the necessity of intoning every note, which the ancient musics perhaps could have had less need of doing. And so (even though I would not be so bold as to claim that this was the type of song used in Greek and Roman plays), I have thus believed it to be the only type that our music can give us to suit our speech.[3]

By the 1630s, a new term—**monody**—had emerged to designate this combination of solo voice and basso continuo. Monody lies partway between song and speech,

---

## Primary Evidence — GIULIO CACCINI ON THE PRINCIPLES OF MONODY

*Monody was practiced for perhaps as long as two decades before it was first notated, or published, in Giulio Caccini's* Le nuove musiche *("New Works of Music") of 1602. When Caccini finally published his collection, he realized its buyers would need some kind of guidance, some word of explanation about these novel works, and his account provides valuable details about the ways in which early monody was performed.*

■ ■ ■

At the time the most excellent *camerata* of the Most Illustrious Signor Giovanni Bardi, Count of Vernio, flourished in Florence, wherein not only a good number of the nobility met, but also the best musicians and clever men, poets, and philosophers of the city. I can truly say, since I attended as well, that I learned more from their learned discussions than I did in more than thirty years of studying counterpoint. This is because these discerning gentlemen always encouraged me and convinced me with the clearest arguments not to value that kind of music which does not allow the words to be understood well and which spoils the meaning and the poetic meter by now lengthening and now cutting the syllables short to fit the counterpoint, and thereby lacerating the poetry. And so I thought to follow that style so praised by Plato and the other philosophers who maintained music to be nothing other than rhythmic speech with pitch added (and not the reverse!), designed to enter into the minds of others and to create those wonderful effects that writers admire, which is something that cannot be achieved with the counterpoint of modern music. In solo singing, especially, with any stringed instrument, the quantity of *passaggi* sung on both long and short syllables meant that not a word could be understood; and in music of every kind, those who provided them would be exalted and praised as great singers by the mob. Seeing, as I am saying, that these kinds of music and musicians were offering no pleasure other than what harmony grants to the ear alone (since the mind cannot be moved by such music without understanding the words), it occurred to me to introduce a kind of music by which anyone could almost speak in music, using (as I have said elsewhere) a certain noble *sprezzatura* in the melody, passing sometimes over some discords while sustaining the pitch of the bass note (except when I wanted to use it in a regular way) and with the middle lines played by the instrument to express some *affetto* as those lines are not of much other use.

In madrigals as in arias I have always achieved the imitation of the ideas of the words, seeking out those notes that are more or less expressive, according to the sentiments of the words. So that they would have especial grace, I concealed as much of the art of counterpoint as I could. I have placed chords on the long syllables and passed over the short ones and also observed this same rule in making *passaggi*. For particular embellishments, however, I have sometimes used a few eighth notes (*crome*) up to the duration of a fourth of a *tactus* or up to a half [of the *tactus*] at the most, largely on short syllables. These can be allowed, because these go by quickly and are not *passaggi* but just an extra graceful touch, and also because good judgment suffers some exception to every rule. But because earlier I have stated that those long turns of the voice are badly used, I must point out that singers do not make *passaggi* because they are necessary to a good singing style, but because, I believe, they titillate the ears of those who understand less well what it means to sing *con affetto*. Because if they knew, then *passaggi* would be abhorred, since nothing is more contrary than they are to expressive singing (which is the reason I have been saying that those long runs are badly used). Therefore, I have introduced them in the kind of music that is less expressive, and used them on long, not short, syllables and in closing cadences.

**Source:** "Prefeace to Le Nuove Musiche" by Giulio Caccini, translated by Margarate Murata, from *Source Readings in Music History: Revised Edition*, edited by Oliver Struck and Leo Treitler. Copyright © 1998 by W.W. Norton & Company, Inc. Copyright renewed 1978 by Oliver Strunk. Reprinted by permission of the publishers.

with singers projecting their texts in a manner that is both lyrical and declamatory, measured and rhythmically fluid. In retrospect, it seems an obvious solution to the problem it solved: how to provide harmonic support to a melodic solo voice while at the same time allowing the singer to declaim a text clearly and with rhythmic freedom. At the time, however, it was a true innovation.

**Listen**

**CD4    Track 4**
**mysearchlab** (with scrolling translation)
GIULIO CACCINI
*Sfogava con le stelle*
Score Anthology I/70

Monody also opened up important new possibilities of performance. Soloists were now free to embellish at will, without rhythmic or motivic regard for any other melodic line. Ornamentation and pure flights of fancy unthinkable in polyphonic textures were now a very real option. All of this could help give the music an air of spontaneity in performance—what Caccini called *sprezzatura*, a certain freedom in the pace and manner of delivery, a kind of noble disregard for the meter and rhythm.

Caccini's monody *Sfogava con le stelle* from *Le nuove musiche* of 1602 illustrates the new practice vividly. The music, following the text, divides into two parts: the first (m. 1–11) is presented from the perspective of a narrator, who sets the scene of a lover venting his grief to the stars. The second (m. 12–57) presents the words of the lover himself, calling on the stars to convince his beloved to return his affections. The rhythms of the opening are slow and measured, and its pitches are confined to a limited range. But once the lover himself begins to declaim *O immagini belle/Dell'idol mio ch'adoro* ("Oh, beautiful images of the one I adore"), the music rises in pitch, velocity, and intensity. Caccini emphasizes key words either by long notes (*adoro*—"adore"— m. 15–16) or by rapid passagework (*ardori*—"passions"—m. 29–30). The vocal line throughout the second half gives the impression of spontaneity, as if the singer is thinking up the words on the spot: the pace of delivery is never predictable. The underlay follows the rhythms of a person speaking, at times slowly or even hesitantly, at other times rushing forward in a torrent.

Caccini's *Sfogava con le stelle* also illustrates another novelty of the *seconda prattica*, the degree of virtuosity it sometimes required of performers. There is, of course, a paradox in the kind of virtuosic flourishes like those on the word *ardori* ("passions," m. 29–31). This gesture certainly provides, following Plato's definition of music, a sense of heightened speech by emphasizing perhaps the single most important word in the entire text. But it also makes the word itself less readily intelligible. Adherents of the new style argued that expressive, passionate texts called for expressive, passionate music. Detractors replied that overly flamboyant music undermined the very premise of the new practice, to free vocal music from anything that might obscure the clear projection of the words.

In any event, the monodies of the early 17th century mark a clear break with earlier practices of the Renaissance. The polyphonic madrigalists of the mid-to-late 16th century had been careful to match the rhythms of words to the rhythms of their music, but they had made relatively little effort to translate the rhythms of entire sentences into music, nor had they allowed for much rhythmic flexibility in performance. The rhythmic intricacies of Renaissance polyphony tend to emerge from the interplay among the various parts; syncopation derives more often from contrasting durations in different parts than from displaced accents within a single line. Renaissance music generally gives the impression of a steady flow, no matter how strong the syncopation or rhythmic variety on a local level. A steady pulse (the *tactus*) governs performance, and although this may change over the course of a work, it usually remains steady for long stretches at a time.

Oddly enough, the *seconda prattica*'s fluid approach to rhythm coincided with the emergence of a much stronger sense of meter in the early Baroque era. Fixed units with strong and weak beats eventually replaced the Renaissance principle of the *tactus*, in

## *Performance Perspective*

# How to Read a Figured Bass

Figured bass notation allows continuo performers considerable freedom to improvise. The Arabic numerals written above the notated bass line in the original (see the illustration) indicate the intervals to be played above that line, which produces the desired harmonies:

- The absence of any numerals signifies that the bass acts as the harmonic root and the performer will supply (typically) intervals a third and fifth above the notated bass, a triad in root position.

- A "6" indicates that the performer is to play an added voice a sixth above the notated bass as well as a third above (implied) to be played. Thus a "6" above a notated "C" in a piece with no key signature would call for the performer to play an "A" and, in between, an "E," creating an A-minor chord. The number "6" thus indicates a chord in first inversion.

- A "6" over a "4" indicates that the "4" replaces the implied, normally unfigured "3." The resulting harmony over a notated bass line "C" in the same piece would be (from bottom to top) C-F-A, an F-major triad in second inversion.

Early figured bass notation differs slightly from later conventions. In the original edition of Caccini's *Le nuove musiche*, for example, the composer uses figures such as "11" and "10," adding an octave to what later practice would notate simply as "4" and "3." (Here, figures such as "7"–"6" and "11"–"10" signify resolving suspensions.) Over time, composers left issues of register, voice leading, rhythm, and melodic figurations increasingly to the performers. Indeed, we speak of a figured bass line being "realized" rather than "played," an important distinction. Even the harmony can be changed at the performer's discretion. In his *New Treatise on Accompaniment* (Paris, 1707), the Frenchman Michel de Saint-Lambert assured performers that

> [Y]ou can sometimes change the chords marked on the notes if you judge that others will suit better. On a bass note of substantial duration, one can put in two or three different chords one after the other, although the text asks for only one, provided that one senses that these chords go with the melodic part. On the other hand one can avoid sounding all the intervals marked in the text, when one finds that the notes are too heavily loaded.[4]

Fifty years later, Carl Philipp Emanuel Bach was urging performers to play "with judgment, often departing from the written text."[5]

**Giulio Caccini, *Sfogava con le stelle*.** Caccini's *Le nuove musiche* of 1602 was the first published collection of monodies. The opening measures of *Sfogava con le stelle* show the careful placement of harmonic changes in the second measure over a single bass note.

**Source:** Giulio Caccini, Le nuove musiche "Sfogava con le stelle", 2 Mus.pr. 1347/Bayerische Staatsbibliothek, Munich

which all beats receive essentially equal emphasis. Most music from the 17th century can be readily notated with bar lines in modern transcriptions, whereas Renaissance music rarely lends itself to such notation.

The increasing prominence of metrical units—fixed patterns of strong and weak beats—also manifested itself in the dance rhythms that permeate a good deal of 17th-century vocal music. Poetic texts that were metrically regular lent themselves to a correspondingly regular musical setting. Thus, alongside free declamation in early monody, we also find an abundance of music—vocal as well as instrumental—that adheres to the principle of periodic phrase structure.

Musically, monodies of the early 17th century strike at least some listeners today as less rich and less varied than their polyphonic counterparts. In the constant struggle to balance lyrical interest and textual intelligibility, monody consistently favored the latter. Peri, Caccini, and other composers of early monodies used chromaticism only sparingly. Their melodic lines are typically more straightforward than what may be found in contemporary polyphonic compositions, and frequent cadences often seem to interrupt the rhythmic flow of the music. But it was precisely these qualities—simplicity and directness, combined with a clear projection of the text—that appealed to contemporary audiences. Monody allowed composers of the early 17th century to synthesize poetry and music in a way that animated the poetry without overwhelming it. Monody also provided a key ingredient for a new genre—opera—by providing a medium for an individual singer on stage to present the words of a single character. And it would soon permit combinations of voices and instruments that would go beyond mere voice doubling.

At the same time, monody did not spell the death of polyphony. On the contrary, the principles of Renaissance counterpoint—particularly the sacred music of Palestrina and his many imitators—continued to flourish well into the 17th century and beyond. Indeed, many more polyphonic a cappella madrigals than monodies were published in the first two decades of the 17th century, and the polyphonic style remained a touchstone of compositional prowess for composers throughout the Baroque era.

In the end, none of the monodists claimed to have truly recreated the music of Greek antiquity. But they firmly believed they had realized its modern equivalent, and the proof of this lay in the reaction of contemporary audiences. In describing a performance of Claudio Monteverdi's opera *Ariadne* in 1608, the composer Marco da Gagliano (1582–1643) declared that Monteverdi had written "the airs so exquisitely that one may truthfully aver that the virtues of ancient music were reborn, for all the audience was visibly moved to tears."[6]

# MUSIC IN THE BAROQUE ERA: A STYLISTIC OVERVIEW

The rise of the *seconda prattica* and monody marked the beginning of a series of stylistic changes that together define the music of the Baroque era. Many of these changes occurred gradually; others, as we have seen, were well underway before 1600. This section briefly summarizes the most important of them, including those associated with the *seconda prattica* just discussed as well as others that we explore in more depth in the chapters to follow.

**The emergence of basso continuo.** In the years around 1600, composers began to write for solo voice and instruments within a new textural framework, in which the melodic line was supported by a group of instruments known as the basso continuo. The basso continuo provided both harmonic and contrapuntal support to the voice, which in turn made it possible for the soloist to project the text at hand with clarity and rhythmic flexibility.

**The coexistence of old and new styles.**   The new style of homophonic writing did not wholly supplant traditional polyphony. Counterpoint persisted throughout the Baroque era in all genres of music, vocal and instrumental, sacred and secular. The terms *prima prattica* and *seconda prattica* were needed because both styles were being used at the same time.

**A shift from modal to tonal writing.**   At the end of the Renaissance, and through much of the 17th century, composers and theorists alike were still writing and thinking in terms of the traditional modes—Dorian, Lydian, Phrygian, and so on. By 1700, these constructs had largely given way to a single type of diatonic scale, with half steps between scale degrees 3–4 and 7–8 (in the major mode) or 2–3 and 7–8 (in the "melodic" minor mode). "Mode" was now reserved to distinguish between the major and minor forms of this one scale, which could be transposed to any desired key (see Focus: "The Emergence of Tonal Harmony").

**A change from intervallic to chordal harmony.**   Although a mid-16th-century work like Palestrina's *Missa Papae Marcelli* (Anthology) can be readily analyzed in terms of modern-day harmonic theory (using concepts like tonic, dominant, and subdominant), it would be anachronistic to do so, for Renaissance theorists and composers conceived of harmony as a by-product of counterpoint—that is, as a by-product of the relationship among the given voices of a work. For music written in the 18th century, however, such an analysis would be entirely appropriate. It was during the 17th century that musicians began to think of harmony more and more in terms of chordal progressions, although counterpoint never lost its prestige in the hierarchy of musical theory or pedagogy.

**Greater rhythmic freedom.**   One of the most striking—and controversial—elements of the music of the *seconda prattica* was its sense of rhythmic freedom, far greater than what had been customary in music of the Renaissance. Singers and instrumentalists could be (and were) called on to sing or play elaborate, complex rhythms that could shift abruptly. This stylistic change was made possible by the move toward homophonic texture, which permitted a far greater range of freedom in the solo voice than had been possible in the essentially equal-voiced textures of the *prima prattica*.

**Increased virtuosity.**   The opportunities for performers to display their talents expanded enormously in the Baroque. Musicians and audiences alike took great delight in the technical challenges of performance. Both Giulio Caccini's *Sfogava con le stelle* from 1602 (Anthology I/69), and Dietrich Buxtehude's Praeludium for Organ, BuxWV 149, from the 1690s (Anthology I/94; see Chapter 10), in spite of their considerable stylistic differences, provide opportunities for soloists to display their talents openly and to great advantage.

**The growing differentiation between vocal and instrumental styles.**   The stress on virtuosity inspired composers to write differently for voices and instruments, and, when writing for instruments, to take into account their specific capabilities.

## SUMMARY OF STYLE DIFFERENCES BETWEEN RENAISSANCE AND BAROQUE MUSIC

| | RENAISSANCE | BAROQUE |
|---|---|---|
| **Style** | One generally consistent style, dubbed in retrospect the *prima prattica.* | Two styles, the *prima prattica* and the newer *seconda prattica.* |
| **Text setting** | Relatively restrained representation of texts; word painting for contrast. | Increasingly free projection of texts with greater attention to the declamation of individual words and, on a larger scale, entire sentences. |
| **Texture** | Polyphonic, with all voices of essentially equal importance. Imitation becomes a pervasive element. | Polyphonic (imitative) or homophonic with a strong sense of polarity between the two outer voices. |
| **Rhythm** | Generally balanced and evenly flowing. A steady pulse (the *tactus*) governs performance, and although this may change within the course of a work, it remains steady for long stretches at a time. | A cultivation of extremes between simplicity and complexity, typically determined in vocal works by the text. The *tactus* gives way to a stronger sense of meter with fixed units of "strong" and "weak" beats. |
| **Melody** | Generally lyrical, rarely virtuosic in an overt manner. | More openly virtuosic, with more opportunities for embellishment by soloists. A growing differentiation between vocal and instrumental idioms. |
| **Harmony** | Primarily modal, with harmony conceived of as a by-product of the interrelationship of voices. Relatively circumscribed treatment of dissonance and voice leading. | Primarily tonal, especially by the end of the 17th century, with harmony conceived of as a progression of vertical sonorities. Relatively freer treatment of dissonance and voice leading. |
| **Form** | Primarily paratactic (A, B, C, D, etc.), with individual subunits of a work more or less sharply demarcated from one another. | Both paratactic and syntactic (i.e., with subunits connected rhythmically, harmonically, and thematically). Formal patterns based on recurring material become increasingly important. |
| **Instrumentation** | Vocal works adhere to the a cappella ideal, with the option of instruments doubling voices. Vocal and instrumental idioms are essentially interchangeable. | Compositions for voices only, instruments only, or for voices and instruments together, with independent instrumental parts complementing rather than doubling vocal lines. Increasingly idiomatic writing for individual instruments. |

The voice, after all, cannot sing a scale as fast as a violinist or oboist can play one, nor can a singer negotiate the same large melodic leaps an instrument can. Whereas the parts of a Renaissance chanson or madrigal might be performed interchangeably by voices and any of a variety of instruments, this kind of flexibility declined gradually over the course of the Baroque. In many instances, lines could be performed only on instruments, and often only on specific instruments.

**The growing importance of instruments and instrumental music.** No other 150-year span in the history of music witnessed the development of so many new instruments and the transformation of so many existing instruments. The Baroque era stands without question as the golden age of organ building and violin making. This period saw great technical improvements in the harpsichord and, in the first half of the 18th century, the earliest pianos. The orchestra itself crystallized as an ensemble of strings, winds, and percussion during this period. And for

## Focus  THE EMERGENCE OF TONAL HARMONY

Renaissance music is based on modes; by the end of the Baroque era, most music rests squarely within a tonal idiom based on the diatonic major and minor scales. The transition from modal to tonal harmony, which began in the 16th century, took place gradually over the course of the Baroque. For most of the 17th century, theorists described both modal and tonal systems as being of more or less equal value. But by the late 17th century, they had shifted their attention mostly away from modes to focus primarily on the diatonic scale in its major and minor forms.

The theoretical debate between advocates of tonal harmony and advocates of modal harmony reached its peak in the early 18th century, by which time the matter had been more or less settled in practice. The conservative north German theorist Johann Heinrich Buttstett (1666–1727) defended the old system in a treatise of 1716 entitled *Ut mi sol, Re fa la: The Eternals of All Music and Harmony; or, A New Exposition on the Old, True, Exclusive, and Eternal Fundamentals of Music.* A year later, Johann Mattheson (1681–1764) responded with a treatise of his own, in which he declared that Buttstett was not describing a theory of "all music" (*tota musica*, as Buttstett had called it in Latin) but rather a theory of "dead music" (the nearly homonymic *todte musica*, in a punning mixture of German and Latin). Mattheson derided Buttstett for being hopelessly old fashioned and clinging to a theoretical framework no longer relevant to the musical practice of the day.

In retrospect, we can see this as a generational conflict. Composers and theorists born in the mid-17th century were reluctant to let go of a system still dominated by medieval modes and accept in its place a single scale—the diatonic—with only two different forms, major and minor. Those born a generation later could not understand the intricacies and subtle advantages of the modal system. In the end, almost every younger composer sided with Mattheson. No less a figure than George Frideric Handel wrote to him that

[A]s concerns the Greek modes, I find that you have said everything that there is to say. Their knowledge is doubtless necessary to those who want to practice and perform ancient music [by this Handel means music of the 16th and 17th centuries], which formerly was composed according to such modes; however, since now we have been freed from the narrow bounds of ancient music, I cannot perceive what use the Greek modes have in today's music.[7]

Modal thinking never died out completely, however. The modes remained a standard feature of counterpoint textbooks, and the "strict style" of Palestrina endured as a model of disciplined form. The modes also retained a strong association with the ideas of the sacred and the past, or some combination of the two. The music of the 19th and 20th centuries abounds in examples of composers writing modally for just this purpose. Beethoven wrote parts of the "Holy Song of Thanksgiving" in his String Quartet, op. 132, in the archaic Lydian mode, even calling attention to this in the score. In the mid-19th century, composers of the "Cecilian movement" used modal writing to conjure up an archaic musical style more evocative of Palestrina than their own era. Several 20th-century English composers, most notably Ralph Vaughan Williams and Benjamin Britten, used modal writing to evoke what they saw as a golden age of English music in the 16th century, the era of Tallis and Byrd, itself grounded in traditional music. Nonchurch modes prevailed in Eastern Europe, northern Africa, and throughout Asia; these were also used by composers to evoke musical cultures outside the West.

---

the first time in the history of music, instrumental virtuosos began to rival vocalists in popularity and financial rewards. All of these developments reflect the growing importance of instrumental music throughout the Baroque era.

**Program music.**   An outgrowth of instrumental music's increasing importance is the rise of **program music** in the years around 1700. This is purely instrumental music that is in some way connected with a story or idea. For example, one of Johann Kuhnau's *Biblical Sonatas* of 1700 (Anthology; see Chapter 10), according to its score, depicts the battle between David and Goliath, the fall of the giant, and the flight of the Philistines.

**The cultivation of contrasting timbres.**   The ideal timbre in late Renaissance music was a blend of essentially uniform sounds, such as a chorus of voices (soprano, alto, tenor, bass) or a set of matched instruments covering different ranges (such as a consort of four recorders, or a "case" of four viols). Baroque musicians and audiences valued contrasts, for example, of melody to accompaniment, voices to instruments, high to low, solo to tutti, loud to soft, or winds to strings.

**The emergence of national styles.**   Renaissance music was for the most part international in style, but national styles of writing began to emerge over the course of the 17th century. The Italian style was associated with the predominance of melody, a sharply profiled rhythmic shape, and a strong sense of meter. Many commentators considered it serious and weighty. Italian notational practice tended to leave the performer considerable room for improvisation. The French style was typically characterized as "sprightly," "bright," and "lively," strongly influenced by the rhythms of dance but tending toward a more fluid sense of melody. French notational practice generally prescribed desired embellishments and grace notes in greater detail than did the Italian. The German style was considered a synthesis of the French and Italian, incorporating elements of both but adding a dimension of contrapuntal gravity.

## SUMMARY

Musicians working in the first decade of the 17th century—the beginning of the Baroque—were keenly aware that music had entered a new era. The emergence of monody opened up possibilities that had been scarcely imaginable only a generation before: opera, madrigals with distinctly separate vocal and instrumental parts, and a nascent conception of chordal harmony, all driven by a fundamentally new attitude toward the relationship between words and music. Over the next 150 years, composers and performers of the Baroque would explore the consequences of these innovations in their ongoing attempts to represent the passions of the human spirit.

**Study** and **Review**
on **mysearchlab.com**

# Vocal Music, 1600–1650

The *seconda prattica* was driven by new attitudes toward text setting in the years around 1600. The transformed genre of the madrigal, the entirely new phenomenon of opera, and the sacred music of this period all manifest the commitment of 17th-century composers to develop new ways of synthesizing text, melody, and rhythm.

## SECULAR SONG

In Italy, composers applied the principles of the new practice to the still popular genre of the madrigal. In France, the influence of monody and basso continuo is reflected in the emergence of a new genre, the *air de cour*.

### Italy: The Madrigal

The madrigal—any through-composed setting of freely structured verse—remained the preeminent genre of secular vocal music in Italy throughout the first half of the 17th century. The genre encompassed traditional a cappella settings as well as the newer monodies for solo voice and basso continuo. The monodic principle is also at work in the **concertato madrigal**, in which voices of any number combine with instruments, either basso continuo alone or basso continuo and other instruments. Concertato madrigals represent a kind of synthesis between the single-voiced monody (with basso continuo) and the multi-voiced a cappella polyphonic madrigal.

The madrigals of Claudio Monteverdi (1567–1643; see Composer Profile), published in nine books, reflect all the manifestations of the genre in the early Baroque. The Madrigals in the first four books (1587, 1590, 1592, 1603) pre-date the rise of monody and are written in the tradition of such mid-to-late 16th-century composers as Willaert, Rore, and Lasso. Basso continuo makes its first appearance in the fifth book (1605), but is structurally essential only in the last five madrigals in the volume. In all the madrigals from Book Six (1614) on, basso continuo is the norm. Indeed, when Monteverdi issued a second edition of Book Four in 1615, 12 years after the first edition, he added a continuo line to each madrigal. Concertato madrigals play an increasingly important role in Monteverdi's output over the final decades of his career, as reflected in the works published in Books Seven (1619), Eight (1638), and Nine (published posthumously in 1651).

Even the early madrigals, written in a traditional polyphonic texture, reflect the emergence of the *seconda prattica*. Monteverdi himself identified

# Claudio Monteverdi (1567–1643)

Monteverdi's career straddled the Renaissance and Baroque, and he mastered both the *prima prattica* and *seconda prattica*. His career falls into two distinct phases, one in Mantua, the other in Venice. In Mantua he served at the court of the Gonzaga dynasty, writing music to order, including his first two operas, *Orfeo* (1607) and *Ariadne* (1608). The success of these works was such that Monteverdi was soon offered the position of maestro di cappella (director of music) at the Basilica of San Marco in Venice. This was arguably the most prestigious position for any musician in all of Italy, and it allowed him the luxury of writing madrigals and dramatic music as well as sacred music. The surviving correspondence paints a vivid picture of a composer who could choose his commissions with care, according to what interested him and how well it paid. When the rulers of Mantua tried to lure Monteverdi back to their court, he replied with a letter declining the offer firmly yet diplomatically. In his position in Venice, Monteverdi pointed out, he was paid twice the salary of his illustrious predecessors, including Adrian Willaert, Cipriano da Rore, and Gioseffo Zarlino; he enjoyed complete control over the hiring and firing or musicians; his duties were relatively light; and he had the opportunity to earn considerable extra money by writing music for various guilds and societies. Perhaps most important of all, he enjoyed the respect of Venice's high society: "Nor is there any gentleman who does not esteem and honor me, and when I undertake to perform anything, whether it be chamber music or church music, I swear to Your Lordship that the whole city comes running."[1]

Monteverdi was constantly trying new styles and new genres. In addition to operas for an elite audience at court (such as *Orfeo*), he also wrote works for the new public opera houses that began to open in Venice at the end of the 1630s. In his later life he introduced a new style of writing he called the *genere concitato* to capture emotions that were agitated or bellicose. His music remained a touchstone for all subsequent 17th-century composers.

# PRINCIPAL WORKS

## Madrigals

Monteverdi's madrigals span almost his entire creative life. Between 1587 and 1638, he published eight numbered books of madrigals along with various miscellaneous collections and pieces. A ninth was published posthumously. The first four books of madrigals are in the traditional polyphonic texture of the Renaissance. Book 5 (1605) introduces basso continuo in its final numbers, and the remaining books all feature basso continuo. These works as a whole reflect a remarkable range of compositional techniques, from polyphony to monody.

## Dramatic Works

An appalling proportion of Monteverdi's dramatic music has disappeared. We know that at least some of it was reused or reworked in surviving madrigals (the *Lamento d'Arianna* is all that survives of the opera *Arianna* from 1608, for example), and we have some of the librettos for works whose music has been lost. But for the most part, scholars can only speculate about more than a dozen missing works for the stage, ranging from operas to *balli*—staged dance spectacles with singing.

The operas that have survived are *Orfeo* (1607), *Il Ritorno d'Ulisse in Patria* ("The Return of Ulysses to His Homeland," 1641), and *L'incoronazione di Poppea* ("The Coronation of Poppea," 1642). Most notable among the

two madrigalists of the mid-16th century—Cipriano de Rore and Adrian Willaert (see Chapter 6)—as the originators of the "new practice," on the grounds that both composers had gone out of their way to make their music project the essence of the words being sung. Monteverdi adhered to this principle throughout his own career as a composer of madrigals.

The most serious public dispute about the *seconda prattica* in fact did not center on any collection of monodies, but rather on certain polyphonic madrigals that would later be published in Monteverdi's Fifth Book of Madrigals. The Italian composer and theorist Giovanni Maria Artusi (ca. 1540–1613) attacked Monteverdi's treatment of dissonance in these works as unacceptable, spelling out his objections

many smaller dramatic works is *Il Combattimento di Tancredi e Clorinda* (1624), whose libretto is drawn from a well-known epic poem of the day, in which the knight Tancred defeats Clorinda—who is disguised as a man—in battle.

## Sacred Music

Monteverdi wrote a variety of Masses, hymns, psalms, and motets. By far his best known sacred work is the *Vespers* of 1610, a cycle of 14 movements that uses a variety of styles, old and new.

**Claudio Monteverdi.** The only indisputably authentic image of Monteverdi appeared on a publication of his music issued shortly after his death. Based on the similarity of that likeness to the portrait here, scholars believe this oil portrait depicts the composer in the mid-1610s, perhaps after he had assumed the position of maestro di cappella at the Basilica of San Marco in Venice.

**Source:** Erich Lessing/Landesmuseum Ferdinandeum, Innsbruck, Austria/Art Resource, NY

| KEY DATES IN THE LIFE OF MONTEVERDI | |
|---|---|
| 1567 | Born in Cremona (northern Italy); baptized May 15. |
| 1582 | First publication, a set of motets for three voices. |
| 1590 | Hired as singer and viol player by the Duke of Mantua; becomes music director at the Mantuan court in 1602. |
| 1605 | Publishes his Fifth Book of Madrigals, which includes several works with basso continuo and a prefatory letter defending the principles of the *seconda prattica*. |
| 1607 | Composes his first opera, *Orfeo,* for the court at Mantua. |
| 1613 | Appointed maestro di cappella at the Basilica of San Marco, Venice. |
| 1643 | Dies in Venice on November 29. |

in considerable detail in a pamphlet issued in 1600 entitled *L'Artusi, ovvero delle imperfettioni della moderna musica* ("The Artusi; or, On the Imperfections of Modern Music"). Artusi knew these madrigals through manuscript copies—Book 5 would not actually be published for another five years—and he took particular exception to Monteverdi's five-voiced *Cruda Amarilli*. He chastised the composer for having violated the precepts of counterpoint as set down by Zarlino. Artusi objected to Monteverdi's practice of repeating suspended notes and of descending after a sharpened tone and rising after a flattened one, pointing specifically to the vertical dissonances in m. 12–13 of *Cruda Amarilli*. He disapproved of the cross-relations between G-F♯ and F♮ in this passage, as well as the unprepared dissonant entry of the A in the highest voice in m. 13 against the G in the bass. He also criticized the work for having more cadences in the twelfth mode (C plagal) than in the seventh mode (G authentic), the mode of its opening and closing. (For more on the system of modes, see Chapters 1 and 4.)

Monteverdi replied with a brief manifesto of his own when his Fifth Book of Madrigals was finally published in 1605. The set opens quite pointedly with *Cruda Amarilli*, the very madrigal Artusi had attacked so sharply. In his introduction to the set, Monteverdi wrote,

> Be not surprised that I am giving these madrigals to the press without first replying to the objections that Artusi made against some very minute portions of them. Being in the service of this Serene Highness of Mantua, I am not master of the time I would require. Nevertheless I wrote a reply to let it be known that I do not do things by chance, and as soon as it is rewritten it will see the light with the title in front, *Seconda prattica overo Perfettione della moderna musica* ["The New Practice; or, The Perfection of Modern Music"]. Some will wonder at this, not believing that there is any other practice than that taught by Zerlino [*sic*]. But let them be assured concerning consonances and dissonances that there is a different way of considering them from that already determined which defends the modern manner of composition with the assent of the reason and the senses. I wanted to say this both so that the expression *Seconda prattica* would not be appropriated by others and so that men of intellect might meanwhile consider other second thoughts concerning harmony. And have faith that the modern composer builds on foundations of truth.[2]

Two years later, the composer's brother, Giulio Cesare Monteverdi (1573–ca. 1630), offered an extended gloss on this brief statement, and although this additional commentary may not have been written by Claudio himself, it was surely approved by him. (It may well be that Claudio was using his younger brother as a kind of front man in this debate, thereby staying above the fray even while responding to his critics.) In this gloss, Giulio argues that in the *seconda prattica*, "the oration is the mistress of the harmony"—that is, the words determine the nature of the music, not vice versa. He goes on to point out that Artusi, in his critique of *Cruda Amarilli*, had paid no attention whatsoever to the madrigal's words, "as though they had nothing to do with the music." And he reiterated Claudio Monteverdi's promise to weigh in with a longer statement justifying the *seconda prattica*. But this work never appeared—Claudio seems to have been too busy writing new music.

The Artusi–Monteverdi controversy exposes the fundamental differences in outlook between advocates of the "old" and the "new" practices. Artusi, representing the traditional approach of an older generation, looks first and foremost at the construction of the music, whereas Monteverdi, 27 years younger, justifies the use of unconventional musical techniques on the basis of the text being set. That Monteverdi felt compelled to respond to Artusi's challenge at all tells us much about the issues at stake. Like many other composers who cultivated the *seconda prattica*, Monteverdi could be thin-skinned in response to questions of technical competence. When he composed *Cruda Amarilli*, he was well aware of having broken with the conventions of counterpoint and harmony as codified by Zarlino. Still, he felt it necessary to defend his compositional practice by appealing to "reason and the senses" and by assuring his critic that this new style of writing rested on "foundations of truth." It is also revealing that the immediate object of debate here—the madrigal *Cruda Amarilli*—is a work for an unaccompanied vocal ensemble written sometime before 1600. The controversies about the nature of the *seconda prattica*, in other words, were already well under way before the emergence of monody and basso continuo. Indeed, some of the a cappella madrigals of the late 16th and early 17th centuries count among the most daring and progressive pieces of the entire Baroque era. The jarring dissonances in the opening measures of Gesualdo's *Moro, lasso, al mio duolo* of 1611 (Example 6–2) and the beginning of Marenzio's *Solo e pensoso* (1599; Anthology) share with *Cruda Amarilli* (and subsequent works by Monteverdi and others) a willingness to project painful emotions through the use of unconventional part writing.

More novel in their time were the concertato madrigals that appeared in ever-greater numbers over the first three decades of the 17th century. Monteverdi's setting of *T'amo mia vita*, published in 1605, exhibits striking differences with Luzasscho Luzasschi's setting of the same text issued only four years earlier (Anthology; see Chapter 6). Thanks to the use of the solo voice, Monteverdi is able to distinguish quite clearly between the narrator's memory of the words he has heard from his beloved ("I love you, my life") and his own injunction to the god of love (Amor), to imprint these words on his heart. The madrigal begins with the remembered words themselves, sung by a solo soprano (representing the beloved's voice) and supported by basso continuo. Only with the entrance of the three lower (men's) voices do we realize the opening line is a quotation, a memory. The effect is quite dramatic, with the contrasting perspectives represented by contrasting sonorities. When the memory returns in m. 9, it is not only the words that come back (*T'amo mia vita*), but also the beloved's voice, for this line is consistently given to the soprano alone in the first half of Monteverdi's setting.

Beginning in m. 40, after the narrator implores the god of love to imprint them on his heart and let his "soul breathe through them alone," Monteverdi incorporates the remembered words into the full texture of all six voices. The soprano sings exactly the same pitches as at the beginning, but her words and the sound of her voice have now been integrated into the body of the whole. Monteverdi projects the text "Let 'I love you, my life,' be my whole life" by folding the falling motive associated with the remembered words into the full texture of the music. Because it is a concertato Madrigal—a work for voice and instruments that function both together and independently of one another—Monteverdi can distinguish solo passages from polyphonic ones and capture the drama of the poetry in ways that Luzasschi's wholly polyphonic setting cannot.

Monteverdi's *Zefiro torna e di soavi accenti*, for two tenors and basso continuo (1632), illustrates just how musically elaborate the concertato madrigal had become by the early 1630s. Most of the work rests on an **ostinato** or **ground bass**, a short phrase repeated over and over again in the lowest voice. This particular phrase, complete in two measures in modern transcription, shares no thematic material with the upper voices but instead provides a structural framework that allows the voices above it to unfold freely without regard to their harmonic underpinnings. The ground bass also provides continuity at those moments when neither of the two tenors is singing (m. 54, 56, 58, 66, etc.). Without the basso continuo, such pauses would simply not be feasible.

The first 11 of the poem's 14 lines are full of pastoral clichés: a gentle wind (the zephyr) blows from the west, branches murmur in the gentle breeze, nymphs dance, the sun rises in a sky of deep blue, etc. The repeating bass reinforces the static nature of this pastoral perfection. Everything is constant and unchanging—a bit too constant and unchanging—and, in fact, the listener may suspect (and even hope) that something is about to happen. In line 12, the poem shifts abruptly to the first

**Listen**

CD4    Track 6
**mysearchlab** (with scrolling translation)
MONTEVERDI
*T'amo mia vita*
Score Anthology I/72

**Listen**

CD4    Track 7
**mysearchlab** (with scrolling translation)
MONTEVERDI
*Zefiro torna e di soavi accenti*
Score Anthology I/73

person: "I alone stand solitary in the lonely forest / The ardor of two beautiful eyes is my torment." The ostinato suddenly breaks off here (m. 113), and the music slows down through a change in mensuration: a breve in the opening section now equals a half note. For the last line of the poem ("As my fate wills it, I sometimes weep, sometimes sing"), Monteverdi forcefully juxtaposes the contrast between joy and sorrow, setting the final statement of the word *piango* ("weep") on a suspension with a jarring dissonance (m. 143–144) whose resolution ushers in the final return of the ground bass with the word *canto* ("I sing").

The use of variation as a structural device is also evident in *Lasciatemi qui solo* ("Leave Me in Solitude Here"), a strophic monody by Francesca Caccini (1587–ca. 1641; see Composer Profile). The text is a lament—once again, a lover has been abandoned—that progresses from sorrow to death. The music's basic structural unit is the nine-measure pattern stated at the outset by the bass. Reinforcing the process of psychological transformation described in the text, Caccini subtly varies both the bass line and the melody in each strophe (m. 1–9, 10–19, 20–29, 30–39, and 40–49) but maintains exactly the same music for the relentless refrain of *lasciatemi morire* ("let me die"). At the very end, however, the longed-for death is now imminent (*Gia sono esangu'e smorto:* "Already I am bloodless and pale"; m. 47–48), and the slight change in the melodic line is full of meaning.

*Tradimento* ("Betrayal"), an **arietta** ("small aria" or song) for soprano and continuo by Barbara Strozzi (1619–1677), illustrates one of the most important of all formal innovations of the Baroque, the **ritornello principle**. A **ritornello** (Italian for "brief return") is an opening musical idea that returns at several points over the course of a work, usually after contrasting material of some kind. Composers used the ritornello principle to establish a framework of both repetition and variation,

((•⊷ **Listen**

CD4　Track 8

**mysearchlab** (with scrolling translation)
FRANCESCA CACCINI
*Lasciatemi qui solo*
Score Anthology I/74

((•⊷ **Listen**

CD4　Track 9

**mysearchlab** (with scrolling translation)
STROZZI
*Tradimento*
Score Anthology I/75

**Barbara Strozzi?** Being a female composer—and a supremely talented one, no less—was not an easy proposition in the 17th century. In 1644, Barbara Strozzi dedicated her first published work, a collection of madrigals, to the Grand Duchess of Tuscany with these words: "To the august name of Your Highness I do reverently consecrate this first work, which I, as a woman, send forth into the light all too anxiously, so that under an oak tree of gold it may rest secure from the lightning bolts of slander prepared for it." The "slander" Strozzi anticipated may have been related to rumors about her chastity, which seems to have been a topic of repeated satire and jest in the late 1630s. One source accused her of having an affair with a castrato; another noted that "it is a fine thing to distribute the flowers after having already surrendered the fruit."

Strozzi's achievements as a composer are all the more impressive in this light. By the end of her life, she had published eight volumes of music, including about 125 individual works, more than all but a few of her male contemporaries. And she accomplished all this without benefit of a secure professional position in music and without extended support from any one patron.

Scholars believe that the unnamed subject of the portrait here, by the artist Bernardo Strozzi (no relation), may be Barbara Strozzi. No other image of her is known to exist.

**Source:** Erich Lessing/Gemaeldegalerie Alte Meister, Staatliche Kunstsammlungen, Dres/Art Resource, NY

and it appears in a great many genres of the Baroque era, vocal as well as instrumental. It would later take on special importance in the genre of the concerto (see Chapter 10).

The ritornello in Strozzi's *Tradimento*—the exclamation "Betrayal!" and the agitated theme associated with it—is both textual and musical. In these recurring outbursts, the scorned lover swears to kill the object of her (or his?) wrath. The ritornello sections offset more inward and less violent reflections: "My sickness has advanced so/That I have discovered that the thought of being [a prisoner of love] makes me contented." But these contrasting emotions are always driven out by thoughts of revenge in the guise of the ritornello ("Betrayal!").

Strozzi's ritornello captures the physical energy of the scorned lover's fury with rapid-fire repeated notes. *Tradimento*'s opening flurry, which outlines a triad and recurs with each statement of the ritornello between strophes and then again at the end, sounds almost like a trumpet fanfare, rousing troops for battle. This *concitato* ("agitated," "warlike") style of writing was developed by Monteverdi for evoking a mood of bellicose agitation or anger, and he used it most famously in his *Combattimento di Tancredi e Clorinda* (1624).

## France: The *Air de cour*

Like their counterparts in the Florentine Camerata, French academicians of the late 16th century sought to re-create the magical powers of ancient music, but in a manner suited to the qualities of the French language. Jean-Antoine de Baïf (1532–1589) and his followers at the Académie de poésie et musique (Academy of Poetry and Music), founded in 1570, developed a system they called *musique mesurée à l'antique* ("music adapted to ancient measure," that is, prosody). Adherents of this approach tried to match French verse to the quantitative principles of Greek and Latin poetry, in which syllables are differentiated by length (duration) rather than

*Aures demulcet, flectit durissima corda,*
*Exhilarat tristes, conciliatque sibi.*

*Et lassus recreat studiorum pondere mentes;*
*Quid mirum a Musis, Musica nomen habet.*

**Party music, 1612.** Music has long been associated with drinking and lascivious behavior, as this scene of student music-making and revelry from 1612 suggests. The harpsichordist and the violinist on the right seem especially interested in the arrival of the young ladies, whom their friend at the door is enthusiastically helping down the steps. The lutenist in the right foreground is repairing a broken string. The others (at least, those who are not drinking) are playing and singing from partbooks. Composers did not hesitate to write music for the student market. In 1626, Johann Hermann Schein issued a collection called *Studenten-Schmauss* ("Student Banquet"), a collection of songs for five voices written to provide "praiseworthy companionship for wine or beer."

**Source:** Kunstsammlungen der Veste Coburg, Germany/Neg#3740, Inv.#VII, 308, 24

# Francesca Caccini (1587–ca. 1641)

As a renowned virtuoso and composer of monodies and operas, Francesca Caccini followed in the footsteps of her father, the composer and singer Giulio Caccini (see Chapter 7). She was the first woman to compose an opera and one of the most celebrated singers of her time. (She was known as *La Cecchina*, the songbird.) She also wrote poetry, both in Italian and Latin, and played the lute. Caccini spent most of her career in or around the Medici court in Florence. By the 1620s, she had become the highest paid musician in the family's service. She wrote music for court performances (particularly intermedi) and a great many songs. Her duties also included teaching music and singing to the women of the court; her *Primo libro delle musiche* (1618) is particularly well suited for teaching. No image of her survives.

Her only surviving opera, *La liberazione di Ruggiero*, pits a young knight, Ruggiero, against Alcina, a seductive sorceress who puts him under a spell. Its performance in Warsaw (1628) was the first for any Italian opera outside Italy. The work has been revived to critical acclaim in both Europe and the United States in recent years.

## PRINCIPAL WORKS

Most of Francesca Caccini's works have been lost. She wrote the music for an estimated 14 court entertainments in Florence during the years 1607 to 1627, including ballets, intermedi, and incidental music to comedies. Her *Primo libro delle musiche* (1618) is a substantial collection of sonnets, madrigals, arias, motets, hymns, and canzonettas, all for solo voice and continuo.

### KEY DATES IN THE LIFE OF FRANCESCA CACCINI

| | |
|---|---|
| 1587 | Born September 18 in Florence. |
| 1600 | Probably performs in her father's operas in Florence, *Euridice* and *Il rapimento di Cefalo*. |
| 1607 | Begins independent service within the Medici court in Florence as a singer, composer, and teacher of music. |
| 1618 | Publishes *Il primo libro delle musiche*, a large collection of monodic songs on both sacred and secular texts. |
| 1625 | Production of her opera *La liberazione di Ruggiero*. |
| 1641 | Dies sometime after June 1641. |

**Listen**

CD4 Track 10
**mysearchlab** (with scrolling translation)
MOULINIÉ
*Enfin la beauté que j'adore*
Score Anthology I/76

by weight (accent). Baïf advocated musical settings in which long and short syllables were consistently declaimed in a ratio of 2:1. The musical accompaniment did not rest on basso continuo—a device that spread only slowly throughout Europe and did not become standard until about 1680—but rather on notated tablature for the lute or other similar instruments. Although this type of notation reduced the need for improvisation, the textural clarity of a solo voice with discreet accompaniment is clearly indebted to the principles of monody.

The most important repertory of secular song in early-17th-century France was the **air de cour** ("courtly air"). Like the madrigal, the *air de cour* was at first polyphonic but eventually evolved into the favored vehicle for solo voice and lute accompaniment. The first collection of this genre, published by Le Roy & Ballard, appeared in 1571. It includes arrangements of earlier four-part compositions as well as new works in the style of the *voix de ville* (simple strophic verse set to chordal accompaniments). Etienne Moulinié's *Enfin la beauté que j'adore* ("At Last, the Beauty Whom I Adore"), published in 1624, resembles many similar *airs de cour* in its fluid, syllabic declamation of text and its harmonic simplicity and melodic grace, avoiding overt displays of virtuosity. Moulinié (ca. 1600–after 1669) served for many years as director of music to Gaston d'Orléans, Louis XIII's younger brother,

## Focus  MUSIC AND THE PASSIONS

The 17th century witnessed the beginnings of what we now think of as modern-day psychology—the study of the human mind and its relationship to the emotions. René Descartes' *The Passions of the Soul* (1649) was the most prominent in a long line of texts that attempted to codify the human passions. Descartes identified six basic affections: admiration (wonder), love, hate, desire, joy, and sadness, and he examined ways in which these states could be induced.

The question of how music might incite such emotions in listeners was a matter of intense debate throughout the Baroque. The theory that an agitated or war-like manner of writing—the **genere concitato**—could evoke feelings of anger and agitation, for example, was part of a broader attempt to find the most effective musical means for portraying human passions. The various ideas about the relationship between music and emotion that emerged over the course of the Baroque are sometimes referred to as the "doctrine of affections," but this designation suggests a far more systematic view of the relationship between music and the passions than really existed.

Most writers of the period adhered to the ancient idea that the passions derived from the physical mixture of the body's four cardinal "humors" or fluids—blood, phlegm, yellow bile, and black bile—each of which governed a particular emotion. In their proper proportion, these were all needed to create a well-balanced disposition. But if one of these elements gained the upper hand, its effect would dominate the whole person. Too much blood (*sanguis* in Latin) made one overly cheerful, or sanguine; too much phlegm made one sluggish, or phlegmatic; too much yellow bile made one angry, or bilious; and too much black bile made one sad, or melancholy.

Certain types of music, it was believed, could excite the body to produce more blood, phlegm, or yellow or black bile, thereby altering the disposition of the listener. The precise mechanism for this was never entirely clear. The German composer and critic Johann Mattheson (1681–1764) suggested that because "joy is an *expansion* of our vital spirits, it follows sensibly and naturally that this affect is best expressed by large and expanded intervals," whereas "sadness . . . is a *contraction* of those same subtle parts of our bodies. It is, therefore, easy to see that the narrowest intervals are the most suitable." Such pronouncements, however, rested more on imagination than scientific observation.

and he was one of many French composers of the early 17th century to cultivate the *air de cour*, along with Pierre Guédron (ca. 1570–ca. 1620) and Antoine Boësset (1586–1643).

# OPERA

Music had played an important role in the theater throughout the Renaissance: plays routinely included songs, dances, and interludes of instrumental music. Shakespeare's dramas, the earliest of which appeared in the 1580s, are full of such musical elements. The so-called **madrigal comedies** of the late 16th century consist of a cycle of madrigals connected by a dramatic theme. The most famous work of this kind, Orazzio Vecchi's *L'Amfiparnaso* of 1597 (the title means roughly "The Slopes of Mount Parnassus"), is a series of 14 madrigals for five voices that draw on the stock characters of the commedia dell'arte, the Italian tradition of improvised comedy: the doddering merchant (Pantalone), the long-winded doctor (Gratiano), and the young lovers (Isabella and Lucio). But these madrigal comedies seem not to have been staged, and even in their most developed form they represent little more than the songs of a play that incorporate narrative or dialogue into their texts.

The chief obstacle to composing an opera—that is, a drama sung in its entirety from beginning to end—was the absence of a technique that would permit a single voice to represent an individual character on stage. Monody overcame that obstacle. And another new technique, **recitative**, permitted solo voices to declaim relatively large quantities of text in a rapid yet comprehensible manner. Recitative is a largely syllabic style of singing in which greater emphasis is given to the declamation of the text than to the creation of a melodic line. With recitative, composers could more nearly approximate the inflections of spoken speech even while indicating specific pitches and rhythms to be sung.

Not surprisingly, the three most important composers associated with the Florentine Camerata and the emergence of the *seconda prattica*—Jacopo Peri, Giulio Caccini, and Emilio de' Cavalieri—played central roles in creating the new genre of opera. Peri and Caccini collaborated at first but later competed with one another, with each claiming to have written the "first" opera, even while acknowledging the contributions of Cavalieri. These are the relevant compositions:

- *Dafne*, music by Giacopo Peri, text by Ottavio Rinuccini. Produced during carnival season of 1598, at the palace of Jacopo Corsi and also at the Medici court, both in Florence. The music is almost entirely lost.

- *Rappresentazione di Anima e di Corpo* ("Representation of the Soul and the Body"), music by Emilio de' Cavalieri, text by Agostino Manni. Produced in Rome, February 1600.

- *Euridice*, music by Peri, text by Rinuccini. Produced in Florence, October 1600; score published in February 1601.

- *Euridice*, music by Giulio Caccini, text by Rinuccini. Produced in its entirety in December 1602 but published January 1601.

Judging from the accounts of eyewitnesses, these earliest operas did not make a particularly strong impression. Although they mix recitative with polyphonic madrigals, arias (settings of strophic texts), choruses, and instrumental interludes, it is recitative that predominates. Effective as it might be for projecting a text, recitative could not provide sufficient musical variety over time to maintain the interest of spectators. At least one member of the original audience that took in Peri's *Euridice* in 1600 found this method of singing tedious, "like the chanting of the Passion" in church.[3]

Having established the new style of recitative, composers now faced the challenge of integrating it into their works in a way that was both musically and dramatically satisfying. Claudio Monteverdi's *Orfeo* of 1607 is generally acknowledged to be the first opera to have achieved this goal. It was certainly not the first opera (as it is sometimes mistakenly called), but it was the first to win critical acclaim. Part of its appeal lies in its keen sense of dramatic pacing, as illustrated in the extended excerpt from Act II in the Anthology.

*Orfeo* takes as its subject the most celebrated musician of ancient myth, Orpheus, whose music was so powerful that it persuaded the gods of the underworld to release Euridice from the realm of the dead. All of Act I and the first half of Act II of *Orfeo* are very much in the pastoral spirit, depicting an idyllic world of shepherds and shepherdesses, a world without care or sorrow. Orpheus himself gives expression to this untainted state in his "Vi ricorda," a strophic aria written in a manner reminiscent of the frottola, alternating between duple and triple meters within the compound meter of 6/8. The whole is introduced by a ritornello, which reappears before every strophe.

With the entrance of the Messenger bearing news of Euridice's death (*Ahi caso acerbo*), the mood shifts suddenly. The unprepared dissonance on the middle syllable of *acerbo* ("harsh") is particularly grating. Orpheus is stunned, but Monteverdi resists depicting this with a sudden outpouring of grief, opting instead for the utterly simple

((•• Listen

**CD4    Track 11**
**mysearchlab** (with scrolling translation)
MONTEVERDI
*Orfeo*
Score Anthology I/77

## Focus WHO'S WHO OF EARLY OPERA

It was in the Florentine home of **GIOVANNI DE' BARDI** (1534–1612), Count of Vernio, that the group calling itself the Camerata met from about 1573 until roughly 1587 to discuss the development of a new style of singing intended to match more closely that of the ancient Greeks. Bardi helped produce the intermedi performed at the wedding celebrations of the Grand Duke Ferdinando I de' Medici in 1589 (see Chapter 7) but left Florence for Rome in 1592.

**VINCENZO GALILEI** (ca. 1520–1591), father of the famous astronomer Galileo Galilei, was an active member of Bardi's Camerata in Florence. A lutenist and composer, he studied with the renowned Gioseffo Zarlino. Galilei published his influential *Dialogo della musica antica et della moderna* ("Dialogue on Ancient and Modern Music") in 1581. In this treatise, he argued for a modern attempt to recapture the essence of Greek drama through the texture of a solo voice accompanied by the lute.

**JACOPO PERI** (1561–1633), nicknamed *Il Zazzerino* ("the fair-haired boy") because of his reddish blond curls, was one of the leading musical figures in Florence, famous as both composer and singer. He was an active member of the Florentine Camerata in the 1580s and composed for and performed in the intermedi of 1589. He is the composer of what is arguably the first opera, *Dafne* (Florence, 1598). The libretto survives but the music is lost. His second opera, *Euridice*, was performed in Florence in October 1600 to celebrate the wedding of Maria de' Medici to Henri IV of France; its music has survived.

Another Florentine, **GIULIO CACCINI** (1545–1618), was one of the most celebrated singers of his time. When he turned to composition, he worked at first in collaboration with Peri, then later became his rival. He rushed his own setting of *Euridice* into print late in 1600 just before Peri's, although Caccini's setting would not actually be performed until 1602. Caccini's daughter Francesca would later rise to fame as a singer and composer.

The nobleman **JACOPO CORSI** (1561–1602) became one of the leading patrons of the arts in Florence after Bardi's departure in 1592. He continued the tradition of the Camerata with a circle that included the poet Rinuccini and the singer-composer Peri. It was under his patronage that Peri's *Dafne* was presented in 1598.

The poet and nobleman **OTTAVIO RINUCCINI** (1562–1621) collaborated with Bardi on the intermedi of 1589. He went on to write librettos for a number of early operas set to music by Peri (*Dafne*, *Euridice*), Caccini (*Euridice*), and Marco da Gagliano (*Dafne*), as well as a number of poems that became the basis of madrigals, including Monteverdi's setting of his *Zefiro torna* (Anthology I/72).

**EMILIO DE' CAVALIERI** (ca. 1550–1602), a Roman nobleman by birth, was active at the court of Florence from the 1580s onward. He helped produce the intermedi of 1589 and Peri's *Euridice* in 1600. He was also a composer in his own right: his *Rappresentatione di Anima et di Corpo . . . per recitar cantando* ("Representation of the Sprit and the Body . . . to Be Recited Through Singing") is one of the earliest dramatic works set entirely to music. First performed in February 1600 in Rome, it mingles monodic recitative with madrigal-like sections. The printed version of the work is also the first publication to feature a figured bass.

---

but all the more moving exclamation on two long notes ("*Ohimè*"). The messenger's narrative illustrates the declamatory powers of the new monodic style splendidly, climbing to a registral high when it quotes Euridice's dying word: "Orfeo."

Monteverdi also makes effective use of instrumentation here, contrasting the brightness of the strings in "Vi ricorda," for example, from the hushed, dark sound of the *organo di legno* (a small organ with wooden pipes), which makes its first appearance with the Messenger. The announcement of death has a distinctive sound.

Timbral contrast is one of many devices Monteverdi used to his advantage over his operatic predecessors. *Orfeo* benefited from the full financial backing of the Mantuan court, which allowed for a large ensemble and elaborate staging. Peri's and Caccini's earlier operas, by contrast, had been produced on relatively small budgets, which limited the number of musicians and the quality of the staging. Monteverdi's score to *Orfeo* calls for almost 40 instruments, an astonishing demand at the time.

- Continuo instruments—at various times, the score calls for harp, chitarrone, harpsichord, *organo di legno* and regal or reed organ, viola da gamba

- Stringed instruments—two *piccoli violini* (small violins), violins, violas, cellos, and bass viols

- Wind instruments—five trumpets, five trombones, two recorders, two cornetts

Monteverdi labels these instruments with extraordinary specificity at various points in his score, creating a distinctive timbre for particular scenes. This is especially evident in the Act III underworld scenes, which are dominated by an ensemble of five trombones, two bass viols, regal, and two cornetts. The low, rasping sound of these instruments gives this sequence a distinctly subterranean quality that perfectly matches the low bass voices of Caron and Pluto, the guardian and god of the underworld, respectively.

Orpheus's celebrated aria in Act III, "Possente spirto" (not included in the Anthology in part because of its length), is a masterpiece of both vocal and instrumental writing. Here,

**Operatic special effects.** The illustration on the left shows the behind-the-scenes machinery used to create the audience's view (shown on the right) of a scene in which the gods float through the clouds. This staging is from Giovanni Legrenzi's opera *Germanico sul Reno,* as performed in 1675 at the Teatro San Salvatore, Venice.

**Source:** Stage machinery (left) and Set design (right) for operas at the San Salvatore theatre in Venice, 1675 (pen & ink wash on paper), Italian School, (17th century) / Bibliotheque de l'Opera Garnier, Paris, France / Archives Charmet / The Bridgeman Art Library

Orpheus uses voice and lyre in turn to persuade Caron to allow him to cross the River Styx and enter the underworld. Each ritornello between the strophes of this plea has its own sound, each magically drawn from the lyre: two violins after the first strophe, two cornetti after the second, two harps after the third. Monteverdi published this aria in two versions, the first unadorned, the second ornamented, to indicate one of many performance options. Although justly renowned, this lengthy aria is in some respects atypical of *Orfeo* as a whole, for it is relatively static. Interestingly, it is only after this aria, with his more spontaneous and unaccompanied outburst on the words *Ahi, sventurato amante* ("Ah, unhappy lover that I am"), that Orpheus achieves his goal. Caron, unmoved by the carefully planned, instrumentally diverse, and artistically ornamented "Posente spirto," is overwhelmed by the passion of the more immediate and direct appeal that follows.

In its fifth and final act, *Orfeo* incorporates what would become a time-honored device in later opera, the *deus ex machina* (literally, "god from a machine"), in which a god (here, Apollo) descends from the skies to rescue the hero. But Monteverdi and his librettist, Alessandro Striggio, avoid an entirely happy ending: instead of restoring Euridice to life yet again, Apollo tells Orfeo that he will see "an image of her loveliness" at all times "in the sun and in the stars." It is a bittersweet conclusion.

From Florence and Mantua, opera soon took root and flourished in other cities on the Italian peninsula. Ruling dynasties saw the genre as a way to promote not only their poetic and musical sophistication but also their technological prowess as well, through dazzling stage displays that we might now think of as special effects. Courts began to commission operas routinely for festivals to celebrate weddings (the tangible joining of dynasties), the birth of heirs, birthdays of monarchs, state visits, coronations, funerals, and military victories.

In Rome, the powerful Barberini family built within the walls of its palace a theater seating no fewer than 3,000 spectators. It opened in 1632 with the opera *Sant' Alessio* ("Saint Alexis"), with music by Stefano Landi (1587–1639) and stage designs by Giovanni Lorenzo Bernini (1598–1680), better known as the architect of Saint Peter's

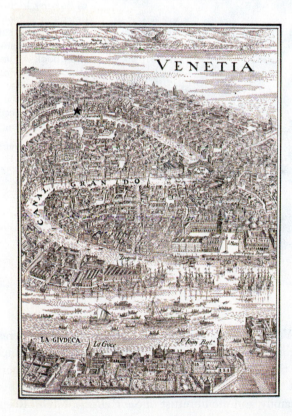

**Venice, 1638.** The city was the heart of the Venetian Republic, which prided itself on its perpetuation of the best traditions of ancient Rome. The Basilica of San Marco, where Monteverdi worked (and before him Adrian Willaert and Andrea and Giovanni Gabrieli) is visible near the center of this image.

**Source:** 19th era 2/Alamy

## Composer Profile

# Heinrich Schütz (1585–1672)

Born exactly 100 years before J. S. Bach, Heinrich Schütz was the leading German composer of the 17th century and a key figure in transmitting the *seconda prattica* north of the Alps. He mastered the polychoral style of the late Renaissance under the tutelage of Giovanni Gabrieli in Venice, adapted the newly developed technique of recitative to the German language, composed the first German opera, and maintained music at the court of Dresden for many years.

In spite of his progressive tendencies, Schütz believed that a proper grounding in counterpoint—the basis of the *prima prattica*—remained an essential element of compositional instruction. In the preface to his *Geistliche Chormusik* ("Sacred Choral Music"), a collection of a cappella motets in the style of the *prima prattica* published in 1648, he wrote,

It is thus that I have been persuaded to undertake a little work such as the present—without *basso continuo*—as a means . . . of admonishing many composers (in particular, the younger generation of Germans) of the need to crack this tough nut [the intricacies of traditional counterpoint] with

their own teeth and to seek out the sweet kernel and foundations of a just counterpoint before progressing to the *stile concertante* [composition with basso continuo]—wishing, in this way, to stand up to their first test. In Italy (true and honest school of all music), when, in my youth, I laid the foundations of my profession, it was normal practice for beginners to start by devising and publishing some little work, sacred or secular, without *basso continuo:* as, probably, is still the custom in these southern climes. I have wished to give this account of my personal experience in the study of music (and for the greater fame of our nation) that it be used by each man as he sees fit, and without wishing to discredit anyone. [4]

Schütz served for more than 50 years as Kapellmeister to the elector of Saxony, but his professional life was far from stable. The Thirty Years' War (1618–1648) forced him to flee Dresden at different times, and he spent extended periods in Denmark and Italy over the course of his career.

**Heinrich Schütz conducts the court chapel of the elector of Saxony.** In this allegorical depiction of Psalm 150 ("Praise the Lord . . . in His sanctuary"), Schütz leads his choristers from a large choir book. An image of King David (author of the Psalms) stands in front of the altar, and an orchestra composed of the instruments listed in Psalm 150 occupies middle balcony just beneath the organ.

**Source:** Choir (engraving) (b/w photo), German School, 17th century) / Private Collection / The Bridgeman Art Library

Basilica in the Vatican. Like a number of subsequent Roman operas, this one centered on a sacred subject. The church—the Jesuits in particular—quickly recognized the power of sung theater to convey moral and spiritual ideas. Singers for Landi's opera were recruited from the Papal Chapel; Pope Urban VIII was himself a member of the Barberini family, and the librettist of *Sant' Alessio*, Giulio Rospigliosi, would later

**Heinrich Schütz.** A portrait by the German painter Christoph Spetner.

**Source:** Lebrecht Music & Arts Photo Library

# PRINCIPAL WORKS

Aside from his early Italian madrigals, the lost opera *Dafne*, and a lost ballet on the legend of Orpheus, Schütz's output is almost entirely sacred, including works in both Latin and German. These are his best known compositions:

- The *Psalmen Davids* (1619), polyphonic choral works based on texts from the Psalms.

- The *Cantiones sacrae* (1625), a collection of 41 sacred motets.

- The *Symphoniae sacrae*, works for various combinations of voices and instruments published in three volumes over a period of 21 years (1629, 1647, 1650).

- The *Musicalische Exequien* (1636), a cycle of music appropriate for funeral services.

- The *Kleine geistliche Konzerte* ("Small Sacred Concertos"), motets for one to five voices with continuo, published in two books (1636, 1639). Of modest scale, they reflect the reduced means of the musical establishment at the Dresden court during the Thirty Years' War.

- The *Geistliche Chormusik* (1648), a set of 29 motets in the *prima prattica*.

- Three Gospel Passions (1664–1666), according to St. Luke, St. John, and St. Matthew, respectively; in addition he composed oratorios celebrating Christmas and Easter. Schütz labeled each of these five works *Historia*.

| KEY DATES IN THE LIFE OF SCHÜTZ | |
|---|---|
| 1585 | Born Köstritz (central Germany) on October 8. |
| 1599 | Becomes a chorister in the court chapel at Kassel. |
| 1609 | Sent to Venice by the landgrave of Hesse-Kassel to study under Giovanni Gabrieli; probably meets and possibly studies with Claudio Monteverdi as well. |
| 1611 | Publishes his first works, a set of five-part Italian madrigals. |
| 1612 | Returns from Venice and becomes court organist in Kassel. |
| 1617 | Appointed Kapellmeister to the elector of Saxony at Dresden; remains employed there for the rest of his career. |
| 1627 | Produces the first German opera, *Dafne* (the music is now lost). |
| 1630s–1640s | Compelled by the ravages of the Thirty Years' War to take extended leaves of absence in Copenhagen and Italy. |
| 1672 | Dies in Dresden on November 6. |

become Pope Clement IX. The themes of these "Roman operas" would soon find a new venue in the oratorio (see Chapter 9).

Not until 1637, however, with the establishment of the first public opera house (in Venice), did the new genre begin to reach beyond the closed circles of court and nobility. Open to any and all who could pay the price of admission, public opera houses were in fact partly supported by the state—a pattern of funding that continues to this day in Europe—but they extended the art of opera to a far wider audience than before.

With the change in audience came changes in production values and musical style. Cost precluded the widespread use of elaborate machinery and staging, which forced increased attention on the singers themselves. In place of lavish scenery, audiences were treated to lavish virtuosity. The musical style began to reflect the tastes of a wider audience, with greater emphasis on melody. Plots shifted from the mythological to the realistic or historical. Comic elements also found their way onto the stage. Composers and librettists who had once written to flatter and suit the monarchy now had to accommodate a wider range of tastes and sensibilities.

A comparison of Monteverdi's *Orfeo*, written for the court of Mantua in 1607, and his *L'incoronazione di Poppea* ("The Coronation of Poppea"), written for the Teatro Grimano in Venice in the season of 1642–1643, illustrates the differences between courtly opera of the early 17th century and public opera of the mid-17th century. *Orfeo*, for all its stylistic variety, is serious from beginning to end, without an ounce of comic relief. *Poppea*, in contrast, mixes high seriousness with comic scenes. It also requires relatively little in the way of chorus and orchestra and has no scenes that call for elaborate sets or machinery. *Poppea*'s very human characters, drawn from history, contrast vividly with the mythic, allegorical characters in *Orfeo*. Nero (Nerone), the emperor of Rome, is married to Octavia (Ottavia) but hopelessly in love with Poppea (Poppaea), who in turn is married to Otho (Ottone), a nobleman. Smitten by his love for Poppea, Nero turns to putty in her hands. At Poppea's urging, he banishes her husband to exile, divorces his own wife, and puts to death the philosopher Seneca for the simple reason that his moralizing is inconvenient for her. Poppea is, in short, a close cousin to Shakespeare's Lady Macbeth, a very realistic personality whose lust for power leads her to cut down every obstacle in her path.

This is scarcely the kind of scenario one finds in courtly opera, in which the heroes and heroines are unfailingly strong and virtuous. But it is precisely the type of story that would have appealed to a less aristocratic audience. Monteverdi was not writing for the lower classes, to be sure—that portion of the public could not afford tickets to the opera and probably would not have attended in any event—but he was writing for the lesser nobility, businessmen, bankers, and the huge influx of visiting dignitaries that came to Venice for carnival season every year. Opera soon became a big business in its own right.

As in *Orfeo*, Monteverdi uses a variety of dramatic and musical strategies to create a story that is consistently fast paced. The prologue to *Poppea* opens with a quarrel between Fortune (Fate) and Virtue, each of whom claims to be the more powerful. Love, a childlike cupid figure, intervenes to remind them that in spite of his small stature, he is in fact far more powerful than either Fate or Virtue, and he shows them the story of Poppea to prove his point.

As the curtain rises on Act I, Otho arrives home late one night to find Nero's bodyguards at his door. His discovery flows seamlessly into a comic dialogue between the two guards, which overlaps the closing lines of Otho's despair as he hides in the shadows. An extended dialogue (Scene iii, Anthology I/77) between Nero and Poppea follows immediately. The juxtaposition of serious and humorous, lyrical and declamatory is readily apparent in this sequence. The boundary between recitative and aria, which would become more pronounced in the opera of the later 17th and 18th centuries, is still quite fluid here.

((•–Listen

CD4     Track 12
**mysearchlab** (with scrolling translation)
MONTEVERDI
*L'incoronazione di Poppea*
Score Anthology I/78

# SACRED MUSIC

Composers applied the principles of the *seconda prattica* to sacred as well as secular music. Monteverdi's *Vespro della Beata Vergine* ("Vespers for the Blessed Virgin") of 1610, for example, is a veritable compendium of compositional techniques that incorporates both old and new styles. This cycle of 14 different movements includes polychoral numbers like *Nisi Dominus* for two, five-part choirs; the notated organ part essentially doubles the voices and does not play a structurally significant role. At the other end of the compositional spectrum is *Duo Seraphim*, a movement for three soloists and basso continuo, with virtuosity every bit as flamboyant as that found in the madrigal *Zefiro torna*. In between are works that blend old-style vocal part writing with instrumental ritornellos (*Ave maris stella*) or with instrumental parts that are structurally essential to the fabric of the work (*Domine ad adjuvandum*).

Heinrich Schütz may or may not have actually studied with Monteverdi in Venice, but he was certainly familiar with the older composer's music. Over the course of his long career, Schütz appropriated the innovations of the early Italian Baroque to write religious music for the chapels at Dresden and other courts. He exploited the German language for its dramatic power and solemnity, at the same time retaining the fervor of early Protestantism and a sense of directness that makes his music readily accessible.

*Singet dem Herren ein neues Lied* ("Sing unto the Lord a New Song") owes much to Monteverdi's style. The two solo violin lines of this work operate at times in counterpoint to the tenor solo, at times as an antiphonal "choir" of their own. Every verse or half verse of the psalm text (Psalm 96: 1–4) is differentiated by a new musical idea, yet the individual sections are connected through a slow but steady increase in register, rhythmic motion, and melodic intensity. In a series of carefully graduated steps, the listener is moved from stasis to a state of spiritual ecstasy at the end.

Like Monteverdi, Schütz never abandoned entirely the strict counterpoint associated with the *prima prattica*. On the contrary, he believed that training in *prima prattica* counterpoint was essential for aspiring composers (see Composer Profile: Heinrich Schütz). Still, even in a polychoral motet like *Saul, was verfolgst du mich?* he incorporates distinct traits of the *seconda prattica*. In a moment of high drama, Saul (later to become the Apostle Paul) is struck blind on the road to Damascus and hears the voice of God calling to him: "Saul, Saul, why dost thou persecute me?" The opening cry rises out of the low depths of the bass, punctuated by the basso continuo, eventually swelling into the combined voices of two, four-part choirs; six soloists; and two additional lines for unspecified treble instruments (usually played by violins). The echo of the cry is not just softer but eerily different in timbre (m. 21–23). God's words to Saul continue with a series of lines distributed among the various vocal and instrumental forces. Solo passages alternate with choral and instrument sections. The words rush ahead at times and hold back at others; certain of them (such as *löcken*, "to kick") are emphasized through the use of melisma; others ("Saul") make their effect through simpler declamation. The cumulative effect is stunning as it captures the reverberations of God's words in Saul's mind at the very moment in which Saul is struck blind.

**Listen**

CD4    Track 13
**mysearchlab** (with scrolling translation)
SCHÜTZ
*Singet dem Herren ein neues Lied*
Score Anthology I/79

**Listen**

CD4    Track 14
**mysearchlab**
SCHÜTZ
*Saul, was verfolgst du mich?*
Score Anthology I/80

## SUMMARY

The first half of the 17th century was a period of rapid and intense change in musical styles. The influence of the *seconda prattica* extended to all genres of vocal music, both secular and sacred, and the new genre of opera moved beyond strictly courtly venues to appeal to a wider public. By 1650, the basso continuo was well on its way to becoming a standard feature of music making throughout the European continent. Further developments in musical style over the next 100 years would build on all these precedents.

**Study** and **Review**
on **mysearchlab.com**

# Vocal Music, 1650–1750

By the middle of the 17th century, opera had established itself as both a critical and commercial success on the Italian peninsula. France began to develop its own traditions of sung drama around this time, and English composers made their first tentative steps in this direction toward the end of the century. But it was the distinctively Italian phenomenon of opera seria that would dominate the theaters of the continent from the 1680s through the whole of the 18th century. Sacred music was also deeply influenced by opera, not only in the new dramatic (but unstaged) genre of the oratorio, but even in such traditional genres as the motet and the Mass. The cantata, in turn, emerged as the principal genre of sacred music in Protestant Germany.

## OPERA

Beyond Italy, opera was slow to develop. France, Spain, and England all enjoyed their own forms of dramatic entertainment, many of which incorporated strong musical elements. But France did not see its first opera until 1662, and even then the new genre failed to win over the court. The reasons were partly political—opera was an imported art, and anti-Italian forces at the court conspired to undermine its introduction into France—but mostly aesthetic. The French nobility found no compelling reason to listen to a drama sung in its entirety from beginning to end. Singing, by its very nature takes longer than speaking, which means an opera necessarily has less text than a play of equivalent duration. And with the possible exception of recitative, a sung text is typically more difficult to understand than a declaimed text. The great French dramatist Pierre Corneille (1606–1684) pointed out with some pride in the preface to one of his plays that he "had taken great care not to let anything be sung that is essential to understanding the drama," on the grounds that different voices singing at once obscure the clarity of the words.[1]

In Spain, opera found similarly inhospitable soil. The celebrated dramatist Pedro Calderón de la Barca (1600–1681), like Corneille, allowed for music in his plays but not at dramatically critical moments. Calderón de la Barca did write the libretto for the first Spanish-language opera, *Celos aun del aire matan* ("Even Groundless Jealousy Can Kill," 1660), by Juan Hidalgo (ca. 1600–1685), but the work had few immediate successors. Attempts at opera in Germany were equally sporadic. As early as 1627, Heinrich Schütz composed an opera— *Dafne* (now lost) to a text by the poet Martin Opitz—but operas in German subsequently languished, not to emerge as a thriving art form until the late 18th century. The few German composers who did write operas preferred on the whole to set Italian texts, with the notable exception of Reinhard Keiser (1674–1739).

In England, the genre of the **masque** enjoyed a certain vogue in the 17th century. This was a form of entertainment rather like the Florentine intermedi, a mixture of declaimed poetry, songs, scenery, dance, and instrumental music. The first opera produced in England was a **pasticcio** (Italian for "hodgepodge"), a work whose individual parts were written by several different composers. But *The Siege of Rhodes*, produced in 1656, was a critical and commercial failure, largely because the English, like the French, resisted the idea of a drama being sung from beginning to end.

Another reason for opera's lack of appeal compared to the ballet in France and the masque in England may have been that opera was mere spectacle, whereas ballet and masque were participatory events, in which the barriers between stage and audience were fluid or even nonexistent. Members of the court did not just watch these entertainments; they mixed with the performers on stage. How could opera compete with the thrill, for a noblewoman, of dancing with Zeus, or for a nobleman, of dancing with Venus? (See the illustration "Dancing with the gods," p. 198.)

## France: *Comédie-ballet* and *Tragédie en musique*

The preferred vehicle for musical theater in France during the first two-thirds of the 17th century was the *ballet de cour*, a genre that arose in the early 1580s. Combining song, dance, and instrumental music, these courtly ballets were heavily allegorical, their heroes almost invariably thinly veiled stand-ins for the reigning monarch. Louis XIV himself—by all accounts an accomplished dancer—took part in a number of productions. (See the illustration "Louis XIV as the Sun King" on p. 189).

It was an Italian immigrant, Jean-Baptiste Lully (1632–1687; born Giovanni Battista Lulli), who established sung drama in France in the guise of the *comédie-ballet*, a new genre that was part opera, part ballet. A superb entrepreneur as well as a gifted composer, Lully skillfully negotiated the royal bureaucracy that controlled theatrical productions in France to advance his career. In 1672, through a series of legal maneuvers aided by his close personal connections with Louis XIV, Lully purchased a patent that gave him the exclusive right to produce sung dramas in France. Then, with the poet Philippe Quinault (1635–1688) and a team of handpicked musicians and stage designers, he created a new operatic genre, the *tragédie en musique* (also known as *tragédie lyrique*), composing and producing one a year between 1673 and 1687. Although supported and financed by the court, these works were accessible to the paying public when performed at the Palais-Royal in Paris, which Lully took over in 1674.

Lully and Quinault drew on classical mythology and chivalric romances for subject matter for their operas, but the plots were widely understood as veiled commentaries (always favorable, of course) on recent events at court. The hero of any given opera was almost invariably understood to be an allegorical counterpart to Louis XIV. In *Armide* (1686), the hero Renaud obeys the call of duty and spurns the enchantment of the sorceress for whom the opera is named.

Structurally, a *tragédie en musique* consists of these parts:

((•—|Listen

**CD4  Tracks 15–16**
**mysearchlab** (with scrolling translation)
LULLY
*Armide*
Score Anthology I/81

- An overture that moves from a slow introduction with dotted rhythms to a fast imitative section. The dotted rhythms, associated with royalty, were an homage to the splendor of the king. This form eventually came to be known as the **French overture** and would be adopted by many composers—Italian and German as well as French—over subsequent decades.

- An allegorical prologue closely connected to some recent event at the court but always flattering to the king, explicitly or implicitly.

## Composer Profile

# Jean-Baptiste Lully (1632–1687)

The founder of the French operatic tradition was an Italian. Giovanni Battista Lulli—better known by the French version of his name, Jean-Baptiste Lully—was born the son of a poor miller in Florence. He did not arrive in France until the age of 14, but he soon won favor at the court through his talents as a dancer, singer, and violinist. By the end of his life he had established himself as a wealthy cavalier at the French court and the most important figure in the musical world of 17th-century France.

An admiring account of a 1668 performance at the court of Versailles of Lully's ballet *Les fêtes de l'Amour et de Bacchus* ("The Festivities of Amor and Bacchus"), which included vocal passages, gives some indication of the esteem in which the composer was held:

It may be said that in this work, the Sieur de Lully has discovered the secret of satisfying and charming everyone, for never was there anything so fine or so well devised. If one takes the dances, there is no step that does not speak of the action the Dancers are to perform, or whose accompanying gestures are not as good as words that may be understood. If one takes the Music, there is nothing which does not perfectly express all the passions, delighting the spirit of the Hearers. But what was never before seen is that pleasing harmony of voices, that symphony [i.e., sounding together] of instruments, that delightful union of different choruses, those sweet songs, those tender and amorous dialogues, those echoes, in short, that admirable conduct in every part, in which it might always be seen from the first words that the Music was increasing, and having begun with a single voice, it concluded with a concert of over one hundred persons, seen all at once upon the same Stage, uniting their instruments, their voices and their steps in a harmony and cadence that brings the Play to an end, leaving everyone in a state of admiration that cannot be adequately expressed.[2]

Lully died in service to his profession. While conducting his ensemble, he accidentally struck his foot with the sharp cane he was using to pound out the beat. The blow must have been severe because gangrene soon set in, and he died of blood poisoning at the age of 54.

Lully was one of the first composers whose music continued to be performed long after his death. His works for the stage were presented repeatedly in Germany, Italy, and England in the 18th century, and they remained popular in France for more than one hundred years.

## PRINCIPAL WORKS

### Ballets

Lully's earliest works for the French court were ballets, many of which incorporated song as well: *Le Bourgeois Gentilhomme* (based on Molière's eponymous play) and *Psyché*.

- Five acts of entirely sung drama, each divided into several different scenes.

- Many *divertissements* (interludes) within individual acts that provide ample opportunities for displays of dancing and choral song. Instrumental music figures prominently in these divertissements in the form of **symphonies**, a term used at the time to describe any music for a large ensemble.

The vocal portions of each opera move fluidly between the declamatory *récit* (recitative) and the lyrical *air* (aria), mixed with occasional duets, trios, and choruses. Lully used measured but highly supple rhythms to project the fluid prosody of the French language. The music is replete with constantly shifting meters that go largely unnoticed in performance because they match the declamation of the text so well.

In the widely admired scene at the end of Act II of *Armide*, the sorceress Armide (Armida) is about to kill the crusadere-knight Renaud (Rinaldo), who is asleep under her spell. But she cannot bring herself to do the deed: she hates Renaud because he is indifferent to her beauty, yet she also loves him. The opera, based on Torquato Tasso's

## Operas

At least half a dozen of Lully's operas stayed in the active repertory of the French stage until the Revolution. Most notable among these are *Cadmus et Hermione*, *Alceste*, *Atys*, *Persée*, *Roland*, and *Armide*.

## Other Genres

In addition to his dramatic works, Lully also wrote a set of trio sonatas, a setting of the Mass, a Te Deum, and a number of motets.

**Jean-Baptiste Lully.** Lully began his steady rise to a position of power at the court of Louis XIV, becoming "Secretary to the King and Superintendent of the King's Music." One contemporary praised his talents as surpassing those of Orpheus.

**Source:** RMN-Grand Palais/Musée Condé, Chantilly, France/Art Resource, NY

| KEY DATES IN THE LIFE OF LULLY | |
|---|---|
| 1632 | Born in Florence (Italy) on November 28, the son of a miller. |
| 1646 | Taken to Paris as a page to a cousin of Louis XIV because of his vocal talent. |
| 1652 | Becomes a ballet dancer in the service of Louis XIV and is soon composing court ballets. |
| 1661 | Appointed superintendent of music at the French court. |
| 1662 | Appointed music master to the French royal family. |
| 1672 | Receives a patent to establish the Royal Academy of Music, essentially an opera house. |
| 1687 | Dies in Paris on March 22. |

epic poem *Gerusalemme liberata* ("Jerusalem Liberated"), will end badly for Armide—Renaud's love for her, induced through subsequent spells, does not last—but for the moment, she is in complete command of everything but herself. The scene divides into two sections: (1) Armide's monologue and (2) a summons to her assisting demons. The opening monologue moves fluidly through a large quantity of text. The declamation here is more melodic than most Italian recitative, and the opening thematic idea will in fact provide the basis for the more dance-like second part of this scene.

Contemporary audiences found this scene spellbinding. "When Armide nerves herself to stab Renaud," commented the French nobleman Jean-Laurent Le Cerf de la Viéville (1674–1707), "I have twenty times seen the entire audience in the grip of fear, neither breathing nor moving, their whole attention in their ears and eyes, until the instrumental air which concludes the scene allowed them to draw breath again, after which they exhaled with a murmur of pleasure and admiration."[3]

Lully's monopoly on sung drama was both a blessing and a curse for the development of French opera. With the best talent of the time at his disposal, he established a model for the genre that would prevail for more than one hundred years. But for

**Lully's *Armide*, Act II, scene 5.** In this scene from the 2008 production at the Théâtre des Champs-Elysée conducted by William Christie, the sorceress Armide (Stéphanie D'Oustrac) is about to kill the sleeping Renaud (Paul Agnew) but pulls back at the last moment, overcome by her tender feelings toward the knight.

**Source:** Collette Masson / Roger-Viollet / The Image Works

the 15 years from 1672, when he secured his royal patent, until his death in 1687, no other composer had any incentive to become proficient at opera. Although composers like André Campra (1660–1744), Marc-Antoine Charpentier (1643–1704), and Marin Marais (1656–1728) later achieved some success in the genre, Lully's operas continued to cast a shadow over the French musical landscape long after his death.

Not until the appearance of the first operas by Jean-Philippe Rameau (1683–1764) in the 1730s did Lully's music find a serious rival on the French stage. Rameau was an unlikely candidate for theatrical success. He had won great fame as a composer of keyboard music and as a theorist, but he did not begin writing operas until he was in his 50s. The great popular success of his opera *Castor et Pollux* (1737) provoked dismay among Lully's admirers (the "Lullistes"), leading to a pamphlet war between them and the followers of Rameau (the "Ramistes"). Like so many of the artistic controversies that arose out of the French court in the 18th century, this one seems to have had less to do with aesthetics than with politics. Rameau himself insisted that he had taken the operas of Lully as his model, but his critics accused him of writing music that was overly intricate and "unnatural," particularly in its rich harmonies. Yet it is precisely this quality that makes his operas so engaging to us today. Ironically, Rameau would be held up as the very embodiment of French music a generation later in yet another controversy, this time between pro-French and pro-Italian operatic camps, the so-called War of the Buffoons (see Chapter 13).

## Italy: Opera seria

**Opera seria** ("serious opera")—so called because of its usually tragic content and in contrast to the later *opera buffa* ("comic opera"; see Chapter 13)—was far and away the most important type of opera cultivated between about 1680 and 1770. Developed in Italy and sung almost exclusively in Italian, opera seria became an international genre, exported to every corner of Europe. The German-born composer George Frideric Handel (see Composer Profile) composed and produced some of the finest examples of the genre in London in the early 18th century. Opera seria underwent many changes over the period in which it flourished, but its central conventions remained more or less constant.

The typical opera seria libretto draws its subject matter from classical antiquity. Rulers are always presented in a favorable light, heroic and magnanimous: they place duty and honor above personal gain. The texts balance the demands of drama and music by alternating action (usually conveyed through recitative) with moments of reflection (conveyed through aria). Librettists therefore crafted their texts in a way that would provide each character with an appropriate number of arias: the more important the role, the more arias. This provided a showcase for the great solo singing that audiences flocked to the theater to hear.

**The Da Capo Aria.** The large majority of the arias in the typical opera seria are **da capo arias**. The name comes from the indication at the end of the second section: *da capo*—literally, "from the head," or, as we would say today, "from the top," that is, the

---

## Primary Evidence    THE PREMISE OF OPERA: A DISSENTING VOICE

*The French nobleman Charles de Marguetel de Saint-Denis, Seigneur de Saint-Evremond (1610–1703), was a soldier and man of letters with strong connections to the British aristocracy. (Like Handel, he would be buried in the Poets' Corner of Westminster Abbey.) In a letter written in 1678 to the Duke of Buckingham, Saint-Evremond takes issue with the very premise of opera: the idea of singing an entire drama from beginning to end. He also criticizes contemporary composers for inserting rather too much of themselves into current operas, at the expense of the drama.*

■ ■ ■

There is another thing in Operas so contrary to Nature, that I cannot be reconciled to it; and that is the singing of the whole Piece, from beginning to end, as if the Persons represented were ridiculously match'd, and had agreed to treat in musick both the most common, and most important affairs of Life. Is it to be imagin'd that a master calls his servant, or sends him on an errand, singing; that one friend imparts a secret to another, singing; that men deliberate in council, singing; that orders in time of battle are given, singing; and that men are melodiously killed with swords and darts? This is the downright way to lose the life of Representation, which without doubt is preferable to that of Harmony: for, Harmony ought to be no more than a bare attendant, and the great matters of the Stage have introduc'd it as pleasing, not as necessary, after they have perform'd all that relates to the Subject and Discourse. Nevertheless, our thoughts run more upon

the Musician than the Hero in the Opera: *Luigi, Cavalli,* and *Cesti,* are still present to our imagination. The mind not being able to conceive a Hero that sings, thinks of the Composer that set the song; and I don't question but that in the Operas at the Palace-Royal, *Lulli* is an hundred times more thought of than *Theseus* or *Cadmus.*

I pretend not, however, to banish all manner of singing from the Stage: there are some things which ought to be sung, and others that may be sung without trespassing against reason or decency: Vows, Prayers, Praises, Sacrifices, and generally all that relates to the service of the Gods, have been sung in all Nations, and in all times; tender and mournful Passions express themselves naturally in a sort of querulous tone; the expressions of Love in its birth; the irresolution of a soul toss'd by different motions, are proper matters for Stanzas, as Stanzas are for Musick. Every one knows that the Chorus was introduc'd upon the Grecian Theatre, and it is not to be denied, but that with equal reason it might be brought upon ours. So far, in my opinion, Musick may be allow'd: all that belongs to Conversation, all that relates to Intrigues and Affairs, all that belongs to Council and Action, is proper for Actors to rehearse, but ridiculous in the mouth of Musicians to sing. The Grecians made admirable Tragedies where they had some singing; the Italians and the French make bad ones, where they sing all.

**Source:** *The Letters of Saint-Evremond,* ed. and trans. John Hayward (London: George Routledge & Sons, 1930), pp. 207–9. Used by permission of the publisher.

beginning. Having finished the B section, the performer goes back to the beginning of A and continues to the end of that section. The A section must always end in the tonic, because in performance, it marks the end of the entire aria.

On paper, this looks like a static, repetitive scheme. In performance, the apparent repetition is in fact no repetition at all. Singers were expected to embellish the A section of an aria on its return, transforming long notes into ornaments or runs, altering entire passages, adding new and spectacularly high (or low) notes, and generally rewriting the music to show off their particular vocal strengths. Any singer who performed the A section the second time around exactly the same as the first would probably be booed off the stage—or worse, pelted with rotten vegetables.

Within each A and B section, the ritornello principle plays a central role, as Ptolemy's aria *L'empio, sleale, indegno*, from Act I of Handel's opera *Giulio Cesare in Egitto* illustrates.

## *Focus*  THE POET OF OPERA SERIA: PIETRO METASTASIO (1698–1782)

Pietro Metastasio was the quintessential librettist of opera seria. In Greek, *metastasio* means "transformation," and that is exactly what this poet brought to the world of the opera libretto in the early 18th century. Born Pietro Antonio Domenico Bonaventura Trapassi (*trapassi* or *trapassamento* also means "transformation" in Italian), the young poet wrote his first tragedy at the age of 15; his first major success as a librettist came in 1723 with *Didone abbandonata* ("Dido Abandoned"), and from then on he was the favorite librettist of his era. Some of the leading composers of 18th-century opera—Leonardo Leo, Johann Adolph Hasse, Niccolò Jommelli, Antonio Caldara, Giovanni Battista Pergolesi, and Christoph Willibald Gluck—used his texts. All told, more than 700 operas are based on Metastasio's librettos. Some of them were set more than 60 times by different composers.

One of Mozart's early oratorios, *La Betulia liberata*, and his last opera, *La Clemenza di Tito* ("The Clemency of Titus"), were both set to adaptations of Metastasian texts. A Metastasio libretto provides a clear delineation between recitative and aria, with ample material for the virtuoso arias that gave composers and soloists the opportunity to show their skill, to the delight of opera audiences.

Metastasio did not always approve of the way his arias were set. "The singers of the present times," he noted late in his life, "wholly forget that their business is to imitate the speech of men, with numbers [i.e., rhythms] and harmony. On the contrary, they believe themselves more perfect, in proportion as their performance is remote from human nature. Their models are Nightingales, Flageolets, Crickets, and Grasshoppers; not the personages they represent or their affections."[4]

**A musical circle at the royal court of Madrid, ca. 1750.** From left to right: Metastasio (with pen in hand), the soprano Teresa Castellini, the famed castrato Farinelli, Jacopo Amigoni (the painter of this group portrait), and Farinelli's dog and pageboy.

**Source:** Portrait Group of the Singer Farinelli and Friends, c. 1750–52 (oil on canvas), Amigoni, Jacopo (1675–1752) / National Gallery of Victoria, Melbourne, Australia / Felton Bequest / The Bridgeman Art Library

## STRUCTURE OF THE DA CAPO ARIA

| Themes | A | | B | | A repeated (da capo) | |
|---|---|---|---|---|---|---|
| Harmony | I | I | (Variable) | | I | I |

Ptolemy (Tolomeo), co-ruler of Egypt with his sister, Cleopatra, is threatened by the arrival of the conquering Julius Caesar (Giulio Cesare). To appease him, Ptolemy has presented him with the severed head of Caesar's Roman rival, Pompey. Caesar is horrified, and when Ptolemy learns that his "gift" has been rejected, he expresses his scorn for Caesar in an aria. *L'empio, sleale, indegno*, opens with an orchestral ritornello that at once establishes the key, mood, and theme of the aria. The opening solo (Solo 1) reiterates the orchestral material in the same key, but now with words. The voice eventually carries the music from E♭ Major to B♭ Major (m. 32). The new key signals the onset of Ritornello 2, a brief return of the instruments alone, offering the singer the opportunity to catch his breath. The soloist reenters in m. 36 and leads the music through a variety of keys before finally bringing it to the dominant at m. 58. This half cadence is a signal to orchestra and audience alike that the **cadenza** is about to begin. From the Italian word for "cadence," the cadenza is a truly soloistic moment, with no accompaniment of the orchestra at all; the soloist instead improvises (or at least gives the appearance of improvising) while putting on a display of virtuosity. Cadenzas are typically indicated in the score of an aria by a simple fermata sign, and the cadenza in the da capo performance of the A section was expected to be even more flamboyant than in the first. After this display of unaccompanied virtuosity, the second solo section concludes on the tonic (m. 61). At this point the third and final ritornello enters to bring this section of the aria—and on its return da capo, the entire aria—to closure on the tonic.

The ritornello principle is reinforced by the tonal structure: the A section begins and ends in the tonic, with a contrasting key in between. The B section, in C minor, beginning at the words *Ma perda pur la vita* is even briefer and consists of a single solo unit; there is no ritornello within this section itself. When considered within the context of the aria as a whole, however, this B section is framed by two ritornello passages: Ritornello 3 from the end of A, and Ritornello 1 from the da capo resumption of the aria's beginning. In a sense, then, the B section as a whole can be seen as a large Solo 3:

((•• Listen

CD5   Tracks 1–3
**mysearchlab** (with scrolling translation)
HANDEL
*Giulio Cesare*
Score Anthology I/82

## HANDEL, *GIULIO CESARE*, ACT I, *L'EMPIO, SLEALE, INDEGNO*: THE A SECTION

| | Rit. 1 | Solo 1 | Rit. 2 | Solo 2 | Cadenza | Rit. 3 |
|---|---|---|---|---|---|---|
| Measure | 1 | 12 | 32 | 36 | 58 | 61 |
| Key | E♭ Major | E♭ Major | B♭ Major | Unstable | V/E♭ Major | E♭ Major |
| Harmony | I | | V | | V/I | I |

## HANDEL, *GIULIO CESARE*, ACT I, *L'EMPIO, SLEALE, INDEGNO*: THE STRUCTURE OF THE WHOLE IN PERFORMANCE

| A | | | | | B | A (da capo) | | | | | |
|---|---|---|---|---|---|---|---|---|---|---|---|
| Rit. 1 | Solo 1 | Rit. 2 | Solo 2 | Rit. 3 | Solo 3 | Rit. 4 | Solo 4 | Rit. 5 | Solo 5 | Rit. 6 | |
| I | | V | | I | vi | I | | V | | I | |

**Recitative.**   By the second half of the 17th century, aria and recitative were becoming increasingly distinct. Opera seria uses *recitativo semplice*—"simple recitative," accompanied only by the basso continuo—for extended passages of prose, as in a monologue or rapid exchanges among characters. This kind of recitative would later come to be called **secco** ("dry") **recitative** because of its timbral simplicity, but it was precisely its sparseness of sound that made this type of recitative so useful in moving a plot forward through large quantities of text. Arias, by contrast, tend to be dramatically static but psychologically quite revealing, allowing characters to reflect on what has just transpired in the recitative. *Recitativo accompagnato*—**accompanied recitative**, supported or

## *Primary Evidence*   FRENCH VERSUS ITALIAN OPERA, 1702

*Comparisons between French and Italian culture in all its aspects, including music, were common in the 17th and 18th centuries. The author of this* Comparison between the French and Italian Music and Operas, *François Raguenet (ca. 1660–1722), was a French priest, physician, and historian. He astutely describes the salient differences between the operas of the two nations. The anonymous translation here is from a contemporary English edition (London, 1709).*

■ ■ ■

Our operas are writ much better than the Italian; they are regular, coherent designs; and, if repeated without the music, they are as entertaining as of our other pieces that are purely dramatick. . . .

On the other hand, the Italian operas are poor, incoherent rhapsodies, without any connexion or design; all their pieces, properly speaking, are patched up with thin, insipid scraps; their scenes consist of some trivial dialogues, or soliloquy, at the end of which they foist in one of their best airs, which concludes the scene. . . .

Besides, our operas have a farther advantage over the Italian, in respect of the voice, and that is the bass, which is so frequent among us, and so rarely to be met with in Italy. . . . When the persons of gods or kings, a Jupiter, Neptune, Priam or Agamemnon, are brought on the stage, our actors, with their deep voices, give 'em an air of majesty, quite different from that of the falsettists or the feign'd basses among the Italians, which have neither depth nor strength. Besides, the blending of the basses with the upper parts forms an agreeable contrast, and makes us perceive the beauties of the one from the opposition they meet with from the other, a pleasure to which the Italians are perfect strangers, the voices of their singers, who are, for the most part, castrati, being perfectly like those of their women.

The Italian language is much more naturally adapted to Musick than ours; their vowels are all sonorous, whereas above half of ours are mute, or at best bear a very small part in pronunciation; so that, in the first place, no cadence, or beautiful passage, can be form'd upon the syllables that consist of those vowels, and, in second place, one cannot hear but half the words, so that we are left to guess at what the French are singing, whereas the Italian is perfectly understood. . . .

The Italians are more bold and hardy in their airs, than the French; they carry their point farther, both in their tender songs and those that are more lively, as well as in their other compositions; nay, they often unite styles, which the French think incompatible. The French, in those compositions that consist of many parts, seldom regard more than that which is principal, whereas the Italians usually study to make all the parts equally shining, and beautiful. In short, the invention of the one is inexhaustible, but the genius of the other is narrow and constrain'd.

It is not to be wonder'd that the Italians think our musick dull and stupefying, that, according to their taste, it appears flat and insipid, if we consider the nature of the French airs compar'd to those of the Italian. The French in their airs aim at the soft, the easie, the flowing, and coherent; the whole air is of the same tone, or if sometimes they venture to vary it, they do it with so many preparations, they so qualifie it, that still the air seems to be as natural and consistent as if they had attempted no change at all; there is nothing bold and adventurous in it; it's all equal and of a piece. But the Italians pass boldly, and in an instant from sharps to flats and from flats to sharps; they venture the boldest cadences, and the most irregular dissonances; and their airs are so out of the way that they resemble the compositions of no other nation in the world.

**Source:** François Raguenet, *A Comparison between the French and Italian Musick and Operas* (London: William Lewis, 1709).

punctuated by the full orchestra rather than the basso continuo alone—was reserved for moments of high emotion and drama, such as Julius Caesar's monologue (*Alma del gran Pompeo*) at the tomb of Pompey in Handel's *Giulio Cesare*.

### Virtuosity and the exit convention.

The da capo aria offered singers the perfect vehicle for demonstrating their vocal prowess. Yet virtuosity—when it comes in the form of very high or low notes, fast passages, or rapid ornaments—can obscure the intelligibility of the words being sung. But because the texts of da capo arias tend to be relatively brief, singers typically articulate the same verbal phrases multiple times, so that an audience that has missed a word or two on the first run-through can pick them up on the second.

The demand for virtuosity also led to personal rivalries among singers, resulting in a staging device known as the **exit convention**. After finishing an aria (presumably to great applause), an opera seria character almost always leaves the stage. This allows for curtain calls, gives the singer who has just finished an aria the chance to recover off-stage, and prevents him or her from upstaging the singer whose turn it is to sing the next aria.

### The castrato.

Soprano singers were so highly prized in the 17th and 18th centuries—for male as well as female roles—that young boys with promising voices would sometimes be castrated, which prevented a change of voice at puberty. The effect of a grown

**Steps to Parnassus.** Johann Joseph Fux's *Gradus ad Parnassum* ("Steps to Parnassus") was the most important contrapuntal treatise of the 18th century. Originally published in Latin (Vienna, 1725), it was later translated into English, French, German, and Italian. The frontispiece of the original edition emphasizes the pedagogical nature of the work. By learning his craft one step at a time, the composer (center) has reached the pinnacle of Mount Parnassus, mythological home of the Muses. Here he receives the laurel crown of triumph from Apollo himself. Pegasus, Apollo's winged horse, rejoices at the accomplishment, while the nine Muses look on with approval.

**Source:** Mark Evan Bonds, UNC Libraries Photographic Services

# George Frideric Handel (1685–1759)

Although Handel and J. S. Bach were born in the same year within one hundred miles of each other, they never met, and their subsequent careers as composers could scarcely have been more different. Bach spent his entire life in central Germany, whereas Handel traveled widely throughout Europe.

After beginning his career near home, Handel moved to Italy in 1706, where he remained for several years, establishing a name for himself as a composer of operas and oratorios. In 1710, he returned to Germany as music director for the elector of Hanover but soon journeyed to England, where a production of his opera *Rinaldo* the following year won great acclaim. In 1712, still in the service of the elector, he took up residence in England, where his music continued to find favor. When the elector ascended the English throne as George I in 1714, Handel was perfectly positioned to enjoy the new king's patronage and support. He associated himself with the newly founded Royal Academy of Music in 1720, but like so many operatic enterprises of the time, it eventually foundered due to financial weakness, political intrigue, and quarrels among performers. Handel later helped found another opera series at the King's Theater in 1729, but like the first undertaking, this one never achieved financial security. It was also involved in a rivalry with a competing company—the Opera of the Nobility—that set many critical tongues wagging. By the mid-1730s, the composer was devoting more and more of his energies to oratorio, and he abandoned opera altogether in 1741.

Handel was one of the first composers whose music has remained steadily popular with the public and has therefore come down to us in an uninterrupted performance tradition. This is not to say that performance styles have gone unchanged: Mozart, for example, was commissioned to "modernize" the orchestration of *Messiah* to include clarinets in the late 1780s, and in the 19th century, Mendelssohn and Brahms would make similar arrangements of other works by Handel.

Handel is buried in the "Poets' Corner" in Westminster Abbey, an honor reflecting both the high esteem in which his contemporaries held him and the idea—relatively new at the time—that composers were artists on the same level as poets. He was also the first composer to be the subject of a separately published biography, John Mainwaring's *Memoirs of the Late G. F. Handel*, published in London in 1760.

In 1784, 25 years after Handel's death, Westminster Abbey was the scene of an enormous festival dedicated to

**George Frideric Handel.** Handel composes at the clavichord, ca. 1730. His head is shaved so as to better accommodate a wig, but he wears a turban here, partly for warmth and partly because the sight of a man's shaved head in public was considered obscene at the time.

**Source:** Alfredo Dagli Orti/The Art Archive/Corbis

his music. The historian Charles Burney wrote the following fond reminiscence of the composer for the occasion:

> The figure of Handel was large, and he was somewhat corpulent and unwieldy in his motions; but his countenance . . . was full of fire and dignity, and as such impressed ideas of superiority and genius. He was impetuous, rough and peremptory in his manners and conversation, but totally devoid of ill-nature or malevolence; indeed, there was an original humor and pleasantry in his most lively sallies of anger or impatience, which, with his broken English, were extremely risible. His natural propensity to wit and humor and happy manner of relating common occurrences in an uncommon way enabled him to throw persons and things into very ridiculous attitudes.[6]

# PRINCIPAL WORKS

## Operas

Handel's *Rinaldo* (1711) was one of the first Italian operas to win public acclaim in London, and the composer was quick to build on this early success. The most acclaimed of his subsequent operas (all in Italian) are *Giulio Cesare* (1724), *Rodelinda* (1725), *Orlando* (1733), *Ariodante* (1735), and *Serse* (1738). Unlike his oratorios, Handel's operas were almost entirely forgotten after his death: only one of them is known to have been performed on a stage anywhere between 1754 and 1920. Thanks to the combined efforts of scholars and musicians, opera lovers have recently begun to rediscover the wonders of this repertory.

## Oratorios, Odes, and Cantatas

Handel wrote Italian oratorios early in his career. *Esther* (1732), his first in English and the first oratorio of any kind performed in London, set off a great wave of enthusiasm for the genre there. Many successes followed: *Saul* (1739), *Israel in Egypt* (1739), *Messiah* (1742), *Samson* (1743), *Semele* (1744), *Hercules* (1745), *Judas Maccabeus* (1747), *Joshua* (1748), and *Jephtha* (1752).

Handel also set to music a number of nonsacred texts—odes and serenades—that are very much in the spirit of the oratorio. Among the more notable of these are *Alexander's Feast* and the *Ode for Saint Cecilia's Day* (both set to texts by the poet John Dryden) and *L'Allegro, il Penseroso ed il Moderato* (to a text by John Milton). Less well known but well worth exploring are the many secular cantatas, mostly early works in Italian and mostly for solo voice and instruments. Handel drew on these compositions later in life and reworked a number of movements for later operas and oratorios.

## Sacred Music

At various times and places, Handel wrote music for the Roman Catholic and Lutheran churches, but the bulk of his sacred music, reflecting his long residence in his adopted home, was for the Anglican church. These works include the Chandos Anthems and music for various royal weddings, coronations, and funerals.

## Orchestral Music

In addition to his concerti grossi and concertos for organ (see Chapter 10), Handel also wrote several orchestral suites that remain great favorites: three suites called *Water Music* (written for a royal procession down the River Thames in 1717) and one entitled *Music for the Royal Fireworks*, composed in 1749 to celebrate the Treaty of Aix-la-Chapelle, which ended the War of Austrian Succession.

## Keyboard and Chamber Music

Handel's works for harpsichord are not as often played or studied today as those by Bach, but they were well known during the composer's lifetime. Most of them fall under the category of suites or variations. They were directed primarily at amateurs, as were the sonatas op. 1 (for flute, recorder, oboe, or violin and basso continuo) and the trio sonatas of op. 2 and op. 5.

| KEY DATES IN THE LIFE OF HANDEL | |
|---|---|
| 1685 | Born in Halle (central Germany) on February 23. |
| 1697 | Becomes assistant organist at Halle Cathedral at the age of 12. |
| 1702 | Enters law school but leaves after a year. |
| 1703 | Moves to Hamburg and plays violin in one of the opera houses there. |
| 1705 | Composes two opere serie, which are produced in Hamburg. |
| 1706 | Travels throughout Italy, where he continues to write operas and composes his first oratorios. |
| 1710 | Returns to Germany as Kapellmeister to the elector of Hanover. |
| 1711 | First visit to England; his opera *Rinaldo* is greeted there with praise. |
| 1712 | Takes up permanent residence in England. |
| 1714 | His German patron, the elector of Hanover, becomes King George I of England. |
| 1720 | Appointed musical director of the new Royal Academy of Music as composer and conductor of operas. |
| 1727 | Becomes a British subject. |
| 1732 | Produces his first English oratorio, *Esther*, to great public acclaim. |
| 1741 | Abandons the stage and turns his attention almost entirely to oratorio. |
| 1742 | *Messiah* is greeted enthusiastically at its premiere in Dublin. |
| 1751 | Undergoes a series of unsuccessful operations to save his failing eyesight; later suffers from total blindness. |
| 1759 | Dies on April 14 and is buried in Westminster Abbey. |

man singing in the soprano range was by all accounts electrifying, for the **castrato** combined the high range of the female voice with the physical power of the male voice. A contemporary observer had this to say about a performance by the famous castrato Farinelli (the stage name of Carlo Broschi, 1705–1782), who was greatly admired by mid-18th-century London operagoers (and his friend Pietro Metastasio):

> [T]he first note he sung was taken with such delicacy, swelled by minute degrees to such an amazing volume, and afterwards diminished in the same manner to a mere point, that it was applauded for full five minutes. After this he set off with such brilliancy and rapidity of execution, that it was difficult for the violins of those days to keep pace with him. . . . But it was not only in speed that he excelled, for he had now every excellence of every great singer united. In his voice, strength, sweetness, and compass; in his style, the tender, the graceful, and the rapid. Indeed he possessed such powers as never met before, or since, in any one human being; powers that were irresistible, and which must have subdued every hearer; the learned and the ignorant, the friend and the foe.[5]

What we now regard as a grotesque practice may have seemed 300 years ago an acceptable sacrifice, considering the compensation. The greatest of the castrati enjoyed celebrity and financial rewards comparable to that of today's pop music stars.

Most important male roles in the typical opera seria went to castrati (and occasionally some of the female roles as well). In the original production of Handel's *Giulio*

**The castrato.** This early 18th-century caricature of the castrato Antonio Maria Bernacchi (1685–1756) lampoons two well-known tendencies of castrati: to put on weight and to sing fantastically elaborate passagework. Here, the music leaps above the bell tower in Venice's St. Mark's Square and explodes in a trill over a nearby building. The music is in fact taken from a melody in the title role of Giovanni Maria Cappelli's *Mitridate re di Ponto* (1723), an opera seria whose libretto would be set to music again almost 50 years later by the young Wolfgang Amadeus Mozart.

**Source:** ecole-du-regard/leemage/Lebrecht Music & Arts Photo Library

*Cesare* in London in 1724, the roles of Julius Caesar, Sextus, Ptolemy, and Nirenus were all performed by castrati. Handel used the tenor or bass range only for minor characters. Today, the castrato roles are given either to women dressed as men or to countertenors (men singing falsetto).

The last major role for a castrato in a new opera was in Giacomo Meyerbeer's *Il Crociato in Egitto*, which premiered in Venice in 1824. The last known castrato—Alessandro Moreschi, a singer in the Vatican choir—died in 1922 a very old man, but he was already an anomaly even in his prime; most castratos had died by the middle of the 19th century. Moreschi made recordings in the early 20th century, but the primitive technology of the period and his advanced age make it very difficult to conclude anything definitive about the quality of castrato singing, at least from these recordings. Modern digital techniques that blend a male (countertenor) and a female (soprano) voice, as in the soundtrack of the movie *Farinelli* (1994), probably give a better sense of what a castrato voice sounded like.

Audiences in the 17th and 18th centuries viewed castrati with a sense of both awe and amusement. These surgically altered singers were the object of humor and satire as well as adulation. The phenomenon of the castrato contributed to a growing image of opera seria as an "unnatural" art form, which in turn led to major changes in the broader genre of opera in the second half of the 18th century (see Chapter 13).

## The business of opera.

The establishment of the first public opera houses in Venice in 1638 profoundly influenced the development of the genre. The new audience was larger and demanded bigger performance spaces. Producers and performers, in turn, had to appeal to the tastes of a broader, more heterogeneous audience. Without the direct support of either the court or the church, opera was forced to establish itself on a for-profit basis.

**Farinelli.** Stefano Dionisi in the title role of the 1994 film *Farinelli.* The sound engineers recreated the castrato singing voice by blending two separate recordings of the same music—one by a man, one by a woman—onto a single soundtrack.

**Source:** Jean-Marie Leroy/Sygma/Corbis

# A CLOSER LOOK

✳ Explore on mysearchlab

**THIS 1740 PAINTING** shows an opera being performed at the Teatro Regio in Turin, in what is now northern Italy. The "Royal Theater" was funded by the Grand Duke of Tuscany, who could enter the hall directly from his palace without going outside. The magnificence of the staging, costumes, singing, and orchestral playing helped the Grand Duke impress visiting dignitaries and thereby enhance his standing within the cultural politics of Europe.

**Source:** The Teatro Reale in Turin (oil on canvas), Oliviero, Pietro Domenico (c. 1672–1754) / Museo Civico, Turin, Italy / The Bridgeman Art Library

The more elite members of the audience sit in stalls or **"boxes"** on the theater's upper levels. Each box was rented privately for an entire season.

The **orchestra** occupies the **pit**, the lowered area between the audience and the stage. Two sets of basso continuo are visible here on each side of the orchestra: one accompanies the recitatives, while the other accompanies arias and other numbers that called for a full orchestra.

**Audience behavior** at operas was more relaxed than today. In this first row, one member of the audience gestures toward the stage. while his neighbor studies the words being sung by following the libretto. His neighbor, in turn, is not even facing the stage but seems more intent on surveying others in attendance. When the Englishman Charles Burney described his travels throughout the musical centers of the continent in the 1770s, he warned his readers that he would "have frequent occasion to mention the noise and inattention at the musical exhibitions in Italy."

A **bailiff** maintains order in the theater. Although his function is largely ceremonial, his physical presence is a reminder to all that this is a royal theater.

A **merchant** sells refreshments to members of the audience. In the Baroque Era, vendors moved up and down the aisles throughout the performance.

**Soloists** sing their parts wearing dazzling costumes, another standard feature in most Baroque operatic productions.

**Stage design** was a major element of the theatrical spectacle. Here, an elaborate backdrop gives the illusion of depth to a fairly small stage.

Opera's major season was Carnival, running from roughly just after Christmas until Lent, which begins in late February or March, 40 days before Easter. Carnival was an enormous draw for visitors from all over Europe: it has been estimated that Venice, a city of about 140,000 in 1700, consistently attracted some 30,000 foreign visitors during this one season every year. These visitors wanted entertainment of all kinds, including opera, and they were willing to pay for it. Small wonder then that Venice should be home to the first public opera house, organized by a group of musicians who put up the necessary capital, rented a theater (San Cassiano), and wrote and performed the music. Other groups of entrepreneurs quickly followed suit, and by the end of the century Venice could boast of no fewer than 16 opera houses.

By then, however, the business had long since been taken over by professional impresarios, the equivalent of modern-day Hollywood producers. It was the impresarios who assembled all the necessary pieces—and the capital—to mount new productions of opera. As a business, opera was both expensive and risky, as this contemporaneous account of the daunting array of expenses faced by a 17th-century impresario suggests:

> The first and greatest of these expenses concerns the remuneration of the singers, the pretensions of these men and women having reached excessive levels (where earlier they were happy to perform irrespective of gain, or at most for honest recognition). It is also necessary to pay the composer. . . . There follow the expenses for the costumes, *mutazioni di scena* [stage sets] and construction of the machines; an agreement must be reached with the *maestro de' balli* [choreographer], and the various instrumentalists and theatrical hands must be paid on a nightly basis. A further expense regards the lighting of the theatre. . . . These are the reasons for which expenses increase year by year, though prices at the door have actually fallen. The very continuation of opera could well be placed in jeopardy if this current state of affairs is not regulated more carefully.[7]

The impresario invested the money to rent the theater, sell tickets, and hire the many artists required to stage an opera, including librettist, composer, singers, players, stage designers, and costume designers. Typically, stalls or boxes were sold for an entire season; other seats, on the ground floor, were available on a night-to-night basis. Not surprisingly, tickets for the opera were expensive. In London in the 1720s, for example, the cost of a single seat at the opera was about two-and-a-half times the cost of a comparable seat for a play.

## England: Masque, Semi-Opera, Opera, and Ballad Opera

Like France, England enjoyed a rich tradition of spoken drama, in which music occupied an important if subordinate role. Plays and masques provided what most Englishmen considered ample opportunity for a combination of drama, song, and ballet. **Masques** began as semi-improvised intrusions into large social festivities by masked and costumed actors; the genre eventually migrated to the stage as a loosely assembled series of vignettes that allowed for a colorful mixture of musical and dramatic elements. The playwright Ben Jonson (ca. 1573–1637) collaborated with the artist and stage designer Inigo Jones to produce more than 30 masques during the first three decades of the 17th century.

What came to be known as **semi-operas** flourished in the second half of the 17th century. These were essentially plays with a large proportion of musical numbers, both vocal and instrumental. The English composer Henry Purcell (see Composer Profile) contributed a number of outstanding works in this genre, most notably *Dioclesian*, *King Arthur*, and *The Fairy Queen*.

But the 17th century was a time of great political unrest in England, and circumstances were not favorable to the introduction of opera from abroad. The Commonwealth (1649–60), under the leadership of the Puritan Oliver Cromwell, took a dim view of secular music in all its various forms. But even with the monarchy restored, England remained resistant to opera. "While other nations bestow the name of opera only on such plays whereof every word is sung," the *Gentlemen's Journal* declared in 1692, "experience hath taught us that our English genius will not relish that perpetual singing." The literary critic John Dennis (1657–1734) railed against the genre even before it arrived in England. In his "Essay on the Operas After the Italian Manner, Which are about to be Establish'd on the English Stage: With Some Reflections on the Damage which they May Bring to the Publick" (1706), Dennis argued that every nationality had its own particular climate, vegetation, and art, and the theatrical genius of the English lay in the realm of spoken drama, not sung drama. It would be as foolish to import Italian opera into England, Dennis maintained, as it would be to start planting olive and orange trees in the English countryside.

Sung throughout, Henry Purcell's opera *Dido and Aeneas* (1689) is thus an anomaly. One of the very few English operas of its time, its origins and performance

## Primary Evidence    A FRENCHMAN'S ACCOUNT OF VENETIAN OPERA, ca. 1672

*The French nobleman Alexandre-Toussaint Limojon, Sieur de Saint-Didier (ca. 1630–89), spent two years in Venice in the early 1670s and wrote a valuable account of the people and manners of the city, including its opera houses. The translation here is from the English edition (The City and Republick of Venice) as published in London in 1699.*

■ ■ ■

At Venice they act in several operas at a time. The theaters are large and stately, the decorations noble and the alterations of them good. But they are very badly illuminated, . . . The ballets or dancing between the acts are generally so pittiful, that they would be much better omitted; for one would imagine these dancers wore lead in their shoes. Yet the assembly bestow their applauses on them, which is merely for want of having seen better. . . .

They that compose the musick of the opera endeavour to conclude the scenes of *the principal* actors with airs that charm and elevate, that so they may acquire the applause of the audience, which succeeds so well to their intentions, that one hears nothing but a thousand "Benissimos" together. Yet nothing is so remarkable as the pleasant benedictions and the ridiculous wishes of the gondoliers in the pit to the women singers, who cry aloud to them, *Sia tu benedetta, benedetto il padre che te generó* ["Bless you, and bless the father who conceived you"]. But these acclamations are not always within the bounds of modesty, for those impudent fellows say whatever they please, as being assur'd to make the assembly rather laugh than angry.

Some gentlemen have shewn themselves so transported and out of all bounds by the charming voices of these girls, as to bend themselves out of their boxes crying, *Ah cara! mi butto, mi butto* ["Ah dear one! I shall jump, I shall jump"], expressing after this manner the raptures of pleasure which these divine voices cause to them. I need not omit the priests in this place, for according to the example of Rome, they are no ways scrupulous of appearing upon the stage in all manner of parts, and by acquiring the character of a good actor they commonly get that of an honest man. I remember once, that one of the spectators discerning a priest in the disguise of an old woman, cry'd aloud, *Ecco, Padre Pierro, che fa la vecchia* ["There, that's Father Peter playing the part of the old woman"]. Nevertheless all things pass with more decency at the opera than at the comedy [i.e., the spoken theater], as being most commonly frequented by the better sort of people. One pays four livres at the door, and two more for a chair in the pitt, which amounts to three shillings and sixpence English, without reckoning the opera-book [i.e., libretto] and the wax-candle every one buys; for without them even those of the country would hardly comprehend any thing of the history [i.e., the plot] or the subject matter of the composition.

**Source:** Alexandre-Toussaint Limojon, Sieur de Saint-Didier, *La Ville et la république de Venise* (Paris, 1680), trans. F. Terne, *The City and Republick of Venice* (London, 1699).

history remain shrouded in mystery. We know it was first performed by the students at a school for young ladies in Chelsea (west of London at the time), but the next known performance, in a drastically altered version, did not occur until 1700, and the earliest surviving musical sources date from well after the composer's death. *Dido and Aeneas* may have been suppressed for political reasons, either by Purcell himself or by the authorities, on the grounds of its potentially unflattering commentary on the dual reign of King William, a foreigner, and Queen Mary, daughter of James II. The plot, after all, deals with a foreign prince (Aeneas) who promises to marry the queen of Carthage (Dido), then reneges and abandons her, driving her to suicide. In fact, William and Mary reigned happily; Purcell wrote two odes to celebrate Queen Mary's birthday (1692; 1694, *Come, Ye Sons of Art*), and one of his last works commemorates her death (the *Funeral Music*, 1695).

The foreign prince, Aeneas, a refugee from fallen Troy, is on his way to Italy with his companions to found the city of Rome in fulfillment of a promise from the gods. They land in Carthage, on the northern coast of Africa, ruled by Queen Dido. Aeneas and Dido are immediately attracted to each other. In spite of knowing his destiny, she lets herself be wooed; he pledges to abandon his promised Rome. But when a witch disguised as Mercury, the messenger of the gods, orders him to leave, he obeys and abandons Dido. She, disconsolate, dies, but not before singing an exquisite lament.

Purcell's opera owes much to the French tradition, beginning with the overture, a slow introduction followed by an imitative fast section. The singing moves rapidly through many short numbers, with a minimum of virtuosity and no da capo arias. Act I opens with Belinda, Dido's confidante, urging her mistress to shake off her anguish; the chorus echoes her thoughts in a kind of communal commentary. Dido responds with a lament over a ground bass, prefiguring her celebrated (but dramatically more static) lament at the very end of the opera. This brief number gives way to an exchange in simple recitative, in which Belinda forces Dido to confront her love of Aeneas. This exchange segues into a song extolling the virtues of a union between Carthage and Troy ("The greatest blessing . . ."), followed by a chorus ("When monarchs unite"). The recitative dialogue between Dido and Belinda resumes, leading in turn to a duet ("Fear no danger to ensue") and chorus.

When opera finally conquered England in 1711, it was through a performance of Handel's *Rinaldo*, an opera seria written in Italian by a German. What had once been scorned was now all the rage, at least among the upper classes. Rival opera companies soon sprang up in London. English-language opera would not establish itself to any appreciable degree for another generation. For the moment, at least, the stage belonged to Handel, Alessandro Scarlatti, Nicola Porpora, Antonio Bononcini, and other foreign-born composers of opera seria.

The English aversion to Italian opera never disappeared entirely, however. In 1728, the playwright John Gay (1685–1732) achieved a rousing success with *The Beggar's Opera*, an English-language play with music that portrayed common criminals rather than mythological figures or historical heroes. Gay set his song texts to existing popular tunes; the German-born Johann Christoph Pepusch (1667–1752) provided the accompaniments and an overture. The arrangements are quite simple, and the dialogue is spoken rather than sung. As the Beggar explains at the outset, "I hope I may be forgiven, that I have not made my Opera throughout unnatural, like those in vogue; for I have no Recitative."

The original libretto of this **ballad opera** features 69 songs, of which 28 have been identified as English ballads; another 23 derive from popular songs of Irish, Scottish, or French origin. The remainder come from works by such composers as Purcell, Handel, and even Frescobaldi. *The Beggar's Opera* is full of political references that delighted

((•—Listen

**CD5    Tracks 4–9**
**mysearchlab**
PURCELL
*Dido and Aeneas*
Score Anthology I/83

((•—Listen

**CD5    Tracks 10–12**
**mysearchlab**
GAY AND PEPUSCH
*The Beggar's Opera*
Score Anthology I/84

# Henry Purcell (ca. 1659–1695)

Considering his stature as one of the greatest of all English composers ever to write for the theater, we know remarkably little about Henry Purcell. We are not sure whether his father was Henry Purcell or his brother Thomas Purcell; both were Gentlemen of the Chapel Royal and active at the English court. Details of Purcell's later life are sketchy. Yet we know that when he died his loss was mourned throughout the English musical world.

Purcell contributed songs and instrumental music to dozens of plays and semi-operas but wrote only one opera, *Dido and Aeneas.* The English musical scene was not hospitable to opera during the 17th century. Commenting on this state of affairs in his letter of dedication to the semi-opera *Dioclesian* (1690), Purcell suggested that an English opera would eventually emerge from a combination of French and Italian characteristics:

> Musick is yet but in its Nonage, a forward Child, which gives hope of what it may be hereafter in *England*, when the Masters of it shall find more Encouragement. 'Tis now learning Italian, which is its best Master, and studying a little of the *French* Air, to give it somewhat more of Gayety and Fashion. Thus being farther from the Sun, we are of later Growth than our Neighbour Countries, and must be content to shake off our Barbarity by degrees.[8]

Purcell himself united the dramatic verve of French *tragédie en musique* with the melodic brilliance of Italian opera seria in *Dido and Aeneas,* based on an episode from Virgil's Latin epic, the *Aeneid* (1st century B.C.E.). That opera's remarkable sense of dramatic pacing leaves us wondering what the history of English opera might have been had its composer lived beyond the age of 36.

# PRINCIPAL WORKS

## Theater Music

Aside from *Dido and Aeneas,* Purcell contributed songs to a great many plays of his day, including dramas by John Dryden, William Congreve, and Thomas D'Urfey as well as various 17th-century adaptations of Shakespeare's plays. *Dioclesian, The Fairy Queen, The Indian Queen,* and *King Arthur* contain enough music to be considered semi-operas rather than merely plays with music.

## Songs

Purcell wrote many songs suited for amateur musicians. The most notable collection is *Orpheus Britannicus,* published posthumously by Purcell's widow.

## Sacred Music

Purcell's duties at Westminster Abbey required him to write many sacred works, particularly anthems. Some of these are in the older polyphonic style, others in a lighter, rhythmically lively style more closely akin to French music of the day.

## Instrumental Music

In addition to the dance and other music contained within his semi-operas and other dramatic works, Purcell composed harpsichord suites and trio sonatas; he was the last in a long line of English composers of viol consort music, including two *In Nomine* pieces.

**Henry Purcell, ca. 1695.** This portrait in black chalk was drawn by John (Johann) Closterman, a German artist who emigrated to England in 1681.

**Source:** INTERFOTO/Personalitites/Alamy

| KEY DATES IN THE LIFE OF PURCELL | |
|---|---|
| ?1659 | Born in London (?). |
| 1669 | Becomes a chorister in the Chapel Royal. |
| 1679 | Succeeds John Blow as organist of Westminster Abbey. |
| 1680 | Writes his first music for the stage. |
| 1689 | Composes *Dido and Aeneas,* his only opera. |
| 1695 | Dies in Westminster (London). |

## Focus   COMPOSERS OF ITALIAN OPERA, 1650–1750

In the generations after Monteverdi, a number of important composers continued to write operas in Italian. Not all of them were Italian themselves—Handel and Hasse were German—but Italian opera's appeal crossed international boundaries, and the genre spread throughout Europe in its language of origin.

**FRANCESCO CAVALLI** (1602–76) studied with Monteverdi and assumed the same post as music director at San Marco in Venice. He wrote more than 40 operas in a style similar to that of Monteverdi's later works, mixing recitative and aria-like passages fluently.

**MARC' ANTONIO CESTI** (1623–69), a pupil of Giacomo Carissimi (discussed subsequently in the section on sacred music), became music director at the Medici court in Florence in 1660. Only about a dozen of his more than 100 operas have survived. His most famous is *Il pomo d'oro* ("The Golden Apple"), a mammoth production in 5 acts, with 66 scenes, 24 different set designs, 48 different singing roles, and numerous ballets. The premiere in Vienna in 1667 was part of the wedding festivities of the Emperor Leopold I of Austria to the Infanta Margherita of Spain. Only a royal court could have mounted such a lavish production.

**ALESSANDRO SCARLATTI** (1660–1725) was one of the first great masters of opera seria. Like Cesti, he studied with Carissimi. He held numerous positions at various courts in Rome and Naples and wrote an estimated 115 operas, of which about 50 have survived.

**GEORGE FRIDERIC HANDEL** (1685–1759; see Composer Profile) learned the craft of opera seria during his early years on the Italian peninsula and played a central role in bringing opera seria to England. His *Rinaldo* (1711) was an instant success and many subsequent works met with equal or even greater acclaim. Foremost among these are *Radamisto* (1720), *Giulio Cesare* (1723), *Rodelinda* (1725), *Tamerlano* (1732), *Ariodante* (1735), and *Serse* (1738).

**JOHANN ADOLPH HASSE** (1699–1783) studied with Alessandro Scarlatti and was the leading exponent of opera seria in German-speaking lands. His musical style was thoroughly Italian; during his lifetime he was widely regarded as the greatest composer in the genre. Nicknamed "Il Sassone" ("the Saxon") after his German place of birth, he was Metastasio's favorite composer.

---

contemporary audiences. Whereas the French overture was always understood to be in honor of the king, the overture to *The Beggar's Opera* quotes the song *Walpole, or the Happy Clown*, a ditty attacking Robert Walpole, prime minister of Great Britain at the time. The drama itself is mock heroic, putting London lowlife through a series of confrontations that parallel the more august dramas of the upper-class stage. The curtain goes up on Mr. Peachum, who in his opening "air" ("Thro' all the employments of life") compares himself to a lawyer, for he both convicts and frees criminals: he is at once a fence for stolen goods and a police informant. In the scenes that follow, Mr. and Mrs. Peachum learn to their horror that their daughter, Polly, has secretly married the highwayman Macheath (Mrs Peachum: "Our Polly is a sad slut"). They are not horrified because Macheath is a criminal but because he is a client of Mr. Peachum, who will no longer be able to do business with him. They are also horrified at the very notion of marriage itself, which they see as something only the "gentry" do. On top of all this, they warn their daughter that she will not be able to support her husband in his "gaming, drinking, and whoring." To the tune known as "Grim King of the ghosts," Polly wonders if "love can be controlled by advice." *The Beggar's Opera* was an enormous commercial success and was soon being performed as far away as Charleston, South Carolina, and Williamsburg, Virginia: it is said to have been George Washington's favorite opera. It continued to be staged in one version or another at least once a year for the rest of the 18th century. The work took on new life in a German adaptation by Bertolt Brecht in 1928 entitled *Die Dreigroschenoper*—"The Threepenny Opera"—with music by Kurt Weill.

# SACRED MUSIC

The demand from religious institutions for new music expanded enormously in the 17th and 18th centuries. The Italian city of Bologna alone had more than 200 churches and chapels, 36 monasteries, and 28 convents by the end of the 18th century. All except the smallest of these had their own chorus and organ. Larger churches, monasteries, and convents routinely presented music by instrumental ensembles as well.

## Music in Convents

Convents took on special importance for music in Italy during the Baroque era. A major increase in the number of these institutions began in the middle of the 16th century and continued well into the 17th. Families sent daughters to convents for a variety of reasons, most commonly economic; the cost of a convent dowry was only a fraction of the cost to marry a daughter into a respectable family. Illegitimate daughters were also frequently sent to convents. By 1600, the city of Milan alone had some 41 convents, and in two-thirds of these, the residents cultivated polyphonic music.

Of the women who published music on the Italian peninsula between 1566 and 1700, more than half were nuns. Isabella Leonarda (1620–1704) was easily the most prominent and prolific of this latter group, publishing some 20 volumes of her own music, mostly sacred vocal but instrumental as well (see Chapter 10).

Visitors frequently commented on the high quality of music making in convents. A Bolognese priest named Sebastiano Locatelli noted that at one convent in Milan in the mid-1660s,

> we could not distinguish if the singing voices were from here on earth or celestial. They sang a *Regina caeli* which showed well that they had learnt from the angel how to salute their Queen. The one who sang best of all was called Donna Angiola; she had a nightingale's throat, and executed trills that lasted so long that it seemed that her soul wanted to deprive itself of breath in order to receive the prize for its labors from Mother Mary who was honored.[9]

For church authorities, the musical renown of the convents was a source of both pride and anxiety. A vehement attack by religious authorities in Milan around 1660 on music making by the nuns at one convent gives some idea of the extent of that renown:

> Music, vocal and instrumental, established for the greater glory of God and His Church, is abused by the nuns of S. Margarita, and serves to foment vice, the corruption of virtue, and irreparable ruin to proper discipline. Not a single prelate, prince, celebrity, or other well-known person arrives in this city who does not immediately arrange for entrance [there], by means of nobles or other highly placed persons, and attempts by all means to be called to the monastery, where in church or in the parlors they are entertained with Italian canzonettas, sonnets, lascivious madrigals . . . indecent acts, and even laments far from monastic modesty. The monastery is more like a seraglio of singers than a cloister of virgins consecrated to God.[10]

Although the authorities often threatened to limit music making in convents— by banning instruments or polyphony, for example—they rarely followed through.

Two sisters in a 17th-century Milanese monastery were, however, prohibited from singing polyphony in the convent for a period of six years after performing secular—and apparently somewhat obscene—songs, a punishment eerily reminiscent of that imposed on Hildegard von Bingen for a different sort of challenge to church authority some five centuries before (see Chapter 1).

## Oratorio

The most significant new genre of sacred music in the Baroque era was the **oratorio**, which offered listeners a sacred counterpart to opera. As an institution, the Roman Catholic church recognized the power of opera to convey moral and spiritual ideals, and in some cities, particularly Rome, the church was quick to commission operas on sacred subjects, such as the lives of individual saints. But the church also condemned opera for its power to dazzle and seduce. Striking a compromise of sorts, the Vatican banned the performance of opera in Catholic-ruled lands across the Continent during the penitential seasons of Advent (the 4 weeks before Christmas) and Lent (the 40 days before Easter) but tolerated it at other times.

Beginning around the middle of the 17th century, this operatic void during Advent and Lent was filled by the new and immediately popular genre of oratorio. The term comes from its original place of performance: in Italian, an *oratorio* is a prayer hall. The prayer hall was a place for contemplation, prayer, and private devotion. In the 16th and early 17th centuries, it was not at all unusual for congregations to hear performances of sacred madrigals and motets in these spaces, and the idea of presenting a dramatic scene from the Bible or from the lives of the saints in this setting began to crystallize in the years around 1650. The result was a genre of sung drama performed without staging or costumes. To compensate for the lack of staged action, a narrator often related connective threads of the plot in recitative. The musical vehicles for projecting the drama, which included recitative, da capo aria, and chorus, were otherwise not much different from those of opera. (Ironically, the best known of all oratorios, Handel's *Messiah*—with no narrator, no characters, and no real plot but instead a collection of biblical texts relating to Christ's coming, death, resurrection, and promised return—is thoroughly atypical of the genre.)

Giacomo Carissimi's *Jephte* (probably written in the second half of the 1640s, certainly before 1650) was one of the most popular of all early oratorios. The Latin-language libretto, based on the book of Judges 11, tells the story of Jephte (also spelled Jephthah), an Israelite general who promises to sacrifice to God the first thing to emerge from his house on his homecoming if God grants him victory in

((•—**Listen**
**CD5 Track 13**
**mysearchlab** (with scrolling translation)
CARISSIMI
*Jephte*
Score Anthology I/85

**". . . no Person to be admitted without Tickets."** The rise of public performances with paid admission created a new need for advertising concerts. This newspaper announcement for the first London performance of Handel's *Messiah,* on 23 March 1743, is typical of its time. Composers often produced their own concerts, and tickets were often to be had directly from the home of the composer, though Handel presumably had servants handle the actual transactions. The "Concerto on the Organ" was one written and performed by Handel himself during the intervals of the oratorio.

**Source:** The New York Public Library/Mariner Books/Art Resource, NY

## Primary Evidence — THE ORATORIO IN ROME

*The performance of an oratorio was both a religious and social event. In his diary entry for March 31, 1715, the German aristocrat Johann Friedrich Armand von Uffenbach describes a performance of Antonio Caldara's oratorio* Abisai *at the palace of Prince Ruspoli, a prominent Roman patron of the arts. Caldara (1670–1736) was a prolific composer of operas (87) and oratorios (32) and one of the most respected musicians of his generation.*

■ ■ ■

In the evening was the great, weekly concert in the palace of Prince Rospoli [i.e., Ruspoli] which, because of the many expenses that he annually allots to it, is the best here; and since he welcomes and permits every foreigner to come in without introduction, we therefore went there together, and were led through a large number of exquisitely furnished rooms to an enormously large and long hall in which, as in the entire house, there is no lack of incomparable paintings and silver work. Everything was most brilliantly illuminated, and on both sides of the entire hall chairs were placed for the listeners; above, however, the place for the musicians was left free where a great number of virtuosos arranged themselves, and three female singers next to a small castrato, belonging to the ambassador Gallas, sat in front. They then gave such an excellent concert, or so-called oratorio, that I was completely delighted and convinced that I had not in my life heard the like, in such perfection. The composition is completely new each time and is composed by the well-known Caldara, papal maestro di cappella, who also conducted here. People listened to the excellent voices so attentively that not a fly stirred, except when a cardinal or a lady arrived, since everyone stood up but afterward sat down again in his old place. I found also that all the voices usually heard in operas fell short of these; particularly the one called Mariotgi had something quite extraordinary and uncommonly pleasing in her singing. The leading soprano was the wife of Caldara; to be sure, she was very finished in music and sang the most difficult things with nothing but great skill, yet to me, because of the weakness of her voice, she did not long please as well as the one described above. At about the middle of the concert they had an intermission, and then liquors, frozen things, confectionery, and coffee were brought around in quantity and presented to everyone. Afterward was performed the other half of the concert, which lasted altogether four hours. I would have remained even fourteen days with great pleasure, for I certainly left with genuine astonishment, and I have never in my life heard anything to compare with this. In the accompaniment there was a violin that was unusually well played, and many other instruments, all played to perfection. It was midnight when we were finished, but sleep did not hinder me from listening to it all to the end with the greatest pleasure. The auditorium was very full, and there were many ladies, also several cardinals, among others the cardinal Ottoboni of Venice who never misses such things. He went as an ordinary abbot, except that he wore red stockings and heels and also a red calotte; and the remaining cardinals also went similarly dressed. After this was over, we went home and dined.

**Source:** Excerpt from *A History of Oratorio*, Vol. I by Howard E. Smithers. Copyright © 1977 by the University of North Carolina Press. Used by permission of the publisher.

an impending battle. Returning home victorious, Jephte is dismayed to see his only daughter emerge first from his house to greet him. She, virtuously, urges him to fulfill his vow. The work ends with an extended lament by the daughter (who has no name, either in the Bible or in this oratorio) and her companions. This lament, in the view of one mid-17th-century Jesuit observer, "is composed with such skill that you would swear that you hear the sobs and moans of the weeping girls."[11] Carissimi (1605–1674) introduces the characters and keeps the plot moving forward in brisk fashion by using a narrator ("Historicus") throughout—at times a bass and at times an alto. Aside from this narrative device, and aside from the fact that it is sung in Latin, *Jephte* is musically indistinguishable from operas of the mid-17th century. Like them, it places a premium on vocal virtuosity and features a quick succession of short movements, some for solo, some for a small group of soloists, others still for chorus.

The new genre of oratorio took root in the Protestant north of Europe as well as in Catholic Italy. German composers like Schütz were especially keen to set the Gospel

**Hogarth's "The Chorus."** This satirical depiction of an oratorio rehearsal, by the English artist William Hogarth (1697–1764), shows a conductor who has become so caught up in the moment that he has knocked off his own headpiece; he has literally flipped his wig. Most of the singers are themselves too absorbed to have noticed: only two see what has happened. The work being performed is *Judith* (1733) by Willem De Fesch (1687–1761), who wrote several oratorios that met with popular success in London.

**Source:** Mary Evans Picture Library/Alamy

narratives of Christ's Passion to music. The chorus played an increasingly important role in these compositions. Johann Sebastian Bach's *Saint Matthew Passion* and *Saint John Passion* are in effect Lutheran oratorios, combining a narrator (the Evangelist), da capo arias, and choruses, many of which incorporate Protestant chorale melodies. Bach never wrote an opera, but his oratorios give us a sense of what an opera by him might have sounded like.

George Frideric Handel cultivated the oratorio with particular zeal from the 1730s onward. This was due in large part to the growing disaffection of London audiences with Italian opera around this time. Handel's later oratorios are all in English. Working with his librettists, he managed to tap into a growing sense of English nationalism, one manifestation of which was a tacit belief that Old Testament events validated English preeminence. His audiences understood Biblical Israel as a metaphor for England, a land they felt was enjoying God's favor in the same way that Israel had in the past. Besides the generically atypical *Messiah*, Handel's most popular oratorios of his late period include *Israel in Egypt*, *Judas Maccabeus*, and *Joshua*.

## Motet and Mass

The same forces that introduced new possibilities for the madrigal also helped expand options in the realm of nondramatic sacred music. The polyphonic motet continued to thrive throughout the Continent. In Italy, Benedetto Marcello (1686–1739) was admired as much for his sacred music as for his operas. A large body of sacred choral music emanated from England in the 17th century from the pen of such composers as Henry Lawes (1596–1662) and his brother William Lawes (1602–45), John Blow (1648–1708), and Henry Purcell. In France, the *grand motet* combined vocal soloists, chorus, and orchestra in a series of contrasting movements to a sacred text in Latin.

Lully, Michel-Richard Delalande (1657–1726), and François Couperin (1668–1733) all contributed to the genre.

Much sacred music from the latter part of the Baroque era strikes many listeners today as operatic in its dazzling virtuosity. But before the early 19th century, no clear distinction was made between sacred and secular musical styles. Johann Sebastian Bach, for example, transformed any number of movements from secular works written in honor of a monarch into sacred works written in honor of God. Like many sacred compositions honoring Saint Cecilia, the patron saint of music, the Kyrie of Alessandro Scarlatti's *Messa di S. Cecilia* is as florid and virtuosic in its own way as any dramatic music of its time (1720).

We should also keep in mind that a good deal of sacred music was tailored to fit quite practical needs. The long orchestral introduction to Handel's *Zadok the Priest*, for example, allowed the royal procession sufficient time to make its way down the long center aisle of Westminster Abbey for the coronation of King George II in 1727. The power of the swelling orchestra, the dramatic entrance of the voices, and the arrival of the new king were of such overwhelming effect that the anthem has been used in every British coronation since then.

## Cantata

Throughout the Baroque era the term **cantata** was applied to many different kinds of vocal works, secular as well as sacred. The word itself derives from the Italian *cantare*, "to sing," and it was used to denote both small- and large-scale works, ranging from a solo singer with basso continuo to a large ensemble of soloists, chorus, and instruments. A cantata could be a single movement or multiple movements. Many 17th-century cantatas are works in the tradition of the solo madrigal.

In 1708, Elisabeth Jacquet de la Guerre (1665–1729; see Composer Profile) published a group of sacred cantatas that included one entitled *Judith*. The libretto is based on the Apochryphal book in which Judith, an Israelite, saves the town of Bethulia (near Jerusalem). She enters the camp of Holofernes, commander-in-chief of the armies of Nebuchadnezzar, with a promise of information to help him seize the town. He drinks too much and falls asleep, at which point Judith, with the help of her maid, decapitates him and uses the head to frighten and disperse the army of Holofernes.

The cantata is performed largely by one singer, with basso continuo. An obbligato violin joins in for instrumental sections called "symphonies" and as part of an accompanied recitative. The singer is a sympathetic narrator who exhorts Judith to accomplish her task. "Le coup est achevé" is a celebratory air sung moments after the fatal blow has been struck. *Judith* is, in effect, a small-scaled oratorio, as French sacred cantatas tended to be.

While French and Italian cantatas were generally nonliturgical in nature, Johann Sebastian Bach wrote the majority of his cantatas for use in Lutheran worship. In fact, he used the designation *cantata* only for his solo cantatas; the broader application of the term originated with 19th-century editors of his works. For works with chorus and orchestra, he more often used terms like *Concerto*, *Motetto*, or *Kirchen-Stück* ("church piece"). The body of works we now think of as Bach's cantatas embody many different traditions and forms, including motet-like movements for chorus, chorale harmonizations, and virtuosic solos and duets, often with the participation of additional solo instruments as well. By Bach's lifetime, a Lutheran service might last up to four hours, contain a "Missa brevis" in Latin (Kyrie and Gloria), organ preludes, chorales, and one or even two cantatas, in addition to the all-important sermon. A cantata was usually performed just before or after the sermon; a second might follow the Lord's Prayer.

((•--Listen
**CD5   Track 14**
**mysearchlab**
HANDEL
*Zadok the Priest*
Score Anthology I/86

((•--Listen
**CD5   Track 15**
**mysearchlab** (with scrolling translation)
JACQUET DE LA GUERRE
*Judith*
Score Anthology I/87

## Composer Profile

# Elisabeth Jacquet de la Guerre (1665–1729)

As a child, Elisabeth Jacquet de la Guerre was a favorite of the French royal court; she would receive royal patronage throughout her life, notably the royal privilege that allowed her to dedicate virtually all of her music to Louis XIV. She married the organist Marin de la Guerre in 1684, and produced her first set of harpsichord pieces three years later. Jacquet de la Guerre was the first Frenchwoman to compose an opera, *Céphale et Procris*, which premiered in 1694 at the Académie Royale in Paris, Lully's old haunting grounds. She later published violin sonatas and trio sonatas. After the death of her husband, son, and other family members, Jacquet de la Guerre began a series of cantata collections, published in 1708, 1711, and 1715; the first two volumes contain sacred works, and the last volume is secular in nature. The only known work of hers after this time, a Te Deum performed in 1721, is lost. Shortly after her death, a commemorative medal was struck in her honor.

## PRINCIPAL WORKS

Aside from *Céphale et Procris*, Jacquet de la Guerre composed an opera-ballet, *Les jeux à l'honneur de la victoire*, performed in 1691 but now lost. Other than a few songs published in collections, Jacquet de la Guerre's vocal legacy rests with the three books of *Cantates françoises*.

**Elisabeth Jacquet de la Guerre at the time of the premiere of her opera *Céphale et Procris*.** This portrait emphasizes the artist's achievements as a composer, showing her with a quill in one hand, a piece of blank paper in the other.

**Source:** Francoise de Troy, "Portrait of Elisabeth-Claude Jacquet de la Guerre" (circa 1694–95), oil on canvas, 47 3/8 in. × 36 3/4 in./ Private Collection, London

### KEY DATES IN THE LIFE OF JACQUET DE LA GUERRE

| | |
|---|---|
| 1665 | Baptized in Paris on March 17. |
| 1673 | Joins the French royal court as a keyboardist, where she remains until 1680. |
| 1694 | Completes first book of *clavecin* pieces. |
| | Her opera *Céphale et Procris* is performed in Paris. |
| 1707 | Publishes sonatas for harpsichord (with optional violin) and violin and *basse continue*. |
| 1708 | Publishes first volume of cantatas; later volumes follow in 1711 and 1715. |
| 1729 | Dies in Paris on June 27. |

*Jesu, der du meine Seele* ("Jesus, Who My Soul"; the libretto is anonymous) was written for the Fourteenth Sunday after Trinity in 1724—not a major event in the church year, by any means. Bach's achievement is all the more remarkable when we consider that he had written another entirely new cantata only the week before and would write yet another the week after. The opening chorus is a tour de force of Baroque compositional techniques, integrating in single movement at least four specific musical devices: ostinato, chorale, ritornello structure, and motet.

((•◦ **Listen**
**CD5 Tracks 16–20**
**mysearchlab** (with scrolling translation)
J. S. BACH
*Jesu, der du meine Seele*, BWV 78
Score Anthology I/88

## Composer Profile

# Johann Sebastian Bach (1685–1750)

Born into a family of musicians in central Germany, Bach synthesized European music of his time without ever really leaving home. He held down a succession of different jobs in his early career, including positions as organist (Mühlhausen), as violinist and concert master to a court orchestra (Weimar), and as court composer (Cöthen). Like any good 18th-century composer, Bach wrote what was demanded of him. Thus a great many of Bach's organ works date from his early years at Mühlhausen, and many of the best known orchestral works, including the Brandenburg Concertos, date from the years in Cöthen.

Bach's final position—as cantor of St. Thomas's Church in Leipzig—required him to produce large quantities of music for worship services, and it was here that he wrote the vast majority of his more than 200 cantatas. Had he spread this output out over his full 27 years in Leipzig, the accomplishment would be remarkable enough. But through detailed studies of paper, handwriting, and other evidence, scholars have been able to demonstrate that Bach actually wrote about 150 cantatas within his first 3 years in Leipzig at the rate of roughly 1 a week. When one considers the tasks involved for Bach—composing the work, writing out the score, supervising the copying of the parts, rehearsing, and performing—and this week after week, all in addition to attending to his duties as a teacher at the church's school, the achievement seems almost superhuman.

In a letter of 1730 to a friend, Bach complained that

(1) the position is not nearly as attractive as it was originally described to me; (2) many of the incidental payments once associated with this position have been abolished; (3) this is a very expensive place in which to live; and (4) the authorities, oddly, are little inclined toward music, and as a result I must live in an environment of constant vexation, envy, and persecution, so much so that with the assistance of the Almighty I find it necessary to seek my fortune elsewhere.

. . . My current position pays about 700 thaler, and whenever there are more funerals than usual, the incidental payments increase accordingly. But if the air is healthful, those payments can decrease, as they did last year when the standard payments for funerals decreased by more than 100 thaler.

In Thuringia I can do more with 400 thaler than I can with twice that amount, given the excessively high cost of living [in Leipzig].[12]

Bach's surviving sons were all successful composers in their own right. Indeed, Carl Philipp Emanuel Bach (1714–1788) would eventually become more famous than his father, even during the elder Bach's lifetime. Johann Christian Bach (1735–1782), sometimes called the "London Bach" because of his eventual home, was one of Mozart's favorite composers. Wilhelm Friedemann Bach (1710–1784), said to be perhaps the most musically gifted of all Bach's sons, met repeated misfortunes in his career and died in poverty.

In contrast to Handel, Bach was largely forgotten as a composer in the decades after his death. Very few of his works were published during his lifetime, and although the *Well-Tempered Clavier* and some other keyboard works continued to circulate in manuscript, the vocal music lay dormant for many years. The first stirrings of a Bach revival came around 1800 with the publication of the first biography of the composer (by Johann Nicolaus Forkel, in 1802) and several of the motets in score. But the big breakthrough came in 1828 when the young Felix Mendelssohn performed the *Saint Matthew Passion* in Leipzig. It was a musical revelation for listeners and composers alike. Western composers began almost without exception to study Bach's music with care and devotion, and his influence remains inescapable even today.

# PRINCIPAL WORKS

## Cantatas

Bach wrote an estimated 280 sacred cantatas, of which about 200 have survived; he also wrote about 30 secular cantatas for royal birthdays, marriages, civic occasions, and university ceremonies.

These works are remarkable in both quantity and quality. Bach's productivity was staggering: he composed the bulk of his sacred cantatas in the span of his first three or four years in Leipzig, producing a new one almost every week. These works appeared in three cycles over the years 1723–1724 (first cycle), 1724–1725 (second cycle), and 1725–1727 (third cycle). Bach began work on each cycle with the First Sunday after Trinity and carried each through to the following Trinity Sunday a year later. For the first cycle, he drew on compositions from his years in Weimar and Cöthen, but for the most part he was writing essentially a new work every Sunday. The second cycle is the most systematic of the three, consisting of chorale cantatas, in which the melody of the closing chorale figures into one or more of the work's other movements as well. Bach also wrote cantatas for special Feast Days such as the Feast of Saint John and the Festival of the Reformation.

Bach drew on three different kinds of sources for his cantata texts: (1) the biblical passages to be read in church that particular day, (2) a chorale text associated with that particular day, and (3) a new poetic interpretation of sentiments consistent with that particular day. A typical cantata mixes all of these elements. (In some cases, the author of the librettos is known—for example, those written by Christian Friedrich Henrici, a Leipzig lawyer who wrote poetry under the name Picander.) Like Schütz and many other Protestant German musicians before him, Bach considered himself an interpreter of the sacred word, using music to convey the spiritual meaning of any given text.

Bach explored a variety of instrumental and vocal forces in his cantatas, as well as a variety of formal plans. Some, like *Jauchzet Gott in allen Landen*, BWV 51, are for soloist; others are for soloists and chorus (like *Jesu, der du meine Seele*). All but the earliest cantatas make use of recitative, and many feature prominent instrumental solo parts in one or more movements, such as the trumpet part in *Jauchzet Gott in allen Landen* or the oboe part in the bass aria of *Jesu, der du meine Seele*.

## Passions

The music for Holy Week—the period leading up to Easter, commemorating the betrayal and crucifixion of Christ—was of particular importance in the German Protestant church. Bach wrote five different settings of the Passion, but only those based on the biblical accounts of Saint Matthew and Saint John survive. These are enormous works featuring a narrator (the Evangelist) and individual characters (Christ, the disciples) who sing texts taken from the gospels. The gospel text settings are interspersed with chorales, recitatives, and arias set to contemporary poetry. In the *Saint Matthew Passion*, Bach sets off the words of Christ by scoring them to a "halo" of stringed accompaniment.

## Mass and Motets

Bach's seven motets are for a cappella chorus, four of them for double chorus. Some of the surviving performance materials indicate that instruments may have doubled the voice parts on occasion. These works were written on commission for special occasions, probably funerals. He also wrote numerous settings of mass movements, but his one integrated cycle, the great Mass in B minor, consists of a variety of movements culled from works written over a period of some two decades.

## Chamber Music

Bach wrote quantities of chamber music for a variety of instruments. Many of these works are now lost, but most notable among those that survive are the sonatas for harpsichord with viola da gamba (3), violin (6), and flute (2). The three sonatas and three partitas for solo violin remain a touchstone of the violin repertory, demanding great virtuosity within a contrapuntal framework remarkable for a single instrument of this kind. The six suites for solo cello are also a staple of that instrument's repertory.

## Orchestral Music

The most famous of Bach's works for orchestra are the six concerti grossi dedicated to the Margrave of Brandenburg, the so-called Brandenburg Concertos. Each is scored differently. The first and third concertos feature no individual soloist, and the third is for strings alone. The second is a brilliantly scored concerto for trumpet, recorder, oboe, violin, and strings. The fourth features a solo violin and two solo recorders. The fifth incorporates an extended solo section (cadenza) for harpsichord, one of three solo instruments in the work, the others being violin and flute. The sixth's unusual scoring calls for low strings (no violins, no violas) to accompany two solo violas and two solo viola da gambas.

Bach also wrote solo concertos for violin, two violins, violin and oboe, and one to four harpsichords. The four orchestral suites all bear evidence of French influence, particularly in their French overtures; the second of these suites features a solo flute throughout.

## Organ Music

Bach generally made a clear distinction between his harpsichord and organ music, almost invariably drawing on the full resources of the latter instrument in ways that

# Johann Sebastian Bach (Continued)

made this music inaccessible to the harpsichord. The organ works span a great many genres, including chorale harmonizations, chorale preludes, toccatas, preludes and fugues, trios, and solo concertos. These last are arrangements of orchestral concertos by Duke Johann Ernst of Saxe-Weimar and by Antonio Vivaldi; BWV 593 is an arrangement of Vivaldi's op. 3, no. 8 (Anthology). Here, as in virtually all other genres, Bach was constantly exploring the works of other composers, both predecessors and contemporaries, to learn new ways of writing music.

## Harpsichord Music

A good deal of the harpsichord music is didactic, intended to serve composers and performers alike: the Two- and Three-Part Inventions, the *Well-Tempered Clavier* (see Chapter 10), the *Clavier-Übung*, and the short pieces from the three *Clavier-Büchlein* ("Little Book of Keyboard Pieces") written for his eldest son, Wilhelm Friedemann Bach, and his second wife, Anna Magdalena Bach. The suite was a genre of special interest to Bach; his keyboard works of this kind include the so-called English and French suites (each a set of six suites), and the six partitas. He also transcribed many orchestral concertos by Vivaldi and others for harpsichord; the *Concerto in the Italian Taste* (better known simply as the Italian Concerto) is an original work for a single keyboard that imitates the tutti and solo alternations so characteristic of Italian concertos of the time.

## Canonic Works and Fugal Works of the Final Decade

In the last decade of his life, Bach devoted increasing attention to canonic and fugal works. The *Musikalisches Opfer* ("Musical Offering") is a set of elaborations on a theme given to him personally by Frederick II ("The Great") of Prussia. Bach had been visiting his son Carl Philipp Emanuel in Potsdam in 1747 when the Prussian ruler asked him to improvise a set of variations on a theme of Frederick's invention. Bach complied but also took the "Royal Theme" back to Leipzig and eventually presented the monarch with a dazzling set of variations, including two ricercars, several canons, and a number of works in a free style.

The *Kunst der Fuge* ("Art of Fugue") is a quasi-encyclopedic compilation of fugues on a single basic theme. The cycle remains unfinished. Legend has it that Bach was struck blind when he entered a countersubject on the notes B-A-C-H (that is, B♭, A, C, B♯, "H" being the German term for B♯), but he had been losing his eyesight for some time. The work is written in open score, with no indication of performance medium, and it has been performed on organ and harpsichord, as well as by instrumental ensembles of all sorts.

The so-called "Goldberg" Variations (Anthology; see Chapter 10), the puzzle canon BWV 1076, and the canonic variations on the Christmas hymn *Vom Himmel hoch* (later reworked by Stravinsky in the 20th century) also belong to the final decade of Bach's life.

**Ostinato.** The ostinato passage in this movement is the four-measure figure in the bass line at the opening of the work that descends by half steps from G to D. This descending chromatic fourth, known as the *passus duriusculus* ("painful passage"), had long been associated with moments of anguish. Purcell had used it in Dido's lament at the end of *Dido and Aeneas*, and Bach himself would later incorporate it into the Credo of his B-Minor Mass for the passage that speaks of Christ's crucifixion. Here it alerts listeners even before a word is sung that the opening movement of this cantata deals with pain and suffering. The ostinato is stated twice in the bass (m. 1–5 and 5–9) and then migrates to other voices: the first oboe (m. 9–12), second oboe (13–16), and then finally to the singers themselves, who enter in imitation (m. 17 ff.). The descending line is then inverted (m. 25 ff.) at the first suggestion of hope in the text ("has through your bitter death . . .") but then reverts to its original descending pattern (m. 28 ff.). The figure continues with similar permutations in almost every measure of the movement.

## KEY DATES IN THE LIFE OF BACH

**1685** Born on March 21 in Eisenach, Germany, the son of a town musician.

**1703** Appointed organist at Arnstadt.

**1705** Walks to Lübeck, some 215 miles away, to hear and meet Dietrich Buxtehude.

**1707** Appointed organist at a larger church in Mühlhausen.

**1708** Appointed court organist and chamber musician (later concertmaster) to the Duke of Weimar.

**1717** Appointed music director at the court of Anhalt-Cöthen; writes many of his works for orchestra (including the Brandenburg Concertos) while in this position.

**1722** Succeeds Johann Kuhnau as cantor of St. Thomas's School in Leipzig; writes most of his cantatas in this position.

**1747** Visits his son Carl Philipp Emanuel in Potsdam and improvises for King Frederick II ("The Great"); the improvisation eventually takes the form of *A Musical Offering*.

**1750** Dies in Leipzig on July 28.

**Johann Sebastian Bach.** To at least some extent, portraits are often self-portraits, in that the subject routinely chooses the backdrop and props. Here, Bach holds in his hand a copy of his *Canon Triplex,* BWV 1076. The choice of works is revealing: this is a puzzle canon whose three notated voices produce six different voices that can be played in an astonishing variety of permutations. Within the portrait itself, the canon is resolved by creating a new voice, through inversion, out of each of the notated parts. The inversion of the uppermost voice enters at a fourth above, the middle voice enters at a fifth above, and the bass (which is similar to the opening of the bass line in the *Goldberg Variations*) enters at a fourth below. Each voice works in counterpoint against not only its own inversion, but against the two other themes and their inversions as well. And this is only one of many possible solutions to this canon.

**Source:** Stadtgeschichtliches Museum Leipzig

**Chorale.** This first movement is also permeated with the melody of the chorale from which the cantata takes its name. The words and melody of *Jesu, der du meine Seele* would have been familiar to any of the parishioners hearing the first performance of this cantata. The melody falls into distinct phrases and is always presented by the soprano (beginning in m. 21). Thus the chorale melody presents a kind of superstructure above the ostinato figure.

**Ritornello structure.** The movement opens with an extended passage for the orchestra alone, with a dotted-rhythm melody running above the ostinato in the bass. This material functions as a ritornello throughout the entire movement, returning between the successive entrances of the chorus. The rhythm of this triple-meter melody is reminiscent of the sarabande, a dance common to many instrumental suites.

## BACH'S *JESU, DER DU MEINE SEELE*, BWV 78: THE RITORNELLO STRUCTURE OF THE FIRST MOVEMENT

| Section | Rit. 1 | Chorus 1 | Rit. 2 | Ch. 2 | Rit. 3 | Ch. 3 | Rit. 4 | Ch. 4 | Rit. 5 | Ch. 5 | Rit. 6 | Ch. 6 | Rit. 7 |
|---------|--------|----------|--------|-------|--------|-------|--------|-------|--------|-------|--------|-------|--------|
| Measure | 1 | 17 | 37 | 49 | 69 | 73 | 85 | 89 | 99 | | 107 | 122 | 129 | 140 |
| Tonality | g | | | d | F | | | Bb | | →g | | | g (G) |

**Motet.**   Finally, by dividing the text into six distinct sections, each with its own thematic material, and each with its own opening points of imitation, Bach in effect employs the structure of the motet for the choral portions of the opening movement. If one were to somehow excise all the statements of the ritornello, in other words, this opening chorus would be able to stand on its own as a choral motet.

Subsequent movements alternate between aria and recitative. The second-movement duet is a masterpiece of word painting. The principal thematic idea takes its cue from the text itself:

*Wir eilen mit schwachen, doch emsigen Schritten,*

We hasten with weak, yet eager steps,

*O Jesu, o Meister, zu helfen zu dir.*

Oh Jesus, oh Master, for help toward thee.

The musical figure Bach uses to present this passage is an upward-moving line that keeps falling back on itself, only to strive ever higher to a constant rhythm of steady eighth notes. The image of "weak, yet eager steps" could scarcely be captured more vividly. The two voices in turn strive with each other to reach their highest pitch.

Formally, Bach constructs this duet as a da capo aria:

## BACH'S *JESU, DER DU MEINE SEELE*, BWV 78: THE DA CAPO ARIA STRUCTURE OF THE SECOND MOVEMENT

| | Section | Measures | Harmony |
|---|---------|----------|---------|
| A | Ritornello 1 | 1–8 | Bb Major |
| | Duet 1 | 9–42 | Bb Major |
| | Ritornello 2 | 43–50 | Bb Major |
| B | Duet 2 | 51–60 | G minor → C minor |
| | Ritornello 3 | 61–64 | C minor |
| | Duet 3 | 65–80 | C minor → D minor |
| | Ritornello 4 | 81–82 | D minor → F Major |
| | Duet 4 | 83–98 | F Major (=V/Bb) |
| | "A" section da capo | | |
| A | See above | [99–148] | Bb Major |

The subsequent recitative and aria pairs for tenor and bass are also full of word painting. In the bass recitative in the fifth movement, for example,

- the words *Wunden* ("wounds"), *Nägel* ("nails"), and *Kron* ("crown") are set to pointed dissonances; on *Grab* ("grave"), the singer descends to a deep register.

- the strings present an agitated sixteenth-note figure to emphasize the word *erschreckliches* ("terrifying") in m. 8–9.

The bass aria is a duet between the vocalist and the oboist. This kind of writing for voice and solo instrument occurs frequently in Bach's music. The cantata concludes with a harmonized setting of the chorale melody *Jesu, der du meine Seele*, which had provided the cantus firmus for the opening movement, rounding out the whole to provide a sense of cyclical symmetry.

# CONCEPTIONS OF THE COMPOSITIONAL PROCESS

Bach's repeated reworkings of his own music remind us that attitudes toward the compositional process in the Baroque era differed markedly from the way most composers approach their work today, but it is very similar to the attitude held by composers in the Renaissance and even the Middle Ages. Almost every composer of the 17th and 18th centuries borrowed musical themes and sometimes entire pieces from others. And almost every composer at some point recycled an earlier work into a new composition. No one considered this dishonest or lazy; rather, it was simply a matter of routine. Originality was valued in composition, but not nearly to the extent that it would be in the 19th century. Thus, although Handel was roundly criticized by 19th- and 20th-century writers for his frequent borrowings, none of his contemporaries seems to have found the practice objectionable. As Johann Mattheson observed in 1739, "Borrowing is permissible; but one must return the object borrowed with interest, i.e., one must so construct and develop imitations that they are prettier and better than the pieces from which they are derived."[13]

Examples of composers who borrowed or reworked earlier compositions—their own or those of others—include the following:

- Monteverdi, who reworked the instrumental overture ("Toccata") to *Orfeo* into the opening chorus ("Domine ad adjuvandum") of *Vespers* of 1610; he also rewrote a canzonetta (*Ci ome d'oro*) as a motet (*Beatus vir*).

- Purcell, who, having written a song for a particular play, would often rewrite the same song to fit into an entirely different play.

- Handel, who reworked movements of his own, as well as movements by Alessandro Stradella and Johann Kaspar Kerll into his oratorio *Israel in Egypt*; he borrowed copiously from Georg Philipp Telemann, Reinhard Keiser, and many other contemporary composers throughout his life.

- J. S. Bach, who reworked Pergolesi's *Stabat mater* into a motet (*Tilge, Höchster, meine Sünden*); he also recast many movements from his own secular cantatas into movements for sacred cantatas.

And while printers and publishers sought monopolies from royalty and local authorities from the 15th century forward, piracy (republishing without permission or a contract to do so) and fraud (intentional misattribution of music to well-known composers) were the primary concerns of the day.

Different forces motivated these borrowings and adaptations. Many composers were writing to deadline: a new cantata due next Sunday, a funeral anthem due tomorrow. Considering the quantity of new music Bach and others in similar positions were expected to produce on an ongoing basis, it is remarkable they did not borrow more often than they actually did. Composers also borrowed in an effort to explore other styles. Bach's reworking of Pergolesi's *Stabat mater* was part of a broader effort to understand and assimilate a different style of composition. Bach had earlier made arrangements (for organ and for harpsichord) of a number of concertos by Vivaldi and others in an attempt to assimilate the new style of writing concertos for solo instruments.

The attitude of Baroque composers toward borrowing and reworking was an extension of a broader way of thinking that lacked the concept of a musical composition as a finished work in a definitive, unalterable state. Most composers of this era took a fairly open-ended approach to their creations for reasons that were partly practical and partly aesthetic. Frescobaldi advised performers that in playing one of his toccatas they could break off at any point they wished. His instrumental pieces were often used in church services, and practical considerations—filling up the time during or after Communion, for example—took precedence over any sense of aesthetic unity or completeness.

We tend to think of musical compositions today as finished works that exist in a definitive form, particularly if they have been published under the composer's

## Primary Evidence    BACH THE MUSICIAN

*In gathering information for the first real biography of J. S. Bach, the composer and critic Johann Nicolaus Forkel (1749–1818) solicited information from many individuals who had known the composer personally, including Bach's son Carl Philipp Emanuel Bach. In this letter of 1774, C. P. E. Bach describes his father as a musician.*

■ ■ ■

The exact tuning of his instruments as well as of the whole orchestra had his greatest attention. No one could tune and quill his instruments to please him. He did everything himself. The placing of an orchestra he understood perfectly. He made good use of any space. He grasped at first glance any peculiarity of a room. . . .

He heard the slightest wrong note even in the largest combinations. As the greatest expert and judge of harmony, he liked best to play the viola, with appropriate loudness and softness. In his youth, and until the approach of old age, he played the violin cleanly and penetratingly, and thus kept the orchestra in better order than he could have done with the harpsichord. He understood to perfection the possibilities of all stringed instruments. This is evidenced by his solos for the violin and for the violoncello without [accompanying] bass. One of the greatest

violinists told me once that he had seen nothing more perfect for learning to be a good violinist, and could suggest nothing better to anyone eager to learn, than the said violin solos without bass.

Thanks to his greatness in harmony [i.e., counterpoint], he accompanied trios on more than one occasion on the spur of the moment and, being in a good humor and knowing that the composer would not take it amiss, and on the basis of a sparsely figured continuo part just set before him, converted them into complete quartets, astounding the composer of the trios.

When he listened to a rich and many-voiced fugue, he could soon say, after the first entries of the subjects, what contrapuntal devices it would be possible to apply, and which of them the composer by rights ought to apply, and on such occasions, when I was standing next to him, and he had voiced his surmises to me, he would joyfully nudge me when his expectations were fulfilled.

**Source:** "Letter to J.N. Forkel" by J.S. Bach from *The New Bach Reader: A Life of Johann Sebastian Bach in Letters and Documents* by Hans. T. David & Arthur Mendel, eds., rev. by Christoph Wolff. Copyright © 1998 by Christoph Wolff. Copyright (c) 1966, 1945 by W.W. Norton & Company, Inc. Copyright (c) 1972 by Mrs. Hans T. David and Arthur Mendel. Reprinted by permission of the publisher.

supervision. But composers of the Baroque era were much more likely to revise, rework, arrange, and otherwise recycle an already finished composition. One of Johann Sebastian Bach's best known cantatas, *Ein feste Burg ist unser Gott* ("A Mighty Fortress Is Our God"), for example, exists in several different versions:

1. *Alles, was von Gott geboren.* ("All That Is Born of God"), BWV 80a (BC A52), a cantata composed in 1715 in Weimar.

2. *Ein feste Burg ist unser Gott.* Only two of the eight movements of this cantata have survived, but from other evidence, we can be fairly sure that Bach took the music for this work, composed between 1721 and 1731 in Leipzig, largely from number 1, underlaying a new text ("Ein feste Burg . . .").

3. *Ein feste Burg ist unser Gott.* A reworking of number 2, done in Leipzig in 1744–1747. Bach replaced the opening chorale of number 2 with a more extended motet-like movement on the chorale's motives and made slight changes of orchestration in some later movements.

4. *Ein feste Burg ist unser Gott.* Sometime after 1747, Wilhelm Friedemann Bach, the composer's oldest son, added parts for three trumpets and timpani to number 3. This is the best-known version of the cantata today.

5. *Gaudete omnes populi* and *Manebit verbum Domini.* W. F. Bach detached the first and fifth movements of number 4, substituted Latin texts, and performed these as separate works in Halle in 1750.

Are these five different works? They are all closely related, yet each is a distinct entity. The very concept of any one of them as a fixed work is problematic. Bach himself viewed his original composition (number 1) as something that could be reused on more than one occasion (numbers 2 and 3). His oldest son, in turn, enriched the orchestration (number 4) and spun off two movements into separate works with Latin texts (number 5).

The example of *Ein feste Burg* is by no means atypical, nor is this phenomenon limited to Bach or the realm of sacred music. When operas were revived or produced for troupes other than those for which they had originally been written, it was not at all unusual for impresarios to commission new or additional arias to suit a different cast of singers. Sometimes the original composers wrote these new arias; on other occasions they were written by a different composer altogether. This practice, moreover, continued well beyond the Baroque era. Mozart, for example, wrote substitute arias for his own *Don Giovanni* when it moved from Prague to Vienna in 1788, and he composed what are known as "insertion arias" for operas by others on many occasions.

## SUMMARY

The synthesis of word, rhythm, and pitch that had been so important in the early decades of the Baroque remained equally important at the end of the era, even if musical styles and genres had changed over time. Yet throughout this same period, composers devoted more and more of their energies to writing music without words at all. And it is to this instrumental repertory that we turn in Chapter 10.

Study and Review on mysearchlab.com

# Instrumental Music, 1600–1750

The same forces that drove changes in vocal music during the Baroque helped transform instrumental music as well. Even though they were working without texts, composers of instrumental music sought to move listeners by writing works that evoked human passions, in keeping with then-current beliefs about the relationship between music and emotion. The new emphasis on homophonic texture, a greater sense of rhythmic and melodic freedom, and a strong desire for timbral contrast animates much of the instrumental music written in the 17th and early 18th centuries.

## INSTRUMENTS OF THE BAROQUE ERA

Over the course of the 17th century, many instruments began to acquire their modern form, including those of the violin family (violin, viola, and cello), the harpsichord, and a variety of winds and brass.

### The Violin

The Baroque violin was outwardly similar to the modern violin, but differed from it in ways that gave it a sweeter, more rounded tone:

- The bass-bar (a piece of wood underneath the surface of the instrument) of the Baroque violin was shorter and lighter than on modern violins, giving it a lighter timbre.

- The angle of the neck as it drops away from the body of the instrument was not nearly as steep as on the modern violin, producing less tension on the strings and, as a result, a softer sound.

- The bridge was lower, further reducing string tension and sound volume.

- The fingerboard was shorter than on the modern violin, reducing the uppermost range of the instrument.

- The bow had not yet acquired a standard form and varied according to region but was in general shorter, with the hair less tensely wound than on the modern bow.

The characteristics that distinguish the modern violin from the Baroque violin did not emerge until the 19th century, when larger concert halls demanded that instruments of all kinds produce a louder, more penetrating sound. As a result, most violins that have survived from the 17th century were modified in the 19th to give them modern characteristics. But in the 20th century, particularly from about 1960 onward, musicians specializing in early music discovered that the sonorities of Baroque violins are well matched to the music of their time. These instruments create a transparent texture that makes it easier to hear inner voices obscured by modern instruments. The effect of hearing Baroque compositions performed on period instruments has often been compared to seeing a painting restored to its original state, cleaned of grime and dust. The colors are brighter, and details that had been lost for centuries are once again apparent.

## Winds, Brass, and Percussion

Early recorders had a cylindrical bore, with a constant diameter along the entire length of the instrument. By the late Renaissance, they were being made with conical bores that narrowed from the top to the bottom. This new design extended the range of the instruments and gave players better control of tuning, especially in the upper register. The transverse flute (today's standard flute, at first made of wood, in which the air stream is directed across rather than along the axis of the instrument) became increasingly prominent during the Baroque, but the recorder predominated for most of the era. The designation *flauto* on Baroque music usually indicates recorder. If composers wanted a transverse flute, they asked for it specifically with the designation *flauto traverso*.

The oboe emerged in the early 17th century as a successor to the shawm, a double-reed instrument of the Renaissance. Like the recorder, the oboe also developed a narrower, tapered bore over the course of time, assuming its modern form in the 19th century. The tone of the Baroque oboe—"quacking" is an unkind but not inaccurate description of it—tends to be less focused than that of the modern instrument yet in its own way richer and more pungent. The oboe d'amore, which had a bulb-shaped bell, emerged in the early 18th century. It had a slightly lower range and a softer, more subdued sound than the oboe. The oboe da caccia, also slightly lower than the standard oboe, would later be supplanted by the English horn.

The bassoon also evolved out of a Renaissance predecessor, the curtal, another double-reed instrument (see the illustration of Renaissance forerunners of the bassoon in Chapter 5). The bassoon was used primarily as a basso continuo instrument until the late 18th century. The chalumeau, a single-reed instrument, emerged in the late 17th century and eventually developed into the clarinet. Composers were slow to incorporate either instrument into the orchestra, however, probably because few players had mastered them and the more common oboe covered a similar range. Isolated works by Handel, Vivaldi, Rameau, and Telemann nevertheless explicitly call for the chalumeau or clarinet.

Brass instruments also developed into their recognizably modern forms during the late Renaissance and early Baroque. The trumpet evolved out of the cornetto (*Zink* in German, not to be confused with the modern-day cornet), a wooden instrument with a cup-shaped mouthpiece. Baroque trumpets were natural instruments; they had no valves and so were limited in the pitches they could play to a series of harmonic overtones. As a result, they were capable of carrying a melody only in their highest register. The valve trumpet, with its full chromatic range, was a 19th-century invention.

The use of trumpets was severely restricted in certain parts of Germany and elsewhere, and the post of town trumpeter was a position of importance in the hierarchy of civic musicians. One had to have a license, in effect, to play the trumpet, at least in public. The trumpeters' guilds kept secret their technique for playing in the highest registers of the instrument—so secret, in fact, that it was lost when the guilds, and

## Focus THE TRADE SECRETS OF VIOLIN MAKING

From the Middle Ages onward, artisans maintained a systematic silence about the secrets of their crafts, passing them on only to their apprentices (often their children) and only by word of mouth. Nowhere was this secretiveness more evident than in the realm of musical instrument making.

Cremona, a small city in northern Italy, emerged as the primary center for the craft of violin making in the 17th century, thanks to the skills of three extraordinary families: Amati, Stradivari, and Guarneri. Andrea Amati (d. 1577) had first introduced violin making to Cremona in the mid-16th century and established the basic proportions of the instruments in the violin family. His grandson Niccolò (1596–1684) made further improvements to the craft. His two most outstanding pupils were Antonio Stradivari (1644–1737; "Stradivarius" is the Latinized form of his name) and Andrea Guarneri (1625–1698), who established workshops of their own. Guarneri's grandson, Giuseppe Antonio Guarneri (1698–1744), would go on to become even more celebrated than his grandfather.

Amati, Stradivari, and Guarneri instruments set the standard for excellence in the art of violin making. No two of these instruments, even from the same workshop, are exactly alike. Makers were constantly tinkering with the precise dimensions of the instruments, the angle and length of the fingerboard, the thickness and placement of the bass-bar underneath the upper surface of the instrument, the shape of the f-holes, and so on. Not until the early 18th century did violins become more or less standardized.

All three workshops produced violas and cellos as well as violins. Indeed, these larger instruments—rarer than violins—command the highest prices on the market today. The rarest and most valuable of all is a Stradivari viola, very few of which were made.

The Cremona masters took many of their trade secrets with them to the grave. In the past 50 years, however, musical instrument makers, historians, and scientists—using sophisticated techniques of chemical analysis and radiography—have begun to penetrate those secrets. We now know that key factors included an instrument's shape, the selection and aging of the wood from which it was made, the technique used for carving the wood, and the characteristics of the varnish that protected it. With the recovery of at least some of the ancient craft, it is now possible to produce very good copies of instruments from the Cremona workshops, but the originals remain superior. One reason may lie in the nature of the wood. With even the most select trees today compromised by air pollution, it may no longer be possible to find wood of the same quality as that used in the original instruments.

their members, eventually died out. Throughout the 19th century and most of the 20th, no one could perform the kind of virtuosic high parts like that in Bach's Second Brandenburg Concerto on a natural trumpet. Around the middle of the 20th century, scholars and performers working together were able to recover this lost art.

The trombone developed out of the Renaissance sackbut. It had a wider bell than the earlier instrument, giving it a more mellow sound. The use of trombones was restricted largely to the church (where they often doubled vocal parts) and the theater, particularly for scenes depicting the underworld. Monteverdi, for example, used trombones to convey a sense of otherworldliness when Orpheus descends to Hades in Act III of *Orfeo*. (This tradition continued well into the 18th century. When the statue on the grave of the Commendatore comes to life in Mozart's *Don Giovanni*—see Chapter 13—it is to the sound of trombones.) Horns, long used in military settings and in the hunt, came into the orchestra around 1700. Players routinely used crooks—small pieces of detachable metal tubing—to play in different keys. Before the introduction of valves, in the 19th century, the number of keys in which hornists could play easily was relatively limited, as were the number of notes that could be played cleanly in each of the scales of those few keys.

Timpani were often used in conjunction with trumpets, probably more often than notated scores suggest. The combination of trumpets and drums was routinely associated with royalty, the military, civic power, or the glorification of God. Timpanists usually played on a pair of drums tuned a fifth apart (tonic and dominant, in modern terms).

## Keyboard Instruments

The keyboard repertory of the Baroque era reflects the growing size and quality of the instruments themselves. The period from the middle of the 16th century through the early decades of the 18th was a golden age of organ and harpsichord making. The technical advances in instrument building were at once inspired by and inspiring to the composers who wrote for the keyboard.

**Clavichord, Harpsichord, Fortepiano.** The clavichord was valued as a particularly expressive instrument because of the control a player could exert over the contact between the striking blade, or tangent, and the string. Because the tangent is attached directly to the key, performers could create a kind of vibrato by moving the finger up and down slightly after a note was struck but still sounding. The Germans called the effect *Bebung*, or "trembling." The clavichord remained an intimate, almost private instrument because of its soft dynamic levels.

Two basic types of harpsichord emerged during the Baroque era, Italian and Flemish. Italian harpsichords generally featured only one keyboard (also called a *manual*), the Flemish two. By the early 18th century, two manuals had become the norm across Europe. Instruments on the whole became larger, louder, and brighter, with an increasing variety of stops. One type of stop, for example, produced a sound like a lute; another produced a nasal sound.

Smaller versions of the harpsichord included the virginal, with a single keyboard and a set of strings aligned—as on the clavichord—at a right angle to the keys, and the spinet, whose strings were aligned diagonally to the keyboard. (Outside of England, the terms were virtually interchangeable.) Like the clavichord, these were instruments for the intimacy of the home, limited in the volume of sound they could produce. They were designed for the pleasure of the performers themselves with perhaps a very small audience gathered around.

For all their versatility, the harpsichord and its plucked string relatives could not produce gradations of volume. Certain stops might be louder than others, but performers had no way to shade from one volume level to another. "The harpsichord is perfect as to its compass and brilliant in itself," the French composer François Couperin (1668–1733) observed in 1713, "but as one can neither swell nor diminish its sounds, I will be forever grateful to those who with infinite pains guided by taste succeed in rendering this instrument capable of expression."[1]

Even as Couperin wrote, instrument makers were at work trying to fulfill his wish. Their chief technical obstacle was to develop a mechanism that would allow a hammer to strike a string with variable force but then immediately fall away without ricocheting, so the string could reverberate freely (a process called *escapement*). The Florentine instrument maker Bartolomeo Cristofori (1655–1730) achieved the earliest breakthrough in this endeavor, building about 20 instruments that he called *gravicembalo col piano e forte* ("harpsichord with soft and loud") between 1709 and 1726. These new instruments—known generally as fortepianos—attracted little attention at the time, however. It was not until about 1760 that the fortepiano began seriously to challenge the preeminence of the harpsichord (see Chapter 12).

**The Organ.** Organ building made great strides during the late 15th and early 16th centuries, but the craft enjoyed its golden age from about 1550 through 1750, particularly in northern Europe, in what is now northern France, Belgium, the Netherlands, northern Germany, Denmark, and Sweden. Important organ builders of this era include Arp Schnitger (1648–1719), who worked in northern Germany, and

Gottfried Silbermann (1683–1753), who was active in southern Germany and what is now eastern France. Silbermann was also known for his harpsichords and early pianos.

The more imposing instruments of this period feature 3 or even 4 manuals, a large independent pedal division, and more than 60 speaking stops. Each of the manuals controlled one or more sets of pipes: the *Hauptwerk* (the Great); the *Brustwerk* (the Chest), placed in front of the organist; and the *Rückpositif* (Chair, so called because it was sometimes placed behind or under the organist's bench).

Churches invested enormous sums of money in their organs. Johann Sebastian Bach, a renowned judge of organs, punctuated his day-to-day duties in Leipzig with trips to towns and cities around central Germany to test out the craftsmanship of newly installed instruments and verify that the makers had fulfilled the terms of their contracts. As his son Carl Philipp Emanuel Bach related in a letter,

> No one has ever tried out organs so severely and yet at the same time as honestly as he. He understood the whole art of organ building in the highest degree. When an organ builder had worked conscientiously, and incurred losses by his work, he would persuade the employers to make amends. No one understood registration at the organ as well as he. Organists were often terrified when he sat down to play on their organs and drew the stops in his own manner, for they thought that the effect could not be good as he was planning it; but then they gradually heard an effect that astounded them. [Here C. P. E. Bach added in the margin of the letter: "These sciences perished with him."]

> The first thing he would do in trying an organ was this: he would say, in jest, "Above all I must know whether the organ has good lungs," and, to find out, he would draw out every speaking stop, and play in the fullest and richest possible texture. At this the organ builders would often grow quite pale with fright.[2]

## The Orchestra

The orchestra in the modern sense of the term—an ensemble of players with more than one to a part, at least in the string section—emerged gradually over the course of the Baroque era. In 17th-century Italy, any large church in a major city maintained its own *cappella* consisting of instrumentalists as well as singers. The size of such ensembles varied according to the importance and resources of the individual church. The largest such ensemble, at San Marco in Venice, kept 35 choristers and 18 instrumentalists on its payroll in 1643; by the early 18th century, the total number had grown to about 70. San Petronio, in Bologna, was somewhat more typical for a large church in a major city, employing 16 singers and 12 instrumentalists in the mid-17th century. Additional musicians were routinely hired for the celebration of major feasts such as Christmas and Easter.

Court orchestras rose to special prominence in France and Germany. The fame of Louis XIV's "24 Violinists of the King"—a core group of 24 string players, augmented by winds and percussion as needed—spread throughout Europe and, like the palace of Versailles itself, became a model for other monarchs to emulate. Visitors to the French court were also impressed by the ensemble's uniformity of attack and its dedication to bowing up and down in unison.

The typical orchestra in a German court was considerably more modest. At Cöthen, for example, J. S. Bach seems to have had only about 18 instrumentalists regularly at his disposal. More were hired for special occasions, but the core ensemble itself was relatively small by today's standards.

**A student orchestra of the 1740s.** Students from the University of Jena's Collegium Musicum perform in the town square in conjunction with a civic ceremony or festivity of some kind. The music is clearly festive in nature, for the large orchestra includes trumpets and timpani. The harpsichordist, at center, conducts from the keyboard. J. S. Bach led a similar ensemble in nearby Leipzig after 1729; indeed, the orchestra here is similar to that called for in Bach's Fourth Orchestral Suite.

**Source:** Museum für Kunst und Gewerbe, Hamburg, Germany/akg-images

## The Public Concert

The public concert—that is, a concert taking place outside the church or theater and open to the public—remained a relatively unusual phenomenon throughout the Baroque era. The notion of a permanent municipal orchestra did not yet exist. Convents and orphanages offered public concerts from time to time, but regular performances in the same locale by the same musicians were quite rare before the 18th century. Taverns and public rooms sometimes sponsored musical performances, and in London, a coal dealer named Thomas Britton offered concerts in his lodgings for a decade or so around 1700. He charged admission and aroused great admiration among his contemporaries for his cultural and entrepreneurial spirit in spite of his modest social standing. Handel is said to have performed at some of these gatherings.

Amateur societies also offered public performances from time to time. In 1702, the composer Georg Philipp Telemann organized the Leipzig Collegium Musicum, consisting primarily of university students, which performed weekly in local coffeehouses. J. S. Bach directed the ensemble during the 1730s and 1740s. The most important venue for public performances in France was the *Concert spirituel* ("spiritual concert") series, founded by Anne Danican Philidor (1681–1728) in 1725. These concerts offered mostly instrumental and sacred music during times when theaters were closed, particularly during Lent. The performers were professional musicians from the opera house and Parisian churches, and the series ran on a subscription basis in various locales under different leadership until 1790.

# INSTRUMENTAL GENRES OF THE BAROQUE ERA

The sonata, concerto, and suite were the most important genres of music for ensembles; the keyboard repertory encompassed sonatas, suites, and a variety of other formal types.

## Sonata

The term **sonata** was used quite broadly in the early Baroque era and did not acquire its modern, more specialized meaning until well into the 18th century. In Italian, *sonata* means simply "that which is sounded," meaning a work played on instruments, as opposed to one that is sung, a *cantata*. The term was something of a catchall for instrumental works of all kinds, including those for a large ensemble with more than one player to a part. In general, a Baroque sonata had no fixed number or order of movements.

Seventeenth-century Italian composers were especially prolific in writing sonatas, often for violin (solo or duo) and basso continuo, and quite virtuosic; their mercurial quality recalls operatic recitative of the period. A Bohemian violinist, Heinrich Ignaz Biber (1644–1704), wrote in this manner, sometimes calling for the violin to be tuned in an unusual manner (*scordatura*, Italian for "mistuning"), a technique still used occasionally by composers as well as traditional musicians.

Isabella Leonarda (1620–1704) came from a prominent family in Novara in the Piedmont region. At age 16 she entered an Ursuline convent, where she remained until her death. Leonarda rose in the leadership ranks of her convent, but her primary efforts went toward the musical education of the women and girls there. (As with other religious institutions in Italy, musical performances were invaluable fundraisers at the time; see Chapter 9.) Leonarda wrote over 200 works, mostly religious vocal pieces for her students, collected into 20 volumes published between ca. 1665 and 1700; she was one of the most published composers of the 17th century.

Leonarda published one collection featuring instrumental music exclusively: the *Sonate à 1. 2. 3. e 4. istromenti*, opus 16 (Bologna, 1693), the first sonatas published by a woman. The twelfth and final sonata in the set is for solo violin and basso continuo. The piece recalls earlier Italian sonatas with its fluidity and formal freedom, its paratactic structure; the changes of tempo and meter are typical of sonatas and concertos of Corelli and others. The music, based on a background progression of D minor → F Major (m. 84) → B♭ (m. 126) → D minor (m. 189), is harmonically rich, although the technical demands on the soloist are fairly limited. It is only in the last forty years or so that musicologists have begun to explore the rich repertory of music produced by and for nuns in earlier times. Convents were an important venue for music-making of all kinds throughout the Baroque era.

By the end of the 17th century, one distinctive type of sonata—the **trio sonata**—had acquired a relatively fixed form. As its name implies, a trio sonata has three notated parts: two higher voices above a basso continuo. The basso continuo, although a single musical line, might be realized by two or even more players. The two upper voices were often written for violins, but composers, publishers, and performers were generally flexible about these designations. Thus the title pages of many published trio sonatas state that the upper voices can be performed by two violins, or two flutes, or two oboes, or any combination of these instruments (violin and oboe, flute and oboe, and so forth). The music, in other words, tends not to be idiomatic to any particular instrument. Because most of these works were written for amateur performers, they tend to be relatively undemanding technically.

By the middle of the 17th century, a distinction had emerged between two different types of trio sonata: the **sonata da camera** and the **sonata da chiesa.** The sonata da camera ("chamber sonata") consists of a suite (collection) of dances. (The genre of the suite is discussed later in this chapter.) The sonata da chiesa ("church sonata") was so called because of its suitability for performance within the liturgy. In his *Dictionnaire de musique* of 1703, Sebastian de Brossard points out that the sonata da chiesa is

((•‣ Listen

**CD5   Track 21**
**mysearchlab**
LEONARDA
Sonata in D minor, op. 16, no. 12
Score Anthology I/89

## Performance Perspective

# The Art of Embellishment

Instrumental soloists, like vocal soloists, were routinely expected to embellish their musical lines during the Baroque era. The illustration here, from a 1710 edition of a sonata for violin and basso continuo by Arcangelo Corelli (op. 5), indicates what that might involve. The bottom line is the basso continuo and the middle line is the violin part as Corelli wrote it. The top line, however, purports to show how Corelli himself, a famous violin virtuoso, actually played the line. It was the slower passages in particular that Corelli embellished. On the page shown here, for example, from the middle of op. 5, no. 1, only the passages marked adagio or grave are embellished.

Embellishment also extended to matters of rhythm. Ample evidence suggests, for example, that performers routinely played two notes of equal value in a single beat as if they had been written with unequal values, the first slightly longer than the second. This practice—known by its French name of *notes inégales* ("unequal notes")—is mentioned in more than 85 French treatises published between roughly 1550 and 1810, as well as in other treatises from elsewhere across the Continent. But exactly how and when to apply it remains open to considerable debate. None of the evidence that historians have culled from the relevant treatises provides an unambiguous answer. Now as then, it is the performer who must decide for any given work how to put the theory of *notes inégales* into practice.

**Source:** Museo internazionale e Biblioteca della musica di Bologna

Arcangelo Corelli "Sonate|für Violine und Basso continuo ad lib.|op. 5" © 2003 by Wiener Urtext Edition, Musikverlag, Ges.m.b.H. & Co., K.G., Wien

"proper for the Church" because it "usually begins with a serious and majestic movement, suited to the dignity and sanctity of the place." The imitative movements that follow sustain this aura of serious dignity. The sequence of movements in Corelli's Trio Sonata, op. 1, no. 5, is typical of the form:

| | |
|---|---|
| Grave | G minor |
| Allegro | B♭ Major (imitative) |
| Adagio/Allegro | G minor/B♭ Major |
| Allegro | B♭ Major (imitative) |

The term *sonata* was also applied to works for solo instrument, including sonatas for solo instrument with basso continuo. These ranged from a single movement to multiple movements. For multimovement sonatas of all kinds, composers sought to provide a variety of tempos and effects, but there was otherwise no fixed pattern for a cycle of movements.

**The guitar as a domestic instrument.** The popularity of the guitar is not a recent phenomenon. The "Spanish" guitar, as it was known in England, was already in wide use by the early 17th century; only in the mid-19th century did it begin to be supplanted by the piano. The ability to sing and accompany oneself on the guitar was long considered a desirable social skill, particularly for young ladies. Here, a young woman from the Lake family has chosen to have herself portrayed with the instrument; this image was made sometime around 1660.

**Source:** Tate, London/Art Resource, NY

## Concerto

Like sonata, the term **concerto** had a wide range of meanings during the Baroque era. In the early 17th century, it was applied to works in which any number or combination of diverse musical forces work together, or "in concert." It did not necessarily apply, as it later would, to the opposition of different forces—soloists against orchestra or singers against instrumentalists—although it certainly did not preclude such contrasts. When Lodovico Grossi da Viadana (ca. 1560–1627) published a collection of sacred monodies in 1602 for one to four vocal soloists with basso continuo, he called the set *Cento concerti ecclesiastici* (One Hundred Church Concertos). And when Heinrich Schütz, later in the same century, published two sets of sacred works for one or two solo voices and small instrumental ensemble, he called them *Kleine geistliche Konzerte* (Small Sacred Concertos).

Only in the last quarter of the 17th century did the opposition between a soloist or soloists and an ensemble emerge as a characteristic feature of the genre, and even then, earlier usage persisted. As late as the 1720s, for example, J. S. Bach gave the designation of "Concerto" to some of his cantatas for soloists, chorus, and orchestra.

The emergence of a genre that highlights the contrasts within its performing forces represents an important new development in the history of music. As with the sonata, several subcategories of concerto had established themselves by the end of the 17th century: the concerto grosso, the solo concerto, and the ripieno concerto.

- The **concerto grosso** features a small group of soloists, the **concertino**, with its own basso continuo, against a larger ensemble known as the **ripieno** (Italian for "full") or **tutti** ("all").

- The **solo concerto** features a single soloist (such as violin, flute, or oboe) or a pair of soloists (two violins or two flutes) against a ripieno ensemble.

- The **ripieno concerto**, which features no soloists at all, reflects the persistence of the earlier understanding of the genre, in which the opposition between contrasting forces within an ensemble plays little or no role. These works have often come down to us with other designations like *sonata* or *sinfonia* as well as *concerto*.

Arcangelo Corelli's concerti grossi are among the earliest works of their kind. Although not published until 1714, a year after the composer's death, at least some of them were circulating in manuscript in Rome as early as the 1680s. Corelli's concerti grossi feature a ripieno of strings and basso continuo with a concertino (solo ensemble) typical of a trio sonata: two violins and basso continuo. The concertino part is continuous and can be performed with or without the ripieno forces. This is demonstrated by the title page of an early publication of Corelli's concerti grossi, op. 6 (by Walsh of London, 1715), which refers to these works as "Great Concertos, or Sonatas" for "two Violins and a Violincello [*sic*] or for two Violins more, a Tenor [i.e., a viola], and a Thorough-Bass: which may be doubled at Pleasure." While part of the strategy behind

## *Focus*  NOTABLE CONCERTO COMPOSERS OF THE BAROQUE ERA

**ARCANGELO CORELLI** (1653–1713), who spent most of his career in Rome, wrote 12 concerti grossi that enjoyed wide distribution in manuscript long before they appeared in print in 1714. A violin virtuoso, Corelli helped establish modern bowing techniques and was one of the first to use double-stopping and chords. According to one contemporary account of his playing, "it was usual for his countenance to be distorted, his eyes to become as red as fire, and his eyeballs to roll as in an agony."[3] Corelli also wrote numerous trio sonatas and sonatas for violin and continuo (see Focus: "The Art of Embellishment").

**GIUSEPPE TORELLI** (1658–1709) worked mostly in Bologna (Italy) but also spent time north of the Alps. His ensemble pieces in op. 5 (published 1692) are among the earliest ripieno concertos. His op. 6 (1698) includes the earliest known concertos, with the solo part (for violin) explicitly marked as such (nos. 6 and 12). He is best remembered for his trumpet concertos, written after 1701.

**FRANCESCO GEMINIANI** (1687–1762) studied with Corelli in Rome and Alessandro Scarlatti in Naples. In 1714, he settled in London and won fame as a violin virtuoso, composer, and teacher. He wrote many concerti grossi in the style of Corelli.

**PIETRO LOCATELLI** (1695–1764) also studied with Corelli and eventually settled in Amsterdam, where he gave regular public concerts. He was renowned as a

virtuoso violinist as well as a composer. His first concerti grossi appeared in print in 1721, and his 24 caprices for violin (1733) were an inspiration to later composers like Paganini in the 19th century.

**ANTONIO VIVALDI** (1678–1741; see Composer Profile in this chapter) was by far the most prolific (and popular) of all concerto composers in his time. He wrote almost 60 ripieno concertos, 350 solo concertos (about two-thirds of which are for solo violin), and 45 double concertos (more than half of which are for two violins).

**GEORGE FRIDERIC HANDEL** (1685–1759; see Composer Profile in Chapter 9) wrote two sets of concerti grossi (op. 3, also known as oboe concertos, and op. 6) as well as two sets of concertos for organ (op. 4 and op. 7), which he performed himself between the acts of opera or oratorio performances in the London theaters.

**JOHANN SEBASTIAN BACH** (1685–1750; see Composer Profile in Chapter 9) studied Vivaldi's concertos carefully and integrated the ritornello principle into a more complex polyphonic texture. His most celebrated concertos are the six dedicated to the Margrave of Brandenburg in 1721 and scored for a variety of solo instruments; one of them (the third) is a ripieno concerto. Bach also wrote three concertos for solo violin, almost a dozen for solo harpsichord, and a half dozen more for two or more harpsichords.

such marketing was clearly commercial (it was much easier to sell music that could be performed by a handful of players rather than by an orchestra plus soloists), the ripieno part provides the necessary element for the timbral variety—the rapid back-and-forth between soloists and ensemble—that gives them their distinctive profile.

The formal structure of these concertos is fluid. The individual movements are not built around recurring themes—ritornelli—like the later concertos of Vivaldi and Bach, but instead move through a series of relatively brief sections that present contrasting thematic ideas in different keys and tempos. The second work of the set (op. 6, no. 2, in F Major) falls into four movements, three of which—the first, third, and fourth—have distinct subsections. The first movement alternates between a Vivace fanfare and an imitative Allegro. It also includes two slow sections—one in the middle (m. 40–51), the other at the end (m. 99–107)—each with its own distinct thematic material. The second movement is a continuous and relatively brief (57 measures) Allegro. The third movement opens with a Grave and moves to a thematically distinct Andante Largo. Harmonically, this movement begins in D minor and ends on C, the dominant of F. It leads without a break into the fourth movement, an Allegro in binary form (consisting, that is, of two repeated sections).

A comparison of Corelli's concerti grossi, written in the 1680s, to Antonio Vivaldi's solo concertos (written in the 1710s) illustrates the development of the Baroque concerto. Vivaldi's concertos reflect the influence of opera (see Chapter 9), making far greater use of the ritornello principle than do Corelli's. In Vivaldi's concertos, ripieno and solo sections are more clearly differentiated, longer, and fewer in number than in any given movement of a Corelli concerto.

Vivaldi's Concerto in A minor for Two Violins, op. 3, no. 8, published in 1711, is typical of many solo concertos written around this time. The solo parts double the tutti in the statements of the ritornello but are otherwise structurally independent, as at the beginning of the Solo I section in the first movement (m. 16), where the tutti support the soloists. In a concerto by Corelli, the ripieno would have dropped out entirely at this point.

((•• Listen
**CD6    Track 2**
**mysearchlab**
VIVALDI
Concerto in A minor, op. 3, no. 8
Score Anthology I/91

**Arcangelo Corelli.** This engraving of Corelli, after a portrait by the Irish painter Hugh Howard, shows the composer in a thoughtful pose, quite in opposition to one contemporary account of him playing the violin with a "distorted" countenance, "his eyes . . . red as fire," and his "eyeballs roll[ing] as in an agony."

**Source:** Arcangelo Corelli "Sonate|für Violine und Basso continuo ad lib.|op. 5" © 2003 by Wiener Urtext Edition, Musikverlag, Ges.m.b.H. & Co., K.G., Wien

Thematically, the opening ritornello of Vivaldi's concerto introduces three of the work's four principal thematic ideas (see Example 10–1). The opening unison **head motif** (1) is typical of many concertos of this era; it presents a memorable, sharply profiled idea that is immediately recognizable whenever it returns over the course of the movement. The middle section of the opening ritornello (2) presents an idea that is more fluid and sequential, while the closing section of the ritornello (3), with its dominant pedal point, clearly signals the arrival of a cadence. These three ideas, taken together, form a self-contained unit consisting of a beginning (1), middle (2), and end (3). Over the course of the movement, however, Vivaldi breaks up the constituent subunits of the ritornello, combining them with a new idea (4) first presented by the solo violins in m. 16.

In the broadest terms, then, the overall form of this movement consists of an alternation of ritornello and solo sections (see the following table). At a more detailed level, however, the form is more complicated than this simple description might suggest. Almost all of the solo and ritornello sections are interrupted at some point by interpolations of an opposing texture. Solo 1, for example, is interrupted by a brief return of tutti texture at m. 22, with a brief restatement of the ritornello's closing idea (3). Ritornello 2, in turn, is interrupted by a brief solo passage in m. 39–41. The

**EXAMPLE 10–1** Vivaldi's Concerto in A minor, op. 3, no. 8: The Principal Thematic Ideas of the First Movement.

| VIVALDI'S CONCERTO IN A MINOR FOR TWO VIOLINS AND ORCHESTRA, OP. 3, NO. 8: THE STRUCTURE OF THE FIRST MOVEMENT | | | |
|---|---|---|---|
| **Section** | **Harmonic Area** | **Measures** | **Thematic Ideas** |
| Ritornello 1 | i | 1–16 | ① ② ③ |
| Solo 1 | I→III | 16–36 | ④ punctuated by ③ |
| Ritornello 2 | III→iv | 37–47 | ② |
| Solo 2 | iv→I | 48–67 | ② punctuated by ① and ③ ④ |
| Ritornello 3 | i | 68–71 | ① |
| Solo 3 | i | 71–78 | ② punctuated by ③ |
| Ritornello 4 | i | 78–93 | ③ |

**Orphan musicians.** The image here depicts a performance given by girls from several different Venetian orphanages in honor of a visiting Russian dignitary in 1782. Orphanages played a significant role in musical life throughout the 16th through 19th centuries, particularly in northern Italy. In an effort to teach orphans a useful trade, a number of these institutions took on the character of a musical conservatory, teaching young boys and girls to sing and play instruments, often at a high level of accomplishment. Antonio Vivaldi taught violin for many years at the Venetian Hospice of Pity for orphaned girls. Its orchestra was famous throughout the Continent, and the city fathers used it repeatedly as a means of both entertaining and impressing visiting dignitaries. The young women there played from behind a veiled screen—disembodied, as it were, so as not to inspire any less-than-spiritual ideas in the minds of the listeners. Accounts of such performances frequently describe the music as angelic.

**Source:** Concert given by the girls of the hospital music societies in the Procuratie, Venice, Bella, Gabriele (1730–1799)/Galleria Querini-Stampalia, Venice, Italy/The Bridgeman Art Library

alternation of ritornello and solo is thus more a general organizational principle than a rigid scheme.

Vivaldi uses harmonic variety to complement the contrasting textures and instrumentation in the first movement of his op. 3, no. 8. Having established a strong sense of the tonic at the beginning of the movement, he moves away from it after the middle of the movement (to III and iv) and then returns to it at the end. Rhythmically, the music pushes forward with a sense of propulsive energy. There are short pauses (the second beat of m. 4 in the violins, for example), but these are typically covered by forward motion in other voices. This technique, which produces a kind of *motoric rhythm*, became increasingly prominent in late Baroque music. German writers of today refer to it as *Fortspinnung*, or "spinning out," a term that aptly describes the way Vivaldi spins out the motivic material in the opening measure into a longer and longer thread before finally cutting it. Other examples of this propulsive technique may be found in the imitative sections of Corelli's Concerto Grosso, op. 6, no. 2 (the beginning of the second movement, in particular), in the arias in Handel's opera *Giulio Cesare* (see Chapter 9), and in the fugues of J. S. Bach's *Well-Tempered Clavier* (Anthology, discussed later).

## Suite

The idea of grouping dance movements in sets of two, three, or even more pieces dates to the Renaissance. In the Baroque era, the **suite** emerged as an even more extended series of dances or dance-inspired movements, usually in the same key, but often varying between major and minor modes. Such groupings went by many different names in the Baroque era, depending on locale. Some works labeled as sonatas are in fact a series of dances (the sonata da camera, for example). The keyboard suite was also known as a *partita* in Germany and Italy, a *lesson* in England, and an *ordre* in France.

Although the number of movements in any given suite is variable, most consist of four to six dances of varying tempo, meter, and character. The basic framework for a suite might consist of two moderately fast movements, followed by a slow movement and, at the end, a lively dance in triple meter, like this:

Allemande (moderate, flowing, duple meter)

Courante (fast, triple meter)

Sarabande (slow, triple meter)

Gigue (fast, often with dotted rhythms, compound meter)

Movements based on other dance forms, such as the minuet, bourrée, or gavotte, might be substituted or added at will (see the following table).

As we saw in Chapter 6, these kinds of dances tend to be in binary form. And binary form, with its built-in repetition, invites variation. Composers usually left the realization of these varied repetitions to the imagination of performers, but occasionally they wrote out altered reprises that constitute, in effect, a variation on the original reprise. This practice is found in the harpsichord suites of Elisabeth Jacquet de la Guerre; it is also a component of the French keyboard chaconne, which alternates between its "A" section and variation-like responses. Composers such as Louis Couperin (ca. 1626–61) and his nephew, François Couperin (discussed later in this chapter), were among the masters of this genre.

Another type of suite, the **variation suite**, is more tightly organized than other examples of the genre. Expanding on the idea of thematically related dances, the variation suite presents a series of contrasting dances based on one basic thematic idea. It is, in effect, a set of variations grouped as a dance suite. Composers who cultivated this approach include Johann Hermann Schein and Samuel Scheidt (who worked in Germany) and Johann Jakob Froberger (who worked in Vienna).

The suite was also a favorite medium for program music—that is, instrumental music meant to express a nonmusical story or idea—much as word painting permitted related effects in vocal music during the Renaissance and Baroque periods. Some of these programmatic works could be quite graphic. A good example is by Johann Kuhnau (1660–1722), J. S. Bach's immediate predecessor as cantor of St. Thomas's Church in Leipzig. In his *Musikalische Vorstellung einiger Biblischer Historien, in 6 Sonaten auf dem Claviere zu spielen* ("Musical Representations of Several Biblical Stories, in Six Sonatas for the Harpsichord"), Kuhnau presented musical depictions of six Bible stories. The

# Antonio Vivaldi (1678–1741)

A near contemporary of Handel and J. S. Bach, Vivaldi was a prolific composer. Known as the "Red Priest"— because he was redheaded and ordained—he served for many years as director of music at Venice's Ospedale della Pietà (Hospice of Pity), a large orphanage for girls (see illustration on page 270). Being the music director of an orphanage might strike us today as a strange job for one of the most famous composers of his time, but the young women at this particular institution were thoroughly trained in musical performance, and to judge from the music Vivaldi wrote for them, they must have been quite talented as well. Although he later worked in Vienna at the court of Charles VI, Vivaldi wrote most of his many concertos while in service to the orphanage in Venice.

Vivaldi's music was widely published and well known throughout Europe during his lifetime. J. S. Bach arranged several of Vivaldi's concertos for the organ, and in the process taught himself how to write concertos "in the Italian taste." Bach and Handel may have had greater facility at counterpoint (Vivaldi tended to rely more on sequential passages), but the Italian was a master of melodic invention and the projection of a sense of drama.

# PRINCIPAL WORKS

## Concertos

An old joke among musicians is that Vivaldi did not write 400 concertos, but rather one concerto 400 times. There is a grain of truth in this witticism, to be sure, but the outward similarities of form and structure in these works mask a rich, almost overwhelming variety of approaches to the genre. Vivaldi wrote for a remarkable range of instruments and instrument combinations, including not only violins, oboes, and flutes, but also more unusual instruments, such as mandolins, lutes, piccolos, and violas d'amore.

## Operas

Vivaldi wrote 46 operas in the opera seria tradition, of which 21 have survived. Rarely performed today, these works were highly regarded by Vivaldi's contemporaries. The success of recent revivals reaffirms this favorable estimation.

## Sacred Music

Vivaldi's *Gloria* is a staple of the choral repertory, but he wrote a great many other works that are equally rewarding. His output includes 12 motets and more than 3 dozen various sacred works, as well as two oratorios.

**Antonio Vivaldi.** This caricature from 1723 by Pier Leone Ghezzi captures a certain levity and mischievousness that characterizes a good bit of Vivaldi's music, which despite its conventional surface is never predictable.

**Source:** Library of Congress

| KEY DATES IN THE LIFE OF VIVALDI | |
|---|---|
| 1678 | Born in Venice on March 4. |
| 1703 | Becomes violin instructor at the Ospedale della Pietà, an orphanage for girls in Venice. |
| 1703 | Takes holy orders and becomes a priest. |
| 1718 | Becomes music director to the court of Mantua. |
| 1727 | Appointed music director to the court of Charles VI in Vienna. |
| 1741 | Dies in Vienna; buried on July 28. |

## BAROQUE DANCE TYPES COMMONLY USED IN SUITES

| Dance Type | Meter | Tempo | Character |
| --- | --- | --- | --- |
| Allemande | 4/4 | Moderate | Flowing; often begins with an upbeat |
| Bourrée | 2/2 | Fast | Units begin on fourth beat |
| Courante | 3/4 or 3/8 | Fast | Begins with an upbeat |
| Double | Variable | Variable | Variation on any immediately preceding dance |
| Gavotte | 4/4 | Fast | Units begin on third beat |
| Gigue | 6/8 | Fast | Often features dotted rhythms |
| Hornpipe | 3/2 | Fast | Cadences on third beat |
| Minuet | 3/4 | Moderate | Stately |
| Passepied | 3/4 or 3/8 | Fast | Light, rapid articulation of notes |
| Polonaise | 3/4 | Moderate | Accents on second beat |
| Sarabande | 3/4 or 3/2 | Slow | No upbeat; noble |
| Siciliano | 6/8 or 12/8 | Moderate | Pastoral; often with dotted rhythms |

first of these illustrates David's battle against Goliath. The score to the various movements of this suite inform us of the precise sequence of events: the Israelites tremble before Goliath; the courageous David comes forward to confront the giant; David slays Goliath. A fast upward scale represents David's slingshot hurling its stone at the giant, and a clumsy dissonant passage depicts Goliath's fall. The Philistines flee in the subsequent figure.

Even more graphic is Marin Marais's *Le Tableau de l'opération de la taille* ("Representation of an Abdominal Surgery"), a suite for viola da gamba and continuo published in 1725. One of the movements depicts a kidney stone being removed, and the score dutifully informs us of exactly when "the incision is made," the moment "the stone is grasped," and the point at which "the blood flows."

More subtle programmatic elements may be found in the instrumental music of the French *clavecinistes* (keyboard composers), particularly François Couperin, who liked to place provocative, often enigmatic titles at the head of individual dance pieces within a suite. He published 4 *livres* for *clavecin* (1713, 1717, 1722, and 1730), comprising 27 consecutively numbered *ordres*, as well as an influential treatise, *L'Art de toucher le clavecin* ("The Art of Playing the Harpsichord," 1716), which includes 8 preludes and an allemande.

The second *ordre* of the 1713 *livre* in D minor contains an astonishing 23 movements; this is typical of Couperin's early *ordres*, which are really collections of pieces arranged by key, rather than integrated suites in a prescribed sequence of movements. Like other *ordres* in the first *livre*, the second suite of Book I features a mixture of standard Baroque dances and programmatic character pieces; the latter would become a prominent piano genre during the 19th century (see Chapter 16). Here, the opening Courante meets the definition of binary dance form: the first half cadences on the dominant, the second half flirts with a cadence in C Major but evades it to finish in the

((•—**Listen**

**CD6 Tracks 3–4**
**mysearchlab**
F. COUPERIN
*Pièces de clavecin*
Score Anthology I/92

tonic. The Sarabande (the third piece in the *ordre*) has the title "La Prude"; this may refer to a specific individual, or a type, or no one in particular. His 24th and 25th *ordres*, published in Book 4, for example, include movements with such intriguing headings as (in English translation):

| | |
|---|---|
| The Elderly Gentlemen | The Mysterious One |
| The Young Gentlemen | The Victorious Muse |
| The Amphibian | The Wandering Shadows |
| The Visionary | |

Couperin revealed something of the origin of these descriptive titles in the preface to the first *livre* of his harpsichord pieces:

> In composing these pieces, I have always had an object in view, furnished by various occasions. Thus the titles reflect my ideas; I may be forgiven for not explaining them all. However, since among these titles there are some which seem to flatter me, it would be as well to point out that the pieces which bear them are a kind of portrait which, under my fingers, have on occasion been found fair enough likenesses, and that the majority of these flattering titles are given to the amiable originals which I wished to represent rather than to the copies which I took from them.[4]

Unlike Italian keyboard music, the highly ornamented French style of the *clavecinistes* was usually indicated by the composer, often in considerable detail. Couperin in fact complained at one point of his "surprise, after the pains that I have taken to indicate the ornaments appropriate to my pieces . . . to hear people who have learnt them without heeding my instructions. Such carelessness is unpardonable, all the more as it is no arbitrary matter to put in such ornaments as one wishes."[5]

The orchestral suite (sometimes referred to as an *ouverture* in France, a term Bach borrowed) was an important genre for larger ensembles of instruments. Together with the ripieno concerto, the suite was the principal genre for nonprogrammatic Baroque orchestral music. (The earliest concert symphonies—those written for the concert hall rather than as overtures to theatrical productions—would not appear until the 1720s.) Opera and ballet provided a significant source of music for orchestral suites written in the 17th and 18th centuries, particularly in France.

At least some orchestral suites were programmatic, however. Among them is an extraordinary work by Jean-Féry Rebel (1661–1747) entitled *Les élémens* ("The Elements," 1737). The first movement, "Chaos," begins with a chord that strikes even 21st-century ears as chaotic. It is a simultaneous sounding of all the notes in a D-minor scale (D-E-F-G-A-B♭-C♯) with the remarkable figuration in the basso continuo of

$$\sharp 7$$
$$\flat 6$$
$$5$$
$$4$$
$$3$$
$$2$$

over a low D. The opening section of the first movement, as Rebel noted in his preface to the score, "represents the confusion that prevails among the elements before that moment in which, subject to invariable laws, they assume the place prescribed for them by the order of Nature." The bass, he goes on to explain, "expresses the Earth through the tied notes, played percussively. The flutes, with their rising and falling lines, imitate the flow and murmuring of water. The air is depicted by long-held notes followed by cadences in the piccolos. And finally, the violins represent the active nature of fire through their vigorous and brilliant strokes. . . . I have dared to connect the idea of the confusion of the elements with a confusion of harmony. . . . These notes proceed to a unison in a progression that is natural, and after a dissonance, we hear a perfect chord [i.e., a unison]." Such a powerful effect would not be attempted again until Joseph Haydn wrote "The Representation of Chaos" to open his 1798 oratorio, *The Creation*.

((•• Listen

CD6   Track 5
mysearchlab
REBEL
*Les élémens*
Score Anthology I/93

## Other Keyboard Genres

Genres of the Baroque era associated primarily or exclusively with keyboard instruments fall into four broad categories: free, vocal based, dance based, and variations.

**Free Genres.**   Free genres are based on no preexistent material and adhere to no particular pattern or structure. They can be predominantly imitative or nonimitative, or they can combine both textures within a single work. The most important

---

*Focus*   MUSICAL RHETORIC

Early Baroque theories of expression had been based on the clear projection of the words being sung, but by the early 1700s, many theorists were advancing a new idea: even without a text, a composition could be considered a musical oration, a speech without words. The principal theme, according to this line of thought, corresponds to the principal theme of an orator's speech. Everything that follows in some way elaborates or comments on this main idea, either through variation or contrast.

The idea of musical rhetoric drew heavily on the traditions of ancient Greek and Roman oratory. Music theorists of the early 18th century developed extended systems of parallels between the structures of verbal and musical "speech." Such basic terms as *period* (from the Latin *periodus*, meaning "sentence"), *phrase*, *antecedent*, and *consequent* were transferred to music from the realm of grammar.

Many writers went even further to establish systems of musical figures, or tropes, comparable to those used in speech. In language, a *figure*, or *trope*, is a manner of expression noticeably different from that used in ordinary speech. John F. Kennedy's celebrated "Ask not what your country can do for you; ask what you can do for your country," for example, is an instance of what ancient Greek rhetoricians classified as *antimetabole*, the juxtaposition of reversed contrasts.

In music, a simple cadence would not in itself constitute a figure, because it is too common; an evaded cadence, however, is unusual enough to call attention to itself. Such

figures could be used in instrumental music and vocal music alike. In vocal music, they are invariably associated with the words being set at that particular moment. We encountered one such figure, the *passus duriusculus* (a descending chromatic fourth), a figure associated primarily with pain and anguish, in the discussion of J. S. Bach's cantata *Jesu, der du meine Seele* (Anthology). Other comparable figures include the following:

- *Pathopoeia*, harsh-sounding accidentals used to create a sensation of sorrow or fear

- *Abruptio*, a sudden and unexpected pause or silence

- *Suspiratio*, the breaking up of a melodic line by rests, often associated with gasping, sighing, or extreme agitation

At least some of the many figures codified in Baroque treatises were known to a broad range of listeners. Other figures are mentioned only once by a single author and seem not to have been so widely recognized. What is particularly significant, though, is not so much the precise definition of individual figures as the growing acknowledgment that instrumental music alone, without the aid of words, might create in listeners the same kinds and degree of effects that had long been considered the exclusive domain of vocal music.

nonimitative free genres of keyboard music in the Baroque era are the toccata, canzona, fantasia, and prelude (Latin, *praeludium*). The most important imitative genres are the ricercar and fugue.

**((•• Listen**

**CD6   Track 6**
**mysearchlab**
FRESCOBALDI
Toccata IX
Score Anthology I/94

The Ninth Toccata from Frescobaldi's *Second Book of Toccatas* (1627), although unusually intricate, is nonetheless representative of the genre as a whole. Rapid passagework combined with freedom of form had been characteristic of the toccata since the genre emerged in the 16th century (see Chapter 6). Highly episodic, Frescobaldi's **toccata** moves rapidly through a variety of textures, registers, rhythms, and meters: some sections last only a few measures. The rhythms are constantly shifting and in certain passages are quite intricate (for example, m. 11, 22, 25); the right and left hands occasionally work in cross-rhythms (m. 56–60, 65); and the passagework, which is distinctly idiomatic to the harpsichord (as opposed to the organ), can be dazzling at times (m. 25–26, 50–54). Small wonder, then, that Frescobaldi should add the remark at the very end of this work: *Non senza fatiga si giunge al fine* ("Not without effort does one arrive at the end").

Already well established as a genre for instrumental ensembles in the 16th century, the **canzona** began to evolve into a keyboard genre in the early 17th century. In the process, it lost its connection with vocal models and became an essentially free composition comparable to the toccata. Canzonas and other keyboard genres were often performed in the church. Frescobaldi's *Fiori musicali* ("Musical Flowers") of 1635, for example, includes a "Canzona [to be played] after the Epistle," a "Toccata [to be played] at the Elevation of the Host," and a "Canzona [to be played] after the Communion."

**((•• Listen**

**CD6   Track 7**
**mysearchlab**
BUXTEHUDE
Praeludium in G minor, BuxWV 149
Score Anthology I/95

Virtuosity and structural openness on an even larger scale than in Frescobaldi's toccatas are evident in Dietrich Buxtehude's Praeludium in G minor for organ

**Girolamo Frescobaldi.** This likeness of the composer is believed to have been made in 1624, three years before the publication of the Second Book of Toccatas (Anthology I/93). Frescobaldi (1583–1643) studied in his native Ferrara with Luzzasco Luzzaschi but spent most of his career in Rome as organist at Saint Peter's.

**Source:** Scala/Ecole des Beaux-Arts, Paris, France/Art Resource, NY

(BuxWV 149), written sometime between 1675 and 1689. (Throughout the Baroque era, *prelude* and *fantasia* were essentially interchangeable terms indicating a work that adhered to no fixed structural pattern.) Except for the very end, the individual sections of Buxtehude's Praeludium are clearly articulated, each with its own distinctive theme and texture. Long imitative sections are typical of the prelude and many other free keyboard genres in the 17th century. But imitation is only one of many textures we are likely to encounter in these characteristically varied and unpredictable works. Buxtehude's Praeludium ends with an extended rhapsody that sounds almost improvisational. The formal structure, in short, is paratactic, with each section more or less self-contained.

Buxtehude's Praeludium exhibits three different kinds of virtuosity:

- Composition, as reflected in the wide range of techniques the composer deploys, from rapid passagework to strict polyphonic imitation

- Performance, as reflected in the extreme technical demands of the writing

- Instrumentation, as reflected in the way it calls on almost all the resources of the organ, from shifts in register to demanding pedalwork

The breadth of sound, intricate pedalwork, and extended imitative passages of this work are characteristic of a northern European tradition of keyboard composition that flourished in the 17th century. This tradition had its roots in the work of Jan Pieterszoon Sweelinck (1562–1621; see Chapter 6). Buxtehude was Sweelinck's greatest successor, and Buxtehude's greatest successor would be Johann Sebastian Bach, who traveled from Arnstadt to Lübeck in 1705 to hear Buxtehude perform.

Other free genres depend primarily on the elaboration of one or more ideas through imitative counterpoint. These include canon, ricercar, and fugue. The **ricercar**

## *Performance Perspective* — Frescobaldi on the Performance of His Toccatas

One of the leading organists of his generation, Girolamo Frescobaldi (1583–1643) broke new ground in writing for the keyboard, placing extraordinary demands on players and listeners alike. Conscious of his music's novelty, the composer prefaced his First Book of Toccatas and Partitas (1615) with detailed instructions on how these works were to be performed. His remarks continue to be an important resource for studying Baroque performance practice.

■ ■ ■

1. This manner of playing must not always follow the same meter; in this respect it is similar to the performance of modern madrigals, whose difficulty is eased by taking the beat slowly at times and fast at others, even by pausing with the singing in accordance with the mood or the meaning of the words.

2. In the toccatas I have seen to it not only that they are rich in varied sections and moods but also that one may play each section separately, so that the player can stop wherever he wishes. . . .

3. The beginnings of the toccatas must be played slowly and arpeggiando. . . .

4. In trills as well as in runs, whether they move by skips or by steps, one must pause on the last note, even when it is an eighth or sixteenth note, or different from the next note. Such a pause will avoid mistaking one passage for another. . . .

**Source**: Frescobaldi, Preface to the *Toccate e partite, primo libro* (1615), in Willi Apel, *The History of Keyboard Music to 1700*, trans. and rev. Hans Tischler (Bloomington: Indiana University Press, 1972), p. 456. Publisher: Bärenreiter-Verlag; used by permission of Bärenreiter Music Corporation, Englewood, NJ.

## BUXTEHUDE'S PRAELUDIUM IN G MINOR, BUXWV 149: THE PARATACTIC STRUCTURE

| Measures | Indicated Tempo | Texture |
|----------|-----------------|---------|
| 1–20 | None | Passagework in hands; ostinato figure in pedals |
| 21–56 | Alla breve | Imitative |
| 57–80 | Allegro | Free; running bass against chords |
| 80–143 | Largo | Imitative; triple meter |
| 144–161 | Largo | Free; quasi improvisatory |

originated as an improvisatory genre for lute in the early 16th century and evolved into an instrumental counterpart to the polyphonic motet by the middle of the century (see Chapter 6). In the 17th century, it underwent yet another transformation, establishing itself primarily as an imitative genre for keyboard instruments. It eventually came to be associated with particularly strict and learned forms of counterpoint in the *stile antico*, or "old style." The two ricercars in J. S. Bach's *Musical Offering*, a cycle of variations on a theme given to the composer by Frederick the Great, are especially demanding in this regard.

The **fugue** emerged in the 17th century as a keyboard genre in which a single thematic idea is subjected to imitative treatment for the entire length of a work. Johann Pachelbel (1652–1706) was one of the first composers to write fugues in this sense. Before the 17th century, the Latin term *fuga* had been used primarily to mean "canon." A *Missa ad fugam* in the Renaissance, for example, was by definition a canonic Mass.

Fugue is a genre rooted in texture rather than a particular medium or form. There is no typical structure, but most fugues share certain basic elements. They usually begin with a single voice that states the theme, or **subject**. A second voice enters in imitation (transposed up a fifth), presenting the same theme (or a slightly altered version of it), even while the first voice continues. When all the voices have entered and stated the subject at least once, we have reached the end of the **exposition** (not to be confused with the exposition of a sonata-form movement; see Chapter 11). From this point on, a fugue can do just about anything. Composers sometimes branch off into long passages in a relatively free style with little or no imitation. At some juncture, however, the fugue subject will reestablish an imitative structure. The nonimitative freestyle passages are called **episodes**, and the subsequent new points of imitation are called **middle entries**. Fugues typically consist of a series of alternating middle entries and episodes, for a fugue with no free sections might sound ponderous, and a fugue with no imitation after the exposition would not sound much like a fugue at all. Toward the end of a fugue, the opening subject may enter in shortened form, with overlapping entries in several voices, increasing the need for a final resolution of the piece's tension. This is one example of the **stretto** technique (from the Italian *stringere*, to draw close).

The two books of Bach's *Well-Tempered Clavier* present a rich variety of imitative and nonimitative keyboard pieces. Each book consists of a series of 24 paired preludes and fugues, with one pair in each of the 24 major and minor keys. No one is exactly certain what the "Well-Tempered" of the title means. Some believe it reflects Bach's advocacy of **equal temperament**, a system of tuning that allowed keyboard players to

((•• Listen

CD6   Track 8
**mysearchlab**

J. S. BACH
*Well-Tempered Clavier*, Book 1,
Prelude and Fugue in C Major
Score Anthology I/96

## Focus NOTABLE KEYBOARD COMPOSERS OF THE BAROQUE ERA

**GIROLAMO FRESCOBALDI** (1583–1643) was born in Ferrara, where he studied with Luzzasco Luzzaschi. Except for a brief period in Florence (1628–1634), Frescobaldi spent most of his life in Rome as organist of St. Peter's. He raised the art of idiomatic composition for the organ and harpsichord to new heights. His music was considered daring for its harmonic boldness and technical difficulty. He cultivated virtually every keyboard genre of his era, including the toccata, fantasia, canzona, ricercar, and, above all, the variation.

**JOHANN HERMANN SCHEIN** (1586–1630) was a friend of Schütz who wrote sacred concertos and other religious works. He is best known, however, for the *Banchetto musicale* (1617), a collection of 20 variation suites, each in the same mode and consisting of four thematically related dance movements.

**SAMUEL SCHEIDT** (1587–1654) is best remembered as the composer of *Tabulatura nova* ("New Tablature"), published in three volumes in 1624 in open score on five-line staves, as opposed to the traditional organ letter tablature or the six-line staves common in other keyboard sources of the time. The set includes chorale preludes, free compositions, and variation sets, and is stylistically indebted to Scheidt's teacher, Sweelinck.

**JOHANN JAKOB FROBERGER** (1616–67) was born in Germany, studied in Rome with Frescobaldi, and eventually settled in Vienna, where he was court organist. He was among the first composers to write extended keyboard suites.

**DIETRICH BUXTEHUDE** (1637–1707) was the most celebrated organist of his day. He spent most of his early career in Denmark. From 1668 onward he held the prestigious post of organist at the Marienkirche in Lübeck, a prosperous port city on the Baltic in what is now northern Germany.

**JOHANN PACHELBEL** (1652–1706), known today almost exclusively for his Canon in D (actually the first part of a Canon and Gigue), was better known during his lifetime as an organist and composer of sacred music, including many sets of chorale variations and chorale preludes. Born in Nuremberg, he held prestigious posts in several German cities, including Eisenach (where J. S. Bach was born in 1685), Erfurt, and Stuttgart, as well as his native Nuremberg.

**FRANÇOIS COUPERIN** (1668–1733), nicknamed "le grand" ("the great") to distinguish him from an uncle with the same name, came from a long line of musicians. Born in Paris, he served most of his adult life as a musician at the courts of Louis XIV and Louis XV. He wrote some 233 pieces for harpsichord and grouped them by tonality in a series of 27 *ordres*, published in four separate books (1713, 1717, 1722, 1730).

**JEAN-PHILIPPE RAMEAU** (1683–1764) inherited Couperin's mantle as the greatest organist and harpsichordist in France. The bulk of Rameau's harpsichord music appeared relatively early in his career (three books, published 1706, 1724, and ca. 1729–30). Like Couperin's suites, Rameau's works include many individual pieces with descriptive and sometimes enigmatic titles.

**JOHANN SEBASTIAN BACH** (1685–1750; see Composer Profile in Chapter 9) wrote many of his harpsichord works, including the *Well-Tempered Clavier*, as didactic exercises for his children and pupils. He also cultivated the suite. His encyclopedic *Clavier-Übung* ends with the massive *Goldberg Variations*. Bach's organ music includes many chorale-based compositions, free works (toccatas, fugues, fantasias), and variations, most notably the Passacaglia in C minor, BWV 582.

play in any key (see Focus: Systems of Temperament). It seems more likely, however, that "Well-Tempered" leaves it to the discretion of the performer to use whatever tuning system is appropriate to the work at hand. Bach's purpose in writing the *Well-Tempered Clavier*, according to this line of thought, was to demonstrate the feasibility of writing and performing works in all 24 keys, leaving the question of tuning to the performer. There were many systems of temperament at the time that could accommodate a wide variety of keys reasonably well, even if Bach's contemporaries disagreed on the precise limitations of reasonableness. Much depended on a performer's willingness to tolerate certain imperfections of certain intervals in certain keys (see Focus: Systems of Temperament).

In any event, Bach organized each book of the *Well-Tempered Clavier* according to the ascending chromatic scale, with major-mode works in each key followed by a corresponding work in the minor mode:

| | |
|---|---|
| Prelude and Fugue in C Major | Prelude and Fugue in E♭ Major |
| Prelude and Fugue in C minor | Prelude and Fugue in E♭ minor |
| Prelude and Fugue in C♯ Major | Prelude and Fugue in E Major |
| Prelude and Fugue in C♯ minor | Prelude and Fugue in E minor |
| Prelude and Fugue in D Major | and so on. |
| Prelude and Fugue in D minor | |

**Listen**

CD6   Track 9

**mysearchlab**

J. S. BACH

*Well-Tempered Clavier*, Book 1, Prelude and Fugue in C# minor

Score Anthology I/96

Reflecting Bach's passion for exploring many possibilities within a self-imposed limitation, all the preludes and fugues are different from one another. The Prelude in C Major (Book I) follows a pattern of broken chords in a manner known as **style brisé** ("broken style"), adopted from the arpeggiated ("broken") chords and figures typically found in lute music. Not coincidentally, this piece remains a favorite among guitar players. The Prelude in C minor (Book I, not in Anthology) is in the style of a keyboard toccata, full of rapid figuration. The Prelude in C♯ minor (Book I) is in the style of a sarabande, a slow dance in triple meter. Some analysts have discerned subtle thematic or motivic links between certain preludes and their associated fugues, but in general these too are musically independent of each other.

Some fugues—especially the longer ones—have more than one subject, and these do not necessarily all appear at the outset. A new subject enters the Fugue in C♯ minor (Book I), for example, in m. 36, still another in m. 49. These incorporate one or more **countersubjects**, thematically distinctive material that is used in counterpoint against the principal subject and plays an important role over the course of the fugue as a whole. In the Fugue in B Major (Book I, not in Anthology), a countersubject appears in the left hand in m. 3–5.

**Vocal-Based Genres.** As in the Renaissance, keyboard arrangements of vocal works, particularly chansons, were popular in the Baroque. By far the most important vocal-based genres of keyboard music in the Baroque era were those based on chorale melodies. Protestant chorales provided northern composers with an almost endless source of material for chorale variations, chorale preludes, and chorale fantasias. Chorale preludes were intended to serve as instrumental introductions to the congregational singing of a chorale in church. Given this function, these works were usually brief and relatively straightforward.

**Listen**

CD6   Track 10

**mysearchlab**

PACHELBEL

Chorale Prelude on the *Magnificat peregrini toni*

Score Anthology I/97

Johann Pachelbel's chorale prelude *Magnificat peregrini toni*, written sometime toward the end of the 17th century, is typical in this regard. The chorale tune had been adopted from the Ninth Psalm Tone of the Roman Catholic liturgy (the *tonus peregrinus*, or "wandering tone," so called because it moves from one recitation tone in its first half to a different one in its second). In Protestant services, this melody was commonly associated with the Magnificat, the words uttered by the Virgin Mary when she feels the Christ Child moving in her womb for the very first time ("My soul doth magnify the Lord," Luke 1: 47–55). In Pachelbel's setting the tune is stated in its entirety in long notes in the upper voice, with the other voices weaving around it. The two measures of introduction present a brief point of imitation on the opening of the theme; once the melody enters in m. 3, the two lower voices engage in

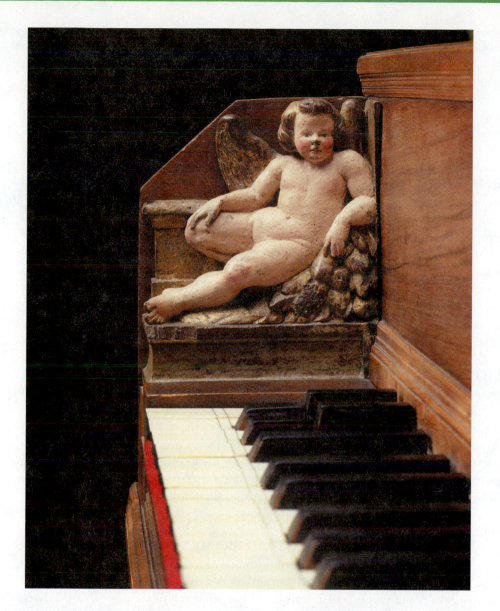

**Split keys.** The lowest range of Baroque keyboard instruments sometimes featured what is called a "broken octave," which used split black keys, thereby giving added range to the instrument without expanding the actual breadth of the keyboard. Split keys were also sometimes used in the middle of the keyboard to accommodate the difference between notes like G♯ and A♭, a distinction that could be crucial in an era before the acceptance of equal temperment. The instrument here is a harpsichord built by an anonymous Italian maker in northern Italy around 1600.

**Source:** National Trust Photographic Library/John Hammond/The Image Works

antiphonal passagework that is flowing but unspectacular; the focus of attention here, after all, is on the melody in the upper voice. The middle voice again introduces a brief point of imitation in m. 9, anticipating the first notes of the second phrase of the chorale melody while the upper voice pauses between the phrases. But once again, the imitation soon breaks off. The rhythmic acceleration in m. 12–13 provides variety, and the chorale prelude ends with a *tièrce de picardie* (**picardy third**)—a major-triad conclusion to a work otherwise in minor mode—in m. 19. Such endings had become commonplace for works in the minor mode by 1700. Evidence suggests that even if a sharpened third was not explicitly notated on the final cadence in a score, performers were expected to provide it—a late vestige of musica ficta (see Chapter 5)

J. S. Bach's chorale prelude on the same melody exhibits a different approach to the genre. Originally part of his cantata BWV 10 (1724), later rearranged for organ (published 1748), this work also places the melody in the upper voice in long note values. The three lower voices, however, are considerably more chromatic and intricate than the lower voices in Pachelbel's setting. The two measures of introduction

((•▸ **Listen**

**CD6   Track 11**
**mysearchlab**
J. S. BACH
Chorale Prelude on *Meine Seele erhebt den Herren*
Score Anthology I/98

## Focus  SYSTEMS OF TEMPERAMENT

The G sharp in a mathematically pure Pythagorean E-Major scale is slightly higher than the A flat in a pure F-minor scale. Vocalists and string players can adjust for this difference, but keyboard players can't, because on a keyboard, G♯ and A♭ are played by the same key. Thus to tune a keyboard in a way that will allow it to play in any of the 24 major and minor keys of the diatonic scale requires a great many slight modifications, or temperaments, away from Pythagorean purity. (While a harpsichord or clavichord could be adjusted for a group of pieces in a particular key, the organ had no such tuning flexibility.) The system of equal temperament in use today emerged only in the 18th century, when it replaced a variety of older systems of tuning and temperament—the most important of which are reviewed here—that had emerged over hundreds of years.

**PYTHAGOREAN INTONATION** Based on the mathematical ratios discovered (according to legend) by the ancient Greek mathematician and philosopher Pythagoras, this system prevailed throughout Europe until the middle of the 16th century. In Pythagorean intonation, all fifths are just, with a mathematically pure ratio of 3:2, as are all fourths, with a mathematically pure ratio of 4:3. Whole-tone intervals are defined as the difference between a fifth and a fourth (that is, 9:8). Once the circle of 12 pure fifths is complete, semitones are narrow (256:243); thirds (81:64) and sixths (27:16) are dissonant.

**JUST INTONATION** This name applies to any type of tuning that features five or more acoustically pure types of intervals within a given octave. If one tunes according to pure fifths (3:2), as in the Pythagorean system, four fifths above C will produce a major third relationship (C to E) that is 81:64 rather than the ideally pure 5:4. Since a scale with perfect fifths will inevitably produce imperfect thirds and sixths, systems of just intonation favor those intervals at the expense of the fifth. Thus, although it is possible to construct systems using 12 pitches with as many as three major and two minor triads with acoustically pure intervals, at least one fifth within a diatonic scale will sound different from the others (and very "out of tune"). Various refinements of just temperament compensate for this phenomenon. Although advocated as early as the 13th century by some English theorists, just systems of temperament did not come into widespread use until the second half of the 16th century.

**MEAN-TONE TEMPERAMENT** This system represents a compromise between the Pythagorean and just systems. Just intonation worked well within a limited range of keys but discouraged modulation to more remote areas. The mean-tone system, which emerged in the second half of the 16th century, allowed for greater tonal variety. Generated through a series of slightly contracted fifths, this system of tuning was probably developed more by ear than by mathematical calculation. It established itself as the predominant system of intonation for keyboard instruments throughout the late Renaissance and Baroque eras. Within a limited range of keys, the meantone system produces a sound that many consider superior for the music of this era. The drawback of mean-tone tuning is that it cannot easily accommodate modulations beyond three fifths up or two fifths down in the circle of fifths.

**EQUAL TEMPERAMENT** This system entailed yet another compromise, leveling *all* intervals to an equal relationship and dividing the octave into 12 half steps of identical size. While some scholars believe that J. S. Bach was advocating this system through his *Well-Tempered Clavier*, others believe he was using a "well temperament" devised by Andreas Werckmeister (1645–1706). Although many objected to the "impure" sound of equally tempered intervals, this system of tuning had become the norm by the end of the 18th century, thanks in large part to its adaptability to every key and every conceivable modulation.

in Pachelbel's version are replaced here by an eight-measure fugal exposition on a chromatic theme unrelated to the chorale. Once the chorale melody enters (m. 9), the imitation in the lower voices continues. The brief pause within the chorale melody—a single measure's rest in Pachelbel's version—expands here to eight full measures, based once again on the independent chromatic motive. Even after the chorale melody concludes, we hear an additional seven measures of imitation, with the piece ending as it had begun, a statement of the chromatic countersubject in the pedals.

The effect of all this is strangely haunting. Yet we can also sympathize with the reaction of his contemporaries who found such preludes disconcerting. Early in his career Bach was taken to task for his overly complicated harmonizations of chorales being sung by parishioners. According to the letter of reprimand, Bach had "made many curious *variationes* in the chorale, and mingled many strange tones in it, and . . . the congregation has been confused by it."[6]

**Dance-Based Genres.** A large percentage of keyboard music is based on the principles of dance, often using binary forms. Other common dance types included the sarabande, allemande, and gavotte. These dance movements were sometimes arranged in ordered sequences as a suite; at other times they were gathered more loosely, as in the *ordres* of François Couperin, collections whose individual units could be played either individually or as a whole.

**Variations.** Variations on bass line patterns—ground basses—were extremely popular in both vocal and instrumental music of the Baroque. These bass lines are not fixed patterns, and they manifest themselves in a variety of ways over time. The use of a **basso ostinato**—an "obstinate bass" that is present at all times and simply will not go away—inspired composers in the art of variation, challenging them to make constant repetition appealing through the use of an ever-changing countermelody above it. The most important of these were the **chaconne** or **passacaglia**, the **passamezzo**, and the **folia**.

**The minuet as dance.** Courtly dancing was one of the requisite social graces for ladies and gentlemen of the upper classes, and tutors helped demonstrate the steps for each dance. The illustration here shows the proper order of steps for the minuet. Dancing of this kind was extremely formal and stylized, and performed much more slowly than a suite's minuet; notice the distance between the two figures.

**Source:** K.8.K.7. Book 2 plate IV The Music Ceremony concluded, the Dance begins : music, dance steps and dancers for a Minuet from Kellom Tomlinson's 'Art of Dancing', engraved by Jan van der Gucht (1697–1776), 18th century (engraving)/British Library, London, UK/© British Library Board. All Rights Reserved/The Bridgeman Art Library

*Chaconne* (*ciaccona* in Italian) and *passacaglia* are more or less interchangeable terms for bass lines that follow the basic chord progression I-V-IV-V. Circling back on itself, with the closing dominant serving as a setup to the opening tonic, this progression could be repeated over and over, as in the ostinato bass in Monteverdi's *Zefiro torna* (see Chapter 8). Chaconne or passacaglia lines could support various melodic patterns, and the harmonic progression could be modified and expanded with additional chords, such as vi or iii just before IV.

The passamezzo, from the Italian dance *pass' e mezzo* (literally, "step and a half"), had two forms, the old passamezzo (*passamezzo antico*) illustrated in Example 10–2, and the new passamezzo (*passamezzo moderno* or*novo*), illustrated in Example 10–3.

The *folia* (the word means "craziness" or "insanity" in Spanish and Portuguese and is related to the English word "folly") was originally a wild and exuberant dance. The bass line associated with it (Example 10–4) follows a pattern similar to that of the *passamezzo moderno*. The most famous example of the folia is in the set of variations that ends Corelli's Sonata for Violin and Continuo, op. 5.

**EXAMPLE 10–2** The old passamezzo (*passamezzo antico*).

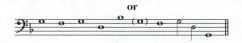

**EXAMPLE 10–3** The new passamezzo (*passamezzo moderno*).

**EXAMPLE 10–4** The folia.

((•●•[Listen

**CD6    Tracks 12–21**
**mysearchlab**
J. S. BACH
*"Goldberg" Variations*
Score Anthology I/99

J. S. Bach's "Goldberg" Variations offer perhaps the most spectacular example in the entire history of music of the elaborations possible within the framework of a simple bass line. For many years, it was believed Bach wrote this set of harpsichord variations on behalf of one of his pupils, Johann Gottlieb Goldberg, who in turn was employed by a certain Baron von Keyserling. Legend has it that the baron had trouble getting to sleep at night and these variations were designed to help him while away the evening hours. But the story is demonstrably false, because Goldberg was only about 14 years old when Bach wrote this work.

The "Goldberg" Variations, like the *Well-Tempered Clavier* and the late, unfinished *Art of the Fugue*, exemplify Bach's passion for writing encyclopedic works. In the *Well-Tempered Clavier* he explored the permutations of free preludes and imitative fugues in every possible key. In the *Art of the Fugue* he would explore various ways in which different fugal devices can be brought to bear on a single subject. In the "Goldberg" Variations he systematically explored the technique of both variation and canon.

The variations take us through an astonishing set of permutations on a single idea. The source of that idea is elusive. Bach's use of the term *aria* to designate the opening

## Focus  RAMEAU'S THEORY OF THE FUNDAMENTAL BASS

The composer and theorist Jean-Philippe Rameau (1683–1764) has justly been called "the creator of the modern science of harmony," for he was the first to codify the modern system of harmony based on triadic chords related to a fundamental bass. The *basse fondamentale*, as Rameau called it, was not the actual notated (figured) bass of any given chord, but its sonorous root. Thus a triad with E in the lowest position and a G and a C above it is to be understood as a chord whose root is actually C, what we would now call a first-inversion chord. An elementary concept nowadays even to the beginning student of harmony, the *basse fondamentale* was a breakthrough in its time, replacing earlier notions of harmony as a by-product of contrapuntal voice leading. Rameau did not invent harmonic thinking, to be sure, but he established the basis on which it could be codified, taught, and debated. For Rameau, harmony was the foundation of all music; melody, he maintained, grew out of harmony.

In the preface to his *Traité de l'harmonie réduite à ses principes naturels* ("A Treatise on Harmony, Reduced to its Natural Principles") of 1722, Rameau emphasized that he wanted to appeal to reason, experience, and authority—more or less in that order. He argued that reason (or science) could divulge the truths of music; that the experience of hearing could help confirm them; and that the "authority of the finest authors in this field" could reinforce reason and experience still further, although Rameau promised not to spare these authorities "when they have erred."[7]

In his desire to reconcile art and science, Rameau sought to discover the physical and quantitative foundations of musical beauty. He justified the priority of the interval of the third, for example, with both mathematical reasoning and experiential evidence. Rameau's goals put him among the vanguard of the thinkers of the Age of Enlightenment, who sought to use observation and reason, as opposed to religion or tradition, to understand the universe and improve the state of humanity.

variation draws our attention to the soprano line, but the theme (Example 10–5) is actually in the bass:

**EXAMPLE 10–5**  The bass line the aria of Bach's "Goldberg" Variations, BVM 988

Bach further conceals the theme with added notes, even on its first presentation in the aria. In the first reprise, the theme's pitches mostly coincide with the longer notes on the downbeats in the bass line (predominantly half notes and dotted half notes); in the second reprise, the notes of the theme do not coincide with the downbeat nearly as often.

Bach uses this bass progression as the foundation for all subsequent variations. In Variation 1, for example, the theme is readily apparent on the downbeat of every measure in the first reprise, but harder to follow in the second reprise.

Another structural device Bach uses throughout this set is a series of canons. Every third variation (Numbers 3, 6, 9, 12, etc.) presents a canon in the two upper voices, creating a trio sonata texture with two high voices and a bass. The bass line operates independently of the canon, although always providing the necessary notes of the theme in the proper order. Each canon, moreover, is written at an interval one step greater than the one before. Thus the first canon (Variation 3) is at the unison: the second voice enters one measure after the first, but at the same pitch. The second canon is composed at the interval of a second

## Performance Perspective

### Bach on the Piano

((•─ Listen on mysearchlab          CD6   Track 17

The Canadian pianist Glenn Gould (1932–82) recorded Bach's *Goldberg Variations* twice, once early in his career (1955) and then again a year before his untimely death, both times on a modern grand piano. It is an excerpt from the second of these recording sessions that is presented here. Both recordings are radically different from virtually all those made by other artists.

To his detractors, Gould was an eccentric: he sang and hummed quite audibly while playing, and he insisted on taking his perpetually squeaky piano bench with him whenever he worked in a recording studio. Pedagogues were horrified by his technique, for he often played with his nose only inches away from the keyboard. And his playing, for many, was just as mannered and exaggerated.

For Gould's admirers, these idiosyncrasies were at the heart of his distinctive musicianship. Gould's performances were like no one else's; his fast tempos were faster, his slow tempos slower, and he had a talent for bringing out the inner voices of a polyphonic texture in a way that few if any other artists on record have ever been able to match. Gould was less interested in period instruments and performance practice than in revealing the inner essence of whatever music he took up, from Sweelinck in the 17th century to Anton Webern in the 20th.

Gould retired from public performance at the age of 31 and from that point on worked only in the recording studio. In his second recording of Bach's "Goldberg" Variations, he displays his characteristically unpredictable musicianship. Even within the theme ("aria") itself, he alters the basic rhythms, dynamics, and articulation set out at the beginning. The theme begins slowly and becomes even slower, yet in the process Gould brings out levels of rhythmic detail and voicing that are lost in

most other performances. And in Variation 4, he brings out the bass line theme with remarkable clarity, even while emphasizing the angular counterpoint of the upper voices.

**Glenn Gould.** The technique was unconventional, the interpretations idiosyncratic, and few critics remained neutral to the playing of Glenn Gould. This photograph from 1965 shows the performer in a recording studio—he had retired from the concert hall the year before—sitting on his ever-present, ever-squeaky bench.

**Source:** The Toronto Star/ZUMA Wire Service/Alamy

(no easy task), with the second voice entering one whole step above the first and a measure behind. The third canon is a canon at the third, and so on.

In a third level of complexity, Bach incorporates a variety of musical styles within the "Goldberg" Variations. Variation 16, for example, which opens the unlabeled second part of the work, is in the style of a French overture. Number 10 is a fugue. Number 7 is a gigue. In addition, the work contains many dazzling passages, as in Variation 14, that require a virtuoso to perform.

As is true of so many works by Bach, the technical intricacies of the "Goldberg" Variations in no way obscure the delightful turns and surprises of the music. We can appreciate the music without knowing how it is put together, but knowing how it is put together can heighten our appreciation of what was, until Beethoven's "Hammerklavier" Sonata of 1819, the longest single work of keyboard music ever published.

## SUMMARY

The quantity and quality of instrumental music written in the Baroque era was without precedent. No previous period in the history of music had seen such an intense cultivation of instrumental genres. In the second half of the 18th century—the Classical era—the genres of sonata, symphony, and concerto would rise to even greater prominence at the hands of such composers as Joseph Haydn and Wolfgang Amadeus Mozart.

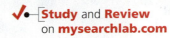

✓• Study and Review
on mysearchlab.com

# Part Four
# The Classical Era

The Classical era in music—roughly 1750 to 1800—corresponds to a period of intense ferment and change in European history. Powerful intellectual currents bearing notions of liberty and progress challenged the established order. Conflict on a global scale among the great powers of Europe undermined the finances of Great Britain and France, loosening Britain's hold on its American colonies and triggering a cataclysmic revolution and the collapse of the monarchy in France. Advances in technology led to the beginning of the Industrial Revolution.

# THE AGE OF ENLIGHTENMENT

The 18th century witnessed the growth of an intellectual outlook that stressed humanity's potential to understand and improve its condition through the application of reason and the power of the individual, granted sufficient liberty, to pursue a life of self-fulfillment. The advocates of this outlook considered it to be enlightened, and the period in which they flourished is known as the Age of Enlightenment.

The German philosopher Immanuel Kant (1724–1804) defined Enlightenment as "man's emergence from his self-imposed immaturity. Immaturity is the inability to use one's understanding without guidance from another. This immaturity is self-imposed when its cause lies not in a lack of understanding, but in a lack of resolve and courage to use it without guidance from another." This call for courage, which Kant summed up in the expression *sapere aude!* ("dare to know!") is an important element of Enlightenment thought. Leading figures of the Enlightenment were ready to follow reason wherever it might take them, even if that meant risking their lives and welfare in attacking such established institutions as the monarchy and the church.

The origins of this remarkable new outlook can be traced to late-17th-century England. The "Glorious Revolution" of 1688 had substantially constrained royal power by means of an elected parliament. In 1690, the English philosopher John Locke published two treatises in which he articulated the principle that government exists as a result of a contract with the governed to protect their natural rights to liberty and property. If the government violates that contract with oppressive policies, the governed have a right to rebel and replace it. The French writer François-Marie Arouet, better known as Voltaire (1694–1778), spent over two years (1726–1729) in exile in England, where he was deeply impressed by the ideas of Locke, the scientific accomplishments

◀ **The composer as cultural hero.** Joseph Haydn last appeared in public at a performance of his oratorio *The Creation* in Vienna on March 27, 1808, just a few days before his 76th birthday. The elderly composer, seated at the center, is being given a scarf for warmth by Princess Marie Hermenegild (wife of Prince Nikolaus Esterházy), scion of the family that Haydn had served for so many years. The gesture is both personal and social: the family that had for so long employed the composer as a member of its household staff now attends to him. The Viennese public, including even the aristocracy and nobility, acknowledged Haydn as a cultural hero. Such a scene would have been unthinkable during the many decades in which Haydn was in daily service to the Esterházy family; by 1808, attitudes toward composers had changed considerably.

**Source:** Alfredo Dagli Orti/Museum der Stadt Wien/The Art Archive at Resource, NY

of Isaac Newton, and the relative freedom of English society, with its emphasis on the dignity of the individual. He returned to France with a firsthand knowledge of English philosophy and social thought and became a leader among a group of French thinkers who called themselves *philosophes* (but whom today we might call social critics). Foremost among these were Charles Montesquieu (1689–1755), Denis Diderot (1713–1784), and the Swiss-born Jean-Jacques Rousseau (1712–1778).

The *philosophes* of the Enlightenment were fundamentally optimistic. Human beings, they believed, were innately good, and society could be perfected if reason was permitted to replace superstition and tradition in the shaping of the social order. Their newfound confidence in reason as a means to self-fulfillment ultimately led to a new outlook on the relationship between the individual and the state, and between the individual and God. The *philosophes* challenged the claim of monarchs to rule by divine right and objected to organized religion for promoting intolerance and diverting attention from the rational pursuit of human and personal betterment in this life.

The political views of the *philosophes*, although generally rooted in the concept of natural rights and the social contract, were varied. They ranged from the reformist ideas of Montesquieu—an admirer of Britain's constitutional monarchy and the first to argue for the separation of powers in government—to the more radical democracy advocated by Rousseau. According to Rousseau, the "noble savage"—humanity in a state of primitive nature before government—was morally superior to the civilized individual hobbled by the arbitrary laws and conventions of society, its division into social classes, and its religions. "Man was born free," Rousseau observed in his *Social Contract* of 1762, "and everywhere he is in chains."

Enlightenment ideals provided an intellectual foundation for the revolutionary movements at the end of the 18th century. The American Declaration of Independence of 1776 is a thoroughly Enlightenment manifesto that asserts as "self-evident" the "truths" that "all men are created equal; that they are endowed by their Creator with

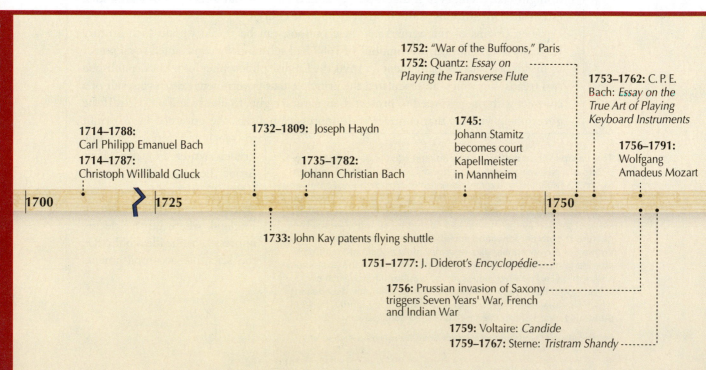

CLASSICAL TIMELINE

MUSICAL LANDMARKS

**1752:** "War of the Buffoons," Paris

**1752:** Quantz: *Essay on Playing the Transverse Flute*

**1753–1762:** C. P. E. Bach: *Essay on the True Art of Playing Keyboard Instruments*

**1714–1788:** Carl Philipp Emanuel Bach

**1714–1787:** Christoph Willibald Gluck

**1732–1809:** Joseph Haydn

**1735–1782:** Johann Christian Bach

**1745:** Johann Stamitz becomes court Kapellmeister in Mannheim

**1756–1791:** Wolfgang Amadeus Mozart

1700    1725    1750

HISTORICAL EVENTS

**1733:** John Kay patents flying shuttle

**1751–1777:** J. Diderot's *Encyclopédie*

**1756:** Prussian invasion of Saxony triggers Seven Years' War, French and Indian War

**1759:** Voltaire: *Candide*

**1759–1767:** Sterne: *Tristram Shandy*

certain unalienable Rights; that among these are life, liberty, and the pursuit of happiness. That to secure these rights, governments are instituted among men, deriving their just powers from the consent of the governed." Each of these assertions is a characteristically Enlightenment proposition: no one would have considered them self-evident 100 years earlier.

Despite the revolutionary implications of their ideas, many Enlightenment thinkers supported Europe's existing monarchies, and even the idea of absolutism (discussed in the Prelude to the Baroque Era). But they advocated an "enlightened" absolutism, led by an "enlightened despot"—a powerful ruler who exercised restraint and who worked consistently for the good of the larger whole, as opposed to his or her self-aggrandizement. Several late-18th-century monarchs sought to apply certain Enlightenment principles along these lines. Both Frederick the Great in Prussia and Catherine the Great in Russia carried on a decades-long correspondence with Voltaire that often touched on ideas about governance; Voltaire even served for a time at Frederick's court in Berlin. In Austria, Joseph II instituted reforms driven by Enlightenment attitudes toward religion, forbidding long services and elaborate music and imposing in their place a form of worship that was simpler, more direct, and less burdened with ritual.

Consistent with their belief in the power of reason to promote progress, the *philosophes* of the Enlightenment were deeply committed to the pursuit of scientific knowledge, not only for its practical applications but also as a key to the understanding of the self. They considered scientific knowledge a principal means of overcoming superstition. Thomas Jefferson (1742–1826), the leading advocate of the Enlightenment in the new United States, established the University of Virginia in the early 19th century on the basis of what he called "the illimitable freedom of the human mind. For here we are not afraid to follow the truth wherever it may lead, nor to tolerate any error so long as reason is free to combat it."

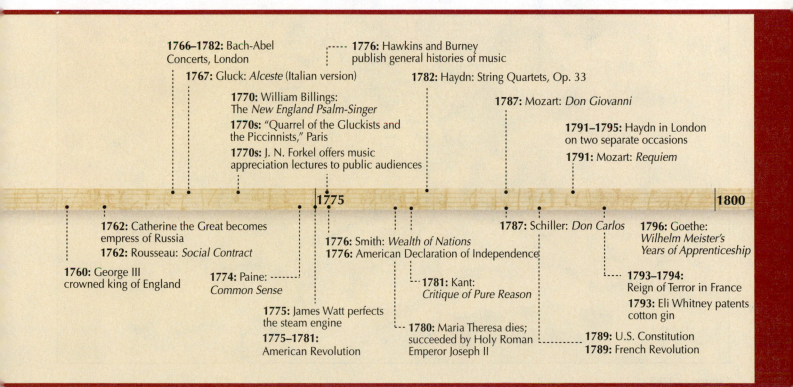

**1766–1782:** Bach-Abel Concerts, London

**1776:** Hawkins and Burney publish general histories of music

**1767:** Gluck: *Alceste* (Italian version)

**1782:** Haydn: String Quartets, Op. 33

**1770:** William Billings: The *New England Psalm-Singer*

**1787:** Mozart: *Don Giovanni*

**1770s:** "Quarrel of the Gluckists and the Piccinnists," Paris

**1791–1795:** Haydn in London on two separate occasions

**1770s:** J. N. Forkel offers music appreciation lectures to public audiences

**1791:** Mozart: *Requiem*

**1775**

**1800**

**1762:** Catherine the Great becomes empress of Russia

**1762:** Rousseau: *Social Contract*

**1760:** George III crowned king of England

**1774:** Paine: *Common Sense*

**1776:** Smith: *Wealth of Nations*

**1776:** American Declaration of Independence

**1775:** James Watt perfects the steam engine

**1775–1781:** American Revolution

**1781:** Kant: *Critique of Pure Reason*

**1780:** Maria Theresa dies; succeeded by Holy Roman Emperor Joseph II

**1787:** Schiller: *Don Carlos*

**1796:** Goethe: *Wilhelm Meister's Years of Apprenticeship*

**1793–1794:** Reign of Terror in France

**1793:** Eli Whitney patents cotton gin

**1789:** U.S. Constitution

**1789:** French Revolution

**KEY FIGURES IN ENLIGHTENMENT THOUGHT**

- *France*: Montesquieu, Voltaire, Rousseau, Diderot
- *Great Britain*: Locke, Smith, Wollstonecraft
- *United States*: Franklin, Paine, Jefferson
- *Germany*: Lessing, Kant, Goethe, Schiller

✳ **Explore** on **mysearchlab**

In order for the fruits of Enlightenment thought to reach the widest possible audience, it had to be synthesized and published. The Enlightenment was the great age of encyclopedias, summaries of known knowledge directed toward a broad reading public. The most important of these was the 33-volume *Encyclopédie*, edited by Diderot and published between 1751 and 1777. This massive compendium, bearing the subtitle *A Systematic Dictionary of Sciences, Arts, and Crafts*, contains approximately 72,000 entries written by more than 140 contributors, including Voltaire, Rousseau, and Diderot himself. Rousseau, who was also a composer, wrote almost all the entries on music for the *Encyclopédie* and would later use them as the basis for his influential dictionary of musical terms, published in 1768. In England, the more modest *Encyclopedia Britannica* first appeared in 1768–1771. The German-language *Brockhaus* encyclopedia began publication in 1796.

# WAR AND REVOLUTION

Throughout the 18th century, the major powers of Europe jockeyed for advantage over one another both at home and in their now far-flung colonies. In 1756, a Prussian invasion of Saxony triggered a global conflict between France and Great Britain over their colonial claims in North America, India, and elsewhere. Known as the Seven

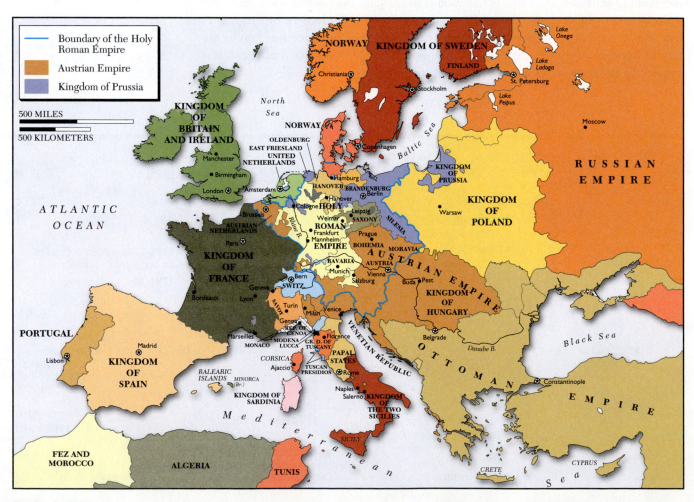

**Europe in 1763**

Years' War in Europe and as the French and Indian War in North America, it ended in defeat for France in 1763, leaving Britain in undisputed control of most of North America east of the Mississippi. The enormous expense of the war, however, strained the finances of both countries. Britain, as a result, sought to impose new taxes in its American colonies, ultimately provoking the American Revolution of 1775–1781 that led to the creation of the United States.

France, left on the verge of bankruptcy by the war, experienced even more catastrophic consequences. After more than a decade of ineffectual attempts to address the financial crisis, Louis XVI was forced in 1789 to summon the Estates General, a representative body that had not met for more than 150 years. Events soon spun out of the king's control. The French Revolution, inspired by Enlightenment doctrines, resulted in the overthrow of the monarchy. Relatively bloodless at first, the revolution turned on itself during the Reign of Terror (1793–1794), during which an estimated 250,000 suspected opponents of the revolution were arrested and about 1,400 executed in public by the guillotine. Louis XVI and his queen, Marie Antoinette, were among the victims.

The violent overthrow of what had long been regarded as Europe's most powerful monarchy shocked the rest of Europe. After 1789, no social or political institution could be taken for granted. Ideas about democracy and public self-determination had been in the air long before: ancient Greece and Rome offered a remote image of

## Focus | MUSIC IN THE FRENCH REVOLUTION

The French Revolution marks a new chapter in the use of music by the state. The ideals of the Revolution—liberty, equality, fraternity—called for an approach to music that was essentially public and nonelitist. The new government encouraged the singing of songs by enthusiastic crowds as a way to spread revolutionary ideology in much the same way that Martin Luther had used the congregational singing of hymns to spread the word of the Reformation in the 16th century. The annual festivals commemorating the anniversary of the revolution made music a participatory event, not merely a spectacle for the entertainment of audiences. These enormous, open-air gatherings featured numerous secular hymns and political songs. Various constitutions of the new state were actually set to music—mostly to well-known tunes—for the express purpose of disseminating their content in a way the common person could understand.

The French Revolution had not one but two anthems. *Ça ira* ("This Shall Be"), with its denunciation of the aristocracy ("We'll string up the aristocrats! Despotism will die, Liberty will triumph. This shall be, this shall be!"), was sung endlessly by the crowds in the streets. *La Marseillaise*, composed in 1792 by Claude-Joseph Rouget de Lisle, an army captain, became the French national anthem on July 14, 1795, the sixth anniversary

of the Revolution. Its capacity to inspire revolutionary ardor led several subsequent regimes—including those of Napoleon, Louis XVIII (after 1815), and Napoleon III (in the 1850s and 1860s)—to ban its performance. It would be reinstated as the French national anthem in 1879.

The new government also transformed the Royal Conservatory of Music into a National Conservatory whose purpose was to train musicians who could compose and perform music for the broader public good. The agenda of the new institution was unabashedly nationalistic. The composer François-Joseph Gossec (1734–1829) argued for the establishment of such a school as a bulwark against those "foreign musicians, who, having no attachment to our country, corrupt our language and pervert our taste. . . . It is therefore advantageous—or to put it better, necessary—that we have a truly national music, and to achieve this end we need an Academy of Music." Gossec later became the conservatory's first director.

In the end, the goals of the French government were far loftier than its accomplishments. Within a few years, Paris was once again attracting foreign musicians of talent, and the emphasis on political music soon declined. But the use of music as a tool of the state would provide a powerful model for subsequent revolutions and regimes throughout the world.

democratic rule, and Britain's monarchs had been ceding power gradually for many years. The American Revolution had provided yet another model for change. Still, the United States was perceived at the time to occupy the edge of a great wilderness, far removed from the centers of civilization. Paris, by contrast, was in many respects the capital of Europe, one of the leading centers of progress in science and the arts.

The French Revolution—with its Enlightenment call for liberty, equality, and fraternity—marked the beginning of a gradual decline in the strict hierarchy of class structure across Europe. The change occurred more rapidly in some places (London, Berlin) than in others (Vienna) but was palpable everywhere. The loosening of social hierarchies meant increased opportunities for individuals of talent, who could choose their occupations with greater freedom than ever before.

The violence of the revolution nevertheless led many to question the Enlightenment ideals that motivated it. After the Terror, it was harder to believe in the inherent goodness of the individual and the perfectibility of society.

# THE INDUSTRIAL REVOLUTION

Another revolution, more subtle but no less significant, was taking place at this time in the world of industry. The Industrial Revolution, as it would later be known, was driven by advances in technology. New machines were making manufacturing more efficient and economical. In the textile industry, John Kay's flying shuttle, patented in 1733, allowed one weaver to do the work of two. The traditional spinning wheel, used in western Europe since the 14th century, could produce only a single thread at a time, but James Hargreaves's spinning jenny, developed during the 1760s, turned out 8 and later 16 threads at once. Eli Whitney's cotton gin (1793) made the cost of producing cotton so economical that the output of cotton from the American South increased tenfold in the years between 1793 and 1800. (Because southern planters relied on slave labor to cultivate cotton, an unfortunate consequence of Whitney's invention was to strengthen the institution of slavery in the South.) All these and other discoveries combined to accelerate the growth of textile mills in England, the United States (beginning in the 1790s), and throughout the Western world.

The most important invention of the Industrial Revolution was the steam engine. The first practical steam engine was invented by Thomas Newcomen and put to use in 1712 to pump water out of underground mines. Improvements by James Watt in the mid-1760s permitted the application of steam power to virtually any industry. Factories that once would have been located near streams and powered by running water could now be located anywhere with access to coal. Within a few short decades, the coal-producing Midlands region of England (including the cities of Manchester, Birmingham, and Sheffield) became the center of a highly industrialized economy that exported textiles, steel, machinery, and finished goods to every corner of the world. Over time, other Western nations would follow England's lead in making the transformation from an agrarian to an industrialized economy.

The social consequences of the Industrial Revolution were profound. Workers operating heavy machinery in large factories increasingly did work that had once been done in the home. Cities grew up around these new factories, often in the most haphazard fashion. Squalid living conditions and poor sanitation were commonplace, as were outbreaks of communicable diseases like tuberculosis, typhoid fever, and cholera. But as national economies increased in size and scope, more and more workers followed job opportunities from the agrarian countryside to the industrialized city.

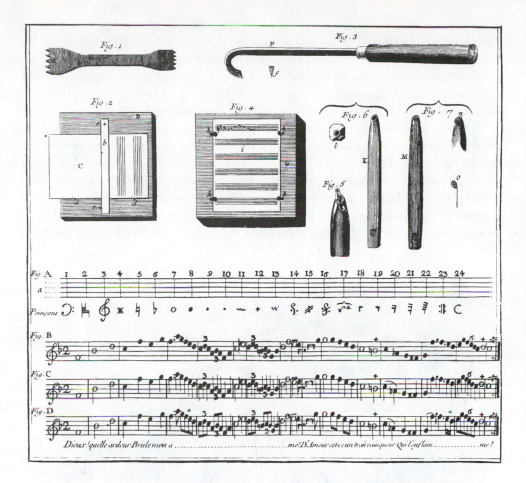

**Music engraving.** Music engraving, although not new in the 18th century, made tremendous advances during this time and became the preferred method for publishing music. It offered the advantages of mass production while at the same time allowing for a considerable degree of freehand notation. This plate from Diderot's *Encyclopédie* illustrates the process of music engraving. The tool labeled Fig. 1 was used to engrave staves. Fig. 2 shows two staves engraved on a metal plate. The straight edge (labeled b) kept the stave engraving tool straight as it was drawn against the plate. Various punches (Fig. 5, Fig. 6, and Fig. 7) produced standard notational elements. The punch labeled Fig. 5, for example, created the treble clef sign. The notes could be either punched or drawn freehand.

**Source:** Library of Congress

# MUSIC IN ENLIGHTENMENT SOCIETY

Both directly and indirectly, music benefited from Enlightenment ideals and the many advances in commerce, technology, and transportation that unfolded over the course of the 18th century. Reflecting the Enlightenment impulse to produce encyclopedic compendiums of knowledge, the first comprehensive histories of music date to the Classical era (see Focus: The First Histories of Music). Technological advances in engraving improved the efficiency of music publishing, and the music trade became truly international in the second half of the 18th century. Improved manufacturing techniques made musical instruments like the piano increasingly affordable to middle- and upper-middle-class households. The growth of cities and entrepreneurial enterprise, particularly in England, was accompanied by an increasing demand for public concerts and an increase in the number of venues in which to hold them.

Audiences also wanted to know more about the music being performed at these concerts. Enterprising publishers filled this need with a steadily increasing number of music periodicals. In the 1770s, the German composer and theorist Johann Nikolaus Forkel (1749–1818) delivered a series of public lectures that represent one of the earliest attempts to educate the general public in what we now think of as music appreciation. Audiences also wanted to learn about composers themselves. John Mainwaring's *Memoirs of the Late G. F. Handel* (1760) was the first separately published biography of a composer. Several biographies of Wolfgang Amadeus Mozart appeared shortly after his death in 1791. This trend reflects the emergence of composers as cultural icons, their growing independence from aristocratic patronage, and their growing dependence on a paying public. When Joseph Haydn arrived in London the same year as Mozart's death, his reputation preceded him. Earlier in his career he had been a liveried servant for his aristocratic employer; now he was welcomed into the highest levels of society. By the time he returned permanently to Vienna in 1795, he had become a cultural hero and national treasure (see "The composer as a cultural hero" on page 289).

Despite these trends, most music continued to be written and performed for the church or for the courts and residences of the nobility and aristocracy during the second half of the 18th century. The variety and quality of music at any given locale thus depended in large part on the tastes and financial resources of the patron who presided over it. Haydn was fortunate to have a princely employer committed to music making of high quality who had the resources to pay for it. He was able to live independently later in his career only because he had become an international celebrity.

JOHN BULL AT THE ITALIAN OPERA.
Design'd and Pub. by T. Rowlandson N. James Street Adelphi Oct. 1811

**Audience participation.** Like every good caricature, this scene from the performance of an Italian opera in London in the late 18th century is based on reality. Several members of the audience are singing along: the gentleman in the front box, in fact, seems to be attracting more attention than the *primo uomo* on stage. The orchestra director looks at the competing singer with despair. The musicians, judging from the expressions on their faces, have seen and heard it all before.

**Source:** Newberry Library/SuperStock

## Focus: THE FIRST HISTORIES OF MUSIC

The first large-scale attempts at a comprehensive history of music appeared during the Classical era. The most important of these are by Giovanni Battista Martini, John Hawkins, Charles Burney, and Johann Nikolaus Forkel.

Martini (1706–1784) never completed his monumental *Storia della musica* ("History of Music"). The three volumes he did complete, published 1757–1781, cover only the ancient world. They are full of speculation about the music of the Egyptians, Hebrews, Greeks, Romans, and other ancient cultures.

Hawkins's *A General History of the Science and Practice of Music*, published in five volumes in 1776, was the first major history of music written in English. Hawkins (1719–1789) was a lawyer by profession. His work is somewhat drier than Burney's, but on the whole fairly reliable and still useful for its portrait of 18th-century concert life in London.

Burney (1726–1814), an organist and composer in his own right, traveled widely to gather material for his four-volume *A General History of Music*, published 1776–1789. Burney's travel diaries and autobiography also make for fascinating reading. His daughter, Fanny Burney (1752–1840), won fame as a novelist and diarist.

Forkel is best known for his early (1801) biography of Johann Sebastian Bach. He completed only two volumes of his *Allgemeine Geschichte der Musik* ("General History of Music"). Published in 1788–1801, these extend only through the middle of the 16th century. They nevertheless exposed German readers to musical repertoires previously unknown to most of them.

Other composers, like Mozart, were not so lucky. Independent by default because he was unable to secure a lucrative appointment, Mozart cobbled together an income from a variety of sources. He taught piano and composition, gave concerts from time to time, wrote works on commission, and sold the rights to works of all kinds to various music publishers. He was finally granted a minor position at the Imperial court in Vienna late in life, but the income it provided was insufficient to support him and his family.

Vienna thrived as a musical center during the Classical era because it was home to many noble and aristocratic families with the resources and the desire to maintain their own musical ensembles. As the capital of the Austrian Empire, it was also home to many foreign embassies, each seeking to impress the others with sophisticated music. Haydn, who had lived in Vienna during the winter months for most of his career, moved there after the death of his long time patron in the 1790s. Mozart moved there in the early 1780s to take advantage of its opportunities and in search of an appointment at the Imperial court. By the time the young Ludwig van Beethoven (1770–1827) arrived in 1792, Vienna had established a well-earned reputation for welcoming musicians and composers of talent. Aristocratic patrons vied for Beethoven's services, in part because they liked his music, and to demonstrate their own cultural sophistication.

# Chapter

# 11

# The Art of the Natural

Like all the other period labels we have encountered so far, the label *Classical* was applied retrospectively. In this case, the designation dates to the middle of the 19th century. It was then that music critics and historians began to look back on the late 18th century as a "golden age" that had produced works of enduring value, hence "classical." Certainly it is easy today to think of the music of composers like Haydn and Mozart in this way. They, however, thought of themselves as modern composers writing in the modern style. And their contemporary audiences had little concern for enduring value. On the contrary, listeners of this time routinely demanded—and got—a steady stream of new music. As in earlier periods, it would have been unusual during the Classical era to hear music written more than a generation before. Haydn and Mozart's contemporaries—and perhaps even the composers themselves—would probably be astonished to know that people are still listening to their works more than two hundred years later.

The term *classical* also evokes Greek antiquity and the aesthetic values associated with it—balance, proportion, clarity, and naturalness. In this sense the term is aptly descriptive, because late-18th-century composers and audiences did indeed value these qualities in music. This was an era that on the whole preferred understatement to overstatement, clarity to obscurity. Although composers had long since given up the idea of recreating the actual music of antiquity, their art reflects the broad ideals and the sculpture and architecture classical of antiquity, which for the most part avoided excessive ornamentation and decoration.

## MUSIC AND THE IDEA OF NATURE

The aesthetic of the Classical era is deeply rooted in ideas about nature and, more specifically, ideas about the relationship between nature and art, the natural and the artificial. Beginning around 1730, a preference for the natural over the excessively artful ("artificial"), became increasingly widespread. The appeal of nature and the natural created a climate in which the ornate gave way to the simple, the opulent to the straightforward. In 1737, for example, the music critic Johann Adolph Scheibe (1708–1776) disparaged the music of Johann Sebastian Bach as "turgid" and "confused." The composer would win wider acclaim, Scheibe maintained, if he did not "darken the beauty" of his works with "an excess of art." Scheibe compared Bach to a now-forgotten poet of the time, a Herr von Lohenstein, and concluded that "turgidity has led them both from the natural to the artificial, and from the lofty to the somber; and in both one admires the onerous labor and uncommon effort—which, however, are vainly employed, since they conflict with Nature."[1]

The ideal work of art, according to the predominant aesthetic of the 18th century, must imitate nature in some way. In the words of the influential French critic Jean-Baptiste Dubos (1670–1742), "Music, like painting, has but a single goal: to present to the mind the truth of nature."[2] Dubos and other similarly minded writers believed that what art could project from nature was first and foremost the human passions. This goal, as we have seen, was also basic to Baroque musical aesthetics. The difference was that by the middle of the 18th century, the emphasis had shifted from the musical expression of the affect inherent in a poetic, dramatic, or religious text to a more straightforward, "natural" representation of the passions. Once again, a critic's comments on the music of Johann Sebastian Bach provide a yardstick by which to measure this changing aesthetic. No less a figure than the critic and composer Johann Mattheson (1681–1754) chastised Bach—although not by name—for his practice of repeating individual words over long stretches of music. Mattheson singled out the cantata *Ich hatte viel Bekümmernis*, BWV 21, for special ridicule with this mocking transcription of the text underlay in one movement:

"I, I, I, I had much grief, I had much grief, in my heart, in my heart. I had much grief, etc., in my heart, etc., etc., I had much grief, etc., in my heart, etc., I had much grief, etc., in my heart etc., etc., etc., etc., etc. I had much grief, etc., in my heart, etc., etc." Then again: "Sighs, tears, sorrow, anguish (rest), sighs, tears, anxious longing, fear and death (rest) gnaw at my oppressed heart, etc." Also: "Come, my Jesus, and refresh (rest) and rejoice with Thy glance (rest), come, my Jesus (rest), come, my Jesus, and refresh and rejoice . . . with Thy glance this soul, etc."[3]

Bach, like many composers of his generation, had repeated the same words many times over to give full expression to their associated musical affect. But during the 18th century, this kind of attention to individual words, basic to so much Baroque vocal music, came to be viewed with increasing distaste. By the time Bach died, even his sons considered his music old-fashioned. It was too ornate, too elaborate—in a word, too artful.

At the same time, 18th-century critics recognized that music, as an art, is distinct from nature, and although it may convey "the truth of nature," as Dubos put it, it requires technique and craft. Music that might seem natural and effortless, in other words, requires considerable art and effort. According to the aesthetic theory of the time, this dichotomy between art and nature plays itself out in the person of the artist, who must combine genius (a natural quality) with technique (a learned, artificial quality) and bring both to bear on the raw material of nature to produce a work of enduring value. Other aspects of this dichotomy can be summarized as follows:

## NATURE VERSUS ART IN 18TH-CENTURY AESTHETICS

| Nature | Art |
| --- | --- |
| Genius | Technique |
| Inspiration | Craft |
| Unconscious | Conscious |
| Effortlessness | Hard work |
| Divine | Human |
| Not teachable | Teachable |

Many accounts of the compositional process from the Classical era reflect these ideas about the connections and tensions between nature and art. In his "Introduction to the Rules of Musick" published at the beginning of his collection *The New England Psalm-Singer* (1770), the Boston-born composer William Billings (1746–1800) sums up the matter quite neatly:

> Perhaps it may be expected by some, that I should say something concerning Rules for Composition; to these I answer that *Nature is the best Dictator*, for all the hard dry studied Rules that ever was prescribed, will not enable any Person to form an Air any more than the bare Knowledge of the four and twenty Letters, and strict Grammatical Rules will qualify a Scholar for composing a Piece of Poetry, or properly adjusting a Tragedy, without a Genius. It must be Nature, Nature must lay the Foundation, Nature must inspire the Thought. But perhaps some may think I mean and intend to throw Art intirely [*sic*] out of the Question, I answer by no Means, for the more Art is display'd, the more Nature is decorated. And in some sorts of Composition, there is dry Study requir'd, and Art very requisite. For instance, in a *Fugue*, where the Parts come in after each other, with the same Notes; but even there, Art is subservient to Genius, for Fancy [i.e., fantasy, imagination] goes first, and strikes out the Work roughly, and Art comes after, and polishes it over. . . . Therefore . . . for me to dictate, or pretend to prescribe Rules of this Nature for others, would not only be very unnecessary, but also a great Piece of Vanity.[4]

Billings goes on to describe in some detail the necessary mechanical rules of music, such as scales, basic harmony, and so on, because a certain familiarity with such conventions is a prerequisite for sharing almost any form of expression. Other composers of the time voiced similar ideas. Haydn drew a sharp distinction between the (natural) invention of a melody and its (artificial) working out. When asked late in his life how he went about composing, Haydn responded,

> I sat down [at the keyboard] and began to fantasize, according to whether my mood was sad or happy, serious or playful. Once I had seized an idea, my entire effort went toward elaborating and sustaining it according to the rules of art. . . . And this is what is lacking among so many of our young composers; they string together one little bit after another, and they break off before they have barely begun, but nothing remains in the heart when one has heard it.[5]

The genius of inspiration—the idea—is an essential first step in the process, but it is not an end in itself. Indeed, Haydn implies it is all too easy to string together a series of appealing—"natural"—melodies, but that such efforts rarely leave a lasting impression on the listener.

# MUSIC IN THE CLASSICAL ERA: A STYLISTIC OVERVIEW

Opinions vary widely as to just when the Classical era began. Some music historians trace its origins as far back as the 1720s, others as late as the 1780s. The date used in this book, 1750, splits the difference between these extremes.

The wide range of opinion about the beginning of the Classical era reflects the mixture of styles prevalent throughout the middle decades of the 18th century. Elements

## Primary Evidence    GENIUS VERSUS TECHNIQUE

*Mozart's most revealing statement on the relationship between genius and technique in composition appears in a letter he wrote from Paris to his father about one of his pupils. The young lady grasps the rules of voice leading and harmony well enough, he reports, but he doubts she will ever have an original idea of her own.*

■  ■  ■

I think I told you in my last letter that the Duc de Guines, whose daughter is my pupil in composition, plays the flute extremely well, and that she plays the harp *magnifique*. She has a great deal of talent and even genius, and in particular a marvelous memory, so that she can play all her pieces, actually about two hundred, by heart. She is, however, extremely doubtful as to whether she has any talent for composition, especially as regards invention or ideas. But her father (who, between ourselves, is somewhat too infatuated with her) declares that she certainly has ideas and that it is only that she is too bashful and has too little self-confidence. Well, we shall see. If she gets no inspirations or ideas (for at present she really has none whatever), then it is to no purpose, for—God knows—I can't give her any. Her father's intention is not to make a great composer of her. "She is not," he said, "to compose operas, arias, concertos, symphonies, but only grand sonatas for her instrument and mine." I gave her a fourth lesson today and, so far as the rules of composition and harmony are concerned, I am fairly well satisfied with her. She filled in quite a good bass line for the first minuet, the melody of which I had given her, and she has already begun to write in three parts. But she very soon gets bored, and I am unable to help her; for as yet I cannot proceed more quickly. It is too soon, even if there really were genius there, but unfortunately there is none. Everything has to be done by rule. She has no ideas whatever, nothing comes. I have tried with her in every possible way. Among other things I hit on the idea of writing down a very simple minuet, in order to see whether she could not compose a variation on it. It was useless. "Well," I thought, "she probably does not know how she ought to begin." So I started to write a variation on the first bar and told her to go on in the same way and to keep to the idea. In the end it went fairly well. When it was finished, I told her to begin something on her own, only the treble part, the melody. Well, she thought and thought for a whole quarter of an hour and nothing came. So I wrote down four bars of a minuet and said to her: "See what an ass I am! I have begun a minuet and cannot even finish the melody. Please be so kind as to finish it for me." She was positive she couldn't, but at last with great difficulty something came, and indeed I was only too glad to see something for once. I then told her to finish the minuet, I mean, the treble only. But for *homework* all I asked her to do was to alter my four bars and compose something of her own. She was to find a new beginning and use, if necessary, the same harmony, provided that the melody should be different. Well, I shall see tomorrow what she has done.

**Source:** Mozart to his father, 14 May 1778; transl. MEB.

---

of Baroque style coexisted with elements of Classical style for some time, often within a single work. Styles also varied widely from region to region within Europe, and even from one work to another by the same composer. One of the hallmarks of the Baroque style, basso continuo, continued to be cultivated throughout the Classical era in sacred music and in secco recitative of all kinds, both sacred and secular. Fugues and dense contrapuntal textures, often associated with the later stages of the Baroque era, abound at the end of the 18th century as well.

The end of the Classical era is equally difficult to pinpoint. Some historians extend the period to the death of Beethoven in 1827; others prefer to treat Beethoven's late style (from about 1815 onward) as part of the Romantic era. Still others have argued that the Classical and Romantic eras together constitute a single stylistic epoch. The

**Harmony as a structural principle.** Johann Philipp Kirnberger's *Die Kunst des reinen Satzes in der Musik* ("The Art of Strict Musical Composition," 1771–1779) devotes considerable attention to the relationship between voice leading and harmony, arguing that "all music which cannot be reduced to a natural progression of both kinds of fundamental chords" — that is, triads and seventh chords — "is composed unintelligibly, hence incorrectly and contrary to the strict style of composition." To illustrate the importance of harmony within even the most contrapuntal structures, Kirnberger reduces the B-minor fugue from Book I of J. S. Bach's *Well-Tempered Clavier* to a series of harmonic progressions. The uppermost system shows Bach's original (mm. 66–67); the middle system shows a skeletal reduction of all parts with a figured bass; the next-to-bottom line shows a slightly different figured bass, including all dissonances; and the bass line at the bottom shows the harmony reduced to its fundamental components as defined by Rameau (triads and chords of the seventh). Although such a reduction might seem unremarkable today, Kirnberger's method manifests a fundamental shift in theoretical thought from the Baroque to the Classical era.

**Source:** Library of Congress

end date used in this book, 1800, is based less on changes of style than on changes in attitudes toward the nature of music, the profession of the composer, and the perceived role of music in society. As we shall see in Chapter 14, these new attitudes fundamentally changed the way music was produced and consumed.

## The Elements of Classical Style

With these qualifications in mind, we can examine the most important stylistic developments in the Classical era. One early marker is the emergence of genuine homophony—in which a subordinate voice or voices support a single prominent melodic line—as opposed to the continuo homophony of the Baroque era. More and more, the bass line ceased to function as an independent voice with its own distinctive profile. Over the course of the Classical era, the basso continuo gradually disappeared. Not coincidentally, the two genres in which it did survive—sacred music and, in opera, secco recitative—were among the most stylistically conservative.

The increasing prevalence of homophony, however, did not mean the end of counterpoint. Many composers continued to cultivate canon and fugue. And even within essentially homophonic textures, more subtle forms of counterpoint became increasingly prevalent in the 1770s and 1780s with the emergence of the **obbligato accompaniment**, in which secondary voices contribute material essential to a work's musical fabric. Although subordinate to the melody, these accompanimental voices provide motific material of their own that is integral to the fabric of the whole. For example, in the opening of Haydn's String Quartet in C Major, op. 33, no. 3 (Anthology; discussed again in Chapter 12), the principal melodic line lies firmly in the first violin part, but the second violin, viola, and cello contribute motives that, although apparently subordinate at first (m. 1–3), become motivically distinctive as they progress (m. 4–6).

Periodic phrase structure, basic to the dance music repertories of earlier eras, became increasingly common in all musical genres of the Classical era. The more or less symmetrical juxtaposition of antecedent and consequent musical statements is found in operas, songs, symphonies, concertos, and all forms of chamber music from the second half of the 18th century. Related to this development was a shift away from paratactic forms, in which discrete thematic ideas follow each other in sequence (A, B, C, D), to syntactic forms, in which a few thematic ideas are manipulated in various ways over an entire movement. The most important new syntactic structure to emerge in the Classical era was sonata form (described later in this chapter), which, like periodic phrase structure, has its roots in earlier dance and dance-related music. Another new syntactic structure, rondo form (described in Chapter 12), became popular in the 1780s, particularly for instrumental finales. Composers regularly exploited both forms, often with great ingenuity and wit, creating patterns that were at once distinctive and easily recognizable.

Another characteristic of Classical style around the middle of the 18th century, was a relative slowing of **harmonic rhythm**—that is, the rate of harmonic change within an individual phrase or series of phrases. In music of the Baroque era, harmonies often change from beat to beat; this rate of change is much less common in music of the Classical era, when harmonies shift less rapidly, changing only once or twice within the course of a given measure. This slower harmonic rhythm reflects the growing emphasis on homophony, which entailed a decrease in the distinctiveness of all voices other than the melody. As composers came to rely increasingly on areas of broad harmonic contrast and repetition in large-scale forms, the polarity between tonic and dominant became particularly strong during the Classical era. In the binary and ritornello structures of the Baroque era, by contrast, the return to the tonic often occurs just before the end of a movement (see, for example, the binary form aria of J. S. Bach's *Goldberg Variations*, Anthology, or the ritornello-based A section of Cleopatra's aria "Non disperar" from Handel's *Giulio Cesare*, Anthology). In the larger-scale structures of the Classical era like sonata form and rondo form, such a brief return of the tonic would sound incomplete and unsatisfying.

## The Illusion of Order

In making such broad generalizations about Classical style, we should keep in mind that Newton's third law of motion applies to musical as well as physical objects: every action produces an equal and opposite reaction. The sense of balance and proportion that characterizes the Classical style is typically countered by an undercurrent of asymmetry and irregularity. Just as syncopation is possible only within a defined metrical pattern, the naturalness favored by 18th-century aesthetics provided a foil for features that might subvert a sense of balance and proportion. The apparent order on the surface of much of this music often covers a more complex subsurface.

This illusion of order is captured in Jean-Honoré Fragonard's well-known painting of 1767 entitled *The Pleasant Dangers of the Swing*. At first glance, the painting appears to depict an orderly scene of simple and innocent playfulness, a young man pushing a young woman on a swing. Closer inspection, however, reveals an undercurrent of

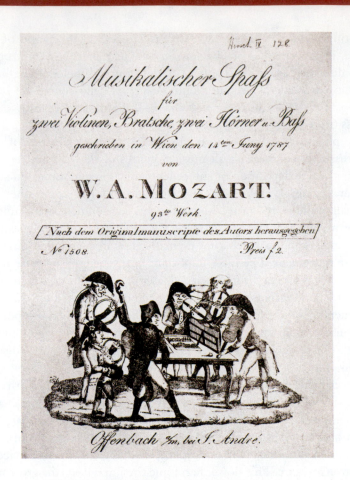

**The original title page from Mozart's "Musical Joke."** "A Musical Joke for Two Violins, Viola, Two Horns, and Bass, written in Vienna on the 14th of June, 1787, by W. A. Mozart. Op. 93," published by Johann André in 1802. The artwork fits the music perfectly, for in this sextet Mozart lampoons many of the conventions of Classical style. The part writing is intentionally faulty at times, rhythms and harmonies are displaced, and the closing fugue never quite gets off the ground. Buyers are nevertheless assured that this publication has been "edited according to the original manuscript of the author." By the end of the 18th century, consumers were beginning to demand editions of works that were accurate and genuine—that is, written by the composer named on the title page and not by someone else. André knew the exact date of composition because he had acquired many of Mozart's manuscripts, including his personal thematic catalog, from the composer's widow, Constanze.

**Source:** Dover Publications, Inc.

sexual tension. Similar contrasting levels operate in music as well: what we hear on the surface may seem orderly and straightforward, yet below the surface—often not so very far down—the music is turbulent and unpredictable. Haydn, Mozart, and their contemporaries wrote music that abounds with irregularity, humor, and irony. The opening of Haydn's String Quartet in C Major, op. 33, no. 3, for example, is anything but regular. The music starts and stops and starts again in unpredictable ways, with gestures that function within—yet at the same time against—the framework of periodic phrase structure. Mozart's Piano Concerto in E♭, K. 271 (Anthology; see Chapter 12), introduces the solo instrument in the second measure, long before any listener of the time would have expected to hear it. And no one at the premiere of Haydn's Symphony no. 103 in E♭ (Anthology) in London in 1795 could possibly have anticipated the very loud and unprepared drumroll with which it begins.

The Classical era is often misunderstood as an age in which composers were somehow shackled by rules. This view, like the label "classical" itself, arose in the 19th century. But there were in fact no rules to follow or break, only conventions to observe or bend. The young Beethoven who arrived in Vienna in 1792 was considerably more conservative than the elderly Haydn, who in his time was renowned for his idiosyncratic wit and unpredictability. During his own lifetime Haydn was repeatedly compared to Laurence Sterne, the author of *Tristram Shandy*, one of the most anarchical works in all of English literature. Sterne uses—and at the same time breaks—every known convention of narrative, repeatedly making his readers aware they are reading a book, and that he—Sterne—is manipulating their reactions. Much of the music written during the Classical era, as we will see, adopts this same approach. In a style that was supposedly natural—at least on the surface—we are repeatedly reminded of the artifice behind the effect.

**The illusion of order.** In his *Les hasards heureux de l'escarpolette* ("The Pleasant Dangers of the Swing") of 1767, Jean-Honoré Fragonard (1732–1806), a contemporary of Haydn, captures perfectly the kind of artistic playfulness and ambiguity so typical of late 18th-century art. The image works on several levels: it is at once innocent, erotic, and comic. The virtuous-looking young man on the right pushes the young lady on the swing (he uses ropes, for it would be improper actually to touch her). His earnestness contrasts with the rapture of the young man—a rival for her affections?—spying voyeuristically on the scene from the bushes on the left. How are we to understand the young lady's strange expression? Is she aware of the man on the left? Has she lost her shoe by accident, or kicked it off deliberately? And if deliberately, is it to reward or punish her concealed admirer? Much of the music of the Classical era moves back and forth between order and disruption in an analogous manner. The music of Haydn, in particular, is often simultaneously regular and irregular, serious and humorous.

**Source:** The Swing (oil on canvas), Fragonard, Jean-Honore (1732-1806) (after)/Musee Lambinet, Versailles, France/Giraudon/The Bridgeman Art Library

# STYLE AND FORM IN THE MID-18TH CENTURY

The hallmarks of Classical style began to emerge as early as the 1720s and became increasingly evident around the middle of the century. Music historians have used several terms to describe the stylistically diverse music of the decades between the 1720s and the 1750s. Some call it *Preclassical*, but this term carries an unfortunate (if unintended) value judgment, suggesting that the music of this time is somehow not yet up to the standards of the full-fledged Classical style. Others, borrowing from art history, use the terms **Galant** and **Rococo**. Both imply a sense of grace and elegance, aptly capturing the more transparent textures evident in many works of this time.

Another term, **Empfindsamkeit**—German for "sensibility"—describes a characteristic aesthetic associated with the new style. In the 18th century, to be a person of sensibility or "sentiment," as it was also called, was to be attuned to nuance and detail, delighting in small things. The author Laurence Sterne mocked this aesthetic in his 1768 novel *A Sentimental Journey through France and Italy*, in which the central character is so sensitive to details that he remains blind to larger and more consequential events. The term is nevertheless fitting for much of the music written around the middle of the 18th century, which tends to focus on detail and avoid thick textures and grandiose gestures.

## Sonata Form

The most important formal innovation of the Classical era was **sonata form**. Although the term dates from the middle of the 19th century, the form itself had become commonplace by the end of the 18th century. It applies to the organization of individual movements in a variety of genres, including sonatas, quartets, and symphonies—not to any sonata, quartet, or symphony as a whole.

Sonata form is essentially an expanded binary form that always modulates within the first reprise and usually involves more than one theme. The first reprise is called the **exposition** because it exposes the thematic ideas that will be manipulated in the second reprise. The exposition begins with one or more themes in the tonic, or primary key area (P), followed by a transitional (T) modulation to one or more themes in the secondary key area (S), usually the dominant (if the movement is in a major key) or the relative major (if the movement is in a minor key). The thematic material first stated in the primary key area is conventionally labeled P (or 1P, 2P, and so on, if there are multiple themes in this key). The thematic material first stated in the secondary key area is conventionally labeled S (or 1S, 2S, and so on). The transitional material, which can have its own themes, is conventionally labeled T.

The first part of the second reprise is called the **development** because it develops the thematic ideas of the exposition. Harmonically, the development tends to be unstable and can move to almost any key other than the tonic. The harmonic instability and unpredictability of the development is counterbalanced by the **recapitulation**—the second part of the second reprise—which reestablishes the tonic. The onset of the recapitulation is usually marked by a simultaneous return to the tonic key and a restatement of the opening theme of the exposition (1P). A recapitulation typically follows the order of the exposition—sometimes closely, sometimes freely—but always with one important difference: the thematic material (S) that was first stated in the secondary key is now restated in the tonic. In other words, the recapitulation, unlike the exposition, does not modulate, but remains in the tonic, providing a sense of harmonic balance and stability. The effect is to resolve the movement's harmonic contrasts and bring it to a satisfying close. Some sonatas conclude with a *coda* (Italian for "tail") after the recapitulation. Codas, like tails, range from short to long, but they always end on the tonic.

A typical sonata-form movement, then, might be diagrammed as follows:

| SONATA FORM | | | | |
|---|---|---|---|---|
| Section | Exposition | Development | Recapitulation | (Coda) |
| Themes | ‖: 1P 2P . . . T 1S 2S . . . | :‖: any theme(s) from exposition | 1P 2P . . . T 1S 2S . . . :‖ | |
| Key | I or | unstable | I or | I or |
| | i →V or III | | i | i |

In practice, no two manifestations of sonata form are entirely alike. The only constant elements are the modulation from a primary to a secondary key area in the exposition, a departure from these harmonic areas in the development, and the simultaneous return of the opening idea and the primary key area in the recapitulation. These predictable conventions provided listeners with easily recognized signposts by which they could orient themselves within a sonata form movement.

The first movement of Georg Matthias Monn's Symphony in B Major is an early example of sonata form. Probably written around 1740, the symphony exhibits both Baroque and Classical features. The first movement begins with two four-measure

| Section | Exposition | | | | | Development | | | Recapitulation | | | |
|---|---|---|---|---|---|---|---|---|---|---|---|---|
| **THE FIRST MOVEMENT OF MONN'S SYMPHONY IN B MAJOR** | | | | | | | | | | | | |
| Themes | ‖:1P | 2P | T | 1S | :‖: | 1P | 2P | | 1P | 2P | T | 1S :‖ |
| Measure | 1 | 9 | 19 | 26 | | 32 | 39 | | 59 | 67 | 79 | 86 |
| Key | I | | V | | | V | ii (unstable) | | I | | | |

phrases in which the figure stated in the first phrase by the first violins is repeated in the second phrase by the second violins. This kind of periodic phrase structure can be found in the music of both eras; but the bass line is decidedly un-Baroque, in that it provides harmonic underpinning but very little in the way of an independent voice. With its steady drumlike rhythm and repetition of single notes for up to two measures, the bass line also acts to slow the harmonic rhythm of the movement.

The exposition sets out two different themes in the tonic (1P and 2P), another within the transition from the tonic to the secondary key area (T), and another (1S) in the secondary key area, F♯ major, the dominant of B. The development begins with 1P but now in the dominant. (Note that themes retain the identity assigned them in the exposition throughout a movement as a whole, regardless of the key in which they might subsequently appear.) The development then circulates through a series of harmonies, none of which establishes an area of clear stability. From m. 39 until the end of the development, a variant of the musical idea 2P predominates. At m. 59, the recapitulation begins with the return of the opening theme (1P) in its original key. At m. 67, we hear what is recognizably 2P, but in a different form. Beginning in m. 79 we hear a variant of the transitional theme (T), which this time remains in the tonic, leading to a restatement of 1S (m. 86), likewise in the tonic. The movement has no coda: the end of the recapitulation corresponds to the end of the exposition.

Not all binary form movements from this period bear the hallmarks of sonata form. Most of Domenico Scarlatti's one-movement sonatas for keyboard lack a clear recapitulation. The Sonata in D Major, K. 492, written in the 1750s toward the end of the composer's life (1685–1757), features two areas of harmonic stability (tonic and dominant) in the first reprise but lacks a clear return of the opening idea in the tonic within the second reprise. The material originally presented in the dominant, however, is restated in the tonic in the second reprise, beginning in m. 91.

Like the first movement of Monn's symphony, Scarlatti's sonata features mixed elements of Baroque and Classical styles. The periodic phrase structure, relatively slow harmonic rhythm, and transparent textures look forward, whereas the virtuosic runs (m. 35–42, 91–97) and sequential passages (m. 10–16, 36–42, etc.) are more characteristic of the earlier part of the 18th century.

The first movement of Johann Stamitz's Symphony in D Major, op. 3, no. 2 (ca. 1752–55) offers yet another example of the way in which mid-18th-century composers integrated both other and newer stylistic elements. It exhibits elements of both sonata form and ritornello structure. From the perspective of sonata form, the movement features a modulation from a primary to a secondary key area, followed by a period of harmonic instability and a return to the tonic at the end. The first modulation begins in m. 18, ending in the dominant, A Major, which is confirmed by a distinctive second theme area (m. 37); this element suggests sonata form (or at least something other than a concerto grosso). Yet the lack of repeat signs (found in the previous two pieces) makes interpretation as a Classical sonata form problematic. The return of the opening theme (m. 103) does not coincide with the return of the tonic, and in this

((•• **Listen**

CD7   Track 1

**mysearchlab**

MONN
Symphony in B Major
Score Anthology II/100

((•• **Listen**

CD7   Track 2

**mysearchlab**

DOMENICO SCARLATTI
Sonata in D Major, K. 492
Score Anthology II/101

((•• **Listen**

CD7   Track 3

**mysearchlab**

STAMITZ
Symphony in D Major, op. 3, no. 2
Score Anthology II/102

### RELATIONSHIP OF RITORNELLO STRUCTURE AND SONATA FORM IN THE FIRST MOVEMENT OF STAMITZ'S SYMPHONY IN D MAJOR, OP. 3, NO. 2

| Ritornello structure | Ritornello I | | | | | | Ritornello II | | | Ritornello III | | | |
|---|---|---|---|---|---|---|---|---|---|---|---|---|---|
| "Sonata form" | "Exposition" | | | | | | "Development" | | | "Recapitulation" | | | |
| Themes | 1P | 2P | 1T | 2T | 1S | 2S | 1P | 2P | 2T | 1S | 2S | 1P | 2P |
| Measure | 5 | 13 | 18 | 29 | 37 | 44 | 53 | 61 | 77 | 87 | 94 | 103 | 111 |
| Key | I | | | V | | | V | (IV-V) | | I | | | |

**Listen**
**CD7    Track 4**
**mysearchlab**
J. C. BACH
Sonata in D Major, op. 5, no. 2
Score Anthology II/103

sense, the recapitulation is diffused; the section that leads up to it is more transitional than developmental. From the perspective of ritornello structure, the movement states its opening theme (the ritornello) twice in the tonic (at m. 5 and m. 103) and once in the dominant (m. 53), with areas of harmonic instability and opposition between. Many movements from the mid-18th century feature such mixed elements of old (ritornello) and new (sonata) forms. Even in the later decades of the 18th century, composers frequently departed from the standard conventions of sonata form.

By the 1760s, sonata form had established itself as the broad structural framework for the first movements of most instrumental works, and for some slow movements and many finales as well. Except for concertos, the influence of ritornello structure had largely disappeared. The opening movement of Johann Christian Bach's Keyboard Sonata in D Major, op. 5, no. 2, first published in 1766, is typical for its time, and not just from the standpoint of form. The simple, straightforward melodies, textures, and rhythms create a movement that is unpretentious in the best sense of the word. The first movement of this sonata exemplifies what 18th-century critics perceived as a natural form of expression that was unforced, without overt displays of contrapuntal, rhythmic, or textural artifice.

The sharp contrast between this movement by J. C. Bach and a work like his father Johann Sebastian Bach's "Goldberg" Variations, written only 25 years earlier, illustrates the generation gap that divided Classical from Baroque style. In the opening air of the "Goldberg" Variations, the theme is in the bass and remains there through all subsequent variations; the melody in the soprano is of only momentary significance. In the opening measures of the son's work, by contrast, the lowest voice consists of repeated figurations on a series of triadic harmonies. This **Alberti bass**—so called because it was a favorite device of an otherwise obscure Italian composer named Domenico Alberti (1710–ca. 1740)—provides harmonic support for the melody in the upper voice but is not itself very engaging. The frequent repetition of the same broken chord necessarily leads to a harmonic rhythm slower than that typically found in music from the Baroque era. J. C. Bach's sonata also avoids the kind of sequential repetition so basic to much of his father's music.

Typically for music of the 1760s, the dimensions of J. C. Bach's movement are relatively small. The exposition presents only one theme in the primary key area (1P, m. 1–8), and the transitional theme (T) suggests a move away from the tonic as early as its second measure (with the A♯ in the bass at the end of m. 10) before cadencing clearly on V of V in m. 18. The first theme in the secondary key area (1S, beginning in m. 19) presents a strong contrast to the opening theme, and the exposition as a whole ends with a clearly articulated cadence (m. 42). During the development, the themes appear in fragments. The last portion of 1S, for example, enters at the beginning

## Focus | MANNHEIM'S "ORCHESTRA OF GENERALS"

Johann Stamitz (1717–1757) wrote his Symphony op. 3, no. 2, for his orchestra at the court of Mannheim, in southwestern Germany. The ensemble was renowned for its virtuosos. The critic and historian Charles Burney, who experienced firsthand almost every major ensemble of his time, wrote that this orchestra had "more solo players and good composers . . . than perhaps . . . any other orchestra in Europe; it is an army of generals, equally fit to plan a battle as to fight it." Another contemporary observer, C. D. F. Schubart, observed that "its forte is like thunder, its crescendo like a waterfall, its diminuendo is like a distant plashing brook, its piano like a breath of spring." In the 1770s, Mozart sought to find a position at the Mannheim court. He failed, but he did meet Constanze Weber, his future wife, there.

In the early 20th century, the German music historian Hugo Riemann championed the composers of what he called the "Mannheim School"—Stamitz, Franz Xaver Richter (1709–1789), Ignaz Holzbauer (1711–1783), and others—for their forward-looking orchestral scoring: extended crescendos (evident in Stamitz's symphony in the opening measures), tremolos, and an advanced integration of winds and strings. More recent research has shown that many of these devices originated in Italy and were transmitted to Mannheim through prominent operatic composers of the day.

**The castle at Mannheim.** Now the central building of the city's university, this imposing structure was the home of Europe's most renowned orchestra in the middle of the 18th century.

**Source:** Werner Dieterich Image Broker/Newscom

of the development in m. 43, and the beginning of T can be heard in m. 48. In m. 60, the harmony reaches what later theorists would call a "point of furthest remove" from the tonic, in this case B minor. The music then gathers itself for a retransition back to the tonic and the opening theme, which arrive simultaneously and with great emphasis at m. 73, the beginning of the recapitulation. In typical sonata form fashion, the themes are presented in the same order as in the exposition, but this time all in the tonic and with only small variations and embellishments.

Sonata form appealed to composers and listeners alike. Composers used it as a framework for large-scale movements incorporating multiple and often contrasting thematic ideas. Audiences, too, benefited from hearing ideas presented in a more or less predictable order and fashion. An 18th-century listener hearing a work like J. C. Bach's Sonata op. 5, no. 2, for the first time, for example, could readily apprehend

# Composer Profile

## Carl Philipp Emanuel Bach (1714–1788) and Johann Christian Bach (1735–1782)

Today, Johann Sebastian Bach's reputation overshadows that of his children, but in the late 18th century this was not the case. Indeed to the extent the senior Bach was known at all, it was primarily as the father of Carl Philipp Emanuel Bach (the "Berlin Bach") and Johann Christian Bach (the "London Bach"). The two were actually half brothers. Carl Philipp was the second surviving son of Maria Barbara Bach, who died in 1720; Johann Christian was the youngest surviving son of Anna Magdalena Bach, whom Johann Sebastian had married in 1721. Both boys, along with their many siblings, learned to perform and compose from their father, but they developed distinctive styles consistent with their times. Carl Philipp, after all, was a near contemporary of Gluck, whereas Johann Christian was actually three years younger than Haydn.

| KEY DATES IN THE LIFE OF CARL PHILIPP EMANUEL BACH | |
|---|---|
| 1714 | Born in Weimar on March 8, second surviving son of J. S. Bach. |
| 1723 | Moves with his family to Leipzig and continues to study music under his father. |
| 1740 | Appointed chamber musician and clavecinist to Frederick the Great at the court in Berlin. |
| 1753–1762 | Publishes his *Essay on the True Art of Playing Keyboard Instruments*. |
| 1767 | Succeeds Telemann as music director of the principal church in Hamburg. |
| 1788 | Dies in Hamburg, December 14. |

**C. P. E. Bach.** Carl Philipp Emanuel Bach (center) drops in on Christoph Christian Sturm, one of the leading clerics in the city of Hamburg, who in turn is having his portrait done by the artist Andreas Stöttrup. Sturm had written a number of poems on religious themes that C. P. E. Bach would later set to music. The scene thus represents a meeting of art, music, and poetry.

**Source:** bpk, Berlin/Art Resource, NY

In 1740, C. P. E. Bach was appointed chamber musician and clavecinist to the court of Frederick II ("The Great") at Potsdam, just outside Berlin. The post gave him the freedom and resources to compose and perform in an almost ideal setting. One of his colleagues was Johann Joachim Quantz, the greatest flutist of his time and a composer of wide renown. In 1752, Quantz published what was then the definitive treatise on flute technique. The following year, C. P. E. Bach published the first volume of a two-volume treatise on harpsichord technique. Both treatises have considerable information on composition and aesthetics. In 1750, C. P. E. Bach sought to succeed his recently deceased father as Kantor of St. Thomas's Church in Leipzig, but the town council there rejected his application. In 1767, he assumed the duties of music director for the city of Hamburg, succeeding another celebrated musician of the time, Georg Philipp Telemann (1681–1767). Bach's responsibilities in this new capacity included providing music for the city's five main churches, so not surprisingly he wrote most of his sacred music during these last years of his life. C. P. E. Bach rivaled his father's prodigiousness, leaving behind more than 200 works for solo harpsichord, more than 50 concertos, 18 symphonies, dozens of chamber works, two oratorios, and 22 Passions.

After a visit to C. P. E. Bach in Hamburg in 1772, the music historian Charles Burney wrote the following account of the composer at the clavichord:

After dinner . . . I prevailed upon him to sit down again to a clavichord, and he played, with little intermission, till near eleven o'clock at night.

During this time, he grew so animated and *possessed*, that he not only played, but looked like one inspired. His eyes were fixed, his under lip fell, and drops of effervescence distilled from his countenance. He said, if he were to be set to work frequently, in this manner, he should grow young again. He is now fifty-nine, rather short in stature, with black hair and eyes, and brown complexion, has a very animated countenance, and is of a cheerful and lively disposition. His performance today convinced me of what I had suggested before from his works; that he is not only one of the greatest composers that ever existed, for keyed instruments, but the best player, in point *of expression*, for others, perhaps, have had as rapid execution: however, he possesses every style; though he chiefly confines himself to the expressive.[6]

**Johann Christian Bach.** Unlike his father, who never traveled outside central and northern Germany, Johann Christian Bach was a true cosmopolite who felt equally at home in Germany, Italy, and England. During his years in London, from 1762 until the end of his life, he enjoyed the patronage of the royal family, particularly Queen Charlotte, wife of George III. This connection led to a commission for the portrait shown here from one of the leading artists of the time, Thomas Gainsborough (1727–1788).

**Source:** Alfredo Dagli Orti/The Art Archive/Corbis

Johann Christian Bach lived for a time in Milan (in northern Italy) but in 1762 moved to London, where he served as music master to Queen Charlotte, the wife of King George III. His graceful compositions, most of which are within the technical grasp of amateur performers, enjoyed great popularity in their time. The "London Bach" wrote in almost every genre of his era: opera, oratorio, sacred music, symphony, chamber music, and above all keyboard music. When the young Mozart visited the English capital with his father Leopold in 1764–1765, J. C. Bach played a key role in introducing them to fellow musicians and influential patrons.

## PRINCIPAL WORKS OF CARL PHILIPP EMANUEL BACH

C. P. E. Bach composed in almost all the same genres as his father, but was perhaps most prolific in his works for keyboard. These include sonatas, concertos, trio sonatas, and many individual pieces such as rondos, fantasias, and dance movements. He also wrote symphonies, songs, and many large-scale works for chorus and orchestra, including passions, oratorios, and motets.

## PRINCIPAL WORKS OF JOHANN CHRISTIAN BACH

J. C. Bach was renowned in his lifetime not only as a composer of keyboard music, particularly sonatas and concertos, but also as one of the leading composers of opera seria, of which he wrote more than a dozen. He wrote symphonies, concertos, and much sacred music as well.

| KEY DATES IN THE LIFE OF JOHANN CHRISTIAN BACH | |
|---|---|
| 1735 | Born in Leipzig on September 5, the 11th and youngest surviving son of J. S. Bach. |
| 1750 | After his father's death, continues his musical studies with his brother Carl Philipp Emanuel Bach, in Berlin. |
| 1754 | Appointed music director to Count Antonio Litta in Milan, Italy. |
| 1762 | Moves to England and is soon appointed music master to Queen Charlotte. |
| 1782 | Dies in London, January 1. |

the overall structure of the opening movement based on its adherence to the conventions of sonata form. In this sense, sonata form functions more as a broad outline than a strict plan, rather like the form of a murder mystery, with its predictable sequence of characters and events: a crime, followed by a series of clues unraveled by an investigator sorting through a string of suspects, and ending with a solution. Yet no two sonata form movements are exactly alike, just as no two murder mysteries follow exactly the same plot, even though they follow the same general and predictable outline.

## The Fantasia

To appreciate the function of formal conventions in a structure like sonata form, it helps to consider the one genre without any: the fantasia. For a composer to designate a work or movement a fantasia was to alert listeners that it would provide them with no predictable framework. In the 18th century, theorists often claimed the fantasia had "no theme." This is not literally true, of course, in that every fantasia has at least one theme, and most of them have quite a few. What theorists meant by this claim is that the fantasia typically lacks a *central* theme around which the work as a whole is organized. Eighteenth-century theorists also liked to compare the fantasia to that part of the compositional process identified with inspiration, the invention of ideas. Haydn himself said that when he began to compose, he sat down at the keyboard and *fantasized* until he latched on to a theme.

In this sense, the fantasia is like a search for themes, often opening with rhapsodic, quasi-improvisatory flourishes on the triad. At the beginning of Carl Philipp Emanuel Bach's Fantasia in C minor (originally published as the finale to a three-movement keyboard sonata in 1753), we hear a series of broken arpeggios and seemingly aimless passagework. The music conveys a mood of inwardness and contemplation. Indeed, it struck the poet Heinrich Wilhelm von Gerstenberg as grappling with issues of life and death, inspiring him to set an elaborate text to this music based on the celebrated soliloquy in Shakespeare's *Hamlet* ("To be, or not to be: that is the question . . ."). Gerstenberg later set a second text to this same music, this one based on the dramatic moment when Socrates drinks poison rather than compromise his ethical principles. Again, the emotion is one of gravity: in both instances, Gerstenberg evokes what are quite literally life-or-death situations. One reason for the serious reaction this work provoked is its dramatic trajectory: it begins with a mood of resigned contemplation, becomes agitated, recedes to a lyrical tone (the Largo section), and concludes with agitated force (Allegro moderato).

Like many fantasias of the time, C. P. E. Bach's is full of abrupt changes and unexpected events. Such musical rhetoric reflects similar forces in the German literary movement known as *Empfindsamkeit*. This term, usually translated as "sensibility" or "expressivity," was first applied to German literary works of the third quarter of the 18th century, and later to the English novel (as "sentimentality" or "sensitivity"). *Empfindsamkeit* refers to keen awareness of and empathy for the experience of others, rather than the mawkishness associated with these terms today. It was seen as a reaction to, or at least as a compensation for, the rationalism of 18th-century Enlightenment and manifested itself in music through an unusual degree of attention to small-scale gestures, unexpected rests, rapidly shifting moods, and rhythmic freedom. C. P. E. Bach's Fantasia exemplifies this style of writing. It features long stretches without any bar lines, emphasizing the rhythmic freedom with which it is to be performed. The notated meter at the opening—allegro moderato—seems almost irrelevant. Only in the middle section do we hear a recognizable theme in a recognizable meter, but this proves transitory.

((•─ **Listen**
**CD7    Track 5**
**mysearchlab**
C. P. E. BACH
Fantasia in C minor
Score Anthology II/104

# SUMMARY

What we now think of as the Classical style developed gradually over the course of several decades during the middle of the 18th century: many works from this period resist easy stylistic classification. But by the 1760s, an aesthetic of naturalness had come to predominate, favoring lighter textures, slower harmonic rhythms, and periodic phrase structure.

✔•─Study and Review
on mysearchlab.com

| SUMMARY OF STYLE DIFFERENCES BETWEEN MUSIC OF THE BAROQUE AND CLASSICAL ERAS | | |
|---|---|---|
| | **BAROQUE** | **CLASSICAL** |
| **Style** | Two styles, the *prima prattica* and the newer *seconda prattica*. | Sacred music tends to be somewhat more conservative, preserving basso continuo and imitative writing, but most music is written in what was then called the modern style. |
| **Text Setting** | Relatively freer projection of texts with greater attention to the declamation of individual words. | Greater emphasis on sense of natural declamation; less focus on the projection of individual words. |
| **Texture** | Polyphonic (in the *prima prattica*) or homophonic (in the *seconda prattica*) with a strong sense of polarity between the two outer voices ("continuo homophony"). | Predominantly homophonic, especially in the early years of the Classical era, although with increasing use of nonimitative counterpoint ("obbligato accompaniment") in later decades. |
| **Rhythm** | A cultivation of extremes between simplicity and complexity, typically determined in vocal works by the text. The tactus gives way to a stronger sense of meter with fixed units of "strong" and "weak" beats. | Periodic phrase structure predominates, but this supposedly natural symmetry is often inflected by subtle irregularities. |
| **Melody** | More openly virtuosic, with more opportunities for embellishment by soloists. A growing differentiation between vocal and instrumental idioms. | Predominantly lyrical, with emphasis on periodic phrase structure. Virtuosity remains an option, but an aesthetic of naturalness predominates. |
| **Harmony** | Primarily tonal, especially by the end of the 17th century, with harmony conceived of as a progression of vertical sonorities. Relatively freer treatment of dissonance and voice leading. | A relatively slower harmonic rhythm, with limited and carefully controlled use of dissonance. The growing polarity of tonic and dominant allows composers to create movement-length forms on the basis of large-scale areas of harmonic stability. |
| **Form** | Both paratactic and syntactic, that is, with subunits connected rhythmically, harmonically, and thematically. Increasing use of ostinato patterns, binary form, and the ritornello principle. | Syntactic forms predominate, particularly binary form and its outgrowth, sonata form; rondo form becomes increasingly popular in finales after 1780. The only significant paratactic form is the set of variations on a theme. |
| **Instrumentation** | Composers have the option of either a cappella or concertato scoring, the latter with independent instrumental parts that complement rather than double the vocal lines. Vocal and instrumental idioms become increasingly differentiated. | A clear distinction between vocal and instrumental parts becomes the norm. The nucleus of the modern orchestra (strings, winds, brass, percussion) emerges as the standard ensemble for large instrumental works. |

# Instrumental Music in the Classical Era

Public demand for instrumental music grew steadily over the course of the Classical era, driven in part by the increasing internationalization of the music publishing trade, in part by the growing affluence of middle- and upper-middle-class musical amateurs. These amateurs sought out the latest chamber music, and publishers made a profit selling it to them. A string quartet by Mozart printed in Vienna would now be readily available in, say, London or Paris. And composers kept publishers and musicians alike supplied with a remarkable outpouring of new works.

## THE LANGUAGE OF INSTRUMENTAL MUSIC

Since antiquity, theorists and musicians had considered vocal music superior to purely instrumental music. Most Enlightenment thinkers who had something to say about music concurred: Jean-Jacques Rousseau, for example, writing in the 1760s, criticized instrumental music on much the same grounds as Plato had more than two thousand years before. Without words, Rousseau argued, music could please the senses, but it could not embody concepts or reason:

> The words to be sung usually provide us with the means to determine the object being imitated, and it is through the touching sounds of the human voice that this image awakens in the depth of our souls the sentiment it is intended to arouse. Who does not feel how far the pure symphony [instrumental music]—which seeks merely to make instruments sound brilliant—is from this energy? Can all the trifles of [the celebrated virtuoso] Monsieur Mondonville's violin move me as much as two sounds from [the celebrated diva] Madame Le Maure's voice? The symphony animates the song and adds to its expression but cannot supplant it. To understand what all the tumult of sonatas might mean . . . we would have to follow the lead of the coarse painter who was obliged to write underneath that which he had drawn such statements as "This is a tree," or "This is a man," or "This is a horse." I shall never forget the exclamation of the celebrated Fontenelle, who, finding himself exhausted by these eternal symphonies, cried out in a fit of impatience: "Sonata, what do you want of me?"[1]

The German philosopher Immanuel Kant likewise deemed instrumental music to be "more pleasure than culture."

**Thomas Jefferson, music collector.** In addition to being author of the Declaration of Independence, president of the United States, and founder of the University of Virginia, Thomas Jefferson was also an accomplished violinist. "Music," he once declared, "is the favorite passion of my soul." This note, probably a copy of one sent to a London music dealer, asks for more sonatas by the Italian composer Carlo Antonio Campioni (1720–1788). Jefferson writes: "On this paper is noted the beginning of the several compositions of Campioni which are in possession of T. Jefferson. He would be glad to have everything else he has composed of Solos, Duets, or Trios. Printed copies would be preferred; but if not to be had, he would have them in manuscript."

In Jefferson's time (and for many decades afterward) there were virtually no thematic catalogs available for any composers (see Appendix 1). Jefferson's laborious set of incipits—the first few m. of each piece—cost him time, but he had no other way to identify Campioni's works precisely. European publishers placed arbitrary opus numbers on whatever group of works they had before them. Thus Campioni's Trio Sonatas, op. 4, as published by Walsh of London around 1762 are altogether different from his Trio Sonatas, op. 4, as published by Hummel of Amsterdam at around the same time. Musicians in the United States relied almost entirely on European publishers for printed music, especially for chamber and orchestral works.

**Source:** Monticello Music Collection on the deposit from the Thomas Jefferson Foundation (3177-o), Special Collections, University of Virginia Library

At the same time, instrumental music was winning newfound respect. Although it lacked vocal music's ability to convey meaning, commentators agreed that it nonetheless constituted a "language of the heart," governed by its own rules of syntax and rhetoric. The idea that instrumental music was a language in its own right had first appeared in the early 1700s (see Focus: Musical Rhetoric, in Chapter 10). By the second half of the century, this idea had become commonplace.

The image of music as a language shaped the way in which composers, theorists, and listeners thought about the art. In one of the era's most detailed treatises on composition, Heinrich Christoph Koch (1749–1816) compared the construction of a melody to the construction of a sentence. Just as a linguistic sentence consists of a subject and predicate, a musical "sentence" (a melody) consists of a "subject" (a short two- or four-measure phrase) followed by a "predicate" (a consequent two- or four-measure phrase). In a series of examples, Koch shows a variety of techniques for expanding a simple musical sentence like the one in Example 12–1a. In Example 12–1b, for example, he substitutes a more elaborate predicate for the original. And in Example 12–1c, he substitutes expanded versions of both subject and predicate. He then goes on to show how to join musical sentences into larger units of musical syntax—paragraphs—that cohere by virtue of their common melodic material.

**EXAMPLE 12–1** Examples of simple and expanded phrases in a musical "sentence," from Koch's *Introductory Essay on Composition*, vol. 2 (Leipzig, 1787).

According to Koch and other theorists, a composer writing a movement of music must carefully combine elements to produce "unity in variety"—that is, a sufficient degree of contrast within an integrated whole. To burden a short movement with too many "completely different melodic units," Koch argued, would create so much variety that it "would destroy a still more basic element of the piece, namely its unity and symmetry."

What is at issue here is the way composers might repeat, vary, and contrast melodic elements over an entire movement within the constraints of a syntactic structure like sonata form. The quality of "unity in variety" is fundamental to the way composers approached all movement-length forms during the Classical era. Without sufficient unity, a work would sound incoherent; without sufficient variety, it would sound tedious. Only the fantasia, which lacks a central theme (see Chapter 11), was exempt from the demands of unity in variety.

A key concept in the Classical analysis of instrumental music in rhetorical terms is that of the *Hauptsatz* (literally "head sentence" in German, or in idiomatic English, "topic sentence"). The inner coherence of an instrumental work, according to Koch and his contemporaries, depends on the way the composer manipulates and sustains the *Hauptsatz*. They compared its function to that of a gospel reading for a church sermon. Just as all the points in a well-structured sermon must relate either directly or indirectly to the reading, so must all the thematic material in an instrumental movement relate directly or indirectly to the *Hauptsatz* (see Primary Evidence: The Musical Theme as a Topic Sentence).

# FORM AND GENRE IN INSTRUMENTAL MUSIC

The most important instrumental genres of the Classical era—sonata, string quartet, symphony, concerto—consist of three or four movements that provided distinct contrasts of tempo. First and last movements are normally fast; the middle movement (or one of the middle movements) is slower. Slow movements can take many forms: sonata form, theme and variations, and ternary (ABA) are the most common.

In four-movement cycles, one of the interior movements (usually the third) is typically a **minuet**. This kind of movement is often rollicking and sometimes downright boisterous, adding a touch of levity to an otherwise predominantly serious work. Derived from a Baroque dance form, the minuet is always in triple meter and almost always consists of two juxtaposed binary forms. The first of these binary forms is called the **minuet proper**, and the second is called the **trio**. At the end of the trio, the minuet proper is repeated, as in a da capo aria. The trio often presents a contrasting mood and typically has a distinct theme or themes of its own; it might also be in a different key or mode.

Finales, too, can take on a variety of forms, the most common of which are sonata form and (particularly from the 1780s onward) **rondo**, a type of movement associated largely with finales and found in many different instrumental genres, including symphonies, string quartets, concertos, and sonatas. Like the minuet, the rondo derives from a Baroque dance form, in this case a lively round dance. Rondos appear in many guises, but they always involve the alternation of a recurring theme with contrasting material. In the simplest terms, this pattern can be diagrammed as ABACADA, with A representing the opening, recurring idea (often called the **refrain**), and B, C, and D representing contrasting ideas (known as **episodes**, or **couplets**).

## Primary Evidence — THE MUSICAL THEME AS A TOPIC SENTENCE

*Johann Philipp Kirnberger (1721–83), a pupil of J. S. Bach, wrote important treatises on composition, counterpoint, and harmony. Here he explains the importance of a musical movement's opening theme—its* Hauptsatz, *or topic sentence—and the theme's relationship to subsequent ideas within the movement.*

■ ■ ■

A *Hauptsatz* is a period within a musical work that incorporates the expression and the whole essence of the melody. It appears not only at the beginning of a movement, but is repeated frequently, in different keys and with different variations. The *Hauptsatz* is generally called the "theme," and [Johann] Mattheson compares it not inappropriately to the [scriptural] text that provides the basis of a sermon, which must contain in a few words that which the discourse will develop more fully.

Music is actually the language of sentiment, whose expression is always concise, for sentiment in itself is something simple, something that can be presented in a few brief utterances. Thus, a very short melodic phrase of two, three, or four measures can express a sentiment so definitely and correctly that the listener understands exactly the emotional state of the person who is singing. If, then, a musical work had no other purpose than to present a sentiment clearly, such a brief phrase, if well thought out, would suffice. But this is not the goal of music; it should engage the listener for a period of time in the same emotional state. This cannot be achieved through the mere repetition of the same phrase, no matter how splendid it may be, for the repetition of the same thing becomes boring and destroys the attentiveness of the listener. Therefore, one had to invent a type of melody in which one and the same sentiment, with appropriate variety and different modifications, could be repeated often enough to make the appropriate impression upon the listener.

It is in this manner that the form of most of our usual current musical works has arisen: concertos, symphonies, arias, duets, trios, fugues, etc. They all have this in common: they are based on a *Hauptsatz* presented in a main period, brief and appropriate to the expression of a sentiment; this *Hauptsatz* is supported or interrupted by smaller, interpolated ideas [*Zwischengedanken*—literally "in-between thoughts"] appropriate to it; this *Hauptsatz* and these interpolated ideas are repeated often enough, in different harmonies and keys, and with small melodic variations, so that the spirit of the listener is sufficiently captivated.

**Source:** Johann Philipp Kirnberger, "Hauptsatz," in Johann Georg Sulzer, ed., *Allgemeine Theorie der schönen Künste* (Leipzig: Weidmann, 1771–74). Transl. MEB.

The opening theme, or refrain, of a rondo movement is typically brief and catchy. It is almost always a closed, self-contained unit consisting of an antecedent and consequent phrase with a cadence in the tonic. The first contrasting episode, or couplet, tends to be brief, with an early return to the refrain. Longer digressions from the refrain usually appear later in a movement.

As with sonata form, composers used the basic rondo structure as a point of departure. They sometimes, for example, bundled more than one contrasting episode between refrains to create a pattern like ABACDAEFBA. They also overlaid aspects of sonata form on the rondo to create what eventually came to be known as **sonata-rondo form**. In this synthesis, the first episode (B) is presented in a secondary key, like a theme in the secondary key area of a sonata-form exposition; when this theme reappears toward the end of the movement, it is transposed to the tonic, as in a sonata-form recapitulation. In general terms, then, a sonata-rondo form might look like this:

| SONATA-RONDO FORM | | | | | | | |
|---|---|---|---|---|---|---|---|
| Theme | A | B | A | C | A | B | A |
| Key | I | V | I | X (unstable) | I | I | I |

In practice, rondo and sonata-rondo movements rarely follow these patterns in any strict manner. Rondo and sonata-rondo, like sonata form, provided composers with a general framework for the presentation of ideas, not an unchangeable design.

## Sonata

The sonata remained the quintessential domestic genre of instrumental music in the Classical era. The keyboard sonata, in particular, flourished throughout the second half of the 18th century, thanks to the growing affordability and availability of the piano (see Performance Perspective: The Fortepiano).

The keyboard sonata by Johann Christian Bach (op. 5, no. 2; Anthology II/102), discussed in Chapter 11, is typical of the genre at midcentury. It is light-textured and small in scale, can be played equally well on harpsichord or piano, and places only limited technical demands on the performer.

The same cannot be said of Haydn's Sonata in C minor, Hob. XVI:20, published in 1771, only five years after Bach's. This three-movement work reflects the increasing scale of late-century sonatas. Compared to Bach's it is longer, more varied musically and emotionally, and more demanding of the performer. Given its many rapid shifts between *forte* and *piano*, the work is clearly intended for the fortepiano (or clavichord) rather than the harpsichord. A harpsichord, for example, would be incapable of the rapid dynamic changes in m. 13–14.

The first eight measures of the sonata also illustrate Haydn's ability to create irregular patterns even within the constraints of periodic phrase structure. The opening two measures present a standard tonic to dominant progression, leading the listener familiar with this kind of pattern to expect the next two measures to lead back from the dominant to the tonic, completing a closed unit. But Haydn delays the **half cadence** (a cadence on the dominant) by repeating the turning figure sequentially to create an antecedent phrase of four rather than two measures. The next two measures (5–6) reiterate the tonic, but this time in a lower register—register will be an important compositional element in this movement—and after a surprise flourish in m. 6,

((•● Listen

**CD7    Track 6**
**mysearchlab**
HAYDN
Piano Sonata in C minor, Hob. XVI:20
Score Anthology II/105

the music returns to the tonic in m. 8. This initial point of harmonic and rhythmic closure, however, is not very strong. The composer does not yet want the music to come to a complete stop, so he creates the expectation of continuity by placing the tonic cadence on the third beat of the measure rather than the downbeat and also by leaving it harmonically "empty"—that is, as unharmonized octave Cs. We may be at the end of a sentence, Haydn is telling us, or even of a paragraph, but certainly not the end of a chapter or an entire work. In one sense, then, this opening eight-measure unit fulfills all our expectations about melodic and rhythmic structure: the first four measures take us from the tonic to the dominant, and the second four bring us back to the tonic. Yet Haydn has manipulated the inner workings of this larger progression in ways that are full of small surprises. Again, the music is rather like Fragonard's painting of the girl on the swing—it seems simple on the surface but on close inspection reveals subtle complications.

Haydn's sonata also features a style of writing that some commentators today refer to as **Sturm und Drang** ("storm and stress"). The term comes from the title of a play written in the late 18th century and applies to a small but significant body of music written during the late 1760s and early 1770s by such composers as Haydn, Mozart, Gluck, and Johann Baptist Vanhal (1739–1813). The characteristics of *Sturm und Drang* music include a prominent use of the minor mode, large melodic leaps, jagged syncopations, and sudden dynamic contrasts. The overall result is a sense of heightened emotional intensity and drama. Haydn wrote several works that fit this description during the late 1760s and early 1770s, including, in addition to the Piano Sonata in C minor, the Symphonies nos. 45 in F♯ minor ("Farewell") and 49 in F minor and the String Quartet in F minor, op. 20, no. 5. Mozart's Symphony in G minor, K. 183, and his Quartet in D minor, K. 173, both of which were written in the early 1770s, also fit the *Sturm und Drang* profile.

## String Quartet

Although composers had written chamber works for four instruments during the Baroque era—some trio sonatas, for example, fall into this category—the string quartet is new to the Classical era. Two features in particular distinguish it from most earlier genres. Its performance forces—two violins, a viola, and a violoncello—are all from the same family, giving it a homogeneous timbre, and it has no basso continuo line. Although manuscript copies of some early string quartets include a figured bass, the cello and viola lines together provide the necessary harmonic underpinning that in earlier times would have been supplied by the basso continuo.

The limited timbral variety of the string quartet posed a special challenge to composers but also contributed to the genre's prestige. Contemporaries compared a good quartet to an intimate conversation among a close group of friends, in which the participants exchange ideas. It was a domestic genre, designed for performance in the house or salon to a small and select audience. During the Classical era, string quartets were rarely performed at public concerts. Some of Haydn's string quartets may have been performed publicly in London in the 1790s, but this would have been an exception.

String quartets of the Classical era typically consist of three, four, or five movements, with the four-movement format emerging as the standard in Haydn's works around the late 1760s. Mozart, too, preferred four movements, although other popular composers of the day—notably Carl Dittersdorf (1739–99) and Ignace Pleyel (1757–1831)—favored three (usually in the sequence fast-slow-fast).

## Performance Perspective

# The Fortepiano

Malcolm Bilson's performance on a fortepiano of the first movement of Haydn's Sonata in C minor, Hob. XVI:20, illustrates the striking difference in sound between the instrument during Haydn's lifetime and the modern-day piano. Bilson plays on an original fortepiano made by the Schantz brothers; we know that Haydn purchased an instrument from this Viennese workshop about 1788. Compared to the modern grand piano, the instrument is smaller in every respect, with a span of about only five octaves and a narrower dynamic range. Yet the fortepiano features a lighter mechanism and a more transparent sound: what it lacks in power it makes up for in finesse, and many players today prefer this kind of instrument for repertory of the late 18th and early 19th centuries.

There were many varieties of fortepiano during Haydn's lifetime. The two most important types were the English and the Viennese (or German). The English pianos manufactured by Broadwood used an intermediate lever to throw the hammer at each set of three strings with considerable force. The resulting sound was distinctively loud, a feature Haydn exploited to great effect in the sonatas he wrote in London in 1791–95.

The Viennese pianos manufactured by such firms as Stein and Walter provided three strings only for the highest notes, two for the rest. Their sound, as a result, was not as powerful as that of the English instruments, but they were more responsive to the player's touch. The most valued feature of the Stein piano was its superior escapement action, which allowed each hammer to return to its original position almost immediately after striking the string. This in turn allowed performers to play rapid and repeated notes more easily than on English instruments. Mozart sent a glowing report of a new Stein instrument's light action to his father in 1777:

Before I had seen any pianofortes made by Stein, those made by Späth had been my favorites. But now I prefer Stein's, for they dampen the sound much better. . . . When I hit a key forcefully, the sound vanishes at once, regardless of whether I hold my finger on the key or lift it. I can attack the keys in any way I wish; the tone is always consistent. It does not mangle, get louder or softer, and it certainly does not fail to sound altogether.

In a word, everything is even. Granted, he will not sell such a pianoforte for less than 300 gulden, but the care and energy he puts into them are priceless. His instruments distinguish themselves from all others in that they are made with an escapement. Only one in a hundred persons cares about this. But without an escapement it is impossible for a pianoforte to avoid jangling or reverberating unduly. When one strikes the keys, Stein's hammers fall back the moment after they have struck the strings, whether one holds the key down or releases it. When he has made such an instrument (as he told me himself) he sits down at it and tries all kinds of passages, runs, and leaps, and he whittles away and works on the instrument until it can do everything. For he works for the benefit of music and not for his personal benefit alone, otherwise he would be finished with his work right away.[2]

**Piano by Johann Andreas Stein, Augsburg, 1790.** Mozart praised the responsive action of Stein's pianos, which had a keyboard of 61 notes, from the F two-and-a-half octaves below middle C to the F two-and-a-half octaves above. The dampers were controlled by a sideways-moving lever operated by the player's right knee.

**Source:** Library of Congress

## Focus  TO REPEAT OR NOT TO REPEAT?

Early examples of sonata-form movements regularly include repeat signs at the end of both the first reprise (the exposition) and the second reprise (the development and recapitulation). Over the course of his long career, however, Haydn gradually stopped calling for a repeat of the second reprise, starting a trend that would continue into the 19th century. By the 1820s, for example, Beethoven was inclined to drop the repeat sign even for the exposition sections of his sonata-form movements.

Today, many performers of Classical-era instrumental music observe some repeat signs when they are present in the music but ignore others. In sonata-form movements, for example, the exposition is routinely repeated, but it has become common to ignore the repeat of the second reprise. But the gradual decline in the use of the repeat sign by composers themselves suggests the signs should be respected when present. When composers didn't want a reprise repeated, in other words, they said so. Some composers, for example, would occasionally indicate that the two reprises of a minuet proper should not be repeated when the minuet proper is played da capo. Performers today tend to abbreviate this return automatically, but when 18th-century composers did not want such repetitions in performance, they explicitly indicated as much.

Impatience with what sometimes seems excessive repetition, however, is not unique to performers today, as is evident from the comments of André Grétry (1741–1813), one of the leading operatic composers of his day:

A sonata is a discourse, an oration. What are we to think of a man who, dividing his discourse in half, repeats each half? "I was at your house this morning; yes, I was at your house this morning to talk with you about something; to talk with you about something." . . . I speak above all of the long reprises that constitute the halves of a [musical] oration. Reprises may have been good at the birth of music, at a time when the listener did not comprehend everything until the second time around. I know that an oration is often divided into two sections; but one certainly does not present each one twice.[3]

The quartets of Haydn and Mozart surpass those of their contemporaries in textural richness and technical difficulty, qualities that did not always impress critics. Mozart's quartets in particular came under fire for being overly elaborate and complex. One anonymous critic, for example, although professing admiration for the composer, complained that Mozart, "in order to become a new creator, aims too high in his artful and truly beautiful writing, so that little is gained for feeling and for the heart. His new quartets for two violins, viola, and cello, which he has dedicated to Haydn, are certainly too highly seasoned—and what palate can endure this for long?"[4]

The first movement of Haydn's String Quartet in C Major, op. 33, no. 3 illustrates the characteristic textural richness of his quartets. The repeated notes in the second violin and viola parts in the opening measures seem at first to be preparing us for the entry of a more engaging melodic line, which does indeed begin to emerge in the first violin in m. 2. Yet the surprising changes of pitch in this seemingly innocuous pulsing figure give it a growing significance: the C and E in the opening measures shift to F and D in m. 7, and B♭ and D in m. 13. What appears to be a subordinate figure, at first static in its pitch and rhythm, gradually emerges as a motivic idea in its own right, blurring the boundary between melody and accompaniment. That boundary is similarly ambiguous in the interaction between the first violin and the cello from m. 18 to 26. Are the two parts exchanging the melody from measure to measure, or is the cello figure merely accompanying the longer note values of the violin's melody? What these examples illustrate is the truly obligatory nature of the obbligato accompaniment in this quartet. Blending counterpoint with

((•• Listen

**CD7    Tracks 7–10**
**mysearchlab**
HAYDN
String Quartet in C Major, op. 33, no. 3
Score Anthology II/106

homophony, Haydn has created a texture in which accompaniment and melody are inextricably linked.

The lively second movement of this quartet, which Haydn labeled "scherzo," follows the typical structure of a minuet, with m. 1 to 34 constituting the minuet proper, m. 35 to 51 the trio. (Why Haydn chose to call this movement and its counterparts in the other quartets in op. 33 scherzos rather than minuets is not clear; he returned to the designation "minuet" in his subsequent quartets.) The duet between the first and second violin in the trio provides another example of the blending of homophony and counterpoint. The first violin clearly carries the melody within this simple two-voiced texture, but the second violin line provides nonimitative counterpoint to the melody.

The slow third movement of Haydn's quartet is in **sonata form with varied reprise**. In this variant of sonata form, the exposition is not repeated note for note, but instead written out and changed in subtle ways. The varied reprise in this particular movement begins with the return to the tonic in m. 30 and a restatement of the opening theme with new melodic embellishments, especially in the first violin. The modulation to the dominant, confirmed in m. 14 in the first statement of the exposition, is repeated in the second statement in m. 43, again with an elaboration in the first violin part. The effect is similar to that of a da capo aria, in which the singer was expected to embellish a reprise the second time through. In this case, however, Haydn specified the embellishments, rather than leaving them up to the performer. After a short development section (m. 59–64), the music returns to the tonic (m. 65) at the onset of the recapitulation, which repeats the themes of the exposition, but this time all in the tonic.

The last movement, a rondo, illustrates one of Haydn's favorite devices in this form—to incorporate thematic material from the opening refrain (the A section) within a contrasting episode. The A section (m. 1–22) and the B section (m. 23–36) are clearly distinct. The material in m. 37 to 72, however, which leads back to a second statement of A, is as long as the A and B sections combined and based on material from A. By manipulating harmonies and fragmenting the thematic material into increasingly small units, Haydn makes the return to A at m. 72 a significant event, even though it offers no thematic contrast to what precedes it. What, then, is the formal status of the material in m. 37 to 72? Because it is based on thematic material from A, it could be considered a statement of A within a typical rondo structure. Functionally, however, it is more like an extended retransition—a return to the opening idea—or even (in sonata-form terms) a development section. The finale as a whole can also be analyzed as a type of sonata-rondo form, as in the following diagram:

| SONATA-RONDO FORM IN THE FOURTH MOVEMENT OF HAYDN'S STRING QUARTET IN C MAJOR, OP. 33, NO. 3 | | | | | | | | |
|---|---|---|---|---|---|---|---|---|
| Theme | A | B | retransition | A | B | retransition | A | Coda |
| Measure | 1 | 23 | 37 | 72 | 93 | 107 | 125 | 147 |
| Key | I | vi | x (unstable) | I | i | x → V | I | |

These overlapping interpretations of a single movement reflect the way Haydn, like many composers of the Classical era, manipulated established conventions, working within the parameters of these forms but never constrained by them.

## Symphony

In the early decades of the 18th century, the terms "symphony" and "overture" were synonymous. Sometime around the 1720s, however, these one- or three-movement works (fast-slow-fast) began to be performed outside the theater, independent of any opera or oratorio for which they had originally been written. The earliest independently composed symphonies are believed to have been written in the 1720s by the Italian composer Giovanni Battista Sammartini (1701–75). The concert symphony was cultivated intensely throughout the Classical era: composers across Europe wrote a staggering number of such works for performance at courts, in churches, and increasingly in public concerts (see Focus: The Rise of the Public Orchestral Concert). One recent scholar has catalogued more than 12,000 symphonies written between roughly 1720 and 1810.

The quality of orchestras varied widely across Europe, but their average size grew steadily during the second half of the 18th century. Haydn's symphonies, which span some four decades from the 1750s through the 1790s, reflect this trend. His early symphonies typically call for strings (first and second violins, violas, cellos, double basses) and two oboes, with an occasional flute (sometimes two) or a pair of bassoons, or both. Relatively few of these early symphonies call for horns, trumpets, or timpani. From the

---

### Focus   CYCLICAL COHERENCE

**Cyclical coherence**—sometimes called *cyclical unity*—refers to the manner in which the various movements of a sonata, quartet, symphony, or any other instrumental genre relate to one another. At the most basic level, the movements of any Classical era work almost always cohere on the basis of their performance forces and tonal relationships. The performance forces stay the same from movement to movement and the key at the beginning and end are almost invariably the same, although the mode (major or minor) may be different.

Beyond these basics, however, there are no consistent patterns in the way movements relate to one another as part of a larger whole. Sometimes we find composers explicitly repeating themes from one movement to another. Haydn did this in the last two movements of his Symphony no. 46 in B Major (1772), and Beethoven would do much the same thing in his Fifth Symphony from 1808. But these are exceptions, not the rule. Cyclical coherence generally expresses itself more subtly in Classical-era works.

Haydn's String Quartet, op. 33, no. 3, provides a case in point. On a fairly obvious level, three of the four movements feature birdlike themes (movement 1, opening measures; movement 2, in the trio; movement 4, throughout). These themes account for this quartet's nickname, "The Bird" (a nickname that, like almost every other connected to Haydn's works, did not come from the composer himself). More subtly, the opening themes of the two outer movements are characterized by an unusual amount of repetition on a single note or a single figure. More subtly still, the unusual voicing of the first movement's opening is replicated in the first measures of the scherzo: both movements begin with a first inversion of a C-major chord. By itself, this parallel might be coincidental, but it seems less so when we observe that the second phrase of each movement (m. 7 in the first movement, m. 5 in the scherzo) begins with a D-minor triad, again in first inversion. And just as the first movement veers unexpectedly to a B♭/D dyad in m. 13, so too does the scherzo move without preparation to a B♭ triad in m. 15.

Was Haydn aware of these connections? Probably, although we cannot be certain. But does it matter? A work of art is inevitably the result of thought processes that are both conscious and unconscious. A more important question is whether such connections are significant enough to enrich our understanding and appreciation of a work, and here there is ample room for reasonable disagreement. A determined analyst will likely find connections between movements in any given cycle that a more skeptical observer will deny. As is often the case in matters of aesthetic judgment, there are no right and wrong answers for questions like these.

late 1760s on, two horns became standard. By the mid-1780s, trumpets and timpani were routinely added to the mix. Haydn was relatively slow to accept clarinets into the orchestra, but in his last four symphonies, written in the mid-1790s, he included them as well. Mozart, by contrast, had scored clarinets into his symphonies of the late 1780s, and the Belgian composer François-Joseph Gossec (1734–1829) had been using them since the 1770s.

Like other composers, Haydn also used special instruments or combinations of instruments from time to time to give a distinctive color to individual symphonies. In his Symphony no. 22 in E♭ Major (nicknamed "The Philosopher" by a later generation of listeners), for example, he substitutes two English horns for the oboes. His Symphony no. 39 in G minor, from the late 1760s, uses four horns. And in his Symphony no. 100 in G Major of 1794 ("Military"), he incorporates a number of so-called Turkish instruments for special effect at certain points: the bass drum, cymbal, tambourine, and triangle, were widely associated with the style of Turkish music and were, in effect, "outdoor" instruments, rarely heard in the concert hall.

Although we tend to think of the Classical symphony as a sequence of four movements (fast-slow-minuet-fast), these works, the early ones in particular, actually display considerable variety in the sequence and number of movements. Many of Haydn's early symphonies, for example, have only three movements, a pattern derived from one of the genre's antecedents in the theater—the so-called **Italian overture**—which

## Focus | THE RISE OF THE PUBLIC ORCHESTRAL CONCERT

The first regularly scheduled public concerts of orchestral music date to the Classical era. The range and nature of offerings, however, varied from city to city.

**London,** with a variety of concert-producing organizations, enjoyed Europe's most active and publicly accessible musical life. The Bach-Abel Concerts, organized jointly by Johann Christian Bach and Carl Friedrich Abel, flourished from 1766 to 1782. The Concerts of Ancient Music, founded in 1776, were unusual for their time in that they played no music less than 20 years old and were particularly committed to music by Handel. The Professional Concerts (1783–93) were organized by the Italian Muzio Clementi and the Germans Wilhelm Cramer and Johann Peter Salomon. In 1786, Salomon formed his own organization and 5 years later brought Haydn to London. Occasional concerts organized for special events provided yet another venue for the public consumption of music. Less formal but no less important were the many performances held in the city's "pleasure gardens"—a sort of genteel amusement park—that appealed to a still wider audience.

The focus of musical life in **Paris** continued to be the court and the residences of the aristocracy. The public *Concerts spirituel* series and the *Concerts de la Loge Olympique* were nevertheless important institutions in prerevolutionary Paris. It was for the latter of these that Haydn was commissioned to write his "Paris" symphonies (nos. 82–87) in 1785–86.

**Vienna,** where private orchestras thrived in the 1780s and 1790s, followed much the same pattern as Paris. There were, however, a few regular public concert series, and occasional concerts open to a paying public also became increasingly common during this period. Mozart, for example, organized and performed in a number of such concerts in the 1780s, often playing his own piano concertos. His father, Leopold Mozart, reported approvingly to his daughter after one such event that "a great many members of the aristocracy were present. Each person pays a gold sovereign or three ducats for these concerts. Your brother is giving them in the Mehlgrube [a local theater] and pays only half a gold sovereign each time he uses the hall. The concert was magnificent and the orchestra played splendidly."[5]

In **Berlin,** concert life outside the court was relatively slow to develop. The opera was open to the public, but instrumental music enjoyed little support. A civic choral society, the *Singakademie*, played an important role in reviving the music of Johann Sebastian Bach in the early 19th century and provided a model for other German cities to follow in establishing their own amateur musical societies.

**Two ways of holding the violin.** Leopold Mozart's *Treatise on the Fundamental Principles of Violin Playing* was the standard violin manual of its day. Published six months after the birth of his son, Wolfgang, this book would go through multiple editions and be translated into several different languages by the end of the 18th century.

The frontispiece shows Leopold himself demonstrating the "relaxed" position of holding the instrument. "Here the violin . . . is held chest-high, slanting. . . . This position is undoubtedly natural and pleasant to the eyes of the onlookers but somewhat difficult and inconvenient for the player as, during quick movements of the hand in the high position, the violin has no support . . ." This position is still used today in bluegrass and old-time fiddling in the United States.

Another plate from the treatise shows the alternative method of holding the instrument, one that more closely resembles modern technique, "whereby the violin remains unmoved in its place even during the strongest movements of the ascending and descending hand." The ever-increasing demands on violinists to shift positions rapidly on the fingerboard eventually led to the almost exclusive adoption of this position among concert violinists.

**Source:** The New York Public Library/Art Resource, NY

consisted of three movements in the order fast-slow-fast. (Many Classical-era operas featured overtures of this kind.) In addition, the finales of early symphonies are not always fast: some are minuets or in the minuet style. A look at the movement structure of Haydn's first 27 symphonies (before 1768; see table on page 327) indicates the extent of their variety.

The now familiar four-movement structure became standard for the symphony after about 1770. This structure can be summarized as follows:

- *First movement.* Typically the weightiest of the four, it sets the expressive tone for the symphony as a whole. It is usually in sonata form, sometimes with a slow introduction.

- *Slow movement.* Usually the second movement, but sometimes exchanges place with the minuet movement to come third. Slow movements take a variety of forms, including sonata form, sonata form without a development (sometimes called "slow movement sonata form"), theme and variations, or some variety of ABA. Slow movements are usually in a key other than the tonic—most commonly the subdominant—providing tonal contrast with the rest of the cycle.

# A CLOSER LOOK

✱Explore on mysearchlab

Charles Hague (1769–1821) was a violinist, impresario, and later professor of music at Cambridge University. He was a former pupil of Johann Peter Salomon, the violinist-impresario who had brought Haydn to London in 1791.

The Red Lion was an inn with a large public space in the town of Cambridge. It survived into the 1960s, when it was demolished to make room for a shopping mall.

Public concerts tended to be either one-time ad hoc affairs or part of a larger series for which audience members bought subscriptions. Hague organized this particular series and performed in it, both as a violin soloist (in the concerto by Geminiani) and from the first violin stand as concert master (in the orchestral works). He probably also performed in the chamber pieces by Boccherini and Le Claire.

The first half of the program features an overture (or possibly a symphony: the terms were interchangeable at the time) for orchestra, a "lesson" (probably a sonata) for solo piano, a song for voice and piano, and a string quintet.

The second half of the program features a violin concerto, another song, a duet for violins, and an unnamed symphony by Haydn, probably one of the twelve he had written for London a few years before. The placement of Haydn's symphony at the very end of the program testifies to the popularity and drawing power of the composer's works.

## MR. HAGUE's
## Ninth Subscription Concert
### Of VOCAL and INSTRUMENTAL MUSIC,
#### WILL BE PERFORMED
### At the RED LION in the PETTY CURY,
On MONDAY Evening, May 1ſt, 1797.

**PART I.**
Overture—*Bergbi.*
Leſſon on the Grand Piano Forte,
Miſs A. Hague.
Song, MR. TAYLOR—*Storace.*
Quintetto—*Boccherini.*

SONG—*Storace.*

Tell ſapſies Oak laſt in the dell,
Where tangled brakes its beauties ſpoil,
And every inſtant ſhoot repel,
Damps hopeleſs o'er th' exhauſted ſoil.
At length the Woodman clears around,
Where'er the noxious thickets ſpreads
And high, reviving o'er the ground,
The foreſt Monarch lifts his head.

SONG—*Carnaby.*

I ſought my fair throughout the valley,
And by'd me to her fav'rite brook ;
The pink, the violet, and lily
Adorn and flouriſh round her crook.
My fable, in accents moving,
Attun'd her lay, and then the ſong—
Where is my Coſin roving ?

**PART II.**
Violin Concerto, *Mr. Hague–Geminiani.*
Song, MASTER WAGSTAFF—*Carnaby.*
Duetto for Two Violins—*Le Claire.*

Symphony—*Haydn.*

Oh, how my heart, tranſported, flutter'd,
When ſhe confeſs'd her love ſo true :
Such ſoothing words, ſo ſweetly utter'd,
New joy inſpir'd—to her I flew :
I kneel, I ſigh'd, a falling tear
Proclaim'd my love ſincere—
Ah ! could I then be roving ?
The world itſelf ſhall fade and periſh,
E'er I my fable forſake ;
With love and truth my fair I'll cheriſh,
Her joys and miſeries partake,—
She bluſh'd and ſmil'd with grace ſerene :
I then addreſs'd fair Beauty's Queen—
Adieu to all my roving.

The Concert will begin at Half paſt Seven o'clock.
Admittance to Non-Subſcribers, *Three Shillings* each Concert.

The program is quite long by today's standards. Audiences were freer to come and go, however, and the strictures of concert decorum were not nearly so rigid. It is safe to say that the Red Lion Inn did a brisk business in food and drink not only before and after the concert but during it as well.

**Interior of a brass instrument workshop in Paris, ca. 1760.** The scale of this workshop is small compared to the instrument factories of the mid-19th century. In the 18th century, instruments were made by licensed masters who took on journeymen and apprentices learning their trade. Workshops like this one had no external source of power. Pounding, shaping, and polishing were all done entirely by hand.

**Source:** Dover Publications, Inc.

## THE VARIETY OF MOVEMENT STRUCTURES IN HAYDN'S EARLY SYMPHONIES (BEFORE CA. 1768)

| Three Movements | | | |
|---|---|---|---|
| F-S-F (8) | F-S-M (2) | S-F-M (1) | S/F-M-F (1) |
| 1, 2, 10, 12, 16, 17, 19, 27 | 9, 26 | 18 | 25 |
| **Four Movements** | | | |
| F-S-M-F (7) | S-F-M-F (5) | S/F-S-M-F (2) | S/F/S-M-S-F (1) |
| 3, 8, 13, 14, 20, 23, 24 | 4, 5, 11, 21, 22 | 6, 7 | 15 |

F = fast movement; S = slow movement; S/F = fast movement with a slow introduction; M = minuet.

- *Minuet*. A dance-inspired movement in minuet form, usually the third movement. Symphonic minuets are often more rhythmically irregular (and certainly faster) than minuets written expressly for dancing.

- *Finale*. Last movement, usually relatively light, often in sonata form, rondo, or sonata-rondo form.

By the early 1770s, the concert symphony had begun to distinguish itself from other genres of instrumental music by its lofty tone as well as the number of performers it required. The first movements of "the best chamber symphonies," according to the composer and critic Johann Abraham Peter Schulz (1747–1800),

contain grand and bold ideas, free handling of compositional techniques, apparent irregularity in the melody and harmony, strongly-marked rhythms of various sorts, powerful bass melodies and unisons, concerting middle voices, free imitations, often a theme handled fugally, sudden transitions and shifts from one key to another, which are the more striking the weaker the connection is, bold shadings of *forte* and *piano*, and particularly the *crescendo*, which has the greatest effect when used with a rising melody and its climax. To this is added the art of weaving all the voices in and out of one another in such a way that all parts, when played together, create a single melody that is incapable of accompaniment, but rather one in which every voice is making its own particular contribution to the whole. Such an Allegro in a symphony is like a Pindaric ode: it elevates and moves the soul of the listener in the same way, and it requires the same spirit, the same sublime imagination, and the same knowledge of art to be fully appreciated.[6]

Schulz went on to point out that the symphony as a whole "is especially suited to the expression of the grand, the solemn, and the sublime." Like his contemporaries, Schulz avoided using the term "beautiful" in accounts of this genre. Critics of the time defined as beautiful anything that was pleasing and "agreeable" (to use a favorite 18th-century term). The sublime, however, was associated with that which was imposing, powerful, and perhaps even a bit frightening. A favorite example of the sublime in nature for 18th-century critics was a storm at sea, because it combined beauty with power and unpredictability. The sublime, in this view, appeals to a level of the soul that is above and beyond reason. The merely beautiful might be worthy of contemplation, but the truly sublime inspires awe.

((•Listen
**CD7   Track 11**
**mysearchlab**
HAYDN
Symphony no. 103 in E♭ Major
Score Anthology II/107

The powerful, sudden, and wholly unexpected drumroll that opens Haydn's Symphony no. 103 in E♭ Major illustrates what critics like Schulz had in mind when they wrote of the sublime in music. It would have struck contemporary listeners as loud, bizarre, and portentous, surely a signal announcing some great event, but what kind of event? It gets our attention but not necessarily our sympathy. The musical idea that follows is dark, fragmented, and difficult to grasp, like a painting of a scene shrouded in mist. Only later will we realize that what we are hearing at this point is a premonition of themes to come.

The opening theme in the low strings reinforces the mysterious air of this slow introduction. The first two measures sound very much like the opening of the *Dies irae* ("Day of wrath") from the plainchant Mass for the Dead (see Example 12–2). (Thirty-five years later, Hector Berlioz would use the complete *Dies irae* melody in the finale of his *Symphonie fantastique*; see Chapter 15.)

The slow introduction ends with what contemporary audiences must surely have perceived as a bizarre pounding on the notes G and A♭ (m. 35–39). But what sounds dark and ominous at the end of the slow introduction is immediately transformed into a bright and airy theme at the beginning of the Allegro con spirito that follows. Progressions like this—from somber to bright, dark to light, obscurity to clarity—are another manifestation of what 18th-century critics considered sublime. The sudden deflection from the dominant of C minor to E♭ Major is likewise another portent of things to come, this time of the many other sudden and unexpected modulations that abound in this sonata-form first movement. The return of the slow movement's opening in the coda of the first movement (at m. 202) is even more unexpected.

**EXAMPLE 12–2** Plainchant Sequence *Dies irae* from the Mass for the Dead.

Day of wrath, day that will dissolve the world in ashes

**Haydn corrects Beethoven's counterpoint exercises.** Most of Beethoven's studies with Haydn in 1792–93 involved exercises in strict counterpoint, a reflection of the enduring importance of counterpoint in the Western musical tradition. Haydn taught it in virtually the same way it is taught today. He provided his student, in this case Beethoven, with a cantus firmus voice (marked "C.f." at the left-hand side of three of the four systems here), and the student filled in the remaining voices. The cantus firmus alternates between alto and tenor in the exercises. Haydn has marked infelicities of voice leading with an "x" above the staves at various points, and to the right of the uppermost example he has written out a preferred solution. When he did these exercises, Beethoven was 23 years old and had already published several compositions of his own. He would later study counterpoint with two other teachers as well.

**Source:** Dover Publications, Inc.

In addition to their inherent musical qualities, slow introductions served a practical purpose: to dampen the noise of the audience. In Haydn's time, audiences did not sit in breathless attention awaiting the beginning of a work. But with a slow introduction like that of his Symphony no. 103, Haydn could write an opening theme in the Allegro con spirito that would otherwise be barely audible. (Beethoven would later use two loud chords at the beginning of his "Eroica" Symphony to set up the soft main theme that follows; see Chapter 15.)

As is typical of slow introductions in general, the introduction to Symphony no. 103 follows no established conventions of form; instead, it represents something along the lines of a fantasia. It nonetheless introduces important elements that are re-worked during the ensuing sonata-form structure that make up the bulk of the first movement. The down-and-up half-step motion of the *Dies irae*–like theme in the introduction, for example, resurfaces in the opening theme of the Allegro con spirito. The opening drumroll itself prefigures a remarkable number of themes in the first movement (and the symphony as a whole) that incorporate repeated notes. Among these are the principal theme of the sonata-form section of the movement (m. 40–41) and the transitional theme beginning at m. 59–60. The opening idea of the finale also features repeated notes, as does the theme of the second reprise of the minuet.

## Concerto

As in the Baroque era, the concerto was the principal genre for instrumental virtuosos to showcase their talents during the Classical era. Concertos for keyboard—harpsichord or piano—were an important new addition to the repertory of the late Baroque and early Classical eras. Johann Sebastian Bach was one of the first to write concertos for

## Composer Profile

# Joseph Haydn (1732–1809)

Haydn's father made wagon wheels for a living, but his family and their neighbors in the village in which he was born recognized the boy's musical talent and sent him to Vienna when he was eight years old. There he sang in the choir at St. Stephen's Cathedral and absorbed the repertory of the late Baroque and early Classical eras. When Haydn's voice broke, he was no longer of any use to the chorus at St. Stephen's and was, by his own account, thrown out on the street. He survived by giving music lessons and eventually drew the attention of the aristocratic Morzin family, who hired him as their music director in 1758. Three years later, he was lured away by Prince Paul Anton Esterházy, who was in the process of assembling what by all accounts was one of the best orchestras in Europe at the time. Prince Paul Anton died in 1762, but his brother and successor, Prince Nikolaus, was willing to spend even *more* money on music.

Haydn was thus in an ideal position to create new music. Late in life, he told one of his biographers, "My Prince was satisfied with all of my works and I received applause. As the director of an orchestra, I could make experiments, observe what elicited or weakened an impression, and thus correct, add, delete, take risks. I was cut off from the world, no one in my vicinity could cause me to doubt myself or pester me, and so I had to become original." A lesser composer might easily have fallen into a comfortable routine, churning out symphonies, sonatas, and quartets according to his patron's requirements, but Haydn imposed astonishing demands on himself. Beyond certain outward similarities, every one of his works seems to define its own issues and standards.

Haydn's first contract with the Esterházy family required him to "compose such music as His Serene Highness may command, and neither to communicate such compositions to any other person, nor to allow them to be copied, but he shall retain them for the exclusive use of His Highness, and not compose for any other person without the knowledge and gracious permission of His Highness." He was obliged to "appear daily . . . in the antechamber before and after midday, and inquire whether His Highness is pleased to order a performance of the orchestra." Haydn was also required "to instruct the female vocalists, in order that they may not forget in the country what they have been taught with much trouble and expense in Vienna."[7]

In spite of all this, Haydn soon became more famous than even he himself realized. Unscrupulous publishers in Paris pirated his music or placed his name on music that others had written. Haydn nevertheless spent most of his professional life writing music on demand. When his prince became obsessed with the baryton, a curious instrument rather like a viola da gamba, Haydn set to work writing literally dozens of trios for baryton, viola, and cello. When the prince was bitten by the opera bug and built a new opera house a few years later, Haydn dutifully composed new operas year after year.

The death of Prince Nikolaus in 1790 opened a new chapter in the composer's life. Johann Peter Salomon, a German-born impresario living in London, persuaded Haydn to make two extended tours to England, where he composed symphonies, songs, and a number of works for piano. After he returned to Vienna for good in 1795, he produced two highly successful oratorios (*The Creation* and *The Seasons*), a handful of Masses, and several of his finest string quartets.

A note on the composer's name: Although baptized "Franz Joseph Haydn," he never used his first name, even in legal documents. (The same is true for Wilhelm Richard Wagner, Fortunino Giuseppe Verdi, and a host of other composers.) Haydn's last name was often misspelled in his own lifetime—as "Hayden," "Haidn," or, as it appeared on his first contract with the Esterházy family, "Heyden"—but always in a manner consistent with the correct pronunciation (roughly, *hidin'*, with the accent on the first syllable).

# PRINCIPAL WORKS

## Symphonies

Haydn's 106 authentic symphonies span almost his entire career. Some of the early ones are openly programmatic (nos. 6, 7, and 8 bear the subtitles "Morning," "Noon," and "Night," respectively). Others are based on plainchant themes: the Symphony no. 26, for example, uses themes from a widely performed plainchant setting of the Lamentations of Jeremiah. Still others are downright bizarre. The most famous of these is the so-called "Farewell" Symphony in F♯ minor—one of only two known 18th-century symphonies in this key—in which the musicians exit one by one in the finale. Haydn was apparently trying to remind Prince Nikolaus that his musicians had stayed too long at Esterháza in the summer of 1772 and were eager to return to their families in Eisenstadt.

Many of Haydn's "London" symphonies (nos. 93–104) feature a gimmick guaranteed to resonate with the widest possible audience. Examples include the drum stroke in the slow movement of the "Surprise" Symphony (no. 94), the tick-tock of the slow movement of the "Clock" (no. 101), and the opening of the slow movement of Symphony no. 98, which begins like "God Save the King," only to continue in a different fashion. At the premiere, some members of the audience must surely have begun to rise when they heard it, only to sit down foolishly a moment later.

## String Quartets

Haydn played an important role in the emergence of the string quartet as a genre during the 1750s and 1760s. Even his earliest quartets (from the mid-1750s) have no need of a supporting basso continuo: the four voices alone combine to create the necessary sonorities and harmonies. Altogether, he wrote 67 complete and indisputably authentic string quartets. The set known as "Opus 3" is probably not by Haydn.

**Haydn composes.** This image of Haydn is consistent with his own account of his working methods. "I sat down [at the keyboard] and began to fantasize, according to whether my mood was sad or happy, serious or playful. Once I had seized an idea, my entire effort went toward elaborating and sustaining it according to the rules of art." The blank music paper underneath the inkwell, juxtaposed with the work now on the stand, suggests a work in progress.

**Source:** DeAgostini/SuperStock

## Keyboard Sonatas

Haydn's career coincides with the rise of the piano as the principal instrument of domestic music making. The earliest of his 36 surviving sonatas were written with the harpsichord in mind, but from the mid-1760s onward, he was clearly attracted to the piano's greater dynamic range.

## Sacred Music

When he returned from England to Vienna in 1795, Haydn was still officially in the employ of the Esterházy family, even though his orchestra had long since disbanded. For several years in a row, Prince Nikolaus's successor commissioned Haydn to write a setting of the Mass Ordinary in honor of his wife's birthday. These late Masses contain some stunning vocal writing and music every bit as dramatic as the late symphonies. *The Creation*, an oratorio, also dates from this last period of Haydn's career.

| KEY DATES IN THE LIFE OF HAYDN | |
|---|---|
| **1732** | Born in Rohrau (Austria) on March 31. |
| **1740** | Sent to Vienna, where he sings in the choir at St. Stephen's Cathedral. |
| **1748** | Forced to leave St. Stephen's; ekes out a living giving music lessons; composes first works. |
| **1758** | Appointed music director to Count Morzin in what is now the Czech Republic. |
| **1761** | Appointed assistant music director to Prince Paul Anton Esterházy in Eisenstadt. |
| **1766** | Becomes music director to Prince Nikolaus, Paul Anton's successor. |
| **1790** | Prince Nikolaus dies; Haydn leaves for England. |
| **1791–1792** | First English tour. Feted as a genius; receives an honorary degree from Oxford University. |
| **1793–1794** | Back in Vienna, gives lessons in harmony, counterpoint, and composition to Beethoven. |
| **1794–1795** | Second English tour; finishes the last of his 12 "London" symphonies. |
| **1796–1801** | Writes his final works, including the last quartets, two oratorios, and several Masses. |
| **1801** | Suffers the first of several strokes. |
| **1809** | Dies in Vienna on May 31. |

## Primary Evidence  HAYDN IN LONDON

*Written a week after Haydn's arrival in England, this fascinating letter to Maria Anna von Genzinger, a talented pianist who lived in Vienna, reminds us of the physical and emotional distance the composer had traveled from his native Austria. When Haydn arrived in London, he was already a celebrity. He granted interviews to three newspapers and received invitations to dine at the highest levels of English society. Only a few months before, he had been going about his daily routine in remote Esterháza.*

■ ■ ■

London, 8th January 1791

Nobly born, Gracious Lady!

I hope that you will have received my last letter from Calais. I should have written you immediately after my arrival in London, but I wanted to wait a few days so as to be able to write about several things at once. So I can tell you that on . . . New Year's Day, after attending early Mass, I boarded the ship at 7:30 A.M. and at 5 in the afternoon I arrived, thank God! safe and sound in Dower [i.e., Dover]. At the beginning, for the first 4 whole hours, we had almost no wind, and the ship went so slowly that in these 4 hours we went no further than one single English mile, and there are 24 between Calais and Dower. Our ship's captain, in an evil temper, said that if the wind did not change, we should have to spend the whole night at sea. Fortunately, however, towards 11:30 o'clock a wind arose and blew so favorably that by 4 o'clock we covered 22 miles. Since the tide, which had just begun to ebb, prevented our large vessel from reaching the pier, 2 smaller ships came out to meet us as we were still fairly far out at sea, and into these we and our luggage were transferred, and thus at last, though exposed to a middling gale, we landed safely. The large vessel stood out to sea five hours longer, till the tide turned and it could finally dock. Some of the passengers were afraid to board the little boats and stayed on board, but I followed the example of the greater number. I remained on deck during the whole passage, so as to gaze my fill at that mighty monster, the ocean. So long as it was calm, I wasn't afraid at all, but towards the end, when the wind grew stronger and stronger, and I saw the monstrous high waves rushing at us, I became a little frightened, and a little indisposed, too. But I overcame it all and arrived safely, without vomiting, on shore. Most of the passengers were ill, and looked like ghosts, but since I went on to London, I didn't feel the effects of the journey at once; but then I needed 2 days to recover. Now, however, I am fresh and well again, and busy looking at this endlessly huge city of London, whose various beauties and marvels quite astonished me. I immediately paid the necessary calls, such as to the Neapolitan Ambassador and to our own; both called on me in return 2 days later, and 4 days ago I luncheoned with the former—N.B. at 6 o'clock in the evening, as is the custom here.

My arrival caused a great sensation throughout the whole city, and I went the round of all the newspapers for 3 successive days. Everyone wants to know me. I had to dine out 6 times up to now, and if I wished, I could dine out every day; but first I must consider my health, and 2nd my work. Except for the nobility, I admit no callers till 2 o'clock in the afternoon, and at 4 o'clock I dine at home with Mon. Salomon. I have nice and comfortable, but expensive, lodgings. My landlord is Italian, and also a cook, and serves me 4 very respectable meals; we each pay 1 fl. 30 kr. a day excluding wine and beer, but everything is terribly expensive here. Yesterday I was invited to a grand amateur concert, but I arrived a bit late, and when I showed my ticket they wouldn't let me in but led me to an antechamber, where I had to wait till the piece which was then being played in the hall was over. Then they opened the door, and I was conducted, on the arm of the *entrepreneur*, up the center of the hall to the front of the orchestra, amid universal applause, and there I was stared at and greeted by a great number of English compliments. I was assured that such honors had not been conferred on anyone for 50 years. After the concert I was taken to a handsome adjoining room, where a table for 200 persons, with many places set, was prepared for all the amateurs; I was supposed to be seated at the head of the table, but since I had dined out on that day and had eaten more than usual, I declined this honor, with the excuse that I was not feeling very well, but despite this I had to drink the harmonious health, in Burgundy, of all the gentlemen present; they all returned the toast, and then allowed me to be taken home. All this, my gracious lady, was very flattering to me, and yet I wished I could fly for a time to Vienna, to have more quiet in which to work, for the noise that the common people make as they sell their wares in the street is intolerable. At present I am working on symphonies, because the libretto of the opera is not yet decided on, but in order to have more quiet I shall have to rent a room far from the center of town. I would gladly write you in more detail, but I am afraid of missing the mail-coach. Meanwhile I am, with kindest regards to your husband, *Fräulein* Pepi, and all the others, most respectfully,

*Your Grace's most sincere and obedient servant,*

JOSEPH HAYDN

**Source**: *The Collected Correspondence and London Notebooks of Joseph Haydn* edited and translated by H.C. Robbine Landon. Copyright © 1959 by H.C. Robbins Landon. Reprinted by permission of Georges Borchardt, Inc., for H.C. Robbins Landon.

the harpsichord, and his sons followed in his footsteps. Like the sonata (but unlike the symphony after about 1770), most concertos of the Classical era are in three movements (fast-slow-fast), without a minuet.

The ideals of spontaneity and improvisation play an important role in the genre of the concerto. Cadenzas in every movement, particularly the first, were expected to be (or at least appear to be) moments of intense improvisation, giving performers free rein to exercise their fancy. Although Mozart wrote out many of his own cadenzas, these were presumably intended for friends or students. Not until Beethoven's last piano concerto, written in 1809, did composers begin to write obligatory cadenzas, and even then only sporadically.

The first movements of many concertos of the Classic era, including Mozart's piano concertos, employ a variant of sonata form called **double-exposition concerto form**. As the name implies, this structural convention presents two expositions, the first for the full orchestra (the tutti exposition) and the second for the soloist (the solo exposition). The tutti exposition does not modulate and remains essentially in the tonic throughout. The solo exposition begins in the tonic and then moves to the secondary key area, as in a conventional sonata-form exposition (I to V or i to III). Development and recapitulation proceed along the lines of conventional sonata form, at least harmonically, with the addition of an opportunity for a solo cadenza toward the end of the recapitulation.

The first movement of Mozart's Piano Concerto in D Major, K. 107, no. 1, based on the first movement of Johann Christian Bach's Keyboard Sonata in D Major, op. 5, no. 2 (discussed in Chapter 11), illustrates the relationship between sonata form and double-exposition concerto form. (It also reflects Mozart's admiration for J. C. Bach as well as the widespread practice of composing a new work on the basis of an established model.) For the first eight measures, Mozart closely follows Bach's sonata (Anthology II/102), adding additional accompaniment in the inner voices (second violins and violas) but making no structural changes. At the beginning of the transition, however (m. 9), when the sonata modulates to the dominant, the concerto stays in the tonic. Mozart then abbreviates much of what J. C. Bach had presented in the secondary key area, adding a cadential figure of his own (m. 24–28) to close out the tutti exposition. All this time the soloist has been playing as a member of the basso continuo, filling in harmonies according to Mozart's figured bass.

| DOUBLE-EXPOSITION CONCERTO FORM | | | | |
|---|---|---|---|---|
| Section | Tutti exposition | Solo exposition | Development | Recapitulation | Cadenza & coda |
| Key | tonic | tonic → secondary | unstable | tonic | tonic |

The soloist assumes an altogether different function in the solo exposition, which begins at m. 29. Now the melody moves to the piano, the accompaniment moves to the strings, and the basso continuo drops out altogether. In the solo exposition Mozart also follows Bach's sonata much more closely, modulating to the dominant on the transitional theme (m. 37–46) and staying there to introduce all the themes Bach had presented in the secondary key area. (In retrospect, we can now see why Mozart abbreviated the tutti exposition: the music would have stayed in the tonic for far too long in proportion to the movement as a whole.)

**A keyboard concerto, 1777.** Although women rarely enjoyed easy access to formal instruction in composition, they could—and did—excel as performers, especially in singing and in playing the harpsichord and piano. Vienna was particularly rich in women keyboard virtuosos during the last three decades of the 18th century. The setting here happens to be domestic: a small and exclusive audience in a private setting. Some in the audience are listening, others conversing.

**Source:** akg-images

((•●[Listen

CD7    Track 12
**mysearchlab**
MOZART
Piano Concerto in D Major, K. 107, no. 1
Score Anthology II/108

((•●[Listen

CD8    Track 1
**mysearchlab**
MOZART
Piano Concerto in D minor, K. 466
Score Anthology II/109

The first movement of this concerto can also be analyzed in terms of ritornello structure, a formal principle that Mozart never wholly abandoned in his concertos. As in a Baroque concerto, the movement as a whole consists of alternating tutti and solo sections. The contrasting tutti and solo sections are easy to identify in the score with a quick look at the keyboard part: figured bass notation—indicating that the solo instrument is acting as a basso continuo—signals a tutti section; the absence of figured bass notation signals a solo section. Mozart appears to have composed the cadential figure first heard at m. 24–28 precisely in order to demarcate tutti from solo sections. These tutti sections are brief in comparison to the solo sections, but they articulate important structural divisions within the whole. In the diagram here, the labels applied to the themes in the tutti exposition (which does not modulate) are based on the appearances of these themes as they appear within the solo exposition (which does modulate).

The first movement of Mozart's Piano Concerto in D minor, K. 466 conveys a strong sense of drama and tension on multiple fronts: in mode (minor vs. major), timbre (winds vs. strings; soloist vs. orchestra), and texture (tutti vs. solo sections). The pianist enters as a soloist at the beginning of the solo exposition with a new, previously unheard theme; this is typical of Mozart's concertos. It has a dreamy, lyrical quality that contrasts starkly with the brooding, agitated opening theme first heard in the low strings. The conflict plays itself out over the course of the movement: at times the orchestra takes the lead, with the soloist complementing the ensemble (as, for example, in the passage beginning at m. 91); at other times, the pianist takes the lead and the orchestra falls in to support the soloist (as, for example, in the passage beginning at m. 128). The arrival of the cadenza is announced by the convention of a fully-voiced second-inversion tonic chord (m. 365), and the soloist in turn announces

## THE STRUCTURE OF MOZART'S PIANO CONCERTO IN D MAJOR, K. 107, NO. 1, FIRST MOVEMENT

| Ritornello structure | Rit. I | | Solo 1 | | | | | | Rit. 2 | |
|---|---|---|---|---|---|---|---|---|---|---|
| Double-exposition concerto form | Tutti exposition | | Solo exposition | | | | | | | |
| Theme | P [T 1S 5S] | | P | T | 1S | 2S | 3S | 4S | 5S | |
| Measure | 1 9 17 24 | | 29 | 37 | 47 | 54 | 59 | 62 | 70 | |
| Key | I | | I | → | V | | | | | |

→ continued below

| Ritornello structure | Solo 2 | | | | Rit. 3 | Solo 3 | Rit. 4 |
|---|---|---|---|---|---|---|---|
| Double-exposition concerto form | Development | | Recapitulation | | | Cadenza | Coda |
| Theme | 1S  T  4S  1S | | P  T  1S  2S  3S  4S | | | (improvisation on earlier themes) | 5S |
| Measure | 75  80  84  93 | | 105  113  120  128  132  135  143 | | | 147 | 148 |
| Key | unstable  V | | I | | | | |

the end of the cadenza with a long trill leading to the tonic. Once the ensemble returns, the soloist functions as a member of the basso continuo for the remainder of the movement.

## SUMMARY

Composers of instrumental music working in the second half of the late 18th century developed or refined a variety of genres and forms that would remain in use throughout the 19th and even 20th centuries. The string quartet and symphony took their place alongside such established genres as the sonata and concerto. Sonata form, rondo, and double-exposition concerto form provided broad frameworks for the presentation of musical ideas. By 1800, instrumental music had established itself as a language without words. Theorists borrowed from the terminology of grammar and rhetoric (period, phrase, antecedent, consequent) to suggest that even without words, music could function as a language in its own right.

✓● Study and Review on mysearchlab.com

# Vocal Music in the Classical Era

In spite of the rising status of instrumental music in the Classical era, vocal music retained its traditional position of aesthetic supremacy. Without a text, instrumental music was perceived as appealing only to the emotions as the "language of the heart)." Bolstered by a text, vocal music—sacred or secular—could appeal to both heart and mind at once.

The opera house, in particular, was a center of intense musical activity—and controversy—at any court or in any city with claims to cultural prominence. Opera's high status in the cultural hierarchy made it a subject of great critical interest and a magnet for the most talented singers, composers, stage designers, and poets of the day. Like movie stars today, these people often found themselves the focus of gossip and adulation.

Unfortunately, very few operas of the Classical era are performed with any regularity today. Other than the operas of Mozart and a handful by Christoph Willibald Gluck (1714–1787), the bulk of this enormous repertory remains largely unknown, even to opera enthusiasts. Yet in their day the works of the leading opera composers—Johann Adolph Hasse (1699–1783), Baldassare Galuppi (1706–1785), Niccolò Jommelli (1714–1774), Tomasso Traetta (1727–1779), Niccolò Piccinni (1728–1800), François-Joseph Gossec (1734–1829), André-Ernest-Modeste Grétry (1741–1813), Domenico Cimarosa (1749–1801), and Antonio Salieri (1750–1825)—were familiar to almost every music lover.

## THE RISE OF OPERA BUFFA

As early as the 1720s, a new style of opera was beginning to emerge in Italy. **Opera buffa**—comic opera—featured many elements not found in opera seria. Its subject matter was humorous rather than serious. The libretto of the typical opera buffa centered on everyday characters rather than heroes, rulers, and gods. Singers included basses (largely absent in opera seria) but not castrati. Opera buffa gave more emphasis to ensemble singing (duets, trios, quartets), again in contrast to opera seria, which featured mostly solo arias. Opera buffa also avoided da capo arias and other opportunities for elaborate vocal improvisations. Melodies were on the whole simple and straightforward, with increasing evidence of periodic phrase structure.

The origins of opera buffa lie in the tradition of the **intermezzo**, a work originally performed between the acts of a larger (serious) opera. Giovanni Battista Pergolesi's intermezzo *La serva padrona* ("The Maidservant as Mistress") was written in 1733 and first performed in Naples between the acts of an opera seria also written by Pergolesi. Over time, this intermezzo and others like it became so well known that they were presented alone rather than between the acts of larger works, thus giving rise to opera buffa as a separate genre.

((•—Listen

**CD8    Track 2**
**mysearchlab** (with scrolling translation)
PERGOLESI
*La serva padrona*
Score Anthology II/110

*La serva padrona* tells the story of a maidservant who, through guile and cunning, becomes mistress of the household in which she had been employed. In contrast to the elaborate cast of characters found in many opere serie of the time, Pergolesi's intermezzo makes do with only two singers: Uberto (a bass), the master of the house, and Serpina (a soprano), the maidservant. (The character of Vespone, a manservant, is entirely mute and limited to mime.) The orchestra consists of string and basso continuo; the texture is homophonic with a great deal of doubling of voice part by the orchestra, although there are a few moments of independence. In the first of two acts, Serpina is hoping to raise her station by marrying her master (although she is in fact his former ward), but the negotiation between them becomes a psychological game: can Uberto marry and still retain his self-respect, and can Serpina marry and still retain her power over him?

In the duet that closes the act, "Lo conosco a quegl' occhietti" (I see it in your eyes), the two "discuss" the question in comic style. Serpina opens with a melody (G Major) that modulates to D Major; Uberto's reply (in D Major) uses thematic material derived from Serpina's opening. The development of the melody through the repetition of short simple phrases is a formula that gives opera buffa much of its character; what better way to suggest stubbornness on the part of both characters? The octaves (Serpina: "furbi, ladri," m. 10; Uberto: "troppo," m. 20) provide simple but effective comic emphasis. Uberto's suffering is evident in his interjected minor-mode chromatic lines (m. 40, etc.). The concluding section features more argumentative (or playful) exchanges between the protagonists; when the two actually repeat one another and the octaves return in the tonic, the discussion reaches its (unsettled) end. The harmonic and motivic changes reinforce the development of the characters as the duet progresses. The work as a whole points toward the lighter style of the mid-18th century and a more psychologically realistic portrayal of everyday characters on stage.

# OPERA WARS

Admired in some quarters, reviled in others, opera buffa provoked controversy throughout Europe. Advocates considered it a breath of fresh air that would reinvigorate opera, a genre many thought had grown stale; opponents considered it an affront to established traditions.

The debate raged with particular virulence in France. The dispute known as the War of the Buffoons (*Guerre des Bouffons*) was ignited in 1752 by the debut of Pergolesi's *La serva padrona* in Paris, in a performance by a troupe calling itself the Bouffons ("The Comedians"). In an era when political dissent was severely limited, this dispute had implications far beyond the issues at hand. Competing social groups used opera as a pretext to jockey for political and cultural prestige without directly confronting established authority. The War of the Buffoons pitted partisans of King Louis XV against those of Queen Marie, defenders of French culture against advocates of Italian style, and the entrenched aristocracy against the intellectual bourgeoisie. The king and his conservative followers sought to uphold the traditions of the French *tragédie lyrique* as represented by the stately, serious works of Lully and Rameau (see Chapter 9). Their opponents sought to use the model of opera buffa to promote a new, lighter style of musical theater in France. The philosopher and amateur composer Jean-Jacques Rousseau weighed in with his own *Le devin du village* ("The Village Soothsayer") of 1752, an opera in French that drew on the conventions of Italian opera buffa. With its simple, unpretentious music about a shepherd and a shepherdess, the work was immensely popular.

**A riot at Covent Garden Theater.** Although today we tend to think of opera as an elite art, earlier audiences in many locales considered it popular entertainment. In London, the King's Theatre catered to a higher social class, but Drury Lane and Covent Garden attracted a more diverse audience. Here, at Covent Garden, members of the audience storm the stage because of management's refusal to admit spectators at half price after the intermission. The musicians are beating a hasty retreat for the door leading under the stage. The opera being performed, *Artaxerxes* by Thomas Arne (1710–88), was one of many 18th-century works based on so-called Turkish themes (the era's term for anything Middle Eastern). At the time, Britain and other European nations were consolidating their empires abroad, and the public was fascinated with representations of exotic locales and peoples.

**Source:** Riot at Covent Garden (engraving) (b/w photo), English School, (18th century)/Private Collection/The Bridgeman Art Library

Opera nevertheless remained a forum for public controversy in prerevolutionary Paris. In the late 1770s, another heated debate erupted, this one dubbed the "Quarrel of the Gluckists and Piccinnists." Once again the dispute pitted Italian against French culture, though in this case the composers at the center of the dispute—Christoph Willibald Gluck and Niccolò Piccinni—were both foreigners. Piccinni was an Italian who came to Paris in 1776; Gluck, who was born in the Bohemian region of the Austrian Empire and spent most of his professional life in Italy and Vienna, had moved to Paris in 1773. The Parisian music-loving public saw Gluck as a worthy successor to Lully and Rameau in the French tradition of *tragédie lyrique*; Piccinni, in turn, was perceived to represent the Italian tradition of opera seria. Benjamin Franklin, the American envoy to France at the time, found the intensity of the debate both amusing and bewildering, comparing it to a debate among flies that consumes most of their short lives:

> We have been shown numberless skeletons of a kind of little fly, called an ephemera, whose successive generations, we are told, were bred and expired within the day. I happened to see a living company of them on a leaf, who appeared to be engaged in conversation. You know I understand all the inferior

animal tongues. . . . I listened through curiosity to the discourse of these little creatures; but as they, in their national vivacity, spoke three or four together, I could make but little of their conversation. I found, however, by some broken expressions that I heard now and then, they were disputing warmly on the merit of two foreign musicians, one a *cousin*, the other a *moscheto* [French and Italian, respectively, for "mosquito"]; in which dispute they spent their time, seemingly as regardless of the shortness of life as if they had been sure of living a month. Happy people! thought I, you live certainly under a wise, just, and mild government, since you have no public grievances to complain of, nor any subject of contention but the perfections and imperfections of foreign music.[1]

To an outsider like Franklin, the issues that separated the two sides of this debate were trivial; his own nation was fighting for its independence when he wrote these lines. But within the upper classes of French society, the debate was quite serious indeed.

# GLUCK AND THE REFORM OF OPERA

While the new genre of opera buffa challenged its dominance from without, opera seria was also facing challenges from within. A growing number of poets, composers, and critics maintained that the time-honored conventions of opera seria, designed to showcase the virtuosity of individual singers, were unnatural impediments to dramatic action. One critic, for example, writing in 1755, criticized the opening ritornello of most arias as "tediously prolix" and "often superfluous." "For can anything be more improbable," he asked, "than that, in an air expressive of wrath, an actor should calmly wait with his hand stuck in his sword belt until the ritornello be over, to give vent to a passion that is supposed to be boiling in his breast?"[2] Other writers pointed out that virtuoso settings of texts—in which a single syllable might endure for dozens of notes—compromised both the intelligibility and dramatic weight of the words.

In response to these concerns, several composers deliberately set out to make opera seria more natural and dramatically coherent. The most notable composers working in this direction included Niccolò Jommelli, Tomasso Traetta, and Christoph Willibald Gluck (see "Composer Profile: Christoph Willibald Gluck").

In the preface to his opera *Alceste* (1769), Gluck spelled out the basic principles behind his efforts to eliminate the "abuses" that he maintained had "disfigured" Italian opera (see Primary Evidence: Gluck's Operatic Manifesto). In many respects, Gluck's aesthetic closely resembles the principles of the Florentine camerata (see Chapter 7), whose members insisted that the words should be the mistress of the music and not vice versa. The music of opera, in Gluck's view, should never serve a purely musical purpose but instead always help further the dramatic action. Many of the characteristic features that distinguish so-called reform opera from opera seria follow from this fundamental premise. These features include the following:

- no da capo arias

- little or no opportunity for vocal improvisation or virtuosic displays of vocal agility or power

- no long melismas

- a more predominantly syllabic setting of the text to make the words more intelligible

- far less repetition of text within an aria

- a blurring of the distinction between recitative and aria, declamatory and lyrical passages, with altogether less recitative

- accompanied rather than secco recitative

- simpler, more flowing melodic lines

- an overture that is linked by theme or mood to the ensuing action

- more prominence for the chorus, giving it, in imitation of classical Greek drama, an important role commenting on the events unfolding on the stage

## *Primary Evidence*    GLUCK'S OPERATIC MANIFESTO

*Gluck's preface to the published score of* Alceste *is a manifesto of his artistic beliefs, setting out the principles by which he sought to "restrict the music to its true purpose of serving to give expression to the poetry."* Alceste *was sufficiently different from all previous operas, in Gluck's own view, as to warrant careful explanation.*

■ ■ ■

When I began to write the music for *Alceste*, I resolved to free it from all the abuses which have crept in either through ill-advised vanity on the part of the singers or through excessive complaisance on the part of composers, with the result that for some time Italian opera has been disfigured and from being the most splendid and most beautiful of all stage performances has been made the most ridiculous and the most wearisome. I sought to restrict the music to its true purpose of serving to give expression to the poetry and to strengthen the dramatic situations, without interrupting the action or hampering it with unnecessary and superfluous ornamentations. I believed that it should achieve the same effect as lively colors and a well-balanced contrast of light and shade on a very correct and well-disposed painting, so animating the figures without altering their contours. So I have tried to avoid interrupting an actor in the warmth of dialogue with a boring intermezzo or stopping him in the midst of his discourse, merely so that the flexibility of his voice might show to advantage in a long passage, or that the orchestra might give him time to collect his breath for a cadenza. I did not think I should hurry quickly through the second part of an air, which is perhaps the most passionate and most important, in order to have room to repeat the words of the first part regularly four times or to end the aria quite regardless of its meaning, in order to give the singer an opportunity of showing how he can render a passage with so-and-so many variations at will; in short, I have sought to eliminate all these abuses, against which sound common sense and reason have so long protested in vain.

I imagined that the overture should prepare the spectators for the action, which is to be presented, and give an indication of its subject; that the instrumental music should vary according to the interest and passion aroused, and that between the aria and the recitative there should not be too great a disparity, lest the flow of the period be spoiled and rendered meaningless, the movement be interrupted inopportunely, or the warmth of the action be dissipated. I believed further that I should devote my greatest effort to seeking to achieve a noble simplicity; and I have avoided parading difficulties at the expense of clarity. I have not placed any value on novelty, if it did not emerge naturally from the situation and the expression; and there is no rule I would not have felt in duty bound to break in order to achieve the desired effect.

These are my principles. Happily all my intentions fitted admirably with the libretto, in which the famous author [Ranieri d' Calzabigi, the librettist], having devised a new plan for the lyrical drama, had replaced florid descriptions, superfluous comparisons, sententious and frigid moralization with the language of the heart, with strong passions, interesting situations and an ever-varied spectacle. My maxims have been vindicated by success, and the universal approval expressed in such an enlightened city [Vienna] has convinced me that simplicity, truth and lack of affectation are the sole principles of beauty in all artistic creations.

**Source:** Hedwig and E. H. Mueller von Asow, eds., *The Collected Correspondence and Papers of C. W. Gluck* (London: Barrie and Rockliff, 1962), pp. 22–4.

Gluck's *Alceste* translates all of these principles into music. The overture, which sets the tone for the action to come, flows directly into the opening scene. Aria and recitative are for the most part readily distinguishable, but the boundaries between the two are far less pronounced than in opera seria. And although the vocal roles for the soloists are demanding, they are by no means ostentatious. The chorus plays a prominent role throughout the entire opera, reacting to the events as they unfold on stage.

Very much in the tradition of opera seria, the libretto is based on a Greek legend, that of Queen Alceste's extraordinary devotion to her husband, King Admetus of Thessaly. When the dying Admetus learns from an oracle that he will be saved if another mortal agrees to die in his place, Alceste resolves to sacrifice herself for him. Admetus recovers and Alceste is summoned to the underworld, but Hercules, with the blessing of Apollo, brings her back and she is restored to life. Unlike other operas based on Greek drama, Gluck's *Alceste* does not require a "happy ending" tacked on (compare his *Orfeo ed Euridice*), although Euripides' *Alcestis* has both darker and lighter elements not found in the libretto.

In the excerpt that appears in the Anthology (from Act II, scene iii) Admetus learns that Alceste is the one who will die for him and he pleads with her to change her mind. (The opera was originally performed in Italian in Vienna in 1767; the excerpt in the Anthology is from the French version Gluck prepared for performance in Paris in 1776.) In this scene, Gluck skillfully weaves together accompanied recitative, chorus, aria, and duet into a musically continuous dramatic sequence.

((•─ Listen
CD8    Track 3
**mysearchlab** (with scrolling translation)
GLUCK
*Alceste*
Score Anthology II/111

- Accompanied recitative (m. 486–524). In the opening dialogue, Admète (French for Admetus) pleads with Alceste to reveal who has agreed to die for him. She resists but in the end admits that she herself is the victim.

- Chorus (m. 525–38). At the climactic moment when Alceste reveals that she is to be the sacrificial victim, the chorus interjects with an outcry of "*O Dieux!*" ("O ye gods!"). This is in keeping with principles of ancient Greek tragedy, in which the chorus reflects the perspective of the community as a whole, transcending that of any individual character. After Admète registers his own astonishment, the chorus sings a lament for Admète and praises Alceste for her courage and love toward her husband.

- Accompanied recitative (m. 538–90). The dialogue resumes. Admète admonishes Alceste, telling her she will be breaking her marriage vows by abandoning him if she dies and leaves him alone. He calls on the gods to intercede. Alceste answers these protestations calmly, ending the dialogue (m. 589–90) with the pleading phrase "*Ah, cher époux*" ("Ah, dear husband").

- Aria (m. 591–638): Without fanfare or ritornello, the accompanied recitative flows into an aria, sung by Admète, who proclaims his love for Alceste and tells her that he cannot live without her. The aria does not adhere to conventional structure, except to repeat text. There is no suggestion of a da capo aria; the music instead follows the sense of the text. In m. 623, for example, when Admète declares that death is his only salvation, the music shifts abruptly from andante and 3/4 time to alla breve presto. Even the text repetitions are handled in a dramatic manner (compare the music on "Barbare," upbeat to m. 591, then upbeat to m. 615).

- Interruption (m. 638–39). Just before the end of Admète's aria, Alceste interrupts with a simple but dramatic repetition of her earlier plea, "*Ah, cher époux.*"

## Composer Profile

# Christoph Willibald Gluck (1714–1787)

Like Handel before him, Gluck was a cosmopolitan composer who seemed to be at home almost anywhere in Europe. He was born in the Upper Palatinate region of Bavaria, moving as a child with his family to Bohemia, then part of the Austrian Empire of the Hapsburgs. He settled in Milan in 1737, where he studied and wrote music and subsequently received commissions to write operas for Dresden, London, Copenhagen, Vienna, Prague, and Paris, where his former student Marie Antoinette became his patron. Gluck achieved extraordinary success in Paris, presenting many of his Italian operas in revised French versions.

Like other 18th-century composers, however, Gluck composed on commission, and even in the midst of writing the most famous of his reform operas (*Orfeo ed Euridice*, 1762; *Alceste*, 1767; *Iphigénie en Aulide*, 1774; *Iphigénie en Tauride*, 1779), he continued to write opere serie as the occasion demanded. Although he wrote some trio sonatas that were widely performed in his day, Gluck devoted himself mostly to opera and was known then and is remembered now as one of the greatest of all composers for the stage. In the 19th century, Richard Wagner (see Chapter 17) looked upon Gluck, not Mozart, as his principal forerunner, because Gluck, like Wagner, was striving for a synthesis of music and drama. Gluck's operas would serve as models for 19th-century French grand opera and have remained in the repertory continuously to the present day.

## PRINCIPAL WORKS

Aside from a set of six trio sonatas and some ballets, Gluck's output is almost entirely vocal. He wrote dozens of operas, some in Italian, some in French; many exist in versions in both languages. His most acclaimed operas include *Demofoonte* (1742), *Orfeo ed Euridice* (1762), *Alceste* (1767), *Iphigénie en Aulide* (1774), *Armide* (1777), and *Iphigénie en Tauride* (1779).

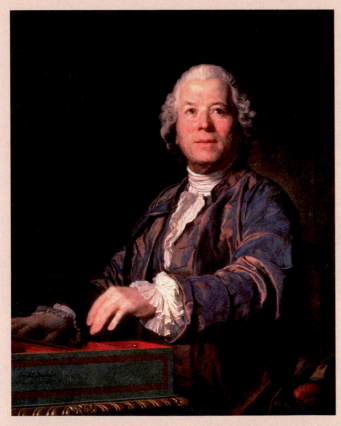

**Gluck composes.** Gluck is seated at the clavichord, a small, intimate instrument traditionally associated with the studio rather than the salon or concert hall. His gaze—directed upward to the muses for inspiration—tells us he is composing and not performing. Note the similarity of this image to Haydn composing at the keyboard (Chapter 12).

**Source:** Christoph Willibald Gluck (1714–87) at the spinet, 1775 (oil on canvas), Duplessis, Joseph Siffred (1725–1802)/Kunsthistorisches Museum, Vienna, Austria/The Bridgeman Art Library

| KEY DATES IN THE LIFE OF GLUCK | |
|---|---|
| 1714 | Born in Erasbach (now in Germany) on July 2. |
| 1736 | Moves to Vienna, plays violin for Prince Lobkowitz (a member of the same family that would support Beethoven), and later travels extensively in Italy. |
| 1741 | Composes his first opera, *Artaserse,* in the tradition of opera seria. Travels extensively, including important stays in Paris and London. |
| 1762 | Premiere of *Orfeo ed Euridice,* in Vienna. |
| 1767 | Premiere of *Alceste,* in Vienna. |
| 1773 | Moves temporarily to Paris; becomes embroiled in the "Quarrel of the Gluckists and Piccinists." |
| 1779 | With his new opera *Echo et Narcisse* a failure and in poor health, returns to Vienna. |
| 1787 | Dies in Vienna on November 15. |

- Return of the aria's opening section (m. 639–44). The tempo shifts to moderato, the meter back to 3/4, and Admète closes by repeating the key phrase from the opening part of his aria just before leaving the stage: "Je ne puis vivre, tu le sais, tu n'en doutes pas" (I cannot live [without you], you know it, you have no doubt of that). By returning to earlier material at the end of the aria, Gluck is to some extent following the conventions of the da capo aria, including even the exit convention. But the differences here are more revealing than the similarities: the return is extremely brief, and virtuosity for its own sake plays no role at all. The repetition reinforces the text, reminding us that in spite of Admète's desire to die, his overwhelming emotion is one of grief at the thought of losing Alceste.

Gluck's approach to opera was soon imitated by other composers seeking a more natural approach to the genre. Still, conventional opera seria did not disappear overnight. On the contrary, it continued to flourish well into the 19th century. Mozart's last completed opera, *La Clemenza di Tito* (1791), for example, was an opera seria, with the title role written for a castrato. Gioacchino Rossini (1792–1868) was still writing in the genre in the 1820s. Even Gluck himself wrote several opere serie in the last decades of his life. Note that the principles of Gluck's manifesto are open to varied interpretation. *Alceste*, for example, is full of ballets. Do these sometimes lengthy numbers unnaturally interrupt the flow of the drama, or do they intensify it? There is no hard and fast answer.

# MOZART AND THE SYNTHESIS OF OPERATIC STYLES

Of all the genres in which Mozart worked—and he wrote in virtually every genre of his day—his operas are justly celebrated as his greatest achievements. And of all the opera composers of his day, he stands out for two accomplishments in particular: his ability to create psychologically complex characters and his ability to synthesize and transcend the boundaries of buffa, seria, and other operatic styles. Mozart was a keen student of human behavior, with a sharp and sometimes wicked sense of humor. The characters in his most celebrated operas—nobles and commoners alike—are believable, three-dimensional human beings, not the heroic but essentially two-dimensional nobles who populate an opera seria like Handel's *Giulio Cesare*, or even Gluck's *Alceste*, or the stock servants and peasants who predominate in the typical opera buffa. (See Composer Profile: Wolfgang Amadeus Mozart.)

In his early operas, those written before he moved to Vienna in 1781, Mozart tried his hand at a variety of styles and traditions, including opera seria (both conventional and in Gluck's reform style), opera buffa, and *Singspiele* (German-language plays with songs, akin to modern-day musicals). He was thus ideally positioned to synthesize the previously separate serious and comic strands of musical drama, which he did in four late operas: *Le Nozze di Figaro*, *Don Giovanni*, *Così fan tutte*, and *Die Zauberflöte*. The first three, which he wrote in collaboration with the librettist Lorenzo da Ponte (1749–1838), are generally considered his greatest, in no small part because their texts and music probe so deeply into that great central human concern: love and war between the sexes.

The plot of *Don Giovanni* is based on the legend of Don Juan, a nobleman and notorious libertine. Da Ponte's libretto is both comic and serious; he called it a *dramma giocoso*, a "comic drama." The plot pits men against women, nobles against commoners, individuals against the community. The title character is at once malevolent and alluring, a man who openly flaunts conventional morality, pursuing instead his own pleasure

((•• **Listen**

**CD8   Tracks 4–7**
**mysearchlab**
MOZART
*Don Giovanni*, K. 527
Score Anthology II/112

under the guise of "liberty." At the beginning of the opera he slays the Commendatore (Commandant), the father of Donna Anna, a woman who has just fought off Don Giovanni's attempted assault. At the end of the opera, the statue of the Commendatore consigns the unrepentant Don Giovanni to the flames of hell.

The overture and first three scenes of *Don Giovanni*, which together constitute some 20 minutes of continuous music and seamless dramatic action, demonstrate the way Mozart integrates buffa and seria elements. True to the principles of Gluck's operatic creed, Mozart uses the overture (not in the Anthology) to set the tone of the opera as a whole, with its unpredictable juxtaposition of tragedy and farce. The opening, with its slow tempo and heavy dotted rhythms, conveys a sense of ominous foreboding, heightened by the sinuous chromaticism that follows; the impression is given that this is a deeply serious opera. But at the beginning of the longer, sonata-form second section (m. 31), the tempo becomes faster and the mood changes abruptly from gravity to gaiety. In a broad sense, these contrasting sections symbolize the Commendatore and Don Giovanni, who will soon defend (quite literally) their completely opposite moral poles: the world of the Commendatore in which law prevails, crime is punished, and damnation is the sure consequence for unrepented sin; and the world of Don Giovanni, in which pleasure and licentiousness prevail.

The overture segues directly into the first scene. Leporello, the servant of Don Giovanni, stands guard outside a nobleman's house while his master attempts to seduce yet another woman. Even before Leporello sings a single note, the music announces he is a commoner: the opening theme, which Leporello picks up when he begins his aria-monologue, bounces back and forth between tonic and dominant. There is nothing sophisticated about this theme harmonically, rhythmically, or melodically. Leporello is complaining to himself about the wicked ways of his master while at the same time longing to be a "gentleman" himself. With its relentlessly syllabic text underlay and vehement repetitions of "No, no, no," the aria sounds appropriately comical.

But as in the overture, the juxtaposition of comedy and tragedy occurs without warning. Leporello's monologue segues into a frantic duet between two members of an altogether different class: the noblewoman Donna Anna and the nobleman Don Giovanni. Donna Anna pursues the unknown man (Don Giovanni), who attempts to escape unrecognized. Almost at once, the duet becomes a trio when Leporello joins their elaborately agitated exchange with more of his melodically simple line, this time commenting on the action and predicting that his master's philandering will bring his own ruin.

A new dramatic unit begins with the arrival of the Commendatore, Donna Anna's father. He demands a duel with the unknown intruder. Don Giovanni reluctantly accepts and deals the Commendatore a mortal wound. Again, Leporello comments on the scene as it transpires before him, this time with an even greater sense of gloom. There follows a brief dialogue in secco recitative between Don Giovanni and Leporello, after which they exit. We then move directly into another dramatic unit, still with no real break in the music. Donna Anna returns, having summoned the aid of her kindhearted but rather boring fiancé, Don Ottavio. During the accompanied recitative that follows, they discover her father's body and she faints. Don Ottavio revives her so efficiently, however, that she is soon able to launch into her part of a powerfully dramatic duet ("Fuggi, crudele, fuggi") at the end of which they swear together to avenge her father's death. The music, agitated and virtuosic, comes from the world of opera seria. Mozart fuses the reflective power of aria (Donna Anna's shock at the death of her father) with the interchange of duet (Don Ottavio's promise of consolation and revenge), all interrupted at unpredictable moments by powerful outbursts of accompanied recitative.

Clearly, Mozart wanted to create a sense of dramatic continuity for the entire opening sequence of events, for it is only now, at the end of this extended duet, that he gives the audience its first opportunity to applaud. The arias and ensembles are not, as is so often the case in opera seria, reflections on events that have already happened: they are part of the action, and they propel it forward. The events of the drama, in other words, move through the music.

One of the devices Mozart uses to structure this extended series of units is tonality (see the table titled "Mozart's *Don Giovanni*: The Structure of the Opening Sequence"). The sequence begins and ends in D minor, and the choice of key in between is closely coordinated with the drama unfolding on stage. Each dramatic unit has its own distinctive key, different from yet related to the one before and the one after.

The integration of music and drama is evident as well in the two subsequent numbers. The first of these, "Ah, chi mi dice mai" ("Ah, who shall ever tell me"), begins like an aria. Donna Elvira, who had been seduced and abandoned by Don Giovanni long before the curtain has gone up, is asking herself if she will ever again find that "barbarian," promising to "cut out his heart" if she does. Her demanding vocal line, full of large leaps and covering a wide range, is that of a character who would be at home in an opera seria. As she is singing, Don Giovanni and Leporello see her from a distance,

## MOZART'S *DON GIOVANNI*: THE STRUCTURE OF THE OPENING SEQUENCE

| | Vocal Number | Key | Type | Dramatic Action |
|---|---|---|---|---|
| Overture | | D minor/major | Instrumental | Slow introduction and sonata form. Leads directly into Scene i. |
| Scene i | 1: Introduction | F Major | Aria | Leporello alone. |
| | | B♭ Major | Duet/Trio | Don Giovanni and Donna Anna enter. The two noble characters struggle, singing in counterpoint. Leporello stands safely apart, commenting, in the bass, in his own diatonic and decidedly nonimitative way. |
| | | G minor | Duet | The Commendatore enters and Donna Anna exits. The Commendatore challenges Don Giovanni to a duel. |
| | | D minor | Instrumental | Sword fight between the Commendatore and Don Giovanni |
| | | F minor | Trio | Slow death of the Commendatore. The Commendatore, Don Giovanni, and Leporello each expresses his own thoughts in what amounts to three simultaneous monologues. Leads directly into Scene ii. |
| Scene ii | | G Major | Secco recitative | Don Giovanni and Leporello alone. Exit from stage, but with an immediate musical segue into Scene iii. |
| | | B♭ Major | | |
| Scene iii | | D Major | Secco recitative | Donna Anna returns with Don Ottavio and servants. |
| | 2: Recitative and duet | G minor | Accompanied recitative | Donna Anna reacts to her father's death; Don Ottavio directs removal of the corpse. |
| | | D minor | Duet | (a) Alternation between Donna Anna, who swears revenge, and Don Ottavio, who offers consolation; (b) Both characters swear revenge in true duet fashion, singing simultaneously. |

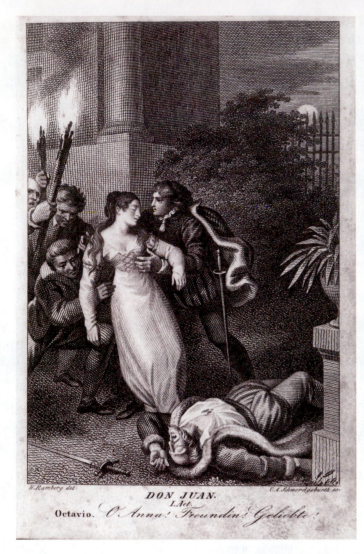

**Two scenes from Mozart's _Don Giovanni_.** These two scenes from Act I of _Don Giovanni_ were engraved by Johann Heinrich Ramberg in 1825. The illustration on the left captures the moment when Donna Anna faints at the sight of the father, who has just been murdered in a duel with an unknown assailant—Don Giovanni, as it turns out. Don Ottavio comforts her as servants rush onto the scene. The illustration on the right shows Leporello beginning his "Catalogue Aria," singing to Donna Elvira from the long list of Don Giovanni's prior loves. The moment depicted here follows the escape from the scene of Don Giovanni, who is visible at the back, between the balcony with flowers and the statue of the god of love showing his disgust.

**Source:** Library of Congress

and the aria becomes a trio. Don Giovanni does not at first recognize her (a curious reversal from the previous scene in which he escaped unrecognized) and so is unaware it is he she is raging about. With another seduction clearly in mind, he steps forward to console her. The moment they recognize each other, the ensemble ends. The music changes without a pause to secco recitative, and the drama presses on. Once again Mozart deprives the audience of an opportunity to applaud. Instead, we watch Donna Elvira's astonishment turn to rage as Don Giovanni slips away, leaving Leporello to deal with her. In his ensuing aria, "Madamina! il catalogo è questo" ("Madam! Here is the catalogue"), Leporello tries to assuage Donna Elvira with evidence that she is "neither the first nor the last" of Don Giovanni's conquests. He shows her a catalogue he has kept of all of them. In the first part of the aria Leporello enumerates his master's seductions by country; in the second part he describes them by type (old or young, fair-haired or dark-haired, large or small). The music reflects this shift of focus. The first part is allegro; the second part, with its own theme, moves at a more leisurely tempo (Andante con moto).

Although we have no letters describing the creation of *Don Giovanni* in any detail, Mozart's comments on one of his earlier operas, *Idomeneo*, give us some idea of the kinds of factors he took into account when setting a dramatic text to music. In a letter to his father dated November 15, 1780, for example, he mused about the detrimental effect an aria would have during a particularly turbulent moment in the drama:

> In the last scene of Act II, [the character] Idomeneo has [in the libretto] an aria . . . between the choruses. It will be better to have just recitative here, of a kind in which the instruments can be put to work. For in this scene, which will be the finest in the whole opera . . . there will be such noise and confusion on the stage that an aria would cut a poor figure at this particular point. Beyond this, there is the thunderstorm, which is not likely to subside because of an aria being sung by Herr Raaf, is it?[5]

Mozart's concern for the careful ordering of tonal areas within larger scenes is evident in another letter to his father, written from Munich in 1781 while he was at work on *Die Entführung aus dem Serail* ("The Abduction from the Seraglio").

> In working out the aria I have . . . allowed Fischer's beautiful deep notes to glow. . . . And because Osmin's rage increases throughout, the allegro assai (which comes just at the moment when the aria seems to have reached its end) is of necessity in a totally different meter and key, thereby allowing it to make the best possible effect. For a man who finds himself in such a towering rage will overstep all bounds of order, moderation, and propriety and completely forget himself; and in just this manner, so must the music, too, forget itself. But because the passions, whether violent or not, must never be expressed to the point of arousing disgust, and as music, even in the most hair-raising situations, must never offend the ear, but must please the listener, or in other words must always remain *music*, so I have chosen a key that is not foreign to F (the key of the aria) but one related to it—not the nearest, D minor, but the more remote A minor.[6]

## SACRED MUSIC

Almost every major composer of the Classical era wrote music for the church. Within the boundaries of the Holy Roman Empire, however, political factors limited the possible outlets for sacred music after 1780, when the Emperor Joseph II became the empire's sole ruler. Influenced by Enlightenment principles, the emperor instituted extensive reforms intended to limit the hereditary privileges of the nobility, strengthen the state bureaucracy, and restrict the influence of the church. His ecclesiastical reforms extended to music. Elaborate Masses requiring full orchestra, chorus, and soloists were no longer welcomed. Instead, the court encouraged simpler, more chordal settings of the liturgy. As a result, many composers—including Haydn and Mozart—largely abandoned the field of sacred music altogether until after Joseph II's death in 1790, when the restrictions were relaxed and eventually dropped altogether. Even then, however,

## Composer Profile

# Wolfgang Amadeus Mozart (1756–1791)

Wolfgang's father, Leopold, was a competent composer in his own right and renowned in his day as the author of the most important treatise of his time on violin method. Wolfgang was a child prodigy who began composing before he was 5. Leopold soon began taking Wolfgang and his talented sister Anna (also a keyboard player) on concert tours throughout Europe. Posterity has not been kind to Leopold for this, condemning him, probably with some justification, for exploiting his children. On the other hand, these tours took Wolfgang to almost every musically important city in Europe and provided him with the best education a young musician of the time could have received.

Mozart astonished audiences on these tours. One English witness recounted handing the 8-year-old prodigy

> a manuscript duet, which was composed by an English gentleman to some favourite words in Metastasio's opera of *Demofoonte*. The whole score was in five parts, viz. accompaniments for a first and second violin, the two vocal parts, and a bass. I shall here likewise mention, that the parts for the first and second voice were written in what the Italians stile the *Contralto* clef. My intention in carrying with me this manuscript composition was to have an irrefutable proof of his abilities, as a player at sight, it being absolutely impossible that he could have ever seen the music before. The score was no sooner put upon his desk, than he began to play the symphony in a most masterly manner, as well as in the time and style which corresponded with the intention of the composer. I mention this circumstance, because the greatest masters often fail in these particulars on the first trial.[3]

In addition to performing, Mozart also heard a great deal of music. In Rome, for example, he heard Gregorio Allegri's *Miserere*, an early-17th-century work for double choir that had traditionally been reserved for exclusive performance by the papal choir. Afterward, Mozart wrote out the work from memory. In this way, city by city, country by country, the young composer absorbed almost everything Europe had to offer in the way of music. As a result, he could later claim, matter-of-factly and without boasting, that he "could write in any style" he chose.

Although we tend to regard Mozart as a figure of almost godlike stature, he was in fact extremely earthy at times. Letters to his cousin Bäsle are full of what would today be called bathroom humor. (Mozart maintained a lifelong obsession with bodily functions.) He made rude comments (in private) about the Archbishop of Salzburg and seldom had anything good to say about contemporary composers: Haydn was an exception.

Like many child movie stars today, Mozart had difficulty adjusting to adulthood. He had to teach composition to supplement his income, and his efforts to secure a steady position at the Habsburg court in Vienna did not bear fruit until the last years of his life, when he was given a minor, essentially part-time position that entailed little more than writing new dances for New Year's galas and other celebrations.

Why was Mozart not more popular in his own time? He was certainly well known, and some of his music—most notably his operas *Le Nozze di Figaro* and *Don Giovanni*—were tremendously successful. But much of his music was perceived to be too complicated, too full of artifice. "Too many notes," the Emperor Joseph II is said to have complained after hearing one of Mozart's operas. Other composers, although they held Mozart in high regard, agreed that the complexity of his music sometimes put it beyond the grasp of contemporary audiences. When the composer Carl von Dittersdorf offered a set of string quartets in 1781 to the same publishing firm that had published some of Mozart quartets three years earlier, he predicted that *his* quartets would earn the firm more money. Why? Because although Mozart's quartets "deserved the highest praise," their "overwhelming and unrelenting artfulness" made them unappealing to a wider public.

Ironically, Mozart's popularity seems to have been on the rise just before he died. *Die Zauberflöte* (1791), a play with many musical numbers, was a great hit, and he was finally beginning to make inroads at the Habsburg court.

There is a myth about Mozart that composition was effortless for him. Like most myths, it is based on an element of truth. Mozart wrote an astonishing quantity of music, especially considering that he died just short of his 36th birthday. He often packed more melodies into a single movement than most composers of his day used in an entire composition. From time to time in his letters, he mentions works he has already composed in his head but "not yet written down." He is said to have composed the overture to *Don Giovanni* the night before the first performance. And unlike Beethoven a generation later, he did not labor through multiple drafts of a single idea. However, he abandoned an enormous number of works before making very much progress on them. One recent scholar has estimated that for every work he completed he abandoned two.

# PRINCIPAL WORKS

## Symphonies

Unlike Haydn, who had a standing orchestra at his disposal, Mozart had no incentive to compose symphonies regularly. He apparently composed his last three symphonies (nos. 39, 40, 41), all in 1788, with an eye toward the kind of trip to London that Haydn would undertake a few years later. In many respects, these last three symphonies are even larger and more ambitious than Haydn's "London" symphonies. Mozart was much quicker than Haydn to integrate the clarinet into the orchestra. With the finale of the Symphony no. 41 in C Major, K. 551 ("Jupiter"), he established the important precedent for later composers, most notably Beethoven, of placing a symphony's emotional and intellectual weight more in the finale than the first movement.

## String Quartets and Quintets

Mozart wrote 27 string quartets, including 6 dedicated to Haydn and published in 1785. The cello part is especially prominent in Mozart's last 3 quartets (K. 575, 589, 590), which he apparently intended to dedicate to the king of Prussia, who was an accomplished cellist.

Mozart turned to the string quintet (a quartet with a second viola) relatively late in life. His two works in this genre in G minor (K. 515) and C Major (K. 516), are worthy counterparts to his last two symphonies in the same keys (K. 550 and K. 551).

## Solo and Chamber Works for Piano

In addition to 19 sonatas for solo piano, Mozart also wrote several keyboard duets, variations, fantasias, rondos, and minuets. He also wrote 36 sonatas for violin and piano, 6 piano trios, 2 piano quartets, and a quintet for piano and winds.

## Concertos

Mozart wrote the bulk of his 23 original piano concertos during his years in Vienna, where they provided a way to showcase his talents both as a composer and performer. His correspondence reveals that he calculated the effects of these works on his audience. After finishing a set of 3 concertos in Vienna, for example, he wrote to his father in Salzburg that the works were "a happy medium between what is too easy and too difficult" for listeners. "They are very brilliant, pleasing to the ear, and natural, without being vapid. There are passages here and there from which connoisseurs alone can derive satisfaction; but these passages are written in such a way that the less learned cannot fail to be pleased, though without knowing why."[4] Mozart also wrote 5 concertos for violin, 4 for horn, 1 for clarinet, 1 for bassoon, 2 for flute, and 1 for flute and harp.

**The Mozart family.** This portrait of Mozart's family was painted around 1780, shortly before his departure from Salzburg to Vienna. The family would never again be together for more than brief visits thereafter. Leopold Mozart (1719–1787), holding the violin, presides. Mozart's sister Anna (1751–1829) sits with her brother at the piano. Nannerl, as her family called her, was also a noted keyboard performer. Mozart was the first composer to write music for four hands that required the performers to cross hands, as he and Nannerl are doing here. Maria Anna Mozart—Leopold's wife and Wolfgang and Nannerl's mother—died in 1778, but this painting reproduces a portrait of her hanging on the wall. A statue of Apollo holding a lyre occupies a place of prominence in an alcove in the wall.

**Source:** Erich Lessing/Mozart House, Salzburg, Austria/Art Resource, NY

# Wolfgang Amadeus Mozart (Continued)

## Operas

Mozart explored every subgenre of opera available to him in his time. *Idomeneo*, K. 366, written for the court at Munich in 1781 and later revived in Vienna, reflects the influence of Gluck's operas. *La Clemenza di Tito*, K. 621, commissioned for the coronation of Emperor Leopold II in Prague in 1791, is in the tradition of opera seria; its text is an adaptation of a much earlier libretto by Metastasio (see Chapter 9). The male lead in both of these works featured a castrato. Mozart's *Singspiele*—German-language plays with songs—include *Die Entführung aus dem Serail* ("The Abduction from the Seraglio"), K. 384, and *Die Zauberflöte* ("The Magic Flute"), K. 620. The latter is a fairy-tale opera that had a wide-reaching influence on 19th-century German opera. The three operas Mozart wrote in collaboration with the librettist Lorenzo da Ponte—*Le nozze di Figaro* ("The Marriage of Figaro"), K. 492, *Don Giovanni*, K. 527, and *Così fan tutte* ("All Women Do It Like That"), K. 588—represent an intriguing mixture of buffa and seria styles.

## Masses and Other Sacred Works

Mozart's duties in Salzburg in the 1760s and 1770s required him to write considerable quantities of sacred music: settings of the Mass and Vespers as well as shorter texts, such as psalms and offertories. But the 1780s were not hospitable to sacred music in Vienna. Emperor Joseph II, in an attempt to reduce the influence of the church, issued decrees limiting the scope of sacred music. In the last year of his life, Mozart received a private commission to write a Requiem but died before he could finish it. His widow, Constanze, approached several of Mozart's pupils to finish the work so she could receive payment, making it difficult to know who composed various parts of it. Most of it, however, is demonstrably by Mozart himself, and these sections include some of his most moving music.

| KEY DATES IN THE LIFE OF MOZART | |
|---|---|
| 1756 | Born in Salzburg (Austria) on January 27. |
| 1763–1771 | Undertakes a series of trips with his father to England, Holland, France, Germany, and especially Italy. |
| 1769 | Appointed concertmaster at the court in Salzburg. |
| 1770s | Continues travels across the European continent but is unable to secure a satisfactory position. |
| 1779 | Returns to Salzburg to his previous position as concertmaster and becomes court organist as well, but he detests the provinciality of his native town. |
| 1781 | Against the protests of his father, moves to Vienna to seek a position there, earning money by giving concerts and lessons, and through sales of his published works. |
| 1782 | Marries Constanze Weber. |
| 1785 | Dedicates a set of six string quartets to his friend Joseph Haydn. |
| 1791 | Dies in Vienna on December 5. |

the church continued to struggle with the proper role of music in the liturgy. By the end of the 19th century, the Vatican was trying to steer its followers away from elaborate concert-style Masses on the grounds that they were overly secular.

In their orchestration, melodic style, and demand for vocal virtuosity, the sacred works of Haydn, Mozart, and others are indeed sometimes hard to distinguish from their secular theatrical works. On the whole, however, church music remained relatively conservative during the Classical era, retaining the basso continuo long after it had been abandoned in the concert hall, and well after it was still necessary from a strictly technical point of view. Sacred music also preserved more of the tradition of strict counterpoint than was customary in either the theater or the chamber. Certain sections of the Mass, such as the end of the Gloria and Credo, were often set as elaborate fugues in what was called the *stile antico*, the "old style," featuring subjects in long note values and written in *alla breve* meter.

The Introit of Mozart's unfinished *Requiem*, K. 626, is a good example of the synthesis of older and newer styles often found in the sacred music of the Classical era. For this movement, Mozart drew on the opening chorus from Handel's *Funeral Anthem for Queen Caroline*, written in 1737 and available to Mozart in Vienna through Baron Gottfried van Swieten, a nobleman who took a special interest in the works of Handel and J. S. Bach. (Van Swieten had once commissioned from Mozart an arrangement of Handel's *Messiah* that includes clarinets and horns.) For the section beginning with the words "Te decet hymnus Deus in Sion" ("To thee, Lord in Zion, we sing a hymn"), Mozart brings in an even older source of sacred music, Gregorian chant. Here, in the

((•– **Listen**

**CD8    Tracks 8–9**

**mysearchlab** (with scrolling translation)
MOZART
Requiem, K. 626
Score Anthology II/113

**Women as musical performers in the church.** The priest is celebrating Mass at the high altar, but almost every eye in the (largely male) congregation is riveted on the female soloist. Even the musicians (especially the trumpeter in the opposite gallery) seem lost in admiration. The appeal is both physical and aural. This illustration first appeared in a Protestant tract in 1784 and reflects the view among at least some Protestant denominations that music in church, when performed by women, distracted the congregation from the liturgy. The Catholic church, in contrast, was more open to women performers, particularly in the Austrian Empire before 1790. The Empress Maria Theresa herself once sang the soprano part in a Mass written by Michael Haydn (Joseph's brother), and Mozart apparently wrote the virtuosic soprano line in his Mass in C minor, K. 427 (417a) for his wife, Constanze.

**Source:** Bildarchiv der Österreichische Nationalbibliothek

soprano, he introduces the Ninth Psalm Tone, also associated in German-speaking lands with the Magnificat, another hymn of praise to God. (This is the same melody Pachelbel and Bach used in their organ chorale preludes; see Chapter 10.) The concluding "Dona eis pacem" ("Grant them peace") section brings back the opening theme ("Requiem aeternam") but now combines it with a new countersubject. Mozart's *Requiem* has been surrounded in controversy since its first performance. It was known at the time that Mozart had died before he could complete the work, yet it was in his widow's interest to portray the efforts of the various collaborators who finished it—mostly students of her late husband—as inconsequential. Scholars have been trying to sort out Mozart's work from those of others since at least the 1820s. There is no dispute, however, about the authorship of the opening half of the work, including the Introit, because it has been preserved in manuscript in the composer's own hand.

## SONG

If the sonata was the quintessential domestic instrumental genre in the Classical era, the song was the quintessential domestic vocal genre. Songs were financially lucrative for composers and publishers alike, and the Classical song repertory is enormous, even if most of it remains unexplored today.

**An 18th-century ballad singer.** Thomas Rowlandson's watercolor of a ballad singer (1789) captures the ease and naturalness of public singing in an earlier age. The woman holds in her hands the words of the latest ballad and is probably singing them to a well-known tune. Onlookers stop to listen, and some may give money at the end of the song.

**Source:** The Ballad Singer (pen & ink and w/c on paper), Rowlandson, Thomas (1756–1827)/Private Collection/ Photo © Agnew's, London, UK/The Bridgeman Art Library

Johann Friedrich Reichardt's "Italien" (Italy) offers a good example of the kind of song writing that flourished throughout the Classical era. The setting is strophic and almost entirely syllabic. Both the vocal and piano parts are straightforward and technically undemanding. The vocal line barely exceeds an octave in range and is mostly doubled by the piano. The text, also known as "Kennst du das Land" (Do you know the land), is from Goethe's widely read novel *Wilhelm Meisters Lehrjahre* ("Wilhelm Meister's Years of Apprenticeship"), the story of a young man's coming of age. Wilhelm is an aspiring actor who falls in with an odd assortment of characters, one of whom is a mysterious young girl named Mignon. She has no family, and Wilhelm becomes something of a father figure to her, but there is a powerful erotic tension beneath the surface of their relationship. From time to time throughout the novel, Mignon sings songs, of which Goethe gives only the words. Reichardt (1752–1814) was one of the first composers to set these texts to music, and Goethe expressed his pleasure with these settings. (They even collaborated on some *Singspiele*.) As we shall see (Chapter 16), many later composers were also drawn to this text, as well as others by Goethe.

William Billings (1746–1800), a native of Boston, was one of the first American-born composers to achieve international fame, though it came after his death. He was largely self-taught, and his musical style, although indebted to English precedents, exhibits a certain roughness that gives it great energy. Billings's part-song *Chester* ("Let tyrants shake their iron rod/And slav'ry clank her galling Chains/we fear them not we trust in God/New England's God for ever reigns") became an unofficial anthem of the American Revolution. His hymn "Africa" was printed in his first collection, *The New-England Psalm-Singer* (1770), without text; he later added a text by the great English hymnodist Isaac Watts when "Africa" was republished in *The Singing Master's Assistant* (1778). As with other Billings choruses, the four-part texture is often expanded

**Listen**

CD8    Track 10
**mysearchlab** (with scrolling translation)
REICHARDT
*Italien*
Score Anthology II/114

**Listen**

CD8    Track 11
**mysearchlab**
BILLINGS
*Africa*
Score Anthology II/115

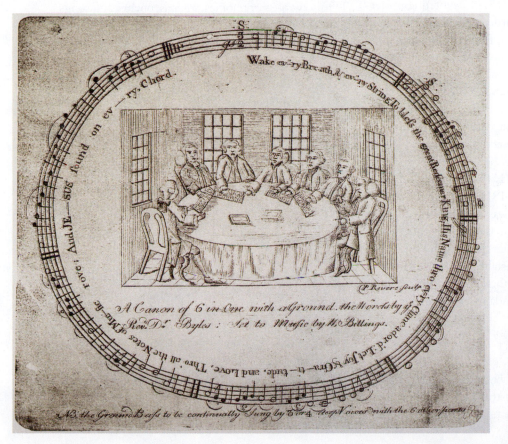

**Social song.** This frontispiece to William Billings's *The New-England Psalm-Singer* (1770) was engraved by the silversmith Paul Revere (1735–1818), better known for his ride from Boston to Lexington on April 18, 1775. It shows a group around a table performing the canon "Wake Ev'ry Breath." Music was an important element in most social gatherings, both in Europe and in the colonies of North America. The performance here is not in a church, but in a home.

in performance to six parts by doubling the treble and tenor lines at the octave. Billings also composed many "social songs," intended to be sung at a social gathering like the one depicted on the frontispiece to his first collection, reproduced on p. 353. Social singing was a tradition brought to the American colonies from England, which had long cultivated part-songs of various kinds. In addition to anthems and hymns, lighter part-songs such as catches and glees were part of the repertoire, while the texts of canons usually addressed moral or religious subjects.

## SUMMARY

Vocal music—opera, sacred music, and song—maintained its traditional position of aesthetic superiority throughout the Classical era. Opera, in particular, was considered the highest of all musical genres and became increasingly accessible to a wider public, particularly in cities like London and Vienna. Although opera seria remained the favored subgenre at European courts, opera buffa appealed to a wider audience. Mozart, in particular, was able to integrate seria and buffa styles in a series of operas that fundamentally shaped the future of the genre.

 **Study** and **Review** on **mysearchlab.com**

# MAJOR COMPOSERS OF THE CLASSICAL ERA

## FRANCE

The celebrated Swiss-French philosopher and novelist **Jean-Jacques Rousseau** (1712–1778) devoted considerable energies to music. As an ardent advocate of Italian music, he was rather an outcast in France. He wrote most of the articles on music for the *Encyclopedia* and an important dictionary of musical terms (1768). His opera *Le devin du village* (*The Village Soothsayer*, 1752) enjoyed great popularity in France well into the 19th century. Rousseau advocated a natural style in music that excluded elements he considered artificial, such as counterpoint and overly elaborate harmony or dissonance.

**François-Joseph Gossec** (1734–1829) and **André-Ernest-Modeste Grétry** (1741–1813) both gained fame as composers of opera. Gossec, who was Belgian but spent most of his life in Paris, was also active in the establishment of the Paris Conservatory in the years after the French Revolution. Grétry was widely credited with establishing the tradition of French comic opera that would thrive in the 19th century under such composers as Auber, Adam, and Boieldieu.

## GREAT BRITAIN

**Charles Avison** (1709–1770) is best remembered for his many concertos for a variety of instruments. **Thomas Arne** (1710–1788), the composer of the tune to "Rule, Britannia,"

also wrote many masques and operas. **William Boyce** (1711–1779) published *Cathedral Music*, a monumental collection of sacred works in three volumes, from 1760 to 1778. He also wrote symphonies, sonatas, operas, and songs.

## ITALY

Although born in the same year as Handel and J. S. Bach, **Domenico Scarlatti** (1685–1757) wrote in a style that in many ways looks forward to the lighter textures of the Classical era. Only a small fraction of his nearly 600 sonatas were published during his lifetime. These single-movement works, mostly in binary form, range from the technically simple to the highly demanding. The son of Alessandro Scarlatti (see Chapter 9), he spent his last three decades in the service of the Spanish court in Madrid, were he wrote the bulk of his harpsichord music.

**Baldassare Galuppi** (1706–1785), **Niccolò Jommelli** (1714–1774), and **Tomasso Traetta** (1727–1779) were hailed in their time as masters of Italian opera. Galuppi has been called "the father of Italian comic opera"; Jommelli and Traetta preceded Gluck in the movement to reform opera (see Chapter 13). **Domenico Cimarosa** (1749–1801) composed almost 80 operas in the span of 29 years. He served for almost a decade as court composer in St. Petersburg, Russia.

Giovanni Battista Sammartini (1701–1775), his brother Giuseppe Sammartini (ca. 1693–ca. 1750), and Luigi Boccherini (1743–1805) are best remembered for their instrumental music. G. B. Sammartini was active in Milan and was one of Gluck's teachers. His most important works are his concert symphonies, some of which date from the 1730s, making them among the earliest works of this kind. Giuseppe Sammartini lived for many years in London, where he played oboe and conducted various ensembles. Boccherini, the leading cello virtuoso of his day, spent many years in the service of the Spanish court in Madrid. Among his many chamber works are 125 string quintets, works of great beauty and formal ingenuity.

Antonio Salieri (1750–1825) and Muzio Clementi (1752–1832), born in Italy, gained fame elsewhere. Salieri was court composer in Vienna and wrote many operas. Clementi spent most of his adult life in England, gaining renown as a piano virtuoso, composer, publisher, and piano manufacturer. His most celebrated compositions are the sonatas for piano.

## THE AUSTRIAN EMPIRE

Christoph Willibald Gluck (see Composer Profile in Chapter 13), Joseph Haydn (see Composer Profile in Chapter 12), and Wolfgang Amadeus Mozart (see Composer Profile in Chapter 13) are the most prominent among a remarkable number of musicians born or raised in the Austrian empire during the 18th century. Georg Matthias Monn (1717–1750) wrote many instrumental works that fall stylistically somewhere between Baroque and Classical (see Chapter 10 and Anthology). Monn's Harpsichord Concerto would later be transcribed by Arnold Schoenberg for cello and orchestra (1933). Johann Georg Albrechtsberger (1736–1809) was a prolific composer of sacred music as well as chamber music; Beethoven studied counterpoint with him in the 1790s. Carl Ditters von Dittersdorf (1739–1799) was similarly prolific. His works include a series of 12 programmatic symphonies based on episodes from Ovid's *Metamorphoses*. Michael Haydn (1737–1806), the younger brother of Joseph Haydn, worked largely in Salzburg and was a close friend of the Mozart family. A symphony long attributed to Mozart (no. 37) was actually written by Michael Haydn. The Viennese composer Johann Baptist Vanhal (or Wanhal) (1739–1813) suffered a similar misattribution;

until the 20th century several of his symphonies were wrongly thought to be by Joseph Haydn.

## GERMANY

In Prussia, Princess Anna Amalia (1723–1787) and her brother, Frederick II ("The Great," 1712–1786), sponsored a remarkably active musical life at the court in Potsdam, just outside Berlin. The princess composed several instrumental works and chorales but is best remembered for assembling an astonishing musical library that included many works by J. S. Bach. Frederick was an accomplished flutist and wrote a number of flute sonatas and concertos. His court flutist, Johann Joachim Quantz (1697–1773), contributed even more music for this instrument and wrote an important treatise on playing the flute. Another important court employee was Carl Philipp Emanuel Bach. His younger brother Johann Christian Bach enjoyed the favor of the English court in London. (See Chapter 11 for a Composer Profile on the Bach brothers.)

A native of Hamburg, Johann Adolph Hasse (1699–1783) gained renown as a composer of Italian operas that were popular throughout Europe. He also wrote many oratorios, Masses, and other sacred works. He spent his later years at the Saxon court at Dresden.

Johann Stamitz (1717–1757) was the most prominent composer for and musical director of the Mannheim orchestra, the remarkable musical establishment assembled and funded by the elector Carl Theodor from the 1740s into the 1780s (see Chapter 11). Stamitz was one of the first composers to write a symphony that used clarinets and among the first to consistently employ the four-movement format in his symphonies. His sons Carl (1745–1801) and Anton (1750–1796) were composers at the same court.

## NORTH AMERICA

Musical life in England's American colonies, and later in the United States, during the Classical era was dominated by European music. William Billings (1746–1800) of Boston was one of the country's first native-born composers. He wrote and published a great deal of sacred music that was extremely popular in its time.

# Part Five
# The 19th Century

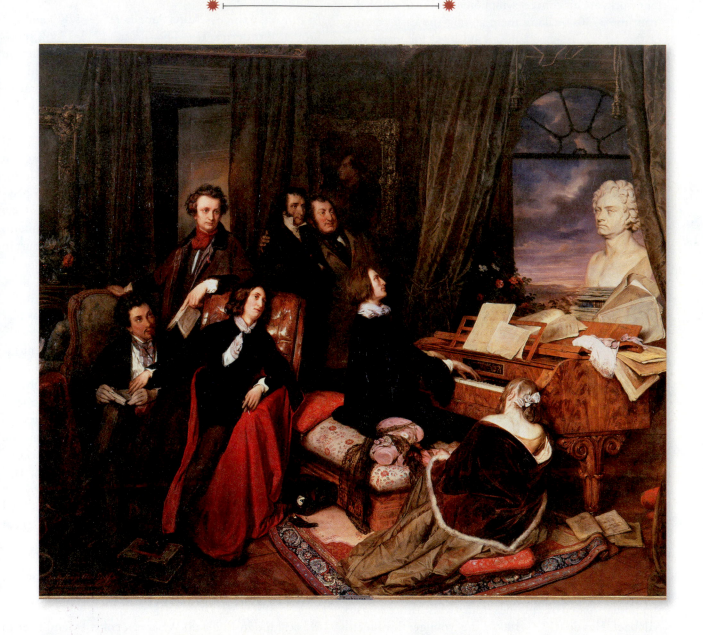

# Prelude

The 19th century was a period of unprecedented change in Western society. The population of the world's major powers increased by more than 150 percent, and the political boundaries of Europe were redrawn several times over. Many European nations established overseas empires, and the United States grew from an outpost at the edge of civilization to a world power reaching from the Atlantic to the Pacific. Technological developments fundamentally altered commerce, travel, and systems of communication.

## PROGRESS AND DISLOCATION

The Industrial Revolution that began in the 18th century accelerated rapidly in the 19th, with profound social, economic, and political consequences. Technological advances in transportation and communication—particularly the railroad and telegraph—changed daily life in basic ways. In 1825, it took a day and a half to travel the almost 200 miles between New York City and Boston by horse-drawn coach; in 1850, the same trip could be completed by rail in under six hours. By 1840, the British rail system was carrying some 18 million passengers a year. The American transcontinental railroad, opened in 1869, connected the western territories of the United States to the nation's northeastern urban-industrial core. The development of metal-hulled, coal-powered steamships produced a comparable revolution in maritime travel and commerce. In 1830, it cost the equivalent of about $800 in today's money to transport one ton of goods from Australia to England; in 1870, the same ton of freight could be transported for about $7.50.

New modes of communication were equally far-reaching. From the beginning of history until the invention of the telegraph in 1837, a message could travel no faster than the

◀ **Music and literature.** This idealized scene, painted in 1840 by the German artist Josef Danhauser, captures the new relationship of music and literature in the 19th century. A number of celebrated figures listen to Franz Liszt perform. Seated on the far left are Alexandre Dumas, author of *The Three Musketeers* and *The Count of Monte Cristo*, and the novelist George Sand. In keeping with the male persona of her pen name (her real name was Amandine-Aurore-Lucile Dudevant) she is dressed in men's clothing and smoking a cigar. Standing behind Sand and Dumas is Victor Hugo, best known as the author of *Notre Dame de Paris* and *Les Misérables*; his drama *Le roi s'amuse* was the basis for the libretto to Verdi's *Rigoletto* (see Chapter 17). Standing against the wall, in front of a portrait of Lord Byron, the quintessential Romantic poet, are Niccolò Paganini (left) and Gioacchino Rossini (right). Paganini was to the violin what Liszt was to the piano, both as a composer and as a performer. Rossini had retired from opera by the time this painting was done, but his Parisian salon continued to attract the leading figures in all the arts. On the floor leaning her head against the piano is Liszt's mistress, Marie d'Agoult (1805–1876). Like her friend George Sand, she was a writer, and she also wrote under a male pen name (Daniel Stern). She bore three children by Liszt, including a daughter, Cosima, who married Richard Wagner. With her back turned to us, Marie d'Agoult alone is focused on Liszt. The others gaze into space. Liszt himself seems to be looking past the bust of Beethoven on the piano to the infinite sky beyond. The painting as a whole, by showing literary and musical figures together, represents music's ability to unite the arts. But it also illustrates music's ability to transcend the word—Dumas, Hugo, and Sand, the three literary figures, have all been interrupted in their reading—and to direct attention to a higher realm.

**Source:** Juergen Liepe/bpk, Berlin/Art Resource, NY

messenger who carried it. Now signals could be transmitted through wires almost instantaneously over great distances, even between Europe and the Americas, once the first transatlantic cable had been laid in 1866. The invention of the telephone in 1876 made it possible to transmit sound over comparably long distances, and the invention of the phonograph in 1877 made it possible to record, preserve, and reproduce sound for the first time in history. Recording technology has shaped the production and consumption of music ever since.

Science and technology combined to change daily life in other areas as well. New fertilizers and new machines like reapers and tractors increased agricultural yields. In medicine, Edward Jenner developed a vaccine for smallpox, and Louis Pasteur demonstrated that microorganisms could cause disease. Anesthesia and the sterilization of medical instruments became routine elements of surgery during the second half of the 19th century, and in the 1890s, Wilhelm Roentgen's work on X-rays opened up an entirely new approach to the diagnosis and treatment of diseases and injuries. Public health also improved, at least in certain locales. Major cities in Europe and the United States began constructing water and sewage systems, substantially reducing the spread of disease.

These and other technological advances—the invention of the sewing machine in the 1850s and the incandescent light bulb in 1879, for example—fed a growing belief in the inevitability of progress, the conviction that every passing year would bring new improvements to life. But for much of the population, this progress came at a heavy price. Industrialization produced disorienting social change. Europe's population increased dramatically during the 19th century (see graph). Millions migrated from the countryside in search of work, swelling the populations of the newly industrialized cities. Many factory workers lived in overcrowded, unsanitary housing and worked in dangerous conditions for low wages and with little or no job security.

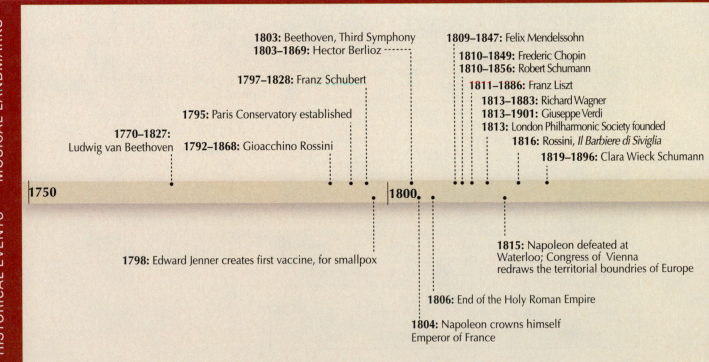

**19TH CENTURY TIMELINE**

**MUSICAL LANDMARKS**

1803: Beethoven, Third Symphony
1803–1869: Hector Berlioz

1797–1828: Franz Schubert

1795: Paris Conservatory established

1770–1827: Ludwig van Beethoven

1792–1868: Gioacchino Rossini

1809–1847: Felix Mendelssohn
1810–1849: Frederic Chopin
1810–1856: Robert Schumann
1811–1886: Franz Liszt
1813–1883: Richard Wagner
1813–1901: Giuseppe Verdi
1813: London Philharmonic Society founded
1816: Rossini, *Il Barbiere di Siviglia*
1819–1896: Clara Wieck Schumann

1750 — 1800

**HISTORICAL EVENTS**

1798: Edward Jenner creates first vaccine, for smallpox

1815: Napoleon defeated at Waterloo; Congress of Vienna redraws the territorial boundries of Europe

1806: End of the Holy Roman Empire

1804: Napoleon crowns himself Emperor of France

**The 19th-Century Population Explosion in Europe and the United States**

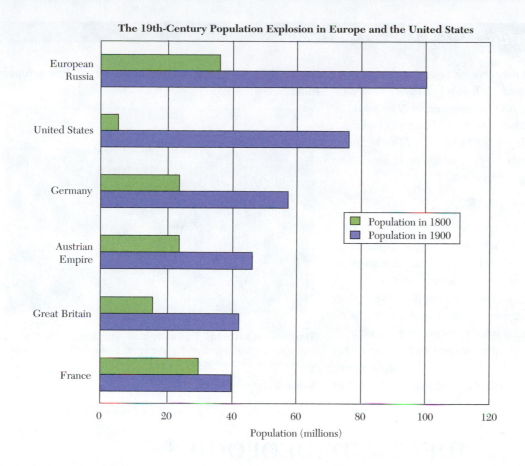

Population (millions)

Legend:
- Population in 1800 (green)
- Population in 1900 (purple)

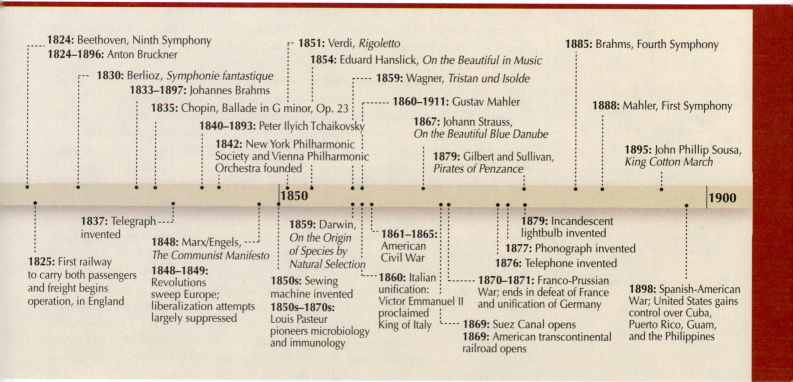

**1824:** Beethoven, Ninth Symphony
**1824–1896:** Anton Bruckner
**1830:** Berlioz, *Symphonie fantastique*
**1833–1897:** Johannes Brahms
**1835:** Chopin, Ballade in G minor, Op. 23
**1840–1893:** Peter Ilyich Tchaikovsky
**1842:** New York Philharmonic Society and Vienna Philharmonic Orchestra founded

**1851:** Verdi, *Rigoletto*
**1854:** Eduard Hanslick, *On the Beautiful in Music*
**1859:** Wagner, *Tristan und Isolde*
**1860–1911:** Gustav Mahler
**1867:** Johann Strauss, *On the Beautiful Blue Danube*
**1879:** Gilbert and Sullivan, *Pirates of Penzance*

**1885:** Brahms, Fourth Symphony
**1888:** Mahler, First Symphony
**1895:** John Phillip Sousa, *King Cotton March*

**1850**                    **1900**

**1837:** Telegraph invented
**1825:** First railway to carry both passengers and freight begins operation, in England
**1848:** Marx/Engels, *The Communist Manifesto*
**1848–1849:** Revolutions sweep Europe; liberalization attempts largely suppressed
**1859:** Darwin, *On the Origin of Species by Natural Selection*
**1850s:** Sewing machine invented
**1850s–1870s:** Louis Pasteur pioneers microbiology and immunology
**1861–1865:** American Civil War
**1860:** Italian unification: Victor Emmanuel II proclaimed King of Italy
**1879:** Incandescent lightbulb invented
**1877:** Phonograph invented
**1876:** Telephone invented
**1870–1871:** Franco-Prussian War; ends in defeat of France and unification of Germany
**1869:** Suez Canal opens
**1869:** American transcontinental railroad opens
**1898:** Spanish-American War; United States gains control over Cuba, Puerto Rico, Guam, and the Philippines

## Primary Evidence    TWENTY MILES AN HOUR

*The railroad changed not only commerce and transportation but the very concept of speed itself, as suggested by Thomas Creevey's diary account of his first train ride, in November 1829. Creevey (1768–1838), a Member of Parliament who at first opposed the building of the Liverpool & Manchester Railroad, was invited to take his first rail trip on it; like others, he reported a range of responses.*

■ ■ ■

I had the satisfaction, for I can't call it pleasure, of taking a trip of five miles on it, which we did in just a quarter of an hour—that is, 20 miles an hour. . . . But the quickest motion is to me frightful: The machine was really flying, and it is impossible to divest yourself of the notion of instant death to all upon the least accident happening. It gave me a headache which has not left me yet. . . . Altogether I am extremely glad indeed to have seen this miracle, and to have travelled in it. Had I thought worse of it than I do, I should have had the curiosity to try it, but having done so I am quite satisfied with my first achievement being my last.

**Stephenson's Rocket.** This early steam locomotive won a major British competition for the most powerful and efficient engine of its kind in 1829.

**Source:** Mary Evans Picture Library/Alamy

# IDEAS AND IDEOLOGIES

In the wake of the French Revolution, the rationality of the Enlightenment gradually gave way to a new mode of thought loosely known as **Romanticism**. The term has been used to mean so many different things—one scholar working in the middle of the 20th century counted no fewer than 11,396 definitions—that a concise definition of Romanticism seems impossible. Still, it provides a convenient shorthand for a new aesthetic and philosophical outlook that took hold in the early 19th century.

In general, the Romantic outlook respected reason but, in contrast to the rationalism of the Enlightenment philosophes, did not believe reason could solve all human problems. Romantics valued the individual and the subjective over the universal, the emotional and spiritual over the rational. They revered nature and glorified the creative genius of the artist for the glimpse it offered of a world quite different from the world of reason. In this respect the Romantic outlook favored music, particularly instrumental music, because it was by far the most abstract of the arts and as such allowed for the greatest play of the imagination.

Romanticism often went hand in hand with nationalism, another relatively new ideology in the early 19th century. Across the European continent, more and more peoples began to embrace the idea that their true identity derived from a common language and culture, including shared literary and musical traditions. The social and political aspirations of marginalized ethnic groups—including Poles in the Russian Empire, Hungarians in the Austrian Empire, and Greeks in the Ottoman Empire—rose steadily over the course of the 19th century. Populations with a common language but divided by national boundaries sought to unite politically. For centuries, "Germany" and "Italy" had been abstractions, not actual nations, but both emerged as functioning states in the second half of the 19th century.

---

### MAJOR LITERARY FIGURES OF THE 19TH CENTURY

- Blake
- Wordsworth
- Byron
- Shelley
- Tennyson
- Austen
- Dickens
- Thackeray
- Hugo
- Balzac
- Flaubert
- Goethe
- Whitman
- Dickinson
- Poe
- Melville
- James

✳ Explore on **mysearchlab**

Enlightenment ideals of equality, religious toleration, economic freedom, and representative government lived on in another important early-19th-century ideology, that of political liberalism. Liberals sought to promote constitutional government and laissez-faire economic policies based on the ideas of the Enlightenment-era economist Adam Smith. For the most part, liberals represented the interests of the increasingly prominent wealthy middle class against the traditional power of monarchs and aristocrats.

By the middle of the 19th century, the social dislocations and poverty associated with the early stages of industrial capitalism were nourishing other ideological movements—socialism and Marxism—that posed a more potent challenge than liberalism to the established order throughout Europe. Karl Marx's (1818–1883) advocacy of radical social reform and the elimination of capitalism would inspire revolutionary movements for a century and a half. Less radical approaches to social reform led to the establishment of trade unions throughout Europe and the Americas.

Science, in addition to the technological wonders it spawned, also confronted Western society with troubling new implications. Charles Darwin's (1809–1882) theory of evolution by natural selection, combined with evidence from geology of the great age of the earth, was as unsettling to long-held assumptions about humanity's origins as was the Copernican theory some three centuries earlier to long-held assumptions about the place of the earth in the solar system. Darwin's theory was soon taken out of its biological context and applied to segments of human society rather than to organisms and species. According to this social Darwinism, human progress depends on what the economist and philosopher Herbert Spencer (1820–1903) called "the survival of the fittest." Social Darwinists used this slogan to justify social inequality and to argue against state assistance to the needy.

> ### MAJOR ARTISTS OF THE 19TH CENTURY
>
> - Constable
> - Turner
> - Goya
> - Friedrich
> - Delacroix
> - Rodin
> - Manet
> - Degas
> - Renoir
> - Gaugin
> - van Gogh
> - Cézanne
> - Rousseau
> - Whistler
> - Homer
> - Eakins
> - Sargent
>
>
> ✳ Explore on mysearchlab

# REACTION, REFORM, AND REVOLUTION

After the failure of a succession of governments in France in the years following the Revolution of 1789, Napoleon Bonaparte (1769–1821), a Corsican artillery officer, took control of the French army and government, crowning himself emperor in 1804. In a series of military campaigns and in the name of the values of the Revolution, he conquered most of the European continent. But after a string of defeats, beginning in Moscow in 1812 and ending at Waterloo in 1815, he was forced into exile. In 1814, the chief European powers—Austria, Great Britain, Prussia, Russia, and France—met in Vienna to redraw the boundaries of the Continent.

The Congress of Vienna, as this gathering was known, restored many of the hereditary kingdoms overthrown by Napoleon's conquests. But revolutionary aspirations—often combined with nationalist claims—continued to smolder. These suppressed aspirations erupted in the Revolutions of 1848–1849, which broke out in France but soon spread to Prussia, Saxony, Bohemia, Austria, and many smaller states to the east and south. The composer Richard Wagner (1813–1883) fought on the barricades in Dresden against the regime that employed him as a conductor at the Dresden Opera; authorities issued a warrant for his arrest, but he managed to escape to Switzerland.

Although these revolutions had been quelled by 1849, pressure continued for more representative government. By the end of the 19th century, France, Germany, and Italy all enjoyed parliamentary democracies of one form or another. Great Britain, which was spared the trauma of revolution in 1848, had passed a reform act in 1832 (The Great Reform Act) that lowered the qualifications for voters to own property, thereby expanding the number of eligible voters by about 50 percent. Subsequent laws widened eligibility still further.

**Revolutionaries defending the barricade at the corner of Kronenstrasse and Friedrichstrasse, Berlin, in 1848.** Throughout 1848 and 1849, citizens of many major European cities fought in a similar fashion against their ruling governments. Note that the image here includes women and children as well as young men, who have armed themselves with makeshift weapons.

**Source:** bpk, Berlin/Art Resource, NY

In Germany and Italy, the Revolutions of 1848–1849 also served as a catalyst for national unification. For centuries, both regions had been divided into many independent or semi-independent states, each with its own ruler, laws, and currency. Through sustained military and diplomatic campaigns, the Prussian chancellor Otto von Bismarck (1815–1898) engineered the political unification of most German states into a single entity, a task that was completed with the defeat of France in the Franco-Prussian War of 1870–1871 and the installation of Wilhelm I as emperor of a united Germany. In Italy, unification followed the defeat of the Austrian forces that had occupied much of the northern Italian peninsula for many decades. Victor Emmanuel was crowned king of Italy in 1860. The occupation of Rome by Italian troops in 1870 marked the end of the Papacy as a territorial power.

The early 19th century marked a decline in Europe's imperial expansion into other areas of the globe. Indeed, in the late 18th and early 19th centuries, Britain and Spain lost many of their American colonies to independence movements. In the late 19th century, however, European nations, including Belgium, Portugal, Spain, and Italy as well as Great Britain, France, and Germany, began to stake claims across the globe. This "new imperialism," as it has been called, represented the high tide of European influence in the world. By the early 20th century, Great Britain alone controlled about one-fifth of the world's land area and 25 percent of the world's population. The United States, which had spread rapidly across the entire North American continent in the early 19th century, joined the ranks of the colonial powers with the acquisition of Alaska from Russia in 1867 and the acquisition of the Philippines, Puerto Rico, and other territories in the Pacific and Caribbean following the Spanish-American War of 1898.

In the late 19th century, economic hardship, religious persecution, and population growth combined to impel millions of Europeans, especially from southern and eastern Europe, to leave their homes and seek opportunity in other parts of the world. Most of these migrants went to the United States and other countries in the Western Hemisphere. The United States alone absorbed an influx of more than 20 million people between 1870 and 1910, drawn by the nation's open spaces and rapidly growing factories. In 1900, the second largest city in the nation, Chicago, boasted a population of almost 1.7 million, of whom 1.3 million were either immigrants or the children of immigrants. Within the United States people were likewise on the move, drawn from the countryside to opportunities in the cities.

# THE MUSICAL WORLD OF THE 19TH CENTURY

The wide-ranging political, social, and economic changes that occurred during the 19th century had correspondingly wide-ranging consequences for the arts. From a strictly commercial point of view, music achieved a scale never before imagined, thanks

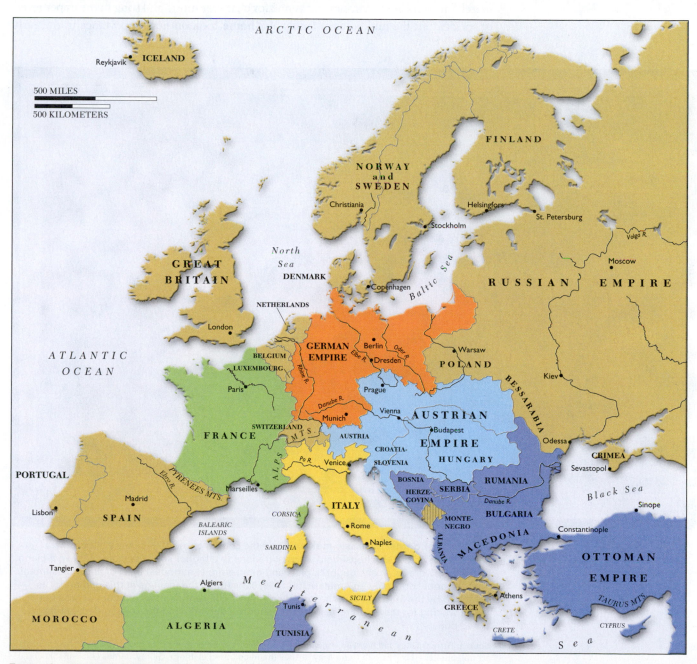

**Europe in 1871, after Italian and German Unifications.**

to advances in music printing, the manufacture of instruments, the growth of public concerts, music journalism, music education, transportation, and the enormous growth of populations in general.

Political change also had a direct effect on the way composers made a living. The established order of Europe did not collapse with the French Revolution of 1789, but it did begin to erode. The power of the nobility gradually gave way to the power of the wealthy—some of whom were members of the old guard, but many of whom had created their own wealth through commerce and industry. By the middle of the 19th century, private orchestras had all but disappeared: aristocratic patrons like those in whose palaces Haydn and Beethoven had given the premieres of various symphonies, could no longer maintain them. Concerts became increasingly public as more and more cities established civic orchestras. The salons of aristocrats and wealthy professionals and merchants remained an important venue for chamber music and song in the upper levels of society, but the middle-class family and home took on new importance in the early

**The perils of domestic music making.** Over the course of the 19th century, it became a social necessity for any household with aspirations to a higher social standing to own a piano. Daughters were routinely taught to play, and often sing, at a modest level of accomplishment. This cartoon, "drawn by an Amateur" in 1809, caricatures the feelings at this gathering, as exhibited by the family group, the audience with its different degrees of attentiveness (no doubt waiting for the liquid refreshment about to be served), and the bedraggled, perhaps bored dog.

**Source:** Farmer Giles and his Wife showing off their daughter Betty to their neighbours on her return from school, published by Hannah Humphrey in 1809 (hand-coloured etching), Gillray, James (1757-1815) / © Courtesy of the Warden and Scholars of New College, Oxford / The Bridgeman Art Library

19th century as a source of private music making. The ability to read and perform music, in the minds of many, was a sign of a well-rounded education. Middle-class families took pains to see that their children, especially their daughters, could play the piano and sing.

As aristocratic patronage declined, the sale of published music became an increasingly important source of income for composers. Technological advances in paper manufacturing and lithography substantially lowered the cost of music printing, and advances in communication and transportation further expanded the market for new compositions. Still, few composers could rely exclusively on music sales; most had to find additional work to make ends meet. Franz Schubert taught school, Hector Berlioz and Robert Schumann worked as music critics, and Frédéric Chopin taught piano. Almost all composers performed or conducted as well. Gustav Mahler, for example, conducted nine months out of the year and was able to focus on his own compositions only during summer holidays. Among the handful of artists able to devote themselves more or less exclusively to their own compositions were Gioacchino Rossini (whose success was so great that he was able to retire at the age of 37), and Giuseppe Verdi and Johannes Brahms, both of whom also conducted, but not out of financial necessity.

No matter how they earned their living, composers benefited from the immense growth in the production and consumption of music across all levels of society. Public education became increasingly widespread over the course of the century, with a corresponding increase in musical literacy as well as general literacy. This helped make the 19th century the era of the amateur musical society. Even small cities that lacked a civic orchestra usually had a variety of amateur musical organizations. Brass bands were a source of considerable pride for many small villages, particularly in England and Wales. Choral societies became popular in Great Britain and Germany, spawning a vast repertory of choral music—most of it a cappella—by such major composers as Mendelssohn, Schumann, Liszt, and Brahms. Although this music is seldom performed today, it sold well in its time. Amateurs also gathered at music festivals to perform large-scale works, particularly symphonies and oratorios. These festivals were participatory events, not passive spectacles, and their success was measured not so much in terms of musical quality (which by all accounts varied greatly), but by the number and diversity of the participants, who often traveled a considerable distance to attend.

In addition to the intrinsic joy of performing, many amateur performers were motivated by the belief in music making as a wholesome and uplifting pursuit that could strengthen social bonds. Indeed, many factory owners encouraged workers to form musical groups for precisely this purpose, as the following passage suggests:

> The Messrs. William, George and Joseph Strutt of Derby, men of great wealth and acquirements, employ nearly the whole population of Belper. . . . To give a higher taste to the work-people at Belper, Mr. John Strutt has formed a musical society by selecting forty persons, or more, from his mills and workshops, making a band of instrumental performers and a choir of singers. These persons are regularly trained by masters and taught to play and sing in the best manner. Whatever time is consumed in their studies is reckoned into their working hours. On the night of a general muster, you may see five or six of the forge-men, in their leather aprons, blasting their terrific notes upon ophicleides [forerunners of the tuba] and trombones.[1]

The contrast with the workplace today is striking. Employers still sometimes use music to enhance productivity, but they pipe it in. For employees, it is something they listen to while at work, not a diversion from work.

## Primary Evidence — MUSIC AND THE STATE

*For most European governments, the identification and fostering of musical talent was a matter of national importance not to be left to the whims of economic circumstance. The Czech composer Antonín Dvořák (1841–1904) was one of many composers and musicians who benefited from this outlook. The government in his native Bohemia supported several outstanding conservatories, often providing promising students—Dvořák was one of them—with full scholarships. When Dvořák visited the United States in the 1890s, he was struck by the lack of state support for music education. In this extract from an article he wrote for* Harper's New Monthly Magazine *in 1895, he criticizes this lack of support as shortsighted, comparing it unfavorably to the system that nurtured him.*

◼ ◼ ◼

Not long ago a young man came to me and showed me his compositions. His talent seemed so promising that I at once offered him a scholarship in our school [the private National Conservatory of Music, in New York, where Dvořák was teaching at the time]; but he sorrowfully confessed that he could not afford to become my pupil, because he had to earn his living by keeping books in Brooklyn. Even if he came on but two afternoons in the week, or on Saturday afternoon only, he said, he would lose his employment, on which he and others had to depend. I urged him to arrange the matter with his employer, but he only received the answer: "If you want to play, you can't keep books. You will have to drop one or the other." He dropped his music.

In any other country the state would have made some provision for such a deserving scholar, so that he could have pursued his natural calling without having to starve. With us in Bohemia the Diet each year votes a special sum of money for just such purposes, and the imperial government in Vienna on occasion furnishes other funds for talented artists. Had it not been for such support I should not have been able to pursue my studies when I was a young man. Owing to the fact that, upon the kind recommendation of such men as Brahms, Hanslick, and Herbeck, the Minister of Public Education in Vienna on five successive years sent me sums ranging from four to six hundred florins, I was able to pursue my work and to get my compositions published, so that at the end of that time I was able to stand on my own feet. This has filled me with lasting gratitude towards my country.

Such an attitude of the state towards deserving artists is not only a kind but a wise one. For it cannot be emphasized too strongly that art, as such, does not "pay," to use an American expression—at least, not in the beginning—and that the art that has to pay its own way is apt to become vitiated and cheap.

**Source:** Antonín Dvořák, "Music in America," *Harper's New Monthly Magazine* 90 (1895): 429–34.

National governments recognized the role of music in the politics of culture and began to assume responsibility for musical education. Virtually every state recognized that it needed a body of civic-minded musicians, composers, and music educators, and that it should establish the institutions to educate such individuals. The Paris Conservatory, established in its modern guise in the 1790s, provided a model for dozens of imitators across the Continent, including Bologna (1804), Milan (1808), Naples (1808), Prague (1811), London (1822), Brussels (1832), Berlin (1850), and St. Petersburg (1862). The conservatories of Vienna (1817) and Leipzig (1843) were private, as were all the earliest such institutions in the United States. Those that endured include the Peabody Conservatory of Music (Baltimore, 1857), the Oberlin Conservatory (Oberlin, Ohio, 1865), the New England Conservatory of Music (Boston, 1867), the Chicago Musical College (1867), and the Cincinnati Conservatory (1867). Colleges and universities first established schools and departments of music in the last three decades of the century. Not until 1892 did a state-supported institution of higher learning—the University of Michigan, in Ann Arbor—establish its own school of music. Unlike most European nations, the United States never embraced the idea of a national conservatory. This was due in part to the nation's decentralized system of higher education, in part to the perception that music is less important to national development than such disciplines as engineering, medicine, and the law (see Primary Evidence: Music and the State).

# The Age of the Tone Poet

The greatest changes in music during the early decades of the 19th century were not primarily in matters of style but rather in modes of perception. Composers and audiences alike began to conceive of music and hear it—particularly instrumental music—in a radically new manner. Before 1800, most critics had considered instrumental music inferior to vocal music because although it could express emotions and move the passions, it could not convey ideas or concepts (see Chapter 12). This consensus, however, began to erode rapidly in the mid-1790s with a new generation of poets and critics, including Friedrich Schlegel (1772–1829), Ludwig Tieck (1773–1853), and E. T. A. Hoffmann (1776–1822). The abstract nature of music, they maintained, was an asset, not a liability. Instrumental music, *because* it was free from the confining strictures of language, was capable of conveying ideas and emotions too profound for mere words.

Composers both shaped and responded to this changing perception of music's powers. They began to see and portray themselves in an entirely new way. Beethoven dubbed himself a "tone poet," an artist who creates poetry with notes rather than words. The public, in turn, began to see great composers as divinely inspired high priests of art who could provide glimpses into a loftier, more spiritual world. Eventually, the idolization of instrumental music triggered a backlash among composers and critics who favored vocal music. Echoing claims that date back to the early Baroque, they argued that opera in particular occupied a higher aesthetic plane than instrumental music alone because it represented a synthesis of all the arts.

## Chapter Outline

- Romanticism and the New Prestige of Instrumental Music
- The Composer as High Priest
- Originality and Historical Self-Consciousness
- The New Dichotomy between Absolute and Program Music
- Nationalism
- The Growing Division between Art and Popular Music
- Music in the 19th Century: A Stylistic Overview

## ROMANTICISM AND THE NEW PRESTIGE OF INSTRUMENTAL MUSIC

The term *romantic* derives from the name of a literary genre—the romance—that first emerged in the medieval era. A romance tells a long story in verse or prose. (As such, the genre is a forerunner to the novel, and indeed the word for "novel" in both French and German is *roman*.) Unlike other literary forms, such as epic or lyric poetry, the romance is largely free of structural or narrative conventions. It was because of this association with relatively freer narrative expression that the genre gave its name to an artistic movement—Romanticism—that values imagination and personal expression.

With its stress on imagination, Romanticism values thought that lies beyond reason and words (in contrast to the rationalism of the Enlightenment); it embraces the spiritual and even mystical aspects of life and art. And for many 19th-century artists and critics who thought of themselves as Romantics, the art form that most nearly approximates the disembodied realm of abstraction was instrumental music. Other art forms of the time, such as painting and poetry, are consistently tied in some way to an identifiable object, setting, or event. Purely instrumental music, by contrast, moves beyond the realm of the physical to the realm of the spiritual and infinite.

The novelist and playwright Ludwig Tieck was one of the first to give voice to this new outlook. In 1799, he maintained that Johann Friedrich Reichardt's purely instrumental overture to *Macbeth* was superior to Shakespeare's original play (see Primary Evidence: The Perceived Superiority of Instrumental Music). In 1810, E. T. A. Hoffmann proclaimed instrumental music to be "the most romantic of all the arts—one might almost say, the only genuinely romantic one—for its sole subject is the infinite." Hoffmann identified Haydn, Mozart, and Beethoven as "Romantic composers," not on the basis of their musical style but because their music provided a glimpse into the realm of "the spirit world" (see Primary Evidence: E. T. A. Hoffmann's Review of Beethoven's Fifth Symphony in Chapter 15). Eight years later, the German philosopher Arthur Schopenhauer (1788–1860) argued that "if music is too closely united to the words, it is striving to speak a language which is not its own." For it is not in the nature of music to "express this or that particular and definite joy, this or that sorrow, or pain, or horror, or delight, or merriment, or peace of mind," but rather "joy, sorrow, pain, horror, delight, merriment, peace of mind *themselves*, to a certain extent in the abstract, their essential nature, without accessories, and therefore without their motives."[1] Music, in other words, should not descend to the level of words.

# THE COMPOSER AS HIGH PRIEST

With art in general and music in particular now perceived as a window to the realm of the infinite and spiritual, the social status of composers rose enormously. In the Classical era, the composer had been viewed essentially as an artisan providing goods made to order. By the 1830s, the composer had taken on the aura of a divinely inspired creator, a demigod. There was much talk in the early 19th century about "Art-Religion." This referred not so much to the worship of art as to the revelation of the divine through the medium of art. Composers emerged as the high priests of this new religion, for they dealt with the most abstract (and thus the most revealing) of all the arts.

The composer, according to Schopenhauer, was like a clairvoyant or sleepwalker, someone who in a half-conscious, half-dreaming state "reveals the innermost nature of the world in a language his reasoning faculty does not understand." Critics and artists of the 18th century, as we saw in Chapter 11, drew a distinction between natural, divinely inspired genius and the teachable techniques—the art—through which that genius found expression. In the 19th century, the distinction between genius and technique became a chasm that only artistic geniuses could bridge—and even then they were not expected to understand the process. If music could provide a glimpse of the infinite, then the distance between inspiration and technique could be neither described nor measured.

This image of the composer as sleepwalker abounds in accounts of the Polish composer Frédéric Chopin's performances of his own music. An English critic writing in 1848 described how "the performer seems to abandon himself to the impulses of his fancy and feeling, to indulge in a reverie and to pour out unconsciously, as it were, the thoughts and emotions that pass through his mind."[3] Robert Schumann described

## Primary Evidence — THE PERCEIVED SUPERIORITY OF INSTRUMENTAL MUSIC

*In a remarkable essay entitled "Symphonies," Ludwig Tieck (1773–1853) argued that Johann Friedrich Reichardt's overture to a German-language stage production of Shakespeare's* Macbeth *was superior to the drama itself. (Symphony and overture were still interchangeable terms in the late 18th century.) Tieck chose the Reichardt work because it was well known in its time, and it allowed him to draw a sharp contrast between the power of instrumental music (the overture) and the poetry of the subsequent play, which struck him as relatively pedestrian in comparison.*

■ ■ ■

In instrumental music . . . the art is independent and free, it writes its own laws only for itself, it fantasizes freely and without purpose and nevertheless fulfills and attains the highest. It follows entirely its own dark drives and expresses the deepest, the most [unforeseen] miraculous with its [seeming] trivialities. The full choruses, polyphonic pieces that are elaborated with great art, are the triumph of vocal music. The highest victory, the most beautiful prize of instruments are the symphonies.

These symphonies can present a colorful, varied, complicated and so beautifully developed drama such as the poet can never produce, for they reveal in an enigmatic language that which is most enigmatic. They do not depend on any laws of probability, they do not need to be affiliated with any story or any character . . . they remain in their purely poetic world. They thereby avoid all means for transporting us, for delighting us. From beginning to end, the thing itself is their object. The goal itself is present at every moment, beginning and ending the artwork. . . .

I remember in particular one such pleasure given to me by music recently on a trip. I went to the theater; *Macbeth* was to be given. A famous musician [Johann Friedrich Reichardt] had created a particular symphony [i.e., overture] for this wonderful tragedy. It delighted and intoxicated me so much, that I still cannot forget the great impressions it made on my spirit. I cannot describe how wonderfully allegorical this great composition struck me, and yet full of highly individualized images, just as the true, highest allegory similarly loses cold universality through itself, and which we find only with poets who have not yet grown to a stature commensurate with their art. I saw in the music the dark, foggy moor, in whose twilight muddled circles of witches passed in and out of one another, with the ever-thickening clouds all the while sinking ever closer and more poisonously to the earth. Horrible voices cry and moan through the desolation, and like ghosts, there is a trembling throughout all this chaos; a laughing, gruesome *Schadenfreude* appears in the distance. The forms take on more definite outlines, horrifying shapes stride meaningfully across the heath, the clouds break. Now the eye sees a revolting fiend that lies in its black cave, bound with heavy chains. He strives with all his power, with all his strength, to rid himself of these chains, but he is still restrained. Around him begins the magic dance of all the ghosts, all the ghouls. With weeping melancholy, the eye trembles in the distance, hoping that the chains will restrain the terrible one, that they will not break. But the commotion grows louder and more horrible, and with a terrifying scream, with the innermost rage the monster breaks loose and jumps with a wild leap into the ghouls. There is a wailing and exultation intermixed. The victory is decided, hell triumphs. The chaos now becomes even more chaotic and becomes truly horrible. Everything flees in terror and returns. The triumphant song of the damned ends the [overture].

After this great phenomenon, many scenes of the drama struck me as tired and empty, for the most terrifying and revolting had already been announced in a grander and more poetic fashion. All I did was to keep thinking back to the music. The drama oppressed my spirit and disturbed my memories, for with the close of this symphony everything was completely finished for me. I know of no master and no work of music that would have aroused this in me, in that I could have perceived the restless, ever more enraged drive of all the soul's power, this terrible, dizzying shift of all musical pulses. The drama should have closed with this great artwork, and in one's fantasies, one could not conceive of or wish for anything higher. For this symphony was the more poetic incarnation of the drama, the most audacious presentation of a lost, lamentable human life that was stormed and conquered by all that is monstrous.

**Source:** Ludwig Tieck, "Symphonien" (1799), from Wilhelm Heinrich Wackenroder and Ludwig Tieck, *Phantasien über die Kunst für Freunde der Kunst,* in Wilhelm Heinrich Wackenroder, *Sämtliche Werke und Briefe: Historisch-kritische Ausgabe,* ed. Silvio Vietta and Richard Littlejohns, 2 vols. (Heidelberg: Carl Winter Universitätsverlag, 1991), I, 245–54. Transl. MEB.

the "unforgettable picture" of Chopin "sitting at the piano like a dreamy clairvoyant," playing in such a way that "the dreams he had created seemed to appear before us."[4] Such accounts were new to the 19th century.

The listening public sought insight into the working methods of composers as never before. Beethoven's sketches commanded high prices in the marketplace. Autograph scores of his works sold well, too, but the sketches held a special fascination for critics and collectors because they offered a glimpse into the "half-conscious, half-dreaming" essence of the creative process. The German scholar Gustav Nottebohm (1817–1882), who studied composition with both Mendelssohn and Schumann in his youth, took it upon himself to gather and examine as many of Beethoven's sketches as he could lay his hands on, and his findings remain useful to scholars even today. The sketches show—sometimes in considerable detail—the sequence of steps by which Beethoven developed seemingly insignificant ideas into powerful, original works of art. Yet in a strange way, the publication of Beethoven's sketchbooks actually made the composer's creative process even more mysterious, for although the record of that process—the sketches—had been preserved, the process of composition itself remained unfathomable.

The public also wanted to know more about the composers themselves, and their biographies began to appear in great numbers. Book-length accounts of any composer's life were rare before 1800, but 19th-century writers produced a long series of biographies about such figures as J. S. Bach (by Johann Nikolaus Forkel in 1802, then by Philipp Spitta in 1873–1880), Handel (Friedrich Chrysander, 1858–1867), Mozart (Otto Jahn, 1856–1859), and Beethoven (Alexander Wheelock Thayer, 1866–1879).

Composers, too, were more likely to write about themselves and their art. Berlioz, Schumann, Liszt, and Wagner all wrote prose as well as music. In earlier eras, audiences had been too small and listeners on the whole not sufficiently curious enough to make such publications profitable. It had been assumed, moreover, that a composer was obligated to make his music sufficiently intelligible and accessible for listeners to understand without the need of outside help. In the 19th century, however, the idea began to take hold that the composer, as a demigod or high priest, did not always "speak" in an immediately comprehensible manner—hence the need for explanatory texts. Beethoven's symphonies were among the first works to elicit this kind of attention. E. T. A. Hoffmann's lengthy review of the Fifth Symphony in 1810 is an early testament to the musical public's desire to understand a work of music at a deeper level (see Primary Evidence: E. T. A. Hoffmann's Review of Beethoven's Fifth Symphony in Chapter 15). A decade later, the Berlin music critic Adolf Bernhard Marx (1795–1866) would pen a series of essays on all of Beethoven's symphonies. Hector Berlioz's own essays on these works were eventually published in book form and sold widely. Later in the century, Wagner's music dramas also demanded, and received, book-length guides for the listening public.

Composers were also far more likely than ever before to incorporate autobiographical elements into their music. Robert Schumann encoded the names of at least two of the women in his life into his piano cycle *Carnaval* (1835; Anthology II/132, discussed in Chapter 16). Berlioz called his first symphony "Episode in the Life of an Artist." (The title by which it is known today—*Symphonie fantastique*—was for many years only its subtitle.) The very notion of writing a work of music *about* an artist is quintessentially Romantic, and although Berlioz never named the artist of the title, there can be no doubt it was he. He also wrote an elaborate prose program for the work that is transparently autobiographical (see Primary Evidence: Berlioz's Program for the *Symphonie fantastique* in Chapter 15).

Given the new perception of the composer as a divinely inspired creator, it is scarcely surprising that performers and listeners would begin to place more weight on the accuracy and authority of published scores. Performers began to question whether the editions from which they were performing actually represented the intentions of the composer. Publishers, taking note of this demand, represented their editions as the most reliable available—sometimes truthfully, sometimes not. Authoritative editions of composers' collected works began to appear for the first time in the 19th century, including the complete works of Beethoven, Schubert, Schumann, and Wagner.

The most revered composers became cultural heroes, bringing honor to their native cities, which, in turn, felt obligated to erect statues in their honor. Salzburg erected its statue of Mozart in 1842, Leipzig completed its monument to J. S. Bach in 1843, and Bonn unveiled its statue of Beethoven in 1845. The funerals of Haydn (1809) and Beethoven (1827) in Vienna were state occasions. Later in the century, Wagner became a cult figure whose influence extended far beyond music. His most devoted followers adopted not only his radical political views but even his vegetarian dietary practices.

# ORIGINALITY AND HISTORICAL SELF-CONSCIOUSNESS

Artists and critics of the 19th century were obsessed with the idea of originality. They firmly believed that every work of art must be new and different. Whereas earlier composers had often recycled themes or even entire movements into new works (see Conceptions of the Compositional Process in Chapter 9), composers of the 19th century were far less inclined to engage in this practice. Critics began to condemn any work that bore too strong a resemblance to any other work, especially one by a different composer. To copy Haydn, Mozart, or even Beethoven was considered unacceptable for any composer who aspired to greatness. Earlier composers, by contrast, would have been pleased to have their style likened to that of an acknowledged master. Now composers sought to find their own distinctive voice and express it in music unlike any heard before.

Not surprisingly, composers who wrote about their own work tended to portray themselves as revolutionaries, as radicals who rejected the music of the past. Many critics took up this same approach, arguing that established conventions of form, genre, and harmony were restrictive in and of themselves. As we have seen in Chapter 11, earlier composers routinely integrated originality and convention. The Romantics nevertheless chose to interpret and portray their innovations as a rejection of convention, as an act of artistic liberation. Virtually every Romantic artist saw himself or herself blazing a unique path to truth.

In an odd way, however, the cult of originality made composers more aware of the musical past than their predecessors had been. One could not be original, after all, in a vacuum. Composers studied earlier music carefully with an eye toward doing something different. The music of the past dominated the concert hall and opera house as never before. Prior to 1800, it would have been unusual to hear the music of a composer from a previous generation. There were exceptions, of course. Lully's operas were still favorites in Paris one hundred years after his death and Handel's oratorios continued to be performed regularly in England throughout the Classical era and beyond. In the early 19th century, however, works by earlier composers became staples in the active repertory, beginning with the later symphonies and quartets of Haydn and Mozart and the operas of Gluck and Mozart. By the end of the century, it would

**The virtuoso as idol.** Throughout the 19th century, the great musical virtuosos and composers were perceived as endowed with divine, superhuman powers. This satirical drawing of the great Polish composer and pianist Ignace Jan Paderewski (1860–1941) from ca. 1895 also reminds us that the public's fascination with long-haired musicians began long before the Beatles. One newspaper of the time reported that "three New York ladies have embroidered musical phrases from [Paderewski's] Minuet on their stockings." In his 1892–1893 concert tour of the United States, Paderewski traveled in his own private railcar along with his secretary, valet, manager, chef, two porters, his Steinway piano, and his piano tuner. The grotesquely exaggerated hand stretch, covering the entire keyboard, betrays the mixture of awe and derision with which the public viewed its virtuosos: awe at their seemingly superhuman powers, derision at their "trained seal" status.

**Source:** Lebrecht Music & Arts Photo Library

have been difficult to find a concert without at least one work from an earlier era. With newer and older works now on the same program, younger composers were inevitably compared not only to their contemporaries, but to masters of earlier times as well. This could be discouraging. When the young Robert Schumann finally managed to get two movements of a never-to-be-finished symphony performed in the early 1830s, his music had to share the program with Beethoven's Seventh Symphony, a work written some 20 years before. Comparisons with the past made the drive for originality all the more compelling and all the more challenging.

By the middle of the 19th century, consciousness of the past took on a new form, that of **historicism**, in which composers openly embraced the forms and styles of earlier generations while presenting them in original ways. Anton Bruckner (1824–1896), for example, whose symphonies used some of the most advanced chromatic harmonies of his era, wrote a number of sacred choral works and Masses in an intentionally anachronistic idiom, one that the unsuspecting ear might mistake briefly for that of Palestrina (see Chapter 17, Anthology). Brahms, appropriating a theme from a cantata by J. S. Bach, openly incorporated the archaic form of the passacaglia into the finale of his Fourth Symphony (see Chapter 18, Anthology).

Interest in earlier music led musicians and scholars to seek out forgotten repertories, leading to the recovery of quantities of music from the medieval era, the Renaissance, and the Baroque period. In 1828, Felix Mendelssohn became the first musician to conduct J. S. Bach's *Saint Matthew Passion* since Bach's death. Mendelssohn's rediscovery inspired the editing and publication of other works by Bach as well. By the end of the century, almost all of Bach's music had been carefully edited and published in a sumptuous edition. Handel, Schütz, and earlier composers such as Lassus and Palestrina enjoyed the same process of rediscovery in the 19th century.

# THE NEW DICHOTOMY BETWEEN ABSOLUTE AND PROGRAM MUSIC

The growing prestige of instrumental music as an abstract art created a critical backlash around the middle of the 19th century. The composers and critics involved in this reaction maintained that music could achieve its highest potential only through a synthesis with other arts, including the arts of the word. Richard Wagner led the attack on what he derisively termed **absolute music**, meaning music that was cut off from the larger world of words and ideas. (The prefix *ab* in *absolute* derives from the Latin word for "separate" or "disconnected.") Wagner's criticism of absolute music echoed the view of 18th-century critics toward instrumental music: he valued its ability to move the passions but considered it too abstract to carry true meaning. Only with the "fertilizing seed" of the word, Wagner argued, could music realize its full potential. This could take the form of a program or programmatic text—like that which Berlioz wrote for his *Symphonie fantastique*—or better still, a text to be sung. Even Beethoven, Wagner argued, had recognized the limitations of purely instrumental music and for this reason had introduced voices into the finale of his Ninth Symphony. Franz Liszt similarly argued that, with the benefit of a written program outlining the "ideas that he [the composer] sought to embody in his work," a purely instrumental composition could be "elevated to definite impressions" and not limited to the "vague impressions" provoked by absolute music (see Primary Evidence: Liszt on the Superiority of Program Music).

The term *absolute* was soon embraced as a label for purely instrumental music even by its proponents, but with a different, positive, interpretation. By this line of thought, pure instrumental music was absolute in its ability to transcend earthly life, rising above mundane, everyday existence. This usage reflected a sense in which *absolute* was equated with a quality of transcendence: that which was absolute stood above all else. The most influential advocate of this view of absolute music in the middle of the 19th century was the Viennese critic Eduard Hanslick (1825–1904). Hanslick argued that the content of music does not and cannot extend beyond the notes themselves but consists instead of "forms animated through tones." Music's independence from earthly life is the quality that makes it most moving (see Primary Evidence: Hanslick on the Superiority of Absolute Music).

Unlike Wagner and Liszt, who wrote forcefully in favor of program music, no composer of any stature who favored absolute music took pen to paper in its defense. Johannes Brahms, for example, one of the most prominent practitioners of absolute music, preferred "to polemicize with works of music rather than with words," as one of his close associates put it.[5] The debate itself was charged with political overtones. Wagner and Liszt claimed for themselves the mantle of progressivism, calling their work "The Music of the Future," whereas Hanslick (and by association, composers like Brahms) were associated with the forces of conservatism.

As often happens in ideological battles, however, the basic issues receded in importance over time. By the last quarter of the 19th century, both sides had begun to suspect that they were debating a distinction without a difference. To the question "Does instrumental music have any meaning beyond itself?" both sides would answer "yes," although they differed on just how that meaning could manifest itself. A new generation of composers, critics, and audiences saw merit in both points of view. Many composers were ambivalent on the matter or changed their opinions gradually. Even Wagner began to realize that absolute music was really not so empty after all. And Liszt, the great champion of program music, issued one of his most significant works, the Sonata in B minor, with a generic title; he refused repeated request to provide

## Primary Evidence — LISZT ON THE SUPERIORITY OF PROGRAM MUSIC

*Franz Liszt, along with Richard Wagner, was a leader in the battle to legitimize program music. In an essay he wrote in 1855 on Berlioz's symphony* Harold en Italie, *he identifies the key distinction between the "purely musical composer" (that is, one dedicated to the idea of absolute music) and the more engaged composer who wrestles with ideas extending beyond music.*

■ ■ ■

The purely musical composer, who places value and emphasis only on the formal shaping of his material, does not have the capacity to derive new formulations from this [musical] material or to breathe new powers into it. For there is no spiritual necessity that compels him to discover new means, he is not driven and compelled by any glowing passion that wills itself toward the light! It is for this reason that those who are called upon to enrich form [i.e., composers of program music] are those who would extend it, make it adaptable, and use it as merely one medium of expression shaped according to the demands of those ideas which are to be expressed. The formalists [i.e., "purely musical" composers], by contrast, are capable of nothing better or cleverer than to use, propagate, rearrange, and occasionally rework that which has already been achieved by these others.

The purpose of the program is merely to indicate, in a preliminary sort of way, those spiritual states of mind that drove the composer to the creation of his work, the ideas that he sought to embody in his work. It is childishly pointless and usually impossible to draft programs after the fact in an attempt to clarify the emotional content of an instrumental poem, for to do so would necessarily destroy the magic and desecrate the feelings and tear apart the finest spun webs of the soul, precisely because such works assumed their shape according to their form and not through words, images, or ideas. At the same time, the master is master of his own work, which he may have created under the influence of distinct impression, which he then later wishes to bring into the complete and full consciousness of his listeners.

Altogether then, the pure symphonist takes his listeners into ideal regions and leaves it to each individual's fantasy just how to conceive of these regions and adorn them. In such instances it is very dangerous for us to impose on our neighbor the same scene and sequence of ideas into which our own imagination feels itself transported. Better to let each listener take silent joy in the revelations and visions for which there are no names and no designations. But the poeticizing symphonist, who takes it upon himself to convey clearly an image distinctly present in his own mind, a succession of spiritual states that appear unambiguously and distinctly within his consciousness—why should he not strive to be fully understood by the aid of a program? . . .

In so-called Classical music, the recurrence and thematic development of themes are determined by formal rules that are considered inviolable, even though its composers possessed no other prescription for these processes than their own fantasies. These composers arranged the formal layout of their works in a manner that some would now proclaim as law. In program music, by contrast, the recurrence, variation, and modification of motifs are determined by their relationship to a poetic idea. Here one theme does not beget another according to any formal laws; the motives are not a consequence of stereotypical similarities or contrasts of timbre; coloration in itself does not determine the grouping of ideas. Although certainly not ignored, all exclusively musical considerations are subordinated to the treatment of the subject at hand. Accordingly, the plot and subject of this symphonic genre demand an engagement that goes beyond the technical treatment of the musical material. The vague impressions of the soul are elevated to definite impressions through a defined plan, which is taken in by the ear in much the same manner in which a cycle of paintings is taken in by the eye. The artist who favors this kind of artwork enjoys the advantage of being able to connect with a poetic process all those affects which an orchestra can express with such great power.

**Source:** Franz Liszt, "Berlioz und seine Haroldsymphonie," *Neue Zeitschrift für Musik* 43 (1855): 51–52. Transl. MEB

indications about any extramusical "meaning" the work might have. Berlioz tried for many years—unsuccessfully—to suppress the detailed program of his *Symphonie fantastique*; Brahms, who remained aloof from open debate on the issue, incorporated certain programmatic elements into at least some of his works, although he never revealed these connections to a wider public.

## Primary Evidence    HANSLICK ON THE SUPERIORITY OF ABSOLUTE MUSIC

*Eduard Hanslick's* On the Beautiful in Music, *first published in 1854, was the manifesto of the musical conservatives who believed in the sanctity of absolute music. Hanslick (1825–1904) argued that music could not in its own right express emotions. By this he did not mean that music is incapable of moving the listener, but rather that beauty in music flows from its ability to project "forms animated through sound."*

■ ■ ■

The nature of beauty in a musical composition is specifically musical. By this we understand a beauty that is independent and in no need of any external content. It is a beauty that lies entirely in the notes and in their artistic interweaving. The meaningful connections of inherently pleasing sounds, their concords and discords, their departure and arrival, their eruption and subsiding—this is what comes before our spiritual perception in free forms and pleases us as beautiful.

If we now ask what is to be expressed with this musical material, the answer is: Musical Ideas. A complete musical idea is already self-sufficient beauty; it is an end in itself and in no way merely a means or the material for the presentation of emotions or thoughts.

*The sole and exclusive content and object of music are forms animated through tones.*

The manner in which music can bring forth beautiful forms without any particular affective content can be illustrated in a general way by a branch of ornamentation in the visual arts: the arabesque. We take in sweeping lines; at times they dip gently, at times they strive boldly upward; they discover and leave one another; they correspond in their curves large and small, seemingly incommensurable yet always well proportioned. Everywhere there is a welcoming counterpart or pendant, a gathering of small details and yet a whole. Let us contemplate this arabesque not as if it were something dead and static, but rather as something constantly in the process of creating itself before our eyes. How the broad and fine lines surprise the eye at every moment, pursuing one another, raising themselves from small curves to a magnificent height, then sinking again, then expanding, coming together and in ingenious alternation of rest and tension! The image as a whole thus becomes higher and more noble. If we think of this living arabesque as the active emanation of an artistic spirit who ceaselessly pours into the arteries of this motion his fantasy—does not this impression approximate quite closely that of music? . . .

It is extraordinarily difficult to describe this self-sufficiently beautiful in music, this specifically musical beauty. Because music has no prototype in nature and expresses no conceptual content, it can be discussed only either in dry technical terms or through poetic fictions. Its kingdom is truly "not of this world." All the fantastic descriptions, characterizations, and paraphrases of a musical work are figurative or wrong. What in accounts of every other art is merely descriptive is already metaphorical in music. Music demands to be perceived simply as music; it can be understood and enjoyed only in terms of its own self. . . .

The concept of "form" is realized in music in an entirely distinctive manner. The forms created out of tones are not empty but full; they are not merely the outlines of a vacuum, but rather a spirit that creates itself from within. In contrast to the arabesque, music is nevertheless in fact an image, albeit one whose object we cannot express through words and comprehend through concepts. In music we find sense and order, but these are musical; music is a language that we speak and understand yet are incapable of translating. That one speaks of "thoughts" in musical works represents a profound insight, and as in speech, a trained judgement easily distinguishes genuine thoughts from empty phrases. In just this way, we recognize the rationally self-contained quality of a group of notes in that we call this grouping a "sentence." We feel precisely where its sense is completed, just as in a logical sentence, even though the truths of the two propositions are entirely incommensurable.

**Source:** Eduard Hanslick, *Vom musikalisch-Schönen* (Leipzig: R. Weigel, 1854). Transl. MEB.

The question of instrumental music's meaning nevertheless remained a central topic of debate throughout the second half of the 19th century. The literary critic Walter Pater (1839–1894) summed up the matter neatly when he declared that music's ability to embody form without the burden of specific content was the envy of poetry and painting, and that "all art constantly aspires towards the condition of music."[6] Such an attitude acknowledges music's unique ability to transcend the representation of objects or ideas while also allowing for the incorporation of nonmusical elements.

# NATIONALISM

Nationalist sentiments and aspirations in particular lent themselves to musical expression particularly well. Even purely instrumental music could be interpreted politically. Chopin, for example, whose native Poland was under Russian control, made a nationalistic statement with the mazurkas and polonaises—both traditional Polish dance forms—that he wrote while living in Paris as part of the Polish exile community. This nationalistic element was not lost on listeners. Schumann pointed out as early as 1837 that if the czar of Russia "knew what a dangerous enemy threatened him in Chopin's works, in the simple tunes of his mazurkas, he would forbid this music. Chopin's works are cannons buried in flowers."[7] And as the American critic James Huneker declared at the end of the century, "the most profound truths, the most blasphemous things, the most terrible ideas, may be incorporated within the walls of a symphony, and the police may be none the wiser. It is its freedom from the meddlesome hand of the censor that makes of music a playground for great brave souls."[8]

A number of Russian composers were themselves seeking a distinctively Russian musical idiom based on the melodic and harmonic inflections of indigenous folk musics. In 1836, Mikhail Glinka (1804–1857) wrote an opera—*A Life for the Tsar* (also known as *Ivan Susanin*)—that was an early landmark in this endeavor. Based on a story from Russian history, it has a Russian libretto, and the score, although following the conventions of contemporary Italian opera, incorporates elements from Russian folk music. Glinka's precedent inspired many later Russian composers, most notably Alexander Borodin (1833–1887) and Modeste Mussorgsky (1839–1881). Borodin's orchestral work *In the Steppes of Central Asia*, for example, incorporates folk songs and employs features associated with Asian music, such as the pentatonic scale. Mussorgsky's opera *Boris Godunov* (1869; revised 1872), like Glinka's *A Life for the Tsar*, draws its story from Russian history and includes folk songs and folk-song-like elements in its music. Throughout Europe and the Americas, many 19th-century composers cultivated styles of writing that in some way drew on the folk idioms of their respective nationalities: Verdi in Italy, Wagner in Germany, Dvořák in Bohemia (now part of the Czech Republic), and Gottschalk in the United States (see Chapter 16).

Composers sometimes used folk music from lands not their own to add an exotic flavor to their music, to pay homage to another nationality, or to indulge in the general Romantic interest in folk culture. The Italian composer Giuseppe Verdi, for example, incorporated what he thought to be "Egyptian" musical elements into his opera *Aida* (1871), which is set in ancient Egypt; the work was written to commemorate the opening of the Suez Canal and had its first performance in Cairo. Brahms, who came from the northern German city of Hamburg, used a "Hungarian" idiom in his various Hungarian Dances. Dvořák incorporated what he considered elements of Native American music into his Symphony no. 9, subtitled "From the New World." He did this in part to encourage American composers to forge their own national idiom (see Chapter 18).

# THE GROWING DIVISION BETWEEN ART AND POPULAR MUSIC

It was during the 19th century that musicians, composers, and the music-consuming public began to draw a distinction between **art music** and **popular music**. The terms, it turns out, are misleading and impossible to define musically in any consistent way (see Appendix 4: The Concepts of "Popular" and "Art" Music ). Still, their emergence reflects real changes in social attitudes toward music and the economics of the music business.

Before the 19th century, composers routinely wrote music to suit their immediate audiences. Mozart, for example, wrote two entirely different works for the stage in the final months of his life: *Die Zauberflöte* ("The Magic Flute"), a *Singspiel* for a middle-class theater in Vienna, and *La Clemenza di Tito* ("The Clemency of Titus"), an opera seria commissioned for the celebrations surrounding the coronation in Prague of Emperor Leopold II as king of Bohemia. *La Clemenza di Tito*, although admired in its time and into the 19th century, never had a substantial audience. At least some numbers from *Die Zauberflöte*, however, became so popular that to this day many Germans believe they are folk songs and are surprised to discover they were actually written by Mozart. In Mozart's time, these two works were performed before audiences of different social levels in decidedly different kinds of theaters. By the end of the 19th century, however, a given opera house might well be presenting both works to essentially the same audience. The works themselves had not changed, but the attitudes toward them had.

This shift in attitudes can be traced to changing assumptions about the nature and purpose of music. Accepting their status in the Romantic imagination as high priests of the new religion of art, at least some 19th-century composers no longer felt obliged to take their audiences into account, at least not directly. Listeners, in turn, came increasingly to accept that it was their responsibility to understand a composer's music, not the composer's responsibility to make it accessible to them. At the same time, undemanding music was becoming increasingly accessible to the broad public. One audience saw music as a means to spiritual enlightenment, the other as a means of entertainment.

Economic factors reinforced this division. With the decline of royal and aristocratic patronage and the growth of an educated middle class, orchestras and opera houses became increasingly reliant on income from ticket sales, which in turn drove them to offer music with broad popular appeal. Publishers, too, recognized that there was serious money to be made in music that could be easily performed and readily absorbed. Before the 19th century, this kind of music would have been part of the unwritten tradition, transmitted orally. The development of recording technology in the 20th century would make this "popular" music ever more pervasive as a commodity that could be bought and sold.

Concert manners—a revealing index of attitudes toward music—also changed considerably over the course of the 19th century. In earlier times, audiences felt free to respond openly at musical performances whenever moved to do so. Mozart, writing to his father from Paris in 1778, describes how he had marked a crescendo in an orchestral work in such a way as to solicit applause from the audience. The audience, he reports, had responded on cue. "What a fuss the oxen here make of this trick!" Mozart observed, half amused, half pleased with the effect. What is particularly revealing in his comment is the assumption that listeners would express their delight without inhibition in the middle of a performance. Such outbursts are still common today at jazz, rock, and country music concerts but not in the realm of the concert halls where Mozart's music is now performed.

By 1900, a little more than one hundred years after Mozart's death, outbursts in the middle of a concert performance had become rare, and even applause between movements was becoming the exception rather than the rule. The new behavior was certainly more considerate toward fellow listeners, but it put a damper on spontaneity. For all practical purposes, the concert hall had become a temple, a sanctuary that fostered devotion and contemplation. The rituals of concert decorum that made music easier to hear by reducing distractions also made the listening experience more passive and self-conscious. In the dance hall and music hall, in contrast, audiences continued to respond to performances spontaneously and vocally; at homes, singing societies, and in other establishments, amateurs played on the piano and sang choruses and songs.

**The expansion of musical literacy.** With a look of weary resignation, the tavern keeper realizes that removing the music stands has not discouraged his clients from continuing with their music making. (The dog seems particularly distressed about this.) Instruction in basic music literacy became a standard part of school curricula in many European nations after 1800, and these amateurs are reading music, not performing from memory. The part-song for men's chorus, a now largely forgotten genre, was popular in the 19th century. Schubert, Schumann, and Brahms all contributed to it. The guitar was ubiquitous in domestic music making; its portability gave it an advantage over the piano. Transported to a comparable scene from today, this group would no doubt be listening to recorded music.

**Source:** Bildarchiv der Oesterreichischen Nationalbibliothek

The growing rift between art and popular repertories in the 19th century has revealing parallels in the world of drama. For most of the century, Shakespeare's plays were routinely altered to appeal to the widest possible public. No one paid much attention to the edition being used in performance, and scenes from different plays were often presented in quick succession (under such titles as "Gems from Shakespeare's Dramas"), with jugglers, dancers, and acrobats entertaining audiences between the unconnected scenes. In one form or another, Shakespeare's plays remained sufficiently popular to draw audiences from all levels of society: the episode in Mark Twain's *Huckleberry Finn* in which two vagabonds stage hilariously inaccurate versions of various scenes from Shakespeare for a country audience willing to pay money to see them reflects this popularity. By the end of the century, however, Shakespeare's plays were being performed from carefully edited, authentic versions before respectful audiences without supplementary entertainments. Shakespeare had become serious art, Culture with a capital C.

The distinction between art and entertainment was not yet firmly established in the concert hall in the early 19th century. At the premiere of Beethoven's Violin Concerto in Vienna on December 23, 1806, the first movement was followed by an intermission, which began only after the soloist had played a short piece of his own while holding his instrument upside down. By the end of the 19th century, such relaxed informality had disappeared. The mixed concert that included songs, choruses, and instrumental works for orchestra, chamber ensemble, and soloists, had also fallen by the wayside. Programs became increasingly homogeneous and as a result appealed to an increasingly narrower audience.

Still, we should not underestimate the wide appeal through most of the century of what we now think of as serious genres. Some of Verdi's music achieved extraordinary popularity among people who probably never set foot in an opera house but who heard the music sung in the streets or performed in arrangements for any of a variety of instruments. Verdi's own account of a rehearsal for the premiere of his early *Nabucco* (1842) illustrates this phenomenon:

> The artists were singing as badly as they knew how, and the orchestra seemed to be bent only upon drowning the noise of the workmen who were busy making alterations in the building. Presently the chorus began to sing, as carelessly as before, the [chorus] "Va pensiero," but before they had got through half-a-dozen bars, the theatre was still as a church. The men had left off their work, one by one, and there they were, sitting about on the ladders and scaffolding, listening! When the number was finished they broke out into the noisiest applause I have ever heard, crying *Bravo, bravo, viva il maestro!* ["Long live the master!"], and beating on the woodwork with their tools. Then I knew what the future had in store for me.[9]

It is difficult to imagine a comparable reaction among stagehands at an opera house today preparing the set for any recently composed work.

# MUSIC IN THE 19TH CENTURY: A STYLISTIC OVERVIEW

The growing drive toward originality opened up a wide variety of options in every element of music: texture, melody, harmony, rhythm, and form. Almost every major composer sought to cultivate a style that was uniquely his or her own.

Textures ranged from the simple homophony of a song like Schubert's *Wanderers Nachtlied* (Anthology, discussed in Chapter 16) to the extreme complexity of a Mahler symphony (Anthology, discussed in Chapter 18). Beethoven introduced a rich array of textures in his late quartets that later composers would explore further. In his String Quartet, op. 130, for example (Anthology, discussed in Chapter 16), all four voices contribute on an essentially equal basis to the fabric of the whole in a way that sounds more like an intimate conversation among friends—the metaphor 18th-century observers had used to characterize the ideal string quartet—than any previous work in the genre.

Melodic structures similarly range from the simple to the complex. Periodic phrase structure persists but becomes increasingly less apparent and regular over the course of the century. The principal theme of the first movement of Berlioz's *Symphonie fantastique* (Example 14–1) reflects this trend. It begins with a clear antecedent-consequent structure based on units of 4 + 4 but then dissolves into a series of repeated

**EXAMPLE 14–1** Berlioz, *Symphonie fantastique*, first movement, m. 72–111: the initial appearance of the principal melody.

fragments that enter at ever higher pitches, mirroring the obsessive mental state of the artist who is the subject of the symphony's program. The harmonic direction, rhythmic structure, and thematic content do not follow any conventional pattern after the first eight measures.

Over the course of the century, harmonies became increasingly chromatic, a trend that can be traced in settings of the same poem, Goethe's "Kennst du das Land," by four different composers: Johann Friedrich Reichardt (1795; Anthology II/114, discussed in Chapter 13), Franz Schubert (1815; Anthology II/124a), Robert Schumann (1849; Anthology II/124b), and Hugo Wolf (1888; Anthology II/124c; the l9th-century settings are discussed in Chapter 16). Reichardt's setting is almost purely diatonic, whereas those by Schubert and Schumann feature chromatic passages and unexpected key contrasts while staying within a diatonic idiom. Wolf's setting, however, changes key signature 8 times within its 122 measures. By the end of the 19th century, chromaticism was no longer reserved for inflections between various points of stability. It had become a legitimate idiom in its own right: open-ended, ambiguous, and unstable in the best sense of all these terms. Franz Liszt's *Nuages Gris* ("Gray Clouds") from 1881 (Anthology II/133, discussed in Chapter 16) exemplifies this new approach.

As harmonies became increasingly chromatic, rhythm became increasingly complex. Even the initially regular rhythm of the principal idea in the first movement of Berlioz's *Symphonie fantastique* (Example 14–1) is accompanied by a metrically irregular, impulsive figure. On the final page of his Ballade in G minor, op. 23 (Anthology II/130, discussed in Chapter 16), Chopin introduces passages in rhythmic groupings of 29 and 39 notes over the span of two measures each, followed by groupings of 21 and 28 notes within individual measures (m. 246–255). Such passages cannot be played with rhythmic exactitude; instead, Chopin uses these large groupings to indicate that performers can present them freely and not in strict meter.

Composers continued to structure works according to such formal conventions of the Classical era as sonata form, scherzo (minuet), and rondo, but because of the demand for originality and innovation, they often downplayed or disguised their presence. How could a composer of genius, after all, write an original work whose formal outline could be found in a compositional textbook? Sonata form maintained its central importance in instrumental music, even for composers as disparate as Johannes Brahms and Gustav Mahler. Yet both composers were also inclined to alter the outlines of the form to make it at times unrecognizable, at least on the surface. Thus in many 19th-century sonata-form movements, particularly those written toward the end of the century, the distinctions between exposition and development or between development and recapitulation can be hard to hear.

Cyclical coherence became increasingly important to composers for multi-movement instrumental works. Compared to the subtle connections late-18th-century composers sometimes created between movements (see Chapter 12), the connections between movements in 19th-century works tend to be more overt. Probably the best-known example of such an overt thematic link is the short-short-short-long rhythmic motif that opens Beethoven's Fifth Symphony and is repeated in various transformations in every movement. The idea that a multi-movement cycle should be built around a central thematic idea reflects the increasingly prevalent view that artworks should appear organic, as if they grew from a single seed. E. T. A. Hoffmann, for example, praised Beethoven's Fifth Symphony for the unity that underlies its seeming chaos. Only on closer examination, he pointed out, would listeners discover that the symphony, like a "beautiful tree" with all its "buds and leaves, blossoms and fruits" had grown "out of a single seed." Wagner's music dramas, with their interconnected network of thematic motifs (see Chapter 17), are a late-19th-century manifestation of this organic analogy.

Published music also became more technically demanding over the course of the 19th century. Some of the most important music from this period lies beyond the technical ability of all but the most skillful performers. Orchestral writing became so intricate that conductors became a necessity. Up until the 1820s, most orchestras were conducted by the concertmaster—the principal first violinist—or the keyboard player within the basso continuo. But the increasing complexities of orchestral textures, the tendency toward more fluid changes in tempo, and the growing intricacies of rhythm created a need for a single individual—someone not playing an instrument—to coordinate and direct the ensemble. The intricate textures of works such as the finale of Brahms's Fourth Symphony (Anthology II/146, discussed in Chapter 18), the opening wind and violin figures in Mendelssohn's *Overture to A Midsummer Night's Dream* (Anthology II/119, discussed in Chapter 15), and the constantly changing and elastic tempos of the slow movement from Mahler's First Symphony (Anthology II/148, discussed in Chapter 18) demand the kind of coordination possible only with a conductor.

Orchestral rehearsals, long an exception, also became the rule. Above one particularly demanding orchestral passage in the first movement of his *Symphonie fantastique* (1830), Berlioz entered this note: "The following eleven measures are extremely difficult. I cannot recommend strongly enough to conductors that this passage be rehearsed many times and with the greatest care. . . . It would be good to have the first and second violins study their parts alone at first, then with the rest of the orchestra."[10] Here, in effect, Berlioz has invented the sectional rehearsal.

## SUMMARY

Stylistic changes between the music of the Classical era and the music of the early 19th century were neither sudden nor pronounced. Rapidly changing attitudes toward the nature and function of music in the early decades of the new century, however, exercised a profound long-term influence on the development of musical styles. Composers, seeking an original voice, developed idioms that were distinctively individual. The range of compositional choices expanded enormously in all elements of music.

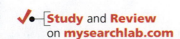
Study and Review on mysearchlab.com

## SUMMARY OF STYLE DIFFERENCES BETWEEN MUSIC OF THE CLASSICAL ERA AND 19TH CENTURY

| | CLASSICAL | 19TH CENTURY |
|---|---|---|
| **Style** | Sacred music tends to be somewhat more conservative, preserving basso continuo and much imitative writing, but most music is written in what was thought of at the time as the modern style. | Composers seek to develop a distinctly personal style; originality becomes paramount in all genres. |
| **Text setting** | Greater emphasis on sense of natural declamation, less focus on the projection of individual words. | A wide range of options from the simple to the ornate emerges. |
| **Texture** | Predominantly homophonic, especially in the early years of the Classical era, although with increasing use of nonimitative counterpoint (obbligato accompaniment) in later decades. | The polyphonic and homophonic coexist, with composers drawing on whichever approach best suits their immediate needs. |
| **Rhythm** | Periodic phrase structure predominates, but this supposedly natural symmetry is often inflected by subtle irregularities. | Periodic phrase structure continues in the works of certain repertories (dance, march), but on the whole becomes increasingly less obvious over the course of the century. |
| **Melody** | Predominantly lyrical, with emphasis on periodic phrase structure. Virtuosity remains an option, but an aesthetic of "naturalness" predominates. | Ranges from the simple to the complex. |
| **Harmony** | A relatively slower harmonic rhythm on the whole, with relatively limited and carefully controlled use of dissonance. The growing polarity of tonic and dominant allows composers to create movement-length forms on the basis of large-scale areas of harmonic stability. | Becomes increasingly chromatic over the course of the century, which makes harmonic simplicity unusual. |
| **Form** | Syntactic forms predominate, particularly binary form and its outgrowth, sonata form; rondo form becomes increasingly popular in finales from the 1780s onward. The only paratactic form of significance is the set of variations on a theme. | The large-scale formal conventions of the Classic era continue in use, but often in a manner that obscures their presence. Cyclical coherence becomes an increasingly important issue within multi-movement works. |
| **Instrumentation** | A clear distinction between vocal and instrumental parts becomes the norm. The nucleus of the modern orchestra (strings, winds, brass, percussion) emerges as the standard ensemble for large instrumental works. | The distinction between vocal and instrumental writing becomes even more pronounced. The orchestra grows in both size and instrumental variety. |

# Orchestral Music, 1800–1850

In the first half of the 19th century, the symphony and concerto became increasingly substantial in length and tone, and the concert overture provided an important new genre of program music. Performed by a large body of musicians before a large audience, these genres distinguished themselves both in scope and content from the more private spheres of chamber music, song, and short pieces for solo piano.

## BIGGER HALLS, BIGGER AUDIENCES, AND LOUDER INSTRUMENTS

With the decline of royal and aristocratic patronage in the first half of the 19th century, orchestral music became an increasingly public genre. Concert impresarios, dependent on ticket sales for revenue, sought bigger venues to boost profits. Audiences grew in size, and concert halls grew larger to accommodate them. Whereas most 18th-century symphony audiences had numbered around two to four hundred, many concert halls built during the 19th century could seat one thousand or more, and the audiences that filled them were more socially diverse than before.

These economic trends had important aesthetic implications for orchestral music. The larger halls required a new approach to orchestral sound. Ensembles grew substantially in size, particularly the string sections. Stringed instruments themselves were modified to increase the volume of sound they produced. These changes included raising the height of the bridge, lengthening the fingerboard, and increasing the angle at which it drops away from the body of the instrument. The result was a louder, more aggressive sound. Longer and heavier bows also contributed to an increase in dynamic potential. Between 1820 and 1850, most older violins, violas, and cellos were modified according to these new specifications.

Wind instruments also helped change the sound of the orchestra. The clarinet established itself as a standard orchestral instrument in the early years of the 19th century, and by the 1820s the trombone, long a fixture of the opera house, was becoming increasingly common in the concert hall. Technical developments in the flute created an instrument with a greater volume of sound and a more even tone. The "Boehm flute," named after its creator, Theobald Boehm (1794–1881), went into large-scale production in the 1840s and had become standard by the 1870s. Its all-metal design featured a cylindrical bore, larger holes, and a mechanism of padded keys, all of which helped to make the flute a more versatile instrument.

The development of valve technology for brass instruments beginning about 1815 further increased the possibilities for orchestration and texture.

Keyed valves allowed players to adjust an instrument's tubing length more easily, thereby permitting them to play chromatic intervals more cleanly across the instrument's full range. Before valves, French horn players, for example, could not have played a line with nondiatonic notes without switching instruments, from, say, a horn in B to a horn in C, something not possible in a short space of time. With valves, by contrast, they could play a long melodic line with several nondiatonic notes evenly on a single instrument. By about 1850, valved instruments—including trumpets and tubas as well as French horns—had become standard. This technological change in turn allowed composers to integrate brass more fully into the texture of the orchestra.

# THE SYMPHONY

By 1800, the symphony had established itself as the most prestigious of all instrumental genres, in part because of its size and length—four movements for a large orchestra—and in part because of its distinctly public nature.

Standard scoring around 1800, the year of Beethoven's First Symphony, consisted of double winds (flutes, oboes, clarinets, bassoons), two horns, two trumpets, timpani, and strings. New instruments were introduced into the genre steadily over the course of the century. Trombones, which had traditionally been restricted to the realms of church and theater, appear in the finale of Beethoven's Fifth Symphony, the "Storm" movement of his Sixth, and the finale of his Ninth. Instruments normally reserved for special effect, such as the piccolo, contrabassoon, bass drum, triangle, and cymbals (as, for example, in Haydn's Symphony no. 100 ("Military") and the finale of Beethoven's Ninth) became increasingly common. With so many timbral options, sonority itself became a distinctive feature of the genre, which made every major 19th-century symphonist feel compelled to some extent to create a distinctive orchestral sound.

Because the symphony required the more or less equal participation of many instruments in a large ensemble, critics came to view it metaphorically as an expression of communal spirit. The theorist Heinrich Christoph Koch, for example, wrote in 1802 that the symphony had "as its goal, like the chorus, the expression of a sentiment of an entire multitude."[1] The critic Gottfried Wilhelm Fink, writing a generation later (1835), called the symphony "a story, developed within a psychological context, of some particular emotional state of a large body of people."[2] Shortly before his death in 1883, Wagner distinguished between Beethoven's sonatas and quartets, in which "Beethoven makes music," and his symphonies, in which "the entire world makes music through him."[3] And in 1907, Gustav Mahler declared that a symphony must "belike the universe" and "embrace everything."[4]

The understanding of the symphony as a genre of universal import helps explain the readiness of 19th-century commentators to associate specific symphonies with extramusical ideas. Sometimes composers themselves provided these associations with a title (like Beethoven, who called his third symphony *Eroica*, or "heroic") or with a detailed program distributed at performances (like Berlioz for his *Symphonie fantastique*). But even works with no such explicit extramusical theme were presumed nonetheless to have some transcendent meaning. Beethoven, for example, gave no hint of any programmatic idea on the score for his Fifth Symphony. The public, however, was quick to accept what Anton Schindler, Beethoven's personal secretary, claimed was Beethoven's explanation for the symphony's famous opening—"Thus fate knocks at the door"—despite Schindler's questionable veracity. E. T. A. Hoffmann and others had already perceived in this symphony an allegory of struggle leading to victory, and Schindler's supposedly eyewitness account merely reinforced this perception.

## Beethoven's Symphonies

Beethoven's nine symphonies encompass a wide range of compositional approaches. Indeed, his symphonies are so varied that it is impossible to single out any one of them as typical. Almost all of them explore some fundamentally new approach to the genre. With the Third Symphony, for example, he extended the reach of the genre into the moral, social, and philosophical realms for the first time. The work's title, *Eroica*, evokes the ethical and political ideals associated with the French Revolution. Beethoven composed it in 1803 when Napoleon Bonaparte was beginning his conquest of Europe. The composer, who initially idealized Napoleon as an enlightened ruler, intended at one point to call the work "Grand Symphony Entitled Bonaparte"—see illustration—but changed his mind in a rage when he learned that Napoleon had

**Beethoven cancels the original title of the *Eroica* Symphony.** Beethoven, who initially idealized Napoleon Bonaparte as an enlightened ruler, became enraged when he learned that Napoleon had accepted the title of emperor. From the title page of the autograph score of the *Eroica* Symphony, it is clear that Beethoven crossed out the words *intitolata Buonaparte* after *Sinfonia grande* ("Grand Symphony entitled Bonaparte"). In his typically sloppy fashion, though, Beethoven left just enough of the words around their edges to make the original still readable. The title page shows an odd mix of Italian (the title itself) and French ("Louis van Beethoven"). Both were more fashionable than German at the time. Only later in life would Beethoven begin to give titles, tempos, and expressive markings in his native language. This reflects the rise of German as a literary language as well as a growing German nationalism, which first emerged around 1810 in part as a response to Napoleon's invasion of German-speaking lands.

**Source:** Erich Lessing/Gesellschaft der Musikfreunde, Vienna, Austria/Art Resource, NY

crowned himself emperor in 1804. In the second movement, labeled "Funeral March," Beethoven seems to confront death itself.

The Fifth Symphony (1808)—with its thematic transformation of a prominent rhythmic motive (the famous short-short-short-LONG of the work's opening), its blurring of movement boundaries (between the two final movements), and the return of an extended passage from one movement (the third) within the course of another (the fourth)—makes explicit strategies of cyclical coherence that had long been latent in earlier music. In the Sixth Symphony (*Pastoral*; 1808), Beethoven explores the potential of instrumental music to represent objects and ideas. Each of the work's five movements bears a programmatic title related to images and feelings inspired by the countryside. The verbal clues about the music's meaning range from the vague to the astonishingly specific. The first movement, for example, bears only the heading "Awakening of Happy Thoughts Upon Arriving in the Countryside," but the slow movement "Scene by the Brook" ends with an evocation of birdcalls that Beethoven actually labels by species: nightingale, cuckoo, and quail. The Seventh Symphony (1812), perhaps the most popular of all Beethoven's symphonies in the 19th century, eschews programmatic headings but explores orchestral sonorities and rhythms with unparalleled intensity.

With the Ninth Symphony (1824), Beethoven fused vocal forces into a symphonic framework. The use of a chorus and soloists to sing a portion of Friedrich Schiller's poem *An die Freude* ("To Joy") in the last movement was unusual and controversial at the time. As we have seen, it suggested to some critics an acknowledgment of the expressive limits of purely instrumental, or absolute, music. But like the Third Symphony, it confirmed the status of the symphony as a vehicle for the expression of ideas extending well beyond music.

While all of Beethoven's symphonies are innovative to varying degrees, the *Eroica* stands out as a work of singular historical significance. First performed in 1805 in the Viennese palace of its dedicatee, Prince Lobkowitz, it broke new ground in many respects. The first movement, in sonata form, is of an unprecedented length; at 691 measures it dwarfs any previous sonata-form first movement. In the slow movement, Beethoven became the first composer to make symphonic use of the **march**, a military form in duple meter characterized by a strong, repetitive beat for keeping soldiers in orderly formation. The third movement of the *Eroica* epitomizes the transformation of the 18th-century minuet—a courtly dance—into the **scherzo** (Italian for "joke"). Although the term had been used for dance-inspired movements before, the designation became standard in the 19th century. Like the *Eroica*'s third movement, scherzos tend to be faster and longer than minuets. This particular scherzo has a written-out return of the opening section; that is, it is not a straightforward da capo form after the middle-section trio. The finale, consisting of a series of variations on a theme, is proportionately substantial and complex yet at the same time readily accessible. The work as a whole, moreover, has an overarching musical trajectory, reflected in the similarity between the opening themes of the first movement and the finale. The finale, in other words, is more than the last movement of the work: it represents a culmination of the whole. Critics seeking to describe the effect of this musical trajectory have consistently described it as a passage from struggle (first movement) and death (second movement) to rebirth (third movement) and triumph (fourth movement). That this work could evoke such profound associations is both a tribute to the power of Beethoven's music and a reflection of the high regard for instrumental music as a vehicle for the expression of abstract ideas in the Romantic aesthetic.

((•—Listen
**CD9 Tracks 1–2**
**mysearchlab**
BEETHOVEN
Symphony no. 3, op.55 (*Eroica*)
Score Anthology II/116

## Primary Evidence  E. T. A. HOFFMANN'S REVIEW OF BEETHOVEN'S FIFTH SYMPHONY

*Ernst Theodor Amadeus Hoffmann (1776–1822), better known as the author of the children's tale* The Nutcracker, *was also a composer whose works include several operas and a symphony. His critical writing, however, is his greatest legacy in music. His widely read review of Beethoven's Fifth Symphony, in particular, has been extraordinarily influential. Unusually long and detailed—more so than any earlier review—it combines technical analysis with descriptive accounts of the power of the music. The excerpt here is from the opening of the review. In it Hoffmann extols instrumental, that is, "pure" music, as the most romantic of all the arts.*

■ ■ ■

When music is spoken of as an independent art, does not the term properly apply only to instrumental music, which scorns all aid, all admixture of other arts (poetry), and gives pure expression to its own peculiar artistic nature? It is the most romantic of all arts, one might almost say the only one that is genuinely romantic, since its only subject-matter is infinity. Orpheus's lyre opened the gates of Orcus. Music reveals to man an unknown realm, a world quite separate from the outer sensual world surrounding him, a world in which he leaves behind all precise feelings in order to embrace an inexpressible longing. . . .

In singing, where the poetry suggests precise moods through words, the magical power of music acts like the philosopher's miraculous elixir, a few drops of which make any drink so much more wonderfully delicious. Any passion—love, hate, anger, despair, etc.—presented to us in an opera is clothed by music in the purple shimmer of romanticism, so that even our mundane sensations take us out of the everyday into the realm of the infinite. Such is the power of music's spell that it grows ever stronger and can only burst the fetters of any other art.

It is certainly not merely an improvement in the means of expression (perfection of instruments, greater virtuosity of players), but also a deeper awareness of the peculiar nature of music, that has enabled great composers to raise instrumental music to its present level.

Mozart and Haydn, the creators of modern instrumental music, first showed us the art in its full glory; but the one who regarded it with total devotion and penetrated to its innermost nature is Beethoven. The instrumental compositions of all three masters breathe the same romantic spirit for the very reason that they all intimately grasp the essential nature of the art; yet the character of their compositions is markedly different. . . .

Haydn romantically apprehends the humanity in human life; he is more congenial, more comprehensible to the majority.

Mozart takes more as his province the superhuman, magical quality residing in the inner self.

Beethoven's music sets in motion the machinery of awe, of fear, of terror, of pain, and awakens that infinite yearning which is the essence of romanticism. He is therefore a purely romantic composer. Might this not explain why his vocal music is less successful, since it does not permit a mood of vague yearning but can only depict from the realm of the infinite those feelings capable of being described in words?

**Source:** *Allgemeine musikalische Zeitung* (Leipzig), 1810, trans. Martyn Clarke. In David Charlton, ed., *E.T.A. Hoffmann's Musical Writings* (Cambridge: Cambridge University Press, 1989), pp. 96–7, 98.

The two loud tonic chords at the opening of the first movement (Allegro con brio) provide the briefest of introductions and serve a double function: to catch the audience's attention and to allow Beethoven to introduce the principal theme at a soft volume. The metrically regular triadic opening of this theme (m. 3–6) contrasts with its syncopated, chromatic continuation (m. 7–10). The transition section (m. 45–83) is unusually long, occupying roughly 25 percent of the exposition. It contains three distinct thematic ideas, each of which will be developed later in the movement. The first idea in this secondary key area (the dominant, B♭ Major), beginning in m. 83, offers a distinct but brief contrast to the turbulence of the opening and the transition. Momentum soon builds, however, culminating in a series of syncopated chords (m. 123–131) just before the end of the exposition.

Within the development, the **fugato**—a passage that begins like a fugue but does not sustain itself after a series of initial entries—starting at m. 236 leads to a thematic standstill in a series of loud repeated chords (m. 248–283). Syncopation is empha-sized at the expense of melody. The theme beginning in m. 284 that follows these chords is one we have not heard before. The introduction of an entirely new theme in the development of a sonata-form movement was not without precedent: Haydn had done this in his *Farewell* Symphony of 1772. Beethoven, however, expands on this device in an innovative way by working his new theme into the remainder of the movement and restating it prominently in the coda.

Beethoven has additional surprises in store before the recapitulation. The long passage on the dominant between m. 338 and 358 seems to signal the end of the development section and the beginning of the retransition to the tonic. But Beethoven avoids the tonic and instead extends the development still further. The true retransition begins at m. 382 with a thinning out of the orchestral texture over an extended $V^9$ harmony. Then, in a quiet yet deeply bizarre gesture, Beethoven has a solo horn enter with the opening theme in the tonic (m. 395) while the strings are still sounding a dominant harmony. In effect, Beethoven has deliberately written an apparent mistake into the score, making it seem to an unsuspecting listener that one of the hornists has come in too early.

The recapitulation itself, which begins at m. 398, is highly unstable at first, moving from the tonic to the supertonic (F Major) after only 11 measures. The harmony finally settles firmly on the tonic with the full orchestral passage that begins in m. 430. From this point onward, the recapitulation is fairly stable. The coda, which begins in m. 557, is substantial. It amounts, in effect, to a second development section, during which the new theme introduced in m. 284 is finally restated in the tonic (beginning at m. 589).

Beethoven's second movement—the "Funeral March"—bears all the characteristic features of that genre: minor mode, slow tempo (Adagio assai), the imitation of muffled drums in the double basses, dotted rhythms in the melody, and a subsequent alternation between minor- and major-mode themes. As the diagram here indicates, the movement is structured to feature the prominent return of the mournful opening figure (A) at key points between other ideas; in other words, this Marcia funebre is very rondo-like, albeit in a much slower tempo than most rondos (see Chapter 12).

The coda of the second movement begins with a ticktock-like figure in the violins that may well represent the passing of time, a reminder of human mortality. The highly syncopated music that follows has a dreamlike quality quite different from the turbulent syncopations of the first movement. In the closing bars the opening theme returns, but it's fragmented in a way that suggests the gasping breath of the dying.

## The Symphony after Beethoven

With its vocal finale, Beethoven's Ninth Symphony provoked a crisis of confidence among composers. How, they wondered, could anyone surpass Beethoven's accom-plishments in this genre? By 1830, the future of instrumental music—the symphony in particular—had become a topic of intense debate. In 1835, Robert Schumann wrote

| BEETHOVEN'S *EROICA* SYMPHONY: THE STRUCTURE OF THE SECOND MOVEMENT | | | | | | |
|---|---|---|---|---|---|---|
| Section | A¹ | B | A² | C | A³ | Coda |
| Measure | 1 | 69 | 105 | 114 | 173 | 209 |
| Key | C minor | C Major | C minor | unstable | C minor | A♭ Major → C minor |

*Performance Perspective*

# Beethoven's *Eroica* Symphony on Period Instruments
## CD9 Tracks 3–4

This recording of the first two movements from the *Eroica*, made in 1993 by the Orchestre Révolutionnaire et Romantique and conducted by John Eliot Gardiner, is performed by an ensemble playing on instruments from Beethoven's own time or on modern copies of such instruments. The sound is markedly different from that of a standard modern-day orchestra. The strings in this recording are fewer in number (10 first violins, 8 second violins, 5 violas, 6 cellos, 3 double basses) and less penetrating in tone by virtue of gut strings and a lower bridge (see p. 383); the performers also use rather less vibrato than is customary nowadays. By way of comparison, the leading orchestras of today normally use a string section of at least 12 first violins, 12 second violins, 10 violas, 10 cellos, and 8 double basses.

The winds, too, differ in structure and sound from their modern-day equivalents. The flutes are wooden rather than metal and feature a conical rather than cylindrical bore. The resulting sound is softer and less resonant but for many listeners more "pure." The oboes, clarinets, and bassoons likewise have a more rounded sound than their modern counterparts, and the wind players also use much less vibrato than their counterparts in a standard modern orchestra. The natural horns and trumpets, without valves, sound a bit rougher around the edges but offer a more open tone. The timpani (kettledrums) are smaller and played with wooden or leather-covered stick-heads, as opposed to the more common felt stick-heads of today. The 18th-century sound is more focused and penetrating.

Orchestral textures as a whole tend to be more transparent: it is generally easier to pick out individual lines and voices in performances by a period-instrument ensemble than in performances by a modern-day orchestra. The overall volume of sound is lower—there are fewer players, and their instruments are individually less powerful—yet it should be kept in mind that concert halls in the early 19th century were considerably smaller than those of today.

Are performances on period instruments superior to those on modern instruments? Most critics would agree that instruments alone do not ensure quality—musicianship remains an essential element to any performance. Beyond this, there is widespread disagreement. Those who advocate the use of period instruments argue that such performances allow the music to be heard with the kind of sound the composers themselves would have recognized. Others maintain that today's larger concert halls were not built for smaller ensembles: period ensembles in such a setting sound feebler than they would have to Beethoven's contemporaries. An even more basic objection is that the very concept of "authenticity" is itself deeply problematic. Performance practices of earlier times varied widely even within a given locale and time, and making music involves the kind of imagination and originality that was rarely put down in writing, either in notation or in prose accounts of performance. Yet all would agree that the revival of period instruments, which grew gradually over the course of the 20th century and accelerated enormously after 1970, has increased the range of performance options available to performers and listeners alike.

**John Eliot Gardiner rehearses.** A leading figure in today's world of period-instrument ensembles, Gardiner (b. 1943) founded the Monteverdi Choir in 1964, the English Baroque Soloists in 1978, and the Orchestre Révolutionnaire et Romantique in 1989. In these and other similar ensembles, it is not only the instruments that differ from their modern equivalents but also the techniques musicians use to play them. Here, for example, the violinist is holding her instrument in a manner that was typical throughout the 18th century and much of the 19th. Her technique closely resembles one of those recommended by Leopold Mozart in his 18th-century treatise on playing the violin (see p. 325).

**Source:** peter Mares/lebrecht Music & Arts/alamy

Composer
Profile

# Ludwig van Beethoven (1770–1827)

Beethoven's contemporaries were quick to note the striking contrast between the man and his music. "Whoever sees Beethoven for the first time and knows nothing about him." wrote an observer in 1797, "would surely take him for a malicious, ill-natured, quarrelsome drunkard who has no feeling for music. . . . On the other hand, he who sees him for the first time surrounded by his fame and his glory will surely see musical talent in every feature of an ugly face."[5]

Beethoven's tendency to isolate himself from society grew with his increasing deafness, the first signs of which he acknowledged privately around the age of 30. It is unclear exactly what caused this deafness, but in the remarkable document known as the "Heiligenstadt Testament"—which Beethoven wrote in 1802 and kept hidden until his death in 1827—he reveals the pain it caused him.

Oh you men who think or say that I am malevolent, stubborn or misanthropic, how greatly do you wrong me. You do not know the secret cause which makes me seem that way to you. . . . But, think that for 6 years now I have been hopelessly afflicted, made worse by senseless physicians, from year to year deceived with hopes of improvement, finally compelled to face the prospect of *a lasting malady*. . . . If at times I tried to forget all this, oh how harshly was I flung back by the doubly sad experience of my bad hearing. Yet it was impossible for me to say to people, "Speak louder, shout, for I am deaf." Ah, how could I possibly admit an infirmity in the *one sense* which ought to be more perfect in me than in others, a sense which I once possessed in the highest perfection, a perfection such as few in my profession enjoy or ever have enjoyed.

His despair, he goes on, drove him almost to suicide. "It was only *my art* that held me back," he concedes. "Ah, it seemed to me impossible to leave the world until I had brought forth all that I felt was within me."[6]

Another document found with the Heiligenstadt Testament after Beethoven's death—a letter dated only July 6 to an unknown woman he addresses as "Immortal Beloved"—provides insight into a different side of the composer's character. The identity of the intended recipient, she either returned the letter or Beethoven never sent it, has been a matter of considerable contention. The American scholar Maynard Solomon has demonstrated convincingly that the letter dates to 1812 and the woman in question is Antonie Brentano (1780–1869). Unfortunately for Beethoven, Brentano was the wife of a prosperous Viennese merchant, hence the repeated references to the impossibility of a physical relationship. "Yes," he writes, "I am resolved to wander so long in distant lands from you until I can fly to your arms and say that I am really at home with you, and can send my soul enwrapped in you into the land of the spirits—Yes, unhappily it must be so."[7]

As if to compensate for the isolation his deafness forced on him, Beethoven's art engages life to the fullest. Some of his most famous works manifest a sense of struggle to overcome an adversity imposed by fate. The Third, Fifth, and Ninth Symphonies, in particular, follow a trajectory that has been compared to a journey from strife to victory, from darkness to light. A portrait commissioned by the composer a few years after the Heiligenstadt Testament certainly conveys this idea, showing Beethoven with his back to a scene of stormy darkness moving toward a sun-drenched field (see "Beethoven as Orpheus," page 391).

Born in Bonn in 1770, Beethoven grew up in a musical household. His father was a singer at the court there, and his grandfather had been Kapellmeister. But his father was alcoholic, and the young Beethoven had to take on adult responsibilities at an early age. He was appointed assistant organist at the court in 1782 and also played viola in the theater orchestra. Recognizing the young man's talent as a composer, the elector of Bonn (the city's ruler) arranged for him to go to Vienna to study with Haydn in 1792. Count Ferdinand Waldstein, another early supporter of the young composer, wrote prophetically in Beethoven's notebook before his departure for Vienna: "With the help of assiduous labor, you shall receive Mozart's spirit from Haydn's hands."[8] Mozart had died less than a year before (in December 1791).

Although the image of Beethoven receiving the spirit of Mozart from the hands of Haydn has become fixed in the public imagination, the composer himself did not create an immediate sensation when he arrived in Vienna, nor did he get along particularly well with Haydn. When Beethoven sent supposedly new works back to Bonn a few years later, these were exposed as compositions that he had mostly already written before he had left for Vienna. Beethoven nevertheless managed to attract the attention of an important group of aristocratic patrons in Vienna who would provide him with financial support in various ways for most of his life. When Jerome Bonaparte, Napoleon's brother, offered Beethoven a lucrative position as Kapellmeister in Kassel in 1808, a group of these aristocrats pooled their resources to keep the composer in Vienna by creating what amounted to a trust fund for him, a large sum of money that generated enough interest to provide a regular income. The last 15 years of Beethoven's life were not happy, however. Inflation ate into his income, he suffered from chronic poor health (his liver, pancreas, and intestines seem to have given him particular problems), his deafness became increasingly worse, and he became embroiled in a bitter custody battle with his sister-in-law over her son Karl, whose father was Beethoven's deceased brother. Beethoven held his sister-in-law in low regard, as did the courts, which awarded him custody of the boy in 1816. But Beethoven was not well prepared to become the single parent of a teenager, and constant struggles involving the boy over the next decade, both in and out of court, took their toll both emotionally and financially.

With so many physical ailments in his final decade, Beethoven was constantly in search of new doctors and new cures. Yet he seems to have maintained a healthy sense of ironic detachment and even humor in the face of all this. His letters and the records of his conversations (visitors wrote their comments in conversation books for the deaf composer to read) show him careening from expressions of deep physical and emotional pain to attention to the mundane details of daily life, like making sure he would have meat in the evening's soup. Most of his voluminous correspondence with publishers revolves around fees and printer's errors, yet in rare moments of openness, as in a letter of September 1824, he could also step back to survey his own output as a composer:

All too burdened with work and poor health as I am, it is necessary to have a certain amount of patience with me. I am here [in Baden, a spa outside Vienna] because of my health, or more accurately because of my illnesses. But there is already improvement. Apollo and the Muses will not yet turn me over to the Grim Reaper, for I still owe them a great deal, and before I depart for the Elysian fields [home of the deceased Greek heroes] I must leave behind what the spirit provides me and commands me to finish. It really seems to me as if I had written hardly any music at all. I wish you all good success in your exertions on behalf of art, for it is art and science alone that point toward a higher life and give us the hope of attaining that life.[9]

It is commonly (but erroneously) believed that Beethoven's music was misunderstood in his own lifetime. On the contrary, his music was extremely popular. Some of his more unconventional works, such as the *Eroica* Symphony, were not well understood at first, but this may have been because they were poorly performed as much as anything else. By 1810, Beethoven was already recognized as the greatest living composer of instrumental music. When he died in 1827, he had become a national hero. Throngs of mourners attended his funeral, hoping to catch a last glimpse of the great tone poet.

**Beethoven as Orpheus.** Anyone who sat for a portrait in Beethoven's time took great care in selecting and arranging the setting and surrounding objects. A portrait, after all, was one of the principal means by which one projected one's self to society as a whole. (People often pose for photographic portraits in the same way today.) This portrait, painted in 1804 or 1805, shows Beethoven with his back to a scene of darkness and turmoil moving toward green, sunlit fields. In his left hand he holds a lyre-guitar, a fashionable instrument of the day. The lyre is traditionally associated with Apollo and (especially) Orpheus, who had great musical powers, so the implication here is that Beethoven is a modern-day Orpheus. Only a few years later, E. T. A. Hoffmann would open his celebrated review of Beethoven's Fifth Symphony by reminding readers how the lyre of Orpheus—instrumental music—had opened up a spirit realm otherwise closed to mortals. Not coincidentally, this portrait presents a much more handsome-looking Beethoven than any other contemporary likeness.

**Source:** Ludwig van Beethoven (1770–1827), 1804 (oil on canvas) Mähler or Maehler, Willibrord Joseph (1778–1860)/Historisches Museum der Stadt, Vienna, Austria/The Bridgeman Art Library

# Ludwig van Beethoven (1770–1827) (Continued)

## BEETHOVEN'S THREE STYLES

Around the middle of the 19th century, critics and historians began to divide Beethoven's musical works into three broad style periods: early (to about 1802), middle (from roughly 1802 until 1815), and late (1815–1827). Although some disagreement has arisen about just when each of these periods begins and where certain works fit, this division has proved remarkably useful over time because it does reflect certain broad changes in Beethoven's style.

### Early Period

Like any aspiring composer, Beethoven took the works of acknowledged masters, especially Mozart and Haydn, as his model. Still, such early works as the Piano Sonatas, op. 10 and op. 13 (*Pathétique*) or the Second Symphony are hardly mere imitations of earlier composers or styles. We hear in them an original voice that is unquestionably Beethoven's.

### Middle Period

On the whole, however, it is the works of the middle period that are generally recognized as quintessentially Beethovenian: the *Waldstein* and *Appassionata* Piano Sonatas, the *Razumovsky* String Quartets, the Third through Eighth Symphonies, the Third through Fifth Piano Concertos, the Violin Concerto, and the opera *Fidelio*. The middle period style is often called "heroic" because of its evocation of struggle and triumph, as in such works as the Third Symphony (subtitled *heroic*), the Fifth Symphony, and the Third *Leonore* Overture.

### Late Period

In the last 12 years of his life, Beethoven became increasingly withdrawn from society and his music became increasingly introspective. With only occasional exceptions (most notably the Ninth Symphony), he abandoned the heroic style for one that many subsequent critics have found to be more enigmatic yet no less moving. Above all, the late works are characterized by an exploration of musical extremes in such areas as form, proportion, texture, and harmony. The finale of the Ninth Symphony, for example, conforms to no conventional pattern at all, and with its unprecedented choral conclusion it incorporates voices into what had been a purely instrumental genre. Exploring extremes of length, Beethoven wrote some of his longest works—the Ninth Symphony, the *Hammerklavier* Piano Sonata op. 106—as

well as some of his briefest, such as the almost cryptic piano works he (ironically) labeled *Bagatelles*, or "little bits of nothing." In the late style we also find extremes of texture, ranging from the simple to the extraordinarily complex. Many movements have the directness of song (such as the *Cavatina* from the String Quartet op. 130); others explore the intricacies of fugue at great length. Finally, in the late period, Beethoven exhibits an increasing sense of harmonic freedom and a kind of raw emotion in tone that is something new in music. In the middle of the *Cavatina* in the String Quartet op. 130, for example, Beethoven moves from E♭ to C♭ Major and tells the first violinist to play the lyrical melody in a manner that is *beklemmt*—literally, "caught in a vise." And indeed, the music sounds like an operatic heroine so emotionally devastated that she is gasping for breath. Beauty is no longer the primary consideration. What is primary now is psychological truth.

## PRINCIPAL WORKS

### Symphonies

Although the first two symphonies are distinctive in their own right, they operate within the traditions of the genre as transmitted by Haydn and Mozart. In contrast, the Third Symphony—the *Eroica*—is a truly revolutionary work, not only because of its size (almost twice as long as any symphony before) but also because of its structural complexity, its treatment of the orchestra, the weight of its finale, and what might be called its ethical dimension, its engagement with the idea of heroism. (Beethoven's symphonies are considered at length in this chapter.)

### Piano Sonatas

Like the symphonies, Beethoven's 32 piano sonatas explore a remarkable variety of styles. Many of these works are known by nicknames that have no connection with the composer. Op. 27, no. 1, for example, became the *Moonlight* Sonata because it reminded one critic of moonlight on a lake. The designation *Appassionata* for op. 57 derives from the passionate tone of the outer movements of the work. The name of the *Tempest* Sonata (op. 31, no. 2) comes from Anton Schindler (1795–1864), Beethoven's personal secretary, who fabricated many stories about the composer. Schindler claimed that when he asked Beethoven about the poetic program behind this sonata, the composer growled, "Go read Shakespeare's *Tempest*." (Even if the report is true, did Beethoven mean it seriously?) Other nicknames have a more solid foundation. The *Waldstein* Sonata (op. 53; discussed in Chapter 16) is in fact dedicated to Count Waldstein. And Beethoven himself, in an indisputable example of the effect of events in his life on his work, named Sonata op. 81a *Les Adieux* ("The Farewell") to commemorate the departure, exile, and return of his pupil and patron, Archduke Rudolph, who had been forced into exile by the arrival of French troops in Vienna. The late sonatas (opp. 101, 106, 109, 110, 111) enjoy a special place in the piano repertory. Op. 106 (the *Hammerklavier*) has been called the "Mount Everest of the Piano" because of its size and technical difficulty, particularly in the fugal finale. The last of these sonatas, op. 111, is in two movements, which prompted the original publisher to inquire whether or not the composer had neglected to send him the finale.

## String Quartets and Other Chamber Works

Beethoven wrote his first set of string quartets, op. 18, under the shadow of Haydn, the acknowledged master of the genre at the time. At least one of these works, however (op. 18, no. 5), takes a quartet by Mozart (K. 464) as its model. Beethoven's next set of quartets, published in 1808 as op. 59, is altogether different: larger, more difficult, and full of the heroic style associated with the Third and Fifth Symphonies. The three works as a whole are known as the *Razumovsky* Quartets by virtue of their dedicatee, the Russian ambassador to the Austrian Empire, who was also one of Beethoven's most important patrons in Vienna. All of the subsequent quartets were substantial enough to be issued individually. The *Harp* Quartet, op. 74 (so called because of its many arpeggiated pizzicato figures in the first movement) still belongs to the middle period, but op. 95 (1810) cannot be classified so easily. Many critics consider it one of the first works in the late style.

The five late quartets (opp. 127, 130, 131, 132, and 135) constitute some of the most demanding music of the 19th century, both technically and aesthetically. Indeed, for much of the 19th century, these works were seen as manifestations of Beethoven's extreme sense of isolation from the external world and were more respected than loved. In the 20th century they came to be appreciated as probing explorations of the human psyche, providing inspiration for such diverse composers as Schoenberg, Bartók, Stravinsky, and Carter.

In addition to the string quartets, Beethoven also wrote ten sonatas for violin and piano, five for cello and piano, six piano trios, five string trios, and various other chamber works in a variety of combinations for strings, winds, and piano. All of these were popular in their day and have endured as staples of the chamber repertoire.

## Vocal Music

Beethoven wrote a great deal more vocal music than most people realize. Several dozen songs, more than 100 folk-song arrangements, two substantial settings of the Mass ordinary, several secular cantatas and miscellaneous works for chorus and orchestra, an oratorio (*Christ on the Mount of Olives*), an opera (*Fidelio*, originally entitled *Leonore* and revised several times), and almost 50 canons for various numbers of voices. Given this considerable output, it must have galled Beethoven that his contemporaries almost always qualified their praise by calling him the greatest living composer of *instrumental* music.

| KEY DATES IN THE LIFE OF BEETHOVEN | |
|---|---|
| 1770 | Born December 16 in Bonn (Germany). |
| 1782 | Appointed assistant organist at the court in Bonn. |
| 1792 | With financial support from the elector of Bonn and other benefactors, goes to Vienna to study with Haydn. |
| 1801 | Acknowledges to a few close friends the onset of deafness. |
| 1802 | Writes the Heiligenstadt Testament, revealing his tumultuous inner life and near suicidal despair over his growing deafness. |
| 1809 | Declines offer from the king of Westphalia to become music director to the court there; leverages the offer to secure a fixed annual income from the pooled resources of several Viennese patrons, on the condition that he stay in Vienna. |
| 1812 | Writes passionate love letter to the "Immortal Beloved," probably Antonie Brentano. |
| 1815 | With increasing deafness, withdraws into an ever-smaller circle of friends and assistants. |
| 1816–1820s | Fights a bitter legal battle with his sister-in-law over the custody of his nephew Karl. The struggle occupies a great deal of the composer's time and energy. |
| 1827 | Dies in Vienna on March 26. |

**Beethoven's sketches for the Ninth Symphony.** Because so many of Beethoven's composition sketchbooks have survived, we know more about his working methods than those of almost any other composer before the 20th century. Some of these sketchbooks are small enough to fit in one's pocket, which is where Beethoven liked to keep them. He would jot down ideas as they came to him on walks, in coffee houses, or wherever he might find himself. Larger sketchbooks record the composer's efforts to shape thematic ideas into more promising form. Beethoven wrestled with dozens of different versions of the "Ode to Joy" theme from the finale of his Ninth Symphony before finally arriving at the tune that seems so simple and natural. Still other sketchbooks preserve Beethoven's struggle to shape a work or movement in its larger form.

**Source:** bpk, Berlin/Art Resource, NY

that after Beethoven's Ninth, there was reason to believe the dimensions and goals of the symphony had been exhausted. Schumann declared Felix Mendelssohn to have won "crown and scepter over all other instrumental composers of the day," but noted that even Mendelssohn had "apparently realized that there was nothing more to be gained" in the symphony and was now working principally within the realm of the concert overture, "in which the idea of the symphony is confined to a smaller orbit."[10] (The *Overture to a Midsummer Night's Dream*, discussed in the next section, is the kind of work Schumann had in mind here.)

Richard Wagner maintained that the Ninth Symphony effectively marked the end of the genre. With it Beethoven had demonstrated what Wagner considered the "futility" of absolute music. Any composer tempted to write a symphony now would have no choice but to copy Beethoven by including voices and text, thereby committing the sin of unoriginality, or retreat to the inadequacy of a purely instrumental format. In contrast to Wagner, other composers saw the Ninth as an aberration, a onetime experiment, and indeed, the surviving sketches for the symphony Beethoven was working on when he died suggest it would have been purely instrumental.

As it turned out, it was the French composer Hector Berlioz (1803–1869) who would be most widely acclaimed as Beethoven's true heir, not because he imitated Beethoven, but because each of his three symphonies was so strikingly original and different from anything heard before. With his brilliant and original orchestration,

## Focus  NOTABLE COMPOSERS OF SYMPHONIES, 1800–1850

Beethoven and Berlioz were not the only composers of symphonies in the first half of the 19th century. Other prominent composers cultivated this genre as well.

**FRANZ SCHUBERT** (1797–1828), by his own admission, labored under Beethoven's shadow in the realm of the symphony yet managed to produce several remarkable works of his own, including the "Unfinished" in B minor and the "Great" C-Major Symphony (so-called to distinguish it from a smaller work by Schubert in the same key). Yet neither of these symphonies was known publicly during the composer's lifetime. Robert Schumann discovered the "Great" C-Major Symphony while visiting Schubert's brother in Vienna in 1839, and the "Unfinished" did not resurface until the mid-1860s.

**FELIX MENDELSSOHN** (1809–1849) wrote a series of string symphonies in his youth and reorchestrated one of them as his First Symphony in 1824. His Second Symphony, called *Lobgesang* ("Song of Praise"), follows the pattern of Beethoven's Ninth with three instrumental movements and a vocal finale for soloists and chorus. His Third and Fourth Symphonies, known as the "Scottish" and "Italian," reflect the impressions of his travels. His Fifth Symphony ("Reformation") is actually a much earlier

work than its number would imply. It features Luther's hymn *Ein feste Burg ist unser Gott* (A Mighty Fortress Is Our God) in its instrumental female.

**ROBERT SCHUMANN** (1810–1856) composed four symphonies, all of them purely instrumental, between 1841 and 1850. While none has an explicit program, Schumann gave descriptive titles to the first ("Spring") and third ("Rhenish"—that is, having to do with the Rhine region). The "Rhenish" includes a folk-like dance in its third movement and a wonderfully dark, contrapuntal slow movement in which the low brass and strings predominate. Its finale, like the finale of the Second Symphony, recalls and transforms musical ideas from earlier movements.

**LUDWIG SPOHR** (1784–1859) enjoyed wide renown during his lifetime as a symphonist. He cultivated the programmatic symphony more than any other major composer of his generation. Most notable among these is his "Historical Symphony," with the first movement reflecting the style of "The Bach-Handel Period (1720)," the slow second movement "The Haydn-Mozart Period (1780)," the scherzo "The Beethoven Period (1810)," and the finale "The Latest Period (1840)."

---

his fresh approach to the grand scale of the genre, and his ability to blend music and narrative, he demonstrated for subsequent composers that it was possible to follow Beethoven's spirit of originality without directly imitating him. The symphonies of Liszt and Mahler, in particular, are deeply indebted to the legacy of Berlioz.

All three of Berlioz's symphonies are programmatic to varying degrees. The first of them, the *Symphonie fantastique* of 1830, as already mentioned, is based on a detailed program of Berlioz's own invention. Inspired by the composer's infatuation with an actress named Harriet Smithson, the program relates the increasing emotional turmoil of a young musician as he realizes the woman he loves is spurning him (see Primary Evidence: Berlioz's Program for the *Symphonie fantastique*). The emotional trajectory of the symphony is thus almost the reverse of Beethoven's Ninth. Beethoven's symphony moves from a turbulent first movement to a joyous finale; the *Symphonie fantastique*, in contrast, moves from a joyous first movement, which evokes of the young musician's first infatuation, to a dark finale, labeled "Dream of a Witches' Sabbath," which evokes the image of the musician's beloved dancing demonically at his funeral. The sounding of the *Dies irae* ("Day of Wrath") from the well-known plainchant Mass for the Dead within the finale serves as a dark counterpoint to Beethoven's theme for the vocal setting of Schiller's "Ode to Joy" in the finale of the Ninth. Instead of a vision of heaven, we are given a vision of hell and the triumph of evil.

Not everyone found Berlioz's program for his *Symphonie fantastique* helpful. Robert Schumann, in an otherwise favorable review of the work, argued that the movement

## Primary Evidence BERLIOZ'S PROGRAM FOR THE *SYMPHONIE FANTASTIQUE*

*Berlioz was for many years adamant about the importance of the program: "At concerts where this symphony is to be performed," he once declared, "it is essential that this program be distributed in advance in order to provide an overview of the dramatic structure of this work." The program exists in two versions. The one given here is from the published score of 1845; a later edition presents the entire story as an opium-inspired dream that is part of an unsuccessful suicide attempt. In the end, however, Berlioz rejected both programs, wearied no doubt by the lavish attention given his prose at the expense of his music. The frequent ellipses in the program are Berlioz's own. The ranz des vaches is a shepherd's call, frequently associated with reed instruments in orchestral compositions of this era. The Dies irae in the last movement is a chant sung during the Mass for the Dead. The text is apocalyptic. It is safe to say that every member of Berlioz's original audience would have recognized this melody (and its implicit text) at once.*

■ ■ ■

(1) Dreams—Passions. The author imagines that a young musician, afflicted with that malady of the spirit called the *vague des passions* by one well-known writer, sees for the first time a woman who embodies all the charms of the ideal being of his dreams, and he falls hopelessly in love with her. By bizarre peculiarity, the image of the beloved always presents itself to the soul of the artist united with a musical idea that incorporates a certain character he bestows to her, passionate but at the same time noble and shy.

This melodic image and its source pursue him ceaselessly as a double *idée fixe*. This is the reason for the persistent appearance, in every movement of the symphony, of the melody that begins the opening Allegro. The transition from this state of melancholic reverie, interrupted by a few spasms of unfounded joy, to one of delirious passion, with its animations of fury, jealousy, its return to tenderness, its tears, its religious consolations—this is the subject of the first movement.

(2) A Ball. The artist finds himself in the most varied situations in the middle of the tumult of a party, in the peaceful contemplation of the beauties of nature. But everywhere—in the city, in the countryside—the cherished image of his beloved presents itself to him and troubles his spirit.

(3) Scene in the Countryside. Finding himself in the countryside one evening, he hears in the distance two shepherds conversing with each other through a *ranz des vaches*. The pastoral duet, the scenic setting, the light rustling of the trees sweetly swayed by the wind, some reasons for hope that have lately come to his knowledge—all unite to fill his heart with unaccustomed tranquility and lend a brighter color to his fancies. He reflects upon his isolation; he hopes that he will not be lonely too much longer. . . . But if she should be deceiving him! . . . This mixture of hope and fear, these thoughts of happiness troubled by certain dark presentiments constitute the subject of the Adagio movement. At the end, one of the shepherds resumes the *ranz des vaches*; the other no longer responds. . . . Distant noise of thunder . . . solitude . . . silence. . . .

(4) March to the Scaffold. Convinced that his love has been ignored, the artist poisons himself with opium. The dose of the narcotic is too weak to kill him and plunges him into a sleep accompanied by the most horrible visions. He dreams that he has killed the woman he loved, that he is condemned, led to the scaffold, and is to witness his own execution. The procession moves to the sound of a march at times somber and fierce, at times brilliant and solemn, in which the muffled noise of the heavy footsteps is followed without any transition by the noisiest outbursts. At the end of the march, the first four measures of the *idée fixe* reappear like a final thought of love interrupted by the fatal blow [of the guillotine].

(5) Dream of a Witches' Sabbath. He sees himself at the Sabbath, in the middle of a frightening troupe of ghosts, sorcerers, monsters of every kind, all gathered for his funeral rites. Strange noises, groans, bursts of laughter, distant cries to which other cries seem to respond. The beloved melody reappears, but it has lost its noble and shy character. It is nothing more than the melody of a common dance, trivial and grotesque; it is she who comes to join the Sabbath. . . . A roar of joy at her arrival. . . . She throws herself into the diabolical orgy. . . . Funeral knell, burlesque parody of the *Dies irae*. Witches' Round Dance. The dance and *Dies irae* combined.

titles alone would have been sufficient, and that "word of mouth would have served to hand down the more circumstantial account, which would certainly arouse interest because of the personality of the composer, who lived through the events of the symphony himself." German listeners in particular, Schumann argued, disliked having their thoughts "so rudely directed," all the more so given their "delicacy of feeling and aversion to personal revelation." But Berlioz, Schumann rationalized, "was writing primarily for his French compatriots, who are not greatly impressed by refinements of modesty. I can imagine them, leaflet in hand, reading and applauding their countryman who has depicted it all so well; the music by itself does not interest them."[11]

## Primary Evidence — HEINRICH HEINE ON BERLIOZ, HARRIET SMITHSON, AND THE *SYMPHONIE FANTASTIQUE*

*The German poet Heinrich Heine (1797–1856) spent most of his adult life in self-imposed exile in Paris. His "Letters on the French Stage" (1837) include an intriguing anecdote about Berlioz. The account probably doctors the truth—no evidence indicates that Berlioz ever played the timpani in the Conservatory orchestra, for example—but it captures the spirit of the* Symphonie fantastique *and Berlioz's passion for the young woman who inspired it.*

■ ■ ■

It is a shame he has had his hair cut. I will always remember him the way I saw him for the first time, six years ago, with his antediluvian hair style, his hair standing on end, over his forehead like a forest growing on the edge of a steep cliff. The setting was the Conservatory of Music, during a performance of a great symphony by him. . . . The best part of the work was a Witches' Sabbath, in which the Devil said Mass and Catholic church music was parodied with the most terrifying, bloodiest foolery. It is a farce in which all the secret serpents that we carry in our hearts come gladly hissing up to the surface. The fellow sitting next to me, a talkative young man, pointed out to me the composer, who was sitting at the far end of the concert hall in a corner of the orchestra, playing the timpani. For the timpani is his instrument. "Do you see there in the stage-box," my neighbor said to me, "that fat Englishwoman? That is Miss Smithson; Monsieur Berlioz has been madly in love with her for three years, and it is this passion we have to thank for the symphony we are now hearing." And in fact, Miss Smithson, the famous actress from Covent Garden, was sitting in the stage-box. Berlioz kept looking directly at her, and every time their gazes met, he would pound away on his drum as if possessed. Miss Smithson has since become Madame Berlioz, and her husband has gotten his hair cut. When I heard the Symphony once again at the Conservatory this past winter, Berlioz was sitting there again as the timpanist in the back of the orchestra, the fat Englishwoman was again sitting in the stage-box, their gazes met once again . . . but this time he no longer beat the drum so furiously.

**Harriet Smithson, the inspiration for the *idée fixe* in Berlioz's *Symphonie fantastique*.** Harriet Smithson (1800–1854) was an Irish actress and a member of a theatrical troupe that performed Shakespeare's plays in English in Paris in the late 1820s. Berlioz fell in love with her and worshipped her from afar for several years before actually meeting her. They married in 1833 but separated definitively in 1844. The day after her death, Berlioz remarried.

**Source:** Portrait of Harriet Smithson (1800–54) (oil on canvas), French School, (19th century)/Private Collection, Lauros/Giraudon/The Bridgeman Art Library International

**Source:** The Art Gallery Collection/Alamy Limited

# Hector Berlioz (1803–1869)

Berlioz, admired today as one of the most original of 19th-century composers, was an outsider almost all of his life. Born in a rural province of southern France, he had to fight to make his way in the bitterly partisan world of Parisian musical politics. By the time he won the grudging admiration of his countrymen, he was nearing the end of his life, and he was never embraced in his native France the way he was in Germany.

Berlioz's father, a physician, sent his son to Paris to study medicine. The young Hector wrote home regularly to report on the progress of his course work and just as regularly to ask for more money. In fact, however, the youth had largely given up attending classes and was busy immersing himself in the local musical scene. This charade could not continue indefinitely, of course, and Berlioz eventually found himself on his own. In 1826, he enrolled in the Paris Conservatory, whose teachers considered him talented but willful and undisciplined. Every year the Conservatory held a contest among its composition students for an award—the coveted Prix de Rome—that automatically opened doors of opportunity for the winner. Berlioz yearned for the prize but failed to win it several years in a row. Finally, in desperation, he resigned himself to writing in a style he knew the judges would like, and he won in 1830.

During this same period, Berlioz was composing the stunningly original *Symphonie fantastique*. The woman who inspired this work, the subject of its thematic *idée fixe* and the object of Berlioz's infatuation, was the Irish actress Harriet Smithson, whom he first saw in a performance of Shakespeare's *Hamlet* in 1827. He eventually met and married her, but the marriage did not last.

The Prix de Rome required winners to spend two years in Italy, and shortly after the premiere of the *Symphonie fantastique* in December 1830, Berlioz left for what he called his "exile" there. He no longer wanted to go, for it meant being away from his beloved Harriet, not to mention such important musical events as the Parisian premiere of Beethoven's Ninth Symphony. Felix Mendelssohn, also in Rome at the time, wrote home with this amusing impression of his French colleague:

Berlioz consumes himself without a spark of talent; he gropes in the dark, thinking himself the creator of a new world. All the while he writes the most grotesque things, dreaming and thinking of nothing but Beethoven, Schiller, and Goethe. At the same time, he is possessed of boundless vanity and looks down grandly on Mozart and Haydn.... But just as I am about to strangle him, he waxes enthusiastic about Gluck, and on that point I must agree with him.[13]

After his return to Paris in 1832, Berlioz struggled to get a commission from the Opéra, the city's most prestigious musical institution, but the politics of artistic patronage conspired against him on repeated occasions. He turned to music journalism to supplement his income, and his reviews still make fascinating reading.

**The shock of the loud: Berlioz conducts (1846).** Like any caricature, this one builds on an element of truth. Audiences in the 19th century found Berlioz's orchestras enormous, his music staggeringly loud. Berlioz was also among the first virtuoso conductors. Until roughly 1830, ensembles had been led by the principal first violinist, the concertmaster, or by a keyboard player seated at the piano or harpsichord. By 1850, the conductor had come to be seen as a true interpreter of the music at hand, not merely as someone who kept the ensemble together. Weber, Mendelssohn, and Ludwig Spohr, like Berlioz, were esteemed as both conductors and composers.

**Source:** The Art Gallery Collection/Alamy Limited

In later decades, Berlioz received greater acclaim from abroad, particularly from Germany and Russia, than at home in France. In 1843, he published a ground-breaking textbook on orchestration that took into account the new possibilities of the orchestra's changing instruments. The text would later be revised by that other 19th-century master of orchestration, Richard Strauss, and it is still in use in many music conservatories.

# PRINCIPAL WORKS

## Symphonies and Concert Overtures

Berlioz's three major symphonies rank among the greatest works of their kind in the 19th century. Each is utterly different from the other, but all have a literary foundation: The *Symphonie fantastique* (1830) follows a prose program of Berlioz's own invention. *Harold en Italie* (1834) draws on Byron's epic poem *Childe Harold's Pilgrimage*, and *Roméo et Juliette* (1839) is based on Shakespeare's *Romeo and Juliet*. It was the novelty and variety of these various approaches to the genre that led Berlioz's German contemporaries to hail him as Beethoven's true successor.

The works of a variety of authors, from Shakespeare to Sir Walter Scott, inspired Berlioz's concert overtures. These include *Waverly* (1828), *Les francs-juges* (1828), *King Lear* (1831), *Rob Roy* (1832), and *Le Corsaire* (1844). Building on Beethoven's accomplishments in this genre, Berlioz's overtures are important forerunners to the symphonic poems that Liszt and Richard Strauss would compose later in the century.

## Operas

Although admired, Berlioz's two operas have never achieved widespread popularity. *Benvenuto Cellini* (1838) traces the life of the celebrated Renaissance sculptor. *Les Troyens* (The Trojans, 1859) is based on the story of the Trojan War. Only the second half of this work was ever performed during Berlioz's lifetime; the complete opera was not produced in its original French until 1920, and then not in Paris, but in Rouen.

## Vocal Music

Berlioz wrote several unstaged vocal works that are difficult to classify but always dramatic in spirit. These include the massive *Requiem* (1837), which calls for antiphonal orchestras and choruses; *L'Enfance du Christ* (The Infancy of Christ, 1854), a "sacred trilogy"; and *La Damnation de Faust* (1846), an *opéra en concert* (concert opera). *Lélio, or the Return to Life* (1831), a sequel to the *Symphonie fantastique*, is a unique mixture of orchestral music, chorus, song, and melodrama. In 1841, building on the tradition of the French chanson, Berlioz invented a new genre with his song cycle for voice and orchestra, *Les nuits d'été* (Summer Nights, 1841).

| KEY DATES IN THE LIFE OF BERLIOZ | |
|---|---|
| 1803 | Born at Côte-Saint-André (southern France) on December 11. |
| 1821 | Goes to Paris to study medicine so he might follow in the footsteps of his father, a physician. |
| 1826 | Abandons medicine and enrolls in the Paris Conservatory, where he is as unhappy with the instructors as they are with him. |
| 1826–1829 | Applies unsuccessfully for the coveted Prix de Rome; all three of his compositions for this competition are rejected. |
| 1830 | Wins the Prix de Rome with a more conventional composition. |
| 1833 | Marries Harriet Smithson, an Irish actress whom he has worshipped from a safe distance for many years and who was the inspiration for his *Symphonie fantastique* (1830). The marriage is a disaster, however, and ends in separation in 1844. He remarries after her death in 1854. |
| 1842 | Makes the first of several successful tours of Germany, where his symphonies are greeted with greater enthusiasm than in France. |
| 1843 | Publishes his *Treatise on Instrumentation and Orchestration*, a work that would subsequently go through many editions and be translated into many languages. |
| 1852 | Appointed librarian of the Paris Conservatory, an honorary post but one that acknowledges his place in the musical world of France. |
| 1869 | Dies in Paris on March 8. |

Whatever their response to the program, listeners were universally impressed by the work's orchestration. More than any composer before or since, Berlioz expanded the sound of the orchestra. The instruments called for in the *Symphonie fantastique* of 1830 were extraordinary in both number and variety:

| | |
|---|---|
| 2 Flutes (one doubling on piccolo) | Timpani |
| 2 Oboes (one doubling on English horn) | Bass drum |
| 2 Clarinets in B♭, A, C, E♭ | Snare drum |
| 4 Bassoons | Cymbals |
| 4 Horns in E♭, E, F, B♭, C | Bells |
| 2 Cornets in B♭, A, G | 2 Harps |
| 2 Trumpets in C, B♭, E♭ | Strings (at least 15 first violins and 15 second violins, 10 violas, 11 cellos, and 9 double basses, according to the composer) |
| 3 Trombones | |
| 2 Ophicleides [a forerunner of the tuba] | |

Berlioz's handling of the orchestra was also unusually forward looking for 1830. At the beginning of the *Symphonie fantastique*, for example, he calls for the high winds to play *pp*, then *ppp*, and then to decrescendo, presumably to an inaudible level. And in the fourth movement, the "March to the Scaffold," he introduces a brass sound never before heard in the concert hall: massive, forceful, and rhythmically charged. Berlioz also peppers his scores with instructions of a hitherto unknown specificity. In the *Symphonie fantastique*, for example, he marked exactly what kind of stick head— wood, leather, or felt—percussionists should use in any given passage. Previously this kind of choice would have been up to the individual performer.

The *Symphonie fantastique* is also notable for its realism: Berlioz avoids prettifying ugly or grotesque themes, representing them instead with what were, for the time, harsh-sounding musical devices. The last movement, "Dream of a Witches' Sabbath," for example, opens with an extended diminished seventh chord, a dissonance that may seem rather tame (even clichéd) today, but that would have sounded jarring at the time, conjuring for listeners a world of dark spirits. In m. 11, Berlioz briefly dispenses almost completely with triadic harmony in his effort to conjure the chaos and depravity of the imagined gathering of witches. The strings play a series of fourths mediated by an occasional third (C-F-B-E/G-C-F-B/D-G-C), rather like the tuning of a guitar, the only instrument Berlioz himself ever mastered. The moment is fleeting, but it signals the beginning of an assault on what had been the foundation of Western harmony for at least two centuries. The return of the *idée fixe*, the theme associated with the beloved, in m. 40 on the E♭ clarinet is also fittingly grotesque. The beloved, according to the program, has lost her noble and shy character and assumed the form of a witch.

# THE CONCERT OVERTURE

The **concert overture** grew out of the 18th-century tradition of performing opera overtures in the concert hall independently of the operas for which they had been written. Mozart, for example, wrote an alternate ending to his overture to *Don Giovanni* so it could be performed outside the theater. But because most listeners of the time would have known the plot of *Don Giovanni*, they associated the drama with the overture; these connections were further reinforced by the overture's use of music that appears within the opera itself.

By the early 19th century, then, the overture had emerged as a work of instrumental music in a single movement connected in some way with a known plot. Overtures themselves became increasingly dramatic, none more so than Beethoven's *Leonore* Overture no. 3 (op. 72a, 1806), one of four different overtures Beethoven wrote for his opera *Fidelio* (entitled *Leonore* in its original version). The plot of *Fidelio* involves faithful love and political injustice. Florestan, imprisoned for his political beliefs by Don Pizarro, a wicked governor, languishes in jail. To free him, his wife, Leonore, disguises herself as a man, takes the name Fidelio ("Faithful One"), and gains the confidence of Florestan's jailer. After long months of menial work, she is finally allowed to take a few scraps of bread and some water to the dungeon that houses the "most dangerous" of all the jail's prisoners, Florestan. But just as she is about to spring her husband free, Don Pizarro appears, intent on killing Florestan. Leonore intervenes and reveals her true identity. Just then an enlightened state minister arrives, saves the couple, frees the rest of the prisoners, and punishes Pizarro.

Beethoven's *Leonore* Overture no. 3 wordlessly encapsulates this drama. It opens with a darkly chromatic slow introduction in C minor before moving to a buoyant Allegro in C Major. The end of the turbulent development reenacts the arrival of the minister with an offstage trumpet fanfare, and the recapitulation provides the climactic moment of triumph. The blaze of C Major at the end of the overture reflects the release of all the political prisoners.

Why did Beethoven reject this overture? It is certainly one of his most dramatic instrumental works, but in a way, it was perhaps *too* dramatic. By encapsulating the emotional trajectory of the entire story—gloom, hope, despair, rescue, jubilation—Beethoven had created an overture that he may have felt made the opera itself something of an anticlimax. We can only speculate, but perhaps he felt the same way about this overture that Ludwig Tieck did about Reichardt's overture to Shakespeare's *Macbeth* (see Primary Evidence: The Perceived Superiority of Instrumental Music in Chapter 14). The instrumental overture had outgrown its function as a mere introduction, and so Beethoven chose to publish it as a separate work. In its place, he composed a much shorter, less dramatic, but more effective overture for *Fidelio*, the one played before the opera in performances today.

Functionally, then, the *Leonore* Overture no. 3 had been transformed from an introduction to a dramatic work intended for performance in the opera house to a drama in its own right intended for performance in the concert hall. And it was this transformation that gave rise to a new genre: the concert overture, a single-movement work that is in some way associated with a drama, poem, place, event, or mood.

Inspired by Beethoven's example, other composers began writing overtures expressly for the concert hall. Felix Mendelssohn wrote his *Overture to A Midsummer Night's Dream* when he was 17 years old as a stand-alone work; only later did he compose additional movements to make the work suitable as incidental music for a theatrical production of Shakespeare's play. Unlike Beethoven's *Leonore* Overture no. 3, the piece does not recount the drama in brief. Instead, Mendelssohn presents a succession of themes representing the play's main characters. The opening five measures, given entirely to the winds, draw us into the enchanted forest that is the setting for much of the play. The scurrying high-pitched figure in the strings that begins in m. 5 conjures up the kingdom of the fairies, led by Oberon and Titania, whereas the pompous theme that begins at m. 62 suits Theseus, the human ruler. The first theme in the secondary key area (beginning at m. 130) corresponds to the young humans—two women and two men—who over the course of the play, through magic, will fall in and out of love with one another in various combinations. Finally, the exposition's closing theme (beginning at m. 195) is clearly associated with the "rude mechanicals," the

((•─ Listen
**CD9  Track 4**
**mysearchlab**
MENDELSSOHN
*Overture to A Midsummer Night's Dream*
Score Anthology II/118

artisans who present a play-within-a-play. One of these artisans, Bottom the weaver, at one point in the play appears with the head of an ass, a transformation reflected in the music by an unmistakable braying sound at m. 200 and elsewhere. In the development section (beginning at m. 250), the scurrying theme associated with fairies predominates. One of the ways Mendelssohn captures the sometimes chaotic magical spirit of the midsummer night's forest here is through the simultaneous use of disparate dynamics. At m. 294, for example, he brings in the horns *fortissimo, con tutta la forza* ("with all possible force"), even as the strings and high winds maintain their elfin *pianissimo* figures.

Mendelssohn himself outlined the work's thematic associations in a remarkable letter of February 15, 1833, to his publisher. The composer is reluctant to equate the music and the stage action directly, yet he cannot deny they are connected. He coyly explains his music by altering the sequence of events in the drama to correspond with the sequence of events in his composition. Shakespeare's drama does not open with the fairies, for example, but rather with a scene at the court of Theseus.

**Shakespeare's *Midsummer Night's Dream*, Act IV, scene 1.** Titania, queen of the Fairies, has been cast under a magical spell and is attracted to Bottom, a mortal whose head has been transformed into that of a donkey. She asks if he would like to hear music. Bottom says he would and declares that he has "a reasonable good ear for music."

**Source:** INTERFOTO/Fine Arts/Alamy

It is not possible for me to indicate the course of ideas in this composition for the printed concert program, for this course of ideas *is* my overture. The piece is nevertheless closely associated with the play, and thus it might perhaps be quite appropriate to indicate to the public the main events of the drama, to remind them of Shakespeare's play. . . . I believe it would suffice to recall how the elf-royalty, Oberon and Titania, appear with all their train throughout the play, at one moment here, at another there; then comes Duke Theseus of Athens, who goes hunting in the forest with his bride-to-be; then the two pairs of tender lovers, who lose and find one another; and finally the troop of clumsy, coarse tradesmen, who pursue their heavy-handed amusements; then the elves once again, who tease all of them—it is precisely out of all this that the work is constructed. When at the end everything is resolved and the main characters depart fortunate and happy, the elves follow them, bless the house, and disappear as the morning dawns. So ends the play, and my overture too. I would prefer it if on the printed program you would summarize only this content and said nothing further about my music, so that it can simply speak for itself, if it is good; and if it is not good, then no explanation will help at all.[12]

Mendelssohn, in other words, admits to broad parallels between his music and the play, but not to explicit thematic connections. His ambivalence reflects the feelings of many composers about the question of "meaning" in their music. Clearly, Mendelssohn wanted his listeners to associate his overture with Shakespeare's play, but he also wanted them to accept his composition on its own terms, as music. Whatever Mendelssohn felt, audiences liked to hear explicit thematic connections of the kind he tried to play down. An *Overture to A Midsummer Night's Dream*, it seems, is easier to focus on than the same work with an abstract title like Overture in E Major.

Mendelssohn wrote many other popular concert overtures in addition to the *Overture to A Midsummer Night's Dream*. These include *The Hebrides* (also known as *Fingal's Cave*), which conjures up a landscape off the Scottish coast; *Calm Seas and a Prosperous Voyage*, which is based on a poem of the same title by Goethe; and *The Fair Melusine*, which reflects a folktale about a mermaid who takes on human form.

Over the course of the 19th century, a great many commentators created programs for instrumental works that had none, often in an attempt to make the difficult and highly abstract art of instrumental music more approachable to untrained listeners. The need for such clues was driven at least in part by the growing formal, harmonic, and rhythmic complexity of the music. Listeners perplexed by Mahler's First Symphony in the last decade of the 19th century, for example, accused the composer of having suppressed the work's program (which in fact is precisely what he had done). The work would have been far more intelligible, they insisted, had its story been revealed to them.

# THE CONCERTO

The 19th century was the age of the great instrumental composer-virtuoso. The violinist Niccolò Paganini (1782–1840), Joseph Joachim (1831–1907), and Pablo de Sarasate (1844–1908) all wrote concertos for themselves, as did the pianists Beethoven, Chopin, Mendelssohn, Clara Schumann, Brahms, Liszt, and Grieg. As with Vivaldi and Mozart, the concerto provided the ideal vehicle for a composer-performer to show off his or her talents in both fields at once.

## Composer Profile

# Felix Mendelssohn (1809–1847)

Mendelssohn was born into a prominent family whose fame was unconnected to music. His grandfather, Moses Mendelssohn, was one of the leading philosophers of his day, and his father, Abraham Mendelssohn, was a very successful banker in Berlin. Abraham converted to Christianity and added "Bartholdy" to the family's name, hence the designation Felix Mendelssohn Bartholdy (often with an erroneous hyphen).

Felix was the greatest child prodigy of his age, both as a composer and as a pianist. The prestigious Singakademie of Berlin performed his setting of the 19th Psalm in 1819, and the young child traveled across Europe in much the same way as Mozart had half a century before. By the time he was 17, he had already written the Octet for strings, op. 20 and the *Overture to a Midsummer Night's Dream*, op. 21. He also excelled as a conductor. In 1828, on the hundredth anniversary of its premiere, he led a hugely successful performance of J. S. Bach's *Saint Matthew Passion*, a then-forgotten work he had helped rediscover.

Mendelssohn was closely attached to his sister, Fanny (1805–1847), who was a talented pianist and composer in her own right. After her marriage in 1829, she published several books of songs and many short piano pieces under the name Fanny Mendelssohn Hensel. She shared her brother's interest in the music of J. S. Bach and remained his closest musical confidante until her sudden death at the age of 41. Biographers have speculated, in fact, that her brother's intense grief hastened his own sudden demise later that same year.

Mendelssohn's death occasioned prolonged public mourning across Europe, and numerous writers speculated on the bleak future of music without him. Within a decade, however, he had become the favorite target of ridicule by musicians who thought of themselves as progressive. To these figures, particularly Wagner, Mendelssohn represented the most conservative elements of music. In the 1930s and 1940s, Mendelssohn became the object of vicious attacks from Germany's Nazi regime because of his Jewish ancestry.

Mendelssohn's music can seem almost too beautiful at times, too effortless. And against the paradigm of Beethoven and other 19th-century composers, Mendelssohn might appear more a member of the establishment, both personally and professionally. He never rebelled against anything and was the darling of both Prussian and English royalty, and in this respect he does

**Felix Mendelssohn.** In contrast to the many likenesses of Beethoven that portray him as a fiery individualist, this image of Mendelssohn done by J. W. Childe in 1829 portrays the composer as a gentleman. Mendelssohn's lack of personal rebelliousness has contributed to his image as a conservative who was unwilling to assault tradition in the manner of his near-contemporaries Berlioz, Liszt, and Wagner. Mendelssohn is shown here on the first of his ten trips to England, where he was idolized both as a composer and as a conductor.

**Source:** Ruth Schacht. Musikabteilung, Mendelssohn-Archiv/bpk, Berlin/ Art Resource, NY

not fit the popular image of the Romantic composer. Yet his private letters reveal a far more complex personality than is generally recognized.

# PRINCIPAL WORKS

## Symphonies and Other Orchestral Works

Mendelssohn wrote several symphonies for strings in his youth and arranged one of them for full orchestra in 1824 as his First Symphony, op. 11. Later, however, he repudiated this and several other works in the genre, including his *Reformation* Symphony (1832), whose finale includes the melody from Martin Luther's famous hymn "A Mighty Fortress Is Our God." Mendelssohn allowed only a few performances of the *Italian* Symphony in the mid-1830s, which has since become his most popular, and appears never to have been completely satisfied with it. The *Scottish* Symphony, op. 56 (1842), was the one work in the genre Mendelssohn allowed to be published. (Although first performed as a symphony, the *Lobgesang* of 1840 was later redesignated a symphony-cantata.)

The concert overtures have fared even better with audiences than the symphonies. Three of them—*The Hebrides* (also known as *Fingal's Cave*), *A Midsummer Night's Dream*, and *The Fair Melusine*—are staples of the orchestral repertory today. In these works, Mendelssohn combined programmatic elements with symphonic writing on a smaller scale, and his contributions in this area exercised a profound influence on later composers of symphonic poems. The Violin Concerto in E minor, op. 64, remains a touchstone of the repertory. The two piano concertos, widely performed in their time, have not fared as well.

## Chamber Works

Aside from the youthful Octet op. 20, Mendelssohn's chamber music—piano trios, string quartets, and string quintets—is not performed as much as it deserves. The early string quartets, opp. 12 and 13, are among the few works of their kind written under the direct influence of Beethoven's late quartets. The later chamber music, in particular, features a distinctly personal idiom that integrates counterpoint and lyricism.

## Piano Works

The 48 *Lieder ohne Worte* ("Songs without Words"), published in 48 separate books, were enormously successful in their time. The piano sonatas and various other miniatures combine brilliance with substance.

## Vocal Music

The oratorios *Paulus* (1836) and *Elijah* (1846) enjoyed extraordinary popularity in the 19th century, particularly in England. Choral societies there were quick to add these works to their repertories alongside the oratorios of Handel, which served as Mendelssohn's principal model in the genre. The choral writing, inspired by Bach as well as Handel, is among the most powerful and moving of the entire 19th-century repertory. Mendelssohn also wrote many works for a cappella chorus, some of them in a deliberately archaic style, evoking the music of earlier composers such as Palestrina and Bach.

| KEY DATES IN THE LIFE OF MENDELSSOHN | |
|---|---|
| 1809 | Born February 3 in Hamburg. |
| 1819 | Becomes a member of the Berlin Singakademie; its director, Carl Friedrich Zelter, introduces the young Mendelssohn to Goethe in 1821, initiating a friendship that would continue until the poet's death in 1832. |
| 1826 | Composes his *Overture to A Midsummer Night's Dream*. |
| 1828 | Conducts Bach's *Saint Matthew Passion* with the Berlin Singakademie on March 11, almost exactly one hundred years after the work's premiere; the work, essentially unknown to 19th-century audiences, sparks renewed interest in Bach's music. |
| 1829 | Makes the first of ten trips to England, where he becomes the most beloved composer of his generation, helped in part by the favor and patronage of Queen Victoria and Prince Albert. |
| 1836 | Becomes conductor of the Leipzig Gewandhaus Orchestra, which he builds into the leading orchestra of Europe. Also initiates a series of "historical concerts" with music by composers of previous generations. |
| 1843 | Helps establish the Leipzig Conservatory, which soon becomes the leading institution of its kind in Germany and second in prestige only to the Paris Conservatory. |
| 1847 | Dies in Leipzig after a brief illness on November 4. |

Most 19th-century concertos maintained the three-movement, fast-slow-fast format of the Classical era. With the decline of basso continuo in the late 18th century, however, the role of the soloist in the concerto changed significantly. No longer obligated to support or play along with the ensemble during tutti sections, the soloist instead waited in silence before making a grand entrance. Unlike the symphony and concert overture, the concerto remained a mostly nonprogrammatic genre, at least on the surface. Few composers openly associated their concertos with extramusical ideas, yet audiences could not help but hear drama in the interplay between soloist and orchestra.

The interplay between soloist and orchestra in the second movement of Beethoven's Fourth Piano Concerto, op. 58, illustrates this kind of drama quite vividly. The soloist and the orchestra—limited in this movement to the strings—engage in an extended dialogue that moves from confrontation to resolution. The strings open with a loud unison figure characterized by dotted rhythms and staccato articulation. The piano responds with an utterly different kind of statement, a lyrical, hymnlike theme that Beethoven marks *molto cantabile*. To underscore the timbral difference between soloist and orchestra, Beethoven calls on the pianist to play the entire movement *una corda* ("one string")—that is, using one of the foot pedals to shift the entire keyboard action so the hammers strike only a single string. Orchestra and soloist alternately present their respective ideas. Neither gives ground at first, but the tutti eventually diminishes in volume. At m. 47, the soloist moves on to a new idea, a soaring melody that sounds very much like a singer's aria. This gives way to a dramatic series of simultaneous runs and trills in an extended (and written-out) cadenza. Beethoven asks the soloist to increase the sound first to two strings, then to the full complement of three, before receding back to the original una corda sound. (This effect is no longer possible on the modern piano, so the performer must simulate the changes in tone.)

At least some listeners have interpreted this movement as a musical reenactment of part of the myth of Orpheus and Euridice. According to this idea, m. 1–5 and 14–18 represent Orpheus descending into the underworld and confronting Charon; m. 19–46 represent him charming Charon with music; m. 47–54 represent him crossing the river Styx to the underworld to retrieve Euridice; m. 55–63 (the solo cadenza) represent his doubts about whether Euridice is still behind him as he ascends back to the world of the living; and finally, the empty-sounding final cadence reflects his despair at the second loss of his beloved. Although Beethoven himself left no direct evidence to support this interpretation, accounts by friends and acquaintances suggest that it is at least plausible. And as a painting he commissioned of himself suggests (see "Beethoven as Orpheus"), Beethoven apparently did think of himself as a modern-day Orpheus.

In its breadth of sound and susceptibility to programmatic interpretation, this movement also illustrates the growing influence of the symphony on the concerto in the 19th century. A result of this trend was to increase the role of the orchestra without diminishing the demand for soloistic virtuosity. This is evident in Beethoven's four other piano concertos, his Violin Concerto, op. 61, and his "Triple Concerto" for cello, violin, and piano, op. 56. The trend toward symphonic scale and tone would continue throughout the first half of the 19th century in the concertos of Felix Mendelssohn (two for piano, one for violin), Robert Schumann (one each for piano, violin, and cello), and Johannes Brahms (two for piano, one for violin, one for violin and cello together). Indeed, Brahms's First Piano Concerto, op. 15 (1854) started life as a symphony; only after he began to expand on its basic ideas did Brahms decide to fashion it into a concerto. Less symphonic in tone but no less impressive in scope and scale are the concertos by Frédéric Chopin (two for piano), Niccolò Paganini (four for violin), and Ignaz Moscheles (eight for piano), which on the whole tend to distinguish more clearly between the roles of the soloist as virtuoso and the orchestra as an accompanimental ensemble.

((•• Listen

**CD10    Track 1**
**mysearchlab**
BEETHOVEN
Piano Concerto no. 4, op. 58
Score Anthology II/119

## Primary Evidence    MENDELSSOHN IN LONDON

*Thanks in part to the patronage of the royal family, Mendelssohn enjoyed immediate and great success in England. Indeed, the popularity of his music endured there long after it had begun to wane on the Continent. Mendelssohn's letters, which have yet to be published in their entirety, offer fascinating insights into the composer's thoughts and 19th-century musical life in general. Here, in a letter to his mother written from London in 1842, Mendelssohn describes his hectic but exhilarating life in the British capital.*

■ ■ ■

If today's letter seems rather tired and creaky, then it reflects my feelings. They really have been driving me a little too hard here. When I was playing the organ the other day in Christ Church in Newgate Street, I thought for a moment I was going to suffocate, so great was the commotion and pressing of the crowd around the organ bench. And a few days after that, when I had to play before an audience of 3,000 in Exeter Hall, they cheered me with "Hurrahs" and waved their handkerchiefs and stamped their feet until the whole place rang with it. I didn't notice any problems at the time, but the next morning my head felt dizzy, as though I had not slept. And then there is the pretty and charming Queen Victoria, who is so girlishly and shyly friendly and polite, who speaks German so well, and who knows all my things so well—the four books of *Songs without Words*, and those with words, and the Symphony, and the *Song of Praise*. Yesterday evening I was at the Palace, where the Queen and Prince Albert were almost entirely alone by themselves. She sat down beside the piano while I played to her seven *Songs without Words*, then the Serenade, then two fantasias on *Rule Britannia* and on Lützow's *wilde Jagd* and *Gaudeamus igitur*. The last was a bit difficult, but I could hardly decline, and because she had given me these themes I could therefore play them. There is also a beautiful, magnificent gallery in Buckingham Palace, where she drank tea and where there is a picture of two pigs by Paul Potter, and several others that struck me as not bad at all. Also, the people here like my A-minor Symphony [the *Italian*] very much. They welcomed us with a pleasant friendliness and thoughtfulness that surpassed anything I have ever experienced in the way of hospitality. At times all this makes my head spin and makes me a bit giddy, and I have to take myself firmly in hand so as not to lose my composure.

**Source:** Mendelssohn, letter to his mother, London, June 21, 1842. Transl. MEB

## SUMMARY

The dimensions of orchestral music expanded in almost every conceivable respect in the first half of the 19th century. Orchestras grew in size and volume, symphonies and concertos became longer, and instrumental music in general took on the task of transcending the realm of mere sound. Beethoven's symphonies, in particular, served as a catalyst in transforming attitudes toward the scope of instrumental music, demonstrating to the listening public the ability of music to convey ideas and images without a text. Following Beethoven's lead, later composers like Mendelssohn also developed the emerging genre of the concert overture, a programmatic orchestral work in a single movement. Before 1800, vocal music had always been considered aesthetically superior to instrumental music. By the 1830s, this was no longer the case. Precisely because of its independence from words, instrumental music—above all, the symphony—was increasingly perceived as the highest form of the musical art.

✓ Study and Review on **mysearchlab.com**

# Piano Music, Chamber Music, Song

((•▪Listen

**CD9    Track 5**
**mysearchlab**
BEETHOVEN
Piano Sonata in C Major, op. 53
("Waldstein")
Score Anthology II/120

In contrast to orchestral genres, the repertories of piano music, chamber music, and song occupied a more private sphere. These smaller-scale genres were performed largely in social gatherings in homes or salons rather than in public concerts. The phenomenon of the solo piano recital before a paying public did not begin to emerge until the end of the 1830s.

## BEETHOVEN'S PIANO SONATAS AND STRING QUARTETS

The gulf between music written for amateurs and that written for professionals widened steadily over the course of the 19th century. Beethoven's piano sonatas, although widely admired, were repeatedly criticized during his lifetime for their technical difficulty. His Sonata in C Major, op. 53, completed in 1804 and dedicated to Count Waldstein (an early patron from Bonn) may seem relatively undemanding compared to his later works, but its rapid passagework and broken octave scales put it beyond the reach of most amateurs at the time it was written. In a break with what had become standard practice in the Classical era, the exposition of the first movement modulates to the mediant (E Major, which later becomes E minor) instead of the dominant (G Major). This kind of modulation reflects the increasing chromaticism of 19th-century harmonic practice and the consequent erosion of the polarity between tonic and dominant that had characterized the formal structures of the mid- to late 18th century. Later composers working within the conventions of sonata form would often modulate to keys other than the dominant or relative major.

While looking forward in terms of its technical demands and harmonic structure, the "Waldstein" Sonata also looks back for thematic inspiration, illustrating Beethoven's ability to transform a predecessor's idea into an entirely new creation. The opening bears striking parallels to Haydn's String Quartet, op. 33, no. 3 (Anthology II/105, discussed in Chapter 12). Like Haydn's quartet, Beethoven's sonata is in the key of C Major, begins with a series of repeated notes, introduces its thematic idea in fragments, and repeats this idea on a series of unusual scale degrees before finally reestablishing the tonic (m. 14). We do not know if Beethoven was conscious of these underlying connections, but we do know that he studied the works of Haydn and Mozart carefully, even copying out entire quartets or quartet movements on occasion to better understand their craft of composition.

Like his piano sonatas, Beethoven's string quartets also reflect the trend toward increasing technical difficulty. Good amateurs could readily have performed the six quartets he published as op. 18 in 1801, but not the three substantially longer quartets of op. 59, which appeared in 1808. Beethoven's late quartets—opp. 127, 130, 132, and 135, composed between 1824 and 1826—are among the most challenging works he wrote in any genre, for performers and listeners alike. Contemporary listeners had never heard anything quite like the opening of the Quartet in B♭ Major, op. 130. The music is full of unexpected starts and stops. What appears at first to be a slow introduction, for example, turns out to be an integral part of the sonata-form exposition. And instead of modulating to the expected dominant (F) in the exposition, Beethoven dramatically overshoots it (m. 51) and lands instead in the unlikely key of G♭ (♭VI, m. 55).

Subsequent movements are similarly full of formal and technical surprises. The second-movement scherzo, marked Presto, runs less than two minutes in many performances, even those that observe all of Beethoven's repeat signs. (The first movement, in contrast, usually runs between 12 and 13 minutes.) The third movement, marked Andante con moto, ma non troppo, is a study in equal-voiced texture. In the opening measures, for example, melody and accompaniment are nearly indistinguishable. The fourth movement, a German dance (Alla danza tedesca), also features unusual textures, especially toward the end (m. 129–140). Here the melodic line bounces from instrument to instrument, each playing solo but completing together a continuous line of melody. Some later writers have compared this technique to pointillism in painting, a device developed in the late 19th century in which recognizable images are created from a pattern of tiny, discrete dots of color.

The fifth movement of this quartet, labeled "Cavatina," is of particular interest. In Italian opera, **cavatina** designated any introductory aria sung by a main character. In Germany, however, the term was reserved largely for simple arias of an introspective quality, free of virtuosic display, and it is clearly this kind of cavatina that Beethoven had in mind here. This movement is in effect an aria without words, with the first violin openly imitating a solo voice. Many composers had written aria-like string quartet movements before; what makes this one different is the interplay of the ensemble as a whole. The other three voices create a texture that is at once homophonic and contrapuntal. The soloist, moreover, "sings" in a voice that is almost sobbing, choking—as Beethoven marks it, *beklemmt* ("as if caught in a vise"). Violinists produce this effect by reducing pressure on the bow, letting it ride lightly across the string. The resulting tone is neither full nor beautiful but all the more emotionally charged.

The original finale of op. 130 was an enormous fugue that Beethoven later published as a separate work with its own opus number, the *Grosse Fuge* ("Great Fugue," op. 133). This work has justly been called Beethoven's equivalent to *The Art of Fugue*, Johann Sebastian Bach's compilation of fugues on a single theme. It is no coincidence that it should have originally been intended to provide the capstone to a work so thoroughly occupied with issues of texture. In its place, Beethoven wrote a shorter finale in which an apparently simple opening, based on a kind of folklike dance, becomes increasingly complex, with a remarkable multiplicity of textures.

# SONG

Like many of his later compositions, Beethoven's String Quartet op. 130 was not particularly well received at first. Most contemporary performers and listeners preferred less demanding music. This explains in part the enormous popularity of the genre of song for solo voice and piano in the first half of the 19th century.

((•• [Listen

**CD10   Tracks 2–4**
**mysearchlab**
BEETHOVEN
String Quartet in B♭ Major, op. 130
Score Anthology II/121

German composers cultivated this genre with such intensity that it is often designated by its German name, the **Lied** (pronounced "leet"; the plural, **Lieder**, is pronounced like the English word "leader"). Several important factors converged to give the Lied its newfound prominence:

- the rise of German poetry
- the growing availability of the piano
- the idealization of domesticity and the family

For much of the 18th century, German was not widely considered a literary or cultured language, not even in Germany itself. Frederick II ("The Great"), king of Prussia from 1740 until 1786, conducted official business in French, not German. Beginning around 1750, however, the works of several remarkable poets and playwrights began to change attitudes toward the German language. These writers included Gotthold Ephraim Lessing (1729–1781), Friedrich Klopstock (1724–1803), Johann Wolfgang Goethe (1749–1832), and Friedrich Schiller (1759–1805). Goethe, who is often likened to Shakespeare, played an especially important role in establishing German as a literary language. Schiller was almost as significant an influence, and the works of the two together galvanized German letters. Composers were drawn to their poetry as a source of texts to be set to music.

The second factor, the growing availability of the piano, reflects advances in piano design and production in the early decades of the 19th century. These advances substantially reduced manufacturing costs, making the instrument increasingly affordable to middle-class families (see Focus: The Piano). With its varied shades of dynamics, wide register, and resonant tone, the piano was the ideal instrument to accompany the voice.

The idealization of domesticity and the family, in turn, provided the perfect context in which songs for a single voice and piano could be performed and heard. The period of European history between 1815 and 1848—that is, between the Congress of Vienna and the Revolutions of 1848—was one of relative stability. After the upheavals of the Napoleonic Wars, European society seemed happy to turn away from heroic, revolutionary ideologies and withdraw into itself. The family became a new center of attention, idealized as a sort of miniature society in its own right. Aesthetic emphasis in the late 1810s and 1820s shifted from the grandiose to the intimate. This increased the appeal of domestic genres of music like the Lied, which lent itself to performance at home. The result was a growing demand for new songs.

Performed by only two musicians in a room of modest size before a select audience (if any audience at all), the song is a genre in which the slightest inflections of harmony, dynamics, and register can have great effect. In contrast to a monumental genre like the symphony, the song calls for heightened sensitivity from composers, performers, and listeners. Its popularity reflects a belief that simplicity can be profound, that a universe of emotions can be encapsulated within a work of small dimensions.

From the perspective of form, songs generally fall into one of three categories: strophic, modified strophic, or through composed. In **strophic form**, the simplest of the three, each verse (strophe) of a poem is set to the same music. In **modified strophic form**, the music varies from strophe to strophe, but the basic theme remains recognizably the same, much as in a set of variations, with melodic embellishment or alteration of texture, harmony, or rhythm. A **through-composed song**, by contrast, has no recognizable pattern of repetition, and often no repetition at all.

**Music in the home.** The private home was ideally suited for piano music and song. Two technological factors combined to foster domestic music making: the declining cost of pianos and the declining cost of printed music. This illustration, from the title page to Wilhelm Heinrich Riehl's anthology entitled *Hausmusik* ("Home Music") of 1856, exemplifies the culture of domestic music making in this era. The grandmother prefers the warmth of the tile oven, but everyone else (including the dogs) gathers around the piano. Music—represented by the piano—is as much a focal point of family activity as the hearth or the dinner table visible in the background. Buoyed by the demand this cultural phenomenon created, the publishers of accompanied songs and short, easy piano pieces flourished.

**Source:** akg-images/Newscom

((•• **Listen**

**CD10    Tracks 5–7**
**mysearchlab** (with scrolling translation)
SCHUBERT
*Erlkönig, Prometheus,* and *Wanderers Nachtlied*
Score Anthology II/122

Song composers in the 19th century were judged according to the extent to which their music enhanced the words of the poems they set. The repetitive rhythmic insistence of Franz Schubert's *Erlkönig* ("Elf-king") reflects the content and iambic meter of Goethe's strophic poem. Schubert, however, goes beyond this rhythmic device to magnify the poem's emotional force in a setting that hovers somewhere between through-composed and modified-strophic form. *Erlkönig* tells a chilling tale of a father riding home with his feverish son in his arms. The boy hears the Elf-king calling to him with seductive blandishments and cries out in fear as his father tries vainly to calm him. When they arrive, the boy is dead in his father's arms. The poem has four voices— a narrator, the Elf-king, the boy, and the father—and Schubert gives each of them a distinctive character through the strategic use of key, mode, texture, and register.

Free verse, as is found in a poem like Goethe's *Prometheus*, calls for a flexible musical structure. Schubert's through-composed setting emphasizes the declamatory tone and irregular rhythms of the poetry. The music and the text are equally dramatic. In Greek myth it was Prometheus who, against the will of Zeus, gave fire to humanity. As punishment for this transgression, Prometheus was chained to a rock, where every day an eagle came to eat out his liver, which grew back every night. In the poem the unrepentant Prometheus hurls scorn and defiance on Zeus. Schubert's setting conveys this defiance through a variety of musical means: dotted rhythms, rumbling tremolos, fully-voiced chords, sudden contrasts of dynamic, and long declamatory passages marked "Recit." (for recitative), which are to be sung in the rhythmically free style characteristic of operatic recitative.

A brief poem of a single strophe like Goethe's *Wanderers Nachtlied* ("Wanderer's Night Song") elicited from Schubert an intense attention to detail. The limited melodic motion and straightforward rhythms of the opening capture the sense of calm that pervades the text ("Above all summits is calm . . .") and make the subsequent syncopation (m. 5–8) all the more pronounced. The repeated horn-call-like figures in m. 9–13 take on added importance through repetition. In so brief a setting, every gesture carries added weight. Even the one-measure epilogue in the piano (m. 14) resonates with significance, given the remarkably small scale of this work.

## *Focus*  THE PIANO

The piano grew in almost every respect over the course of the 19th century. By 1900, its compass had increased from 5 octaves to the now-standard 88 keys. A substantial increase in the size of the frame and various improvements in escapement action made it possible for a single instrument to combine both lightness and power. Leather hammer coverings were eventually replaced with felt, producing a thicker, heavier sound. Improvements in damper pedals and the addition of a shifting pedal to allow hammers to strike only one string for each note (una corda) increased timbral variety. The introduction of a one-piece cast-iron frame increased both durability and sound volume.

When pianos began to be mass produced in the second quarter of the 19th century, their cost dropped, and by the 1850s they had become standard fixtures in middle- and upper-class homes. Every home with any pretensions to culture had one, and every daughter in such a home was almost certain to have been subjected to piano lessons at some point in her upbringing. As a result, the market for piano teachers and piano music was enormous. The popularity of the instrument also made it feasible for composers (and publishers) to disseminate music in other genres—operas, symphonies, concertos, and even string quartets—in the form of piano reductions.

Atelier des caissiers-monteurs.

**A piano factory.** The mass manufacture of pianos in the 19th century made the instruments considerably more affordable. The upright models being assembled here in the Parisian piano factory of Pleyel around 1845 were designed to fit into the smaller spaces of middle-class homes. The contrast of scale with 18th-century methods of instrument production is striking (see illustration, "Interior of a brass instrument workshop in Paris, ca. 1760" in Chapter 12).

**Source:** Mary Evan Picture Library/Alamy

Schubert also helped establish the genre of the **song cycle**, a collection of songs ordered in such a way as to convey at least the outline of a story or idea. His *Die schöne Müllerin* ("The Beautiful Daughter of the Miller"), to texts by Wilhelm Müller, is a series of 20 songs that tell the story of a journeyman miller who falls in love with his master's daughter but is spurned and eventually commits suicide. Other cycles, such as Robert Schumann's *Dichterliebe*, op. 48, a setting of poems by Heinrich Heine, are more loosely structured in terms of text but carefully organized in terms of tonality and other musical parameters.

Different composers were often drawn to the same text, bringing to it a variety of interpretations that reflect changing styles and expanding musical options. For example, Johann Friedrich Reichardt's late-18th-century setting of Goethe's poem "Kennst du das Land?" ("Do You Know the Land?") under the title "Italien" (Anthology II/114, discussed in Chapter 13) is relatively straightforward, with a limited melodic range and folklike diatonicism. Later settings—like those by Schubert, Schumann, and Hugo Wolf—have more intricate vocal lines, richer textures, and increasingly chromatic harmonies that reflect the 19th century's ever-expanding harmonic vocabulary. Wolf's setting, in particular, illustrates the move away from the aesthetic of simplicity among composers of the latter part of the 19th century. His "Mignon," composed in 1888, focuses on the second part of each strophe ("Kennst du es [ihn] wohl? Dahin!"), initiated by the accompaniment (marked *Belebt*—"lively"—in m. 21, 58, and 99), to provide structural background through repetition and melodic climax. The first half of each strophe is more freely composed, with multiple changes of tempo, key, and dynamic level, building in intensity until the final strophe, in which Mignon pleads with Wilhelm, "Dahin! Dahin geht unser Weg! o Vater, lass uns ziehn!" (The version included on the CD set is Wolf's second of two orchestrations [1893] of "Mignon.")

This genre was also popular in the United States, where songs for voice and piano were cultivated with special intensity. Particularly in the first half of the 19th century, Americans had relatively little opportunity to hear large professional musical ensembles, increasing the appeal of music that could be performed in a domestic setting. By far the most important 19th-century American songwriter was Stephen Foster (1826–1864). Born in Pennsylvania, he initially worked as a bookkeeper but eventually supported himself entirely from the sale of his music, the first American composer to do so. Although he spent most of his adult life in Cincinnati, Pittsburgh, and New York City, he is indelibly associated with the pre–Civil War South because of his contribution to the subgenre of the **minstrel song**. Typically performed by white musicians in blackface, minstrel songs purported to represent African American slave life. There were black troupes, but most of these formed after the Civil War. A minstrel ensemble generally included a tambourine, castanets ("bones"), banjo, and fiddle. The shows often portrayed African Americans with demeaning caricatures and exaggerated dialect, helping reinforce and perpetuate racial stereotypes. Foster's songs, although sentimental (in the modern sense), usually portrayed his subjects with compassion and dignity. At least some of these songs have been performed by such 20th-century African-American singers as Paul Robeson and Roland Hayes. The minstrel tradition, moreover, to the extent that it indeed featured and popularized music with characteristically African-American syncopations, was one of the roots of ragtime, a genre that

((•—[Listen

**CD10     Tracks 8–10**
**mysearchlab** (with scrolling translation)
SCHUBERT, ROBERT SCHUMANN, AND WOLF
Settings of Goethe's *Kennst du das Land?*
Score Anthology II/123

**African-American minstrels, ca. 1860s.**
A rare photograph of four African-American musicians from some time around the 1860s, playing the tambourine, violin, banjo, and castanets ("bones").

**Source:** James Bollman

# Franz Schubert (1797–1828)

Schubert was born into a musical family and received his early training from his father (a schoolmaster), his brother, and the organist of his parish church. In 1808, he gained a place in the Imperial court choir, and with it, admission to the prestigious Imperial and Royal City College. While there, he studied composition with Antonio Salieri, the court Kapellmeister.

As a composer, Schubert followed very much in the footsteps of Mozart in Vienna: he never managed to secure a position as a composer at the court in spite of his talent; he was forced to give music lessons to make ends meet; and he died young, at the age of 31. Unlike Mozart, however, Schubert never achieved operatic success, in spite of repeated efforts to write a theater hit. His greatest talents lay in the realm of song, where he had an extraordinary ability to match texts with melodies ranging from the lyrical to the dramatic, the simple to the intricate. He found ample opportunity to perform his songs within his circle of friends, which included many poets and singers. His reputation as a songwriter attracted the attention of Beethoven and helped secure him a more or less open arrangement with the Viennese publisher Cappi and Diabelli to publish any new songs he might compose. Unfortunately, this fame and the potential for financial security it promised came only a few years before the composer's untimely death.

Schubert was incredibly prolific. In the year 1815 alone, he composed no fewer than 144 songs. In the 1820s, he turned more and more toward instrumental music, particularly piano sonatas, quartets, piano trios, and symphonies. He composed more songs toward the end of his life, however, and the publisher Haslinger issued a posthumous set under the title of *Schwanengesang* ("Swansong").

For almost a century and a half, the predominant image of Schubert was that of a dreamy, introverted Romantic who was more or less indifferent to events and persons around him and who lived only for his music. The recent work of several musicologists, however, has given us a far more complex image of the composer. Schubert was apparently an intensely sensual man of uncertain sexual orientation. He belonged to a group of artists who called themselves "The Nonsense Society" and who enjoyed playing practical jokes and creating enigmatic images of one another. One of these, a watercolor titled *Der Sündenfall* ("The Original Sin"), is reproduced here.

# PRINCIPAL WORKS

## Symphonies

Schubert took Haydn, Mozart, and, later, Beethoven, as models for his instrumental music, confessing to a friend in 1824 that he was working his way toward a large-scale symphony by composing string quartets. At the time, in fact, he had already completed the two remarkable movements of his so-called *Unfinished* Symphony in B minor (D. 759) and sketched portions of a third. In the last year of his life, he completed his Symphony in C Major (D. 944, "the *Great*"), a masterpiece that points toward a remarkably distinctive approach based less on principles

**Schubert in his circle of friends.** This curious watercolor—*The Original Sin* ("Der Sündenfall"), by Leopold Kupelwieser (1821)—shows a gathering of Schubert's circle of friends engaged in a pantomime. Kupelwieser, the artist, stands by the door, posing as the "Tree of Knowledge," while the poet Franz von Schober plays the part of a serpent. The couple in front of him represents Adam and Eve, who are about to be driven from the Garden of Eden. Schubert, seated at the keyboard in the foreground, has interrupted his playing to look on. But why are so few members of the audience actually looking at the pantomime? The figure opposite Schubert is the poet Joseph Spaun, who gazes intently over the piano's music stand at the composer, seemingly oblivious to the pantomime. The similarity in posture between Schubert and the dog behind him is too obvious to be coincidental, but what is its significance? On the whole, this watercolor gives a sense of the kind of obscure symbolism favored by Schubert's circle, many of whom belonged to a group that called itself the "Nonsense Society."

**Source:** The family of Franz Peter Schubert (1797–1828) playing games, Kupelwieser, Leopold (1796–1862)/Wien Museum Karlsplatz, Vienna, Austria/The Bridgeman Art Library

of thematic manipulation and counterpoint than on melody, color, and large-scale harmonic design. Both the *Great* and the *Unfinished* remained essentially unknown, however, until their rediscovery and first public performances in 1839 and 1865, respectively. As with Mozart, we can only speculate about the kinds of works Schubert might have written had he lived longer.

## String Quartets and Other Chamber Works

Two of Schubert's best known chamber works incorporate slow movements related to his songs. The 12th of the 15 string quartets, D. 810, is known as *Death and the Maiden* because its slow movement is a set of variations on Schubert's own song of the same name. The *Trout* Quintet, D. 667, for violin, viola, cello, double bass, and piano, features a set of variations on his song *Die Forelle* ("The Trout"). The two late piano trios are remarkably expansive works that point toward the scope of his Symphony in C Major, "the Great."

## Piano Sonatas and Miscellaneous Works for Piano

As a composer of instrumental music, Schubert is inevitably compared to Beethoven, but Schubert's distinctive voice is abundantly evident in his works. By his late 20s—which is to say, toward the end of his life—he had even managed to achieve a distinctive approach toward sonata form, based on the large-scale juxtaposition of broad harmonic areas, as opposed to Beethoven's characteristic intensive manipulation and fragmentation of thematic ideas. The *Wanderer* Fantasy, D. 760, consists of four movements played without interruption, all of them based on a theme derived from Schubert's song of the same name. Miscellaneous works for solo piano include marches and dances, as well as the *Impromptus* and *Moments musicaux*, both of which bear a certain resemblance to song in both tone and form. Performers of four-hand piano music particularly prize Schubert's contributions to that repertory.

## Songs

Had Schubert written only a handful of the hundreds of songs he did, he would still be honored as the greatest composer of all time in this genre. His choice of poetry varies widely from some of the best ever written in the German language (by Goethe and Schiller) to some that is mediocre at best. Whatever their quality, however, Schubert always managed to elevate the texts he set. A few dozen songs have emerged as perennial favorites, such as *Gretchen am Spinnrade* (set to a text from Goethe's *Faust*), *Der Lindenbaum*, *An Schwager Kronos*, and *Die Forelle*. The two song cycles, *Die schöne Müllerin* ("The Beautiful Daughter of the Miller") and *Die Wintereise* ("The Winter Journey"), have also achieved enduring popularity, in part because they combine the miniature essence of the genre with a larger scale plot. His less well-known songs and many part-songs deserve greater exposure than they have had. Recordings today group many songs together, encouraging listeners to play through many at a time. Schubert, however, intended them, like all miniatures, to be savored individually.

| KEY DATES IN THE LIFE OF SCHUBERT | |
|---|---|
| 1797 | Born January 31 in Lichtenthal (now a part of Vienna). |
| 1808 | Becomes a singer in the Imperial court choir at Vienna; later receives composition lessons from Antonio Salieri, the court Kapellmeister. |
| 1813 | Becomes an elementary school teacher in the school his father directs. |
| 1815 | Composes the song *Erlkönig,* later published in 1821 as his op. 1. Prepublication performances establish a reputation that leads to the sale of a remarkable 300 copies within the first 18 months. |
| 1820s | Tries repeatedly, without success, to secure a position at the court in Vienna. Meager income from private lessons and sales of his songs leaves him always on the edge of poverty. |
| 1828 | Dies in Vienna on November 19 and is buried near Beethoven, testifying to the belated recognition of his enormous talent. |

became immensely popular in the early 20th century (see Chapter 24). Among Foster's most famous minstrel songs are *Oh! Susanna*, *My Old Kentucky Home*, *Camptown Races*, *Old Folks at Home*, and *Massa's in the Cold, Cold Ground*.

Foster also wrote many **parlor songs** (so called because of their place of performance, the 19th-century equivalent of today's living room). The texts are invariably strophic and sentimental, as in Foster's *Beautiful Dreamer*. The simplicity and melodic straightforwardness of these songs is very much in keeping with the aesthetic of the German Lied in the first half of the century, with its emphasis on naturalness and directness. Although billed as his last song on early editions—the work was first published after the composer's death—*Beautiful Dreamer* was in fact written in 1862, when Foster was still turning out songs at the rate of about two a month.

The *mélodie*, as the song was known in France, was cultivated by such composers as Berlioz, Charles Gounod (1818–1893), Jules Massenet (1842–1912), Ernest Chausson (1855–1899), and above all Gabriel Fauré (1845–1924). Berlioz's *Nuits d'été* ("Summer Nights") of 1840–1841 is the earliest French song cycle, and when the composer orchestrated the set in 1856, it marked the beginning of a new genre, the orchestral song. This type of composition would later be cultivated by the Austrian composers Gustav Mahler and Hugo Wolf, both of whom orchestrated their Lieder with piano accompaniment (as had Berlioz with *Nuits d'été*); see the earlier discussion of Wolf's "Mignon").

In Russia, the most important composers of song included Mikhail Glinka (1804–1857), Alexander Dargomyzhsky (1813–1869), and Modeste Mussorgsky (1839–1881). Russian composers often incorporated folklike elements into their songs,

**Music marketing.** Jenny Lind (1820–1887), widely regarded as the greatest singer of her generation, toured the United States from 1850 to 1852 under the sponsorship of P. T. Barnum, who is better remembered today for his circuses than his concerts. According to his contract with Lind for her first American tour, Barnum was to pay her $1,000 for every performance, plus expenses. But when Lind discovered the first concert grossed $28,000, she demanded $1,000 per concert, plus half the receipts over $3,000, plus expenses, and Barnum capitulated. The tour ultimately grossed more than $712,000, earning Lind $175,000. At the time, the president of the United States earned $25,000 a year.

Lind was still a legend long after she had retired from the stage. This image of her appeared on a card distributed in the 1880s with packs of cigarettes, in much the same way that cards with the image of baseball players would later be included in packs of bubble gum.

**Source:** Mary Evans Picture Library/Alamy

((•—Listen

**CD10   Track 11**
**mysearchlab**
FOSTER
*Beautiful Dreamer*
Score Anthology II/124

repeating or varying slightly a folklike melody, for example, or using characteristically Russian chromatic and modal inflections. Mussorgsky's *V chetyrjokh stenakh* ("In Four Walls"), from the song cycle *Bez solnca* (1874, "Sunless"), illustrates the ever-expanding presence of chromaticism in music from the later decades of the 19th century, as well as Mussorgsky's penchant for a naturalistic kind of declamation that fits well with his often dark and brooding texts. (Performers who are native speakers of Russian can add an extra bite to the text with clear pronunciation of its frequently complex consonants and consonant combinations.) The recitative-like declamation elicits a chordal piano part, sprinkled with brief parallel countermelodies.

((•—Listen

CD10    Track 12
**mysearchlab** (with scrolling translation)
MUSSORGSKY
*V chetyrjokh stenakh*
Score Anthology II/125

# THE CHARACTER PIECE

The **character piece**, a new genre associated almost exclusively with the piano, is the instrumental counterpart to the song. A work of relatively small dimension, it seeks to portray and explore the mood or "character" of a particular person, idea, situation,

## Primary Evidence    THE SALON

*The salon was a vital forum for music making in the 19th century, particularly chamber music, piano music, and song. The setting—the residence of a wealthy host or hostess—was small enough to be intimate yet large enough to exercise influence on a city's broader musical life. On occasion, a host or hostess might engage a single artist to perform for the assembled guests: many contemporary accounts of Chopin's playing derive from performances he gave in salons. Countess Marie d'Agoult, Liszt's longtime companion, recalls the more common system for arranging the musical entertainment in a Parisian salon in the mid-1820s. Anyone throwing a party catered the artists, in effect, along with the food. In this case, the musical caterer was Rossini.*

■  ■  ■

Composers and singers still had their place apart; in spite of the eagerness to have them, they appeared in the salons only on the footing of inferiors. If someone wanted to give a fine concert, he sent to Rossini, who, for a recognized fee—it was small enough, only 1,500 francs if I recollect rightly—undertook to arrange the program and to see to its carrying out, thus relieving the master of the house of all embarrassments in the way of choice of artists, of rehearsals, and so on. The great maestro himself sat at the piano all evening accompanying the singers. Generally he added an instrumental virtuoso—Herz or Moscheles, Lafont or Bériot, Nadermann (the leading Paris harpist), Tulou (the king's first flute), or the wonder of the musical world, the little Liszt. At the appointed

**A Parisian salon.** The pianist Henri Herz (1803–1888) in a Parisian salon of the 1840s. Music (center), drawing (far left), and conversation (far right) were staples of salon gatherings.

**Source:** Bibliothèque Nationale de France

hour they arrived in a body, entering by a side door; in a body they sat near the piano; and in a body they departed, after having received the compliments of the master of the house and of a few professed dilettantes. The next day the master sent Rossini his fee and believed he had discharged his obligations toward them and him.

**Source:** Marie d'Agoult, *Mes Souvenirs,* quoted in Arthur Loesser, *Men, Women, and Pianos: A Social History* (New York: Simon & Schuster, 1954), p. 344.

or emotion. Sometimes these are specified, sometimes not. The character piece tends to be brief, sectional, and fairly simple in construction. Many follow an ABA, AAB, or ABB pattern.

By its very nature, the character piece operates on the border between programmatic and absolute music. Mendelssohn's provocatively titled *Lieder ohne Worte* ("Songs without Words,") invite—indeed challenge—performers and listeners to imagine the nature of the words that the composer so pointedly omits. Mendelssohn himself was reluctant to elaborate on these works, letting them suggest the possibility of concrete interpretation while remaining abstract. In an eloquent answer to a friend who had asked for descriptive titles for several of these pieces, Mendelssohn emphasized the inadequacy of words to capture the spirit of music:

There is so much talk about music, and so little is said. I believe that words are not at all up to it, and if I should find that they were adequate I would stop making music altogether. People usually complain that music is so ambiguous, and what they are supposed to think when they hear it is so unclear, while words are understood by everyone. But for me it is exactly the opposite—and not just with entire discourses, but also with individual words; these, too, seem to be so ambiguous, so indefinite, in comparison with good music, which fills one's soul with a thousand better things than words. What the music I love expresses to me are thoughts not too *indefinite* for words, but rather too *definite*.

Thus, I find in all attempts to put these thoughts into words something correct, but also always something insufficient, something not universal; and this is also how I feel about your suggestions [to provide titles for the individual "Songs without Words"]. This is not your fault, but rather the fault of the words, which simply cannot do any better. So if you ask me what I was thinking of, I will say: just the song as it stands there. And if I happen to have had a specific word or specific words in mind for one or another of these songs, I can never divulge them to anyone, because the same word means one thing to one person and something else to another, because only the song can say the same thing, can arouse the same feelings in one person as in another—a feeling which is not, however, expressed by the same words. . . .

Will you accept this as my answer to your question? It is at any rate the only one I know how to give—though these, too, are nothing but ambiguous words.[1]

((•—[Listen

**CD10    Track 13**
**mysearchlab**
FANNY MENDELSSOHN HENSEL
Piano Trio in D minor, op. 11
Score Anthology II/126

Felix's sister Fanny Mendelssohn Hensel (her married name from 1829) composed numerous character piano pieces as well, including sets of *Lieder ohne Worte*. In her Piano Trio in D minor, op. 11 (1846), she extends the idea a step further by labeling its third movement *Lied*, that is, a "Song without Words" for piano, violin, and cello. Using modified strophic form, she alters the melody each time it returns, allowing each instrument to have a turn at taking the lead and changing the notes and harmonies slightly each time. The melody itself conforms to a poetic meter, trochaic tetrameter: each "line" consists of four units ("tetra"="four"), each of which is a trochee (LONG-short). Henry Wadsworth Longfellow's *Song of Hiawatha* is a well-known poem written in this meter, and its words can in fact be superimposed on the opening theme of this movement quite easily:

**By** the **shores** of **Git**che **Gu**mee
**By** the **shin**ing **Big**-Sea-**Wa**ter,
**Stood** the **wig**wam **of** Nokomis,
**Daugh**ter **of** the **Moon**, Nokomis.

Dance, like poetry, also relies on meter, and Chopin's Mazurka op. 17, no. 4 (1833), is one of many 19th-century character pieces modeled on a particular dance rhythm—in this case, the **mazurka**, a Polish peasant dance in triple meter, often with an accent on the second or third beat. The work is harmonically ambiguous in several ways. It opens with three three-note chords that do not follow a harmonic progression in any conventional sense. The focus, instead, appears to be the motion of the middle note in each chord, the only one of the three to change. The progression B-C-D within the framework of the F and A in the outer voices prefigures a harmony that will prove repeatedly elusive. The cadence at the end of m. 4 can be read as an F-major chord in first inversion (A-C-F), but the absence of B♭ gives the work more a modal sound, either Lydian (a scale on F without the B♭) or Aeolian (a scale on A with no accidentals). The chromatic descent of linked thirds beginning in m. 9 (F♯—D♯ followed by F♮—D♮) further undermines the sense of a strong tonal center. Chopin creates the expectation of a strong cadence on A minor at the downbeat to m. 13 but delays it until m. 20. And even then, he gives us just enough stability in A minor to make us think we know where we are going and the piece has a tonal center. The middle section of this work, by contrast (m. 61–92), hammers away at A-Major triads so relentlessly that it seems to take all the energy it can muster to move to a dominant harmony even briefly. But with the return of the opening section at m. 93, we are thrust back into the realm of harmonic ambiguity. At the end of the piece, Chopin repeats the opening sequence of harmonically ambiguous chords followed by an A-C-F triad, giving us a conclusion

((•• [Listen
**CD10    Track 14**
**mysearchlab**
CHOPIN
Mazurka in A minor, op.17, no. 4
Score Anthology II/127

## Focus   OVERCOMING OBSTACLES: FANNY MENDELSSOHN HENSEL

As a composer, Fanny Mendelssohn Hensel (1805–1847) faced two major obstacles. The first was the immense fame of her younger brother, an international celebrity as both a performer and composer while still in his teens. In spite of her considerable accomplishments as a pianist (she could play Bach's *Well-Tempered Clavier* from memory by age 13) and composer, Fanny was inevitably known as "Felix's sister." The second obstacle was her sex. Fanny grew up in an era when musical composition was not considered an appropriate profession for women, and she grew up in a family in which women were not expected to pursue a vocation of any kind. Her father, Abraham Mendelssohn, wrote to her in 1820—she was 15 at the time—that while Felix might pursue a musical career, music "for you will always remain but an ornament; never can or should it become the foundation of your existence." This helps explain why for most of her life Fanny published her music under her brother's name. Only later—just a year before her death, as it turned out—did she begin issuing compositions under her own name.

Only recently have critics and historians begun to discover the full range of Fanny's talents as a composer of more than 200 songs, over 100 works for piano (including *Das Jahr* a cycle commemorating the months of the year), more than two dozen works for chorus (among them biblical cantatas), and works for a variety of chamber ensembles (including the Piano Trio in D minor, op. 11, and two string quartets).

**Fanny Mendelssohn Hensel.**

**Source:** Abigail Lebrecht/Lebrecht Music & Arts Photo Library

but no harmonic closure. A harmonically ambiguous opening had many distinguished precedents. One need think only of such works as Mozart's 'Dissonant' Quartet, K. 465, or Haydn's Symphony no. 103 ("Drumroll"; Anthology). But a harmonically ambiguous close like this one was a phenomenon essentially new to the 19th century.

As a work for solo instrument, this mazurka and other character pieces like it allowed for considerable rhythmic freedom in performance. By all accounts, Chopin himself took many rhythmic liberties when playing his own music, so many that Berlioz accused him of not being able to play in time. The noted conductor Sir Charles Hallé (1819–1895) described in greater detail what it was that so aroused the ire of Berlioz:

> I once ventured to observe to him [Chopin] that most of his Mazurkas (those dainty jewels), when played by himself, appeared to be written not in 3/4 but in 4/4 time, the result of his dwelling so much longer on the first note in the bar. He denied it strenuously, until I made him play one of them and counted audibly four in the bar, which fitted perfectly. Then he laughed and explained that it was the national character of the dance which created the oddity. The more remarkable fact was that you received the impression of a 3/4 rhythm whilst listening to common time. Of course this was not the case with every mazurka, but with many.[2]

Chopin and other pianists of the day also made considerable use of **tempo rubato** (literally, "robbed time"), a performance tradition that involved subtle accelerations and decelerations in tempo and at times complete independence of the hands, with the "singing" hand moving in a freer rhythm against the steady beat of the accompaniment. Carl Mikuli, one of Chopin's students, described his teacher's playing in this way:

> In keeping time Chopin was inexorable, and some readers will be surprised to learn that the metronome never left his piano. Even in his much maligned *tempo rubato*, the hand responsible for the accompaniment would keep strict time while the other hand, singing the melody, would free the essence of the musical thought from all rhythmic fetters, either by lingering hesitantly or by eagerly anticipating the movement with a certain impatient vehemence akin to passionate speech.[3]

((•━ **Listen**

**CD11 Tracks 1–4**
**mysearchlab**
CHOPIN
Preludes, op. 28
Score Anthology II/128

((•━ **Listen**

**CD11 Track 5**
**mysearchlab**
CHOPIN
Ballade in G minor, op. 23
Score Anthology II/129

Character pieces were usually too brief to be published separately, and so works like Chopin's nocturnes, polonaises, and waltzes, or Mendelssohn's *Songs without Words* were issued typically in collections of three, four, or more individual pieces. Occasionally, however, composers organized a set of character pieces as a coherent cycle. Chopin's 24 preludes, for example, follow the circle of fifths to move systematically through the 24 major and their relative minor keys of the 12-note scale (from C Major and A minor to G Major and E minor, and so forth). The homage to J. S. Bach's *Well-Tempered Clavier* is unmistakable (Anthology; see Chapter 10), although Chopin's ordering differs from Bach's. The first prelude, in C Major, imitates the broken chordal writing in the corresponding prelude of the first book of Bach's collection and uses harmonic progressions to create a sense of overall shape. And even though Chopin's preludes lack fugues, many of them explore unusual possibilities of voice leading. In the A-minor Prelude, for example, a back-and-forth half-step motion in one voice is framed by another voice making leaps of a tenth.

Although composers in the generations after Beethoven never abandoned the multimovement sonata entirely, it gradually gave way to larger scale forms in a single movement such as the ballade, cultivated by Chopin, Liszt, Brahms, and Fauré, and the scherzo, cultivated by Chopin and Brahms. At least some of these longer character pieces were substantial enough to be published separately. Chopin's Ballade in G minor, op. 23, written between 1831 and 1835, is an extended work with many elements of sonata form. After a brief introduction (m. 1–7), Chopin establishes two main key areas, G minor (m. 8–44) and E♭ major (m. 68–93), connected by a transition section (m. 45–67). Although the modulation here is from i to VI rather than the more typical i to III, the form of this opening corresponds to the conventions of a sonata-form exposition. Then, as in the development section of a sonata-form movement, Chopin takes the two main ideas through a variety of new key areas and manipulates them thematically before introducing a new idea (m. 138). The recapitulation deviates from the conventions of sonata form in that the theme originally presented in E♭ major returns in that same key (m. 166) rather than in the tonic. Only later does the first theme finally return to reestablish the tonic (m. 194). A coda (m. 208–264) introduces yet another new theme. Given so many deviations from the conventions of sonata form, it would be misleading to say that Chopin's G-minor Ballade is "in sonata form." At the same time, it would be wrong to deny altogether that it reflects the influence of sonata form. Many 19th-century instrumental works share this kind of formal ambiguity, simultaneously operating within and pushing beyond the conventions of established forms.

It was long believed that Chopin based each of his four ballades on one of the poetic ballads of the 19th-century Polish poet Adam Mickiewicz, but no evidence supports this belief. The G-minor Ballade nevertheless projects a strong sense of narrative direction. The powerful unison opening is a call to attention, and the rhythmic regularity of the subsequent moderato (m. 8–32) conveys a sense of metered verse. Each section of the work embodies a particular affect, moving from the resigned (m. 8–32) to lyrical (m. 68–93), to ecstatic (m. 106–124), to agitated (m. 124–137), to waltzlike (m. 138–154), to furious (m. 208–242). The catastrophic conclusion (m. 244 to the end), with its abrupt finish, brings to mind the abrupt and tragic end of Goethe's well-known poetic ballad *Erlkönig* (see Anthology II/123a for Schubert's setting). Indeed, the work as a whole conveys a strong sense of the kind of creative improvisation associated with the ballad. Like the singer of ballads as described by Goethe, Chopin "has so thoroughly internalized his pregnant subject—his characters, their actions, their emotions—that he does not know how he will bring it to light. . . . He can begin lyrically, epically, dramatically and proceed, changing the forms of presentation at will, either hastening to the end or delaying it at length."[6]

Ambiguity and complexity were not the only interests of 19th-century composers; there was an ever-increasing number of good amateur players for whom to write music. Franz Liszt evokes a fashionable dance of the period with his *Galop de bal* (ca. 1840). It places relatively limited demands on the performer and with its relentless accents captures the physical frenzy of the ballroom (see "Dance fever, 1839," in this chapter). Other composers also wrote music in a disarmingly simple style. Robert Schumann's cycle of character pieces entitled *Kinderszenen* ("Scenes from Childhood"), op. 15 (1838), evoke the ancient idea that truth is to be found in the unspoiled innocence of childhood. *Träumerei* ("Reveries") and *Der Dichter spricht* ("The Poet Speaks") are two well-known works from this set: they are technically quite straightforward yet every bit as profound as the more openly virtuosic and sophisticated character pieces of their time.

Schumann's *Carnaval*, op. 9 (1835), is a cycle of character pieces ranging from the simple to the complex, linked by the common theme of Carnival, the brief season of revelry immediately preceding the penitential season Lent. During Carnival, whose

((•• Listen

CD11    Track 6
**mysearchlab**
LISZT
*Galop de bal*
Score Anthology II/130

((•• Listen

CD11    Tracks 7–11
**mysearchlab**
ROBERT SCHUMANN
*Carnaval*, op. 9
Score Anthology II/131

# Frédéric Chopin (1810–1849)

The son of a French father and a Polish mother, Chopin never felt quite at home anywhere. Poland had lost its always precarious independence in the late 18th century and during Chopin's youth was mostly under Russian domination. After early training in his homeland, Chopin set out on a European tour in 1830. Kept abroad by an ultimately abortive nationalist uprising in Poland, Chopin settled in France, never to return to his homeland. Polish nationalism continued to smolder after the uprising, particularly among the nation's exile community. Chopin's own deep affection for his native land is reflected in his cultivation of such national dances as the polonaise and mazurka.

Thanks in part to the large number of Polish expatriates in Paris, Chopin was able to circulate in the highest levels of Parisian society. He made a good living from teaching and the sale of his music, as well as from the occasional public concert, although he avoided these as much as he could, especially in his later years. His fame allowed him to charge far more than the going rate for piano lessons. In 1837, he began a decade-long liaison with the novelist Amandine-Aurore Lucile Dudevant (1801–1876), better known by her pen name, George Sand. The relationship eventually went sour, but for a time at least, Sand helped provide Chopin more freedom and time to compose than he would have had otherwise. In 1838–1839, the two wintered on the island of Majorca, off the Spanish coast in the Mediterranean. During their stay, Chopin took ill and was diagnosed with tuberculosis by local doctors. Chopin refused to believe them. In a letter to a friend, he wrote,

> I have been sick as a dog these last two weeks; I caught cold in spite of 18 degrees of heat [65 degrees Fahrenheit], roses, oranges, palms, figs, and three most famous doctors of the island. One sniffed at what I spat up, the second tapped where I spat it from, the third poked around and listened how I spat. One said I had died, the second that I am dying, the third that I shall die. . . . I could scarcely keep them from bleeding me. . . . All this has affected the Preludes [op. 24], and God knows when you will get them. . . . Don't tell people that I've been ill; or they'll make up a tale.[4]

Despite his poor health, Chopin continued to compose steadily until the last months of his life. On tour in England and Scotland during the early fall of 1848, he described what would prove to be his final decline:

> Things are getting worse with me every day. I feel weaker; I cannot compose, not for want of inclination, but for physical reasons, and because I am every week in a different place. . . . I am all morning unable to do anything, and when I have dressed myself I feel again so fatigued that I must rest. After dinner, I must sit for two hours with the gentlemen, hear what they say in French, and see how much they can drink. Meanwhile I feel bored to death. I think of something totally different, and then go to the drawing room, where I require all my strength to revive, for all are anxious to hear me [play the piano]. Afterwards my good Daniel [his servant] carries me upstairs to my bedroom, undresses me, puts me to bed, leaves the candle burning, and then I am again at liberty to sigh and dream until morning, to pass the next day just like the preceding one.[5]

# PRINCIPAL WORKS

## Solo Piano

The bulk of Chopin's output consists of works for solo piano. In addition to the mazurkas and preludes already discussed, these include the following:

- *Nocturnes.* These "night pieces," characterized by lyrical melody and a relatively clear homophonic texture, follow no particular fixed form. The genre itself was relatively new, related to the tradition of the serenade, an "evening song" performed outside a loved one's window. The nocturne as a character piece was first introduced into the piano repertory by the Irish composer John Field (1782–1837).

- *Etudes.* Chopin's two books of "Studies," op. 10 and op. 25, each consisting of 12 numbers, reflect the composer's devotion to strict technique and his abhorrence of the standard finger exercises that were so common in his time. Each of the etudes addresses a particular technical challenge—such as scalar runs, three-against-two rhythms, or rapid broken arpeggiations—but presents that challenge in a form that sounds like anything but a mechanical exercise.

- *Polonaises.* Chopin created many highly stylized versions of this Polish dance. The polonaises have generally heavier textures than those of Chopin's other music.

- *Waltzes.* These, too, are stylized pieces, not meant for dancing. They vary widely in character, tempo, and dimension.

- *Sonatas.* The earliest, op. 4, is a youthful work, but the two later ones are substantial four-movement works. Robert Schumann, in an otherwise favorable review of these later works shortly after their publication, questioned their cyclical coherence and accused Chopin of having smuggled "four of his dearest children" into a single work under the guise of composing a "sonata." With their uncharacteristically dense textures, these show Beethoven's influence more than any of Chopin's other works.

- *Ballades.* The four ballades are among the most celebrated works of the 19th-century piano repertory. Technically demanding and inherently dramatic, each gives the impression of telling a different kind of story. Long thought to be associated with the ballads of the Polish poet Adam Mickiewicz (1798–1855), these works adopt a distinctly narrative approach with clearly delineated episodes of contrasting character.

- *Scherzos.* The four scherzos are large-scale works, like the ballades, but without their narrative qualities. The scherzos also feature more repetition of extended sections. As is characteristic of the scherzo form, they are in triple meter and approximately ABA form. But although *scherzo* many mean "joke" in Italian, these works are not particularly joking.

- *Impromptus.* These few works (there are only three) are lighter in tone, as their name suggests, than those in the other genres Chopin cultivated. The *Fantasie-Impromptu* of 1835 remained unpublished during the composer's lifetime but has become a perennial favorite since then.

- *Individual piano pieces.* In addition to pieces in the genres just listed, Chopin also wrote several independent works of substantial proportion. These include the *Barcarolle*, the *Berceuse* ("Cradle Song," a fascinating compositional study on a gently rocking ostinato bass figure, in keeping with the title), the *Bolero* (inspired by Spanish music), and the *Fantasie*.

## Other Works

All of Chopin's other works involve the piano with other forces. These include two piano concertos, the Sonata for Cello (op. 65), The Piano Trio (op. 8), and some posthumously published songs on Polish texts.

**Chopin.** One of the earliest known photographic images of any composer, this daguerreotype, made in 1849, reveals weariness from the tuberculosis that had sickened Chopin for so long and that would kill him a few months later.

**Source:** Peter Barritt/SuperStock

| KEY DATES IN THE LIFE OF CHOPIN | |
|---|---|
| 1810 | Born near Warsaw on February 22. |
| 1825 | Publishes first piano works. |
| 1831 | After touring central Europe, gives first concert in Paris and soon afterward settles there, living off lessons, performances, and the publication of his works. |
| 1837 | Meets the novelist George Sand and begins a decade-long relationship with her. |
| 1838 | Suffering from tuberculosis, spends the winter with Sand on the island of Majorca in the Mediterranean. |
| 1849 | Dies in Paris on October 17 and is buried between Cherubini and Bellini. |

only high-profile manifestation in the United States today is the Mardi Gras celebration in New Orleans, conventional social standards are set aside. In Schumann's time it was perfectly acceptable—and indeed expected—for people to go about in costume and do behind masks what they could only dream of doing openly.

Like the season for which it is named, many of the movements of Schumann's *Carnaval* contain elements of intrigue, impersonation, excess, and downright nonsense. Why Schumann chose the French form of the word for the title, rather than his native German, is one of the many mysteries of this work that have never been adequately explained. Indeed, the entire cycle is based on a riddle, whose key is given in the movement entitled "Sphinxes." In Greek mythology, the sphinx was a creature who posed

*Der große Galop von Joh. Strauß.*

**Dance fever, 1839.** *The Grand Galop of Johann Strauss,* engraving by A. Geiger after J. C. Schöller. The "Grand Galop" was a favorite finale of dance events, a group activity in which partners could hold one another tightly while moving at dizzying speeds. The pace was clearly too much for the couple in the left foreground of this illustration. A pileup looms behind them as they stumble to the ground. (Is she more upset to have fallen or to have discovered her partner was wearing a toupee?) The single young men clustered in the middle look on with envy. The orchestra, conducted by Johann Strauss the elder (1804–1849, father of the "Waltz King"), plays on the balcony, with the bass drum occupying a place of special prominence.

**Source:** Alfredo Dagli Orti/Museum der Stadt Wien/The Art Archive at Art Resource, NY

a riddle to passersby, killing those who couldn't solve it. Here, Schumann presents a series of brief motivic ideas in archaic breves. The key to the riddle is to be found in the German names for the notes of each motivic idea. Adding "s" to any note name in German designates it as flat. Thus E♭ is "Es" and A♭ is "As." In addition, German designates B♮ with the letter "H." With this in mind, we can see that one of the sequences (E♭-C-B-A) spells "Schumann" in an abbreviated form, and the other two (A♭-C-B and A-E♭-C-B) spell "Asch":

|      |      |        |        |
|------|------|--------|--------|
| E♭   | C    | B      | A      |
| Es   | C    | H      | A      |
| **S** | **C** | **h(um)** | **a(nn)** |

|      |      |     |
|------|------|-----|
| A♭   | C    | B   |
| As   | C    | H   |
| **As** | **c** | **h** |

|      |      |      |      |
|------|------|------|------|
| A    | E♭   | C    | B    |
| A    | Es   | C    | H    |
| **A** | **s** | **c** | **h** |

"Asch" was the hometown of Ernestine von Fricken, who was Schumann's fiancée when he wrote *Carnaval*. The use of notes in this way to spell names or other words has a long tradition in Western music. Josquin, for example, did it in the 16th century with the cantus firmus of his *Missa Hercules Dux Ferrariae* (see Chapter 5), and J. S. Bach did it in the 18th century when he spelled his name in a countersubject in his *The Art of Fugue* (see Chapter 9).

Among the riddles Schumann poses with these Sphinxes is to find all the ways in which he embeds them within the individual pieces in *Carnaval*. The opening notes in the upper part of "Papillons," for example, are A, E♭, C, and C♭ (= B♭ = H). The opening of "Chiarina" is A♭, C, B♭ (= H). It turns out—and this presents another riddle—that Schumann never uses the first Sphinx, the one derived from his own name. And in still another riddle, he leaves unstated whether or not the Sphinxes themselves are to be played in performances of the work.

As the Sphinxes suggest, *Carnaval* is an autobiographical work, rather like Berlioz's *Symphonie fantastique*. Schumann uses the mask of music to say things he would not otherwise have ventured to acknowledge openly. Consider, for example, the trio of movements labeled "Chiarina," "Chopin," and "Estrella." Chiarina was the nickname of the 15-year-old Clara Wieck, the daughter of his own piano teacher. Schumann would later marry Clara, but when he wrote *Carnaval* he was engaged to Ernestine, whose nickname was Estrella. In a gesture clearly anticipating the inevitable end of his engagement to Ernestine, Schumann marks "Estrella" to be played *con affetto* ("with affection," or "tenderly") and, in pointed contrast, marks "Chiarina" to be played *passionate* ("passionately"). The two women in question surely grasped the significance of these indications. The two movements are mediated by one named after Chopin, a composer Schumann greatly admired, who had paid personal visits to both Clara and Robert in September 1835. The admiration was mutual: Chopin dedicated his Second Ballade for piano to Schumann in 1840. In an imitation of Chopin's style, the piece titled "Chopin" has a graceful and soaring melodic line, an elaborately arpeggiated accompaniment, and a clear homophonic texture, and it offers plenty of opportunity for *tempo rubato* in performance.

Like the song, the character piece became increasingly chromatic in the latter part of the 19th century. Liszt's *Nuages gris* ("Gray Clouds"), written in 1881 but unpublished at the composer's death five years later, opens with a rising fourth, followed by

((•⟶ **Listen**
**CD11   Track 12**
**mysearchlab**
LISZT
*Nuages gris*
Score Anthology II/132

## Composer Profile

# Robert Schumann (1810–1856)

A pianist by training, Schumann quite naturally began his compositional career with a series of piano works. But in 1840, he shifted almost exclusively to song and in 1841, to orchestral music; chamber music followed in 1842, oratorio in 1843. These successive pursuits of a single genre have sometimes been interpreted as evidence of a manic-depressive personality and a foreshadowing of the debilitating mental illness of his last years. It seems equally plausible that these periods of intense engagement with a particular genre were the result of Schumann's systematic effort to broaden his scope as a composer.

Schumann was also one of the most influential critics in the history of music. His collected journalistic writings fill two thick volumes and have shaped the way we think and write about music today. He founded and edited for a decade the *Neue Zeitschrift für Musik* ("New Journal of Music"), which quickly established itself as the most important journal of its kind and is still published today. Schumann and his colleagues took on the more conservative elements of the musical establishment with an "us versus them" attitude, dubbing themselves the *Davidsbund*, the "Band of David," because they saw themselves fighting the numerically superior but aesthetically deficient "Philistines." Schumann was one of the first to extol Berlioz's *Symphonie fantastique*, and he was the first major critic to recognize publicly the compositional genius of both Chopin and Brahms.

To give voice to different points of view in his reviews, and in general to represent different aspects of his own persona, Schumann invented several fictional characters: the exuberant, extroverted Florestan; the more circumspect and introverted Eusebius; and the sagacious Magister Raro, who sometimes mediates between the other two. Schumann attributes the opening of his review of *the Symphonie fantastique*, for example, to Florestan, and its detailed account of the work's technical structure to Eusebius. All three characters are drawn from the fiction of Schumann's favorite novelist, Jean Paul (Johann Paul Friedrich Richter, 1763–1825).

Schumann's last years were turbulent. He accepted the directorship of the municipal orchestra at Düsseldorf in 1850, but the arrangement was mutually unsatisfactory. Advancing signs of mental instability forced him to resign in 1853, and thereafter his condition deteriorated rapidly. In 1854, he attempted suicide by throwing himself into the Rhine and was confined to an institution. In his last months he rarely recognized visitors.

# PRINCIPAL WORKS

## Symphonies and Other Orchestral Works

Like almost every other composer of his generation, Robert Schumann struggled against Beethoven's legacy in the symphony, eventually opting for a smaller scale, less monumental approach to the genre. His four numbered symphonies have gained in prestige over the years. The myth that Schumann was an incompetent orchestrator is also beginning to disappear, thanks to recent performances on period instruments, which reveal a clarity of texture and counterpoint that had been obscured by later transformations of the orchestra, not to mention numerous retouchings at the hands of conductors like Felix Weingartner and Gustav Mahler. Schumann's

**Robert and Clara Schumann (1850).** Schumann married Clara Wieck (1819–96), the daughter of his piano teacher, in 1840. (For a profile of Clara Wieck Schumann, see Chapter 17.) By the time this photograph was made ten years later, she had become one of the most renowned piano virtuosos of her time. She sacrificed much of her early career to help raise their children but was able to concertize more extensively from about 1845 onward. Clara's innate grace and Robert's innate awkwardness are amply evident in this revealing dual portrait. Even before his final illness, Robert was a notoriously uncomfortable conversationalist, whereas Clara, by all accounts, could captivate any gathering. Upright pianos like the one in this picture were a 19th-century innovation that lowered costs and made it possible to fit pianos into small spaces.

**Source:** Hervé/Musee d'Orsay, Paris, France/RMN-Grand Palais/ Art Resource, NY

other works for orchestra include the *Overture, Scherzo, and Finale*, op. 52, several concert overtures, and the ever-popular Piano Concerto in A minor, op. 54, written for and widely performed by his wife, Clara Wieck Schumann. The Cello Concerto in A minor, op. 129, is one of the few late works to have gained general acclaim.

## Chamber Music

In 1842, his "year of chamber music," Schumann wrote three string quartets, op. 41; the Piano Quartet, op. 47; and the Piano Quintet, op. 44. To this remarkably intensive output, he later added three piano trios and various other works for combinations of piano and strings or winds.

## Piano Music

Schumann's piano music, particularly the early works from the 1830s, established his reputation as a composer, and these works remain central to the piano repertory. Outstanding among them are *Papillons* ("Butterflies"), op. 2; the *Davidsbündlertänze* ("Dances for the Brotherhood of David"), op. 7; *Carnaval*, op. 9 (discussed in this chapter); the *Symphonic Etudes*, op. 13, a set of etude variations on an original theme; and *Kreisleriana*, op. 16, evoking the mystical world of E. T. A. Hoffmann's fictional Kapellmeister, Johannes Kreisler. Perhaps surpassing even these in greatness, however, is the monumental *Fantasie*, op. 17, the proceeds from which Schumann donated to the erection of a statue of Beethoven in Bonn.

## Songs

Marriage to Clara in 1840 coincided with a remarkable outpouring of song, including the cycles *Liederkreis*, op. 24, and *Dichterliebe* ("Poet's Love"), op. 48, both to texts by Heinrich Heine; another *Liederkreis*, op. 39 (to texts by Joseph von Eichendorff); and *Frauenliebe und-leben* ("Woman's Love and Life"), op. 42, to texts by Adelbert von Chamisso. *Dichterliebe*, in particular, explores the many subtle techniques by which a series of miniatures can be linked in a larger cycle. Stylistically, Schumann's songs continue the tradition cultivated by Schubert, albeit with the more pronounced chromaticism we would expect from a later composer. Schumann also gave the piano a more prominent role. Although instrumental preludes had long been a common feature in songs, Schumann cultivated the idea of allowing the piano to continue after the voice has stopped, providing a kind of wordless commentary on the text that has gone before.

## Vocal Music

Most of Schumann's choral music is forgotten today, but in its time, the oratorio *Das Paradies und die Peri* was hugely popular, as were a number of compositions for men's, women's, and mixed choruses, both with and without orchestra. The decline in the reputation of these works is in part social, for Schumann's music provided important repertory for the widespread choral societies of his time. He himself founded and conducted one such group in Dresden in the late 1840s. With the decline of such choral societies in the 20th century, this and similar music by Schubert, Mendelssohn, and even Brahms has unfortunately fallen into obscurity.

| KEY DATES IN THE LIFE OF ROBERT SCHUMANN | |
|---|---|
| 1810 | Born in Zwickau (Saxony, in central Germany) on June 8. |
| 1828 | Studies law at Leipzig, later at Heidelberg, but eventually abandons law for music. |
| 1830 | Moves to Leipzig and lives with his piano teacher, Friedrich Wieck. |
| 1832 | Injures his hands through a device intended to promote independence of the fingers; forced to abandon a performance career, he turns increasingly to journalism and composition. |
| 1834 | Co-founds the *Neue Zeitschrift für Musik*. |
| 1840 | Marries Clara Wieck. |
| 1841 | Produces or begins five major works for orchestra. |
| 1842 | Writes three string quartets, a piano quartet, and a piano quintet. |
| 1850 | Moves to Düsseldorf to become the city's musical director. |
| 1853 | Meets the 20-year-old Johannes Brahms and proclaims the young composer's talent to the world in the celebrated essay "New Paths." First signs of growing mental instability. |
| 1854 | Attempts suicide and is confined to an asylum at Endenich, near Bonn. |
| 1856 | Dies at Endenich on July 2. |

**The title page to Louis Moreau Gottschalk's *The Banjo* (1855).** The fanciful artwork, with its rustic lettering, conjures up images of the American backwoods, in keeping with the work's subtitle, "An American Sketch." Note the international distribution of this seemingly provincial work: France, Spain, England, Germany, Italy, and Portugal. The banjo was probably African-American in origin, but minstrelsy had made it popular among all Americans. "The piano may do for love-sick girls who lace themselves to skeletons, and lunch on chalk, pickles, and slate pencils," Mark Twain wrote in 1865. "But give me the banjo. . . . When you want *genuine music*—music that will come right home to you like a bad quarter, suffuse your system like strychnine whisky, go right through you like Brandreth's pills, ramify your whole constitution like the measles, and break out on your hide like the pin-feather pimples on a pickled goose—when you want all this, just smash your piano, and invoke the glory-beaming banjo!" Gottschalk's *The Banjo* replicates the sounds of this quintessentially American instrument.

**Source:** Dover Publications, Inc.

a rising augmented fourth and a descending triad. In this context, the G-minor triad in m. 2 certainly does not sound like a tonic triad. Liszt inserts chromatic inflections throughout that obscure the work's tonal identity; in m. 21–32, the opening figure returns in the left hand as the melody cadences on notes of the G minor triad. Immediately thereafter, the left hand figure turns into an unstable ostinato, and a chromatic ascent in octaves leaves off with on the leading tone, F♯, unresolved (m. 44). Even the final chords fail to confirm any tonality; the leading-tone resolution is undermined by the harmony, notably the G-B♮ dyad with an open A♭ chord in the lower voices that concludes the piece. The music seems to float like the clouds evoked in its title, with little sense of any forward motion. In this respect, it anticipates the Impressionist style of the late 19th and early 20th centuries (see Chapter 20).

## THE VIRTUOSO SHOWPIECE

Virtuosity was not a new phenomenon in the 19th century: singers and instrumentalists had long been dazzling audiences through improvisation and the performance of notated music far beyond the technical range of average musicians. During the middle third of the century, however, more and more composers began writing music of this kind. The **etude** (the French word for "study") became a public genre, to be performed and heard outside the practice studio, and a number of character pieces of the time display an increasing tendency toward musical showmanship. One cannot hear such pieces without being aware of the immense technical abilities involved in bringing them to life.

The composers who wrote these virtuoso showpieces were usually performers themselves, and many of them cultivated an aura of mystique, encouraging audiences to view them as super-human, endowed with unearthly talents. Rumor had it that the Italian composer and violinist Niccolò Paganini (1782–1840) had made a pact with the devil to win his extraordinary skills as a virtuoso. Paganini did nothing to dispel this story. His 24 Caprices, op. 1 (published in 1820 but probably written at least a decade before) are themselves homage to a set of 24 caprices published by Pietro Locatelli, an earlier violin virtuoso, in 1733. The last of Paganini's 24 Caprices makes an unusually wide array of technical demands on the violinist. Formally, it is a set of variations on a theme, with each variation highlighting a particular technique:

**Listen**

**CD11  Track 13**
**mysearchlab**
PAGANINI
Caprice in A minor, op.1, no. 24
Score Anthology II/133

- **Variation 1:** Spiccato arpeggiation (bouncing the bow lightly on the string).

- **Variation 2:** Bariolage, the rapid and repeated alternation between two adjacent strings, one open, the other fingered.

- **Variation 3:** Octaves. Because the violin does not feature fixed pitches, like a piano, octaves require absolutely perfect placement of two fingers in relation to each other.

- **Variation 4:** High chromatic passages. The higher the hand moves on the fingerboard, the smaller the physical space between the finger placements of the individual notes.

- **Variation 5:** String crossing. This variation requires the player to move quite rapidly across strings.

- **Variation 6:** Thirds and octaves. Again, both pitches must be perfectly fingered.

- **Variation 7:** Bowing. The player must pick up and replace the bow in a downstroke rapidly in succession while playing a triplet figure that moves through all registers of the instrument.

- **Variation 8:** Triple stopping. The performer rolls a series of chords on three different notes, each played on a different string.

- **Variation 9:** Left-hand pizzicato. The player must alternate rapidly between notes played with the bow and notes plucked with the left hand (not the right hand, as in normal pizzicato).

- **Variation 10:** High position. The performer must execute rapid runs in a very high register.

- **Variation 11:** Successive double stops.

- **Finale:** Long runs and successive double stops.

This particular caprice was so appealing that a long list of composers would draw on it in one form or another: Franz Liszt made a piano transcription of it, Robert Schumann added a piano accompaniment to Paganini's violin line, and Johannes Brahms wrote a set of variations on it. In the 20th century Sergei Rachmaninoff used it as the basis for his *Rhapsody on a Theme of Paganini* (1934) for piano and orchestra. More recently still, the Polish composer Witold Lutoslawski made this theme the centerpiece of his *Paganini Variations* for piano and orchestra (1978).

## Composer Profile

# Franz Liszt (1811–1886)

Liszt is a figure who seems to pop up everywhere. He crossed paths with virtually every major musician in the generations from Beethoven through Brahms and played an important role in the careers of such diverse figures as Berlioz, Paganini, Chopin, and Wagner. He was extraordinarily generous with his time and energy toward younger composers and performers. He was also a man of enormous contradictions. Liszt cultivated his image as a Hungarian composer (his *Hungarian Rhapsodies* for piano are perennial favorites), but his native language was German, and he learned Hungarian only toward the end of his life. After living a life full of earthly pleasures, he took holy orders in his mid-50s and assumed a new identity as Abbé Liszt.

Physical appearance was part of his mystique: the imposing height, aquiline nose, swept back hair, and graceful hands all contributed to an air of suavity and mystery that captivated audiences. He revolutionized the art of the recital and gave the phenomenon its very name. *Recitals* had previously been confined to the sphere of oratory (as in a "recital of facts"). Playing on the image of music as a language in its own right, Liszt transferred the term to musical performance. He also turned the piano sideways on the stage so the audience could see his dramatic profile. When possible, he even placed two pianos on stage facing one another and alternated between them so all members of the audience could see his hands (and profile) at some point. His consistently spoke of being "transported" by his playing. So great were the passions generated by Liszt's performances that the poet Heinrich Heine coined the term "Lisztomania" to describe a condition having "every resemblance to an infectious disease."[7]

# PRINCIPAL WORKS

## Symphonies and Symphonic Poems

Liszt's two symphonies represent a synthesis of symphony and symphonic poem. The *Faust-Symphonie* of 1854 (revised 1857) consists of what he called three "character pieces" reflecting the three central figures in Goethe's *Faust*: Faust, Gretchen, and Mephistopheles. In this work, Liszt used what would later come to be known through Wagner's music dramas as *Leitmotivs*, a network of interrelated musical ideas that convey some sort of extramusical idea. The symphony concludes with a brief section for tenor and chorus based on the closing scene from Part II of Goethe's *Faust*. The *Symphonie zu Dantes Divina commedia* of 1856, also in three movements, similarly concludes with a brief vocal section that culminates a trajectory leading from struggle (*Inferno*, *Purgatorio*) to paradise. Liszt called his early one-movement works for orchestra *overtures* because at the time of their composition there was no better designation by which to describe them. In the mid-1850s, however, he coined the terms *symphonic poem* and *tone poem* to convey their alliance with some kind of literary program or idea.

## Piano Works

Liszt's piano music covers an enormous range, from large-scale works like the Sonata in B minor to miniatures, most of it beyond the technical reach of amateurs. Many of the character pieces relate to texts, like the *Sonnets after Petrarch*, or to places, like the *Années des pèlerinages* ("Years of Pilgrimage"), which take the listener on a series of wide-ranging journeys. Programmatic ideas behind

Paganini's counterpart on the piano was Franz Liszt, whose technical prowess was unrivalled even in an age of great virtuosos. Chopin is said to have expressed envy at Liszt's ability to play his own—Chopin's—etudes with such facility. Liszt wrote a good many etudes of his own, including a set entitled *Etudes d'exécution transcendante* (1838; revised 1851), that is, etudes requiring a technique transcending the ordinary. The first of these, in C Major, clearly fits into the tradition of C Major works that open large, systematically ordered sets, such as Bach's C Major Prelude in the *Well-Tempered Clavier* (Anthology I/95), Chopin's C Major Prelude in his Preludes, op. 24 (Anthology II/129),

**Franz Liszt, 1858.** Photograph by Franz Hanfstägl.

**Source:** Bettmann/Corbis

| KEY DATES IN THE LIFE OF LISZT | |
|---|---|
| 1811 | Born near Ödenburg (Hungary), in what was then part of the Austrian Empire. |
| 1821 | Moves with family to Vienna and begins study of the piano with Carl Czerny, one of the leading virtuosos of his day and a friend of Beethoven. |
| 1827 | Moves to Paris and continues to amaze audiences with his dazzling performances on the piano. |
| 1830s | Concertizes extensively and publishes many works for piano. |
| 1848 | Becomes music director at the court of Weimar and turns more and more to writing for the orchestra. |
| 1861 | Moves to Rome but continues extensive travels. |
| 1865 | Receives minor holy orders by decree of Pope Pius IX and becomes an abbot. |
| 1870 | Daughter Cosima marries Richard Wagner, further intensifying his already well established support of that composer. |
| 1886 | Dies in Bayreuth on July 31. |

Liszt's piano music are as likely to be sacred ("Saint Francis of Assisi Preaches to the Birds") as demonic (the various "Mephisto" Waltzes). The *Transcendental etudes* are even more technically difficult than Chopin's *Etudes*. Liszt also transcribed for solo piano all of Beethoven's symphonies and numerous songs by Schubert. His paraphrases on contemporary operas were in great demand during his lifetime.

## Vocal Music

The four Masses, Requiem, 3 oratorios, and numerous works for chorus and orchestra, although they constitute an important portion of the composer's output, are for the most part forgotten today. Liszt's more than 60 songs for voice and piano occasionally find their way into performances but largely await rediscovery.

and the opening C Major Etude in Chopin's Etudes for piano, op. 10. Liszt follows the same organizational pattern in these etudes that Chopin had used in his Preludes: a circle of descending fifths in the major keys, with each major-mode work followed by one in the relative minor. But from the perspective of technical demands, Liszt's opening salvo in these "Transcendental" Etudes leaves all earlier works in its wake. Robert Schumann, reviewing an earlier version of Liszt's set, called them "studies in storm and dread, fit for 10 or 12 players in the world." Weaker players, Schumann added, "would arouse only laughter with these works."

**Paganini weaves his magic.** Paganini never did anything to contradict the rumors that he had made a pact with the devil to gain his extraordinary skills as a violin virtuoso; the story only added to the artist's mystique. The orchestra players here look on in amazement. Note the high hand position on the fingerboard: part of Paganini's virtuosity lay in his ability to play fluently in the uppermost range of the instrument.

**Source:** V&A Image/London/Art Resource, NY

**Louis Moreau Gottschalk.** Gottschalk's artistry and good looks were a source of constant commentary in the American press wherever he performed. He concertized widely in North America, South America, the Caribbean, and Europe. A showman as well as a musician, he always made a ceremony of taking off his white gloves before he played in public.

Beethoven—in the form of a bust—looms over all. The conspicuous placement of the piano's brand name is no coincidence: Gottschalk was paid to endorse this particular brand of piano. Chickering was one of hundreds of American piano firms that thrived in the 19th and early 20th centuries but eventually went out of business or were absorbed by larger companies.

**Source:** The New York Public Library/Art Resource, NY

# A CLOSER LOOK

✳ Explore on mysearchlab

**A CIVIL WAR CONCERT TOUR** After almost six years in Latin America, mostly in the Caribbean, Gottschalk returned to the United States early in 1862. He concertized extensively throughout the north that year. On one of his tours, he covered some 15,000 miles by train and gave 85 concerts over the course of 18 weeks. He performed his newly composed *Union*, with its "patriotic airs" of *Yankee Doodle, Hail Columbia,* and *The Star-Spangled Banner,* at virtually every opportunity. In his diary, Gottschalk recorded his impressions of various stops on his tours.

**7. Early December:** Madison, Wisconsin. "This town is hardly more than twelve years old, and nevertheless is already remarkable. The cathedral (Catholic) and the marble capitol are superb."

**4. June 6:** Portland, Maine. "The hall contains twenty-five hundred persons, and is one of the finest in the world for its acoustic properties. The public are desirous that I should return and give another concert. Extraordinary enthusiasm."

**3. April 18:** On the way east from Chicago, Gottschalk witnesses a convoy of wounded soliders recently arrived from the Battle of Shiloh, in Tennessee. "I have never in my life seen a more heart-rending sight than the spectacle of these heroic victims of our monstrous war."

**5. June 28:** Springfield, Massachusetts. "Visited a large manufactory of guns belonging to the government, where as many as twelve hundred rifles are made daily by a machine. Three thousand workmen are employed here."

**8. December 15:** Indianapolis: "Whistling is here applause carried to its highest point… Another annoyance is the people who arrive late at the concert, and who traverse the hall in the middle of a piece, marching as if they were marking time for a battalion of raw recruits."

**1. February 22:** New York City. Gottschalk premieres *Union* to great acclaim on Washington's birthday.

**2. Spring:** In St. Louis, Gottschalk observes that "the Germans (they are numerous here, as throughout the West) have organized a Philharmonic Society, which performs the works of Beethoven, Mendelssohn, Schumann, and Wagner."

**6. November 26:** Toledo. Gottschalk is unimpressed with Toledo. "Nothing interesting. Audience stupid. In the Artist's Room there was a bill attached to the wall: 'If, before commencing the concert, the performers do not pay the rent of the hall, the porter has orders from the proprietors to turn off the gas'."

CANADA

U.S.A.

Portland, ME   4

Madison, WI   7

Springfield, MA   5

Chicago, IL   3   6

New York, NY   1

Indianapolis, IN   8

Toledo, OH

2

Washington, DC

N

St. Louis, MI

Confederate States of America

In *Union* (1862), Louis Moreau Gottschalk (1829–1869) combines virtuosity and nationalism in spectacular fashion. Although born and raised in New Orleans, Gottschalk was a staunch Unionist from the very start of the American Civil War. This "concert paraphrase" incorporates three "national airs" associated with the Northern cause: *The Star-Spangled Banner*, *Yankee Doodle*, and *Hail, Columbia*. The first of these would become the country's official national anthem in 1931, while the second has always been associated with the United States. *Hail, Columbia* was just as popular in the 19th century but for reasons that remain unclear dropped out of favor in the years around World War I. But at the time of the Civil War, it functioned as an unofficial national anthem. *Union* was a favorite number during Gottschalk's 1863 concert tours of northern cities. After a performance in Philadelphia, he noted in his diary that the piece had elicited "unheard of enthusiasm . . . Recalls, encores, hurrahs, etc.!"[8]

Virtuosity of this kind provoked both wonderment and scorn in the 19th century. Many critics dismissed such bravura works on the grounds that they were "merely" virtuosic, as if virtuosity were somehow not a musical quality. But audiences clearly responded (and continue to respond) to this repertory, especially when performed by a musician in complete command of the required skills.

## SUMMARY

Chamber music, song, and music for solo piano found a ready market in 19th-century households. The growing affordability of the piano made this instrument the new focus of music making in the home. Sonatas and other works for solo piano, as well as songs for voice and piano, became a staple of the domestic repertory. The emergence of German as a literary language gave composers new texts to set by such prestigious poets as Goethe and Schiller. The character piece for piano, in turn, provided an instrumental counterpart to song, a miniature genre with strong suggestions of programmatic content but without an explicit text. Virtuoso showpieces highlighted the performer's ability to play works whose technical demands lay far beyond the capacities of the average player.

# Dramatic and Choral Music

In spite of the growing significance of instrumental music in the 19th century, the large-scale genres of vocal music—opera, operetta, and sacred music—maintained their traditional aesthetic prestige. For many if not most critics and listeners, opera remained the pinnacle of the musical art, for it combined drama (the libretto), music (the score), and the visual arts (scenery, costume) in a single genre. It continued to attract the finest singers and many of the most talented composers of the day, and it was by far the most financially lucrative of all genres. Through ticket sales, printed scores, and the prospect of future commissions, a hit opera was a composer's surest path to fame and success. Operetta, a lighter form of sung drama, usually with spoken dialogue, commanded an even wider following among the public. Sacred music, in turn, became increasingly varied in scope, ranging from monumental settings of the Mass and Requiem in the most modern style to smaller scale motets strongly influenced by the idiom of the late Renaissance.

## OPERA

Since its emergence in the early 17th century, composers of opera had struggled to reconcile the demands of music against the demands of drama: purely musical considerations did not always mesh with dramatic realism or the clear declamation of texts. Over the course of the 19th century, particularly from the 1840s onward, composers of all nationalities pursued new approaches to reconciling these often conflicting demands. By the end of the century, their efforts had fundamentally changed the genre of opera, but in ways that were different in Italy, France, and Germany.

### Italy in the Early 19th Century: Rossini

The first three decades of the 19th century are often referred to as the "Age of Beethoven," but it would be more accurate to call this period the "Age of Rossini and Beethoven." Like Beethoven in the realm of instrumental music, Gioacchino Rossini (1792–1868) enjoyed unquestioned preeminence in the world of opera in the first half of the 19th century. Rossini helped establish a style of Italian opera known as **bel canto**—literally, "beautiful singing." The term refers to a vocal technique that emphasizes lyrical melodic lines, legato phrasing, and a seemingly effortless vocal technique, even in passages of great technical difficulty. Orchestral accompaniment in 19th-century bel canto opera is typically discreet, limited to harmonic underpinning with little or no counterpoint. The emphasis throughout is on the voice. Although not every aria or every role in a bel canto opera conforms to this style, the ideal of beautiful production lies at the aesthetic core of all these works.

**((•• Listen**

**CD12    Tracks 1-2**
**mysearchlab**
ROSSINI
*Il Barbiere di Siviglia*
Score Anthology II/136

Rossini's *Il Barbiere di Siviglia* ("The Barber of Seville," 1816), the most popular of his many operas, integrates the traditions of opera buffa into the style of bel canto. The barber of the title is Figaro, a buffa-like character whose profession brings him into contact with people at the highest levels of Seville's society, making him an ideal go-between: a "factotum," as he calls himself. Over the course of the opera, Count Almaviva (disguised as a student) uses Figaro to help him win the hand of Rosina, who is being pursued at the same time by a certain Doctor Bartolo, who, awkwardly enough, also happens to be her legal guardian. The drama unfolds in a series of madcap antics full of mistaken identities, disguises, and secret notes.

In this opera the music illustrates the essential nature of the characters in ways that the text alone cannot. Figaro's opening number, for example, *Largo al factotum* ("Make way for the factotum"), does a marvelous job introducing the title character. He half complains, half boasts that his services are in such demand among people of quality that he is always busy. Constantly repeating the same lines of text, Figaro works himself into a frenzy, imitating people calling him—"Figaro! Figaro!"—in that famous three-note melody (beginning at m. 187) that has come to be indelibly associated with his character. "One at a time!" he half shouts to himself in response.

Rosina's *Una voce poco fa* ("A voice a short while ago") is very much in the bel canto tradition and draws an equally sharp characterization. Like many arias of this period, it consists of two sections, a slow opening and a lively conclusion, known as the **cabaletta**. Rosina sings while writing a letter to Lindoro, who is in fact Count Almaviva in disguise. After declaring Lindoro her chosen suitor, she professes to be "docile, respectful, and obedient." The music, however, gives the lie to this claim, changing from reserved to lively and spontaneous in the cabaletta as she goes on to sing, "But if you push me the wrong way, I'll be a viper, and the last laugh will be on you." By the time she returns to professing her docility, the feistiness of the music has infected the orchestra, leaving no doubt that the music, not the words, represents Rosina's true character.

## Italy at Midcentury: Verdi

**((•• Listen**

**CD11    Tracks 16-18**
**mysearchlab** (with scrolling translation)
VERDI
*Rigoletto*
Score Anthology II/137

In the generations after Rossini, composers devoted increasing attention to issues of dramatic integrity. Giuseppe Verdi (1813–1901) was the leading composer of Italian opera in the middle of the 19th century, and his *Rigoletto* exemplifies several key characteristics of a new approach to the genre: dramatic realism, the use of the *scena* (scene) as the unit of dramatic organization, and dramatically justified virtuosity.

**Dramatic Realism.**   Verdi was fiercely committed to the idea of realism on the stage and struggled throughout his life to find librettos of high literary quality. For *Rigoletto*, he used an adaptation of the play *Le roi s'amuse* ("The King Amuses Himself") by the French writer Victor Hugo (1802–1885), one of the greatest playwrights of his age. Verdi worked closely with the Italian dramatist Francesco Piave (1810–1876) to adapt Hugo's stage play into a suitable libretto. The opera's plot revolves around the Duke of Mantua, a notorious womanizer; his humpbacked court jester, Rigoletto; Rigoletto's daughter and only child, Gilda; and a wronged father's curse. The Duke's courtiers resent Rigoletto's malicious wit and plot to humiliate him. Rigoletto has been keeping Gilda in seclusion, allowing her out only on Sunday to attend church.

# Gioacchino Rossini (1792–1868)

Born into a family of musicians—his father was a town trumpeter, his mother a soprano on the stage—Rossini was internationally famous as an opera composer by the age of 21. Between 1815 and 1823, he composed 20 new operas, including a critically acclaimed setting of Shakespeare's *Othello* in 1816. He toured the Continent extensively, scoring successes in Vienna, Paris, and London. In 1829, he won renewed acclaim with his opera *Guillaume Tell* ("William Tell"). For reasons that remain unclear, he then abruptly retired from the world of opera at the age of 37, composing only a few nonoperatic pieces thereafter. He spent the remainder of his life in Florence, Bologna, and Paris, where he became a fixture in the salons.

## PRINCIPAL WORKS

Except for works written during his student years, Rossini's output consists almost entirely of operas and cantatas. He wrote opere serie (*Tancredi*, *Otello*, *Semiramide*) as well as opere buffe (*Il Barbiere di Siviglia*, *La Cenerentola*, the latter based on the story of Cinderella). *Guillaume Tell*, regarded by many as Rossini's masterpiece, fuses Italian lyricism into the tradition of French grand opera.

**Rossini in 1862.**

**Source:** Peter Joslin/ArenaPAL/Topham/The Image Works

Eт. CARJAT.

| KEY DATES IN THE LIFE OF ROSSINI | |
|---|---|
| 1792 | Born in Pesaro (northern Italy) on February 29. |
| 1813 | Achieves his first major operatic success with *Tancredi,* an opera seria. |
| 1816 | Premiere of *Il Barbiere di Siviglia,* his most famous work. |
| 1829 | Premiere of *Guillaume Tell,* his last opera, after which he abruptly retires from the world of opera. |
| 1868 | Dies in Paris on November 13. |

The courtiers discover her, but mistake her for Rigoletto's mistress, and plot to abduct her for the Duke's pleasure. But the Duke, disguised as a young student, has already approached her on her Sunday outings and has determined that she will be his next conquest. In the opening sequence, Rigoletto belittles Count Monterone, who has come to denounce the Duke for seducing his daughter. As he is led off to prison, Monterone turns on Rigoletto and the courtiers and hurls a curse at them all, but singling out Rigoletto in particular. When the courtiers abduct Gilda and bring her to the Duke, Rigoletto attributes his misfortune to Monterone's curse. Discovering the Duke has had his way with Gilda, Rigoletto hires an assassin to kill his master. But Gilda, in love with the Duke despite his faithlessness, saves his life by sacrificing herself at the last moment to the assassin's knife. When Rigoletto realizes what has happened, he cries out in despair, "Ah, the curse!"

Verdi and Piave encountered serious obstacles from state censors in their effort to bring *Rigoletto* to the stage in Venice. Both Hugo's play and Piave's adaptation present

## Primary Evidence   STENDHAL DESCRIBES A PERFORMANCE OF AN OPERA BY ROSSINI

*The novelist Stendhal (Marie-Henri Beyle; 1783–1842) was a keen observer of contemporary manners, including the world of music. His description of this unnamed opera by Rossini captures the spirit of the Paris Opéra in the 1820s.*

■ ■ ■

As the overture begins, you could hear a pin drop; as it bangs its way triumphantly to an end, the din bursts with unbelievable violence. It is extolled to high heaven; or alternately, it is whistled, nay rather *howled* into eternity with merciless shrieks and ululations. There is no parallel in Paris, where cautious vanity anxiously eyes a neighboring vanity beside it; these are men possessed of seven devils, determined at all costs, by dint of shrieking, stamping, and battering with their canes against the backs of the seats in front, to enforce the triumph of *their* opinion, and above all, to prove that, come what may, *none but their opinion* is correct—for, in all the world, there is no intolerance like that of a man of artistic sensibility. . . .

Each *aria* of the new opera, in its turn, is listened to in perfect silence; after which, the cataclysm is let loose once more; and the bellowing of a storm-tormented sea is nothing but the feeblest comparison. The audience makes its opinion of the singers on the one hand, and of the composer on the other, distinctly audible. There are cries of *Bravo Davide! Bravo Pisaroni!*, or on other occasions, the whole theatre will echo with demonic shrieks of *Bravo maestro!* Rossini rises from his seat at the piano, his handsome face assuming an unwonted expression of gravity. He bows thrice, submitting to storms of applause, and deafened by a most unlikely variety of acclamations, for whole sentences of adulation may be flung at his unresisting head; after which, the company proceeds to the next item.

**Source:** Stendhal, *The Life of Rossini;* trans. Richard N. Coa (London: Calder, 1956). pp. 118–19.

royalty in an unflattering light, featuring, as they do, a philandering ruler who hides behind the protection of his lofty position in society. Almost as problematic was the character of Rigoletto himself. In an age when the physically disabled were thought unsuitable subjects for a drama, it was daring indeed to feature a hunchback in an opera's title role.

**Larger Units of Dramatic Organization.**   Although Verdi uses many of the traditional elements of Italian opera (such as arias, duets, choruses, and accompanied recitative), he consistently incorporates these into a larger dramatic units. Verdi was not the first to take this approach to dramatic organization. It was already being used by Gluck and Mozart in the 18th century and was particularly prominent, as we saw in Chapter 13, in the opening sequence of Mozart's *Don Giovanni* (Anthology). It is also found in works by Rossini and his contemporaries, such as Gaetano Donizetti (1797–1848) and Vincenzo Bellini (1801–1835). But Verdi and other midcentury composers expanded on this approach to create increasingly extended spans of music and drama uninterrupted by scenery changes or obvious opportunities for applause.

In *Rigoletto* this approach enhances the sense of dramatic realism. Verdi's means of expression are remarkably economical. Avoiding an extended overture, he opens instead with a brief, somber instrumental Prelude that sets the tone of this deeply tragic opera. The opening bars introduce the motif associated with Monterone's curse, and although we do not yet know its meaning, we recognize at once the dark character of the music. The effect is similar to that of the theme that begins the overture to Mozart's *Don Giovanni*, a theme later associated with the Commendatore's death and subsequent vengeance. Indeed, *Rigoletto* is in many ways Verdi's homage to Mozart's opera. Both concern the fate of a libertine and his victims.

The curtain rises to reveal a scene of dancing, drinking, and revelry in the ballroom of the Duke's palace, labeled simply "N[umber] 2. Introduction." This extended opening unit of music unfolds continuously, yet consists of eight interconnected subsections. In each of these, the music underscores the dramatic action:

1. The opening dance, although not given a label in the score, has the same kind of frenzied beat associated with the *galop* (see Anthology). The incessant accentuation on every note conjures up a sense of intense physical activity.

2. When the Duke and one of his courtiers enter, the music shifts to a dance that has a lighter texture with emphasis only on beats 1 and 3 of a four-beat measure. This change allows the recitative-like patter of the voices to emerge clearly over the orchestra.

3. The Duke's first aria (*Questa o quella*) is also the first moment in the opera in which the voice carries the melody completely. The texture here is utterly homophonic, with the orchestra providing a demure accompaniment. Verdi's critics carped that this kind of accompaniment was "organ barrel grinder music," a complaint that, even if true, is irrelevant given the extraordinary beauty of Verdi's melodies. Verdi, moreover, used this style only when it was dramatically justified. Here, the Duke is bragging about his sexual prowess: why should he share the spotlight with the orchestra or anyone else? The dramatic setting demands a straightforward aria, and it is precisely the compelling simplicity of this number that makes it so powerful. The Duke sings two musically identical strophes, ending with a vocal cadenza that matches perfectly the boastful nature of his words.

4. With the entrance of the Countess of Ceprano—a woman the Duke has had his eye on for some time—the music changes to a minuet played by an onstage string ensemble. This decidedly old-fashioned dance fits perfectly with the Countess's traditional character: she resists the Duke's advances and insists she must remain with her husband.

5. When the Duke leaves with the reluctant Countess, Rigoletto and the courtiers ridicule her husband, who anxiously follows after his wife and the Duke. One of the festive dance melodies from the opening returns briefly here. Rigoletto exits and the onstage ensemble strikes up a new melody, which Verdi labels a *perigordino*, an Italian dance in 6/8 meter whose frenzied character is very different from that of the preceding minuet. This purely instrumental passage allows for a brief ballet.

6. The opening galop-like dance resumes briefly with the entrance of Marullo, a courtier who brings "great news." Rigoletto, he reports, has a secret lover. As in segment 2, Marullo's recitative-like delivery is accompanied by a lighter texture and a less insistent rhythm.

## Primary Evidence — VERDI REACTS TO THE CENSORS' PROPOSED CHANGES TO THE LIBRETTO OF *RIGOLETTO*

*Verdi had to fight many battles with censors throughout his artistic career. Government officials were quick to realize the political potential of the genre of opera, and various state offices kept close watch over the librettos, the music, and the staging of new works. Venice, like most of Italy, was at the time under the direct or indirect control of the Austrian Empire, and an opera like* Rigoletto, *depicting a dissolute monarch, was inevitably subjected to intense scrutiny. Censors demanded that many elements of the plot be altered: among other changes, the character of the Duke was to be made more sympathetic, and Rigoletto was to lose his humpback. In this letter of December 14, 1850, to Carlo Marzari, president of La Fenice (the Venetian theater that had commissioned Verdi's new work), Verdi reacts angrily to the proposed changes.*

■ ■ ■

I have taken very little time to re-examine the new libretto: but I have seen enough to realize that, reduced to the present condition, it lacks character and importance; further, the dramatic moments have become very cool indeed. . . . In the fifth scene of Act I, all that anger vented by the courtiers against Triboletto [the original name of the jester, later changed to Rigoletto] makes no sense. The old man's malediction [curse], so terrible and sublime in the original, becomes ridiculous here, because the motive for his malediction is not so important any more, and because this is no longer a subject speaking so boldly to his king. Without this malediction what purpose, what significance does the play have? The Duke is a nonentity: the Duke must absolutely be a libertine; otherwise, Triboletto's fear that his daughter might leave her hiding place is ungrounded: and the play impossible. How does it happen that the Duke, in the last act, goes to a remote tavern all alone, without an invitation, without an appointment? I don't understand why the sack was taken out! Of what consequence was the sack to the police? Are they afraid of its effect? Forgive me, but what makes them think they know more about the subject than I do? Who is entitled to be a Maestro? Who is entitled to say, this will be effective, that won't? A difficulty of that kind arose on account of the horn in *Ernani* [one of Verdi's earlier operas]. Well then, did anyone laugh at the sound of that horn? Take away that sack, and it becomes improbable that Triboletto should speak to a corpse for half an hour, till a flash of lightning reveals it to be that of his daughter. Finally, I note that they have avoided making Triboletto ugly and humpbacked!! A singing humpback? Why not! . . . Will it be effective? I don't know; but if I don't know, neither does, I repeat, the person who suggested the change. As a matter of fact, I think it is a very fine thing to depict this extremely deformed and ridiculous character who is inwardly impassioned and full of love. I chose the subject expressly because of these qualities, and if these original traits are removed, I can no longer set it to music. If I'm told that my notes will suit the present drama just as well, I answer that I have no understanding for these arguments, and I frankly state that, good or bad, I never write music at random and I always manage to give it character.

In short, what was an original, powerful play has been turned into something very common and cold. I very much regret that the Board of Directors has not answered my last letter. I can only repeat and request that what I wrote in it should be carried out, for upon my artist's conscience I cannot set this libretto to music.

**Source:** *Letters of Composers through Six Centuries,* ed. Piero Weiss (Philadelphia: Chilton, 1967), pp. 217–18.

7. The Duke, Rigoletto, and Count Ceprano return, and with them the opening galop-like theme. The Duke rebukes Rigoletto for his excessive jesting about the Count. The chorus of courtiers joins in, and in a general frenzy all agree to get their revenge on Rigoletto.

8. The choral frenzy ends abruptly with the entrance of Monterone. He has come to find his daughter, who at some earlier point had been abducted by the Duke. The music now shifts ominously to accompanied recitative: Monterone lays down his accusation and Rigoletto taunts him. Monterone, in response, lays a curse on the entire court, particularly on Rigoletto. The curtain closes on a scene of general confusion and distress.

Every dramatic turn on the stage, every arrival or departure of a main character, is articulated through a change in the music. The action continues without interruption from the beginning to the end of the entire scene. The next unit of action (Act I, Scene 7; not in Anthology), a dialogue between Rigoletto and the assassin Sparafucile,

**Costume designs for the premiere of Verdi's *Rigoletto* (1851).** Stage and costume design were matters of great importance to 19th-century opera producers and audiences. The costume designs shown here give some idea of the variety available to each major character in Verdi's *Rigoletto* at its world premiere in Venice in 1851. Gilda's first costume is actually that from the end of Act III, when she appears at the tavern disguised as a man. Rigoletto is shown in his two guises, with and without his jester's costume. Note that the jester's hunchback is played down in this setting; many subsequent productions have emphasized this characteristic feature far more strongly, but Verdi had already gone through considerable difficulties in persuading the censors to accept the very idea of a hunchback appearing on the stage (see Primary Evidence: Verdi Reacts to the Censors' Proposed Changes to the Libretto of *Rigoletto*).

**Source:** DeAgostini/SuperStock

functions as a transition to the subsequent "Scene and Duet" (Act I, Scene 8), which is far more complicated. The "scene" is a monologue in which Rigoletto muses on his deformity, his malicious wit, and his contempt for the Duke and his courtiers. In his extended duet with Gilda, Rigoletto reveals another, more compassionate side to his character (see the table titled "**Verdi's *Rigoletto*: The Structure of Act I, Scene 8**").

The final duet within the duet has its own internal structure (see the table titled "**Verdi's *Rigoletto*: The Structure of the Closing Duet in Act I, Scene 8**"). It is, in effect, a series of variations on a single theme and follows the traditional pattern of love duets: he sings, she sings, and then finally they both sing, and in this respect, Verdi adheres to convention. But he also slips in important plot developments within the course of this duet. At m. 279, Rigoletto hears a prowler—the Duke, it turns out—and interrupts himself to launch into an agitated inquisition of Gilda's nursemaid, Giovanna. Thus we have a dramatic dialogue in the middle of the duet (Rigoletto: "No one has followed her from church?" Giovanna, lying: "Never!" and so on). Meanwhile, the Duke himself has been listening in on all this and realizes the woman he has been pursuing (Gilda) is the daughter of his court jester (Rigoletto) and interjects a few asides to express his astonishment at this revelation. With his fears calmed, Rigoletto resumes

| VERDI'S *RIGOLETTO*: THE STRUCTURE OF ACT I, SCENE 8 | | | | |
|---|---|---|---|---|
| | **Measure** | **Tempo** | **Text** | **Dramatic Action** |
| **Scene** | 1–11 | Adagio | "Pari siamo . . ." | Rigoletto muses on the similarities between himself and Sparafucile, the assassin. |
| | 12–14 | Adagio | "Quel vecchio maledivami!" | Rigoletto: "That old man has laid a curse on me!" Return of the "curse" motif. |
| | 15–29 | Allegro/ Adagio | "O uomini! o natura!" | Curses his deformity and fate. |
| | 30–40 | Moderato | "Questo padrone mio . . ." | Rigoletto thinks of the Duke, who is "young, powerful, and handsome." |
| | 41–51 | Allegro | "Oh dannazione!" | Curses the Duke and all the members of his court. "If I am evil, it is only because of you!" |
| | 52–57 | Andante | | "But here I change into another man." Rigoletto arrives home. |
| | 58–68 | Andante/ Allegro | "Quel vecchio . . ." | Unwelcome memory of Monterone's curse. |
| **Duet** | 69–116 | Allegro | "Figlia!" | Gilda enters, and Rigoletto embraces her. |
| | 117–124 | Adagio | "Se mi volete . . ." | Rigoletto reminds Gilda never to leave the house; he has never revealed to her his true identity as jester; she knows him only as her father. |
| | 125–202 | Andante | "Deh non parlare" | Rigoletto tells Gilda that she is his sole consolation in life; Gilda is moved by his suffering. |
| | 203–242 | Andante | "Già da tre lune" | Gilda asks why she must always remain at home, allowed to leave only to attend church on Sunday. Rigoletto, constantly fearful that she will be abducted, thinks he hears a prowler; it is Giovanna, the family's servant. |
| | 243–343 | Allegro | "Ah! veglia, o donna . . ." | Rigoletto implores Giovanna to protect Gilda. |

| | VERDI'S *RIGOLETTO*: STRUCTURE OF THE CLOSING DUET IN ACT 1, SCENE 8, M. 243–343 | | | | | |
|---|---|---|---|---|---|---|
| **Tempo** | Allegro moderato assai | | | Allegro Più mosso | Tempo 1 | Più mosso |
| **Voices** | Rigoletto (solo) | Gilda (solo) | Rigoletto (solo) | Rigoletto, Gilda, Duke, Giovanna; free material, quasi recitative | Rigoletto and Gilda (duet) | Cabaletta to the duet |
| **Measure** | 243 | 259 | 274 | 278 | 303 | 318 |
| **Harmony** | E♭ Major | A♭ Major | E♭ Major | D♭ minor/B♭ Major | E♭ Major | E♭ Major |
| **Dramatic action** | Rigoletto implores Giovanna to protect Gilda. | Gilda: "What love, what affection." | Rigoletto resumes but is interrupted. | Rigoletto hears someone prowling (the Duke), who in turn now realizes that Gilda, the object of his latest adventure, is the daughter of his jester, Rigoletto. | Rigoletto and Gilda resume Gilda's "lassù in ciel" is a premonition of her dying words in Act III. | Rigoletto and Gilda bid farewell. |

his duet with Gilda, who sings a glorious descant to his original melody (m. 303). The protracted farewell provides the traditional cabaletta, an extended concluding section that accelerates as it nears the end of this very long unit of music.

**Dramatically Justified Virtuosity.** The music in *Rigoletto* requires virtuoso singing, but Verdi never introduces virtuosity for its own sake. Arias never interrupt the flow of the drama, though drama sometimes interrupts an aria. The style of virtuosity, moreover, reflects each character's nature: the Duke's brilliant vocal displays, for example, fit his pompous strutting, just as Gilda's soaring yet delicate and airy lines help project her fragile innocence and key moments of emotional ecstasy.

The celebrated Quartet from Act III, *Bella figlia dell'amore* ("Beautiful daughter of love"), illustrates Verdi's remarkable ability to convey contrasting emotions simultaneously. Verdi is the only composer ever to have rivaled Mozart in this regard. Scene 2 has just concluded with one of the most famous arias in all of opera, the Duke's *La donn' è mobile*, yet another self-justification for his philandering ("Women are always changing," he sings, "like a feather in the wind"). The subsequent Quartet (Anthology II/138b) presents two scenes simultaneously. One is going on inside the tavern, the other outside. Inside, the Duke is trying to seduce Maddalena, Sparafucile's sister; she resists but finds him charming nonetheless. Through a window, Gilda and Rigoletto watch what is happening. Rigoletto asks his daughter if she does not finally realize what a scoundrel the Duke is; she looks on in stunned disbelief and anguish. Verdi meshes the contrasting emotions of these four characters in a manner that is astonishingly intricate without sounding complex. The music seems to fall into place quite simply, even though it is four-part nonimitative counterpoint.

## Opera and Politics

As in previous eras, the influence of opera extended beyond the purely musical into the realm of social and political expression. The opera house was a meeting place for socialites and businesspeople and a forum for the often symbolic dramatization of political and moral ideas. State censors scrutinized *Rigoletto* for subversive ideas because they knew that composers, librettists, and audiences were prone to interpret events on

# Giuseppe Verdi (1813–1901)

Little in Verdi's early life suggests his later greatness. He showed musical talent as a child but failed the entrance examination for the Milan Conservatory. He turned instead to private teachers and immersed himself in the study of harmony and counterpoint. Verdi then secured a series of conducting posts in his native Busseto, a relatively small community. His first opera, *Oberto*, scored a success at one of Europe's leading opera houses, La Scala in Milan, in 1840, opening further opportunities in the theater. Two years later, Verdi enjoyed even greater success with *Nabucco* (1842). The opera's chorus of the captive Israelites in Babylon (*Va, pensiero*) became one of the unofficial anthems of the simmering Italian uprising against the occupying Austrian forces, helping secure Verdi's place, at age 30, within the great tradition of Italian opera.

Several of Verdi's operas constituted thinly veiled appeals for the unification of Italy, which at the time was still a loose confederation of small states, many of them under the domination of the Austrians. Italian patriots seeking independence from the Austrians and unity for the Italian people used Verdi's name as an acronym for "**V**ittorio **E**manuele, **R**e **d'I**talia" ("Victor Emanuel, King of Italy"). This slogan, innocent enough on the surface ("We are only celebrating our favorite composer of opera!"), was in fact a deeply subversive rallying cry for Italian nationalists. Verdi himself became swept up in the political struggles of the day when he was voted into the newly constituted Italian parliament in 1860. He served until 1865 but by his own admission did not take an active role:

> For two long years I was absent from the Chamber and afterwards I attended only rarely. Several times I was about to hand in my resignation but some obstacle always came up at the last moment and I'm still a deputy against every wish and every desire, without having the slightest inclination nor aptitude nor talent. There you have it. Anyone who wishes or who has to write my biography as Member of Parliament has only to print in large letters in the middle on a blank sheet of paper: "The 450 are really only 449 because Verdi as a deputy doesn't exist."[1]

The remainder of Verdi's long life revolved around a series of commissions. He was at home in both Italy and France but spent the majority of his time in Milan. In addition to his Italian works for the stage, he produced two grand operas in French, *Les Vêpres siciliennes* (1855) and *Don Carlos* (1867). The influence of French grand opera is also evident in *Aida* (1871, in Italian), commissioned to celebrate the opening of the Suez Canal. After being coaxed out of retirement, Verdi produced two operas that many consider his finest: *Otello* (1887) and *Falstaff* (1893), the latter produced when Verdi was 80.

**Verdi.** When preparing a new opera for production, Verdi's attention to detail was legendary. He coached the singers, kept or supervised the production of copious notes on staging and scenery, and devoted great care to historical detail. Although he could not attend the premiere of *Aida* in Cairo in 1871, he made sure the stage designs were supervised by August Mariette, a renowned Egyptologist of the day.

**Source:** Library of Congress

Visitors who recorded their impressions of Verdi almost invariably spoke of the man's modesty and self-effacing nature. A few years before his death, he established a home for retired musicians unable to support themselves and consigned all his royalties for 30 years after his death to this institution.

# PRINCIPAL WORKS

## Operas

The operas fall roughly into three periods. The works through the 1840s (including *Oberto, Nabucco, Ernani, Macbeth,* and *Luisa Miller*) build on traditions established by his predecessors. The middle-period works, beginning with *Rigoletto* (1851), include some of the composer's most popular operas—*Il Trovatore, La Traviata, Un ballo in maschera, La forza del destino,* and *Aïda*—which all remain staples of the operatic repertory. But Verdi was never content to remain within established formulas, and he was consistently able to make the operatic conventions of his day sound fresh and original. His style ranged from the utterly straightforward (homophonic texture, strophic form) to the astonishingly complex (polyphonic textures, through-composed forms). In his late works—*Otello* (1887) and *Falstaff* (1893)—he integrated the orchestra into the vocal texture to an unprecedented degree and at the same time developed a formal approach that considerably reduced the number of such recognizable units as arias and duets. Many contemporaries saw this change as a concession to Wagner's principles of music drama (discussed later). But anyone familiar with Verdi's earlier works can recognize the continuing development of tendencies already present in his earlier works.

## Sacred Music

After writing a few small sacred pieces in his early years, Verdi turned almost exclusively to opera. But after his initial retirement from the stage with *Aïda* in 1871, he returned to choral music on sacred themes. When Rossini died in 1868, Verdi conceived of asking 13 different Italian composers to contribute 1 movement each to a setting of the Requiem Mass. Verdi wrote the last movement, "Libera me," but the plan did not otherwise bear fruit. When he learned of the death of Alessandro Manzoni (1785–1873), poet and novelist, Verdi resolved to complete the Requiem himself. The result, his *Messa da Requiem*, premiered one year to the day after Manzoni's death. Its theatricality—the furor of the "Dies irae" is particularly famous—has led more than one wit to term it "Verdi's best opera." The *Four Sacred Pieces* were published in 1898; the first of these, *Ave Maria*, is composed on what the composer called the "enigmatic scale"—of C-D♭-E-F♯-G♯-A♯-B-C—which is neither major nor minor nor even wholly diatonic, given the interval of three half steps between D♭ and E. Even the 85-year-old Verdi was open to chromatic experimentation.

| KEY DATES IN LIFE OF VERDI | |
|---|---|
| 1813 | Born near Busseto (northern Italy) on October 10. |
| 1832 | Applies to the Milan Conservatory but is rejected for lack of technical knowledge; studies privately instead. |
| 1839 | His first opera, *Oberto,* is greeted warmly at La Scala in Milan, one of Italy's leading opera houses. |
| 1840s | Establishes his reputation in Italy with a series of operatic successes, most notably *Nabucco, Macbeth,* and *Luisa Miller.* |
| 1850s and 1860s | Achieves international fame with *Rigoletto* (1851), *Il Trovatore* (1853), *La Traviata* (1853), *Un ballo in maschera* (1859), and *Don Carlos* (1867, in French). |
| 1871 | Premiere of *Aïda,* commissioned for the opening of the Suez Canal and first performed in Cairo. |
| 1887 | Persuaded to come out of retirement to write two last operas on Shakespearean themes: *Otello* (1887) and *Falstaff* (1893). |
| 1901 | Dies in Milan on January 27. |

the stage as a kind of allegorical commentary on current events. Early in the century, Beethoven struggled with Viennese authorities over his politically charged *Fidelio*, which advocated freedom of political speech. Daniel-François-Esprit Auber's *La muette de Portici* ("The Deaf Girl of Portici") was the likely catalyst for a popular uprising that erupted in Brussels when it was performed there in 1830. The plot, about a peasant revolt in Naples in 1647, was apparently enough to ignite the smoldering passions of the Brussels populace. Verdi's *Un ballo in maschera* ("A Masked Ball") in 1859 encountered even more resistance from the censors in Naples than *Rigoletto* had received from the censors in Venice. The Neapolitan censors prohibited the performance of the opera because it was based on the real-life assassination of King Gustavus III of Sweden. Only when Verdi and his librettist changed the time and place of the opera's setting to remote colonial Massachusetts and the victim to a fictitious Earl of Warwick did the censors relent. And when George Bernard Shaw interpreted Wagner's *Der Ring des Nibelungen* as an allegory for the struggles during the 19th century among the competing forces of capitalism, socialism, and anarchy, his views were taken very seriously indeed.

## France: Grand Opéra and Opéra Comique

French opera of the 19th century divides into two broad categories, each with its own tradition. **Grand opéra** emphasized story lines drawn from historical subjects and typically featured lavishly expensive stage designs, ballets, and large choral numbers. Works written in the tradition of grand opéra tend to be long and are almost invariably in five acts. Although always sung in French, they were written by composers from across the Continent: the Italians Rossini and Gaspare Spontini (1774–1851), the German Giacomo Meyerbeer (1791–1864, born Jakob Beer), and the French Daniel-François-Esprit Auber (1782–1871) and Jacques-François-Fromental-Elie Halévy (1799–1862). Meyerbeer was acknowledged as the unrivaled master of the genre. A protégé of Rossini, he wrote works that appealed to the public love of spectacle combined with frequent evocations of the supernatural, especially in his most

**The quartet from Act III of Verdi's *Rigoletto*.** This ensemble manifests one of the powers of opera to do what spoken drama cannot: convey contrasting emotions simultaneously. Inside the tavern, the Duke is seducing Maddalena (the sister of and co-conspirator with the assassin Sparafucile); outside, Gilda watches and listens in horror while her father, Rigoletto, asks if she is not now convinced that the man she loves (the Duke) is in fact a libertine. The room above (only the bottom of the window is visible here) is where the Duke will retire for the night and sing the reprise of his famous aria *La donn' è mobile*. Near the end of the opera, when Rigoletto hears the Duke singing again, he thinks at first it is a dream; but he quickly discovers it is in fact his daughter who has been murdered and not the Duke.

**Source:** Mary Evans Picture Library/The Image Works

popular work, *Robert le diable* ("Robert the Devil," 1831). Grand opéra was a true institution of the political establishment. Commissions were given as much on the basis of personal contacts as on talent; intrigue was rampant.

The city's other two leading opera houses, the Opéra Comique and the Théâtre Lyrique, offered alternatives to the grand style. In spite of its name, the genre known as **opéra comique** was not always comic. But it allowed for spoken dialogue and placed far less emphasis on ballet, stage design, and crowd scenes. Composers like Charles Gounod (1818–1893), Bizet, and Jules Massenet (1842–1912) all contributed to this genre. Among the works still performed today are Gounod's *Faust*, Bizet's *Carmen*, and Massenet's *Manon*. The fate of Bizet's *Carmen* illustrates the gulf between the two worlds of French opera. In its original form, the work could not be presented at the prestigious Opéra. But shortly after Bizet's death, his friend Ernest Guiraud set the spoken dialogues to music in the form of recitative and added a ballet scene to Act IV, drawing on music from other works by Bizet. In this guise—and still translated into Italian—*Carmen* became one of the most popular operas of all time.

## Germany: Weber to Wagner

German opera had been slow to develop before the 19th century. Italians and French had dominated the German stage, both as composers and as performers. Most of the dramatic works even of the German-speaking composers Haydn and Mozart had Italian texts. The most important exceptions were Mozart's *Die Entführung aus dem Serail* ("The Abduction from the Seraglio") and *Die Zauberflöte* ("The Magic Flute"). Like Beethoven's later *Fidelio*, these works were *Singspiele*—that is, written in German, with spoken dialogue and only occasional accompanied recitatives.

Carl Maria von Weber (1786–1826) caused a sensation in 1821 with yet another work of this kind, *Der Freischütz*, the story of a hunter who strikes a bargain with the devil to win a shooting contest that in turn will allow him to marry the woman he loves. *Freischütz* is something of a Faust story with a happy ending, and Weber's setting captured the imagination of his contemporaries. The "Wolf's Glen Scene" at the end of Act II won special praise, with its electrifying combination of music and special effects, including diminished sevenths played on low tremolo strings, an offstage chorus, shadowy figures, and a burning wagon wheel careening across the stage. The use of spoken dialogue accompanied by the orchestra was known as **melodrama** (that is, dramatic speech with musical underpinning). Opera-length works of this kind had been staged since the 18th century. Audiences also responded to the folklike arias, choruses, and dance scenes elsewhere in *Freischütz*. Weber's sudden death at the age of 39 cut short what would have certainly been a brilliant career, but his works inspired the next generation of German composers to write stage works in their native tongue.

The most important of Weber's successors was Richard Wagner (1813–1883). Like so many composers of his generation, Wagner was committed to making opera more dramatically realistic, but the approach he eventually settled on differed radically from that of Weber, Verdi, or for that matter any other figure in the history of the genre.

Wagner rejected traditional opera on the grounds that in it the libretto, the drama, served as little more than a pretext for the music, and more specifically, for virtuosic singing. Traditional opera, according to Wagner, suffered from a fatal flaw: neither of its constituent elements—text and music—could stand on its own, without the other. In other words, a staged, spoken performance of a typical opera libretto would be dramatically unsatisfactory, whereas a performance of an opera's score, without its text, would be musically incoherent. Even a composer as great as Mozart, Wagner

**The "Wolf's Glen Scene" from Weber's *Der Freischütz*.** This illustration from the 1820s depicts the opera's central moment, when Max (left), the unlucky hunter, casts seven magic bullets under the guidance of the evil spirit Samiel (top right). The scene was renowned for its combination of scenic and musical effects, most notably its extensive use of unharmonized chromaticism and diminished seventh chords, both of which filled contemporary listeners with a sense of mystery, horror, and the supernatural.

**Source:** Mary Evans Picture Library/Alamy

maintained, could not overcome this fundamental problem. The "error of opera," he declared, was that "a means of expression"—the music—had become an end in its own right while the goal of that expression—the drama—"had been made a means." The challenge for composers, Wagner maintained, was to integrate drama and music in a way that would work to the advantage of both.

## The Elements of Wagnerian Music Drama

Accomplishing this integration, correcting the "error of opera," was easier said than done. Wagner struggled with this problem for decades but eventually arrived at a solution he considered so revolutionary that it represented not merely a new kind of opera, but an entirely new genre altogether, the **music drama**. In spite of its outward similarity to opera, Wagnerian music drama rests on premises and elements not ordinarily found in earlier forms of opera.

**The Ideal of the *Gesamtkunstwerk*.**   Wagner summarized his approach to his art with an imposing term—*Gesamtkunstwerk*—a compound based on three German words:

- *Gesamt*, meaning "synthesized, unified, whole, complete, self-contained"
- *Kunst*, meaning "art" (that is, the arts in general, including music, poetry, and gesture or movement)
- *Werk*, meaning "work" (of art)

For Wagner, the *Gesamtkunstwerk* was a work that synthesized all the arts. It could be argued, of course, that opera had all along been integrating music, drama, poetry, gesture, architecture, and painting—the latter two through stage design. Wagner anticipated this charge by arguing that these various arts merely coexisted in the opera house, and not even very well. A true *Gesamtkunstwerk* was one in which all the requisite elements were at once both self-sufficient yet inextricable from one another. Thus the music should cohere as in a symphony by Beethoven, the drama should be as compelling as a drama by Goethe, and these two elements, music and drama, should be mutually motivating.

**Drama as "Deeds of Music Made Visible."** Wagner's breakthrough came with his realization that the drama being acted out on the stage could be treated as a visible and verbal manifestation of the drama being acted out by the instruments of the orchestra. He recognized that purely instrumental music was inherently dramatic but only in an abstract way. Inspired by such works as Beethoven's Third and Fifth Symphonies, and particularly the *Leonore* Overture no. 3 (see Chapter 15), Wagner sought to transfer the power of instrumental music into the theater by establishing "genuine drama on the basis of absolute music." In music drama, the music alone, separate from the text, should have its own dramatic coherence and trajectory. In a particularly memorable turn of phrase, Wagner called the drama—the events transpiring on the stage—"deeds of music made visible." What happens on the stage, in other

---

## Primary Evidence — GEORGE BERNARD SHAW ON THE ADVANTAGES OF OPERA OVER DRAMA

*The playwright George Bernard Shaw (1856–1950) worked for many years as a music critic. His writings are always witty and often insightful. This passage, from an essay written in 1894, goes to the heart of Wagner's ability to integrate music and words and the advantages of music drama over traditional spoken drama; Shaw seems at odds with Johann Mattheson's opinions concerning Baroque text setting (see Chapter 11).*

■ ■ ■

Wagner regarded all Beethoven's important instrumental works as tone poems; and he himself, though he wrote so much for the orchestra alone in the course of his music dramas, never wrote, or could write, a note of absolute music. The fact is, there is a great deal of feeling, highly poetic and highly dramatic, which cannot be expressed by mere words—because words are the counters of thinking, not of feeling—but which can be supremely expressed by music. The poet tries to make words serve his purpose by arranging them musically, but is hampered by the certainty of becoming absurd if he does not make his musically arranged words mean something to the intellect as well as to the feeling.

For example, the unfortunate Shakespeare could not make Juliet say:

O Romeo, Romeo, Romeo, Romeo, Romeo;

and so on for twenty lines. He had to make her, in an extremity of unnaturalness, begin to argue the case in a sort of amatory legal fashion, thus:

O Romeo, Romeo, wherefore art thou Romeo?
Deny thy father and refuse thy name,
Or, if thou wilt not, etc., etc., etc.

It is verbally decorative; but it is not love. And again:

Parting is such sweet sorrow
That I shall say goodnight till it be morrow;

which is a most ingenious conceit, but one which a woman would no more utter at such a moment than she would prove the rope ladder to be the shortest way out because any two sides of a triangle are together greater than the third.

Now these difficulties do not exist for the tone poet. He can make Isolde say nothing but "Tristan, Tristan, Tristan, Tristan, Tristan," and Tristan nothing but "Isolde, Isolde, Isolde, Isolde, Isolde," to their hearts' content without creating the smallest demand for more definite explanations; and as for the number of times a tenor and soprano can repeat "Addio, addio, addio," there is no limit to it.

**Source:** Reproduced in *Shaw on Music,* ed. Eric Bentley, pp. 114–15, which in turn quotes *The World,* January 17, 1894.

words, is a tangible reflection of what is going on in the orchestra pit. By the same token, what happens in the orchestra pit is the musical manifestation of the actions on stage. Ideally, then, we should be able to follow the course of a Wagnerian music drama through the music alone, by tracing the fate of its various musical ideas. These musical ideas would eventually come to be known as *Leitmotivs*.

**The Leitmotiv.**   Literally, a "leading motive," a **Leitmotiv** is a brief musical idea connected to some person, event, or idea in a music drama. Opera composers had long used specific musical motifs as tags for specific dramatic themes, bringing them in repeatedly at appropriate points in a plot. The curse motif in Verdi's *Rigoletto* is a perfect example of this well-established practice of musical reminiscence. We hear it at the beginning of the Prelude as a kind of premonition, ominous and important but as yet unspecific; we realize its meaning when it accompanies the moment Monterone curses the jester; and we hear it again every time Rigoletto thinks about that fateful moment.

The occasional return of an isolated idea or two, however, cannot ensure the musical coherence of a work as sizable as an opera. To do that, Wagner expanded on the technique of reminiscence to create complex webs of musically interrelated and constantly changing motifs. What distinguishes Leitmotiv from reminiscence in Wagner's music dramas is (1) the musical metamorphosis of these ideas over time according to the dramatic situation, and (2) the musical and dramatic interrelationship of these motifs within a broad network of thematic ideas. A Leitmotiv, then, is a musical figure capable of growth, development, and transformation.

The network of Leitmotivs in Wagner's *Tristan und Isolde* illustrates the way these thematic ideas work. Based on an ancient legend that had circulated in various forms throughout northern Europe, *Tristan und Isolde* tells a story of ill-fated love. Tristan, a knight in the service of King Mark, has been given the task of bringing the Irish princess Isolde back to Cornwall, on the western coast of England, where she is to marry Mark, against her will. But Tristan and Isolde have already met: she had nursed

((•• **Listen**
**CD12    Tracks 3-4**
**mysearchlab**
WAGNER
*Tristan und Isolde*
Score Anthology II/138

**Tristan und Isolde, Act II.** Isolde awaits Tristan's clandestine return. The stage design here is by Alfred Roller, created for the Vienna Opera in 1902, in a production conducted by Gustav Mahler.
**Source:** akg-images/Newscom

him back to health some years before, and Tristan now feels torn between his debt to her and his allegiance to King Mark. The two vow to drink poison and kill themselves before their ship lands in Cornwall, but Brangaene, Isolde's maidservant, substitutes a love potion for the poison. Tristan and Isolde fall madly in love, yet they must hide their passion from all others, especially King Mark. In Act II, the lovers contrive a pretext to meet alone: Tristan drops back from a hunting party and returns to the castle under cover of night. But their deception is revealed, a fight ensues, and in the closing Act III, Tristan dies of the new wounds he has suffered. Isolde, overcome with grief, sinks lifeless upon his corpse, uniting the two lovers in death.

In their simplest forms, the motifs in this opera have a one-to-one relationship with corresponding onstage actions. Wagner makes sure, for example, that we will associate the motif in Example 17–1 with the potion that causes Tristan and Isolde to fall in love. We hear it first at the beginning of the Prelude, but as with the curse motif that begins the Prelude to *Rigoletto*, we do not yet know its implications. But the symbolic associations of the motif become clear when the theme recurs in Act I at the moment when Tristan and Isolde (thinking they are about to die) drink the love potion. They do not die, of course, but are instead seized by passionate feelings for one another. Wagner has thereby established a direct connection between the music and the drama. What happens on stage—the drinking of the potion—is a visible manifestation of the music, which captures the sense of longing that seizes lovers at that inexplicable moment when they fall in love.

What conveys that sense of longing in this Leitmotiv is its celebrated dissonance, beginning with what has come to be known as the "Tristan chord" (F-B-D♯-G♯ on the downbeat of m. 2 in Example 17–1). Commentators have often cited the progression from this chord to the end of the motif as signaling the beginning of the end of traditional harmony. Although the progression can be described, technically, as a movement from an augmented ("French") sixth (F-B-D♯-A) to V⁷ in the key of A minor (E-G♯-D-B), such an account scarcely captures the sense of harmonic instability this opening chord creates. The rhythmic emphasis on the dissonant G♯, which is held for almost an entire measure before resolving upward to A, was especially grating to contemporary ears. That this should be the very first harmony heard in the entire work made the dissonance all the more striking: although the unison opening of m. 1, played by the cellos, had suggested the key of A minor, it had not really established any firm sense of a tonal center. That the downbeat of the succeeding measure (m. 3) should also be dissonant compounded the perception of harmonic groundlessness. The concluding V⁷ chord itself, moreover, remains unresolved, leading to a long silence, followed by a series of upwardly moving chromatic progressions that similarly fail to resolve. This absence of harmonic resolution caused a sensation in Wagner's time, giving the "Tristan chord" its well-deserved notoriety.

Within the course of the Prelude, Wagner goes on to fragment, extend, transpose, invert, and otherwise manipulate this basic idea over and over again. The rising minor chromatic third first heard in m. 2–3 assumes special importance. Following the model

**EXAMPLE 17–1** The "love potion" motif, with the "Tristan chord" highlighted

"Tristan" chord

# Richard Wagner (1813–1883)

"Wagner," one historian recently observed, "is the most controversial artistic figure of all time." Such a claim might well seem like an exaggeration at first, but it is difficult to think of any other artist who has aroused such powerful feelings of support and opposition over such a long period of time. Musically, politically, and personally, Wagner has been worshiped by some, reviled by others. Indeed it is often said there are only two other figures in the history of the world about whom more has been written: Jesus Christ and Napoleon. This probably *is* an exaggeration, but the frequency with which this claim is repeated reflects the never-ending fascination with the figure of Wagner, whose cultural importance goes far beyond the world of music.

Born in Leipzig, Wagner aspired early to a career as a composer and conductor. He immersed himself in the music of Beethoven and put bread on his table by writing music criticism. A series of increasingly prestigious positions as a conductor of opera in Germany culminated in his appointment as Kapellmeister in Dresden in 1843. Wagner would have been assured success had he stayed in this prestigious position the rest of his life, for he had outstanding resources at his disposal there.

The Revolution of 1848 changed everything. Wagner fought on the barricades, in effect seeking to overthrow the very regime that employed him. A warrant was issued for his arrest and he fled to Switzerland, where he lived in exile for the next decade, composing, among other works, *Tristan und Isolde*. He eventually won the support of King Ludwig II of Bavaria, who spared no expense to support the composer and his art. It was around this time, in the mid-1860s, that Wagner became intimate with Cosima Liszt von Bülow, the daughter of Franz Liszt and the wife of the conductor Hans von Bülow. Wagner, Cosima, and von Bülow lived for a time in a bizarre ménage à trois, with all three devoted to Wagner's art. Eventually, Cosima divorced von Bülow and married Wagner, by whom she had already borne three children.

The final phase of Wagner's life centered around Bayreuth, a small city roughly halfway between Munich and Berlin, the respective capitals of Bavaria and Prussia. "Germany" had only recently become a political reality, and it was Wagner's aim to build in Bayreuth a *Festspielhaus*—a "festival drama house"—that would unify Germany culturally as well. Wagner oversaw every detail of the building and the performances to be held within it. Thus, when the

*Ring* received its premiere there in 1876, Wagner could legitimately claim not only to have written the libretto and the music, but to have built the opera house as well. He died in Venice in 1883.

As a critic, Wagner was one of the most prolific and influential of all composers who have also written about music. In addition to his early reviews, he wrote program notes, pamphlets, numerous essays, an autobiography, and an especially important (if long-winded) three-volume treatise entitled *Opera and Drama* (1850).

**Richard Wagner at his home in Bayreuth.** This richly symbolic scene shows Wagner in the last year of his life at the center of an admiring circle of intimates, all eyes on him. The composer, standing, is reading from the libretto of his latest (and last) work, *Parsifal*, which received its premiere in Bayreuth in 1882, the same year in which this group portrait was executed. On the wall above his left shoulder is a portrait of the great German philosopher Arthur Schopenhauer, who had singled out music as the greatest of all the arts because it alone could capture the essence of the universe. Wagner's position suggests that he and his works embody Schopenhauer's ideas. Sitting to the composer's right is his wife, Cosima Liszt Bülow Wagner. A portrait of Cosima leans against the back wall, above her head. On the floor behind her is a painting of one of the sets from *Parsifal*, the Temple of the Grail. The first figure to Wagner's left is his father-in-law, Franz Liszt, who seems to be conducting an imaginary orchestra from a manuscript, probably the score of *Parsifal*, in his lap. Wagner's hands overlap Liszt's, symbolizing the important links—both familial and artistic—between these two musical giants of the 19th century. The third seated figure, Hans von Wolzogen, was a disciple of Wagner who wrote many pamphlets identifying the Leitmotivs in Wagner's music dramas.

**Source:** Richard Wagner with Franz Liszt and Liszt's daughter Cosima (oil on canvas), German School, (19th century)/Richard Wagner Museum, Bayreuth, Bavaria, Germany/The Bridgeman Art Library

As an individual, Wagner is one of the least appealing composers in the history of music. He was vain and selfish, almost never paid his debts on time, and was deeply anti-Semitic. During the Third Reich, Hitler gave Wagner special prominence in the pantheon of German composers. The composer's virulent nationalism and anti-Semitism meshed well with the ideals of Nazi Germany, and to this day, performances of Wagner's music are for all practical purposes banned in Israel. The posthumous use of any composer's work remains problematic, however. In Germany, almost every political faction from the far left to the far right has appropriated the music of Beethoven at one time or another. Whether or not this has or should change our opinion of Beethoven and his works remains an open question.

The painting by W. Beckmann reproduced here shows Wagner at home in Bayreuth surrounded by family and other intimates.

# PRINCIPAL WORKS

In his early years, Wagner wrote in a variety of genres, including song, sonata, and quartet; he even tried his hand at the symphony on more than one occasion. But the young composer soon recognized that his talents and interests lay in the realm of theater music, and from the 1840s onward, almost all his most significant works are operas—or, as he called his later works, "music dramas." Dates in parentheses here represent the date of first performances.

## Early Operas

Wagner used a number of models for his early operas, drawing particularly on the works of Rossini, Donizetti, Weber, and Heinrich Marschner for *Die Feen*, a fairy-tale opera; *Das Liebesverbot*, a comic opera based on Shakespeare's *Measure for Measure*; and *Rienzi*, a grand opera based on a contemporary novel about a tribune of the Roman Empire.

## The Romantic Operas

*Der fliegende Holländer* ("The Flying Dutchman," 1843) is based on the Norse legend of the sea captain who is condemned to eternal wandering and who will find rest, and death, only through the love of a woman. Every seven years, the Dutchman lands ashore to seek his salvation, which he ultimately finds in a woman named Senta. The most famous number in the opera is Senta's ballad in Act II, in which she tells the story of the Dutchman and becomes transported by her own narrative.

*Tannhäuser* (1845) is an opera about the minnesingers, medieval Germany's equivalent of the French troubadours and trouvères (see Chapter 1). Once again, Wagner deals with the redemptive power of a woman's love and the title character's struggle between sensual pleasure and religious faith.

*Lohengrin* (1850) also draws on Germanic legend. Lohengrin, a knight of mysterious origins, makes a dramatic appearance just in time to defend the honor of Elizabeth, who has been falsely accused of murdering her brother. Lohengrin makes only one demand of Elizabeth: that she accept him for who he is and not demand to know his name or his lineage. Elizabeth accepts this condition, and Lohengrin defeats her accuser in a duel, thereby winning her hand in marriage. But plotting by the defeated accuser and his sister eventually drives Elizabeth mad with curiosity, and she puts the fateful question to Lohengrin just before they are to be married. (The famous wedding march known as *Here Comes the Bride* is from this opera.) In *Lohengrin*, we sense that Wagner is on the edge of making the breakthrough from traditional opera to the music drama.

## The Music Dramas

*Tristan und Isolde* (1859) draws on a medieval legend to tell the story of the tragic love triangle of Tristan, Isolde, and King Mark. As in so many of Wagner's works, redemption comes only through death.

*Die Meistersinger von Nürnberg* (1868), like *Tannhäuser*, deals with the minnesingers of medieval Germany, but in a much more lighthearted vein. In this thinly veiled account of Wagner's own battle with his critics, Beckmesser, a pedant, insists that songs must always be written according to the rules while other characters show him just how dry and stale such an approach is. Wagner weaves a love story around all of this, but for once no one dies in the end.

Wagner worked on the libretto for *Der Ring des Nibelungen* ("The Ring of the Nibelungs," 1876) from the late 1840s through the mid-1850s before setting the text to music. He interrupted his work for some seven

## Composer Profile

# Richard Wagner (1813–1883) (Continued)

years in the late 1850s and early 1860s to compose *Tristan* and *Meistersinger*. Although some of the works in the *Ring* cycle were premiered individually, the cycle as a whole received its debut at the newly opened Festspielhaus in Bayreuth in 1876. The plot, based on various legends from Norse mythology, is intricate and highly symbolic, revolving around a web of conflicts that pits love against both power and duty. The *Ring* consists of four separate works performed ideally on four successive days: *Das Rheingold, Die Walküre, Siegfried,* and *Götterdämmerung.*

In *Parsifal* (1882), Wagner turned again to medieval legend. The title character is the "perfect" fool, an innocent who discovers the truths of life, self-denial, and love (both sacred and profane) through the Fellowship of the Grail. It was Wagner's wish that *Parsifal* never be performed anywhere except at Bayreuth. Fortunately, this wish has been disregarded.

### KEY DATES IN THE LIFE OF WAGNER

| | |
|---|---|
| 1813 | Born in Leipzig (Germany) on May 22. |
| 1831 | Studies composition with Theodor Weinlig, cantor of the *Thomasschule* and thus an indirect successor to J. S. Bach. |
| 1832 | Publishes first composition, a piano sonata, and writes a symphony, both strongly influenced by the music of Beethoven. |
| 1833–1843 | Takes on a series of increasingly responsible positions in German opera houses (Würzburg, Königsberg, Riga), with a three-week stint in debtors' prison (1840). |
| 1843 | Appointed music director at the Royal Opera House in Dresden, one of the most coveted positions of its kind in Germany. |
| 1848–1849 | Participates actively in the Revolution; a warrant is issued for his arrest, and he flees to Switzerland. |
| 1850s | While in exile, writes *Tristan und Isolde*, begins composing *Der Ring des Nibelungen*, and writes several important treatises on music. |
| 1864 | Receives support from the new king of Bavaria, Ludwig II ("Mad Ludwig"), who supports Wagner financially with public funds, much to the dismay of the Bavarians and the members of Ludwig's court. |
| 1868 | First contact with the philosopher Friedrich Nietzsche, who at first supports Wagner and later turns against him. |
| 1870 | Marries Cosima Liszt von Bülow, who keeps a detailed diary that records the remainder of the composer's life in astonishing detail. |
| 1872 | Cornerstone laid for the Festspielhaus in Bayreuth. The central work on the dedicatory concert is Beethoven's Ninth Symphony, the work Wagner considered the cornerstone for the "Music of the Future." |
| 1876 | The Bayreuth Festspielhaus opens with the first complete performance of the *Ring* cycle. |
| 1883 | Dies in Venice on February 13. |

of thematic elaboration provided by the instrumental music of Beethoven, Wagner manipulates a fragment of this theme (Example 17–2a, first measure; Example 17–2b) by using repetition, harmonic and melodic variation, and silence to enrich each successive statement. The Prelude as a whole follows no established convention of large-scale form. Instead, the music seems to propel itself forward through a series of constant transformations. The rising three-note figure that first appears in the cellos in m. 17, for example (Example 17–2, m. 2), represents a metamorphosis of the rising

RICHARD WAGNER, ᵇʸ GILL.

**Wagner assaults the modern ear.** Much of the controversy surrounding Wagner's music in his own lifetime centered on his penchant for massive orchestration and highly chromatic harmonies. As one irate listener wrote to the editors of the English journal *Musical World* in 1876, "Enough already has been done in the present century to lead the public away from the laws of nature. It may be original to have interminable successions of discords which don't resolve, but it is a matter of taste whether such proceedings are an improvement on the pleasurable sensations of man. Vinegar, mustard, and cayenne-pepper are necessary condiments in the culinary art, but I question whether even the Wagnerites would care to make their dinner of these articles only. When sound taste begins to fail, eccentricity will take its place. Let the young student beware of its malignant influence."

**Source:** Leonard de Selva/Corbis

minor chromatic third from m. 2–3. This new idea, in turn, is further fragmented and manipulated (m. 36–37). The orchestra, all the while, builds gradually in size and volume, reaching a high point of sorts with the fortissimo statement of yet another version of the cello's theme at m. 74. But a crashing dissonance (m. 83) turns out to be the true climax, for it ushers in a return to the quiet tension of the opening (m. 85). There is no sense of resolution here: the music closes pianissimo and leads without a pause into the opening scene of Act I.

Having developed at least some of the intrinsically musical potential of the Prelude's central thematic idea, Wagner establishes its dramatic significance by bringing it back toward the end of Act I, at the crucial moment when Tristan and Isolde drink what they believe is a death potion. But what makes the technique of Leitmotiv different from the convention of isolated reminiscences is the manner in which the thematic transformations of these motifs relate to the events of the drama. When we listen to Act II more closely, we realize the distinctive chromatic rise in the "love potion" motif has actually

**EXAMPLE 17–2** Subsequent transformations of the "love potion" motif

(a)

(b)

been present for quite some time in a variety of guises—sometimes rising, sometimes falling—going all the way back to the Prelude to Act I. We hear these kinds of transformations in Act II, for example, when Brangaene laments having switched potions (m. 351–353), and then again even more tellingly shortly afterward (m. 380–382), when Isolde explains it was the power of love that caused the potion to transform itself. Here, underneath Isolde's declamation (beginning at m. 385), the orchestra spins out a series of thematic variants based on the characteristic rising chromatic third we first heard in the work's opening measures. Isolde now views the love potion quite differently, and the orchestra reflects this by presenting the motif within the guise of a softer, more lyrical tone. In Wagnerian terms, Isolde gives voice to what the orchestra is already expressing through music alone.

The motif known as "love's longing" (Example 17–3) represents yet another manipulation of the rising chromatic third. Here, the melodic trajectory is reversed: the chromatic line moves downward and is supported by a clearly outlined triadic base. The feeling here is more confident, more directional, as befits the dramatic situation. This motif dominates the tension that builds toward an event Isolde knows will happen: Tristan's return. Still another metamorphosis of this motif (Example 17–4) emerges when Tristan finally arrives: the theme becomes ecstatic in mood, rising in its opening to a high note before descending, rather than descending from the very start. Such changes, subtle but effective, have led more than one commentator to accord this idea a separate identity, associating it with the idea of "bliss," which is of course the desired consequence of longing. The musical and dramatic parallels function in tandem.

Another prominent Leitmotiv in *Tristan und Isolde* is associated with death (*Tod* in the German text). Like the "love potion" motif, the "death" motif (Example 17–5) is chromatic and harmonically unusual. (Wagner often used chromatic themes or unusual harmonic progressions to evoke conditions of pain, such as love and death.) Although the "death" motif manifests itself in many different ways, its characteristic harmonic feature is the juxtaposition of two otherwise distant chords (such as A♭ major and A major, as in Example 17–5, or C major and A♭ major in Example 17–6), combined with a distinctive dotted rhythm.

Having established these and other motifs in the listener's mind, Wagner is free to use them in any number of ways, some of them obvious, some of them not. Near

**EXAMPLE 17–3** "Love's longing"

**EXAMPLE 17–4** "Bliss"

the end of Act II, Scene 1, for example, when Isolde extinguishes her torch, signaling Tristan to leave the hunting party and return to the castle, Wagner embeds the "death" motif in the orchestra, beginning at m. 485; the texture is so thick at this point that the motif is not evident in the piano reduction of the score in the anthology. What is the connection between this moment and death? Once Tristan returns, the lovers will consummate their passion, which in turn will lead to their deaths. By linking the extinguishing of the torch to the "death" motif, Wagner is telling us, in musical terms, that the act carries ultimately fatal consequences.

More mundane elements of the plot receive appropriately mundane music. The "hero's call" motif with which Tristan's crew acclaims him in Act I (Example 17–7) is based on pointedly conventional harmonic and melodic progressions. The phrase is intentionally trite, and when Tristan hears it, he remains unmoved. His men literally sing his praises, but he himself is torn between loyalty to King Mark (to whom he is delivering Isolde) and a mixture of love and guilt toward Isolde. This "hero's call" motif, then, means nothing to Tristan, because it concerns only his public persona: it is associated with crowds, daylight, and the realm of reason. Its musical squareness provides an effective contrast with the private world of Tristan and Isolde's passion, which occupies the spheres of darkness and intimacy.

**EXAMPLE 17–5** "Death"

Death-destined head! Death-destined heart!

**EXAMPLE 17–6** Transformation of the "death" motif

Life and death are subordinate [to love]

**EXAMPLE 17–7** "Hero's call"

Hail to our hero, Tristan, who knows how to exact tribute!

When the lovers are finally reunited in Act II, Isolde reminds Tristan in jest of how he had once loved the day, and the mock-heroic tone she briefly assumes (m. 776) recalls the music of this "hero's call" motif. After so much chromaticism, the music seems trite and distant from the passion of the moment. At an even more subtle level, Wagner transforms the very opening of this motif (a fifth down, then up a third stepwise) into a very different kind of idea used throughout much of Act II and associated with the idea of day. When the characters on stage speak of the day (*Tag*) or daylight (*Tageslicht*), we hear variants of this "hero's call" motif so consistently and repeatedly (particularly from m. 809 onward) that we might well label this manifestation of the motif the "day" motif.

The labels we have been using to identify these Leitmotivs, although useful for analyzing Wagner's music, can lead us to think of them (incorrectly) as fixed entities, both musically and in terms of their dramatic associations. Probably for this reason, Wagner himself almost never explicitly identified any of these themes. It would be tedious, pointless, and ultimately impossible to ascribe an individual name to every different manifestation of every motif, in any event. More important is to recognize how Wagner works his Leitmotivs into an ever-evolving web of complementary and contrasting musical and dramatic relationships that can sustain a work lasting many hours in performance.

**The Relationship of Voice and Orchestra.** Wagner's Leitmotivs are sometimes sung, but more often they appear in the orchestra alone. In traditional opera, in contrast, the voice carries the melody while the orchestra provides the accompaniment. Constant repetition of text is likewise common in traditional opera. Indeed text set to ornate vocal lines often has to be repeated if it is to be understood. Wagner abhorred this practice, and it was his desire to make the text intelligible that prompted him to shift the melodic element from the voice to the orchestra. Doing so allowed him to have the characters on stage sing in a declamatory manner lying between aria and recitative. A typical Wagnerian vocal line, considered without any accompaniment at all, is not nearly as lyrical as a vocal line by Verdi, but the texture of Wagner's writing allows the words to come through with remarkable clarity. His design for the opera house in Bayreuth (illustrated on p. 459) also helps the vocal line to project through and above a large orchestra.

**The Structure of the Dramatic Text.** Unlike most composers of opera, Wagner wrote his own librettos, developing in his mind (and occasionally committing to paper) the musical motifs to be associated with particular moments of the drama. Wagner was also careful to avoid distinctions between verse and prose in his librettos. Traditionally, arias had been written in metrical verse, recitative in prose. In his effort to eliminate what he considered the arbitrary and disturbing disjunction between recitative and aria, Wagner wrote his librettos in a consistently free poetic style that avoided any

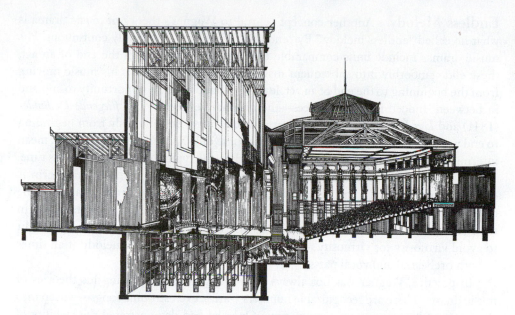

**Cross-section of the Bayreuth Festspielhaus.** In addition to writing his own librettos and music, Wagner designed his own theater, the "Festival Drama House," in Bayreuth, a small municipality halfway between Munich and Berlin. The design puts most of the orchestra beneath the stage. This ingenious device brings the audience closer to the stage and also projects the sound of the orchestra more directly toward the audience, creating a better blend of voices and the orchestra within the hall. The acoustics in Bayreuth have long been considered ideal for the integration of orchestral and vocal lines so characteristic of Wagner's music dramas.

**Source:** Reproduced with the permission of the Special Collections Library, The Pennsylvania State University Libraries

suggestion of metrical (and thus also melodic and musical) regularity. He did not, however, turn to entirely free verse, employing instead an alliterative poetic device called *Stabrheim* that had been cultivated in certain repertoires of German poetry of the Middle Ages. *Stabrheim* literally means "staff rhyme"—staff in the sense of a shepherd's crook, something that gathers together loose elements. What it gathers, though, is not rhyme (which typically occurs within an established metrical pattern) but rather the initial or internal sounds of two or more different words. For example, here are the words Isolde uses to command her servant to extinguish the light in Act II of *Tristan und Isolde* (beginning at m. 304):

> Lösche des Lichtes letzten Schein!
> Dass ganz sie sich neige, winke der Nacht!
> Schon goss sie ihr Schweigen durch Hain und Haus,
> schon füllt sie das Herz mit wonnigem Graus.
> O lösche das Licht nun aus,
> lösche den scheuchenden Schein!
> Lass' meinen Liebsten ein!

> (Extinguish the last glow of the light!
> So that night might approach fully, give her [the night] a signal!
> She has already poured her silence on field and house,
> She already fills the heart with blissful horror.
> Oh, extinguish the light,
> Put out the frightening glow!
> Let my lover in!)

This passage is typical of Wagner's texts in that it rhymes at certain points (Haus/Graus/aus; Schein/mein) and, although it avoids any fixed, predictable rhythm, does verge at times on metrical regularity. As is characteristic of *Stabrheim*, its rhyme and meter are fluid, which is precisely the quality Wagner sought to bring out in the music to which these words would be declaimed. While the internal alliteration has its (intentional) bumps along the way, Anglo-Saxon and early English poetry made use of a similar approach.

**Endless Melody.**   Another concept central to Wagner's theory of music drama is what he called "endless melody." By "endless," Wagner meant fluidly continuous. His music dramas include units comparable to arias, but at least until the end of an act, these elide smoothly into subsequent material. Wagner thus keeps his music moving from the beginning to the end of an act, leaving the audience no opportunity to applaud in between. Indeed in two instances—the original version of *Der fliegende Holländer* (1841) and *Das Rheingold* (1854)—an entire work moves continuously from beginning to end without a break. "Endless" does not, as some of Wagner's critics suggested, mean interminable. His music dramas are no longer than the typical grand operas of his time.

By "melody," Wagner had in mind something different from what the term is commonly understood to mean. He differentiated "true melody" from what might be called filler. He abhorred the empty figuration that played such an important role in the Italian opera of his time and even in the instrumental music of Mozart. He sought to avoid virtuosity for virtuosity's sake, stressing the need for true melody at all times in both orchestral and vocal parts.

In practice, Wagner was not always entirely rigorous in applying his theories of music drama. There are recognizable numbers—arias, even strophic songs—woven into the fabric of his music from time to time. Once he had demonstrated the viability of his new approach, he seems to have felt free to use more traditional forms in his later music dramas. Wotan's farewell to Brünnhilde at the end of *Die Walküre*, the soaring love duet between Siegfried and Brünnhilde at the end of *Siegfried*, and the trio of revenge in Act II of *Götterdämmerung* are all in the tradition of 19th-century Italian and French opera. The playwright George Bernard Shaw (1856–1950), an ardent Wagnerite, placed the whole of *Götterdämmerung*, with its vast sets, large choral numbers, and extended ensembles, squarely within the tradition of grand opera.

On the whole, however, Wagner's method of integrating music and text opened important new vistas for opera. His influence extended well beyond his lifetime, leaving a deep imprint on the operas of Richard Strauss, Arnold Schoenberg, Alban Berg, and even Giacomo Puccini (see Chapter 21).

# OPERETTA

Around the middle of the 19th century, the lighter genre of **operetta** began to establish itself. As the diminutive suffix suggests, this form of musical theater operated on a smaller scale than opera. It usually mixed spoken dialogue with sung numbers and dealt invariably with humorous and lighthearted subjects. Operetta was also more likely than opera to be composed or at least performed in the vernacular. Thus separate traditions of operetta developed in France, Germany, Italy, and even England, scarcely a bastion of operatic composition in the 19th century.

Operetta grew out of the long tradition of songs with plays. In 18th-century Germany, these were known as *Singspiele* (literally, "song plays") and included such works as Mozart's *Die Entführung aus dem Seraglio* and *Die Zauberflöte*, both of which were written to German texts. This tradition continued with later works like Johann Strauss's *Die Fledermaus* ("The Bat," 1874) and Franz Léhar's *Die lustige Witwe* ("The Merry Widow," 1905). In France, the operettas of Jacques Offenbach (1819–1880) were enormously popular. A transplanted German, Offenbach wrote more than 90 works of this kind, the most famous of which is *Orphée aux enfers* ("Orpheus in the Underworld," 1858), a farce on the ancient Greek legend in which Eurydice is quite happy to be in Hades. The work includes the famous "can-can" music danced by spirits of the underworld.

No English composer for the stage has achieved the enduring renown of Sir Arthur Sullivan (1842–1900), who, in partnership with the librettist Sir William S. Gilbert (1836–1911), created a long string of box office successes that continue to fill theaters today. Gilbert and Sullivan's *Pirates of Penzance* (1879) illustrates both the similarities and differences between 19th-century opera and operetta. It draws heavily on the principal forms of opera, with numbers that are easily recognizable as arias, duets, ensembles, and even accompanied recitatives. At the same time, the work manages to poke fun at almost every one of these very same conventions. The General's famous patter song ("I am the Very Model of a Modern Major General") is entertaining enough in its own right and even more so when we realize it is a parody of a model established by Rossini. In addition to the humor inherent in the song's rapid declamation, it is also incongruous to see a supposedly noble figure of authority like a general performing in a manner usually reserved for servants like Leporello in Mozart's *Don Giovanni* or Rossini's Figaro.

Still, the distinction between opera and operetta was not always clear, even in the 19th century. The New York orchestra rehearsing the world premiere of *The Pirates of Penzance* threatened to go on strike on the grounds that the new work was an opera rather than an operetta and the musicians should therefore be paid on a higher scale. But a strike was averted and *Pirates* opened to great acclaim. Within 18 months it had been performed not only in such major cities as Boston, Philadelphia, Chicago, St. Louis, and New Orleans, but also in smaller cities in New Jersey, Pennsylvania, Ohio, Indiana, Michigan, Missouri, Tennessee, Kentucky, Kansas, Nebraska, Iowa, Minnesota, and Wisconsin.

((•─|Listen
CD12     Tracks 5-6
mysearchlab
GILBERT AND SULLIVAN
*Pirates of Penzance*
Score Anthology II/139

# CHORAL MUSIC

With the growth of musical literacy, composers and publishers found a ready market for secular choral music, often in the form of four-part songs written expressly for amateur choruses. These could be for all-female, all-male, or mixed voices. Such groups were in part social, in part musical. Most communities of any size, particularly in German-speaking lands, could boast of at least one singing club (*Singverein*).

It was for such a group that Clara Wieck Schumann (see Composer Profile) wrote *Drei gemischte Chöre* (Three Mixed Choruses, to texts by Emanuel Geibel, 1848), from which "Vorwärts" (Forwards) is taken. ("Vorwärts" is the universal German cry into battle, whatever the mission and whenever and wherever it might take place.) The text was written in 1840, when stirrings against autocratic post-Napoleonic governments were being felt. Schumann's setting, composed as the 1848–49 revolutions were on the verge of breaking out, is full of fervor; does not simply repeat the music for all five strophes. The composer structures the music as ABA1B1A2; the repeated final phrase ("Wer den Himmel will gewinnen, /Muss ein rechter Kämpfer sein!"—Who would win the heavens must be a true fighter!) features a climactic high note on "Himmel" (heavens) and a brief staggered entry for further emphasis prior to the close of the piece. It should be noted that the choruses remained in manuscript and were not published until 1988, which certainly kept Schumann out of political difficulty at the time.

((•─|Listen
CD12     Track 7
mysearchlab (with scrolling translation)
CLARA WIECK SCHUMANN
*Vorwärts!*
Score Anthology II/140

The growing importance of instrumental music and the fierce debate about the nature of opera during the 19th century have tended to obscure the many important works of sacred music written during this time. As with other genres, settings of the Mass grew considerably in length: Beethoven's *Missa solemnis*, op. 123, and Bruckner's Mass in F minor both run well over an hour in performance. Schubert, Weber, Mendelssohn, Schumann, and Liszt also contributed to this repertory. Settings of the Requiem enjoyed special favor in the 19th century, most notably at the hands of Berlioz, Verdi, and Fauré. The first two are particularly theatrical, combining chorus and orchestra (and in Berlioz's work, multiple orchestras) to great effect.

The oratorio also flourished, allowing composers a chance to write sacred vocal music to librettos of their own choosing. The oratorios of Handel remained the model for virtually all 19th-century composers, including Beethoven (*Christ on the Mount of Olives*), Mendelssohn (*Elijah, Paulus*), Berlioz (*L'enfance du Christ*), and Brahms (*A German Requiem*, set to biblical texts). These works combine large choruses (almost always with at least one extended fugue), solo arias, and solo ensembles, mixed with recitative.

Over the course of the 19th century, the Catholic church became increasingly uncomfortable with what it perceived to be the overly virtuosic and operatic nature of

## Composer Profile

# Clara Wieck Schumann (1819–1896)

Clara Wieck Schumann was one of the most celebrated piano virtuosos of the 19th century, and her work as a composer has been recognized more and more in recent decades. Her partnership with Robert Schumann reflects the evolving pattern of relationships between men and women in 19th-century society. The two married out of love, against her father's wishes, and they forged a musical partnership throughout their 16 years of marriage, which ended only with Robert's death in 1856. They concertized widely—Robert conducting, Clara performing on the piano—throughout Europe. Indeed, in many respects Clara was more famous as a virtuoso than Robert was as a composer.

Clara was the daughter of Robert's piano instructor, Friedrich Wieck, but the courtship was not an easy one. Wieck did not want his daughter to marry a composer and journalist, particularly one of such limited financial means as Schumann. In the middle of an extended series of legal battles with her father, the couple eloped. Until her father eventually reconciled himself to the marriage, Clara found herself in often heartbreaking conflict with him. At one point she had to go to court to get back from him a piano she herself had paid for. She nevertheless concertized widely, and her performances of Beethoven's sonatas and concertos, Chopin's piano pieces, and her husband's compositions were legendary in their time. She developed a close relationship with Johannes Brahms, 14 years younger, who helped her manage her affairs during the difficult last years of her husband's life. After his death, she resumed her concert touring; later in life, she edited the first complete edition of her husband's works.

For a photo of Clara Schumann with her husband Robert, see page 426.

## PRINCIPAL WORKS OF CLARA WIECK SCHUMANN

Clara Schumann worked in many of the same genres as Robert Schumann, even before their marriage. She composed songs, part-songs, and several works of chamber music, the most notable of which is the Piano Trio in G minor, op. 17 (1846). She also wrote a Piano Concerto in A minor in 1836, ten years before her future husband's piano concerto in the same key.

### KEY DATES IN THE LIFE OF CLARA WIECK SCHUMANN

| | |
|---|---|
| 1819 | Born in Leipzig on September 13. |
| 1828 | After studying piano with her father, gives her first public recital. |
| 1832–1839 | Gives concert tours throughout Germany, Austria, and France. |
| 1840 | Against her father's wishes, marries Schumann; concertizing over the next 16 years includes an extended tour of Russia. |
| 1856 | Moves to Berlin with her children after her husband's death; continues concertizing. |
| 1878–1882 | Directs the piano division of the Hoch Conservatory of Music in Frankfurt. |
| 1896 | Dies in Frankfurt on May 20. |

**Anton Bruckner.** In addition to his sacred vocal works, Bruckner composed nine numbered symphonies (along with several that remained unnumbered), often employing an advanced chromatic idiom. He taught harmony and composition for many decades at the University of Vienna and was was widely regarded as one of the greatest organists of his generation; his improvisatory talents won special praise.

**Source:** Peratoner, Ferry (Beraton) (1866–1900)/The Art Gallery Collection/Alamy

music written for the liturgy. These misgivings are reminiscent of the objections raised at the Council of Trent in the mid-16th century about the "profane" nature of sacred music (see Chapter 6). A number of 19th-century composers allied themselves to what came to be known as the **Caecilian movement**, named after the patron saint of music, which sought to restore Gregorian chant and the style of 16th-century a cappella polyphony as the ideals of church music. During the 1830s, the Benedictine monks of Solesmes, France, began to prepare critical editions of Gregorian chant, and a number of composers cultivated a self-consciously archaic style modeled on the polyphonic sacred works of the late Renaissance. Bruckner's motet *Virga Jesse floruit*, for example, is indebted to what was broadly known as the "Palestrina style" in its rhythms and textures, even if its harmonies are highly chromatic from time to time. No one would mistake this for a work by Palestrina, yet Palestrina's influence is undeniably evident in this and many other sacred works of the period.

((•—**Listen**

**CD12    Track 8**
**mysearchlab** (with scrolling translation)
BRUCKNER
*Virga Jesse floruit*
Score Anthology II/141

# SUMMARY

Opera more than maintained its hold on the musical world of the 19th century. In Italy, Giuseppe Verdi developed an approach to opera that strove to create a greater sense of dramatic realism by integrating text and music to an unprecedented degree. In Germany, Richard Wagner sought to fuse operatic and symphonic idioms in a new genre he called the music drama, in which the dramatic coherence of the music coming from the orchestral pit was as important as the dramatic coherence of the words and gestures unfolding on the stage. Operetta, a lighter form of opera with spoken dialogue between the musical numbers, attracted even wider audiences. And although the importance of the church as a patron of new music declined somewhat in the 19th century, composers of this era produced a remarkable range and quantity of sacred music, from monumental works in the most advanced idiom to small-scale compositions reflecting the influence of Renaissance masters.

✓•—**Study** and **Review**
on **mysearchlab.com**

# Orchestral Music, 1850–1900

Orchestral music flourished in the second half of the 19th century. The civic orchestra, a permanent ensemble located in a single city and giving a regular schedule of public concerts season after season, became the predominant musical institution for orchestral music in this period. Such ensembles had been rare in earlier times. The orchestra Haydn conducted in England in the 1790s was assembled expressly for him and disbanded after he left; London had no organization providing regular concerts until the establishment of the Philharmonic Society in 1813. Vienna—home to Mozart, Beethoven, and other prominent composers—offered only occasional concerts performed by mostly ad hoc ensembles until the establishment of the Vienna Philharmonic in 1842. The New York Philharmonic was likewise established in 1842. The leading orchestra of Paris in the 1820s and 1830s was that of the Conservatory. But by the end of the century, every city with any claim to cultural significance could boast its own opera company and civic orchestra. Smaller cities often housed both in a single building, whereas larger, more affluent cities built separate structures for each.

## MUSIC FOR DANCING AND MARCHING

The concert hall was not the only important venue for orchestral music in the 19th century. Others included the dance hall, music hall, and parade ground. Dance halls and music halls served up food, drink, and music in varying proportions to clients from all classes of society. Dance, which offered unmarried couples the opportunity for physical contact at a time when it was otherwise frowned on, was a vital element in the rituals of courtship, and music was indispensable for dance. The most popular dances in the 19th century were the quadrille (a type of square dance); the polka (a lively dance in duple meter); and, above all, the waltz, which originated in Vienna in the last decades of the 18th century and swept all Europe in the first decades of the 19th century. Much of its popularity was due to the nature of the dance itself. It was one of the first socially acceptable dances that allowed partners to hold each other in a relatively close embrace, with the man's hand on his partner's back. George Gordon, Lord Byron, captured the mania for the dance in 1812 in these lines from his "The Waltz: An Apostrophic Hymn":

> Endearing Waltz!—to thy more melting tune
> Bow Irish jig and ancient rigadoon.

Scotch reels, avaunt! And country-dance, forego
Your future claims to each fantastic toe!
Waltz—Waltz alone—both legs and arms demands,
Liberal of feet and lavish of her hands;
Hands which may freely range in public sight
Where ne'er before—but—pray "put out the light." . . .

"How uneasy an English mother would be to see her daughter so familiarly treated," Charles Burney remarked in an entry on the "Waltz" for an English encyclopedia that appeared in 1819, "and still more so to witness the obliging matter in which the freedom is returned by the females."

The popularity of the waltz was boosted by the memorable music written for it by such composers as Joseph Lanner (1801–1843) and the two Johann Strausses, father (1804–1849) and son (1825–1899). All three hailed from Vienna, a city that became inextricably linked in the public mind with the waltz. The younger Strauss's *An der schönen blauen Donau* ("On the Beautiful Blue Danube," 1867) is representative of the genre. It consists of an extended introduction followed by a series of individual waltzes (numbered 1, 2, 3, etc.), most in binary form, each with its own thematic idea, and some with their own introductions (marked *Intrada* ["entry"] in the score). This modular structure allowed ensembles to repeat any individual waltz as often as desired. At the same time, Strauss was careful to integrate the sequence of dances into a coherent whole. The introduction (notated in A major but heard as the dominant of D) establishes the tonic key of D major for most of the waltzes. The fourth waltz modulates to F major for the sake of harmonic variety, and an extended coda brings the work to a close in the tonic and reprises the theme of the opening waltz.

Typically for dance music, each of the individual waltzes within *An der schönen blauen Donau* is built on units of 4 or 8 measures, which join to create larger units of 16 or 32 measures, and most of the waltzes follow a simple ABA pattern. This kind of rhythmic and structural predictability was essential for the function of social dance and would become the basis for many forms of dance or dance-related genres in the 20th century, including ragtime, the blues, and even rock and roll.

Music halls offered a mixture of instrumental and vocal works together with comedy, vaudeville routines, and animal acts. *Ta-Ra-Ra-Boom-de-ay*, still used in circuses today, is a typical music hall song of the 1890s. It was described by one critic of the time as

a senseless ditty with a dismal yet fascinating melody. . . . "Ta-Ra-Ra-Boom-de-ay" drove all London mad, and the rest of the world marveled at its madness. It became an epidemic. Babies lisped it, school children sang it, tottering old men and staid old ladies hummed it, and street boys whistled and shrieked it. Costers [street vendors] . . . stamped, kicked, and yelled it until they were hoarse and feeble from sheer exhaustion. Street organs and German bands played nothing else: it was taken up and echoed from town to village, and the cry throughout the land from cockcrow till midnight was "Ta-Ra-Ra-Boom-de-ay."[1]

The **march**, like dance music, was written to coordinate physical movement—in this case, the movement of soldiers. In the hands of such masters as the American

((•⸱ **Listen**
**CD12  Track 9**
**mysearchlab**
JOHANN STRAUSS, JR.
*An der schönen blauen Donau*
Score Anthology II/142

((•⸱ **Listen**
**CD12  Track 10**
**mysearchlab**
SOUSA
*Washington Post*
Score Anthology II/143

**Music and industry.** In 19th- and early-20th-century America, businesses routinely commissioned musical works to commemorate special events. John Philip Sousa's *King Cotton March* (1895) was commissioned by an industrial trade fair, the Cotton States and International Exposition, held in Atlanta in 1895. Note the enormous variety of instruments for which the work has been arranged: two mandolins and piano, two mandolins and guitar, zither solo, etc.

**Source:** Hartman Center for Sales, Advertising & Marketing History

**A women's banjo, mandolin, and guitar ensemble, ca. 1890.** Every American high school and college has its musical organizations, but few can boast of an ensemble like this particular group, probably from a college toward the end of the 19th century. This group might well have included in its repertory one of the many arrangements of John Philip Sousa's *King Cotton March.*

**Source:** James Bollman

composer John Philip Sousa (1854–1932), however, it became a genre for the bandstand and even eventually the concert hall. Like Strauss's waltzes, Sousa's marches are invariably modular in structure and build on units of 4, 8, 16, and 32 measures. But Sousa's marches are less concerned with issues of tonal closure; in fact, he often ends

## Focus | MUSIC PERIODICALS OF THE 19TH CENTURY

The number of journals devoted specifically to music grew exponentially in the 19th century. The public that bought tickets to the ballet, opera, and the symphony orchestra was eager to learn about the music they were hearing and keep up with the latest developments in the art through reviews of the latest performances and publications. For historians today, these journals provide an important record of day-to-day musical life in previous times. The more important include the following:

- *Allgemeine musikalische Zeitung* (Leipzig, 1798–1848; 1863–1865; 1866–1882). The "General Musical News," originally published by the firm Breitkopf & Härtel, reported musical events from across Europe and published many important reviews and essays, including E. T. A. Hoffmann's famous review of Beethoven's Fifth Symphony (see Primary Evidence feature, Chapter 15).

- *Neue Zeitschrift für Musik* (also Leipzig, 1834–). Founded and first edited by Robert Schumann, the "New Journal of Music" offered direct competition to the *Allgemeine musikalische Zeitung*, which Schumann and his circle perceived as stuffy and old fashioned. The *Neue Zeitschrift für Musik*, which has continued under various different names to the present day, was the forum for most of Schumann's writings on music, including his celebrated review of Berlioz's *Symphonie fantastique* and his essay of extravagant praise for the young Johannes Brahms (see Primary Evidence: Schumann Proclaims the Young Brahms a Musical Messiah, later in this chapter).

- *The Musical Times* (London, 1844–) provides a fascinating mirror of musical life in Great Britain. The advertisements alone reveal much about the changing nature of music from the mid-19th century to the present day.

- *Dwight's Journal of Music* (Boston, 1852–1881), founded and edited by John Sullivan Dwight, documents the growth of music in the United States.

his marches in the subdominant: his *Washington Post* (1889) begins in F major and closes in B♭ Major. While the 6/8 time signature may seem odd for a march (usually in a duple or quadruple meter), the effect is that each beat equals a triplet in eighth notes; the modular measure groupings further subdivide into (2 + 2 triplets) = 12/8, conducted as 4/4. Sousa wrote this and many of his other marches for the United States Marine Band, which he conducted from 1880 until 1892; he subsequently formed his own private band and toured with it throughout the United States and Europe. The nonimitative counterpoint (see, for example, the passage beginning at m. 68) is typical of the march repertory but often lost in piano transcriptions. Sousa was a master of orchestration and frequently made adjustments to his scores as conditions demanded or allowed. The score of *Washington Post*, for example, includes an optional part (shaded in gray in the edition used in the anthology) for harp, a clear indication that Sousa's marches were intended as much for the concert hall as for the parade ground.

# THE BALLET

Accounts of theatrical dance go back as far as the Renaissance, and ballet had played an important role in opera since the very beginnings of that genre around 1600. Ballet nevertheless assumed unprecedented importance in the 19th century. It began to provide the main attraction for entire evenings of public entertainment in Paris in the 1870s. Ballet offered yet another approach to that enduring artistic dilemma: how to reconcile the abstract with the concrete. Ballet is less abstract than purely instrumental music, but without words it avoids the specificity of opera. Audiences are free to interpret the dancers' movements as direct representations of emotions or actions, or they can view these gestures abstractly, as movements that are beautiful in their own right.

The 19th century witnessed many technical innovations in ballet, including a more athletic kind of movement, as well as dancing *en pointe* (on the tips of the toes). Costumes became shorter, and eventually skintight, showcasing the human form. On the whole, choreography avoided realism, combining massive formations of dancers (as in Hollywood musicals of the 1930s and 1940s) with a focus on a principal female soloist, the *prima ballerina*. Male dancers remained secondary until the early 20th century. In their time, the ballerinas Marie Taglioni, Fanny Elssler, Fanny Cerrito, Carolotta Frisi, and Lucille Grahn were as admired as the most celebrated singers and instrumental virtuosos.

France, which had always been preeminent in the field of dance, continued to lead the way in the 19th century as ballet became an increasingly public genre, moving outside the patronage of the courts. The most prominent French ballet composers of the period were Adolphe Adam (1803–1856) and Léo Delibes (1836–1891). Adam's *Giselle* (1841) and Delibes's *Coppélia* (1870) remain staples of the ballet repertoire.

In the last third of the century, the Russian composer Peter Ilyich Tchaikovsky (1840–1893) emerged as the preeminent ballet composer. Tchaikovsky's lyrical melodies and rich orchestrations combined to make his *Swan Lake* (1876), *Sleeping Beauty* (1889), and *The Nutcracker* (1892) among the most enduringly popular works of their kind. The plot of *Swan Lake* revolves around the lovers Siegfried, a young prince, and Odette, a young princess who has been kidnapped by the evil sorcerer von Rothbart. To keep her for himself, Rothbart has cast a spell on Odette: by day,

((•–[ **Listen**
**CD12    Track 11**
**mysearchlab**
TCHAIKOVSKY
*Swan Lake*
Score Anthology II/144

**Tchaikovsky's *Swan Lake*.** Prince Siegfried and Odette, the princess who has been transformed into a swan by an evil sorcerer. This image is from the Bolshoi Ballet's 2005 Moscow production.
**Source:** ITAR-TASS Photo Agency/Alamy

## Composer Profile

# Peter Ilyich Tchaikovsky (1840–1893)

Tchaikovsky was a late bloomer. He did not enter a musical conservatory until the age of 21, having already secured a position as a government clerk. Within five years, however, he was teaching harmony at the Moscow Conservatory. A wealthy widow, Nadezhda von Meck, provided him with a long series of generous commissions that allowed him to resign his teaching position in 1878 and devote himself entirely to composition. He was an intensely private individual who acknowledged his homosexuality within his immediate circle but otherwise kept it concealed for fear of public condemnation. The strain of this concealment, some have speculated, contributed to his repeated bouts of depression.

Tchaikovsky embraced his Russian heritage but did not make a display of it, unlike some of his contemporaries, who made a point of writing explicitly nationalistic music. Stylistically, he was an internationalist, blending Russian, French, Italian, and German traditions with his remarkable gift for melody. As a conductor, he traveled widely across Europe and even made a brief tour of the United States in 1891. His highly popular Piano Concerto no. 1 received its premiere in Boston in 1875.

The circumstances surrounding Tchaikovsky's death have long been controversial. He died apparently of cholera during an epidemic of the disease in St. Petersburg. Some maintain that he knowingly drank contaminated water, effectively committing suicide, but nothing in his correspondence suggests that he was unusually depressed at the time.

preferring the more traditional designation of "overture" for these works. The celebrated *1812 Overture*, written to commemorate the Russian victory over Napoleon's invading army, incorporates the French and Russian national anthems and concludes with a blast of cannons. The First Piano Concerto and the Violin Concerto are among the most enduringly popular works of their kind.

**Tchaikovsky.** When the composer toured the United States in 1891, he helped inaugurate the newly built Carnegie Hall in New York City.

**Source:** Library of Congress

## PRINCIPAL WORKS

### Ballets and Operas

Even had he written nothing else, Tchaikovsky's ballets would be enough to justify his fame as a composer. *Swan Lake* (1876), *Sleeping Beauty* (1889), and *The Nutcracker* (1892) all became immediate staples of the repertory. Tchaikovsky's most notable operas are *Eugene Onegin* (1879) and *Queen of Spades* (1890).

### Symphonies, Overtures, Concertos

The six completed symphonies are remarkable for their lyricism, orchestration, and dramatic tone. Formally, they broke little new ground, although the last, the *Pathétique*, has a waltz-like second movement in 5/4 and ends with a long slow movement full of heroic resignation rather than triumph. Tchaikovsky also cultivated the symphonic poem,

| KEY DATES IN THE LIFE OF TCHAIKOVSKY | |
|---|---|
| 1840 | Born in Votinsk, Russia, the son of a mining inspector in the Ural Mountains. |
| 1850 | Moves with his family to St. Petersburg, capital of Russia. |
| 1861 | Enters the St. Petersburg Conservatory; studies composition with Anton Rubinstein. |
| 1866 | Appointed professor of harmony at Moscow Conservatory. |
| 1876 | Attends the opening of Wagner's Festspielhaus at Bayreuth and writes musical criticism for a Moscow newspaper. |
| 1878 | Resigns from the Moscow Conservatory and devotes himself entirely to composition. |
| 1891 | Makes concert tour of the United States, where he conducts at the inauguration of Carnegie Hall, New York, on May 5. |
| 1893 | Dies in St. Petersburg on November 6. |

she is a swan, and by night she returns to her human form. Siegfried discovers Odette among a flock of swans in the forest and falls in love with her, but she forbids him from killing Rothbart before the spell over her is broken. In the end, however, Odette realizes that the spell will continue as long as she lives, and so in the finale she leaps to her death (Figure 23 in the score); Siegfried follows her, and Rothbart collapses, powerless. The opening minor-mode theme, a Leitmotif associated throughout with the swans, now appears in an apotheosis of major, performed by the full orchestra (Figure 26). Tchaikovsky's music provides clear points of reference for the most dramatic moments of the tale, but choreographers have always had the freedom to interpret the wordless depiction of this drama in a variety of ways. A comparison of various productions of this finale reveals the wide of range of choreographic possibilities.

# THE SYMPHONIC POEM

By 1850, Berlioz, Mendelssohn, and Schumann had all contributed important works to the symphonic repertory. Yet widespread skepticism remained about the continuing viability of the genre. Richard Wagner had proclaimed the death of the symphony and many composers, like him, avoided the genre altogether. Others, like Brahms, as we will see, took it on despite its historical freight. Still others negotiated a middle ground in the genre of the symphonic poem.

Liszt coined the term **symphonic poem** (*Symphonische Dichtung*) in 1854 as a new name for what had traditionally been called a concert overture (see Chapter 15). By the 1830s, the traditional designation had become a misnomer because works in this genre were no longer overtures in any meaningful sense of the word. Although usually programmatic and only one movement long, they were written expressly for the concert hall, not as an opening for a play or opera. The new term caught on quickly because it captured the main characteristics of the genre: symphonic and poetic. The "poetic" element lay in the program or the evocative title given these works; the "symphonic" element lay in the resources of the full orchestra. The programmatic source for a symphonic poem could range from the vague to the specific and might be reflected in the music in anything from a very general to a very particular way. A list of the extra-musical associations for Liszt's 13 symphonic poems (see Focus: The Programmatic Sources for Liszt's Symphonic Poems) gives some idea of the variety of programmatic sources composers turned to for inspiration.

Richard Strauss (1864–1949) succeeded Liszt as the acknowledged master of the symphonic poem, combining his gifts as an orchestrator with his genius for joining symphonic forms and story lines. Strauss's symphonic poems include *Also sprach Zarathustra* (loosely based on a treatise of the same name by the poet and philosopher Friedrich Nietzsche), *Don Juan* (based on a poem by Nicholaus Lenau), *Don Quixote* (based on the novel by Cervantes), and the quasi-autobiographical *Ein Heldenleben* ("A Hero's Life").

These expansive, opulent works epitomize the late 19th century's love of grandeur, particularly in their exploitation of the ever-expanding resources of the modern orchestra. It was Strauss who revised Berlioz's influential treatise on orchestration (see Composer Profile: Hector Berlioz, in Chapter 15) and he did so in part to account for the expanded size of the orchestra and the new instruments that had been added to it since Berlioz's day, such as the tuba and saxophone. The forces Strauss calls for in his symphonic poems represent the orchestra at its peak—or, as

## Focus THE PROGRAMMATIC SOURCES FOR LISZT'S SYMPHONIC POEMS

Liszt drew on a variety of extramusical sources for his symphonic poems, from specific poems to historical events to general ideas.

| Title | Extramusical Associations |
| --- | --- |
| *Ce qu'on entend sur la montagne* (1849) | Poem by Victor Hugo ("That Which Is Heard on the Mountain") |
| *Tasso* (1849) | Poem by Johann Wolfgang Goethe |
| *Heroïde funèbre* (1850) | Funeral march |
| *Prometheus* (1850) | The myth of Prometheus |
| *Mazeppa* (1851) | Poem by Victor Hugo |
| *Festklänge* (1853) | Marriage celebration ("Festival Sounds") |
| *Orpheus* (1854) | The myth of Orpheus |
| *Les préludes* (1848; revised 1854) | Poem by Alphonse de Lamartine |
| *Hungaria* (1854) | The dream of an independent Hungary |
| *Die Ideale* (1857) | Poem by Friedrich Schiller ("The Ideals") |
| *Die Hunnenschlacht* (1857) | Painting by Wilhelm von Kaulbach ("The Battle of the Huns") |
| *Hamlet* (1857) | Shakespeare's play |
| *Von der Wiege bis zum Grabe* (1882) | Painting by Mihály Zichy ("From Cradle to Grave") |

some critics would have it, at its most overblown. In *Don Juan* (1889), for example, he called for the following:

| | |
| --- | --- |
| 3 Flutes (one doubling on piccolo) | 3 Trombones |
| 2 Oboes | Tuba |
| English horn | 3 Timpani |
| 2 Clarinets | Triangle |
| 2 Bassoons | Cymbals |
| Contrabassoon | Glockenspiel |
| 4 Horns | Harp |
| 3 Trumpets | Strings |

Strauss was careful to use these forces judiciously, frequently dividing them into smaller units and reserving the full ensemble for special effect.

# THE SYMPHONY

The symphony enjoyed renewed vigor in the second half of the 19th century. Many of the most prominent composers of instrumental music turned to this genre, creating works of unparalleled breadth and scope. The growing size of the orchestra, the increasing number of civic orchestras and standing concert series, and the inherently public nature of the genre all helped reinforce the symphony's standing as the largest, most ambitious, and most prestigious of all instrumental genres.

In an effort to take the genre of the symphony in new directions, several prominent composers created works that draw on elements from other genres. Outstanding examples include hybrids with the concerto (Berlioz's *Harold en Italie*, Lalo's *Symphonie espagnole*); cantata (Mendelssohn's *Lobgesang*, Félicien David's *Le Desert* and *Christophe Colombe*—the latter two bearing the designation *ode-symphonie*); opera (Berlioz's *Roméo et Juliette*); and even the symphonic poem (Liszt's *Faust-Symphonie*, each of whose three movements the composer called a "Character Sketch"—the first for Faust, the second for Gretchen, the third for Mephistopheles).

The symphonic character of many pieces lying nominally outside the genre is also evident in works such as Rimsky-Korsakov's *Sadko* (1867; revised 1869 and 1891), subtitled "Symphonic Pictures," and Debussy's *La Mer* (1898), subtitled "Three Symphonic Sketches," in which the remnants of symphonic form are clearly discernible: a slow introduction to a fast opening movement, followed by a scherzo and a fast culminating finale. Symphonic form and breadth are also frequently evident in concertos. The concertos of Schumann, Brahms, and Dvořák—for example—all display a symphonic tone, avoiding virtuosity for its own sake and more fully integrating soloist and orchestra than earlier concertos.

## The Challenge of the Past: Brahms

Still other composers, most notably Johannes Brahms and Antonín Dvořák, continued to write symphonies in the traditional four-movement pattern. Brahms in particular embraced his musical heritage, openly aligning himself with the traditions of composers like Bach, Haydn, Mozart, Beethoven, Schubert, and Schumann. But he did so with considerable ambivalence, for like all 19th-century composers, he felt compelled to demonstrate creative originality. Approaching the age of 40, Brahms despaired of ever writing a symphony. When asked whether he would, he confided to a friend, "You have no idea how it feels . . . when one always hears such a giant marching along behind." The "giant" was of course Beethoven. In his First Symphony, Brahms introduced a triumphant lyrical theme in the finale that closely resembles the "Ode to Joy" in the finale of Beethoven's Ninth. When someone pointed this resemblance out to the composer, Brahms is said to have replied, "Yes indeed, and what's really remarkable is that every jackass notices it at once."

Despite the inhibiting effect of Beethoven's long shadow, Brahms was able to write four symphonies that each bear his own distinct stamp. As with Beethoven, his symphonies have no common formula; each takes a different conceptual approach to the genre. In general, Brahms sought to avoid making the symphony even more monumental than it had already become. The relatively diminutive inner movements of his First Symphony, for example, serve almost as interludes to the outer movements, and the last movement of the Second Symphony breaks with the tradition of the finale as a grandiose symphonic culmination.

The imposing set of variations in the finale of his Fourth Symphony, however, stands well within a tradition set down in the last movement of Beethoven's *Eroica*. But here, Brahms reaches past Beethoven to an even earlier tradition, that of J. S. Bach. On one level, the structure of this finale is quite simple: it is a series of 30 variations, each eight measures long and based on the same eight-measure theme. Within this relatively simple, potentially restrictive, framework, Brahms introduces a stunning variety of thematic ideas, textures, harmonies, and colors. The theme is based on the ostinato subject of the finale of Bach's Cantata no. 150, a work that Brahms knew well. (Bach used the ostinato technique in a similar fashion in the first movement of Cantata no. 78, *Anthology*, discussed in Chapter 9).

((•⋅ Listen
**CD13    Track 1**
**mysearchlab**
BRAHMS
Symphony no. 4
Score Anthology II/145

Bach's ostinato theme (Example 18–1) is not particularly distinctive; it fills in the interval of a fifth and ends with an octave leap on the dominant, which in turn sets up the repetition of the theme. Brahms (Example 18–2) extends the theme to eight measures (one note per measure), moves the melodic idea to the uppermost voice,

**EXAMPLE 18–1** Ostinato theme of Bach, Cantata no. 150, finale (transposed).

**EXAMPLE 18–2** Brahms's ostinato theme for the finale of his Symphony no. 4.

## Primary Evidence — SCHUMANN PROCLAIMS THE YOUNG BRAHMS A MUSICAL MESSIAH (1853)

*In what would turn out to be his last published piece of musical criticism, Robert Schumann introduced the musical world to a still unknown 20-year-old composer named Johannes Brahms. Schumann begins by reviewing the most promising young composers of the age and then poses the question of who might follow in the steps of Beethoven.*

■ ■ ■

After such an antecedent there would and must appear quite suddenly one who was called to articulate the highest expression of the age in an ideal manner, one who would bring us mastery not in a process of step-by-step development, but would instead spring fully-armored, like Minerva, from the head of Cronus. And he has come, a new blood at whose cradle the graces and heroes stood guard. His name is Johannes Brahms; he came from Hamburg, where, working in dark stillness, he was nevertheless educated by an excellent and enthusiastic teacher [Eduard Marxsen] in the most difficult elements of the art, and he was recently recommended to me by a venerated and well-known master [Joseph Joachim]. Even in his external appearance, he carried with him all the characteristics that proclaimed to us: This is One who has been called. Sitting at the piano, he began to reveal the most wonderful regions. We were drawn into an increasingly magic circle. There we heard the most genial playing, which made an orchestra out of the piano, with lamenting and jubilant voices. There were sonatas, more like disguised symphonies; songs, whose poetry one would understand without knowing the words, although there was through all of them a profound vocal line; individual piano pieces, some of a demonic nature in the most daring form; then sonatas for violin and piano; quartets for stringed instruments; and each so different from the other that they all seemed to flow out of different sources. . . .

If he lowers his magic staff where the massed forces of chorus and orchestra give their powers, then we shall yet have even more wondrous glimpses into the secrets of the spiritual world. May the highest spirit of genius strengthen him for this. The prospect for this exists, given that another spirit of genius already lives within him, the spirit of modesty. His colleagues greet him on his first journey through the world, where wounds, perhaps, await him, but also laurels and palms. We welcome him as a strong combatant. There dwells in every age a secret society of kindred souls. Close the circle tighter, ye who belong to it, so that the truth of art might glow ever more clearly, spreading joy and blessings everywhere!

**Source:** Robert Schumann "Neue Bahnen" ("New Paths"), *Neue Zeitschrift für Musik* (1853). Transl. MEB.

## Composer Profile

# Johannes Brahms (1833–1897)

Brahms was once caricatured in silhouette walking next to a hedgehog, an image that captures the composer's personality perfectly. Brahms was an intensely private man. Among his close friends, he was known for his warmth and dry sense of humor, but to the public, he remained reclusive and cold. He zealously collected sketches by Beethoven and other composers, but he wanted no one to pry into his own workshop. When he realized he was dying of cancer, he destroyed his remaining sketches and drafts. He wanted his art to speak for itself.

Like Beethoven, Brahms was from the northern part of Germany—Hamburg—and chose to spend most of his adult life in Vienna. The decisive moment of his career came at the age of 20, when Robert Schumann declared him the new messiah of music (see Primary Evidence: Schumann Proclaims the Young Brahms a Musical Messiah). This pronouncement proved both a blessing and a curse. Thanks to Schumann's stature, it gave Brahms immediate recognition, but its extraordinary language burdened him with unrealistic expectations. Critics predisposed to dislike his music (that is, the followers of Liszt and Wagner) were quick to belittle Brahms's first works for falling short of those expectations.

Stung by these early assaults, Brahms soon developed a thick skin. For the rest of his life, he more or less ignored his critics and moved forward as he alone saw fit. His music cannot be easily classified as either "progressive" or "conservative." In many ways, it was both at the same time. In the 20th century, Arnold Schoenberg, one of the most radical composers of his generation, hailed Brahms as one of the most progressive composers of the late 19th century, primarily because of Brahms's ability to reveal the rich potential of a seemingly simple germinal idea. Many critics in Brahms's own lifetime found his music texturally and harmonically complicated, structurally intricate, and difficult to comprehend.

Brahms was nevertheless deeply committed to building on and rejuvenating the works of the great composers of the past, from the recent Schumann, Beethoven, Mozart, and Haydn to the more distant Bach, Handel, and Schütz of the Baroque era, and the even more distant Palestrina of the Renaissance. In an era remarkable for its emphasis on novelty and originality, Brahms thus embraced the musical past. In contrast to Liszt and Wagner, he refused to accept that music could or should be subordinate to any other art.

In keeping with these beliefs, Brahms composed numerous works in the traditional genres of instrumental music. He also applied the principles of sonata form more openly than almost any other composer of the late 19th century. This is not to say that Brahms's sonata-form movements are predictable—he manipulated the conventions of the form in the same spirit as had Haydn and Beethoven.

Brahms found another outlet for his historicism as a music editor. He prepared many new editions (often without credit or payment) of music by Couperin, Handel, Bach, Mozart, Schubert, and Schumann. His friends included many prominent music scholars who were helping launch the first substantial effort to publish critical editions of past composers. Among these scholars were Philipp Spitta, who wrote the first full-scale biography of J. S. Bach and was a driving force in the first complete edition of Bach's music; Friedrich Chrysander, Handel's biographer and editor of his music; and Gustav Nottebohm, renowned for his work on Beethoven's sketches. (Brahms once created a fake sketch by Beethoven and surreptitiously paid a Viennese street vendor to use the sheet as a wrapper for some cheese Nottebohm was buying.)

**Brahms (right) and Johann Strauss, Jr. (1894).** Brahms admired the art of the "Waltz King" deeply. He once wrote the opening theme of the *Blue Danube Waltz* on a lady's fan and underneath it added the words "Leider nicht von Brahms" ("Not by Brahms, unfortunately"). The contrast between these two men in appearance and style of dress is striking, especially when we realize the dapper Strauss was almost eight years older than Brahms. When this photograph was taken, Strauss was 69 and Brahms was 61.

**Source:** Bettmann/Corbis

# PRINCIPAL WORKS

## Symphonies and Other Orchestral Works

Brahms struggled off and on for more than 20 years to write a first symphony. Throughout the 1860s and early 1870s he produced a small but steady stream of orchestral works. These include the two Serenades (1858, 1860), and the *Variations on a Theme of Haydn* (1873; more recent scholarship has revealed that the tune is in fact probably not by Haydn, although Brahms had every reason to think it was). After finally finishing his First Symphony in 1876, he produced three more in relatively quick order: no. 2 in D Major (1877), no. 3 in F Major (1883), and no. 4 in E minor (1885). Each is different from the others, yet all four fall squarely within the symphonic tradition.

Brahms's later orchestral works include two overtures: the *Academic Festival Overture* (1880), written as a thankful gift to the University of Breslau for conferring an honorary doctorate on him, and the *Tragic Overture* (1881), a work for the concert hall. "One laughs, one cries," Brahms noted of these two works.

## Concertos

Although few in number, Brahms's concertos helped define the genre in the second half of the 19th century. The two piano concertos (1854, 1881), the Violin Concerto (1878), and the "Double" Concerto for violin and cello (1887) are all symphonic in scope and tone. These works demand great virtuosity on the part of the soloist, yet the solo part never seems arbitrarily difficult.

## Chamber Works

Brahms cultivated chamber music with an intensity unmatched by any other composer of his generation. His output includes three violin sonatas; two cello sonatas; two clarinet sonatas; three piano trios; trios for horn, cello, and piano and for clarinet, cello, and piano; three string quartets; three piano quartets; a piano quintet; a clarinet quintet; and two string sextets. All of these works are technically demanding and lie well beyond the range of the average amateur musician.

## Piano Music

Brahms established his early reputation both as a pianist and as a composer. His op. 1, in fact, is a piano sonata with strong echoes of Beethoven's *Hammerklavier* Sonata, op. 106. But with op. 5, he abandoned the solo piano sonata and turned instead to variations, producing sets based on themes by Schumann, by Handel, and by Paganini. Later in life, he cultivated the character piece, even though he gave these generic names such as Capriccio, Rhapsody, Intermezzo, or the utterly neutral designation of *Klavierstück* ("Piano Piece"). Brahms pointedly avoided references to external ideas or objects in these works, presumably to distance himself from other 19th-century composers for the piano like Gottschalk and Liszt, who applied programmatic ideas to otherwise straightforward etudes. Brahms's late piano pieces include some of his most beautiful and moving compositions.

## Songs

Considering how many songs Brahms wrote, it is surprising that so relatively few remain in the active repertory today. In addition to the standard settings for voice and piano, there are also a number of vocal duets and quartets. Brahms also arranged a number of German folk songs for publication.

## Vocal Music

The *German Requiem* (1868), written to texts selected from the Bible, is a staple of the choral repertory. Less well-known but every bit as appealing are such works as the *Alto Rhapsody* (1869) and *Nänie* (1881). Brahms also wrote music for men's, women's, and mixed choruses that is little known but deserves wider exposure. He also wrote his share of occasional music, such as the *Triumphlied* of 1871 to celebrate the German victory in the Franco-Prussian War of 1870–1871.

| KEY DATES IN THE LIFE OF BRAHMS | |
|---|---|
| **1833** | Born in Hamburg (Germany), May 7. |
| **1847** | Gives first public concert as a pianist. |
| **1853** | On tour with the violin virtuoso Joseph Joachim, meets both Liszt and Schumann. Schumann introduces the young Brahms to the world as the new messiah of music. |
| **1862** | Moves to Vienna, where he spends most of the remaining years of his life. Makes his living subsequently almost exclusively from conducting and from sales of his own compositions. |
| **1876** | Finishes First Symphony; declines an honorary doctorate from Cambridge University but accepts one from Breslau University. |
| **1897** | Dies in Vienna on April 3 and is buried alongside Beethoven and Schubert in Vienna's Central Cemetery. |

and adds a striking dissonance by sharpening the second iteration of the fourth scale degree (A#). He further deviates from Bach's theme by ending on the first scale degree. The resulting harmonic closure increases the challenge of composing a continuous movement from a string of such sequences, but it is a challenge Brahms confronts with zeal. By the time we reach the middle of this movement, we have to remind ourselves that it is in fact a set of variations on a theme. The division between Variations 6 and 7 (m. 49–56 and 57–64) is almost imperceptible even when we listen for it. The movement nevertheless holds consistently to the repeating eight-measure structure all the way through Variation 30. Only the coda, beginning in m. 253 after a few introductory measures, is freely composed.

Within this self-imposed structure of variations on a theme, Brahms integrates another formal principle, that of tripartite (ABA¹) form (variations 1–15; 16–23; 24–coda). There is an unmistakable sense of transition in Variations 10 and 11 (m. 81–88, 89–96) and a clear change of mood with Variation 12 (m. 97–104); then the meter changes, the music is marked *dolce* for the first time, and the timbre of the solo flute dominates the substantially thinned texture. The impression of change is reinforced in Variation 13 (m. 105–112) with a shift to E Major. Variation 16 marks the onset of what corresponds to the B section, and Variation 24 sounds very much like the beginning of a recomposed A section. The material after Variation 30, as already noted, constitutes a freely composed coda.

With this finale of his last symphony, Brahms seems to be reminding the musical world that old forms are capable of rejuvenation, that it is possible to search for the new without abandoning tradition entirely. The Baroque technique of basing a set of variations on an ostinato (which Brahms labeled a chaconne) provides a most compelling structure for the composer; in its ostensibly simple construction, this movement is firmly rooted in tradition, but in its harmony, orchestration, and sense of flow, it is distinctly progressive.

## Nationalism: Dvořák

With its perceived ability to give voice to communal feeling (see Chapter 15), the symphony proved itself a particularly fertile genre for composers seeking to introduce nationalistic elements into their music. In Russia, such composers as Nikolai Rimsky-Korsakov, Peter Ilyich Tchaikovsky, Dmitri Balakirev, and Aleksandr Borodin were quick to incorporate into their symphonies such nationalistic elements as modal inflections, folk-inspired rhythms, and the rich tradition of the Russian brass ensemble.

Several important American composers also used the symphony as a vehicle for nationalistic expression. Anthony Philip Heinrich, who emigrated to the United States from Bohemia in the first decade of the 19th century, incorporated such tunes as *Yankee Doodle* and *Hail, Columbia* into his *Columbiad: Grand American National Chivalrous Symphony* (1837). Like Dvořák many decades later, Heinrich was fascinated with the music of Native Americans, as is reflected in his *Manitou Mysteries, or The Voice of the Great Spirit*, subtitled *Gran sinfonia misteriosa-indiana* (1845). Despite its unusual title, the work follows a traditional four-movement format, with a rondo finale. Louis Moreau Gottschalk's *La Nuit des tropiques: Symphony No. 1* (1859), by contrast, is a two-movement work that integrates rumba and fugue toward the end of its finale. The *Gaelic* Symphony by Amy Beach (1896) uses Irish melodies, in keeping with the fin-de-siècle cultural revival known as the "Celtic twilight." These and other American symphonies of the 19th century remain little known but are well worth investigating.

((•–Listen

**CD12    Track 12**
**mysearchlab**
DVOŘÁK
Symphony no. 9 ("From the
New World")
Score Anthology II/146

Ironically, the best-known "American" symphony from the second half of the 19th century was written by a Czech, Antonín Dvořák (1841–1904). During an extended sojourn in the United States (1892–1895), he composed his Symphony no. 9 in E minor and subtitled it "From the New World." Its themes are supposedly based on or inspired by Native American ("Indian") and African-American ("Negro") musical idioms. Dvořák motivations here seem to have been in part didactic: he hoped to show American composers how they might use indigenous musical materials to create a distinctively American style, thereby weaning themselves from the European tradition.

Dvořák urged American composers to model orchestral music on the music of African Americans and Native Americans. "These are the folk songs of America," he wrote, "and your composers must turn to them. All the great musicians have borrowed from the songs of the common people. . . . In the Negro melodies of America I discover all that is needed for a great and noble school of music. . . . It is music that suits itself to any mood or any purpose. There is nothing in the whole range of composition that cannot be supplied with themes from this source. The American musician understands these tunes and they move sentiment in him. They appeal to his imagination because of their associations."[2]

In his Symphony no. 9, Dvořák synthesizes the traditions of both the Old and New Worlds. Structurally, the work follows the standard pattern of four movements: a sonata-form first movement with an extended slow introduction; a pastoral slow movement (the Largo); a fast, dance-like third movement in triple meter; and a rousing finale that breaks through from minor to major. Within each of these individual movements, however, Dvořák incorporates what he considered to be characteristic elements of indigenous American music. The principal theme of the Largo, for example (beginning at m. 7), is largely **pentatonic**—that is, based on a scale of only five notes. Although frequently associated with the music of East Asia, pentatonic scales figure large in many traditional ("folk") idioms of the West as well, and when Europeans like Dvořák heard Native Americans making music, they tended to hear the melodies as characteristically pentatonic. The opening phrase on the English horn (which sounds a fifth lower than notated) uses primarily the pitches D♭, E♭, F, A♭, and B♭. The C♮ that first appears in m. 11 functions as a leading tone to the tonic, but the scale of the melody pointedly avoids the fourth scale degree in the key of D♭ (that is, G♭), thereby lending a strongly pentatonic coloring to the theme. The melody of the contrasting section in C♯ minor (beginning at m. 46), played on flutes and oboes, is also constructed on a pentatonic scale (C♯-D♯-E-G♯-B), again omitting the fourth scale degree (F♯).

The orchestration and harmonization of both these melodies contribute to the pastoral tone of the movement. The English horn and oboe are both reed instruments and thus connected, at least indirectly, to the shepherd's reed pipe; the flute, too, is an instrument associated with the idealized serenity of the countryside. The drone bass underneath both melodies, reminiscent of a bagpipe, further contributes to this air of calm. But pastoral scenes are almost inevitably disrupted at some point, and Dvořák's Largo holds true to form: the C♯ minor section introduces a dark and at times threatening tone to the whole. The extended section over a "walking bass" (beginning at m. 54) includes still more pentatonically inflected melodies. The idea in the flute incorporates the so-called "Scotch snap," a short note on the accented beat followed by a longer note. In m. 60, for example, the sixteenth note in the flute is followed by a dotted quarter tied to a half, emphasizing rhythmically the melodic absence of the fourth scale degree in the melodic fragment E-F♯-G♯-B-C♯. Yet another interruption, a lively major-mode section (beginning at m. 90) leads to a portentous reference back to the main theme of the first movement (m. 96)—Dvořák

## Composer Profile

# Antonín Dvořák (1841–1904)

In 1857, Antonín Dvořák moved to Prague to focus on composition studies. He began to gain recognition, first with the help of his fellow Bohemian, Bedřich Smetana, who performed his music in Prague, and later through the support of Johannes Brahms, who had been introduced to Dvořák's work while serving on a panel that awarded governmental stipends for music. Emulating his own experience with Schumann, Brahms recommended Dvořák to the German publisher Simrock, who issued the first set of *Slavonic Dances* (1878), Dvořák's first major success, which led to international attention and performances. Although he was advised to move to Vienna and write an opera in German; Dvořák, a Czech nationalist who resented the Habsburg view of his native land's culture as parochial, did neither.

To build his reputation, Dvořák spent the next years touring throughout Europe, especially England, and had an audience with the emperor in Vienna. By the time his popular *Carnival Overture* was premiered in 1891, he had been appointed professor of composition at the Prague Conservatory. But Dvořák soon accepted the directorship of the National Conservatory of Music of America in New York, where he remained from 1892 to 1895. He conducted at Chicago's World Columbian Exposition, and vacationed with his family at a Czech-speaking colony in Spillville, Iowa. Back in New York, he was apparently introduced to the African-American spiritual by his composition student Harry Thacker Burleigh; contact with this music and that of Native Americans, combined with his personal experiences as a musical nationalist, led him to urge American composers to develop a distinctly national style by drawing on these indigenous idioms. Upon the premiere of his Symphony no. 9 by the New York Philharmonic in 1893, he chose to argue his point in a letter to the *New York Herald*:

> [T]he new American school of music must strike its roots deeply into its own soil. There is no longer any reason why young Americans who have talent should go to Europe for their education. . . . The country [i.e., the United States] is full of melody, original, sympathetic and varying in mood, color and character to suit every phase of composition. It is a rich field. America can have great and noble music of her own, growing out of the very soil and partaking

of its nature—the natural voice of a free and vigorous race.[3]

The success of the "New World" Symphony as "American music" testified to Dvořák's ability to capture a national spirit that by rights was not "natural" to him.

Dvořák returned to Prague, where he resumed his duties at the Prague Conservatory and composed successful operas, symphonic poems, and his most popular work after the Ninth Symphony, the Cello Concerto in B minor (1895), given its premiere in London in 1896; Brahms said of this work, "Had I known that one could write a cello concerto like this, I would have written one long ago!" Dvořák served as the conservatory's director from 1901 until his death.

# PRINCIPAL WORKS

## Symphonies and Other Orchestral Works

Until quite recently, Dvořák was considered to have written five symphonies, which were published accordingly. After the four earlier works were "rediscovered" after his death, the symphonies originally numbered 1 through 5 were renumbered nos. 6, 7, 5, 8, and 9, respectively. As in other genres, the early works reflect various influences—Schubert, Beethoven, Wagner, Liszt—that he gradually integrated into a Czech nationalist style, akin to but more easygoing and fluid than Brahms, and by no means superficially "folksy": there are many darker passages in these works. He also composed a cycle of symphonic poems based primarily on Czech folklore (1896–97), concert overtures, the Symphonic Variations, the String Serenade, and the two series of *Slavonic Dances*. Concertos for violin and piano solo preceded the cello concerto; he also orchestrated a number of his piano and chamber pieces, including the "American Suite" for piano and *Silent Woods* for cello and piano.

## Chamber Works and Piano Music

Dvořák wrote a considerable amount of chamber music, demonstrating a considerable melodic gift. In addition to 14 string quartets, he composed 4 piano trios, 2 piano quartets, 2 piano quintets, and smaller pieces. His solo and duet piano works were often based on familiar genres (minuet, Scottish, march, humoresque, impromptu) as well as Czech idioms (dumka, furiant, polka); he also published two solo piano cycles.

## Operas

Unlike Brahms, Dvořák ventured into musical theater, the most lucrative venue for a composer at the time. Like so many others, he was caught up in the Wagnerian music drama as a young composer, but soon put that influence to rest, looking to Russian models. His two major successes, *The Devil and Kate* and *Rusalka*, came late in his career, as did a major failure, *Armida* (1903–1904, based on the same source that Gluck used; see Chapter 13).

## Songs

Dvořák's song cycles range from the early *Cypresses* (an unsuccessful wooing present to the sister of the woman he would eventually marry), *Evening Songs, Gypsy Melodies* (which he set in German), and the *Biblical Songs*, written after the deaths of his friends Tchaikovsky and Hans von Bülow. Almost all his other songs were based on folk poetry or written in a folk music style. As with any song written in a less common language, performances of Dvořák's songs are rare outside his native land.

## Vocal Music

Modern choral ensembles are more likely to encounter Dvořák's works. As with other foreign composers (including Handel and Mendelssohn), he found England to be receptive to him; even more significant is that his best-known choral works are Latin settings: the *Stabat Mater*, the Mass in D Major, the Requiem Mass, and the *Te Deum*.

**Antonín Dvořák.**

**Source:** akg-images/Newscom

| KEY DATES IN THE LIFE OF DVOŘÁK | |
|---|---|
| 1841 | Born in Nelahozeves, near Kralupy (Austrian Empire; now Czech Republic), September 8. |
| 1857 | Moves to Prague, where he studies music, joins the Provisional Theatre orchestra, and receives his first important performances. |
| 1878 | Brahms introduces him to the Berlin publisher Simrock, who publishes Dvořák's music until 1890, when Dvořák ends relationship. |
| 1884–1891 | Tours throughout Europe and especially England as composer and conductor. |
| 1892–1895 | Based in New York as director of the National Conservatory of Music in America; becomes acquainted with the music of Native Americans and African Americans. |
| 1893 | Begins his campaign to encourage American composers to draw from the traditional music of their own country as a resource; Symphony no. 9 ("From the New World") is premiered on December 16 in New York. |
| 1895 | Returns to Prague, where he resumes teaching at the Conservatory, becoming its director in 1901. |
| 1904 | Dies in Prague on May 1 after becoming ill at the first performance of his *Armida* and is buried in the city's Vyšehrad Castle cemetery. |

carefully integrates all four movements of the symphony—before the original mood of calm is restored with the return of the English horn theme in the tonic (m. 101).

Dvořák himself pointed to Henry Wadsworth Longfellow's *The Song of Hiawatha* as the source of inspiration for this movement, though it is not altogether clear whether Dvořák meant a particular passage in this long poem or the mood of the poem as a whole. The composer denied from the outset that the work was primarily based on what were called "Negro melodies." As one critic of the time noted, "The composer has not taken the external forms of plantation music, but has used his own themes suggested by the southern music. Now and then the motifs and the rhythms strongly suggest the origin of the symphony."[4] But the association with a genuine spiritual was reinforced in the public mind in 1922, when the American composer William Arms Fisher, a Dvořák student, set the Largo's English horn theme to a text he had written in the style of a Negro spiritual ("Goin' home, goin' home, I'm a-goin' home/Quiet like, some still day, I jes' goin' home"). This "neo-spiritual" and its many arrangements continue to fuel the still widely held belief that Dvořák did use an old spiritual as the basis for the Largo.

Dvořák's "New World" Symphony evoked an ongoing debate about the identity of "American music" at the end of the 19th century. It was widely assumed that composers in the United States were obligated to develop a distinctively national style, but what form would that style take? Many of these composers had learned their craft in Europe or at the very least looked to European composers as models. The idea that music of the disenfranchised—African Americans and Native Americans—might provide the basis of a national musical style unleashed a stream of controversy. Many critics thought this music unworthy of the concert hall, and they often expressed their opinions with elements of undisguised racism. But the debate about what constitutes "American music" was on, and it would continue for some time. Perhaps the critic of the *New York Daily Tribune* summed it up best in 1894 when he observed that the "New World" Symphony, along with several other recent compositions by Dvořák, had captured "something which sounds native in a style which is pleasant and natural in the ears of the people, the vast, vague, varied people of America."[5]

**The world turned upside down.** Gustav Mahler once revealed that this well-known woodcut had inspired the slow movement of his First Symphony. The image is one of a world turned upside down: animals bury the hunter. The weeping and mourning are of course deeply ironic and provide an important clue to the nature of the third movement's funeral march, which is at times sincere, at times sardonic.

**Source:** ArenaPal/The Image Works

# The Collision of High and Low: Mahler

Straddling the 19th and 20th centuries are the symphonies of Gustav Mahler (1860–1911). Although his later symphonies, particularly the Ninth (1910) and unfinished Tenth, anticipate 20th-century idioms and approaches to the genre, his First Symphony (1888) is a decidedly 19th-century work. Like many of Beethoven's symphonies, it follows a trajectory from struggle to triumph.

The funereal third movement of Mahler's First Symphony careens wildly from the beautiful to the grotesque, the sincere to the ironic. Mahler himself once suggested that the entire movement was inspired by a well-known illustration, reproduced here, showing wild animals bearing a hunter to his grave. By writing a funeral march into his symphony, Mahler is of course directly linking it to the funeral march in the second movement of Beethoven's *Eroica*. But the ironic tone of this music, inspired by a grotesque ceremony in which the hunted bury the hunter, mocks the somberness of the earlier work. The solemn tread of the timpani in the opening measures of the movement combined with its slow tempo, low register, and minor mode all announce that this will be a funeral march befitting the slow movement of a symphony. The instrument playing the melody is a solo double bass, and it is playing in a torturously high range for that instrument. The tone is not deep and resonant, but pinched and forced. Odder still, the melody turns out be a minor-mode variant of the children's tune *Frère Jacques* (or *Bruder Martin*, as it is known in German-speaking lands). A children's play song in minor in the slow movement of a symphony? We can begin to understand why so many contemporary critics found Mahler's music perplexing and at times exasperating.

Still other critics (many of them motivated by anti-Semitism) criticized the passage immediately following the funeral march for its "Jewish" or "eastern" qualities. The sound world evoked here (beginning in m. 39) is that of the *klezmorim*, the professional Jewish musicians of eastern Europe, who performed what we refer to today as **klezmer** music, characterized by a steady oompah sound in the bass (here, in low strings, bass drum, and cymbals) and rhythmically free winds above. Chromatic passages in thirds, exaggerated accents, repeated half steps back and forth, and the prominence of the shrill-sounding E♭ clarinet all contribute to what many critics dismissed as the music of peasants, not suited to the lofty realm of the symphony. After a brief return of the *Bruder Martin* theme (m. 71), the mood shifts yet again, introducing a passage of lyrical beauty accompanied now by the harp (beginning in m. 83). Mahler uses here a melody from a song he himself had written several years before entitled *The Two Blue Eyes of My Beloved*, and the tone is decidedly sincere: the composer indicates this section is to be played "very simply and unadorned, like a folk melody," in contrast to the klezmer-like passages, which he directs at one point to be played "like a parody" (m. 45).

All these contrasts are intentionally jarring, and Mahler uses them to drive home his belief that a symphony can and should encompass the banal and mundane as well as the beautiful. The contrast between the funeral marches of Beethoven's Third Symphony and Mahler's First manifests the enormous changes music had experienced in less than a century. Beethoven's music is earnest, sincere, unselfconscious; Mahler's, by contrast, combines hauntingly beautiful melodies with passages that fairly drip with irony. Mahler's subsequent symphonies manifest similar contrasts of tone—at times deadly serious, at times lighthearted and remote. All of his symphonies are large-scale works: unlike Mendelssohn, Schumann, and Brahms, he built on the monumental aspect of the genre as embodied above all in Beethoven's Ninth Symphony, but also in Schubert's *Great* C-Major Symphony, D. 944, and the symphonies of Bruckner.

((•• Listen

**CD13   Track 2**
**mysearchlab**
MAHLER
Symphony no. 1
Score Anthology II/147

## Composer Profile

# Gustav Mahler (1860–1911)

When Gustav Mahler was a child, he was reportedly asked what he wanted to be when he grew up. "A martyr" was the young boy's reply. Mahler certainly got his wish. In spite of his acknowledged brilliance as a conductor, he would eventually be driven from his post as music director of the Vienna Opera, and his contemporaries would dismiss his compositions, mostly symphonies and songs, as little more than a harmless sideshow. "My time will yet come," Mahler predicted, and again correctly. For almost five decades after his death, the composer's symphonies were considered monstrous curiosities, championed only by a small group of devoted followers. Thanks to the advent of long-playing records and such outstanding conductors as Jascha Horenstein, John Barbirolli, and above all Leonard Bernstein, Mahler's music began to gain a huge following in the early 1960s. Today he is acknowledged as one of the towering figures of late-19th- and early-20th-century music.

This belated recognition has much to do with the nature of Mahler's music, which most of his contemporaries found to be a confused mixture of incompatible styles and idioms. But it is precisely this juxtaposition of the serious and comic, the sublime and the banal that seems so appealing today. This deep sense of conflict is very much an extension of Mahler's own personality: he struggled throughout his life with the question of life after death, and in one way or another translated this issue into all of his symphonies. He was also torn between his Jewish heritage and the Catholic faith, to which he converted in 1897. There has been considerable debate about the sincerity of this conversion. Anti-Semitism was so rampant in Austria that Mahler would not, as a Jew, have been able to assume the directorship of so prestigious an institution as the Vienna Opera. At the same time, the theological promise of life after death made Christianity deeply appealing to Mahler. He ended his life as a pantheist, finding manifestations of God and eternal life in all things.

Mahler's extended tours of the United States in the years 1907 to 1911 reflect the growing cultural power of the United States in the late 19th and early 20th centuries. Organizations like the Metropolitan Opera and the New York Philharmonic now had the financial resources to attract musicians of the highest stature from across the Atlantic. Although Mahler struggled constantly with the management of both institutions, he helped raise the artistic standards of American musical life immeasurably.

# PRINCIPAL WORKS

## Symphonies

Like Beethoven, Mahler consistently rethought the nature of the genre every time he began a new symphony. These works nevertheless fall into several broad categories:

- The *Wunderhorn* Symphonies (nos. 1–4). Each of these incorporates thematic material from at least one of his *Wunderhorn* songs (see later), and three of the four incorporate voices as well. The First, the only purely instrumental work of the group, follows the pattern of struggle to triumph established in Beethoven's Fifth and Ninth Symphonies, as does the second (*Resurrection*), which includes a grandiose choral finale. The fourth and fifth movements of the Third Symphony are vocal, but the slow finale is instrumental. The Fourth Symphony's finale is a *Wunderhorn* song for voice and orchestra, but the entire work operates on a smaller scale than any of the previous three.

**Working holiday.** Mahler is shown here on holiday in the Austrian Alps in the summer of 1908 with the younger of his two daughters, Anna (1904–1988), who would go on to become an accomplished sculptor. Because he devoted most of the year to conducting, Mahler could focus on composing only during the summer. He typically wrote new works while on holiday and left matters of revision and orchestration for fall, winter, and spring.

**Source:** akg-images/Newscom

- The Middle-Period Symphonies (nos. 5–7). These are strictly instrumental works, independent of earlier songs. The Fifth follows a trajectory from struggle to triumph; the Sixth (*Tragic*) is equally heroic but ends in the minor mode. The Seventh ends with an almost maniacally joyful rondo in C Major, but only after working its way through an inner movement that Mahler marks *schattenhaft* ("shadowy").

- The "Symphony of a Thousand" (no. 8). So-called (with some exaggeration) because of its large performance forces, this work is unique within Mahler's output. The symphony is in two movements, each with soloists and chorus. The first is a setting of the Latin hymn *Veni creator spiritus* ("Come creator spirit"), the second a setting of scenes from the end of Part II of Goethe's *Faust*, concluding with the celebrated line "The eternal-feminine draws us ever onward" (*Das Ewig-Weiblich zieht uns hinan*). These seemingly disparate texts are in fact closely related, as are the musical themes of these two enormous movements.

- The Late Symphonies (nos. 9 and 10 and *Das Lied von der Erde*). These works mark a turn away from the triumphalism of most earlier works. An air of quiet resignation dominates all of these late works, including even their finales. Mahler had a fear of writing a Ninth Symphony, knowing that Beethoven, Schubert, and Bruckner had all died without completing a Tenth. Mahler thought to avoid this by not numbering what would have been his ninth symphony, calling it instead *Das Lied von der Erde* ("The Song of the Earth"), a "Symphonic Song Cycle for Tenor and Alto" based on a German translation of Chinese poetry. His subsequent Ninth Symphony, however, would indeed prove to be his last finished work. Both *Das Lied* and the Ninth end with long, slow elegiac movements, and the last measure of *Das Lied* remains harmonically open, a C-Major triad juxtaposed with the note A. Several subsequent composer-scholars have produced their own completions of the Tenth, left unfinished at the composer's death.

**"Noise" invades the symphony.** Mahler's use of cowbells, an anvil, and bunched twigs (applied to the timpani) in his Sixth Symphony of 1905 evoked howls of derision in many critical circles. (The sleigh bells had been used in the Fourth Symphony; the ratchet is fictional.) The caption reads: "Heavens, I've forgotten the automobile horn! I'll have to write another symphony."

**Source:** Lebrecht Music & Arts/The Image Works

## Songs

Mahler stands at the end of the entire 19th-century tradition of song, integrating Schubert's lyricism with the chromaticism of Wagner and Wolf. In addition to numerous miscellaneous songs for voice and piano, Mahler wrote three major cycles for voice and orchestra: *Des Knaben Wunderhorn* ("Youth's Magic Horn") and *Lieder eines fahrenden Gesellen* ("Songs of a Wayfarer") are settings of German folk poetry, whereas the *Kindertotenlieder* ("Songs on the Death of Children") are based on texts by the poet Friedrich Rückert.

## Gustav Mahler (1860–1911) *(Continued)*

| KEY DATES IN THE LIFE OF MAHLER | |
|---|---|
| 1860 | Born in Kalischt, Bohemia (then part of Austrian Empire; now in the Czech Republic) on July 7. |
| 1880–1888 | Obtains increasingly responsible conducting positions in a number of opera houses, including Ljubliana, Olmütz, Kassel, and Leipzig. |
| 1888 | Appointed music director at the Royal Opera in Budapest. Conducts from fall through spring and devotes summer vacations to composing. |
| 1897 | Appointed music director of the Vienna Court Opera, the most prestigious institution of its kind in the Austrian Empire and arguably in all of Europe. |
| 1901 | Marries Alma Schindler (1879–1964), an aspiring composer of songs; Mahler at first prohibits her from composing, then relents and promotes her music enthusiastically. |
| 1907 | Forced out of his position as music director of the Vienna Court Opera in spite of critical acclaim for his artistic accomplishments; accepts offer to become principal conductor of the Metropolitan Opera in New York. |
| 1908 | Appointed principal conductor of the New York Philharmonic Society. |
| 1911 | After several years of slowly declining health, dies in Vienna. |

## SUMMARY

Music for the orchestra assumed many forms in the second half of the 19th century: functional music for dancing and marching, the stylized dance of the ballet, the programmatic symphonic poem, and—in its most expansive manifestation—the symphony, a genre capable of being presented or interpreted with or without programmatic associations. Civic orchestras proliferated toward the end of the century, further strengthening the importance of the symphony and symphonic poem within the social network of music.

✔●─ **Study** and **Review** on **mysearchlab.com**

# MAJOR COMPOSERS OF THE 19TH CENTURY

## FRANCE

**Berlioz** (see Composer Profile, Chapter 15) and the Polish expatriate **Chopin** (see Composer Profile, Chapter 16) were the most prominent of many illustrious French composers in the 19th century. **Luigi Cherubini** (1760–1842) was highly esteemed for his operas and sacred music. **Charles Gounod** (1818–1893), **Georges Bizet** (1838–1875), and **Jules Massenet** (1842–1912) were among the leading theatrical composers of France in the second half of the century. Gounod's best known work is *Faust*; Bizet's fame rests largely on *Carmen*, one of the most popular operas of all time. Massenet's *Manon* and *Werther* continue to be staged today.

**César Franck** (1822–1890) was born in Liège (now a part of Belgium) but became a French citizen in 1873. He was one of the great organ virtuosos of his century. His one symphony, in D minor, is a staple of the concert repertory. **Camille Saint-Saëns** (1835–1921) worked in virtually every genre of his era and was immensely prolific. He lived such a long life that, despite the immense vitality of his work, he eventually came to be identified with musical conservatism in France. His Symphony no. 3, which includes a prominent part for the organ, remains popular, as does his opera *Samson et Dalila*.

**Eduard Lalo** (1823–1892) is best remembered today as the composer of the *Symphonie espagnole*, for violin and orchestra; his opera *Le Roi d'Ys* is occasionally performed as well. **Gabriel Fauré** (1845–1924) ranks as one of the great song composers of the 19th century; his chamber music and choral music, especially the Requiem, are also significant. **Vincent d'Indy** (1851–1931) and **Ernest Chausson** (1855–1899) both wrote masterfully for the orchestra. Like many of their French contemporaries, they also fell under the spell of Wagner, succumbing to what came to be known in France as *Wagnerisme*. D'Indy is best remembered for his *Symphony on a French Mountain Air*, which incorporates a French folk song. He also wrote an important composition manual and founded the Schola Cantorum in 1896 in an attempt to revive the plainchant repertory. Chausson's most frequently performed works are his *Poème* for violin and orchestra and his one symphony.

## GREAT BRITAIN

The piano virtuoso and composer **John Field** (1782–1837) was born in Dublin but spent most of his adult life on the Continent. His nocturnes influenced the young Chopin. **Charles Villiers Stanford** (1852–1924), also born in Ireland, and **Charles H. H. Parry** (1848–1918) contributed much to the repertory of sacred music. **Sir Arthur Sullivan** (1842–1900) is best known for his collaborations with the lyricist William Schwenk Gilbert (1836–1911). Together, Gilbert and Sullivan wrote a string of enormously successful operettas, the most beloved of which are *H.M.S. Pinafore*, *The Pirates of Penzance*, *Iolanthe*, *The Mikado*, *The Yeomen of the Guard*, and *The Gondoliers*. Sullivan also wrote the music to the hymn *Onward, Christian Soldiers*.

## ITALY

Only slightly younger than **Rossini** (see Composer Profile, Chapter 17), **Gaetano Donizetti** (1797–1848) and **Vincenzo Bellini** (1801–1835) also worked largely in the field of opera, emerging from Rossini's shadow after his abrupt retirement in 1829. Donizetti's most celebrated operas include *L'Elisir d'amore*, *Lucrezia Borgia*, *Lucia di Lammermoor*, and *Don Pasquale*. Bellini's most frequently performed works for the stage are *Il Pirata*, *La Straniera*, *La Sonnambula*, and—above all—*Norma*. Italian opera composers working in the wake of **Verdi** (see Composer Profile, Chapter 17) include **Pietro Mascagni** (1863–1945) and **Ruggiero Leoncavallo** (1858–1919). They are inseparably linked in the mind of the musical public by two one-act operas that are frequently performed on the same bill: Mascagni's *Cavalleria rusticana* and Leoncavallo's *I Pagliacci*.

## SPAIN

**Fernando Sor** (1778–1839), the most celebrated guitar virtuoso of the 19th century, wrote many short pieces for that instrument. **Pablo de Sarasate** (1844–1908) was to the violin what Sor was to the guitar; his most popular work is *Zigeunerweisen*, on gypsy-style themes. **Isaac Albéniz**

(1860–1909) and **Enrique Granados** (1867–1916) count among Spain's first nationalistically inclined composers; both also won fame as pianists. Albéniz's best known work is *Iberia*, a suite for piano. Granados's most popular composition is his piano suite *Goyescas*, each of whose movements is associated with a specific painting or etching by the Spanish artist Francisco Goya.

# GERMANY AND AUSTRIA

**Beethoven** (see Composer Profile, Chapter 15) cast a long shadow over his contemporaries. Most prominent among these are two who are best known today for their work in opera: **Carl Maria von Weber** (1786–1826) and **Heinrich Marschner** (1795–1861). Both created works rich in special effects and fairy-tale atmospheres. In addition to *Der Freischütz* (see Chapter 17), Weber also wrote *Euryanthe* and *Oberon*. Marschner gained fame through such works as *Der Vampyr* ("The Vampire") and *Hans Heiling*. Both composers exercised considerable influence on **Wagner** (see Composer Profile, Chapter 17).

**Ludwig Spohr** (1784–1859) worked in a variety of genres, composing six symphonies, ten operas, and four oratorios. He was regarded as one of the leading musicians of his day, excelling as violinist, conductor, and composer. Like **Mendelssohn** (see Composer Profile, Chapter 15), **Schumann** (see Composer Profile, Chapter 16), and **Brahms** (see Composer Profile, Chapter 18), Spohr wrote a number of important symphonies, as did the Austrian **Anton Bruckner** (1824–1896). Bruckner was associated in the public mind with Wagner because of his penchant for large orchestras and advanced chromaticism, but Bruckner devoted himself largely to symphonies (nine of them numbered) and sacred music. **Carl Loewe** (1796–1869) and **Hugo Wolf** (1860–1903) are best known for their songs. Loewe, a near contemporary of **Schubert** (see Composer Profile, Chapter 16), cultivated the ballad with particular intensity.

**Richard Strauss** (1864–1949) belongs equally to the 19th and 20th centuries. Along with **Mahler** (see Composer Profile, Chapter 18), Strauss was deeply influenced by the works of **Liszt** (see Composer Profile, Chapter 16), Wagner, and Bruckner. Strauss was also one of the great conductors of his generation. He favored the genres of opera and symphonic poem in particular. His works for the stage include *Elektra*, *Salome*, and *Der Rosenkavalier*. At the time of its premiere in 1907, *Salome* was considered particularly daring, not only because of its advanced chromaticism but also its erotically charged subject matter. Most of Strauss's symphonic poems date from the earlier decades of his career: among the most often performed are *Till Eulenspiegel's Merry Pranks*, *Don Juan*, *Death and Transfiguration*, *Thus Spake Zarathustra*, and *Don Quixote*, the last a series of "variations on a knightly theme" for solo cello and orchestra. Even Strauss's most bitter critics conceded that he was one of the greatest orchestrators of all time, and it is only fitting that he should have produced a new edition of Berlioz's *Treatise on Orchestration*, bringing it up to date to reflect more recent developments in the orchestra.

# SCANDINAVIA

**Niels Gade** (1817–1890) was a protégé of Felix Mendelssohn, who conducted Gade's First Symphony in Leipzig in 1843. Gade went on to become a leading figure in Denmark's musical life. The Norwegian **Edvard Grieg** (1841–1907), one of the celebrated piano virtuosos of his day, achieved renown not only through his performances, but also through his own compositions. His Piano Concerto remains a favorite in the repertory of 19th-century concertos.

# BOHEMIA

**Dvořák** (Composer Profile, Chapter 18) and **Bedřich Smetana** (1824–1884), both natives of Bohemia (now part of the Czech Republic), grew up in what at the time was part of the Austrian Empire. Smetana's *The Bartered Bride* was the first Czech opera to register international success; his cycle of symphonic poems, *Má Vlast* ("My Country"), continues to enjoy great popularity.

# RUSSIA

**Mikhail Glinka** (1804–1857) was one of the first Russian composers to gain international fame. While studying in Italy as a young man, he experienced "musical homesickness," the desire to hear music that was distinctively Russian. His two great operas, *A Life for the Tsar* and *Ruslan and Ludmila*, inspired several subsequent generations of Russian composers, including the group known as "The Five": **Mily Balakirev** (1836–1910), **César Cui** (1835–1919), **Alexander Borodin**

(1833–1887), **Modeste Mussorgsky** (1839–1881), and **Nikolai Rimsky-Korsakov** (1844–1908). Many Russian composers considered **Tchaikovsky** (see Composer Profile, Chapter 18) too foreign in training and outlook to belong to this group of nationalists. Russian musical idioms are especially evident in such works as Balakirev's symphonic poem *Islamey*; Borodin's *In the Steppes of Central Asia* (also a symphonic poem) and his opera *Prince Igor*; and Mussorgsky's operatic masterpiece *Boris Godunov* and his celebrated piano suite *Pictures at an Exhibition* (later orchestrated by Maurice Ravel). Rimsky-Korsakov, the dean of Russian composers at the end of the century, won renown with such orchestral works as *Scheherezade* and the *Le Coq d'or* suite, and also wrote an important treatise on orchestration. As an educator, he lent guidance and support to a great many younger Russian composers, including Igor Stravinsky.

## UNITED STATES

**Lowell Mason** (1792–1872) wrote many hymns and sacred works still in use today, but his greatest legacy is as an educator. Mason worked tirelessly to ensure that children be taught to read music in the schools; his efforts paralleled a similar movement in Europe. Mason himself eventually became superintendent of music in the Boston public school system, but his impact extended far beyond New England.

**Dan Emmett** (1815–1904) played in minstrel bands and wrote both the words and music to *Dixie*, the unofficial anthem of the Confederate States of America during the Civil War. **Stephen Foster** (1826–1864) was unquestionably the greatest of all 19th-century songwriters in America. He earned his early reputation as a composer of minstrel songs (discussed in Chapter 16). Foster's first great hit, *Old Folks at Home* ("Way Down upon the Swanee River . . .") sold some forty thousand copies in its first year. Several of his songs became so popular that many people still believe them to be folk songs.

**Anthony Philip Heinrich** (1781–1861), Bohemian by birth, was one of the first composers to write in a self-consciously American idiom, often drawing on Native-American themes. He wrote hugely ambitious works with such titles as *Complaint of Logan the Mingo Chief*, *Last of His Race* and *The Mastodon: A Grand Symphony in Three Parts for Full Orchestra*, whose finale bears the title "Shenandoah, a Celebrated Oneida Chief." **Louis Moreau Gottschalk** (1829–1869) also worked American inflections into many of his works, including *The Banjo* (Anthology). A showman as well as a musician, he always made a ceremony of taking off his white gloves before he played in public.

Many composers born in the United States went to Europe for their training, among them **John Knowles Paine** (1839–1906)—who taught at Harvard—and **Horatio Parker** (1863–1919)—whose pupils at Yale included the young Charles Ives (see Composer Profile, Chapter 20). Another New Englander, **Amy Beach** (1867–1944), was the first American woman to gain recognition as a significant composer of large-scale orchestral works. Her compositions include the *Gaelic Symphony*, based on Irish folk melodies, and a Mass in E♭.

# Part Six
# The 20th Century

# Prelude

The most striking aspect of music in the 20th century is its stylistic diversity. By the end of the century, composers, performers, and listeners had more access to more different kinds of music than ever before, thanks largely to technological advances in travel and communication. Either firsthand or through recordings, people could experience entire repertories of music that in previous eras would have remained unknown to them. Musical styles that had once existed only in the form of unwritten folk traditions could now be disseminated through recordings and broadcasts. These in turn expanded the musical vocabulary of composers working within the written tradition. The spirit of the age was one of innovation, and in pursuit of innovation a number of prominent composers rejected tonality, up until this time one of the most basic premises in all of Western music. Still other composers embraced tradition. The result, by the end of the century, was a musical landscape that was either hopelessly fragmented or abundantly diverse, depending on one's point of view.

This diversity reflects 20th-century society as a whole, which was itself far more inclusive in its approach to previously marginalized groups than any society had been in the past. In the United States, women gained the right to vote in 1920, and the civil rights movement of the 1950s and 1960s ended the legal segregation that had relegated African Americans to second-class citizenship.

The world itself was far more diverse in 2000 than it had been 100 years earlier. The sprawling overseas empires of the United Kingdom, France, Spain, Portugal, Belgium, and the Netherlands disappeared almost completely in the years between 1945 and 1970. Even in Europe, new states asserted their independence from traditional rulers: Norway (from Sweden, 1905), Finland (from Russia, in 1917), and Ireland (from the United Kingdom, in 1921). The right of self-determination was one of the guiding forces behind the Treaty of Versailles after World War I, which led to the establishment of such nations as Czechoslovakia (which later split into two separate states, the Czech Republic and Slovakia), Poland (reestablished after World I, with new boundaries pushed westward after World War II), and the Baltic republics of Estonia, Latvia, and Lithuania (annexed by the Soviet Union in 1940

◀ **The 20th Century.** Roy Lichtenstein's *Reverie* (1965) evokes many of the issues central to the history of music in the 20th century: **(1) "High" vs. "Low" Art.** Liechtenstein uses the style of comic-book art on a work that now hangs in New York's Museum of Modern Art. By crossing the supposed boundaries between "serious" and "popular" art, Lichtenstein calls into question the legitimacy of these very categories. Many 20th-century composers, including John Cage, Leonard Bernstein, and the Beatles, raised similar issues in their music. **(2) Technology.** The microphone suggests that this "reverie" is being performed in front of an audience and perhaps recorded. Amplification and recording technologies changed the nature of music in fundamental ways over the course of the 20th century. **(3) Authenticity.** The singer looks the part—dreamy, distracted, far away, in short with all the qualities one associates with a reverie. But how authentic is the emotion? Is a cliché any less real because it is a cliché? **(4) Post-modernism.** A movement in all the arts during the last third of the 20th century, post-modernism distances itself from the quintessentially modernist drive toward novelty; the use of older styles, often in a deliberately self-conscious fashion, is a hallmark of post-modernism.

**Source:** The Estate of Roy Lichtenstein/Smithsonian American Art Museum, Washington, DC/Art Resource, NY

but reestablished as independent nations in the early 1990s). The number of sovereign nations in the world as a whole grew from 55 in 1900 to 192 in 2000.[1]

Wars, revolutions, and long-term international conflicts changed the political landscape of the globe repeatedly during the 20th century. In 1914, the growing territorial rivalries among the European powers—France and Great Britain in western Europe, Germany and Austria-Hungary in central Europe, and Russia to the east—culminated in World War I, which would leave some 10 million dead in its wake. The United States joined the conflict against Germany and Austria-Hungary in 1917 and helped turn the tide of battle. The Treaty of Versailles (1919), which redrew the map of Europe, laid the groundwork for the League of Nations, headquartered in Geneva.

World War I also helped precipitate the Russian Revolution. In March 1917, after teetering on the edge of dissolution for more than a decade, the Russian monarchy collapsed. The provisional government that replaced it was in turn overthrown by Nikolai Lenin's Bolshevik party in October of that same year. Lenin thereby succeeded in establishing the renamed Soviet Union as the first communist state, ruled in theory by the people themselves—the proletariat—but in fact controlled by a handful of party bureaucrats.

By the mid-1920s, most of the world had entered what would become a long-term economic depression. Economic uncertainty in Germany undermined that nation's fledgling attempt at democratic rule and contributed to Adolf Hitler's rise to power in the early 1930s. The United States, which enjoyed an economic boom during the 1920s, plunged into the Great Depression following a precipitous collapse in prices on the New York Stock Exchange in October 1929. By 1932, one-third of the American work force was unemployed.

War broke out again in 1939 when Hitler's Germany invaded Poland. World War II (1939–1945), which pitted the Axis powers (Germany, Italy, Japan) against the Allies

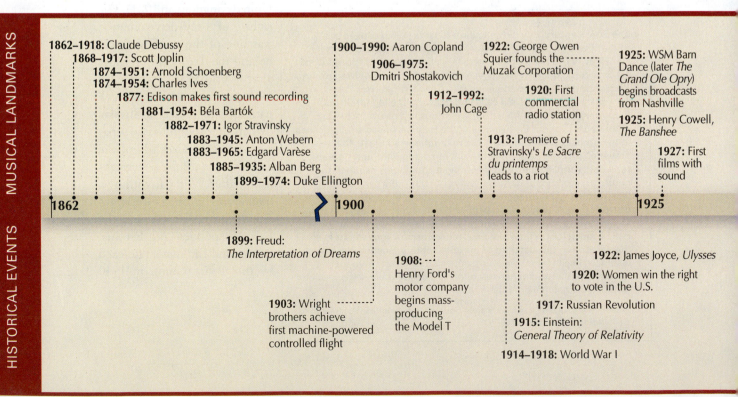

**20TH CENTURY TIMELINE**

**MUSICAL LANDMARKS**

1862–1918: Claude Debussy
1868–1917: Scott Joplin
1874–1951: Arnold Schoenberg
1874–1954: Charles Ives
1877: Edison makes first sound recording
1881–1954: Béla Bartók
1882–1971: Igor Stravinsky
1883–1945: Anton Webern
1883–1965: Edgard Varèse
1885–1935: Alban Berg
1899–1974: Duke Ellington

1900–1990: Aaron Copland
1906–1975: Dmitri Shostakovich
1912–1992: John Cage

1922: George Owen Squier founds the Muzak Corporation
1920: First commercial radio station
1913: Premiere of Stravinsky's *Le Sacre du printemps* leads to a riot

1925: WSM Barn Dance (later *The Grand Ole Opry*) begins broadcasts from Nashville
1925: Henry Cowell, *The Banshee*
1927: First films with sound

**1862** — **1900** — **1925**

**HISTORICAL EVENTS**

1899: Freud: *The Interpretation of Dreams*

1903: Wright brothers achieve first machine-powered controlled flight

1908: Henry Ford's motor company begins mass-producing the Model T

1922: James Joyce, *Ulysses*
1920: Women win the right to vote in the U.S.
1917: Russian Revolution
1915: Einstein: *General Theory of Relativity*
1914–1918: World War I

(Great Britain, France, and, from 1941, the Soviet Union and the United States), was the bloodiest and most far-flung conflict in history. It left an estimated 50 million dead, provided cover for the attempted extermination of all the Jews by the German Nazi regime, and ended with the detonation of two atomic bombs over Japan in August 1945. The United Nations was founded that same year to help avoid international conflicts.

Although the United States and the Soviet Union fought as allies against Germany, they rapidly became enemies after the end of World War II. The Soviet Union translated its battlefield victories in eastern Europe into a sphere of influence that gave it control over the satellite states of Poland, East Germany, Czechoslovakia, Hungary, Romania, and Bulgaria (Yugoslavia broke with the Soviet Union in 1948, and Albania turned to communist China for support in 1961). Tensions between the communist nations of this "Eastern bloc" (led by the Soviet Union) and the "Western bloc" (led by the United States) threatened to explode into war at many points in the four decades after World War II. However, the threat of mutual annihilation through nuclear weapons helped prevent a third world war. Because the two superpowers—the United States and the Soviet Union—never confronted one another directly on the battlefield, this period came to be known as the cold war. One of the most striking symbols of this era was the Berlin Wall, erected by East German authorities in 1961 to prevent the mass exodus of their population to the West.

The cold war featured many indirect confrontations between the two superpowers. Among the most significant of these were the Korean War (1950–1953) and Vietnam War (1964–1973), in both of which the United States and its allies fought proxies of the Soviet Union. Both wars reflected the American strategy of containment, by which Western nations sought to limit the global spread of communism.

Confronted with a collapsing economy in the mid-1980s, Premier Mikhail Gorbachev (b. 1931) sought to promote economic reform and greater political

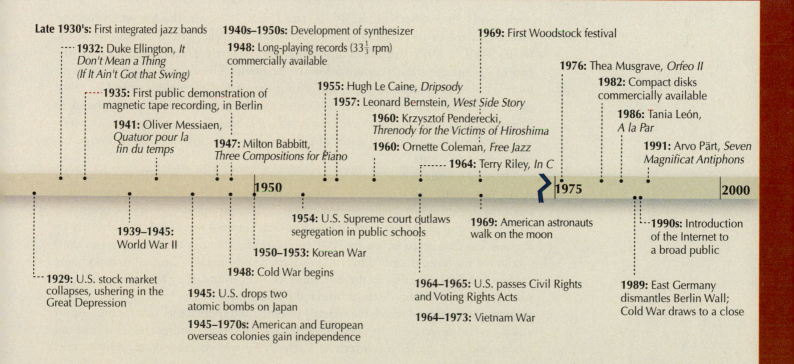

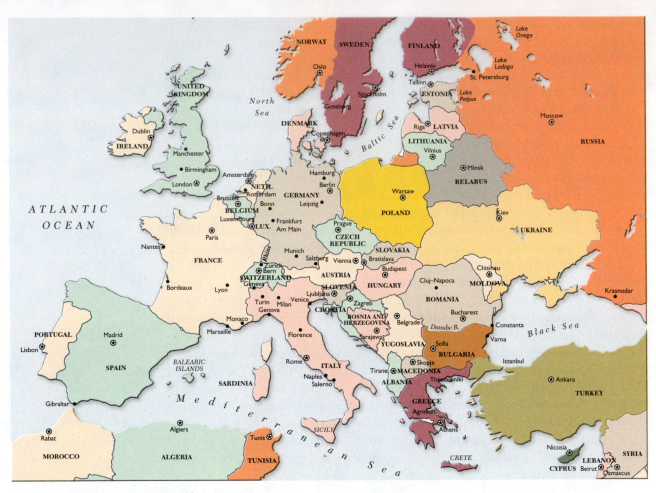

**Europe at the end of the 20th century.**

openness in the Soviet Union. By the late 1980s, however, the Soviet Union was losing control of its satellite states in Eastern Europe. The dismantling of the Berlin Wall in 1989 and the reunification of Germany a year later signaled the end of Communist Party domination of the Soviet Union and most other communist states in Eastern Europe, and with it the end of the cold war. In late 1991, the Soviet Union officially disbanded into a loose Commonwealth of Independent States (CIS), the largest of which were Russia, Ukraine, Belarus, Georgia, Armenia, and Kazakhstan. The Baltic states of Estonia, Latvia, and Lithuania reemerged as independent nations.

Parallel to these political and economic upheavals, a revolution no less profound was taking place in the fields of transportation and communication. Technological advances made the world an ever smaller place during the 20th century. In 1900, it took seven days to travel by ship from New York to London. One hundred years later, the same trip by air took less than seven hours. By 2000, commercial airlines in the United States alone accounted for more than 600 billion passenger miles annually. Ground transportation changed no less radically. At the beginning of the century, the railroad provided the principal means of long-distance overland travel. Horse-drawn vehicles were still the primary means of local travel; the recently invented automobile was only for the wealthy and paved roads were few. By 2000, 85 percent of American families owned at least one automobile, and the federal Interstate Highway System covered almost 43,000 miles across all 50 states.

Advances in communication were even more sweeping:

- **Telephone:** In 1915, the average American made 40 phone calls a year; by 2000, the number had grown to 2,300, many of them from mobile phones. Facsimile transmissions over telephone wires, first introduced in 1966, provided a means of almost instantaneous written communication.

- **Film:** Thomas Edison had developed the first moving pictures in 1891 (he called his device a "projecting kinetoscope"), but the first commercially marketed films were not released until 1902. Films with sound ("talkies") arrived in 1927, and the first major feature films in color were produced in the late 1930s.

- **Radio:** Invented by the Italian Guglielmo Marconi in 1894, the radio was used in the early decades of the 20th century mainly for voice broadcasting by the military, ships, businesses, and private citizens. After the first commercial radio broadcasting license was issued in the United States in 1920, the industry began two decades of exponential growth. FM radio began commercial broadcasting in 1939. In 2000, there were some 10,300 commercial radio stations nationwide, and 99 percent of American households owned at least one radio. Satellite radio became a viable option, and stations began broadcasting on the Internet.

- **Television:** The television, invented in 1927, proliferated in the second half of the century. In 1950, 9 percent of households in the United States owned a television; by 1955, this figure had increased to 64.5 percent, and by 1965, it was 92.6 percent. Cable television, widely available by the early 1980s, expanded the number of available channels from a mere handful to dozens; satellite technology in the 1990s pushed the number into the hundreds.

- **Computer:** First developed during World War II, computers were used almost exclusively in business and industry through the 1960s. In 1981, the personal computer was introduced to the general public and soon became a common amenity. The Internet and e-mail became widely available in the early 1990s.

# THE IMPACT OF RECORDED SOUND

The emergence of sound recording in the late 19th century marks the most important development in the transmission of music since the introduction of music printing by movable type in the early 16th century. Thomas Edison created the first viable recording—his recitation of "Mary Had a Little Lamb"—in his laboratory in Menlo Park, New Jersey, in 1877. Edison's metal (later, wax) cylinders eventually gave way to the shellac disk, played on a turntable moving at the rate of 78 revolutions per minute (rpm). By 1910, these 78 rpm disks had become standard features of well-to-do households. In retrospect, the sound quality seems poor, the format bulky and cumbersome: each disk held no more than five minutes of music per side. And in an era before the invention of the microphone, the challenges of recording a large ensemble were considerable. Still, the very notion of being able to listen to an orchestral rendition of a complete symphony by Beethoven or an aria by Verdi in one's home at a time of one's own choosing represented a stunning advance. The great Italian tenor Enrico Caruso (1873–1921) was one of the recording industry's first superstars: at the peak of his career, he was earning $115,000 a year from recordings alone, the equivalent of almost

**Little Nipper.** Recorded sound is so common today that we can scarcely imagine how astonishing it must have been to hear disembodied music for the first time. The 1896 logo for the Victor Talking Machine Company, "His Master's Voice," captures the combined sense of bafflement and fascination that humans of the time shared with dogs.

**Source:** US Patent & Trademark Office

**The technology of early sound recording.** Until the development of useful microphones in the mid-1920s, amplification remained a fundamental obstacle to making recordings. Orchestras had to work in cramped settings and rely on megaphone-like devices to convey the music directly onto disk. Tapes and the possibilities of editing would not emerge until the 1940s. In this image from 1919, the English composer Edward Elgar conducts his Cello Concerto; the soloist is his compatriot Beatrice Harrison (1892–1965), the first woman cellist ever to give a solo performance at Carnegie Hall in New York.

**Source:** Hulton-Deutsch Collection/Corbis

$2 million today. His success on the stage fueled sales of his recordings, and the popularity of his recordings further boosted his success on the stage.

Recordings had an enormous impact on composers as well, shrinking the distance between musical cultures. Lacking access to recordings, the only way Claude Debussy could hear a Javanese gamelan in Paris in the late 19th century was to witness a performance of an ensemble specially organized for the world's fair that took place there in 1889 (and which also gave us the Eiffel Tower). One hundred years later, a composer in Paris could place an order through the Internet for compact disk recordings of three dozen different gamelan ensembles and have them delivered to her door within a few days. Recording technology also changed the very notion of what constitutes a work of music. By the 1960s, composers as diverse as Milton Babbitt and John Lennon and Paul McCartney of the Beatles were creating works that could not be performed by musicians in a live setting but existed solely in recorded form.

# MODERNISM: THE SHOCK OF THE NEW

**Modernism** was a phenomenon that affected all the arts in the 20th century, including literature and painting as well as music. It is not a style in its own right but rather an attitude, one that gave rise to a variety of important styles. Modernism is the self-conscious striving for novelty at almost any cost, based on a conviction that the new must be as different as possible from the old. Since at least the Renaissance, artists have consciously sought to create new kinds of art, and in this sense modernism has long been a driving force in the creative process. But in the 20th century, the quest for novelty took on unprecedented centrality, involving the outright rejection of what had long been fundamental elements: rhyme and meter in poetry, linear narrative in literature (see Primary Evidence: Literary Modernism), representation and perspective in painting, and ornament in architecture. Each generation had what it thought of as its **avant-garde**. The term is French for "vanguard," the first troops to engage the enemy in battle. As such it conjures the image of a small band of artists waging war against the conservative tastes of resistant audiences. In all the arts in the 20th century, the avant-gardists (modernists) considered it their duty to lead art in new directions.

In music, the most obvious manifestations of modernism were the abandonment of conventional forms and of tonality. Musical modernism produced a succession of new approaches—impressionism, expressionism, atonality, serial composition, aleatory music—that confronted listeners with the challenge of the New. Even the less overtly confrontational idioms of neoclassicism, minimalism, and postmodernism can be understood as manifestations of modernism, insisting on a distinction between new and old even while accepting certain elements of the old. The most extreme forms of modernism sought to erase all links to the past. "Creators must look straight ahead," the composer and conductor Pierre Boulez (b. 1925) once declared. "It is not enough to deface the

| MILESTONES OF SOUND RECORDING AND BROADCAST TECHNOLOGY | |
|---|---|
| 1877 | Recording on cylinders, invented by Thomas Edison. |
| 1897 | Shellac disk recordings, rotating on a turntable at 78 revolutions per minute (rpm), begin to enjoy wide distribution, driving Edison's cylinders out of the market. |
| 1920 | KDKA in Pittsburgh begins operation as the nation's first commercial radio station. |
| 1927 | The first commercial film with spoken dialogue—*The Jazz Singer,* starring Al Jolson—is released, signaling the end of the silent film era. Recorded music soon becomes an integral part of the film industry. |
| 1935 | Magnetic tape recording is introduced publicly in Berlin; part of the Nazi secret war effort, it is uncovered by the Allies at war's end. |
| 1948 | The 12-inch 33 rpm long-playing record is introduced; the LP holds 23 minutes per side, in contrast to the 5-minute capacity of the 12-inch 78 rpm record. |
| 1949 | The first 7-inch 45 rpm record is introduced; each side of the disk holds up to 5 minutes of music, making this format an ideal medium for the distribution of popular songs. |
| 1958 | Stereo recordings enter the commercial market. |
| 1963 | Cassette tape, a format offering unprecedented portability, becomes available commercially. |
| 1982 | Compact disks become commercially available and within 6 years surpass sales of LPs. They have a capacity of 80 minutes. |
| 1990s | The Internet becomes a major vehicle for transmitting music. |

Mona Lisa because that does not kill the Mona Lisa. All the art of the past must be destroyed." On another occasion, and in a more conciliatory mood, Boulez maintained that "history as it is made by great composers is not a history of conservation but of destruction—even while cherishing what is being destroyed."

In the process of destroying the past, cherished or not, composers had to confront the music of that past at every turn. Novelty, after all, could only be measured against what had already been done. John Cage, perhaps the most quintessentially modernist of all 20th-century composers, summed up this paradox neatly in the form of an anecdote:

> Once in Amsterdam, a Dutch musician said to me, "It must be very difficult for you in America to write music, for you are so far away from the centers of tradition." I had to say, "It must be very difficult for you in Europe to write music, for you are so close to centers of tradition."[2]

The gulf between new and old became wider and wider as the century progressed. To be sure, audiences had confronted so-called difficult music before the 20th century, but in the early decades of the century a number of younger composers posed an unprecedented challenge when they started writing music without a tonal center. Most

## Primary Evidence — LITERARY MODERNISM: THE STREAM OF CONSCIOUSNESS

*In the early decades of the 20th century, modernist writers abandoned the idea of a logical, directed narrative. Several of them, including James Joyce (1882–1941), Ezra Pound (1885–1972), and T. S. Eliot (1888–1965), opted for what came to be known as a stream of consciousness style, in which the prose resembles the fragmented manner in which most people think their private thoughts. Although carefully crafted, this style sometimes gives the impression of randomness. The selection here, from Joyce's* Ulysses *(1922), is from the "Sirens" episode, which bears strong parallels to the account of Odysseus and the sirens in Homer's* Odyssey. *Joyce's character Leopold Bloom, eating his lunch in a Dublin bar, listens to Simon Daedalus sing an aria from Friedrich von Flotow's opera* Martha *(sung in English as "When first I saw that form endearing"). Bloom is moved by the music for it evokes multiple complications in his own life, and toward the end of this passage he wraps his fingers in an elastic band. The act faintly echoes Odysseus's command to his men that they bind him to the mast of their ship so he might hear the song of the sirens without being lured to his death (see p. 13).*

■ ■ ■

The harping chords of prelude closed. A chord long-drawn, expectant drew a voice away.

—*When first I saw that form endearing.*
Richie turned.
—Si Dedalus' voice, he said.
Braintipped, cheek touched with flame, they listened feeling that flow endearing flow over skin limbs human heart soul spine. Bloom signed to Pat, bald Pat is a waiter hard of hearing, to set ajar the door of the bar. The door of the bar. So. That will do. Pat, waiter, waited, waiting to hear, for he was hard of hear by the door.
—*Sorrow from me seemed to depart.*
Through the hush of air a voice sang to them, low, not rain, not leaves in murmur, like no voice of strings of reeds or what doyoucallthem dulcimers, touching their still ears with words, still hearts of their each his remembered lives. Good, good to hear: sorrow from them each seemed to from both depart when first they heard. When first they saw, lost Richie, Poldy, mercy of beauty, heard from a person wouldn't expect it in the least, her first merciful lovesoft oftloved word.

Love that is singing: love's old sweet song. Bloom unwound slowly the elastic band of his packet. Love's old sweet *sonnez la* gold. Bloom wound a skein round four forkfingers, stretched it, relaxed, and wound it round his troubled double, fourfold, in octave, gyved them fast.

**Source:** James Joyce, *Ulysses* (New York: Vintage, 1961), pp. 273–4.

listeners found the new idiom difficult to follow, and many reacted with overt hostility. Arnold Schoenberg and his followers in Vienna, weary of having their concerts disrupted, formed their own Society for Private Musical Performances, withdrawing themselves from public scrutiny altogether. Audiences became less confrontational after World War II as the rage of earlier listeners eventually cooled, partly through acceptance of new sounds but also partly through indifference. More and more people began to think of so-called classical music as music by dead composers. It is a sad but undeniable fact that by the end of the 20th century, Béla Bartók's *Concerto for Orchestra* (1944) remained the most recent major orchestral work to have entered the standard concert hall repertory.

For much of the 20th century, what came to be known as "difficult" music, while not particularly popular with the general listening public, nevertheless enjoyed a certain prestige within the community of musical artists. A great many composers took comfort in Ralph Waldo Emerson's pronouncement that "To be great is to be misunderstood." Popular success, in fact, became suspect in certain circles. This is especially evident in the case of a composer like Leonard Bernstein, who wrote "difficult" music as well as music of wide appeal, most notably his Broadway musicals *Candide* and *West Side Story*.

**Modernism in painting: Cubism.** Modernist developments in music in the first decade of the 20th century have striking parallels in other arts. Atonality, for example, has often been compared to cubism, an artistic movement of the same period that went out of its way to violate the conventions of representation, especially perspective. Cubism emerged between 1907 and 1914 in the work of Pablo Picasso (1881–1973) and Georges Bracque (1882–1963), contemporary with the earliest atonal works by Schoenberg and his pupils. In cubism, objects that are often only barely recognizable appear disassembled and reassembled with all sides of an object showing at once, as if on a flat plane. As in this 1911 painting by Picasso—*Man with a Violin*—no one perspective has priority, just as no one pitch has priority in atonal music. The effect can be disturbing or refreshing—or both at the same time.

**Source:** The Philadelphia Museum of Art/Artist's Rights Society/Art Resource, NY

Even when criticizing the isolation of avant-garde music in the mid-1960s, Bernstein felt compelled to adopt an apologetic tone:

> As of this writing, God forgive me, I have far more pleasure in following the musical adventures of Simon & Garfunkel or of The Association singing "Along Comes Mary" than I have in most of what is being written now by the whole community of "avant garde" composers. . . . Pop music seems to be the only area where there is to be found unabashed vitality, the fun of invention, the feeling of fresh air. Everything else suddenly seems old-fashioned: electronic music, serialism, chance music—they have already acquired the musty odor of academicism.[3]

Bernstein's remark is deeply revealing. As a conductor, he was open to new music of many different styles, yet as a composer he experienced a certain degree of disdain from colleagues who accused him of selling out to popular tastes: Bernstein knew that his comments were likely to antagonize a good many of his peers. To be popular, in the view of these avant-gardists, was to be shallow. Compositional complexity was a correlative of quality, and if the public didn't "get it," the fault lay with the public. "I can't be responsible for the audience," the British composer Harrison Birtwistle (b. 1934) pointed out late in the 20th century. "I'm not running a restaurant."[4]

The widespread acceptance of such a perspective was new in the 20th century. Earlier composers—Haydn and Verdi, for example—had seen little if any conflict between popularity and musical integrity. But in the end it is pointless to blame either composers or listeners for this state of affairs. Audiences have always listened to the music that moves them, and at no point in history were there ever so many listeners, or so large a menu of musical styles from which to choose, as at the end of the 20th century.

---

**MAJOR VISUAL ARTISTS THE 20TH CENTURY**

- Pablo Picasso
- Wassily Kandinsky
- Oskar Kokoschka
- Salvador Dali
- Jackson Pollock
- Andy Warhol

 **Explore** on **mysearchlab**

# The Growth of Pluralism

The diversity of 20th-century musical styles was a source of both pleasure and anxiety for composers and listeners alike. The proliferation of styles during this era can be viewed from several different perspectives, each of which reflects broader trends in society as a whole.

## FROM HOMOGENEITY TO DIVERSITY

At the beginning of the 20th century, Western nations dominated much of the globe, and Western peoples presumed for themselves a corresponding cultural superiority. The United States proudly proclaimed itself a social melting pot in which people from all over the world could blend into an already established homogeneous society. By the end of the century, the melting pot metaphor had changed to that of a mosaic—that is, many individually distinct units combining to create a larger whole. The shift in imagery is revealing, for the mosaic metaphor rejects the idea that diverse cultures can (or should) be homogenized into a single mainstream. What had previously been seen as fragmentation, a source of weakness, was now recognized as diversity, a source of strength.

Attitudes toward music in Western culture of the 20th century reflect a similar transformation in outlook. In the early and middle decades of the century, music that did not conform to the mainstream idiom of tonal music was widely condemned. The tonally unconventional works of Arnold Schoenberg and the rhythmically unconventional works of Igor Stravinsky were seen in part as a rebellion against the social status quo (which in a sense they were); performances of this music occasionally led to riots in the concert hall. Rhythmically charged music like ragtime (in the 1900s and 1910s), jazz (1920s and 1930s), and rock and roll (1950s and 1960s) also touched off their share of controversy. Part of this animosity was motivated by racial prejudices and generational conflicts, but, as in the case of Schoenberg and Stravinsky, the music offended listeners because it was perceived to threaten the existing social order, a concern that cultural observers have expressed at many times throughout history. Plato, for example, had warned more than two thousand years before that "a new type of music is something to beware of as a hazard of all our fortunes. For the modes of music are never disturbed without unsettling of the most fundamental political and social conventions." This mistrust of new music was still common in the first half of the 20th century.

In the later decades of the century, however, audiences became more and more inclined to take a pluralistic, live-and-let-live attitude, embracing the music they liked and simply ignoring any they found objectionable.

## Chapter Outline

**"The next concert by Schoenberg in Vienna."** Schoenberg continues to conduct even though pandemonium has broken out. The figure on the floor at the bottom center appears to be Schubert, suggesting that Schoenberg's music is an affront not only to his contemporaries but to Viennese composers of the past as well. The image caricatures an actual event, the Viennese "Scandal Concert" of March 31, 1913, in which a performance of Alban Berg's *Altenberg Lieder,* op. 4, led to an open revolt of the audience. One of the organizers of the concert was arrested for striking the operetta composer Oscar Straus, who at the trial glibly remarked that the punch to his head "seemed to be the most harmonious sound of the entire evening."

**Source:** Die Zeit/Austrian Archives

Performances of innovative music stopped being a matter of controversy. Indeed, it became increasingly difficult for composers to shock listeners at all. Aside from lyrics and stage antics, there seemed to be very little that would move listeners to disrupt a performance or call for a ban on sales of recordings. Rap music came under fire in the 1990s because of its words, not its musical style. Just as the image of the melting pot had given way to that of a mosaic, the illusion of a musical mainstream had evaporated to leave a sense of tolerance toward many varied musical styles. By the 1980s, Western society as a whole was embracing a greater diversity of musical idioms than at any point in its past: country music (including bluegrass) and rock (the two most popular), rhythm & blues (encompassing soul, hip-hop, and traditional blues), jazz and big band, classical, gospel and hymns, songs from musicals and operettas, easy listening ("mood music"), ethnic or world music (particularly Latin), and folk (American traditional).

Technology such as television—an invention of the mid-20th century—offers a key to understanding the transformation of attitudes toward music. In the 1950s, most Americans could tune in only two or three national networks; any additional channels they could receive were likely to be local ones. When Elvis Presley and the Beatles appeared on *The Ed Sullivan Show* for the first time, in 1964, their audiences included viewers of all ages, from children to adults. This weekly show was designed to offer something for everyone: comedians, acrobats, magicians, and musicians of all kinds, from Maria Callas performing Puccini's *Tosca* to Bo Diddley singing "Bo Diddley." The shows with Elvis Presley in 1956 were seen by one out of every three Americans, and one of the Beatles's three 1964 broadcasts garnered the largest single audience in television history up to that point. Not everyone approved of the latest developments in music, but almost everyone knew what they were.

By the mid-1980s, this was no longer the case. Much as radio stations were already developing highly focused niche audiences before World War II, the rise of cable television now made the concept of the network variety show obsolete. With so many channels to choose from, viewers could focus not only on specific shows but entire networks devoted to specialized interests: sports, cooking, comedy, and so on. On the one hand, such diversity gave individual viewers a greater freedom of choice; on the other hand, this diversity has eroded a sense of shared culture. In the 1950s and 1960s, it was almost impossible for adults of all ages to avoid seeing Elvis and the Beatles, because so many of them watched *The Ed Sullivan Show* every Sunday night, no matter who the guests on any given broadcast happened to be. By the 1980s, viewers who wanted to watch the latest music videos chose MTV or VH1. With so many television and radio broadcasts available, musical groups were no longer competing for a common audience, and listeners were content to leave one another more or less alone; it became relatively easy for listeners of one generation to be wholly unaware of the music of another. A dominant culture with a dominant set of norms was replaced by cultural pluralism. At the end of the century, the Internet had pushed traditional notions of shared culture even further to the brink; individuals were now able to offer their work directly to a global audience (see Epilogue).

The multiplicity of musical styles in the 20th century can be found even within the works of individual composers. Here are some examples:

- **Scott Joplin** (1868–1917), known during his life as the "King of Ragtime" because of his enormously popular piano rags (see Chapter 24), integrated the style of ragtime into the classical genre of opera. Although a concert production of his *Treemonisha* (1911) failed to arouse great interest during Joplin's lifetime, the work was successfully revived in a staged performance in 1972 and won a special posthumous Pulitzer Prize in 1976.

- **George Gershwin** (1898–1937) moved easily between popular song ("Swanee," "Let's Call the Whole Thing Off") and the traditional genres of the opera house and concert hall with works that frequently incorporate jazz idioms (see Chapter 24). *Rhapsody in Blue* (1924) is in effect a one-movement concerto for piano and jazz orchestra, and the opera *Porgy and Bess* (1935) draws on African-American sources.

- **Duke Ellington** (1899–1974) defies categorization (see Chapter 24). He wrote popular songs, dance numbers for big bands, sacred music, and works for orchestra. Songs like "Sophisticated Lady" and "It Don't Mean a Thing (If It Ain't Got That Swing)" stand side by side in his output with works like *Harlem*, commissioned by Arturo Toscanini for the NBC Symphony Orchestra, and *Black, Brown, and Beige*, a symphonic poem that runs some 45 minutes in performance.

- **Frank Zappa** (1940–1993) pursued an astonishing variety of musical styles, writing for orchestras as well as for rock bands. His "Dog Breath Variations," for example, began life on *Uncle Meat* (1969), an album recorded with his rock group, the Mothers of Invention; Zappa subsequently refashioned the work on two occasions, once for orchestra and once for a smaller wind ensemble.

- **Jim Morrison** (1943–1971) crossed many boundaries both as a performer and as a composer. His 1967 recording of the "Alabama Song" from Kurt Weill's *Aufstieg und Fall der Stadt Mahagonny* (Anthology, discussed in Chapter 22) introduced an entire generation of rock aficionados to a German opera written in the 1920s. Morrison's 11-minute "The End," released on the same album (*The Doors*), extended both the textual and musical expectations of what a rock group could do.

- **Wynton Marsalis** (b. 1961) has used his virtuosic trumpet skills to accompany Sarah Vaughan and Dizzy Gillespie and collaborate with the operatic soprano Kathleen Battle, country singer Willie Nelson, and poet Maya Angelou. He has led the Lincoln Center Jazz Orchestra, recorded classical trumpet concertos, and composed music for several modern dance companies. He has written two major oratorios—*Blood on the Fields* (1994; Pulitzer Prize in Music, 1997) and *All Rise* (1999)—and recorded numerous albums, including the provocative *The Majesty of the Blues*, with its strong stance favoring early jazz. Marsalis heads Jazz at Lincoln Center, which since 1995 has held equal status with the Center's New York Philharmonic, Metropolitan Opera, and New York City Ballet.

In spite of such personal diversity, marketing dictated that musical works—which is to say, recordings—be packaged in such a way as to target specific audiences and tastes. The Grammy Awards, presented annually by the National Academy of Recording Arts and Sciences, provide a good index of how the music industry promotes its products. The proliferation of award categories for the Grammys in recent years suggests that almost every category of music eventually breeds its own subcategories; for example, gospel music, generally viewed as a "single" genre, is divided by the academy into no fewer than seven different categories: traditional, pop/contemporary, Southern/country/bluegrass, traditional soul, contemporary soul, contemporary rhythm and blues (that is, hip-hop), and rock. A separate evening of Latin Grammy awards appeals to yet another demographic. Such distinctions inevitably shape the way we hear these and other kinds of music.

Marketing also plays a basic role in what kinds of music listeners hear in the first place. Laurie Anderson's (b. 1947) minimalist "O Superman (For Massenet)" became a number two hit in the United Kingdom in 1981. Polish composer Henryk Gorecki (b. 1933) rocketed to fame in the mid-1990s when his neo-modal Third Symphony (with soprano, 1976) was marketed in England as a pop recording in 1992; it rose to number six on the charts. When Samuel Barber's highly chromatic *Adagio for Strings* (originally composed in 1936) appeared on Hollywood film soundtracks—*Elephant Man* (1980) and *Platoon* (1986), among others—it became a worldwide hit with listeners who had never before heard of Barber.

# THE PAST CONFRONTS THE PRESENT

The listening public's interest in new idioms was not confined to new music. The rediscovery of what has come to be known as early music—generally speaking, music written before 1700—opened up an entirely new section of the musical menu. Earlier repertories that had for all practical purposes been inaccessible to the music public became readily available through scores, performances, and above all recordings. The works of Du Fay, Josquin, and Monteverdi, for example, had all languished in obscurity for centuries and were virtually unknown in 1900; by 2000, some of them had become very well known indeed.

Arnold Dolmetsch (1858–1940) was in many respects the father of what in his time was called the early music movement. He was one of the first and certainly the most visible of a number of musicians in the late 19th and early 20th centuries who began performing on instruments that had remained essentially dormant for a century or more, such as the harpsichord, clavichord, spinet, viola da gamba, viola d'amore, and a variety of wind and percussion instruments. Although amateurish by today's standards, Dolmetsch's work was profoundly important in laying the foundation for the post–World War II revival of interest in music of the medieval, Renaissance, and Baroque eras. In the years between 1950 and 1980, a number of outstanding groups sprang up that specialized in what came to be known as period instruments, either originals or accurate copies of instruments contemporary to the repertory being performed. At first the music and instruments were so strange and novel to audiences that they often required commentary from the performers. But before long, the work of musicians like Nikolaus Harnoncourt, David Munrow, and Roger Norrington had become so well known that explanations were no longer necessary. Indeed, Norrington extended the concept of period instruments into the repertory of the mid- and even late-19th century with the symphonies of Brahms.

By the late 1970s, Josquin, Du Fay, and Machaut had joined Bach, Beethoven, and Brahms in the record (and later CD) stores. Even Gregorian chant hit the charts in the mid-1990s. In a sense, then, a great deal of supposedly new music in the 20th century was in fact extremely old, but the style of it was new to listeners. Composers of the late 20th century thus had to struggle for recognition not only within the realm of contemporary music and the standard repertory (from Bach onward), but against extremely old works as well. To a certain extent, the early music movement has satisfied the desire of listeners for new repertories without recourse to newly composed music.

Some composers found new sounds in instruments of the past. Although the harpsichord had never disappeared entirely, it enjoyed a renaissance in the early 20th century through works like Manuel de Falla's Harpsichord Concerto. Many popular recording artists, among them the Beatles and singer Tori Amos, also made use of the instrument in their recordings. Paul Hindemith, in turn, wrote several pieces for the viola d'amore, an instrument that had not been in general use since the Baroque era. Sonorities, forms, and styles of earlier times inspired still other composers of the 20th century. Many works by the Estonian composer Arvo Pärt (b. 1935), for example,

## *Primary Evidence*     "THIS UGLY GAME OF IDOLIZING THE PAST"

*In response to a questionnaire distributed in 1984 by the International Music Council, the eminent German avant-garde composer Karlheinz Stockhausen (1928–2007) railed against the preoccupation of artists and the recording industry with music of the past to the exclusion of music of the present. At no time before the present, Stockhausen argued, has the public ever been so absorbed with music of prior generations and so unconcerned with new music. Here he proposes a program of change, supporting "musical evolution" rather than "idolizing the past."*

■ ■ ■

What can be done: Shake up the leading interpreters in the world, ask them to refuse to serve any longer the machinery of composer-stripping, financial exploitation of dead composers through established gangs of cultural manipulation and "music marketing"; insist that they serve musical evolution: help vulnerable new musical organisms rather than living from a 300-year-old bank account of musical literature; spend at least 50 percent of their time rehearsing and performing new works; fight for progress and refuse to continue this ugly game of idolizing the past.

By using the new technologies of audio engineering, including the manipulation of sounds recorded on magnetic tape, Karlheinz Stockhausen and other composers of his generation sought to distance themselves from established musical timbres and traditions.

**Source:** akg-images/Harald Fronzeck/Newscom

are indebted to the textures and sonorities of 13th-century polyphony (see Anthology). The American composer Ellen Taaffe Zwillich (b. 1939), in turn, has written works from time to time that openly evoke the forms and styles of the Baroque, such as her *Concerto Grosso* (1985) and *Partita* for violin and string orchestra (2000).

# RECORDED VERSUS LIVE MUSIC

Until the late 19th century, music had always been a quintessentially social art, one that brought people together in the same space to share the experience of performing and hearing music. A person could read a novel or contemplate a painting in solitude, but listening to anyone other than one's own self was possible only in places where others were making music. People who wanted to appreciate and enjoy music played an instrument or sang, and they often learned to read musical notation. In 1900, almost every village of any size had a community band, chorus, or both; music lessons were a standard feature of a middle-class childhood, and families that could afford a piano had one more often than not.

Some middle-class families also owned what was then a new invention: a phonograph. With this device, for the first time in history, a single performance could be preserved and repeated almost indefinitely, and a work of music could be heard outside the presence of a performing musician. Over the course of the 20th century, the phonograph was supplemented by radio, television, video- and audiotape, the compact disc, and other recording technologies that the inventors of the first phonograph could scarcely have dreamed of. Recording technology transformed the manner in which music was both produced and consumed. As a result, today a greater selection of music is more readily available to more people in more places than ever before.

This technological evolution had the unintended consequence of turning music into an increasingly less social experience. Whereas in 1900, the phonograph's megaphone filled a room with sound, making listeners of everyone present, in 2000, the preferred music source of millions was the earphone-equipped personal playback device. The availability of recorded music in general also made music a more passive experience. Making music for oneself and one's friends became a far less common activity than it once was, and the number of community choruses and bands declined markedly.

We are so accustomed to sound recordings today that it is difficult to recapture the sense of alienation this technology created when it was new. In the early 20th century, many believed that something intangible had been lost and that recordings had changed the very nature of the musical experience for the worse. The absence of a performer, some felt, robbed music of its expressive and emotional power. The opportunity to hear a given piece as often as desired, whenever desired, was thought to reduce the immediacy of the musical experience. In 1929, the American Federation of Musicians issued a plea against "Canned Music" (see the illustration "Canned Music on Trial"), which today may strike us as self-serving and quaint. Nevertheless, the experience of listening to live music is different from that of listening to recorded music in ways that cannot be measured or identified, at least not yet.

An outspoken advocate of recorded music, the Canadian pianist Glenn Gould (1932–1982) shunned public performances for most of his mature career, arguing that he "could better serve music in a recording studio than in a concert hall."[5] Although Gould's stance may have been extreme, his point remains an important one. The musical possibilities of the recording studio are in many respects considerably greater than those of the live stage. In the studio it is possible to overdub tracks and modify sounds

SQUEAK

SQUEAK

SQUEAK

SCRATCH!

# CANNED MUSIC

*Big Noise* BRAND

GUARANTEED TO PRODUCE NO INTELLECTUAL OR EMOTIONAL REACTION WHATEVER

## OYEZ! OYEZ! OYEZ!

## CANNED MUSIC ON TRIAL

THIS is the case of Art vs. Mechanical Music in Theatres. The defendant stands accused before the American people of attempted corruption of musical appreciation and discouragement of musical education.

Theatres in many cities are offering synchronized mechanical music as a substitute for Real Music. If the theatre-going public accepts this vitiation of its entertainment program a deplorable decline in the Art of Music is inevitable.

Musical authorities know that the soul of the Art is lost in mechanization. It cannot be otherwise because the quality of music is dependent upon the present mood of the artist, upon the human contact, without which the essence of intellectual stimulation and emotional rapture is lost.

### Is Music Worth Saving?

No great volume of evidence is required to answer this question. Music is a well-nigh universally beloved art. From the beginning of history men have turned to musical expression to lighten the burdens of life, to make them happier. Aborigines, lowest in the scale of savagery, chant their song to tribal Gods and play upon pipes and shark-skin drums. Musical development has kept pace with good taste and ethics throughout the ages, and has influenced the gentler nature of man more powerfully perhaps than any other factor.

Has it remained for the Great Age of Science to snub the Art by setting up in its place a pale and feeble shadow of itself?

**"Canned Music on Trial" (1929).** The introduction of recorded sound created enormous anxiety for musicians. Although some profited from the new technology, many more were driven from their jobs. In the era of silent films, for example, a pianist, organist, or even a small orchestra might provide live music to accompany the images on screen. After 1927, such opportunities became increasingly rare. The American Federation of Musicians appealed to the public to resist "canned" music on the grounds that mechanization destroys the soul of art. The objection seems slightly odd today, accustomed as we are to recorded sound, but this advertisement reminds us that the perception of music changed fundamentally during the 20th century.

**Source:** Hartman Center for Sales, Advertising & Marketing History

in myriad ways. It is even possible to make music without any performer at all—at least in the traditional sense—by using prerecorded sounds such as the singing of birds or whales, or with a preprogrammed electronic synthesizer, or by sampling snippets of other recordings.

The ready availability of recordings also altered listener expectations, making many listeners less tolerant of wrong notes, flawed tuning, or other imperfections in live performances. By the end of the century, more and more live performances were integrating recorded sounds, even to the point of overdubbing the lead singers themselves. The distinctions between recorded and live music became increasingly fuzzy in the last decades of the 20th century.

# AUTHENTICITY

The idea of performing a work of music in a manner that reflected the composer's original intentions became more important than ever. Reasonably good editions prepared in the 19th century were replaced with scrupulously prepared editions in the 20th (see Appendix 2: Evaluating Musical Editions). Editorial techniques rose to a level worthy of biblical scholars, and in many respects the output of Bach, Mozart, and Beethoven, among others, was treated as if it were holy writ. Many performers took up the cause of historical authenticity as well, not only by using period instruments, but by performing them in a manner consistent with practices that were current in the composer's own time. These techniques included different kinds of vibrato, articulation, and attack, as well as various approaches to tempo, dynamics, and phrasing. These historically informed performances were a revelation to listeners. The way Bach's cantatas and Handel's oratorios were performed at the end of the 20th century was substantially different from the way they had been presented in 1900, or even 1950—and, most would agree, far more representative of what the composers originally intended.

But historical authenticity exacted a price. Repertories shrank in scope. Large orchestras were less inclined to play Bach's Brandenburg Concertos and Orchestral Suites in the second half of the 20th century than they had been in the first because these works were not written for modern instruments or such large ensembles. Pianists

## Primary Evidence — AUTHENTIC SPONTANEITY

*Many critics have dismissed much of the popular repertory as trivial and shallow because of its supposed simplicity. But equating complexity with quality and simplicity with cheapness denies the driving force that ultimately gives music its ability to move the human spirit. Rock music, for example, is often deprecated for its harmonic, rhythmic, textural, and textual simplicity and for its unrefined directness of emotion. Yet these are the very same qualities valued in the song repertory of the late 18th and early 19th centuries. With its loud volume, insistent rhythms, and glorification of the sensuous, rock music often generates an experience that can overwhelm the listener. As the music critic and journalist Robert Palmer (1945–1997) reminds us, however, the rock concert is in many respects the closest thing we have nowadays to the Dionysian frenzies of ancient Greece, wild celebrations of physical and spiritual ecstasy in the name of Dionysus, the god of wine.*

■ ■ ■

And that's the beauty of rock and roll. The lifestyle can be perilous, the rate of attrition remains high, but the survivors can go on practicing and perfecting their craft while the younger generation's best and brightest assume the Dionysian mantle and get on with the main program, which is liberation through ecstasy. Somewhere, in some sleazy bar or grimy practice room or suburban garage, young musicians wielding guitars or turntables, drum kits or beat boxes, sequencers or samplers, are creating the music for tomorrow's rock and roll revelry. Now that women have belatedly been accepted as guitarists, bassists, drummers, songwriter-auteurs, and "not just another pretty face," we're witnessing the birth of a whole new style of rock and roll frenzy and transcendence. Even the media overkill surrounding the much-hyped "riot grrrls" can't rob the term of its Dionysiac import. Don't let the faux-Apollonians fool you. As rockers, we are heirs to one of our civilization's richest, most time-honored spiritual traditions.

We must never forget our glorious Dionysian heritage.

**Source:** Robert Palmer, *Rock & Roll: An Unruly History* (New York: Harmony Books, 1995), p. 155.

were less likely to perform the music of Bach, or even Haydn and Mozart, in their recitals in 2000 than 50 years before because the modern piano is not the instrument for which those composers wrote. Except for encore pieces, instrumentalists of all kinds dropped most arrangements of works not originally composed for their instruments from their repertories. Concerts and recordings became far less heterogeneous in the second half of the 20th century. Orchestras differentiated more and more between "standard" and "pops" concerts, with increasingly little repertory crossing boundaries. This kind of division discouraged breadth of taste. The exigencies of marketing to specific audiences dictated that recordings and concerts contain, in effect, only a single type of music rather than a variety.

In other repertories, authenticity took on a different form. Many jazz and rock vocalists cultivated a sound considered emotionally authentic precisely because it ran counter to the standards of cultivated voice production. Voices that might have been considered strained, distorted, or out of tune in an earlier era were no longer automatically dismissed as inferior. To the contrary, a "realistic" sound, unvarnished by training and practice, was taken to be a reflection of the performer's emotional authenticity. The emotional ideal of most rock music demanded a correspondingly authentic, or at least seemingly authentic, style of singing (see Primary Evidence: Authentic Spontaneity).

# MUSIC IN 20TH-CENTURY SOCIETY

Technological advances in the reproduction and dissemination of sound created a wealth of new potentials—and pitfalls—for music in 20th-century society. Music was used on a scale and in places that could not have been imagined a century before. Indeed, the largest single event in human history, the Live Aid concert held July 13, 1985, to raise money for famine relief in Ethiopia, was focused on music. The concert featured almost one hundred different artists and groups, including Bob Dylan, Joan Baez, Phil Collins, U2, Mick Jagger, Eric Clapton, Neil Young, David Bowie, Paul McCartney, Elton John, the Beach Boys, the Who, Sting, and the Four Tops. It was staged simultaneously in London (Wembley Stadium) and Philadelphia (John F. Kennedy Stadium) and broadcast live over 14 satellites to an estimated 1.6 billion people in 160 countries. Music was a powerful unifying force in this global undertaking: "Maybe for the first time since Man left the African Rift Valley we began to talk in a common language, and that language, bizarrely, turned out to be pop music," proclaimed organizer Bob Geldof a decade after the event.[6]

In truth, there was nothing at all bizarre about the idea of music uniting people of different nationalities or of using music to raise money for worthy charities. Haydn had conducted a number of performances in London in the 1790s to support needy musicians in their old age, and Liszt had given recitals in 1838 to benefit victims of a recent flood on the Danube River. But 20th-century technology made it possible to disseminate music, and raise money, on an unprecedented scale.

## Music and the State

Since the time of Plato (see Prologue), governments have recognized the ability of music to move the emotions of entire populations, and with the increased reach the new technologies of amplification, recording, and broadcasting made possible, music took on an even more significant role in political life in the 20th century. Instrumental music was particularly susceptible to varied political interpretation. The fate of Beethoven's symphonies in 20th-century Europe offers a good case in point. They were used by every element of the German political spectrum, from the extreme right (Nazis) to the extreme left (communists) and every party in between, before, during, and after World War II. Ironically, they were even used by Germany's enemies: the opening motif of the Fifth Symphony served as a sonic icon of Allied resistance throughout World War II and was used in coded messages. German troops found it difficult to suppress this use among partisan resisters, who could rightly claim they were just "whistling a little Beethoven." Nazi Germany was quick to suppress jazz, because of its African-American origins, and all music by Jewish composers (including Mendelssohn): none of this music, it was maintained, belonged to the "natural" idioms of the Aryan nations.

The Soviet Union also struggled with nontraditional musical styles. In the decade after the revolution of 1917, the communist government encouraged experimentation, and the avant-garde flourished. But by the early 1930s, the regime had changed its stance. Josef Stalin encouraged native composers to produce music that was accessible to the masses and that was informed, at least to some degree, by folk music. Absolute music—particularly abstract, complex music—came under special censure as "formalist" on the grounds that it seemed to be written without regard toward its emotional

## *Focus*  SONGS ABOUT THE ATOM BOMB

Almost every major event in human history has inspired songs—the beginnings or ends of wars, the death of great leaders, or new inventions like the telephone, airplane, and automobile. As the following list suggests, the atomic bomb inspired many songs:

Karl and Harty, *When the Atom Bomb Fell* (1945)

Slim Gaillard Quartette, *Atomic Cocktail* (1945)

The Buchanan Brothers, *Atomic Power* (1946)

The Golden Gate Quartet, *Atom and Evil* (1946)

The Sons of the Pioneers, *Old Man Atom* (1947)

Jackie Doll and his Pickled Peppers, *When They Drop the Atomic Bomb* (1951)

Billy Hughes and the Rhythm Buckaroos, *Atomic Sermon* (1953)

Sonny Russell, *50 Megatons* (1956)

The Commodores, *Uranium* (1957)

The Five Stars, *Atom Bomb Baby* (1957)

Skip Stanley, *Satellite Baby* (1957)

Bob Dylan, *A Hard Rain's A-Gonna Fall* (1963)

Barry McGuire, *Eve of Destruction* (1965)

Tom Lehrer, *So Long, Mom (A Song for World War III)* (1966)

An American nuclear bomb test on the Bikini Atoll in the South Pacific, 1946.

**Source:** ClassicStock/Alamy

Using humor and pathos, some songwriters took an approach that entertained but also helped listeners cope with the terrifying prospect of nuclear war; other songwriters (Dylan, McGuire) took a more sober approach.

effect on average citizens. The composers Dimitri Shostakovich and Serge Prokofiev, among others, came under attack from the government at various times during the period 1930 to 1970 for writing overly formalist music. Political leaders discouraged and openly derided serial composition (see Chapter 21). As late as the 1960s, the premier of the Soviet Union, Nikita Khrushchev, condemned this technique of composition as a threat to the "wholesomeness" of socialist ideals, declaring, "Our people can't use this garbage as a tool of their ideology."

Others, however, continued the long tradition of using music to assert their opposition to the status quo. Kurt Weill and his librettist Bertolt Brecht collaborated to produce a series of stage works ridiculing capitalism and middle-class values; Alban Berg took up the cause of society's outcasts with his opera *Wozzeck* (Anthology, discussed in Chapter 21).

American leaders never became embroiled in musical politics to the same degree as in Europe. No president ever offered an opinion for or against serial composition, and the government as a whole never invested very heavily in any of the arts. Efforts to establish a national conservatory of music in the 1920s failed for lack of funds and were never seriously revived. The founding of the National Endowment for the Arts in the early 1960s represented a modest step in the direction of government patronage of the arts. Yet while this agency helped many programs and individuals, its funding for music was never substantial enough to provoke a national political debate over any music it did fund.

Music nevertheless played a potent role in the American political landscape of the 20th century. A politician's choice of music revealed much about his or her identity. Harry Truman's campaign for the presidency in 1948 was accompanied by the Eubie Blake song "I'm Just Wild about Harry." When Bill Clinton accepted the presidential nomination of the Democratic Party in 1992, the loudspeakers blared out Fleetwood Mac's 1977 hit "Don't Stop (Thinking about Tomorrow)." The moment was revealing in more than one respect. The traditional music played at every Democratic Party convention since the 1930s had been a Depression-era song, "Happy Days Are Here Again," performed by a live band of brass and woodwinds. By embracing a rock song and the (recorded) music of a new generation, Clinton helped define himself as a New Democrat. Candidate Clinton used music again later in the campaign when he played a jazz number on the saxophone on a late-night talk show. Had he sat at the piano and played Schoenberg's Piano Suite, op. 25, he would have sent a very different message to viewers.

## Music and Race

Music played a vital role in the ongoing struggle for racial justice throughout the world, particularly in the United States. Ragtime, jazz, and rhythm and blues (the basis for rock and roll, which evolved into rock) were closely associated with African-American culture when they first arrived on the musical scene, yet all were embraced and cultivated by white people as well. All three genres still had to overcome considerable resistance, much of it blatantly or subtly racist. But the appeal of this music ultimately transcended racial lines, even if the process was slow.

There can be no doubt that Elvis Presley's enormous success was helped by his being white and therefore vastly more marketable to a white public in the middle 1950s than the black artists of the time who performed in much the same style (Little Richard, James Brown, Richard Berry). Presley's remake of a rhythm and blues hit like "Hound Dog" by Big Mama Thornton received greater exposure and higher sales; a less provocative white singer, Pat Boone, did the same with Fats Domino's "Ain't That a Shame" and "I'll Be Home" by the Flamingos. African-American artists such as

**A 1938 jam session.** Jazz, more than any other kind of music, promoted racial integration for audiences as well as performers, although the process was subtle. Here the celebrated clarinetist Artie Shaw jams with Duke Ellington and drummer Chick Webb in 1938. At the time, most American institutions, including the military and schools—not to mention housing, restaurants, and hotels—were segregated either by law or in practice.

**Source:** Frank Driggs Collection/Contributor/Archive Photos/Getty Images

Chuck Berry had to adapt their music and stage presentation to be accepted by white audiences; Chubby Checker recorded "dance craze" songs that crossed racial lines but were more successful in the white-dominated Top 40 charts than in the black-dominated rhythm and blues charts.

From the 1920s through the 1940s, all African-American popular artists were relegated by major labels to the less widely distributed category of "race records," without serious attempts to reach a wider market. Beginning in the 1950s black musicians were being marketed aggressively in the economic mainstream, no longer labeled or segregated (officially, at least) as race records. Black musicians had to wait for greater support until the 1960s, when major record labels owned by African Americans established themselves in the market.

Ragtime, jazz, rock—all of these increasingly brought black and white performers and audiences together at a time when American society and most of its institutions were racially segregated. Integrated ensembles were almost unknown in the 1920s and still rare in the 1930s. The African-American singer Billie Holiday, appearing in Detroit with Count Basie's jazz band in 1936, recalled that she had been compelled to apply what she called "dark grease paint" to her face because the theater's management was afraid her light complexion might cause her to appear "too yellow to sing with all the black men in the band."[7] By the late 1930s, however, the white clarinetist Benny Goodman's bands featured four African-American musicians: pianist Teddy Wilson, vibraphonist Lionel Hampton, guitarist Charlie Christian, and arranger Fletcher Henderson. Other white jazzmen like Artie Shaw, Charlie Barnet, and Woody Herman soon followed Goodman's lead in hiring African Americans. The African-American composer and bandleader Duke Ellington likewise began integrating white musicians into his group in the late 1930s.

With the progress of the civil rights movement beginning in the 1940s and the end of legal segregation in the 1960s, the black-white divide in jazz and rock, although it remained present, became less pronounced. When rap music, a new idiom rooted in the black experience, emerged in the 1990s, it encountered, like its predecessors, a round of racially tinged criticism. And like its predecessors, it too was soon adopted by white musicians.

## Music and Protest

The music of three protest movements in the 20th century stands out in particular: the labor movement, especially in the decades 1910 to 1950; the civil rights movement of the 1950s and 1960s; and the anti-Vietnam War movement from the mid-1960s through the early 1970s.

Group song helped labor unions create and sustain a sense of solidarity. The International Workers of the World (IWW, also known as the "Wobblies") issued its first songbook in 1909. Over the next 70 years, the *Little Red Song Book: Songs to Fan the Flames of Discontent* would go through 35 editions.

It is difficult to imagine the civil rights movement of the 1950s and 1960s without the songs that became a basic tool for protesters marching for racial equality. "We Shall Overcome," a hymn transformed into a striker's song by the 1940s, became the unofficial anthem of the movement and was sung at almost every rally, protest, and meeting. The text alone is fairly straightforward; it is the music that gives this song its true power. The low, confident beginning, the soaring rise in the middle, the return to the opening register at the close—all these combine to make a powerful musical statement. Other modern folk songs came to be associated with the movement as well: "If I Had a Hammer" (by Pete Seeger and Lee Hays of the Weavers), "The Times They Are A-Changin'" (by Bob Dylan), and "We'll Never Turn Back" (by Bertha Gober).

Protesters against American military involvement in Vietnam in the 1960s and early 1970s also used music as a means of galvanizing support for their cause. Some of the more notable songs of this kind included "I Feel Like I'm Fixin' to Die Rag" (1965) by Country Joe [McDonald] and the Fish; "War" (1970) by Edwin Starr; and "What's Going On" (1971) by Marvin Gaye. Less well remembered are the songs supporting the war, such as Barry Sadler's "Ballad of the Green Berets" (1966). With its minimal amplification and snare drum accompaniment, this strophic song topped the U.S. sales charts for five weeks, sold more than nine million copies, and became the theme song for a movie starring John Wayne.

Protest messages did not depend on texts alone. Jimi Hendrix's distorted rendition of "The Star-Spangled Banner" on an electric guitar at the Woodstock Festival in 1969, although wordless, was universally understood as an act of protest. The melodic distortions, heavy electro-acoustic feedback, and free flights of improvisation helped turn the national anthem into a statement of dissent.

## Music Therapy

Music has been used to cure illnesses since ancient times, as suggested by the biblical story of David curing Saul of his melancholy by playing the harp (see p. 3). It was not until the 20th century, however, that music therapy established itself as an acknowledged protocol for the treatment of psychological, physical, and cognitive problems. Doctors treating wounded and traumatized soldiers after World War I noticed that patients exposed to music or given a chance to make music tended to recover more rapidly and more fully than those who were not. The first professional association of music therapists in the United States was established in 1950, the outgrowth of an expanding body of scientific literature that had substantiated the positive effects of music on the physical and mental health of individuals.

In clinical settings, music therapy has proved particularly important in helping patients suffering from neurological disorders like Alzheimer's and Parkinson's diseases. Scientists believe that music's therapeutic effects relate to its ability to enhance the processes by which the brain reorganizes cerebral functions that have been damaged by disease or injury. By the 1990s, music therapy workshops were also being used as agents of social change, as at the Pavarotti Music Center, a grammar school in Mostar, Bosnia-Herzegovina. Initially funded by the singer Luciano Pavarotti (1915–2007), the Center applied music making to the bridging of divides, both ethnic and religious, between longtime antagonists (1997–2003).

## Ambient Music

The primary purpose of **ambient music**—background music—is to shape actions and attitudes within a given space without being itself a focus of attention. Music had been used to create moods and influence human behavior long before the 20th century, but the idea of placing it in the background, and not as the immediate focus of listeners' attention, was first introduced by Erik Satie (1866–1925) in the form of **musique d'ameublement** (furnishing music). He wrote a small number of pieces thus designated for various ensembles, with descriptions referring to "arrival of the guests . . . to be played in a vestibule"; "phonic tiling—can be played during lunch or a civil marriage"; and "wallpaper in a prefect's office." Over the course of the 20th century, Satie's humorous titles would become more serious than he could have ever imagined.

George Owen Squier (1865–1934) was the first to recognize the commercial applications of ambient music. In 1922 he founded what eventually became the Muzak Corporation, marketing the service to private homes; but Squier soon discovered that carefully programmed music—mostly soft-edged arrangements of well-known tunes—could increase productivity in the workplace and make customers spend more time in retail outlets or less time in restaurants, thereby boosting revenue. Audio "architects" became adept at designing playlists to meet the needs of any given business. Although few listeners were aware of the presence of ambient music at any given moment, by the end of the century it had become the most widely heard source of music in the world, with more than 100 million listeners daily. And almost none of them, as its critics pointed out, could turn this music off.

Satie's idea of creating new works designed to function specifically as ambient music caught the imagination of a number of talented composers in the last quarter of the 20th century. This kind of ambient music is characterized by widely spaced textures, consistently soft dynamics, and an extremely subdued sense of rhythm or pulse. The English composer Brian Eno (b. 1948) maintained that his *Music for Airports* (1978) was "intended to induce calm and a space to think. Ambient music must be able to accommodate many levels of listening attention without enforcing one in particular; it must be as ignorable as it is interesting."[8] Eno's half-joking, half-serious title reflects the ways in which the use of ambient music has altered the tacit assumptions about conventional ways of listening, whether in a concert hall or in the privacy of one's home through a recording. In recent years, ambient music in the style of Eno's *Music for Airports* has actually been used in airports.

# MUSIC IN THE 20TH CENTURY: A STYLISTIC OVERVIEW

The history of Western music in this era follows a trajectory of ever-expanding possibilities. Anyone writing music in this era could choose from an unprecedented array of options in every element of the art. Indeed, styles varied so markedly from genre to genre, within genres, and even within the work of many individual composers that it is no longer possible to identify a lowest common denominator of style.

Textures in 20th-century music ranged from the extremely simple to complex. No single genre or style can be associated exclusively with any particular texture.

Rhythm, like other musical elements, manifested itself in a variety of possibilities. Dance music, as in all previous eras, relied on a steady beat. Ragtime, jazz, country music, and rock all evolved from dance idioms and accordingly built on a steady rhythm. Ragtime and jazz tended toward syncopated rhythms, sometimes quite intricate. In contrast, some art music consciously avoided the steady meters of dance-related music.

Like melody, musical textures in the 20th century ranged from the extremely simple to complex. No single genre or style can be associated exclusively with any particular texture. Melody varied greatly according to genre, the intended audience, and the function of the work at hand. The melodic variety evident in much music of the late 19th century continued to grow, supplemented by increasing use of nondiatonic scales such as whole tone, pentatonic, and octatonic. At the same time, many composers at the end of the century were still writing in a diatonic idiom not terribly different from that of Mozart and Haydn. But this was a choice made consciously and not for lack of options.

## SUMMARY OF STYLE DIFFERENCES BETWEEN MUSIC OF THE 19TH CENTURY AND 20TH CENTURY

| | 19TH CENTURY | 20TH CENTURY |
|---|---|---|
| **Style** | Composers seek to develop a distinctly personal style; originality becomes paramount in all genres. | An even greater variety of compositional styles; originality remains paramount in most genres. |
| **Texture** | The polyphonic and homophonic coexist, with composers drawing on whichever approach best suits their immediate needs. | A wide range of options, from monophony to complex polyphony. |
| **Rhythm** | Periodic phrase structure continues in the works of certain repertories (dance, march), but on the whole becomes increasingly less obvious over the course of the century. | A continuation and intensification of 19th-century tendencies; post–World War II extremes range from repetitive music to the conceptual use of silence. |
| **Melody** | Ranges from the simple to the complex. | From the simple to the complex, with added possibilities derived from nondiatonic scales, such as whole tone, pentatonic, and microtonal. |
| **Harmony** | Becomes increasingly chromatic over the course of the century, which in turn makes harmonic simplicity a potentially unusual feature. | In addition to inherited idioms, atonality—the absence of a tonal center—emerges as one of many compositional options. |
| **Form** | The large-scale formal conventions of the Classical era continue in use but often in a manner that obscures their presence. Cyclical coherence becomes an increasingly important issue within multimovement works. | Conventional forms remain important in the work of some composers; others avoid these forms at all costs. |
| **Instrumentation** | The distinction between vocal and instrumental writing becomes even more pronounced. The orchestra grows in both size and instrumental variety. | Along with new and previously excluded acoustic instruments, amplification and the electronic production of sound open new dimensions in timbre; through the use of a synthesizer, any audible wavelength can be reproduced precisely. |

Harmony was widely perceived in the first two-thirds of the 20th century as the defining element of style, in spite of important developments in other areas. It emerged as the chief battleground in the debate over musical modernism, by which critics tended to categorize composers according to their preferred harmonic idiom; when a new piece was performed, accounts invariably mentioned its place on the spectrum between tonality and atonality. Atonal music (discussed in Chapter 21) is characterized by the lack of any tonal center. It emerged early in the century in the works of several innovative composers. Indeed, the controversy over harmony in the early decades of the 20th century bears many remarkable similarities to the debate over the merits of the *prima prattica* and the *seconda prattica* in the years around 1600 (see Chapter 8). In both instances, new and old styles continued to flourish side by side. Harmony based on the whole-tone scale and quartal harmonies expanded tonal possibilities even further.

Form also ranged from the simple to the complex. Composers who chose to work within the tonal idiom were generally more inclined to use such traditional forms as sonata form, rondo, and ABA. Those working outside the tonal idiom typically preferred to use dynamics, texture, and orchestration rather than harmony and thematic ideas as the basis of large-scale structures. Serial composition (see Chapter 21), based on the manipulation of a basic series of notes (and, later, rhythmic and other elements) throughout a work, provided important structural alternatives for composers working outside the tonal idiom. Minimalism (see Chapter 23) and aleatoric music (see Chapter 23) offered some of the more radical new approaches to form.

Instrumentation featured the greater use of a variety of percussion. Beyond the realm of acoustic instruments, electronically generated sounds through such instruments as the electric guitar, the synthesizer, and the computer were added (see Chapter 23). The synthesizer and computer provided composers the opportunity to control with precision the basic elements of pitch, vibrato, and timbre.

# SUMMARY

As in the early decades of the Baroque era, composers working at the end of the 19th century and the beginning of the 20th had the option of writing in both "old" and "new" styles. However, thanks to the rapid emergence and evolution of new technologies in sound recording, radio and television broadcasting, and computers, the range of idioms available to composers expanded dramatically over the course of the 20th century. The result, by the end of the century, was a stylistic pluralism that made it impossible to identify anything resembling a musical mainstream.

✓●─ **Study** and **Review**
on **mysearchlab.com**

# The Search for New Sounds, 1890–1945

The two generations of composers working between approximately 1890 and 1945 confronted and challenged many of the most basic stylistic premises of Western music, including triadic harmony, traditional forms, and conventional timbres. The result of these challenges was a variety of new approaches to self-expression through sound.

## IMPRESSIONISM

The movement known as **impressionism** represents one of the earliest attempts to explore fundamentally new approaches to music. The term was first used in painting to designate the style of a group of artists (including Claude Monet, Edouard Manet, Pierre-Auguste Renoir, and Edgar Degas) who used an accumulation of short brush strokes instead of a continuous line to produce not so much a representation of an object as a sensation—an impression—of it. The movement took its name from the title of Monet's painting *Impression: Sunrise* (1872; see illustration).

In impressionist painting, color takes precedence over line. Similarly, the impressionist style in music gives greater emphasis to color (timbre) than to line (melody) than in any previous style of writing. The number of composers thought of today as impressionists is relatively small—the most prominent are Claude Debussy (1862–1918) and Maurice Ravel (1875–1937)—but their influence on later composers and later styles was considerable.

Musical impressionism can be broadly characterized as follows:

- *Form:* Impressionist music for the most part avoids the kind of goal-oriented structures that had dominated music of the preceding century or more. These works flow instead from one moment to the next, building and receding in tension but without the same sense of striving toward resolution. They tend to be structured less around harmony and thematic ideas than around masses of sound.

- *Harmony:* Although impressionist composers never abandoned tonality, they used ninth, eleventh, and thirteenth chords to an unprecedented degree. They also drew occasionally on nondiatonic scales such as the whole tone and pentatonic, creating sounds evocative of East Asia.

- *Voice leading:* Individual voices often move without strict regard to the traditional rules of voice leading. Parallel fourths, fifths, and octaves contribute to the distinctive sound of impressionism.

**Impressionism.** Impressionist paintings command big money in the auction house nowadays, but the style was widely rejected when it first came onto the scene in Paris in the mid-1870s. One critic, writing of an exhibition in which this 1872 painting—Claude Monet's *Impression: soleil levant* (Impression: Sunrise)— appeared, complained that Monet, Renoir, Cezanne, and others were "impressionists in that they do not render a landscape, but the sensation produced by the landscape. The word itself has passed into their language: in the catalogue, the *Sunrise* by Monet is called not landscape, but *Impression.* Thus they take leave of reality and enter the realms of idealism." Another critic of the time was even less charitable: "Wallpaper in its embryonic state is more finished than that seascape." Musical impressionism, similarly concerned more with color than with line, also met with resistance for a time; one critic declared that Debussy's *Prélude à l'Après-midi d'un faune* was "to a work of music what an artist's palette is to a finished painting."

**Source:** The Art Gallery Collection/Alamy

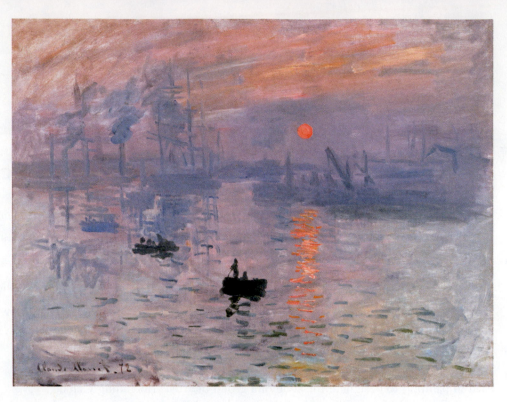

- *Rhythm:* The rhythms of impressionist music tend to be fluid, often avoiding any definite sense of meter and preferring instead an elusive sense of motion that at times moves forward and at times seems to hang in suspension.

- *Timbre:* Impressionist composers drew new sounds out of the piano and orchestra alike. Debussy once declared that Beethoven had written for the piano in an overly percussive style; he advocated instead a style that treats the piano as an "instrument without hammers," with a tone that is more lyrical, intimate, and sensuous.[1] Debussy and Ravel were both renowned for their orchestrations, which rely frequently on techniques that distribute thematic ideas throughout the entire fabric of the orchestra.

Debussy hated the term impressionism, particularly when used to describe his music. He insisted he was more concerned with making "something new—realities— as it were: what imbeciles call 'impressionism.'"[2] His objection rests on the belief that our sensory perceptions, our impressions of the world, construct their own kind of reality, an alternative to a conscious and supposedly objective, external reality that may not even exist in the first place. This attitude was not a new one: the Romantics of the early 19th century had embraced the idea of music as a means of conveying an alternate reality, but the impressionists extended the inward turn of the eye (and ear) still further.

Debussy's music also resonates with the French poetry of his day. Poets like Charles Baudelaire (1821–1867), Stéphane Mallarmé (1842–1898), Paul Verlaine (1844–1896), and Arthur Rimbaud (1854–1891) relished the sound of language for sound's sake and were not constrained by syntax or logic. These poets, who became known as symbolists, envied music's ability to suggest without stating, to construct forms without the burden of representation, and they sought to recreate this in their poetry. In place of narrative in their works—a linear progression of ideas—we find a succession of images, often connected only loosely. In place of description, we find symbols, allusions, suggestions.

Debussy's music takes a comparable approach to sound. His *Prélude à l'Après-midi d'un faune* ("Prelude to an Afternoon of a Faun," 1894) was actually inspired by a symbolist poem, Stéphane Mallarmé's *L'Après-midi d'un faune* (1876). Evocative and at times obscure, Mallarmé's poem captures the ruminations of a mythological faun, a half man, half goat who remembers—or did he only dream about?—his erotically charged encounter with a pair of wood nymphs. The opening line reads, "Those nymphs, I want to make them permanent," and the rest of the poem floats between dream and consciousness. Illusion and reality are indistinguishable.

Critics have drawn many indirect and a few direct connections between Mallarmé's poetry and Debussy's music. The faun's instrument is traditionally the flute, and it is this instrument that opens Debussy's work. The languorous chromatic line falls and rises like the faun's own fantasy. Debussy himself was evasive about further particulars, however, stating merely that his piece conveyed "a general impression of the poem, because if music were to follow more closely it would run out of breath, like a dray horse competing for the Grand Prize with a thoroughbred."[3] Yet the consistent opposition between flute and strings and the points of structural articulation (m. 30–31, 37, 55, 79, 94) resonates subtly with both the design and content of Mallarmé's poem.

It is also unclear why Debussy called this the "Prelude" to the faun's afternoon. At one point he had announced a forthcoming work entitled *Prélude, interludes et paraphrase finale pour l'Après-midi d'un faune*, and it would seem that the first of these, the prelude, was the only movement the composer actually completed. In a way, though, the title fits the enigmatic nature of the poetry.

Debussy's work puzzled more traditionally minded listeners of his time. They found the lack of clearly defined themes, the successions of seventh chords (m. 48–49), and the parallel fifths (m. 102) primitive in the worst sense of the word. Almost 30 years after the work's premiere, even Camille Saint-Saëns (1835–1921), one of the leading French composers of his generation, wrote privately to a friend that he could make little sense of it:

> The need to be new at any price is an illness of our era. In earlier times, in all the arts, even in the industrial arts, all artists used the same formulas, yet none of this prevented those artists of the first order from affirming their personalities. . . . But if one has no personality, then the quest for originality can lead only to the baroque, to twaddle, to clatter. . . . True, one can adjust to anything, to obscenity, even to crime itself; but it is precisely these kinds of things that one should not get used to. It has now gone well beyond accommodation. The public . . . now applauds a work in which the trumpets violently present to your ears a succession of fourths and fifths. It is a return to the earliest attempts at harmony. This is no longer music.
>
> The *Prélude à l'Après-midi d'un faune* has a pleasing sonority, but one finds in it scarcely anything that could properly be called a musical idea. It is to a work of music what an artist's palette is to a finished painting. Debussy has not created a style; he has cultivated an absence of style, of logic, and of common sense.[4]

But others found in this "absence of style" an inspiration, a new approach to music that opened the door to writing in a manner that was decidedly modern. Although no single work can be said to represent the birth of modernism, Debussy's *Prélude à l'Après-midi d'un faune* epitomizes the assault on traditional elements and attitudes that characterizes a great deal of music written at the end of the 19th century and the beginning of the 20th.

## CHALLENGES TO TONALITY

(((•◦—Listen
**CD13    Track 4**
**mysearchlab**
DEBUSSY
*Voiles*
Score Anthology II/149

For all its chromaticism and harmonic ambiguities, Debussy's *Prélude à l'Après-midi d'un faune* stands well within the tonal tradition: it ends squarely in the key of E Major. But his later *Voiles*, published in 1910 in the first book of his *Préludes* for piano, goes beyond the traditions of even advanced chromatic harmony. *Voiles* is full of parallel octaves and fifths, and its harmonies are obstinately nondirectional. Its supple rhythms add to a sensation of constant fluidity, as does its form. Although the work seems to follow a general ABA outline, we hear no clear delineation for the beginning of the middle section (m. 22 or 42?) or the return of A (m. 48 or 58?). Here as elsewhere, Debussy's music is delightfully ambiguous. Even the title has two possible meanings: "sails" or "veils."

*Voiles* also illustrates the increasing use of nontraditional scale forms in the early decades of the 20th century. Debussy constructs the melodic ideas of this work primarily from **whole-tone** and **pentatonic scales**:

- Based on six notes, each a whole tone apart (Example 20–1), the whole-tone scale subverts some of the most basic elements of diatonic harmony: it cannot be used to construct major and minor triads. In *Voiles*, Debussy uses a whole-tone scale. Here again, the effect is one of a freely floating tonality with no clear center, very much in keeping with the work's evocative title. The opening figure is based on a scale without half steps.

- Although frequently associated with East Asian music, pentatonic scales (Example 20–2)—scales based on five notes—are found in many traditional ("folk") idioms of the West as well. Debussy uses one such scale in the inner section of *Voiles*, beginning toward the end of m. 42.

A growing number of composers in the early 20th century also turned—or perhaps more appropriately, returned—to modal scales. Since about the end of the 17th century, modal scales—Dorian, Lydian, Phrygian, and so on (see Chapters 4, 6, and 7)—had been

**EXAMPLE 20–1**  Whole-tone scale

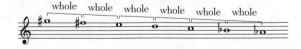

**EXAMPLE 20–2**  Pentatonic scale

used relatively little, especially outside the realm of sacred music. But composers of Debussy's generation began to draw on these modes in an attempt to break away from conventional major and minor scales. Ironically, these archaic modes gave this new music a distinctively modern sound. English composers like Ralph Vaughan Williams and Benjamin Britten were particularly attracted to modal writing, as was the song-writing team of John Lennon and Paul McCartney, whose *Norwegian Wood* (1966) uses the Mixolydian mode.

The **octatonic** scale was another important source of new sounds for composers of the early 20th century. It alternates between half and whole steps and contains within itself all possible intervals, from the minor second to the major seventh. Although the octatonic scale had been used on occasion in the 19th century for coloristic effect (by Liszt, Mussorgsky, and Rimsky-Korsakov, among others), it became an important element for such later composers as Alexander Scriabin, Debussy, Stravinsky, Maurice Ravel, and Béla Bartók. Because of its symmetrical construction and strict alternation between half and whole steps, this scale, too, tends to subvert the idea of a tonal center. Bartók's short piano piece *Diminished Fifth*, from Book 4 of his *Mikrokosmos*, repeatedly juxtaposes two **tetrachords** (four-note units) that together make up the octatonic scale outlined in Example 20–3.

(((•—|Listen
**CD13    Track 5**
**mysearchlab**
BARTÓK
*Diminished Fifth*
Score Anthology II/150

The possibilities of harmonies based on unconventional scales were almost limitless. In 1947, the composer and critic Nicolas Slonimsky published a systematic list of more than a thousand different kinds of scales, some based on as few as 2 notes, others containing as many as 12. Relatively few of the scales in Slonimsky's *Thesaurus of Scales and Melodic Patterns* were used in practice, but the exercise of compiling so many different possibilities in a single source exemplifies the attitude of experimentation that characterizes so much of the 20th century's music.

In Russia, Alexander Scriabin (1872–1915) promoted the possibilities of what he called his "mystic chord," which he believed would give his music an unusually ethereal tone. The chord (Example 20–4) consists of augmented and diminished fourths.

In the United States, Charles Ives (1874–1954), independently of Scriabin, was also experimenting with the idea of **quartal harmonies**, chords built on the interval of a fourth rather than a third. His song *The Cage* (1906) is based entirely on such chords. The unsettling text, about a leopard pacing in his cage, receives an appropriately repetitive and unsettling melody whose relentless up-and-down progression creates a kind of cage in its own right. The accompaniment provides little sense of direction, at least not within the expected conventions of triadic harmony. This brief song, in effect, is in no key at all.

(((•—|Listen
**CD13    Track 6**
**mysearchlab**
IVES
*The Cage*
Score Anthology II/151

**EXAMPLE 20–3** Octatonic scale used in m. 1–5 of Béla Bartók, *Diminished Fifth*

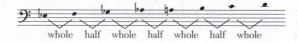

**EXAMPLE 20–4** Scriabin's "mystic chord"

### Composer Profile

# Claude Debussy (1862–1918)

Debussy's life straddled two centuries—he was born during the American Civil War and died a few months before the end of World War I—yet he is widely regarded as the first great composer of the 20th century. The inevitable association with the label of impressionism tends to obscure the genuine novelties of his music: no other single figure of his era did more to expand the possibilities of form, harmony, voice leading, and timbre.

In all this, Debussy developed a style of writing that provided a model for countless subsequent composers seeking to overthrow the cultural domination of 19th-century German music, particularly that of Beethoven, Brahms, and Wagner. Yet he remained curiously aloof from the musical scene of his day. He held no formal posts after his youth, appeared in public only sporadically as a pianist or conductor, and left behind no direct pupils. He nevertheless had many imitators (*Debussyistes*, as they were known), and his death was widely mourned throughout the musical world. Prominent composers, including Igor Stravinsky, Béla Bartók, Paul Dukas, Manuel de Falla, Maurice Ravel, and Erik Satie, contributed short pieces to the commemorative volume issued as *Le tombeau de Claude Debussy* in 1920.

## PRINCIPAL WORKS

### Piano Music

The *Suite bergamasque* (1890–1905) includes the celebrated *Claire de lune*. Debussy wrote *The Children's Corner* (1908) in a deceptively simple style: like all great works for children, it offers something to young and old alike. Its title and the titles of its individual movements are all in English, a nod to the propensity of affluent French families to hire English nannies. Each of the 24 *Préludes* (in 2 books, 1910 and 1913) bears a descriptive title that appears at the end of each piece: *The Sunken Cathedral*

**Debussy and Stravinsky.** This photo, taken around 1912 by the composer Erik Satie, documents a meeting of two of the greatest composers of the 20th century. Stravinsky, 20 years younger than his French colleague, owed much to Debussy's style, particularly in matters of form and timbre. Debussy, in turn, consulted Stravinsky about the orchestration of his ballet *Jeux*, which, like Stravinsky's *Le Sacre du printemps*, was produced for the Ballets Russes of the Russian impresario Sergei Diaghilev. Debussy acknowledged Stravinsky's present of a score of *Le Sacre* with these words: "It is a special satisfaction to tell you how much you have enlarged the boundaries of the permissible in the empire of sound."

**Source:** Bettmann/Corbis

and *The Girl with the Flaxen Hair* are two of many well-known works in this set. Each of the 12 *Etudes* (1915), implicit homages to Chopin, addresses a particular technical challenge (repeated notes, arpeggios, octaves, etc.) without sounding like an exercise.

Ives's *The Things Our Fathers Loved* (1917), a song written to a text by the composer himself, plays with traditional harmony in a different way by stringing together a series of tunes from popular songs but joining and harmonizing them in an extremely unusual manner, often in the "wrong" key. *Dixie*, at the very beginning, merges imperceptibly into *My Old Kentucky Home*, followed by *On the Banks of the Wabash* (at the words "I hear the organ on the Main Street corner"), the hymn tune *Nettleton* ("Aunt

## Orchestral Music

Debussy was a master of orchestration from the very beginning. His *Prélude à l'Après-midi d'un faune* (1894), *Nocturnes* (1899), *La Mer* ("The Sea," 1905), and *Images* (1908) are all staples of the orchestral repertory. He avoided the symphony as a genre, even though traces of the form are evident in the three-movement cycle *La Mer*.

## Dramatic Music

Although *Pelléas et Mélisande* (1902) is the only opera Debussy actually completed, he labored on several others throughout his life, including settings of two stories by Edgar Allan Poe, *The Devil in the Belfry* and *The Fall of the House of Usher*. *Jeux* (1913), a ballet with a scenario that takes place on a tennis court, was written for Diaghilev's Ballets Russes (see Focus: Sergei Diaghilev) and performed in the same year as Stravinsky's *Le Sacre du printemps*.

## Chamber Music

Debussy's String Quartet (1893) is the most frequently performed of all French quartets. Toward the end of his life, Debussy set out to write a series of six sonatas for different combinations of instruments. Unfortunately, by the time of his death he had completed only three of these works: the Sonata for Flute, Viola, and Harp (1915); the Cello Sonata (1915); and the Violin Sonata (1917).

## Songs

Debussy's songs continue the rich tradition of the French *mélodie* fostered before him by Berlioz, Fauré, Gounod, Franck, and Massenet, among others. Debussy was particularly drawn to the texts of such symbolist poets as Charles Baudelaire, Paul Verlaine, and Stéphane Mallarmé. He cultivated melodic lines that combine sinuous melody with a declamatory style; the piano is an equal partner throughout.

| KEY DATES IN THE LIFE OF DEBUSSY | |
|---|---|
| 1862 | Born in the Parisian suburb of St.-Germain-en-Laye, August 22. |
| 1872 | Admitted to the Paris Conservatory at the age of 10. |
| 1880 | Becomes the piano teacher for the children of Nadezhda von Meck, the patroness of Tchaikovsky; travels through Switzerland, Italy, and Russia, where he becomes familiar with the works of Mussorgsky. |
| 1884 | Wins the Prix de Rome, the highest compositional prize of the Paris Conservatory. |
| 1888 | Visits Bayreuth and falls briefly under the spell of Wagner's music, but struggles against this tradition over the decade, even though its influences remain evident in his only completed opera, *Pelléas et Mélisande*. |
| 1889 | Hears Javanese gamelan at the Paris Exposition and begins to experiment with new, non-Western approaches to timbre, form, and harmony. |
| 1901 | Begins writing music criticism for a Parisian journal in an attempt to pay debts. |
| 1907 | Begins a series of tours throughout Europe as a conductor and pianist. |
| 1918 | Dies in Paris on March 25. |

Sarah humming Gospels"), *The Battle Cry of Freedom* ("The village cornet band, playing in the square. The town's Red, White and Blue"), *In the Sweet Bye and Bye* ("Now! Hear the songs!") through the end of the text. The harmonizations of these tunes, all of them familiar to Ives's contemporaries, create a strange sense of distance. The familiar becomes unfamiliar, and the way in which one melodic fragment flows into the next, always to words from a different source, seems very much in keeping with the

## Composer Profile

# Charles Ives (1874–1954)

Ives was a true American original whose music incorporates many of the idioms blended in the melting pot of late-19th-century American society. As a youth in Danbury, Connecticut, he absorbed a wide variety of musical traditions: the orchestral repertory of the concert hall, hymns in church, band music at community gatherings like the Fourth of July, and popular songs in the parlors of the town's homes. Ives worked all of these styles into his own music at various times, often in the same work. And all this was merely a part-time hobby, for Ives's real profession was in the insurance business.

George Ives, the composer's father and first teacher, was a bandmaster in the Civil War and a musical eccentric in his own right who at times experimented with polytonality and quarter-tone tuning. At Yale, Charles Ives studied with a very different kind of teacher, Horatio Parker, one of the leading American composers of his era but for all intents and purposes a European composer in outlook and idiom. German trained, Parker wrote in the style of Mendelssohn, Schumann, and Brahms, and Ives absorbed the finer points of this tradition. But Ives's String Quartet no. 1, written as an undergraduate, shows his interest in other idioms as well. Subtitled *A Revival Service*, it is full of references to popular hymns of the day. The first movement is based on the hymn tune *From Greenland's Icy Mountains* by another American composer, Lowell Mason.

After graduation, Ives entered the insurance business but continued to write music in his spare time. If a composer "has a nice wife and some nice children," he once asked, "how can he let them starve on his dissonances?"[7] But he more or less stopped composing in his early to mid-40s after his health began to fail, writing only a small number of songs after his heart attack. Ives achieved only modest fame as a composer during his lifetime, in part because of the advanced idiom of his style, in part because he never really promoted himself. Many of his more

**Ives the Revolutionary: graduation portrait, Yale University, 1898.** Beneath the conventional clothing and demeanor lay an undergraduate seething at the strictures of musical convention. Ives had studied music at Yale with Horatio Parker, who was only 11 years older than Ives but already one of the most celebrated American composers of his generation. Parker was of the Old School—which is to say, the school of German tradition; Ives, in turn, came to Yale having already experimented with polytonality and quarter-tone tunings. The relationship of pupil and teacher was predictably strained.

**Source:** Lebrecht Music & Arts Photo Library/The Image Works

important works were not performed publicly until long after they had been composed. The String Quartet no. 2, for example, was written in 1913 but not performed in public until 1946, and his Symphony no. 2 (1902) had to

literary technique of the stream of consciousness developed by the modernist author James Joyce. The net result is a song that insists on its modernity even while celebrating (and quoting from) songs of the past.

The conflict between traditional and nontraditional harmonies is particularly acute in Ives's *The Unanswered Question* (1908), in which the solo trumpet and the small ensemble of flutes seem to occupy an entirely different sphere from the

wait almost 50 years for its premiere in 1951. He won the 1947 Pulitzer Prize for his Symphony no. 3 (1904), a year after its long-awaited premiere. But Ives's fame and influence have grown steadily since the 1950s, and in many ways his music was an inspiration to later composers, in part for his readiness to combine contrasting idioms, and in part because of his irreverence toward the seriousness of "high art."

# PRINCIPAL WORKS
## Orchestral Music

In spite of their eccentricities, the five symphonies (four with numbers, one titled *Holidays*) stand well within the tradition of the genre as an expression of broad, communal sentiment. The first dates from Ives's college years, the last from 1916; each differs from the others in style and the balance between philosophical depth and the familiar reference, sometimes poignant, at other times comic. Even in the final years of his life he talked of writing an enormously ambitious "Universe Symphony," which he described as "a striving to . . . contemplate in tones rather than in music . . . to paint the creation, the mysterious beginnings of all things, known through God to man, to trace with tonal imprints the vastness, the evolution of all life, in nature of humanity from the great roots of life to the spiritual eternities, from the great unknown to the great unknown."[8] Ives also wrote a number of programmatic works for orchestra, including *Three Places in New England* and *The Unanswered Question*.

## Piano and Chamber Music

Ives wrote a *Three-Page Sonata* for piano in 1905 and his Sonata no. 1 in 1909. His Sonata no. 2—subtitled *Concord, Mass., 1840–1860* and inspired by the writings of fellow New Englanders Emerson, Hawthorne, the Alcotts, and Thoreau—is widely regarded as one of his finest works in any genre. Ives published the work at his own expense in 1919. In addition to two string quartets, Ives also wrote four violin sonatas; a trio for violin, clarinet, and piano; and a piano trio.

## Vocal Music

In 1922 Ives collected and published at his own expense a volume entitled *114 Songs* for distribution to friends free of charge. These works, like his many compositions for chorus, range from exceedingly simple to exceedingly complex, spanning his entire career.

| KEY DATES IN THE LIFE OF IVES | |
|---|---|
| 1874 | Born October 20 in Danbury, Connecticut. |
| 1894 | Enters Yale University, where he studies composition with Horatio Parker, one of the leading American composers of the day. |
| 1898 | Graduates from Yale and enters the insurance business. |
| 1907 | Establishes an insurance firm of his own in partnership with George Myrick and plays an important role in developing the modern industry of life insurance. |
| 1918 | Suffers heart attack and begins a long period of ill health that will last until his death. |
| 1922 | Publishes and distributes to friends, at his own expense, *114 Songs*. |
| 1947 | Receives the Pulitzer Prize for his Third Symphony, written in 1911. |
| 1954 | Dies May 19 in New York City. |

strings, which speak in slow, measured, choralelike tones, using the tonal language of conventional triads. Dissonance in the strings is carefully controlled and resolved: the entire string part, in fact, looks and sounds almost like a student essay in species counterpoint, not terribly different from the kind of exercises Beethoven had worked out under the critical eye of Haydn (see Chapter 12). The solo trumpet, by contrast, repeatedly poses a five-note figure that implies no harmonic center at all

(B♭–C♯–E–E♭–C, or, in some instances, ending with a B♮ instead of a C). The winds, in turn, are even more tonally diffused and grow rhythmically more independent. The work ends with a serene, perfect authentic G-Major triad, yet the sensation it creates is not one of resolution.

In his foreword to the score of *The Unanswered Question*, Ives gave some hint as to the symbolism behind these contrasting elements:

> The strings play *ppp* throughout with no change in tempo. They are to stand for "The Silence of the Druids—Who Know, See and Hear Nothing." The trumpet intones "The Perennial Question of Existence," and repeatedly states it in the same tone of voice each time. But the hunt for "The Invisible Answer" undertaken by the flutes, and other human beings, becomes gradually more active, faster and louder through an *animando* [animatedly] to a *con fuoco* [with fire]. This part need not be played in the exact time position indicated. It is played in somewhat of an impromptu way; if there be no conductor, one of the flute players may direct their playing. "The Fighting Answerers," as the time goes on, and after a "secret conference," seem to realize a futility, and begin to mock "The Question"—the strife is over for the moment. After they disappear, "The Question" is asked for the last time, and "The Silences" are heard beyond in "Undisturbed Solitude."[5]

It is revealing that Ives should choose to represent this metaphysical debate through a simultaneous contrast of the musical old (conventional harmony and regular rhythms within a single tempo) and the musical new (unconventional harmony and irregular rhythms within shifting tempos). Like other modernist composers of the early 20th century, Ives felt the need to challenge listeners out of what he perceived to be their all-too-comfortable habit of listening to "beautiful" music—listeners who, like the Druids of *The Unanswered Question*, are content within themselves and oblivious to all that is around them. Ives elsewhere wrote,

> [B]eauty in music is too often confused with something that lets the ear lie back in an easy chair. Many sounds that we are used to do not bother us, and for that reason we are inclined to call them beautiful. Frequently—possibly almost invariably—analytical and impersonal tests will show, we believe, that when a new or unfamiliar work is accepted as beautiful on its first hearing, its fundamental quality is one that tends to put the mind to sleep. A narcotic is not always unnecessary, but it is seldom a basis of progress—that is, wholesome evolution in any creative experience.[6]

Ives was profoundly disturbed by what he perceived as the tendency of most music to take the easy path of sentimentality and convention. After hearing a performance by the Kneisel Quartet, one of the premier chamber ensembles of the early 20th century, he declared, "[They] played so exquisitely 'nice' that I lost some respect for those four instruments. A whole evening of mellifluous sounds, perfect cadences, perfect ladies, perfect programs, and not a dissonant cuss word to stop the anemia and beauty during the whole evening." In his own Second String Quartet, Ives said he wanted to make "those men fiddlers get up and do something like men," and he peppered the score with such half-facetious indications as "Largo sweetota" and "Allegro con fisto swato."

As is so often the case with "nationalist" composers, Ives's music is considered so quintessentially American that the nationalist surface of his work has often deflected attention from more fundamental elements of his approach to music. At least one European contemporary, however, Arnold Schoenberg (see Chapter 21), understood Ives's attitude. Writing as an exile in Los Angeles in 1945, Schoenberg noted that "There is a great man living in this country—a composer. He has solved the problem of how to preserve one's self and to learn. He responds to negligence by contempt. He is not forced to accept praise or blame. His name is Ives."[9]

# RADICAL PRIMITIVISM

Modernism's rejection of tradition assumed many forms in the early 20th century. One of the most powerful of these was **primitivism**, sometimes referred to more specifically as radical primitivism. *Primitive* is often used as a derogatory term, but as an aesthetic movement in the early 20th century, primitivism was considered a positive, purifying force in all the arts. The impetus behind primitivism was a rejection of the self-imposed, arbitrary conventions of Western culture. Primitive peoples, what the Enlightenment philosopher Jean-Jacques Rousseau had called "noble savages," were uneducated and unrefined and for that very reason all the more genuine and pure. The primitive was regarded as a source of both beauty and strength, representing a stage of civilization unthreatened by decadence and self-consciousness. In painting, primitivism manifested itself in the work of the group of artists known as the *fauves*— the "wild beasts"—who used a seemingly crude kind of draftsmanship, coupled with bold, unrealistic colors. These artists owed much to Paul Gauguin (1848–1903), who had abandoned his career as a Parisian stockbroker to move to Tahiti in the South Pacific, where he devoted his life to painting; and to Henri Rousseau (1844–1910), another Frenchman who painted in a style critics initially derided as childlike and

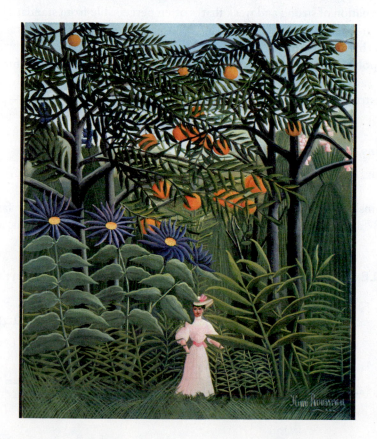

**Primitivism in painting.** Musical primitivism had parallels in the visual arts. Henri Rousseau (1844–1910) painted fantastical visions that often juxtapose humans and nature. Here, in *Femme se promenant dans une forêt exotique* (*Woman Walking in an Exotic Forest*), completed in 1905, the exotic nature of the subject, the simplicity of line, and the bold colors of the flowers all suggest that true power resides not in the civilized woman—a small, isolated, and partly hidden figure in this painting—but in the tropical forest with its improbably oversized plants. Like Stravinsky's music for *Le Sacre du printemps,* Rousseau's art is sophisticated, even while conveying a sense of raw power, unrefined and elemental.

**Source:** Woman Walking in an Exotic Forest, 1905 (oil on canvas), Rousseau, Henri J.F. (Le Douanier) (1844–1910)/ The Barnes Foundation, Merion, Pennsylvania, USA/ The Bridgeman Art Library

simplistic. But Rousseau's striking use of line and color—as in his *Femme se promenant dans une forêt exotique* (*Woman Walking in an Exotic Forest*), see page 525—was soon recognized for its boldness.

Musical primitivism manifested itself in many ways over the course of the 20th century, particularly in the work of composers who sought to elevate rhythm to a level of unprecedented importance. Rhythm, after all, is the most basic of all musical elements, for music can exist without harmony and even without melody, but not without rhythm. Composers associated with primitivism also tended to abandon or substantially alter such "civilized"—arbitrary—concepts as voice leading, triadic harmony, and the major and minor forms of the diatonic scale.

All of these traits are evident in Igor Stravinsky's ballet *Le Sacre du printemps* ("The Rite of Spring," 1913), subtitled "Pictures from Pagan Russia." By rejecting traditional harmonic progressions, timbres, and above all rhythms, Stravinsky was able to create a score that reflected the same kind of raw, elemental relationship between humans and nature that is represented on stage through the story of the dance. The ballet's scenario centers on a pre-Christian ritual that welcomes the coming of spring and offers in thanks to the gods a human sacrifice—primitive and uncivilized to be sure, but consequently all the more elemental and powerful. Stravinsky elevated the role of rhythm in this ritual in a number of ways, sometimes through complexity, sometimes through simplicity. Just before the moment of sacrifice at the end of the piece, audiences hear a passage in which the meter shifts no fewer than 8 times in the span of only 12 measures (Example 20–5).

In Part I (Adoration of the Earth), the passage beginning at m. 88 is equally unpredictable, even though it is based on a series of repeating eighth-note chords. Stravinsky strips the music of all harmonic and melodic variety. The orchestra, in effect, functions as a kind of giant, polychordal drum, repeating the same chord 32 times in succession (Example 20–6). By marking each iteration with a down bow, Stravinsky eliminates the slight alternation of strong and weak that is often perceptible from standard back-and-forth (down-up) bowing, and by placing accents at irregular intervals, he eradicates any sense of a rhythmic pattern.

The **polytonal** harmony of this same passage (Example 20–6) posed further challenges to early listeners. Contrasting triads are juxtaposed simultaneously, with each of four instrumental groups—two sets of horns, high strings, low strings—playing its own chord:

| | |
|---|---|
| **Violins, violas, horns 1–4** | E♭[7] chord (E♭-G-B♭-D♭) |
| **Cellos, basses, horns 5–8** | E Major chord (F♭-A♭-C♭ = E-G♯-B) |

Stravinsky juxtaposes arpeggiated chords in an even more jarring fashion: an implied B♭[7] arpeggio in the English horn, against C major in the bassoons, against an

**Listen**
CD13   Track 9
**mysearchlab**
STRAVINSKY
*Le Sacre du printemps*
Score Anthology II/153

**EXAMPLE 20–5** Stravinsky, *Le Sacre du printemps*, Sacrificial Dance (rhythm only)

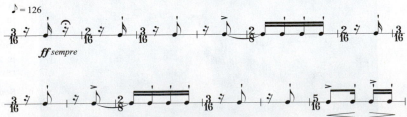

alternation of E major and E minor in the cellos (Example 20–7). Each chord is perfectly tonal within itself, but the simultaneous sounding of these chords rubbed many ears the wrong way, at least on first hearing in 1913. Within a decade, however, the elemental power of the score had won over a large following of critics and listeners alike.

For all its appeal to the aesthetics of primitivism, Stravinsky's *Le Sacre du printemps* is technically quite advanced and very much a product of the early 20th century. The

**EXAMPLE 20–6** Measures 1–8 after no. 13

**EXAMPLE 20–7** Measures 1–4 after no. 14

orchestra is enormous, even by the standards of its time, and represents the product of hundreds of years of development and innovation:

*Woodwinds*
1 piccolo
3 flutes, 1 doubling on second piccolo
1 alto flute
1 English horn
4 oboes, 1 doubling on second
   English horn
1 E♭ clarinet
3 clarinets, 1 doubling on second bass
   clarinet
1 bass clarinet
4 bassoons, 1 doubling on second
   contrabassoon
1 contrabassoon

*Brass*
8 French horns, 2 doubling on tenor tubas
1 high trumpet (D trumpet)
4 trumpets
1 bass trumpet
3 trombones
2 bass tubas

*Percussion*
Timpani, bass drum, cymbals, gong,
   güiro, tambourine, triangle

*Strings*
First violins, second violins, violas, cellos,
   double bass

But Stravinsky often uses these instruments in unconventional ways to create an *impression* of rawness. The very opening of the ballet illustrates this point quite well. The high range of the bassoon makes the instrument sound strained, and the disconnected entrances of the other winds contribute to a sensation of hearing the orchestra in an inarticulate, almost chaotic state. We do not hear the traditions of Bach, Beethoven, or Brahms in these measures, but a more elemental, unrefined means of expression.

Textures in *Le Sacre du printemps* are correspondingly complex. The passage beginning at figure 11, for example, presents no fewer than 18 distinct and rhythmically unique ideas all at the same time:

- Flutes and piccolos (5 rhythmically independent ideas)
- Oboes and English horn (2)
- Clarinets (4)
- Bassoons (1)
- Horns (1)
- Piccolo trumpet (1)
- Solo violin (1)
- Violas (1)
- Cellos (1)
- Double basses (1)

Although composers had created layered textures many times before, no one had ever constructed anything quite this intricate. For most orchestras, the challenge of performing passages like this lies not in the pitches, but rather in the coordination of so many rhythmically independent parts.

The audience rioted at the premiere of *Le Sacre du printemps* in Paris in May 1913. As the composer himself later recalled,

The complexity of my score had demanded a great number of rehearsals, which [Pierre] Monteux had conducted with his usual skill and attention. As for the actual performance, I am not in a position to judge, as I left the auditorium [to stand backstage in the wings] at the first bars of the prelude, which had at once evoked derisive laughter. I was disgusted. These demonstrations, at first isolated, soon became general, provoking counter-demonstrations and very quickly developing into a terrific uproar. During the whole performance

I was at [the choreographer Vaslav] Nijinsky's side in the wings. He was standing on a chair, screaming "sixteen, seventeen, eighteen"—they had their own method of counting to keep time. Naturally, the poor dancers could hear nothing by reason of the row in the auditorium and the sound of their own dance steps. I had to hold Nijinsky by his clothes, for he was furious, and ready to dash on to the stage at any moment and create a scandal. [The impresario Sergei] Diaghilev kept ordering the electricians to turn the lights on or off, hoping in that way to put a stop to the noise. That is all I can remember about that first performance. Oddly enough, at the dress rehearsal, to which we had, as usual, invited a number of actors, painters, musicians, writers, and the most cultured representatives of society, everything had gone off peacefully, and I was very far from expecting such an outburst.[10]

The noted Parisian critic Pierre Lalo spoke for many of his contemporaries when he characterized the work in these terms:

The essential characteristic of *Le Sacre du printemps* is that it is the most dissonant and the most discordant composition that has ever been written. . . . Never before has the system and cult of the wrong note been applied with such industry, zeal, and obstinacy. From the first measure of the work to the last, whatever note one expects is never the note that follows; instead, we get the note next to it, that is, the note that should not come. Whatever the previous chord, the chord one actually hears, and this chord and this note are used expressly to produce the impression of falseness that is acute and almost excruciating. When two themes are superimposed, the composer scarcely uses themes that might work together; quite to the contrary, he chooses themes whose superimposition produces the most irritating friction and grating that can be imagined.[11]

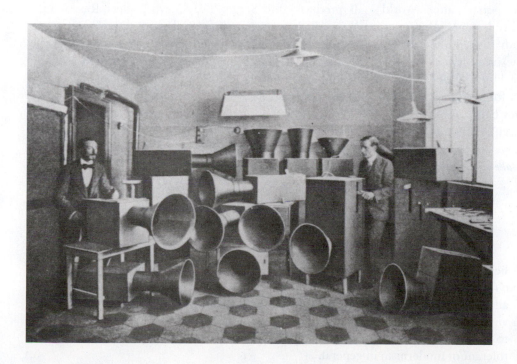

**The art of noises.** One of the more curious manifestations of musical modernism was the movement known as Futurism, led by the Italian composer Luigi Russolo (1885–1947). Russolo, shown here on the left, was determined to break down what he considered the artificial barriers between music and noise. To this end, he designed a great many "Noise-Makers" (*Intonarumori*—in Italian, *rumor* is the word for "noise"). During the 1910s and 1920s Russolo mounted a series of concerts using these instruments in works with such colorful titles as *The Gathering of Automobiles and Airplanes* and *The Awakening of a City.*

**Source:** Hulton Archive/Stringer/Getty Images

## Composer Profile

# Igor Stravinsky (1882–1971)

Stravinsky occupies a central place in the history of 20th-century music not only because of the quality of his works but also because of their remarkable range and variety. He was a true cosmopolitan who at various times called Russia, France, Switzerland, and the United States home. Like almost every composer of his generation, he absorbed the chromaticism and bombast of late Romanticism, but he went on to explore other idioms as well, including primitivism, Neoclassicism and, in the last 15 years of his life, even serial composition. His detractors called him a "musical chameleon," but the epithet does not give due credit to his remarkable ability to assimilate new styles and approaches to music. The phases of his career break down roughly in this way:

- *Russian period.* Like almost every other composer of his generation, Stravinsky began writing in a style of advanced chromaticism. The early ballets written for Diaghilev—*L'oiseau de feu* ("The Firebird"), *Petrouchka*—belong very much to the traditions of the 19th century. *Le Sacre du printemps* and *Les Noces* ("The Wedding") both mark a turn to primitivism; in their modal inflections, polytonality, and impulsive rhythmic vitality, both capture the spirit of what Stravinsky called "Pagan Russia."

- *Neoclassical period.* In the period after World War I, Stravinsky changed styles, moving toward a greater economy of both means and expression (see Chapter 22). The intensity of *Le Sacre* gave way to the cool detachment ("objectivity") of the Octet, the Concerto for Piano and Winds, *Pulcinella* (another Diaghilev ballet, based on pre-existent 18th-century material), the *Symphony in C*, the *Symphony in Three Movements*, the *Symphony of Psalms*, and the opera *The Rake's Progress*.

- *Serialist period.* Prompted in part by his personal assistant, Robert Craft, Stravinsky began studying serial music in the early 1950s and was drawn to the works of Anton Webern in particular. His own serial compositions using this technique include the ballet *Agon* (1957, only partly serial), *Threni* (1958), and the *Requiem Canticles* (1966).

Even during his lifetime Stravinsky was widely considered one of the century's two greatest composers (the other was Schoenberg). He always seemed to stay one step ahead of everyone else, reinventing himself at various points along the way. In spite of his avowed modernism (more than one critic dubbed him "Modernsky"), his music found a relatively wide following among concertgoers. Although he had no direct students, his influence on subsequent generations of composers was profound. (For a photo of Stravinsky, see p. 520.)

# PRINCIPAL WORKS
## Ballets and Other Orchestral Works

Stravinsky made his early mark in the world through his ballets, particularly *L'oiseau de feu* (1910), *Petrouchka* (1911), *Le Sacre du printemps* (1913), and *Les Noces* (1920), all produced for Sergei Diaghilev's Ballets Russes in Paris. All three use striking orchestral effects, and the combined brilliance of their music and choreography soon propelled Stravinsky into the forefront of modernist composers. His later ballets include *Apollon Musagète* (1928), commissioned by the Elizabeth Sprague Coolidge Foundation and premiered in Washington, DC, at the Library of Congress; *Perséphone* (1934), with recitation and chorus, to a text by André Gide; *Jeu de cartes* ("Card Game," 1937); and *Orpheus* (1948).

But the riot soon turned to Stravinsky's advantage. It certainly provided good publicity, and within a few short months, audiences across Europe were greeting *Le Sacre du printemps* with great enthusiasm. The initial rejection of the work served to rally all artists of modernist tendencies. They saw in this incident a vindication of artistic vision in the face of conservative public tastes. Audiences, in turn, became less likely to express disapproval in such a disruptive fashion and began to become increasingly tolerant of modernism in general.

The reputation of the ballets tends to overshadow that of the symphonies, all of which are significant works in the history of the genre: the *Symphony for Winds* (1920, written in memory of Debussy), the *Symphony in C* (1940), the *Symphony in Three Movements* (1945), and above all the *Symphony of Psalms* (1930) for chorus and orchestra, commissioned by the Boston Symphony Orchestra. Stravinsky also wrote several significant (and quite individual) concertos: for piano and winds (1924), for violin (1931), for clarinet and swing band (the *Ebony Concerto*, 1946), for chamber orchestra (the Dumbarton Oaks Concerto, 1938), and for string orchestra (the Concerto in D, 1947).

## Vocal and Dramatic Works

*L'Histoire du soldat* ("The Soldier's Tale," 1918) is scored for narrator and seven instrumentalists and written in Stravinsky's Neo-classical style, as is the "opera-oratorio" *Oedipus Rex* (1927), based on Sophocles' drama, which can be performed either in concert or as a theatrical piece. *The Rake's Progress* (1951), acknowledged by most to be Stravinsky's greatest opera, set to an English-language libretto by W. H. Auden and Chester Kallman, was inspired by a series of engravings by the 18th-century English artist William Hogarth; the work traces the decline and fall of a libertine.

## Chamber Works

In addition to the Octet (1923), Stravinsky wrote a number of small-scale works for chamber ensembles: the *Duo concertante* for violin and piano; The Septet for piano, strings, and winds (1954); and an instrumental arrangement of three madrigals by the Renaissance composer Gesualdo (1960).

| KEY DATES IN THE LIFE OF STRAVINSKY | |
|---|---|
| 1882 | Born June 17, son of the famous bassist Feodor Stravinsky, in Oranieneburg, near St. Petersburg. |
| 1903 | While studying law, begins private lessons with Nikolai Rimsky-Korsakov, the leading Russian composer of his day. |
| 1910 | Premiere of the ballet *L'oiseau de feu* in Paris, commissioned by the Russian impresario Sergei Diaghilev. |
| 1911 | Moves to Paris and produces a string of stunningly successful ballets for Diaghilev: *Petrouchka* (1911), *Le Sacre du printemps* (1913), *Le Rossignol* (1914), *Pulcinella* (1920), *Les Noces* (1923). |
| 1925 | First American tour; he receives many commissions from American patrons and institutions from this point onward. |
| 1934 | Becomes a French citizen. |
| 1939 | Leaves France, settles in Hollywood, and becomes an American citizen in 1945. |
| 1939–1940 | Delivers (in French) the Charles Eliot Norton Lectures at Harvard University, largely ghostwritten by the composer Roland-Alexis Manuel Lévy. |
| 1950–1962 | Tours and conducts widely, including a return to the Soviet Union in 1962, where he is welcomed warmly. |
| 1971 | Dies in New York on April 6 and is buried in Venice, near Diaghilev. |

# NATIONALISM

Musical nationalism, like primitivism, was driven by a desire to assert cultural identity through a musical idiom connected to the people. Already evident in the 19th century (see Chapters 14 and 18), musical nationalism took on new importance in the 20th with the growing political and cultural aspirations of ethnic groups throughout Europe and the Americas. A "nation" in this sense is a community that may or may not

## Focus  SERGEI DIAGHILEV

Few nonmusicians exerted such an enormous effect on 20th-century music. As a producer, an impresario, Sergei Diaghilev (1872–1929) assembled teams of artists that included painters, dancers, choreographers, conductors, and composers. Finding just the right mix of talent could yield impressive results, and Diaghilev scored success after success in the first three decades of the 20th century. The "Russian Ballet" did in fact consist largely (but not exclusively) of Russian dancers, but the list of other artists Diaghilev engaged at various times includes many of the early 20th century's most distinguished figures:

- **Composers** Erik Satie, Igor Stravinsky, Sergei Prokofiev, Claude Debussy, Maurice Ravel, Darius Milhaud, Francis Poulenc, Manuel de Falla

- **Artists and stage designers** Pablo Picasso, Léon Bakst, Juan Gris, Georges Braque, Max Ernst, Juan Miró, Giorgio de Chirico

- **Dancers** Vaslav Nijinsky, Tamara Karsavina, Léonide Massine, George Balanchine, Anna Pavlova, Serge Lifar

Diaghilev's troupe cultivated many different styles of dance, but he is best remembered for his abandonment of the classical traditions of dance, moving away from graceful movements and women dancing *en pointe* (on the point of their toes) and toward a more vigorous, athletic kind of dance. The choreography for Stravinsky's *Le Sacre du printemps* exemplifies this new approach to ballet.

**Sergei Diaghilev, ca. 1916.** The Russian impresario found great success in Paris through his collaborations with Stravinsky and other artists, including composers, poets, painters, and choreographers.

**Source:** Lebrecht Music & Arts Photo Library

coincide with the political boundaries of a given state: the members of this community are bound by varying combinations of ethnicity, cultural beliefs, customs, traditions, language, and music. The Austro-Hungarian Empire, ruled by the Habsburg dynasty from its German-speaking capital of Vienna, provides a good example of the potential contrasts (and conflicts) between the political entity of the state and the many cultures within it. In 1900, it extended across portions or all of what are now Austria, Hungary, the Czech Republic, Slovakia, Croatia, Slovenia, Bosnia, Herzegovina, Serbia, Romania, the Ukraine, Poland, and even Italy. The central government recognized no fewer than 11 official languages: German, Hungarian, Czech, Slovak, Croatian, Slovene, Serbian, Romanian, Ukrainian, Polish, and Italian.

Music played an important role for each of these cultural and linguistic groups to assert its ethnic identity.

When Béla Bartók set out into the field to record the melodies sung and played by peasants (see the photograph in Composer Profile: Béla Bartók), he was thus attempting to capture not only a repertory of songs but also the very identity of the ethnic groups singing them. Bartók and others like him were driven in part by the belief that folk song represents the untarnished purity of preindustrial society. "Folk music," the

English folk song collector Cecil Sharp declared, "is the ungarbled and ingenuous expression of the human mind, and on that account it must reflect the essential and basic qualities of the human mind." After collecting folk songs throughout the British Isles for several decades, Sharp (1859–1924) transferred his base of operations to the Appalachian region of the United States in the belief that only in the backwoods and mountains of a former colony could he find what he considered to be the true spirit of the English peoples. The English composer Ralph Vaughan Williams (1872–1958) made his own intensive study of English folk song and frequently incorporated such melodies into his own music.

For modernist composers, folk music offered important stylistic alternatives to the traditions of conventional melody and harmony. Bartók and his colleague Zoltán Kodály (1882–1967) found an altogether different set of melodic possibilities in the folk music of various ethnic groups they collected throughout central and eastern Europe. The two made frequent use of distinctively ethnic characteristics in their own music. They often incorporated irregular rhythms and meters and generally avoided the conventions of functional harmony, preferring instead to substitute intervals of the second, fourth, and seventh in favor of the traditional triad. They also drew on a variety of nondiatonic scales, including whole tone and pentatonic.

Bartók in particular favored the kind of irregular meters that characterize a good deal of the folk music of eastern Europe. The first of his *Six Dances in Bulgarian Rhythm* from his *Mikrokosmos*, Book 6, for example, is built on a metrical pattern notated as follows:

$$\frac{4 + 2 + 3}{8}$$

This kind of meter is sometimes referred to as complex meter, and although it ostensibly had its origins in folk music, it found its way into much modernist music as well.

Nor were Bartók and Kodaly alone in such ventures. Stravinsky, as we have seen, drew on recent Russian scholarship of the time and adapted several published folk melodies to great effect in *Le Sacre du printemps*. Charles Ives worked many traditional American melodies not only into his songs, but also his symphonies and string quartets. George Gershwin, in turn, regarded jazz as "an American folk music; not the only one but a very powerful one which is probably in the blood and feeling of the American people more than any other style." Gershwin's *Rhapsody in Blue* (1924), for piano and orchestra, was one of the earliest of many works by American composers to integrate the jazz idiom into the repertory of the concert hall.

In Brazil, Heitor Villa-Lobos (1887–1959) recorded and collected popular tunes throughout his native land and used many of their melodies and rhythms in his own compositions. His nine *Bachianas Brasileiras*, written for various instruments and ensembles, integrate characteristically Brazilian musical elements with the traditions of J. S. Bach. In this regard, these works are party neo-classical (see Chapter 22) and partly modernist. The *Bachianas Brasileiras* no. 4 (1930), originally written for piano and later orchestrated by the composer, illustrates both of these tendencies. The formal structure of the work follows the pattern of a Baroque suite: it opens with a Preludio (*Preludio*) that is reminiscent of the broken chordal style typical of many Bach preludes. The second-movement Chorale (*Coral: Canto de Sorato*) features the texture and rhythms of a Bach-like chorale but with decidedly modernist harmonies and interjections; the melody derives from a Catholic religious song sung in northeastern Brazil. The third-movement *Aria* is based on a folksong from the same region

((•• Listen
CD13    Track 9
mysearchlab
BARTÓK
*Six Dances in Bulgarian Rhythm*
Score Anthology II/154

((•• Listen
CD13    Track 10
mysearchlab
VILLA-LOBOS
*Bachianas Brasileiras no.4*
Score Anthology II/155

## Composer Profile

# Béla Bartók (1881–1945)

Alongside his conventional training as a pianist and composer, Béla Bartók developed an intense interest in the folk musics of central and eastern Europe. He took advantage of recent developments in recording technology to make what we would now call field recordings, and his published transcriptions attempt to capture nuances of singing and playing not normally notated in concert repertory. Bartók had a keen ear for the more fluid sense of pitch and meter in the unwritten tradition, along with its flexible rhythms and distinctive timbres.

This kind of music eventually worked its influence on Bartók's own compositions. He wrote his earliest works in the style of Brahms, but from about 1905 onward most of his music incorporates at least some elements that give it an ethnic sound. For Bartók, the idioms of the people offered a source of inspiration and tradition that was at once genuine and a departure from the established (and predominantly German) tradition of Bach, Haydn, Mozart, Beethoven, and Brahms. Bartók sometimes used folk tunes more or less directly, adding harmonies; on other occasions he created original tunes with folklike inflections.

Bartók emigrated to the United States in 1940, but beyond a small group of dedicated enthusiasts, his music did not generate much immediate interest in North America. His *Concerto for Orchestra* (1944), however, commissioned by Serge Koussevitsky, the conductor of the Boston Symphony Orchestra, soon established itself as one of the most popular of all 20th-century orchestral works. Already ill, the composer died of leukemia less than a year after its premiere.

**Bartók records in the field (1908).** Bartók was one of the first researchers to make field recordings of folk musicians. His recordings and transcriptions of music from across eastern Europe remain a valuable source of information for ethnographers. In Bartók's day, the musical traditions of the remote villages he visited were still relatively untouched by the growing influence of urbanization, radio, and recorded sound. The villagers are dressed in their Sunday finest: this is, after all, a memorable day in the life of the village. But their garb manifests a more subtle problem faced by field workers who go out to collect "authentic" data. The formality of the occasion might well affect the nature of the performance. Would a villager dressed in his Sunday finest sing for an outsider with a strange recording device in exactly the same way as when dressed in ordinary work clothes singing in an everyday setting?

**Source:** Alfredo Dagli Orti/The Art Archive/Corbis

# PRINCIPAL WORKS

## Orchestral Works

The *Music for Strings, Percussion, and Celesta* (1937) and *Concerto for Orchestra* (1944) are two of the most popular of all 20th-century orchestral works. The Violin Concerto (1939) and the Third Piano Concerto (1945) have also established themselves in the repertory. Other works for orchestra include the Concerto for Two Pianos and Orchestra (1942, an arrangement of his own Sonata for Two Pianos and Percussion) and the Viola Concerto (1945, completed by his pupil Tibor Serly).

of the country. The concluding *Dansa: Miudinho* is a whirlwind toccata-like finale that evokes the rapid gigues that Bach occasionally used as a finale to his keyboard partitas. Villa-Lobos quotes no specific tunes here, but the Latin dance rhythms are unmistakable. Along the way, a slower-moving theme stands out against the rapidly moving voices in a manner reminiscent of Bach's treatment of the chorale melody in the opening movement of Cantata 78.

## Vocal and Dramatic Works

*Bluebeard's Castle* (1911), an opera in one act, and especially the ballets *The Wooden Prince* (1917) and *The Miraculous Mandarin* (1919) are admired but have not achieved the popularity of some of the orchestral works.

## Chamber Music

The six string quartets rank among the greatest in the literature. As in the case of Beethoven, we can trace the composer's development from early to late styles in these works, which explore an astonishing variety of forms, tones, and instrumental techniques. Bartók's two sonatas for violin and piano, as well as a sonata for solo violin, are also significant additions to the repertory.

## Piano Music

In the tradition of J. S. Bach, Bartók wrote many pedagogical works for his own children and pupils, most notably *Mikrokosmos*, a set of 153 progressive works, many of them influenced by his work as a collector of traditional musics. His *Allegro barbaro* and his many Hungarian and Romanian dances for piano also incorporate folklike elements.

| KEY DATES IN THE LIFE OF BARTÓK | |
| --- | --- |
| 1881 | Born March 25 in Nagyszentmiklós, in the Transylvania region of Hungary (now Romania). |
| 1899 | Enters the Royal Academy of Music in Budapest and studies both piano and composition. |
| 1905 | Begins collaboration with the composer Zoltán Kodály to collect folk music of central and eastern Europe; continues to travel to remote regions to record and transcribe the songs and instrumental music of many different ethnic groups. |
| 1907 | Appointed piano instructor at Royal Academy of Music, Budapest. |
| 1922 | Tours London and Paris, performing his own music and accompanying a number of noted violinists. |
| 1927–1928 | Makes his first tours of the United States and the Soviet Union. |
| 1934 | Commissioned by the Hungarian Academy of Sciences to prepare an edition of some thirteen thousand Hungarian folk songs; the work would be completed and published posthumously. |
| 1940 | Emigrates to the United States and settles in New York; receives an honorary degree from Columbia University. |
| 1941 | Takes position as research fellow at Columbia to pursue folk song studies; receives several major commissions for new compositions. |
| 1945 | Dies in New York on September 26. |

# NEW TIMBRES

In addition to rhythm and pitch, many modernist composers of the early 20th century sought novelty in timbre, through new instruments or new ways of playing old instruments.

Although the 20th century brought relatively few technical changes to the piano itself, composers developed many novel ways of using the existing instrument. One

((•• Listen
CD13    Track 11
mysearchlab
COWELL
*The Banshee*
Score Anthology II/156

new technique involved direct contact with the piano strings, bypassing the keys, with the piano top open or removed altogether. In *The Banshee* (1925), for example, the American composer Henry Cowell (1897–1965) calls on the performer to manipulate by hand the strings inside the instrument. The work actually requires two performers, although the sole responsibility of the one at the keyboard is to keep the damper pedal down throughout the entire work. The other player stands in the crook of the instrument and touches the strings. Cowell's explanation of the special performance symbols for the work takes up almost as much space as the score itself. The opening of the piece calls for the standing player to "sweep with the flesh of the finger from the lowest string up to the note given," ending with another lengthwise sweep of the finger on the string of that highest note. Different sounds are gradually introduced: the sweep concludes with a pluck of strings, then with a sweep along the strings of three notes together, then sweeping with the back of the fingernails instead of the fleshy part of the finger, and so on. The unearthly effect is unlike anything anyone had heard from a piano before this time. The eerie quality of the sound fits with the work's title. In Cowell's own words, a banshee is "a woman of the Inner World . . . who is charged with the duty of taking your soul into the Inner World when you die. . . . She has to come to the outer plane for this purpose, and she finds the outer plane very uncomfortable and unpleasant, so you will hear her wailing at the time of a death in your family."[12]

In some of his other works for piano, like *Advertisement* (1914), Cowell pioneered the use of tone clusters, directing that adjacent keys be struck with the forearm, flat of the hand, or some object of an appropriate shape, such as a block of wood. This technique foreshadowed the sounds of the "prepared piano" devised by one of Cowell's

**Henry Cowell.** In addition to composing and performing, Cowell was a renowned writer on music and made important recordings of music from outside the Western art tradition. He was an early champion of the music of Charles Ives and later held teaching positions at Peabody Conservatory (1951–1956) and Columbia University (1949–1965). In the opinion of John Cage, Cowell provided the "open sesame" for new music.

**Source:** Everett Collection

pupils, John Cage (see Chapter 23), who in the 1940s began placing objects like paper clips and pieces of rubber and wood on the strings to produce unusual sounds.

Edgard Varèse's *Ionisation* (1931) is another seminal work reflecting the growing range of sounds available to 20th-century composers. The title comes from the world of particle physics, and the timbre is appropriately abstract and challenging. *Ionisation* is the first major composition to have been written entirely for percussion. Most of the 37 instruments have no definite pitch at all: 4 tam-tams, gong, cymbals, 3 different sizes of bass drum, bongos, snare drums, güiro ("scraper"), slapsticks, Chinese blocks, claves ("rhythm sticks"), triangle, maracas ("shakers"), sleigh bells, castanets, tambourine, anvils, and 2 sirens. Previously, these sounds would have been used for special effects and ethnic references: church bells (Berlioz), working anvils (Verdi and Wagner operas), castanets and tambourines for Hispanic-flavored music (Bizet), or cowbells (Mahler symphonies). The entrance of pitched instruments (piano, celesta, chimes) toward the end of *Ionisation* creates a strange sensation, for by this point listeners have somehow grown accustomed to the sound of no pitches of any kind. Much as happens with the "Tristan chord" in pieces discussed earlier, the familiar is made unfamiliar, or at least awkward, in context.

When analysts speak of the different "themes" and "subjects" in this work, then, they are talking almost exclusively about rhythms and timbres, not pitch. We are so accustomed to hearing musical structures on the basis of pitch and harmony that the formal element of repetition in this particular work is often not readily apparent on first hearing. The first subject, for example, which appears after an eight-measure introduction, returns in modified form, then again in fragmentary form toward the very end.

Like a good many modernist pieces, *Ionisation* alienated its share of critics. One of them—writing anonymously—had this to say about the work's premiere, in New York's Carnegie Hall, in 1933:

> Varèse's latest effort, played twice, contains almost nothing of traditional tonal quality, being scored for various gatling-gun species of percussion, a dolorous and quaintly modulated siren, sleigh bells and an ingenious instrument that imitated the voice of an anguished bull. Toward the end of this strange work, which moved even earnest devotees of the musically esoteric to smiles, there was a slight undercurrent of the lyrical in some muted tones of a piano and a celesta.[13]

Although such reviews make for entertaining reading today, we should not lose sight of the genuine difficulties posed by a work like *Ionisation*. No one had ever heard a work of this size written almost entirely without fixed pitches, and it conformed to no established convention of form or genre.

In an interview given in 1924, almost a decade before writing *Ionisation*, Varèse explained the motivation behind his search for new musical timbres. He wondered aloud why stringed instruments were "still the kings of the orchestras" even though they had not advanced technologically in any significant way for more than two centuries. Only by custom, he declared, that this family of instruments continued to dominate orchestral sound. Varèse called for "an entirely new medium of expression," and he would spend the rest of his professional life exploring the possibilities of new timbres.[14] He worked with Bell Laboratories at various times. . . . [etc.]

In his ongoing research in the possibilities of new timbres, including percussion, Varèse also worked with Bell Laboratories at various times to develop the possibilities of electronic music; his 1958 *Poème électronique*, put together with the aid of Iannis

**Edgard Varèse.** Earlier composers had often portrayed themselves seated at the keyboard, surrounded by notated scores of their most recent works. For this photographic portrait from the 1950s, Varèse gave strategic prominence to the open-reel tape deck, immediately identifying himself as a musician even while setting himself apart from composers of previous generations.

**Source:** Bettmann/Corbis

Xenakis (see Chapter 23), was written specifically for the striking World's Fair building in Brussels designed by Le Corbusier. Heard on 11 channels over 425 loudspeakers in the Philips Pavilion, the combination represents a unique blend of music and architecture. "I refuse to submit myself only to sounds that have already been heard," he once declared.[15] "I do not write experimental music. My experimenting is done before I make the music. Afterwards, it is the listener who must experiment."[16]

Varèse wrote relatively little music, yet his influence on 20th-century composition was enormous. During his lifetime, he was highly regarded by avant-garde composers but little known outside this circle until the 1950s, when his contributions to the art of music first began to gain widespread recognition, particularly from such younger composers as Pierre Boulez, Karlheinz Stockhausen, and Frank Zappa.

## SUMMARY

The early decades of the 20th century witnessed a series of radical challenges to established musical conventions. Claude Debussy, Igor Stravinsky, and Charles Ives, each in his own way, developed strikingly original approaches to such basic elements of music as melody, harmony, rhythm, and form. Primitivism emerged as a driving force in all the arts, but nowhere more strongly than in music, which embraced the elemental rhythms of Stravinsky's ballets and the motoric rhythms of works by Prokofiev and others. The musical idioms of eastern European peoples recorded by Béla Bartók and others provided an important source of inspiration to composers looking for new sounds. Still other composers, like Henry Cowell and Edgard Varèse, extended the range of timbres inherited from the 19th century, either through performing on old instruments in new ways or through the cultivation of instruments that had not previously been used in the concert hall. The sound of the early 20th century, in short, was decidedly new.

# Beyond Tonality

In the early decades of the 20th century, no element of musical modernism was more contentious than tonality. By 1910, the advanced chromaticism of Wagner's *Tristan und Isolde* (see Chapter 17) seemed tame. Composers like Gustav Mahler, Richard Strauss, and Claude Debussy—all born in the 1860s—were extending the reach of chromaticism to an unprecedented extent. Arnold Schoenberg, born in 1874, carried these tendencies still further and eventually established a harmonic idiom in which the idea of a tonal center played no role at all.

## ATONALITY

The dividing line between extreme chromaticism and **atonality**—the absence of a tonal center altogether—is often difficult to identify. None of the elements characteristic of extended chromatic harmony was new in the 20th century, after all. Augmented triads, extended sonorities built on thirds (9th, 11th, and 13th chords), unresolved dissonances, nonharmonic tones, nonfunctional bass lines, enharmonicism, fleeting or merely implied tonicization, parallel voice leading—all of these can be found in the music of the mid-to-late 19th century. What *was* new at this time was the substantially greater prominence given to all these kinds of features.

The opening of Schoenberg's Chamber Symphony in E Major, op. 9 (1906) provides a good illustration of the limits of traditional chromatic tonality (Example 21–1). The initial chord builds up gradually out of a series of fourths rather than thirds (G-C-F-B♭-E♭-A♭). This sonority resolves to an F-major chord in m. 4 through an augmented sixth chord on G♭ (a French sixth) that includes an additional A♭. The goal of this progression is clearly tonal: there is nothing ambiguous about the second chord in m. 4. But the manner in which the music arrives at this harmony makes the triadic sonority seem all the more isolated and out of place, as if it is the consonance that is dissonant. The tonal basis of the work is further confused by the following four measures, which open with a different series of fourths (D-G-C-F-B♭-E♭) that then moves through a series of whole-tone chords in descending parallel motion. The sense of a goal-oriented functional harmony is so remote here that its very presence is called into doubt. Once again, the resolution (vii⁷/E with an added D♮, moving to E Major first inversion) sounds almost out of place, even though it is technically correct according to the standards of traditional harmony and voice leading. The resolution seems to echo the "Tristan" chord, which by this point had first been heard more than half a century before.

Schoenberg recognized that chromatic harmony was approaching the point at which distinctions between dissonance and consonance had become almost meaningless. At some point, he reasoned, the extended avoidance of a tonal

**EXAMPLE 21–1** Schoenberg, Chamber Symphony in E Major, op. 9 (1906), m. 1–10.

center becomes the absence of a tonal center. Indeed, he seems to have bid a symbolic farewell to tonality itself the year before in the third movement of his Second String Quartet, op. 10 (1908), in which the relentless repetition of tonic and dominant harmonies over the children's song *Ach, Du lieber Augustin* (better known in English as "Did you ever see a lassie go this way and that way?") dissolves into banality. Schoenberg wanted to wean the public from tonality and explore the "air of other planets," to quote the words sung by the solo soprano in the same quartet. The public, for the most part, was reluctant to travel with him.

Partly independently, partly in conjunction with his pupil-colleagues Anton Webern and Alban Berg, Schoenberg persisted in advancing what he called "the emancipation of the dissonance." In a truly atonal idiom, Schoenberg argued, dissonances would no longer be considered a "spicy addition to dull sounds" but instead the "natural and logical outgrowths" of a musical "organism."[1] Schoenberg hated the term *atonality*, on the grounds that it defined an idiom in terms of what it was not. "I am a musician," Schoenberg declared, "and I have nothing to do with the atonal. Atonal might well mean simply: something that corresponds in no way to the essential nature of tones. . . . A piece of music will always be tonal, at least in the sense that there must be some kind of a relationship from one tone to the next."[2] He advocated calling such music *pantonal*, but the term never caught on.

The impetus toward atonality was more than merely technical. Schoenberg, Webern, and Berg were searching for a new way of writing music whose emotional impact would be more direct and immediate than anything available in the vocabulary of extended chromaticism. Atonality, as it turned out, was particularly well suited to the aesthetics of **expressionism**, a broad artistic movement of the time that sought to give voice (expression) to the unconscious, to make manifest humanity's deepest and often darkest

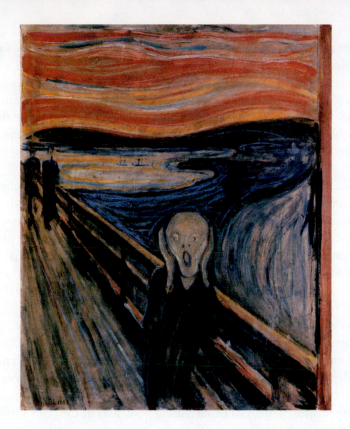

**Expressionism in painting.** Edvard Munch (1863–1944), *The Scream* (1893): The image has become a cultural cliché but still has the power to move those who take the trouble to look at it with fresh eyes. Munch's style here anticipates expressionism, an artistic movement that sought to bring to the surface unconscious thoughts and visceral emotions. One of the image's four versions sold for almost $120 million at auction in May 2012.

**Source:** Scala/Art Resource, NY/© 2011 The Munch Museum/ The Munch-Ellingsen Group/Artists Rights Society (ARS), NY

emotions. Expressionism is related to primitivism in that both attempt to strip away the veneer of so-called civilized behavior and reveal the innermost recesses of human emotion. In Freudian terms, expressionist art bypasses the ego—the conscious self—and aims straight for the id—the unconscious repository of basic instincts and drives. Expressionism in all its forms—in literature, painting, cinema, and music—strives for psychological truth. Beauty, at least in any conventional sense of the concept, is irrelevant; the externalization of emotion takes precedence.

The quintessential act of expressionism is the scream (see *The Scream*), an utterance that is not a word, a product of civilization, but rather an intense, spontaneous reaction to something that has caused pain or fear. Indeed, the Austrian poet and critic Hermann Bahr (1863–1934) defined expressionism precisely in terms of this act: "Man screams from the depths of his soul; the whole era becomes a single, piercing shriek. Art also screams, into the deep darkness, screams for help, screams for the spirit. This is expressionism."[3]

Schoenberg, who was deeply sympathetic to expressionist art, and whose own paintings are very much within the expressionist idiom, was drawn to the surreal, violent, and eerie imagery in Albert Giraud's *Pierrot lunaire* (1883), a cycle of poems that had recently been translated from their original French into German. He was especially pleased to receive a commission from the actress/singer/artist Albertine Zehme (1857–1946) to set a group of 21 poems taken from the larger selection that she had already used in spoken recitals accompanied by piano music. Schoenberg enjoyed the composition process immensely, aided by Zehme's willingness to allow for more than piano accompaniment; the resulting 1912 setting of this cycle for soprano and instrumental ensemble is one of the most widely admired works of musical expressionism and one of the earliest works of atonal music to achieve a wide following.

((•●─Listen
**CD13 Tracks 12–14**
**mysearchlab** (with scrolling translation)
SCHOENBERG
*Pierrot lunaire*
Score Anthology II/157

Pierrot is one of the stock masked characters from the *commedia dell'arte*, and *Pierrot lunaire* draws on the mask as a metaphor for the human manners that conceal deeper emotions. Pierrot himself is the melancholy, moonstruck clown who lives in a state of constant longing. The atonality of no. 7 ("The Sick Moon") makes the moon seem far more ill than any tonal idiom could. The music projects the violence of the text in no. 14 ("The Cross")—whose first line reads "Holy crosses are the verses on which poets bleed to death"—by having the voice make leaps of ninths, diminished and augmented octaves, and other nontriadic intervals, thereby undermining any sense of a tonal center.

By setting a series of relatively short poems in *Pierrot lunaire*, Schoenberg was able to circumvent one of the more pressing challenges of writing within the new atonal idiom: how to construct large-scale musical forms in the absence of tonality. The tonal system, after all, had provided the basic framework for most musical forms for several centuries. It is no coincidence, then, that most of the atonal works from the early decades of the century are relatively brief, and that many of them are vocal. The texts of these works provide a certain degree of structural coherence in the absence of traditional tonality.

**Sprechstimme**, the style of singing called for throughout *Pierrot lunaire*, reinforces the surreal quality of the text and music. *Sprechstimme* (literally, "speech-voice," with "voice" understood here in the sense of "singing") is neither speech nor song, but a means of declamation somewhere between the two. When using *Sprechstimme*, the vocalist must articulate specified pitches and rhythms, and in this respect it is more like singing than speech. Instead of sustaining a pitch as in the conventional method of singing, however, the performer allows the pitch to drop rather in the same way one's voice drops with the enunciation of a spoken word. *Sprechstimme* is indicated by means of standard notes with a small "x" through the stem. The effect is unique: as song, it falls short of lyricism, and intentionally so; as speech, it constitutes a purposefully exaggerated, overblown kind of delivery. It occupies a kind of twilight zone between speech and song that calls attention to the essentially artificial distinction between the two.

Schoenberg did not invent *Sprechstimme*. It had been in use in the theater since at least the 1890s. Cabaret singers had long cultivated a style of singing that was half-spoken and half-sung, and Schoenberg himself used it in his oratorio *Gurrelieder* (1900–01). But in *Pierrot lunaire*, the device helps create a heightened sense of surrealism, a feeling that the speaker-singer is somehow distanced from the text she is delivering. Many commentators have in fact detected a certain degree of irony in the work, arguing, in effect, that its extreme emotionalism can also be interpreted as a parody of extreme emotionalism. This kind of irony would be fitting in a work that draws so deeply on the traditions of the *commedia dell'arte*, a style of performance in which the performers are constantly calling attention to the fact that they are performers.

The atonal idiom of *Pierrot lunaire* also provided Schoenberg with an effective foil for the limited use of tonality. The final number of the cycle (no. 21, "O Ancient Scent") speaks of the intoxicating "ancient scent" that comes "from the time of fairy tales," and throughout this finale, the composer's music is more nearly tonal for longer stretches than at any other point in the entire cycle. At the very end of *Pierrot*, the moonstruck clown wistfully longs for the age of tonality, the age of childhood and fairy tales, but seems to realize this is only a dream, that there is no turning back now. The voice descends so low at the very end that the final words—half spoken, half sung in *Sprechstimme*—are almost inaudible. The contrast with the closing numbers of the previous two parts, the eeriness of no. 7 and the violent expressionism of no. 14, could not be greater. The dream is over, the nightmare and screams of expressionism exhausted, and a return to the past impossible.

## Primary Evidence   THE LAST WORD IN MUSICAL ANARCHY

*Schoenberg's* Pierrot lunaire (1912) *posed a challenge to many if not most of its first listeners. The American music critic Arthur M. Abell (1868–1958) filed this review from the work's London premiere.*

■ ■ ■

To arouse any kind of a sensation in these days of such enormous overproduction in every branch of music is of itself an extraordinary feat. Arnold Schoenberg may be either crazy as a loon, in which case we may assume that his efforts are prompted by honest conviction, or he may be a very clever trickster who is apparently determined to cause a sensation at any cost, finding, seemingly, the cheapest and surest way to be by writing music that in its hideousness and illogical, ear splitting ugliness defies description. At any rate, he is just at present the most talked of musical personality of the day, not excepting Richard Strauss. And he has succeeded in twice filling Choralion Hall and each time the audiences were made up chiefly of professional musicians and critics. His music to Albert Giraud's fantastical poems entitled "The Songs of Pierrot Lunaire," is the last word in cacophony and musical anarchy. Some day it may be pointed out as of historical interest, because representing the turning point, for the outraged muse surely can endure no more of this; such noise must drive even the moonstruck Pierrot back to the realm of real music. Albertine Zehme, a well known Berlin actress, dressed in a Pierrot costume, recited the "Three Times Seven" poems, as the program announced, while a musical, or rather unmusical, ensemble consisting of a piano, violin, viola, cello, piccolo and clarinet, stationed behind a black screen and invisible to the audience, discoursed the most ear splitting combinations of tones that ever desecrated the walls of a Berlin music hall. Schoenberg has thrown overboard all of the sheet anchors of the art of music. Melody he eschews in every form; tonality he knows not and such a word as harmony is not in his vocabulary. He purposely and habitually takes false basses and the screeching of the fiddle, piccolo and clarinet baffled description. The remarkable part of this whole farce is that Schoenberg is taken seriously. A musically cultured audience sits through such an atrocity with hardly a protest. The grotesque sounds which emerged from behind the black screen occasionally called forth outbursts of merriment, but the audience was as a whole very well behaved. The critics have written columns about Schoenberg. To be sure, they condemn him almost to a man, but they give him space—from four to five times the space that other more deserving composers get and they do this for the same reason that I am now doing it, because there is an element of interest for the readers of their papers in the whole scheme. As I said before, Schoenberg has succeeded in causing a veritable sensation. He even has adherents who rally round his standard and swear by his muse, declaring that this is music of the future. Otto Taubmann, the critic of the *Börsen Courier*, expressed the feelings of all sane musicians when he wrote, "If this is music of the future, then I pray my Creator not to let me live to hear it again."

**Source:** Arthur M. Abell, review in *The Musical Courier,* November 6, 1912.

**The first interpreters.** In this photograph of the performers of the 1912 premiere of *Pierrot lunaire*, Albertine Zehme (center) is flanked on her right by Arnold Schoenberg and on her left by Eduard Steuermann, pianist and Schoenberg pupil.

**Source:** Arnold Schoenberg and Pierrot Lunaire Ensemble. Berlin 1912. © Arnold Schoenberg Center

Early composers writing atonal works without a text had to find other means to structure them. Anton Webern's *Five Pieces for String Quartet*, op. 5 (1908), is a series of miniatures that concentrates its resources into a remarkably intense form of expression. Like most atonal works, it uses a limited number of building blocks that usually consist of four or five notes—sometimes fewer, sometimes

((•• **Listen**
**CD13    Track 15**
**mysearchlab**
WEBERN
*Five Pieces for String Quartet,*
op. 5, no. 4
Score Anthology II/158

# Arnold Schoenberg (1874–1951)

Schoenberg was a tortured soul, an outsider who longed to be accepted yet never felt comfortable within the establishment. Widely perceived as a radical, he saw himself as a traditionalist extending the heritage of Bach, Beethoven, and Brahms. Born Jewish, he converted to Christianity, then later back to Judaism. An Austrian by birth, he moved back and forth between Vienna and Berlin, finally emigrating to the United States when the Nazis assumed power in Germany. (It was in the United States that he changed the spelling of his name from Schönberg to Schoenberg.)

His work falls into three broad periods:

- *Early (advanced chromaticism).* Schoenberg's early works explore the outer limits and reaches of chromaticism. Lush harmonies, thick textures, and an almost constant avoidance of cadences characterize such works as *Verklärte Nacht* ("Transfigured Night"), a tone poem for string sextet; *Gurrelieder*, an oratorio of enormous proportions; the Quartet in D minor, in one large movement; the Chamber Symphony no. 1 in E Major, op. 9; and many songs.

- *Middle (atonal).* Around 1908, Schoenberg abandoned tonality altogether and declared the "emancipation of the dissonance." Principal works of the atonal period include the String Quartet no. 2 (whose finale features a solo soprano singing the words "I breathe the air of other planets"); the Piano Pieces op. 11 and op. 19; *Pierrot lunaire*; the monodrama *Erwartung* ("Expectation," for soprano and orchestra); the unfinished oratorio *Jakobsleiter* ("Jacob's Ladder"); and the *Five Orchestral Pieces*, op. 16.

- *Late (serial).* Dissatisfied with the lack of a more structured formal principle by which to organize his atonal works, Schoenberg eventually developed the method of 12-tone serial composition (discussed later) in which no note is repeated until all other 11 pitches of the scale have been stated. His earliest attempts at serial composition date from around 1920, and within a few years he was applying this method in almost all his music. The principal serial works include the String Quartets nos. 3 and 4, the *Variations for Orchestra*, the opera *Moses und Aron*, and the String Trio.

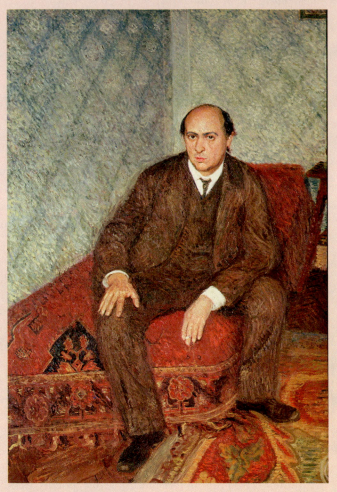

**A portrait of Schoenberg by the Viennese painter Richard Gerstl (1883–1908).** Around or shortly after the time he made this portrait, Gerstl began having an affair with Schoenberg's wife. When their liaison ended and Mathilde Schoenberg returned to her husband in 1908, Gerstl committed suicide. The events bear strong similarities to the plot of Schoenberg's opera *Die glückliche Hand* ("The Magic Touch") of 1913.

**Source:** Portrait of Arnold Shoenberg (1874–1951), c. 1905–6, Gerstl, Richard (1883–1908)/Wien Museum Karlsplatz, Vienna, Austria/ The Bridgeman Art Library

With Stravinsky, Schoenberg was widely regarded as one of the two great composers of the 20th century. No one, however, ever accused him of being a "musical chameleon," as Stravinsky had been called. Even those who did not care for his music respected his uncompromising pursuit of artistic principles. His influence, moreover, extended well beyond his two most famous pupils, Anton Webern and Alban Berg. Every subsequent generation of composers has studied Schoenberg's music carefully, and in this sense he stands as one of—and arguably *the*—most influential composers of the entire century.

# PRINCIPAL WORKS

## Dramatic Works

The unfinished opera *Moses und Aron*, based on the book of Exodus, is in many respects Schoenberg's masterpiece; it is also a veiled autobiography of the composer himself. Moses, the lawgiver, strives to elevate the people of Israel by transmitting the word of God. But Moses (a *Sprechstimme* role in the opera) cannot persuade with the fluency and eloquence of the young Aaron (a lyric tenor). Many critics have seen in this constellation a parallel with Schoenberg and his pupil Berg, whose atonal and 12-tone music was for most listeners more lyrical and accessible than Schoenberg's. Late in his life, Schoenberg also turned to the genre of the monologue with orchestra in such works as *Kol nidre*, the *Ode to Napoleon*, and *A Survivor from Warsaw*.

## Orchestral Music

The *Five Orchestral Pieces* and the *Variations for Orchestra* are atonal and serial, respectively. The Violin Concerto and Piano Concerto are later compositions.

## Piano Music

*The Three Piano Pieces*, op. 11, and *Six Piano Pieces*, op. 19, are brief but important works in the development of the atonal idiom. Schoenberg turned to the piano again in developing his 12-tone method of composition, most notably in the Piano Suite, op. 25, which openly adopts the forms, but not the style, of a Baroque dance suite (see Chapter 10). The Piano Pieces op. 33a and 33b use combinatoriality (see Chapter 23).

## Chamber Music

*Verklärte Nacht*, for string sextet (later arranged for string orchestra), is a tone poem based on the story of a woman's confession of infidelity. Written in a lush, post-Wagnerian style, it is the most frequently performed of all Schoenberg's works. The five string quartets (1897, 1905, 1908, 1927, 1936; the first is not numbered) offer a good way to trace the various periods of Schoenberg's compositional career, as do the two chamber symphonies (1906, 1939).

## Writings

Schoenberg's writings are among the most important in the field of 20th-century theory. He wrote a massive treatise on harmony, and through his lectures, teaching, and analytical essays he exerted considerable influence on subsequent generations of composers, theorists, and listeners. Several of these essays were collected and published in English as *Style and Idea* (1950; expanded edition, 1975, reprinted 1984).

| KEY DATES IN THE LIFE OF SCHOENBERG | |
|---|---|
| 1874 | Born in Vienna on September 13. |
| 1894 | Begins private composition lessons with Alexander Zemlinsky; performs in local music halls to earn money. |
| 1910 | Appointed teacher of composition at the Vienna Academy. |
| 1911 | Finishes his *Harmonielehre*, dedicated to the recently deceased Gustav Mahler, one of his early supporters; moves to Berlin, where he teaches at the Stern Conservatory. |
| 1912 | Premiere of *Pierrot lunaire,* which causes a sensation. |
| 1918 | After serving in the Austrian military during World War I, settles once again in Vienna and organizes the Society for Private Musical Performances, to which only selected listeners are invited. |
| 1925 | Appointed professor at the Prussian Academy of Arts in Berlin. |
| 1933 | Dismissed from his position in Berlin because of his Jewish ancestry and emigrates to France and then the United States, where, after a year in Boston, he settles in Los Angeles. |
| 1935 | Appointed professor of music at the University of Southern California; begins teaching a year later at the University of California at Los Angeles; becomes an American citizen in 1941. |
| 1951 | Dies on July 13 in Los Angeles. |

more, but rarely very many more. These units tend to avoid triads, both in their linear (melodic) and vertical (harmonic) alignments. Webern, like Schoenberg and Berg, saw himself as a traditionalist who continued in the manner of Beethoven and Brahms by manipulating motivic ideas in a process that Schoenberg called "developing variation." Although the extreme brevity of the movements in Webern's op. 5 makes it difficult to hear this process, at least on first listening, this music does in fact rest on the manipulation of a few thematic ideas that are laid out at the beginning and sustained through to the end. The work's unusual voicings and textures, and Webern's avoidance of any strong sense of meter over extended periods, make it all the more challenging to discern structure in a work in which no one pitch emerges as more important than any other. Fortunately, set theory, which was developed in the third quarter of the 20th century by the American scholar Allen Forte, provides us with a framework for identifying the constituent elements that go into most atonal music and helps us realize that in spite of its surface challenges, this music is in at least some respects quite traditional (see Focus: Set Theory and the Analysis of Atonal Music).

By far the most successful atonal work of the early 20th century—both critically and commercially—was Alban Berg's opera *Wozzeck*, completed in 1922 and premiered in Berlin in 1925. The libretto, drawn from selected scenes of the drama *Woyzeck* by the Austrian playwright Georg Büchner (1813–1837), traces the mental and physical deterioration of a simple army soldier, who is treated abysmally by everyone: his captain, his doctor, and the woman by whom he has fathered a child. In the end, he goes mad and murders Marie, the mother of his young son.

Berg used a series of traditional instrumental forms to structure his opera. He identified them himself as follows:

### ACT I: FIVE CHARACTER PIECES (EXPOSITION)

Scene 1: Wozzeck and the Captain—Suite

Scene 2: Wozzeck and Andres—Rhapsody on Three Chords

Scene 3: Wozzeck and Marie—March (Drum Major) and Lullaby (Marie's Child)

Scene 4: Wozzeck and the Doctor—Passacaglia

Scene 5: Marie and the Drum Major—Quasi Rondo

### ACT II: SYMPHONY IN FIVE MOVEMENTS (PERIPETEIA OR DEVELOPMENT)

Scene 1: Marie alone—Sonata-form Movement

Scene 2: Captain, Doctor, Wozzeck—Invention and Fugue on Three Themes

Scene 3: Marie and Wozzeck—Largo in the Instrumentation of Schoenberg's Chamber Symphony, op. 9

Scene 4: Wozzeck and Others in the Tavern—Scherzo

Scene 5: Wozzeck and Drum Major in the Barracks—Rondo Marziale

### ACT III: SIX INVENTIONS (CATASTROPHE OR DENOUEMENT)

Scene 1: Marie and Child—Inventions on a Theme

Scene 2: Wozzeck and Marie by the Pond—Invention on One Note

Scene 3: Wozzeck and Others in the Tavern—Inventions on a Rhythm

((•• Listen

**CD14    Track 1**
**mysearchlab** (with scrolling translation)
BERG
*Wozzeck*
Score Anthology II/159

Scene 4: Wozzeck, Later the Doctor and Captain—Invention on
a Six-Note Chord

Scene 5: Child, Other Children—Invention on an Eighth-Note Rhythm
(Perpetuum Mobile)

Berg insisted, however, that "there must not be anyone in the audience who . . .
notices anything about these various fugues, inventions, suites and sonata movements,
variations and passacaglias. Nobody must be filled with anything except the idea of the

## Focus  SET THEORY AND THE ANALYSIS OF ATONAL MUSIC

Atonal music—works like Webern's Five Pieces for String Quartet, neither tonal nor 12-tone—seemed for a long time resistant to anything approaching systematic analysis. The American theorist Allen Forte (b. 1926) was the most prominent among a number of critics working in the 1950s and 1960s to develop a method for examining this kind of music. In what came to be called *set theory*, Forte proposed a system for identifying and clarifying the relationship of the relatively small units (*cells* or *sets*) that together provide the building blocks for a typical atonal composition. These sets can consist of anywhere between two and ten pitch classes. (A pitch class is any manifestation of a particular pitch, regardless of register; thus the pitch class A–F can be used for units that go either down a major third or up a minor sixth—or down a tenth, and so on.) A finite number of set types—220 to be exact—can be created out of all the various combinations of pitch classes (see table).

| Number of Pitches in Set | Name of Type of Set | Number of Possible Combinations |
|---|---|---|
| 2 | Dyad | 6 |
| 3 | Trichord | 12 |
| 4 | Tetrachord | 29 |
| 5 | Pentachord | 38 |
| 6 | Hexachord | 50 |
| 7 | Septachord | 38 |
| 8 | Octachord | 29 |
| 9 | Nonachord | 12 |
| 10 | Decachord | 6 |
| | | Total: 220 |

In analysis, these combinations of differing size are identified by a series of numbers reflecting the prime form of the set, beginning with 0 (the lowest note of the set) and moving upward by half step, in much the same way that 12-tone rows are identified numerically. Another important principle of the prime set form is that the pitch class numbers are ordered with smallest interval first (that is, are "packed" to the left); thus, the tetrachord set C-D♯-F-G would be reinterpreted as D♯-F-G-C, and then transposed to C-D-E-A. This prime set form is designated 0–2–4–9 because D is two half steps above C, E is four half steps above C, and A is nine half steps above C. Sets can be presented either simultaneously (as a "chord") or successively (as a "melody"). Example 21–2 shows the two tetrachords of the opening set of Webern's op. 5, no. 4 (without transposition).

Looking at the score, we can see that set A is presented in the two upper voices in m. 1, and set B is at the beginning of m. 2. The pitches of set A recur on the final half beat of m. 2; set B appears as a melodic line in the first violin in m. 3–4, and then again in the second violin (m. 4) transposed down a fifth. Identifying pitch-class sets can be a hit-or-miss process at times: some sets occur only once or twice in a piece and cannot really be considered to have structural importance. The identification of sets can nevertheless be extremely helpful for making audibly coherent a work of music that might otherwise seem shapeless, even after repeated hearings.

**EXAMPLE 21–2** Two tetrachords from the opening of Webern's Five Pieces for String Quartet, op. 5, no. 4.

## Composer Profile

# Anton Webern (1883–1945)

Webern's music tends to be extremely concentrated and brief. The orchestral *Passacaglia*, op. 1, lasts about ten minutes in performance, but no subsequent work has more than five minutes of continuous music. A set of his complete works issued on long-playing records in the 1960s took up only four disks. This aphoristic quality strips music to its bare essentials. In much of his work, Webern never calls for a dynamic level louder than *piano*, and he uses silence more often and more effectively than any composer before him. Listening to this music is like listening to a brilliant speaker who wastes no words and speaks in a whisper: we strain to hear every detail, every nuance.

Born into an aristocratic family, the future composer completed a doctoral degree in historical musicology at the University of Vienna in 1906. His dissertation was on the second volume (1555) of the *Choralis Constantius* by the Renaissance composer Heinrich Isaac (see Chapters 5 and 6). Webern was fascinated by the constructive techniques of Renaissance music, particularly its elaborate canons. During this time, he also studied composition privately with Arnold Schoenberg, and together teacher and pupil explored the possibilities of atonal composition and, later, serial composition.

Webern's death is shrouded in mystery. While visiting his daughter and son-in-law in a small Austrian village shortly after the end of World War II, he stepped outside to enjoy his first cigar in months, only to be shot and killed by an American sentry who was part of the Allied

**Anton Webern and Alban Berg.** Anton Webern (right) and Alban Berg were Arnold Schoenberg's two most prominent students and colleagues. At the time this photograph was taken in 1912, both had essentially broken their musical ties with tonality and had begun to explore the possibilities of the atonal idiom.

**Source:** Lebrecht Music & Arts Photo Library

opera." The congruence of musical and dramatic form within each scene and across each act is extremely effective.

The opening scene of Act I, a suite, provides a good illustration of the manner in which the character of individual dances is matched to the dramatic dialogue. Berg uses here exactly the same device used by Verdi in the opening scene of *Rigoletto* (see Chapter 17): a series of dances, each with a particular symbolic meaning. The curtain goes up on a scene that is at once both mundane and chilling. We see Wozzeck shaving the Captain. With a flick of the wrist Wozzeck could kill him, and indeed the thought occurs to him as, in the process of trying to engage the laconic soldier in conversation, the Captain crosses the line by reminding Wozzeck of his illegitimate child. The scene is constructed as a suite, a series of dances (or rather, dance rhythms) that relate precisely to the nature of the conversation.

- *Prelude* (m. 1): The Captain, who, as we later realize, is obsessed with the passage of time, reminds Wozzeck to proceed slowly, "one step at a time."[4] In the course of urging calm, the Captain himself becomes quite agitated.

force occupying Austria at the time. The soldier claimed self-defense and pointed out that Webern was outside after curfew, but it seems unlikely that the diminutive, middle-aged Webern could have posed any threat.

# PRINCIPAL WORKS

## Orchestral Music

The *Passacaglia*, op. 1, reveals Webern's early interest in strict forms and his gift for orchestration. His *Variations*, op. 30, rewards careful analysis for the elaborate application of 12-tone devices. Webern's scoring for orchestra is extraordinarily transparent; he once said the sound of a full orchestra caused him physical pain.

## Chamber Music

Webern preferred to work within the smaller scale genres of string quartet and song; even his one symphony is scored for a chamber ensemble and is quite brief. The Five Movements for String Quartet, op. 5, are celebrated for their conciseness and economy of expression, as are the Six Bagatelles, op. 9. The String Quartet, op. 28, is a 12-tone work.

## Vocal Music

Webern, along with his teacher Schoenberg, worked through many of the problems of atonality within the genre of song. He favored contemporary poets such as Stefan George, Georg Trakl, and Rainer Maria Rilke; he wrote several texts of his own as well. From 1926 onward, however, he set exclusively the texts of Hildegard Jone (1891–1963), a fellow Austrian whose texts greatly appealed to Webern's sense of an inherent connection between nature and art. Jone's poetry also provided the texts for the two cantatas.

| KEY DATES IN THE LIFE OF WEBERN | |
|---|---|
| 1883 | Born December 3 in Vienna. |
| 1906 | Receives Ph.D. in musicology from the University of Vienna with a dissertation on the Renaissance composer Heinrich Isaac. |
| 1908–1914 | Conducts theater orchestras in various cities in Austria and Germany. |
| 1915–1916 | Serves as a volunteer in the Austrian Army in World War I but is discharged because of poor eyesight. |
| 1918 | Helps run the Society for Private Musical Performance until its demise in 1921; begins giving private lessons in composition. |
| 1926 | Meets the poet Hildegard Jone and from this point on sets only her texts to music. |
| 1933 | The Nazis prohibit performances of Webern's music, and he is forced to lecture in secret and work as a proofreader for his Viennese publisher, Universal Edition. |
| 1945 | Dies September 15 in Mittersill, Austria, shot by an American soldier. |

- *Pavane* (m. 30): The Captain broods on eternity and mortality. This section ends with a cadenza for the viola.

- *Gigue* (m. 65): The Captain has not been able to engage Wozzeck in a conversation on morality, so he turns instead to the weather ("I believe the wind is from South-North"), but even these absurdities fail to capture Wozzeck's attention. The music ends with a cadenza for bassoon.

- *Gavotte* (m. 115): Returns to the idea of morality and scores a hit when he declares that Wozzeck's child was born out of wedlock, "without the blessings of the church."

- *Double I* (m. 127): Wozzeck finally responds and quotes Christ's words "Let the little children come unto me." At Double II (m. 133), the Captain's erratic rhythm takes over when he insists he had not been talking about Wozzeck at all. Suddenly it is the Captain who does not want to talk.

- *Air* (m. 136): Wozzeck erupts in a passion of genuine emotion, a lyrical outburst. "We poor people," he sings, and the music to these words will return often in the course of the opera. Morality, he proclaims, is a function of affluence.

- *Prelude (reprise)* (m. 154): The Captain, quite shaken, tries to regain his original air of calm. The music of the opening returns, and he resumes his verbal harassment of Wozzeck as if nothing had happened in the meantime.

In addition to introducing the opera's central character, this opening scene also introduces one of the work's principal ideas: the consequences of emotional repression. At first, Wozzeck assumes the guise of an automaton, answering each of the Captain's provocative questions with a monotonous and unthinking "Yes, Captain." Only when the Captain touches on the question of Wozzeck's child do we begin to see the soldier's true feelings emerge; but because they are so raw and powerful, the Captain quickly seeks to put them back in place, insisting (quite absurdly) that he had not even been talking to Wozzeck at all during this time.

Some critics, predictably, lambasted Berg's *Wozzeck*. Paul Zschorlich, writing in the *Deutsche Zeitung* of Berlin on December 15, 1925, commented as such:

> As I left the opera house last night I had the feeling that I was coming out of a public institution dedicated not to art, but rather out of a public asylum for the insane. On the stage, in the orchestra, in the hall, nothing but crazies. Among them were tightly-knit units in defiant cadres: the shock troops of atonalists, the dervishes of Arnold Schoenberg. . . . Alban Berg's *Wozzeck* was the battlecry. The work of a Chinaman from Vienna. For these massive onslaughts of instruments have nothing to do with European music and its development. . . . In Berg's music there is not even a trace of melody. There are only crumbs, scraps,

## *Focus*  OPERA IN THE EARLY 20TH CENTURY

In the early decades of the 20th century, opera continued to thrive in the hands of such composers as Richard Strauss, Alban Berg, Giaccomo Puccini, and Leoš Janáček. From the perspective of form, most of these composers were descendants of Wagner in one way or another, emphasizing musicodramatic continuity even while preserving (in most cases) units still recognizable as arias, duets, and so on. Stylistically, opera was as diverse as the music of the 20th century itself, ranging from the atonal expressionism of Schoenberg's *Die glückliche Hand* (1913), to the tonal lyricism of Puccini's *Turandot* (1926), to the jazz-inspired harmonies and rhythms of Gershwin's *Porgy and Bess* (1935).

Among the more notable operatic composers of this period are the following:

Giaccomo Puccini—*La bohème* (1896), *Tosca* (1900), *Madama Butterfly* (1904), *La fanciulla del West* (1910), *Turandot* (1926)

Leoš Janáček— *Jenůfa* (1904); *Kátya Kabanová* (1921), *The Makropoulos Affair* (1926), *From the House of the Dead* (1928)

Richard Strauss—*Salome* (1905), *Elektra* (1909), *Der Rosenkavalier* (1911)

Arnold Schoenberg—*Erwartung* (1909), *Die glückliche Hand* (1913), *Moses und Aron* (1932)

Alban Berg—*Wozzeck* (1925), *Lulu* (1937)

Paul Hindemith—*Cardillac* (1926, rev. 1952), *Mathis der Maler* (1935)

Kurt Weill—*Die Dreigroschenoper* (1928), *Aufstieg und Fall der Stadt Mahagonny* (1929–1930)

George Gershwin—*Porgy and Bess* (1935)

Igor Stravinsky—*Oedipus Rex* (1927), *The Rake's Progress* (1951)

hiccups, and burps. The work cannot be discussed from a harmonic perspective, because everything sounds wrong. . . . The perpetrator of this work . . . relies firmly on the stupidity and wretchedness of his fellow beings, and for the rest relies on God Almighty and Universal Edition [the publisher of *Wozzeck*]. I consider Alban Berg a musical swindler and a composer who poses a threat to the public at large. Indeed, one must go still further than this. Unheard-of events demand new methods. The question we must seriously consider is this: Is it possible to treat music in a criminal manner, and if so, to what extent? For in the realm of music, we are dealing here with a capital offense.[5]

*Wozzeck* nevertheless became a critical and commercial success almost overnight, opening to great acclaim in 17 cities in Germany between 1926 and 1933. Audiences in Prague, Petrograd (St. Petersburg), Paris, Philadelphia, and New York welcomed the work enthusiastically. When the National Socialists under Adolf Hitler came to power in Germany in 1933, however, Berg's music—along with all other atonal music—was repressed and eventually banned from public performance. In the years after World War II, *Wozzeck* quickly reestablished itself as a staple of the operatic repertory.

# SERIAL COMPOSITION

For more than a decade, between roughly 1908 and the early 1920s, Schoenberg, Webern, Berg, and others struggled to find a means of creating large-scale atonal structures. Berg's use of traditional instrumental forms in *Wozzeck* was part of this effort, but the new idiom of atonality required a correspondingly new approach to form as well.

In response to this need, Schoenberg developed the technique of **serial composition** in the early 1920s. Serial composition is based on the premise that an established unit of music—most often a **row**, or **series** (hence the term "serial"), of 12 different pitches—can be varied repeatedly in such a way as to provide the structural basis for an entire work. A composer using this approach could integrate the row and any of its many possible permutations into established formal conventions—variations, sonata-form movements, rondos, and so on—but such forms were not essential to the structural integrity of the work, which was ensured by the constant presence of the row in one guise or another. Serial composition provided composers seeking to break away from traditional tonality with the means to construct large-scale forms that were structurally coherent despite the absence of a tonal center.

Twelve-tone serial composition, also known as **dodecaphony** (from the Greek *dodeca*, meaning "12"), uses as its basic unit a row of 12 different pitches drawn from the 12 pitches of the chromatic octave (C, C♯, D, D♯, etc., up through B). Schoenberg identified three principal functions of the 12-tone row: (1) to avoid creating the impression of a principal note, which in turn might suggest a "tonic" key area; (2) to unify the composition motivically; and (3) to "emancipate" the dissonance—that is, to eradicate any distinction between consonance and dissonance (see Primary Evidence: Schoenberg on the Three Functions of the 12-Tone Row). It is important to distinguish between the theory and practice of 12-tone composition. In theory, 479,001,600 different basic rows are possible (this number is 12! or $12 \times 11 \times 10 \times 9 \times 8 \times 7 \times 6 \times 5 \times 4 \times 3 \times 2 \times 1$). In practice, composers pay careful attention to the musical qualities of the row, generally avoiding intervals or sequences of intervals that might suggest a key area, such as a succession of thirds or of pitches in a diatonic scale. In the strictest applications of 12-tone composition, no pitch is repeated until all other 11 pitches have been stated in that particular iteration of the row.

In practice, composers applied this system with considerable flexibility, often repeating a particular pitch before moving on to another one.

There are four basic forms of any given row, each of which can be transposed to start on any of the 12 chromatic pitches in the diatonic scale:

- Prime (P) is the basic form of the row.

- Inversion (I) is the row played upside down: a rise of a major third in the prime form of the row becomes a fall of a major third; a fall of a minor second in the prime form becomes a rise of a minor second, and so on.

- Retrograde (R) is the row played backward, beginning with the last note and ending with the first.

- Retrograde Inversion (RI) is the inverted form of the row played backward.

((•• Listen
**CD14    Track 2**
**mysearchlab**
SCHOENBERG
*Piano Suite,* op. 25
Score Anthology II/160

These different permutations of a single row are readily evident in Schoenberg's Piano Suite, op. 25, an early serial work, written in 1923. The prime form of the row consists of the pitches E-F-G-C#-F#-D#-G#-D-B-C-A-B♭. A **matrix** shows at a glance all the 48 possibilities of this row in the transposed versions of P, I, R, and RI (Example 21–3).

**EXAMPLE 21–3**  The matrix of the row for Schoenberg's Piano Suite, op. 25. The prime form in its original transposition (P-0) reads from left to right across the top row.

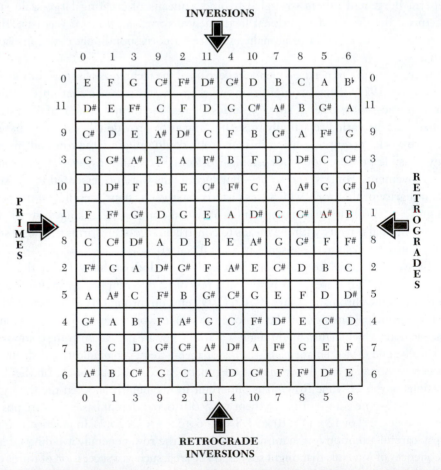

**Source:** Arnold Schoenberg, Piano Suite, op. 25 (Vienna: Universal Edition © 1926, renewed 1953). From *Materials and Techniques of Twentieth-Century Music* by Stefan Kostka, 2nd ed., Prentice Hall, © 1999, p. 201. Reprinted by permission of Pearson Education, Inc., Upper Saddle River, NJ.

By convention, the **pitch class** on which each form of the row begins is designated by a number. (Theorists use the term *pitch class* to designate any set of notes—any A, any B, any C, and so on—regardless of register.) The prime form of the row would thus be P-0 (no matter which pitch class the actual row begins with); the Inverted form beginning on 4 (that is, four half steps above the original note of P-0) would be I-4; the Retrograde Inverted form beginning on 8 would be RI-8; and so on. By the same token, the pitches of the rows themselves can also be designated numerically. Thus the basic row of Schoenberg's op. 25 (P-0) can be identified as 0–1–3–9–2–11–4–10–7–8–5–6; each of these numbers can in turn represent a transposition of the basic row and its permutations. (Some analysts use the series of numbers 1 through 12, but most American writers on music have tended toward the system using 0 through 11, as atonal set theory does, and it is this latter system that is used here.)

At first glance, such a compositional system might seem like little more than the equivalent of a musical crossword puzzle. But it is important to remember that all forms of composition, and especially the so-called strict forms such as canon and fugue, involve self-imposed limitations. Such limitations, moreover, have nothing to do with the inherent quality of a work. There are good fugues and bad fugues, and the same is true of 12-tone compositions.

It is equally important to remember that in spite of all these limitations, the composer retains enormous control over the course of a serial work, because the number of ways in which the row can be permuted and combined with other iterations of the same row is virtually infinite. In fact, the matrix of any given row is far more than most composers ever need or use. Typically, only a small fraction of the 48 possible combinations of a row will actually come into play. In his Piano Suite, op. 25, to remain with the previous example, Schoenberg limited himself to just eight different versions of the row, as outlined in Example 21-4.

Schoenberg's Piano Suite offers a particularly clear example of how serial music works, in part because it is one of the composer's earliest attempts at a large-scale serial work. All six movements—Prelude, Gavotte, Musette, Intermezzo, Minuet, Gigue—are based on different manifestations of the same row. The prime form of the row (P-0) is presented in the upper voice (right hand) of the Prelude's first three measures. But what is going on in the left hand? Careful scrutiny of the first four pitches there (B♭, C♭, D♭, G) reveals they are the first four notes of the same series transposed up a tritone (P-6) to begin on the note B♭ (= A♯). The relationship of the pitches is identical to that of the upper voice: up a half step (B♭-C♭ = A♯-B), and then up a whole step (C♭-D♭ = B-C♯; the disposition of register is of no importance in identifying rows), then a tritone leap (D♭-G = C♯-G). The relationship is not audible on the surface (at least not to most people), yet the structure is every bit as present as the harmony of a I–IV–V progression in tonal work.

Matters become slightly more complicated in m. 2–3 in the left hand, where we see multiple pitches sounded simultaneously within the same row. Here, Schoenberg in effect divides the row in two: the "middle voice" (the upper line in the left hand) continues with the fifth through eighth pitches of the P-6 form of the row (C-A-D-G♯ = 2–11–4–10 [see the bottom line of the matrix on p. 552]); the left hand at the same time is playing the ninth through twelfth pitches of this same form of the row (F-F♯-D♯-E = 7–8–5–6). The repetition of the B♭ in m. 3 is "permitted" because no other pitches have sounded in that particular voice. Once that voice leaves B♭, that pitch does not return until all other 11 have sounded in that particular voice. ("Permitted" is in quotation marks here because composers can of course do whatever they like, including bending or breaking their own self-imposed limitations.)

## *Primary Evidence*    SCHOENBERG ON THE THREE FUNCTIONS OF THE 12-TONE ROW

*In addition to composing, Schoenberg wrote a good deal about his own music and the music of others. He was a teacher at heart, and he tried throughout his life to make the logic of his music as accessible as possible. Here he identifies the three basic functions of the 12-tone row.*

▪ ▪ ▪

The construction of a basic set of 12 tones derives from the intention to postpone the repetition of every tone as long as possible. I have stated in my *Harmonielehre* that the emphasis given to a tone by a premature repetition is capable of heightening it to the rank of a tonic. But the regular application of a set of twelve tones emphasizes all the other tones in the same manner, thus depriving one single tone of the privilege of supremacy. It seemed in the first stages immensely important to avoid a similarity with tonality. The feeling was correct that those free combinations of simultaneously sounding tones—those "chords"—would fit into a tonality. Today's ear has become as tolerant to these dissonances as musicians were to Mozart's dissonances. It is in fact correct to contend that the emancipation of the dissonance is at present accomplished and that twelve-tone music in the near future will no longer be rejected because of "discords."

The other function is the unifying effect of the set. Through the necessity of using besides the basic set, its retrograde, its inversion, and its retrograde inversion, the repetition of tones will occur oftener than expected. But every tone appears always in the neighbourhood of two other tones in an unchanging combination which produces an intimate relationship most similar to the relationship of a third and a fifth to its root. It is, of course, a mere relation, but its recurrence can produce psychological effects of a great resemblance to those closer relations.

Such features will appear in every motif, in every theme, in every melody and, though rhythm and phrasing might make it distinctly another melody, it will still have some relationship with all the rest. The unification is here also the result of the relation to a common factor.

The third advantage of composition with a set of twelve tones is that the appearance of dissonances is regulated. Dissonances are not used here as in many other contemporary compositions as an addition to make consonances more "spicy." For the appearance of such dissonant tones there is no conceivable rule, no logic, and no other justification than the dictatorship of taste. If dissonances other than the catalogued ones are admitted at all in music, it seems that the way of referring them all to the order of the basic set is the most logical and controllable procedure toward this end.

**Source:** Arnold Schoenberg, "Composition with Twelve Tones (2)," ca. 1948, in *Style and Idea: Selected Writings of Arnold Schoenberg*, ed. Leonard Stein, trans. Leo Black. (Berkeley and Los Angeles: University of California Press, 1984), pp. 246–7.

**EXAMPLE 21–4**  Forms of the row actually used in Schoenberg's Piano Suite, op. 25.

The distribution of material between right and left hands in the opening of the Minuet is fairly complicated, but if we pay close attention to the voice leading, we can see how consistently Schoenberg applies the serial process (Example 21–5). The presentation of rows in the Trio of this same movement is more straightforward, but this portion of the movement is also canonic, which provides us with a healthy reminder that serial composition does not by any means dictate all aspects of musical form. Indeed, the canonic element of this Trio is more clearly audible on the surface (through the agency of rhythm) than is the 12-tone construction itself. The analysis of 12-tone music may begin with an identification of rows but it does not end there. Other elements, such as rhythm, register, dynamics, and timbre, must also be taken into account.

For Schoenberg, the idea behind serial composition was deeply rooted in tradition. He maintained that every worthy piece of music, regardless of idiom, was a "working out" of a basic musical idea. This idea was more than just a theme: it could incorporate harmonic, contrapuntal, rhythmic, registral, timbral, and dynamic elements as well. All of Schoenberg's music manifests this basic process of what he called "developing variation," the process by which an idea grows and evolves over the course of a movement or entire work. It was in this sense that Schoenberg saw himself as the heir to the traditions of Beethoven and Brahms, who had also created large-scale musical structures through the unfolding of relatively simple motives and ideas.

What Schoenberg felt was necessary in new music, however, was the cultivation of what he called "musical prose," a style of writing in which musical ideas proceed in a style analogous to prose, as opposed to rhymed, metered poetry. Using Johann Strauss's *The Blue Danube Waltz* (Anthology) as an example, Schoenberg showed how Strauss's melody was immediately comprehensible and memorable because of its regular rhythmical patterns (its phrase structure) and its sense of musical "rhyme" (consequent phrases satisfying the expectations of antecedent phrases). Schoenberg argued that in musical prose, little if anything should be repeated exactly or within a readily predictable pattern; instead the composer should "jump quickly to the remoter stages of development" and take for granted that "the educated listener is able to discover the intervening stages for himself."[6] Schoenberg's own 12-tone music exemplifies this approach: the multiple permutations of the prime form of the row are always present even if they are not easy to hear at first. In one of his most widely read essays, "Brahms the Progressive," Schoenberg sought to demonstrate that Brahms was already moving toward the idea of musical prose before Schoenberg himself had even begun to compose. For all his revolutionary innovations, Schoenberg saw himself as part of a long tradition of music extending from Bach through Beethoven and Brahms. He even predicted to one of his pupils in 1921 that dodecaphony would "assure the supremacy of German music for the next hundred years."[7]

**EXAMPLE 21–5** Schoenberg, Piano Suite, op. 25, opening of Minuet.

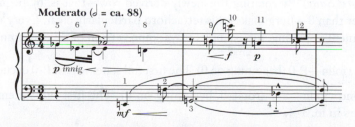

**Source:** Arnold Schoenberg, Piano Suite, op. 25 (Vienna: Universal Edition © 1926, renewed 1953). Reprinted with permission. From Glenn Watkins, *Soundings: Music in the Twentieth Century* (Schirmer Books, 1988), p. 331. Used by permission of Belmont Music Publishers, Pacific Palisades, CA 90272.

Schoenberg's premise of music as the temporal unfolding and growth of an idea continues the 19th-century tradition of **organicism**, which lies at the heart of an enormous amount of theoretical and analytical work in the 20th century. The primary goal of organicist analysis is to demonstrate the manner in which the many different elements immediately audible on the musical surface—contrasts in theme, timbre, harmony, rhythm, and so on—manifest a deeper coherence. By this line of thought, the musical work constitutes a living organism, as it were, and the challenge of analysis is to identify what we might now thing of as the DNA of the work at hand, the blueprint behind the finished composition.

Dodecaphony is a technique, not a style. Schoenberg, Webern, and Berg each developed their own personal ways of applying it, even though their followers lumped them together under the rubric of the "Second Viennese School" (following the earlier triumvirate of Haydn, Mozart, and Beethoven, who also worked in Vienna). As with any school of composers, common interests and differences exist side by side. Their interrelationships could be complex at times: respect and even love mingled with a palpable sense of rivalry. Schoenberg, for example, once accused Webern of stealing his ideas.

Webern's application of serial technique was the most complex and concentrated of the three. Many listeners perceive his music as cryptic and aphoristic; it has been said that his compositions are to music what haiku is to poetry. He tended to work with subunits of the 12-tone row, small motifs of three or four notes. Very often, the first few notes of a row will be transformed in some way to create the remainder of the row. The row of his String Quartet, for example, consists of three different statements of the same pitch-class set—one of which spells out the notes "B-A-C-H." He relished the challenge of synthesizing serial technique with such contrapuntal and constructivist devices as canons, mirror canons, and passacaglias.

Berg tended to take a more liberal approach to serial composition than either Schoenberg or Webern. The first movement of his *Lyric Suite* for string quartet, for example, uses three different (yet related) rows, and not all of its six movements are serial: only the outer movements are entirely dodecaphonic. The third movement is serial in its outer sections but not in its trio, and only the trios of the fifth movement are written using the 12-tone method. Berg manipulates the basic row of the work (Example 21–6a) in ingenious ways. He divides it into two **hexachords** (groups of six notes, Example 21–6b) and derives two "new" rows from these notes by rearranging their order (Examples 21–6c and d).

The tonal implications of Example 21–6b are particularly clear; this is the kind of row that Schoenberg and Webern avoided. For the third movement, Berg exchanges the pitches 3 (A) and 9 (G♭) in P-0 (Example 21–6a) and transposes the whole up a fourth to create a "new" primary row for this movement. The importance of this change is that it creates a row (Example 21–6d) in which the notes A-B♭-B-F appear in succession: this tetrachord held intense personal meaning for the composer because its notes spelled out the initials of his lover and himself (see Focus: The "Secret Program" of Berg's *Lyric Suite*). By rotating this newly derived row—that is, by beginning it on a pitch other than 0—Berg makes this tetrachord particularly clear. Every voice in the third movement's opening, for example, plays some version of this grouping:

- First violin—P-0 (beginning on 0). The first full statement of P-0 occurs in m. 2–3.

- Second violin—P-7 (rotated, beginning on 9). The first full statement of P-7 occurs in m. 3–4.

- Viola—P-10 (rotated, beginning on 3). The first full statement of P-10 occurs in m. 3.

((••)) **Listen**

**CD14    Track 4**
**mysearchlab**
BERG
*Lyric Suite*
Score Anthology II/161

**EXAMPLE 21–6** Berg, *Lyric Suite*, the row (a) and three derivations (b, c, and d).

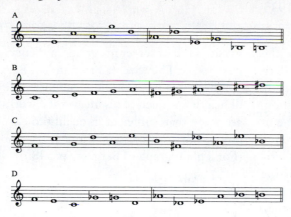

*Focus*  THE "SECRET PROGRAM" OF BERG'S *LYRIC SUITE*

On a purely musical level, the quotation of the opening of Wagner's *Tristan und Isolde* in the finale of Berg's *Lyric Suite* is at once surprising, amusing, and revealing about the relationship between tonality and atonality: what had represented the extremes of chromatic harmony in 1859 now sounded positively tame. But there is yet another level of meaning at work here, for the entire *Lyric Suite* is a coded love letter from Berg to his mistress, Hanna Fuchs-Robettin.

The headings of the six movements trace the progression of the affair:

1. Allegretto gioviale        "Jovial"

2. Andante amoroso        "Amorous"

3. Allegro misterioso/Trio estatico        "Mysterious, ecstatic"

4. Adagio appassionato        "Passionate"

5. Presto delirando/Tenebroso        "Delirious, gloomy"

6. Largo desolato        "Desolate"

But the programmatic elements go even further in shaping the music. Berg used the notes A–B♭ (in German, A–B, for "Alban Berg") and B–F (in German, H–F, for "Hanna Fuchs") in much the same way that Schumann had used notes spelling the names of significant people in his life in *Carnaval* almost a hundred years before (see Chapter 16). The opening motif of the third movement plays on these four notes, which appear for the first time together in this movement. The formal proportions and metronome markings of the entire work revolve around the numbers 23 and 10, which Berg associated with himself and his lover. The third movement consists of a scherzo-like A section of 69 measures (23 × 3) and a B section (trio) of 23 measures. The written-out return of the A section presents the music in shortened form (46 measures = 23 × 2) and in retrograde, as if to negate the declaration of love in the "Ecstatic Trio."

How do we know all this? In 1977, the American composer and Berg scholar George Perle uncovered Berg's annotated score in Mifflinburg, Pennsylvania, in the possession of Hanna Fuchs-Robettin's daughter. There, Perle found a first edition of the *Lyric Suite* that Berg himself had annotated as a "key" to the program. In this context, the *Tristan* reference toward the end of the work—the musical emblem of another ill-fated love affair—begins to make even more sense. The *Lyric Suite*, moreover, is not alone in its secret program. Similar encryptions are also found in Berg's Violin Concerto, his Chamber Concerto, and his second and final opera, *Lulu*.

# Alban Berg (1885–1935)

Of the three members of the Second Viennese School, Berg stands out as the composer whose music is in many ways the most accessible. In spite of early opposition, his atonal opera *Wozzeck* has established itself as one of the only operas of its kind that can draw audiences in the same way as the operas of Verdi and Wagner. Berg's lyrical gifts and his uncanny ability to capture the dramatic moment with just the right sound contribute to his stature as one of the great opera composers of music history. As did Schoenberg and Webern, Berg began composing in a lush, post-Wagnerian style of extreme chromaticism, broke with the principles of tonality more or less completely around 1909, and then adopted the serial method in the mid-1920s. In his application of 12-tone technique, Berg tended to be rather more free than Schoenberg and especially Webern, yet he was particularly attracted to the idea of retrograding large sections of music, as in the return of the A section of the third movement of the *Lyric Suite*. This kind of large-scale retrograde structure is often associated in his music with some kind of emotional negation or reversal. Indeed, his music is full of secret programs and encrypted messages (see Focus: The "Secret Program" of Berg's *Lyric Suite*).

Berg was not a prolific composer. He suffered from ill health for much of his life, yet the works he left behind are more than sufficient in quality to ensure his place as one of the great masters of the atonal and serial idioms. (For a photograph of Berg, see p. 548.)

# PRINCIPAL WORKS

## Dramatic Works

*Wozzeck* remains the most frequently performed of all atonal operas, indeed perhaps of all atonal works of any kind. Its ability to draw even listeners otherwise hostile to this idiom has proven extraordinary. *Lulu*, Berg's other 12-tone opera, is even more ambitious but remained unfinished at the composer's death. It was completed by the Austrian composer and scholar Friedrich Cerha and premiered in its full form in 1979.

## Orchestral Music

The 12-tone Violin Concerto is one of the few works of its kind that have thrived in the concert hall. Berg also made several arrangements of music from his *Lyric Suite*, *Wozzeck*, and *Lulu* that helped expose these larger works to a greater number of listeners.

## Chamber Music

In addition to one string quartet (op. 3) and the *Lyric Suite*, Berg wrote an important Chamber Concerto for piano, violin, and 13 wind instruments, based in part on serial principles and featuring a middle movement (*Adagio*) in "perfect" arch form, or palindrome—120 measures followed by the mirror image of those same 120 measures.

## Songs

Most of Berg's songs are early works for piano and voice. The *Five Orchestra Songs on Postcard Text by Peter Altenberg* (1912) display the composer's uncanny ability to shape texts and orchestral colors with melodic lines.

| KEY DATES IN THE LIFE OF BERG | |
|---|---|
| 1885 | Born in Vienna on February 9. |
| 1904 | Begins compositional studies with Arnold Schoenberg. |
| 1913 | The premiere of Berg's *Altenberg Lieder,* op. 4, creates an uproar in the concert hall. |
| 1915 | Drafted into the Austrian army but declared unfit for active service because of severe and chronic asthma. |
| 1918 | Helps establish, with Schoenberg and Webern, the Society for Private Musical Performances. |
| 1925 | Premiere of *Wozzeck* in Berlin; in spite of many scathing reviews, the work soon gains acceptance and assures Berg's financial security for his remaining years. |
| 1930 | Appointed to the Prussian Academy of Arts, a testimony to the impact of *Wozzeck* on his contemporaries. |
| 1935 | Dies December 24 in Vienna from blood poisoning induced by an infected bee sting. |

These three forms of the row, along with I-5, are the only ones Berg uses in this section. The *Trio estatico* ("ecstatic trio") is freely composed; the return of the opening section at m. 93 presents the opening section in a large-scale retrograde. The inverse relationship of opening and closing becomes especially clear when we compare the first and last few measures of the movement.

## SUMMARY

The boundaries between extreme chromaticism and atonality became blurred in the music of certain composers working in the early decades of the 20th century, most notably Arnold Schoenberg, Anton Webern, and Alban Berg. Dissatisfied with the difficulties of creating coherent large-scale works in the absence of tonality, Schoenberg developed the idea of serial composition in the early 1920s, based on transpositions and permutations of a basic row or series of notes. Webern and Berg developed serial composition in their own individual ways. Although many composers and listeners refused to embrace these new idioms, the abandonment of tonality introduced a new range of musical options that would be widely explored in subsequent decades.

Study and Review on mysearchlab.com

# Chapter
# 22

# The Tonal Tradition

For all the importance of atonality and serial composition in the 20th century, many of the era's leading composers continued to work largely if not entirely within the tonal tradition. Stravinsky, Bartók, Prokofiev, Shostakovich, Copland, and others all extended the bounds of the traditional harmonic idiom but for the most part retained the idea of a tonal center. For some composers, this was almost a matter of faith. The noted German composer Paul Hindemith (1895–1963) believed that

> Music, as long as it exists, will always take its departure from the major triad and return to it. The musician cannot escape it any more than the painter his primary colors or the architect his three dimensions. In composition, the triad or its direct extensions can never be avoided for more than a short time without completely confusing the listener. If the whim of an architect should produce a building in which all those parts which are normally vertical and horizontal (the floors, the walls, and the ceilings) were at an oblique angle, a visitor would not tarry long in this perhaps "interesting" but useless structure. It is the force of gravity, and no will of ours, that makes us adjust ourselves horizontally and vertically. In the world of tones, the triad corresponds to the force of gravity. It serves as our constant guiding point, our unit of measure, and our goal, even in those sections of compositions which avoid it.[1]

Others were even blunter in their rejection of atonality. The American composer Alan Hovhaness (1911–2000) argued, "[A]tonality is against nature. There is a center to everything that exists. The planets have the sun, the moon, the earth. . . . All music with a center is tonal. Music without a center is fine for a moment or two, but it soon sounds all the same."[2]

## NEOCLASSICISM AND THE "NEW OBJECTIVITY"

Atonality, primitivism, and expressionism fostered their own counterreactions in the early decades of the 20th century. The most important of these was an aesthetic movement known as **Neoclassicism**, the deliberate imitation of an earlier style within a contemporary context. ("Classic" in this sense refers to anything from the distant past, not specifically to the Classical era or to so-called classical music in general.) The idea of writing in a manner openly influenced by a much earlier style was not an invention of the 20th century.

Still, the movement known as Neoclassicism took on a special significance by virtue of its pointed rejection of modernist developments. Neoclassicism is characterized by the following:

- A return to the tonal idiom, often chromatically inflected but not nearly to the extent found in the music of Wagner, Hugo Wolf, or Richard Strauss

- A return to conventional genres and forms, particularly those of the Baroque and Classical eras, such as suite, sonata, concerto, and concerto grosso, along with their commensurate conventions of large-scale structure, such as the ritornello principle, sonata form, rondo, and theme and variations

- A return to the ideal of absolute music—that is, music not connected with a text or program of any kind

- A general tendency toward transparent textures, lighter orchestration, and smaller ensembles in general

- Conciseness of expression, avoiding grandiose or bombastic gestures

Neoclassicism reached its height in the 1920s and 1930s, in the wake of World War I. Disillusioned by this devastating conflict, many artists and audiences took pleasure in the vaguely nostalgic sense evoked by the Neoclassical idiom. "Back to Bach" and "The New Simplicity" became slogans. This new music did not sound like Bach, of course, nor was it necessarily harmonically simple; but it certainly sounded more *like* Bach (or other earlier composers) than works of the day that rejected the premise of triadic harmony.

The finale to the Concertino for Harp and Orchestra (1927) by the French composer Germaine Tailleferre (1892–1982) offers a good example of Neoclassicism. The *-ino* at the end of "Concertino" indicates at once that this is a work of smaller dimensions, for a medium-sized orchestra, and its three movements run only about 16 minutes in performance. The harmonic idiom is a mixture of old and new, with a strong sense of the tonic, but without the tonic-dominant polarity that characterizes the style of the eighteenth century. The score features numerous modal and non-tonic inflections. The textures tend to be light and transparent, even in the fugal section (beginning at Figure 6 in the score) and the form—a rondo—is decidedly traditional. Tailleferre builds the opening theme on a clear antecedent-consequent structure, which further reinforces the "classical" element of the neoclassical. But no one would mistake this movement for something written 150 years—or even 50 years—before.

Stravinsky also embraced the Neoclassicist idiom in the 1920s. His ballet *Pulcinella* (1920) is based on themes from early-18th-century works attributed to the 18th-century Italian composer Giovanni Battista Pergolesi (see Chapter 13); it was later discovered the music had in fact been written by a lesser-known composer of that time, but the important point is that Stravinsky drew on material from a much earlier era. Other Neoclassical works by Stravinsky include the Concerto for Piano and Winds (1924) and the *Symphony in C* (1940; note the designation of key). Like *Pulcinella*, these works evoke pointedly old-fashioned idioms even while incorporating features that make them unmistakable products of their time. Other composers associated with Neoclassicism include Paul Hindemith and Aaron Copland (1900–1990), whose ballet *Appalachian Spring* includes an elaborate and decidedly tonal fantasy on a Shaker hymn tune.

Related to Neoclassicism is an outlook known as the "new objectivity." Today, we might think of it as the aesthetic of "cool": music that is detached, unsentimental,

((•—Listen

CD 14    Track 5
mysearchlab
TAILLEFERRE
*Concertino for Harp and Orchestra*
Score Anthology II/162

and perhaps slightly hard-edged. Part of Neoclassicism's appeal lay in its tendency toward understatement: if the quintessential act of expressionism is the scream, then the quintessential act of the "new objectivity" is the raised eyebrow. To view something objectively, we must step outside ourselves and consider it as something quite separate from us, in a word, as an object. This is precisely how Stravinsky described his Octet for Winds of 1923 (see Primary Evidence: Stravinsky on Musical "Objectivity"). The style of the explanatory prose itself is clinical, with clipped rhythms and a quasi-scientific tone. Stravinsky even goes so far as to deny the presence of emotional content within the work, although this may be meant ironically—irony being a favorite device of Neoclassicism in all the arts.

A similar attitude of detachment is evident in many of the works of the German composer Kurt Weill (1900–1950), who collaborated with the playwright Bertolt Brecht (1898–1956) on several stage works in the late 1920s and early 1930s. These productions often emphasized the distance between characters, their words, their music, and the audience. Speaking in the third person (a verbal technique of distancing), the composer announced, "Brecht and Weill have investigated the question of music's

## Primary Evidence | STRAVINSKY ON MUSICAL "OBJECTIVITY"

*The clinical, almost robotic tone of Stravinsky's description of his Octet for Winds (1923) parallels his argument that the work is not "emotive," but is based instead on self-contained "objective elements." This music, according to the composer, has no room for "nuances" that cannot be notated precisely. How seriously can we take all this? Is it really possible to have music that can be performed without expressive nuance? Or is Stravinsky pulling our collective leg? Did such thinking anticipate the zealously detailed markings on scores written later in the century and their composers' heightened expectations of their realization?*

■ ■ ■

My *Octuor* is a musical object. . . .

My *Octuor* is not an "emotive" work but a musical composition based on objective elements which are sufficient in themselves. . . .

I have excluded from this work all sorts of nuances, which I have replaced by the play of these volumes.

I have excluded all nuances between the *forte* and the *piano*; I have left only the *forte* and the *piano*.

Therefore the *forte* and the *piano* are in my work only the dynamic limit which determines the function of the volumes in play. . . .

To interpret a piece is to realize its portrait, and what I demand is the realization of the piece itself and not of its portrait.

It is a fact that all music suffers, in time, a deformation through its execution; this fact would not be regretted if

that deformation were done in a manner that would not be in contradiction to the spirit of the work.

A work created with a spirit in which the emotive basis is the nuance is soon deformed in all directions; it soon becomes amorphous, its future is anarchic and its executants become its interpreters. The nuance is a very uncertain basis for a musical composition because its limitations cannot be, even in particular cases, established in a fixed manner.

On the other hand, a musical composition in which the emotive basis resides not in the nuance but in the very form of the composition will risk little in the hand of its executants.

I admit the commercial exploitation of a musical composition, but I do not admit its emotive exploitation. To the author belongs the emotive exploitation of his ideas, the result of which is the composition; to the executant belongs the presentation of that composition in the way designated to him by its own form. . . .

This sort of music has no other aim than to be sufficient in itself. In general, I consider that music is only able to solve musical problems; and nothing else, neither the literary nor the picturesque, can be in music of any real interest. The play of the musical elements is the thing.

**Source:** Igor Stravinsky, "Some Ideas about My Octuor" (1923), in Eric Walter White, *Stravinsky: The Composer and His Works* (Berkeley: University of California Press, 1966), pp. 528–31.

role in the theater. They have concluded that music cannot further the action of a play or create its background. Instead, it achieves its proper value when it interrupts the action at the right moments."[3]

Weill's first major collaboration with Brecht was *Die Dreigroschenoper* ("The Threepenny Opera") of 1927, an up-to-date re-telling of John Gay's *The Beggar's Opera* (see Chapter 9). Their second collaboration was *Aufstieg und Fall der Stadt Mahagonny* ("Rise and Fall of the City of Mahagonny," 1928–1929), a satire on capitalism that takes place in the fictional city of Mahagonny, where the only crime is poverty. Everything is legal as long as it can be paid for. The "Alabama Song," sung by Jenny (a prostitute) and her six cohorts, assumes the outward form of a traditional aria, with a declamatory introduction and a soaring conclusion, but the words are surreal, a parody of pidgin English ("Oh! Moon of Alabama we now must say goodbye, / We've lost our good old mama and must have whisky oh you know why")[4] and, oddly enough for an opera otherwise in German, the text of this particular number is in English. All this creates a sense of distance—objectivity—that is magnified by the discordant sound of the honky-tonk–style accompaniment, using the American foxtrot rhythms that Europeans had made their own after World War I.

**CD14    Track 6**
WEILL
*Aufstieg und Fall der Stadt Mahagonny*
Score Anthology II/163

# ORCHESTRAL MUSIC

The genres of symphony and symphonic poem continued to flourish in the 20th century. The symphony retained its essential character as a large-scale work in multiple movements, and many of the most prominent composers of the century turned to this genre at one time or another. It proved an especially important vehicle for musical nationalism. Prokofiev and another Russian composer, Dmitri Shostakovich (1906–1975), used folk or folk-like inflections in many of their symphonies, as did the Finnish composer Jean Sibelius; the English composer Ralph Vaughan Williams (1872–1958); the Americans Charles Ives, Roy Harris (1898–1979), and Aaron Copland (1900–1990); and the Mexican composer Carlos Chavez (1899–1978). Neoclassicists were also attracted to the symphony. Examples include Prokofiev's overtly retrospective *Classical Symphony*, op. 25, and Stravinsky's *Symphony in C* (1940) and *Symphony in Three Movements* (1945), which are among the composer's most important orchestral works.

Despite this continued vitality, the symphony no longer occupied the position of central importance it had in the 19th century. The idea of musical pluralism extended to genres as well as styles, and aspiring composers of instrumental music in the 20th century were no longer expected to prove their abilities by writing a symphony. Atonal and serial composers, focused as they were on breaking with the past, largely avoided the genre, in part because it carried with it such an imposing tradition. The use of atonality, moreover, posed problems of large-scale formal organization that were difficult to solve at first; most early atonal works, as we have already seen, operated on a fairly small scale. Anton Webern's Symphony, op. 21 (1928), a 12-tone work, is really more an anti-symphony, written for chamber ensemble (one player to a part) rather than orchestra, and in two movements rather than the customary four. Like nearly all of Webern's music, the work is quite brief: the entire symphony takes less than ten minutes to perform.

The symphonic poem, like the symphony, appealed primarily to composers whose style remained within the tonal idiom. After completing the *Prélude à l'Après-midi d'un faune* (see Chapter 20), Debussy would go on to write *Nocturnes* and *La mer* ("The Sea"), a three-movement work that resembles a symphony in all but name, but whose programmatic movement headings evoke specific images of the sea. His last orchestral triptych was *Images* (1912). Other composers who cultivated the symphonic poem include the following:

Paul Dukas—*The Sorcerer's Apprentice* (1897)

Arnold Schoenberg—*Pelleas und Melisande* (1903)

Alexander Scriabin—*Poem of Ecstasy* (1908), *Prometheus* (1910)

Jean Sibelius—*Finlandia* (1899), *Tapiola* (1926)

Charles Ives—*Holidays* (1904, 1909–1913), *Three Places in New England* (1911–1914)

Gustav Holst—*The Planets* (1917)

Sergei Rachmaninoff—*The Isle of the Dead* (1909)

Arthur Honegger—*Pacific 231* (1923), *Rugby* (1928)

Ottorino Respighi—*The Fountains of Rome* (1917), *The Pines of Rome* (1924)

Darius Milhaud—*The Ox on the Roof* (1919), *The Creation of the World* (1923)

George Gershwin—*An American in Paris* (1928)

((•—Listen
CD14    Track 7
**mysearchlab**
BARTÓK
*Music for Strings, Percussion, and Celesta*
Score Anthology II/164

Still other composers wrote large-scale works for orchestra that avoided programmatic and generic associations altogether. Béla Bartók's *Music for Strings, Percussion, and Celesta* (1936) suggests no programmatic elements and avoids aligning itself with the tradition of the symphony, even though its four movements follow an essentially symphonic format. The work is written for an unusual combination of instruments: a double string orchestra (including harp), celesta (a keyboard instrument that mimics the sound of small bells), and a battery of percussion instruments (timpani, piano, xylophone, bass drum, side drum, cymbals, tam-tam).

The work is tightly integrated, with all four movements deriving their principal thematic ideas from the fugue subject of the opening movement, a theme built on the eight chromatic pitches between A and E with three different meters over the course of its four measures. The music remains tonally centered throughout, but not always within the framework of triadic harmony. Bartók frequently uses themes that employ all the chromatic pitches within a limited range. The opening phrase of the first movement's fugue touches on every chromatic note between A and E in a way that avoids any sense of triadic harmony, even while grounding the theme itself on A. The theme that enters at m. 6 of the third movement, to take another example, is similarly chromatic within a narrow range; its rhythms and articulations reflect the quasi-improvisatory performance style of much eastern European folksong without actually quoting from a recorded folk song. The underlying drone to this melody (m. 6–16) is not a perfect fifth but rather a tritone on C and F♯, the same pitches on which the work as a whole will end. Once again, Bartók has provided his music with a tonal center, but not one based on a triad.

The third movement of *Music for Strings, Percussion, and Celesta* is full of unusual sonorities. It opens with an extended solo on a single note in the upper reaches of the xylophone—a note so high, in fact, that its pitch (f³, that is, the F three octaves above middle C) can scarcely be perceived as a pitch at all. The repetitions of this echo follow the Fibonacci series, after the initial sounding {1, 1, 2, 3, 5, 8}, followed by the palindromic completion {5, 3, 2, 1, 1}. The xylophone is soon joined by timpani playing glissando rolls. The movement as a whole is structured around the principle of a symmetrical or **arch form**, by which the music progresses toward a

THE 20TH CENTURY ✳ 565

midpoint and then more or less retraces its steps. This particular movement centers on m. 49–50, which present an essentially retrograde form of m. 47–48. The music "turns" this moment. On the whole, the movement can be broken down as follows:

| BARTÓK'S *MUSIC FOR STRINGS, PERCUSSION, AND CELESTA*: THE PALINDROMIC STRUCTURE OF THE THIRD MOVEMENT | | | | | | | | | |
|---|---|---|---|---|---|---|---|---|---|
| | A | B | C | D | E | D | C | B | A |
| Measure | 1 | 6 | 20 | 35 | 45 | 65 | 75 | 77 | 80 |

The proportions are not strict—Bartók was seldom pedantic about such matters—but the overall impression is one of growth, development, climax, and return to an original state. A glance at the opening and closing measures shows the gradual addition of instruments from xylophone to timpani and cello; the movement ends with instruments dropping out: first the violas, then xylophone, then timpani. The idea of symmetry operates at various points throughout this movement on a smaller scale as well. The opening rhythm of the xylophone gesture, for example, is symmetrical in its own right, with its midpoint at the downbeat of m. 3.

# FILM MUSIC

Film music was a new genre altogether in the 20th century. Although motion pictures first appeared in 1891, they did not begin to feature sound until 1927. Dialogue in silent movies was limited to what could be displayed in writing on the screen, with live music provided in the theater by an organist, pianist, small instrumental ensemble, or even (for especially important showings) an orchestra. Published anthologies from the early decades of the 20th century provided these musicians with a series of musical excerpts tied to general moods; much of the music is drawn from the classical repertory, particularly Beethoven, Liszt, and Wagner. With the advent of "talkies," however, recorded music could be incorporated directly into the film itself, and producers soon discovered it was cheaper and more effective to commission music that would correspond precisely to the events and emotions being portrayed on the screen than to provide live music for every showing.

The challenge of writing for film was similar to that of writing for opera, with the key difference that composers were almost always asked to write music to fit a scene that had already been shot and whose timing was thus fixed. By the middle of the 1930s a number of highly skilled composers were taking on this challenge. Among the more prominent composers who ventured into the world of cinema were the Englishmen Ralph Vaughan Williams, William Walton, and Benjamin Britten; the Frenchmen Darius Milhaud and Georges Auric; and the Americans Bernard Herrmann (1911–1975), Elmer Bernstein (1922–2004), Henry Mancini (1924–1994), and John Williams (b. 1932). From the 1930s onward, émigré composers from central and eastern Europe were particularly successful in this field. In fact, some of the most seemingly quintessential American films were set to music by artists who had spent relatively little time in the United States. The music for the Civil War epic *Gone with the Wind* (1939), for example, is by the Austrian Max Steiner (1888–1971); Russian-born Dimitri Tiomkin (1899–1979) created the score for one of the most famous of all Westerns, *High Noon* (1952). Erich Wolfgang Korngold (1897–1957), a brilliant child prodigy and a composer of symphonies and operas in his native Vienna, spent much of his life after 1934 in Hollywood, where he produced the music for such films as *The Adventures of Robin Hood* (1938) and *The Sea Hawk* (1940). Arnold Schoenberg even composed an *Accompaniment to a Cinematographic Scene* for orchestra (1929–1930), which has yet to have a film made for it.

Film music also provided the basis for a number of larger, independent works: Ralph Vaughan Williams reworked his music from the film *Scott of the Antarctic* (1948) into his Seventh Symphony (*Sinfonia antarctica*); Benjamin Britten originally wrote the music that would become *The Young Person's Guide to the Orchestra* for an instructional film entitled *The Instruments of the Orchestra* (1945); and Sergei Prokofiev's cantata *Alexander Nevsky* uses music from the original film of that name (1938).

The film *Alexander Nevsky*, directed by Sergei Eisenstein, is based on the true story of Grand Duke Alexander of Novgorod, who defeated the Swedes on the River Neva (hence "Nevsky" is his popular name) in the year 1240 and went on to repel an army of Teutonic knights in 1242 in a battle that took place on the frozen surface of Lake Chudskoye. In the film's climactic scene, the ice breaks and swallows the invaders. In 1939, Prokofiev turned his brilliant score for this movie into a cantata for mezzo-soprano, chorus, and large orchestra. The rousing fourth movement of this work ("Arise, People of Russia") represents the hopes of those people before the battle. Like much of the rest of the score, it integrates folksong-like melodies (of Prokofiev's own invention) with a harmonic idiom that is essentially triadic. The occasional modal and chromatic inflections are extremely limited, for this was music written to appeal to mass audiences and their spirit of patriotism. This kind of writing was actively promoted by Soviet authorities as **socialist realism**, a readily accessible style that evokes the music of the people in an overwhelmingly optimistic tone (see Primary Evidence: Socialist Realism).

The Soviet government was quick to recognize the potential of film and film music to galvanize patriotic fervor. The state itself financed Eisenstein's *Alexander Nevsky* in the late 1930s at a time when German invasion appeared imminent: the

(((•─ **Listen**

**CD14    Track 8**
**mysearchlab**
PROKOFIEV
*Alexander Nevsky*
Score Anthology II/165

**Alexander Nevsky.** Prokofiev's music for Sergei Eisenstein's 1938 film *Alexander Nevsky* includes an extended number accompanying the central battle between the Russian troops and the invading Teutonic Knights. At the climax of this 13th-century battle, fought on a frozen lake, the icy surface opens and swallows the invaders. The film reflects the growing tensions of the late 1930s between the Soviet Union and Germany. With the Hitler-Stalin Non-Aggression Pact of 1939, Stalin ordered that the film be shelved; when Germany invaded the Soviet Union in 1940, he ordered the film to be re-released to rouse popular support against this invasion from the west.

**Source:** Bettmann/Corbis

**ALEXANDER NEVSKY**  Directed by Sergei Eisenstein
Produced by Mosfilm, Moscow, U.S.S.R.
Distributed by Amkino Corp.    printed in U. S. A.

## Primary Evidence  SOCIALIST REALISM

*The leadership of the Soviet Union worked for decades to encourage composers to write in a style accessible to a wide audience. Socialist realism involved writing in a fundamentally tonal idiom, using folksong or folksong-like melodies whenever possible and employing programmatic music favorable to the ideals of communism. Conversely, the authorities discouraged what they called "formalism"—abstract, nonprogrammatic music, particularly in an atonal or serial idiom—on the grounds that these techniques were not rooted in the arts of the people. In the pronouncement here, Tikhon Khrennikov (1913–2007), a prominent Russian composer who served as musical adviser to the Red Army during World War II and was secretary general of the Union of Soviet Composers during the late 1940s and early 1950s, denounces the "decadent" tendencies of Western music. Khrennikov reserves special scorn for his own countrymen who have turned away from writing music for "the people" in favor of a more intellectual style.*

■ ■ ■

It was established that repeated directives of the Party on the problems of art were not carried out by the majority of Soviet composers. All the conversations about "reconstruction," about switching of composers to folkways, to realism, remained empty declarations. Almost all composers who worked in the field of large forms kept aloof from the people, and did not enjoy popularity with the broad audiences. The people knew only songs, marches and film music, but remained indifferent towards most symphonic and chamber music. . . .

The Central Committee of the All-Union Communist Party (Bolsheviks) points out in its Resolution that formalistic distortions and anti-democratic tendencies have found their fullest expression in the works of such composers as Shostakovich, Prokofiev, Khachaturian, Popov, Miaskovsky, Shebalin, and others. In the music of these composers we witness a revival of anti-realistic decadent influences calculated to destroy the principles of classical music. These tendencies are peculiar to the bourgeois movement of the era of imperialism: the rejection of melodiousness in music, neglect of vocal forms, infatuation with rhythmic and orchestral effects, the piling-up of noisy ear-splitting harmonies, intentional illogicality and unemotionality of music. All these tendencies lead in actual fact to the liquidation of music as one of the strongest expressions of human feelings and thoughts. . . .

When occasionally [these composers] turned toward folk melodies they arranged them in an overcomplex decadent manner alien to folk art. . . .

All these creative faults are typical expressions of formalism.

Formalism is a revelation of emptiness and lack of ideas in art. The rejection of ideas in art leads to the preachment of "art for art's sake," to a cult of "pure" form, a cult of technical devices as a goal in itself, a hypertrophy of certain elements of the musical speech at the price of a loss of integrity and harmoniousness of art.

**Source:** Tikhon Khrennikov, quoted in Nicolas Slonimsky, *Music Since 1900*, 4th ed. Macmillan Reference U.S.A., © 1971. Reprinted by permission of The Gale Group.

---

film's plot is deeply nationalistic and transparently anti-German. Soldiers of the Red Army were actually used as extras in the movie. But after signing the Non-Aggression Pact with Hitler in 1939 (the same agreement whose secret appendix also spelled out the later dismemberment of Poland by both Germany and the Soviet Union), Stalin had the film removed from circulation, only to have it rushed back into theaters after Germany's surprise invasion of the Soviet Union in June 1941. The film's powerful images were made all the more evocative by Prokofiev's stirring score.

## BALLET

Ballet enjoyed two "golden ages" in the 20th century. The first came in Paris in the years before World War I through the work of Sergei Diaghilev's Ballets Russes (see Chapter 20) and the American Isadora Duncan (1877–1927), another pioneer of modern dance. The second took place in the middle of the century in New York City through the work of choreographers like the Russian émigré George Balanchine (1904–1983), who had choreographed for Serge Diaghilev (see Chapter 20); Martha Graham (1893–1991)

**((•—Listen**

CD14   Track 9
**mysearchlab**

TRADITIONAL
*Bonaparte's Retreat*
Score Anthology II/166a

**((•—Listen**

CD14   Track 10
**mysearchlab**

COPLAND
*Rodeo*
Score Anthology II/166b

and Agnes de Mille (1909–1993), both of whom worked with Aaron Copland; Merce Cunningham (1919–2009), who danced for Graham and then collaborated for many decades with John Cage; and Jerome Robbins (1918–1998), who choreographed the original stage and film versions of Leonard Bernstein's *West Side Story* (discussed later in this chapter) and who worked alongside Balanchine in the New York City Ballet.

Copland was the premiere American composer of ballet. *Billy the Kid* (1938) was followed by *Rodeo*, commissioned and premiered by Agnes de Mille and the Ballet Russe de Monte Carlo in 1942. The scenario is far more lighthearted than its predecessor: a cowgirl refuses to "dress like a girl" simply to gain the attention of a champion wrangler; when a more traditional rancher's daughter seems to be gaining the young man's affection, the cowgirl shows up in a dress for the square dance finale, "Hoe-down," and win the wrangler's heart. (The discomfort of the cowgirl with traditional gender roles was said to be autobiographical for de Mille.) De Mille choreographed the entire ballet before Copland had written a note, and requested that the composer incorporate traditional tunes into the score. In the case of "Hoe-down," Copland turned to a recently-issued anthology of American folk music edited by Alan and John Lomax called *Our Singing Country* (1941). This collection included a fiddle tune, "Bonaparte's Retreat" (or simply "Bonyparte"), transcribed by Ruth Crawford Seeger (see Chapter 23) from a recorded performance by "Fiddler Bill" Stepp in eastern Kentucky in 1937. Copland makes the melody his own, thanks to colorful elements such as the "tuning up" at the beginning, the tension between conjunct and disjunct melodic lines, Stravinsky-like accents applied to the principal tune in the violins (which sound like "fiddles" in cross-tuning), and the beautiful depiction of (temporary) technological breakdown after m. 207. When the next opportunity for a ballet came along, Copland wrote one for the dancer Martha Graham; originally entitled *Ballet for Martha*, it eventually became *Appalachian Spring* (1944), another work on a distinctively American theme.

**The American dancer Agnes de Mille in the role of the Cowgirl in the premiere of Copland's *Rodeo* (1942).** De Mille (1905–1993) was also the choreographer for this production, which blended modern ballet with square dancing. She later choreographed Broadway musicals, including *Oklahoma!* (1943), *Carousel* (1945), *Brigadoon* (1947), *Gentlemen Prefer Blondes* (1949), and *Paint Your Wagon* (1951). Together with her friend Martha Graham, de Mille is widely regarded as one of the most influential figures in 20th-century American ballet.

**Source:** Maurice Seymour/Lebrecht Music & Arts Photo Library

**William H. ("Fiddler Bill") Stepp.** Stepp (1875–1947) was among a group of Kentucky fiddlers recorded by the Library of Congress's Archive of Folk Culture in the 1930s; other Stepp recordings include "The Drunken Hiccups," "Callahan," "Silver Strand," and "The Ways of the World."

**Source:** Courtesy Shanachie Records

**Composer Profile**

# Aaron Copland (1900–1990)

Copland belonged to the generation of American composers that came of age in the 1920s and 1930s, a generation consumed with the idea of American music. Like so many of his contemporary colleagues, he was trained in the European tradition, studying composition with Nadia Boulanger in Paris and analyzing, under her guidance, a wide range of music by such composers as Monteverdi, Bach, Mahler, and Stravinsky. Some of Copland's music is extremely demanding for listeners and performers alike. Examples include the *Piano Variations* (1930), the freely serial Piano Quartet (1950), and the *Piano Fantasy* (1957). Yet he never lost what might be called a populist touch, more evident in such works as *Appalachian Spring*, *Billy the Kid*, *Rodeo*, *Lincoln Portrait*, and *Fanfare for the Common Man*. He also wrote music for a number of Hollywood films, including *Our Town* and *Of Mice and Men*. The appeal of Copland's music transcends generations. The filmmaker Spike Lee used several of his works in the soundtrack to *He Got Game* (1998). "When I listen to Copland's music," Lee explained, "I hear America, and basketball is America. It's like he wrote the score for this film."[5]

Over the last 40 years of his life, Copland was showered with a string of honors and awards: a Pulitzer Prize for *Appalachian Spring*, an Oscar for the score of the movie *The Heiress* (1950), the Presidential Medal of Freedom (1964), and a long series of honorary degrees from American universities. His unwillingness to "name names" of supposed Communists at the McCarthy hearings in 1953 led to personal difficulties for a number of years, but his reputation was fully restored by the 1960s.[6]

In addition to his work as a composer, Copland was also a superb lecturer and writer on music. His *What to Listen for in Music* remains a model of its kind, and his many essays for the journal *Modern Music* from the 1920s and 1930s have admirably withstood the test of time.

## PRINCIPAL WORKS

Copland's best known works are his ballets, particularly *Billy the Kid* (1938, for the choreographer Lincoln Kirstein), *Rodeo* (1942, for Agnes de Mille), and *Appalachian Spring* (1944, for Martha Graham). His *Lincoln Portrait* (1942), for narrator and orchestra, is also frequently performed, as is his *Fanfare for the Common Man* (1942).

The *Twelve Poems of Emily Dickinson* (1950) are widely admired. The *Old American Songs* (1950, 1952) are

**Aaron Copland.** The composer addresses the Cultural and Scientific Conference for World Peace, New York City, 1949. In his speech, Copland advocated music as a way of bridging political differences between nations. Dmitri Shostakovich would give a rather different address to this same conference (see p. 574). Leonard McCombe/Time & Life Images/Getty Images

arrangements of American folksongs and as such another manifestation of Copland's populist side.

*Vitebsk* (1929), for piano trio, is a "Study on a Jewish Theme." The Piano Quartet (1950) and Nonet for Strings (1960) reflect the more demanding aspects of Copland's musical personality, as do the *Piano Variations* of 1930.

| KEY DATES IN THE LIFE OF COPLAND | |
|---|---|
| 1900 | Born November 14 in Brooklyn, New York. |
| 1921–1924 | Studies in Paris with Nadia Boulanger. |
| 1924 | Returns to New York and becomes a leading member of what was known as the "New Music" scene. |
| 1940 | Becomes head of the composition department at the Berkshire Music Center at Tanglewood in Lenox, Massachusetts, a position he would hold every summer through 1965. |
| 1951–1952 | Delivers the Charles Eliot Norton lectures at Harvard, later published as *Music and Imagination*. |
| 1960s | Tours, conducts, and lectures extensively throughout the United States and Europe. |
| 1990 | Dies December 2 in North Tarrytown, New York. |

# CHAMBER MUSIC

Chamber music appealed to composers working in a broad variety of styles. The string quartet maintained its traditional status as the most prestigious of all chamber genres: Schoenberg, Webern, and Berg all wrote atonal and serial works for this medium; Bartók and Shostakovich produced an impressive body of quartets within an essentially tonal idiom.

Other composers explored less conventional groupings of instruments, sometimes out of necessity. The French composer Olivier Messiaen (1908–1992) wrote his *Quatuor pour la fin du temps* ("Quartet for the End of Time") to be performed by fellow inmates in a prisoner-of-war camp in Germany during the early years of World War II: the only instruments at his disposal were a clarinet, a violin, a cello, and a rickety piano. Although many inmates interpreted its title as an allusion to the end of their time in prison, the composer himself insisted the true inspiration for the work came from Chapter 10 of the New Testament book of Revelation, in which an angel causes time to cease at the end of the world. Messiaen compared the opening movement, "Liturgy of Crystal," to "the harmonious silence of the firmament." The **harmonics** in the cello help create a particularly light, ethereal timbre: by touching the string lightly wherever a lozenge-shaped note is indicated, the cellist creates a pitch—a harmonic overtone—that actually sounds two octaves higher than the notated pitch.

But the "End of Time" in the work's title is most directly evident in its organization of rhythm. The four voices operate on entirely different rhythmic levels: the violin and clarinet—which by the composer's own account reflect the songs of a nightingale and blackbird, respectively—are free, random, unpredictable. The cello and piano, by contrast, adhere to strict rhythmic and melodic patterns. The cello presents a 15-note melody eight and a half times over the course of the movement (Example 22–1). But because the melody begins before the downbeat and ends after it, these repetitions are rhythmically different with every iteration of the theme.

The rhythmic pattern of the melody is palindromic—the same forward as backward—or as Messiaen himself called it, **nonretrogradable rhythm**. This is not obvious at first because the note values begin in the middle of the rhythmic

((•– **Listen**
CD14 Track 11
**mysearchlab**

MESSIAEN
*Quatuor pour la fin du temps*
Score Anthology II/167

**Olivier Messiaen.** A gifted performer as well as a composer, Messiaen served for more than 60 years as principal organist at a major Parisian church. He also found time to collect birdsongs from many parts of the world and incorporated some of them into his music, including his *Quatuor pour la fin du temps* (Anthology). "I have a passion for ornithology," Messiaen once declared. "Just as Bartók scoured Hungary for folksongs, so have I traveled for many years throughout the provinces of France transcribing the songs of the birds. It is an immense and endless labor. But it has given me the right to be a musician. What joy to hear a new melody, a new style, in a new landscape!"

**Source:** Portrait of Olivier Messiaen, French composer and organist (photo)/Haags Gemeentemuseum, The Hague, Netherlands/The Bridgeman Art Library

sequence: time, after all, has been going on before the piece begins. There are several ways to construct a palindromic sequence out of this line. If we count eighth-note values beginning six notes from the end of Example 22–1, for example, we find the following pattern, which is identical forward and backward:

1 1 3 1 1 4 4 3 4 4 1 1 3 1 1

Hearing such rhythms as palindromes seems far more difficult than apprehending the manipulations of a 12-tone row, especially a rhythmic pattern of this length; rhythm in music is always perceived as moving ahead (forward) in time. Messiaen establishes an overall pattern of repetition with this rhythm, in tandem with the repeating pitch content.

**EXAMPLE 22–1** Messiaen, *Quatuor pour la fin du temps*, first movement, cello line (sounding pitch), m. 2–8.

**Source:** Olivier Messiaen, *Quatuor pour la fin du temps*. In Anthony Pople, *Messiaen: Quatuor pour la fin du temps* (Cambridge University Press, 1998), p. 21. Reprinted by permission of BMG Music Publishing Ltd./Durand.

The piano's rhythm of 17 note values, although not palindromic, is also repeated many times. As in the case of the cello, the rhythmic pattern begins and ends in the middle of two different measures and thus shifts constantly in relation to the bar line. Thematically, the piano repeats a sequence of 29 chords throughout, but the thematic and rhythmic patterns do not coincide. This structure resembles that of the medieval isorhythm (see Chapter 3), in which a melodic pattern (*color*) is played against an independent rhythmic pattern (*talea*). Although Messiaen himself was well aware of isorhythm, he maintained that his more immediate sources were the rhythmic structures of certain modes of Hindu music.

From a harmonic perspective, many of the piano's 29 chords (see Example 22–2) incorporate triadic harmonies. The many additional nonharmonic tones, however, make the music sound almost atonal at times. The inner voices of chords 9 through

**EXAMPLE 22–2** Messiaen, *Quatuor pour la fin du temps*, first movement, sequence of 29 chords in the piano part.

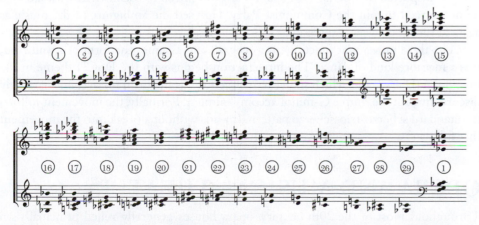

**Source:** Olivier Messiaen, *Quatuor pour la fin du temps*. In Anthony Pople, *Messiaen: Quatuor pour la fin du temps* (Cambridge University Press, 1998), Ex. 1.3 p. 22. Reprinted with permission of Cambridge University Press.

12, for example, present a series of first-inversion harmonies on G♭ Major, G major, A♭ Major, and A Major, but the nonharmonic notes of the outer voices mask the sound of these triads. At the same time, the insistent F in the bass, which has been present since the very first chord, grounds the music around a semblance of a tonal center. Messiaen himself described the opening sonority as a "chord on the dominant"—in this case, of B♭ major, the tonality implied by the key signature—even though it does not function as such in the traditional sense.

The String Quartet no. 8 of the Russian composer Dmitri Shostakovich is also heavily autobiographical. "When I die," Shostakovich wrote to a friend, "it's hardly likely that someone will write a quartet dedicated to my memory. So I decided to write it myself." The work is saturated with a musical motif the composer himself identified as his musical monogram: the notes D-E♭-C-B, which in the German system of notation (see Chapter 16) spell D-S (or Es = E♭)-C-H (= B♮), shorthand for **D**mitri **Sch**ostakovich, the German transliteration of the composer's name. The piece as a whole is full of quotations from Shostakovich's operas, symphonies, and chamber works; it also includes snippets from Siegfried's funeral music in Wagner's *Götterdämmerung* and from the first movement of Tchaikovsky's Sixth Symphony. The latter two are directly associated with the idea of death, as is the recurring *Dies irae* plainchant melody, the same tune used by Berlioz in the finale of his *Symphonie fantastique* (see Chapter 14).

Shostakovich dedicated his Eighth Quartet "to the memory of the victims of fascism and war"—that is, to the victims of the struggle against Nazi Germany in World War II—a sentiment wholly acceptable to Soviet authorities. But several of the composer's friends have since asserted the work was Shostakovich's "suicide note," that the composer planned to swallow an overdose of sleeping pills after finishing this quartet. He was depressed at having been forced to join the Communist Party; he had also recently been diagnosed with myelitis, an illness affecting the spinal cord. As is so often the case with Shostakovich, truth and fiction are difficult to separate. Eyewitness accounts of events in his life are not always reliable, many of them never having been committed to paper until after the composer's death. The music itself, however, clearly connects the images of Shostakovich (through the many quotations of his own music and of his musical monogram) and death (through the quotation of death-related music by other composers). In the final movement, the DSCH motif appears as a counterpoint to a quotation from the last scene of Shostakovich's opera *Lady Macbeth of the Mtsensk District* (1934, banned by the Soviet government) in which prisoners are being transported to Siberia. This could easily have been Shostakovich's own fate had he not agreed to join the Communist Party. He used the ambiguity of the music as a shield for his own self-expression.

The third movement functions as a scherzo and assumes the form of a waltz, but it is a macabre kind of dance. The introduction begins with the DSCH theme in the first violin (D-E♭-C-B♮), which soon (m. 20) reenters as the main motive, now jarringly discordant with the simple G-minor accompaniment. Formally, the movement follows the standard scherzo-trio-scherzo pattern. It leads without a break into the movement that follows.

# OPERA AND MUSICAL THEATER

Throughout most of the 20th century, opera houses generally relied principally on works of the past: Mozart, Rossini, Verdi, Wagner, Bizet, and Puccini constituted the core repertory. New operas in English that attracted wide followings nevertheless

((•—Listen

**CD14 Track 12**
**mysearchlab**

SHOSTAKOVICH
String Quartet no. 8
Score Anthology II/168

appeared at a steady rate from the pens of such composers as Benjamin Britten, Michael Tippett, Gian Carlo Menotti, Philip Glass, John Adams, Jack Beeson, and Harrison Birtwistle. Abroad, the works of Luigi Dallapiccola, Hans Werner Henze, Einojuhani Rautavaara, Alberto Ginastera, Aulis Sallinen, Krzysztof Penderecki, and Alfred Schnittke expanded the range of topics and styles in opera. The revival of even earlier repertories, particularly the operas of Monteverdi and Handel, offered another kind of novelty to the public as well.

The most vital form of new musical drama throughout the 20th century, however, was the Broadway musical, a genre that took its name from the New York City street on which many of the most prominent musical theaters are located. A direct descendant of the Singspiel or operetta—plays with a large number of songs—the Broadway musical is a commercial venture that requires considerable capital. A hit show can bring handsome returns to investors, driving theaters to produce musicals that can attract audiences willing to pay high prices for good seats. Some shows have had runs that would be the envy of any opera: Andrew Lloyd Webber's *Cats* ran for some 7,485 performances between 1982 and 2000; revivals of earlier musicals like Richard Rodgers's *Oklahoma!* and Jerome Kern's *Show Boat* testify to the continuing appeal of older repertory.

The plots of many early musicals were no more than a framework for a **revue**, a successor to music hall and vaudeville performances in which a potpourri of acts followed in quick succession; song and dance were the dominant components of these shows. Although theatrical presentations continued to segregate performers and audiences, African Americans at the turn of the 20th century began to produce musical comedies on Broadway that drew white audiences (and on occasion integrated casts). Many of the offensive stereotyped images perpetrated by the minstrel shows endured, but African-American musical and dance idioms were combined with more standard Broadway fare to produce a successful synthesis. Many stars emerged from these shows, including Ernest Hogan, Will Marion Cook, Bob Cole, George Walker, and Bert Williams (who later starred in *Ziegfeld's Follies*). After a hiatus of African-American shows in the 1910s, the genre was revived in *Shuffle Along* (1921) by Sissle and Blake, featuring Josephine Baker, Paul Robeson, and "I'm Just Wild about Harry"; *Blackbirds of 1928* by Fields and McHugh, featuring Adelaide Hall, Bill "Bojangles" Robinson, and "I Can't Give You Anything but Love"; and *Hot Chocolates* (1929), a collaboration between Andy Razaf, Harry Brooks, and Thomas "Fats" Waller (1904–1943), a brilliant songwriter, pianist, and entertainer who played an jazz-inflected style of ragtime known as "stride piano." (Ragtime and jazz are discussed in Chapter 24.)

*Hot Chocolates*, which started life as a Harlem nightclub revue, is now best known for the song "Ain't Misbehavin'," later the eponymous title of a successful Broadway revue of Waller songs in 1978. Among the original cast of *Hot Chocolates* were the multitalented Cab Calloway and the trumpeter and bandleader Louis Armstrong (1901–1971). Although Calloway sang "Ain't Misbehavin'" in the show, Armstrong made his own recording with his "orchestra" (11 players) the same year the show opened. In Armstrong's version, the song (in the standard AABA song form) is played through three times: first as an ensemble, then sung by Armstrong in the improvisational style he was famous for, then as a platform for an skillful Armstrong solo.

Many of the most successful musicals of the 20th century, like their operatic counterparts in the 19th century, combined entertainment with social commentary. Here are some outstanding examples:

- *South Pacific* (1948, music by Richard Rodgers, lyrics by Oscar Hammerstein II), which addresses interracial love against the backdrop of World War II.

((•─ **Listen**

**CD14    Track 13**
**mysearchlab**
WALLER
*Ain't Misbehavin'*
Score Anthology II/169

# Dmitri Shostakovich (1906–1975)

Shostakovich remains one of the great enigmas of 20th-century music. He labored for most of his life under the repressive regime of the Soviet Union and had to be extremely careful about what he said and wrote, both in words and in music. We are not even sure if he wrote the book that claims to be his memoir. The key question about *Testimony*, first published in the West in 1979 is the degree to which the composer differed with the communist regime. Like other citizens of the Soviet Union, he could not voice negative opinions openly without risking punishment, and this makes it difficult to distinguish between what he believed and what he was compelled to say. Shostakovich himself acknowledged the "validity" of Soviet attacks on his "decadence" and "formalism," for example, and dubbed his Fifth Symphony his "creative answer to justified criticism." But are we to take all this at face value? Historians continue to debate the point, often quite heatedly. Indeed, the furor over biography has lately tended to overshadow discussions of the music, most of which has yet to be discovered by the wider music-loving public.

Perhaps no other major composer of the 20th century was as indebted to Beethoven. Shostakovich was attracted to the same genres—symphony, sonata, concerto, quartet, opera—and much of his music follows the same emotional trajectory characteristic of much of Beethoven's music: struggle leading either to triumph or resignation. Shostakovich never abandoned tonality, yet his idiom is distinctly innovative for its time.

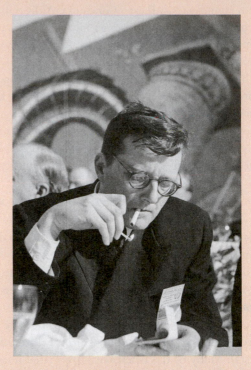

**Dmitri Shostakovich in New York, 1949.** Shostakovich was a Soviet delegate to the Cultural and Scientific Conference for World Peace, held at the Waldorf-Astoria Hotel in New York City in March, 1949. This gathering of some 800 artists and Scientists sought to defuse the rapidly escalating tensions between the United States and the Soviet Union. Shostakovich was allowed to travel to the United States for this conference with the understanding that he would deliver a speech condemning Western "warmongers." Just how much he believed personally in the content of this speech remains a matter of debate among scholars.

**Source:** Leonard McCombe/Time & Life Pictures/Getty Images

- *My Fair Lady* (1956, music by Frederick Loewe, lyrics by Alan Jay Lerner), based on George Bernard Shaw's play *Pygmalion*, which deals with class warfare as waged through the weapon of language.

- *Miss Saigon* (1989, music by Claude-Michel Schönberg, lyrics by Richard Maltby, Jr., and Alain Boublil), based loosely on Puccini's *Madame Butterfly*, which considers the aftermath of the American military involvement in Vietnam.

- *Rent* (1996, music and lyrics by Jonathan Larson), a reinterpretation of Puccini's *La Bohème* that confronts the problem of AIDS.

# PRINCIPAL WORKS

## Orchestral Music

The 15 symphonies are among the most impressive body of works of their kind by any 20th-century composer. They range from the heroic (nos. 5 and 7) to the resigned (nos. 13, 14, 15). The concertos (two each for piano, for violin, and for cello) are among Shostakovich's most popular compositions.

## Chamber Music

The 15 quartets, written between 1938 and 1974, exhibit a remarkable range of styles, tones, structures, and instrumental techniques. They are becoming better known to audiences over time. The Piano Trio and Piano Quintet are already widely performed.

## Piano Music

The *24 Preludes and Fugues* are modeled in certain respects on Bach's *Well-Tempered Clavier* and deserve wider performance, as do the many miscellaneous works for solo piano, such as the Preludes, the two sonatas, and the *Aphorisms*.

## Operas

*Lady Macbeth of the Mtsensk District* (1934) drew the ire of Soviet authorities, not only because of its dissonant musical idiom, but also because it presented such dramatic themes as murder, suicide, and adultery, behaviors inconsistent with what the regime perceived to be the ideals of Soviet art. Shostakovich's earlier opera, *The Nose* (1930), reveals the composer's deep sense of the humorous and grotesque.

| KEY DATES IN THE LIFE OF SHOSTAKOVICH | |
|---|---|
| 1906 | Born September 25 in St. Petersburg (Russia). |
| 1919 | Enters the conservatory in his native city and studies piano and composition. |
| 1926 | Achieves international reputation with the premiere of his First Symphony. |
| 1936 | The opera *Lady Macbeth of the Mtsensk District* elicits a furious assault from Soviet authorities, who condemn the work as decadent, a "bedlam of noise." Rehabilitates himself with Soviet authorities with his Fifth Symphony and later (1942) with his Seventh Symphony, which supposedly depicts the defeat of the German army at the hands of the Soviets. |
| 1949 | Serves as a delegate to the Cultural and Scientific Congress for World Peace, in New York, but the U.S. State Department forces the entire Soviet delegation to leave the country prematurely. |
| 1957 | Elected as a secretary of the Union of Soviet Composers. |
| 1959 | Tours the United States and attends the world premiere of his Cello Concerto in Philadelphia. |
| 1962 | Pressured by the Soviet government to alter the text of his Symphony no. 13, commemorating the death of Jews in Kiev during World War II. |
| 1966 | Awarded two of the Soviet Union's highest honors, the Hero of Socialist Labor and the Order of Lenin. |
| 1975 | Dies August 9 in Moscow. |

Leonard Bernstein's *West Side Story* (1957) focuses on the problem of gang warfare between Puerto Ricans (the Sharks) and whites (the Jets) in New York City. The libretto, by Stephen Sondheim (who would go on to compose many hit musicals of his own), was unusually gritty and realistic by the standards of its time. It draws liberally on Shakespeare's *Romeo and Juliet*, featuring a pair of lovers from rival groups and ending in the death of one of them.

The *Quintet* is an ensemble very much in the tradition of *Bella figlia dell'amore* from Act III of Verdi's *Rigoletto* (see Chapter 17). Dramatically, both revolve around the feeling of anticipation: the Sharks and Jets await their climactic conflict, while the

CD14  Track 14
BERNSTEIN
*West Side Story*
Score Anthology II/170

sultry Anita knows she will get "her kicks" that night ("He'll walk in hot and tired, so what? Don't matter if he's tired, as long as he's hot.");[7] the music of the two gangs and Anita are closely related thematically. At the same time, the two lovers, Tony and Maria, await their meeting ("Tonight, tonight won't be just any night."). The number builds gradually and becomes increasingly contrapuntal as it progresses, with a lyrical love duet between Tony and Maria that unfolds above the animosity of the rival choruses. Bernstein uses a jazz-like orchestration, a rapid alternation of duple and triple meters, and even *Sprechstimme* at one point to give the music a decidedly modern sound. But the overall shape of the movement—contrasting emotions expressed simultaneously—owes much to the traditions of 19th-century opera.

## SUMMARY

The tonal idiom thrived throughout the whole of the 20th century in every genre of music, particularly the symphony and symphonic poem, the new genre of film music, ballet, song, and musical theater. Some composers were content to remain within the idiom of extended chromaticism inherited from the late 19th century. Others expanded the limits of tonality beyond triadic harmonies and the diatonic scale. Yet all these composers remained committed to the principle of writing works with a tonal center of some kind. Tonal and atonal music thus coexisted in much the same way that the *prima prattica* and *seconda prattica* had flourished side by side in the 17th century.

# New Currents after 1945

The end of World War II marked a decisive turning point not only in world history but in music as well. The war had been a catastrophic experience: the majority of the 50 million killed in the conflict were civilians and included the estimated 6 million Jewish victims of the Nazi Holocaust. (The total population systematically murdered in Europe by the Axis powers was between 9 million and 11 million persons.) The atomic bombs dropped on Japan in 1945 opened an era in which humans became capable of destroying virtually all life on earth. People everywhere sought to turn away from these horrors and make a fresh start; artists in all fields were no exception. In the light of the recent past, the New became all the more appealing, setting off what amounted to a second, postwar wave of modernism. Composers at the cutting edge of novelty elicited increasingly novel sounds in a variety of ways, by using traditional media like the orchestra, new compositional techniques, and at times new sources of sound itself.

## NEW SOUNDS FROM OLD INSTRUMENTS

In his *Threnody for the Victims of Hiroshima* (1960), the Polish composer Krzysztof Penderecki (b. 1933) used an orchestra consisting exclusively of stringed instruments—24 violins, 10 violas, 10 cellos, and 8 double basses—to create a world of sound that was startlingly new and unconventional. At times the string players are asked to create sharp, percussive sounds by snapping strings against the fingerboard; at other times they strike the body of the instrument with the fingertips. Penderecki grants considerable freedom to the performers: at several points in the score, he directs individual musicians to play "the highest note possible"; in other passages he directs different groups of instruments to play with vibrato at different rates of speed, indicated only generally by the size of the wavy line in the score, with the precise speed left up to individual players. On still other occasions, individual members of the ensemble may choose from a group of four different notational sequences and perform their chosen group "as rapidly as possible." The score features no metrical indications or bar lines: Penderecki indicates durations by timings that run underneath the bottom of each system of the score.

Other elements of the score, however, are extremely precise. Penderecki uses **microtones**—intervals smaller than a half step in the diatonic scale—at many points in the score. Western musicians had long been aware of microtones, but principally as a theoretical idea (see Prologue: Antiquity). It was not until the 20th century that composers like Ives, Bartók, Berg, Copland, and Ligeti began to use them in their works. Penderecki's *Threnody* explores these possibilities to

**Krzysztof Penderecki.** A composer of extraordinary breadth, Penderecki (pronounced "Pen-de-*ret*-ski) has written works in a variety of idioms and genres, from opera and oratorio to symphony, concerto, and string quartet. His uncompromising, avant-garde style of the 1960s, exemplified by his *Threnody for the Victims of Hiroshima*, has given way in recent decades to a more tonally oriented style that some critics have called "romantic." Penderecki has held several guest professorships in Germany and the United States and is also highly regarded as a conductor.

Source: Album/Prisma/Newscom

an unprecedented degree, concluding with a massive quarter-tone cluster of tones and microtones spanning 2 octaves and played by all 52 instruments.

Structurally, *Threnody* also offers a mixture of precision and imprecision. Like Varèse's *Ionisation* (see Chapter 20), the work is organized around sonorities, dynamics, and textures rather than themes or key areas. Although it resists ready-made formal analysis, *Threnody*'s ever-changing surface suggests a division into five large sections:

1. m. 1–5      High register, varying vibrato
2. m. 6–9      Pizzicato and bowed passages played on the tailpiece
3. m. 10–25    Expanding and contracting tone clusters
4. m. 26–62    Percussive, pointilistic sounds, with much tremolo
5. m. 63–end   Gradual return of tone clusters

((•• **Listen**

**CD14    Track 15**
**mysearchlab**
PENDERECKI
*Threnody for the Victims of Hiroshima*
Score Anthology II/171

Penderecki had originally called this work *8'37"*, a decidedly neutral title that reveals nothing more than the length of its performance; this may have been in homage to John Cage's *4'33"*. After he had heard the premiere of the work, however, he felt that this indication was too abstract and did not adequately reflect the work's emotional power. Sometime around 1961 he decided to dedicate it to the victims of Hiroshima and renamed it. He was by no means the first composer to alter a work's original title, as Beethoven's renaming of his "Buonaparte" Symphony as the "Eroica" reminds us (see in Chapter 15).

# COMBINATORIALITY

In the late 1920s, Arnold Schoenberg had discovered that certain 12-tone rows embody special features. He pointed out that a limited number of rows were **combinatorial**. A row is combinatorial if one of its hexachords—its first six or last six notes, commonly referred to as hexachords A and B—can be combined with one of the hexachords of an inverted, retrograde, or retrograde inverted form of the same row without producing any duplication of pitches.

**EXAMPLE 23–1** Row forms used in Babbitt's *Three Compositions for Piano*, no. 1

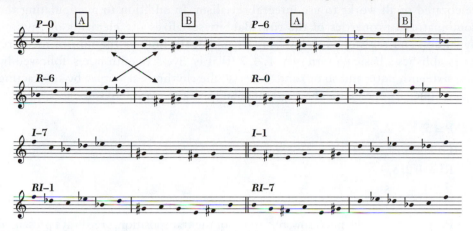

**Source:** © Copyright 1957 by Boelke Bomart, Inc. Used by permission.

The row for the first of Milton Babbitt's *Three Compositions for Piano* (1947) illustrates this property (see Example 23–1). Here, P-0 is combinatorial with R-6. In other words, hexachord A of P-0 combines with hexachord B of R-6 to produce all 12 pitches. The order of the pitches is different than in P-0, but combinatoriality is concerned only with the content of the individual (and combined) hexachords, not the actual sequence of the pitches. The complementary hexachords of the two forms (hexachord B of P-0 and hexachord A of R-6) are also combinatorial.

Schoenberg first developed the use of combinatorial rows in his *Variations for Orchestra*, op. 31 (1928), and in his *Piano Pieces*, op. 33a (1929). Combinatoriality eventually became his preferred method of 12-tone composition; Berg and Webern never really embraced the technique.

Schoenberg's students and followers in the United States took up the idea with special fervor in the years after World War II. Combinatoriality allowed these composers to align different set forms to sound at the same time without risking simultaneous or nearly simultaneous iterations of the same pitch class. By exploiting the combinatorial properties of this row, Babbitt and others were able to create multiple statements of the 12-tone row not only horizontally (in individual voices) but also vertically through the alignment of two different forms of the row sounding simultaneously. In the opening measures of the *Three Compositions for Piano*, no. 1, for example, we find the basic row both horizontally and vertically:

- Horizontally—the left hand in m. 1–2 presents P-0 in its entirety; the right hand presents P-6 in its entirety.

- Vertically—taking both voices together, all 12 pitches appear in m. 1; all 12 appear again in m. 2, in m. 3, and so on.

# INTEGRAL SERIALISM

In the years immediately after World War II, Olivier Messiaen (1908–1992) and Milton Babbitt (1916–2011), working independently of each other, developed ways of extending the parameters of serial composition beyond pitch to include such elements as rhythm and dynamics as well. This approach soon became known as **integral serialism** or **total serialism**.

((•—**Listen**

**CD15    Track 1**
**mysearchlab**
BABBITT
*Three Compositions for Piano*
Score Anthology II/172

Babbitt's *Three Compositions for Piano* (1947) is one of the earliest and most celebrated of all works to use integral serialism. In addition to manipulating the combinatorial properties of the row, Babbitt serializes the elements of rhythm, dynamics, and register as well. Using the sixteenth note as the unit of measure, he establishes a basic pattern of 5, 1, 4, 2 (that is, five sixteenth notes, followed by one sixteenth note, and so on) and "inverts" the rhythmic structure by subtracting these values from 6. Thus the rhythmic matrix of the work looks like this:

P = 5, 1, 4, 2
I = 1, 5, 2, 4
RI = 4, 2, 5, 1
R = 2, 4, 1, 5

Prime forms of the pitch row, regardless of the transposition, are always presented in the P rhythm (5, 1, 4, 2), inverted forms of the pitch row in the I rhythm (1, 5, 2, 4), retrograde inverted forms in the RI rhythm, and retrograde forms in the R rhythm. Rhythmic durations are articulated by disrupting the pattern of continuous sixteenth notes, either through rests or through slurred notes that create rhythms of longer duration. The grouping of 5 in the left hand in m. 1, for example, is created by the added duration on the fifth note after the four initial sixteenths, whereas the subsequent "1" is articulated through the eighth-note rest at the end of m. 1.

Dynamics are also determined by precompositional choices.

P = *mp* (*pp* in m. 49–56)
I = *f* (*mp* in m. 49–56)
RI = *p* (*ppp* in m. 49–56)
R = *mf* (*p* in m. 49–56)

The structure of the work as a whole is highly symmetrical. This is most immediately evident in a comparison of its opening and closing sections:
Section 1 (m. 1–8):

| | | | | |
|------|------|------|------|------|
| R.H. | P-6 | R-0 | RI-7 | I-1 |
| L.H. | P-0 | RI-1 | I-7 | R-6 |

Section 6 (m. 49–56):

| | | | | |
|------|------|------|------|------|
| R.H. | P-0 | RI-1 | I-7 | R-6 |
| L.H. | RI-7 | I-1 | P-6 | R-0 |

Close examination reveals comparable (and more intricate) symmetries between sections 2 (m. 9–18) and 5 (m. 39–48) and between sections 3 (m. 19–28) and 4 (m. 29–38).

Messiaen's *Mode de valeurs et d'intensités* ("Mode of Durations and Intensities"), published in 1949, is not quite as systematic, but it treats both pitch and rhythm in a quasi-serial fashion. He uses 3 different 12-tone rows, each in its own register (high, medium, low), spanning a total of 36 different notes. Each of these 36 notes, in turn, is assigned a unique rhythmic value, from a 30-second note to a dotted whole note. Dynamic markings (from *ppp* to *fff*) and articulation (accent, staccato, a short vertical line, a wedge, or no marking at all) are aligned with specific notes as well, although not in a unique one-to-one correspondence.

Messiaen himself did not pursue integral serialism or even serialism itself much further in subsequent years, but his work in this area exercised great influence on a generation of younger composers, most notably Pierre Boulez (b. 1925) and Karlheinz Stockhausen (1928–2007). In the end, however, integral serialism proved more important as a concept than as an application. In later years, Boulez considered this approach as part of a larger attempt to work through the burdens of tradition—tonal as well as atonal, serial as well as nonserial:

> After the war [World War II], we felt that music, like the world around us, was in a state of chaos. Our problem was to make a new musical language, seeking out what was good from the past, and rejecting what was bad. Around 1950, and for the following three years, we went through a period of seeking out total control over music. The serial process, which originated with Schoenberg and was refined in Webern, pointed out the way. What we were doing, by total serialization, was to annihilate the will of the composer in favor of a predetermining system. . . . But total control, like the total lack of control, can lead to chaos. Gaining this control was a necessary step in our development, because of our need to transubstantiate our musical heritage. But once there, we were at the zero point as composers. Now we could begin. Our process since about 1955 has been to enlarge and generalize what we had acquired through the period of atomization. In that way, we could gain a freedom through conquest, not merely through *laissez-faire*.[1]

Advocates of serialism originally hailed it as the salvation of music, a way out of the perceived dead ends of tonality, extreme chromaticism, and atonality. In retrospect, it is easy to see that serialism was in fact only one of many alternatives that emerged for composers in the 20th century. In the decades immediately after 1945, however, its significance seemed far more central, and today it is difficult to appreciate just how vital the idea of serialism was in the minds of mid-20th-century composers. Even Stravinsky—long perceived as the polar opposite of Schoenberg—turned to 12-tone techniques in the mid-1950s and early 1960s, applying the kind of serial rotation Crawford had used in the *String Quartet 1931*. In the minds of many, Stravinsky's use validated the triumph of serial composition in 20th-century music.

By the end of the 20th century, however, serialism's prestige had declined greatly. Composition students continued to learn it as a technique, but only as one of many. By the 1980s, a new generation of composers was beginning to perceive serial composition as outmoded. Once again, what had been radical at the time of its first appearance had become old-fashioned within only a generation or two.

Still, our appreciation of this music will be enhanced if we understand that its aesthetic principles supported attempts of composers to construct coherent, large-scale forms without recourse to tonality, to move beyond the exigencies of advanced chromaticism, and to create a new kind of sound as satisfying as it is demanding.

# ALEATORY MUSIC

Whereas integral serialism stressed a high degree of structure and control, **aleatory music** took precisely the opposite approach, with chance playing a leading role. The term *aleatory* comes from the Latin *alea* meaning "die" (the singular of "dice"), and aleatory music involves (at least metaphorically) a "roll of the dice"—that is, chance. The idea of writing music by chance, even by a literal throw of the dice, was by no means new in the 20th century. Mozart and other composers of the Classical era were fascinated by the possibility of creating works based on modular units chosen at random from an extensive array of possibilities. The idea of aleatory (or aleatoric) music enjoyed a healthy revival in the 1950s and 1960s through such composers as John Cage, Karlheinz Stockhausen, and Pauline Oliveros.

Aleatory music typically fixes one or more elements of the musical experience and leaves others to what might be called chance operations or events. In Terry Riley's *In C* (1964; Anthology II/180, discussed later in this chapter), for example, a group of musicians play written-out melodic gestures in a specific sequence within an ongoing pulse, but each performer is free to move on to the next gesture as he or she sees fit. Thus the composer determines the pitches to be played, but the instrumentation, rhythm, dynamics, and large-scale form are left to the performers. John Cage, in the score of his *Imaginary Landscape No. 4* (1951), for 12 radios, 24 players, and a conductor, specifies rhythm and dynamics with great precision but leaves the sound content entirely to chance. Cage calls for two performers on each radio, one controlling the frequency, the other the volume, with the conductor giving cues for each. The duration of the work, the volume, and the points of entry are all fixed, but what is actually heard at any given moment from any of the 12 radios is entirely unpredictable, from rock to talk to classical to static.

Cage's *4′33″* remains the most celebrated and controversial work of aleatory music ever written. It was premiered by Cage's longtime collaborator, the pianist David Tudor, on August 29, 1952, at the appropriately named Maverick Concert Hall in Woodstock, New York (near the site of the celebrated 1969 rock festival). The score, which consists of a single page without musical notation of any kind, indicates that the work consists of three movements of unspecified length. For each movement, the direction to the performer—"on any instrument"—is the same: "Tacet." In other words, the performer does not play at all in any of the three movements. At its premiere, Cage notes on the score, the performer had indicated the beginning of each movement by closing the lid on the piano's keyboard, the ending of each movement by opening it. Cage gives the work no title but merely notes that at this same performance, Tudor had presented this work over the span of 4 minutes and 33 seconds, and it is from this comment that the work has taken its title. Thus, even the one point that many people believe is prescribed—the length of the work—is in fact left to chance.

*4′33″* was inspired in part by the "white paintings" by one of Cage's friends, the artist Robert Rauschenberg. These so-called blank canvases are by their very nature never truly blank, of course. Every canvas has its own unique colors and textures, and each canvas is constantly changing because of the way it reflects the light of its surroundings. In much the same way, Cage's *4′ 33″* challenges the notion that there is such a thing as silence—the musical equivalent of a blank canvas—and by extension, the very idea of music itself. By listening to a supposedly silent work, we become acutely aware of the sounds around us: breathing, coughing, a room's ventilation system, a dog barking in the distance. We are listening to a work that is not silent at all and changes constantly and differs from performance to performance. These kinds of sounds, moreover, are always a part of the listening experience: if we choose to shut them out, it is because we have been conditioned to do so. As Cage suggests in his interview with William Duckworth (see Primary Evidence: John Cage on *4′ 33″* ), "[This piece] opens you up to any possibility *only* when nothing is taken as the basis." Since its premiere, many have interpreted Cage's work as the epitome of the modernist composer's contempt for the audience. Others have reveled in its profoundly provocative absurdity.

# A CLOSER LOOK

 ✳ Explore on mysearchlab

**THE SCORE OF CAGE'S** most famous work—a single page—makes the work even more problematic than most music-lovers realize.

This is only one of several different scores Cage prepared of the work; no two are identical, and Cage's account of the premiere's timings are inconsistent. Whether these inconsistencies were intentional or not remains unclear.

The work consists of three movements. For each the performer is instructed to remain silent. The marking "tacet" (Latin for "is silent") is familiar to percussionists, trombonists, and any other ensemble player who does not participate in one or more movements of a multi-movement work.

The work's title is variable, changing with the length of each performance. Thus, a performance of this work might last four minutes and 33 seconds, but that is not a parameter stipulated by the composer.

Irwin Kremen (b. 1925), a visual artist known for his collages, met John Cage at Black Mountain College in western North Carolina, where Cage, Tudor, Kremen, and other avant-garde artists gathered over the course of several summers in the early 1950s. Kremen later earned a Ph.D. in clinical psychology and joined the faculty at Duke University, where he taught until his retirement in 1992.

David Tudor (1926–1996) premiered the work at the Maverick Theater near Woodstock, New York, on August 29, 1952. The program that night concluded with a performance of Cowell's *The Banshee*.

The issue of the work's copyright remains contentious. In 2002 the publisher C. F. Peters sued the British composer Mike Batt (b. 1949, best known for his work with the pop group The Wombles) for a track on a CD Batt had released with his rock group The Planets called "A One Minute Silence." Peters argued that the concept of a silent piece was Cage's intellectual property. The matter was settled out of court, reportedly for a six-figure sum.

I

TACET

II

TACET

III

TACET

NOTE: The title of this work is the total length in minutes and seconds of its performance. At Woodstock, N.Y., August 29, 1952, the title was 4' 33" and the three parts were 33", 2' 40", and 1' 20". It was performed by David Tudor, pianist, who indicated the beginnings of parts by closing, the endings by opening, the keyboard lid. However, the work may be performed by any instrumentalist or combination of instrumentalists and last any length of time.

FOR IRWIN KREMEN                    JOHN CAGE

**The woods are alive with the sound of music.** The Maverick Concert Hall in rural Ulster County, New York, about 100 miles north of New York City, was the site of the premiere of John Cage's 4'33" on August 29, 1952. Built in 1916 and now on the Register of National Historic Places, the hall features a performance space whose open design minimizes differences between "inside" and "outside." The Maverick Concerts series, the nation's oldest continuous summer chamber music festival, will celebrate its 100th anniversary in 2016.
Margot Granitsas / The Image Works

# ELECTRONIC MUSIC

Electronic music was a fundamentally new phenomenon in the 20th century. In its purest form, it requires no performer: the sounds are produced by a machine, and the recorded version *is* the work. The ideal apparatus allows composers to manipulate all possible frequencies at all possible amplitudes with all possible durations. No sound—including those inaudible to the human ear—is impossible.

Electronic instruments first emerged in the 1920s. The theremin, named after its Russian-born inventor, Léon Theremin (Lev Termen, 1896–1993), was one of the first such instruments to attract widespread attention. It produced a single tone whose pitch and volume could be controlled by the motion of the player's hands around its antenna. Its eerie, other-worldly sound made it a favorite instrument of composers writing scores for science fiction movies, such as *The Day the Earth Stood Still* (1951) and *It Came from Outer Space* (1953), not to mention the television cartoon series *The Jetsons* (1962) and the Beach Boys' 1966 hit *Good Vibrations*.

Far more significant was the development of electronic music synthesizers in the late 1940s and 1950s. These instruments made it possible for composers to create, modify, and control the entire spectrum of sound for the first time in history. The only real variants in a purely electronic composition are the quality of the sound system on which a work is reproduced and the acoustics of the space in which the work is presented. Milton Babbitt, one of the first major composers to exploit the possibilities of this new technology, praised the ability of these machines to realize complex rhythms to a degree not possible in most live performances.

Electronic music can be categorized into three major subcategories: musique concrète, synthesized electronic music, and computer music. Any and all of the three can be combined with live performers.

**Musique concrète** is a French term used to denote music in which the sonic material to be manipulated is a recorded sound taken from everyday life (the sounds are thus real, or "concrete"). The sources of the sound might include a passing train, speaking voices, or burning charcoal. These concrete sounds are manipulated by tape splicing, mixing, and superimposing to create a larger whole.

In the late 1940s, the French composer Pierre Schaeffer (1910–1995) was one of the first to explore the possibilities of musique concrète. Others who took up this approach include Karlheinz Stockhausen (1928–2007), who composed the powerful *Gesang der Jünglinge* (1956), John Cage, Luciano Berio, and Steve Reich. In *Different Trains* (1988), Reich incorporates recordings of railway sounds and the voices of his wartime governess, a railway porter, and three Holocaust survivors into a work for string quartet that reflects on the different implications of train travel during World War II.

The Canadian composer Hugh Le Caine's *Dripsody* (1955) derives entirely from the briefest moment of sound: a single falling drop of water. By running this single recorded sound over and over again through a variable-speed tape recorder, Le Caine (1914–1977) was able to create an astonishing variety of sounds never before heard. But the work is far more than interesting sonic effects: it has a definite shape, a trajectory that projects a sense of drama and development. The ending of the work, playing on the sound of the proverbial dripping faucet, is eerily reminiscent of Haydn's String Quartet op. 33, no. 2, which leaves the unsuspecting listener uncertain just when the work has ended.

Musique concrète raises provocative questions about distinctions between music and sound in general, and between music and speech. In an earlier era, music was tacitly understood to be a special type of sound, created for its own sake either with the voice or musical instruments (or both) and distinctly different from sounds that are mere by-products of daily life. But the composers who have manipulated everyday sounds have called into question this basic assumption.

**Synthesized electronic music** consists of sounds generated and manipulated entirely by electronic means, through an electronic oscillator or a modifying device like a synthesizer. Basic sine waves can be modified by modulators, filters, and reverberators, all of which in one way or another change the color of a tone by altering its overtones. Babbitt, Stockhausen, Le Caine, and Morton Subotnick (b. 1933) are three prominent composers associated with this kind of electronic music. As a member of the faculty at Princeton University, Babbitt had access to the RCA Mark II Sound Synthesizer in the Columbia-Princeton Electronic Music Center in New York City in the late 1950s and early 1960s. The machine, although expensive, slow, and cumbersome to operate by

((•⁃ **Listen**

**CD15    Track 2**
**mysearchlab**
LE CAINE
*Dripsody*
Score Anthology II/173

## Primary Evidence    "WHO CARES IF YOU LISTEN?"

*When Milton Babbitt's essay "Who Cares If You Listen?" first appeared in 1958 it soon became the flashpoint of a larger debate about the difficulties audiences were experiencing with modern music. The provocative title—imposed on the author by the editors of High Fidelity—suggests that Babbitt and his colleagues had no concern for listeners. But Babbitt's real argument is that some composers need to be able to work in an environment that allows them to explore new ideas the same way scientists conduct experiments in their laboratories. Such an environment, Babbitt argued, is to be found in the university. There, free from commercial pressures, composers would be able to help music develop beyond its current state.*

■ ■ ■

This article might have been entitled "The Composer as Specialist" or, alternatively, and perhaps less contentiously, "The Composer as Anachronism." For I am concerned with stating an attitude towards the indisputable facts of the status and condition of the composer of what we will, for the moment, designate as "serious," "advanced," contemporary music. This composer expends an enormous amount of time and energy—and, usually, considerable money—on the creation of a commodity which has little, no, or negative commodity value. He is, in essence, a "vanity" composer. The general public is largely unaware of and uninterested in his music. The majority of performers shuns and resents it. Consequently, the music is little performed, and then primarily at poorly attended concerts before an audience consisting in the main of fellow professionals. At best, the music would appear to be for, of, and by specialists. . . .

Nor do I see how or why the situation should be otherwise. Why should the layman be other than bored and puzzled by what he is unable to understand, music or anything else? It is only the translation of this boredom and puzzlement into resentment and denunciation that seems to me indefensible. After all, the public does have its own music, its ubiquitous music: music to eat by, to read by, to dance by, and to be impressed by. Why refuse to recognize the possibility that contemporary music has reached a stage long since attained by other forms of activity? The time has passed when the normally well-educated man without special preparation could understand the most advanced work in, for example, mathematics, philosophy, and physics. Advanced music, to the extent that it reflects the knowledge and originality of the informed composer, scarcely can be expected to appear more intelligible than these arts and sciences to the person whose musical education usually has been even less extensive than his background in other fields. But to this, a double standard is invoked, with the words "music is music," implying also that "music is *just* music." Why not, then, equate the activities of the radio repairman with those of the theoretical physicist, on the basis of the dictum that "physics is physics"? It is not difficult to find statements like the following, from the *New York Times* of September 8, 1957: "The scientific level of the conference is so high . . . that there are in the world only 120 mathematicians specializing in the field who could contribute." Specialized music, on the other hand, far from signifying "height" of musical level, has been charged with "decadence," even as evidence of an insidious "conspiracy."

It often has been remarked that only in politics and the "arts" does the layman regard himself as an expert, with the right to have his opinion heard. In the realm of politics he knows that this right, in the form of a vote, is guaranteed by fiat. Comparably, in the realm of public music, the concertgoer is secure in the knowledge that the amenities of concertgoing protect his firmly stated "I didn't like it" from further scrutiny. Imagine, if you can, a layman chancing upon a lecture on "Pointwise Periodic Homeomorphisms." At the conclusion, he announces: "I didn't like it." Social conventions being what they are in such circles, someone might dare inquire: "Why not?" Under duress, our layman discloses precise reasons for his failure to enjoy himself; he found the hall chilly, the lecturer's voice unpleasant, and he was suffering the digestive aftermath of a poor dinner. His interlocutor understandably disqualifies these reasons as irrelevant to the content and value of the lecture, and the development of mathematics is left undisturbed. If the concertgoer is at all versed in the ways of musical lifesmanship, he also will offer reasons for his "I didn't like it"—in the form of assertions that the work in question is "inexpressive," "undramatic," "lacking in poetry," etc., etc., tapping that store of vacuous equivalents hallowed by time for: "I don't like it, and I cannot or will not state why." The concertgoer's critical authority is established beyond the possibility of further inquiry.

I say all this not to present a picture of a virtuous music in a sinful world, but to point up the problems

## Primary Evidence *continued*

of a special music in an alien and inapposite world. And so, I dare suggest that the composer would do himself and his music an immediate and eventual service by total, resolute, and voluntary withdrawal from this public world to one of private performance and electronic media, with its very real possibility of complete elimination of the public and social aspects of musical composition. By so doing, the separation between the domains would be defined beyond any possibility of confusion of categories, and the composer would be free to pursue a private life of professional achievement, as opposed to a public life of unprofessional compromise and exhibitionism. . . .

Granting to music the position accorded other arts and sciences promises the sole substantial means of survival for the music I have been describing. Admittedly, if this music is not supported, the whistling repertory of the man in the street will be little affected, the concert-going activity of the conspicuous consumer of musical culture will be little disturbed. But music will cease to evolve, and, in that important sense, will cease to live.

**Source:** Milton Babbitt, "Who Cares If You Listen?" *High Fidelity*, vol. 8, no. 2 (1958): 38–40. Copyright Hachette Filipacchi Magazines, Inc. Reprinted by permission of the author.

today's standards, was in its time a breakthrough that allowed Babbitt to produce a new kind of music. The introduction of portable synthesizers in the mid-1960s and the rise of the personal computer in the 1980s allowed virtually anyone to pursue this kind of composition. MIDI (Musical Instrument Digital Interface) emerged in the early 1980s as the standard computer language for driving electronic synthesizers, which in turn produce sound. MIDI allows composers to control pitch, rhythm, dynamics, vibrato, and timbre in a remarkably sophisticated manner. Acoustic instruments may also be adapted for use as MIDI controllers, and interactive works involving live performers and electronic equipment have become a staple of this repertory (see the following discussion). MIDI has eliminated the need for much (but not all) programming associated with electronic and computer music.

One of the earliest and still best known works of synthesized electronic music is the soundtrack to the MGM film *Forbidden Planet* (1956), composed by the husband-and-wife team of Louis Barron (1920–1989) and Bebe Barron (1925–2008). A science fiction adaptation of Shakespeare's *The Tempest*, this was the first commercially released film to feature an entirely electronic soundtrack. The eerie soundscape resonated with the story's setting on a bleak and distant planet. Instead of a lushly orchestrated score, audiences heard stark, disembodied sounds created in a recording studio the Barrons had set up in their New York apartment, consisting of oscillators, mixers, filters, and tape recorders. By later standards, the equipment was primitive, but the sound, generated entirely by electrical sources, was distinctively new.

**Computer music** is music that has been generated, transformed, fully composed, or performed by a computer program. In its earliest form, computer music involved allowing a computer to determine how a work would unfold. Lejaren Hiller's *Illiac Suite* for string quartet (1957) is generally acknowledged to be the first work in which the computer actually emulated the process of composition itself. Hiller (1924–1994), working with the scientist Leonard Issacson, created the work on an Illiac computer at the University of Illinois, programming the machine to create a series of movements in specific styles, ranging from strict counterpoint to 12-tone to random. Hiller later collaborated with John Cage to produce *HPSCHD* (1967–1969), a multimedia, 5-hour

# John Cage (1912–1992)

"Everything we do is music," Cage once declared, and in many respects his music was devoted to making life itself an art form. He did not see himself as a high priest of art but rather as a facilitator between listeners and sounds. Profoundly influenced by Zen Buddhism and its renunciation of striving and the will, Cage maintained his "purpose is to eliminate purpose," and many of his works from the late 1940s on seem to avoid or challenge the traditional stance of the composer as an omnipotent creator of a small musical world.

Cage's output falls into several broad categories:

- *Works for percussion, including prepared piano.* The composer's early output includes a number of works for standard and nonstandard percussion instruments. A student of Henry Cowell (see Chapter 20), Cage extended his teacher's novel approach to the piano by calling for fitting the instrument's strings with such objects as screws, rubber bands, and coins, producing a range of timbres as oddly familiar as they are strange.

- *Aleatory works.* In addition to *4' 33"*, Cage wrote many works based on the element of chance. Several relate directly to the *I Ching,* also known as the *Book of Changes,* a system of interpreting the interplay of strong and weak forces based on the throw of dice. Cage's *Imaginary Landscape no. 4* (1951) calls for 12 radios tuned to 12 different stations playing simultaneously. The instructions to the performers are precise, but the results are naturally unpredictable. *0' 00"* (1962) consists of an amplified projection

**John Cage.** Many of Cage's works from the 1960s and 1970s were multimedia productions created with other artists. Two of his longtime collaborators were the dancer and choreographer Merce Cunningham (1919–2009) and the pianist and composer David Tudor (1926–1996). In this live performance of Cage's *Variations V,* Cage is seated at the far left in the foreground, manipulating electronic sound equipment along with Tudor (center) and (at the far right) the composer Gordon Mumma (b. 1935). Members of the Merce Cunningham Dance Company perform behind them, with images projected against the backdrop. In this work, Cage called for the dancers to perform within a matrix of strategically placed microphones, making the sounds of the dancers' movements an integral part of the performance.

**Source:** Herve Gloaguen/Gamma-Rapho/Getty Images

of a "disciplined action": in one of his many performances of this work, the composer sliced vegetables, placed them in a blender, and drank the mix while standing very close to a microphone.

collage of musical quotations from Mozart, Beethoven, Schoenberg, and others, the sounds of 52 tape recorders and 7 harpsichordists, all structured according to computerized models and accompanied by 6,400 slides (5,000 from NASA, the rest abstract designs), and 40 films, producing a simultaneous or an asynchronous and exuberant anarchy of activity. By the 1990s, digitized computer technology had largely replaced the tape recorder (thus bypassing the physical limitations of tape) and electronic synthesis (allowing for more sophisticated manipulation of sounds).

Seeking a remedy for the inherently variable and unpredictable nature of performance, composers of many different orientations welcomed electronic music as a way of achieving total control over the finished product. Viennese composer Ernst Krenek praised the "electronic medium, earlier denounced as a mechanistic degradation of music," for its ability to lend itself "to a kind of controlled compositional

- *Electronic works.* Cage was part of the first generation able to explore the possibilities of electronically generated sound. *Fontana Mix* (1959) combines aleatory principles with taped music, the mix being determined by the combination of various transparencies on which are graphically notated changes in amplitude, frequency, timbre, and so on.

- *Writings.* Cage's book *Silence* (1961) was the first of several influential collections of essays, diary entries, and experimental writing. He invented a poetic form of acrostic called the mesostic (in which lines intersect other lines, rather than meeting at the ends), and created visual and plastic art, including the 1969 type-superimposed-on-plexiglass sculpture *Not Wanting to Say Anything About Marcel,* dedicated to Marcel Duchamp. Despite these artistic forays and his expertise in mycology, Cage never broke his promise to Arnold Schoenberg to devote his life to music.

Cage and his music consistently polarized listeners. Most of the audience at New York's Lincoln Center walked out of his *Atlas eclipticalis* (whose score superimposes transparent staff paper on star charts to determine pitches) when it was performed by the New York Philharmonic in 1964; even members of the orchestra hissed the composer. But Cage's provocative music and writings remained fresh over time, and toward the end of his life he was showered with honors. He delivered the prestigious Charles Eliot Norton lectures at Harvard University in 1988, continuing in the tradition of Stravinsky, Hindemith, Copland, Boulez, Bernstein, and Berio. Some saw genius in his works, others charlatanism, but all were provoked by them to rethink the nature of music and its relationship to the world around us.

| KEY DATES IN THE LIFE OF CAGE | |
|---|---|
| 1912 | Born September 5 in Los Angeles. |
| 1930 | After visiting Europe returns to the United States and studies piano and composition with Henry Cowell. |
| 1934 | Studies harmony and counterpoint with Arnold Schoenberg at UCLA. |
| 1938 | Begins a lifelong personal and artistic association with the dancer Merce Cunningham, collaborating on a series of "happenings," performances that combine music, dance, poetry, film, and other forms of expression. |
| 1954 | Concert tour of Europe with the pianist David Tudor. |
| 1961 | Publishes *Silence,* the first of his many books on music. |
| 1972 | Sixtieth birthday is marked by concerts at the New School for Social Research and at Lincoln Center. |
| 1988–1989 | Delivers the Norton Lectures at Harvard University. |
| 1992 | Dies August 12 in New York City. |

improvisation much more readily than the realm of live sound because the composer can mould the sound material while he is creating it."[2] Around the middle of the century, in fact, some composers believed that electronic music would sweep away the established instruments and performance venues of most, or even all, music in Western society. Babbitt, for one, declared in 1958 that "the composer would do himself and his music an immediate and eventual service by total, resolute, and voluntary withdrawal from this public world to one of private performance and electronic media, with its very real possibility of complete elimination of the public and social aspects of musical composition" (see Primary Evidence: "Who Cares If You Listen?"). Although the assertion may seem startling today, it reflects the ideals of many midcentury composers who sought a purity of expression they felt could not be achieved through the inconsistent and unpredictable agency of performers.

**"I could specify something and hear it instantly." Milton Babbitt at the RCA Mark II Sound Synthesizer, Columbia-Princeton Studios, New York City, late 1950s.** By today's standards, this synthesizer is limited. But in its time, it was one of the most advanced machines of its kind, and there were only a handful like it anywhere in the world. On several occasions, Babbitt praised the ability of machines like this one to realize rhythms to a degree not possible in most "live" performances. But the apparatus, containing 750 vacuum tubes, was cumbersome to control. "It had a paper drive," Babbitt recalled later, "and getting the paper through the machine and punching the holes was difficult. We were punching in binary. The machine was totally zero, nothing predetermined, and any number we punched could refer to any dimension of the machine. . . . It was basically just a complex switching device to an enormous and complicated analogue studio hooked to a tape machine. And yet for me it was so wonderful because I could specify something and hear it instantly." A sequencer (which generated a loop of pitches automatically and continuously) was of special appeal to integral serialist composers like Babbitt. The Mark II declined in use after the mid-1970s, its pride of place taken over by less cumbersome analog synthesizer types such as the voltage-controlled modular Buchla and the keyboard-controlled Moog.

**Source:** Bruce H Frisch/Photo Researchers/Getty images

By century's end, however, it was clear that electronic music was not about to replace live performers. Instead, like serial composition, it would provide composers with another option for creating music, enriching the musical landscape with its possibilities without eliminating earlier practices.

In retrospect, electronic music achieved its greatest impact when composers began to integrate it with live performance. Babbitt's *Philomel* (1963) calls for a soprano soloist to perform live against a recorded tape running at the same time. By the 1980s, rock music and other types of concerts were routinely combining taped (or digitally recorded) and live music; a notated score of much popular music and jazz is in fact nothing more than an approximate transcription of an electronic original. The essential work exists not in the form of a notated score, but rather as a recording. The Pulitzer Prize Committee recognized this in 2004, no longer requiring a score to be submitted for consideration of a work (see Focus: The Pulitzer Prize in Music; for more on this change, see the Epilogue).

The recording studio also benefited from the technologies of electronic music. As early as the 1950s, technology had given artists the freedom to vary such elements as dynamics (by altering levels of amplification) and resonance (by altering reverberation).

**Modernism in painting: Abstract expressionism.** Abstract expressionism is nonrepresentational, making its effect through the interplay of shapes and colors. This painting—Number 1, 1950 (*Lavender Mist*)—is by Jackson Pollock, one of the leading abstract expressionist painters of his generation. Pollock began working in his "drip and splash" style in the late 1940s, applying paint with objects other than brushes and often simply by pouring it onto his canvases. The resulting style avoids any single point of emphasis and any hierarchy of shapes or forms. The immediacy and raw energy conveyed by this technique have often been compared to the literary and musical manifestations of expressionism.

**Source:** National Gallery of Art, Washington DC, USA / The Bridgeman Art Library / © 2012 The Pollock-Krasner Foundation / Artists Rights Society (ARS), New York

Overdubbing (originally known as "sound on sound") allowed musicians to superimpose an additional voice or voices over an existing one; each of these "voices" was called a "track." Popular music, particularly rock, embraced these techniques with extraordinary enthusiasm. Electronic technology was also applied to standard instruments of the rock band in live performances, most notably the piano and the guitar. By the late 1960s, the synthesizer had become a staple of rock bands and many jazz ensembles.

# MINIMALISM

**Minimalism** is a term first applied to new music in the early 1960s. It takes its name from an approach to painting that started around the same time and that featured multiple and slightly varied repetitions of small units, such as geometric patterns or a particular figure. In music as in painting, minimalism was a reaction against opulence and complexity. Whereas painting functions in space, music operates through time, and this allowed composers to explore the possibilities of repetition in an altogether different dimension, with small motives repeated and changed only gradually over long stretches of time. In this sense, minimalism is something of a misnomer, because it often involves works of considerable length. Musical minimalism was by no means a new phenomenon in the 20th century: the age-old tradition of church bell change-ringing uses a few fixed pitches (one from each of three or more bells), repeated at different speeds in such a way that the resulting permutations create an apparently infinite number of combinations. But it was not until the 1960s that composers like Terry Riley (b. 1935), Steve Reich (b. 1936), and Philip Glass (b. 1937) began to apply this idea to large-scale works of music.

The score of Riley's *In C* (1964) consists of 53 brief thematic fragments to be played in any combination of any kind of instruments, although the composer recommends a group of about 35 if possible. Each player performs these ideas in the

((• **Listen**
**CD15    Track 3**
**mysearchlab**
RILEY
*In C*
Score Anthology II/174

## Focus | THE PULITZER PRIZE IN MUSIC

The Pulitzer Prize in Music is awarded annually for a "distinguished musical composition of significant dimension by an American that has had its first performance in the United States during the year." Like any award, the acknowledgment is to some extent arbitrary, yet the roster of winners since the inception of the award in 1943 provides an index of the enormous diversity of American music since that time. Award winners have ranged from Aaron Copland's ballet *Appalachian Spring* (1945) to Elliott Carter's String Quartet no. 3 (1973) to Wynton Marsalis's *Blood on the Fields* (1994), an oratorio for vocalists and jazz ensemble. The list is also notable for the absence of prominent composers such as Leonard Bernstein, Morton Feldman, George Rochberg, Lou Harrison, Vincent Persichetti, Steve Reich, Philip Glass, and above all, John Cage. That there is considerable cynicism regarding this or similar prizes can be understood when, as occurred in 1965, the Pulitzer jury awarded the prize to Duke Ellington, but the Pulitzer Board refused to accept the ruling and awarded no prize that year.

1943    *Secular Cantata no. 2. A Free Song* by William Schuman

1944    *Symphony no. 4. op. 34* by Howard Hanson

1945    *Appalachian Spring* by Aaron Copland

1946    *The Canticle of the Sun* by Leo Sowerby

1947    *Symphony no. 3* by Charles Ives

1948    *Symphony no. 3* by Walter Piston

1949    Music for the film *Louisiana Story* by Virgil Thomson

1950    Music in *The Consul* by Gian Carlo Menotti

1951    Music in *Giants in the Earth* by Douglas S. Moore

1952    *Symphony Concertante* by Gail Kubik

1953    (No Award)

1954    *Concerto for Two Pianos and Orchestra* by Quincy Porter

1955    *The Saint of Bleecker Street* by Gian Carlo Menotti

1956    *Symphony no. 3* by Ernst Toch

1957    *Meditation on Ecclesiastes* by Norman Dello Joio

1958    *Vanessa* by Samuel Barber

1959    *Concerto for Piano and Orchestra* by John LaMontaine

1960    *Second String Quartet* by Elliott Carter

1961    *Symphony no. 7* by Walter Piston

1962    *The Crucible* by Robert Ward

1963    *Piano Concerto no. 1* by Samuel Barber

1964    (No Award)

1965    (No Award)

1966    *Variations for Orchestra* by Leslie Bassett

1967    *Quartet no. 3* by Leon Kirchner

1968    *Echoes of Time and the River* by George Crumb

1969    *String Quartet no. 3* by Karel Husa

1970    *Time's Encomium* by Charles Wuorinen

1971    *Synchronisms no. 6 for Piano and Electronic Sound* (1970) by Mario Davidovsky

1972    *Windows* by Jacob Druckman

1973    *String Quartet no. 3* by Elliott Carter

1974    *Notturno* by Donald Martino

1975    *From the Diary of Virginia Woolf* by Dominick Argento

1976    *Air Music* by Ned Rorem

1977    *Visions of Terror and Wonder* by Richard Wernick

1978    *Déja Vu for Percussion Quartet and Orchestra* by Michael Colgrass

1979    *Aftertones of Infinity* by Joseph Schwantner

1980    *In Memory of a Summer Day* by David Del Tredici

1981    (No Award)

1982    *Concerto for Orchestra* by Roger Sessions

1983    *Symphony no. I (Three Movements for Orchestra)* by Ellen Taaffe Zwilich

1984    *"Canti del Sole" for Tenor and Orchestra* by Bernard Rands

1985    *Symphony, RiverRun* by Stephen Albert

1986    *Wind Quintet IV* by George Perle

1987    *The Flight into Egypt* by John Harbison

1988    *12 New Etudes for Piano* by William Bolcom

1989    *Whispers Out of Time* by Roger Reynolds

## Focus *continued*

| | | | |
|---|---|---|---|
| **1990** | *"Duplicates": A Concerto for Two Pianos and Orchestra* by Mel Powell | **2001** | *Symphony no. 2 for String Orchestra* by John Corigliano |
| **1991** | *Symphony* by Shulamit Ran | **2002** | *Ice Field* by Henry Brant |
| **1992** | *The Face of the Night, The Heart of the Dark* by Wayne Peterson | **2003** | *On the Transmigration of Souls* by John Adams |
| **1993** | *Trombone Concerto* by Christopher Rouse | **2004** | *Tempest Fantasy* by Paul Moravec |
| **1994** | *Of Reminiscences and Reflections* by Gunther Schuller | **2005** | *Second Concerto for Orchestra* by Steven Stucky |
| **1995** | *Stringmusic* by Morton Gould | **2006** | *Piano Concerto: "Chiara in Mano"* by Yehudi Wyner |
| **1996** | *Lilacs, for Voice and Orchestra* by George Walker | **2007** | *Sound Grammar* by Ornette Coleman |
| **1997** | *Blood on the Fields* by Wynton Marsalis | **2008** | *The Little Match Girl Passion* by David Lang |
| **1998** | *String Quartet #2 (musica instrumentalis)* by Aaron Jay Kernis | **2009** | *Double Sextet* by Steve Reich |
| | | **2010** | *Violin Concerto* by Jennifer Higdon |
| **1999** | *Concerto for Flute, Strings and Percussion* by Melinda Wagner | **2011** | *Madame White Snake* by Zhou Long |
| **2000** | *Life Is a Dream, Opera in Three Acts: Act II, Concert Version* by Lewis Spratlan | **2012** | *Silent Night: Opera in Two Acts* by Kevin Puts |

same sequence but is free to repeat each unit as often as he or she sees fit. "There is no fixed rule as to the number of repetitions a pattern may have,"[3] the composer notes in the score, although if a performance runs between 45 and 90 minutes, then each performer would ordinarily repeat each pattern for somewhere between 40 and 90 seconds. "One of the joys of *In C*," the composer noted in his performing directions to the score, "is the interaction of the players in polyrhythmic combinations that spontaneously arise between patterns. Some quite fantastic shapes will arise and disintegrate as the group moves through the piece when it is properly played." The one constant element of the piece is an ostinato C octave played on the high range of a piano or mallet instrument. If a performance of *In C* runs to 90 minutes, this would mean repeating this particular figure as many as 15,000 times in succession. This might sound like a recipe for monotony, but the process of unfolding is such that the work remains constantly in motion and gradually transforms itself into whatever the performers decide it will become.

What kind of a work is *In C*? It resists classification. It bears many hallmarks of jazz (individual "riffs," enormous latitude for improvisation), yet it is essentially a canon at the unison. Riley notes that "all performers must play strictly in rhythm," and he even recommends that musicians "rehearse patterns in unison before attempting to play the piece to determine that everyone is playing correctly." In many respects, *In C* harks back to the compositional principles and performance practices of an earlier period of time: its open-ended instrumentation and the tremendous freedom given to performers seem in some respects more typical of the Renaissance or Baroque than the 20th century. "At the time I wrote *In C*, I was almost ready to drop out of music," the composer once explained. "Classical music was very mental; the mind governed

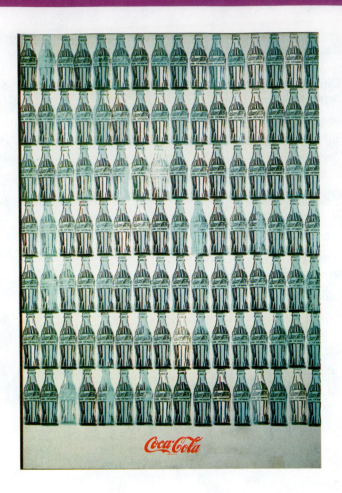

**Minimalism in painting.** "Art," Andy Warhol once famously observed, "is what you can get away with." His *Green Coca-Cola Bottles* (1962) combines the daily objects of pop art with the subtle variations of minimalism. What at first glance seems to be unchanging repetition is in fact a series of similar but not identical objects; no two are exactly alike. Like minimalist music, minimalist art focuses our attention on small-scale changes of detail.

**Source:** Whitney Museum of American Art/Artist's Rights Society/Coca-Cola Company

## *Primary Evidence*   MUSIC AS A GRADUAL PROCESS

*Steve Reich, a composer widely associated with the development of minimalism in the early 1960s, has written frequently about the relationship of composer, performer, and listener. The comments here, from an essay of 1968 entitled "Music as a Gradual Process," address the idea that processes in music should unfold slowly enough so as to be perceptible to listeners.*

■ ■ ■

I am interested in perceptible processes. I want to be able to hear the process happening throughout the sounding music.

To facilitate closely detailed listening a musical process should happen extremely gradually.

Listening to an extremely gradual musical process opens my ears to *it*, but *it* always extends farther than I can hear, and that makes it interesting to listen to that musical process again. That area of every gradual (completely controlled) musical process, where one hears the details of the sound moving out away from intentions, occurring for their own acoustic reasons, is *it*.

I begin to perceive these minute details when I can sustain close attention and a gradual process invites my sustained attention. By "gradual" I mean extremely gradual; a process happening so slowly and gradually that listening to it resembles watching a minute hand on a watch—you can perceive it moving after you stay with it a little while.

. . . While performing and listening to gradual musical processes one can participate in a particular liberating and impersonal kind of ritual. Focusing in on the musical process makes possible that shift of attention away from *he* and *she* and *you* and *me* outwards towards *it*.

**Source:** Steve Reich, "Music as a Gradual Process" (1968). From Steve Reich, *Writings About Music* (New York: New York University Press, 1973). © 1974 Steve Reich.

the musical activity. I think the shift in what this music [*In C*] was doing was letting the heart back into the game. I wanted to make the score so minimal that it wasn't important anymore."[4]

Another manifestation of minimalism involves what has come to be known as **phase music** or **process music**, in which we can clearly hear the process by which the elements of a work gradually transform themselves into something new and different. In the 1960s and early 1970s, Steve Reich applied this principle to musique concrète (*It's Gonna Rain*, *Come Out*, both based on manipulations of the spoken word on tape), music for live performers interacting with electronics (*Violin Phase*, *Pendulum Music*), and works for live performers (*Four Organs*, *Drumming*, *Music for Pieces of Wood*).

*Nagoya Marimbas* (1994), for two marimbas, takes its name from the Japanese city in which the work premiered. The work opens with a pentatonic opening phrase (on the pitches A, B, D, E, and G) repeated 25 times by Marimba 1, first by itself (3 times), then against a series of ever-changing contrapuntal figures based on the same pitches played by Marimba 2. When the meter shifts—briefly to 4/4 but then to 3/4, we hear a new and larger set of pitches (now with an added F).

((•−|**Listen**
**CD15    Track 4**
**mysearchlab**
Score Anthology II/175

## *Focus*    MUSIC EDUCATION IN THE 20TH CENTURY

Music education became an integral element of most elementary school curricula throughout the Western world during the course of the 20th century; rhythm bands, choral groups, and instrumental ensembles flourished at many schools. At the secondary level, most schools were able to establish one or more musical groups, such as a chorus, wind band, or orchestra. Although funding for these groups could become precarious at times, these ensembles have continued to provide an important component of musical education down to the present day. Research studies repeatedly confirmed the intellectual, social, and physical benefits of music making in early childhood.

Three important figures stand out in the development of music education in the 20th century:

- Zoltán Kodály (1882–1967), a Hungarian composer, was an inveterate collector of folksongs, and he believed that folksong should be the basis for the musical education of very young children. The "Kodály Method" moves children through a carefully graded sequence of skills, moving from simple to increasingly complex intervals and rhythms.

- The German composer Carl Orff (1895–1982) gave the impetus to what came to be called the *Schulwerk* ("School Work"), an approach centered more on instruments than singing, with a special emphasis on dance. After learning a few basic patterns, beginning

with rhythms and simple melodic cells, students are encouraged to improvise on their own.

- The Japanese violinist Sin'ichi Suzuki (1898–1998) developed a method of musical education that emphasizes group participation (including parents as well as children), physical activity, and frequent repetition of a small number of basic units. The "Suzuki Method" originated with the violin but eventually extended to other instruments as well. It has exposed thousands of children across the world to music making at a very young age.

By the end of the century, music education efforts were increasingly focused toward very young children. In 1998, Florida governor Lawton Chiles signed into law a bill requiring all state-funded child-care centers and preschools to play classical music and read to children for 30 minutes each day (the so-called Beethoven's Babies Law). A year later, Georgia governor Zell Miller negotiated a public-private partnership with Sony to send new mothers home from the hospital with a free copy of a classical music CD. The original *Build Your Baby's Brain Through the Power of Music!* included selections by Mozart, Handel, Beethoven, Schubert, and Bach. Sony has since issued a series of more specialized disks, focusing on the individual powers of Mozart, Beethoven, Bach, and, most recently, the Baroque. Other companies have focused attention on the mother-to-be or the daily activities of infancy. The effect of neonatal, even prenatal, exposure to classical music continues to occupy researchers.

The piece continues to expand slowly in this way, adding more pitches incrementally, extending its register in both directions, and becoming increasingly complex in the rhythmic interplay of the voices. The timbral varieties are minimal when compared to a work for orchestra or even a work for string quartet. Yet the scale of contrast compels us to focus all the more on its timbral subtleties, which are no less effective because of what only seems to be a limited range. "Limited" is a relative concept.

# POSTMODERNISM

In 1979, the distinguished American composer Charles Wuorinen (b. 1938) published a treatise on composition that opened with these words:

> Most of the Western music we know from the past is representative of the tonal system. . . . But while the tonal system, in an atrophied or vestigial form, is still used today in popular and commercial music, and even occasionally in the works of backward-looking serious composers, it is no longer employed by serious composers in the mainstream.[5]

Wuorinen's thoroughly modernist pronouncement is typical of the generation of composers who came of age in the 1950s and 1960s: it rests on the assumption that a chasm exists between "high" and "low" art, between "forward-looking" and "backward-looking" composers, and that no forward-looking serious composer would write in a tonal idiom, a stylistic remnant of the past. By the last quarter of the 20th century, however, **postmodernism** had made Wuorinen's claim seem remarkably dated.

Postmodernism, like modernism itself, is an aesthetic attitude rather than a particular style. It embraces the past (including modernism) but often in an eclectic manner, synthesizing a variety of styles and techniques in a single work. All approaches are equally valid within the postmodernist aesthetic. Postmodernist composers felt obliged neither to avoid nor to use traditional forms and genres. On an even broader scale, postmodernism often abandons the pretension of art as an invariably serious enterprise.

Postmodernism emerged gradually over the last third of the 20th century, becoming particularly conspicuous in the field of architecture. For several decades in the mid-20th century, "serious" architects (to borrow Wuorinen's term) prided themselves on the elegant simplicity of steel-and-glass skyscrapers that conspicuously avoided anything that smacked of ornament. The mantra of such architects was the famous dictum of their early 20th-century Viennese colleague Adolf Loos: "Ornament is crime." When the Seagram Building, designed by Mies van der Rohe and Philip Johnson, opened in New York in 1958, critics hailed the purity and simplicity of its design as cool, impersonal, aloof. By the 1970s, however, at least some architects were beginning to rebel against the rigidity of such design. The "cool" of the late 1950s was increasingly perceived as cold. In the mid-1980s, the same Philip Johnson designed the quintessentially postmodern AT&T Building, also in Manhattan. It embraces the modern—most of the building conforms to the steel-and-glass formula—but its pediment evokes a Chippendale-style chest of drawers. The very top of this modernist skyscraper is ornamental, whimsical, and draws on an idiom of the past. Postmodernism never hesitates to draw attention to the artificiality of art.

By the end of the 20th century, postmodernism had become the predominant aesthetic in the concert hall. For the first time in several decades, audiences were hearing substantial quantities of new music that could no longer be described as

**Postmodern architecture.** In postmodern architecture, as in postmodernism in general, modernism coexists with ornamentation, humor, and overt references to past styles. The glass-and-stone body of Philip Johnson's AT&T Building (1978) in New York City is decidedly modern in its austere functionality, but the ornamental scrolled top provides a postmodern touch. It offers a whimsical and even ironic commentary on what lies beneath; to many observers, the building as a whole resembles a Chippendale-style chest of drawers.

**Source:** Ted Thai/Time & Life Pictures/Getty Images

modernist or avant-garde. Some critics called this approach "the new lyricism" or "the new Romanticism." Shock was suddenly passé. *The People United Will Never Be Defeated* (1976) by the American composer Frederick Rzewski (b. 1938), for example, uses a decidedly tonal Chilean revolutionary song as the basis of a set of 36 variations, a decidedly old-fashioned form. Rzewski thus places his work conspicuously within the tradition of Bach's *Goldberg Variations* and Beethoven's *Diabelli Variations*. He uses a variety of stylistic and technical approaches in these variations; the set as a whole constitutes a veritable history of pianistic writing—some traditional, some not, some tonal, some not. This eclectic mixture of styles is typical of postmodernism, which in many respects represents a culmination of the 20th century's characteristic pluralism. In the postmodern outlook, the very concept of a musical mainstream becomes irrelevant.

Like many composers of her generation, Thea Musgrave (b. 1928) cultivated but eventually moved beyond modernism, atonality, and serialism. Born in Scotland, she studied with Nadia Boulanger and eventually took a teaching position at the University of California, Santa Barbara. Her *Orfeo II* (1976), scored for solo flute and string ensemble, moves freely between tonal and atonal idioms. Long passages of its opening section ("Orfeo Laments") are centered on G and D. It would be misleading to say the music is *in* either of these keys, but it has a strong sense of a tonal center.

((•⊷ **Listen**
**CD15      Track 5**
**mysearchlab**
MUSGRAVE
*Orfeo II*
Score Anthology II/176

**Thea Musgrave.** The composer rehearses her opera *Pontalba* (2003), with Robert Lyall, conductor of the New Orleans Opera Association. Musgrave was commissioned to write the work to celebrate the 200th anniversary of the Louisiana Purchase, and she chose to tell the story through the real-life character of Micaela Almonester, a New Orleans woman who became the Baroness de Pontalba. Musgrave has also written operas about Mary, Queen of Scots, Simon Bolivar, and Harriet Tubman—all of them, in the composer's own words, "feisty people."

**Source:** Cheryl Gerber/AP Photos

The tonality is reinforced rhythmically by the steady, repeated pattern of eighth notes in the opening in the lower voices, almost in the fashion of a Baroque ground bass.

At figure 4, the first violin intones the opening phrase of the most famous aria from Christoph Willibald Gluck's opera *Orfeo* of 1762, *Che farò senza Euridice?* ("What shall I do without Euridice?"), Orpheus's moving lament at the loss of his beloved wife (Example 23–2). This reminiscence from another musical world, the middle of the 18th century, has an eerie effect within the context of Musgrave's *Orfeo II.* When it appears in the first violin at figure 4, it sounds like (and is) a fleeting memory. The

**EXAMPLE 23–2** Gluck, *Orfeo ed Euridice*, "Che farò senza Euridice?"

What shall I do without Euridice? Where shall I go without my beloved?

flute soloist, representing Orpheus, listens to the fragments of this melody and tries to imitate them (just after figure 10 through figure 14) but cannot sustain the line. Orpheus's inability to recover the tonal melody parallels his inability to recover the dead Euridice.

References to past idioms, although frequently used in postmodern music, are not essential to its aesthetic. But what happens when modernism confronts popular music in the same work? Tania León's (b. 1943) *A la par* (1986), a three-movement work for percussion, offers one possible scenario. The second movement, "Guaguancó," mixes the rhythms of a Cuban popular dance with atonal harmonies. León calls this her attempt "to express the dichotomy between the folk-music traditions of my native Cuba and the Classical European training I received at the Havana Conservatory." In this particular movement, the repeated melodic-rhythmic figure in the bass line can be heard as representing the vernacular idioms of Cuban dance, while the other instrumental lines reflect the idiom of European modernism. Listen for the repeated melodic and rhythmic figure in the lower register of the piano. This kind of figure is typical of the Afro-Cuban dance known as the *guaguancó*.

The Spanish title *A la par* translates loosely as "at the same time as" or "on a par with," and it is a fitting description of the relationship between popular and modernist styles. Even though they are often quite distinct—each goes its own way—they nevertheless complement one another to create a whole larger than the sum of its parts. Every instrument seems to occupy its own space, yet in the end, everything is indeed *a la par*.

While León has turned to popular music for inspiration, others have turned to music of a much earlier era. Arvo Pärt (b. 1935), born in Estonia, wrote music using serialist and other modernist techniques during the early part of his career; the

((•∙ **Listen**
**CD15     Track 6**
**mysearchlab**
LEÓN
*A la par: Guaguancó*
Score Anthology II/177

**Tania León.** In addition to composing, Tania León has conducted several of the world's leading orchestras, including the Leipzig Gewandhaus and the New York Philharmonic.

**Source:** Michael Provost

## Focus | THE BUSINESS OF COMPOSING IN THE 20TH CENTURY

Thanks to the introduction of meaningful international copyright laws, composers and recording artists of the early 20th century could make a decent living from their art if they pursued their careers over many years. By the late 20th century, the market potential of recorded sound was so great that composers could sometimes make a fortune from one recording of a single hit song.

Not surprisingly, a great deal of 20th-century musical talent gravitated toward the recording studio. And over the course of time, that studio became increasingly accessible. For most of the century, a recording was a major milestone for any composer, musician, or musical group. The barriers to be crossed were substantial: one had to secure a contract, rent a recording studio, and pay for pressings, packaging, and distribution. By the last decade of the century, the process had become so simple that musicians could record a CD in the privacy of their own homes and distribute the music almost instantly over the Internet. Even the music itself could be created by means of machines with few (if any) actual performers. Synthesizers that had taken up the space of half a basketball court in 1960 could now fit inside a laptop computer.

Composers of the 20th century also benefited from a new source of patronage: the university. Supported by a salary based on teaching, university composers were free to write the kind of music they wished to write, without commercial pressures. The arguments for and against such an arrangement have raged endlessly. Critics maintain that this "ivory tower" setting contributes to a sense of isolation between composer and society. Aaron Copland, for one, observed that it was not "healthy" for "the whole composing community to move within university walls," on the grounds that such individuals would find themselves cut off from stimuli that would otherwise enlarge their capacities as artists.[6] Others, like Milton Babbitt, argued that the university setting allowed at least a few composers to pursue more experimental kinds of composition, in the same way that many scientists pursue knowledge for its own sake rather than for its direct commercial applications (see Primary Evidence: "Who Cares If You Listen?"). Both sides would agree, however, that the phenomenon of the university composer has added even more diversity to the 20th-century musical scene, even as economic realities have curtailed the availability of such opportunities.

((•• Listen

CD15    Track 7
mysearchlab (with scrolling translation)
PÄRT
O Weisheit
Score Anthology II/178

unpredictability of official Soviet reactions to his work led to a pattern of lengthy compositional silence interrupted by bursts of activity. His reputation began to go beyond Soviet borders with *Fratres* (chamber ensemble, 1976) and *Cantus in Memoriam for Benjamin Britten* (string orchestra and bell, 1977). Pärt emigrated in 1980 and began to write music that reflected his fascination with bells and their overtones in the form of triads.

The *Seven Magnificat Antiphons* for four-part chamber choir (1988) is one of many works by Pärt on liturgical texts. The texts, in German, are from the so-called "O" antiphons, traditionally sung as plainchant in the original Latin at Vespers during the last seven days of Advent. The first of these, *O Weisheit* ("Oh, Wisdom"), is based on a remarkably limited range of pitches. The two outer voices are both divided and intone an open fifth (A-E in the soprano) and a fourth (E-A in the bass); they always sing together, replicating, as it were, the sound of a bell with its overtones brought to the audible surface. The two inner voices are only slightly more wide-ranging in pitch. The divided altos sing only the notes of the tonic A-Major triad (A-C♯-E), moving between a fourth (E-A) and a slightly lower third (C♯-E). The divided tenors have the greatest range of pitches: dyads on C♯-E, on D-F♯, and B-D. The rhythms are correspondingly few, consisting solely of half-note and whole-notes at a fairly slow tempo, with the text set syllabically throughout and no change at all from the dynamic of *piano*. Given such narrow parameters, one might well expect a work of limited range. But the results are surprising. The occasional dissonances are all the more piquant,

**Arvo Pärt.** Born in Estonia, the composer emigrated to the West in 1980 and has lived in Berlin since 1981. Here he accepts the 2011 Composer of the Year at the Classic BRIT Awards at Royal Albert Hall, London.

**Source:** SEAN DEMPSEY/PA Photos/ Landov

and the changing pitches in the middle voices generate changes in overtones similar to that of a bell which, having been struck, appears to change pitch while the overtones resonate in varying combinations with one another. Pärt's composition is at once an homage to earlier traditions of polyphony and a distinctively modern piece. He does not "rediscover" consonance (which was never really lost), but he does change our perspectives on it.

## SUMMARY

The decades immediately after World War II witnessed a second wave of modernism. Combinatoriality and integral serialism manifested a widespread desire to make a fresh start and explore new systems of composition that had not been widely used before the war. Aleatory music—music of chance—fulfilled these desires in an even more radical fashion, whereas electronic music opened up new possibilities of timbre and form in a way that gave the composer complete or nearly complete control over the musical work. By the late 1960s, however, at least some composers were beginning to turn away from the modernist aesthetic to embrace postmodernism, a more eclectic outlook that accepted the traditions of the past, including tonality, conventional forms, and established genres, as well as modernism itself. Minimalism, based on the extended manipulation of a limited number of musical ideas, offered yet another idiom running counter to the second wave of modernism. As will be seen in Chapter 24, other forms of music with origins outside the Western art music world came to dominate in the marketplace, developing in a variety of directions over the second half of the century and contributing to a musical scene that by the year 2000 was more diverse than at any previous time in the history of Western music.

**Study** and **Review** on **mysearchlab.com**

# Chapter

# 24

# Popular Music

Distinctions between "popular" and "art" music can be both problematic and useful. It is often difficult and sometimes impossible to separate the two categories neatly (see Appendix 4: "The Concepts of 'Popular' and 'Art' Music"), and yet these concepts highlight key differences between two broad kinds of music in ways that can help us trace their historical development more readily. Popular music tends to have a wider appeal than "art" or "classical" music; in the 20th century and beyond, it is more likely to be transmitted in ways that bypass or minimize the significance of notation and the medium of print. Popular music did not begin in the 20th century—any number of works considered earlier in this book might well be considered "popular"—but the advent of sound recording, radio transmission, television, and other electronic media over the last 125 years has made this kind of music commercially lucrative (and thus attractive to musicians) to an extent that would have been unthinkable in earlier times. These same media have helped increase public exposure to art music as well, although the number of similarly lucrative classical "hits" is small in comparison to the total variety of classical music recorded and broadcast.

Popular music in the 20th century has played a particularly important role in the musical culture of the United States, where repeated waves of immigration and westward expansion have created an unusually rich and diverse musical culture. Virtually all popular music of the United States in the 20th century can trace its origins to elsewhere, and often to multiple points of origin, because musical styles have constantly absorbed influences from throughout the world. The resulting diversity of this country, so crucial to its cultural identity, makes it all the more difficult to summarize American popular music in such a short space. Size is one immediate obstacle: how does one tackle regional differences when the regions themselves are larger than most other nations? The music of a resident population inevitably changes when new groups of people with their own languages and cultures arrive on the scene. Internal relocations from one region of the country to another (for religious, social, or economic reasons) have caused American popular culture to shift and blend anew. Technology, in turn, has made the transmission of music so fast and so portable that any style can quickly become international in its reach. Through recordings, what had once been known only through oral tradition could now be transmitted around the world in virtually no time at all.

## HYMNODY AND ITS LEGACY

Europeans who came to North America from the 16th century onward did so in search of economic gain, freedom from religious persecution, or some combination of the two. Except for the Quakers (who do not use music in their worship services), all of these groups continued the European traditions of sacred music. Indeed, it is no coincidence that the first book printed in British North America, the *Bay Psalm Book* (1640), was a collection of metrical Psalm texts intended to be sung. And it is no coincidence that in its earliest editions this book contained no notated music, because the congregations for whom it was intended already knew these tunes by heart; it is in this sense that this music might be considered "popular." (Later editions of the *Bay Psalm Book*, starting in 1698, would be published with music.)

Other factors encouraged the composition of hymns. So-called singing schools began to crop up in New England in the 1720s, in which musicians would educate their students on the principles of score reading and singing; William Billings (see Chapter 13) operated such a school. A series of "Great Awakenings" brought open-air evangelism (advocated by American Congregationalist minister Jonathan Edwards and by John Wesley and other Methodists) to religious worship. These eras (ca. 1730–1760, ca. 1800–1830, ca. 1850–1900) produced new markets for hymnals and other religious songbooks. At the turn of the 19th century, singing-school teachers eased the learning process by inventing **shape-note singing**, replacing pitch staff reading with sol-fa syllables (recalling the Guidonian system), indicated by differing note head shapes (Example 24–1):

**EXAMPLE 24–1** The sol-fa syllables used in shape-note singing (four-shape system).

fa   sol   la   fa   sol   la   mi   fa

Inspired by Billings's *The New England Psalm Singer* (1770) and similar collections, editors began compiling "sacred harp" collections, a reference to David the psalmist. The "sacred harp" tradition calls for a leader to cue a congregation by "lining out" each line of text in advance, creating a **call and response** texture. The three most famous collections of this kind were the *Southern Harmony and Musical Companion* (1835, last revised 1854), its successor the *Christian Harmony*, using seven-shape notation (1866, now in two competing versions), and the *Sacred Harp* (1844), which was eventually published in four competing versions due to controversies over content. The most recently revised of these, the 1991 Denson volume, still contains 14 Billings tunes.

In 1867, three northern abolitionists published *Slave Songs of the United States*, an important vehicle for the preservation of African-American religious song from the antebellum era. Each of the 136 songs was presented as a melody with words; while the

**The Fisk University Jubilee Singers.** The nine original members, shown here, sang for President Ulysses S. Grant, Queen Victoria, and many other dignitaries on their extended concert tours in the 1870s. This student ensemble continues to concertize widely today.

**Source:** Picture history/Newscom

rhythms and pitches were probably homogenized to "European" standards, the power of text and music was not lost. In 1871, a group of students at Fisk University, a school for emancipated slaves founded in Nashville in 1866 formed and ensemble that called itself the Fisk University Jubilee Singers. The group began fundraising tours for their university in Europe and the United States, singing four-part harmonizations of these and other "slave songs."

Although many of these songs (and others borrowed from the oral traditions of African-American worship) would come to be known as **spirituals** or be categorized as **gospel music**, the terms were not originally limited to African-American music. Both Caucasian and African-American religious worship were similarly ecstatic in nature during the height of the third Great Awakening. Churches, however, remained largely segregated, and practices varied widely. Some Caucasian-American congregations retained the sacred harp style, while others continued or resumed reliance on hymnals directed at specific Protestant denominations. As the variety of gospel music categories in the Grammy Awards (see Chapter 19) suggests, African-American gospel music has continued to experience musical interchange with secular music since the beginning of the 20th century.

Hymnody provided a rich source of material for a good deal of art music as well, including such works as Charles Ives's song "The Things Our Fathers Loved" (see Chapter 20). African-American composers of the 20th century like Henry T. Burleigh, William Grant Still, Margaret Bonds, J. Rosamond Johnson, Julia Perry, R. Nathaniel Dett, and Undine Smith Moore set spirituals as art songs; performers such as Roland Hayes, Marian Anderson, and Paul Robeson sang and recorded them. The same composers often wrote original songs with the flavor of the spiritual, or incorporated them into orchestral works.

# RAGTIME AND BLUES

Styles and repertories that developed largely through unwritten traditions found new audiences in the early 20th century through the media of sound recordings, radio, and printed music. Audiences that previously had little or no direct contact with such styles as ragtime, blues, jazz, and country music now had ample opportunity to hear this music.

## Ragtime

**Ragtime**, which grew out of the largely unwritten tradition of African-American dance, flourished at the end of the 19th century and in the early decades of the 20th century. The music is usually in duple meter and based on units of 8 or 16 measures. Syncopation is prevalent throughout, thrown into relief by the steadiness of the bass line typically heard in the banjo music of minstrel shows (see Chapter 16). A "rag"—that is, a piece in ragtime style—typically follows the form of a march: three or four different sections, each with its own theme, each running to 16 measures, with connecting material between sections. In ragtime, the opening section is often repeated after the second theme. The structure of Scott Joplin's "Maple Leaf Rag," for example, follows the typical ragtime pattern of AA BB A CC DD.

Joplin himself was quite particular about how his music should be played. In 1908 he issued a primer on the subject, *The School of Ragtime*, in which he noted the following:

It is evident that, by giving each note its proper time and by scrupulously observing the ties, you will get the effect. So many are careless in these respects. Play slowly until you catch the swing, and never play ragtime fast at

((•⁃[ Listen
**CD15   Track 8**
**mysearchlab**
JOPLIN
*Maple Leaf Rag*
Score Anthology II/179

any time. We wish to say here, that the Joplin ragtime is destroyed by careless or imperfect rendering, and very often good players lose the effect entirely, by playing too fast.[1]

Like its successors jazz and rock, ragtime met with considerable resistance, with complaints about its syncopated ("loose") rhythms and the purportedly loose morals of those who played it and listened to it. One commentator, writing on the eve of World War I, called ragtime "a pernicious evil and enemy of true art," and urged readers to

> take a united stand against the Ragtime Evil as we would against bad literature, and horrors of war or intemperance and other socially destructive evils. In Christian homes, where purity of morals is stressed, ragtime should find no resting place. Avaunt with ragtime rot! Let us purge America and the Divine Art of Music from this polluting nuisance.[2]

Middle- and upper-class white listeners nevertheless responded to ragtime enthusiastically. Many welcomed it as spontaneous and genuine, in contrast to what they considered the overly refined and decadent idioms of the concert hall and opera house. Since at least the 1880s, there had been a growing sense that many of the most prominent composers—Wagner, Brahms, Debussy—had become too self-conscious and removed from the more elemental connections of music and time, music and the body. Music with a simpler, infectious beat, more direct harmonies, and more straightforward form was seen as a salvation from the hyper-intellectualized, overly sophisticated styles of the late 19th century, and even more so from the musical modernism emerging in the early 20th century.

As in the case of hymnody, ragtime inspired composers of art music as well. This distinctly American idiom soon captured the imagination of European artists as well: Charles Ives wrote a set of ragtime dances for small orchestra, and Igor Stravinsky composed a short piece he called *Ragtime for Eleven Instruments* (1917). Claude Debussy's "Golliwog's Cakewalk," from his *Children's Corner Suite* (1908), captures the rhythms of the style perfectly, even if the harmonies are at times distinctly chromatic. The cakewalk was a strutting dance that figured prominently in minstrel shows of the 19th and early 20th centuries and was itself a source of the ragtime style. Debussy adds a touch of irony to his work by incorporating into it (m. 61–63) an oblique reference to the celebrated "Tristan" chord of Wagner's *Tristan und Isolde* (see Chapter 17). He instructs the performer to play this passage haltingly, and "with great emotion," only to answer the quotation with a series of jaunty, disjointed eighth notes.

There are rhythmic elements in "Golliwog's Cakewalk" with wider stylistic implications as well. Using the jaunty 2/4 metric frame of ragtime as a foundation (four eighth-notes per measure), Debussy employs accent shifts throughout. An accent on the third 8th note (m. 2 and 3) shifts to an even more dramatic *fortissimo* to the fourth 8th note (m. 4). Amid the steady left hand in m. 5–8 there is another accent shift, from the third 8th note (m. 6) to the second 8th note (m. 8). These shifts amuse, but they also keep the listener from getting too comfortable within a "fixed" meter. In m. 41, the accompaniment becomes the entire texture, with no actual "melody" until the "Tristan" quotations (beginning m. 61 ff.). After the quotations, the opening three notes of the primary melody (m. 85 ff.) are isolated and shifted by one 16th into a downbeat figure before returning to their proper place in the return (m. 90ff.). The remainder of the piece recapitulates the opening section.

((•● **Listen**
**CD15    Track 9**
**mysearchlab**
DEBUSSY
*Golliwog's Cakewalk*
Score Anthology II/180

# Scott Joplin (1868–1917)

Scott Joplin was not the first African-American composer, nor was he the first composer of ragtime music, but he was without question the most famous on both counts in his time. As a musician, he was largely self-taught and earned his early living by playing the piano in saloons, brothels, and music halls. His "Maple Leaf Rag" propelled him to instant fame: published in 1899, the piece sold 75,000 copies in its first six months and would eventually become the first million-seller hit in any musical genre or medium.

In spite of this and other successes, Joplin struggled to achieve his greatest dream: to integrate ragtime into the established forms of opera. The music to his first opera, *A Guest of Honor*, is lost, and if the work was performed publicly at all, it received little notice. Joplin published a piano-vocal score of a second opera, *Treemonisha*, at his own expense in 1911, but it was not well received in an under-rehearsed backers' audition in Harlem in 1915. Its first staged performance did not take place until 1972, when it opened to rave reviews in Atlanta, GA.

Today we would call Joplin a **crossover** artist, taking one musical style into unfamiliar territory and creating a new subgenre. The black audiences of his own time seem not to have been prepared to hear a synthesis of popular African-American music with opera, although African-American musicals were filled with similar music. While Joplin's lack of success may have also been due to racial prejudices, many ragtime composers were white, as was his most sympathetic publisher. His style influenced many other composers, although Irving Berlin's huge hit, "Alexander's Ragtime Band" (1911) was less a rag than a relatively unsyncopated march. Ragtime had ceased to be popular by the time of Joplin's death.

Pianists began a revival of Joplin's music in the 1960s; this culminated in arrangements being successfully employed in the soundtrack to the movie *The Sting*. Today, his piano pieces are acknowledged, as one critic has observed, as the American counterparts to Chopin's mazurkas and Brahms's waltzes, both in musical quality and in the manner in which each captures the spirit of its time and place.

## PRINCIPAL WORKS

Aside from two operas (see above), various songs, waltzes, and marches, Joplin's output consists of about 50 piano rags.

| KEY DATES IN THE LIFE OF JOPLIN | |
|---|---|
| 1868 | Born November 24 in Texarkana, Texas. |
| 1882 | Leaves home and earns a living in St. Louis and other towns by playing the piano in brothels, saloons, and variety halls. |
| 1896 | Settles in Sedalia, Missouri; enrolls in harmony and composition courses at George R. Smith College for Negroes. |
| 1899 | Publishes "Maple Leaf Rag" and achieves immediate fame. |
| 1907 | Moves to New York City; begins work on his opera *Treemonisha* two years later. |
| 1911 | Publishes *Treemonisha* at his own expense; the work is performed in concert in 1915 but does not reach the stage until 1972. |
| 1917 | Dies April 1 in New York City. |

**Scott Joplin.** A drawing of the composer and the title page from an early edition of his "Maple Leaf Rag." Joplin rocketed to fame with the publication of this work in 1899. Legend has it that the publisher, John Stark, heard Joplin playing it in the Maple Leaf Club, a saloon in Sedalia, Missouri, and later offered him $50 plus royalties on the work. "Maple Leaf Rag" eventually sold more than a million copies.

**Source:** (left) Scherl/SZ Photo/The Image Works; (right) Frank Driggs Collection/Contributor/Getty Images

# Blues

The broad repertory of music known as the **blues** was a particularly important force in American music, both as a genre in its own right and later for its enormous impact on the development of jazz. The text of a blues song is by definition a lament, bemoaning poverty, social injustice, fatigue, or, most famously of all, lost love. This type of song originated in the South among formerly enslaved African Americans and their descendants (although rural Caucasian-American musicians may have influenced the music also). Recordings played an especially important role in the dissemination of this style: early recorded examples preserve the artistry of such individuals as "Blind Lemon" Jefferson (1894–1929), Blind Willie Johnson (1897–1945), and Robert Johnson (1911–1938).

At the same time, a more urban style of blues was evolving, influenced on one hand by the vaudeville and tent tour circuits (providing more variety in the accompaniment) and on the other by songwriters who found in the blues a new and fruitful style to pursue. Ma Rainey (1886–1939) and Bessie Smith (1895–1937) were among the first to record this new "theatrical" blues style.

The first to establish a reputation as a blues composer of this kind was William Christopher Handy (1873–1958). The son of recently emancipated slaves, Handy was born in Florence, Alabama. He worked for a time as a schoolteacher but eventually became a professional musician, traveling throughout the South. It was not an easy life. In his autobiography, Handy (known as "The Father of the Blues") describes a period of homelessness in St. Louis when he took on a series of menial jobs, and his "St. Louis Blues" (1914) was one of the earliest published blues numbers and among the most frequently recorded works of its kind. "I have always imagined that a good bit of that hardship went into the making of 'St. Louis Blues'," he noted. "I like to think that the song reflects a life filled with hard times as well as good times."[3]

"St. Louis Blues" is constructed on a standard pattern known as the **12-bar blues form**. This consists of a series of variations on a repeated harmonic pattern of 12 measures in 4/4 time. Each of these 12-measure units is known generically as a **chorus** and is in turn divided into three groups of four measures each. The harmonic progression in "St. Louis Blues" follows a harmonic pattern typical for the blues:

| Measure number | 1 | 2 | 3 | 4 | 5 | 6 | 7 | 8 | 9 | 10 | 11 | 12 |
|---|---|---|---|---|---|---|---|---|---|---|---|---|
| Harmony | I | | | | IV | | I | | V | | I | |

Like a great many blues number, "St. Louis Blues" opens with a **vamp**, a short progression of chords (and in this particular case, a melody as well) whose function is to introduce the basic harmonies, tempo, and mood of the whole. The vamp in "St. Louis Blues" is unusual in that it contrasts markedly with the chorus that follows. Handy explained this striking feature in his autobiography:

When "St. Louis Blues" was written the tango was in vogue. I tricked the dancers by arranging a tango introduction, breaking abruptly then into a low-down blues. My eyes swept the floor anxiously, then suddenly I saw lightning strike. The dancers seemed electrified. Something within them came suddenly to life. An instinct that wanted so much to live, to fling its arms and to spread joy, took them by the heels. By this I was convinced that my new song was accepted.[4]

((•─ Listen
CD15    Track 10
**mysearchlab**
W. C. HANDY
*St. Louis Blues*
Score Anthology II/181

## Performance Perspective

### A Blues Performance with Two Star Soloists

Listen on **mysearchlab**
CD 15   Track 10

A classic collaboration on a recording of W. C. Handy's "St. Louis Blues" illustrates the extraordinary flexibility not only of the blues, but of jazz in general. The notated score gives only the barest of outlines for what the blues actually sound like in performance. Harmonies can be altered, enriched, or made to move at a faster speed, and melodies can easily be changed to accommodate the text. In performance, a blues song is fluid in spite of its underlying form. Vocalists are free to improvise, and the text, even if metered, can be declaimed irregularly, stretching the music to accommodate any number of syllables at any given point. The characteristic sound of the blues is shaped by the **blue note**, the slightly lowered third or seventh degree in the major scale. (For an especially clear example of this, listen to the first "ain't" in "It Don't Mean a Thing" as performed by Duke Ellington's band.)

When Bessie Smith (1895–1937) recorded "St. Louis Blues" in 1925 with the trumpeter Louis Armstrong, she omitted the vamp and altered many of the words in Handy's published score. The melodic line in this performance often bears only the faintest resemblance to the notated melody: Smith's plaintive sound and the slow tempo create something more nearly akin at times to speech. The simplicity of the arrangement—a reed organ (harmonium) provides the only accompaniment—focuses attention on the ongoing dialogue of the two soloists: Armstrong's mournful trumpet responds to each phrase of Smith's singing. This recording, which was marketed by Columbia as a "race record" (that is, music recorded by and marketed to African Americans), helped further solidify Smith's reputation as "Empress of the Blues" and helped make her the highest-paid African-American entertainer in the United States at the time.

**Bessie Smith.** Her 1925 recording of "St. Louis Blues" with Louis Armstrong was so successful that the song's composer, W. C. Handy, later produced a short film (*St. Louis Blues*) in which Smith sings this number. The 1929 film features an entirely African-American cast and represents an early instance of a musician recording her art on film. "Talkies"—films with recorded soundtracks and thus music as well—had been introduced only two years before.

**Source:** Frank Driggs Collection/Archive Photos/Getty Images

Elements of the blues, notably the emphasis on certain scale degrees and the bending of pitch, soon became basic to other musical genres. Jazz counted on blues as one of the crucial sources of its development (see discussion later in this chapter). Composers of dance and theater music also incorporated these elements. But the most versatile of these composers, who brought the crossover blend of blues, early jazz, and "concert hall" music to a peak of popularity, was George Gershwin (1898–1937), who began his career as a Tin Pan Alley song-plugger (an in-store or publisher's pianist who played through sheet music for potential customers) and writer. He began to write piano pieces ("Rialto Ripples," 1917), songs for other shows ("The Real American Folk Song is a Rag," 1918) hit songs ("Swanee," 1919), and musicals, mostly with his brother Ira (1896–1983), starting with *Lady Be Good* (1924) and including *Funny Face* (1927), *Girl Crazy* (1930), and *Of Thee I Sing* (1932; Pulitzer Prize for Best Play). Gershwin also wrote large-scale works with orchestra reflecting the crossover style, including *Rhapsody in Blue* (1924, with piano), *Concerto in F* (1925, with piano) *An American in Paris*, and the opera *Porgy and Bess* (1935).

Among Gershwin's small group of piano solos are the Three Preludes, composed and premiered in 1926 by the composer. Actually, five preludes were originally presented, but two were eliminated before publication. In fact, Gershwin had planned for a set of 24 preludes, after the examples of Bach and (more precisely) Chopin. The second, *Andante con moto e poco rubato* in E major, was described by Gershwin as a "blues lullaby"; a comparison with Chopin's Prelude in A minor, op. 28, no. 1 (see Chapter 16) shows that this piece is clearly an homage to the Polish master.

CD15   Track 11
GEORGE GERSHWIN
*Prelude no. 2*
Score Anthology II/182

# POPULAR SONG

Even as many composers of the mid-20th century developed new harmonic idioms—both tonal and atonal—others continued to work within the boundaries of traditional triadic harmony. This trend is seen most remarkably in the genre of song, particularly in the United States. This country produced an unparalleled abundance of outstanding songwriters in the 20th century, most of whom also worked in the musical theater and film. Most prominent among many are Irving Berlin (1888–1989), Cole Porter (1891–1964), George Gershwin (1898–1937), Hoagy Carmichael (1899–1991), and Richard Rodgers (1902–1979). All but Carmichael achieved success on Broadway and in the movies. Berlin and Porter are remarkable for having written their own lyrics as well. Berlin came to the United States as a child from his native Russia; Porter and Carmichael were both natives of Indiana; Gershwin, born in New York City, collaborated extensively with his brother Ira as lyricist; and Rodgers, also a New Yorker, teamed with lyricists Lorenz Hart and later Oscar Hammerstein II to write an astonishing string of Broadway hits. Although they are generally classified as popular rather than art music, the songs of these and other song composers in fact stand in a direct line of descent from those of Schubert, Schumann, Brahms, and Wolf.

Porter's "Night and Day" and Ellington's "Sophisticated Lady," to take but two examples, reflect the traditions of the 19th-century song in remarkable ways. The harmonic vocabularies of these works, although essentially tonal, are richly chromatic and far from straightforward. The poetry is elegant and witty, the melodies unforgettable, and the union of the two represents the genre at its best. In Porter's "Night and Day," sung by Ella Fitzgerald, the juxtaposition of the wandering chromatic line in the bass against the repeated B♭ of the voice establishes the underlying tension between longing and insistency. Finally, after 35 iterations of B♭, the vocal line itself begins to rise and fall chromatically, gradually, languorously; the longing has become infectious. We do not feel a strong sense of tonic until the word "one" in the clinching phrase ". . . you are the one"[5] (m. 23). In m. 52, the music moves to a remote key (G♭ = ♭III), the repeated notes grow into a back-and-forth of a whole step (m. 57), and the tonic finally returns after a circuitous passage through a series of chromatic harmonies. Unlike Wagner in Act II of *Tristan und Isolde* (see Chapter 17) or Leonard Bernstein in the "Quintet" from *West Side Story* (see Chapter 22), Porter erases the differences between night and day: the lover here is indifferent to the setting and rising of the sun.

Ellington's "Sophisticated Lady" uses advanced melodic and harmonic chromaticism to project the idea of a woman who has assumed a worldly attitude toward life and love. This chromaticism as well as the rhythmic freedom of Sarah Vaughan's interpretation emphasize the woman's exterior life of glamour and uncaring attitude

((•• Listen
CD15   Track 12
mysearchlab
COLE PORTER
*Night and Day*
Score Anthology II/183

((•• Listen
CD15   Track 13
mysearchlab
DUKE ELLINGTON
*Sophisticated Lady*
Score Anthology II/184

**Ella Fitzgerald in rehearsal.** "Lady Ella" (1917–1996) was among those who participated in the Jazz at the Philharmonic (JATP) concerts produced by Norman Granz. The superlative roster of musicians involved in JATP led to many invitations to perform abroad. Here, the group has just arrived in Stockholm (one of Europe's most jazz-enthusiastic cities) for a six-week concert gig. From left to right: Fitzgerald, Oscar Peterson (piano), Roy Eldridge (trumpet), and, standing in back, Max Roach (drums).

**Source:** Bettmann/Corbis

("Smoking, drinking, never thinking of tomorrow, nonchalant . . .").[6] Only with the final word of the text—"cry"—does the music arrive at its long-avoided resolution on the tonic. The chromaticism, in the end, is revealed as a mask that hides the woman's true feelings.

Like many songs of this era, "Night and Day" and "Sophisticated Lady" have been subjected to countless arrangements, vocal and instrumental. Porter's "Night and Day" was first recorded by Fred Astaire for the movie *The Gay Divorcee* (1934), a comedy that revolves around mistaken identity and provides a platform for much singing and dancing. Within three months of the film's premiere, more than 30 artists had recorded the song. Within 25 years, the number had surpassed a hundred. And no two recordings are alike: the performance tradition of a song like "Night and Day" allows—and in fact encourages—performers to take considerable liberties with its rhythm, text, orchestration, harmonies, words, and even its melody. Astaire's version sounds very different from Frank Sinatra's, which in turn sounds very different from Ella Fitzgerald's. Nor can any of these renditions really be said to represent the composer's original intentions, because Cole Porter did not really conceive of the song as a fixed entity so much as a starting point for different performances, arrangements, and interpretations. The notion of an "authentic" version of this song is somehow faintly ridiculous. Is it Cole Porter's original manuscript? The first edition? The first recording? As in jazz, improvisatory freedom plays such a basic role in this kind of music that the idea of an authentic notated text loses all relevance.

## Focus  NOTABLE SONG COMPOSERS OF THE 20TH CENTURY

- **IRVING BERLIN** (1888–1989): "Alexander's Ragtime Band," "Always," "Blue Skies," "Puttin' on the Ritz," "How Deep Is the Ocean," "Marie," "God Bless America," "White Christmas," "There's No Business Like Show Business," "Easter Parade"

- **COLE PORTER** (1891–1964): "Night and Day," "Anything Goes," "All through the Night," "Love for Sale," "Begin the Beguine," "Just One of Those Things," "I've Got You under My Skin," "Don't Fence Me In," "In the Still of the Night"

- **GEORGE GERSHWIN** (1898–1937): "Swanee," "Strike Up the Band," "I Got Rhythm," "Someone to Watch over Me," "Embraceable You," "Fascinatin' Rhythm," "Love Is Here to Stay," "Let's Call the Whole Thing Off," "They Can't Take That Away from Me," and the opera *Porgy and Bess*, which includes "Summertime," "I Got Plenty o' Nuttin,'" "It Ain't Necessarily So," "Bess, You Is My Woman Now," and "A Woman Is a Sometime Thing"

- **HOAGY CARMICHAEL** (1899–1991): "Stardust," "Georgia on My Mind"

- **RICHARD RODGERS** (1902–1979): Songs from the musicals *Oklahoma!*, *South Pacific*, *Carousel*, *The King and I*, *The Sound of Music*, and *Flower Drum Song*

- **HAROLD ARLEN** (1905–1986): "Stormy Weather," "It's Only a Paper Moon," and the songs for *The Wizard of Oz*, including "Over the Rainbow"

- **HENRY MANCINI** (1924–1994): "Moon River," "Days of Wine and Roses," and the soundtracks for the *Pink Panther* movies

- **BURT BACHARACH** (b. 1928): "Raindrops Keep Fallin' on My Head," "Walk on By," "What the World Needs Now," "Do You Know the Way to San Jose?"

- **BOB DYLAN** (b. 1941): "Blowin' in the Wind," "The Times They Are A-Changing," "Mr. Tambourine Man," "Like a Rolling Stone," "Just Like a Woman," and the album *Blood on the Tracks*

- **JOHN LENNON** (1940–1980) and **PAUL MCCARTNEY**(b. 1942): "I Want to Hold Your Hand," "Yesterday," "Ticket to Ride, "Revolution," "Let It Be," and the album *Sergeant Pepper's Lonely Hearts Club Band*

- **CAROLE KING** (b. 1942): "Natural Woman," "Up on the Roof," "I Feel the Earth Move," "Will You Still Love Me Tomorrow?"

- **PAUL SIMON** (b. 1942): "Sounds of Silence," "Mrs. Robinson," "Bridge over Troubled Waters," and the album *Graceland*

- **JONI MITCHELL** (b. 1943): "Woodstock," "Big Yellow Taxi," "Chelsea Morning," "From Both Sides Now," "Help Me," "You Turn Me On, I'm a Radio," "Free Man in Paris"

- **ELTON JOHN** (b. 1947): "Your Song," "Rocket Man," "I Guess That's Why They Call It the Blues," "Candle in the Wind"

- **JAMES TAYLOR** (b. 1948): "Carolina in My Mind," "Country Road," "Fire and Rain," "Lo and Behold," "Mexico," "Your Smiling Face"

- **ALLAN MENKEN** (b. 1949): Songs from *Little Shop of Horrors*, *The Little Mermaid*, *Beauty and the Beast*, and *Aladdin*

**Joni Mitchell performs in concert, September 7, 1979.** Mitchell (b. 1943), a native of Saskatchewan, moved to the United States in 1965 and within two years had begun a career as a songwriter, singer, and performer in a modern folk style. Her early work was of the personal/confessional variety; albums from *Clouds* (1969) to the live *Miles of Aisles* (1974) exhibited increasing range in subject matter as well as popular success. Beginning with *The Hissing of Summer Lawns* (1975), Mitchell began to experiment with rock- and jazz-influenced arrangements and electronic instrumentation, and her lyrics were increasingly political. *Mingus* was a collaboration with the bassist/composer Charles Mingus, completed shortly after his death. Thereafter, Mitchell continued to release recordings that mixed her approaches, but after 1998's *Taming the Tiger*, she stopped recording new material, a hiatus recently broken with *Shine* (2007). In addition to Mitchell's songwriting, her unique and rich guitar style, based on open tunings, is a trademark of her musicianship.

**Source:** Michael Wheatley/Alamy

# JAZZ: TO 1945

The rhythmic liveliness so characteristic of ragtime, combined with the use of expressive pitch distortion so typical of the blues, were particularly important forces in the development of **jazz**. The term (often spelled "jass" in the early decades of the 20th century) has been used to cover such an enormous range of musical styles that attempts at a concise definition seem futile. The trumpeter Louis Armstrong (1901–1971) once famously answered the question "What is jazz?" by saying, "Man, man, if you gotta ask, you'll never know." Armstrong's response is at once evasive and revealing: he recognized that the term cannot be confined to a list of specific musical characteristics. Along these lines, more than one jazz musician has defined the art "not as a what, but a how." Jazz, in this view, is not so much a style of playing as an attitude, an approach toward music that embraces improvisation and rhythmic and intonational freedom, along with a general acceptance that the musical work exists in performance rather than in the form of a written score. Jazz musicians worked as hard as any other musicians to perfect their craft, of course, but the element of spontaneity (or at least apparent spontaneity) has always played a key role in the world of jazz.

Like ragtime, jazz originated in the largely unwritten traditions of African-American dance and song, combined with other diverse influences such as marching band music, hymnody, and improvisatory storytelling. In the 1920s, it appealed as modernist art by virtue of its emphasis on rhythm, its freedom of improvisation, and what was perceived to be a kind of purity of expression, spontaneous and seemingly devoid of calculated artifice.

Although jazz developed in many places in the early 20th century, New Orleans is generally regarded as the most important center for this kind of music. It was there that Louis Armstrong grew up and learned to play the cornet and trumpet under the tutelage of the great cornettist Joe "King" Oliver (1885–1938). Armstrong and Oliver later developed an intricate duet style that sounded improvised but was in fact carefully worked out. This kind of careful arrangement, infused with a sense of improvisation, is amply evident in Oliver's "Snake Rag," recorded in 1923, with Oliver and Armstrong on cornets, Lil Hardin (Armstrong's future wife) on piano, and the Dodds brothers, Johnny and Warren ("Baby") on clarinet and drums. The instrumentation is typical of Dixieland jazz, a sound and style that had developed in New Orleans in the early years of the 20th century. The Dixieland sound, said to have evolved out of the bands that accompanied funeral processions in New Orleans, is characterized by an ensemble in which the trumpet carries the melodic lead, the clarinet provides rapid counterpoint to the melodic line, the trombone helps carry the bass line, and the piano and drum set work together to emphasize the strong beats in duple meter, with the piano providing triadic harmonies on the off beats. An additional trumpet, a saxophone, banjo, and double bass often figure in Dixieland ensembles as well. Also typical of the Dixieland style (and for that matter, many other varieties of jazz) is the steady succession of soloists, each of whom improvises on at least one unit of the 12-bar blues chorus.

After a brief stint with Oliver in Chicago, Armstrong moved to New York in 1924, joining both the Fletcher Henderson Orchestra (primarily a dance orchestra) and Clarence Williams's Blues Five (which often served to back blues singers such as Bessie Smith). He returned to Chicago to begin leading his own groups, the Hot Five and Hot Seven; as the primary soloist, Armstrong recorded solos of considerable virtuosity and inventiveness, and his reputation as the greatest jazz soloist of his era was firmly established. From then on, he moved between Chicago and New York, joining the pit orchestra for Fats Waller's 1929 *Hot Chocolates* (and recording the show's

((•— **Listen**
**CD15   Track 14**
**mysearchlab**
JOE OLIVER
*Snake Rag*
Score Anthology II/185

**Louis Armstrong.** After his enormously successful recording of "St. Louis Blues" with Bessie Smith in 1925, Armstrong would release at least six subsequent renditions of that song with various groups between 1929 and 1960. A recent (2004) film entitled *St. Louis Blues,* starring Sean Patrick Thomas, traces Armstrong's life from his impoverished childhood in New Orleans to worldwide fame.

**Source:** Hulton Archive/Getty Images

"Ain't Misbehavin'"; see Chapter 22). By 1930, Louis Armstrong and His Orchestra had become the ensemble (usually 10 or so musicians) in which he would make his continuing contributions to jazz.

Duke Ellington's "It Don't Mean a Thing (If It Ain't Got That Swing)," written in 1932, represents jazz in the "Swing Era" of the 1930s and 1940s. Swing rhythm features a hard meter but a subtle avoidance of cadences and downbeats, with the soloist placing notes either just ahead or just behind the beat in a way that heightened the music's rhythmic suppleness. Swing was also dominated by the sound of what were called big bands, relatively large ensembles consisting of piano, drums, double bass, and a large complement of winds: saxophones (often five—two altos, two tenors, one baritone) and groups of three or four trumpets, trombones, and clarinets. Many of these bands also featured a vocal soloist: Ella Fitzgerald began her career with Chick Webb's band, and Frank Sinatra rose to prominence with the bands of Harry James and Tommy Dorsey. Each group sought to establish its own distinctive sound through its orchestration, often dictated by the leader's instrument and tastes—Duke Ellington's piano, Harry James's trumpet, Glenn Miller's trombone, Artie Shaw's clarinet, and, in the crossover Western swing style, Bob Wills's violin.

Formally, the original song version of Ellington's "It Don't Mean a Thing" consists of an eight-measure instrumental introduction, followed by a two-measure vamp that can be repeated indefinitely before the entrance of the voice. The **verse** ("What good is melody . . .")[7] consists of 16 measures (2 × 8) that end on a half cadence leading to the song's chorus or principal melody. The chorus itself consists of four units of 8 measures each whose thematic content follows the pattern AABA. This pattern is so common in 20th-century song that it has come to be known as **song form**. The contrasting B section (here, from the words "It makes no diff'rence" through "ev'rything you got") is often known as the **bridge** because it connects statements of the A theme.

When Ellington recorded this number with his band in 1932, he substantially reworked the form of the piece. The recorded version omits the introduction and begins with 10 measures of the vamp, in which the singer (Ivie Anderson) uses her voice as an instrument, singing syncopated nonsense syllables against the steady beat of the bass in a technique first popularized by Armstrong and Fitzgerald—**scat singing**. The 32-measure verse, expanded from the song's 16-measure version, is allotted to a solo muted trombone. The voice, in turn, presents the chorus in its full 32-measure form.

((•• Listen

**CD15    Track 15**
**mysearchlab**
DUKE ELLINGTON
*It Don't Mean a Thing*
Score Anthology II/186

At this point, the instruments take over with a series of quasi-improvised solos. In rehearsal, Ellington and his group would have planned who would play these solos and in what order. Beyond this, each instrumentalist was free to improvise at will, knowing in advance the basic chord progressions with which the band would support him or her. In this particular performance, we hear only one extended solo, given to the saxophonist (Johnny Hodges), who varies thematic elements of both verse and chorus. The full band then plays the opening of the chorus; the vocalist returns with the bridge passage, and the work concludes with the syncopated "doo-wah" fragmented on the muted brass.

Other performances of this same work by Ellington vary the number and sequence of the soloists, the order in which verse and chorus are first presented, the final cadence, and countless other features, large and small. Jazz performances by their very nature represent a fusion of composed and improvised elements; only the limitations of a 78 rpm disk dictated the length of the 1932 performance found in the CD set.

As jazz ensembles became increasingly larger and their instrumental arrangements correspondingly complex, some listeners bewailed a loss of spontaneity. The noted critic Winthrop Sargeant took Ellington to task in 1943 for allegedly losing touch with the musical roots of jazz and having abandoned its "elemental" nature (see Primary Evidence: Jazz and the Question of Stylistic "Purity"). But Sargeant was guilty of assuming that jazz had always had and would always retain what he perceived to be a kind of stylistic purity, untouched by the same forces of musical change that had shaped every other form of Western music since the Middle Ages.

# JAZZ: AFTER 1945

In the decade after World War II, a variety of jazz musicians began moving beyond established concepts of tonality, rhythm, and form. Foremost among these artists were the bassist Charles Mingus (1922–1979), the trumpeters Dizzy Gillespie (1917–1993) and Miles Davis (1926–1991), the saxophonists Charlie Parker (1920–1955) and John Coltrane (1926–1967), and the pianists Thelonious Monk (1917–1982) and Bud Powell (1924–1996).

A new style called **bebop** featured fast tempos, irregular chordal progressions, complex harmonies, and asymmetrical, often jagged melodies. Gillespie and Parker were the most celebrated of the bebop artists, renowned for their extraordinary improvisational abilities. At times both musicians also incorporated elements of what came to be known as Afro-Cuban jazz, which featured an expanded percussion section and emphasized ostinato figures and complex polyrhythms. Miles Davis's album *The Birth of the Cool* (1949) featured a style in which vibrato in the winds was held to a minimum, creating a distinctively "cool" sound that avoided the sentimentality and fullness so characteristic of the Big Band sound.

Davis was among those who, in the 1950s, contributed to a "modal" approach to jazz improvisation in which scales or harmonic patterns became the underpinning for improvisation, rather than existing songs or standard progressions, without the pressure of bebop's harmonic complexities, and with the opportunity to "stretch" out in improvisational exploration, rather than having to "exchange choruses" on a regular basis. With tape recording and the long-playing record now commonplace technologies, jazz recording gained new freedom during this era as well. The most successful synthesis of these elements was Davis's 1959 recording *Kind of Blue*, which featured an all-star group of sidemen: Julian "Cannonball" Adderly, John Coltrane, Bill Evans (who was later credited as co-composer on one piece), Paul Chambers, Jimmy Cobb,

**Primary Evidence** JAZZ AND THE QUESTION OF STYLISTIC "PURITY" (1943)

*Winthrop Sargeant, a highly influential music critic of the mid-20th century, was deeply sympathetic to jazz (he wrote a book on the subject in 1938), but his sympathy had a patronizing edge. The appeal of jazz, Sargeant argued, lay in its directness and simplicity. He was alarmed that jazz in its so-called pure form was beginning to mix too much with other styles of composition and thereby lose its essential, primitive, quality. What bothered Sargeant was what would trouble many others over subsequent decades, whether they admitted it or not: jazz was evolving in new directions, not remaining what it had once been. Ellington responded gracefully but with force.*

■ ■ ■

## SARGEANT'S CRITIQUE

The mistake of the fashionable jazz aesthetes has been to take jazz out of the simple sidewalk and dance hall milieu where it belongs and pretend that it is a complex, civilized art. In its own surroundings, jazz need make no apologies. It is the most vital folk music of our time; it is distinctly and indigenously American, and it speaks a new, infectious dialect that is fresher than anything of the sort Europe has evolved in centuries. It is, I think, something of a pity that, in a watered-down commercial form, jazz has virtually drowned out every other form of American popular music. . . . Curiously enough, the mass-produced, commercialized product is also tending to swamp what is left of real, improvised jazz. It is already obvious that the fresh, ingenuous type of jazz the Negroes of New Orleans and Chicago played a generation ago is unlikely ever to be heard again except in phonograph records. Thus, the original spring of jazz has run dry—and for very logical reasons. The musical dialect of jazz, like verbal dialects, owes its development to its remoteness from standardized education. One of its most important ingredients has been the rather colorful awkwardness—the lack of technical polish—with which it is played. And that awkwardness, when genuine, is the fruit of ignorance.

Jazz appeared in the first place because the poor Southern Negro couldn't get a regular musical education, and decided to make his own homemade kind of music without it. His ingenuity has proved him to be one of the world's most gifted instinctive musicians. But as his lot improves, and with it his facilities for musical education, he is bound to be attracted by the bigger scope and intricacy of civilized concert music. Give him the chance to study, and the Negro will soon turn from boogie woogie to Beethoven.

## ELLINGTON'S RESPONSE

Mr. Sargeant has evidently not been exposed to some of the more intelligent jazz, nor is he aware of the amazing musical background of some of our foremost composers and arrangers, in the popular field. . . .

He says that "harmony in jazz is restricted to four or five monotonous patterns," and names the blues, to substantiate this strange statement. I would be interested in knowing how he has managed to arrive at his classifications. Everyone knows that the blues is built upon a set pattern, as is, for example, the sonnet form in poetry. Yet this hasn't seemed to limit poetry to four or five monotonous patterns, nor do I think is jazz so limited. . . .

Most of all, I was struck by Mr. Sargeant's concluding statement, that given a chance to study, the Negro will soon turn from boogie woogie to Beethoven. Maybe so, but what a shame! There is so much that is good in a musical expression in the popular field.

**Source:** Winthrop Sargeant, "Is Jazz Music?" *American Mercury* 57 (1943): 403–9; Duke Ellington, "Defense of Jazz," *American Mercury* 57 (1944): 124. Reprinted with permission of the Enoch Pratt Free Library, in accordance with the terms of the bequest of H. L. Mencken.

and (on one track) Wynton Kelly. It is noteworthy that tempos in the five compositions are indicated either as "moderately" or "slowly."

The best known tracks are "All Blues," a relaxed blues in 6/4, and "So What," a call-and-response between the bass (a nine-note solo) and the others (a two-chord reply mimicking "So what?"), with a 32-measure cycling of two scales; there is also a fairly traditional blues number ("Freddie Freeloader"). "Flamenco Sketches" is based on a repeated chord on C, while each soloist works through a series of five scales until satisfied. Finally, "Blue in Green" (recorded without Adderly), following a four-bar introduction by the pianist Evans, uses a 10-measure progression of chords

((•●|**Listen**
**CD15   Track 16**
**mysearchlab**
MILES DAVIS
*Blue in Green*
Score Anthology II/187

## Composer Profile

# Duke Ellington (1899–1974)

Ellington always struggled with musical labels. He resisted being categorized as a "jazz musician" and wrote in a variety of styles reflecting, at various times, the influences of the big band sound, swing, bop, cool jazz, rock, and

**Duke Ellington and His Orchestra, 1943.** Ellington was able to keep his big band in operation from 1923 until his death, although there were many lean years. The first nadir occurred around the time this photograph was taken, during the American Federation of Musicians' strike against recording companies (1942–1943); the strike eliminated royalty payments and forced many other bands to fold.

**Source:** Michael Ochs Archives/Corbis

many kinds of classical music. In his own way, Ellington synthesized as many styles as Stravinsky. But in the case of Ellington, critics were slow to accept this variety. When "The Duke" began to explore larger forms and more classically inspired idioms, disappointed listeners accused him of "abandoning jazz." Ellington himself insisted that "there are simply two kinds of music, the good kind and the other kind."[8]

In any event, Ellington was widely hailed in the 1930s as the leading jazz composer of his time. For almost 50 years, he was able to assemble and direct a remarkable group of musicians who toured the country and eventually the world. They could (and did) function as a dance band, but they went far beyond this. Their celebrated Carnegie Hall concert of 1943 included the premiere of *Black, Brown, and Beige*, a tone poem tracing the history of African Americans and suggesting, metaphorically, their eventual integration of American society. The concert concluded with the presentation of a plaque signed by Kurt Weill, Aaron Copland, Marian Anderson, Leopold Stokowski, and others. The entire event symbolized a bridging of both racial and musical barriers, although many of Ellington's subsequent audiences, particularly in the South, would remain segregated until the 1960s.

Like his near contemporary, Aaron Copland, Ellington was hugely feted toward the end of his life,

(starting and ending on A) on which the soloists improvise (Davis twice, Coltrane twice, Davis twice). This pattern alternates with Evans performing the progression transposed a whole step down (to G), which occurs after the first Davis set and the Coltrane set (now "double time, rubato"); after the second Davis set, Evans's transposed double-time rubato version is played through twice before a cadence on D (an echo of the piano introduction). The relative rigor of "Blue in Green" (improvisation based on a timed progression) is an antidote to the freedom of "Flamenco Sketches" (unlimited improvisation based on a series of scales); the mix of these with two tunes with catchy riffs and an otherwise straightforward blues resulted in a recording that not only outsold all other jazz albums, but had as much influence as any post–World War II jazz recording.

During the 1950s, Davis began exploring the possibilities of combining two mainstream idioms of music—jazz and classical—to create what came to be known as **third-stream music**. This approach attempted to find an independent path that bridged jazz improvisation and harmony with instruments and voice-leading techniques

## KEY DATES IN THE LIFE OF ELLINGTON

| | |
|---|---|
| **1899** | Born Edward Kennedy Ellington on April 29 in Washington, D.C.; later nicknamed "Duke" because of his personal elegance and bearing. |
| **1923** | Moves to New York City and forms his first band. |
| **1939** | Begins collaborating with the songwriter and arranger Billy Strayhorn; together the two create some of the band's most memorable hits. |
| **1943** | First of several concerts at Carnegie Hall. |
| **1965** | First of a series of "Sacred Concerts," events for which Ellington wrote new music to sacred texts. |
| **1970** | Tours Soviet Union under the sponsorship of the U.S. Department of State as a "goodwill ambassador." |
| **1974** | Dies in New York on May 24. |

receiving the Presidential Medal of Freedom (1969) and some 17 honorary degrees. The U.S. State Department sponsored a tour of the Soviet Union in 1970 at a period of intense tension between the two superpowers. In spite—or more likely because—of the Soviet government's tendency to discourage jazz, Ellington and his group were wildly received there: at some concerts, tickets sold for eight times their face value.[9]

# PRINCIPAL WORKS

## Songs

Ellington's most celebrated songs (many of which he wrote in collaboration with his colleague Billy Strayhorn) include "Mood Indigo," "Don't Get Around Much Anymore," "I Got it Bad (And That Ain't Good)," "Prelude to a Kiss," and "Satin Doll." Ellington made multiple arrangements of all his songs, both with and without lyrics.

## Instrumental Music

*Harlem* and *Black, Brown, and Beige* are tone poems that take as their subject the history of African Americans. Ellington also wrote extended works that highlighted his own instrumentalists, such as *Echoes of Harlem* and *Concerto for Cootie*, both created for his principal trumpeter, Cootie Williams. His film scores include *Anatomy of a Murder* (1959) and *Paris Blues* (1961).

(particularly counterpoint) more commonly associated with classical music. The Modern Jazz Quartet, Dave Brubeck, Bill Evans, and Stan Getz were among the many other artists working in this vein throughout the 1950s and into subsequent decades. Gunther Schuller (b. 1925), a composer and horn player who coined the term in 1957, collaborated with many of the leading practitioners; Schuller later went on to become President of the New England Conservatory in Boston. Wynton Marsalis's *Blood on the Fields* (1994), a three-hour jazz oratorio for an ensemble of three vocalists and 15 instrumentalists, represents a more recent manifestation of third-stream music. In this work, Marsalis (b. 1961) traces the experience of two African Americans in their struggle from slavery to freedom. *Blood on the Fields* won the Pulitzer Prize in Music in 1997 (see Chapter 23).

Davis also played a central role in the emergence of a style known as **fusion**. With the growing popularity of hard rock in the 1960s, Davis—along with Cecil Taylor (b. 1933), Herbie Hancock (b. 1940), and Chick Corea (b. 1941)—developed a type of jazz that used the textures, rhythms, and sonorities of rock and soul music, using

**Miles Davis performs in West Germany, ca. 1956–1957.** By this time, Davis had a quintet that included John Coltrane and Paul Chambers, both of whom would appear in *Kind of Blue* (1959). In 1957 he recorded the soundtrack for Louis Malle's *Ascenseur pour l'Échafaud* ("Elevator to the Gallows") in Paris.

**Source:** Michael Ochs Archives/Corbis

such typical rock instruments as electric guitars and electric piano. Groups like the Mahavishnu Orchestra and Weather Report (both offshoots of the late 1960s Davis band) were among the most innovative ensembles of their kind in the 1970s.

By far the most radical and controversial of all jazz styles after World War II was the approach known as **free jazz**. Although improvisation had long been one of the characteristic features of jazz, free jazz extended the boundaries of the concept, eliminating such standard elements as improvisations on a given theme, fixed meters, chord progressions, and even tonality itself.

Dissatisfied with traditional forms of jazz and seeking a more distinctively Afro-centric voice, the saxophonist Ornette Coleman (b. 1930) assembled in 1960 a group of eight musicians—a double quartet, each consisting of a reed instrument (saxophone or bass clarinet), trumpet, bass, and drums—that included the saxophonist Eric Dolphy, trumpeters Don Cherry and Freddie Hubbard, and bassist Charlie Haden. The group began to improvise without a central theme, and the resulting "collective improvisation," as Coleman called it, runs 38 minutes without a pause. It was recorded in a single take, without splices or edits. The music blurs the line between solo and accompaniment, another important distinction in more traditional jazz. It uses no established themes, chord patterns, or chorus lengths, and moves freely in and out of tonality. "The most important thing," Coleman wrote in the liner notes for the album, "was for us to play together, all at the same time, without getting in each other's way, and also to have enough room for each player to ad lib alone—and to follow this idea for the duration of the album. When the soloist played something that suggested a musical idea or direction to me, I played that behind him in my style. He continued his own way in his solo, of course."[10] As if to underline the interrelationship of modernist arts, the album cover of *Free Jazz* featured an abstract painting by the American artist Jackson Pollock (see Chapter 23).

*Free Jazz* created a firestorm of controversy among critics and listeners, many of whom accused Coleman of creating music that was not jazz at all. Others maintained that he had over-intellectualized the art. The terms of the debate are eerily reminiscent

**Ornette Coleman in concert, 1982.** Coleman's critical reception ranges from high praise to accusations of iconoclasticism. The "free nature" of his approach is hardly anarchic; his music is often composed in advance, his playing influenced by blues and bebop. His collaborators have included Charlie Haden, Don Cherry, Scott LaFaro, Freddie Hubbard, Eric Dolphy, Pat Metheny, Jackie McLean, Geri Allen, and James Blood Ulmer.

**Source:** Marc PoKempner/Alamy Limited

of those in the exchange between Winthrop Sargeant and Duke Ellington in the 1940s (see Primary Evidence: Jazz and the Question of Stylistic "Purity"). It was a tribute to the quality of Coleman's creativity that he received the 2007 Pulitzer Prize in music for his *Sound Grammar* (2005).

# COUNTRY MUSIC

Like jazz, country music embraces a variety of styles and represents the synthesis of many different musical traditions, most of them unwritten. The most important of these are Anglo-American folksong, hymnody, and traditional dance tunes. As early as the 17th century, country dancing in England was a lively type of social dance accompanied by one or two fiddles. Unlike courtly dance, these steps—reels, jigs, hornpipes, and the like—were often fast and physical. Transplanted to North America, these musical traditions were cultivated with particular intensity in the rural South, especially in the Appalachian region. The singing and playing style of country music was decidedly uncultivated; its energetic and sometimes rough-edged quality gave it an emotionally authentic quality. There were also influences borrowed from and by African-American musicians, some of whom played in a similar style (in a segregated setting).

When this music began to be recorded for commercial purposes in the 1920s, it was marketed as "hillbilly music," but the term was viewed with the same wariness by its practitioners as "race record" was by its African-American counterparts. Eventually the term "old-time" or "old-timey" became the accepted nomenclature. Unlike piano rags and popular songs of the early 20th century, country music was played by "string bands," using the fiddle, banjo, guitar, mandolin, autoharp, and/or double bass—all of them readily mobile and capable of being played outdoors, in contrast to the piano, a parlor instrument associated more closely with the urban middle classes. The musicians themselves were quick to emphasize their rustic integrity and humble origins in the names of their bands: George Daniell's Hill Billies, The Skillet Lickers, and Uncle Dave Macon and His Fruit Jar Drinkers (so named because moonshine, whisky brewed illegally in the backwoods, was commonly consumed from of jars made for home canning of fruits).

**Thomas Hart Benton,** *The Sources of Country Music* **(1975).** Benton's mural, commissioned by the Country Music Hall of Fame in Nashville, Tennessee, captures the inherent contradictions between the sources and later development of the art. All of Benton's sources are true enough—the church choir, the dulcimer player, the dancers moving to the sound of the fiddle, the African-American banjo player, the cowboy strumming his guitar, the train racing across the landscape—but the image omits important technological components that have since become just as powerful in the development of the art: the radio, recordings, television, and film.

**Source:** Country Music Hall of Fame and Museum

As with traditional musicians throughout the world, country musicians were for the most part not professionally trained. One of the first big stars, Jimmie Rodgers (1897–1933), known as "America's Blue Yodeler," was a railroad worker from Mississippi who heard country blues singing and learned to play guitar while employed on a New Orleans–based line. When he contracted tuberculosis, Rodgers decided to pursue a career in entertainment. He left railroad work permanently in 1927 and soon found himself making records for the Victor Talking Machine Company. When the first of his "Blue Yodel" recordings ("T for Texas") became a hit, his reputation was established. During his short career, he toured with Will Rogers and made a brief film, *The Singing Brakeman*, playing on his other nickname. Rodgers recorded approximately 100 "sides," most notably the series of 13 "Blue Yodels" that produced some of his biggest hits. One of the most intriguing, "Blue Yodel # 9 (Standing on the Corner)," was a collaboration with Louis Armstrong and Lillian Hardin Armstrong. Recorded in 1930, it marks a rare moment during the segregated era when extraordinary musicians whose lives had taught them to value character over color came together to produce a crossover recording of such magnitude. Although Rodgers did not live to see the full impact of his contributions, his status as one of country music's seminal musicians is undisputed.

With the rise of radio in the 1920s, the popularity of country music began to extend well beyond the South. On November 28, 1925, station WSM in Nashville, Tennessee, began broadcasting a local program called *The WSM Barn Dance*; its first performer—77-year-old "Uncle" Jimmy Thompson who claimed he could "fiddle the bugs off a 'tater vine"—was old enough to have fought in the Civil War.[11] The show changed its name to *The Grand Ole Opry* in 1928 to emphasize its distinction from the "high" art of grand opera. Yet as an institution, The Grand Ole Opry functioned very much like the great opera houses of Europe, for its impresarios launched many a career. By the late 1930s its weekly show, now performed before a large studio audience, was being broadcast nationwide. As the singer Loretta Lynn (b. 1935) put it, "If you've never played on *The Grand Ole Opry*, you haven't quite made it yet."[12]

Recordings changed country music in other ways as well. Throughout the 1930s, a number of scholars went into rural parts of the country to record

**Jimmie Rodgers and the Carter Family, Louisville, KY, ca. 1930.** Mississippi's "Singing Brakeman" and the Virginia folk revivalists (left to right: Maybelle, Alvin P., and Sara Carter) made a number of country music recordings that had immense influence on later musicians. Maybelle Carter also developed a much-emulated guitar style (playing melodies in the lower strings). Her daughter, June Carter (1929–2003), married Johnny Cash (1932–2003), a highly successful songwriter and performer in his own right. Together, they continued the legacy of the first Carter generation.

**Source:** Michael Ochs Archives/Corbis

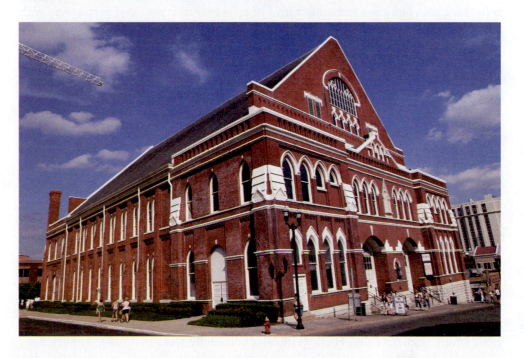

**The Grand Ole Opry.** Ryman Auditorium, a onetime church, served as the site for the Grand Ole Opry broadcasts on WSM in downtown Nashville, Tennessee, from 1943 to 1974. When the new Opry opened outside of the city, the Ryman fell into disrepair; a series of 1992 concerts by Emmylou Harris revived interest in the hall, and in 1994 it reopened as a performance space and small museum. The Opry now holds its winter season at Ryman.

**Source:** Jason Moore/ZUMA/Corbis

"old-time" musicians. Among those most active in making such recordings were John A. Lomax (1867–1948) and his son Alan Lomax (1915–2002). The elder Lomax began his career with a publication of material he had collected directly from the singers (*Cowboy Songs and Other Frontier Ballads*, 1910). Over the next 30 years, he became noted for his studies and field recordings, especially those made at southern "prison farms" whose inmates were mostly African Americans. He helped Hudie Ledbetter (Lead Belly, ca. 1888–1949) launch a career as a singer-guitarist. Alan Lomax, who had begun working with his father in the 1930s, would pursue an international career, collecting traditional music in Great Britain, Italy, Spain, and the West Indies as well as the United States. It was the younger Lomax who made the 1937 field recording of fiddler W. H. Stepp's playing "Bonaparte's Retreat" that would appear in his *Our Singing Country* (1941); this publication, as noted earlier (see Chapter 22), was Aaron Copland's source for the opening theme of the "Hoe-down" finale of his ballet *Rodeo*.

"Foggy Mountain Breakdown," as recorded by Lester Flatt (1914–1979), Earl Scruggs (1924–2012), and the Foggy Mountain Boys in 1949, represents the country music subgenre of **bluegrass**. The style's name derives from the band in which Flatt and Scruggs first met, Bill Monroe and his Blue Grass Boys. The characteristic sound of bluegrass is an acoustic string ensemble of banjo, guitar, fiddle, and double bass. The banjo is picked (as opposed to strummed), and vocals tend to be pitched in the upper end of the singer's register, creating what has been described as a "high, lonesome sound." The characteristic syncopation of bluegrass anticipates the downbeat slightly, in contrast to jazz, in which performers often play just slightly behind the beat. The resulting rhythms are propulsive and infectious—"folk music with overdrive" as one commentator described it. In "Foggy Mountain Breakdown," Scruggs demonstrates his renowned technique of three-finger banjo picking. The virtuosity is dazzling, even within the relatively simple harmonic and metrical confines of this particular number. The piece also reveals formal similarities with the basic patterns of many blues and jazz numbers: soloists take turns improvising variations on a given theme or harmonic pattern. Like jazz, bluegrass and other forms of country music provided performers with a framework for improvisation.

The later fortunes of Flatt and Scruggs exemplify the development of country music over the decades that followed. The two toured and recorded successfully for many years, and their music attracted an even wider following through television and films. Their "Ballad of Jed Clampett" won fame as the theme song for the television series *The Beverly Hillbillies* (1962–1971), and "Foggy Mountain Breakdown" figured prominently in the blockbuster film *Bonnie & Clyde* (1968). But Flatt and Scruggs split up as a duo in 1969 over musical differences. Scruggs, the younger of the two, had pushed Flatt to explore new repertories, including such numbers as Bob Dylan's folk-rock song "Like a Rolling Stone." Flatt disliked performing such nontraditional repertory and established his own group, called Nashville Grass. Scruggs formed the Earl Scruggs Review with his sons, one of whom played electric guitar, and moved beyond the traditional bluegrass sound. He later won a Grammy Award for Best Country Instrumental Performance with a rerecording of "Foggy Mountain Breakdown" for the 2000 film *O Brother, Where Art Thou?*

Like jazz, country music evolved in many directions. Bluegrass itself was a relatively late phenomenon that first emerged in the 1940s. Other subgenres of country music included cowboy music (Gene Autry, Roy Rogers), western swing (Bob Wills), honky-tonk (Ernest Tubb, Hank Williams), rockabilly (Johnny Cash), country rock (Emmylou Harris), outlaw (Willie Nelson), and so-called new country (Garth Brooks). Comparable genres emerged in other regions such as Texas (Tejano) and Louisiana (Cajun and zydeco).

No musical style or genre has ever been immune from change, and country music has been no exception. Like jazz, country music has struggled with issues of stylistic "purity." For many of its followers, "true" country music is unadulterated by the pressures of commercialism and the technology of the recording studio. But the ideal of a wholly rural music untouched by the influences of electronic media and the marketplace ignores the reality of stars such as Hank Williams (1923–1953),

((•—[Listen
**CD15** **Track 17**
**mysearchlab**
FLATT AND SCRUGGS
*Foggy Mountain Breakdown*
Score Anthology II/188

a performer and songwriter in the honky-tonk mode whose music was both a blend of country and non-country styles and whose turbulent life was anything but pastoral. The "down-home" image of country music is not without foundation: many artists did in fact grow up in households and communities that cultivated "old-time" music. But none of them has remained unaffected by the power of radio, recordings, and the recording studio, not to mention the stylistic give and take between country music and a variety of other styles.

# THE FOLK REVIVAL

Partly in reaction against the loud volume, insistent rhythms, and increasingly technological elements of rock and roll in the late 1950s and early 1960s, a number of musicians and their listening public gravitated toward a more natural sound, untouched (or at least less obviously touched) by electronic manipulation. A broad category of music loosely known as "folk music" rode an enormous wave of popularity at this time. The repertory was derived from or created in the spirit of the traditional songs that had been cultivated by country musicians in previous decades. The folk sound rested on acoustic (not electric) guitars, limited use (or absence) of percussion instruments, and lyrical melody and texts that harkened back to an earlier era, extolling the virtues of simplicity and the enduring themes of love and loss. From the early 1950s into the 1970s, groups like the Weavers; the Kingston Trio; Peter, Paul and Mary; and Simon and Garfunkel, and individual artists like Bob Dylan, Joan Baez, Judy Collins, Joni Mitchell, John Denver, Gordon Lightfoot, and James Taylor more than held their own in the charts against Elvis, the Beatles, and the Rolling Stones.

The quintessential American folk musician is Pete Seeger (b. 1919), whose stepmother Ruth Crawford Seeger (see Chapter 23) was instrumental in preserving American folksong as an educational resource. He has been tireless as a folksong revivalist and supporter of social causes, taking over the mantle of Woody Guthrie (1912–1967, composer of "This Land Is Your Land") as a "singer to all the people" who brought songs of human dignity from all over the world to his audiences with just his voice and a banjo. As a member of the Weavers, he had several hit songs; but his career hit a roadblock when he was subpoenaed to testify in 1955 before the House Un-American Activities Committee about his earlier membership in the Communist Party of the United States. As he testified to the committee, "I resent very much and very deeply the implication . . . [that] . . . because my opinions may be different from yours [the committee members], that I am any less of an American than anybody else. I love my country very deeply."[13] He was subsequently blacklisted from all media outlets until the late 1960s, although his songs were covered successfully during this period by groups such as Peter, Paul and Mary and the Byrds.

The relationship of the folksong to its sources remains much in dispute. Folk music, like traditional country music, operates under the (usually unspoken) premise that orally transmitted music is unadulterated by such commercial influences as radio and recordings and therefore has a greater value than music composed and performed by musicians who can read musical notation and are familiar with the immense capabilities of the recording studio. The untrained musician is somehow superior to those who have been trained (once again, shades of Sargeant and Ellington). In reality, few if any country musicians of the past 50 years have remained entirely free of the influences of the recording and broadcasting industries.

**Pete Seeger testifies before HUAC, 1955.**
Seeger, like Aaron Copland, did not "name names" when he testified before Congress. With his attorney, Paul Ross (left), Seeger responded to questions from the House Un-American Activities Committee by insisting they were unconstitutional invasions of privacy. As a result, he was given a year's probation; the sentence was overturned in 1962, but he continued to be blacklisted by major media outlets until the late 1960s.

**Source:** Bettmann/Corbis

The ballad "Tom Dooley" illustrates the complexity of the relationship between the oral traditions of earlier times and the later realities of recording and broadcasting. "Tom Dooley" was originally a true folk ballad, a musical broadside that related the murder of one Laura Foster in 1865 in western North Carolina, allegedly at the hands of her lover, Tom Dooley. In 1938, the folklorist Frank Warner was traveling in that area and took down the song as performed in unaccompanied form by a local resident named Frank Proffitt, who had learned the song from his father, who in turn had learned it from his mother, who had witnessed the hanging of Tom Dooley. Warner passed his transcription on to his colleague Alan Lomax, who in 1947 published it in a collection called *Folk Song U.S.A.*, crediting Warner as the collector. Eleven years later, the Kingston Trio made and recorded their own arrangement of "Tom Dooley," and scored their first big hit, selling over four million copies of the song by 1962. Warner and Lomax contacted Proffitt, and the three filed suit against the Kingston Trio. The case was settled out of court, and those associated with *Folk Song U.S.A.* began to receive small royalties on the Kingston Trio's recording after 1962. As one authority on intellectual property noted later, the Kingston Trio "could have stayed out of trouble by learning the song from a **public domain** version,"[14] referring to work not under copyright and therefore available for all to use without charge. But expert testimony confirmed that it was the copyrighted published version that had provided the basis for the Kingston Trio's recorded version, and the group (and its record label) had little choice but to acquiesce.

The process of collecting and publishing folk music seems poised at times to turn the concept of oral tradition upside down: should true (public domain) folksongs be allowed to be made private property, or should they be declared a permanent part of the public domain? A typical example of this situation involves "Buffalo Skinners," a ballad about the experience of hired hands working for a corrupt boss "on the plains of the buffalo." Versions of this song have been performed, arranged, recorded, and (in some cases) copyrighted by Woody Guthrie, Arlo Guthrie, Pete Seeger, Roger (Jim) McGuinn, Bob Dylan, Cisco Houston, Ramblin' Jack Elliot, Jim Kweskin, and John Renbourn. The song was not new when John Lomax published it in *Cowboy Songs and Other Frontier Ballads* (1910) nor when it was rearranged for publication in Silber and Robinson's *Songs of the Great American West* (1967).

Other artists wrote new works in the style of folk music. Bob Dylan (b. 1941), who at first considered himself a disciple of Woody Guthrie, initially wrote songs that drew on the traditional repertory through their uncomplicated, sometimes technically "incorrect" harmonies and less-than-perfect metrical blends of music and text. Dylan's singing style borrowed extensively from old-time and blues performers: he avoided any sense of traditional vocal beauty, cultivating instead a sound that was rough-hewn, half sung, half declaimed, and sometimes glaringly out of tune. No matter how many hours and studio recording takes were actually required to capture a song, Dylan still took as an ideal the impression of unvarnished immediacy.

As Dylan began to direct his energies against the political and social status quo, the absence of vocal beauty became its own act of resistance against The Establishment. It was not merely with his lyrics that Dylan protested; the voice itself was by extension the angry voice of the people, uncultivated and for that very reason all the more genuine and sincere. Dylan was also a traditionalist in using song as a vehicle of social protest. Ballads in 18th-century England had often protested against unpopular laws or court verdicts, and Dylan extended his work to protest against racial injustice, nuclear proliferation, and governmental repression.

Dylan eventually moved away from folk-inspired protest music when he saw the success the California folk-rock band The Byrds had with his "Mr. Tambourine Man"; in one critic's words, he put down his acoustic and plugged in his electric guitar. His followers felt betrayed at first, but most of them (and many new fans) eventually supported the decision, which in a way symbolized the end of the folk revival. As with other composer/performers who have survived the instability of musical fashion, Dylan's music has reflected a variety of styles—rock, country music, protest song, gospel, love song, blues—at different times and in different mixtures. His chameleon-like artistic path has scampered in many directions, only to return to a previous style; it is fair to say, however, that few were prepared to hear him actually croon on his 1969 country music album, *Nashville Skyline*.

# RHYTHM & BLUES, ROCK, AND RAP

Rhythm and blues ("R&B"), rock-and-roll (later known simply as "rock") and rap music were three of the more prominent styles to emerge out of various combinations of popular styles in the middle of the 20th century. R&B grew out of a piano-based fusion of ragtime, blues, and jazz that came to be known as **boogie-woogie**. It featured "walking" bass lines in left-hand octaves (usually broken up and syncopated) or other ostinato figures, with the right hand playing chords, melody, or improvisational passages. Favoring slow tempos, R&B grafted onto this style various other features of jazz, incorporating instruments like the bass and drums along with the concept of "soloing," which in R&B could mean a guitarist, a harmonica player, or a reed or brass instrumentalist. Performers like Howlin' Wolf (Chester Arthur Burnett, 1910–1976), Muddy Waters (McKinley Morganfield, 1915–1983), and B. B. King (b. 1925) used a generally louder sound (eventually amplified electrically) for new effects and greater vocal power.

Rock-and-roll used many of these same techniques, often with a rapid tempo and a strong backbeat. Singers typically rejected refinement in favor of immediacy, often

**The Byrds with Bob Dylan, Los Angeles, 1965.** While Dylan had already recorded some songs with an electric backup, the success of the Byrds' cover of his "Mr. Tambourine Man" (released April 1965) convinced him to follow their path in his own way. Three months later, he became a "rock star" with his "Like a Rolling Stone." Members of the Byrds had made similar transitions: singer Gene Clark had been a member of the New Christy Minstrels (a hootenanny revival group), while Jim (later Roger) McGuinn— a sideman with the Chad Mitchell Trio—Judy Collins, and Simon and Garfunkel, brought the sound of the electric 12-string guitar (six courses, two strings apiece, like the Renaissance lute) to rock music.

**Source:** Michael Ochs Archives/Corbis

((•⬤ **Listen**
**CD15    Track 18**
**mysearchlab**
CHUCK BERRY
*Roll Over, Beethoven*
Score Anthology II/189

using an assertive, "unpretty" singing style and pointedly using words like "ain't" and "nohow." Backup singers often reinforced the rhythm with nonsense syllables like "shu-bop shu-bop" and "doo-lang doo-lang." But the formula for a memorable rock song remained essentially the same as that for any song from any period: a good tune and resonant lyrics.

Chuck Berry's "Roll Over, Beethoven" (1956) is typical of many early rock-and-roll songs of the 1950s and early 1960s. Its melodic range is limited; its formal structure and rhythms are repetitive; its essential harmonies are confined to the tonic, dominant, and subdominant—and for all these reasons, the work is mesmerizing. The lyrics themselves, urging the most revered of all classical composers to turn over in his grave, evoke a cultural war between so-called high and low art, contemplation and activity, old and young. (The lyrics are also historically revealing: "Dig these rhythm and blues!") The song spoke directly to a generation of teenagers and retains its elemental force today. Formally, "Roll Over, Beethoven" follows the 12-bar blues form. The published lead sheet provides only the barest outline of the melody, harmonies, and words; a great many aspects of the music are left to the discretion of the performer or performers.

After the first few years of the 1960s, rock (as was now coming to be known) began moving in many different directions. The Beatles, building on the traditions of Elvis Presley, Little Richard, and others—emerged on the American scene in 1963 and paved the way for what would be called the "British Invasion" of similar groups, including the Dave Clark Five, the Rolling Stones, the Animals, and the Who. In 1970, the Who released the first significant rock opera, *Tommy*, which was transformed first into a film and later into a stage musical. Other sub-genres of rock included folk-rock, surf rock, blues rock, and hard (or acid) rock. Surf rock was a curious mixture of styles: in some cases, it relied on close, sometimes intricate harmonies and counterpoint, as heard in Brian Wilson's music for the Beach Boys; on other occasions, a bold melody on lead guitar and an impression of surfing action (including wave sound effects) defined the style. Blues and blues rock were favored by British groups who studied the

**Chuck Berry.** This image of Chuck Berry performing his signature duck walk captures two contradictory streams in the emergence of rock during the mid-1950s. What appealed to youth—and what parents found so threatening about this music—was its physical presence, its pounding rhythm, and the suggestive movements associated with it on the stage. The coat-and-tie outfit was a calculated effort to counter this. Berry was one of the first African-American rock-and-roll artists to be marketed directly to white youth, and the respectable clothing helped penetrate that market. In fact, this outfit remained standard for many rockers well into the 1960s. The Beatles, the Rolling Stones, and even the Doors made early appearances in such attire, and the male participants in Dick Clark's long-running *American Bandstand* television show were required to wear ties until the late 1960s.

**Source:** Michael Ochs Archives/Getty Images

music of rediscovered African-American songwriters and placed them in more modern contexts, whether in a post-1940s-style band (Alexis Koerner, John Mayall) or within an electric guitar–dominated context (Cream, the Yardbirds). Hard rock or acid rock was characterized by a louder, more aggressive sound, often involving sonic distortion. Preeminent among these groups were Jefferson Airplane, the Grateful Dead, the Jimi Hendrix Experience, and Jim Morrison and the Doors.

Within a few years of their 1964 *Ed Sullivan Show* debut, the Beatles had expanded the boundaries of rock to include orchestral and non-Western instruments, more sophisticated and enigmatic texts, a broader range of harmonies and forms, and an increasingly sophisticated use of recording technology to create works that in effect could not be performed in a live setting in any recognizable fashion.

The manipulation of sound in the Beatles' "Strawberry Fields Forever" (1967), for example, is so basic to the work that the song can be legitimately considered an example of electronic music. Beyond standard techniques of amplification, resonance, and overdubbing, "Strawberry Fields Forever" features electronic manipulation of the vocals that causes the pitch to drop, thereby contributing to the dreamy, otherworldly quality of the sound. The technique is essentially the same as that used by Le Caine in his *Dripsody* (see Chapter 23). The cymbals and other percussion instruments were dubbed backward in places, creating a strange, unsettling effect. George Martin, the Beatles' producer at the time, deserves almost as much credit for these innovations as the Beatles themselves. "Strawberry Fields Forever" also features unusual harmonic, rhythmic, instrumental, and lyrical effects:

- *Harmony*. The opening harmonic progression, for example, moves from A to E minor to F♯ Major to D and only then back to A, and at the words "nothing is real," we hear a ♭V–VI progression.

- *Rhythm and tempo*. These are irregular at many points, set in a manner that speeds up and slows down quite unpredictably, with the instruments underneath playing cross rhythms against the voice, all of which captures the essence of the words perfectly. (This technique also helped to splice together adjoining parts of two takes that were not quite in tune with one another.)

- *Instrumentation.* In addition to the standard guitars and drums, the work uses orchestral instruments such as flutes and cellos, as well as a non-Western instrument (the svaramandal, an Indian harp).

- *Lyrics.* These are largely unrhymed and unmetrical in structure, the words are elliptical, elusive, partly nonsensical in content (or perhaps not), but in any case markedly different from the typical lyrics of rock songs at that time.

Such techniques are even more abundant in the Beatles' landmark album, *Sergeant Pepper's Lonely Hearts Club Band*, released in 1967. This concept album, centered on the idea of a fictional band, was one of the first to be issued with a complete set of printed lyrics. The music moved well beyond standard harmonies and forms, borrowing from several non-rock genres; it spawned a subgenre of its own known as progressive rock. From the late 1960s through the early 1980s, groups like Frank Zappa and the Mothers of Invention, Pink Floyd, the Moody Blues, Jethro Tull, Yes, Genesis, Emerson, Lake and Palmer, and Tangerine Dream cultivated a type of rock that consistently emphasized unconventional harmonies, complex rhythms, polyphonic textures, and unusual sonorities. No resource was off limits: Gentle Giant's "On Reflection" (1975) begins as a four-part fugue, reminiscent of a 14th-century caccia; Pink Floyd, in true musique concrète fashion, occasionally integrated into their music recorded sounds made from household objects. Rock styles proliferated still further in the closing decades of the 20th century. Heavy metal bands from the late 1960s onward, like Led Zeppelin, Kiss, and Guns n' Roses, emphasized an unprecedented volume of sound.

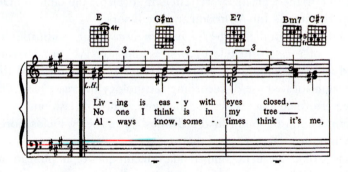

**Representing the composer's intentions?** Until relatively recently, a composer's intentions were preserved primarily in the written or published score, or through some combination of the two. The rise of recorded music in the 20th century created new ways for composers to realize their works. John Lennon and Paul McCartney's song "Strawberry Fields Forever" (1967) was created in the recording studio: there were few if any written sketches and no "autograph score," only studio takes and retakes. The published version of the song, shown here, thus represents little more than a transcription made by an anonymous professional arranger hired by the publisher. The song's recorded performance is the real "published" score, designated by the Ⓟ (phonogram) symbol; the studio outtakes are the aural "sketches," never intended for publication (although often made available surreptitiously).

Disco, popular in the 1970s and 1980s, was developed to meet the needs of a new kind of popular dancing. It featured a relentless 4/4 beat (minus the backbeat of most postwar popular music) and sweeping melody, often played by violins. Disco evolved into several subgenres (among them "acid house," later simply house) that reflected different audience's lifestyles. Techno relied heavily on electronic and digital manipulation and made little or no effort to mimic traditional instruments in the process. By the 1990s disco-related music had become ubiquitous (although accented backbeats had been restored). Those unsympathetic to these styles went in disparate directions, producing melodic music recalling the popular music of the pre-rock era; adopting an unforgiving "back to basics" approach (grunge); or just turning off the electricity (unplugged acoustic concerts). And, much like rock music of the 1960s and 1970s, no issue was off-limits as lyrical content.

In the 1950s, African-American musicians continued to suffer the indignity of watching their popular songs sell far more copies when performed by Caucasian-Americans with the backing of the largest record companies, while black labels were neither able to advertise their wares to the same degree nor break through racial barriers at most radio stations and performing venues. So in 1959, Berry Gordy, Jr. (b. 1929), founded a record label, Tamla; the following year he created Motown Records, named for his home city of Detroit ("Motortown").

Motown flourished in Detroit, with African-American groups like the Temptations, Diana Ross and the Supremes, the Four Tops, and Smoky Robinson and the Miracles and individual artists like Stevie Wonder and Marvin Gaye. The Motown sound was characterized by close vocal harmony, soaring melody, call and response, and a steady beat; the house band that supported the singers was led by musicians of

**The Supremes, 1965.** The Supremes (left to right: Florence Ballard, Diana Ross, Mary Wilson) symbolize the crossover success Motown Records' owner Berry Gordy, Jr., had in bringing African-American music to an integrated audience. The three women were dressed in gowns, wore fashionable wigs, and moved with carefully choreographed grace. The vocal arrangements borrowed from 1950s doo-wop, even as a more modern rhythm and blues style was employed. Diane (later Diana) Ross became the lead singer with her more mainstream pop voice; she was increasingly featured in the staging of their shows, and in 1967 the group renamed itself Diana Ross and the Supremes.

**Source:** Bettmann/Corbis

great skill and taste, the composers and producers were gifted and prolific. As in rock music of the era, the repeated riff (a short motif, whether in the bass part or as a melodic feature) became a signature element. This crossover style proved extremely successful with all audiences, and for the first time, popular African-American music was providing a financial windfall for African Americans without the aid, well-intentioned or exploitative, of others.

The Motown style gave way to others, some more or less related to it than others. Soul music, with its roots in gospel and rhythm and blues, flourished from the early 1960s on, recorded primarily in Memphis, Tennessee, and in Muscle Shoals (Florence), Alabama. Among many others, Aretha Franklin, who came out of the church gospel tradition, brought that sound and a personal conviction to a more syncopated, energetic beat. Horns also began to reappear in the arrangements. Soul would develop a number of subgenres: psychedelic, which loosened up the song form and reflected greater social and political consciousness; funk, which relied increasingly on repetitive figures and more exaggerated syncopation; Philadelphia, which revived the 1950s group vocal sound in a more sophisticated context of lush orchestrations; and genres influenced by rock, jazz, disco, and, since the 1980s, hip-hop music.

**Hip-hop** evolved out of Jamaican roots and began with words being shouted over a disk on a turntable being manipulated by a disk jockey. But a steady rhythmic element, known as the "beat," came to the fore; patterns were devised from live, electronic, and sampled sources, the last borrowing from other popular music styles and using MIDI and other devices to create repetitive patterns. (This at times secretive practice initially raised issues of copyright, but such borrowing is now in the open and considered as much homage as a musical issue.) Over that wall of hip-hop sound, **rap** emerged, derived in part from the Jamaican practice of toasting and the American "talking blues"; both concentrated on creating and performing texts spontaneously while music was being played. Rappers soon synthesized the beats with rhymed poetry, using a vocal technique not unlike *Sprechstimme*. Initially dominated by male African Americans and criticized for the violent and misogynistic content of its lyrics more than any perceived musical deficiency, rap has become a genre open to both sexes and all races.

## SUMMARY

The proliferation of approaches found in 20th-century art music was mirrored in the rise of many new popular genres: gospel, ragtime, blues, jazz, country music, folk music, rhythm & blues, rock, and rap are only a few of the more prominent categories that flourished in the 20th century. These genres were transmitted largely outside the realm of notation, and their reach beyond live audiences was greatly aided by technological advances in recording and broadcasting, both radio and television.

✓ ● ⌐**Study** and **Review**
└ on **mysearchlab.com**

# MAJOR COMPOSERS OF THE 20TH CENTURY

## FRANCE

**Erik Satie** (1866–1925) was an iconoclast and an inspiration to many later composers, most notably **Claude Debussy** (see Composer Profile, Chapter 20). Satie cultivated mostly smaller forms, and many of his works are hauntingly beautiful. Others are openly challenging, even absurdist. His *Three Pieces in the Form of a Pear*, for piano, was a response to critics who said he had no sense of form; he indicated that another one of his piano pieces, *Vexations*, was to be played 840 times in succession (premiere, 1963). Satie collaborated with Sergei Diaghilev to produce the ballet *Parade* in 1917. His reminiscences, published in 1912, bear the title *Memoirs of an Amnesiac*.

**Paul Dukas** (1865–1935) is best remembered for his tone poem *The Sorcerer's Apprentice* (made famous by Mickey Mouse in Walt Disney's *Fantasia* and *Fantasia 2000*). An important critic, and teacher as well as a composer, Dukas destroyed many of his works shortly before his death, leaving posterity relatively little to appreciate of his output. **Maurice Ravel** (1877–1937), along with Debussy, was the most outstanding exponent of impressionism. His piano music, particularly *Gaspard de la nuit* and *Miroirs*, is of outstandingly high quality. The celebrated *Boléro* manifests Ravel's talents as an orchestrator; his orchestral version of Mussorgsky's *Pictures at an Exhibition* is in fact better known than the piano original. Ravel also wrote two operas, several ballets (most notably *Daphnis et Chloé*), two piano concertos (one for the left hand alone, written for a pianist who had lost his right arm during World War I), a string quartet, and a number of songs for voice and orchestra.

The composers **Darius Milhaud** (1892–1975), **Francis Poulenc** (1899–1963), **Georges Auric** (1899–1983), **Arthur Honegger** (1892–1955), **Germaine Tailleferre** (1892–1983), and **Louis Durey** (1888–1979) were dubbed "Les Six" ("The Six") by the journalist Henri Collet in 1920. These six composers were only loosely connected in their individual styles, but all were united in their attempts to write in a distinctively French manner, to draw on subjects from everyday life, and to integrate styles from outside the so-called classical tradition into their music. Milhaud was a prolific and wide-ranging composer whose output encompassed chamber music (his 18 string quartets deserve to be better known), piano music, symphony, opera, and even electronic music. His *Création du monde* and *Le Boeuf sur le toit* use jazz elements to great effect. A brilliant pianist, Poulenc developed a highly idiomatic style for the instrument. His early works include a ballet for Diaghilev, *Les Biches* (1924). He later wrote a religious opera, *Dialogue of the Carmelites* (1957), that has held its own on the stage. Poulenc's *Gloria* is also frequently performed, as are many of his fine songs for voice and piano. Auric was a child prodigy: by the time he was 16 he had already written nearly three hundred songs. He wrote several ballets for Diaghilev, the best known of which is *Les Matelots* (1925). In 1946, he wrote the film score for Jean Cocteau's classic film *Beauty and the Beast*. Honegger is perhaps best known for *Pacific 231*, a musical portrayal of a steam locomotive, but he also wrote many works for the stage and for chorus. The cantatas *Le Roi David* (1921) and *Jeanne d'Arc au bûcher* (1938) are widely admired, as are his five symphonies and his many sonatas for various instruments. The only woman composer of Les Six, Tailleferre studied orchestration with Ravel and wrote in a number of genres, both instrumental and vocal. Her *Concertino for Harp and Orchestra* was commissioned and premiered by the Boston Symphony Orchestra in 1927. Durey worked primarily in the area of chamber music and song but eventually turned to using music as a means toward political ends. He was active in the French Communist Party for many years, and his *The Long March* (1949), for tenor solo, chorus, and orchestra, uses a text by Mao Tse-tung.

**Edgard Varèse** (see Chapter 20) and **Olivier Messiaen** (1908–1992) were important figures to an entire generation of composers coming of age after World War II. Most prominent among these was **Pierre Boulez** (b. 1925), who, along with the German Karlheinz Stockhausen and the American Milton Babbitt, was one of the first composers to embrace total serialism. From 1971 to 1977, Boulez served as music director of the New York Philharmonic and introduced an unprecedented quantity of new or recent music into that orchestra's repertory. From the early 1970s until 1992, he also directed France's Institute for Research and Coordination in Acoustics/Music (IRCAM), a major government-funded center for musical research and performance.

## GREAT BRITAIN

**Edward Elgar** (1857–1934) is best known for his *Pomp and Circumstance March no. 2* (the theme song of graduations), but his style was on the whole far more chromatic.

He was widely considered the leading English composer of his day. His concertos for violin and for cello, the oratorio *The Dream of Gerontius*, and the orchestral "Enigma" Variations remain in the repertory today. **Frederick Delius** (1862–1934), regarded as the finest English composer of the impressionist style, lived for a time in Florida but spent most of his life in France. His orchestrations are particularly noteworthy in such works as *Brigg Fair*, *Appalachia*, and *On Hearing the First Cuckoo in Spring*. His *Mass of Life* is an enormous work for soloists, chorus, and orchestra, set to texts by the German philosopher and poet Friedrich Nietzsche.

**Ralph Vaughan Williams** (1872–1958) was a leader in the 20th-century renaissance of English music. He was an active member of the English Folk Song Society, and many of his works incorporate folk tunes or folk-like tunes. A number of his compositions evoke the modal counterpoint of another golden age of English music, the 16th century. His *Fantasia on a Theme by Tallis* for strings and his *5 Variants of "Dives and Lazarus"* are good examples of this kind of sound. Vaughan Williams's nine symphonies are significant contributions to the genre in the 20th century; he also wrote a substantial quantity of choral music that continues to be performed today, including several outstanding hymns. **Gustav Holst** (1874–1934) is best remembered for his suite *The Planets* (1916), brilliantly scored for an enormous orchestra, but his other works—for chorus and for orchestra alike—deserve wider exposure. **William Walton** (1902–1983) gained international attention with his witty music for *Façade*, a monologue with an equally witty libretto by the poet Edith Sitwell. But Walton went on to demonstrate mastery over a variety of styles and genres, from oratorio (*Belshazzar's Feast*) to concerto (one apiece for violin, viola, and cello) to film music. **Michael Tippett** (1905–1998) composed several successful operas (including *Midsummer Marriage*, *King Priam*, and *The Knot Garden*), but his most widely acclaimed work is *A Child of Our Time* (1941), written in the tradition of Bach's Passions but substituting African-American spirituals for Lutheran chorales. Tippett's four symphonies are also worthy of note. **Benjamin Britten** (1913–1976) is acknowledged as the greatest composer of opera in the English language since Henry Purcell. *Peter Grimes*, *Billy Budd*, and *The Turn of the Screw* have all become standards of the opera house. *The Young Person's Guide to the Orchestra* (1946) is a series of variations and a fugue on a theme by Purcell; each variation highlights a particular instrument or group of instruments in the orchestra. Britten's many vocal works retain a distinctly English sound, yet their appeal extends far beyond his native land; his masterpiece may well be the *War Requiem*. The music of **Peter Maxwell Davies** (b. 1934) synthesizes many different styles and idioms. His *Tenebrae pro Gesualdo* explores the chromaticism of the late Renaissance composer, and his opera *Taverner* centers on the 16th-century English composer. But Davies's most celebrated work by far is *Eight Songs for a Mad King* (1969), which calls for the instrumentalists to sit in birdcages, a reference to King George III's bullfinches and a metaphor for his mental imprisonment. **Harrison Birtwistle** (b. 1934) established his reputation with the opera *Punch and Judy* (1966–1967), a re-creation of the classic puppet show using live performers. Birtwistle writes for most instrumental and vocal media, but his operas have gained the most attention, including *Down by the Greenwood Side* (1968–1969), (1973–1984), *Gawain* (1990–1992), and *The Last Supper* (1998–1999).

**Thea Musgrave** (b. 1928), a native of Scotland, studied with both Nadia Boulanger and Aaron Copland. Her music has been enormously successful on both sides of the Atlantic. Well known for her many operas, including *The Voice of Ariadne* (1973), *Mary, Queen of Scots* (1977), and *Harriet, The Woman Called Moses* (1984), Musgrave has taught at Queens College in New York since 1987. **Andrew Lloyd Webber** (b. 1948), the most financially successful theatrical composer ever, has demonstrated time and again the appeal of modern musical theater, tackling an eclectic variety of subject matter and styles in hits such as *Jesus Christ Superstar*, *Evita*, *Cats*, *Phantom of the Opera*, and *Sunset Boulevard*.

# ITALY

**Giacomo Puccini** (1858–1924) was widely hailed as the successor to Verdi in the tradition of Italian opera. He scored international successes with such works as *La Bohème* (1896, the point of departure for the 1996 Broadway musical *Rent*), *Madama Butterfly* (1904), *Tosca* (1901), and *Turandot* (unfinished at the composer's death, it was completed and premiered in 1926). Although his music is more chromatic and on the whole more polyphonic than Verdi's, Puccini was an equal master of lyricism. No subsequent Italian composer has captured the stage to the same degree.

**Ottorino Respighi** (1879–1936) and **Gian Francesco Malipiero** (1882–1973) are generally regarded as Neoclassicists, although this label does not do justice to the full variety of their music. Respighi's three sets of *Ancient Airs and Dances* (1916, 1923, 1931), based on chansons and dance music of the Italian Renaissance, exposed many listeners for the first time to the delights of this earlier music. Malipiero was the moving force behind the first modern edition of Monteverdi's complete works.

**Luigi Dallapiccola** (1904–1975) was one of the first Italian composers to embrace dodecaphonic composition. Many of his works are overtly political. The *Canti di Prigionia* (1941, "Songs of Prison"), for example, sets texts by three famous prisoners: Mary Stuart (Queen of Scots), Boethius, and Savonarola (a monk and Florentine leader who was martyred for his reformist beliefs). The opera *Il Prigioniero* (1948) addresses similar themes. Dallapiccola taught and traveled widely in the United States after World War II. **Luigi Nono** (1924–1990) was another composer who connected his music with politics. He embraced dodecaphonic composition and married Schoenberg's daughter Nuria. His later works incorporated aleatory and electronic techniques as well. His most significant composition, *Intolleranza* (1960, revised 1970), sets texts by Brecht, Sartre, and others in a condemnation of social inequity and imperialism. **Luciano Berio** (1925–2003) was the most prominent composer of the Italian avant-garde. His music is eclectic and consistently provocative. Berio's best known work is *Sinfonia* (1968) for voices and orchestra, which uses a number of collage-like techniques. Section II is a tribute to the memory of Martin Luther King, Jr., in which, as the composer explains, the eight voices "exchang[e] among themselves the sounds constituting the name of the black martyr until the point when his name is clearly enunciated." Section III uses the entire third movement of Mahler's Second Symphony as an underpinning above which Berio sets a dazzling array of thematic references to the works of other composers, from Bach to Boulez. He is also known for a series of challenging solo pieces, each called *Sequenza*.

# SPAIN

**Manuel de Falla** (1876–1946) combined the musical idioms of his native Spain with an impressionistic style. He spent the years 1907 to 1914 in Paris and enjoyed the support of Debussy, Dukas, and Ravel, among others. He returned to Spain in 1914 but left for Argentina at the end of the Spanish Civil War in 1939. His most frequently performed works include *Nights in the Gardens of Spain* for piano and orchestra, the ballets *The Three-Cornered Hat* and *El Amor brujo*, and the *Siete canciones populares españolas*.

# GREECE

**Iannis Xenakis** (1922–2001) began his academic work in Athens as an engineering student, but he then went to Paris to study composition with Messiaen. He combined these two fields when he helped the celebrated architect Le Corbusier create the Philips Pavilion for the 1958 Brussels World's Fair, for which both he and Edgard Varèse supplied electronic music. As a composer, Xenakis rejected both serialism and aleatory music, opting instead for an approach determined in large part by mathematical calculations.

# GERMANY AND AUSTRIA

Composition in German-speaking countries was by no means dominated by atonalists and serialists in the first half of the 20th century. **Arnold Schoenberg, Alban Berg,** and **Anton Webern** (see Composer Profiles, Chapter 21) remain among the most celebrated composers of their era, but **Paul Hindemith** (1895–1963) achieved comparable renown as the leading German figure in the Neoclassical movement. A prolific composer in virtually every genre, he never abandoned tonality, although his works expand the concept of consonance well beyond that of earlier generations. Forced to resign his teaching position at the Berlin Academy of Music because of his refusal to divorce his Jewish wife, the couple emigrated first to Switzerland and then to the United States, becoming American citizens in 1946. Hindemith taught composition for many years at Yale University. His best known works include the symphonic suite derived from his opera *Mathis der Maler, Ludus tonalis* (a 20th-century counterpart to Bach's *Well-Tempered Clavier*), and the *Symphonic Metamorphosis on Themes by Weber.* He also wrote many sonatas and concertos for a variety of instruments. His song cycle *Das Marienleben* is a staple of the repertory.

**Kurt Weill** (1900–1950) wrote *The Threepenny Opera* (a thoroughly modernized version of the Gay and Pepusch classic from the 1720s) and *Rise and Fall of the City of Mahagonny* (Anthology) in collaboration with the poet and playwright Bertolt Brecht (1898–1956). Both works seek to realize Brecht's idea of "epic theater," in which emotional distance between the viewer and the events on stage is cultivated: the audience is repeatedly made aware of the artifice behind the illusion. With the rise of the Nazis to power in 1933, Weill emigrated to France and then to the United States, where he wrote several Broadway musicals.

Hans Werner Henze (b. 1926) is an eclectic, extremely prolific, and at times controversial composer. He intended his oratorio *The Raft of the Medusa* (1968), depicting the aftermath of on an infamous 1816 shipwreck of a French frigate, to be a memorial to Che Guevara, but some performers refused to perform with a portrait of Guevara hanging over them; the scandal helped make Henze an international figure (the work was finally premiered in 1971). Unlike his fellow Marxist Nono, Henze's politics did not inspire an especially radical compositional style. Karlheinz Stockhausen (1928–2007) was a leading figure in the German avant-garde after World War II, leading the way for a new generation of composers seeking to distance themselves from the music of the war and prewar years. He embraced serialism, total serialism, electronic music, aleatory music, and spatially organized music with an unswerving confidence. He combined his compositional energies with an immense talent for organization and showmanship in the best sense of the word.

# SCANDINAVIA

Carl Nielsen (1865–1931) cultivated the symphony (he wrote six of them) as well as the concerto (one apiece for violin, flute, clarinet). His harmonic idiom is more dissonant than Mahler's, but his music displays a comparable, sometimes Neoclassical sense of contrapuntal grandeur mixed with humor. The Finnish composer Jean Sibelius (1865–1957) also straddles the 19th and 20th centuries. Several of his best known works, such as *En Saga* and *Finlandia*, are overtly patriotic. After brief tours in Germany and the United States (where Yale University awarded him an honorary degree in 1914), he spent the remaining years of his life in semi-seclusion and gave up composing altogether in 1929. His most important works are the seven symphonies, the last of which are written in an advanced chromatic idiom.

# HUNGARY

Zoltán Kodály (1882–1967) collaborated with Béla Bartók (see Composer Profile, Chapter 20) in collecting folk music of eastern Europe, and his compositions reflect elements of this music as well. Kodály's best known work is the *Psalmus Hungaricus* (1923), written for the festivities celebrating the 50th anniversary of the union of the cities Buda and Pest. The orchestral suite from his opera *Háry János* is also frequently performed. But he is probably best remembered for developing the Kodály Method of teaching music to young children (see Focus: Music Education in the 20th Century in Chapter 23).

György Ligeti (1923–2006) left Budapest in 1956 in the wake of the failed uprising against the Soviet Union and settled in Germany. His *Atmosphères* for orchestra (1961), used in Stanley Kubrick's film *2001: A Space Odyssey*, makes for a good introduction to the work of this remarkably versatile composer.

# CZECHOSLOVAKIA/ CZECH REPUBLIC

Leoš Janáček (1854–1928), although born even before Mahler, did not begin to write his most important music until around 1900. It was then that he began to develop a theory of "speech melody" in which vocal lines more nearly resemble the natural contours of spoken language. His operas *Jenůfa*, *Kátya Kabanová*, *The Cunning Little Vixen* and *The Makropoulos Affair* have all held the stage in Europe and to a lesser degree North America. His *Slavonic Mass* is also an important work. Alois Hába (1893–1973) began exploring the possibilities of microtonal music around 1920, dividing all half steps into two. He also developed what he called "nonthematic music," in which all voices are melodically unrelated. His String Quartet no. 3 (1922) uses both these techniques.

# POLAND

Karol Szymanowski (1882–1937) absorbed a variety of styles: German late Romanticism (Richard Strauss), Russian mysticism (Scriabin), and impressionism (Debussy). His works, although tonal, flirt with atonality at times but always sustain lyrical interest and are almost invariably virtuosic. He wrote many works for solo piano (including a number of mazurkas), for piano and orchestra, and for orchestra, including three symphonies. He was an important influence for the remarkable generation of Polish composers who followed: **Witold Lutoslawski** (1913–1994), **Krzysztof Penderecki** (b. 1933), and **Henryk Gorecki** (b. 1933). Lutoslawski's earlier works are rather in the style of Bartók, drawing on Polish folk sources; he later explored ideas of aleatory and dodecaphonic composition. Penderecki (pronounced "Pen-de-*ret*-ski") has been particularly interested in exploring new possibilities of timbre, as is evident in his most celebrated work, *Threnody for the Victims of Hiroshima* (discussed in Chapter 23). He has written in many genres, for instruments and voices alike. After laboring in relative obscurity for many years, Gorecki ("Go-*ret*-ski") rocketed to fame in 1994 with his Symphony no. 3, a work he had written in 1976.

# RUSSIA AND THE SOVIET UNION

**Alexander Scriabin** (1872–1915) is noted for his many piano miniatures, ten piano sonatas, and his large-scale orchestral works, especially *Le Poème de l'extase* ("Poem of Ecstasy") and *Prometheus, or the Poem of Fire*, the latter of which includes a part for a "color organ" designed to convert specific pitches or keys into colors (C major as red, F♯ major as blue, etc.). Productions of this work during the composer's life were unsuccessful for technological reasons. Scriabin's sense of advanced chromaticism eventually merged into a kind of free atonality around 1908. Despite his early death, Scriabin's "mystic chord" was a crucial influence on many atonalists seeking an organizing pitch principle, including Ruth Crawford.

**Sergei Rachmaninoff** (1873–1943), by contrast, continued in the 19th-century tradition of Tchaikovsky and Rimsky-Korsakov. He was hardly a modernist when compared with his countryman and younger colleague **Igor Stravinsky** (see Composer Profile, Chapter 20). Rachmaninoff's most popular works are the Piano Concertos nos. 2 and 3, the *Preludes* and *Études-Tableaux* for piano, and the *Rhapsody on a Theme of Paganini* for piano and orchestra. An internationally renowned pianist and conductor, he fled Russia after the Revolution in 1917 and eventually settled in Los Angeles. **Sergei Prokofiev** (1891–1953) spent much of his early career in France after the Revolution of 1917 but returned to the Soviet Union in 1932 and spent the rest of his life there working in an uneasy relationship with the regime. The communist authorities at first looked to Prokofiev as a kind of prodigal son who had voluntarily returned home from the "decadent" West, and the government bestowed many honors on him. That same government would later attack Prokofiev and his colleague **Dmitri Shostakovich** (see Composer Profile, Chapter 22) for their "decadence" and "formalism."

**Aram Khachaturian** (1903–1978), an Armenian, is noted for his use of exotic tone colors: the frenetic "Sabre Dance" from the ballet *Gayane* is a well-known example of his ability to incorporate timbres and modes that sound vaguely Asian yet still within the Western tradition. **Alfred Schnittke** (1934–1998) was an ethnic German born in Russia. His works cover a wide range of styles and media, from electronic music to more traditional genres such as concertos, suites, symphonies, and operas. His *Requiem* (1975) is particularly noteworthy. **Arvo Pärt** (b. 1935), born in Estonia, emigrated to Vienna in 1980, later moving to Berlin. Since the 1970s, he has applied the concept of *tintinnabuli* to produce triadically-based, chant-like music full of changing overtones associated with the sound of bells. He is especially fond of setting Latin and Church Slavonic texts.

# LATIN AMERICA

Like his near contemporaries Bartók and Vaughan Williams, the Brazilian **Heitor Villa-Lobos** (1887–1959) traveled throughout his native land to collect folksongs. He avoided direct quotation of these materials in his compositions, preferring instead to use them as a source of inspiration for his own ideas. In the celebrated *Bachianas Brasileiras*, a series of works for a variety of different instruments, he used such themes within a polyphonic texture reminiscent of Bach. **Carlos Chavez** (1899–1978) was the preeminent Mexican composer of his era. He, too, collected and drew on native musical sources for inspiration. His single best known work is the *Sinfonia India* of 1936. The Argentinian composer **Alberto Ginastera** (1916–1983) also drew on native idioms but cultivated a variety of other styles as well. His Second Piano Concerto (1972) is based on a 12-tone row derived from the dissonant chord in the finale of Beethoven's Ninth Symphony. **Mauricio Kagel** (1931–2008), also from Argentina, has produced provocative works that are as much theater as music, even when performed in the concert hall.

# UNITED STATES

Foremost among American modernists in the 20th century were **Charles Ives** (see Composer Profile, Chapter 20) and three Californians: **Henry Cowell** (1897–1965), **Harry Partch** (1901–1974), and **John Cage** (see Composer Profile, Chapter 23). Cowell, according to his student Cage, provided the "open sesame" for new music in America, experimenting with tone clusters and new timbres long before they became fashionable. Cowell was also an early champion of the music of Ives, at a time when few people knew the elder composer's work. Partch rejected almost every element of Western music and sought new models of sound in the music of ancient Greece and Asia; he also created an array of new musical instruments, including what he called a "gourd tree" and "cloud chamber bowls."

Often classified as "romantics" or "conservatives" (but perhaps Neoclassical in the essence of their styles), composers like **Virgil Thomson** (1896–1989), **Roy Harris** (1898–1979), and **Samuel Barber** (1910–1981) remained within the extended tonal idiom at a time when many of their contemporaries were embracing atonality and (later) serialism. Thomson is particularly known for his operas, which include *Four Saints in Three Acts* (to a libretto by Gertrude Stein) and *The Mother of Us All* (to a libretto, also by Stein, about Susan B. Anthony and the struggle for women's suffrage). He was also one of the finest music critics of his time. Harris is remembered primarily for his symphonies, most of which reflect some aspect of the American experience (no. 4 is the *Folksong Symphony*, with chorus; no. 6 the *Gettysburg Address*). Barber's lyricism, which won great praise in his time, is evident in his *Adagio for Strings* (taken from his second string quartet), his Violin Concerto, the opera *Vanessa*, and the song cycle *Knoxville: Summer of 1915* (for soprano and orchestra, to texts by James Agee).

**Gian Carlo Menotti** (1911–2007) was born in Italy but spent most of his life in the United States. He is noted particularly for his operas *The Medium*, *The Telephone*, *The Consul*, and *Amahl and the Night Visitors*. His style is unpretentious but dramatically effective and generally within the technical reach of amateur opera companies. **Vincent Persichetti** (1915–1987) wrote in an idiom that was at once both modern and lyrical. His output includes nine symphonies and a number of concertos and sonatas.

Of the many American (and non-American) composers who took up jazz elements and mixed them into concert hall repertory, the most notable was **Leonard Bernstein** (1918–1990), who wrote his undergraduate thesis at Harvard on the use of jazz in classical music and went on to compose a number of works that did just that, including the musical *West Side Story* (1957). His other works include the operetta *Candide*, the *Chichester Psalms*, and three symphonies, notably no. 3 (*Kaddish*). In 1958, he became the first American-born permanent conductor of the New York Philharmonic Orchestra and used the position as a forum for a series of acclaimed broadcasts aimed at children. He was the first conductor to record all of Mahler's symphonies, and his recordings sold widely. His 1976 Norton Lectures were published in both book and video formats entitled *The Unanswered Question*.

Other composers developed an idiom not as immediately accessible to the wider public. **Roger Sessions** (1896–1985) wrote an opera at the age of 12 and entered Harvard University two years later; he was appointed to the faculty of Smith College at age 21. After eight years in Europe he returned to the United States to teach at UC Berkeley, Princeton, and Harvard. He established a reputation as a "composer's composer," one whose works were greatly admired by his colleagues yet never gained a wide following among audiences at large. His most important compositions are the eight symphonies, the

Violin Concerto, the three piano sonatas, the opera *Montezuma*, and the suite from his incidental music to the play *The Black Maskers*. **Elliott Carter** (1908–2012) is another composer whose music is enormously admired by a devoted group of followers. He won the Pulitzer Prize twice, for his Second String Quartet in 1960 and again for his Third String Quartet in 1973. His early music tends toward the Neoclassical, but he later embraced serial composition. His music tends to be highly polyphonic and metrically complex.

**Milton Babbitt** (1916–2011) was at the forefront of two important developments around midcentury: total serialism and electronic music. His *Three Compositions for Piano* (Anthology) was the first work by any composer to serialize pitch and nonpitch elements alike, including rhythm, timbre, and dynamics. His *All Set* (1957) is a 12-tone work for jazz ensemble. Babbitt taught composition for many years at Princeton University and exercised a profound influence on subsequent generations of American composers. **George Crumb** (b. 1929), a native of West Virginia, taught at the University of Pennsylvania. His compositions explore a remarkable variety of timbres and constructive devices, and the graphic presentation of his scores is paramount in their interpretation. His most noted works include *Makrokosmos* for piano, *Echoes of Time and the River* (for which he won the Pulitzer Prize in 1968), *Black Angels* (for amplified string quartet), and *Ancient Voices of Children* (for soprano, boy soprano, and seven instrumentalists). In his vocal music, Crumb has frequently set texts of the poet Federico García Lorca.

Minimalists **Terry Riley** (b. 1935), **Steve Reich** (b. 1936), and **Philip Glass** (b. 1937) have all learned from John Cage and explored the musical implications of the dictum "less is more." All three of these younger composers have formed groups that perform their music in live concerts. Riley played in jazz ensembles in his early career, and his landmark work, *In C* (discussed in this chapter), is based on the impulse toward improvisation. Reich studied composition at Mills College with Darius Milhaud and Luciano Berio before moving back to his native New York, where he has flourished as an independent composer. Glass won critical acclaim for his opera *Einstein on the Beach* in 1975, as well as the subsequent operas *Satyagraha* (1980) and *Akhnaten* (1983). His repetitive use of small units and his approach to form, rhythm, and texture have been shaped in part by his assimilation of certain Indian and African musical idioms. A younger generation has taken the minimalist approach in different direction; one of the best known is **John Adams** (b. 1947), who has demonstrated a flair for dramatic works (*Nixon in China*, *The Death of Klinghoffer*) as well as orchestral pieces (*The Wound-Dresser*, *Harmonium*). He won the Pulitzer Prize in Music in 2003 for *On the Transmigration of Souls*, composed in remembrance of the events of September 11, 2001.

A number of American women composers rose to great prominence in the second half of the century. **Pauline Oliveros** (b. 1932), born in Houston, has been a driving force behind the production and performance of new music in the San Francisco Bay Area for several decades. Some of her works involve group participation, blurring the distinction between performers and listeners. She has written for unconventional ensembles (for example, garden hoses and sprinklers) and for conventional ensembles in unconventional ways (for example, works in which the singers in a mixed chorus make all kinds of sounds with their mouths and hands); she has also composed for electronic media. **Joan Tower** (b. 1938), a native of New York, was a founding member of the Da Capo Chamber Players, one of the leading ensembles of its kind, specializing in contemporary music. She has received numerous grants and awards for her compositions, which have won a wide audience. **Ellen Taaffe Zwilich** (b. 1939) was the first woman ever to receive a D.M.A. (Doctor of Musical Arts) in composition from the Juilliard School (in 1975) and received the Pulitzer Prize in Music for her Symphony no. 1 in 1983.

**Tania León** (b. 1943) grew up in Havana and emigrated to the United States in 1967. She served as the first music director of the Dance Theater of Harlem and has conducted orchestras in the United States and abroad. Her opera *Scourge of Hyacinths* (1994) received performances in Europe and North America and has won widespread acclaim; her libretto is based on a radio play by the Nigerian Nobel-winning playwright Wole Soyinka. Her music reflects the diversity of her ancestry in a variety of cultures, including French, Spanish, Chinese, African, and Cuban. **Libby Larsen** (b. 1950) has established herself as one of the leading composers of concert and choral music. Academically trained (she holds a Ph.D. in composition from the University of Minnesota), she has remained largely independent of university positions, writing instead on commission from major orchestras and other ensembles. Women who have been active in the world of experimental and electronic music include **Sorrel Hays** (b. 1941), **Alice Shields** (b. 1943), **Laurie Spiegel** (b. 1945), **Laurie Anderson** (b. 1947), **Joan LaBarbara** (b. 1947), and **Eve Beglarian** (b. 1958).

# Epilogue

## MUSIC IN THE NEW MILLENNIUM

The 21st century is too young to have defined itself musically: for the moment at least, the pluralism and rapid changes of the late 20th century continue. Musical genres and subgenres emerge and fade at a remarkable rate. New techniques explode into prominence, blend with other styles, fade, revive, and recombine with still newer styles.

The aesthetic principles of postmodernism prevail on the concert scene today, with new compositions integrating a wide range of idioms. Three works written since 2000 reflect this broad trend: Corey Dargel's *On This Date Every Year* (2010), a song for baritone, violin, and tape; Gabriela Lena Frank's *Leyendas: An Andean Walkabout*, for string quartet (2001); and Lisa Bielawa's Double Violin Concerto (2008).

Born in 1977 in McAllen, Texas, the composer, poet, and singer Corey Dargel studied composition at Oberlin College with Pauline Oliveros and John Luther Adams. He now lives in New York City.

Jim Baldassare

Corey Dargel's *On this Date Every Year*, (Listen on mysearchlab, CD 15, track 19, Score Anthology II/191) a song for baritone, violin, and digital looping, straddles the conventional divisions between "art" and "popular" music in ways that make such distinctions seem pointless. The song is part of *Every Day Is the Same Day: A Song Cycle about Clinical Depression*, a genre that evokes the traditions of earlier song cycles by Schubert and

Schumann, who created narrative trajectories in collections of songs through a common poetic theme, musical means, or some combination of the two. Digital looping is a technology that allows a live musician (in this case, a violinist) to record a loop of his or her own making on the spot and use it over and over again as often as desired. Unlike a tape loop, which must be prepared in advance if used in live performance, a digitial loop can be created and used seamlessly within the course of a live performance. In *On This Date Every Year*, the violinist plays live against an accumulating series of different three-measure fragments created only moments before and are repeated within the performance itself. Each loop consists of 15 beats, amounting to three measures notated in 5/4 meter. Once five voices have sounded for a short time—baritone, live violin, and three digital loops—the score calls for the live violinst to continue playing against the loops with music that will not be recorded and reused. After a cadence, the live violinist resumes as a soloist and the process begins again, with a series of newly created loops. The baritone, in the meantime, sings both with and outside all this. In the final cycle of the song, we eventually hear an accumulation of eight voices: six digital loops, the live violin, and the baritone. The slowing-down of rhythms, the expansion of register, and a growing range of timbres (through double-stopping and harmonics) create an eerily tranquil, even other-worldly conclusion to a song whose text (also by Dargel) is deeply unsettling. The 5/4 meter and the quirky rhythms of voice and violin within that meter make the projection of the text seem all the more spontaneous and yet somehow at the same time all the more detached.

Gabriela Lena Frank's *Leyendas: An Andean Walkabout* (2001), (Listen on mysearchlab, CD 15, Track 20, Score Anthology II/192) owes much to the rich traditions of the string quartet genre, which is to say, it moves the genre forward in the way that Haydn, Mozart, Beethoven, Brahms, and Bartók, among others, always tried to push the possibilities of this small, homogeneous ensemble of instruments beyond what others had done before. The piece, as the composer herself has observed, "draws inspiration from the idea of *mestizaje* as envisioned by the Peruvian writer José María Arguedas, whereby cultures co-exist without the subjugation

639

A native of Berkeley, California, Gabriela Lena Frank studied music at Rice University and received a D.M.A. in composition at the University of Michigan in 2001, where she studied with William Albright and William Bolcom, among others. She now lives in the San Francisco Bay Area.

Burr/PictureGroup/AP Photos

of one by the other." Each of the work's six movements bears a descriptive title that links it with various cultures of the Andean region. The fourth movement, "Chasqui," as the composer describes it, "depicts a legendary runner from the Inca era who delivered messages between towns separated by the Andean peaks."[1]

With or without a title, the movement certainly conveys a sense of enormous speed and energy. The constantly shifting meters and rhythms never fall into any kind of predictable pattern, yet the music flows in a seemingly effortless fashion, even though the work is extremely difficult to play. In several passages (e.g., m. 11, 144) the violins are called upon to imitate the sound of the plucked *charanco* (*charango*), a small lute-like instrument common in the Andes. At other points Frank asks each of the instruments to imitate the sound of the *quena*, a traditional Andean flute, at times in duet (violins: m. 76–95; viola and cello: m. 104–126), marking one passage "fluttertongue," as if to recreate the sound of a rapidly vibrating tongue along the mouthpiece of that instrument. The movement owes much to the quartets of Bartók as well, not only in its incorporation of folk idioms and instruments, but also in its use of strings snapped on the fingerboard to create a sharp, percussive sound (the "Bartók snap," m. 70, 159, etc.). The work ends with a root-position C-minor chord, a clear tonal ending to a movement that has otherwise carefully avoided any sense of strong tonal center.

Born in San Francisco, Lisa Bielewa studied literature as an undergraduate at Yale University and moved to New York City in 1990. She has toured with the Philip Glass Ensemble since 1992 and has promoted performances of music by young composers through the MATA Festival, which she co-founded in 1997.

Amy Sussman/Getty Images Entertainment/Getty Images

Lisa Bielawa's three-movement Double Violin Concerto (2008) (Listen on mysearchlab, CD 15, Track 21, Score Anthology II/193) also pushes the boundaries of its genre: its second movement ("Song") sets an English translation of a passage from the prologue to Goethe's *Faust*. The text, declaimed in the original by a character playing the role of a theater director, urges a poet and an actor to use all the mechanical resources at their disposal ("Do not spare our machinery. / Employ the sun and moon, do not hold back!"). But what does this have to do with a concerto for two violins? Through her music, Bielawa seems to be making much the same point as the theater director: art rests on artifice and should not deny its essentially constructed—artificial—nature. The final portion of the text ("Leave the great world . . .") is actually spoken later in the play by the evil spirit Mephistopheles, yet the implied transposition to the theater director makes great sense, for the theater fashions "little worlds within the bigger one," creating, in effect, an alternate reality through artifice. The concert hall and the genre of the concerto do the same thing, and if a violin soloist sings while playing, that simply illustrates the limitless boundaries of art.

The resources—the "machinery"—of the Bielawa's Double Violin Concerto are relatively modest but used in creative ways. The orchestra consists two flutes (one doubling on piccolo), two oboes (one doubling on English horn), two bassoons, two horns, two trumpets, a trombone, an accordion, and strings. And is not just the soloists who are allowed to improvse, but the orchestral players as well at many points throughout. The two solo violin parts are labeled "Colin" and "Carla" for the performers for which they were written: Colin Jacobsen and Carla Kihlstedt. In the second movement, "Carla" plays an instrument strung entirely with E strings and tuned to the pitches B♭, A, F, and the same F tuned about a quarter-tone higher. (See the "Performance Notes" in the score.) This "arpeggio" on open E-strings is most readily audible at the very opening of the movement, when Carla plays unaccompanied. "Carla" also sings while playing her solo violin part, yet another act of artifice and virtuosity. "Colin" also has the option to join in with a vocalization doubling his violin part at an octave below (m. 31, 127). The music is full of small details and big surprises, none more unexpected than its ending.

All three of these contemporary composers are acutely aware of their position within the history of music. In their own ways, they all draw attention to the nature of art, which by its very nature is artificial and yet also constructs "little worlds within the bigger one." This is, in a way, the essence of postmodern art: it makes no pretense to be anything other than artifice, a construct.

Musical institutions of the new millennium continue to evolve as well. The recording industry, which had enjoyed eight decades of uninterrupted growth during the 20th century, had to confront declining sales for the first time in its history, beginning around 1999. It has recently begun to rebound after refashioning itself in response to the inescapable reality of the Internet: digital sales eclipsed physical sales for the first time in 2011.[2] Through the Internet, the public now has access to more varied repertories, styles, and performers than ever before. Civic orchestras, which rose to prominence in the late 19th century, are adopting creative strategies to retain audiences and attract new listeners. Concert venues accommodate increasingly diverse kinds of performances. In the 1930s and 1940s, when Benny Goodman's band and Duke Ellington's band performed at what had been a bastion of classical music—Carnegie Hall—critics hailed the events as landmarks in the history of jazz. In 2002, by contrast, when the hip-hop band Roots played in Avery Fisher Hall at Lincoln Center, the home of the New York Philharmonic Orchestra, the event created scarcely a stir.

Even the governing board of the Pulitzer Prize in Journalism and the Arts has changed its criteria for what it considers a "distinguished musical composition of significant dimension" (see p. 592). In June 2004, the board announced that nominees for the award in music would no longer be required to submit a score and a live recording of the work under consideration; now, only a recording is needed. The change reflects an important shift in attitudes. In the past, a "distinguished musical composition of significant dimension" was assumed to be—and was for the most part equated with—the notated score of that work. Given

the importance of improvisational and electronic music throughout the second half of the 20th century, it could be argued that the change was in fact long overdue. The idea that a composition does not necessarily involve notation allowed jazz saxophonist Ornette Coleman to win the 2007 Pulitzer Prize in Music for his 2005 live concert recording released under the title *Sound Grammar*.

As styles continue to proliferate, some artists are combining them in ways that break down the borders between them. So-called crossover acts, intended to appeal to the audiences for more than one genre, are now so common that the term has begun to lose meaning. The African-American jazz violinist Regina Carter (b. 1966) exemplifies the trend toward a deepening synthesis of musical traditions. In December 2001, she was invited by the city of Genoa, Italy, to play on the violin known as "The Cannon," a 250-year-old instrument once owned and used by the 19th-century virtuoso Niccolò Paganini. Carter and her group played a mixture of jazz numbers, improvisations, and arrangements of popular songs. At one point, she wove allusions to works by Johann Sebastian Bach and Arvo Pärt (see chapter 23) into a cadenza within her own arrangement of *Don't Explain*, a popular song written in the mid-1940s by Billie Holiday (1915–1959).

The gradual erosion of meaningful distinctions between the genres of opera and musical offers yet another example of how genres can change and merge over time. Gian Carlo Menotti composed several operas for Broadway in the late 1940 and 1950, and received two Pulitzer Prizes in Music for *The Consul* (1950) and *The Saint of Bleecker Street* (1955). Baz Luhrmann's 1990 production of Puccini's *La Bohème*, revived in 2002 for Broadway, presented the opera in its original Italian (with English translations running at the top and bottom of the stage) but with amplified sound. Elton John and Tim Rice's 1999 reworking of Verdi's *Aïda* was more radical, using the plot of Verdi's opera as the basis for an entirely new score. In 2003, the Italian rock musician Lucio Dalla premiered a reworking of Puccini's *Tosca* as *Tosca: Desperate Love*, in which singers perform against a recorded soundtrack. Some critics see the work as a "dumbing down" of traditional opera; others consider it part of a necessary transformation of a genre in danger of becoming ossified. This is not to say that transformations and reworkings of long-established operas will eventually supplant more traditional productions and venues. What seems more likely is that such works will add to the growing range of musical choices available to audiences.

Still, the history of music teaches us that no one can predict music's future. We know from the past that music will change in ways we cannot today envision. Composers, performers, and audiences of the early 19th century could

the chance that one or both of these crafts might some-day fall into the hands of an extraterrestrial civilization, the National Aeronautics and Space Administration (NASA) included in the payload a series of photographs of life on earth, texts, recordings of many sounds from earth (wind, water, animals), greetings in multiple languages, and a variety of musical selections from cultures around the world. The musical selections are as follows:

- J. S. Bach, Brandenburg Concerto no. 2, first movement
- Java, court gamelan, *Kinds of Flowers*, recorded by Robert Brown
- Senegal, percussion, recorded by Charles Duvelle
- Zaire, Pygmy girls' initiation song, recorded by Colin Turnbull
- Australia, Aborigine songs, *Morning Star* and *Devil Bird*, recorded by Sandra LeBrun Holmes
- Mexico, *El Cascabel*, performed by Lorenzo Barcelata and the Mariachi México
- Chuck Berry, *Johnny B. Goode*
- New Guinea, men's house song, recorded by Robert MacLennan
- Japan, shakuhachi, *Tsuru No Sugomori* ("Crane's Nest"), performed by Goro Yamaguchi
- J. S. Bach, Gavotte en rondeaux from the Partita no. 3 in E major for Violin, performed by Arthur Grumiaux
- W. A. Mozart, *The Magic Flute*, Queen of the Night's aria (no. 14)
- Georgian S.S.R., chorus, *Tchakrulo*, collected by Radio Moscow
- Peru, panpipes and drum, collected by Casa de la Cultura, Lima
- *Melancholy Blues*, performed by Louis Armstrong and his Hot Seven
- Azerbaijan S.S.R., bagpipes, recorded by Radio Moscow
- Igor Stravinsky, *Rite of Spring*, Sacrificial Dance
- J. S. Bach, *The Well-Tempered Clavier*, Book 2, Prelude and Fugue in C, no. 1
- Ludwig van Beethoven, Symphony no. 5, first movement
- Bulgaria, *Izlel je Delyo Hagdutin*, sung by Valya Balkanska

Voyager 2 launches from the Cape Canaveral Air Force Station, Florida, carrying a payload that includes a variety of musical selections, on the chance that extraterrestrial life will some day recover the recording and the machine with which to play it.
NASA Images

not have imagined the phonograph. Their grandchildren at the beginning of the 20th century, although familiar with recorded sound, could not have imagined the digital manipulation of sound. Even as recently as the 1960s, few would have predicted a medium with the potential and international scope of the Internet, which has provided artists with the ability to reach potential audiences directly, bypassing many traditional marketing approaches. And so, almost certainly, our children and grandchildren a hundred years from now will be listening to music in ways that are unimaginable to us today—even as they enjoy the opportunity to explore the "golden oldies" of the early 21st century and thereby learn a little about us and our musical tastes.

Whatever form it takes, music will remain one of humanity's defining characteristics. Indeed the music of Bach, Beethoven, and Chuck Berry, among others, is now at this very moment on its way out of our solar system, representing humanity to the universe. In August and September 1977, the United States launched two essentially identical spacecrafts to explore the outer planets and beyond. On

- Navajo Indians, *Night Chant*, recorded by Willard Rhodes

- A. Holborne, instrumental selections from *The Fairie Round*

- Solomon Islands, panpipes, collected by the Solomon Islands Broadcasting Service

- Peru, wedding song, recorded by John Cohen

- China, ch'in, *Flowing Streams*, performed by Kuan P'ing-hu

- India, raga, *Jaat Kahan Ho*, sung by Surshri Kesar Bai Kerkar

- *Dark Was the Night*, written and performed by Blind Willie Johnson

- Ludwig van Beethoven, String Quartet in B, op. 130, Cavatina

What any extraterrestrial creatures will make of this assortment is anyone's guess. But it will surely make clear to them music's central importance to the human race.

# Appendix 1

## A GUIDE TO SELECTED RESEARCH MATERIALS IN MUSIC HISTORY

The literature on music can sometimes seem overwhelmingly vast, but with the help of a few key sources, you can navigate it confidently.

Two good brief guides to research in music are Jane Gottlieb, *Music Library and Research Skills* (Upper Saddle River, NJ: Prentice Hall, 2008); and Laurie J. Sampsel, *Music Research: A Handbook*, 2nd ed. (New York: Oxford University Press, 2013).

The standard bibliography of resource materials in the field is Vincent H. Duckles and Ida Reed, *Music Reference and Research Materials: An Annotated Bibliography*, 5th ed. (New York: Schirmer Books, 1997). Although now somewhat out of date, it provides a good overview of the various categories of music reference materials, beginning with dictionaries and proceeding through music histories, guides to musicology, bibliographies of music and works about music, journal indexes, catalogs of music libraries, and more. The rest of this appendix provides only a brief overview of what can be found in abundance in *Music Reference and Research Materials*.

### Dictionaries and Encyclopedias

The basic English-language encyclopedia of music is *The New Grove Dictionary of Music and Musicians*, 2nd ed. (New York: Grove's Dictionaries, 2000). First published in 3 volumes in the late 19th century, *Grove* has grown to a substantial 29 volumes and is also available online (www.grovemusic.com). It has entries for musical terms, individual composer biographies, and biographies of other important figures in music history. Every composer biography includes a list of works with essential information—such as date of composition, date of first performance, and date of publication—on all the music a composer wrote.

The most important biographical dictionary is *Baker's Biographical Dictionary of Musicians* (New York: Schirmer Books, 2001). Thoroughly revised by the late Nicolas Slonimsky, the entries in this six-volume work are more concise than the biographical entries in *The New Grove*.

Still more concise biographies can be found in a one-volume reference, *The Harvard Biographical Dictionary of Music* (Cambridge, MA: Harvard University Press, 1996).

The standard one-volume reference source for musical terms is *The Harvard Dictionary of Music* (Cambridge, MA: Harvard University Press, 2003).

### Journals

Journals (also known as periodicals) are collections of scholarly articles that appear on a regular schedule (such as monthly, three times a year, or yearly). A typical issue contains articles by several authors on a variety of subjects. Just how varied the subject matter is depends on the particular publication. The *Journal of the American Musicological Society*, for example, has a broad scope: a single issue might include an essay on the dissemination of Gregorian chant, another on the cantatas of Bach, and yet another on Wagner's early operas. A journal like *19th-Century Music*, in contrast, publishes articles only on the music of a single century, and a journal like *Opera Quarterly* focuses on a single genre.

Many journals also include book reviews. The purpose of these reviews is not so much to persuade people to buy (or not to buy) a particular book, but rather to move forward scholarly debate on a particular subject. If the author of a new book makes a particularly startling claim about, say, the circumstances of Mozart's death, a book reviewer has the obligation not only to summarize the argument, but also to evaluate it. In this way, book reviews constitute an important part of an ongoing dialogue among scholars.

Some of the more important journals in the field of music history include the following:

| | |
|---|---|
| *Acta Musicologica* | *Music Theory Spectrum* |
| *American Music* | *Music & Letters* |
| *Early Music* | *Musical Quarterly* |
| *Journal of Music Theory* | *19th-Century Music* |
| *Journal of Musicology* | *Notes: The Journal of the Music Library Association* |
| *Journal of the American Musicological Society* | *Popular Music* |
| *Journal of the Society of American Music* | |

## Journal Indexes

Several excellent indexes, all of them regularly updated and available in both printed and online editions, provide a guide to the abundant information available in music journals:

- The *Music Index* lists the articles in a wide range of music periodicals published since 1949 categorized by subject and author (http://www.ebscohost.com/public/music-index).

- The *RILM Abstracts of Music Literature* covers books as well as journals published since 1969. (*RILM* is the acronym for *Répertoire International de Littérature Musicale*, or "International Repertory of Musical Literature.") More scholarly and international in scope than *Music Index*, it also includes abstracts—brief summaries—of every book or article it indexes (www.rilm.org).

- The *Arts & Humanities Citation Index (A&HCI)*, which first appeared in 1980, indexes journal articles in a variety of fields, including music. In addition to the standard author and subject indexes, *A&HCI* also indexes every footnote appearing in each of these journal articles. This allows researchers to trace citations to a particularly central source or work. If, for example, you have identified a particular book or article as an important source for a topic you are researching, you can use *A&HCI* to find out what recent journal articles have cited that same source or work. This can often lead you to important new sources that you might not otherwise have found. For online access to *A&HCI*, consult your local library.

- *JSTOR* (www.jstor.org) is one of many online search engines for scholarly journals past and present. Check your library's online catalog for this and other options.

## Dissertations

A dissertation is a book-length work written by a graduate student to earn a doctoral degree—in music either a doctor of philosophy (Ph.D.) or doctor of musical arts (D.M.A.). Dissertations usually have a narrow focus. The standard guide to dissertations in music is Charles Adkins, *Doctoral Dissertations in Musicology*, available in printed form but more up to date in its online form (www.ams-net.org/ddm).

## Printed Library Catalogs

With the advent of computer catalogs, library card catalogs are easy to overlook, but they remain essential for the serious music scholar. A great deal of material in all disciplines issued before the 1970s has not yet found its way into any database. Some very large libraries, such as the New York Public Library and the British Library, have made the contents of their collections accessible through printed library catalogs. The New York Public Library's *Dictionary Catalog of the Music Collection* (Boston: G.K. Hall, 1964–1976), for example, consists of page after page of photographed catalog cards, most of which are still not represented in that institution's computer database. Other major collections have made their card catalogs available in a similar format; see Duckles and Reed's *Music Reference and Research Materials* for a list of the most important of these.

## Union Catalogs

A union catalog shows the holdings of more than one library. The most important of these specifically for music-related materials is the *Répertoire international des Sources Musicales* ("International Repertoire of Musical Sources"), better known as *RISM*. This essential resource for anyone working with music written before 1800 lists the holdings of music manuscripts, prints, and books to be found in libraries throughout the world. The many volumes within this multifaceted series are indexed in Duckles and Reed's *Music Reference and Research Materials*.

Two catalogs that include music among many other disciplines are these:

- WorldCat (www.worldcat.org), the world's largest online union catalog.

- *National Union Catalog of Pre-1956 Imprints* (London: Mansell, 1968–1981), a printed catalog of 754 volumes covering materials published prior to 1956. This catalog shows holdings from libraries throughout North America and is particularly useful for older materials that may not appear in any online databases.

## Thematic Catalogs

Thematic catalogs are an invaluable resource for research in music. A thematic catalog of the works of a particular composer lists the entire output of that individual and gives details on each work, including an *incipit* (the first few notes of the work or movement in musical notation, enough to identify it unambiguously), the location of the autograph score (if it still exists), first and early editions, and a bibliography of writings about a particular work. The best source for thematic catalogs is the works lists in the composer biographies in *The New Grove*.

## Style Manuals

Any standard style manual—such as Kate L. Turabian's *A Manual for Writers of Term Papers, Theses, and Dissertations*, 6th ed. (Chicago: University of Chicago Press, 1996) or the Modern Language Association's *MLA Handbook for Writers of Research Papers*, 6th ed. (New York: Modern Language Association of America, 2003)—can help you prepare a research paper. But music, like any discipline, has a specialized vocabulary and specialized stylistic conventions, and three useful guides address these:

- Jonathan Bellman, *A Short Guide to Writing about Music*, 2nd ed. (New York: Pearson Longman, 2007).

- D. Kern Holoman, *Writing about Music: A Style Sheet*, 2nd ed. (Berkeley and Los Angeles: University of California Press, 2008).

- Richard J. Wingell, *Writing about Music: An Introductory Guide*, 4th ed. (Upper Saddle River, NJ: Prentice Hall, 2009).

# Appendix 2

✹━━━━━━━━✹

# EVALUATING MUSICAL EDITIONS

When you study or perform a work of music, which edition should you use? If only one is available, the question is easy to answer. But often, particularly in the case of major composers, we have many editions from which to choose. If you're using the library, you might be tempted to use the first edition you find, but then you'd be relying on luck, because the quality of musical editions varies greatly.

A good edition of music conveys as closely as possible the composer's intentions. Editors sift through a variety of musical sources and other evidence to determine those intentions. In the edition they identify their sources and make clear their reasons for choosing a particular reading in cases where the correct reading is in dispute. Ideally, they also include a **critical report** that establishes the relationship among those sources and the basis for their editorial choices. Critical reports are either appended to the back of a volume or issued as a separate volume.

The original manuscript score of a work in the composer's own hand—known as the **holograph, autograph score**, or simply **autograph**—is usually the most reliable guide to a composer's intentions. The autograph score of many works, however, has not survived. And even when it is available, it is by no means infallible. Composers, after all, make mistakes. Considering how complicated and intricate a four-movement symphony is, for example, it shouldn't be surprising that the composer of one might occasionally write, say, a natural sign where a sharp sign was clearly intended. Editors would not be doing their job simply to perpetuate such mistakes. Composers also take shortcuts, such as marking the phrasing of a frequently repeated figure only the first two or three times it occurs. Editors then must decide whether or not to apply that same phrasing to all subsequent occurrences. Composers also change their minds. The autograph score and the first edition of Mozart's six string quartets dedicated to Haydn are significantly different. Mozart was almost certainly involved with the production of this first edition, and in the process of seeing it into print, he appears to have had second thoughts about certain details of tempo, articulation, and other matters. Mozart's participation in the publication process makes the first edition an authoritative source, in this case one that is arguably more important than the autograph.

Yet even an authoritative first edition is not necessarily the last word. Hector Berlioz, for instance, tinkered with matters of orchestration repeatedly after hearing his works in performance, even after a work had been published, and he wrote about these changes in some of his letters. Anton Bruckner, in turn, undertook massive revisions of many of his symphonies. Which version represents a composer's final thoughts on any given passage? Conscientious editors have to identify and evaluate carefully all relevant sources of a particular work—autograph, early copies, first editions, later editions, comments in the composer's correspondence—to make a **critical edition** of that work. What is critical about these editions is the editor's attitude toward all the sources. Editors do not merely accept, uncritically, whatever sources happen to be the earliest or most widely disseminated, but rather subject each source to careful scrutiny.

For an example of what can result from uncritical editing, consider the case of the six string quartets by Joseph Haydn now known as Opus 33. The autograph score of these quartets no longer exists. Haydn probably gave it to his Viennese publisher, Artaria, who used it to engrave the first edition in 1782. This edition consisted of a set of parts; no full score of the work was issued until the early 19th century. The publisher then probably either threw the manuscript away or reused it for packaging. (Composer's autographs were not perceived as valuable until a decade or so later, and even then publishers continued to be astonishingly cavalier with them.) Artaria's first edition, then, is the most reliable source we have for Opus 33. We know through Haydn's correspondence that he worked with Artaria in producing this edition, and for this reason we can call it an authoritative source. Surviving copies of this edition, however, are exceedingly rare, probably because few were printed and because people would have used them mostly at home the way we use sheet music today.

Another edition, published a few years later by Hummel of Amsterdam, in contrast, seems to have been widely available. This edition was the first to designate the quartets as Opus 33. It is, however, thoroughly unreliable, beginning with the opus number, which is different from the one that appears on Artaria's authoritative edition. Haydn had nothing to do with the Hummel edition; he received no payment for it and would certainly have been outraged to have his work pirated. Although it was considered unethical in Haydn's time for a publisher to print a living composer's music without any payment, the practice was nonetheless common until the emergence of effective copyright laws in the late 19th century.

What, then, was the source for Hummel's edition? We cannot know for sure, but it was clearly corrupt, both ethically and textually. One possible scenario is that these corruptions originated with one of Haydn's copyists, who in an attempt to earn some extra money made an unauthorized additional copy, which he then sold to any unscrupulous publisher, like Hummel, who was willing to pay the right price. Haydn was aware of this practice and complained about it on more than one occasion, but he could do little to stop it. Because these unauthorized copies had to be made quickly and surreptitiously, they were likely to contain errors. Another possible scenario is that the corruption came from Hummel himself or someone working for him. Troubled by the strange opening in the first movement of op. 33, no. 1 (Example A2–1), Hummel may have "corrected" it by filling in what he thought were missing harmonies (Example A2–2). The result is musically disastrous.

Unfortunately, bad editions have a way of perpetuating themselves. The least expensive and most widely available edition of the Opus 33 quartets today is a reprint, an exact photographic reproduction, of an edition of these works published in the late 19th century, prepared by a German scholar named Wilhelm Altmann. This is an uncritical edition: Altmann provides no indication of his sources. It is, however, clearly based on Hummel's unreliable early-19th-century edition. And because it is considerably less expensive, musicians are more likely to buy Altmann's edition than a critical edition of the quartets published as part of Haydn's complete works by the Haydn-Institut in Cologne, Germany. Thus Hummel's corrupt edition remains with us even today.

A note of caution: Many editions of music proclaim themselves as "Urtext" editions. *Urtext* is a German word that means "original text." Some of these self-proclaimed Urtext editions are in fact very carefully prepared critical editions, but others are not. The word itself has been used so indiscriminately that it is difficult to know when it really means something and when it is being used as a label to sell an item. Be critical in choosing an edition.

**EXAMPLE A2–1** The opening of the first movement of Haydn's String Quartet op. 33, no. 1, as it appears in Artaria's authoritative first edition.

**EXAMPLE A2–2** The opening of the first movement of Haydn's String Quartet op. 33, no. 1, as it appears in Hummel's edition.

# Appendix 3

## WRITING ABOUT MUSIC

"Don't write about the music," the jazz musician Miles Davis once advised. "The music speaks for itself."[1] Anyone who has ever tried to describe a piece of music in words knows exactly what Davis meant. Yet writing about music— the most abstract and elusive of all the arts—can help us better appreciate its subtlety and magic. Our words will never replace the music, but they can help us understand it.

Writing about the emotional power of music poses particular challenges. It is not easy to put into words the passion we feel when we hear a work of music that moves us, and no two listeners respond identically to the same performance. Gushing accounts are rarely helpful. To write that a specific passage is "powerful and awesome" does not, by itself, tell us anything; we need some justification for such a statement, some explanation of what it is that makes the passage remarkable.

To avoid such difficulties, some writers avoid the subjective and emotional aspects of music and restrict themselves to objective issues like harmony and form. But if writing that focuses on the emotional aspects of music can be overblown, writing that focuses solely on its technical aspects can be dry and tedious. The playwright George Bernard Shaw (1856–1950), who supported himself as a music critic early in his career, skewered this sort of analysis in the following passage, which begins with a hypothetical description of Mozart's Symphony in G minor, K. 550:

> Here is the sort of thing: "The principal subject, hitherto only heard in the treble, is transferred to the bass (Ex. 28), the violins playing a new counterpoint to it instead of the original mere accompaniment figure of the first part. Then the parts are reversed, the violins taking the subject and the basses the counterpoint figure, and so on till we come to a close on the dominant of D minor, a nearly related key (commencement of Ex. 29), and then comes the passage by which we return to the first subject in its original form and key."

How succulent this is; and how full of Mesopotamian words like "the dominant of D minor"! I will now, ladies and gentlemen, give you my celebrated "analysis" of Hamlet's soliloquy on suicide ["To be or not to be . . ."] in the same scientific style. "Shakespeare, dispensing with the customary exordium, announces his subject at once in the infinitive, in which mood it is presently repeated after a short connecting passage in which, brief as it is, we recognize the alternative and negative forms on which so much of the significance of repetition depends. Here we reach a colon; a pointed pository phrase, in which the accent falls decisively on the relative pronoun, brings us to the first full stop."

I break off here, because, to confess the truth, my grammar is giving out. But I want to know whether it is just that a literary critic should be forbidden to make his living in this way on pain of being interviewed by two doctors and a magistrate, and hauled off to Bedlam [an infamous mental institution in London] forthwith; whilst the more a musical critic does it, the deeper the veneration he inspires.[2]

The technical and emotional elements of music go hand in hand: no work of music is completely devoid of emotion, and every work of music is built on technical foundations of some kind (even John Cage's *4'33"*). Composers fuse the technical and emotional in their work; a writer's job is to analyze and describe how these two elements function in tandem.

# Appendix 4

✳————————————✳

# THE CONCEPTS OF "POPULAR" AND "ART" MUSIC

Consciously or unconsciously, we often distinguish between music written for a serious purpose ("art" or "classical" music) and music whose function is primarily to entertain and that appeals to a broader public ("popular" music). Such distinctions have a long heritage in Western thought. Aristotle noted that certain rhythms "are noticeably vulgar in their emotional effects while others better suit free-born persons" (see Prologue: Antiquity). And Johannes de Grocheo, writing around 1300, recommended that the motet "not be performed in the presence of common people, for they would not perceive its subtlety, nor take pleasure in its sound." He urged that motets be performed only "in the presence of learned persons and those who seek after subtleties in art" (see Chapter 2). The categories of art and popular music remain very much with us today and are fundamental to the way in which music is marketed.

Yet the distinction between popular and art music is conceptually fuzzy and impossible to define in any consistent way. To begin with, the two categories are not mutually exclusive. Just because a work of music is popular does not mean it cannot be a work of art, and just because it is a work of art does not mean it cannot be popular.

However art music is defined—as music that has survived the test of time, for example, or music with some serious purpose, or music written for an elite audience—we have no clear way to distinguish it stylistically from popular music. Works can easily shift from one category to the other over time. Take, for example, *The Beggar's Opera* (Anthology) by Pepusch and Gay in the 1730s. It was written, adapted, and readapted in many different guises over the course of the 18th century and composed in a style as different as possible from the prevailing serious opera of the upper classes. Yet it is now included in every discussion of opera from the period (as it is in Chapter 9 of this book). The same holds true for Mozart's *Magic Flute*, which premiered in 1791 in a theater that catered to a decidedly middle-brow, if not low-brow, public but is now performed routinely in every major opera house in the world. In the 20th century, Kurt Weill and Berthold Brecht adapted Gay's *The Beggar's Opera* into *Die Dreigroschenoper* ("Threepenny Opera"), a biting social satire. One number in particular from this work, *Mack the Knife*, became quite popular. Louis Armstrong and Frank Sinatra, for example, both recorded very different arrangements of it. Similarly the Doors, a rock group, included on one of their albums a rendition of the *Alabama Song* (Anthology) from another Weill/Brecht production, *The Rise and Fall of the City of Mahagonny*. And the Beatles, who were consistently marketed as popular musicians, produced music of enormous stylistic variety, ranging from the rock-and-roll *I Wanna Hold Your Hand* to *Revolution No. 9*, a montage of electronically manipulated sound clips that reflected trends in the world of avant-garde electronic music at the time.

Recognizing the inadequacy of the terms *art* and *popular*, some commentators have attempted to distinguish instead between "cultivated" and "vernacular" styles, but this distinction also breaks down on close inspection. Rock music, an ostensibly vernacular genre, is today produced and recorded with the most sophisticated audio equipment available; bands rehearse endlessly, and individual performers practice with as much intensity as any other kind of musician. Although vernacular music may convey an impression of spontaneity, it is often as carefully thought out—as cultivated—as any music in the ostensibly cultivated category.

But if no consistent difference exists stylistically between art and popular music, or cultivated and vernacular music, there is a difference in the attitudes composers, performers, and audiences bring to bear on music they assign (consciously or unconsciously) to one category or the other. Popular music is usually associated with a relatively relaxed approach toward the work at hand. Compare any two performances of almost any popular song and you will quickly realize they can differ enormously. Performers routinely change words, harmonies, instrumentation, and even melody and form. Listeners, in turn, not only accept but welcome such changes. Ella Fitzgerald's rendition of

Cole Porter's *Night and Day* differs markedly from Frank Sinatra's, and both take liberties with Porter's original. Sinatra, for example, begins one of his many recordings of the work with the chorus, ignoring the opening verse entirely. But even Porter, as a composer, expected performers to make such alterations.

Yet even here, differences in attitude cannot be assigned exclusively to one kind of music or another. Probably no one would think of 18th-century opera seria as popular music (see Chapter 9), yet composers, performers, and audiences all expected singers in this repertory to embellish da capo arias.

On the whole, however, such practices and attitudes are far less common within the repertory we tend to think of as art music or classical music, particularly in works written after the early 19th century. As we saw in Chapter 14, the respect and deference toward the composer's intentions that now characterize our attitude toward art music dates to roughly 1800, that is, to the generation of Beethoven. Mozart, a few decades earlier, had readily agreed to rewrite the music of several roles in *Don Giovanni*. He had originally composed the work for a specific cast of singers in Prague but willingly made significant changes to accommodate the strengths of the different cast that performed it in Vienna. Over the course of the 19th century, this kind of alteration became increasingly rare. Opera houses began to accommodate the composer, not the other way around.

From the 19th century onward, tradition has taught performers to approach certain repertories with a sense of veneration. Musicians go to great lengths to ascertain and execute the composer's intentions as accurately as possible, using the best edition available (see Appendix 2). Within this tradition, performers rarely change words, harmonies, form, or instrumentation. When Leonard Bernstein substituted a single word in the finale of Beethoven's Ninth Symphony at the Berlin Wall in 1989—changing *Freude* (joy) to *Freiheit* (freedom)—critics debated the alteration at great length. Some considered it appropriate to the circumstances; others found it sacrilegious, a defilement of Beethoven's original score. What is significant is that this alteration of a single word aroused so much attention.

Works that have at various times been considered both classical and popular can also tell us something about the essence of this distinction. Performers have long felt at liberty to make fundamental changes to Gilbert and Sullivan's *Pirates of Penzance* (Anthology I/140), altering words, music, and orchestration to suit their immediate times, needs, and resources. One recent American production, for example, substituted "Coast Guard" for the original "Customs House" in order to make a particular passage more comprehensible to its audience. Joseph Papp's Broadway production of 1980 used electric guitars and synthesizers in addition to a standard orchestra. Unlike Bernstein's alteration of Beethoven's Ninth, however, these and other changes, because they are consistent with a long tradition of performance practice, elicited virtually no comment. In contrast, scholars are now preparing a critical edition of

the work in an attempt to reconstruct the original version from autograph sources and the earliest editions.

Music of all kinds can be fruitfully studied and performed from both an art and popular point of view. Neither is superior to the other. Both are legitimate, and both represent valid ways of making—and listening to—music.

# Appendix 5

✳ |————————| ✳

## THE ORDINARY OF THE MASS

The ritual of the Mass,[3] as celebrated in the Catholic Church since the medieval era, consists of certain unvarying elements—the Ordinary—and certain elements used in connection with specific seasons, weeks, or days—the Propers. The Ordinary, in other words, is that portion of the Mass that remains constant, whereas the Propers change throughout the year. Until the mid-1960s, all the elements of the Mass, both Ordinary and Propers, were always said (or sung) in Latin; most Catholic churches now use the vernacular, that is, the everyday language of the country in which the Mass is being celebrated. (Protestant sects, many of which retained the Mass in whole or in part, switched to the vernacular early on, during the Reformation in the 16th century.)

A Mass can be performed with no singing at all, but the five parts of the Ordinary that are typically set to music and have posed a challenge to generations of composers are these:

- The Kyrie, a supplication for mercy ("Lord have mercy upon us"). Its text is actually in ancient Greek, not Latin.

- The Gloria, a hymn of praise to the Holy Trinity (God the Father, God the Son, God the Holy Spirit).

- The Credo (creed), a statement of faith, detailing the essential elements of church doctrine.

- The Sanctus, a hymn of consecration at the moment when the Communion wine and bread are blessed.

- The Agnus Dei, a prayer for peace.

## Kyrie

| | |
|---|---|
| Kyrie eleison. | Lord, have mercy. |
| Christe eleison. | Christ, have mercy. |
| Kyrie eleison. | Lord, have mercy. |

## Gloria

| | |
|---|---|
| Gloria in excelsis Deo. | Glory to God in the highest. |
| Et in terra pax hominibus bonae voluntatis | And on earth peace to people of good will. |
| Laudamus te. | We praise You. |
| Benedicimus te. | We bless You. |
| Adoramus te. | We worship You. |
| Glorificamus te. | We glorify You. |
| Gratiam agimus tibi propter magnam gloriam tuam | We give thanks to You for thy great glory, |
| Domine Deus, Rex coelestis. | Lord God, heavenly King. |
| Deus Pater omnipotens. | God the father almighty. |
| Domine Fili unigenite, Jesu Christe. | O Lord, the only begotten Son, Jesus Christ. |
| Domine Deus, Agnus Dei, Filius Patris | Lord God, Lamb of God, Son of the Father |
| Qui tollis peccata mundi, | Who takest away the sins of the world |
| miserere nobis. | have mercy upon us. |
| Qui tollis peccata mundi, | Who takest away the sins of the world |
| suscipe deprecationem nostram. | Receive our prayer. |
| Qui sedes ad dexteram Patris | Who sittest at the right hand of the Father |
| miserere nobis. | have mercy upon us. |

Quoniam tu solus sanctus.
Tu solus Dominus.
Tu solus altissimus,
Jesu Christe.
Cum Sancto Spiritu,
in gloria Dei Patris.

Amen.

For thou only art holy.
Thou only art the Lord.
Thou only art most high,
O Jesus Christ.
With the Holy Spirit,
in the glory of God the
Father.
Amen.

## Credo

Credo in unum Deum,
Patrem omnipotentem,
factorem caeli et terre,
visibilium omnium,
et invisibilium.
Et in unum Dominum
Jesum Christum,
Filium Dei unigenitum:

et ex Patre natum ante
omnia saecula;
Deum de Deo, lumen de
lumine,
Deum verum de Deo vero;
genitum, non factum,
consubstantialem Patri;

per quem omnia facta sunt.

Qui propter nos homines,
et propter nostram salutem,
descendit de caelis.
Et incarnatus est
de Spiritu Sancto
ex Maria Virgine;
et homo factus est.
Crucifixus etiam pro nobis,

sub Pontio Pilato passus,

et sepultus est.
Et resurrexit tertia die,

secundum Scripturas.

Et ascendit in caelum,
sedet ad dexteram Patris.

Et iterum venturus est

I believe in one God,
the Father almighty,
maker of heaven and earth,
and of all things visible
and invisible.
And in one Lord
Jesus Christ,
the only begotten Son of
God,
born of the Father
before all ages;
God of God, light of
light,
true God of true God;
begotten not made;
being of one substance
with the Father;
by whom all things were
made.
Who for us men,
and for our salvation,
came down from heaven;
and was incarnate
by the Holy Spirit, of
the Virgin Mary;
and was made man.
He was crucified also
for us,
suffered under Pontius
Pilate,
and was buried.
And the third day he rose
again
according to the
Scriptures;
and ascended into heaven.
He sitteth at the right
hand of the Father;
and he shall come again

cum gloria judicare
vivos et mortuos:
cujus regni non erit finis.

Et in Spiritum
Sanctum Dominum
et vivificantem,
qui ex Patre Filioque procedit.

Qui cum Patre et Filio

simul adoratur et
conglorificatur;
qui locutus est per Prophetas.

Et unam, sanctam,
catholicam et
apostolicam Ecclesiam.
Confiteor unum baptisma
in remissionem peccatorum.
Et exspecto
resurrectionem mortuorum,
et vitam venturi saeculi. Amen.

with glory to judge the
living and the dead;
and his kingdom shall
have no end.
And [I believe] in the
Holy Ghost,
the Lord and giver of life,
who proceeds from the
Father and the Son,
who together with the
Father and the Son
is adored and
glorified;
who spoke by the
Prophets.
And [I believe in] one
holy catholic and
apostolic Church.
I confess one baptism
for the remission of sins.
And I await the
resurrection of the dead,
and the life of the world
to come. Amen.

## Sanctus

Sanctus, sanctus, sanctus
Dominus Deus Sabaoth.
Pleni sunt caeli et
terra gloria tua:
Hosanna in excelsis.
Benedictus qui venit
in nomine Domini:
Hosanna in excelsis.

Holy, holy, holy,
Lord God of hosts.
Heaven and earth are
full of thy glory.
Hosanna in the highest.
Blessed is he that cometh
in the name of the Lord.
Hosanna in the highest.

## Agnus Dei

Agnus Dei,
qui tollis peccata mundi,

miserere nobis.
Agnus Dei,
qui tollis peccata mundi,

miserere nobis.
Agnus Dei,
qui tollis peccata mundi,

dona nobis pacem.

Lamb of God,
who takest away the sins
of the world,
have mercy on us.
Lamb of God,
who takest away the sins
of the world,
have mercy on us.
Lamb of God,
who takest away the sins
of the world,
Grant us peace.

# Glossary

**Absolute music**   Instrumental music without a program or any other indication of a possible extramusical content.

**Accompanied recitative**   Type of recitative accompanied by the orchestra.

**Affect**   Predominant emotion of a text or musical work.

*Air de cour*   Literally, "courtly air"; genre of secular song in late-16th-century and early-17th-century France that could be either polyphonic or homophonic (voice and lute).

**Alberti bass**   Type of accompanimental figure used in much music of the Classical era and featuring frequent repetitions of a broken triad. The device is named after Domenico Alberti (1710–ca. 1740), an otherwise obscure Italian composer who favored its use.

**Aleatory music**   From the Latin *alea* ("die," the singular of "dice"), music of chance, leaving one or more elements of performance to randomly determined or indeterminate circumstances such as a roll of the dice, sounds that happen to be present at given moment, or actions determined at the whim of the performer.

**Ambient music**   Background music, the sonic equivalent of architecture, whose primary purpose is to shape actions and attitudes rather than to be the focus of the listener's attention.

**Ambitus**   Range of a given melody or mode.

**Antecedent and consequent**   Terms borrowed from grammar to describe the relationship of units within a phrase of music. The **antecedent** phrase comes first (*ante* = "before") and in its most basic form moves from tonic to dominant. The **consequent** phrase follows, and in its most basic form moves from dominant to tonic. See also **periodic phrase structure.**

**Anthem**   Designation given to many motet-like works on English texts from the 16th century onward. The full anthem is for chorus throughout. The verse anthem alternates choral passages with passages for solo voice and instrumental accompaniment.

**Antiphon**   Type of plainchant sung before (and sometimes after) the recitation of a psalm or other type of chant.

**Antiphonal**   Type of performance featuring repeated alternation between two voices or groups of voices.

**Antiphoner** (*Antiphonale*)   The liturgical book containing the texts (and, if notated, the chants) of the Mass Propers.

**Arch form**   Symmetrical structure within which a unit of music progresses toward a midpoint and then more or less retraces its steps.

**Aria**   A composition for voice, often with instrumental accompaniment and often part of a larger work. The term is also sometimes used in its original Italian sense to indicate a melody or tune of any kind.

**Arietta**   A song or aria of relatively small dimension.

*Ars nova*   Literally, *The New Art*; the title of an early-14th-century theoretical treatise attributed to Philippe de Vitry and used, by extension, to describe French music of the period as well.

**Art music**   A term used to distinguish certain repertories as belonging to a tradition transmitted through notated music; also sometimes called "classical" music. See Appendix 4.

**Atonality**   Melodic and harmonic idiom first cultivated in the early decades of the 20th century, characterized by the absence of a tonal center.

**Augmentation**   Process by which the rhythmic value of a line is systematically increased.

**Authentic mode**   Any of the melodic modes with an ambitus running an octave above the final note.

**Autograph** or **Autograph score**   Score written in the composer's own hand; also known as a holograph.

**Avant-garde**   From the French term for military vanguard, an elite group of artists considered far in advance of all others, leading the way to the future. The term, widely used in all the arts of the 20th century, is particularly associated with the phenomenon of modernism.

**Ballade**   (1) One of the *formes fixes* in the music of the 14th and 15th centuries. The texts usually consist of three strophes of seven or eight lines, the last of which is a refrain. The rhyme scheme varies, but typical patterns include ababccdD, ababbcbC, ababcdE, and ababcdeF (the upper-case letter indicates the refrain, which remains constant from strophe to strophe). (2) Narrative poem, often set to music in the 19th century. (3) Instrumental work that reflects the narrative character of its poetic counterpart.

**Ballad opera**   Type of opera popular in England during the 18th century, featuring contemporary songs (including, but not limited to ballads) mixed with dialogue.

**Ballata** (plural, **ballate**)   Italian poetic and musical form of the 14th and early 15th centuries, formally similar to the French virelai of the same period. The form of the ballata is AbbaA, with a refrain (A) framing the internal lines of each strophe and returning unchanged in each strophe, both musically and textually.

**Bar form**   Form associated with the repertory of the medieval minnesinger, consisting of two *Stollen* followed by an *Abgesang* (AAB).

**Basse danse**   Type of dance popular in the 15th and early 16th centuries. The notated sources preserve only a series of long notes around which other instruments were expected to improvise their own contrapuntal lines.

**Basso continuo**   Literally, the "continuous bass"; the bass line of any work from the 17th or 18th century that incorporates not only the bass line itself but also the harmonies to be realized above that line. The term is also used to describe the performers playing this part: at a bare minimum, this would consist of a chordal instrument (such as organ or lute), ideally supported by one or more instruments capable of sustaining a bass line (such as viol or bassoon).

**Basso ostinato** Literally, "obstinate bass"; a bass pattern repeated many times within the course of a movement or work.

**Bebop** In jazz, a style featuring fast tempos, irregular chordal progressions, complex harmonies, and asymmetrical, often jagged melodies.

**Bel canto** Italian for "beautiful singing," a term used to describe a style of Italian opera in the first half of the 19th century that emphasized lyrical melodic lines, legato phrasing, and a seemingly effortless vocal technique, even in passages of great technical difficulty. The emphasis throughout is on the voice: orchestral accompaniment in 19th-century bel canto opera is typically discreet, limited to harmonic underpinning with little or no counterpoint.

**Binary form** Any musical form that consists of two parts.

**Bluegrass** Style of country music that emerged in the 1940s, typically performed by an ensemble of banjo, acoustic guitar, fiddle, and double bass. The banjo is picked (as opposed to strummed), and vocals tend to be pitched in the upper end of the singer's register; the characteristic syncopation of the style anticipates the downbeat slightly, in contrast to jazz, in which performers often play just slightly behind the beat.

**Blue note** In blues and jazz, the slightly lowered third or seventh degree in the major scale; in natural minor, the slightly lowered third or seventh degree; in any scale, the slightly lowered diminished fifth (resolving to a fourth).

**Blues** Style of song that originated in the American South among African Americans who were slaves and the descendants of slaves. The standard **12-bar blues form** rests on a repeated harmonic pattern of 12 measures in 4/4 time, which in turn is divided into 3 groups of 4 measures each.

**Boogie-woogie** Jazz piano style drawn from blues and ragtime, featuring syncopated "walking" or other ostinato bass lines in the left hand while the right hand plays melodic chords or improvisational passages.

**Bourrée** Lively dance in duple meter with a prominent upbeat at the beginning of each section.

**Branle** "Line dance," sometimes in duple meter (*branle simple*), sometimes in triple (*branle gay*).

**Breve** In Franconian notation, the note value that subdivides the long.

**Bridge** In popular song of the 20th century, the contrasting B section that connects statements of the A theme.

**Cabaletta** Fast closing section of an aria.

**Caccia** (plural, **cacce**) Poetic and musical form cultivated in 14th- and early-15th-century Italy, sometimes monophonic but more frequently for three voices, often with two canonic upper voices. The texts typically deal with hunting.

**Cadence** Point of musical closure indicated by pitch, harmony, rhythm, or any combination of these elements.

**Cadenza** Solo passage in a concerto movement or in an aria, usually toward the end, in which the soloist displays his or her virtuosic talents by embellishing themes heard earlier in the movement or aria; the orchestra remains silent throughout.

**Caecilian movement** Tendency among certain 19th-century composers to restore Gregorian chant and the style of 16th-century a cappella polyphony as the ideals of church music.

**Call and response** Musical texture in which a soloist (leader, minister) sings or cues ("lines out") a phrase to be answered by the choir (ensemble, congregation).

**Canon** (1) Polyphonic work written in such a way that the imitating voice or voices follow the line of the original either exactly (a strict canon) or with small modifications (a free canon). (2) Rule or direction given at the beginning of such a composition to indicate the manner in which it is to be realized (e.g., the points at which the successive voices are to enter).

**Cantata** In its broadest sense, a work to be sung (the Italian word *cantare* means "to sing"). More specifically, the term is used to denote a vocal work, usually sacred, for performance forces of varying size, from soloist and basso continuo to soloists, chorus, and orchestra.

**Cantilena motet** Type of 15th-century motet that features a florid, lyrical top voice over slower moving lower voices.

**Cantus firmus** (plural, **cantus firmi**) "Fixed melody" that serves as the basis of a composition. A cantus firmus can be newly composed for a work but is most often derived from an existing composition.

**Canzona** Instrumental work of the late Renaissance or Baroque originally based on a vocal model, such as the chanson, but later often composed independently of any vocal model.

**Castrato** Castrated male singer whose voice has never broken and who therefore sings in the soprano or alto range. Castrati were common in opere serie of the 17th and 18th centuries.

*Cauda* The long melisma at the end of a conductus.

**Cavatina** In Italian opera of the 19th century, the introductory aria sung by a main character. In German opera of the same period, a type of aria characterized by an introspective quality, free of virtuosic display.

**Chaconne** Type of bass pattern used throughout the Baroque.

**Character piece** Brief work for solo piano that seeks to portray the mood or "character" of a particular person, idea, situation, or emotion. These are sometimes specified, sometimes not. The character piece, which first appeared in the early 19th century, tends to be brief, sectional, and fairly simple in construction.

**Chorale** A hymn, either in its harmonized form or as a melody alone. Chorales are associated particularly with the congregational music of the Protestant Reformation.

**Chorus** In popular song of the 20th century, the principal tune or section.

**Clausula** (plural, **clausulae**) Passages of measured organum that could be substituted at will into the appropriate textual section of a larger existing work of organum.

**Coda** From the Italian word for "tail," a closing section of a work or movement.

*Color* Melodic pattern of an isorhythmic tenor.

**Combinatorial** Quality of certain 12-tone rows in which the hexachord of a row—its first six or last six notes—can be combined with one of the hexachords of an inverted, retrograde, or retrograde inverted form of the same row without producing any duplication of pitches.

**Computer music** Music generated, transformed, composed, and/or performed by a computer.

**Concertato madrigal** Type of madrigal that emerged in the early 17th century, using instruments (basso continuo with or without additional instruments) independently of the vocal part or parts.

**Concertino** Small group of soloists within a concerto grosso, often consisting of two violins and basso continuo.

**Concerto** Term used in the 17th century to indicate broadly any work consisting of multiple forces, such as voices and instruments. From the 18th century onward, the term was reserved primarily for works featuring a soloist or soloists contrasted against a larger ensemble.

**Concerto grosso** Type of Baroque concerto typically featuring soloists (the concertino) and a larger ensemble (the ripieno). The term also encompasses the ripieno concerto, a work for large ensemble with no soloists.

**Concert overture** Single-movement work for orchestra associated with a programmatic idea of some kind. The genre grew out of the 18th-century tradition of performing opera overtures in the concert hall; the concert overture is, in effect, an overture without an opera.

**Concitato** See *genere concitato.*

**Conductus** (plural, **conductus or conducti**) Genre of vocal monophony or polyphony cultivated in the 12th and 13th centuries. Conductus of one, two, three, or occasionally four voices were not based on borrowed musical material of any kind; their texts consist of freely composed poetry written in metered verse that lend themselves to syllabic and strongly metrical musical settings. In the polyphonic conductus, all voices move in roughly the same rhythm.

**Conjunct motion** Melodic motion exclusively or predominantly by half or whole steps.

**Consequent** See **Antecedent and consequent.**

**Consort** Small ensemble of matched instruments with ranges from soprano to bass, in emulation of vocal groups.

**Contenance angloise** Literally, "the English guise"; term used by the French poet Martin le Franc in 1442 to describe the music of Dunstable, Binchois, and Du Fay. This "new way of composing with lively consonances" probably refers to the triadic sonorities and panconsonance of their music.

**Contratenor** Literally "against the tenor"; name first given in the 14th century to a voice line moving in the same range as the tenor.

**Copyright** According to legal registration, the sole or shared ownership of any work of music or other art, often but not necessarily including the creator.

**Countersubject** Contrapuntal theme played against the subject of a fugue.

**Couplet** In a rondo, a contrasting theme (B, C, D, etc.) within the pattern ABACADA. Also called an **episode.**

**Critical edition** Edition prepared by an editor who critically evaluates the relative merits of all sources for a work, such as the composer's autograph score, authorized copies, first and early editions, and later revisions by the composer. A critical edition is usually issued with a critical report.

**Critical report** Editor's report on all significant discrepancies between the critical edition and the various sources (autograph score, first edition, etc.) used to create that edition.

**Crossover** A term used from the mid-twentieth century onward to describe a musical style transferred to genre or medium in which it is not normally used; often used to indicate the use of an "art" style in "popular" music or vice versa.

**Cross-relation** Simultaneous or nearly simultaneous sounding of two pitches a half step apart.

**Cyclical coherence** Manner in which the various movements of a multi-movement cycle (sonata, quartet, symphony, etc.) are related to one another through thematic ideas, distinctive textures, or other musical elements.

**Cyclic Mass** Cycle of all movements of the Mass Ordinary integrated by a common cantus firmus or other musical device.

**Da capo aria** Type of aria consisting of three sections: an opening A section, a contrasting B section, and a return of the A section. In performance, singers were expected to embellish and elaborate the notated music, particularly in the return of A.

**Development** In sonata form, the section following the exposition and preceding the recapitulation, so called because it develops the ideas originally presented in the exposition. The typical development manipulates themes, moves through a variety of keys, and avoids the tonic.

**Diastematic neumes** Neumes that indicate the relative relationship of notes (higher, lower, same) according to their vertical placement on the page. In early plainchant notation, diastematic neumes (also known as heightened neumes) were written without staff lines of any kind.

**Discant organum** See **measured organum.**

**Dissonant counterpoint** Species counterpoint emphasizing dissonant harmony and voice leading rather than consonance.

**Divine Office** (or **Office**) Series of eight services held daily in monastic communities from dawn through the middle of the night, consisting musically of the chanting of psalms and hymns.

**Doctrine of ethos** In ancient Greece, the belief that music had the power to elevate or debase the soul, to enlighten or degrade the mind, and to arouse in listeners certain kinds of emotions and behaviors.

**Dodecaphony** From the Greek *dodeca*, meaning "12." A method of serial composition based on a series or row of 12 pitches drawn from the chromatic octave (C, C♯, D, D♯, etc., up through B).

**Double-exposition concerto form** Type of sonata form found in many concertos of the late 18th and 19th centuries, in which the opening tutti exposition remains in the tonic and the subsequent solo exposition modulates from the tonic to a secondary key area.

**Double leading-tone cadence** Type of cadence favored in the 14th and early 15th centuries that featured two leading tones a fourth or a fifth apart resolving upward by a half step.

**Duplum** From the Latin word for "second," the added second voice in organum and polyphony of the 12th and 13th centuries.

**Empfindsamkeit** The German word for "sensibility," used by some music historians to identify an aesthetic attitude prevalent in the mid-18th century and reflected in much music of that time as well. The style of *Empfindsamkeit* is associated with music that focuses on detail and avoids thick textures and grandiose gestures.

**Episode** (1) Nonimitative section within a fugue. (2) In a rondo, an extended passage that appears between entrances of the main theme (the refrain); also known as a **couplet.**

**Equal temperament** System of tuning that came into widespread use over the course of the 18th century, based on a division of the octave into 12 absolutely equal semitones.

**Etude** A work for solo instrument, originally designed to improve or expand technique in private; by the 19th century, a piece of great difficulty to be played for public approval.

**Exit convention** Convention of opera seria in which the singer who has just finished an aria leaves the stage.

**Exposition** (1) In a fugue, the opening section that introduces the subject in all voices. (2) In a sonata-form movement, the opening section that presents the principal themes of the movement over the course of a harmonic plan that typically moves from tonic to dominant or (in minor-mode works) from tonic to relative major.

**Expressionism** Broad artistic movement of the early 20th century that sought to give voice to the unconscious, to make manifest humanity's deepest and often darkest emotions. In Freudian terms, expressionist art bypasses the ego and aims straight for the id, the unconscious repository of primal urges.

**Faburden** Style of three-voice writing found in some English music of the 15th and 16th centuries, featuring one notated and two implied lines. The uppermost voice moves parallel to the notated voice at the interval of a fourth above; the lowermost voice moves in thirds and fifths below the notated line.

**Fantasia** Type of work that follows no structures of large-scale convention but follows instead (or at least gives the impression of following) the composer's free flight of fantasy.

**Fauxbourdon** Style of three-voice writing popular in the 15th century in which two voices are notated and a third, implied voice (the fauxbourdon) runs parallel to the uppermost notated line at the interval of a fourth below.

**Figured bass** Notational convention of the basso continuo in the 17th and 18th centuries using numbers ("figures") to indicate the desired intervals—and thus the harmonies—to be played above a given bass line.

**Finalis** Characteristic final note of a given mode.

**Florentine Camerata** Group of artists and noblemen who met in Florence between roughly 1573 and 1587 to discuss, among other things, the possible means of recreating the music of ancient Greece.

**Folia** Type of bass pattern used throughout the Baroque.

***Formes fixes*** Literally, "fixed forms"; the poetic and musical structural patterns in French music of the 14th and 15th centuries. The most important of the *formes fixes* were the ballade, virelai, and rondeau.

**Franconian notation** Earliest system of mensural notation, used in the second half of the 13th century and ascribed to Franco of Cologne. Franconian notation assigned specific durational values for the first time to specific note forms.

**Free jazz** Subgenre of jazz that emerged in the early 1960s, characterized by extreme improvisation, often without a central theme, fixed meters, chord progressions, or even tonality itself.

**Free organum** See **unmeasured organum.**

**French overture** Type of overture that begins with a slow introduction featuring dotted rhythms and moves to a fast imitative section. Commonly used in French operas and opere serie of the 17th and 18th centuries.

**Frottola** (plural, **frottole**) Secular Italian vocal genre of the late 15th and early 16th centuries. The texture tends to be chordal and the texts are often lighthearted, comic, or ironic.

**Fugato** Passage within a work or movement that begins like a fugue but does not sustain itself after a series of initial entries.

**Fugue** Type of composition that incorporates a series of imitative entries, usually on a single theme but capable of accommodating multiple themes as well.

**Fusion** A type of jazz that borrows the textures, rhythms, and sonorities of rock and soul music, using instruments such as electric guitars and electric piano.

**Galant** Term used by some historians to describe the musical style of the mid-18th century, emphasizing the music's lightness and grace.

**Galliarde** Type of dance, similar to the saltarello but even more vigorous, with larger leaps by the dancers.

**Gamut** In medieval theory, the entire range of available pitches, conceived of as a series of seven interlocking hexachords beginning on C, F, or G (see Example 1–4).

***Genere concitato*** Literally, the "agitated" or "warlike" manner; a style of writing, developed by Monteverdi, for evoking a mood of agitation or anger, often through the use of rapid repeated notes and fanfare-like figures.

***Gesamtkunstwerk*** German for "integrated art work"; Richard Wagner's ideal of the highest form of art, synthesizing music, drama, and gesture.

**Gospel music** Hymns and other songs associated with American Christianity; more recently, a specific reference to African African Christian music.

**Gradual (*Graduale*)** (1) The liturgical book containing the texts (and, if notated, the chants) of the Mass Ordinary. (2) The second element of the Mass Propers.

**Grand opéra** Type of French-language opera prevalent in the 19th century, usually in five acts, with elaborate staging, costumes, and ballet, often based on historic subjects.

**Gregorian chant** Name often given to plainchant in honor of Pope Gregory I (later Saint Gregory), long believed to have been the originator of the repertory.

**Ground bass** Short bass pattern that, repeated many times over the course of a movement or work, provides the structural basis for the voice or voices above it.

**Guidonian hand** Mnemonic device attributed to the medieval theorist Guido d'Arezzo, used to teach solmization syllables.

**Half cadence** Cadence on the dominant.

**Harmonic rhythm** Rate of harmonic change within a given passage of music. A passage is said to have a slow harmonic rhythm if it maintains the same harmony over a relatively long span of time, such as a full measure or half a measure, depending on meter and tempo.

**Harmonics** Effect created by a technique of string playing in which the performer touches the bowed string lightly at a designated point. The resulting sound is a harmonic overtone two octaves higher than the notated pitch, and the sound is light and ethereal.

**Head motif** Thematic idea that occurs at the beginning of a movement or work and returns prominently throughout the course of the music that follows.

**Heightened neume** See **diastematic neume.**

**Hemiola** Brief passage of duple-meter rhythms within an otherwise triple-meter context.

**Hexachord** Any grouping of 6 pitches. Through the Baroque era, a hexachord was conceived of as a series of 6 ascending notes, all separated by whole steps except the third and fourth notes, which are separated by a half step. In 20th-century dodecaphony (12-tone serial music), a hexachord is half of a 12-tone row.

**Hip-hop** Originally a popular dance music based on "beats," combinations of musical samples and sounds produced in the recording studio; in combination with an adaptation of Jamaican "toasting" (speaking over the music), hip-hop is referred to as rap music.

**Historicism** Approach to artistic creation that openly embraces the forms and styles of earlier generations even while presenting them in original ways.

**Hocket** Passage featuring rapid-fire voice exchange, a favorite device of 14th- and early-15th-century composers.

**Holograph** Score written in the composer's own hand; also known as an autograph score or simply as an autograph.

**Homophony** Type of texture in which a principal melodic line is accompanied by a clearly subordinate voice or voices.

**Humanism** A philosophical movement of the Renaissance committed to independent reasoning (without, however, rejecting faith), the study of ancient literature in its original language, and a reliance on original sources rather than secondhand commentary. Humanism was the successor to medieval scholasticism, which relied almost entirely on abstract thought and the accumulation of wisdom through disputation rather than empirical evidence or observation.

**Hymn** Setting of a sacred but nonliturgical text, usually strophic and predominantly syllabic.

**Idealism** System of thought based on the premise that objects in the physical world are a reflection of ideas in the mind. The rise of Idealism in the late 18th and early 19th centuries played a key role in the rising status of instrumental music.

**Impressionism** Musical style that flourished in the period 1890 to 1920, associated chiefly with the French composer Claude Debussy and characterized by a blurring of distinct harmonies, rhythms, timbres, and forms.

**Intabulation** Arrangement for keyboard or for a plucked stringed instrument—lute, guitar, vihuela, cittern, pandora—of a work originally written for voices.

**Integral serialism** System of serial composition in which elements beyond pitch, such as rhythm and dynamics, are also subjected to serial treatment. Also known as **total serialism.**

**Intermedio** (plural, **intermedi**) Dramatic work, often with music, performed between the acts of a larger theatrical presentation such as a play or opera.

**Intermezzo** Sung dramatic work staged between the acts of a larger opera, usually an opera seria.

**Inversion** Mirror image of a melodic line. The inversion of a line that moves up a major third and then down a minor second would be a line that moves down a major third and then up a minor second.

**Isomelic** From the Greek *iso* ("the same") and *melic* ("melodic"), a term coined by 20th-century scholars to describe music of the Renaissance in which one or more voices in the various sections of a polyphonic work present a series of variations on the work's opening idea.

**Isorhythm** Term coined in the 20th century to describe the rhythmic and melodic structure of certain tenor lines in polyphony of the 14th and 15th centuries. An isorhythmic tenor features a rhythmic pattern (the *talea*) and a melodic pattern (the *color*), each of which is repeated at least once. The *talea* and *color* may be of equal duration, but more often they are not.

**Italian overture** Type of overture found in many operas and oratorios of the 18th century consisting of three movements in the sequence fast-slow-fast.

**Jazz** Musical style that emerged in the early decades of the 20th century in the American South, covering a wide range of substyles connected by an approach toward music that embraces improvisation and rhythmic and intonational freedom, along with a general acceptance that the musical work exists in performance rather than in the form of a written score.

*Jubilus* In plainchant settings of the Alleluia within the Propers of the Mass, the long melisma on the final syllable of the word *Alleluia*.

**Klezmer** Type of instrumental music originally cultivated in the 19th century by the *klezmorim*, the professional Jewish musicians of eastern Europe, and characterized by a steady bass and rhythmically free winds above, often with chromatic passages in thirds, exaggerated accents, and repeated half steps back and forth.

**Leitmotiv** German for "leading motif," a brief musical idea connected to some person, event, or idea in a music drama. The Leitmotiv distinguishes itself from the earlier device of the musical reminiscence by virtue of its malleability and its context within a network of related musical ideas. It was first pioneered in the music dramas of Richard Wagner.

*Liber usualis* Literally, "Book of Use"; anthology of many different kinds of plainchant for both the Mass and the Office.

**Lied** (pronounced "leet"; the plural, **Lieder**, is pronounced like the English word "leader") German term for the genre of song.

**Ligatures** Notational signs used in plainchant and polyphony through the Renaissance to represent two or more pitches within a single unit. In mensural notation, ligatures were often used to indicate rhythmic values.

**Liturgical drama** A liturgical passage in chant presented in a quasi-theatrical manner during the service, with individual portrayals of the protagonists.

**Long** In Franconian notation, longest standard note value.

**Lute song** Type of strophic secular song cultivated in England during the early 17th century for lute and voices (usually four). The lute could substitute for or double as many as three of the four voices.

**Madrigal** Poetic and musical form first used in 14th-century Italy and then taken up later again in the 16th century. (1) The texts of 14th-century Italian madrigals usually consist of two or three strophes, each with three lines, plus a two-line ritornello (refrain) at the very end. (2) The 16th-century Italian madrigal is a poem of a single strophe using a free rhyme scheme and meter, such as an alternation of 7- and 11-syllable lines.

**Madrigal comedy** Series of polyphonic madrigals loosely connected through plot and characters. The genre enjoyed its heyday in the closing decades of the 16th century.

**Mannerism** Term used to describe an artistic style prevalent in the works of certain artists of the 16th and early 17th centuries—both in painting and in music—that emphasized unusual degrees of distortion, exaggeration, and unsettling juxtaposition for dramatic effect. In music, these devices could include extreme dissonance, unusual harmonic progressions, and exaggerated word painting.

**March** Genre of music originally intended to keep soldiers in formation during movement, characterized by duple meter and a steady tempo.

**Masque** Theatrical genre of 17th-century England featuring a mixture of declaimed poetry, songs, scenery, dance, and instrumental music.

**Mass** The central service of the traditional Christian liturgy, a ritualistic celebration of Christ's Last Supper with his disciples. The liturgy of the Mass consists of the Ordinary (fixed texts said or sung at every Mass) and the Propers (texts that vary according to the date within the liturgical year, such as a particular feast day or season).

**Matrix**   An interlocking numerical grid showing all four forms of a tone row at all transpositions.

**Mazurka**   A Polish peasant dance in triple meter, often with the accent on the second or third beat; also a type of character piece based on this metric pattern.

**Mean-tone tuning**   System of tuning used widely in the Renaissance and Baroque eras in which perfect fifths were altered in such a way to make major and minor thirds more pleasing to the ear.

**Measured organum**   Type of organum in which all voices move at about the same speed. Also known as **discant organum.**

**Melisma**   Florid musical setting of several notes per syllable of text. The term is primarily used in connection with medieval plainchant.

**Melismatic organum**   Type of organum in which multiple notes in the added voice(s) run against the individual notes of an original chant.

*Mélodie*   French for "melody," also used for the genre of song in France from the 19th century onward.

**Melodrama**   A staged musical work or number in which a spoken voice is accompanied by the orchestra.

**Mensural notation**   System of musical notation that first emerged in the mid-13th century, in which rhythmic durations were indicated by distinct note shapes as opposed to ligatures. In its broadest sense, mensural notation is still in use today, but the term is generally understood to refer to the various forms of mensural notation used between approximately 1250 and 1600.

**Mensuration signs**   Notational devices used at the beginning of a work to indicate the mensural relationship of note values, such as the number of semibreves per breve or the number of minims to a semibreve.

**Meta-art**   The application of a mathematical, computer-generated, or other process to achieve artistic expression in any medium.

**Microtones**   Intervals smaller than a half step within the diatonic scale.

**Middle entries**   Those sections within a fugue that present a point of imitation, in contrast to **episodes,** which feature little or no imitation.

**Minim**   In Petronian notation, the note value that subdivides the semibreve.

**Minimalism**   Artistic movement that emerged in the early 1960s, relying on multiple repetitions of small units that differ only slightly or are varied only gradually over long stretches of time.

**Minnesinger**   Medieval German poet-composer-performer who sang songs of love.

**Minstrel song**   Type of song typically performed in the 19th and early 20th centuries by white performers in blackface. The songs themselves purportedly represent the perspectives of African American slaves or their descendants.

**Minuet**   Dance form that became a common feature in instrumental cycles of the Baroque and Classical eras. The typical minuet consists of two binary forms, the first known as the *minuet proper,* the second as the *trio.* The minuet proper is repeated at the end of the trio.

**Minuet proper**   In a minuet, the opening and closing section (A) within a basic ABA form.

**Mode**   (1) Melodic mode—a scale type characterized by a specific pattern of whole steps and half steps. Melodies in any of the eight so-called church modes of the medieval era end on a characteristic pitch (the **finalis,** or final) and move up and down within a particular range (ambitus). (2) Rhythmic mode—in the medieval era, one of six consistent patterns of repeated units of long and short durations. (3) Since the early 18th century, one of the two principal forms—major and minor—of the diatonic scale.

**Modernism**   Artistic movement of the early 20th century that emphasized novelty at almost any cost, based on the conviction that the New must be as different as possible from the Old. Modernism in music frequently involved a rejection of tonality, conventional forms, and established genres.

**Modified strophic form**   Type of strophic form in which the music varies to some degree from strophe to strophe—through melodic embellishment, for example, or alteration of texture or harmony—but remains otherwise recognizably the same.

**Monody**   Any work of the 17th century consisting of a solo voice supported by basso continuo.

**Monophony**   Musical texture of a single voice or line, without accompaniment of any kind.

**Moresca**   "Moorish" dance, supposedly influenced by the Arabic cultures of northern Africa and Spain.

**Motet**   Polyphonic vocal work, usually sacred.

**Motetus**   In the 13th-century motet, the voice added above the tenor. Its counterpart in organum was known as the **duplum,** but with an underlaid text of its own in motets, this part became known as the motetus.

**Motoric rhythm**   Music in a rapid tempo and nonlegato, with notes struck on a constant rhythmic subdivision of the beat.

*Musica ficta*   Convention of the late medieval and Renaissance eras in which certain notes were sharped or flattened in performance according to various conventions, such as creating cadential leading tones or avoiding cross-relations between voices.

*Musica reservata*   Term used in the 16th and early 17th centuries to describe certain kinds of music "reserved" for connoisseurs and not intended for wide-scale distribution. These works were demanding for performers and listeners alike and often included unconventional elements of notation, chromaticism, or the use of ancient Greek genera.

**Music drama (***Musikdrama***)**   Term coined by Richard Wagner to distinguish traditional opera from what he felt to be his fundamentally new approach to sung drama. The music drama is characterized by the ideal of the *Gesamtkunstwerk,* in which music, words, and gesture are all inextricably linked yet at the same time self-sufficient.

**Musique concrète**   French term for "concrete music," used to denote music in which the sonic material to be manipulated is a recorded sound taken from everyday life. The sounds are thus real, or "concrete." Also known as electroacoustic music.

**Musique d'ameublement (Fr., furnishing music)**   Music designed by Erik Satie as background to other activities, the aural equivalent of wallpaper; a forerunner of Muzak and **ambient music.**

**Mutation**   In solmization, the process by which singers would shift from one hexachord to another.

**Neoclassicism**   Style that emerged in the 1910s and 1920s, characterized by a return to the tonal idiom, conventional genres and forms, the ideal of absolute music, conciseness of expression, and a general tendency toward transparent textures, lighter orchestration, and small ensembles.

**Neumatic** Musical setting of two or more notes (i.e., a neume) per syllable of text. The term is used primarily in connection with plainchant.

**Neume** Sign used in early chant notation to indicate pitch.

**Nonretrogradable rhythm** Olivier Messiaen's term for a palindromic rhythmic unit—that is, one that is the same forward as backward and whose retrograde form is therefore identical to its original form.

**Obbligato accompaniment** Style of homophony associated particularly with music of the later decades of the 18th century in which the accompanying voices contribute material essential to a work's musical fabric.

**Octatonic scale** Scale that alternates between half and whole steps and contains within itself all possible intervals, from the minor second to the major seventh.

**Office** See **Divine Office.**

**Opera** In the narrowest sense, a drama sung entirely from beginning to end. In a looser sense, any drama consisting primarily of singing, as opposed to speaking.

**Opera buffa** Literally "comic opera," a subgenre of opera that emerged in Italy out of the tradition of the intermezzo, based on humorous subjects and featuring everyday characters rather than the heroes, rulers, and gods typically found in opera seria.

**Opéra comique** Type of opera in 19th-century France that incorporated spoken dialogue as well as music. In spite of its name, the subject matter of the genre was not always comic.

**Opera seria** Literally, "serious opera." Type of opera cultivated in the period ca. 1680 to 1810, particularly in Italy. Its characteristic features were a strict division between recitative and aria, an emphasis on virtuoso singing, particularly in da capo arias, and the use of castrati. The librettos were typically drawn from ancient history or mythology.

**Operetta** Lighter type of opera that emerged in the mid-19th century out of the traditions of the singspiel and the opéra comique. Operettas mix spoken dialogue with sung numbers and deal invariably with humorous and light-hearted subjects.

**Oratorio** Genre of vocal music similar to opera in its musical elements (recitatives, arias, choruses, etc.) but performed without staging or costumes. Most oratorios revolve around religious subjects, but some are written on secular themes.

**Organicism** A theoretical and analytical approach to music that attempts to demonstrate that elements audible on the surface manifest a deeper coherence, the work being treated as a "living form."

**Organum (plural, organa)** Polyphonic work of the 9th to 12th centuries consisting of an original plainchant melody in one voice along with at least one additional voice above or below.

**Ostinato** Figure presented repeatedly in succession.

**Overture** Single-movement orchestral work, either independent or as the prelude to a sung drama.

**Panconsonance** Style of writing associated with Dunstable and Du Fay in the early 15th century that makes ample use of triads and restricts the use of dissonance considerably, compared to the idioms of the 14th century.

**Parallel organum** Type of organum in which the added voice or voices run parallel to an established plainchant melody at a constant interval.

**Paraphrase** Free variation of an existing melodic line or polyphonic network.

**Paratactic form** Any structure that consists of a series of more or less discrete units unrelated to one another musically. Paratactic form can be represented schematically as A, B, C, D, E, and so on.

**Parisian chanson** Term coined by 20th-century scholars to describe a type of song that emerged in the French capital during the 1520s, featuring predominantly chordal textures.

**Parlor song** So called because of its preferred place of performance in the 19th-century home, a type of song whose texts are invariably strophic and sentimental and whose music is melodically and harmonically straightforward.

**Passacaglia** Type of bass pattern used throughout the Baroque.

**Passamezzo** (1) Type of bass pattern used throughout the Baroque. (2) Dance similar to the pavane, but with a lighter step.

**Pasticcio** Work whose individual units are written by several different composers.

**Pavane** Slow, courtly dance in duple meter.

**Pentatonic scale** Any scale based on five notes.

**Periodic phrase structure** Form consisting of many modular units of equal length, initially associated with dance music. See also **antecedent and consequent.**

**Pervading imitation** Compositional technique in which a series of musical ideas are stated imitatively in all voices across the course of an entire work or section of a work. The technique first began to be cultivated in a widespread manner in the second half of the 15th century.

**Petronian notation** System of mensural notation used in the late 13th and early 14th centuries, ascribed to Petrus de Cruce and based on the principles of Franconian notation, but including the shorter note values of the minim and semiminim and allowing for as many as nine semibreves within the duration of a single breve.

**Phase music or process music** Subgenre of minimalism in which the listener can clearly hear the process by which the elements of a work gradually transform themselves into something new and different.

**Picardy third** See *tierce de picardie.*

**Pitch class** Any set of notes associated with a particular note regardless of register: any A, any B, any C, and so on.

**Plagal mode** Any of the melodic modes with an ambitus running roughly a fifth above and a fourth below the final note.

**Plainchant** Monophonic music of the medieval Christian church.

**Point of imitation** Unit of music in which all the voices of a polyphonic composition take up more or less the same musical idea in succession. Points of imitation are a by-product of pervading imitation.

**Popular music** A term used to distinguish certain repertories of broad public appeal and that do not rely primarily on notated music for their transmission. See Appendix 4.

**Polyphony** Musical texture of two or more voices essentially equal in importance.

**Polytextual motet** Any motet with multiple texts performed simultaneously. The polytextual motet was cultivated most intensely in the 13th century.

**Polytonality** Simultaneous juxtaposition of contrasting triads or keys.

**Postmodernism** Aesthetic attitude that emerged in the last third of the 20th century, embracing the past (including modernism) but often in an eclectic manner, synthesizing a variety of approaches in a single work. Postmodernist composers felt obliged neither to avoid nor use tonality or atonality, conventional forms, and established genres.

**Prepared piano**  Instrument with sounds altered by inserting foreign objects (bolts, weather stripping, screws, wool, bamboo, coins) into selected strings. The prepared piano is played primarily on the keyboard, while the "string piano" and other extended techniques involve playing directly on the strings.

*Prima prattica*  Term coined in the early 17th century to describe an older attitude toward text setting in which the projection of a sung text was subordinated to the established conventions of good counterpoint. The *prima prattica* is closely associated (but not synonymous) with polyphony. Literally, the "first practice," so called because it existed before the emergence of the *seconda prattica*, the "second" (or newer) practice.

**Primitivism**  Aesthetic movement of all the arts in the early 20th century that consciously avoided the cultivated traditions of Western art. In music, primitivism gave special importance to rhythm, the most basic of all musical elements, and abandoned or substantially altered such arbitrary (so-called civilized) concepts as voice leading, triadic harmony, and the major and minor forms of the diatonic scale.

**Process music**  See **Phase music**.

**Program music**  Any instrumental work that in one way or another—through a title or accompanying poetry or prose—is connected with a story or idea that lies outside the music itself.

*Prosula* (plural, *prosulae*)  Type of trope in which words were added to an existing chant.

**Psalm tone**  Plainchant formula used to recite the psalms.

**Public domain**  Term applied to any creation (music, literature, artwork, invention, phrase, etc.) that never was or is no longer the property of an individual or organization; the main issue behind copyrighting "traditional" or "folk" music.

**Quadruplum**  From the Latin word for "fourth," the added fourth voice in organum and polyphony of the 12th and 13th centuries.

**Quartal harmonies**  Chords built on the interval of a fourth rather than a third.

**Quattrocento**  Italian term for the 15th century (literally, "the 1400s").

**Ragtime**  Style that grew out of traditions of African American dance and flourished at the end of the 19th century and in the early decades of the 20th. Ragtime music is usually in duple meter and based on units of 8 or 16 measures. Syncopation is prevalent throughout, thrown into relief by the steadiness of the bass line.

**Rap**  See **Hip-hop**.

**Recapitulation**  In sonata form, the section following the development. In its simplest form, the recapitulation begins with a return of the opening idea of the movement in the tonic key; it continues by restating the entire exposition in the tonic, without modulation. In practice, recapitulations are not nearly so regular and often incorporate substantial changes in relation to the exposition.

**Recitation tone**  In plainchant, and particularly in psalm tones, a central pitch used repeatedly in immediate succession to declaim large quantities of text.

**Recitative**  Style of singing characterized by syllabic declamation, with greater emphasis on the projection of the text at hand than on melody, more nearly approximating the inflections of speech even while adhering to the basic musical elements of pitch and rhythm.

**Refrain**  (1) In the broadest sense, any theme and/or text that returns repeatedly over the course of a work after contrasting material. (2) In a rondo, the recurring theme (A) within the pattern ABACADA.

**Reprise**  Unit of music to be repeated in performance immediately after it has been first presented. A binary form often consists of two reprises.

**Respond**  Refrain portion of a responsorial chant, sung before the verse.

**Responsorial chant**  Any of the plainchants, such as the Gradual, Alleluia, and Tract, in which the chorus and soloist alternate.

**Retrograde**  Melodic line presented backward, that is, from its end to its beginning.

**Revue**  A theatrical presentation of a potpourri of acts following one another in quick succession, dominated by but not limited to song and dance; a successor to music hall and vaudeville performances.

**Rhythm and blues**  Popular music synthesis of electrified blues and boogie-woogie that in its up-tempo form is analogous to early rock and roll.

**Rhythmic mode**  See **mode**.

**Ricercar**  In the early 16th century, a freely composed work that was improvisatory and preludial in character, often for lute or keyboard. By the mid-16th century, the term had become identified with polyphonic works for keyboard or for instrumental ensembles. By the 18th century, the term was associated with fugues that used a large number or variety of contrapuntal devices.

**Ripieno**  Literally, "full"; designation used in the Baroque era for the large ensemble within a concerto grosso.

**Ripieno concerto**  Type of concerto for large ensemble, without soloists.

**Ritornello**  Literally, a "brief return"; musical idea that returns at several points over the course of a work, usually after contrasting material of some kind. The **ritornello principle** is the structural basis by which composers construct large-scale forms around successive returns of an opening idea. This principle is especially important in the genre of the concerto.

**Rococo**  Term borrowed from art history and used by some music historians to describe the musical style of the mid-18th century, emphasizing qualities of lightness and grace.

**Romanticism**  Mode of thought that emerged in the late 18th and early 19th centuries and placed unprecedented importance on imagination and subjectivity over reason and objectivity.

**Rondeau** (plural, **rondeaux**)  One of the *formes fixes* used in music of the 14th and 15th centuries. Each strophe consists of eight lines of text set to music following the rhyme scheme ABaAabAB (uppercase letters indicate refrains, which remain constant from strophe to strophe).

**Rondellus**  Type of polyphonic composition cultivated in the medieval era, in which the voices exchange extended phrases repeatedly (e.g., A over B, followed by B over A, followed by A over B, etc.).

**Rondo**  A type of movement associated largely with finales and found in many different instrumental genres of the late 18th and 19th centuries. It is composed in **rondo form**, a structure derived from dance music ("round dance") in which the basic pattern in its simplest form is ABACA, with the recurring theme (A) constituting the **refrain** and the contrasting themes (B, C, etc.) constituting the **episodes** or **couplets**.

**Root position triad** Triad whose root or fundamental pitch appears in the lowest-sounding voice.

**Row** In serial composition, another name for the series of 12 different pitch classes.

**Rubato** See **Tempo rubato.**

**Saltarello** Lively dance that often follows a slower one.

**Scat singing** Technique of singing in which the voice mimics an instrument, singing syncopated nonsense syllables against the steady beat of the bass.

**Scherzo** From the Italian word for "joke," a movement type that emerged in the early 19th century and eventually supplanted the minuet within such multi-movement cycles as symphonies, quartets, and sonatas. Like the minuet, the scherzo is in ABA form; in contrast to the minuet, the scherzo is typically faster and at times humorous or even grotesque in its gestures.

**Secco recitative** Literally, "dry recitative," accompanied by basso continuo alone; also known as *recitativo semplice* ("simple recitative").

*Seconda prattica* Term coined in the early 17th century to describe a new attitude toward text setting in which all musical means were subordinated to the effective delivery of the text being sung. The *seconda prattica* is closely associated (but not synonymous) with the emerging practice of monody. Literally, the "second practice," so called because it appeared after the *prima prattica*, the "first" (or older) practice.

**Semibreve** In Franconian notation, the note value that subdivides the breve.

**Semiminim** In Petronian notation, half the note value of a minim.

**Semi-opera** Type of theatrical entertainment that flourished in England during the second half of the 17th century. These were essentially plays with a large proportion of musical numbers, both vocal and instrumental.

**Sequence** (1) Element of the Mass Propers, authorized for special feast days, appearing after the Alleluia. (2) Any musical idea repeated on successively different pitches.

**Serial composition** Method of composition based on the repeated manipulation of an established row (series) of pitches and/or rhythms and/or dynamics. Transpositions and permutations of the series (inversion, retrograde, retrograde inversion) provide variety. Dodecaphony is the most common form of serial composition, based on a row of 12 different pitch classes.

**Series** In serial composition, another name for the row of 12 different pitch classes.

**Shape-note singing** Religious music read from a system combining standard notation with a set of differently shaped note heads related to solfège.

*Singspiel* (plural, *Singspiele*) "Singing play"; German-language spoken drama with interpolated musical numbers (arias, duets, trios, etc.). The singspiel of the 18th century was an important forerunner of the later operetta and musical.

**Socialist realism** Aesthetic doctrine espoused by Soviet bloc authorities in the 20th century to encourage artists to produce works in a readily accessible style. In music, works written under the influence of socialist realism typically incorporate folk or folklike elements and project an overwhelmingly optimistic tone.

**Solmization syllables** Syllables associated with the pitches of a hexachord, in ascending order: *ut, re, mi, fa, sol, la*.

**Solo concerto** Type of concerto featuring a soloist and a larger ensemble, as opposed to a ripieno concerto.

**Sonata** Literally, "that which is sounded" (i.e., played on instruments). Term used in the Renaissance and Baroque in the broadest sense to indicate a work for an instrument or instruments of any combination. From the 18th century onward, the term was used to indicate a work for one or more solo instruments, usually in three or four movements.

**Sonata da camera** Literally, "sonata of the chamber"; type of sonata featuring a series of dance-related movements, popular in the Baroque era.

**Sonata da chiesa** Literally, "sonata of the church"; type of sonata featuring a slow first movement and at least one additional imitative movement, popular in the Baroque era.

**Sonata form** Structural convention frequently found in first movements, slow movements, and finales of instrumental works, particularly from the second half of the 18th century and all of the 19th century. A movement in sonata form incorporates an **exposition**, a **development**, and a **recapitulation**. An introduction and coda are sometimes added but are not essential elements of the form.

**Sonata form with varied reprise** Type of sonata form in which the exposition is not repeated note for note but instead written out and changed in subtle ways.

**Sonata-rondo form** Type of rondo (ABACABA) in which B corresponds to the secondary key area of a sonata-form movement; that is, it is presented first in a contrasting key and then (toward the end) in the tonic, as in a sonata-form recapitulation.

**Song cycle** Collection of songs ordered in such a way as to convey at least the outline of a story or idea.

**Song form** A common form in popular song of the 20th century, featuring alternating units, often of eight measures each, following such thematic patterns as AABA, ABAB, etc.

**Spiritual** African American hymn developed from pre–Civil War songs; a primary influence on African American popular as well as religious music.

*Sprechstimme* Literally, "speech-voice," with "voice" understood here in the sense of "singing." A style of vocal declamation that lies midway between speech and song, cultivated particularly in the early 19th century by such composers as Arnold Schoenberg and Alban Berg.

**Stop** On an organ, a lever that controls the flow of air through sets or combinations of sets of pipes, thereby altering the timbre of the instrument's sound.

**Stretto** Overlapping entries in several voices of a fugue subject in shortened form, designed to increase the need for a final resolution of the fugue's tension.

**Strophic** (1) In poetry, any text made up of stanzas (strophes), each of which has the same number of lines and follows the same rhyme scheme and meter. (2) In music, any setting of a strophic text in which each strophe is sung to the same music.

*Sturm und Drang* Literally, "storm and stress"; designation, given by 20th-century scholars, to a style of writing that appears in certain works by Haydn, Mozart, Gluck, and others in the late 1760s and early 1770s. The characteristics of *Sturm und Drang* music include a predilection for the minor mode and such extreme gestures as large melodic leaps, jagged syncopations, and sudden dynamic contrasts.

**Style brisé** Literally, "broken style"; style of writing for the keyboard that imitates the broken (arpeggiated) chords often played on a lute or guitar.

**Subject** Theme of a fugue.

**Suite** In the music of the Baroque and Classical eras, a series of dance or dance-like movements. Later, a collection of any kind of individual movements not falling into the standard pattern of the sonata, symphony, or other established genres.

**Syllabic** Musical setting of one note per syllable of text.

**Symphonic poem** Term coined by Franz Liszt in 1854 to replace the generic name of what had previously been called the **concert overture**, a one-movement work for orchestra with some kind of programmatic association.

**Symphony** (1) In the 17th and early 18th centuries, a work or movement for large instrumental ensemble. (2) In the 18th century, an overture to an opera or stage play. (3) From about 1720 onward, a multimovement work for instrumental ensemble.

**Syntactic form** Any formal structure that maintains one or more thematic ideas consistently across the course of an entire movement or work. Syntactic form involves an interrelationship of musical units in the same way that syntax relates to the functional relationship of a sentence's verbal units (nouns, verbs, etc.). Syntactic form is the opposite of paratactic form, in which the units of a movement are thematically unrelated.

**Synthesized electronic music** Music consisting of sounds generated and manipulated entirely by electronic means, through an electronic oscillator or a modifying device like a synthesizer.

**Tactus** From the Latin word for "touch," the basic unit of temporal measurement used in Renaissance music. One theorist of the late 15th century claimed the rate of the *tactus* was equivalent to the heartbeat of an adult man breathing at a normal speed—that is, roughly 60 to 70 times per minute.

**Talea** Rhythmic pattern of an isorhythmic tenor.

**Temperament** Manner of adjusting ("tempering") the intervals of a scale.

**Tempo rubato** Literally, "robbed time"; practice of performing with subtle accelerations and decelerations of tempo not otherwise indicated in a score.

**Tenor** (1) The high voice range of the adult male, running roughly from the G above middle C to the B slightly more than an octave below middle C. (2) In medieval and Renaissance music, the vocal part that "holds" (Latin, *tenere*) the chant melody.

**Tenorlied** Type of secular song cultivated in Germany in the 16th century in which the principal melody appears in the tenor voice, with three contrapuntal voices surrounding it.

**Tetrachord** Any grouping of four pitches, in particular, the interlocking descending successions of notes in the ancient Greek musical system.

**Third-stream music** A style that bridges jazz improvisation and harmony with instruments and voice-leading techniques (particularly counterpoint) more commonly associated with classical music.

**Through-composed** Term used to describe any form in which each section is based on thematic material different from that presented in other sections. In the song repertory, the term refers to settings that are not strophic, in which new music accompanies each new section of text.

**Tierce de picardie** Literally, "Picardy third"; major third at the end of a work otherwise in minor mode. The raised third was not always notated but instead left to the discretion of the performer.

**Toccata** Type of work for keyboard that is freely constructed, based on no preexistent material, and typically features rapid passagework.

**Total serialism** See **integral serialism**.

**Trecento** Italian term for the 14th century (literally, "the 1300s").

**Triad** Chord of three notes whose adjacent pitches are separated by intervals of a major or minor third.

**Trio** (1) Any work for three voices or instruments. (2) In a minuet or scherzo, the contrasting middle section (B) within a basic ABA form.

**Trio sonata** Type of sonata for two instruments of a high range (violins, flutes, oboes, etc.) and basso continuo, popular throughout the 18th century.

**Triplum** From the Latin word for "third," the added third voice in organum and polyphony of the 12th and 13th centuries.

**Trope** Musical or textual addition to an existing plainchant. Tropes could be added to the beginning or end of a chant, or they could be interpolated into the chant itself.

**Troping** Process of creating a trope.

**Troubadours** (fem., **trobairitz**), **trouvères** The mostly wandering minstrels—often composer, poet, and performer in the same person—who entertained the courts of the nobility in southern (troubadour) and northern (trouvère) France in the 12th and 13th centuries.

**Tutti** Literally, "all"; term used to indicate the large ensemble within a concerto grosso. Also used to designate the sections of the work played by this ensemble.

**12-bar blues form** A series of variations on a repeated harmonic pattern of 12 measures in 4/4 time; the most common harmonic pattern is I-IV-I-V-I.

**Unmeasured organum** A type of organum in which the added voice(s) move rapidly against the slower-moving notes of original chant. Also known as **free organum**.

**Vamp** In popular song of the 20th century, a short progression of chords that can be repeated indefinitely before the entrance of the voice.

**Variation suite** Set of contrasting dance-related movements based on one basic thematic idea.

**Verse** In popular song of the 20th century, the opening section that leads into the song's chorus or principal melody.

**Villancico** Principal genre of Spanish song in the Renaissance. The term was first used in the late 15th century to identify a poetic form equivalent to the French virelai (AbbaA).

**Villanella** General term used to describe a variety of Italian song types of the 16th and early 17th centuries. These songs were often to bawdy texts and featured predominantly chordal textures.

**Virelai** One of the *formes fixes* in the music of the 14th and 15th centuries. Each strophe consists of a variable number of lines but always begins and ends with the refrain, an unchanging unit of text and music. The general pattern of rhyme is AbbaA (the uppercase letter indicates the refrain).

**Vocalize** To sing a melodic line to a vowel sound, without a text.

**Voice leading** Manner in which two or more voices move in relationship to one another.

**Volta** Vigorous "turning" dance (*voltare* means "to turn" in Italian), often in compound duple meter.

**Whole-tone scale** Scale of six notes, each a whole tone apart.

**Word painting** Use of musical elements to imitate the meaning of a specific passage of the text being sung at that moment, such as a falling melodic line to indicate descent, a leap to indicate jumping, and so on.

# Source Notes

## Prologue

1. Aristotle, *Problemata* 19.20 (919a), trans. E. M. Forster, in *The Works of Aristotle*, ed. W. D. Ross, vol. 7 (Oxford: Clarendon Press, 1927), p. 145.
2. Apuleius, *The Golden Ass*, Book 11, Chapter 47, trans. P. G. Walsh (Oxford: Clarendon Press, 1994), p. 224.
3. Warren D. Anderson, *Ethos and Education in Greek Music* (Cambridge, MA: Harvard University Press, 1966), p. 127.
4. Plato, *Republic*, Book 4, 424b–c, in *The Collected Dialogues of Plato*, ed. Edith Hamilton and Huntington Cairns (New York: Pantheon Books, 1961).

## Chapter 1

1. Quotation from Saint Basil, *Homily on Psalm 1*, trans. James McKinnon, in *Music in Early Christian Literature*, ed. James McKinnon (Cambridge: Cambridge University Press, 1987), p.65. Reprinted with the permission of Cambridge University Press.
2. Isidore of Seville, *Etymologies*, Book 3, section 15, trans. Helen Dill Goode and Gertrude C.Drake (Colorado Springs: Colorado Music Press, 1980), p. 13.
3. Kenneth Clark, *Civilization* (New York: Harper & Row, 1969), p. 19. Law of 789.
4. Quotation from Hildegard von Bingen, "Epistle 47: To the Prelates of Mainz," in Oliver Strunk, *Source Readings in Music History*, 2nd ed. (New York: Norton, 1998), pp. 183–6. Copyright 1998 W. W. Norton & Company, Inc. Used by permission.

## Chapter 2

1. Quotation from John, in *Hucbald, Guido, and John on Music; Three Medieval Treatises*, trans. Warren Babb, ed. Claude Palisca (New Haven, CT: Yale University Press, 1978), p. 160. Copyright Yale University Press, 1978. Used by permission of the publisher.

## Chapter 3

1. Pseudo-Basil, *Commentary on Isaiah*, V, in *Music in Early Christian Literature*, ed. James McKinnon (Cambridge: Cambridge University Press, 1987), pp. 70–1.

## Chapter 4

1. Edward Lowinsky, "Music of the Renaissance as Viewed by Renaissance Musicians," in his *Music in the Culture of the Renaissance and Other Essays*, vol. 1, edited and with an introd. by Bonnie J. Blackburn; with forewords by Howard Mayer Brown and Ellen T. Harris; 2 vols. (Chicago: University of Chicago Press, 1989), I, 97. Copyright The University of Chicago, 1989. Reprinted with permission of the University of Chicago Press.
2. Ibid., p. 90.
3. Ibid., p. 91.
4. Ibid., p. 91.
5. Ibid., p. 92.
6. Bartolomé Ramos de Pareja, *Musica Practica*, ed. and trans. Clement Miller (Neuhausen-Stuttgart: American Institute of Musicology/Hänssler-Verlag, 1993), p. 55.
7. Lowinsky, "Music of the Renaissance," p. 105, citing in turn Nicholaus Burtius's pamphlet of 1487 against Ramos entitled (in translation) "Against a Spanish Prevaricator of the Truth." Reprinted with permission of the University of Chicago Press.
8. Vincenzo Galilei, *Dialogo dell musica antica e della moderna* (1581), ed. Fabio Fano (Milan: Alessandro Minuziano, 1947), p. 55.

9. Paul Johnson, *The Renaissance: A Short History* (New York: Modern Library, 2000), p. 96.
10. Quotation from Martin Luther writing about Josquin, in *The New Grove Dictionary of Music and Musicians*, 2nd ed. (29 volumes), edited by John Tyrrell, executive editor, copyright 2003 by Oxford University Press, Inc. Used by permission of Oxford University Press, Inc.
11. Quotation from a courtier of Duke Ercole d'Este of Ferrara, in Lewis Lockwood "Josquin at Ferrara: New Documents and Letters," in Edward E. Lowinsky, ed., *Josquin Des Prez* (New York and Oxford: Oxford University Press, 1976), pp. 132–133. Reprinted by permission of Oxford University Press.

## Chapter 5

1. Pietro Aron, *Thoscanello de la Musica* (Venice, 1523), Chapter 41.
2. Gioseffo Zarlino, *Le istitutioni armoniche*, rev. ed. (Venice, 1589), Book III, p. 252.
3. Thomas Morley, *A Plain and Easy Introduction to Practical Music* (1597), ed. R. Alec Harman (New York: Norton, 1952), p.167.

## Chapter 6

1. Jane Bowers, "The Emergence of Women Composers in Italy, 1566–1700," in *Women Making Music: The Western Art Tradition, 1150–1950*, ed. Jane Bowers and Judith Tick (Urbana and Chicago: University of Illinois Press, 1985), p. 140.
2. Thomas Morley, *A Plain and Easy Introduction to Practical Music* (1597), ed. R. Alec Harman (London: Dent, 1952), p. 293.
3. Johannes Riedel, *The Lutheran Chorale and Its Basic Traditions* (Minneapolis: Augsburg, 1967), p. 47.
4. Walter E. Buszin, "Luther on Music," *Musical Quarterly* 32 (1946): 88.
5. Council of Trent, "Canon on Music to Be Used at Mass," September 1562, quoted in Gustave Reese, *Music in the Renaissance*, 2nd ed. (New York: Norton, 1959), p. 449.
6. Nicola Vicentino, *L'Antica musica*, quoted in Henry Kaufman, *The Life and Works of Nicola Vicentino* (Rome: American Institute of Musicology, 1966), pp. 38–9.
7. The Swiss humanist Samuel Quickelberg, quoted in Jerome Roche, *Lassus* (London: Oxford University Press, 1982), p. 16.
8. Peter Bergquist, "The Poems of Orlando di Lasso's *Prophetiae Sibyllarum* and Their Sources," *Journal of the American Musicological Society* 32 (1979): 533.
9. Thomas Morely, *A Plain and Easy Introduction to Practical Music* (1597), ed. R. Alec Harman (New York: Norton, 1952), p. 296.

## Chapter 7

1. Nicola Vicentino, *Ancient Music Adapted to Modern Practice* (1555), trans. Maria Rika Maniates, ed. Claude Palisca (New Haven, CT: Yale University Press, 1996), p. 150.
2. Vincenzo Galilei, *Dialogo della music antica e della moderna* (1581), ed. Fabio Feno (Milan: Alessandro Minuziano, 1947), p. 127.
3. Quotation from Jacopo Peri, preface to *Euridice* (1600), in Tim Carter, *Composing Opera: From Dafne to Ulisse Errante* (Kraków, Poland: Musica Iagellonica, 1994), pp. 25, 27, 29. Used by permission.
4. Robert Donington, *A Performer's Guide to Baroque Music* (London: Faber, 1978), pp. 210–11.
5. Ibid.

6. Piero Weiss and Richard Taruskin, eds., *Music in the Western World: A History in Documents* (New York: Schirmer, 1984), p. 176.

7. Joel Lester, "The Recognition of Major and Minor Keys in Germany Theory: 1680–1730," *Journal of Music Theory* 2 (1978): 91–2, citing in turn Handel's letter published in Mattheson's *Critica musica* III (1725).

**Chapter 8**

1. Claudio Monteverdi, letter of 13 March 1620, in his *Lettere*, ed. Éva Lax (Florence: Olschki, 1994), p. 93.

2. Quotation from Claudio Monteverdi, introduction of Fifth Book of Madrigals (1605), in Claude V. Palisca, "The Artusi-Monteverdi Controversy," in *The New Monteverdi Companion*, ed. Denis Arnold & Nigel Fortune (London: Faber & Faber, 1985), pp. 151–2. Used by permission of the publisher.

3. Tim Carter, "The Seventeenth Century," in Roger Parker, ed., *The Oxford Illustrated History of Opera* (Oxford and New York: Oxford University Press, 1994), p. 7.

4. Heinrich Schütz, preface to *Geistliche Chormusik* (1648), trans. David Bryant, in Lorenzo Bianconi, *Music in the Seventeenth Century* (Cambridge: Cambridge University Press, 1987), pp. 297–8. (Modifications to translation by MEB.)

**Chapter 9**

1. Pierre Corneille, *Writings on the Theatre*, ed. H. T. Barnwell (Oxford: Blackwell, 1965), p. 144.

2. Jean-Laurent Le Cerf de la Viéville, *Comparaison de la musique italienne et de la musique française* (Brussels, 1704–1706), trans. in Caroline Wood and Graham Sadler, *French Baroque Opera: A Reader* (Aldershot: Ashgate, 2000), p. 39.

3. Quotation from A. Félibien, *Rélation de la feste de Versailles du 18e juillet 1668* (Paris, 1668), trans. in *The Early Baroque Era*, ed. Curtis Price, p. 243. © Reprinted by permission of Pearson Education, Inc. Upper Saddle River, NJ.

4. Charles Burney, *Memoirs of the Life and Writing of the Abate Metastasio*, 3 vols. (London: G.G. and J. Robinson, 1796), II, 135.

5. Charles Burney, *The Present State of Music in France and Italy* (London: T. Becket, 1773), p. 216–7.

6. Charles Burney, *An Account of the Musical Performances in Westminster Abbey . . . in Commemoration of Handel* (London: T. Payne, 1785), p. 31–2.

7. Cristoforo Ivanovich, *Memorie teatrali di Venezia* (Venice, 1681), transl. in Lorenzo Bianconi, *Music in the Seventeenth Century* (Cambridge: Cambridge University Press, 1987), p. 308–9.

8. Robert Kendrick, *Celestial Sirens* (Oxford: Clarendon Press, 1996), pp. 106–7.

9. Athanasius Kircher, *Musurgia universalis*, 2 vols. (Rome, 1650), I, 603; translation from Claude Palisca, *Baroque Music*, 3rd ed. (Englewood Cliffs, NJ: Prentice Hall, 1991), p. 125.

10. Athanasius Kircher, *Musurgia universalis* (1650); translation from Claude V. Palisca, *Baroque Music*, 2nd. edn. (Englewood Cliffs, NJ: Prentice-Hall, 1981), p. 125.

11. J. S. Bach to Georg Erdmann, 28 October 1730.

12. J. Peter Burkholder, "Borrowing," *The New Grove Dictionary of Music and Musicians*, 2nd edn., ed. Stanley Sadie (New York: Grove's Dictionaries, 2000).

**Chapter 10**

1. Charles P. Fisher, "Piano," *The New Harvard Dictionary of Music*, ed. Don Michael Randel (Cambridge, MA: Harvard University Press, 1986), p. 631.

2. *The New Bach Reader: A Life of Johann Sebastian Bach in Letters and Documents*, edited by Hans T. David and Arthur Mendel; revised and enlarged by Christoph Wolff (New York: Norton, 1998), p. 396. Copyright 1998 Christoph Wolff. Used by permission of W. W. Norton & Company, Inc.

3. John Hawkins, *A General History of the Science and Practice of Music*, 5 vols. (London: T. Payne, 1776), IV, 310.

4. Quotation from Edward Higginbottom, "François Couperin," *The New Grove Dictionary of Music and Musicians*, 2nd ed. Stanley Sadie (29 Volumes), edited by John Tyrrell, executive editor, copyright 2003 by Oxford University Press, Inc. Used by permission of Oxford University Press, Inc.

5. Preface to *Troisième livre de pieces de clavecin*, in Colin Lawson and Robin Stowell, *The Historical Performance of Music: An Introduction* (Cambridge UK: Cambridge University Press, 1999), p. 68.

6. *The New Bach Reader: A Life of Johann Sebastian Bach in Letters and Documents*, edited by Hans T. David and Arthur Mendel; revised and enlarged by Christoph Wolff (New York: Norton, 1998), p. 46. Copyright 1998 Christoph Wolff. Used by permission of W. W. Norton & Company, Inc.

7. Jean-Philippe Rameau, *Treatise on Harmony*, trans. and ed. Philip Gossett (New York: Dover, 1971), p. xxxvi.

**Chapter 11**

1. Quotation from Johann Adolph Scheibe, *Der critische Musikus*, 14 May 1737, trans. in *The New Bach Reader: A Life of Johann Sebastian Bach in Letters and Documents*, edited by Hans T. David and Arthur Mendel; revised and enlarged by Christoph Wolff (New York: Norton, 1998), p. 338. Copyright 1998 by Christoph Wolff. Used by permission of W. W. Norton & Company, Inc.

2. Jean-Baptiste Dubos, *Réflexions critiques sur la poésie et sur la peinture*, 3 vols. (Paris, 1719), II, 113.

3. Quotation from Johann Mattheson parody of BWV 21 text, trans. in *The New Bach Reader: A Life of Johann Sebastian Bach in Letters and Documents*, edited by Hans T. David and Arthur Mendel; revised and enlarged by Christoph Wolff (New York: Norton, 1998), p. 325. Copyright 1998 Christoph Wolff. Used by permission of W. W. Norton & Company, Inc.

4. William Billings, "Introduction to the Rules of Musick," from his *The New England Psalm-Singer* (1770), in *The Complete Works of William Billings*, vol. 1, p. 32, ed. Karl Kroeger (©1981 American Musicological Society and the Colonial Society of Massachusetts).

5. Georg August Griesinger, *Biographische Notizen über Joseph Haydn*, ed. Karl-Heinz Köhler (Leipzig: Reclam, 1975; 1st edition 1810), p. 78.

6. Charles Burney, *The Present State of Music in Germany, the Netherlands, and United Provinces*, 2nd ed., 2 vols. (London: T. Becket, 1775), II, 270–71.

**Chapter 12**

1. Jean-Jacques Rousseau, *Dictionnaire de musique* (Paris: Veuve Duchesne, 1768), article "Sonate."

2. Mozart, letter to his father, October 17, 1777, in Wolfgang Amadeus Mozart, *Briefe und Aufzeichnungen*, ed. W. A. Bauer and O. E. Deutsch, vol. 2 (Kassel: Bärenreiter, 1962), p. 68.

3. André-Ernest-Modeste Grétry, *Mémoires, ou Essais sur la musique*, 3 vols. (Paris: Imprimerie de la République, 1797), III, 356–7.

4. Cramer's *Magazin der Musik*, 23 April 1787.

5. Leopold Mozart, letter of 16 February 1785 to Maria Anna Mozart.

6. Johann Abraham Peter Schulz, "Sinfonie," in Johann Georg Sulzer's *Allgemeine Theorie der schönen Künste* (Leipzig, 1771–1774).

7. Karl Geiringer, *Haydn: A Creative Life in Music*, 3rd ed. (Berkeley and Los Angeles: University of California Press, 1982), pp. 65–7.

**Chapter 13**

1. Benjamin Franklin, *Writings*, vol. 7, ed. Albert Henry Smyth (New York: Macmillan, 1907), p. 207.

2. Francesco Algarotti, *An Essay on the Opera* (Glasgow: R. Urie, 1768), p. 41. Algarotti's treatise had first appeared in Italian in 1755.

3. Daines Barrington, "An Account of a Very Remarkable Young Musician," 28 September 1769 (published in Deutsch, *Mozart: A Documentary Biography*, p. 96).
4. Mozart, letter of 15 November 1780.
5. Mozart, letter of 26 September 1781.
6. Mozart, letter of 28 December 1782.

## Chapter 14

1. William Gardiner, *Music and Friends*, 3 vols. (London: Longman, 1838), II, 511–12.
2. Arthur Schopenhauer, *The World as Will and Idea*, trans. R. B. Haldane and J. Kemp, 2 vols. (London: Kegan Paul, Trench, Trubner & Co., 1896), I, 338.
3. George Hogarth, *Daily News*, 19 July 1848, quoted in Jean-Jacques Eigeldinger, *Chopin, Pianist and Teacher as Seen by His Pupils*, trans. Krysia Osostowicz and Naomi Shohet, ed. Roy Howat (Cambridge: Cambridge University Press, 1987), p. 294.
4. Robert Schumann, *Gesammelte Schriften über Musik und Musiker*, 4th ed., 2 vols., ed. F. Gustav Jansen (Leipzig: Breitkopf & Härtel, 1891), II, 23.
5. Max Kalbeck, *Johannes Brahms: Leben und Werk*, 4 vols. (Vienna, Leipzig, and Berlin, 1904–1914), IV, 109.
6. Walter Pater, "The School of Giorgione," "The School of Giorgione," *Fortnightly Review* 22 (October 1877): 528.
7. Robert Schumann, *Gesammelte Schriften über Musik und Musiker*, 5th ed., 2 vols. (Leipzig: Breitkopf & Härtel, 1913), I, 167 (1837).
8. James Gibbons Huneker, *Mezzotints in Music* (New York: G. Scribner's Sons, 1899), p. 122.
9. Marcello Conati, ed., *Encounters with Verdi*, transl. Richard Stokes (Ithaca and London: Cornell University Press and Victor Gollancz Ltd., 1984), p. 238. Used by permission of Cornell University Press.
10. Hector Berlioz, *Symphonie fantastique* (New York: Kalmus, n.d.).

## Chapter 15

1. H. C. Koch, *Musikalisches Lexikon* (Frankfurt/Main: A. Hermann d. J., 1802), article "Sinfonie oder Symphonie."
2. Gottfried Wilhlem Fink, "Ueber die Symphonie, als Beitrag zur Geschichte und Aesthetik derselben," *Allgemeine musikalische Zeitung* 37 (1835): 523.
3. Cosima Wagner, *Die Tagebücher*, vol. 2, ed. Martin Gregor-Dellin and Dietrich Mack (Munich: Piper, 1976), p. 1103 (entry for January 30, 1883).
4. Robert P. Morgan, *Twentieth-Century Music: A History of Musical Style in Modern Europe and America* (New York: Norton, 1991), p. 122.
5. From the Diaries of Carl Friedrich Baron Kübeck von Kubau (1797), cited in H. C. Robbins Landon, *Beethoven: A Documentary Study* (New York: Macmillan, 1970), p. 71.
6. Alexander Wheelock Thayer, *Thayer's Life of Beethoven*, rev. and ed. Elliot Forbes (Princeton, NJ: Princeton University Press, 1967), pp. 304–6.
7. Maynard Solomon, *Beethoven*, 2nd ed. (New York: Schirmer, 1998), pp. 209–11.
8. Thayer, *Thayer's Life of Beethoven*, p. 115.
9. Beethoven to B. Schott's Sons, Mainz, September 17, 1824, in Ludwig van Beethoven, *Briefwechsel: Gesamtausgabe*, ed. Sieghard Brandenburg, vol. 5 (Munich: Henle, 1996).
10. Robert Schumann, "A Symphony by Berlioz" (1835), trans. Edward T. Cone, in Hector Berlioz, *Fantastic Symphony*, ed. Edward T. Cone (New York: Norton, 1971), pp. 227–8.
11. Ibid.
12. Felix Mendelssohn Bartholdy, *Reisebriefe aus den Jahren 1830 bis 1832*, ed. Paul Mendelssohn Bartholdy (Leipzig: Hermann Mendelssohn, 1869), p. 136, letter to his family of March 29, 1831.
13. Mendelssohn, *Briefe an deutsche Verleger* (Berlin: de Gruyter, 1968), pp. 25–6, letter of 15 February 1833.

## Chapter 16

1. Quotation from letter to Gerard Souchay, 15 October 1842, trans. In Oliver Strunk and Leo Treitler, eds., *Source Readings in Music History*, rev. ed. (New York: Norton, 1998), pp. 120–1. Copyright 1998 W. W. Norton & Company, Inc. Used by permission.
2. Sir Charles Hallé, Life and Letters of Sir Charles Hallé (London: Smith, Elder & Co., 1896), p.34.
3. Jean-Jacques Eigeldinger, Chopin: Pianist and Teacher as Seen by his Pupils, trans. Krysia Osostowicz and Naomi Shohet, ed. Roy Howat (Cambridge: Cambridge University Press, 1987), p. 276, quoting in turn Carl Mikuli, Preface to Chopin's Pianoforte-Werke, ed. Mikuli (Leipzig: Kistner, 1880).
4. Quotation from letter from Frédéric Chopin ca. 1838–1839, in *Chopin's Letters*, ed. Henryk Opienski, trans. E. L. Voynich (New York: [no publisher]: 1931; reprinted New York: Vienna House 1971; and 1988: Dover Publications), p. 186. Used by permission of Dover Publications.
5. Quotation from letter from Frédéric Chopin, October 1848, in Tad Szulc, *Chopin in Paris* (Scribner, 1998), p. 381. Used by permission of Janklow & Nesbit Associates, agents for Tad Szulc.
6. Goethe, "Ballade," in Johann Wolfgang Goethe, *Sämtliche Werke*, XIII/1 (Munich: Hanser, 1985), p. 505.
7. Alan Walker, *Franz Liszt*, vol. 1 (New York: Knopf, 1983), p. 371.
8. Louis Moreau Gottschalk, *Notes of a Pianist*, ed. Clara Gottschalk (Philadelphia: Lippincott, 1881), p. 61.

## Chapter 17

1. Quoted in Julian Budden, *Verdi* (London: J. M. Dent, 1985), pp. 84–5, citing in turn *I copialettere di Giuseppe Verdi*, Milan, 1913, pp. 601–2. Used by permission of Oxford University Press, Oxford, U.K.

## Chapter 18

1. Anonymous source of the 1890s, quoted in Archibald Haddon, *The Story of the Music Hall* (London: Fleetway Press, 1935), p. 96.
2. Antonín Dvořák, "On the Real Value of Negro Music," *New York Herald*, 21 May 1893; quoted in Michael Beckerman, "The Master's Little Joke: Antonín Dvořák and the Mask of the Nation," in *Dvořák and His World*, ed. Michael Beckerman (Princeton, NJ: Princeton University Press, 1993), p. 138.
3. Antonín Dvořák, letter to the editor, New York Herald, 28 May 1893; quoted in Michael Beckerman, "The Master's Little Joke: Antonín Dvořák and the Mask of the Nation," in *Dvořák and His World*, ed. Michael Beckerman (Princeton, NJ: Princeton University Press, 1993), p. 137.
4. James Creelman, "Dvořák's Negro Symphony," *Pall Mall Budget*, 21 June 1894; reproduced in *Dvořák and His World*, ed. Michael Beckerman (Princeton, NJ: Princeton University Press, 1993), p. 179.
5. Henry Krehbiel, "Dvořák's American Compositions," *New York Herald*, 31 January 1894; anthologized in *Dvořák and His World*, ed. Michael Beckerman (Princeton University Press, 1993), p. 171.

## Chapter 19

1. http://www.fordemocracy.net/electoral.shtml.
2. John Cage, "History of Experimental Music in the United States" (1959), in Cage, *Silence* (Cambridge, MA: M.I.T. Press, 1966), p. 73.
3. Leonard Bernstein, *The Infinite Variety of Music* (New York: Simon & Schuster, 1966), p. 10.
4. Nicholas Cook, *Music* (New York: Oxford University Press, 1998), p. 40.
5. http://www.sonyclassical.com/artists/gould/bio.html. Accessed April 17, 2008.
6. http://www.herald.co.uk/local_info/live_aid.html. Accessed April 17, 2008.
7. W. Peretti, *The Creation of Jazz* (Urbana: University of Illinois Press, 1992), p. 187.
8. Brian Eno, liner notes to *Music for Airports/Ambient 1*, PVC 7908 (AMB 001), 1978.

## Chapter 20

1. Harold C. Schonberg, *The Great Pianists*, rev. ed. (New York: Simon & Schuster, 1987), p. 477.
2. William W. Austin, *Music in the 20th Century* (New York: Norton, 1966), p. 25.
3. Glenn Watkins, *Soundings: Music in the Twentieth Century* (New York: Schirmer, 1995), p. 13.
4. Letter to Maurice Emmanuel, August 4, 1920, published in *La Revue musicale*, 1947.
5. Quotation from Charles Ives, Foreword to the score of *The Unanswered Question* (New York: Southern Music Publishing, 1953), p. 2. Published by Southern Music for Peer International. Used by permission.
6. Charles Ives, "Essays before a Sonata" (1920), in *Essays before a Sonata and Other Writings*, ed. Howard Boatwright (New York: Norton, 1962), pp. 97–8.
7. Quoted in Jan Swafford, *Charles Ives: A Life with Music* (New York: Norton, 1996), p. 143.
8. Ralph Kirkpatrick, *A Temporary Mimeographed Catalogue of the Music Manuscripts and Related Materials of Charles Edward Ives* (New Haven: Yale University, 1955), p. 27.
9. Arnold Schoenberg, ca. 1945, in a note found by his widow after his death. Quoted in Henry and Sidney Cowell, *Charles Ives and His Music* (New York: Oxford University Press, 1955), p. 114.
10. Igor Stravinsky, *Stravinsky: An Autobiography* (New York: Simon & Schuster, 1936), pp. 72–3.
11. *Le Temps*, Paris, June 3, 1913.
12. Interview with Cowell recorded on *Henry Cowell: Piano Music* (Washington, DC: Smithsonian Folkways, CD SF40801).
13. Review of the Pan-American Association of Composers Concert, March 6, 1933, Carnegie Hall. *Musical Courier*, vol. 106, no. 11 (1933): 12.
14. Quotation from Edgard Varèse in *The Evening Standard* (London), July 31, 1924. Reprinted by permission of *The Evening Standard*.
15. Joseph Machlis, *Introduction to Contemporary Music*, 2nd ed. (New York: Norton, 1979), p. 353.
16. From *Music of Edgar Varèse* (Albany, NY: One Way Records, 1996).

## Chapter 21

1. Arnold Schoenberg, "My Evolution (1949)," in *Style and Idea*, ed. Leonard Stein, trans. Leo Black (Berkeley and Los Angeles: University of California Press, 1984), p. 91.
2. Arnold Schoenberg, *Harmonielehre*, 3rd ed. (Vienna: Universal Edition, 1922), pp. 487–8.
3. Hermann Bahr, quoted in *Art in Theory, 1900–1990: An Anthology of Changing Ideas*, ed. Charles Harrison and Paul Wood (Oxford: Blackwell, 1993), p. 119.
4. Quotations from libretto of *Wozzeck* by Alban Berg. © 1931 by Universal Edition A. G., Wien Copyright renewed. All Rights Reserved. English translation © 1952 by Alfred A. Kalmus, London W1. © renewed. All Rights Reserved. Used by permission of European American Music Distributors LLC, sole US and Canadian agent for Universal Edition A. G., Wien.
5. Quotation from review of *Wozzeck* by Paul Zschorlich, *Deutsche Zeitung* (Berlin, December 15, 1925). Transl. MEB
6. Arnold Schoenberg, "The Orchestral Variations, op. 31: A Radio Talk," *The Score* 27 (July 1960), p. 39.
7. Joseph Rufer, *The Works of Arnold Schönberg*, trans. Dika Newlin (London: Faber and Faber, 1962), p. 45.

## Chapter 22

1. Paul Hindemith, *The Craft of Musical Composition* (1937), trans. Arthur Mendel (New York: Associated Music Publishers, 1941), p. 4.
2. Alan Hovhaness, quoted in David Ewen, *American Composers: A Biographical Dictionary* (New York: G. P. Putnam's Sons, 1982), p. 342.

3. Bryan Simms, ed., *Composers on Modern Musical Culture* (New York: Schirmer, 1999), p. 85.
4. Quotation from lyrics by Bertolt Brecht, "Alabama Song" from Kurt Weill & Bertolt Brecht, *Aufstieg und Fall der Stadt Mahagonny*, © 1929 by European American Music Corporation. © renewed. All Rights Reserved. Used by permission of European American Music Distributors LLC, sole US and Canadian agent for European American Music Corporation.
5. http://www.sonyclassical.com/music/60593.
6. Copland testified in Washington, DC, on May 26, 1953, before the U.S. Senate Permanent Subcommittee on Investigations of the Committee on Government Operations, chaired by Senator Joseph McCarthy (R-Wisconsin). For a transcript of this "executive session," go to www.overgrownpath.com/2004/08/aaron-coplands-mccarthy-hearing.html. Accessed on June 30, 2012.

## Chapter 23

1. Quotation from Pierre Boulez to an unidentified New York journalist, 1963, quoted in Robert Jacobson, *Reverberations: Interviews with the World's Leading Musicians*, pp. 25–26. Copyright © 1974 by Robert Jacobson. Reprinted by permission of HarperCollins Publishers Inc.
2. Ernst Krenek, *Horizons Circled* (Berkeley and Los Angeles: University of California Press, 1974), p. 151.
3. Performance instructions in score of *In C* by Terry Riley. © 1964 Composed by Terry Riley. Published by Ancient Word Music, Administered by Celestial Harmonies.
4. Terry Riley, quoted in Michael Walsh, "The Heart Is Back in the Game," *Time*, September 20, 1982, p. 60.
5. Charles Wuorinen, *Simple Composition* (New York: Longman, 1979), p. 3.
6. Howard Pollack, *Aaron Copland* (New York: Henry Holt, 1999), p. 286.

## Chapter 24

1. Scott Joplin, *The School of Ragtime* (New York: Author, 1908).
2. Leo Oehmler, "Ragtime: A Pernicious Evil and Enemy of True Art," *Musical Observer* (September 1914), p. 15.
3. W. C. Handy, *Father of the Blues: An Autobiography*, ed. Arna Bontemps (New York: Macmillan, 1941), pp. 28–29.
4. W. C. Handy, *Father of the Blues: An Autobiography*, ed. Arna Bontemps (New York: Macmillan, 1941), p. 122.
5. Quotation from lyrics, Cole Porter, "Night and Day." Published by Warner Bros.
6. Quotation from lyrics, Duke Ellington, "Sophisticated Lady." Used by permission of Warner/Chappell Music, Inc.
7. Quotation from lyrics, Edward Kennedy "Duke" Ellington, "It Don't Mean a Thing (If It Ain't Got That Swing)." Used with the permission of Warner/Chappell Music, Inc.
8. *The Duke Ellington Reader*, ed. Mark Tucker (New York: Oxford University Press, 1993), p. 326.
9. John Edward Hasse, *Beyond Category: The Life and Genius of Duke Ellington* (New York: Simon & Schuster, 1993), p. 380.
10. Liner notes to *Free Jazz* (Atlantic 1364), 1960.
11. http://www.southernmusic.net/grandoleopry.htm.
12. http://www.countryreview.com/GrandOleOpry.
13. For the complete transcript of Seeger's testimony, go to http://www.peteseeger.net/HUAC.htm. Accessed June 30, 2012.
14. Peter Irvine, "Folk, Copyright, and the Public Domain," 2003, online at http://www.peterirvinelaw.com/pdf/Folk_Music_Copyright_PD.pdf. Accessed on April 27, 2008.

## Epilogue

1. Gabriela Lena Frank, liner notes to her *Leyendas: An Andean Walkabout*, The Chiara String Quartet (New Voice Singles CNVS 002), 2006.
2. The Nielsen Company and Billboard's 2011 *Music Industry Report* (January 5, 2012). http://narm.com/PDF/NielsenMusic2011YEUpdate.pdf

# Index